MÉXICO

www.visitmexico.com

wake up and smell the savings.

Nothing gets me started like a free hot breakfast. And when I show my AAA card, I get AAA rates.* Throw in all the other extras I appreciate, and my stay's even more tantalizing. Real value from my friends at Hampton. For reservations, call your AAA agent, visit **hampton.com** or call 1-800-hampton.

we love having you here.®

| free high-speed internet | free hot breakfast | preferred hotels |

Connecticut, Massachusetts & Rhode Island

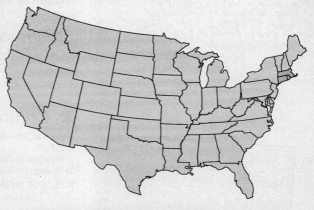

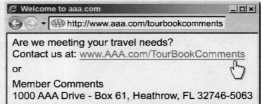

Welcome to aaa.com

http://www.aaa.com/tourbookcomments

Are we meeting your travel needs?
Contact us at: www.AAA.com/TourBookComments

or

Member Comments
1000 AAA Drive - Box 61, Heathrow, FL 32746-5063

Published by AAA Publishing
1000 AAA Drive, Heathrow, FL 32746-5063
Copyright AAA 2010, All rights reserved

The publisher has made every effort to provide accurate, up-to-date information but accepts no responsibility for loss or injury sustained by any person using this book. TourBook® guides are published for the exclusive use of AAA members. Not for sale.

Advertising Rate and Circulation Information: (407) 444-8280

Printed in the USA by Worldcolor, Buffalo, NY

Photo Credit: (Cover & Title Page)
Scituate Lighthouse, Scituate, MA
© Laurence Parent Photography

 Printed on recyclable paper.
Please recycle whenever possible.   Stock #4607   ◆ ◆

This book is printed on paper certified by third-party standards for sustainably-managed forestry and production.

Connecticut,
Massachusetts
&Rhode Island

Featured Information

Rhode Island

4

Now That's *Refreshing*

Discover the pleasure of getting what you expect.

Whether you need a simple night's sleep, a family hotel with breakfast and a pool or an elegant escape for a special occasion, the key is in the AAA Diamond Rating.

For lodging and dining experiences that fit your travel preferences and budget, use the AAA Diamond Ratings to guide your selection.

AAA Diamond Ratings…yours for the choosing.

Find AAA Diamond Rating definitions for lodgings and restaurants in the front of any TourBook® guide and at **AAA.com/Diamonds**.

Refreshingly simple. Refreshingly reliable.

What do these items have in common? AAA members spend less.

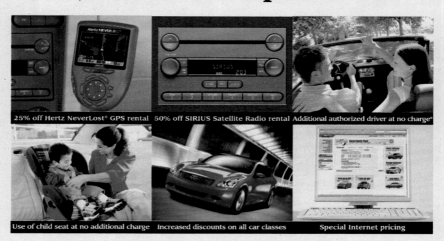

25% off Hertz NeverLost® GPS rental   50% off SIRIUS Satellite Radio rental   Additional authorized driver at no charge*

Use of child seat at no additional charge   Increased discounts on all car classes   Special Internet pricing

Hertz offers AAA members exclusive discounts on a variety of products and services. Benefits include:

- 25% off Hertz NeverLost® GPS rental
- 50% off SIRIUS Satellite Radio rental
- Additional authorized driver at no charge*
- Free use of child seat
- Discounts on all car classes
- Special Internet pricing
- Member Satisfaction Guarantee

SHOW YOUR AAA CARD AND SAVE

THE ONLY CAR RENTAL COMPANY ENDORSED BY AAA

AAA.com/Hertz

FOR YOUR INFORMATION: Advance reservations are required. Discounts and benefits are valid at participating locations in the U.S., Canada and Puerto Rico. One child seat at no additional charge. Hertz NeverLost and SIRIUS Satellite Radio subject to availability. SIRIUS not available in Alaska, Hawaii or Puerto Rico. Discounts valued in local currency upon redemption and exclude applicable taxes and surcharges. Your valid AAA membership card or Hertz/AAA discount card must be presented at time of pickup. SIRIUS is a registered trademark of SIRIUS Satellite Radio, Inc.

*No charge for an additional authorized driver who is a AAA member, holds a major credit card in their name and meets standard rental qualifications.

® Reg. U.S. Pat. Off. © 2009 Hertz System, Inc.

| Visit | Over 1,100 AAA Offices | Click | AAA.com/Hertz | Call | 800-654-3080 |

Attractions, lodgings and restaurants are listed on the basis of merit alone after careful evaluation and approval by one of AAA/CAA's full-time, professionally trained inspectors. Evaluations are unannounced to ensure that we see an establishment just as you would see it.

An establishment's decision to advertise in the TourBook guide has no bearing on its evaluation or rating. Advertising for services or products does not imply AAA endorsement.

Information in this guide was believed accurate at the time of publication. However, since changes inevitably occur between annual editions, we suggest you work with your AAA travel professional or check on AAA.com to confirm prices and schedules.

How the TourBook Guide is Organized

The TourBook guide is organized into three distinct sections.

The **Points of Interest** section helps you plan daily activities and sightseeing excursions and provides details about the city or attraction you are visiting.

The **Lodgings and Restaurants** section helps you select AAA Approved accommodations and dining facilities meeting your specific needs and expectations.

The **Reference** section provides indexes for locating information within this guide and items to aid the trip planning process.

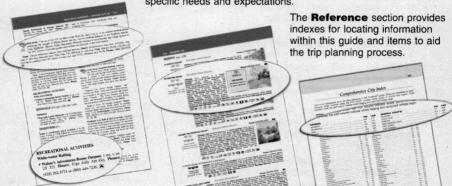

Locating the Attractions, Lodgings and Restaurants

Attractions, lodgings and restaurants are listed under the city in which they physically are located - or in some cases under the nearest recognized city. Most listings are alphabetically organized by state, province, region or island, then by city and establishment name.

A color is assigned to each state or province so that you can match the color bars at the top of the page to switch from the **Points of Interest** section to the **Lodgings and Restaurants** section.

Spotting maps help you physically locate points of interest, lodgings and restaurants in the major destinations.

The Comprehensive City Index located in the **Reference** section contains an A-to-Z list of cities.

Destination Cities and Destination Areas

Destination cities, established based on government models and local expertise, include metropolitan areas plus nearby vicinity cities. **Destination areas** are regions with broad tourist appeal; several cities will comprise the area.

If a city falls within a destination's vicinity, the city name will appear at its alphabetical location in the book, and a cross reference will give you the exact page on which listings for that city begin.

An Orientation map appears at the beginning of each destination section to familiarize you with that destination.

Understanding the Points of Interest Listing

GEM Designation

A ⬦ indicates the attraction has been rated a AAA GEM, a "must see" point of interest that offers a *Great Experience for Members®*. These attractions have been judged to be of exceptional interest and quality by AAA inspectors.

Discount Savings

The [SAVE] icon denotes those attractions offering AAA/CAA, AAA MasterCard, AAA VISA or international Show Your Card & Save discount cardholders a discount off the attraction's standard admission. Present your card at the attraction's admission desk.

A list of participating points of interest appears in the Reference section of this guide.

Shopping establishments preceded by a [SAVE] icon also provide to AAA/CAA members a discount and/or gift with purchase; present your card at the mall's customer service center to receive your benefit.

Exceptions

- Members should inquire in advance concerning the validity of the discount for special rates.
- The [SAVE] discount may not be used in conjunction with other discounts.
- Attractions that already provide a reduced senior or child rate may not honor the [SAVE] discount for those age groups.
- All offers are subject to change and may not apply during special events, particular days or seasons or for the entire validity period of the TourBook guide.

Adventure Travel

There are inherent risks with adventure travel activities like air tours, hiking, skiing and white-water rafting. For your own safety, please read and adhere to all safety instructions. Mentions of these activities are for information only and do **not** imply endorsement by AAA.

BLUE RIDGE PAR

Boone Convention & Visitors Bureau: 208 such as
Howard St., Boone, NC 28607 **Phones:** (828) Laughing
555-5555 or (800) 555-5555

⬦ GEM **RED OAK,** .7 mi. n. of US 421 via Horn in the West Dr
struggle of Daniel Boone and his men to establish free
[SAVE] Hickory Ridge Homestead Museum contains a reconstr
Costumed guides demonstrate the lifestyle of the early

Time: 2 hours minimum. Inquire about weather policies. Ho
June to mid-Aug. Museum open Tues.-Sun. 1-8, mid-June to
mission to museum) $18; $9 (senior citizens and ages 0-12)
Phone: (800) 555-5555. 🎫

typical of th...
onstrate the lifestyle of the early sch... Phon
Time: 2 hours minimum. Inquire about weather
policies. **Hours:** Performances Tues.-Sun. at 8 p.m.,
mid-June to mid-Aug. Museum open Tues.-Sun. 1-8,   Seat
mid-June to mid-Aug. **Cost:** Musical drama (in-   coac
cludes admission to museum) $18; $9 (senior citi-   met
zens and ages 0-12). Museum only $4.50. **Phone:**   Tra
(800) 555-5555. 🎫   late

RECREATIONAL ACTIVITIES

White-water Rafting   "T
- **Wahoo's Adventures-Boone Outpost,** 1 mi. s. on   are
US 321. **Hours:** Trips daily Apr.-Oct. **Phones:**   da
(828) 555-5555 or (800) 555-5555. 🅰   p
a

BOONVILLE (B-4) pop. 1,138, elev. 1,066   T
s
WINERIES
- **RagApple Lassie Vineyards** is at 3724 RagApple
Lassie Ln. **Hours:** Daily noon-6. Closed Easter,
Thanksgiving and Dec. 25. **Phones:** (336)
555-5555 or (866) 555-5555.

BRASSTOWN (F-1)

JOHN C. CAMPBELL FOLK SCHOOL is in the
center of town at 1 Folk School Rd. Visitors observe
students at work in a variety of folk classes including cooking, w...
potter...

RECREATIONAL ACTIVITI

White-water Rafting

- **Wahoo's Adventures-Boone**
US 321. **Hours:** Trips daily
(828) 555-5555 or (800) 555-

Directions

Unless otherwise specified, directions are given from the center of town, using the following highway designations:

I=interstate highway	**US**=federal highway
SR=state route	**CR**=county road
FM=farm to market	**FR**=forest road
Mex.=Mexican highway	**Hwy.**=Canadian or Caribbean highway

Prices and Dates of Operation

Admission prices are quoted without sales tax. Children under the lowest age specified are admitted free when accompanied by an adult. Days, months and age groups written with a hyphen are inclusive.

Prices pertaining to points of interest in the United States are quoted in U.S. dollars; points of interest in Canada are quoted in Canadian dollars; prices for points of interest in Mexico and the Caribbean are quoted as an approximate U.S. dollar equivalent.

Schedules and admission rates may change throughout the validity period of this guide. Check AAA.com for the most current information.

Credit Card Information

Most establishments accept credit cards, but a small number require cash. If you want to use a specific credit card, call ahead to ensure it's accepted.

Icons

Attraction icons represent some of the services and facilities offered:

Camping facilities available

Food available on premises

Recreational activities available

Pets on leash allowed

Picnicking permitted

Bulleted Listings

Gambling establishments within hotels are presented for member information regardless of whether the lodging is AAA Approved.

Recreational activities of a participatory nature (requiring physical exertion or special skills) are not inspected.

Wineries are evaluated by AAA inspectors to ensure they meet listing requirements and offer tours.

All are presented in an abbreviated bulleted format for informational purposes.

Understanding the Lodging Listing

Local Member Value

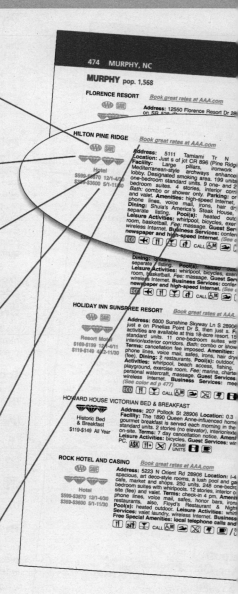

🅐🅐🅐 or 🅒🅐🅐 and SAVE identify hotels that offer members a rate guarantee and up to two free special amenities as part of their Official Appointment partnership with AAA. Rate guarantee: Discounted standard room rate (usually based on last standard room availability) or the lowest public rate available at time of booking for dates of stay. Free special amenity options such as breakfast, local telephone calls, newspaper, room upgrade, preferred room or high-speed Internet are included in the listing.

Diamond Rating

The number of Diamonds informs you of the overall complexity of a lodging's amenities and service. Red indicates an Official Appointment lodging. An fyi in place of Diamonds indicates the property has not been rated but is included as an "information only" service. A detailed description of each rating level appears on page 18.

Classification

All Diamond Rated lodgings are classified using three key elements: style of operation, overall concept and service level. See pages 20-21 for details on our classifications.

Rates

The property's standard 2-person rates and effective dates are shown.

Rates provided to AAA for each lodging represent the publicly available rate or ranges for a standard room. Rates are rounded to the nearest dollar and do not include taxes. U.S., Mexican and Caribbean rates are in U.S. dollars; rates for Canadian lodgings are in Canadian dollars.

Information about cancellation and minimum stay policies is provided in the **Terms** section of the property's listing.

Online Reservations

This notation indicates AAA/CAA members can conveniently check room availability, validate room rates and make reservations for this property in a secure online environment at AAA.com.

Service Availability

Unit types, amenities and room features preceded by the word "Some" indicate the item is available in **some units**, potentially within only one unit. The term "fee" appearing beside an amenity indicates an extra charge applies.

Nationwide Member Value

The blue box in the listing identifies hotel brands that offer an everyday member benefit at all AAA Approved locations. (See page 17 for additional program benefits.)

Spotting Symbol

Black ovals with white numbers are used to locate, or "spot," lodgings on maps we provide for larger cities.

Credit Card Information

Most establishments accept credit cards, but a small number require cash. If you want to use a specific credit card, call ahead to ensure it's accepted.

Icons

Lodging icons represent some of the member values, services and facilities offered. The term "FEE" appearing to the left of an amenity icon indicates an extra charge applies.

The ECO icon indicates lodgings that have been certified by well-established government and/or private eco-certification organizations. For more information about these organizations and their programs, visit AAA.com/eco.

Discounts

(A$K) May offer discount

Member Services

(✦) Airport transportation

(🐾) Pets allowed (call property for restrictions and fees)

(🍽) Restaurant on premises

(🍽→) Restaurant off premises (walking distance)

(24🍽) 24-hour room service

(🍸) Full bar

(👶) Child care

(&M) Accessible features (call property for available services and amenities)

Leisure Activities

(🎰) Full-service casino

(🏊) Pool

(💪) Health club on premises

(💪→) Health club off premises

(🎿) Recreational activities

In-Room Amenities

(🚭) Designated non-smoking rooms

(🎬) Movies

(🧊) Refrigerator

(📟) Microwave

(☕) Coffee maker

(🚫) No air conditioning

(🚫) No TV

(🚫) No cable TV

(🚫) No telephones

Safety Features

(see page 22)
(Mexico and Caribbean only)

(S) Sprinklers

(D) Smoke detectors

Understanding the Restaurant Listing

Official Appointment

AAA or CAA indicates Official Appointment (OA) restaurants. The OA program permits restaurants to display and advertise the AAA or CAA emblem. These establishments are highlighted in red to help you quickly identify them. The AAA or CAA Approved sign helps traveling members find restaurants that want member business.

Local Member Value

SAVE identifies restaurants that offer a Show Your Card & Save® discount to AAA/CAA members.

Diamond Rating

The number of Diamonds informs you of the overall complexity of food, presentation, service and ambience. Red indicates an Official Appointment restaurant. A detailed description of each Diamond level appears on page 19.

Cuisine Type

The cuisine type helps you select a dining facility that caters to your individual taste. AAA currently recognizes more than 120 different cuisine types.

Prices

Prices shown represent the minimum and maximum entree cost per person. Exceptions may include one-of-a-kind or special market priced items. Prices are rounded to the nearest dollar and do not include taxes. U.S., Mexican and Caribbean prices are in U.S. dollars; prices for Canadian restaurants are in Canadian dollars.

Icons

Icons provide additional information about services and facilities.

🄰🄲 No air-conditioning

♿M Accessible features offered

   (call property for available services and amenities)

🚬 Designated smoking section available

Menus

This notation indicates AAA/CAA members can conveniently view the restaurant's menu in a secure online environment at AAA.com.

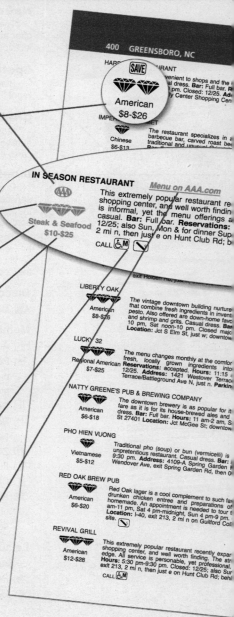

the casual eatery prepares tasty steak, seafood, chicken and salads. **Phone:** 555/555-5555
ons: accepted. **Hours:** 11:15 am-10 pm, Fri & Sat-11 pm, Sun 10:30
01 Friendly Center Rd 27408 **Location:** Jct Wendover Ave, just w; in
ing: on-site.

an-eat buffets for lunch and dinner. Included in the buffet are a **Phone:** 555/555-5555
sushi and dim sum selection. Buffet items include a variety of
also available. Casual dress
Rd 27407

expanded to this newly constructed building, located behind a **Phone:** 555/555-5555 ⟨43⟩
y specialize in all-you-can-eat buffets for lunch. The atmosphere
tting edge. All service is personable, yet professional. Dressy
sted. **Hours:** 11 am-8:30 pm, Thurs & Fri 5 pm-9 pm. Closed
wl Sun. **Address:** 604 Milner Dr 27410 **Location:** I-40, exit 213,
Quaker Village Shopping Center. **Parking:** on-site. **Classic**

Brazilian
Closed: 12/25;
14B, 1.8 mi e on Wendover Ave,

ually upscale dining atmosphere. The menu features dishes **Phone:** 555/555-5555
s, such as in stuffed rainbow trout and lamb with honey-mint
pared with flair, including roasted pulled pork, fried chicken
ar. **Reservations:** accepted. **Hours:** 11:30 am-9:30 pm, Fri-
ys; also Sun. **Address:** 100-D W Washington St 27401
ing: street.

scale eatery, with the focus of the cuisine on incorporating **Phone:** 555/555-5555
al American fare. Casual dress. **Bar:** Full bar.
, Fri & Sat-11 pm, Sun 10 am-10 pm. Closed: 11/26.
Location: Wendover Ave, exit US 220 N/Westover
e.

y menu of burgers, wraps, sandwiches and hearty pub **Phone:** 555/555-5555
utdoor seating is offered during warm weather. Casual
ight. Closed: 11/26, 12/24, 12/25. **Address:** 345 S Elm
ng: street.

stiest and is served with a smile in the comfortable, **Phone:** 555/555-5555
vine. **Hours:** 11 am-3:30 & 5-9:30 pm, Fri-Sun 11 am-
7 **Location:** I-40, exit 214 or 214 B, 1.8 mi ne on
Parking: on-site.

s gourmet sandwiches, fish and chips, the signature **Phone:** 555/555-5555
Angus beef. Sauces, dressings and soups are
te brewery. Casual dress. **Bar:** Full bar. **Hours:** 11
11/26, 12/25. **Address:** 714 Francis King St 27410
just w on Hunt Club Rd, then just n. **Parking:** on-

this newly constructed building, located behind a **Phone:** 555/555-5555
e is informal, yet the menu offerings are cutting
casual. **Bar:** Full bar. **Reservations:** accepted.
Address: 604 Milner Dr 27410 **Location:** I-40,
er Village Shopping Center. **Parking:** on-site.

Spotting Symbol

White ovals with black numbers serve as restaurant locators and are used to locate, or "spot," restaurants on maps for larger cities.

Classifications

If applicable, a restaurant may be defined as:

Classic - renowned and/or landmark restaurant in business longer than 25 years, known for unique style and ambience.

Historic - establishments must meet one of the following criteria:

- Listed on the National Register of Historic Places
- Designated a National Historic Landmark
- Located in a National Register Historic District

Separate criteria designate historic properties in Canada, Mexico and the Caribbean.

Credit Card Information

Most establishments accept credit cards, but a small number require cash. If you want to use a specific credit card, call ahead to ensure it's accepted.

AAA/CAA members can generally expect to pay no more than the maximum regular rate printed in the TourBook guide in each rate range for a standard room. On rare occasions AAA receives or inadvertently publishes incorrect rates.

Obtain current AAA/CAA member rates and make reservations at AAA.com. Rates may vary within the range, depending on season and room type. Listed rates are usually based on last standard room availability.

Discounts

Member discounts, when offered, will apply to rates quoted within the rate range and are applicable at the time of booking. Special rates used in advertising, as well as special short-term promotional rates lower than the lowest listed rate in the range, are not subject to additional member discounts.

Exceptions

Rates for properties operating as concessionaires for the U.S. National Park Service are not guaranteed due to governing regulations. Rates in the Mexico TourBook are not guaranteed and may fluctuate based on the exchange rate of the peso.

Lodgings may temporarily increase room rates, not recognize discounts or modify pricing policies during special events. Examples of special events range from Mardi Gras and the Kentucky Derby (including pre-Derby events) to college football games, holidays, holiday periods and state fairs. Although some special events are listed in AAA/CAA TourBook guides and on AAA.com, it is always wise to check in advance with AAA travel professionals for specific dates.

Meeting Your Travel Needs

AAA is proud to stand behind the Approved hotels, restaurants, attractions and campgrounds listed in the TourBook and CampBook guides. If, however, your visit doesn't meet your expectations, now you can tell us about it immediately. Visit AAA.com/TourBookComments to complete an easy online form, or send written comments to: AAA Member Comments, 1000 AAA Dr., Heathrow, FL 32746.

Get the Room You Reserved

When making your reservation, identify yourself as a AAA or CAA member and request written confirmation to guarantee: type of room, rate, dates of stay, and cancellation and refund policies. At registration, show your membership card.

When you find your room is not as specified, and you have written confirmation of reservations for a certain type of accommodation, you should be given the option of choosing a different room or finding one elsewhere. Should you choose to go elsewhere and a refund is refused or resisted, submit the matter to AAA/CAA within 30 days, along with complete documentation, including your

reasons for refusing the room and copies of your written confirmation and any receipts or canceled checks associated with this problem.

If you are charged more than the maximum rate listed in the TourBook guide for a standard room, question the additional charge. If management refuses to adhere to the published rate, pay for the room and submit your receipt and membership number to AAA/CAA within 30 days. Include all pertinent information: dates of stay, rate paid, itemized paid receipts, number of persons in your party and the room number you occupied, and list any extra room equipment used. A refund of the amount paid in excess of the stated maximum will be made if our investigation indicates that unjustified charging occurred.

Deposit, Refund and Cancellation Policies

Most establishments give full deposit refunds if they have been notified at least 48 hours before the normal check-in time. Listing prose will note if more than 48 hours' notice is required for cancellation. Some properties may charge a cancellation or handling fee. When this applies, "cancellation fee imposed" will appear in the **Terms** section of the listing. If you cancel too late, you have little recourse if a refund is denied.

When an establishment requires full or partial payment in advance and your trip is cut short, a refund may not be given.

When canceling a reservation, phone the lodging immediately. Make a note of the date and time you called, the cancellation number if there is one, and the name of the person who handled the cancellation. If your AAA/CAA club made your reservation, allow them to make the cancellation for you as well, so you will have proof of cancellation.

Check-in and Check-out Times

Check-in and check-out times are shown in the lodging listings, under **Terms**, only if they are before 3 p.m. or after 10 a.m. respectively.

Members Save With Our Partners

Show Your Card & Save

These Show Your Card & Save® partners provide the listed member benefits. Visit AAA.com/Discounts to discover all the great Show Your Card & Save® discounts in your area. Even greater discounts on theme park tickets may be available at your local AAA/CAA club. Discounts apply to a maximum of six tickets for Amtrak, Gray Line and the theme parks. Restaurant savings apply to AAA/CAA members and up to five guests.

SeaWorld, Busch Gardens, Sesame Place

WORLDS OF DISCOVERY

- Save on admission at the gate, at participating offices or online AAA.com/SeaWorld
- Save 10% on up-close dining; visit Guest Relations for details

Six Flags

- Save on admission at the gate, at participating offices or online AAA.com/SixFlags
- Save 10% on merchandise purchases of $15 or more at in-park stores

Universal Orlando Resort and Universal Studios Hollywood

- Save on admission at the gate, at participating offices or online AAA.com/Universal
- Save 10% at select food and merchandise venues in-park and at Universal CityWalk®

The Entertainment Capital of L.A.™

Hard Rock Cafe

- Save 10% on food, non-alcoholic beverages and merchandise at all U.S., Canadian and select international locations

Landry's Seafood House, The Crab House, Chart House, Saltgrass Steak House, Muer Seafood Restaurants and Aquarium Restaurants

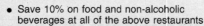

- Save 10% on food and non-alcoholic beverages at all of the above restaurants
- Save 10% on merchandise at Aquarium and Downtown Aquarium restaurants

Amtrak

- 10% discount on rail fare when booked at least 3 days in advance of travel date

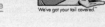

EagleRider

- We Rent Dreams® 12% off motorcycle rentals 1-877-869-5023

Fetch! Pet Care

- Save 10% off pet-sitting and dog-walking services AAA.com/Fetchpetcare 1-877-533-8242 code AAAPETS

We've got your tail covered.™

Grand Canyon Railway

- Save up to 20% on rail fare, hotel accommodations, restaurant and gift shop purchases sold outside of Grand Canyon National Park

GRAND CANYON Railway

Gray Line
AAA.com/GrayLine

- Save 10% on sightseeing tours of 1 day or less worldwide

Hertz

- Exclusive AAA member savings on daily, weekend, weekly and monthly rentals AAA.com/hertz or 1-800-654-3080

Tanger Outlet Centers www.tangeroutlet.com

- Save up to 20% on total purchase at select merchants with FREE coupon booklet
- Member BONUS: FREE $5 gift card for each additional Tanger Outlet Center visited after first within same calendar year
- Show membership card and register at the AAA customer service desk when you visit

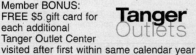

Show Your Card & Save

Preferred Hotels

AAA Preferred Lodging Partners

EXPECT SAVINGS, SELECTION, AND SATISFACTION

- **Best AAA/CAA member rates for your dates of stay.** Provide a valid membership number when placing your reservation and show your card at hotel check-in.
- **Satisfaction guarantee.** Notify the property if you are dissatisfied with any part of your stay. If the matter cannot be resolved, you may be entitled to compensation (see page 15).
- **Seasonal promotions and special member offers.** Visit AAA.com to view current offers.
- **Everyday member benefit.** Look for the blue boxes in the TourBook listings for everyday values offered at all AAA Approved locations. *Offer good at time of publication: Chains and offers may change without notice. Preferred Hotel Partner discounts may vary in Mexico and the Caribbean.*

10% Off Best Available Rates
Best Western International

5% or More Off Best Available Rates
Conrad, DoubleTree, Embassy Suites, Hampton, Hilton, Hilton Garden Inn, Hilton Grand Vacations, Home2 Suites, Homewood Suites, and Waldorf=Astoria Collection

10% Off Best Available Rates
ANdAZ, Grand Hyatt, Hyatt Place, Hyatt Regency, Hyatt Summerfield Suites, and Park Hyatt

5% or More Off Best Available Rates
Courtyard, Fairfield Inn, JW Marriott, Marriott, Renaissance Hotels & Resorts, Residence Inn, SpringHill Suites, and TownePlace Suites

5-15% Off Best Available Rates
aloft, element, Four Points, Le Meridien, Sheraton, St. Regis, The Luxury Collection, Westin, and W Hotels

Visit Over 1,100 AAA Offices **Click** AAA.com **Call** 1-866-AAA-SAVE (222-7283)

Understanding the Diamond Ratings

AAA/CAA inspectors have evaluated and rated each of the 58,000 lodging and restaurant establishments in the TourBook series to ensure quality travel information for our members. All properties must meet AAA's minimum requirements (for lodgings) concerning cleanliness, comfort and security - or - AAA's minimum requirements (for restaurants) pertaining to cleanliness, food preparation and service.

Eligible applicants receive an unannounced evaluation by a AAA/CAA inspector that includes two distinct components:

- **AAA Approval:** The inspector first must determine whether the property meets the criteria required to be AAA Approved. Every establishment that meets these strict guidelines offers AAA members the assurance that, regardless of the Diamond Rating, it provides acceptable quality, cleanliness, service and value.
- **AAA Diamond Rating:** Once an establishment becomes AAA Approved, it is then assigned a rating of one to five Diamonds, indicating the extensiveness of its facilities, amenities and services, from basic to moderate to luxury. These Diamond Ratings guide members in selecting establishments appropriately matched to their needs and expectations.

LODGINGS

1 Diamond

One Diamond lodgings typically appeal to the budget-minded traveler. They provide essential, no-frills accommodations and basic comfort and hospitality.

2 Diamond

Two Diamond lodgings appeal to travelers seeking affordable yet more than the basic accommodations. Facilities, decor and amenities are modestly enhanced.

3 Diamond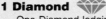

Three Diamond lodgings offer a distinguished style. Properties are multi-faceted, with marked upgrades in physical attributes, amenities and guest comforts.

4 Diamond

Four Diamond lodgings are refined and stylish. Physical attributes are upscale. The fundamental hallmarks at this level include an extensive array of amenities combined with a high degree of hospitality, service and attention to detail.

5 Diamond

Five Diamond lodgings provide the ultimate in luxury and sophistication. Physical attributes are extraordinary in every manner. Service is meticulous, exceeding guest expectations and maintaining impeccable standards of excellence. Extensive personalized services and amenities provide first-class comfort.

The lodging listings with [fyi] in place of Diamonds are included as an *information only* service for members. The icon indicates that a property has not been rated for one or more of the following reasons: too new to rate, under construction, under major renovation, not evaluated, may not meet all AAA requirements.

A property not meeting all AAA requirements is included for either its member value or because it may be the only accommodation available in the area. Listing prose will give insight as to why the [fyi] designation was assigned.

4 Diamond

Four Diamond restaurants provide a distinctive fine-dining experience that is typically expensive. Surroundings are highly refined with upscale enhancements throughout. Highly creative chefs use imaginative presentations to augment fresh, top-quality ingredients. A proficient service staff meets or exceeds guest expectations. A wine steward may offer menu-specific knowledge to guide selection.

5 Diamond

Five Diamond restaurants are luxurious and renowned for consistently providing a world-class experience. Highly acclaimed chefs offer artistic menu selections that are imaginative and unique, using only the finest ingredients available. A maitre d' leads an expert service staff in exceeding guest expectations, attending to every detail in an effortless and unobtrusive manner.

The restaurants with **fyi** in place of Diamonds are included as an *information only* service for members. These listings provide additional dining choices but have not yet been evaluated.

RESTAURANTS

1 Diamond

One Diamond restaurants provide simple, familiar specialty food (such as burgers, chicken, pizza or tacos) at an economical price. Often self-service, basic surroundings complement a no-nonsense approach.

2 Diamond

Two Diamond restaurants offer a familiar, family-oriented experience. Menu selection includes home-style foods and family favorites, often cooked to order, modestly enhanced and reasonably priced. Service is accommodating yet relaxed, a perfect complement to casual surroundings.

3 Diamond

Three Diamond restaurants convey an entry into fine dining and are often positioned as adult-oriented experiences. The atypical menu may feature the latest cooking trends and/or traditional cuisine. Expanded beverage offerings complement the menu. The ambience is well coordinated, comfortable and enhanced by a professional service staff.

Understanding the Lodging Classifications

To ensure that your lodging needs and preferences are met, we recommend that you consider an establishment's classification when making your travel choices. While the quality and comfort at properties with the same Diamond Rating should be consistent (regardless of the classification), there are differences in typical decor/theme elements, range of facilities and service levels.

Lodging Classifications

Bed & Breakfast

Typically smaller scale properties emphasizing a high degree of personal touches that provide guests an "at home" feeling. Guest units tend to be individually decorated. Rooms may not include some modern amenities such as

1884 Paxton House Inn
Thomasville, GA

televisions and telephones, and may have a shared bathroom. Usually owner-operated with a common room or parlor separate from the innkeeper's living quarters, where guests and operators can interact during evening and breakfast hours. Evening office closures are normal. A continental or full, hot breakfast is served and is included in the room rate.

Cabin

Vacation-oriented, typically smaller scale, freestanding units of simple construction— roughly finished logs or stone—and basic design or décor. Often located in wooded, rural, or waterfront locations. As a rule, basic cleaning supplies, kitchen utensils, and complete bed and bath linens are supplied. The guest registration area may be located off site.

Greenbrier Valley Resorts
Gatlinburg, TN

Condominium

Vacation-oriented—commonly for extended-stay purposes—apartment-style accommodations of varying design or décor. Routinely available for rent through a management company, units often contain one or more bedrooms, a living room, full kitchen, and an eating area. Studio-type models combine the

Sands of Kahana
Kahana, Maui, HI

sleeping and living areas into one room. As a rule, basic cleaning supplies, kitchen utensils, and complete bed and bath linens are supplied. The guest registration area may be located off site.

Cottage

Vacation-oriented, typically smaller scale, freestanding units with home style enhancements in architectural design and interior décor. Often located in wooded, rural, or waterfront locations. Units may vary in design and décor. As a rule, basic cleaning supplies, kitchen utensils, and

Paradise Villas, Little Cayman Island

complete bed and bath linens are supplied. The guest registration area may be located off site.

Country Inn

Although similar in definition to a bed and breakfast, country inns are usually larger in scale with spacious public areas and offer a dining facility that serves—at a minimum— breakfast and dinner.

Greenville Inn, Greenville, ME

Hotel

Commonly, a multistory establishment with interior room entrances offering a variety of guest unit styles. The magnitude of the public areas is determined by the overall theme, location and service level, but

The Grand America Hotel
Salt Lake City, UT

may include a variety of facilities such as a restaurant, shops, fitness center, spa, business center, and/or meeting rooms.

Motel

Commonly, a one- or two-story establishment with exterior room entrances and drive up parking. Typically, guest units have one bedroom with a bathroom of similar décor and design. Public areas and facilities are often limited in size and/or availability.

Best Western Deltona Inn, Deltona, FL

Ranch

Typically a working ranch with an obvious rustic, Western theme featuring equestrian-related activities and a variety of guest unit styles.

Lost Valley Ranch, Deckers, CO

Vacation Rental House

Vacation-oriented—commonly for extended-stay purposes—typically larger scale, freestanding, and of varying design or décor. Routinely available for rent through a management company, houses often contain two or more bedrooms, a living room, full kitchen, dining room, and multiple bathrooms. As a rule, basic cleaning supplies, kitchen utensils, and complete bed and bath linens are supplied. The guest registration area may be located off site.

ResortQuest, Hilton Head Island, SC

Lodging Sub-classifications

The following are sub-classifications that may appear along with the classifications listed previously to provide a more specific description of the lodging.

Boutique

Often thematic and typically an informal, yet highly personalized experience; may have a luxurious or quirky style which is fashionable or unique.

Casino

Extensive gambling facilities are available, such as: blackjack, craps, keno, and slot machines. **Note:** This sub-classification will not appear beneath its Diamond Rating in the listing. It will be indicated by a ⚅ icon and will be included in the row of icons following the lodging listing.

Classic

Renowned and landmark properties, older than 50 years, well-known for their unique style and ambience.

Contemporary

Overall design and theme reflects characteristics of the present era's mainstream tastes and style.

Extended Stay

Offers a predominance of long-term accommodations with a designated full-service kitchen area within each unit.

Historic

These properties are typically over 75 years of age and exhibit many features of a historic nature with respect to architecture, design, furnishings, public record, or acclaim. Properties must meet one of the following criteria:

- Maintain the integrity of the historical nature
- Be listed on the National Register of Historic Places
- Have a National Historic Landmark designation or be located in a National Register Historic District

Separate criteria designate historic properties in Canada, Mexico and the Caribbean.

Resort

Recreation-oriented, geared to vacation travelers seeking a specific destination experience. Travel packages, meal plans, themed entertainment, and social and recreational programs are typically available. Recreational facilities are extensive and may include spa treatments, golf, tennis, skiing, fishing, or water sports. Larger resorts may offer a variety of guest accommodations.

Retro

Overall design and theme reflect a contemporary design reinterpreting styles from a bygone era.

Vacation Rental

Typically houses, condos, cottages or cabins; these properties are a "home away from home" offering more room and greater value for the money. In general, they provide the conveniences of home, such as full kitchens and washers/dryers. Located in resort or popular destination areas within close proximity to major points of interest, attractions, or recreation areas, these properties may require a pre-arranged reservation and check-in at an off-site location. Housekeeping services may be limited or not included.

Vintage

Offers a window to the past and provides an experience reflecting a predominance of traits associated with the era of their origin.

Guest Safety

Room Security

In order to be approved for listing in AAA/CAA TourBook guides for the United States and Canada, accommodations must have deadbolt locks on all guest room entry doors and connecting room doors.

If the area outside the guest room door is not visible from inside the room through a window or door panel, viewports must be installed on all guest room entry doors. Bed and breakfast properties and country inns are not required to have viewports. Ground floor and easily accessible sliding doors must be equipped with some type of secondary security locks.

Even with those approval requirements, AAA cannot guarantee guest safety. AAA inspectors view a percentage of rooms at each property since it is not feasible to evaluate every room in every lodging establishment. Therefore, AAA cannot guarantee that there are working locks on all doors and windows in all guest rooms.

Fire Safety

Because of the highly specialized skills needed to conduct professional fire safety inspections, AAA/CAA inspectors cannot assess fire safety.

Properties must meet all federal, state/province and local fire codes. Each guest unit in all U.S. and Canadian lodging properties must be equipped with an operational, single-station smoke detector. A AAA/CAA inspector has evaluated a sampling of the rooms to verify this equipment is in place.

Mexico and the Caribbean

Requirements for some features, such as door locks and smoke detectors/sprinkler systems, differ in Mexico and the Caribbean. If a property met AAA's security requirements at the time of the evaluation, the phrase "Meets AAA guest room security requirements" appears in the listing.

Service Animals

The Americans with Disabilities Act (ADA) prohibits U.S. businesses that serve the public from discriminating against persons with disabilities. Some businesses have mistakenly denied access to persons who use service animals. Businesses must permit entry to guests and their service animals, as well as allow service animals to accompany guests to all public areas of a property.

A property is permitted to ask whether the animal is a service animal or a pet, and whether the guest has a disability. The property may not, however, ask questions about the nature of the disability, the service provided by the animal, or require proof of a disability or certification that the animal is a service animal. These regulations may not apply in Canada, Mexico or the Caribbean.

No fees or deposits, even those normally charged for pets, may be charged for service animals. Service animals fulfill a critical need for their owners—they are not pets.

Frank Frand with his seeing eye dog, Cardinal.

Connecticut

Center of Culture

Feed your creative appetite in museums, theaters, concert halls and craft shops

Take It Easy

Stroll a secluded beach, drive a country road or browse for antiques

Sailing Back in Time

See the sights and learn about history on a narrated cruise

Author, Author

Tour the homes of Mark Twain and Harriet Beecher Stowe

Go Yale!

Its ivy-covered buildings and Gothic dormitories are among New Haven's many charms

Old Lighthouse Museum, Stonington
© Ric Ergenbright
Danita Delimont Stock Photography

Bethlehem / © Kindra Clineff / age fotostock

G ood things come in small
packages.

And packages don't come much
smaller than gracious Connecticut, which
surpasses only Rhode Island and
Delaware in size.

There's the southwestern corner, home
to celebrities and commuters who enjoy
having easy access to the Big Apple

without having to sacrifice privacy and
space.

The fertile Connecticut River Valley
nurtured the talents of authors Harriet
Beecher Stowe and Mark Twain, both of
whom kept homes in Hartford. It also
fueled the eccentricities of actor William
Gillette, whose peculiar 24-room castle
on a hilltop overlooking the river is open
for tours.

A picture postcard of the great outdoors, the wooded Litchfield Hills boast lush, green valleys; the magnificent 250-foot cascade of Kent Falls; and a pair of romantic covered bridges over the peaceful Housatonic River.

New Haven is Connecticut's intellectual hub. Home to prestigious Yale University, the city is the birthplace of the lollipop, the corkscrew and the steamboat.

A rich maritime history punctuates the personality of Mystic, most noted for its re-created mid-1800s seaport.

The state's emerging locale is the Quiet Corner, a collection of tranquil northeastern towns that share an authentic Colonial feel.

Take the time to unwrap Connecticut. It's a worthwhile delight.

Starting in 1810, when the Hartford Fire Insurance Co. was incorporated as the country's first such business, insurance has been key to Connecticut's economy.

Scads of other providers—among them Mutual Insurance Co., Connecticut Mutual Life Insurance Co., Aetna Life Insurance Co., Travelers Insurance and Connecticut General Life Insurance Co.—have been founded in the state to insure everything from cars and houses to health and life.

Can these companies ensure a delightful escape from the day-to-day grind?

Probably not. But it's highly likely that Connecticut can.

The scenery is spectacular. SR 169, one of Connecticut's two national scenic byways, wends through dense forests, quaint towns and acres of farmland between the Massachusetts border and the Quiet Corner region, in the northeastern quadrant. The other so-designated road is Merritt Parkway, a 38-mile route in southwestern Connecticut lined with interesting bridges.

Get in touch with the outdoors at a nature center. They're in Bristol, Canton, Litchfield, Manchester, Mystic, New Canaan, New Haven, Stamford, Westport and Windsor. Factor

in Audubon centers, and you can add Fairfield, Greenwich and Sharon to that lengthy list.

Breathtaking cascades splash splendor into the landscape. Visit Kent to see the impressive Kent Falls, which tumbles 250 feet over rock ledges. For more watery views, take a cruise along the Connecticut River, among the tiny Thimble Islands or in Long Island Sound.

That Mystical Appeal

Aquatic sightseeing also is popular in Mystic, where water defines the city's past. Penguins, beluga whales and sea lions are among the residents at Mystic Aquarium & Institute for Exploration. The houses, shops and buildings that make up Mystic Seaport paint a picture of 19th-century life, while the local maritime museum displays such items as ship models and figureheads.

Nearby Groton sustains this focus in a museum that houses the world's first nuclear-powered submarine.

Other aspects of history are recounted, too. Trace Revolutionary War events at Fort Griswold State Park in Groton, Shaw Mansion in New London and Webb-Deane-Stevens Museum in Wethersfield.

Dutch explorer Adriaen Block maps the Connecticut coastline.
1614

Yale University is founded as the Collegiate School.
1701

Michael Marsland
Yale University

The *Nile* returns to New London after 11 years at sea, the longest whaling voyage on record.
1869

1662
Governor John Winthrop Jr. obtains a royal charter for the colony.

Library of Congress

Connecticut Historical Timeline

1806
Noah Webster, born in West Hartford, publishes the first American dictionary.

Learn about the military at The U.S. Coast Guard Museum in New London or at Military Historians Museum in Westbrook. Explore American Indian heritage at such places as Mashantucket Pequot Museum & Research Center in Ledyard, Mohegan Indian Burial Ground in Norwich and The Institute for American Indian Studies in Washington.

The Constitution State is the birthplace of plenty of creative folks, such as showman P.T. Barnum and the diminutive spotlight of his circus, Gen. Tom Thumb (a.k.a. Charles Thurwood Stratton), both of Bridgeport; composer Charles Ives, of Danbury; author Harriet Beecher Stowe, of Litchfield; and lexicographer Noah Webster, of West Hartford.

Also originating here were numerous inventions, including the Colt revolver, portable typewriter, sewing machine, can opener, lollipop, Frisbee, vacuum cleaner, Polaroid camera, helicopter and color TV.

A Who's Who of Nutmeggers

Noted nutmeggers, as Connecticut residents colloquially are dubbed, include Mark Twain, who lived for 27 years in Hartford; opera singer Marian Anderson, who called Danbury home; and Nobel Prize-winning playwright Eugene O'Neill, who grew up in New London. The castle that is the centerpiece of Gillette Castle State Park was the home of William Gillette. The eccentric actor, who designed unique locks for each of the doors to castle rooms, implored his family not to sell the estate to some "blithering saphead" upon his death.

There are places to view exquisite art. Impressionist pieces by such masters as Mary Cassatt, Edgar Degas and Edouard Manet decorate the walls of Farmington's Hill-Stead Museum. New Britain Museum of American Art includes works by Winslow Homer and James McNeill Whistler. At New Haven's Yale University Art Gallery you'll find paintings by Claude Monet, Pablo Picasso and Vincent van Gogh.

If crafts are more your style, stop by Brookfield Craft Center in Brookfield or Silvermine Guild Arts Center in New Canaan.

In Connecticut, you'll run out of acreage before you deplete your options for fun.

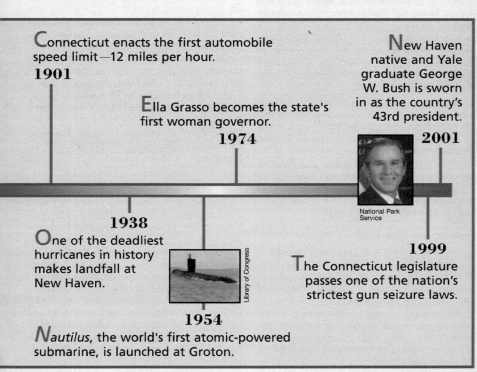

Connecticut enacts the first automobile speed limit—12 miles per hour.
1901

Ella Grasso becomes the state's first woman governor.
1974

New Haven native and Yale graduate George W. Bush is sworn in as the country's 43rd president.
2001

National Park Service

1938
One of the deadliest hurricanes in history makes landfall at New Haven.

Library of Congress

1999
The Connecticut legislature passes one of the nation's strictest gun seizure laws.

1954
Nautilus, the world's first atomic-powered submarine, is launched at Groton.

Recreation

Although small in size, Connecticut is plenty big on recreation.

State parks along the rocky coast boast beautiful sandy beaches. Whether you prefer **swimming** or just sprawling on a towel, Hammonasset Beach, west of Clinton, Rocky Neck, near Niantic, and Sherwood Island, in Westport, all fit the bill.

Long Island Sound is the top destination for water lovers. Forget about your troubles while **boating** in the sparkling blue waters, or cast your **fishing** line to see if the bluefish, striped bass and flounder are biting. You can charter a boat from many towns along the shore.

Also a lure for boaters are the Thimble Islands, a cluster of many tiny islands just offshore from Branford.

Inland, you'll find lots more water—more than 80 lakes and ponds and more than 300 miles of rivers and streams. Avid anglers head to the western upland region and to the Farmington and Housatonic rivers, where bass as well as brown and rainbow trout nearly always are running. Only fly fishing is permitted on the section of the Housatonic in Housatonic Meadows State Park, in Cornwall Bridge.

For a leisurely way to pass the day, try **canoeing** or **kayaking** on the Connecticut or Housatonic rivers. Or just float your woes away while **tubing** on the lazy Farmington River, near New Hartford.

Don an oxygen tank and flippers and go **scuba diving** at Lake Waramaug State Park, in New Preston; Pachaug State Forest, north of Voluntown; Rocky Neck State Park, near Niantic; or Squantz Pond, in New Fairfield.

The Constitution State boasts more than its fair share of waterfalls. **Hiking** trails lead to Chapman Falls, at Devil's Hopyard in East Haddam; Kent Falls, north of Kent on US 7; and Shelter Falls, near Mansfield.

Taking on The Trail

Serious trekkers can take on a stretch of the Appalachian Trail, which follows the Housatonic for a while before veering east to Cornwall, then turning north near Lakeville to the Massachusetts state line.

Other hiking routes lead to vantage points offering spectacular countryside vistas. Neighboring New York, Massachusetts and Rhode Island are visible from the tower atop Talcott Mountain, in Simsbury.

It's also perfectly acceptable to **climb** all over the sleeping giant rock formation at Sleeping Giant State Park, in Hamden. A 1.6-mile trail on the "left hip" of the resting body leads to a four-story observation tower.

Outstanding paths at Canaan Mountain, near Canaan, and Topsmead State Forest, east of Litchfield, attract **horseback riding** enthusiasts. An 8-mile trail from Hamden to Lock 12 Historical Park, in Cheshire, awaits hikers, **bicycling** enthusiasts and inline **skaters.** Mountain biking is among the biggest draws at Nepaug State Forest, east of Torrington.

To maximize any outdoor experience, plan your trip around the Columbus Day holiday, when fall foliage usually is at its most vibrant.

Ready to Chill Out

When the temperature drops, fun-seekers head for the slopes. **Downhill skiing** resorts—Mohawk Mountain, off SR 4 near Cornwall; Mount Southington, near Hartford; Ski Sundown, in New Hartford; and Woodbury Ski Area, in Woodbury—cater to skiers of all abilities.

Cross-country skiing and **snowshoeing** are other winter diversions. Visit Macedonia Brook State Park in Kent, Putnam Memorial State Park in West Redding or Squantz Pond State Park in New Fairfield. Kick your cold-weather thrills up a notch by **snowmobiling** through state forests such as Cockaponset, west of Chester; Natchaug, south of Phoenixville; or Peoples, north of Pleasant Valley. The Connecticut Department of Environmental Protection offers trail maps for the 11 state-owned areas where snowmobiling is permitted; snowmobiles must be registered with the Department of Motor Vehicles.

Recreational Activities

Throughout the TourBook, you may notice a Recreational Activities heading with bulleted listings of recreation-oriented establishments listed underneath. Similar operations also may be mentioned in Destination City recreation sections. Since normal AAA inspection criteria cannot be applied, these establishments are presented only for information. Age, height and weight restrictions may apply. Reservations often are recommended and sometimes are required. Addresses and/or phone numbers are provided so visitors can contact the attraction for additional information.

Fast Facts

POPULATION: 3,405,565.

AREA: 5,009 square miles; ranks 48th.

CAPITAL: Hartford.

HIGHEST POINT: 2,380 ft., Mount Frissell, in Salisbury.

LOWEST POINT: Sea level, Long Island Sound.

TIME ZONE(S): Eastern. DST.

TEEN DRIVING LAWS: Driving is not permitted 11 p.m.-5 a.m. No passengers, with the exception of parents, a licensed driving instructor or an instructor more than 20 years old and with 4 years of licensed, suspension-free driving, are permitted during the first 6 months. In addition to these persons, family members are permitted as passengers during the final 6 months of the first year. The minimum age for an unrestricted driver's license is 18. Phone (860) 263-5700 for more information about Connecticut's driver's license regulations.

MINIMUM AGE FOR GAMBLING: 18 for bingo; 21 for casinos.

SEAT BELT/CHILD RESTRAINT LAWS: Seat belts required for driver and front seat passengers ages 16 and older. Passengers ages 7 until 16 and at least 60 lbs. are required to use a seat belt or child restraint. Child restraints required for passengers under 7 years and less than 60 lbs.

CELL PHONE RESTRICTIONS: All drivers are prohibited from any use of hand-held cell phones, including text messaging. Teen drivers are prohibited from using any type of cell phone. State law also prohibits distracted driving, defined as any activity unrelated to the actual operation of a motor vehicle and interfering with the vehicle's safe operation.

HELMETS FOR MOTORCYCLISTS: Required for riders under 18.

RADAR DETECTORS: Permitted.

MOVE OVER LAW: Driver is required to slow down and vacate the lane nearest police, fire and rescue vehicles, as well as tow trucks, stopped roadside and using audible and/or flashing signals.

FIREARMS LAWS: Vary by state and/or county. Contact the Department of Public Safety, Special Licensing and Firearm Unit, 1111 Country Club Rd., Middletown, CT 06457, (860) 685-8290.

HOLIDAYS: Jan. 1; Martin Luther King Jr. Day, Jan. (3rd Mon.); Lincoln's Birthday, Feb. 12; Presidents Day, Feb. (3rd Mon.); Good Friday; Memorial Day, May (last Mon.); July 4; Labor Day; Columbus Day, Oct. (2nd Mon.); Veterans Day, Nov. 11; Thanksgiving; Christmas, Dec. 25.

TAXES: Connecticut's statewide sales tax is 6 percent. There is an admissions tax of 10 percent on most places of amusement.

INFORMATION CENTERS: The state welcome centers at I-95 northbound at Darien; I-95 southbound at North Stonington; I-84 eastbound at Danbury; I-84 westbound at Willington; and on the Merritt Pkwy. (SR 15) at Greenwich are open daily year-round. A center northbound on I-95 at Westbrook is open daily Memorial Day to Columbus Day; Thurs.-Sun. rest of year. Centers on I-91 northbound at Middletown and southbound at Wallingford are not staffed but have tourism literature available. Visitor information also is available in Terminals A and B of Bradley International Airport, Windsor Locks.

AREA CODE REQUIRED: Whenever you make a local call within Connecticut from a 203, 475, 860 or 959 area code, you must dial the area code as well as the seven-digit telephone number.

FURTHER INFORMATION FOR VISITORS:
Connecticut Commission on Culture & Tourism
One Constitution Plaza
2nd Floor
Hartford, CT 06103
(860) 256-2800 or
(888) 288-4748

RECREATION INFORMATION:
State of Connecticut Department of Environmental Protection
79 Elm St.
Hartford, CT 06106-5127
(860) 424-3000

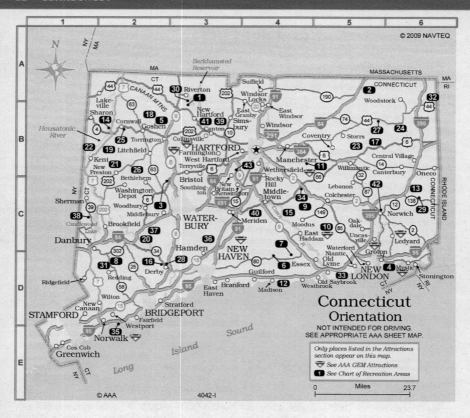

© 2009 NAVTEQ

Connecticut
Orientation

NOT INTENDED FOR DRIVING.
SEE APPROPRIATE AAA SHEET MAP.

Only places listed in the Attractions
section appear on this map.
See AAA GEM Attractions
See Chart of Recreation Areas

0   Miles   23.7

© AAA   4042-I

RECREATION AREAS

RECREATION AREAS	MAP LOCATION	CAMPING	PICNICKING	HIKING TRAILS	BOATING	BOAT RAMP	BOAT RENTAL	FISHING	SWIMMING	PETS ON LEASH	BICYCLE TRAILS	WINTER SPORTS	VISITOR CENTER	LODGE/CABINS	FOOD SERVICE
STATE															
American Legion (A-3) 782 acres 1 mi. n. of Pleasant Valley on West River Rd. Canoeing and kayaking only, cross-country skiing, hunting, snowmobiling.	**1**	●	●	●	●	●		●		●		●			
Bigelow Hollow (A-5) 513 acres 2 mi. n. of Union on SR 197. Cross-country skiing, scuba diving, snowmobiling.	**2**		●	●	●	●	●	●		●		●			
Black Rock (C-2) 444 acres 3 mi. s.w. of Thomaston on US 6.	**3**	●	●	●				●	●	●		●			●
Bluff Point Coastal Reserve (D-6) 806 acres 5 mi. s.e. of Groton off US 1. Saltwater and shell fishing.	**4**		●	●				●		●	●	●			
Burr Pond (B-2) 438 acres 5 mi. n. of Torrington off SR 8.	**5**		●	●	●	●	●	●	●	●		●			●
Chatfield Hollow (D-4) 356 acres 1.5 mi. w. of Killingworth on SR 80. Cross-country skiing.	**6**		●	●				●	●	●					●
Cockaponset (C-4) 15,652 acres 3 mi. w. of Chester on SR 148. Cross-country skiing, horseback riding, hunting, snowmobiling.	**7**		●	●				●	●	●		●			
Collis P. Huntington (D-2) 883 acres n. of Redding on Sunset Hill Rd. Canoeing, cross-country skiing, horseback riding, hunting.	**8**		●	●	●			●		●		●			
Day Pond (C-4) 180 acres .5 mi. n. of Westchester on SR 149. Horse trails.	**9**		●	●				●	●	●		●			
Devil's Hopyard (C-5) 860 acres 3 mi. n. of North Plain off SR 82. Bird-watching.	**10**	●	●	●				●		●		●			
Gay City (B-5) 1,569 acres 8 mi. s.e. of Manchester on SR 85. Ice skating; horse trails.	**11**		●	●				●	●	●		●			
Hammonasset Beach (D-4) 923 acres 2 mi. e. of Madison off US 1; 1 mi. s. off I-95 exit 62. Canoeing and kayaking only.	**12**	●	●	●	●	●		●	●	●		●	●		●
Hopeville Pond (C-6) 554 acres s.e. of Hopeville on SR 201.	**13**	●	●	●	●	●		●	●	●		●			
Housatonic Meadows (B-2) 452 acres 1 mi. n. of Cornwall Bridge on US 7. Canoeing and kayaking only.	**14**	●	●	●	●			●		●		●			
Hurd (C-4) 884 acres w. of Haddam Neck off SR 151. Bird-watching, canoe camping.	**15**	●	●	●				●		●		●			
Indian Well (D-2) 153 acres 2 mi. n.w. of Shelton on SR 110.	**16**		●	●	●	●		●	●	●					
James L. Goodwin (B-5) 2,171 acres 3 miles e. of South Chaplin on US 6. Bird-watching, boating (electric motors only), cross-country skiing; gardens, horse trails.	**17**	●	●	●	●	●		●		●		●	●		
John A. Minetto (B-2) 678 acres 5 mi. n. of Torrington on SR 272. Cross-country skiing, ice skating. Walk-in access only.	**18**		●	●				●		●		●			
Kent Falls (B-2) 275 acres 4 mi. n.e. of Kent on US 7. *(See Kent p. 62)*	**19**		●	●				●		●					
Kettletown (C-2) 492 acres 6 mi. s. of Southbury off I-84 exit 15.	**20**	●	●	●				●	●	●					
Lake Waramaug (B-2) 95 acres 5 mi. n. of New Preston on Lake Waramaug Rd. (SR 478). Canoeing and kayaking only, ice skating, scuba diving.	**21**	●	●	●	●	●	●	●	●	●		●			●
Macedonia Brook (B-1) 2,300 acres 4 mi. n.w. of Kent off SR 341. Cross-country skiing.	**22**	●	●	●				●		●		●			
Mansfield Hollow (B-5) 2,328 acres 1 mi. e. of Mansfield Center off SR 89. Cross-country skiing.	**23**		●	●	●	●		●		●	●	●			
Mashamoquet Brook (B-6) 860 acres 5 mi. s.w. of Putnam on US 44.	**24**	●	●	●				●	●	●					
Mohawk Mountain (B-2) 259 acres 6 mi. w. of Goshen off SR 4. Cross-country and downhill skiing.	**25**		●	●				●		●		●			
Mount Tom (B-2) 232 acres 3.5 mi. w. of Bantam off US 202. Ice skating, scuba diving; observation tower.	**26**		●	●	●		●	●	●	●		●			●
Natchaug (B-5) 12,935 acres 4 mi. s. of Phoenixville on SR 198. Historic. Cross-country skiing, hunting, snowmobiling; horse trails.	**27**	●	●	●				●		●		●	●		

RECREATION AREAS

	MAP LOCATION	CAMPING	PICNICKING	HIKING TRAILS	BOATING	BOAT RAMP	BOAT RENTAL	FISHING	SWIMMING	PETS ON LEASH	BICYCLE TRAILS	WINTER SPORTS	VISITOR CENTER	LODGE/CABINS	FOOD SERVICE
Osbornedale (D-3) 350 acres 1 mi. n.w. of Derby off US 34. Ice skating.	28		•	•				•		•		•	•		
Pachaug (C-6) 23,938 acres 1 mi. n. of Voluntown. Snowmobiling.	29	•	•	•	•	•	•	•	•	•		•	•	•	
Peoples (A-3) 2,942 acres 1 mi. n. of Pleasant Valley on East River Rd. Canoeing, cross-country skiing, kayaking, snowmobiling, tubing.	30		•	•	•			•		•		•			
Putnam Memorial (D-2) 183 acres n. of Redding at jct. SRs 107/58. Historic. Cross-country skiing, ice skating; museum. *(See Redding p. 73)*	31		•	•				•		•		•	•		
Quaddick (A-6) 116 acres 7 mi. n.e. of Putnam off SR 44. Ice skating.	32		•		•	•		•		•		•			
Rocky Neck (D-5) 710 acres 1 mi. e. of South Lyme off I-95 exit 72. Scuba diving; beach.	33	•	•	•				•	•	•					•
Salmon River (C-4) 6,115 acres 1 mi. n. of Westchester, 2 mi. w. of SR 149 on River Rd. Historic. Hunting, snowmobiling.	34		•	•				•		•		•			
Sherwood Island (E-2) 234 acres 2 mi. s. of Westport off I-95 exit 18. Observation platform.	35		•					•	•	•			•		•
Sleeping Giant (C-3) 1,439 acres 3 mi. n. of Hamden off SR 10. Observation tower.	36		•	•				•		•		•			
Southford Falls (C-2) 120 acres 4 mi. s.w. of Southbury on SR 188. Cross-country skiing, ice skating.	37		•	•				•		•		•			
Squantz Pond (C-1) 172 acres 4 mi. n. of New Fairfield on SR 39. Cross-country skiing, ice skating, scuba diving; beach. Leashed pets are allowed Oct. 1 to mid-Apr.	38		•	•	•	•	•	•	•	•		•			•
Stratton Brook (B-3) 148 acres 2 mi. w. of Simsbury on SR 309. Cross-country skiing, ice skating.	39		•	•				•	•	•	•	•	•		
Wadsworth Falls (C-4) 285 acres 3 mi. s.w. of Middlefield on SR 157.	40		•	•				•	•						
OTHER															
Lake McDonough (B-3) 3 mi. n.e. of New Hartford on SR 219.	41		•	•	•	•	•	•	•	•					
Mohegan Park and Memorial Rose Garden (C-5) 380 acres e. of Norwich off SR 32 on Judd Rd. *(See Norwich p. 72)*	42		•	•				•	•						
Stanley Quarter Park (B-4) 225 acres in New Britain, n. of Central Park on Stanley St. Skateboarding; paddleboat rental.	43		•	•				•		•	•	•	•		

Connecticut Temperature Averages
Maximum/Minimum
From the records of The Weather Channel Interactive, Inc.

	JAN	FEB	MAR	APR	MAY	JUNE	JULY	AUG	SEPT	OCT	NOV	DEC
Bridgeport	37 / 23	39 / 25	47 / 32	57 / 41	67 / 51	76 / 60	82 / 66	81 / 65	74 / 58	63 / 46	53 / 38	42 / 28
Hartford	35 / 16	39 / 19	47 / 27	59 / 38	70 / 48	79 / 57	84 / 63	82 / 61	74 / 51	63 / 40	52 / 32	40 / 22
New Haven	35 / 17	37 / 19	46 / 28	57 / 37	68 / 47	77 / 56	83 / 62	81 / 60	73 / 52	62 / 41	50 / 32	39 / 23

Points of Interest

BETHLEHEM (C-2) pop. 3,422, elev. 861'

Once part of Woodbury, Bethlehem was settled in the early 18th century and incorporated in 1787. God-fearing Puritan settlers named more than 30 Connecticut places after the devil, and Bethlehem is no exception: east of town is a ridge known as the Devil's Backbone.

The Bethlehem Fair, at the Bethlehem Fairgrounds off SR 61, is held the Fri.-Sun. following Labor Day and offers stage shows, competitions and demonstrations, dancing and live music; phone (203) 266-5350. Bethlehem's town green and its surrounding buildings are decorated with lights during the Christmas Town Festival, held the first Fri.-Sat. of December. Attendees may listen to holiday storytelling, craft ornaments and observe a candlelight procession; phone (203) 266-5557 for event schedule. Throughout the month, thousands of visitors arrive to mail their Christmas cards with a Bethlehem postmark.

The 400-acre Abbey of Regina Laudis, 273 Flanders Rd., is home to a community of Benedictine nuns. On permanent display is an 18th-century Neapolitan crèche, an elaborate nativity scene containing 63 hand-carved figures. The site's The Gary-The Olivia Performing Arts Center hosts a music festival in June and offers performances late July-early Aug. Phone (203) 266-7637 for the abbey, or (203) 273-5669 for the performing arts center.

SAVE **THE BELLAMY-FERRIDAY HOUSE & GARDEN** is at jct. SRs 61 and 132 at 9 Main St. N. The site was the 18th-century home of Rev. Joseph Bellamy, a prominent Colonial minister. Henry Ferriday of New York later purchased the sprawling farmstead and made it his family's early 20th-century summer home; his daughter, Carolyn Woolsey Ferriday, continued stewardship until bequeathing the property to the state in 1990. The property features American antiques, historic barns and outbuildings and a 1915 formal garden. **Time:** Allow 1 hour minimum. **Hours:** Wed. and Fri.-Sun. 11-4, May-Aug.; Sat.-Sun. 11-4, Sept.-Oct. **Cost:** $7; $6 (senior citizens, educators and students with ID); $4 (ages 6-18); $15 (family, two adults and children). **Phone:** (203) 266-7596.

BRANFORD (D-3) pop. 28,683, elev. 17'

Established in 1644, the coastal village of Branford became a popular Long Island Sound vacation spot at the turn of the 20th century. Short Beach, Branford Point, Indian Neck, Pine Orchard and Stony Creek—granite coves known as the "five fingers" of Branford—lured many summer vacationers. The hundreds of rocky islands just offshore are known collectively as the Thimble Islands; only a few dozen are inhabited.

Harrison House and Museum, 124 Main St., is a 1724 house with period furnishings, local historical items and archives, an herb garden and a barn. Tours are offered Saturday 2 to 5 June through September and by appointment; phone (203) 488-4828.

Branford Chamber of Commerce: 239 N. Main St., P.O. Box 375, Branford, CT 06405. **Phone:** (203) 488-5500.

SEA MIST **THIMBLE ISLANDS CRUISE** departs from the Stony Creek dock, 3 mi. s. of I-95 exit 56 to Leetes Island Rd., following signs. Capt. Mike Infantino takes passengers on a narrated 45 minute tour of the 25 inhabited islands in the Thimble archipelago. Seal watch cruises are offered in March. **Hours:** Tours board on the hour and depart on the quarter-hour Wed.-Mon. 10:15-4:15, July-Aug.; Wed.-Mon. at 10:15, 12:15, 2:15 and 4:15, in June; Fri.-Sun. at 10:15, 12:15, 2:15 and 4:15, in May and Sept.; Sat.-Sun. at noon and 2, in Oct. (weather permitting). **Cost:** Fare $10; $9 (ages 66+); $5 (ages 0-12). **Phone:** (203) 488-8905.

VOLSUNGA IV **THIMBLE ISLANDS CRUISE** departs from the Stony Creek dock, 3 mi. s. of I-95 exit 56 to Leetes Island Rd., following signs. Capt. Bob Milne guides a 45-minute tour of the 25 granite islands in Long Island Sound. **Hours:** Tours leave daily at 11, 1 and 3, in May; Tues.-Fri. at 11, noon, 1 and 3, Sat.-Sun. on the hour 11-4, in June; Tues.-Sun. on the hour 11-4, July-Aug.; Tues.-Sun. at 11, 1 and 3 (also Sat.-Sun. at noon), in Sept.; Sat.-Sun. at 11, 1 and 3, Oct. 1-Oct. 18 (weather permitting). Phone ahead to confirm schedule. **Cost:** Fare $10; $9 (ages 66+); $5 (ages 0-12). The trip is not recommended for children ages 0-2. **Phone:** (203) 481-3345.

BRIDGEPORT (D-2) pop. 139,529, elev. 12'

Residents of the older settlements of Fairfield and Stratford first moved to this harbor on the Pequonnock River in 1639. Known as Newtown, then Stratfield, the community was incorporated as Bridgeport in 1821; by 1836 it had become a city. As in many New England seaport towns, its first economic activity was whaling, which gave way to industry with the coming of the railroad.

Bridgeport was the home of P.T. Barnum and the 1838 birthplace of Charles Thurwood Stratton, who was only 25 inches tall until he was in his teens and 40 inches tall at maturity. Billed as "General" Tom Thumb, Stratton was the main attraction of Barnum's "Greatest Show on Earth."

Another tiny resident of Bridgeport is the monk parakeet, a native of South America. Feral colonies of the bright green birds live along the coast from Norwalk to Branford. Also known as Quaker parrots, these former pets survive the New England winter in communal stick nests that often span 6 feet.

The Port Jefferson Ferry provides daily car ferry service from Bridgeport to Port Jefferson, N.Y.; phone (888) 443-3779.

SAVE **THE BARNUM MUSEUM** is at 820 Main St. Exhibits chronicle the life and times of P.T. Barnum. The three-story museum presents three themes: Barnum the Man; Barnum's American Museum; and Bridgeport & Barnum. A scale model of a miniature five-ring circus is included. A 5-minute introductory film runs continuously. Changing displays also are presented. **Time:** Allow 1 hour minimum. **Hours:** Tues.-Sat. 10-4:30, Sun. noon-4:30. Last admission is 45 minutes before closing. Closed major holidays. **Cost:** $7; $5 (ages 65+ and active military and students with ID); $4 (ages 4-17). **Phone:** (203) 331-1104.

SAVE **CONNECTICUT'S BEARDSLEY ZOO** is in Beardsley Park at 1875 Noble Ave. The 36-acre zoo features more than 300 animals in North and South American outdoor habitats. Endangered species include the Siberian tiger, the Andean spectacled bear and the golden lion tamarin. The zoo features a New England petting farm, an indoor rain forest and a seasonal carousel. **Time:** Allow 2 hours minimum. **Hours:** Daily 9-4. Closed Jan. 1, Thanksgiving and Dec. 25. **Cost:** $11; $9 (ages 3-11 and 62+). **Phone:** (203) 394-6565. 🍴 🅿️

SAVE **THE DISCOVERY MUSEUM AND PLANETARIUM** is 1 mi. s. of Merritt Parkway exit 47 at 4450 Park Ave. Interactive exhibits and a play area invite children to explore the science behind electricity, energy, sound and space. Permanent exhibits include ViewSpace, an internet-fed view from Space Telescope Science Institute in Baltimore, Md. The Henry B. duPont III Planetarium features simulated night sky views. Traveling exhibits change three times a year.

Time: Allow 3 hours minimum. **Hours:** Museum open Tues.-Sat. 10-5, Sun. noon-5 (also Mon. 10-5, July-Aug.), Sept.-June. Planetarium shows Mon.-Fri. at 11, 1, 2 and 3:30, Sat.-Sun. at 1, 2 and 3, July-Aug.; Tues.-Fri. at 1 and 3, Sat.-Sun. at 1, 2 and 3, rest of year. **Cost:** Museum and planetarium $8.50; $7 (ages 5-17, ages 65+ and students with ID). **Phone:** (203) 372-3521. 🍴 🅿️

BRISTOL—*see Hartford p. 55.*

BROOKFIELD (C-2) elev. 285'

In 1743, settlers on the outskirts of Danbury asked for permission to establish a new town with its own meetinghouse, because traveling to church in the winter was a hardship. Eleven years later, the parish of Newbury was formed. In 1788, the General Assembly approved the new name of Brookfield after Thomas Brooks, the parish's first minister.

BROOKFIELD CRAFT CENTER is just s. of US 7 on SR 25 in the historic Mill Building. The craft school is known for its innovative classes and workshops, including such specialized fields as woodworking, glass blowing, boat building and blacksmithing. An exhibition gallery presents the works of metalsmiths, glassblowers, weavers, potters and other artisans. **Hours:** Mon.-Sat. 10-5, Sun. noon-5. Closed major holidays. **Cost:** Free. **Phone:** (203) 775-4526.

WINERIES

• **DiGrazia Vineyards** is .9 mi. e. of jct. SRs 25 and 133, then just s. to 131 Tower Rd. **Hours:** Daily 11-5, May-Dec.; Sat.-Sun. 11-5, rest of year. Closed major holidays. **Phone:** (203) 775-1616.

CANTERBURY (B-5)

The Canterbury Female Boarding School, a private academy for young women, opened in 1831. A year later, when headmistress Prudence Crandall agreed to admit an African-American student named Sarah Harris, local parents withdrew their daughters.

Crandall, a Quaker, saved the school by recruiting other "young ladies of color" from as far away as Boston and New York City. Despite a town boycott—and the passage of a state law prohibiting African Americans from coming into Connecticut to attend school—Crandall continued to teach minority students. She was arrested in 1833 and later won a supreme court case, but an angry mob ransacked the school, forcing its closure. Canterbury became a landmark in the national debate over abolition and integration.

THE PRUDENCE CRANDALL MUSEUM is on the Canterbury Green at SRs 14 and 169. The museum occupies the 1805 house in which Prudence Crandall conducted an academy for young African-American women 1833-34. An elaborate entrance doorway and a second floor Palladian window are among the Federal-style architectural features of the house. Permanent and changing exhibits explore Prudence Crandall's life, women's history and local history.

Time: Allow 1 hour minimum. **Hours:** Wed.-Sat. 10-4, Apr. 1 to mid-Dec. Last ticket sold 30 minutes before closing. Closed Good Friday, Easter, July 4, Veterans Day and Thanksgiving. **Cost:** $6; $4 (ages 6-17, ages 60+ and students with ID). Phone ahead to confirm schedule and rates as changes may occur without notice. **Phone:** (860) 546-7800.

CANTON—*see Hartford p. 55.*

CENTRAL VILLAGE (B-5) elev. 185'

Founded about 1825 on the Moosup River, Central Village features several houses dating from the 18th century.

QUINEBAUG VALLEY TROUT HATCHERY is 1.7 mi. n.w. of I-395 exit 89 via SR 14, following signs to 141 Trout Hatchery Rd. One of the largest fish hatcheries east of the Mississippi, this is the first to use round tanks. About 600,000 trout are raised annually; glass walls in the visitor center allow viewing into the hatchery. Informational exhibits also are displayed. **Hours:** Visitor center open daily 9-3:30. **Cost:** Free. **Phone:** (860) 564-7542.

COLCHESTER (C-5) elev. 472'

WINERIES

• **Priam Vineyards** is 1.7 mi. s. of jct. SRs 2 and 149, then just w. to 11 Shailor Hill Rd. **Hours:** Fri.-Sun. 11-5, Mar.-Dec. **Phone:** (860) 267-8520.

COLLINSVILLE—*see Hartford p. 55.*

CORNWALL (B-2) elev. 437'

The Cornwalls—comprising Cornwall, Cornwall Bridge, Cornwall Center, Cornwall Hollow and West Cornwall—are villages nestled in the Litchfield Hills. The charming scenery has attracted many artists. The West Cornwall Covered Bridge, built in 1864, spans the Housatonic River. It is one of two such bridges in the state open to automobile traffic.

RECREATIONAL ACTIVITIES

Fishing

• **Housatonic River Outfitters** is 3.4 mi. s.w. on Furnace Brook Rd. (SR 4), then 1.2 mi. s.w. to 24 Kent Rd. S. (US 7S) in nearby Cornwall Bridge. Other activities are offered. **Hours:** Trips depart late Mar.-early Oct. **Phone:** (860) 672-1010.

Skiing

• **Mohawk Mountain Ski Area** is .2 mi. n. on Pine St., .8 mi. e. on Cemetery Hill Rd. (SR 4), then just s. to 46 Great Hollow Rd. Other summer and winter activities are offered. **Hours:** Open daily Thanksgiving-early Apr. **Phone:** (860) 672-6100 or (800) 895-5222.

COS COB (E-1)

A summer retreat for New Yorkers, the rural village of Cos Cob developed into an art colony in the late 19th century. The residence of art teacher John Twachtman and the Bush-Holley house became gathering places for artists and writers. The town's name is said to come for the Algonquin word *Cassacubque,* meaning "high rocks."

BUSH-HOLLEY HISTORIC SITE is off I-95 exit 4 to 39 Strickland Rd. The Bush-Holley boarding house was a favorite haunt for members of the Cos Cob art colony, which thrived 1890-1920. The visitor center in an 1805 storehouse features the William Hegarty Gallery, which showcases Greenwich history and artistically significant exhibits. The house, open by guided tour, contains an American Impressionist art collection and historic interiors. A research library is on site.

Hours: Visitor center open Tues.-Sun. noon-4. House tours depart on the hour Wed.-Sun. 1-3, Mar.-Dec.; Fri.-Sun. noon-4, rest of year. Archives Tues.

and Thurs. 10-12:30 and 1-4. Library open Wed.-Thurs. 10-4. Closed major holidays. **Cost:** $10; $8 (ages 65+ and students with ID); free (ages 0-6 and Tues.). **Phone:** (203) 869-6899, ext. 10.

COVENTRY (B-4)

First settled in 1700, Coventry was incorporated in 1711. From this rolling region issued livestock products for the West India trade as well as the Morgan pacing horse that could make the 72-mile trip to Boston in one day and return the next.

Shopping areas: The downtown area features a variety of antique and specialty shops.

NATHAN HALE HOMESTEAD is 4 mi. s. of SR 44 on South St., following signs. Revolutionary War patriot and official State Hero Capt. Nathan Hale was born on this farm in 1755. The family rebuilt the house in 1776, the same year Hale was captured by the British and hanged as a spy. The house is restored and furnished with many Hale family possessions. **Hours:** Guided tours depart on the hour and half-hour Wed. and Fri.-Sun. 11-4, mid-May to mid-Oct. **Cost:** $7; $6 (senior citizens); $4 (ages 6-18 and students with ID); $15 (family, two adults plus children). **Phone:** (860) 742-6917 or (860) 247-8996.

DANBURY (C-1) pop. 74,848, elev. 371'

Founded by eight families in 1684, Danbury included the town of Bethel until 1855. Supplies were stored locally during the Revolution, and in 1777 Gen. William Tryon's British troops burned many of the stores and buildings. Gen. David Wooster led a force in pursuit of the British; he was mortally wounded in one of the ensuing battles and was buried here.

For nearly two centuries Danbury was the hat city of the world. Since the early 1950s Danbury's economic base has undergone a dramatic transition and now comprises a broad range of corporate headquarters and businesses related to metal fabrication and high technology products, pharmaceuticals, biomedical products, paper, publishing, energy and aerospace product development.

Pulitzer Prize-winning composer Charles Ives was born in Danbury, and famed opera singer Marian Anderson made the city her home for 50 years. The Danbury Museum & Historical Society, 43 Main St., offers tours of the Ives Homestead, Anderson Studio, 1785 Rider House, 1790 Dodd Hat Shop and a restored schoolhouse; phone (203) 743-5200. Musical and theatrical performances are presented each summer at Charles Ives Concert Park and at other locations throughout the city.

Greater Danbury Chamber of Commerce: 39 West St., Danbury, CT 06810. **Phone:** (203) 743-5565.

DANBURY RAILWAY MUSEUM is off I-84 exit 5, s. onto Main St. then e. to 120 White St. Housed in Danbury's restored 1903 station and rail yard, the museum depicts the history of railroading in the Northeast. Vintage equipment, photographs, artifacts and scale models are among interpretive displays. A guided tour of the rail yard allows visitors to walk through several trains. The Rail Yard Local train provides a view of the historic rail yard on 25-minute rides, given on weekends. **Time:** Allow 30 minutes minimum. **Hours:** Mon.-Sat. 10-5, Sun. noon-5, Memorial Day-Labor Day; Wed.-Sat. 10-4, Sun. noon-4, rest of year. Turntable rides are available Sat.-Sun., Apr.-Nov. Closed major holidays. **Cost:** $6; $5 (ages 62+); $4 (ages 3-12). Prices increase during special events. **Phone:** (203) 778-8337.

MILITARY MUSEUM OF SOUTHERN NEW ENGLAND is at 125 Park Ave. Displayed outside are tanks, armored vehicles and artillery pieces from World War II and the Korean and Vietnam wars. Inside, life-size dioramas feature medals, photographs, uniforms, heavy fighting vehicles and artillery pieces. **Time:** Allow 1 hour minimum. **Hours:** Tues.-Sat. 10-5, Sun. noon-5, Apr.-Nov.; Fri.-Sat. 10-5, Sun. 1-5, rest of year. Closed Jan. 1, Easter, Thanksgiving and Dec. 25. **Cost:** $6; $4 (ages 5-18, ages 62+ and active military with ID). **Phone:** (203) 790-9277.

DERBY (D-2) pop. 12,391, elev. 16'

First inhabited by Paugassett and Pootatuck Indians, the Derby area was settled by fur traders in 1642. The town's location at the confluence of the Housatonic and Naugatuck rivers made it a center for water-powered manufacturing; Derby's first gristmill was built in 1681. Covering just 5.3 square miles, Derby calls itself "Connecticut's smallest city."

OSBORNE HOMESTEAD MUSEUM is 1.7 mi. w. via SR 34, n. on Lakeview Terr., then w. on Hawthorne Ave., next to Osbornedale State Park *(see Recreation Chart)*. This was the home of early 20th-century businesswoman and conservationist Frances Eliza Osborne Kellogg. The furnished house, built in the mid-1800s and remodeled in the 1920s, contains American and European antiques, delftware and local silverware. Formal gardens, a rock garden, a rose garden and ornamental shrubs adorn the grounds. The Kellogg Environmental Center offers exhibits, programs and nature trails. **Time:** Allow 30 minutes minimum. **Hours:** Thurs.-Fri. 10-3, Sat. 10-4, Sun. noon-4, mid-May to mid-Oct. Holiday tours Thurs.-Sun. 10-4, Fri. after Thanksgiving to mid-Dec. Kellogg Environmental Center open Tues.-Sat. 9-4:30. Phone ahead to confirm schedule. **Cost:** Donations. **Phone:** (203) 922-7832 for the museum, or (203) 734-2513 for the environmental center.

EAST GRANBY—*see Hartford p. 56.*

EAST HADDAM (C-4)

What is claimed to be the world's oldest church bell tolls from the tower of St. Stephen's Episcopal Church. Cast for a Spanish monastery in A.D. 815, the bell was salvaged after Napoleon's troops destroyed the monastery.

The bell arrived in New York on a 19th-century trading vessel as part of a shipload of metal. In 1834 William Pratt, a local resident and ships chandler, claimed the bell and shipped it to East Haddam. Also at St. Stephen's is the small schoolhouse where Nathan Hale taught 1773-74.

Goodspeed Musicals offers nationally acclaimed productions April through December in the 1876 Victorian Goodspeed Opera House, which overlooks the Connecticut River; phone (860) 873-8668 for tickets and information.

EAST HADDAM HISTORICAL SOCIETY MUSEUM is 2.5 mi. e. to 264 Town St. (SR 82). Exhibits include works of sculptor Heinz Warneke, painter W. Langdon Kihn, actor William Gillette and events vital to East Haddam's history. Guided tours are available by appointment. **Time:** Allow 1 hour minimum. **Hours:** Fri.-Sun. 10-4, Memorial Day-Columbus Day. **Cost:** $5; $2 (students with ID); free (ages 0-11). **Phone:** (860) 873-3944.

GILLETTE CASTLE STATE PARK is off SR 82 at 67 River Rd. Overlooking the Connecticut River, the park was the estate of William Gillette, noted actor and playwright renowned for his portrayal of Sherlock Holmes. The focal point of the 184-acre park is the 24-room, 8,500-square-foot mansion, which sits upon a rock formation known as the "Seventh Sister."

Designed to look like a medieval ruin, the fieldstone castle was built 1914-19. Intricate woodwork in the interior includes 47 hand-carved doors, each with a different carved latch. Woodland trails on the grounds cross the stone bridges and trestles of Gillette's narrow-gauge railroad.

Food, picnic areas and camping facilities are available seasonally. **Hours:** Park open daily 8-dusk (weather permitting). Castle open daily 10-4:30, Memorial Day weekend-Columbus Day. **Cost:** Free. Castle $10; $4 (ages 6-12). Phone to confirm prices. Cash only. **Phone:** (860) 526-2336.

EAST HAVEN (D-3) pop. 28,189, elev. 37'

Ironworks were established at the mouth of Lake Saltonstall in 1657, and the town of East Haven was incorporated in 1785. A number of buildings have survived, including the Old Stone Church, circa 1774, and a green where Marquis de Lafayette is said to have camped. The Old Cemetery, in use since 1707, contains the grave of native son John Winthrop, Yale University's first student, who graduated in 1704.

Greater New Haven Convention and Visitors Bureau: 169 Orange St., New Haven, CT 06510. **Phone:** (203) 777-8550 or (800) 332-7829.

SAVE **SHORE LINE TROLLEY MUSEUM** is at 17 River St. near the green, off I-95 exit 51 northbound or exit 52 southbound, following signs. The museum contains a large collection of antique

U.S. and Canadian streetcars, inter-urban and rapid-transit cars. A scenic 3-mile ride aboard an antique trolley car is included with admission.

Time: Allow 1 hour minimum. **Hours:** Daily 10:30-4:30, Memorial Day-Labor Day; Sat.-Sun. and holidays 10:30-4:30, in May and Sept.-Oct; Sun. 10:30-4:30 in Apr. and Nov. Trolley rides depart throughout the day. Santa Claus trolley rides available Sat.-Sun., Thanksgiving-Dec. 25. **Cost:** $8; $6 (ages 62+); $4 (ages 2-15). **Phone:** (203) 467-6927.

EAST WINDSOR—*see Hartford p. 56.*

ESSEX (D-4) pop. 2,573, elev. 32′

Sea captains' houses still line Main Street, keeping Essex much the same as it was during the height of its shipbuilding prosperity about 1815. Among historic buildings are Hill's Academy, one of the earliest educational facilities in the region, and Pratt House, built by one of the earliest settlers. The first American warship, *Oliver Cromwell*, was built in Essex during the Revolutionary War.

CONNECTICUT RIVER MUSEUM is at 67 Main St. on the Connecticut River. Exhibits relate to river steamboats, shipbuilding, archeology and the 1775 *Turtle*, said to be the first American submarine. A collection of boats built and used on the Connecticut River is displayed in the boat house. Changing exhibits are presented. **Time:** Allow 30 minutes minimum. **Hours:** Daily 10-5, Memorial Day-Labor Day; Tues.-Sun. 10-5, rest of year. Closed Thanksgiving and Dec. 25. **Cost:** $8; $7 (ages 65+); $5 (ages 6-12). **Phone:** (860) 767-8269.

ESSEX STEAM TRAIN AND RIVERBOAT is .2 mi. w. of SR 9 exit 3 on Railroad Ave. The company offers a 12-mile sightseeing trip through the Connecticut River Valley. Restored steam trains provide hour-long round trips; all except the last train of the day connect with an optional 1.5-hour riverboat cruise on the Connecticut River. Holiday trips also are available during October's Fall Foliage season and around Christmas.

Time: Allow 1 hour minimum. **Hours:** Departures daily at 11, 12:30, 2 and 3:30, late June-Labor Day; Sat.-Sun. and Memorial Day at 11, 12:30, 2 and 3:30, early May-late June; Fri.-Sun. at 11, 12:30, 2 and 3:30, Fri. after Labor Day-Sept. 30; Thurs.-Mon. and Columbus Day at 11, 12:30, 2 and 3:30, in Oct. **Cost:** Train and riverboat $26; $17 (ages 2-11); $80 (family, two adults and up to six children ages 2-11). Train only $17; $9 (ages 2-11); $50 (family). Parlor car and caboose $5 extra. Open car (seasonal) $3 extra. **Phone:** (860) 767-0103 or (800) 377-3987.

FAIRFIELD (D-2) elev. 52′

Known as Unquowa to the Pequot Indians, the land that is now Fairfield was purchased from them in 1639. During the Revolution the town was looted and burned by the British under the command of Gen. William Tryon in 1779.

Greens

The green, also known as *the common,* is a distinctive feature of many New England towns. Lined with whitewashed Colonial-style structures, this manicured, grassy rectangle of public parkland usually has a bandstand, gazebo or monument.

The green hasn't always been green, however. It wasn't until the early 1800s that New Englanders began restoring what a visitor described as "an uneven and barren sand waste, lying open to the public, traversed by vehicles in all directions."

Consisting of a few acres of common land, the green was a transplanted feature of the 17th-century English village, where common-field husbandry was practiced. With the help of their memories of the mother country and with the anonymous guide "The Ordering of Towns" in hand, colonists planned their towns to radiate outward from the meetinghouse and the meetinghouse lot, which would later be called the green.

Trampled by animals and neglected by the townspeople, the green didn't stay green for long. By 1654 few towns remained clustered around the meetinghouse lot, and the green was often a mudflat rutted by wagon wheels and strewn with rubbish; town officials would fence off surviving patches of grass and rent them as pasture, using the income to maintain the meetinghouse.

In the 1820s a lush green became fashionable again, so New Englanders began to fence the areas off and restore them. Soon the town hall, country store, inn and stately houses were installed around the green, creating the impression of a typical "Colonial" New England town.

While only in his early 20s Fairfield native Capt. Samuel Smedley, who had seized numerous prize ships by the end of the Revolution, inspired a British officer to remark upon capture, "There is little hope of conquering an enemy whose very schoolboys are capable of valor equaling that of trained veterans of naval warfare."

Fairfield Chamber of Commerce: 1597 Post Rd., Fairfield, CT 06824. **Phone:** (203) 255-1011.

CONNECTICUT AUDUBON SOCIETY BIRDCRAFT MUSEUM AND SANCTUARY is at 314 Unquowa Rd. This small natural history museum features wildlife dioramas and hands-on exhibits. Highlights include a honeybee observation hive, a collection of dinosaur footprints and displays about bird diversity. The 6-acre songbird sanctuary protects 120 species of birds. **Hours:** Museum open Tues.-Fri. 9-1. Sanctuary open daily dawn-dusk. **Cost:** $2; $1 (ages 0-14). **Phone:** (203) 259-0416.

CONNECTICUT AUDUBON SOCIETY CENTER AT FAIRFIELD is at 2325 Burr St. Six miles of boardwalk nature trails are included within this 155-acre wildlife sanctuary. The Birds of Prey Compound contains raptors such as falcons, hawks and owls. A nature center is on the premises. Lectures, classes and guided walks are offered. **Time:** Allow 1 hour, 30 minutes minimum. **Hours:** Nature center open Tues.-Sat. 10-3. Sanctuary open daily dawn-dusk. Phone ahead to confirm schedule. **Cost:** Nature center free. Sanctuary $2; $1 (ages 2-18). **Phone:** (203) 259-6305, ext. 109.

FAIRFIELD MUSEUM AND HISTORY CENTER is at 370 Beach Rd. Exhibits feature area history, art and decorative arts. Walking tours and events also are offered. The library has local historical collections. **Hours:** Mon.-Fri. 10-4, Sat.-Sun. noon-4. Library Wed.-Fri. 10-4, Sat.-Sun. noon-4. Closed Jan. 1, Thanksgiving and Dec. 25. **Cost:** $5; $3 (senior citizens and students with ID ages 6-22). **Phone:** (203) 259-1598.

THE GALLERY OF CONTEMPORARY ART AT SACRED HEART UNIVERSITY is at 5151 Park Ave. The gallery mounts five exhibitions each year, including the annual student and faculty exhibit, as well as contemporary professional works in various media. A self-guided "Art Walk" tour begins at the gallery, where maps are available, and showcases contemporary site-specific sculptures on campus.

Note: Parking is free, but visitors must ask about a parking pass at the security booth at the entrance to the college; vehicles not displaying a parking pass are ticketed. **Time:** Allow 1 hour minimum. **Hours:** Gallery open Mon.-Thurs. noon-5, Sun. noon-4; closed between exhibitions, academic holidays and early June to mid-Sept. Grounds open daily dawn-dusk. Phone or check the web site for the exhibition calendar. **Cost:** Free. **Phone:** (203) 365-7650.

OLD TOWN HALL is at 611 Old Post Rd. on the town green. Rebuilt in 1791, the building contains land records and other documents dating from 1648. **Hours:** Mon.-Fri. 8:30-4:30. Closed major holidays. **Cost:** Free. **Phone:** (203) 256-3000.

FARMINGTON—see Hartford p. 56.

GOSHEN (B-2) pop. 2,697, elev. 520'

Synonymous with livestock shows, quilt exhibitions and tractor pulls, Goshen hosts the state's most popular agricultural event, the Goshen Fair, a Labor Day weekend tradition since 1912; (860) 491-3655.

ACTION WILDLIFE FOUNDATION is at 337 Torrington Rd.; 2 mi. e. on SR 4 to jct. SR 63. Set on 116 acres, the farm is home to more than 32 species of animals in natural settings. The grounds also feature a drive-through safari, a petting zoo and a museum with animal dioramas and live reptiles. **Time:** Allow 1 hour minimum. **Hours:** Park 10-5, Mar.-Oct. (weather permitting). Museum open daily 10-5. **Cost:** $10; $8 (ages 0-11). **Phone:** (860) 482-4465. 🍽️ 🪑

GREENWICH (E-1) elev. 550'

Although Adriaen Block established the first settlement in Greenwich in 1614, a permanent community did not come about until 1640, when the land was purchased from the original inhabitants for

25 coats. That land now is graced by large houses with commensurate price tags.

Putnam Cottage, 243 E. Putnam Ave., is where Gen. Israel Putnam escaped from the British in 1779. The cottage has been restored to the Colonial and Revolutionary appearance of its early Knapp Tavern days and contains 17th- and 18th-century furniture, decorative objects and Putnam memorabilia; phone (203) 869-9697 for tour information.

Greenwich Chamber of Commerce: 45 E. Putnam Ave., Suite 121, Greenwich, CT 06830. **Phone:** (203) 869-3500.

AUDUBON CENTER IN GREENWICH is n. off SR 15 exit 28 to jct. John St. and Riversville Rd. The 285-acre preserve features seven miles of hiking trails around a wooded lake. Family programs are available. The nearby Audubon Fairchild Garden offers more nature trails. **Hours:** Center open daily 9-5. Trails open daily dawn-dusk. Closed major holidays. **Cost:** $3; $1.50 (ages 0-17 and 65+). **Phone:** (203) 869-5272.

BRUCE MUSEUM is off I-95 exit 3, then .2 mi. n. to 1 Museum Dr. The multifaceted, family-oriented arts and science museum presents hands-on activities and changing exhibits of fine and decorative arts and artifacts. Permanent displays include an extensive mineral collection, a wildlife diorama, a marine tank, mounted birds and examples of American Indian culture. **Hours:** Tues.-Sat. 10-5, Sun. 1-5. Last admission 30 minutes before closing. Closed major holidays. **Cost:** $7; $6 (ages 65+ and students with ID ages 5-22); donations (Tues.). **Phone:** (203) 869-0376.

GREENWICH LIBRARY is at 101 W. Putnam Ave. The library contains a large art gallery with changing monthly exhibits. Free concerts and book readings are offered. Food is available at breakfast and lunch. **Hours:** Mon.-Fri. 9-9, Sat. 9-5, Sun. 1-5, Sept.-June; Mon.-Thurs. 9-9, Fri.-Sat. 9-5, Sun. 1-5, rest of year. Phone ahead for concert and readings schedule. **Cost:** Free. **Phone:** (203) 622-7900. ⓉⓉ

GROTON (C-5) pop. 10,010, elev. 47′

Groton is the home of the electric boat division of General Dynamics, the nation's largest submarine producer. General Dynamics launched the USS *Nautilus*, the first atomic-powered submarine, on Jan. 21, 1954. Groton also is a center for deep-sea fishing; numerous charters are available.

The Avery Memorial, in the center of town on Poquonnock Street just south of U.S. 1, was erected by descendants of Capt. James Avery on the site of his 1656 homestead. Descendant John D. Rockefeller helped fund the project.

The black granite, 60-foot-long Wall of Honor at Bridge and Thames streets contains the names of the approximately 3,600 American submariners who died in the line of duty during World War II. There are monuments for each of the 52 boats lost.

FORT GRISWOLD BATTLEFIELD STATE PARK is off I-95 exit 87 at Monument St. and Park Ave. The 17-acre park was the scene of a massacre in 1781 when British forces led by Benedict Arnold took the fort and burned New London and Groton. Also in the park is the 1750 Ebenezer Avery House to which the wounded were taken; the house contains period furnishings. **Hours:** Park daily 8-dusk. House open daily 10-5, Memorial Day-Labor Day; Sat.-Sun. 10-5, day after Labor Day-Columbus Day. **Cost:** Free. **Phone:** (860) 444-7591. 🚗 🎁

Groton Monument is off I-95 exit 87 at Monument St. and Park Ave. on the hilltop in Fort Griswold. The 135-foot-tall monument was dedicated in 1830 to victims of the massacre; 88 of the 165 persons in the fort were killed. A tablet shows their names. **Hours:** Wed.-Sun. 9-5, Memorial Day-Labor Day. Park daily 8-dusk. **Cost:** Free. **Phone:** (860) 449-6877.

Monument House Museum is off I-95 exit 87 at Monument St. and Park Ave. in Fort Griswold Battlefield State Park. The house contains relics of the Fort Griswold massacre and the whaling industry as well as period furniture and china. **Hours:** Daily 10-5, Memorial Day-Labor Day; Sat.-Sun. 10-5, day after Labor Day-Columbus Day. **Cost:** Free. **Phone:** (860) 449-6877.

PROJECT OCEANOLOGY AND THE LIGHTHOUSE PROGRAM offers three cruises that depart from the University of Connecticut at 1084 Shennecossett Rd. at Avery Point. The 2.5-hour hands-on educational cruises take place aboard a 55-foot research vessel. On the *EnviroLab* cruises, marine scientists teach passengers how to identify fish, measure lobsters and test seawater. Core samples from the ocean bottom also are taken and examined.

Lighthouse cruises include a boat tour of New London Harbor during which instructors discuss its history from the days of privateering to the present. Instruction in the evolution of navigational aids is capped by a tour of the 1909 New London Ledge Lighthouse, from its foundation to the light four stories above. In winter, Maine seals that call Fishers Island Sound their seasonal home may be observed in their natural habitat during seal-watching tours, which begin with a 20-minute multimedia presentation.

Note: Seal-watching tour passengers should wear deck shoes or boots and dress accordingly to the weather. Binoculars and cameras are permitted. The vessel's cabin is heated. Food is available Mon.-Fri. **Hours:** *EnviroLab* cruises depart daily at 10 and 1, mid-June through Aug. 31. Lighthouse cruises depart Tues., Thurs. and Sat. at 4, June-Aug.; Sat. at 4 in Sept. Seal tours depart at least once per day on Sat. in Feb. and Sat.-Sun. in Mar. **Cost:** Fare $19; $16 (ages 6-12). Prices may vary; phone ahead. Children ages 0-5 are not permitted. Arrival at least a half hour prior to departure time is recommended. Reservations are required. **Phone:** (860) 445-9007 or (800) 364-8472. ⓉⓉ

U.S. NAVY SUBMARINE FORCE MUSEUM, HOME OF USS *NAUTILUS*, is off I-95 exit 86, then n. on SR 12 to just outside the Naval Submarine Base. The world's first nuclear-powered submarine was commissioned in 1954. Four years later, the *Nautilus* completed the first undersea voyage to the North Pole. Models, films and equipment at the museum trace the history and development of the U.S. Submarine Force. Submarines from the Revolutionary War to the present include World War II midget submarines. A highlight is the model of Capt. Nemo's *Nautilus* from Jules Verne's "20,000 Leagues Under the Sea."

On self-guiding tours of the *Nautilus*, visitors receive an audio wand that describes each compartment. Select areas of the submarine, including its torpedo room, officer staterooms, dining areas and control room, may be explored. Occasional submarine test voyages departing from the adjacent Naval Submarine Base along the Thames River may be seen from the *Nautilus* as well as other on-site areas.

Time: Allow 2 hours minimum. **Hours:** Wed.-Mon. 9-5, Tues. 1-5, mid-May to late Oct.; Wed.-Mon. 9-4 (closed Tues.), rest of year. Closed Jan. 1, the last two weeks in Apr. and the first two weeks in Nov. for maintenance, Thanksgiving and Dec. 25. Phone ahead to confirm schedule. **Cost:** Donations. **Phone:** (860) 694-3174 or (800) 343-0079. 🍴

GUILFORD (D-4) elev. 14′

Guilford was settled by the Puritan congregation that followed Rev. Henry Whitfield from England in 1639. About 500 houses dating 1639-1876 are preserved; the shoreline has several striking promontories and bays.

One distinguished Guilford citizen of the mid-18th century, Samuel Hill, ran for office repeatedly from the time he was a young man and gave rise to the expression "run like Sam Hill."

HENRY WHITFIELD STATE MUSEUM is off I-95 exit 58, then 1 mi. s. of US 1 via CR 77 to 248 Old Whitfield St. The museum is housed in what is said to be the oldest building in Connecticut and the oldest stone house in New England. Built in 1639, the building was restored in the 1930s. Visitors can view 17th- through 19th-century furnishings and stroll through a visitor's center, which features changing exhibits.

Hours: Wed. and Sat.-Sun. 10-4, Apr. 1-Dec. 14. Closed Good Friday, Easter, July 4 and Thanksgiving. **Cost:** $4; $3 (ages 65+ and college students with ID); $2.50 (ages 6-17). Phone ahead to confirm schedule and rates as changes may occur without notice. **Phone:** (203) 453-2457.

HYLAND HOUSE is 1 blk. e. of the green at 84 Boston St. An example of early saltbox construction, the 1690 house is furnished with period pieces and accessories. A 30-minute guided tour is available. **Hours:** Tues.-Sat. 10-4:30, Sun. noon-4:30, early June-Labor Day; Sat. 10-4:30, Sun. noon-4:30, day after Labor Day-Columbus Day. **Cost:** Donations. **Phone:** (203) 453-9477.

THOMAS GRISWOLD HOUSE MUSEUM is at 171 Boston St. This classic Colonial saltbox house was built in 1774. The house depicts a lifestyle of the early 1800s, when George Griswold and his family were in residence. **Hours:** Tues.-Sun. 11-4, June-Sept.; Sat.-Sun. 11-4 in Oct.; by appointment, rest of year. **Cost:** $3; $2 (senior citizens and students with ID); free (ages 0-11). **Phone:** (203) 453-3176.

HAMDEN (C-3) elev. 101′

After inventing the cotton gin, Eli Whitney moved to Hamden in 1798 to harness the power of the Mill River. Whitney had obtained a contract to provide 10,000 muskets to the government before ever producing a single firearm. Innovations at his armory included water-driven machinery, the use of interchangeable parts and a model housing project for his workers; the contract was fulfilled in 10 years. Whitney's son later used the Mill River to provide New Haven with its first public water supply.

ELI WHITNEY MUSEUM is 3 mi. s. of SR 15 exit 61 at 915 Whitney Ave. Beside the river that powered Eli Whitney's armory, the museum honors the inventor's contributions to the American industrial revolution and the tradition of Yankee ingenuity. Visitors' creativity is encouraged in a variety of workshops focusing on design and such scientific processes as buoyancy and gravity. Workshop projects include the construction of mazes, miniature architecture and battery-operated vehicles.

Workshop project availability may vary; phone ahead to confirm. **Time:** Allow 30 minutes minimum. **Hours:** Daily 11-4, June 15-Sun. of Labor Day weekend; Wed.-Fri. and Sun. noon-5, Sat. 11-4, rest of year. **Cost:** Projects $6-$12. **Phone:** (203) 777-1833.

DID YOU KNOW

From 1703 to 1875 Connecticut had two capitals: Hartford and New Haven.

Hartford

City Population: 121,578   **Elevation:** 100 ft.

Editor's Picks:

Harriet Beecher Stowe Center..... *(see p. 52)*

Mark Twain House and
Museum .... *(see p. 53)*

Wadsworth Atheneum
Museum of Art .... *(see p. 53)*

Connecticut State Capitol
© Raymond Forbes / age fotostock

Contemporary Hartford is a dynamic blend of the past and future—its Ancient Burying Ground is only blocks away from the boat-shaped headquarters of Phoenix Life Insurance Co., the world's first two-sided building.

Although much of Hartford's reputation rests on the creation and collection of insurance premiums, this state capital can claim a boisterous history. Hartford grew from a Dutch trading post in 1633 into an English settlement founded 1636 by the Rev. Thomas Hooker and Samuel Stone. Its name derives from Stone's birthplace in Hertford, England.

Hartford was the site of one of the first Colonial efforts to resist English rule. In 1687 Sir Edmund Andros, the English governor, demanded that Hartford's citizens relinquish a 25-year-old charter granted by King Charles II that gave the colony its independence; the colonists hid the charter in the trunk of a large oak tree for about 3 days. A round stone marker on Charter Oak Place marks the spot where the oak stood until 1856.

By the 1870s Hartford had the highest per capita income in the country, and philanthropists and world literary figures made their homes here. Mark Twain and Harriet Beecher Stowe were neighbors in the lovely and exclusive Nook Farm area. The newspaper they read, *The Hartford Courant*, was founded in 1764 and today has the oldest continuous name and circulation of any newspaper in the country.

Hartford's path to insurance capital of the world began with the establishment of the Hartford Fire Insurance Co. in 1810; eventually insurance companies expanded both in number and in scope of coverage until they formed today's multibillion-dollar industry. The Travelers Tower is one of the tallest structures in New England at 527 feet. A stunning example of insurance-company architecture is the green-tinted headquarters of the Phoenix Home Life Mutual Insurance Co. at Constitution Plaza.

Education always has been important to Hartford. Founded in 1823, Trinity College, 300 Summit St., has some fine examples of collegiate Gothic architecture on its 96-acre campus. The interior of the chapel has many carvings in stone and wood. Free concerts are offered at the Plumb Memorial Carillon on Wednesday evenings in the summer. The Austin Arts Center features changing exhibitions and theatrical and musical performances. The University of Connecticut School of Law is on 20 picturesque acres near Elizabeth Park. The University of Connecticut is nearby in Storrs.

An ongoing effort to reconnect downtown Hartford with the Connecticut River has resulted in a rejuvenation of the riverfront district. Once a prime part of the city's economy, the river is now used mainly for recreational pursuits. A combination of new and restored riverfront parks on both banks of the river—Charter Oak Landing, Riverside Park and Mortensen Riverfront Plaza in Hartford and Great River Park in East Hartford—provide boat launches, riverwalks and picnic areas.

Getting There — starting on p. 45

Getting Around — starting on p. 45

What To See — starting on p. 45

What To Do — starting on p. 53

Where To Stay — starting on p. 264

Where To Dine — starting on p. 265

Dinosaur State Park, Rocky Hill
© Robert Holmes / Alamy

Expert not just at innovating, Hartford also adopts and adapts. In a creative variation on Yankee hospitality, the city has stationed in downtown the Hartford Guides, roving ambassadors of goodwill in red hats and khaki and white uniforms. Assisting visitors, workers and residents, these professionals offer insights into the city's history and information about its amenities, facilities and events. They can also help in emergencies such as when keys are locked inside the vehicle. After more than 350 years, Hartford continues to stretch the envelope.

Getting There

By Car

Looking at a map, it almost seems as if all roads lead to Hartford. The major north-south highway into the city is I-91, while I-84 runs northeast-southwest. Signage is good with generally adequate warning for exit ramps. Avoid the 7-9 a.m. and 3-6 p.m. rush hours.

Getting Around

Street System

A good map is an absolute necessity for negotiating the Hartford vicinity. At some major intersections downtown traffic is stopped in all four directions and pedestrians may cross on the diagonal.

Parking

Parking downtown is readily available in the numerous garages and lots. Rates range from $16.50 per day in city-operated lots to as much as $5 per hour in privately owned garages with a maximum of $24 per day. On-street parking is nearly impossible to find.

What To See

ANCIENT BURYING GROUND is at 60 Gold St. The city's only cemetery until 1803 forms a green oasis in the middle of downtown. Buried here are 6,000 of the city's early founders; the oldest gravestone dates from 1648. The cemetery is on the north and west sides of the 1807 Center Church, 675 Main St., which traces its history to a meetinghouse established in 1636. The church has six Tiffany windows. Self-guiding brochures are available at the Main Street gate. **Time:** Allow 30 minutes minimum. **Hours:** Cemetery open daily dawn-dusk. Guided tours offered Mon.-Fri. at noon, early July to mid-Aug. (weather permitting). **Phone:** (860) 228-1517 for tour information.

BUSHNELL PARK adjoins the capitol grounds on the n. end. One of the oldest public parks in the country, Bushnell Park contains the Civil War-era Soldiers and Sailors Memorial Arch and the Spanish American War Memorial. The Pump House Gallery (temporarily closed) presents art exhibits; the Per-

Destination Hartford

Connecticut's capital city and its environs have a rich heritage of literature, art and history.

Two of America's most celebrated 19th-century authors—Harriet Beecher Stowe and Samuel Clemens (Mark Twain)—were Hartford neighbors, and Clemens penned the youthful adventures of Tom Sawyer and Huckleberry Finn while living here. Paintings, sculpture and decorative arts spanning more than 5,000 years grace the galleries of a world-class museum. And carefully restored homes depict life during our country's Colonial era.

Connecticut State Capitol, Hartford. (See listing page 52)

Ancient Burying Ground, Hartford. (See listing page 45)

© Richard Cummins / SuperStock

Places included in this AAA Destination City:

*Cathedral of
St. Joseph, Hartford.
(See listing page 49)*

© Andre Jenny

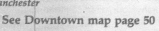

(10) Suffield
(91)

East
Granby   East Windsor

• Simsbury   Windsor
           Locks
(202)
                 Windsor
                              (84)   See Vicinity
Hartford   map page 50

(44)
West   (384) Manchester
Hartford   See Downtown map page 50

Wethersfield
New
• Britain
Kensington (91) Rocky   (2)
(9)   Hill

(691) Middletown

(91)
                            (9)

(95)
                        *Mark Twain House and
                        Museum, Hartford.
                        (See listing page 53)*

© Ruddy Gold / age fotostock

The Informed Traveler

Sales Tax: Connecticut sales tax is 6 percent. Lodging tax in the greater Hartford area is 12 percent. The car rental tax is 9.18 percent with an added $1 per day tourism tax.

WHOM TO CALL

Emergency: 911

Police (non-emergency): (262) 673-2600

Fire (non-emergency): (262) 673-8290

Hospitals: Hartford Hospital, (860) 545-5000; and Saint Francis Hospital and Medical Center, (860) 714-4000.

WHERE TO LOOK

Newspapers

Founded in 1764, *The Hartford Courant* is the morning daily newspaper.

Radio

WDRC (1360 AM) and WTIC (1880 AM) are all-news/weather stations; WPKT (90.5 FM) is a member of National Public Radio.

Visitor Information

Greater Hartford Convention & Visitors Bureau: 31 Pratt St., Fourth Floor, Hartford, CT 06103-1592. **Phone:** (860) 728-6789 or (800) 446-7811.

TRANSPORTATION

Air Travel

Bradley International Airport, 12 miles north on I-91 in Windsor Locks, is serviced by domestic and international airlines.

Public bus transportation is provided daily from the airport into downtown by Connecticut Transit (CTTransit); phone (860) 525-9181, or TTY (860) 727-8196.

Rental Cars

Hertz, at the airport, offers discounts to AAA members; phone (860) 627-3850 or (800) 654-3080.

Rail Service

The Amtrak station, (860) 727-1776 or (800) 872-7245, is downtown in the Union Station Transportation Center at 1 Union Pl.

Buses

Greyhound Lines Inc., (860) 724-7080 or (800) 231-2222, and other intercity buses operate out of the Union Station Transportation Center at 1 Union Pl. Taxis and CTTransit buses also are available.

Taxis

Taxis hired at the airport taxi stand charge $36 to downtown (for up to four people). Cab companies include United Cab Co., (860) 547-1602, and Yellow, (860) 666-6666. Base fare (for up to four people) is $2.75, plus $2.25 per mile or a flat rate of $2.60 per mile for destinations further than 15 miles.

Public Transport

The buses of CTTransit, (860) 525-9181 or TTY (860) 727-8196, run on more than 30 routes servicing Hartford and its surrounding towns. The buses operate daily, with reduced schedules weekends and holidays. Schedule information is available Mon.-Fri. 6 a.m.-11 p.m., Sat. 6 a.m.-9 p.m., Sun. 8-6. An all-day pass is available for $3.25.

formance Pavilion offers summer jazz concerts. The 37-acre park also features a working Stein and Goldstein 1914 carousel with 48 hand-carved wooden horses, two chariots and a 1925 Wurlitzer band organ.

Also on the premises are several statues and the 30-foot-tall marble and stone Corning Fountain. Free brochures for a self-guided "tree walk" are available at the Hartford Welcome Center at 45 Pratt St.

Tours: Guided tours are available. **Hours:** Park open daily 6 a.m.-10 p.m. Gallery open Tues.-Fri. 11:30-2:30 and 5-10, Sat. 5-10. Carousel operates Tues.-Sun. 11-5, May-Aug.; Thurs.-Sun. 11-5, Sept. to mid-Oct. Guided tours depart from the Memorial Arch Thurs. at noon, May-Oct. Art in the Park walking tours are offered Wed. at noon, Sat. at 2, May-Sept. (weather permitting). Guided arch tours depart Thurs. at noon, May-Oct. **Cost:** Park, gallery and arch tours free. Carousel ride $1. **Phone:** (860) 585-5411 for the carousel, or (860) 232-6710 for the gallery. 🍴

BUTLER-McCOOK HOUSE & GARDEN is at 396 Main St. The oldest surviving homestead in Hartford, the 1782 house contains a collection of four generations of 18th- and 19th-century furnishings, art and household items. Highlights include Victorian-era toys and paintings, as well as a period garden. **Tours:** Guided tours are available. **Time:**

Allow 1 hour minimum. **Hours:** Thurs. and Sat. 10-4 (also first Thurs. of the month 4-8, Apr.-Oct.), Sun. 1-4. Last tour departs 30 minutes before closing. **Cost:** $7; $6 (senior citizens); $4 (ages 6-18). **Phone:** (860) 247-8996 or (860) 522-1806.

CATHEDRAL OF ST. JOSEPH is at 140 Farmington Ave. The striking 1962 contemporary structure is noted for 26 huge stained-glass windows that line the nave. Guided tours of the Catholic church are conducted by appointment only. **Time:** Allow 30 minutes minimum. **Hours:** Open Mon.-Fri. 7-2, Sat. 7-5, Sun. 7-1; schedule is abbreviated on holidays, so phone ahead. **Cost:** Free. **Phone:** (860) 249-8431.

SAVE **CONNECTICUT HISTORICAL SOCIETY MUSEUM** is off I-84 exit 46 at 1 Elizabeth St. The museum has changing exhibits about Connecticut history as well as permanent displays containing 17th- through 19th-century Connecticut furniture and decorative arts. A research library also is available.

Time: Allow 1 hour minimum. **Hours:** Museum open Tues.-Fri. noon-5, Sat. 9-5. Research library open Tues.-Sat. 10-5. Last admission for museum and library is 45 minutes before closing. Closed Jan. 1, Easter, July 4, Thanksgiving and Dec. 25. **Cost:** Museum or library $6; $3 (ages 6-17, ages 65+ and students with ID); free (9-1 on first Sat. of the month). Additional fees may apply during special events. **Phone:** (860) 236-5621.

Wadsworth Atheneum Museum of Art / © Omni Photo Communications Inc. / Index Stock Imagery / Photolibrary

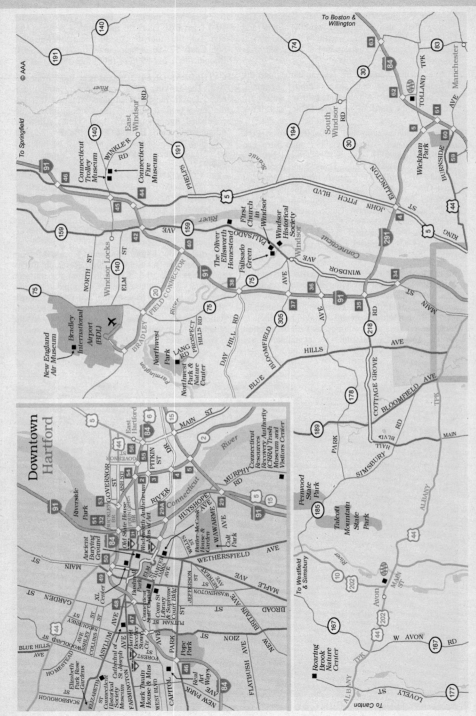

© AAA

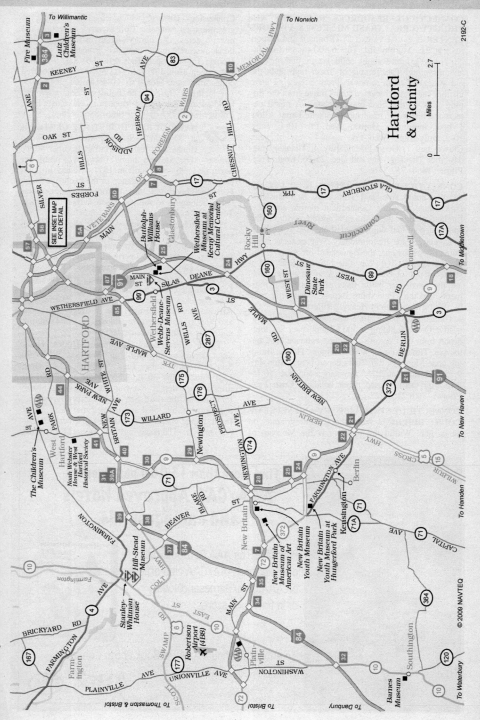

Hartford & Vicinity

N

Miles
0   2.7

2192-C

© 2009 NAVTEQ

CONNECTICUT RESOURCES RECOVERY AU-THORITY (CRRA) TRASH MUSEUM & VISITORS CENTER is e. of I-91 exit 27 (Brainard and Airport rds.) at 211 Murphy Rd. This 6,500-square-foot facility has exhibits about solid waste management and recycling. The Temple of Trash represents the old system of trash removal. From a viewing area, visitors can watch recycled items move from the tipping floor to the final bundling area. A mural depicts the history of trash management. **Time:** Allow 1 hour minimum. **Hours:** Wed.-Fri. 10-4, Tues. 10-2, July-Aug.; Wed.-Fri. noon-4, rest of year. Closed Jan. 1, Good Friday, July 4, Thanksgiving, day after Thanksgiving and Dec. 25-26. **Cost:** Free. **Phone:** (860) 757-7765.

CONNECTICUT STATE CAPITOL is off I-84 exit 48 on Capitol Ave. and Trinity St. near Bushnell Park. Made of white Connecticut marble and New England granite, the building is adorned with Gothic spires, a gold-leaf dome, medallions and bas-reliefs.

Displayed are Revolutionary War general Israel Putnam's tombstone, the figurehead off Adm. David G. Farragut's Civil War flagship *Hartford* and a statue of patriot Nathan Hale. Also on the grounds are the Civil War battle flags of Connecticut regiments and the "Petersburg Express," a mortar used by the 1st Connecticut Heavy Artillery.

Guided tours begin at the west entrance of the Legislative Office Building at 300 Capitol Ave.; Sat. tours depart from the Capitol's southwest entrance off Capitol Ave. **Time:** Allow 1 hour minimum. **Hours:** Building open Mon.-Fri. 8-5. Tours depart hourly Mon.-Fri. 9:15-1:15 (also at 2:15, July-Aug.; and Sat. 10:15-2:15, Apr.-Oct.). Closed major holidays. **Cost:** Free. **Phone:** (860) 240-0222.

CONNECTICUT STATE LIBRARY AND SUPREME COURT BUILDING faces the Capitol grounds on the s. end. Within the building is the Museum of Connecticut History, which contains portraits of governors, an extensive Colt firearms collection and historic items. The library's archives/secured collections research area contains genealogy records. **Hours:** Library open Tues.-Fri. 9-5, Sat. 9-2. Museum open Mon.-Fri. 9-4, Sat. 9-3. Archives/secured collections area Mon.-Fri. 10-4:15, Sat. 9:15-1:45. All facilities closed state holidays, Sat. after Fri. holidays and Sat. before Mon. holidays. **Cost:** Free. **Phone:** (860) 757-6500 or (866) 886-4478.

HARRIET BEECHER STOWE CENTER is at 77 Forest St. near the Mark Twain House. The restored Harriet Beecher Stowe House—Mrs. Stowe's home from 1873 until her death in 1896—was built in 1871. Modest in comparison to her other residence in the exclusive Nook Farm neighborhood, the 14-room house contains items belonging to the renowned author of "Uncle Tom's Cabin."

The kitchen was designed after the model described by Mrs. Stowe and her sister Catherine in their 1869 book "The American Woman's Home." Paintings by the author, period furnishings and eight Victorian gardens can be seen on guided tours.

Built in 1884, the adjacent Katharine Seymour Day House contains a research library housing reference works about 19th-century women's and African-American history, the suffrage movement and Victorian architecture and design. An exhibition gallery is in the visitors center.

Time: Allow 1 hour minimum. **Hours:** House tours depart on the half-hour Wed.-Sat. 9:30-4:30, Sun. noon-4:30 (also Tues. 9:30-4:30, May-Oct.). Last tour begins 30 minutes before closing. Children's tours depart Sat.-Sun. at 2. Living history tours depart the third Sat. at 4. Library is open by appointment. Seasonal and themed tours also are offered; phone ahead for schedule. Closed Jan. 1, Easter, July 4, Thanksgiving and Dec. 24-25. **Cost:**

House tour $9; $8 (ages 65+); $6 (ages 5-16). Children's tour $5 (ages 5-12); $4 (adults). Living history tour $11; $9 (ages 65+), $8 (ages 5-16). **Phone:** (860) 522-9258, ext. 317, or (860) 522-9258, ext. 313 to schedule a library appointment.

MARK TWAIN HOUSE AND MUSEUM is at 351 Farmington Ave. The unusual 19-room Victorian Gothic house was the author's home 1874-91 while he wrote his greatest works, including "The Adventures of Tom Sawyer" and "Adventures of Huckleberry Finn."

Designed by Edward Tuckerman Potter, the magical brick mansion has towering turrets and large porches. In 1881 Twain commissioned Louis Comfort Tiffany and his partners to decorate the interior. Details include elaborate stencils and carved woodwork; some 50,000 items belonging to the author and his family are displayed throughout the house.

A museum center presents changing exhibitions of rare manuscripts, photographs, artifacts and fine and decorative arts, as well as a film biography by director Ken Burns.

Access to the house is by a guided 25-minute Servants' Wing Tour or 45-minute Main House Tour, both requiring climbing stairs. Some areas are wheelchair accessible. **Hours:** Wed.-Mon. 9:30-5:30, (also Tues., Apr.-Dec.). Last tour departs 1 hour before closing. Closed Jan. 1, Easter, July 4, Thanksgiving and Dec. 24-25. **Cost:** Main House Tour $14; $12 (ages 65+); $8 (ages 6-16). Servants' Wing Tour $5; $3 (with Main House Tour). **Phone:** (860) 247-0998.

OLD STATE HOUSE is at 800 Main St. Designed by Charles Bulfinch, this 1796 Federal-style building was the site of the Hartford Convention and the first Amistad trial. Said to be the nation's oldest statehouse, the building served as Connecticut's seat of government until the present capitol building opened in 1878.

Steward's Museum, on the second floor, was established in 1797 and features paintings and curiosities including a two-headed calf and an 8.5-foot alligator. Guided and audio tours are available by reservation. **Time:** Allow 1 hour minimum. **Hours:** Tues.-Sat. 10-5. Last tour departs at 4. Closed July 4 and Dec. 25. **Cost:** $6; $3 (ages 6-17, ages 65+ and students with ID); free (military with ID). **Phone:** (860) 522-6766.

REAL ART WAYS is at 56 Arbor St. The art gallery features contemporary exhibits. Art, poetry, videotape, movie and music events are held at varying times. Performing arts programs and events are offered. **Hours:** Gallery open Tues.-Thurs. and Sun. 2-10, Fri.-Sat. 2-11. **Cost:** Gallery by donation. Performance fees vary; phone ahead. **Phone:** (860) 232-1006.

WADSWORTH ATHENEUM MUSEUM OF ART is at 600 Main St. Founded in 1842, it is said to be the nation's oldest continuously operated public art museum. Nearly 50,000 works are featured, including a large collection of Hudson River School landscape paintings, world renowned Baroque paintings, Impressionist masterpieces, American art spanning five centuries, decorative arts and Wallace Nutting Colonial furniture, a costume and textiles collection and the MATRIX series of contemporary art.

Included in the collection is works by Cole, Church, Caravaggio, Dali, Ernst, Matisse, Monet, O'Keeffe, Picasso, Pollock, van Gogh and Wyeth. The Amistad Center for Art & Culture manages 7,000 works of art, artifacts and archives from the Randolph Linsly Simpson Collection representing over 300 years of African American heritage in America.

Time: Allow 1 hour minimum. **Hours:** Wed.-Fri. 11-5 (also first Thurs. of the month 5-8), Sat.-Sun. 10-5. Guided tours are given Wed.-Sun. at 1 (also Sat.-Sun. at 2:30). Closed Jan. 1, July 4, Thanksgiving and Dec. 25. **Cost:** $10; $8 (ages 62+); $5 (ages 13-18, college students with ID and first Thurs. of the month after 5 p.m.); free (Martin Luther King Jr. Day). Discounted rates available first weekend of each month. **Phone:** (860) 278-2670.

What To Do

Sports and Recreation

The American **Hockey** League's Hartford Wolf Pack, an affiliate of the National Hockey League's New York Rangers, take to the ice mid-October to mid-April at the XL Center; phone (860) 246-7825. **Collegiate athletics** hold court in nearby Storrs *(see p. 76)*, especially when the University of Connecticut's men's and women's basketball teams play; phone (860) 486-2724.

Goodwin Park, 1130 Maple Ave., offers a driving range and 27 holes of **golf, tennis** courts, a fitness **trail** and other facilities; phone (860) 291-7160 for the park, or (860) 956-3601 for golf information.

Shopping

The outdoor Hartford Downtown Farmers' Market, 855 Main St., offers food and locally grown

DID YOU KNOW

First printed in 1764, *The Hartford Courant* is the oldest newspaper in the United States.

seasonal produce Monday, Wednesday and Friday from 9-2, June through November.

In the Farmington area is Westfarms, on New Britain Avenue off I-84 exit 40 (SR 71). The mall contains JCPenney, Lord & Taylor, Macy's and Nordstrom; phone (860) 561-3024. Buckland Hills Mall, I-84 exit 62 at 194 Buckland Hills Dr. in Manchester, contains more than 130 stores, including Dick's Sporting Goods, JCPenney, Macy's and Sears; phone (860) 644-1450.

Old Wethersfield offers shops, restaurants and museums in preserved antebellum houses, warehouses, carriage houses and barns. Old Avon Village, on SR 44 in Avon, offers 65 shops and eateries. Riverdale Farms Shopping, off I-84 exit 39 in Avon, is on a restored, landscaped 19th-century dairy farm; phone (860) 677-6437. Nearly 140 galleries, shops and boutiques can be visited at West Hartford Center, along Farmington Avenue in West Hartford.

Performing Arts

The Tony Award-winning Hartford Stage Company, (860) 527-5151, presents classics and contemporary experimental productions at 50 Church St. TheaterWorks, (860) 527-7838, at 233 Pearl St., presents off-Broadway productions all year. In addition to presentations by local companies, offerings by the 1930s Art Deco Bushnell Center for the Performing Arts include visiting orchestras, plays direct from or on their way to Broadway, lectures, and performances by well-known entertainers; phone (860) 987-5900.

The musical arts are not neglected in Hartford. The Hartford Symphony Orchestra, (860) 244-2999, performs at the Bushnell Center for the Performing Arts. The University of Connecticut's Jorgensen Center for the Performing Arts in Storrs plays host to Broadway musicals, symphony orchestras, dance, opera, pop, country, jazz and cabaret acts September through April; phone (860) 486-4226. At the Comcast Theater, (860) 548-7370, offerings range from productions for children to musicals to performances by superstars.

A variety of performances, lectures and workshops are held at Charter Oak Cultural Center, which is housed in what was once the state's first synagogue, built in 1876; phone (860) 249-1207.

Special Events

Bushnell Park is the site of jazz concerts and other entertainment events in the spring and summer. Nearby West Hartford's Elizabeth Park, the nation's first municipally owned rose garden, also is the site of summer concerts. Riverfront Plaza plays host to concerts, festivals and performances.

In late June the Greater Hartford Rose and Garden Weekend celebrates the blooming of some 15,000 rose bushes. Also in late June, the TPC River Highlands in nearby Cromwell host the PGA Tour's Travelers Championship. Riverfest, a 4th of July celebration, brings crowds to the downtown riverfront for music, entertainment and fireworks. The Podunk Bluegrass Music Festival is held in Martin Park in East Hartford in July.

In late July New Britain's Italian Festival offers arts and crafts, entertainment and food. Southington salutes local agriculture the first two weekends in October during the Apple Harvest Festival.

Middletown plays host to a pair of fall events: the Head of the Connecticut Regatta in early October and the Wesleyan Potters Exhibit in late November and early December. Downtown's Constitution Plaza celebrates the holiday season with the Festival of Light from late November through New Year's Day.

The Hartford Vicinity

BRISTOL (C-3) pop. 60,032, elev. 332'

Bristol complements its manufacturing pursuits with several recreation areas, including Page Park in the Federal Hill section, which has facilities for swimming, tennis, basketball, baseball and skating as well as a playground. Rockwell Park, west of the city, offers swimming and skating.

Bristol's tallest building is the 29-story elevator tower at Otis Research Center near Lake Compounce. The 383-foot test tower, visible from most points in town, was the tallest of its kind in the world until Otis built a second facility in Shibayama, Japan.

Bristol Chamber of Commerce: 200 Main St., Bristol, CT 06010-6562. **Phone:** (860) 584-4718.

AMERICAN CLOCK AND WATCH MUSEUM is 2 blks. s. off US 6 at 100 Maple St. Housed in the 1801 Miles Lewis House, the museum is supplemented by two modern wings. Displayed are more than 2,000 clocks and watches dating from the 1690s. Exhibits include grandfather clocks, shelf clocks, novelties and church-tower clocks. Many strike simultaneously on the hour.

Connecticut Clockmaking and The Industrial Revolution, an 1890 Victorian clock and watch store and a sundial garden, are highlights. **Hours:** Daily 10-5, Apr.-Nov.; Sat.-Sun. 10-4, in Dec. Closed Easter and Thanksgiving. **Cost:** $5; $4 (ages 65+); $2 (ages 8-15); $12 (family). **Phone:** (860) 583-6070.

HARRY BARNES MEMORIAL NATURE CENTER is .5 mi. e. of SR 69 at 175 Shrub Rd. The center comprises 70 acres of forest and field habitat with nature trails, and an interpretive center houses living and preserved animals. Educational programs and displays designed for children also are featured. **Note:** The center is closed for renovations and is scheduled to reopen in winter 2010. The nature trails remain available. Admission prices may vary upon reopening. **Time:** Allow 30 minutes minimum. **Hours:** Wed.-Fri. 3-5, Sat. 10-4. **Cost:** $2; $1 (ages 0-4). **Phone:** (860) 589-6082.

LAKE COMPOUNCE THEME PARK is off I-84 exit 31, then 2 mi. n. on SR 229 following signs. This park, established in 1846, is said to be the oldest continuously operating amusement park in the nation. Rides and attractions include wood and steel roller coasters, a white-water raft ride, Kiddie Land and Splash Harbor Water Park. Boulder Dash is a mountainside roller coaster. Among the more traditional features are a 1927 wooden roller coaster and a 1911 carousel.

Hours: Park opens daily at 11, early June through late Aug.; opens at 11 Sat.-Sun. and Labor Day, Labor Day weekend-second Sun. in Sept.; days and opening times vary, mid-May through early June. Closing times vary; phone ahead. **Cost:** $34.99; $25.99 (under 52 inches tall); $17.99 (ages 61+ and after 5 p.m.); free (ages 0-3). Rates may vary; phone ahead. **Parking:** $7. **Phone:** (860) 583-3300.

THE NEW ENGLAND CAROUSEL MUSEUM is at 95 Riverside Ave. (SR 72). The museum features an array of carousel animals and a replica of an old carving shop, with miniature carousels and a Wurlitzer band organ. Hand-carved European and American carousel pieces also are displayed. **Tours:** Guided tours are available. **Time:** Allow 1 hour minimum. **Hours:** Mon.-Sat. 10-5, Sun. noon-5, Apr.-Nov.; Thurs.-Sat. 10-5, Sun. noon-5, rest of year. Closed major holidays. **Cost:** $5; $4.50 (ages 63+); $2.50 (ages 4-14). **Parking:** Free. **Phone:** (860) 585-5411.

CANTON (B-3) elev. 900'

Formerly a portion of Simsbury, Canton first was called Suffrage because of the hardships overcome by the early settlers in 1740. It separated from the parish of West Simsbury in 1806. The name of the town indicates the state's interest in the China trade at that time.

Local legend claims that the ghostly remains of a paymaster murdered at the Canton Tavern during the Revolution can be seen at night in the form of a galloping headless horseman.

ROARING BROOK NATURE CENTER is 1.5 mi. n.e. of US 44; n. on Lawton Rd. from jct. US 44 and SR 177, following signs to 70 Gracey Rd. The center has 5 miles of self-guiding trails and 115 acres of woodland. The interpretive building houses both permanent and seasonal exhibits, including a small animal collection and a replica of an eastern woodland Indian longhouse.

Programs deal with the natural history of North America; folk concerts are offered weekend evenings in spring, fall and winter. Concerts are held seasonally. **Time:** Allow 1 hour, 30 minutes minimum. **Hours:** Nature center open Tues.-Sat. 10-5, Sun. 1-5 (also Mon. 10-5, July-Aug.). Trails open daily dawn-dusk. Closed Jan. 1, Memorial Day, July 4, Labor Day, Thanksgiving and Dec. 25. **Cost:** $5; $4 (ages 62+); $3 (ages 2-12). **Phone:** (860) 693-0263.

COLLINSVILLE (B-3) pop. 2,686, elev. 317'

On the east bank of the Farmington River, Collinsville is the site of one of the first ax factories in the world. In 1826 Samuel and David Collins and William Wells established the factory from which John Brown obtained pikes for his insurrection at Harper's Ferry.

CANTON HISTORICAL MUSEUM is 1 blk. off SR 179 at 11 Front St. The museum occupies a building of the Collins Axe Co., whose antique products are displayed. Exhibits include a 19th-century general store, post office, printing press and blacksmith and barber shops, as well as vehicles, tools and farm equipment, a working railroad diorama and Victorian fashions, toys and dolls.

Time: Allow 1 hour minimum. **Hours:** Wed.-Sun. 1-4 (also Thurs. 4-8), Apr.-Nov.; Sat.-Sun. 1-5, rest of year. **Cost:** $4; $3 (ages 65+); $2 (ages 6-15). **Phone:** (860) 693-2793.

EAST GRANBY (B-4)

Divided by a mountain of traprock, East Granby was settled in 1710 in a region originally known as Turkey Hills. The country's first commercially successful silver plating process was perfected in 1845 by Asa Rogers for the Cowles Co. Rogers later moved to Hartford and established the Rogers Brothers trademark in 1847.

The Congregational Church, at SRs 20 and 187, was built in 1830 in the Gothic style and bears the distinctive features of a wooden belfry and pinnacles.

OLD NEW-GATE PRISON AND COPPER MINE is .7 mi. w. on SR 20, then 1 mi. n. to 115 Newgate Rd. Opened in 1705, the cold, damp tunnels of this unprofitable copper mine were used as a prison starting in 1773, making it the first state prison in the nation. The prison was abandoned in 1827 and quickly became a tourist attraction. Visitors may explore the underground caverns and ruins of prison buildings on self-guiding tours; the 1790 guardhouse contains historical exhibits.

Hours: Fri.-Sun. 10-4, Memorial Day weekend-Oct. Last admission 30 minutes before closing. **Cost:** $10; $8 (ages 60+ and college students with ID); $6 (ages 6-17). Phone ahead to confirm schedule and rates as changes may occur without notice. **Phone:** (860) 653-3563. 🚻

EAST WINDSOR (B-4) elev. 69'

In 1636 William Pynchon built a warehouse at Warehouse Point to store cargo that could not be transported around Enfield Rapids. Goods were taken by oxcart to Thompsonville, where they were reloaded onto flatboats to complete the journey to Springfield.

CONNECTICUT FIRE MUSEUM is .5 mi. e. of I-91 exit 45 at 58 North Rd. (behind the Connecticut Trolley Museum). The museum houses a collection of antique fire equipment ranging from a circa 1894 fire sleigh to a 1967 Walter crash truck. Fire truck models and memorabilia also are displayed. **Time:** Allow 30 minutes minimum. **Hours:** Mon. and Wed.-Fri. 10-4, Sat. 10-5, Sun. noon-5, mid-June through Labor Day; Sat. 10-5, Sun. noon-5, Mar. 1 to mid-June and day after Labor Day-Oct.; Fri.-Sun. 5-9, mid-Nov. through Dec. 31. Closed Easter, Thanksgiving and Dec. 24-25. **Cost:** (includes Connecticut Trolley Museum) $8; $7 (ages 62+); $5 (ages 2-12). **Phone:** (860) 627-6540.

CONNECTICUT TROLLEY MUSEUM is .5 mi. e. of I-91 exit 45 on SR 140 at 58 North Rd. Operating trolleys and associated rail cars dating 1894-1947 are displayed. Unlimited 3-mile rides on antique trolley cars is offered. **Time:** Allow 1 hour, 30 minutes minimum. **Hours:** Mon. and Wed.-Fri. 10-4, Sat. 10-5, Sun. noon-5, mid-June through Labor Day; Sat. 10-5, Sun. noon-5, Mar. 1 to mid-June and day after Labor Day-Oct.; Fri.-Sun. 5-9, mid-Nov. to Dec. 31. Closed Easter, Thanksgiving and Dec. 24-25. **Cost:** (includes trolley ride and Connecticut Fire Museum) $8; $7 (ages 62+); $5 (ages 2-12). **Phone:** (860) 627-6540.

FARMINGTON (B-3) elev. 245'

Farmington, an aristocratic old town, sits unchanged amid its wealth and culture. The long main street is laid out on a river terrace. To the east is wild hill country; to the west is a river plain.

HILL-STEAD MUSEUM is at 35 Mountain Rd., .2 mi. from the center of town by way of Farmington Ave. and Main St. The collection includes etchings and paintings by Impressionists Mary Cassatt, Edgar Degas, Edouard Manet, Claude Monet and James McNeill Whistler. Chinese porcelains of the Ming and Ching dynasties also are featured as well as other art objects.

Set on 152 acres, which include a sunken garden designed by Beatrix Farrand, the 36-room Colonial Revival house was designed and built in 1901 by Theodate Pope, one of the first female architects in the country. Her father, industrialist Alfred Atmore Pope, used the house as a showplace for his art collection.

Hours: Grounds open daily 7:30-5:30. One-hour guided tours are given every half-hour Tues.-Sun. 10-4, May-Oct.; 11-3, rest of year. Last tour departs 1 hour before closing. Closed Jan. 1, Easter, July 4, Thanksgiving and Dec. 25. **Cost:** $10; $9 (ages 63+); $8 (students with ID); $5 (ages 6-12). **Phone:** (860) 677-4787.

STANLEY-WHITMAN HOUSE is at 37 High St. This well-preserved example of New England framed architecture features an overhanging second story with pendant drops. Capt. John Stanley built the saltbox house in 1719. Details include a central chimney, diamond-paned sash windows and period furnishings. Herb and vegetable gardens reflect foods and medicinal herbs used in Colonial times.

Hours: Guided 30-minute tours are offered Wed.-Sun. noon-4. Last tour leaves 30 minutes before closing. Interactive exhibits Wed.-Fri. 9-4, Sat.-Sun. noon-4. Closed major holidays. **Cost:** $7; $5 (ages 63+); $4 (ages 6-18). **Phone:** (860) 677-9222.

KENSINGTON (C-4) pop. 8,541, elev. 79'

NEW BRITAIN YOUTH MUSEUM AT HUNGERFORD PARK is at 191 Farmington Ave. (SR 372). The museum's seasonally themed indoor local history displays depict the state's four seasons; in summer, children may play at an old-fashioned ice cream parlor exhibit, and an antique country kitchen is available in fall. Other indoor highlights include a puppet theater and the Bears Den slide. The grounds feature forest walking trails, a pond observation station, a wildflower meadow and an outdoor petting zoo at which such animals as cows, llamas, rabbits and sheep may be seen.

Time: Allow 1 hour minimum. **Hours:** Museum open Tues.-Sat. 10-4:30. Public animal programs are offered Sat. at 11, 1:30 and 3:30. **Cost:** $4; $3 (ages 65+); $2 (ages 2-16). Trails free to all. **Phone:** (860) 827-9064.

MANCHESTER (B-4) elev. 117′

From a center of small industry in 1823, Manchester has grown into one of the state's major manufacturing cities, with several of its industries more than a century old. The town produced gunpowder that was used by the Continental Army during the Revolutionary War.

Prosperity skyrocketed after six grandsons of Timothy Cheney founded the Cheney Brothers Silk Co. in 1838; the Cheney Homestead, 106 Hartford Rd., is open to the public. The silk company made Manchester the nation's silk-producing capital and was responsible for the establishment of schools, local utilities and other public services before it went out of business after World War II.

FIRE MUSEUM is off I-384 exit 3 (SR 83) to 230 Pine St. Displays are housed in a restored 1901 Manchester firehouse. Firefighting equipment and memorabilia include early hand pumps, an 1841 steam fire engine, badges, ribbons, Currier and Ives lithographs and a 1911 gas-electric water tower that extends 65 feet when elevated.

Hours: Sat. noon-4, mid-Apr. to mid-Nov.; by appointment rest of year. **Cost:** Donations. **Phone:** (860) 649-9436.

LUTZ CHILDREN'S MUSEUM is at 247 S. Main St. Changing participatory exhibits about art, history, science, nature and ethnology are featured. There is a permanent collection of small native, domestic and exotic live animals. The nearby 53-acre Oak Grove Nature Center contains wildlife habitats in a natural setting. **Time:** Allow 1 hour minimum. **Hours:** Tues.-Fri. 9-5, Sat.-Sun. noon-5. Closed Jan. 1, Easter, Memorial Day, July 4, Labor Day, Thanksgiving and Dec. 25. **Cost:** $5; free (under 1). **Phone:** (860) 643-0949.

WICKHAM PARK is off I-84 exit 60 on US 6/US 44 at 1329 W. Middle Tpke. This 250-acre park has extensive manicured grounds containing seven ornamental gardens as well as an aviary, a nature center and a wetlands preserve. Recreational facilities include play areas, tennis and volleyball courts, softball fields, a Frisbee golf course and walking and fitness trails. **Hours:** Daily 9:30-dusk (weather permitting), first Sat. in Apr.-last Sun. in Oct. **Cost:** Sat.-Sun. and holidays $5 per private vehicle; Mon.-Tues. $3; Wed.-Fri. $4. **Phone:** (860) 528-0856. 🎟

MIDDLETOWN (C-4) pop. 43,167, elev. 55′

From about 1750 until after the Revolution, Middletown was a great trading port and the largest and wealthiest city in Connecticut. Simeon North, the first official pistol maker for the government, built his factory in 1799. The city is now an important research and manufacturing center supporting diversified industries.

CENTER FOR THE ARTS is on the Wesleyan University campus. Three performance halls and two galleries present changing exhibits of contemporary and international art. The Davison Art Center focuses on printmaking and photography; the Ezra and Cecile Zilkha Gallery often presents contemporary paintings and sculpture. **Time:** Allow 30 minutes minimum. **Hours:** Both galleries Tues.-Sun. noon-4, Sept.-May. Closed academic holidays. **Cost:** Free. **Phone:** (860) 685-2500, or (860) 685-3355 for event ticket information.

KIDCITY CHILDREN'S MUSEUM is off SR 9 exit 15, then .2 mi. w. on SR 66 to 119 Washington St. The museum presents a hands-on educational experience for children ages 0-7. Theme rooms such as Main Street and Musical Planet as well as a fishery stimulate play and imagination. **Time:** Allow 30 minutes minimum. **Hours:** Sun.-Tues. 11-5, Wed.-Sat. 9-5. Closed Jan. 1, Easter, Thanksgiving and Dec. 25. **Cost:** $7; free (under 1). **Phone:** (860) 347-0495.

OLIN MEMORIAL LIBRARY is at 252 Church St. on the Wesleyan University campus. Opened in 1928, the library contains more than 1.4 million volumes and numerous portraits. Also on display are book jackets, music memorabilia and 1931 Wedgwood plates. **Time:** Allow 30 minutes minimum. **Hours:** Mon.-Thurs. 8:30 a.m.-2 a.m., Fri. 8:30 a.m.-11:30 p.m., Sat. 10-10, Sun. 10 a.m.-2 a.m. Hours are limited during the summer and semester break; phone ahead. Closed major holidays. **Cost:** Free. **Phone:** (860) 685-2660.

NEW BRITAIN (C-3) pop. 71,538, elev. 199′

Metalworking industries are prevalent in New Britain, known as the "Hardware City." During the 19th and early 20th centuries, the city was at the forefront of industrial enterprise and urban development, as is visible in the Art Deco architecture downtown.

Those who like to golf can play at the 27-hole municipal golf course in Stanley Quarter Park *(see Recreation Chart)*, jct. Hartford Road and Stanley Street north of Central Park; phone (860) 827-1362. From April through September the New Britain Rock Cats, the Class AA affiliate of the Minnesota Twins, entertain baseball fans at New Britain Stadium; phone (860) 224-8383.

NEW BRITAIN MUSEUM OF AMERICAN ART is at 56 Lexington St. A collection of permanent and changing exhibits in 15 galleries encompass more than 8,000 paintings, graphics and sculptures tracing the history of American art from 1740 to the present. Included are murals by Thomas Hart Benton and Graydon Parrish's 9/11 memorial as well as works by Mary Cassatt, John Singleton Copley, Winslow Homer, Gilbert Stuart, James McNeill Whistler and artists of the Hudson River School.

Tours: Guided tours are available. **Time:** Allow 1 hour minimum. **Hours:** Tues.-Wed. and Fri. 11-5, Thurs. 11-8, Sat. 10-5, Sun. noon-5. Guided tours depart Sun. at 1 or by reservation. Closed Jan. 1, July 4, Thanksgiving and Dec. 25. **Cost:** $9; $8 (ages 65+); $7 (students with ID); free (ages 0-12 and on Sat. 10-noon). **Phone:** (860) 229-0257. 🍴

NEW BRITAIN YOUTH MUSEUM is at 30 High St. Children's artifacts and changing regional culture exhibits are featured. Other highlights include a playroom, puppet theatre and a variety of interactive exhibits. **Time:** Allow 30 minutes minimum. **Hours:** Tues. 10-5, Wed.-Fri. noon-5, Sat. 10-4. Closed Jan. 1, July 4, Thanksgiving and Dec. 25. **Cost:** Donations. **Phone:** (860) 225-3020.

ROCKY HILL (B-4) elev. 46′

Giant prehistoric reptiles once roamed the Rocky Hill region, and their footprints and fossils still can be found. Millions of years after the dinosaurs' demise, the town was settled in 1650 as a suburb of Wethersfield. A change in the course of the Connecticut River caused Rocky Hill to become Wethersfield's chief port for a period of time; however, that function since has been relinquished.

DINOSAUR STATE PARK is off I-91 exit 23, then 1 mi. e. to 400 West St. A geodesic dome covers the sandstone trackway in which 500 dinosaur footprints from the Lower Jurassic period have been preserved. The exhibit center includes life-size dioramas and interactive displays. On the grounds are nature trails,

display gardens and the Dinosaur State Park Arboretum, which features living examples of plant species from the age of dinosaurs. A Track Casting area enables guests to make castings of the footprints.

Phone ahead for a list of supplies necessary for Track Casting area. Pets on leash allowed in picnic area only. **Hours:** Grounds open daily 9-4:30. Exhibit center open Tues.-Sun. 9-4:30. Track Casting area daily 9-3:30, May-Oct. Closed Jan. 1, Thanksgiving and Dec. 25. **Cost:** Free. Exhibit center $10; $4 (ages 6-12). **Phone:** (860) 529-8423. 🍴 🐾

SIMSBURY (B-3) elev. 164′

Simsbury, originally named Massacoe, was settled in 1640 by British emigrants from Symondsbury in Dorsetshire, England, who initially had settled in Windsor. The village was incorporated as the town of Simsbury in 1670.

Frightened by the depredations of King Phillip's War, the residents returned to their former town. Later, scouts reported that the village was left in ashes by the king's American Indian warriors. The discovery of copper at nearby East Granby stimulated economic recovery in the area, and Simsbury again flourished.

Panoramas of Farmington Valley to the west are offered by the Heublein Tower at Talcott Mountain State Park.

The International Skating Center of Connecticut, 1375 Hopmeadow St., lets visitors watch Olympic figure skating champions and Olympic hopefuls train and perform in shows; phone (860) 651-5400.

PHELPS TAVERN MUSEUM & HOMESTEAD is at 800 Hopmeadow St. The 1771 Phelps House, used as a tavern 1786-1849, played host to travelers who arrived by horse, stagecoach and canal. The museum includes the tavern room, card room, kitchen, guest

rooms, ballroom and meeting room, all of which contain period furniture and historical and family items. **Tours:** Guided tours are available. **Time:** Allow 1 hour minimum. **Hours:** Tues.-Sat. noon-4. Closed major holidays. **Cost:** $6; $5 (ages 65+); $4 (ages 6-17). **Phone:** (860) 658-2500.

SOUTHINGTON (C-3) elev. 149′

Cement and hardware long have been the major industries in Southington, which was settled in 1696. Several historic houses, many with 18th-century doorways and trim, stand near the green.

Greater Southington Chamber of Commerce: One Factory Sq., Suite 201, Southington, CT 06489. **Phone:** (860) 628-8036.

BARNES MUSEUM is at 85 N. Main St. The house, framed in solid oak, has finely crafted woodwork, stairways and fireplaces. Inside, historic diaries, photographs, periodicals, clothing and other items dating from 1836 are displayed. **Time:** Allow 30 minutes minimum. **Hours:** Guided tours Mon.-Wed. and Fri. 1-5, Thurs. 1-7 (also first and last Sat. of the month 1-5, Sept.-June). Closed major holidays. **Cost:** $5; $4 (ages 60+); $2 (ages 7-18 and students with ID). **Phone:** (860) 628-5426.

SUFFIELD (A-4) elev. 124′

In an area bought from the native inhabitants by John Pynchon in 1670, Suffield thrived on tobacco growing, which was learned from the former owners. As early as 1727 this crop was of such importance that it was legal tender; tobacco remains an important crop today.

PHELPS-HATHEWAY HOUSE & GARDEN is at 55 S. Main St. (SR 75). The home reflects two 18th-century architectural styles. The original portion of the 1761 house is a typical Colonial house, while the north wing, added in 1794, is one of the first examples of the neoclassical style in the Connecticut Valley. The house contains one of the few known signed and dated rooms; on its walls are four French hand-blocked wallpapers of the 1790s.

Time: Allow 30 minutes minimum. **Hours:** Sat.-Sun. 1-4, Memorial Day weekend-Columbus Day weekend. Last tour departs at closing. **Cost:** $7; $6 (ages 65+); $4 (ages 6-18); $15 (family, two adults with children). **Phone:** (860) 668-0055 or (860) 247-8996.

WEST HARTFORD (B-3)
pop. 63,589, elev. 146′

Noah Webster was born in West Hartford in 1758 and remained until 1798. His first small dictionary of the American language (as distinguished from the British) appeared in 1806; the large version in 1828. A 13.5-foot statue of the lexicographer sculpted by Korczak Ziolkowski stands on the town hall lawn.

A 1912 Pope-Hartford Model 28 Roadster is permanently displayed in the AAA Automobile Club of Hartford's West Hartford office at 815 Farmington Ave.; phone (860) 236-3261. The display exemplifies the area's contribution to the advancement of automotive development in the early 1900s.

SAVE **THE CHILDREN'S MUSEUM** is at 950 Trout Brook Dr. A life-size replica of a sperm whale greets visitors to the center, where hands-on exhibits invite children to explore science, nature and astronomy. Permanent exhibits include the Idea Zone, Turtle Town, Critter Crossing, Kids' Corner and Excavation Station. The Gengras Planetarium presents daily star and laser shows; the UTC Wildlife Sanctuary is home to more than 80 species of live animals including lizards, owls, rabbits and snakes, .

Time: Allow 1 hour, 30 minutes minimum. **Hours:** Mon.-Sat. 9-4, Sun. 11-4, July-Aug.; Tues.-Sat. and Mon. holidays 9-4, Sun. 11-4, rest of year. Critter Crossing closed Tues. 10-noon and Wed. 10-11. Closed Easter, Memorial Day, July 4, Labor Day, Thanksgiving and Dec. 25. **Cost:** Exhibits $11; $10 (ages 63+); free (ages 0-1). Exhibits and one show $11; free (ages 0-1 if seated in a lap during show). Additional planetarium or laser show $4.50; free (ages 0-1 if seated in a lap). **Phone:** (860) 231-2824.

ELIZABETH PARK ROSE GARDENS is off I-84 exit 48 at 1555 Asylum Ave. Nearly 15,000 plants boast 650 varieties of roses. Peak blooming season for the rose, annual and perennial gardens is late June to early July; however, the gardens provide continuous color from spring through fall. Lawn bowling can be played in summer, and ice skating is offered in winter. **Hours:** Park open daily dawn-dusk. **Cost:** Free. **Phone:** (860) 231-9443.

NOAH WEBSTER HOUSE & WEST HARTFORD HISTORICAL SOCIETY is at 227 S. Main St. Lexicographer Noah Webster, author of the first American dictionary and the "Blue-Backed Speller," was born here in 1758. The restored farmhouse and an adjoining museum contain period furnishings and changing exhibits; a videotape presentation commemorates Webster's life. Costumed guides conduct tours.

Time: Allow 1 hour minimum. **Hours:** Tours are given Thurs.-Mon. 1-4. Closed major holidays and the first 5 weekdays in Jan. Phone ahead to confirm schedule. **Cost:** $7; $5 (ages 62+); $4 (ages 6-18 and students with ID). **Phone:** (860) 521-5362.

WETHERSFIELD (B-4) pop. 26,271, elev. 36′

Along with Windsor, Wethersfield claims to be the oldest permanent English settlement in Connecticut. One of the first Colonial uprisings against British authority occurred Apr. 11, 1640, when the townspeople held an illegal public election. As a result the Royal Court fined them 5 pounds, but the citizens refused to pay.

Wethersfield became the commercial center for towns along the Connecticut River; ships built, owned and manned by locals sailed along the coast and to the West Indies with goods produced by the rich valley soil. Many structures built prior to 1800 are marked with the date of construction and the names of the original owners. The original Colonial steeple and brickwork of the Meeting House, now the First Church of Christ, remain.

The Cove Warehouse, at the north end of Main Street, was built in the 1600s and remained standing after a flood in 1692 that changed the course of the river; phone (860) 529-7656.

BUTTOLPH-WILLIAMS HOUSE is at 249 Broad St. at Marsh St. The diamond-paned casement windows, weathered clapboards, hewn overhang and period furnishings of this 1711 house epitomize the Puritan pioneering of New England. **Time:** Allow 30 minutes minimum. **Hours:** Mon. and Wed.-Sat. 10-4, Sun. 1-4, May-Oct. Last tour begins 30 minutes before closing. **Cost:** $4; $3 (ages 60+); $2 (ages 5-18 and students with ID); $10 (family, two adults and children). **Phone:** (860) 529-0460.

WEBB-DEANE-STEVENS MUSEUM is .5 mi. w. of I-91 exit 26 at 211 Main St. Three 18th-century houses—reflecting 250 years of the nation's history—include the elegant 1781 home of America's first diplomat, Silas Deane; the 1752 Webb house, site of George Washington's 1781 meeting with French General Comte de Rochambeau to plan a joint campaign to end the American Revolutionary War; and the post-Industrial Revolution household of leatherworker Isaac Stevens. Family artifacts, costumes, textiles and decorative arts are part of the museum collection.

Murals commissioned by Wallace Nutting depict the Battle of Yorktown and other historic sites, and the room in which Washington slept retains its original 18th-century wallpaper. A 1921 Colonial Revival garden has been recreated on the grounds.

Time: Allow 1 hour minimum. **Hours:** Guided tours are offered on the hour Mon. and Wed.-Sat. 10-4, Sun. 1-4, May-Oct.; Sat. 10-4, Sun. 1-4, in Apr. and Nov. Themed holiday tours are offered daily in Dec. Closed Jan. 1, Easter, Memorial Day, July 4, Labor Day, Thanksgiving and Dec. 25. **Cost:** Three-house tour $8; $7 (ages 60+); $4 (ages 5-18 and students with ID); $20 (family, two adults and children). Highlight tour $4; $3 (ages 60+); $2 (ages 5-18 and students with ID); $10 (family, two adults and children). **Phone:** (860) 529-0612.

WETHERSFIELD MUSEUM AT KEENEY MEMORIAL CULTURAL CENTER is at 200 Main St. This center, built in 1893 as a school, houses the Wethersfield Historical Society's museum, which features "Legendary People, Ordinary Lives," an exhibit about local history. Also on display are changing exhibits by local artists. **Time:** Allow 30 minutes minimum. **Hours:** Mon.-Sat. 10-4, Sun. 1-4. Closed major holidays. **Cost:** $5; free (ages 0-15 and Wethersfield residents). **Phone:** (860) 529-7161 or (860) 529-7656.

WINDSOR (B-4) elev. 54′

Windsor shares with Wethersfield a claim to being the oldest town in the state, a controversy that may never be settled. In 1639 Windsor united with Hartford and Wethersfield under the "Fundamental Orders" to form the Colony of Connecticut.

FIRST CHURCH IN WINDSOR is at 107 Palisado Ave. The present building was erected in 1794, but the Congregational organization, having begun in 1630, is among the oldest gathered congregations in North America. The adjoining cemetery, which is not managed by the church, contains tombstones dating from the 1600s.

Hours: Sunday services are held at 8 and 9:30, third weekend in June-Labor Day weekend; at 8 and 10, rest of year. Church open by appointment with a two-week advance request. Cemetery open daily 24 hours. **Cost:** Donations. **Phone:** (860) 688-7229 for the church.

NORTHWEST PARK & NATURE CENTER is off I-91N exit 38 or I-91S exit 38A, 1.5 mi. n. on SR 75, 1.2 mi. w. on Prospect Hill, then 1 mi. n. on Lang Rd. This 473-acre park includes more than 10 miles of trails for hiking, jogging and cross-country skiing. The nature center features a children's tree house and hands-on displays in the Discovery Room. Sheep, goats and chickens live in the adjacent animal barn. The Luddy/Taylor Connecticut Valley Tobacco Museum houses early and modern harvesting equipment in a former curing shed.

Time: Allow 1 hour minimum. **Hours:** Park open daily dawn-dusk. Nature center open Mon.-Sat. 8:30-4:30. Tobacco museum open Tues.-Thurs. and Sat. noon-4, early Mar. to mid-Dec. **Cost:** Free. **Phone:** (860) 285-1886 for the nature center, or (860) 285-1888 for the museum.

THE OLIVER ELLSWORTH HOMESTEAD is at 778 Palisado Ave. The Federalist Colonial home was built in 1781 by Connecticut's first senator and Supreme Court Justice, who played a role in the framing of the U.S. Constitution. Ellsworth is the author of the Judiciary Act, which set the stage for the country's third branch of government. The home features many original artifacts, including china and furniture.

Tours: Guided tours are available. **Time:** Allow 1 hour minimum. **Hours:** Wed., Thurs. and Sat. noon-4, May 15-Oct. 15 (also last Sun. of the month 1-4, July-Sept.). Closed major holidays. **Cost:** Donations. **Phone:** (860) 688-8717.

PALISADO GREEN is on Palisado Ave. (SR 159). The green occupies part of the site of the old stockade built during the 1637 Pequot War. The Founders Monument lists the English settlers who disembarked from the *Mary and John* in 1630. Also on the grounds is a statue of John Mason, an original founder of Windsor. Adjacent is the Palisado Cemetery, which contains tombstones dating from the 1600s. **Hours:** Cemetery open dawn-dusk.

THE VINTAGE RADIO AND COMMUNICATIONS MUSEUM OF CONNECTICUT is .6 mi. n.e. on SR 159 from jct. SR 75, then .4 mi. n.w. to 115 Pierson

Ln. The museum chronicles the evolution of communications technology and allows visitors to tune antique radios, communicate via candlestick telephones, create and send Morse code messages, crank a phonograph and listen to century-old records. Exhibits detail the history and uses of such equipment as telegraphs, telephones and computers as well as the practices of mechanical sound recording, satellite communications and wireless telegraphy. **Time:** Allow 1 hour, 30 minutes minimum. **Hours:** Thurs.-Fri. 10-3, Sat. 10-5, Sun. 1-4. **Cost:** $7; $6 (ages 60+); $5 (students with ID); free (ages 0-4). Cash only. **Phone:** (860) 683-2903.

WINDSOR HISTORICAL SOCIETY is at 96 Palisado Ave. (SR 159). The museum comprises the 1758 John and Sarah Strong House, the 1769 Dr. Hezekiah Chaffee House, two exhibition galleries, the Hands-On-History Learning Center and a research library. **Time:** Allow 1 hour minimum. **Hours:** Tues.-Sat. 10-4. Closed major holidays. **Cost:** Complex $5; $4 (senior citizens and students with ID); free (ages 0-12). **Phone:** (860) 688-3813.

WINDSOR LOCKS (A-4)

pop. 12,043, elev. 49'

To skirt a series of rapids on the Connecticut River, the 6-mile Enfield Canal was built at Windsor in 1829. Horses towed boats weighing up to 70 tons, and three locks accommodated a 30-foot drop in elevation. Trains later supplanted river shipping, but Windsor Locks remains a major transportation hub as the home of Bradley International Airport.

SAVE **NEW ENGLAND AIR MUSEUM** is off I-91 exit 40 just off SR 75 next to Bradley International Airport. Displays include more than 80 vintage and modern aircraft as well as aviation exhibits and memorabilia in three hangars. The 58th Bomb Wing Memorial honors the first men to take the B-29 Superfortress into combat during World War II. **Time:** Allow 1 hour minimum. **Hours:** Daily 10-5. Closed Jan. 1, Thanksgiving and Dec. 25. **Cost:** $10; $9 (ages 65+); $6 (ages 4-11). **Phone:** (860) 623-3305.

Bushnell Park / Ed Homonylo / Getty Images

This ends listings for the Hartford Vicinity.
The following page resumes the alphabetical listings of cities in Connecticut.

KENSINGTON—see Hartford p. 56.

KENT (B-1) pop. 2,858, elev. 395'

Kent was incorporated in 1739 after lots were sold at public auction in Windham. Known as a center for winter sports and hiking, the town also is home to a large art colony. The Housatonic River has cut a gorge through the limestone, and geologists find excellent specimens of marble and schist in the area. Bull's Bridge, built circa 1842, spans the river. It is one of two covered bridges in the state that accommodates automobile traffic.

CONNECTICUT ANTIQUE MACHINERY ASSOCIATION MUSEUM is 1 mi. n. on US 7 on Kent-Cornwall Rd. Nine exhibit buildings house antique machinery, including a three-foot gauge railroad, tractors, steam-powered manufacturing machines and engines used to pump oil. A late 1800s agricultural schoolhouse is on the grounds as well as a mining and mineral museum dedicated to the state's mineral history. During a festival in late September, visitors can see the machines in operation. **Time:** Allow 1 hour minimum. **Hours:** Wed.-Sun. 10-4, May-Oct. **Cost:** Donations. $3; free (ages 0-11). Additional fees may apply during special events. **Phone:** (860) 927-0050.

KENT FALLS STATE PARK is 4 mi. n. on SR 7. A favorite with Impressionist painters at the turn of the 20th century, the 295-acre park contains a spectacular waterfall that plunges 250 feet to the Housatonic River. A half-mile trail with observation decks goes to the falls, while a footpath leads across a covered bridge. An outdoor exhibit features a reproduction of Willard Leroy Metcalf's painting "November Mosaic" in the setting where the artist worked. *See Recreation Chart.*

Time: Allow 30 minutes minimum. **Hours:** Daily 8-dusk. **Cost:** Free. **Parking:** Sat.-Sun. and holidays $20; $14 (state residents). **Phone:** (860) 927-3238. 🅰️

SLOANE-STANLEY MUSEUM is 1 mi. n. of jct. US 7 and SR 341. Displayed are Early American tools and paintings donated by artist and author Eric Sloane. One wing houses a re-creation of Sloane's Warren studio. Next to the museum a small structure depicts the austere conditions of an early frontier cabin. Below the museum are the ruins of a Kent iron furnace, which began producing pig iron in 1826 and continued for almost 70 years.

Hours: Thurs. 10-4, mid-May to late Oct. Last admission 30 minutes before closing. **Cost:** $8; $6 (ages 60+ and college students with ID); $5 (ages 6-17). Phone ahead to confirm schedule and rates as changes may occur without notice. **Phone:** (860) 927-3849 or (860) 256-2800.

LAKEVILLE (A-2) elev. 975'

The Holley-Williams House Museum and Salisbury Cannon Museum, on the north side of US 44 in the Lakeville Historic District, feature hands-on exhibits and living-history tours; phone (860) 435-0566.

(SAVE) **LIME ROCK PARK** is at 60 White Hollow Rd. One of America's oldest continuously operated sports car tracks, it plays host to amateur and professional racing events. The 1.5-mile track allows hillside viewing from the surrounding 325-acre Litchfield Hills. **Hours:** Grounds open Mon.-Sat. 9-5. Racing events are held early Apr. to mid-Oct. Car shows are held on Memorial Day and Labor Day. Camping begins at 6 p.m. the evening before events. **Cost:** $15-$80; free (ages 0-12). **Phone:** (860) 435-5000 or (800) 722-3577. 🍴

LEBANON (C-5) elev. 270'

Lebanon's tree-shaded streets, old houses, spacious lawns and green common give no indication of the Revolutionary War activity that once took place. The town was a cultural center and home to the Trumbull family and its vast West India trade. When the Stamp Act was passed in 1770, trade was devastated and personal fortunes were lost. In April of the same year local freemen drafted a declaration of rights and liberties that foreshadowed the Declaration of Independence.

JONATHAN TRUMBULL HOUSE MUSEUM is off SR 87 on Lebanon Green. The 1735 house was the home of the Revolutionary War governor of Connecticut, said to be the only Colonial governor to support the war. Trumbull was a counselor to George Washington and housed a detachment of Comte de Rochambeau's army.

Behind the house is the Wadsworth Stable. Also featured is the William Beaumont House, which contains displays of surgical instruments. **Hours:** Trumbull House open Wed.-Sun. noon-4, May 15-Oct. 15. Beaumont House open Sat. noon-4, third Sat. in May-Columbus Day weekend. **Cost:** $3; free (ages 0-5). **Phone:** (860) 642-7558.

LEDYARD (C-6)

East of Ledyard, the Pequot Indians called the land Mashantucket, or the "much wooded place." In the 1637 Pequot Wars, most tribal members were forced off their land, and only a few dozen Pequots remained by the early 1800s. Illegal land sales later reduced the reservation to 200 acres. In 1983, the federal government placed 1,250 acres in trust for the Mashantucket Pequots, who now operate one of the largest resort casinos in the world.

MASHANTUCKET PEQUOT MUSEUM & RESEARCH CENTER is e. on SR 2 then s. on SR 214, following signs to 110 Pequot Tr. The center is devoted to the history and culture of the Pequot Indian tribe and other Eastern Woodland tribes. The native and natural history of southern New England from the last ice age to the present is examined through dioramas, interactive displays, audiovisual presentations, archeological collections, artwork and traditional crafts.

An 18th-century farmstead contains a garden and orchard. Exhibits about the impact of the last ice age include a large globe showing glacial movements and a simulated glacial crevasse with wind and ice.

A life-size and re-created 16th-century Pequot village contains scenes with wigwams and clothing made by native craftspersons. Interactive 3-D computers and 13 filmed presentations explain daily life and present historical events. An 18-story tower provides panoramic views of the reservation.

The museum is handicapped-accessible. **Time:** Allow 3 hours minimum. **Hours:** Wed.-Sat. 10-4. Last admission 1 hour before closing. Closed Jan. 1, Thanksgiving Eve and Day, and Dec. 24-25 and 31. **Cost:** $15; $13 (ages 55+); $10 (ages 6-15). **Phone:** (800) 411-9671. *See color ad p. 294.* ⊞

GAMBLING ESTABLISHMENTS

- **Foxwoods Resort Casino** is on SR 2, 7.3 mi. w. of I-95 exit 92; from I-395 exit 79A, s.e. 11 mi. on SR 2. **Hours:** Daily 24 hours. **Phone:** (860) 312-3000 or (800) 752-9244. *See color ad inside front cover.*

LITCHFIELD (B-2) pop. 1,328, elev. 1,100'

Founded in 1719, Litchfield is noted for its many fine Colonial houses, including the birth site of Harriet Beecher Stowe. The town also is the home of the first law school in the country, founded in 1784 by Judge Tapping Reeve. One of Reeve's first law students was his brother-in-law, Aaron Burr, who became Thomas Jefferson's vice president and killed Alexander Hamilton in a duel.

The Livingston Ripley Waterfowl Conservatory, 10 Duck Pond Rd., is home to more than 60 species of waterfowl. Guided tours are offered; phone (860) 567-1691 for information and reservations.

Litchfield Hills/Northwest Connecticut Convention & Visitors Bureau: P.O. Box 968, Litchfield, CT 06759-0968. **Phone:** (860) 567-4506 or (800) 663-1273.

LITCHFIELD HISTORY MUSEUM is at jct. SRs 118 and 63. Several galleries contain paintings, furniture, decorative arts and costumes that tell the story of the town. One exhibition gallery changes annually. A research library is available. **Hours:** Tues.-Sat. 11-5, Sun. 1-5, mid-Apr. through Nov. 30. **Cost:** (includes Tapping Reeve House and Law

School) $5; $3 (ages 60+ and students with ID); free (ages 0-13 and law students with ID). **Phone:** (860) 567-4501.

LOURDES IN LITCHFIELD is .5 mi. e. on SR 118. Built by the Montfort Missionaries, the Shrine of Our Lady of Lourdes is a replica of the grotto in France. On the 35-acre grounds are Stations of the Cross, several small shrines and a picnic area. **Hours:** Grounds open daily dawn-dusk. Mass is conducted during pilgrimage season Tues.-Sun. at 11:30, May-Oct. **Cost:** Donations. **Phone:** (860) 567-1041. ⊞

TAPPING REEVE HOUSE AND LAW SCHOOL is at 82 South St. The renovated house and law school feature an exhibition about America's first school of law and the contributions of its many graduates to the development of politics, law, business and legal education in early 19th-century America. The school began in 1774 under the tutelage of a single student and evolved into an institution that graduated some 1,100 attorneys before it closed in 1833.

Hours: Tues.-Sat. 11-5, Sun. 1-5, mid-Apr. through Nov. 30. **Cost:** (includes Litchfield History Museum) $5; $3 (ages 60+ and students with ID); free (ages 0-13 and law students with ID). **Phone:** (860) 567-4501.

TOPSMEAD STATE FOREST is 2 mi. e. on SR 118, right on E. Litchfield Rd., then right on Buell Rd. The 600-acre forest lies atop a 1,230-foot knoll. Once the summer home of Edith Morton Chase, daughter of the founder of Chase Brass, the forest contains her English Tudor-style cottage, which is furnished with 17th- and 18th-century antiques and surrounded by formal gardens. Walking, sledding and cross-country skiing are possible over several miles of trails, roads and open fields.

Fires are not permitted. **Time:** Allow 30 minutes minimum. **Hours:** Park open daily 8-dusk. Chase House open second and fourth weekends of the month noon-5, June-Oct. **Cost:** Donations. **Phone:** (860) 567-5694. ⊞ 🐾

WHITE MEMORIAL FOUNDATION is 2 mi. s.w. on US 202. The 4,000-acre wildlife sanctuary includes about half of the shoreline of Bantam Lake,

the Bantam River, streams and ponds, a mile-long boardwalk and 35 miles of trails for cross-country skiing, hiking and horseback riding (equipment is not available).

The White Memorial Conservation Center Museum explains the refuge's natural features and wildlife. Guided tours and nature programs are available upon request. **Hours:** Grounds open daily 24 hours. Center open Mon.-Sat. 9-5, Sun. noon-5; closed major holidays. **Cost:** $5; $2.50 (ages 6-12). **Phone:** (860) 567-0857. 🚻 🔺

RECREATIONAL ACTIVITIES
Horseback Riding
- **Lee's Riding Stable** is 2 mi. e. on SR 118 at 57 E. Litchfield Rd. **Hours:** Daily 9-5. Closed Thanksgiving and Dec. 25. **Phone:** (860) 567-0785.

WINERIES
- **Haight Vineyard and Winery** is 1 mi. e. of the green on SR 118, then s. at wine trail sign to 29 Chestnut Hill Rd. **Hours:** Mon.-Sat. 11-5, Sun. noon-5. Closed Easter, Thanksgiving and Dec. 25. **Phone:** (860) 567-4045.

MADISON (D-4) elev. 30'

Madison is the site of Hammonasset Beach State Park *(see Recreation Chart)*, Connecticut's largest waterfront park. The town's historic sites include the 1681 Deacon John Grave House and the 1785 Allis-Bushnell House, which houses the Madison Historical Society and is open in summer as a museum of local history.

MANCHESTER—*see Hartford p. 57.*

MERIDEN (C-4) pop. 58,244, elev. 150'

From the 19th century through the 1970s, Meriden was a leader in the silverware industry. Ashbil Griswold made the first pewterware in 1808, and in 1847 Asa Rogers invented electroplating. Meriden also is known for its vibrant daffodils.

Greater Meriden Chamber of Commerce: 3 Colony St., Suite 301, Meriden, CT 06450. **Phone:** (203) 235-7901.

HUBBARD PARK is 2 mi. w. on I-691, reached via W. Main St. This 1,803-acre park is in the Hanging Hills, which reach an elevation of 1,007 feet. The park was designed by the Olmstead brothers. Of interest are Castle Craig, a stone observation tower, Mirror Lake and Merimere Reservoir. Drives, paths, a nature trail and fishing are available. **Hours:** Park open daily dawn-dusk. Observation tower open daily 10-4:45, May-Oct. **Cost:** Free. **Phone:** (203) 630-4259.

MIDDLEBURY (C-2)

Named for its central location between the settlements of Southbury, Waterbury and Woodbury, the town of Middlebury was established in 1790.

Northwest Connecticut Convention & Visitors Bureau: 21 Church St., Waterbury, CT 06702. **Phone:** (203) 597-9527 or (888) 588-7880.

QUASSY AMUSEMENT PARK is off I-84 exit 16E or 17W on SR 64 at 2132 Middlebury Rd. The 20-acre park on Lake Quassapaug has 24 rides, games, a beach and picnic facilities. Saturation Station is an interactive water play area at sandy Quassy Beach; the beach is on a spring-fed lake.

Hours: Sun.-Thurs. 11-8, Fri.-Sat. 11-10, late May-June 12 and June 22-Aug. 31; Sat.-Sun. noon-6, late Apr.-late May and Sept.-early Oct.; Mon.-Thurs. 10-4, Sat.-Sun. 10-6, June 13-June21. Saturation Station daily 11-7, Memorial Day-Labor Day. **Cost:** Individual ride tickets $3; 25¢ (Fri., May 23-Labor Day). Twelve tickets $27. All-day ride and swim pass (includes beach admission) $21; $17 (under 45 inches tall and senior citizens). Ride pass after 5 p.m. $9. Saturation Station and beach only $10. Carload $20 (Sat. 5-10, May 26-Sept. 1; includes parking). Hours and admission may vary; phone ahead. **Parking:** $5. **Phone:** (203) 758-2913 or (800) 367-7275.

MIDDLETOWN—*see Hartford p. 57.*

MOODUS (C-4) pop. 1,263

Moodus has been a center for twine production for more than a century, but an even older distinction is the strange subterranean rumblings associated with the area. American Indian legend claims the noises are the threats of evil spirits; early settlers believed the noises were the work of the devil.

Legend claims that in 1765 a Dr. Steele from Great Britain disappeared while researching the phenomenon, leaving word that the sounds were caused by two pearls he had discovered. He warned the residents that he had found others in miniature, that, when developed, would produce the same effect.

The "Moodus Noises" did not recur until 1791 when explosions and violent shocks that opened crevices in the earth again racked the area. Modern scientific opinion holds that the sounds are the result of movement along intersecting fractures in the Earth's crust.

Dating from 1816, the Amasa Day House is furnished with three generations of Day family heirlooms. A barn contains a museum; phone (860) 873-8144.

MYSTIC (D-6) pop. 4,001, elev. 9'

The fastest clipper ships in the country were being built in Mystic by the middle of the 19th century. In 1861 the first regular ironclad vessel, the *Galena*, was built in the Mystic shipyards. Houses dating from those maritime days still stand.

Mystic Depot Welcome Center: 2 Roosevelt Ave., Mystic, CT 06355. **Phone:** (860) 572-9578 or (860) 572-1102.

Shopping areas: Olde Mistick Village, off I-95 exit 90 at Coogan Boulevard, offers more than 60 specialty stores and restaurants set in a Colonial New England atmosphere, featuring gardens, a water wheel and duck pond; phone (860) 536-4941. Across the street is the Mystic Factory Outlets, featuring Bass, Izod, Lacoste, London Fog and Van Heusen.

ARGIA MYSTIC CRUISES leaves from Schooner Wharf at 15 Holmes St. The company offers cruises aboard the 81-foot schooner *Argia*.

Hours: Half-day cruises depart daily at 10:20 and 2:20. Two-hour sunset cruises depart daily at 5:30, May-Oct.

Cost: Half-day and sunset fare $42; $39 (ages 60+); $33 (ages 0-18 with adult). Reservations are required. **Phone:** (860) 536-0416.

DENISON HOMESTEAD MUSEUM is off I-95 exit 90, n. on SR 27, e. on Jerry Brown Rd., then s. to 120 Pequotsepos Rd. Dating from 1717, the homestead illustrates home life in New England from the Colonial period to 1941. Heirlooms of six generations of Denisons represent five stylistic periods. **Time:** Allow 1 hour minimum. **Hours:** Mon. to Fri.-Sat. 1-5, Sun. noon-4, mid-June to mid-Oct. Last tour departs 30 minutes before closing. Phone ahead to confirm schedule. **Cost:** $5; $4 (ages 62+ and students with ID); $2 (ages 0-11). **Phone:** (860) 536-9248.

DENISON PEQUOTSEPOS NATURE CENTER is off I-95 exit 90, .5 mi. n. on SR 27, 1 mi. s.e. on Jerry Brown Rd., then .5 mi. s. to 109 Pequotsepos Rd. This nature center features a natural history museum and a 300-acre wildlife sanctuary with 10 miles of well-marked trails, including a path to the Mystic Aquarium. Exhibits include both live and mounted animal specimens native to Connecticut. More than 160 species of birds have been identified within the sanctuary. Programs and events are scheduled throughout the year.

Time: Allow 1 hour minimum. **Hours:** Mon.-Sat. 9-5, Sun. 10-4. Closed Jan. 1, Thanksgiving and Dec. 25. **Cost:** $8; $5 (ages 0-12 and 65+). **Phone:** (860) 536-1216.

MYSTIC AQUARIUM & INSTITUTE FOR EXPLORATION is off I-95 exit 90 at 55 Coogan Blvd. The aquarium is home to more than 12,000 ocean animals, including beluga whales, penguins, sharks, colorful reef fish and rare blue lobsters. Animal contact programs allow visitors to go nose-to-beak with an African penguin, feed rays and wade with a beluga whale. Efforts to care for and conserve these and other animals are explored. Interactive exhibits with reptiles, native invertebrates and cownose rays is offered.

The Marine Theater features California sea lions. The aquarium is one of four sites in North America housing Steller sea lions, the largest of all sea lions. Kodiak, a Steller sea lion weighing more than 1,700 pounds, may be seen in an outdoor exhibit.

The aquarium is home to Dr. Robert Ballard's "Exploring Your National Marine Sanctuaries" research and exhibition center, featuring notable shipwrecks and coral reefs. The XD Motion Theater features the Deep Sea 3-D motion ride, which allows visitors to follow the path of a sperm whale and encounter a giant squid. "Exploring Your National Marine Sanctuaries" explores notable shipwrecks and the oceans' colorful corals.

Time: Allow 2 hours minimum. **Hours:** Daily 9-6, Mar.-Oct.; 9-5, in Nov.; 10-5, Dec.-Feb. Last admission 1 hour before closing. Closed Thanksgiving and Dec. 25. **Cost:** (good for 3 consecutive days with validation) $24; $21 (ages 60+); $18 (ages 3-17). Animal contact programs (includes admission) $79-$149; reservations are advised. Deep

Sea 3-D ride $1; riders must be at least 40 inches tall. **Phone:** (860) 572-5955. [11]

MYSTIC ARTS CENTER is at 9 Water St. on the Mystic River. Oils, watercolors, sculptures and etchings by popular local and regional artists are displayed, in addition to works by landscape painters who settled in the area in the early 20th century and created a thriving art colony. Juried shows throughout the year also feature photography and abstract art. **Time:** Allow 30 minutes minimum. **Hours:** Daily 11-5. Closed Jan. 1, Easter, Thanksgiving and Dec. 25. **Cost:** Donations. **Phone:** (860) 536-7601.

MYSTIC SEAPORT is 1 mi. s. of I-95 exit 90 to 75 Greenmanville Ave., along the Mystic River. Among its 17 acres are over 50 historic houses, shops, galleries and trade buildings that promote an understanding of life in a seaport during the mid-19th century. The last of the wooden whaling ships, the *Charles W. Morgan*, the 1882 training ship *Joseph Conrad* and the fishing schooner *L.A. Dunton* can be boarded by visitors; many other ships and boats are displayed.

Ship models, scrimshaw, figureheads and small boats trace the history of ships, shipbuilding and maritime activities. A children's museum contains toys, clothing and games popular in the 19th century. The 1908 steamboat *Sabino* offers half-hour excursions on the Mystic River.

Time: Allow 2 hours minimum. **Hours:** Museum open daily 9-5, Apr.-Oct.; Tues.-Sun. 10-4 (also Mon. in Nov.), rest of year. Cruise leaves on the half-hour 11:30-3:30, mid-May to Columbus Day. Closed Dec. 24-25. **Cost:** (good for 2 consecutive days with validation) $24; $22 (ages 65+, military and students with ID); $15 (ages 6-17). Cruise $5.50; $4.50 (ages 6-17). **Phone:** (860) 572-0711, (860) 572-5315 or (888) 973-2767. [11]

NEW BRITAIN—*see Hartford p. 57.*

NEW CANAAN (D-1) elev. 340'

Along SR 106 is the main area of the New Canaan Bird Sanctuary and Wildlife Preserve. Smaller areas of the preserve are on Cedar Lane and Wahackme Road; several nature trails are open for hiking daily during daylight hours.

NEW CANAAN HISTORICAL SOCIETY is 2.5 mi. n. of Merritt Pkwy. exit 37 at SR 124. The society consists of six buildings housing museums, collections and a library—the 1764 Hanford-Silliman House Museum; the 1878 John Rogers Studio and Museum; the re-created, 19th-century Tool Museum and Print Shop with the New Canaan Hand Press; 1799 Rock School, 1868 Little Red Schoolhouse and the 1845 Cody Drug Store. The 1825 Town House includes the Costume Museum and a research and genealogical library.

Tours: Guided tours are available. **Hours:** Town House and library open Tues.-Fri. 9:30-4:30, Sat. 9:30-12:30 and 2-4:30. Tool Museum and John Rogers Studio open Tues. 2-4. Rock School open only

for special events. Other buildings open Wed.-Thurs. 2-4, Sept.-June, and by appointment. Reservations are required for tours; phone ahead. Closed major holidays. **Cost:** Donations. **Phone:** (203) 966-1776.

NEW CANAAN NATURE CENTER is 3 mi. n. from Merritt Pkwy. exit 37 at 144 Oenoke Ridge Rd. (off SR 124), .5 mi. n. of the town center. Native plants and animals inhabit the preserve's 40 acres of meadow, woodland, stream, pond and marsh habitats; gardens and displays adjoin nature trails. Environmental tips are shared in exhibits about landscaping. The outdoor Birds of Prey exhibit, consisting of seven aviaries, also is included.

The Discovery Center offers hands-on exhibits, and there also is a public greenhouse. **Hours:** Mon.-Sat. 9-4. Trails open daily dawn-dusk. **Cost:** Donations. **Phone:** (203) 966-9577.

THE PHILIP JOHNSON GLASS HOUSE offers tours departing from the visitor center at 199 Elm St. On the 47-acre site rests the former private residence of architect Philip Johnson, whose stylistic achievements include the Sony Tower and Seagram Building in New York City as well as the Crystal Cathedral in Garden Grove, Calif. The 1949 glass house served as Johnson's home until his death in 2005. As its name implies, the house has a structure consisting of four glass sides, allowing for the scenery from the outdoor pond and woodland area to be seen clearly from indoors. David Whitney, a curator and avid art collector with whom Johnson was friends for nearly 50 years, designed the landscape.

Portraits of Johnson by artist Andy Warhol, pieces contributed by other artists and exhibits honoring the accomplishments of renowned architects as well as outdoor pottery and underground art studios may be seen during 90-minute and 2-hour tours.

Note: Each tour is limited to 10 participants. Tour tickets must be purchased in advance and be presented at the visitor center in order for tour admittance. Photography is not permitted on the 90-minute tour, but is allowed on the 2-hour tour. Limited parking for guests with special needs is available at the visitor center; transportation from the center and to the house is provided to all. Tour participants should arrive at least 20 minutes prior to the beginning of the tour. **Time:** Allow 1 hour, 30 minutes minimum.

Hours: Ninety-minute guided tours depart on the hour Mon. and Wed.-Sat. 10-noon, May-Oct. Two-hour guided tours depart on the hour Mon. and Wed.-Sat. 1-3, Sun. 2-3, May-Oct. Visitor center open Mon.-Sat. 9:30-5:30, Sun. 11:30-5:30, May-Oct. **Cost:** Ninety-minute tour $30. Two-hour tour $45. Reservations are required. **Phone:** (203) 594-9884 for the visitor center, or (866) 811-4111 for tickets.

SILVERMINE GUILD ARTS CENTER is off Merritt Pkwy. exit 38 at 1037 Silvermine Rd. The guild maintains an art school and five galleries that offer exhibits throughout the year, including a summer music series beginning in June and a holiday exhibit beginning in early December. **Hours:** Tues.-Sat. 11-5, Sun. 1-5. Closed major holidays and Dec. 25-31. **Cost:** Donations. **Phone:** (203) 966-9700.

NEW HARTFORD (B-3) elev. 449′

WINERIES

• **Jerram Winery** is 5.6 mi. s./s.w. on US 202 from jct. US 44, then 2 mi. n.e. on SR 219 (Town Hill Rd.) to 535 Town Hill Rd. **Hours:** Daily 11-5, May-Dec.; Sat.-Sun. 11-5, in Jan. and Apr. Closed major holidays. **Phone:** (860) 379-8749.

NEW HAVEN (C-3) pop. 123,626, elev. 33′

New Haven was laid out by the Puritans in 1638 in nine equal squares; the central square, or green, was reserved for the public. Historic buildings are scattered throughout the city.

Termed the "Birthplace of the Nation's Hits," the Shubert Theatre, 247 College St., is where many of the world's most popular actors, musicians and dancers made their debuts; phone (203) 562-5666. Other venues include Yale Repertory Theatre, 1120 Chapel St., (203) 432-1234 or TTY (203) 432-1521; and Long Wharf Theatre, 222 Sargent Dr. at the junction of I-95, I-91 and SR 34, (203) 787-4282 or (800) 782-8497.

New Haven also was the birthplace of 43rd president George W. Bush. Graced by the presence of Yale University, New Haven is a college town as well.

Among interesting items invented in New Haven were the corkscrew, lollipop, steamboat and steel fishhook.

Sightseeing cruises off the coast of New Haven are available from Schooner, Inc., which combines pleasure excursions with education aboard the 91-foot-long *Quinnipiack,* a replica of a Biloxi freight schooner of the late 19th century. The double-mast ship serves as a floating classroom aboard which passengers can assist in its sailing and participate in science experiments from June through October. Chantey and Ale, Brunch, Harbor Discovery, Pirate and Sunset sails are among the specialty cruises offered; phone (203) 865-1737 for reservations.

Greater New Haven Convention and Visitors Bureau: 169 Orange St., New Haven, CT 06510. **Phone:** (203) 777-8550 or (800) 332-7829.

EAST ROCK PARK is 1.3 mi. n. on Church St./Whitney Ave., .3 mi. e. on Willow St. and .2 mi. n.

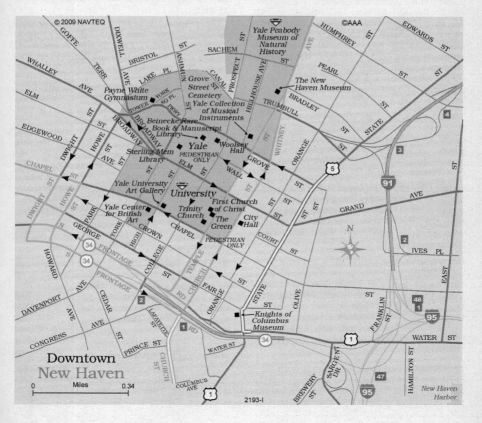

Downtown New Haven

on Orange St. to Cold Spring St. The 425-acre park includes trails and is a notable bird-watching area; visitors may see warblers in April and May. The rock for which the park is named is 365 feet high and 1.5 miles long. Accessible via Davis Road, the summit offers a panorama of Long Island Sound and the city of New Haven. The Civil War Soldiers and Sailors Monument, Indian Head Peak and the Pardee Rose Gardens are in the park.

Nature walks and animal programs at the Trowbridge Environmental Center allow visitors to learn about migrating and resident birds as well as how the area's leafless trees are identified.

Hours: Park open daily dawn-dusk. Summit open daily 8-dusk, Apr.-Oct.; Fri.-Sun. 8-dusk (weather permitting), rest of year. Environmental center open Thurs.-Fri. and some Sat. 10-5. **Cost:** Free. Environmental center program fees vary; phone ahead to verify. **Phone:** (203) 946-6086.

THE GREEN is in the center of the city. Covering 16 acres, it remains as plotted by the original settlers. Three churches on Temple Street, built about 1815, are the only buildings remaining on the green. **Hours:** Green open daily 24 hours. **Cost:** Free.

First Church of Christ is at 311 Temple St. The building is the fourth meeting place on this general site. Its first services were held outdoors in 1638. The spire, Tiffany window and wall tablets are of interest. The church covers part of the old burial ground including 1,500 to 1,700 historic gravestones, the oldest dating from 1687. **Hours:** Guided tours are available Thurs. and Sat. 11-1; crypt tours are available Thurs. and Sat. 11-1, Apr.-Oct. and by appointment. **Cost:** Donations. **Phone:** (203) 787-0121.

Trinity Church is at Temple and Chapel sts. Founded in 1752 on Church Street, the Episcopal congregation built the present church 1812-14. **Hours:** Services Sun. at 7:45, 9 and 11, mid-Sept. to early June; at 7:45 and 10, rest of year. **Cost:** Free. **Phone:** (203) 624-3101.

United Church on the Green is at 270 Temple St. at Elm St. This two-story, brick meetinghouse, built about 1815, contains a Hillebrand tracker-action pipe organ. **Hours:** Open for services Sun. at 10:30; other times by appointment. **Cost:** Free. **Phone:** (203) 787-4195.

GROVE STREET CEMETERY is at Grove St. between Prospect and Ashmun sts. The burial ground contains the graves of Lyman Beecher, James D. Dana, Charles Goodyear, Roger Sherman, Noah Webster, Theodore Winthrop and Eli Whitney. **Hours:** Daily 8-3:30. Guided tours depart Sat. at 11, first and third Sun. at noon, early May-late Nov. (weather permitting). **Cost:** Free. **Phone:** (203) 787-1443.

KNIGHTS OF COLUMBUS MUSEUM is off SR 34 exit 1 to 1 State St. Displays at the museum explain the history of the largest Catholic fraternal organization, established in New Haven in 1882. Galleries

are devoted to founder Father McGivney, the Vatican and Christopher Columbus. A Wall of History details charitable acts. **Time:** Allow 1 hour minimum. **Hours:** Daily 10-5, May 1-Labor Day; Wed.-Sat. 10-5, Sun. 11-5, rest of year. Closed Good Friday, Thanksgiving and Dec. 24-25. **Cost:** Donations. **Phone:** (203) 865-0400.

LIGHTHOUSE POINT PARK is off I-95 exit 50NB, then s. on Townsend Ave. to the end of Lighthouse Rd. The 90-foot-tall New Haven Harbor Lighthouse was built in 1840 and used 1845-77. The lighthouse is not open to the public, but boating, fishing and picnicking are permitted on the grounds; there also is a carousel. Ranger-led programs focus on marine history and ecology. **Hours:** Park open daily 7 a.m.-dusk. Carousel Sat.-Sun. and holidays noon-4, Memorial Day weekend-Labor Day. **Cost:** Free. Carousel fare 50¢. **Parking:** $10 for non-residents, Memorial Day weekend-Labor Day. **Phone:** (203) 946-8005.

[SAVE]   **THE NEW HAVEN MUSEUM** is at 114 Whitney Ave. near Trumbull St. (I-91 exit 3). Permanent and changing exhibits of furniture, paintings, maritime relics and inventions illustrate more than 350 years of New Haven history. The Whitney Library, a genealogical/historical library, also is available.

Time: Allow 1 hour minimum. **Hours:** Museum and library open Tues.-Fri. 10-5, Sat. noon-5. Closed major holidays. **Cost:** Museum or library $4; $3 (ages 62+); $2 (ages 6-16 and students with ID). **Phone:** (203) 562-4183.

WEST ROCK RIDGE STATE PARK is off Merritt Pkwy. exit 60, s. on Dixwell Ave., w. on Benham St., s. on Main St., then s. on Wintergreen to park entrance. The park, a ridge rising 428 feet high and encompassing more than 1,500 acres, offers fishing, hiking, mountain biking and scenic views. The park drive is open seasonally; parking is available at the West Rock Nature Center and at Lake Wintergreen. Of interest is Judges' Cave, named for Colonial judges who hid from British troops after they condemned Charles I to death.

Hours: Park open daily 8-dusk. Path to summit is accessible by vehicles Memorial Day through Oct. 31. **Cost:** Free. **Phone:** (203) 789-7498 to confirm when the gate is open. 🏕️ 🎣 🚫

West Rock Nature Center is off Merritt Pkwy. exit 60, s. on Dixwell Ave., w. on Benham St., s. on Main St., then s. on Wintergreen, just past the West Rock Ridge State Park entrance. A visitor center and nature house sit on 43 acres of woods with trails, ponds and meadows. **Time:** Allow 1 hour minimum. **Hours:** Mon.-Fri. 10-4 or by appointment. Closed major holidays. **Cost:** Free. **Phone:** (203) 946-8016.

[GEM]   **YALE UNIVERSITY** visitor center is at 149 Elm St. Founded in 1701 as the Collegiate School, the university moved in 1716 to New Haven, where it was renamed in honor of its benefactor, Elihu Yale.

Of the school's ivy-covered buildings, 1752 Connecticut Hall is the oldest. Nathan Hale lived and studied here. The Memorial Quadrangle, a block of Gothic-style dormitories, contains both the 216-foot Harkness Tower and the Wrexham Tower, a duplicate of the cathedral tower in Wrexham, Wales.

On Tower Parkway is the Payne Whitney Gymnasium, one of the largest buildings in the world devoted exclusively to sports and physical training. About 1,000 sporting prints from the Garvan Collection are in the gymnasium. Yale Bowl and Athletic Fields are on Derby Avenue. Guided tours of the campus start at the visitor center.

Tours: Guided tours are available. **Hours:** Visitor center open Mon.-Fri. 9-4:30, Sat.-Sun. 11-4. Tours depart Mon.-Fri. at 10:30 and 2, Sat.-Sun. and some holidays at 1:30. Closed Thanksgiving and Dec. 24-Jan. 1. **Cost:** Free. **Phone:** (203) 432-2300 Mon.-Fri. 9-4, Sat.-Sun. 10-4.

Beinecke Rare Book and Manuscript Library is at High and Wall sts. on the Yale campus. The library contains a Gutenberg Bible, books from the 1742 Yale Library, an Audubon "Birds of America" exhibit and changing displays of rare books and manuscripts. **Time:** Allow 1 hour minimum. **Hours:** Mon.-Thurs. 9-7, Fri. 9-5, Sept.-July; Mon.-Fri. 8:30-5, rest of year and during university vacations. Exhibit gallery Mon.-Thurs. 9-7, Fri. 9-5, Sat. noon-5. Closed major holidays. **Cost:** Free. **Phone:** (203) 432-2977.

Sterling Memorial Library is at 120 High St. on the Yale campus. More than ten million volumes and historical manuscripts and the Yale Archives are shelved here. **Hours:** Mon.-Thurs. 8:30-midnight, Fri. 8:30-5, Sat. 10-5, Sun. noon-midnight, Sept. 1 to mid-Dec. and mid-Jan. to mid-May; Mon.-Fri. 8:30-5, Sat. 11-3, mid-Dec. to mid-Jan.; Mon.-Fri. 8:30 a.m.-9:45 p.m., Sat. 10-5, rest of year. Closed academic holidays. **Cost:** Free. **Phone:** (203) 432-2798.

Woolsey Hall is at College and Grove sts. Home to the Yale Symphony Orchestra and Yale School of Music, the hall seats 2,695. It also features the Newberry Memorial organ. The Friday edition of the *New Haven Register* has a listing of current events. **Hours:** Events are scheduled Sept.-May. **Cost:** A fee may be charged. **Phone:** (230) 432-4158 for concert information.

Yale Center for British Art is at 1080 Chapel St. at High St. Displays include British paintings, drawings, prints, books and sculpture. A gift from Paul Mellon, the extensive collection surveys the development of British art, life and thought from the Elizabethan period to the present, stressing the period 1697-1851. Changing exhibits are featured. A research library is on the premises. **Hours:** Tues.-Sat. 10-5, Sun. noon-5. Closed Jan. 1, Memorial Day, July 4, Thanksgiving and Dec. 24-25 and 31. **Cost:** Free. **Phone:** (203) 432-2800 or (877) 274-8278.

Yale Collection of Musical Instruments is at 15 Hillhouse Ave. More than 1,000 Western and non-Western musical instruments include historic violins and other stringed instruments, harpsichords, pianos, trumpets and woodwinds. Formal concerts are offered periodically throughout the year; phone for schedule and ticket information. **Hours:** Tues.-Fri. 1-4, Sun. noon-5, Sept.-June. Closed during university vacations. **Cost:** $2. **Phone:** (203) 432-0822.

 Yale Peabody Museum of Natural History is at 170 Whitney Ave. at Sachem St.; visitor parking is 1 blk. n. at the s. end of Yale lot No. 22. The museum features fossils of dinosaurs and prehistoric mammals, dioramas of North American habitat groups and birds of Connecticut and collections devoted to the Pacific Islands, the Plains Indians, ancient Egypt and Central and South America.

Time: Allow 1 hour minimum. **Hours:** Museum open Mon.-Sat. 10-5, Sun. noon-5. Guided tours depart Sat.-Sun. at 12:30 and 1:30. Closed Jan. 1, Easter, July 4, Thanksgiving, Dec. 24-25 and 31. **Cost:** $7; $6 (ages 66+); $5 (ages 3-18 and college students with ID); free (Thurs. 2-5, Sept.-June). Guided tours free with museum admission. **Parking:** $3. **Phone:** (203) 432-5050.

Yale University Art Gallery is at 1111 Chapel St. between York and High sts. The oldest university art museum in the Western Hemisphere was founded in 1832 with a gift from patriot and artist John Trumbull. The gallery has classical and contemporary pieces, noted collection of early Italian paintings and works by Winslow Homer, Edward Hopper, Henri Matisse, Claude Monet, Pablo Picasso and Vincent van Gogh.

Hours: Tues.-Sat. 10-5 (also Thurs. 5-8, Sept.-June), Sun. 1-6. Closed major holidays. **Cost:** Free. **Phone:** (203) 432-0600.

NEW LONDON (D-5) pop. 25,671, elev. 27'

See map page 70.

New London, founded in 1646 by a group of Puritan families under John Winthrop Jr., became the principal rendezvous of privateers during the Revolution. As such the port was an important objective of Benedict Arnold's Tory force in 1781. The attackers, with the assistance of a 32-vessel fleet, burned wharves, houses and stores.

The whaling industry began in New London in 1784 and grew rapidly until it reached its height in the middle of the 19th century, when about 75 whaling vessels were based at the port. The industry declined in the late 1840s after whale populations were devastated and cheaper substitutes for whale products were found.

The downtown historic district includes Nathan Hale's Schoolhouse, the Captain's Walk and the Greek Revival houses of Whale Oil Row. The Statue of Nathan Hale in Williams Park is a duplicate of the one located in City Hall Park, New York City. The John Winthrop Jr. Monument at Buckley Place off Hempstead Street honors the colony's founder.

The cemetery on Hempstead Street, known as Ye Ancientest Burial Grounds, dates from 1653. Benedict Arnold watched the burning of New London from this point in 1781.

Pequot Avenue Drive leads from Bank Street past two prominent lighthouses to Ocean Beach, along the west bank of the Thames. On private property but visible from Pequot Avenue, the New London Harbor Lighthouse was established in 1760 and re-built in 1801. It is not open to the public. Offshore, the 1909 New London Ledge Lighthouse is notable for its French Second Empire-style corner quoins, pediment dormers and mansard roof.

Ferries depart year-round from State Street for Fisher's Island, N.Y., (631) 788-7463, and from Ferry Street for Orient Point, N.Y., (860) 443-5281. A high-speed ferry also departs New London for Block Island, R.I., from mid-June to early October; phone (860) 444-4624 or (401) 466-2212.

CONNECTICUT COLLEGE ARBORETUM is off Williams St. Walking paths lead through the 20-acre Native Plant Collection, which features 300 types of woody plants, a 4-acre pond, a wildflower garden and many other collections. The 4-acre Caroline Black Garden, off SR 32, displays a diversity of woody plants in a garden setting. **Tours:** Guided tours are available. **Hours:** Grounds open daily dawn-dusk. Guided tours are offered Sun. at 2, May-Oct.; reservations are required. **Cost:** Free. Phone ahead for tour rates. **Phone:** (860) 439-5020.

FORT TRUMBULL STATE PARK is at 90 Walbach St. The historic stronghold to the Thames River, the five-sided fort displays an Egyptian Revival style. Built in 1852, it operated from the Revolutionary War through the Cold War. Visitors may see exhibits in the former officers' quarters, the barracks and the grounds, which feature cannon batteries and a block-house citadel. Pets on a leash allowed in the park

area. **Time:** Allow 1 hour minimum. **Hours:** Park grounds open daily 8-dusk. Fort and visitor center open Wed.-Sun. 9-4, late May-Columbus Day. Fishing pier daily 24 hours. **Cost:** Free. Fort and visitor center $10; $4 (ages 6-12). **Phone:** (860) 444-7591.

HEMPSTED HOUSES are at the jct. of Hempstead, Jay and Truman sts. The houses were built in 1678 and 1759, respectively, and are furnished to represent several generations of Hempstead family life. Both contain many pieces of original furniture. The Nathaniel Hempsted House is an unusual example of Colonial New England stone construction.

Time: Allow 1 hour minimum. **Hours:** Both houses are open Sat.-Sun. noon-4, Memorial Day weekend-June 30 and Sept.-Columbus Day; Fri.-Sun. noon-4, July-Aug. **Cost:** Both houses $7; $6 (ages 65+); $4 (ages 6-18 and students with ID); $15 (family, two adults and children). **Phone:** (860) 443-7949 or (860) 247-8996.

LYMAN ALLYN ART MUSEUM is off I-95 exit 83 to 625 Williams St., across from the Coast Guard Academy and next to Connecticut College. The collection boasts more than 15,000 objects, including contemporary, modern and early American fine arts, American Impressionist paintings and Connecticut decorative arts. The Art Park is an outdoor sculpture park geared for children. Special exhibits are featured.

Hours: Tues.-Sat. 10-5, Sun. 1-5. Closed major holidays. **Cost:** $8; $7 (ages 60+ and students with ID); free (ages 0-11). **Phone:** (860) 443-2545.

MONTE CRISTO COTTAGE is 1.5 mi. s. of US 1 at 325 Pequot Ave. This is the boyhood home of Eugene O'Neill, Nobel Prize winner and one of the nation's great dramatists. The setting for his play "Long Day's Journey into Night," the cottage contains O'Neill memorabilia; a short multimedia presentation introduces visitors to the playwright.

Time: Allow 1 hour minimum. **Hours:** Thurs.-Sat. noon-4, Sun. 1-3, day after Memorial Day-day before Labor Day. Closed major holidays. **Cost:** $7; $5 (ages 65+ and students with ID). **Phone:** (860) 443-5378.

MYSTIC WHALER **CRUISES** sails from City Pier on Water St. Excursions aboard the 83-foot schooner include 5-hour day sails, lobster dinner cruises and multi-day overnight trips. **Hours:** Cruises depart Memorial Day weekend-early Sept. Phone ahead to confirm schedule. **Cost:** Day sails (including lunch) and dinner sails $80; $40 (ages 5-12). Rates may vary; phone ahead. Reservations are required. **Phone:** (860) 447-1249 or (800) 697-8420.

OCEAN BEACH PARK is off I-95 exit 83; 1.5 mi. s. Colman St. to Bank St., .2 mi. e. to Ocean Ave., then 3 mi. to end. This city-owned recreation area includes an Olympic-size pool, kid's spray park, a playground, a carousel, rides and water slides, a video arcade and an 18-hole miniature golf course.

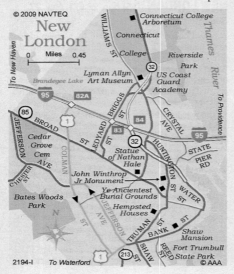

© 2009 NAVTEQ

New London

Connecticut College Arboretum

0   Miles   0.45

Connecticut College

Thames River

WILLIAMS ST

To New Haven

Brandegee Lake

Lyman Allyn Art Museum

Riverside Park

US Coast Guard Academy

To Providence

BROAD

Cedar Grove Cem

JEFFERSON

COLMAN

EDYARD ST

BRIGGS ST

Statue of Nathan Hale

CRYSTAL AVE

STATE PIER RD

HUNTINGTON ST

John Winthrop Jr Monument

CHESTER ST

Bates Woods Park

Ye Ancientest Burial Grounds

Hempstead Houses

WATER ST

JEFFERSON AVE

TRUMAN ST

BANK ST

REED ST

SHAW ST

Shaw Mansion

Fort Trumbull State Park

2194-I   To Waterford   ©AAA

A boardwalk overlooks the large beach and Long Island Sound, and a nature walk leads to an observation platform. Live entertainment is presented Monday through Saturday. Food, picnic facilities, showers and lockers are available.

Hours: Park open daily 8 a.m.-10 p.m., Sat. before Memorial Day-Labor Day; hours for individual facilities vary. **Cost:** Park entrance per private vehicle Sat.-Sun. $18; Mon.-Fri. $14; Tues.-Sat. evenings $5; July 4 $25. Additional fees apply for individual facilities such as pool, water slid or miniature golf and locker rental. Prices may vary; phone ahead. **Phone:** (860) 447-3031 or (800) 510-7263.

SHAW MANSION is at 11 Blinman St. Dating from 1756, the mansion was the home of ship owner Capt. Nathaniel Shaw Jr. and housed the Naval Office for Connecticut during the Revolution. Displays include antique furniture, silver, china and family portraits. Changing exhibits focus on New London County history. Flower gardens can be toured May through September. **Time:** Allow 1 hour minimum. **Hours:** Wed.-Fri. 1-4, Sat. 10-4, Memorial Day-Labor Day. Closed major holidays. **Cost:** $5; $4 (ages 66+). **Phone:** (860) 443-1209.

THE U.S. COAST GUARD MUSEUM is just off I-95 on Mohegan Ave. (SR 32); on the west bank of the Thames River, the museum is located in Waesche Hall at The U.S. Coast Guard Academy. Medals, uniforms, paintings and ship models highlight the Coast Guard's 200-year history. Also on display is the only known first-order Fresnel lenses in the country and a few figureheads. When in port, the training boat *Eagle* can be boarded at the State Pier.

Time: Allow 30 minutes minimum. **Hours:** Pavilion open Wed.-Sun. 10-5, May-Oct. Museum open Mon.-Fri. 9-4:30 (also Sat. 10-4:30, Sun. noon-4:30, Memorial Day weekend-Labor Day). *Eagle* tours, when in port, daily 1-5. Closed major holidays. **Cost:** Free. Photo identification required for admittance to academy grounds. **Phone:** (860) 444-8511. 🍴

NEW PRESTON (B-1) pop. 1,110

Set in the Litchfield Hills, New Preston's main draw is Lake Waramaug, a haven for summer water activities *(see Recreation Chart)*. The top of nearby Pinnacle Mountain offers views of Massachusetts and New York.

WINERIES

- **Hopkins Vineyard** is off SR 45 on Hopkins Rd., on the n. shore of Lake Waramaug. **Hours:** Mon.-Sat. 10-5, Sun. 11-5, May-Dec.; Wed.-Sat. 10-5, Sun. 11-5, Mar.-Apr.; Fri.-Sun. 10-5, rest of year. Closed Jan. 1, Thanksgiving and Dec. 25. **Cost:** Guided tour and tasting $10. **Phone:** (860) 868-7954.

NIANTIC (C-5) pop. 3,085, elev. 20′

An Algonquin tribe, the Niantics were nearly destroyed in the Pequot War of 1637, a conflict between New England Indians and colonial settlers. At one time, Niantic settlements stretched from Connecticut to Rhode Island. After the war, survivors of the Western Niantic tribe were taken in by the Mohegans; the Eastern Niantics later merged with the Narragansetts.

CHILDREN'S MUSEUM OF SOUTHEASTERN CONNECTICUT is at 409 Main St. The hands-on museum allows children ages 8 months to 10 years of age to explore such hands-on exhibits as a fossil dig in an Egyptian pyramid and preparation of flan in a Mexican restaurant. Other activities include a scavenger hunt, photo search, book exploration in a clubhouse, blowing bubbles and finding magnetic surfaces as well as exploration of a fishing boat and real 2-person submarine.

Time: Allow 1 hour minimum. **Hours:** Mon.-Sat. 9:30-5, Sun. noon-5, Memorial Day-Labor Day; Tues.-Sat. 9:30-5, Sun. noon-5, rest of year. Closed Easter, Memorial Day, July 4, Labor Day, Thanksgiving and Dec. 25. **Cost:** $6; free (under 1). **Phone:** (860) 691-1111.

SAVE **THOMAS LEE HOUSE** is off I-95 exit 72 on the Rocky Neck Connector, then .5 mi. e. to 228 W. Main St. Built about 1660, the house is an excellent example of early Colonial architecture and is furnished in period. Many articles date 1670-1800. It is said to be Connecticut's oldest frame house left in its original state. A Colonial herb garden is behind the house; next door is the well-preserved Little Boston School, dating from 1734. An exhibit describes Ezra Lee's service during the Revolutionary War aboard the *Turtle*, said to be the first American submarine. **Hours:** Wed.-Sun. 1-4, late June-day before Labor Day. **Cost:** Donations. **Phone:** (860) 739-6070 or (860) 739-7225. 🏛

NORWALK (E-2) pop. 82,951, elev. 39′

Today a suburb of New York, Norwalk was an agricultural town before the Revolution. In 1779 British soldiers seized the town and burned many buildings. By 1780 a kiln was built uptown, where the stoneware pottery for which Norwalk became recognized was produced. The Industrial Revolution prompted numerous companies to relocate to the area.

Norwalk's city hall complex, 3 blocks north of I-95 exit 16, contains an impressive collection of WPA murals commissioned expressly for the city.

Fairfield County Convention & Visitors Bureau: Gate Lodge at Mathews Park, 297 West Ave., Norwalk, CT 06850. **Phone:** (203) 853-7770 or (800) 473-4868.

Self-guiding tours: A self-guiding tour brochure is available inside Norwalk City Hall, 125 East Ave.; phone (203) 854-3200.

LOCKWOOD-MATHEWS MANSION MUSEUM is at 295 West Ave. via I-95 exit 14 northbound or exit 15 southbound. Built by Civil War financier LeGrand Lockwood, the partially restored 62-room Second Empire chateau contains stenciled walls, inlaid woodwork and a rotunda with a skylight.

Hours: Guided tours of the first and second floors depart on the hour Wed.-Sun. noon-3, Apr. 1-Jan. 1. Closed Thanksgiving and Dec. 24-25. **Cost:** Fee $10; $8 (ages 61); $6 (ages 8-18). **Phone:** (203) 838-9799.

THE MARITIME AQUARIUM AT NORWALK is on the w. bank of the Norwalk River at 10 N. Water St. The 5-acre, restored 19th-century foundry features interactive exhibits about the marine life of Long Island Sound.

Highlights of the complex include an aquarium with more than 1,000 animals native to Long Island Sound; two touch tanks, one with crabs, starfish and other animals, the second with stingrays; a jellyfish encounter; an IMAX theater; "Frogs!" exhibit; sharks, sea turtles, large fish and more. Changing exhibits and educational programs also are featured.

Time: Allow 2 hours, 30 minutes minimum. **Hours:** Daily 10-6, July-Aug.; 10-5, rest of year. Last admission 30 minutes before closing. IMAX films are shown daily; phone for schedule. Closed Thanksgiving and Dec. 25. **Cost:** Aquarium $11.75; $10.75 (ages 65+); $9.75 (ages 2-12). IMAX theater $9-$11.50; $8-$10.50 (ages 65+); $6.50-$9.50 (ages 2-12). Combination ticket (with daytime IMAX showings) $17.25; $16.25 (ages 65+); $15.25 (ages 2-12). Prices may vary; phone ahead to verify. **Parking:** $2-$5. **Phone:** (203) 852-0700.

SHEFFIELD ISLAND can be reached by ferry from Seaport Dock at jct. N. Water and Washington sts. (next to the Maritime Aquarium at Norwalk). A 40-passenger ferry, the *G.W. Tyler*, offers scenic cruises through Norwalk harbor and past several of the Norwalk Islands en route to Sheffield, its outermost.

The cruise lasts 3 hours; the sea route takes 45 minutes each way, and passengers disembark for 1.5 hours to enjoy the island and its nature trail. A guided tour of historic Sheffield Island Lighthouse is included. A lunch box or dinner package is available.

Time: Allow 3 hours minimum. **Hours:** Ferry leaves Norwalk Mon.-Fri. at 11 and 3, Sat.-Sun. and holidays at 11, 2 and 3:30, late June to mid-Sept.; Sat.-Sun. and holidays at 11, 2 and 3:30, early May-late June. Reservations are recommended. Dinner cruise/tours are held Thurs. 6-10, Memorial Day weekend-Sept. 30; reservations are recommended. Reservations for ferry are required. Passengers should arrive 30 minutes before departure. **Cost:** Fare (includes ferry, island visit and lighthouse tour) $20; $18 (ages 65+ Mon.-Wed.); $12 (ages 4-12); $5 (ages 0-3). Dinner package $55; $75 (for lobster meal). Phone to confirm all schedules and prices. **Phone:** (203) 838-9444 Mon.-Fri., or (203) 838-2898 Sat.-Sun. and holidays.

STEPPING STONES MUSEUM FOR CHILDREN is off I-95 exit 14 northbound or 15 southbound to 303 West Ave. in Mathews Park. Five main galleries for ages 1-10 and a toddlers-only gallery offer opportunities to explore art, culture and science. Hands-on exhibits include Build It!, Healthyville, Waterscape

and Rainforest Adventure. Celebration Courtyard provides an outdoor play space under a large open-air tent. The Performance Gallery is an indoor/outdoor theater used for performances and community events.

Time: Allow 1 hour, 30 minutes minimum. **Hours:** Daily 10-5, July 1-Labor Day; Wed.-Sun. 10-5, Tues. 1-5, rest of year. Closed Jan. 1, Easter, Thanksgiving and Dec. 25. **Cost:** $9; $7 (ages 62+); free (ages 0-1). **Phone:** (203) 899-0606.

NORWICH (C-6) pop. 36,117, elev. 33'

Meeting House Rock, Norwichtown Green and the Old Burying Ground on Town Street served as the commons for Norwich's first settlers in the 17th century. The first church was built on the green in 1660.

Three miles north on what is now SR 12, one of the fiercest American Indian battles of the settlement period was fought. Uncas, chief of the Mohegans and friend of the colonists, defeated Miantonomoh, the Narragansett chief. The Royal Mohegan Indian Burial Ground is off SR 32 near Sachem and Washington streets. The burial place contains the remains of Mohegan tribe rulers. The cornerstone for a monument to Chief Uncas was laid in 1833 by Andrew Jackson; the granite shaft was erected in 1842.

The Cathedral of St. Patrick, 213 Broadway, was built in 1879. It contains stained-glass windows, marble furnishings and a hand-carved baldachin; phone (860) 889-8441.

MOHEGAN PARK AND MEMORIAL ROSE GARDEN is e. of SR 32 on Judd Rd. Covering about 380 acres overlooking the city, the park contains the two-acre Memorial Rose Garden, which honors all war veterans. The garden's 2,500 rose bushes, representing 120 varieties, is in full bloom from late June to mid-July. The park features nature trails as well as fishing and swimming in season. *See Recreation Chart.* **Hours:** Daily 10-dusk. **Cost:** Free. **Phone:** (860) 823-3700.

SLATER MEMORIAL MUSEUM AND CONVERSE ART GALLERY is off SR 2 at 108 Crescent St. on the Norwich Free Academy campus. The gallery has a Greek, Roman and Renaissance plaster cast collection; American art and furniture from the 17th century to the present reflecting 350 years of Norwich history; American Indian artifacts; and African, European, Asian and American art. A separate section houses six galleries with rotating exhibits.

Tours: Guided tours are available. **Hours:** Tues.-Fri. 9-4, Sat.-Sun. 1-4. Closed major holidays. **Cost:** $3; $2 (ages 66+ and students with ID); free (ages 0-11). Reservations are required for tours. **Phone:** (860) 887-2506.

OAKDALE (C-5) elev. 281'

THE DINOSAUR PLACE AT NATURE'S ART is at 1650 SR 85. More than 25 life-size dinosaurs are along 1.5 miles of easy walking trails within a 60-acre outdoor park. Youngsters can exercise their imaginations in the hands-on discovery stations and let off steam in Monty's Playground. In the warmer months the 30-plus dynamic dinosaur-themed features of Splashpad stimulate, challenge and cool off children of all ages. Indoors, visitors can dig for gems, pan for "gold" and unearth "dinosaur bones."

Time: Allow 2 hours minimum. **Hours:** Outdoor activities open daily 10-6, mid-Apr. through Oct. 30; Sat.-Sun. 10-6, in Nov. (weather permitting). Indoor activities open daily 10-5, Father's Day-Labor Day; Sat.-Sun. and school holidays 10-5, rest of year. Closed Jan. 1, Easter, Thanksgiving and Dec. 25. **Cost:** Outdoor activities in summer $18.99; $14.99 (ages 60+). Outdoor activities in spring and fall $9.99; $8.99 (ages 60+). Indoor activities have separate fees. **Phone:** (860) 443-4367. 🍴

OLD LYME (D-5) elev. 14'

It has been said that at one time every house in Old Lyme was occupied by a sea captain, and the records indicate that 60 once lived here. These men brought their contact with foreign lands home in the form of treasures and tales. Today Old Lyme's treasure is its art community, which formed the nucleus of the American Impressionism movement in the early 1900s.

FLORENCE GRISWOLD MUSEUM is .2 mi. n. of I-95 exit 70 at 96 Lyme St. Housed in a Georgian mansion that served as an early 20th-century art colony, the museum has a collection of American paintings, works on paper, sculpture, New England decorative arts and furniture. Period rooms offer tools, toys, clothing and household items. The Krieble Art Gallery showcases changing exhibits. **Time:** Allow 30 minutes minimum. **Hours:** Tues.-Sat. 10-5, Sun. 1-5. Closed Easter, July 4, Thanksgiving and Dec. 25. **Cost:** $9; $8 (ages 63+ and students with ID); free (ages 0-12). **Phone:** (860) 434-5542.

LYME ACADEMY COLLEGE OF FINE ARTS is at 84 Lyme St. Changing exhibits of works by local artists and academy students are displayed in the Chauncy Stillman Gallery and the 1817 Sill House, a restored Federal-style mansion. **Time:** Allow 30 minutes minimum. **Hours:** Mon.-Sat. 10-4; otherwise by appointment. Closed major holidays. **Cost:** Donations. **Phone:** (860) 434-5232.

LYME ART ASSOCIATION GALLERY is at US 1 and Lyme St., off I-95 exit 70. The gallery is headquarters for the Lyme Art Association, reputedly the nation's oldest art group to have held continuous exhibitions in its own gallery. The gallery features contemporary representational paintings and sculpture as well as changing exhibitions. **Hours:** Tues.-Sat. 10-5, Sun. 1-5. Closed major holidays and between shows. **Cost:** Donations. **Phone:** (860) 434-7802.

OLD SAYBROOK (D-5) pop. 1,962, elev. 24'

Pashbeshauke, "the place at the river's mouth," was the name American Indians gave to their settlement on the river they called Quonitocutt. Dutch traders lived in the region in the early 1600s, but in 1635 a group of English Puritans led by John Winthrop Jr. routed the Dutch and established a permanent colony. The colony was named Saybrook after William Fiennes, the first Viscount Saye and Sele, and Lord Brooke, heads of the settlers' Saybrook Company.

Years later, when the colony divided into seven communities, the original site became known as Old Saybrook. The first one-man submarine designed for battle, the *Turtle*, was invented in Old Saybrook. Constructed in 1776 by David Bushnell, the *Turtle* was used briefly during the American Revolution.

The General William Hart House, on SR 154 at 350 Main St., was built just a few years before the Revolution. It is typical of residences of well-to-do New Englanders of the period; phone (860) 388-2622.

Old Saybrook Chamber of Commerce: 1 Main St., Old Saybrook, CT 06475-0625. **Phone:** (860) 388-3266.

Self-guiding tours: A brochure describing a self-guiding walking tour contains historical information about Old Saybrook's older homes. The brochure is available at the chamber of commerce.

ONECO (B-6)

When Europeans arrived in southern Connecticut in the early 1600s, they documented more than 20 Pequot Indian villages, including Oneco. A smallpox epidemic killed thousands of Pequots in 1633, and the tribe would be decimated in a war with colonists that ended with the Treaty of Hartford 5 years later. Under the conditions of the treaty, Pequots were forbidden from returning to their homes or using their tribal name; many survivors were sold into slavery.

LUCKY STRIKE MINE is in the River Bend Campground; from I-395 exit 88, 5.5 mi. e. on SR 14A. Visitors can don miner's hats and search for gems, minerals, fossils and shells in a man-made cave, then pan for gemstones at the sluice. **Hours:** Daily 9-5, late Apr. to Columbus Day. **Cost:** Mine $8.50. Gemstone panning and screening $7-$9. Ages 0-7 must be with an adult. **Phone:** (860) 564-3440.

REDDING (D-2) elev. 410'

Redding first was secured for settlement in 1714 by John Read, a lawyer and land speculator who obtained a large grant from an American Indian chief named Chicken. The General Assembly had the land sold at auction, and in 1767 the area became incorporated as a town and was named for the speculator. The area is rich in mineral deposits, and a number of mines have prospered nearby.

PUTNAM MEMORIAL STATE PARK is at jct. SRs 107 and 58. The park contains the 1778 winter quarters of Gen. Israel Putnam and his New England troops. The palisade and blockhouses have been restored; traces of other buildings can be seen. An interpretive trail winds through the area. The park offers hiking, fishing and ice skating. *See Recreation*

Chart. **Hours:** Park daily 8-dusk. Visitor center and museum daily 9-5, Memorial Day-Veterans Day. **Cost:** Free. **Phone:** (203) 938-2285. 🚻 🍴 ⊠

RIDGEFIELD (D-1) pop. 7,212, elev. 725'

Connecticut's only inland battle of the Revolutionary War was fought at the village of Ridgefield on April 27, 1777. Troops led by American generals Benedict Arnold, Gold Selleck Silliman and David Wooster attempted to hold off British forces returning to Long Island Sound from a raid on Danbury. Outnumbered three to one, the patriots were forced to retreat after a fierce day-long fight. Though the British considered it a victory, thousands of revolutionary soldiers would rush to the area within hours, preventing future attacks.

THE ALDRICH CONTEMPORARY ART MUSEUM is at 258 Main St. Changing exhibits of contemporary painting, sculpture and photography are offered. **Tours:** Guided tours are available. **Time:** Allow 1 hour minimum. **Hours:** Tues.-Sun. noon-5. Guided tours depart Sun. at 2. Closed Jan. 1, Thanksgiving and Dec. 25. **Cost:** Museum $7; $4 (ages 65+ and students with ID); free (ages 0-18 and Tues.). **Phone:** (203) 438-4519.

KEELER TAVERN MUSEUM is at jct. SRs 33 and 35 at 132 Main St. The 1713 building has been a farmhouse, a tavern and stagecoach stop, an inn and the summer home of noted architect Cass Gilbert. The building has been restored to its days as an 18th-century tavern and furnished with period pieces. A small cannonball fired by the British during the 1777 Battle of Ridgefield remains lodged in a corner post. Costumed guides conduct tours.

Time: Allow 45 minutes minimum. **Hours:** Guided tours are given Wed. and Sat.-Sun. 1-4, Feb.-Dec. Last tour begins 30 minutes before closing. Closed Easter, July 4, Thanksgiving and Dec. 25. **Cost:** $5; $3 (ages 60+ and students with ID); $2 (ages 0-11). **Phone:** (203) 438-5485.

RIVERTON (A-3)

Surrounded by hills and two state forests, Riverton is in the northwestern corner of the state on the banks of the Farmington River, one of four National Wild and Scenic Rivers in New England. The town maintains its early 1800s appearance. Lambert Hitchcock, known as one of America's greatest chair makers, built his mill in 1826.

ROCKY HILL—*see Hartford p. 58.*

SHARON (B-1)

Parcels for the town of Sharon were sold at auction in 1738; purchasers were required to clear 6 acres, build a house and live there for 3 years. An early success, the settlement was struck in 1732 by a mysterious "nervous fever" that killed at least 100 people and left others bedridden for months. The hardiest colonists survived, and discovery of iron ore in the northwest corner of the state ensured Sharon's economic future.

SHARON AUDUBON CENTER is 2.2 mi. s.e. on CR 41 and SR 4 to 325 Cornwall Bridge Rd. In the Clement R. Ford Home, the center holds nature exhibits, including birds, turtles and snakes; a children's discovery room; and herb and wildflower gardens. The grounds serve as a wildlife sanctuary and offer 11 miles of scenic hiking trails as well as nearly 1,150 acres of forest, meadows and wetlands. Picnicking facilities are available. **Hours:** Trails open daily dawn-dusk. Center open Tues.-Sat. 9-5, Sun. 1-5. Closed major holidays. **Cost:** $3; $1.50 (ages 0-11 and 65+). **Phone:** (860) 364-0520. 🚻

SHERMAN (C-1)

WINERIES

- **White Silo Farm & Winery** is at 32 SR 37 E., just w. of jct. SR 39. **Hours:** Fri.-Sun. and holidays 11-6, May-Dec. or by appointment. **Phone:** (860) 355-0271.

SIMSBURY—*see Hartford p. 58.*

SOUTHINGTON—*see Hartford p. 59.*

STAMFORD (D-1) pop. 117,083, elev. 34'

Siwanoys Indians sold the land now called Stamford to Nathaniel Turner, an agent for the New Haven Colony, in 1640; settlement began the following year. On a wide bay crossed by two tidal inlets, Stamford retains its New England charm despite its growth as a corporate center.

THE BARTLETT ARBORETUM AND GARDENS is 1.6 mi. n. of SR 15 exit 35 at 151 Brookdale Rd. Ten different trails and boardwalk paths lead through the 91-acre grounds. Displays include award-winning trees, charming gardens, wildflower meadows, wetlands, woodlands and varied wildlife and nature habitats. **Tours:** Guided tours are available. **Time:** Allow 1 hour minimum. **Hours:** Grounds open daily 8:30-dusk. Buildings open Mon.-Fri. 8:30-4:30. Closed major holidays. **Cost:** $6; free (ages 0-11 and to all Wed.). **Phone:** (203) 322-6971. 🍴

FIRST PRESBYTERIAN CHURCH is at 1101 Bedford St. This contemporary-style structure was inspired by an early Christian symbol, the fish. Of note are abstract colored-glass windows and a Visser-Rowland Opus 87 organ. Outside, a walk with more than 100 stones depicts the history of religion from the time of Moses and Abraham. Memorial Wall, fronting the church property, traces the history of Stamford. Free concerts are offered at the Maguire Memorial Tower Carillon. **Time:** Allow 30 minutes minimum. **Hours:** Mon.-Fri. 9-5, Sept.-June; Mon.-Fri. 9-3, rest of year. Carillon concert Sun. at 11 (also Thurs. at 7, in July). **Cost:** Free. **Phone:** (203) 324-9522.

STAMFORD MUSEUM AND NATURE CENTER is .7 mi. n. of Merritt Pkwy. exit 35, at High Ridge and Scofieldtown rds. on SR 137. The 118-acre

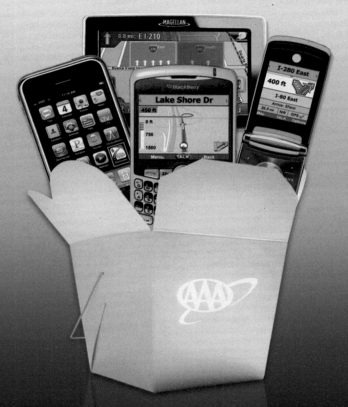

woodland site features a small working New England farm with heirloom breeds of animals, a nature center, an observatory with a 22-inch research telescope, a planetarium, a playground, and galleries for changing exhibitions. Hiking trails and universally accessible paths lead through a vast hardwood forest. **Hours:** Museum open Mon.-Sat. 9-5, Sun. 11-5. Planetarium show second Sun. of the month at 3. Observatory Visitors' Night Fri. 8-10 p.m., Sept.-Apr.; Fri. 8:30-10:30 p.m., rest of year (weather permitting). Closed Jan. 1, Thanksgiving and Dec. 25. **Cost:** $8; $6 (ages 65+ and students with ID); $4 (ages 4-17). Planetarium show $3; $2 (ages 5-17). Observatory $3; $2 (ages 4-17). Children ages 0-4 are not permitted in the planetarium. **Phone:** (203) 322-1646. 🅰️

STONINGTON (D-6) pop. 1,032, elev. 7'

The Pequot Indians controlled the Stonington area until 1637, when an attack on their fort in nearby Mystic by Capt. John Mason opened the area for settlement. Conflict did not end, however. Both Massachusetts and Connecticut claimed the Stonington region until 1662, and the town twice was attacked by the British, once during the Revolutionary War and again during the War of 1812.

With its favorable location as the last protected harbor in Long Island Sound, the town developed as a 19th-century center for sealing and whaling fleets and as a transportation hub; trains from Boston met steamboats from New York for 50 years. Mariners such as Capt. Nat Palmer—who discovered Antarctica on a sealing trip in 1821—sailed from Stonington, which became known as the "Nursery of Seamen." Palmer's clipper ship *Houqua* later broke the speed record to Hong Kong.

The 1852 Capt. Palmer House, a 16-room Victorian mansion on a hill overlooking Stonington Harbor, contains memorabilia pertaining to Palmer's discovery of Antarctica as well as period portraits, furnishings and relics. The building's octagonal cupola affords spectacular views of the area; phone (860) 535-8445.

OLD LIGHTHOUSE MUSEUM is at 7 Water St. The original stone building—the first federal lighthouse—was erected in 1823. Due to erosion, it was moved in 1840 to its current site, where it operated for the next 50 years. Home to the Stonington Historical Society since 1925, the lighthouse contains ship models, whaling and naval battle gear, a China trade exhibit, oil portraits and children's toys. Six rooms of exhibits change yearly.

A trip up a circular, stone stairway to the top of the tower provides views of three states. **Hours:** Daily 10-5, May-Oct.; other times by appointment. **Cost:** (includes the Capt. Palmer House) $8; $5 (ages 6-12). Prices may vary; phone ahead. **Phone:** (860) 535-1440.

STORRS (B-5) pop. 10,996, elev. 640'

Storrs is the home of the University of Connecticut. Founded in 1881 as Storrs Agricultural College, it became the University of Connecticut in 1939. Scattered among the traditional turn-of-the-20th-century buildings are contemporary and modern structures that reflect the university's growth.

Maps and campus information are available at the Lodewick Visitors Center, 115 N. Eagleville Rd.; phone (860) 486-4900. Visitor parking is available in the north and south garages; phone (860) 486-6267 or (860) 486-9088 for hours and pricing information. On campus are several greenhouses, animal barns and a dairy bar featuring the university's homemade ice cream.

Notable buildings include the Atrium Gallery in the Fine Arts Building, phone (860) 486-1511; William Benton Museum of Art, phone (860) 486-4520; Connecticut State Museum of Natural History, phone (860) 486-4460; EEB Conservatory and Greenhouses, phone (860) 486-4052; Connecticut Archaeology Center, phone (860) 486-4460; Ballard Institute & Museum of Puppetry, phone (860) 486-0339; and Homer Babbidge Library, phone (860) 486-2518. The Jorgensen Center for the Performing Arts plays host to professional touring companies such as dance, theater and music as well as festivals and internationally known soloists and symphony orchestras; for performance and ticket information phone (860) 486-4226.

STRATFORD (D-3) pop. 49,976, elev. 21'

Established in 1639, Stratford adjoins Bridgeport *(see place listing p. 35)* on the Housatonic River. In its early years Stratford was noted for its shipbuilding and oyster industries, which still exist.

Bridgeport Regional Business Council: 10 Middle St., 14th Floor, P.O. Box 999, Bridgeport, CT 06601-0999. **Phone:** (203) 335-3800.

BOOTHE MEMORIAL PARK AND MUSEUM is s. off Merritt Pkwy. exit 53, 1 blk. s. on River Rd. (SR 110), then 1 blk. s. on Main St. The park is the site of the 32-acre homestead of the Boothe family, who resided here 1663-1949. Ten of the 20 historic buildings have been restored, including a blacksmith shop, clock tower, trolley station and ice house. Museum buildings display early farm, house and craft implements. The carriage house contains antique buggies and an award-winning rose garden.

Playground facilities is available. **Time:** Allow 2 hours minimum. **Hours:** Park open daily 9-5. Museum open Tues. and Fri. 11-1, Sat.-Sun. 1-4, June-Oct. **Cost:** Free. **Phone:** (203) 381-2046. 🅰️

JUDSON HOUSE AND MUSEUM is at 967 Academy Hill Rd. The 1750 house is a good example of the clapboard-sheathed, post-and-beam construction that was typical of 18th-century New England. It is furnished in period. The adjacent Mitchell Museum contains a genealogy library as well as exhibits from periods of Stratford's history. **Time:** Allow 1 hour, 30 minutes minimum. **Hours:** Wed. and Sun. noon-4, first Sat. in June-Oct. 31; closed July 4. Genealogy library open Tues. and Thurs. 9-2:30. Last admission to house is one hour before closing. **Cost:**

$5; $4 (senior citizens); $2 (students with ID). **Phone:** (203) 378-0630.

NATIONAL HELICOPTER MUSEUM is off I-95 exit 32 to the Stratford Eastbound Railroad Station at 2480 Main St. Exhibits, which explore the development of the helicopter, include photographs and drawings of such prototypes as a boomerang (the first rotary wing) and Leonardo da Vinci's "Helix." A helicopter cockpit, model turbine engine and rotor blade also are displayed. **Time:** Allow 30 minutes minimum. **Hours:** Wed.-Sun. 1-4, Memorial Day weekend to mid-Oct. **Cost:** Donations. **Phone:** (203) 375-8857.

SUFFIELD—*see Hartford p. 59.*

TERRYVILLE (B-3) pop. 5,360, elev. 609′

The Pequabuck Tunnel was considered a railroad marvel in its day. Some 700 men worked at Terryville for 3 years to cut through 3,500 feet of rock; the project was completed in 1910.

LOCK MUSEUM OF AMERICA, INC. is .6 mi. w. of SR 72 at 230 Main St. The museum houses more than 23,000 kinds of locks, including vault locks, door locks, padlocks, handcuffs, a cannon ball safe and early time locks. Three locks made by Stephen Bucknall in 1833 also are displayed. Eight separate rooms—including the Eagle Lock Company, Bank Lock, Corbin-Russwin, Yale and Antique Lock rooms—feature locks and keys manufactured by nearly every lock company in the United States and several from Europe. **Time:** Allow 1 hour minimum. **Hours:** Tues.-Sun. 1:30-4:30, May-Oct. **Cost:** $3; $2.50 (ages 51+); free (ages 0-11). **Phone:** (860) 589-6359.

TORRINGTON (B-2) pop. 35,202, elev. 593′

Settled in 1737, Torrington once was called Wolcottville for the factory established by Frederick and Guy Wolcott in 1813. After Israel Coe began making brass kettles in 1835, the town became an international producer and exporter of brass products. Brass manufacture was supplemented by the production of needles, ball bearings, machinery, roller skates and woolens. The town is still one of the state's largest commercial centers.

THE HOTCHKISS-FYLER HOUSE is at 192 Main St. The Victorian mansion features elaborate woodwork, ornamental plaster and murals. Original family furnishings include antiques, art glass and porcelain collections, Oriental carpets and paintings by Connecticut artists. **Time:** Allow 30 minutes minimum. **Hours:** Tues.-Sat. noon-4, Apr. 15-Oct. 31. Last tour begins 30 minutes before closing. The house also is open two weeks in Dec. during Victorian Christmas.; phone for hours. Closed major holidays. **Cost:** $5; free (ages 0-12). **Phone:** (860) 482-8260.

TORRINGTON HISTORY MUSEUM is adjacent to the Hotchkiss-Fyler House at 208 Main St. Photographs and artifacts depict the city's past, including

Native American settlement, English Colonial history, industrialization, immigration and many unique aspect of the community like abolitionist John Brown. Displays in an 1930s machine shop chronicle the history of the Hendey Machine Company, which produced lathes, shapers and milling machines. **Time:** Allow 30 minutes minimum. **Hours:** Tues.-Sat. noon-4, Apr. 15-Oct. 31. Closed major holidays. **Cost:** $2; free (ages 0-11). Fees are payable at the Hotchkiss-Fyler House. **Phone:** (860) 482-8260.

UNCASVILLE (C-5)

Named for Uncas, 17th-century chief of the Mohegan tribe, Uncasville is home to the 400-acre Mohegan Indian Reservation. Connecticut colonists formally recognized the sovereignty of the Mohegans in 1638, a treaty that remains in effect to the present day. The Mohegan Sun Casino has become one of the largest casino complexes in the world.

The remains of an old Mohegan fort and burial ground can be seen at Fort Shantok State Park, which covers 167 acres on the west bank of the Thames River, 4 miles south off SR 32.

GAMBLING ESTABLISHMENTS

• **Mohegan Sun Casino** is off I-395 exit 79A (SR 2A), then 1 mi. e. to 1 Mohegan Sun Blvd. **Hours:** Daily 24 hours. **Phone:** (888) 226-7711.

WASHINGTON DEPOT (C-2) elev. 479′

In a mountainous region scored by a gorge of the Shepaug River, Washington Depot is noted for its scenery and the large number of country estates in the area.

GUNN MEMORIAL LIBRARY AND MUSEUM is .7 mi. s. on SR 47, on the town green at Wykeham Rd. and SR 47 in Washington. Housed in the former Simeon-Mitchell House, built in 1781, the museum offers exhibits about local history. The Connecticut Room contains genealogical information, photograph albums and books by local authors. The 1908 public library features a ceiling mural by Henry Siddons Mowbray. **Time:** Allow 30 minutes minimum. **Hours:** Library Tues. and Thurs. 9:30-8, Mon. and Fri. 9:30-5, Sat. 9:30-3. Museum Thurs.-Sat. 10-4. Closed major holidays. **Cost:** Donations. **Phone:** (860) 868-7756 for the museum, or (860) 868-7586 for the library.

THE INSTITUTE FOR AMERICAN INDIAN STUDIES is .9 mi. s. on SR 47, 1.3 mi. s. on SR 199, then .1 mi. w. to 38 Curtis Rd. in Washington. Displays of American Indian artifacts and contemporary American Indian art help to reconstruct the past 12,000 years of the area's cultural heritage. A replica of a Northeastern Indian village, a nature trail, a simulated archeological site and changing exhibits highlight aspects of native life, including contemporary themes.

Guided tours are available by appointment. **Hours:** Mon.-Sat. 10-5, Sun. noon-5. Closed Jan. 1,

Easter, Memorial Day, July 4, Thanksgiving and Dec. 25. **Cost:** $5; $4.50 (ages 66+); $3 (ages 6-16). **Phone:** (860) 868-0518.

WATERBURY (C-3) pop. 107,271, elev. 280′

Two scouts reported in 1686 that the Waterbury townsite was so poor that it could accommodate no more than 30 families. Despite that grim assessment, Waterbury rose to become one of the world's major brass centers, supporting considerably more families than the initial estimate. The inscription on the 1915 city hall, *Quid Aere Perennius*, means "What is more lasting than brass?"

Noted American architect Cass Gilbert, designer of the U.S. Supreme Court Building, drew up the plans for the city hall complex, along with four other buildings in Waterbury's historic district on Grand Street.

The Green is on West Main Street. Around this historic spot were clustered the 18-by-16-foot "mansion houses" of the original settlers. A Soldiers' Monument and war memorials were erected in the 19th century. The 1922 Palace Theater, with its elaborate Baroque and Art Nouveau architecture, has been restored as a community arts center; phone (203) 755-4700. Also of interest are the 240-foot Republican American Tower, castle-like St. John's Episcopal Church and the Italian-Renaissance-style Church of the Immaculate Conception. In nearby Cheshire, the Cheshire Community Pool at 520 South Main St. is open to the public year-round; phone (203) 271-3208.

Northwest Connecticut Convention & Visitors Bureau: 21 Church St., Waterbury, CT 06702. **Phone:** (203) 597-9527 or (888) 588-7880.

MATTATUCK MUSEUM is at 144 W. Main St., facing the green. Housed in a former Masonic temple, the museum displays decorative arts, 18th- to 20th-century landscape and portrait paintings and sculpture by Connecticut artists. Local history exhibits also are presented. A second-floor gallery displays contemporary paintings by Connecticut artists. Of interest is Charles Goodyear's rubber desk. A collection of 10,000 buttons is displayed on the third floor in The Waterbury Button Museum.

Time: Allow 1 hour, 30 minutes minimum. **Hours:** Tues.-Sat. 10-5, Sun. noon-5. **Cost:** $5; $4 (ages 65+); free (ages 0-15). **Phone:** (203) 753-0381. 🕍

SAVE **THE TIMEX MUSEUM** is off I-84 exit 22 to 175 Union St. The museum traces the history of Timex and its predecessor, Waterbury Clock Co. A time tunnel leads to an archaeological exhibit about the mysteries of Easter Island. Also included are hands-on exhibits, computer activities and videotape presentations. **Time:** Allow 1 hour minimum. **Hours:** Tues.-Sat. 10-5. Closed major holidays. **Cost:** $6; $5 (ages 65+); $4 (ages 5-12). **Phone:** (203) 755-8463 or (800) 225-7742.

WATERFORD (D-5) elev. 48′

The settlements of Waterford and New London were Siamese twins both historically and geographically for 148 years. Founded in 1646, Waterford did not become a separate town until 1801. A nearby quarry was a source of millstones as early as 1737; the quarry's owner, the governor, eventually gave the lucrative property to his daughter for her dowry. Many of the estates built along the Niantic River by local wealthy families can be seen today.

Excursions on the Sunbeam Fleet, which depart from Mago Point, include fishing trips, a lighthouse cruise and harbor seal cruises; phone (860) 443-7259.

Shopping areas: Crystal Mall, I-95 exit 82 on SR 85, contains JCPenney, Macy's and Sears; phone (860) 442-8500.

HARKNESS MEMORIAL STATE PARK is at Goshen Point off Great Neck Rd. The park comprises 125 acres and features the 42-room Harkness Mansion. **Hours:** Grounds open daily 8-dusk. Mansion tours depart Sat.-Sun. and holidays 10-2, Memorial Day-Labor Day. Last tour departs 45 minutes before closing. **Cost:** Memorial Day-Labor Day Sat.-Sun. and holidays $20 per private vehicle; $14 (state residents); $10 (to all after 4 p.m.). Memorial Day-Labor Day Mon.-Fri. $14 per private vehicle; $10 (residents and to all after 4 p.m.). Free rest of year. **Phone:** (860) 437-1523. 🏕 🍽

HISTORIC JORDAN GREEN is at jct. SRs 156 and 213. The village consists of reconstructed and relocated 18th- and 19th-century buildings. A barn has an extensive collection of farm implements, equipment and artifacts. Other buildings include a 1740 schoolhouse, a blacksmith shop with a working forge, a corn crib and an 1838 house with both Colonial and Victorian furnishings. Apple orchards and an herb garden also are on the grounds.

Time: Allow 30 minutes minimum. **Hours:** Buildings open Wed.-Fri. 1-4, July-Sept. and by appointment. Closed July 4. **Cost:** Donations.

WESTBROOK (D-4) pop. 2,238

Westbrook was founded in 1648 in an area known as Pochoug, an Indian name meaning "at the confluence of two rivers." Westbrook was the birthplace of David Bushnell, a Revolutionary War patriot who is recognized by the U.S. Navy as the inventor of the submarine.

Shopping areas: Westbrook Factory Stores, on SR 153 off I-95 exit 65, offers more than 65 discount outlets including J. Crew and Timberland; phone (860) 399-8656.

MILITARY HISTORIANS MUSEUM is 1 mi. s. of I-95 exit 65 on N. Main St. This museum contains one of the largest collections of military uniforms in the United States. Exhibits devoted to medals and awards, women's uniforms and the instruments and uniforms of military bands are featured.

Several vehicles used in military actions ranging from World War II to Operation Desert Storm are displayed. A reference library is on the premises. **Time:** Allow 30 minutes minimum. **Hours:** Tues.-Fri. 8-2:30; other times by appointment. Closed major holidays. **Cost:** Free. **Phone:** (860) 399-9460.

WEST HARTFORD—*see Hartford p. 59.*

WESTPORT (E-2) pop. 25,749, elev. 26'

The "pedlar ships" that operated in the Westport harbor once brought an aura of romance to the local waters, similar to the effect steamboats had on the Mississippi. The town's scenic coves and hillocks attract artists, actors, writers and New York commuters.

Compo Beach, where local minutemen surprised the British in 1777, still displays the cannons used in that battle. A statue commemorates the event. Sherwood Island State Park *(see Recreation Chart)* has a beach and picnic areas.

CONNECTICUT'S 9-11 LIVING MEMORIAL is off I-95 exit 18 in Sherwood Island State Park. Shrubs and trees surround a large granite stone dedicated to those killed in the terrorist attacks on September 11, 2001. On the edge of the Long Island Sound and facing the Manhattan skyline, the park was used as a staging ground for relief efforts following the tragedy.

Note: Pets are permitted Oct. 1-Apr. 14. Alcohol is not permitted inside the park. **Time:** Allow 30 minutes minimum. **Hours:** Daily 8 a.m.-dusk. **Cost:** Free. Park entrance Sat.-Sun. and holidays, second Sat. in Apr.-third Sun. in Sept. $30 per private vehicle; $20 (with Connecticut registration); $10 (after 4). Park entrance Mon.-Fri., Memorial Day weekend-Labor Day $20 per private vehicle; $14 (with Connecticut registration); $10 (after 4). Free rest of year. Phone to confirm prices. **Phone:** (860) 424-3200. ☎

EARTHPLACE is about 1 mi. n. of US 1 at 10 Woodside Ln. The 62-acre wildlife sanctuary includes woods, fields, streams and wetlands as well as a natural science museum, galleries and an ecology lab. Indoor/outdoor live animal exhibits, a courtyard with native plants and a butterfly garden also are featured. Traversing the grounds are 2.5 miles of accessible trails. **Hours:** Grounds open 7 a.m.-dusk. Museum open Mon.-Sat. 9-5, Sun. 1-4. Closed major holidays. **Cost:** Grounds free. Museum $7; $5 (ages 1-12 and 63+). **Phone:** (203) 227-7253.

WETHERSFIELD—*see Hartford p. 59.*

WILLIMANTIC (B-5) pop. 15,823, elev. 247'

From the Algonquin word for "place of swift running water," Willimantic became a center for water-powered textile mills in the early 19th century.

Although the town calls itself "Thread City," frogs are its mascot. The giant green statues on Frog Bridge—and the bullfrog on the town seal—hark back to a night in 1754 when villagers heard terrible sounds coming from the woods and, fearing attack, barricaded themselves in their homes. In the morning, they found evidence of a great battle; thousands of bullfrogs had fought and died for a foothold in the drought-stricken millpond.

WINDHAM TEXTILE AND HISTORY MUSEUM is at 411 Main St. The museum occupies two 1877 buildings within the mill complex of the former Willimantic Linen Co. Dugan Mill depicts a late 19th-century factory setting, complete with an overseer's office overlooking a fully equipped shop floor. Thread Mill Square II replicates an affluent mill owner's mansion and a worker's house. Dunham Hall Library contains books, manuscripts, photographs and architectural drawings.

Time: Allow 1 hour, 30 minutes minimum. **Hours:** Guided tours are given Fri.-Sun. 1-4, Memorial Day-Columbus Day; Sat. 1-4 and by appointment rest of year. Closed July 4. **Cost:** $5; $3.50 (ages 60+); $3 (ages 5-15). **Phone:** (860) 456-2178.

WILTON (D-2) elev. 186'

Wilton was established in 1726. David Lambert built a large country home here a year later, and the house remained in the family until the early 20th century. Threatened by construction of US 7, the Lambert House was moved to its present location at the corner of SR 7 and 33, where eight historic structures—including a general store, post office and railroad station—have been preserved.

WEIR FARM NATIONAL HISTORIC SITE is .2 mi. w. on SR 102 past jct. US 7, 1.2 mi. w. on Old Branchville Rd., then .7 mi. s. to 735 Nod Hill Rd. Nearly 60 acres are reminiscent of the era highlighted in the paintings of American Impressionist painter J. Alden Weir. The Burlingham House Visitor Center displays historic photographs. A 12-minute video describes Weir's life and times. Changing exhibits of contemporary artists and guided tours of two historic art studios are available.

Self-guiding tours follow footpaths across the site. Picnicking is permitted on the lawn. RVs are not permitted. **Time:** Allow 1 hour minimum. **Hours:** Grounds open daily dawn-dusk. Visitor center open Wed.-Sun. 9-5, May-Oct.; Thurs.-Sun. 10-4, rest of year. Site tours are offered Wed.-Sun. at 11 and 3 (also Wed. and Fri.-Sat. at 1), May-Oct.; Thurs.-Sun. at 11 and 3 (also Fri. at 1), rest of year. Stone wall walking tours are offered Thurs. and Sat. at 1. Closed Jan. 1, Thanksgiving and Dec. 25. **Cost:** Free. **Phone:** (203) 834-1896. ⛺

WINDSOR—*see Hartford p. 60.*

WINDSOR LOCKS—*see Hartford p. 61.*

WOODBURY (C-2) pop. 1,298, elev. 264′

Near the center of Woodbury a large boulder and a plaque honor Chief Pomperaug who once owned this territory. He was buried in 1650, and the town originally bore his name.

In 1672 the Rev. Zechariah Walker and his congregation left Stratford after a church feud and settled in Woodbury. The group established the First Congregational Church, the oldest in Litchfield County. In the south cemetery stands The Fathers' Monument, a granite slab honoring the church's first three pastors; together they served their congregations for 143 years. The ancestors of two Civil War generals, Ulysses S. Grant and William Tecumseh Sherman, also are buried at the site.

GLEBE HOUSE is off SR 6 at 149 Hollow Rd. At this gambrel-roofed farmhouse in 1783, Samuel Seabury was elected as the first American bishop of the Episcopal Church. His position as bishop illustrated the new nation's religious tolerance and the separation of church and state prior to the drafting of the U.S. Constitution.

The Gertrude Jekyll Garden, commissioned in 1926, is the last of three American gardens planned by the noted English horticultural designer. **Time:** Allow 30 minutes minimum. **Hours:** Wed.-Sun. 1-4, May-Oct.; Sat.-Sun. 1-4 in Nov.; other times by appointment. **Cost:** House and garden $5; $2 (ages 6-12). Garden $2. **Phone:** (203) 263-2855.

WOODSTOCK (A-5)

Woodstock's land was purchased in 1686 by a company from Roxbury, Mass. The settlement became part of that state and was named for a town in Oxfordshire, England. Woodstock later was claimed by Connecticut under the Connecticut Charter; early residents included Rev. Jedidiah Morse, father of telegraph inventor Samuel F.B. Morse.

The town's first religious services were held in 1686; the minister preached from a boulder called "Pulpit Rock" to parishioners on the nearby hillside. The site is marked by a commemorative tablet.

ROSELAND COTTAGE (HENRY C. BOWEN HOUSE) is at 556 SR 169, facing Woodstock Common. The Gothic Revival summer house was built in 1846. Known as "The Pink House," the restored cottage contains much of its original furniture. Featured is one of New England's oldest known boxwood parterre gardens.

Highlights include the original icehouse, a garden house and a barn with one of the oldest indoor bowling alleys in the country. **Time:** Allow 1 hour minimum. **Hours:** Guided tours are given on the hour Wed.-Sun. (also July 4 and Columbus Day) 11-5, June 1 to mid-Oct. Last tour begins 1 hour before closing. **Cost:** $8; $7 (ages 66+); $4 (ages 5-12). **Phone:** (860) 928-4074.

Massachusetts

Path to Liberty

The Freedom Trail connects 16 sites important to the American Revolution

The Hills Are Alive

The Berkshire Hills roll through western Massachusetts under a verdant layer of forest

Quaint Seaside Villages

Waves lapping on the sand of Cape Cod calm the nerves of even the most frazzled visitors

Name Dropping

The homes of such well-known people as Norman Rockwell reveal lives touched by greatness

Pilgrims & Witches

Plymouth and Salem preserve a history marked by fortitude and marred by superstition

Edgartown,
Martha's Vineyard
© J. David Andrews
Masterfile

The Old House, Adams National Historical Park, Quincy / National Park Service

Citizens of Massachusetts have worn many hats during the state's long history. Think of the Pilgrims arriving in a strange land, and it's easy to imagine them removing their dour, broad-brimmed hats as they gazed at their new home. Hear the name Salem, and you'll probably picture the pointed black hats that none of the 19 people falsely accused and executed for practicing witchcraft actually wore.

You might envision Paul Revere clutching his three-cornered hat to his head as he sped through the night to warn the minutemen of the advancing British army—arrayed into neat rows of identical cocked hats and red coats—marching toward Concord behind him.

Mortarboards with tassels have covered heads in the Bay State for hundreds of years. There are more than 50 colleges and universities in the Boston

area alone—including Harvard, the oldest university in the nation.

Such literary luminaries as Ralph Waldo Emerson, Henry David Thoreau, Nathaniel Hawthorne, Emily Dickinson and Edgar Allan Poe achieved fame by putting on their thinking caps and writing poems, stories and essays that have entertained and enlightened people around the world.

Then there are those Massachusetts natives who have thrown their hats into the national political ring. Such names as Adams and Kennedy come to mind.

Whatever the hat, there's usually a place associated with it: Thoreau's Walden Pond, Hawthorne's The House of the Seven Gables and Revere's Old North Church are but a few examples. Visit these and you too may feel like tipping your hat to the great men and women of Massachusetts.

Take away Massachusetts and some of the most important chapters in American history would be left blank: no Thanksgiving, no Boston Tea Party, no "shot heard 'round the world," no Battle of Bunker Hill, no Paul Revere, no John Hancock and quite possibly no American Revolution.

For centuries the Bay State has proven to be fertile ground for new ideas and political philosophies that have been admired, debated and—the sincerest form of flattery—duplicated by people across the globe. Scene of the most vehement speeches against taxation without representation, Massachusetts led the way to independence from Britain. And during the Civil War it became a hotbed of anti-slavery sentiment, producing many of the Union's most enthusiastic soldiers. Massachusetts has shaped America's destiny more than once.

A City on a Hill

The English Pilgrims who set sail for America aboard the *Mayflower* dreamed of establishing a religious community that would become a model for pious living. Quoting the Bible, they envisioned "a city on a hill" serving as a shining example to the world. Coincidentally, Massachusetts is an American Indian word meaning "at the great hill."

The Pilgrims settled at Plymouth in 1620 and celebrated the first Thanksgiving a year later. You don't need a time machine to see what everyday life was like for these early immigrants: With the aid of costumed actors, a reconstructed settlement and a little imagination, Plimoth Plantation takes you back to 1627. Moored at State Pier, the *Mayflower II* is a reproduction of their ship, while Plymouth Rock, regarded as the Pilgrims' steppingstone onto the new continent, is preserved not far away.

In 1692 the zeal with which Pilgrims and Puritans strove to create their idealistic city on a hill revealed a dark side. In Salem 19 people were hanged for practicing witchcraft; five more of the accused died in jail, and another was tortured to death. Today several area museums vividly recount the hysteria that resulted in this tragedy.

By the time the infamous witch trials had begun, one Puritan city on *three* hills had surpassed all others to become the largest English settlement in Colonial America. Though founded just 10 years after Plymouth, Boston is more often associated with events of the following century. A lion's share of the path leading to independence from Britain—literally as well as figuratively—passes through

Pilgrims, religious dissenters from England, arrive at Plymouth aboard the *Mayflower*. The following year they celebrate the first Thanksgiving.

1620

Harvard University, the nation's oldest, is founded in Cambridge.

1636

Library of Congress

1692

Nineteen people are hanged as a result of the Salem Witch Trials.

The Boston Massacre occurs when British soldiers fire upon an angry mob, killing five.

1770

Library of Congress

1773

Protesting British taxes, colonists dump British tea into Boston Harbor.

Massachusetts Historical Timeline

downtown Boston. Known as the Freedom Trail, it connects more than a dozen historic sites.

Along this route you'll see the Boston Massacre site, where five colonists were killed by redcoat troops in 1770, and Faneuil Hall, where Samuel Adams passionately called for colonialist freedom. Stroll past Paul Revere's house and the Old North Church and recall his midnight ride to warn Colonial minutemen of approaching British forces. The trail includes Granary Burying Ground, the final resting place of Revere, Adams and Declaration of Independence signer John Hancock.

In nearby Lexington and Concord, Minute Man National Historical Park commemorates the first battle of the American Revolution. It was here, at the North Bridge, that "the shot heard 'round the world" was fired, beginning a running battle that ended at Boston's Bunker Hill.

More Fame to Claim

Past glories and patriotic struggles aren't the only reasons to celebrate Massachusetts. At Boston's New England Aquarium you'll *ooh* and *ahh* over giant tanks brimming with exotic sea life. Peruse a Picasso or marvel at a Monet inside the Museum of Fine Arts, Boston. If roller coasters are more your speed, you won't be disappointed with the selection of hair-raising rides at Six Flags New England in Agawam.

Often eclipsed by its historical attractions, Massachusetts' natural beauty shouldn't be ignored. Outside of Beantown are Cape Cod, Nantucket and Martha's Vineyard, where beach communities, artists' colonies, lighthouses and sandy shores all but define the word "charm." In addition to the picturesque coast, the beautiful Berkshire Hills in western Massachusetts abound with parks and waterfalls. Here the Mohawk Trail connects quaint villages, covered bridges and vantage points offering lovely vistas. Visit in autumn and you'll be treated to the riot-of-color fall foliage display you'd expect in New England.

Visitors might wonder how so many historic landmarks, cultural sites and picturepostcard views could fit into such a small state. Somehow they do.

Recreation

If you yearn to walk in the footsteps of our founding fathers, then you've come to the right place: Massachusetts is chock full of historic sites. But that's not all there is to the

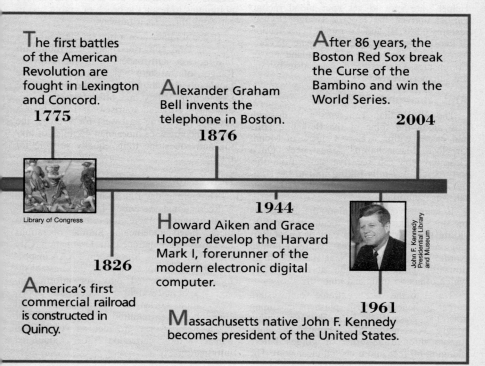

The first battles of the American Revolution are fought in Lexington and Concord.
1775

Library of Congress

Alexander Graham Bell invents the telephone in Boston.
1876

After 86 years, the Boston Red Sox break the Curse of the Bambino and win the World Series.
2004

1944
Howard Aiken and Grace Hopper develop the Harvard Mark I, forerunner of the modern electronic digital computer.

1826
America's first commercial railroad is constructed in Quincy.

John F. Kennedy Presidential Library and Museum

1961
Massachusetts native John F. Kennedy becomes president of the United States.

Bay State. Nature lovers have it good here, too. When all those famous names, dates and places start making your head swim, take a real dip—or a hike—in one of the state's numerous parks. This small state has one of the country's largest state park and forest systems.

Over the River...

Grab a paddle and head to Concord, where canoeing on the Concord River is especially pleasant. You'll pass beneath a replica of the Old North Bridge, where the first shots of the American Revolution were fired. Autumn is the best time to go with the flow here—there are fewer motorboats than in summer and dazzling fall foliage to boot.

Outside the concrete canyons of Boston, the Charles River flows through peaceful countryside. Drop your canoe in at Medfield and you're a far cry from the flotilla of racing sculls and sailboats just a few miles downriver.

If you like your water on the frothier side, then head west to the Berkshires, which have a long history of luring urbanites from seacoast cities. Here white-water rafting is popular along the Deerfield River. Between Florida and Buckland, Class II and III rapids with colorful names such as "Hangover Helper" are sure to get your blood racing. Farther upriver, the Monroe Bridge Dryway features Class III and IV rapids. This section of the Deerfield was diverted to generate electricity, but a deal with New England Power Co. ensures 32 releases of water, usually during summer weekends.

And Through the Woods

The Appalachian Trail cuts a north-south path along the spine of the Berkshire Hills and passes within a stone's throw of Mount Greylock, Massachusetts' tallest peak. On a clear day you can see five states from this lofty perch. A 2-mile hiking trail to the summit ends at the base of an imposing, 100-foot-tall war memorial.

In winter you can explore the Berkshires on skis, thanks to many local cross-country skiing trails. A few miles east of Great Barrington, Butternut Ski Area features groomed Nordic and alpine trails. Near Hancock, more downhill skiing is available at Jiminy Peak, which offers 45 trails and nine lifts.

Travel to the state's extreme southwestern corner to hear the splish-splash of cascading water at Bash Bish Falls. Located within Mount Washington State Forest, the falls tumble through a series of gorges before plunging 60 feet into a crystal-clear pool. The surrounding forest offers hiking trails and wilderness camping.

On the opposite side of Massachusetts, Cape Cod is laced by so many trails that you could hike among the holly trees and salt marshes from one end (Cape Cod Canal) to the other (Provincetown). The Coskata-Coatue Wildlife Refuge on Nantucket Island boasts 10 miles of windswept shoreline along with tidal creeks, salt ponds and forests of pine, oak and holly. Terns, plovers, ducks and geese thrive along the crustacean-rich shallows.

Traprock ridges, historical landmarks and waterfalls border the 200-mile New England National Scenic Trail, which comprises the Metacomet, Monadnock and Mattabesett trails and traverses 39 communities in Massachusetts and Connecticut. Winding through scenery ranging from rural to suburban, the Minuteman Bikeway near Boston is not only a good place for a workout, it's a perfect spot for a history lesson. The trail roughly parallels the route of Paul Revere's famed midnight ride.

A great path for biking, horseback riding and inline skating, the Cape Cod Rail Trail stretches for 22 miles between the towns of Dennis and Wellfleet. You'll have several opportunities to reach the beach or grab a bite to eat along this former railway.

If you'd rather take a ride on the wild side, you can find numerous places for mountain biking, too. Off-roaders love the Holyoke Range of western Massachusetts. These mountains rise abruptly from the floor of the Connecticut Valley and offer fantastic views that have attracted tourists for more than a century. Stretching east-west for 9 miles, the range encompasses more than 45 miles of hiking and equestrian trails equally suitable for biking.

Recreational Activities

Throughout the TourBook, you may notice a Recreational Activities heading with bulleted listings of recreation-oriented establishments listed underneath. Similar operations also may be mentioned in Destination City recreation sections. Since normal AAA inspection criteria cannot be applied, these establishments are presented only for information. Age, height and weight restrictions may apply. Reservations often are recommended and sometimes are required. Addresses and/or phone numbers are provided so visitors can contact the attraction for additional information.

Fast Facts

POPULATION: 6,349,097.

AREA: 8,257 square miles; ranks 45th.

CAPITAL: Boston.

HIGHEST POINT: 3,491 ft., Mount Greylock.

LOWEST POINT: Sea level, Atlantic Ocean.

TIME ZONE(S): Eastern. DST.

TEEN DRIVING LAWS: No passengers under age 18 except family members are permitted for the first 6 months unless supervised by a licensed driver aged 21 or older. Driving is not permitted daily 12:30 a.m.-5 a.m. The minimum age at which passenger restrictions may be lifted is 16 years and 8 months; the minimum age at which nighttime restrictions may be lifted is 17 years and 9 months. Phone (617) 351-4500 for more information about Massachusetts driver's license regulations.

SEAT BELT/CHILD RESTRAINT LAWS: Seat belts are required for driver and all passengers ages 8 and older and over 56 inches tall; child restraints are required for under age 8 and under 57 inches tall.

CELL PHONE RESTRICTIONS: Cell phone use is permitted as long as it does not interfere with the operation of the motor vehicle; the driver also must keep one hand on the steering wheel at all times. However, some jurisdictions in Massachusetts have handheld cell phone bans.

HELMETS FOR MOTORCYCLISTS: Required for all riders.

RADAR DETECTORS: Permitted.

MOVE OVER LAW: Driver is required to slow down and vacate the lane nearest stopped police, fire and rescue vehicles using audible or flashing signals. The law also includes tow trucks.

FIREARMS LAWS: Vary by state and/or county. Contact the Massachusetts State Police, 470 Worcester Rd., Framingham, MA 01702; phone (508) 820-2121.

HOLIDAYS: Jan. 1; Martin Luther King Jr. Day, Jan. (3rd Mon.); Washington's Birthday, Feb. (3rd Mon.); Patriot's Day, April (3rd Mon.); Memorial Day, May (last Mon.); July 4; Labor Day, Sept. (1st Mon.); Columbus Day, Oct. (2nd Mon.); Veterans Day, Nov. 11; Thanksgiving, Nov. (4th Thurs.); Christmas, Dec. 25.

TAXES: The Massachusetts statewide sales tax is 6.25 percent. Lodging taxes range from 5.7 to 9.7 percent.

INFORMATION CENTERS: State welcome centers are maintained at the Massachusetts Turnpike at Lee (eastbound), Natick (eastbound) and Charlton (eastbound and westbound); I-95 at Mansfield (northbound); I-95 at Salisbury (southbound); SR 3 at Plymouth (southbound); I-495 at Chelmsford (northbound); SR 2A/I-91 at Greenfield (westbound); SR 2 at Lancaster (westbound); SR 25 at Plymouth (eastbound); and I-195 at Swansea (eastbound). Massachusetts State House center open daily 9-5.

FURTHER INFORMATION FOR VISITORS:
Massachusetts Office of Travel and Tourism
State Transportation Building
10 Park Plaza, Suite 4510
Boston, MA 02116-3981
(617) 973-8500
(800) 227-6277

RECREATION INFORMATION:
Massachusetts Department of Conservation and Recreation
Division of State Parks and Recreation
251 Causeway St., Suite 600
Boston, MA 02114-2140
(617) 626-1250

FISHING AND HUNTING REGULATIONS:
Division of Fisheries & Wildlife
1 Rabbit Hill Rd.
Westborough, MA 01581
(508) 389-6300

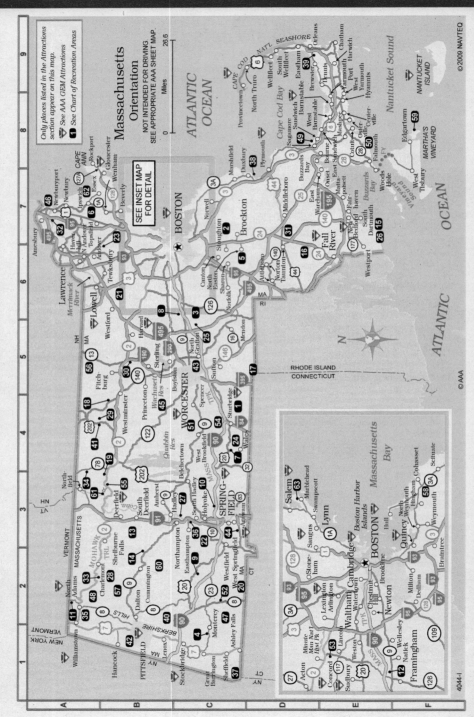

Massachusetts
Orientation

NOT INTENDED FOR DRIVING
SEE APPROPRIATE AAA SHEET MAP.

Only places listed in the Attractions
section appear on this map.

🔻 See AAA GEM Attractions
❶ See Chart of Recreation Areas

SEE INSET MAP
FOR DETAIL

© 2009 NAVTEQ

©AAA

4044-I

RECREATION AREAS

	MAP LOCATION	CAMPING	PICNICKING	HIKING TRAILS	BOATING	BOAT RAMP	BOAT RENTAL	FISHING	SWIMMING	PETS ON LEASH	BICYCLE TRAILS	WINTER SPORTS	VISITOR CENTER	LODGE/CABINS	FOOD SERVICE
NATIONAL PARK AREAS															
Boston Harbor Islands (E-3) 1,200 acres consisting of 34 islands in Boston Harbor. *(See Boston p. 105)*		•	•	•	•			•	•						
Bumpkin Island		•	•	•	•			•							
Georges Island Historic. *(See Fort Warren in Boston p. 106)*			•	•	•			•							•
Grape Island		•	•	•	•			•							
Lovell's Island		•	•	•	•			•	•						
Peddock's Island		•	•	•	•			•							
NATIONAL SEASHORES *(See place listings)*															
Cape Cod National Seashore (C-9) 43,608 acres.			•	•				•	•		•	•	•		
ARMY CORPS OF ENGINEERS															
Buffumville Lake (C-4) 451 acres 4 mi. s. of North Oxford off SR 12.	❶		•	•	•	•		•	•	•	•				
STATE															
Ames Nowell (C-7) 607 acres n.w. of Abington off SR 123 on Linwood St. Horse rental.	❷		•	•	•			•		•	•				
Ashland (C-6) 470 acres 2 mi. s.w. of Ashland on SR 135.	❸		•	•	•	•		•	•	•		•			
Beartown (C-1) 10,897 acres 3 mi. s.e. of Stockbridge on SR 23. Horse rental.	❹	•	•	•	•	•		•	•	•	•				
Borderland (C-6) 1,772 acres on Massapoag Ave. in North Easton.	❺		•	•				•			•	•	•		
Bradley Palmer (A-7) 721 acres s.w. of Topsfield off US 1.	❻		•	•	•			•	•	•	•				
Brimfield (C-4) 3,250 acres 2 mi. s. of Brimfield off US 20. Horse rental.	❼		•	•				•	•	•	•	•			
Callahan (B-6) 820 acres off Millwood St. in Framingham. Horseback riding trails.	❽		•	•				•			•	•			
Chester-Blandford (C-2) 2,308 acres 4 mi. s.e. of Chester on US 20.	❾		•	•				•		•		•			
Chicopee (C-3) 574 acres on Burnett Rd. in Chicopee.	❿		•	•				•	•	•	•				
Clarksburg (A-2) 3,431 acres 3 mi. n. of North Adams on SR 8.	⓫	•	•	•	•			•	•	•		•			
Cochituate (F-1) 1,126 acres off SR 30 in Natick.	⓬		•		•	•	•	•	•						
Conway (B-3) 1,946 acres s. of Conway via SR 116. Horse rental.	⓭			•				•		•		•			
D.A.R. (B-2) 1,517 acres 3 mi. n. of Goshen off SR 9. Horse rental.	⓮	•	•	•	•	•		•	•	•	•	•			
Demarest Lloyd (E-7) 222 acres 3 mi. s. of Dartmouth off US 6 on Barney's Joy Rd.	⓯		•	•				•	•						
Dighton Rock (D-6) 85 acres s. of Berkley on Bay View Ave.	⓰		•	•	•	•		•				•	•		
Douglas (D-5) 4,640 acres 2 mi. w. of Douglas off SR 16. Horse rental.	⓱		•	•	•	•		•	•	•	•	•			
Dunn (A-4) 119 acres e. of Gardner on SR 101.	⓲		•	•	•			•	•				•	•	
Erving (B-4) 4,479 acres 2 mi. n.e. of Erving on SR 2A. Horse rental.	⓳	•	•	•	•	•		•	•	•	•	•			
Granville (C-2) 2,376 acres 1 mi. s.w. of West Granville off SR 57. Horse rental.	⓴	•		•				•			•	•	•		
Great Brook Farm (B-6) 1,000 acres on Lowell Rd. in Carlisle.	㉑		•	•				•			•	•	•		
Hampton Ponds (C-3) 42 acres s.e. of Southampton off SR 10.	㉒	•		•	•	•		•	•	•					

RECREATION AREAS

Recreation Area	Map Location	Camping	Picnicking	Hiking Trails	Boating	Boat Ramp	Boat Rental	Fishing	Swimming	Pets on Leash	Bicycle Trails	Winter Sports	Visitor Center	Lodge/Cabins	Food Service
Harold Parker (B-7) 3,000 acres 2.6 mi. s.e. off SR 114 in North Andover. Horseback riding trails. *(See North Andover p. 153)*	23	•	•	•				•	•	•	•	•			
Holland Pond (C-4) 35 acres 2 mi. n. of Holland off SR 20. Horse rental.	24		•		•	•		•	•	•					
Hopkinton (C-5) 1,450 acres 3 mi. n. of Hopkinton on SR 85. Horse rental.	25		•	•	•	•	•	•	•	•	•				
Horseneck Beach (E-7) 600 acres 14 mi. s. of Fall River on SR 88 at Horseneck Beach.	26	•	•					•	•	•					•
Joseph Allen Skinner (C-3) 390 acres 4 mi. n. on SR 47. Snowmobiling; horse rental. *(See South Hadley p. 199)*	27		•	•						•		•	•		
Kenneth M. Dubuque Memorial (B-2) 7,822 acres off SR 8A near Hawley. Backpack camping; horse rental.	28	•		•	•			•							
Lake Dennison (B-4) 4,221 acres 2 mi. n. of Baldwinsville on US 202.	29	•	•	•	•	•		•	•			•			
Leominster (B-5) 4,300 acres 7 mi. s. of Fitchburg on SR 31. Horse rental.	30	•	•	•				•	•	•		•			
Massasoit (D-7) 1,500 acres 3 mi. w. of Middleboro off SR 18. Horse rental.	31		•	•	•	•		•	•	•	•		•		
Maudslay (A-7) 476 acres on Curzon Mill Rd. in Newburyport. Historic. Horseback riding trails. *(See Newburyport p. 151)*	32		•	•							•	•			
Mohawk Trail (A-2) 6,457 acres 3 mi. w. of Charlemont on SR 2.	33	•	•	•				•	•	•		•		•	
Mount Grace Forest (A-3) 1,689 acres off SR 78 in Warwick. Horse rental.	34		•	•						•	•	•			
Mount Greylock (A-2) 12,500 acres 8.5 mi. s. of North Adams off SR 2. Horse rental. *(See North Adams p. 191)*	35	•	•	•						•	•	•	•	•	•
Mount Tom (C-3) 2,082 acres 4 mi. n. of Holyoke on US 5. *(See Holyoke p. 185)*	36		•	•				•				•	•		
Mount Washington (C-1) 4,169 acres s.w. of South Egremont off SR 41 on Mount Washington Rd. Backpack camping; horse rental, waterfall.	37	•	•	•				•		•	•				
Myles Standish (D-8) 14,651 acres off US 3 on Cranberry Rd. in Carver. Horse rental.	38	•	•	•	•	•		•	•	•	•		•		
Nickerson (D-9) 1,900 acres 1 mi. e. of East Brewster off SR 6A. Horse rental.	39	•	•	•	•	•		•	•	•				•	•
October Mountain (B-2) 16,127 acres 3 mi. n. of Lee on a county road. Horse rental.	40	•		•	•	•		•		•	•				
Otter River (A-4) 12,788 acres 1 mi. n. of Baldwinsville on US 202.	41	•	•	•				•	•	•		•			
Pittsfield (B-1) 10,000 acres 4 mi. n.w. of Pittsfield. Horse rental. *(See Pittsfield p. 193)*	42	•	•	•	•			•	•	•	•	•			
Quinsigamond (C-5) 51 acres 2 mi. e. of Worcester off SR 9.	43		•		•			•	•	•					
Robinson (C-3) 811 acres 2.7 mi. w. of Agawam on North St. (SR 147). Horse rental.	44		•	•				•	•	•	•	•			
Rutland (B-4) 300 acres 3 mi. s.w. of Rutland on SR 122A.	45		•	•	•			•	•	•	•				
Salisbury Beach (A-7) 521 acres 2 mi. e. of Salisbury off SR 1A.	46	•	•		•	•		•	•	•					•
Sandisfield (C-2) 7,785 acres 1 mi. w. of Sandisfield off SR 57. Backpack camping; horse rental.	47		•	•				•	•	•		•			
Savoy Mountain (A-2) 11,118 acres 6 mi. s.e. of North Adams off SR 2. Horse rental.	48	•	•	•	•	•		•	•	•	•			•	
Scusset Beach (D-8) 380 acres off US 6 and SR 3A on Scusset Beach Rd. in Sandwich.	49	•	•	•				•	•	•	•				•

RECREATION AREAS

	MAP LOCATION	CAMPING	PICNICKING	HIKING TRAILS	BOATING	BOAT RAMP	BOAT RENTAL	FISHING	SWIMMING	PETS ON LEASH	BICYCLE TRAILS	WINTER SPORTS	VISITOR CENTER	LODGE/CABINS	FOOD SERVICE
South Cape Beach (E-8) 401 acres s. of Mashpee on Great Oak Rd.	50		•	•				•	•						
Spencer (C-4) 965 acres .5 mi. s. of Spencer on SR 31. Historic. *(See Spencer p. 200)*	51		•	•				•	•	•			•		
Tolland (C-2) 4,893 acres 3 mi. n. of New Boston off SR 8. Horse rental.	52	•	•	•	•	•		•	•	•			•		
Walden Pond (E-1) 462 acres .2 mi. s. of Concord on SR 126. Historic. *(See Concord p. 142)*	53		•	•	•	•		•	•				•		
Wells (C-4) 1,400 acres 2 mi. n. of Sturbridge off SR 49N.	54	•		•	•			•	•	•					
Wendell (B-3) 7,900 acres e. of Farley off SR 2 on Wendell Rd. Horse rental.	55	•	•	•	•			•	•	•	•	•			
Willard Brook (A-5) 2,597 acres 3 mi. e. of Ashby off SR 119. Scenic. Horse rental.	56	•	•	•				•	•	•	•	•		•	
Windsor Forest (B-2) 1,743 acres off SR 116 in Windsor.	57	•	•	•				•	•	•		•			
Wompatuck (F-3) 3,500 acres off SR 228 s.e. of Hingham. Horse rental.	58	•						•		•	•	•	•		
OTHER															
Cape Poge Wildlife Refuge (F-8) 1,000 acres 2.5 mi. s.e. of the Chappaquiddick ferry landing on Chappaquiddick Rd., then .5 mi. e. on Dike Rd. Historic. Scenic. Bird-watching, canoeing, hunting, kayaking; beach. *(See Edgartown p. 186)*	59		•	•	•			•	•	•					
Chesterfield Gorge (B-2) 166 acres 1 mi. s. of Chesterfield via Ireland St. Scenic. Bird-watching, cross-country skiing.	60		•	•					•			•			
Northfield Mountain Recreation and Environmental Center (A-3) 2 mi. n. of SR 2 on SR 63. Cross-country skiing, snowshoeing; riverboat cruises. *(See Northfield p. 192)*	61	•	•	•	•	•	•	•	•			•	•	•	
Richard T. Crane Jr. Memorial Reservation (A-7) 1,399 acres 6 mi. e. of Ipswich via Argilla Rd. *(See Ipswich p. 146)*	62		•	•				•	•						
Winter Island Marine Park (D-3) 20 acres 2 mi. e. of Salem on Winter Island Rd. Historic.	63	•	•		•	•			•	•	•				•

Massachusetts Temperature Averages Maximum/Minimum
From the records of The Weather Channel Interactive, Inc.

	JAN	FEB	MAR	APR	MAY	JUNE	JULY	AUG	SEPT	OCT	NOV	DEC
Boston	36 / 22	39 / 24	46 / 31	56 / 41	67 / 50	77 / 59	82 / 65	80 / 64	73 / 57	62 / 46	52 / 38	42 / 28
Nantucket	39 / 25	39 / 26	44 / 31	51 / 38	60 / 46	69 / 55	75 / 62	76 / 63	70 / 56	61 / 47	53 / 39	44 / 30
Pittsfield	32 / 13	36 / 14	45 / 23	58 / 34	70 / 43	77 / 52	81 / 57	79 / 56	71 / 48	60 / 37	48 / 30	37 / 19
Worcester	31 / 16	34 / 18	43 / 26	54 / 36	66 / 46	74 / 55	79 / 61	77 / 59	69 / 51	58 / 41	47 / 32	36 / 22

Points of Interest

ACTON—*see Boston p. 134.*

AGAWAM (C-3) pop. 28,144

A suburb of Springfield, Agawam was the hometown of Anne Sullivan, tutor and companion of Helen Keller. Robinson State Park *(see Recreation Chart)* is 2.7 miles west on North Street (SR 147).

SIX FLAGS NEW ENGLAND, 1623 Main St. (SR 159), is said to be New England's largest theme and water park. The park features more than 100 rides, shows and attractions, including Superman Ride of Steel, a steel hypercoaster that soars 208 feet in the air at a speed of up to 70 mph.

Other roller coasters include Flashback, a forward and backward looping, twisting steel coaster; Mind Eraser, a suspended steel looping coaster; the traditional wooden coasters Thunderbolt and Cyclone; the floorless roller coaster Batman the Ride; Pandemonium, a family spinning coaster; and Typhoon Water Coaster.

Looney Tunes Movie Town, Wiggles World and Thomas Town offer family entertainment with rides and shows just for kids. Hurricane Harbor is a water park with more than two dozen waterslides, two wave pools, a lazy river and a children's area.

Hours: Park open daily, Memorial Day-Labor Day; Fri.-Sun., mid-Apr. through day before Memorial Day; Sat.-Sun., day after Labor Day-Nov. 1. Phone ahead to confirm schedule. **Cost:** $41.99 (including Hurricane Harbor); $31 (under 54 inches tall); free (ages 0-2). AAA members save on select services and merchandise. See guest relations for details. **Parking:** $15. **Phone:** (413) 786-9300.

AMESBURY—*see Boston p. 134.*

AMHERST (B-3) elev. 255′

Amherst was named for Lord Jeffrey Amherst, a British general in the French and Indian War. In the town's early years the residents made several efforts to industrialize but were most successful with cattle farming. In 1864 the livestock's prizewinning reputation led to the founding of Massachusetts Agricultural College, which later developed into the University of Massachusetts.

In 1821 Amherst College was founded and was dedicated to preparing young men for missionary

work; in the mid-19th century more liberal educational aims were adopted. Among renowned graduates are Henry Ward Beecher and Calvin Coolidge. Also adding to the area's scholarly atmosphere were some of its residents: author Ray Stannard Baker (David Grayson) and poets Emily Dickinson, Robert Frost and Eugene Field.

The Amherst History Museum, 67 Amity St., features guided tours of the Strong House, built about 1750. Historical exhibitions present items from the 18th and 19th centuries; phone (413) 256-0678.

The National Yiddish Book Center at 1021 West St. on the campus of Hampshire College preserves more than 1.5 million books written in Yiddish. The center is housed in a building designed to look like a 19th-century *shtetl,* a cluster of wooden buildings surrounding a synagogue. In addition to Yiddish texts the center houses educational exhibits; phone (413) 256-4900.

Mead Art Museum, 1 block south of SR 9 on the Amherst College campus, contains changing displays of artifacts, paintings and sculpture from the 17th through the 20th century; phone (413) 542-2335.

Amherst Chamber of Commerce: 28 Amity St., Amherst, MA 01002. **Phone:** (413) 253-0700.

AMHERST COLLEGE MUSEUM OF NATURAL HISTORY is on Barrett Hill Rd. on the Amherst College campus off SR 9 (College St.). Rocks, minerals and fossils are displayed, including mammal skeletons from the ice age; Cenozoic mammal fossils; and more than 1,100 slabs of tracks and traces from the Connecticut Valley, which were among the first dinosaur fossils discovered in North America. Limited on-campus parking is available on weekends. **Time:** Allow 1 hour, 30 minutes minimum. **Hours:** Tues.-Sun. 11-4. **Cost:** Free. **Phone:** (413) 542-2165.

EMILY DICKINSON MUSEUM: THE HOMESTEAD & THE EVERGREENS is .1 mi. n.e. on Northampton Rd./SR 115/SR 9, .1 mi. n. on S. Pleasant St., then .2 mi. e. to 280 Main St. The museum includes the Homestead, Emily Dickinson's home and birthplace; and The Evergreens, the next-door home of Dickinson's brother, Austin.

Located in the Homestead, the Tour Center offers an exhibit about Emily Dickinson's poetry and is the starting point for all visits. The 90-minute Emily Dickinson's World tour affords exploration of both historic homes and a full account of Dickinson's life and work; the 45-minute This was a Poet tour introduces visitors to the writer in her own home. A self-guiding audio tour of the grounds also is available.

Note: Only the first floors of the historic houses are wheelchair accessible. **Hours:** Wed.-Sun. 10-5, June-Aug.; 11-4, Mar.-May and Sept.-Dec. Last tour begins 1 hour before closing. Tour schedule may vary; phone ahead. Closed major holidays. **Cost:** Tour Center free. Guided tours $4-$10; free (ages 0-5). Tickets are available on a first-come, first-served basis. **Phone:** (413) 542-8161, or (413) 542-8429 for information about handicap access.

SAVE **THE ERIC CARLE MUSEUM OF PICTURE BOOK ART** is at 125 W. Bay Rd. Named for author and illustrator Eric Carle, this museum features three galleries displaying national and international picture book art. A hands-on art studio, a reading library and an auditorium for lectures and performances also are on-site. Changing exhibitions, special events and programs are offered throughout the year.

Time: Allow 2 hours minimum. **Hours:** Tues.-Fri. (also Mon. in July and Aug. and during school vacation weeks in Feb. and Apr.) 10-4, Sat. 10-5, Sun. noon-5. Closed Jan. 1, July 4, Thanksgiving and Dec. 24-25. **Cost:** $9; $6 (ages 1-18 and 65+); $22.50 (family, two adults and two children). **Phone:** (413) 658-1100. ⊟

JONES LIBRARY INC., 43 Amity St., is a small public library built to resemble a luxurious private home. Several rooms, paneled in walnut and Philippine mahogany, are decorated with Oriental rugs and paintings. The Special Collection section has information about local history and genealogy as well as exhibits about Emily Dickinson, Robert Frost and others. The Burnett Gallery features the works of local artists.

Hours: Library Tues. and Thurs. 9 a.m.-9:30 p.m., Mon. 1-5:30, Wed. 9-5:30, Fri. 9-1, Sun. 1-5, day after Labor Day-May 31; Tues. and Thurs. 9-8:30, Mon. 1-5:30, Wed. 9-5:30, Fri. 9-1, rest of year. Special Collection section Tues.-Thurs. 10-5, Mon. and Sat. 2-5, Fri. 10-1. Closed major holidays. Phone ahead to confirm schedule. **Cost:** Free. **Phone:** (413) 259-3090, or (413) 259-3097 for the Special Collection section.

DID YOU KNOW

The first portable house in America was brought from Windsor to Plymouth in 1724.

ANDOVER—*see Boston p. 135.*

ARLINGTON—*see Boston p. 135.*

ASHLEY FALLS (C-1) elev. 684′

BARTHOLOMEW'S COBBLE is 1 mi. w. on Rannapo Rd., then just s. on Weatogue Rd. The 329-acre reservation on the Housatonic River is named for two rocky knolls consisting mostly of limestone and marble. A wide variety of fern, wildflower and bird species can be seen. The nature preserve has a natural history museum, staffed by a naturalist; hiking trails; and a visitor center. Pets are not permitted. **Hours:** Grounds daily dawn-dusk. Museum daily 9-4:30, Apr.-Nov.; Tues.-Sat. 9-4:30, rest of year. **Cost:** $5; $1 (ages 6-12). **Phone:** (413) 229-8600.

ATTLEBORO (D-6) pop. 42,068, elev. 133′

United Regional Chamber of Commerce: 42 Union St., Attleboro, MA 02703. **Phone:** (508) 222-0801.

ATTLEBORO ARTS MUSEUM, 86 Park St., mounts changing exhibitions of a mixture of local, regional, professional and amateur artists working in various media and genre. **Hours:** Tues.-Sat. 10-5. Closed holidays and holiday weekends. **Cost:** Free. **Phone:** (508) 222-2644.

CAPRON PARK ZOO, 1.5 mi. e. on SR 123E to 201 County St., contains exhibits of wildlife from Asia, Africa, and North and South America, including rare and endangered species. Educational programs are offered. **Hours:** Daily 10-5, early Apr.-late Oct.; 10-4, rest of year. Last admission 1 hour before closing. Closed Jan. 1, Thanksgiving and Dec. 25. **Cost:** $5.50; $3.75 (ages 3-12 and 65+). **Phone:** (774) 203-1840.

NATIONAL SHRINE OF OUR LADY OF LA SALETTE, 947 Park St. (SR 118), is staffed by the Missionaries of Our Lady of La Salette. Within this Marian shrine are statuary gardens, a church and a retreat house. Visitors flock to the ☂Christmas Festival of Lights, when more than 250,000 lights illuminate the grounds during the winter holiday season. **Hours:** Shrine open daily 9-8. Festival of Lights is presented nightly 5-9, Thanksgiving-Jan. 1. Phone ahead to confirm schedule. **Cost:** Free. **Phone:** (508) 222-5410.

BARNSTABLE—*see Cape Cod p. 164.*

BELCHERTOWN (C-3) pop. 2,626, elev. 476′

CHARLES L. McLAUGHLIN TROUT HATCHERY is 3.75 mi. e. on SR 9, then .5 mi. s. to 90 East St. The hatchery, which raises rainbow, brown and brook trout, is part of the 1,000-acre Swift River Wildlife Management Area. Visitors can feed the fish with food pellets bought from machines in the hatchery. **Hours:** Daily 9-3:45. **Cost:** Free. **Phone:** (413) 323-7671.

BERKSHIRES

In westernmost Massachusetts lies an area of rivers, lakes and hills known as the Berkshires. The serenity and separateness of the area shaped and influenced both settlers and visitors. For theologian Jonathan Edwards and Mother Lee's Shakers, this region served as part of their separate journeys to find and serve God. For writers Edith Wharton, Herman Melville and Nathaniel Hawthorne, the Berkshires nurtured great literary works, such as Melville's "Moby Dick," which he wrote while living in Pittsfield.

Strung along US 7, the major towns of the Berkshires offer a long procession of events, theater, dance, music, museums and historical sites. Recreational opportunities for downhill and cross-country skiing, bicycling, canoeing, fishing and hiking are abundant. Rounding out these offerings are the natural beauty of the fall foliage as well as numerous winter ski resorts and country inns.

Places and towns listed individually are Ashley Falls, Dalton, Great Barrington, Hancock, Lenox, North Adams, Pittsfield, Stockbridge and Williamstown.

Berkshire Visitors Bureau: 3 Hoosac St., Adams, MA 01220. **Phone:** (413) 743-4500 or (800) 237-5747.

BEVERLY—*see Boston p. 135.*

Smithsonian
National Museum of American History
Kenneth E. Behring Center

See how we got here.

Immerse yourself in the newly renovated museum and explore how transportation has changed America. National Museum of American History, Washington, D.C.

http://americanhistory.si.edu/onthemove

AMERICA
ON THE MOVE

Boston

City Population: 589,141   **Elevation:** 20 ft.

Editor's Picks:

Faneuil Hall ....*(see p. 108)*

Museum of Fine Arts, Boston.... *(see p. 110)*

USS *Constitution* ....*(see p. 107)*

Find more AAA top picks at AAA.com

© Greg Probst / Panoramic Images

Over time, Boston promoters have bestowed many names upon the city, including the "Athens of America," "The Cradle of Modern America" and the particularly vainglorious "Hub of the Universe." But, as the birthplace of numerous cultural, intellectual and technological revolutions, Boston merits acclaim. Even the loftiest of praises bestowed upon this East Coast city have persisted, at least for the last *few* centuries.

Sumus primi, or "We are first," is another proud, but well-suited, description for the Greater Boston area. The phrase—the motto of Boston Latin, the country's oldest continuing public school—succinctly conveys 300-plus years of Boston-bred organizations, inventions and pioneering ideas. In a metropolis where firsts are commonplace, the expression fits like a well-insulated glove—the kind you'll definitely need when visiting New England during its frosty winter.

Even on chilly days, coffee- and hot chocolate-guzzling visitors roam the nation's first public park, the Boston Common. Here ice-skaters clad in cozy scarves and knit caps welcome Jack Frost's glacial touch, coasting across the frozen Frog Pond from November to mid-March. When sandal season arrives, munching picnickers recline beneath dazzling blue skies, their views of dawdling clouds interrupted occasionally by soaring Frisbees and colorful kites. This grassy area became common land for Puritans who arrived in 1630 and settled on a hilly peninsula the American Indians called *Shawmut,* or "Living Waters." Cows grazed on "the common," and the verdant expanse later served as a military training field. In the 1860s the Oneida Football Club, considered by some to be the nation's first organized football team, played ball here. In the last

century such imitable figures as Martin Luther King Jr., Pope John Paul II and Gloria Steinem have inspired crowds gathered at this lush civic centerpiece.

Continue along the Emerald Necklace—Boston's linear system of urban green space designed by Frederick Law Olmsted—to the majestic Public Garden. Walk across a whimsical, miniaturized version of the London Bridge surrounded by Victorian garden designs and tulip, elm and maple trees sheltering plump, inquisitive squirrels. The park's iconic swan boats (operated by the same family since the 1870s) cruise about the botanical garden's sunlight-flecked lagoon, with area students pedaling photo-happy tourists past mallard ducks and graceful swans.

Established in 1837, the fragrant Public Garden also is home to several sculptures. Near the Arlington Street gate, artists with grass-stained jeans and furrowed brows busily sketch an arresting equestrian statue of George Washington. (Erected in 1869, Thomas Ball's creation is one of the earliest depictions of the first president on horseback.) Elsewhere in the garden eager children clamber about nine bronze, winged figures that celebrate Robert McCloskey's picture book "Make Way for Ducklings."

*G*etting *T*here — *starting on p. 102*

*G*etting *A*round — *starting on p. 102*

*W*hat *T*o *S*ee — *starting on p. 104*

*W*hat *T*o *D*o — *starting on p. 113*

*W*here *T*o *S*tay — *starting on p. 353*

*W*here *T*o *D*ine — *starting on p. 366*

*E*ssential *E*xperiences — *visit AAA.com*

*E*ditor's *E*vent *P*icks — *visit AAA.com*

You may recognize the bronze relief sculpture located at the northeast corner of the Boston Common, opposite the present State House. (The 1713 Old State House, the city's oldest surviving public building, is on Court Street.) Honoring the Civil War's first African-American military unit recruited in the North and the regiment's commanding officer, Boston Brahmin Robert Gould Shaw, the memorial appears in the credits of the 1989 film "Glory." The movie earned three Academy Awards for its depiction of the 54th Massachusetts Volunteer Infantry Regiment, which led the July 18, 1863, assault on the Confederate stronghold Fort Wagner. Sgt. William Harvey Carney, who bravely protected the American flag during the bloody battle in which more than half of his compatriots were lost, often is regarded as the first African-American Medal of Honor recipient.

Harborfest / Greater Boston Convention & Visitors Bureau

The striking monument fashioned by Augustus Saint-Gaudens is the starting point for the Black Heritage Trail. Learn about Boston's 19th-century African-American community on a self-guiding tour, or let a National Park Service ranger lead the way. Abolitionist William Lloyd Garrison founded the New England Anti-Slavery Society in 1832 at the African Meeting House, the oldest existing church in the country built by free African-Americans. You'll find this historic structure, along with several other Black Heritage Trail sites, in Beacon Hill. Gas lamps still light narrow passageways and quaintly uneven brick sidewalks once traversed by such influential citizens as Louisa May Alcott and Robert Frost.

Venture through the neighborhood today and you're likely to rub elbows with politicians and celebrities amid a mishmash of splendid old row houses and antique shops, posh clothing boutiques and gourmet markets. To start your day, devour a stack of fluffy blueberry pancakes at The Paramount on Charles Street; the casual eatery has been serving up simple, scrumptious and well-priced meals since 1937. As night falls, stop for a brewski at the Beacon Street pub (originally known as the Bull & Finch) that inspired the Emmy-winning TV show "Cheers."

The city embraces numerous neighborhoods such as the Back Bay, Charlestown and the South End. Furthermore, Greater Boston comprises many abutting, but separate, municipalities as well as a score of outer suburbs, from Braintree to Newton to Woburn. Cambridge—sometimes mistaken by the uninitiated to be part of Boston—is home to Harvard University, the oldest institution of higher education in the nation. The city also produced the first book printed in what is now the United States. The Howard Johnson chain got its start in nearby Quincy, as did Dunkin' Donuts. After enjoying a cup of Joe and some sugary goodness at the original

© age fotostock
SuperStock

John F. Kennedy Presidential Library and Museum, Boston.
(See listing page 109)

Destination Boston

Y ou'd better pack your walking shoes, because Boston is best explored on foot. Here, a jaunt around town is like opening an American history textbook.

F ollow the red line marking the Freedom Trail. You'll pass Boston Common, the Old North Church, Paul Revere's house and Bunker Hill, to name a few of the city's most significant historical sites.

© age fotostock / SuperStock

Old State House, Boston.
(See listing page 112)

P laces included in this AAA Destination City:

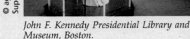

NEW HAMPSHIRE
MASSACHUSETTS

3

3

Westford .

2

Acton .

495

Sudbury .

9

Natick .
Framingham •

90

495

The Witch House, Salem.
(See listing page 158)

© culliganphoto / Alamy

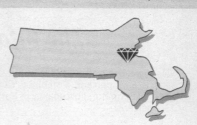

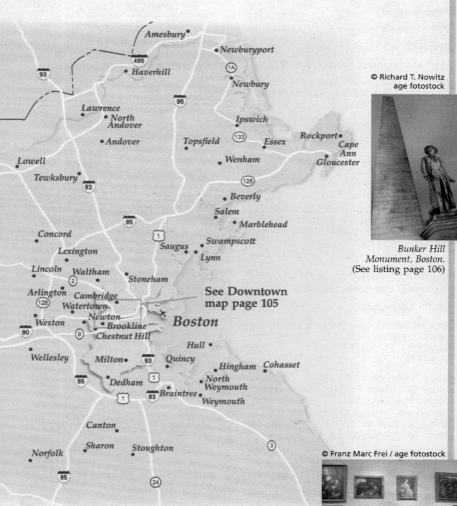

Amesbury

Newburyport

495

93

Haverhill

1A

Newbury

95

Lawrence

North
Andover

Ipswich

Andover

Topsfield

133

Essex

Rockport

Cape
Ann

Lowell

Wenham

Gloucester

Tewksbury

93

128

93

Beverly

95

Salem

Marblehead

Concord

Saugus

Swampscott

Lexington

1

Lynn

Lincoln

Waltham

2

Stoneham

Arlington

128

Cambridge

Watertown

See Downtown
map page 105

Weston

Newton

90

9

Brookline

Boston

Chestnut Hill

Wellesley

Milton

93

Hull

Quincy

Hingham

Cohasset

95

Dedham

1

North
Weymouth

1

93

Braintree

Weymouth

Canton

Sharon

Stoughton

3

Norfolk

95

24

© Richard T. Nowitz
age fotostock

Bunker Hill
Monument, Boston.
(See listing page 106)

© Franz Marc Frei / age fotostock

Museum of Fine Arts, Boston.
(See listing page 110)

The Informed Traveler

Sales Tax: The state sales tax in Massachusetts is 6.25 percent. Combined city and state taxes on hotel occupancy in Boston is 13.7 percent.

WHOM TO CALL

Emergency: 911

Police (non-emergency): (617) 343-4200

Fire: (617) 343-3550

Time and Temperature: (617) 637-1234

Hospitals: Beth Israel Deaconess Medical Center, (617) 667-7000; Boston Medical Center, (617) 638-8000; Faulkner Hospital, (617) 983-7000; Massachusetts General Hospital, (617) 726-2000; Tufts-New England Medical Center, (617) 636-5000.

WHERE TO LOOK

Newspapers

The daily newspapers are the morning *Boston Herald* and *The Boston Globe*. The *Christian Science Monitor* is published weekly.

Radio

Boston radio station WBUR (90.9 FM) is a member of National Public Radio.

Visitor Information

Greater Boston Convention & Visitors Bureau: 2 Copley Place, Suite 105, Boston, MA 02116. **Phone:** (617) 536-4100 or (888) 733-2678.

An information center on the Tremont Street side of the Boston Common is open Mon.-Sat. 8:30-5, Sun. 9-5. Visitor information also is available in the center court at the Prudential Center, 800 Boylston St., Mon.-Sat. 9-6, Sun. 10-6.

The National Park Service Visitor Center, on the Freedom Trail at 15 State St., is open daily 9-5. Closed Jan. 1, Thanksgiving and Dec. 25.

Panorama: The Official Guide to Boston and *Boston Phoenix* provide information about events and attractions. The convention and visitors bureau has information about special events; phone (888) 733-2678.

WHAT TO PACK

Boston's latitude leaves the city vulnerable to both polar and tropical air masses. Low-pressure storm systems frequently follow tracks that take them near Boston, while the Atlantic Ocean has a moderating influence on both summer and winter temperature extremes. The four seasons are quite distinct here.

New England winters are not for the fainthearted. Boston experiences its fair share of snow, sleet and icy winds, and the Charles River normally freezes over. Coastal storms, or northeasters, can produce tremendous amounts of snow or rain. Summers are warm but not usually uncomfortable, although occasional heat waves send temperatures and humidity soaring.

Spring and early fall are pleasant times to visit. Although bitterly cold weather can last well into March, spring eventually arrives. May, when many of the spring flowers are in bloom, is a lovely month. Autumn visitors will be greeted with crisp, clear air and resplendent fall colors, starting in September and peaking by mid-October. *For additional information see temperature chart p. 91.*

Boston's dress code ranges from the conservative attire of downtown's Old Guard establishments to the casual accoutrements worn at Cambridge's student enclaves. The most important thing to remember is that the city's variable weather requires a flexible wardrobe. In winter bring a heavy coat and a pair of sturdy boots or shoes for negotiating icy sidewalks. An umbrella will come in handy at almost any time of year.

Dunkin' Donuts store (543 Southern Artery), visit Adams National Historical Park, which shelters the birthplaces of John and John Quincy Adams.

Even newcomers will find it easy to get around the area with Boston's straightforward public transportation system—a stress-free alternative to navigating the Hub's maze of narrow roads by car. The launching point for the nation's first subway line is just around the corner from the gold-domed Massachusetts State House. On the line's inaugural day in 1897, more than 100,000 people are said to have taken the 3.5-minute trip, which traveled from Park Street to Boylston Street beneath Tremont Street.

Take a ride on the Green Line to the New England Conservatory of Music, where you can applaud a string ensemble at the oldest independent school of music in the United States. If the crack of the bat is music to your ears, take the subway (locals just call it the "T") to Fenway Park, the *second* home of the Boston Red Sox. At their first stadium, the bygone Huntington Avenue Grounds, the Sox (then known as the Boston Americans) defeated the Pittsburgh Pirates during game 8 of the first modern World Series in October 1903.

Much of Boston proper exists because of a series of 19th-century land reclamation projects. To really appreciate the nuances of this compact, multifaceted locale, investigate Boston ("America's Walking City") on foot. For a leisurely stroll, travel east from the Park Street "T" station on Winter Street. As a tribute to the first president, the lane (as do most other Boston thoroughfares) changes its name

as it crosses over Washington Street. Continue down *Summer* Street to spend a few greenbacks in Downtown Crossing, a bustling retail destination since the 1800s. The oldest U.S. off-price retailer, Filene's Basement, originated here, holding the first of its now famed stampede-like bridal gown sales in 1947. (**Note:** The Basement's Downtown Crossing location is closed for renovations until sometime in 2011.)

Perhaps the best (and most popular) way to get to know Boston is to traverse the Freedom Trail, a red line connecting 16 historic sites from Boston Common through downtown and the North End. Along the way you can board the USS *Constitution,* the oldest commissioned vessel afloat in the world. Pick up a few keepsakes at Faneuil Hall—where such political leaders as Samuel Adams and James Otis garnered support for the American Revolution. While you're there, head upstairs to learn about the nation's first chartered military organization, the Ancient and Honorable Artillery Company. Afterward, peruse the rest of the festive marketplace, which includes an assortment of pushcarts as well as Quincy Market's aromatic food stalls.

Whether it's your first trip to Boston or your fifth, you'll no doubt take more than just a few souvenirs home with you. If you're lucky enough to experience Boston's treasures—from First Night festivities to Boston cream pies to its colorful array of residents—you'll leave with a better understanding of both this enduring city's vast heritage and the nation's.

Fenway Park / © Raymond Forbes / age fotostock

Getting There

By Car

The spokes of major highways converging on Greater Boston from three sides make it seem that all roads lead to the Hub. Three interstate highways offer a direct approach to the city and its suburbs. From the north I-95 merges with SR 128 at Peabody before skirting the western edge of the metropolitan area; south of Boston I-95 branches southwest and heads toward Providence.

Also from the north I-93 angles down through Medford and Somerville, merges with US 1 at Charlestown, crosses the Charles River (via the cable-stayed Leonard P. Zakim Bunker Hill Bridge) and passes under downtown. I-93/US1 then proceeds through South Boston, parallels the western shore of Massachusetts Bay and passes through Quincy before turning west and running into I-95 near Norwood. SR 3, the route to Cape Cod, branches southeast off I-93 near Braintree.

The major east-west highway into Boston is the Massachusetts Turnpike (I-90), which runs into I-93/US1 just south of downtown. Paralleling this toll route to the south is SR 9, serving the suburbs of Wellesley, Newton and Brookline. Another east-west artery, SR 2, passes just south of Concord and then heads southeast into Cambridge.

The Boston Big Dig project has reorganized the highways into and through Boston. First-time and returning visitors should review the Boston map prior to venturing into the city.

Air Travel

Logan International Airport occupies a peninsula just south of East Boston, 3 miles east of downtown across Boston Inner Harbor. Logan functions as New England's hub airport and serves most major airlines. Drivers should depart by the main exit and take the Boston Expressway to the Sumner Tunnel (toll $3.50), which crosses the harbor into downtown. Drivers traveling south of the city via I-93 or west on I-90 should follow signs for the Ted Williams Tunnel (toll $3.50).

As tunnel traffic jams are all too common, the quickest and easiest way to reach downtown is by subway. Free shuttle service runs from all five terminals to the Airport "T" station on the Blue Line. From there it's about a 20-minute ride to downtown's State Street or Government Center stations. Shuttles run every 8-12 minutes daily 4 a.m.-1 a.m.; phone (617) 561-1800 or (800) 235-6426.

Combined bus and subway fare to downtown is $2. Logan Express shuttles depart from Terminal B to the outer suburbs of Braintree, Framingham, Peabody and Woburn. Buses leave the airport daily 6:30 a.m.-11 p.m.; phone (800) 235-6426.

The Water Shuttle is another convenient way to cross the harbor, departing from the Logan dock and arriving 10 minutes later at Long Wharf in the Financial District. Shuttle bus 66 provides free, frequent service from airport terminals to the dock.

Boat departures from Logan are Mon.-Fri. 7 a.m.-8 p.m., Sat.-Sun. 10-6 (weather permitting), except on holidays. The fare is $10; phone (617) 422-0392 or (617) 222-6999. Commuter boats also run to Quincy and Hingham from Long Wharf.

Taxi fares to downtown and to Cambridge run about $20, depending on traffic congestion. Flat-rate fares are in effect beyond a 12-mile radius of downtown; ask the cab driver or Logan dispatcher for the exact fare in advance. City buses will drop off passengers at downtown hotels; bus stop signs are located outside each terminal.

Boston is served by most major rental car agencies. Arrangements should be made before leaving on a trip; local AAA clubs can provide this assistance and additional information. Hertz provides discounts to AAA members; phone (617) 338-1512 or (800) 654-3080. Rates do not include the per-day charge for full insurance coverage.

Rail Service

Amtrak offers service to and from New York, Philadelphia and Washington, D.C., out of Boston's South Station at Atlantic Avenue and Summer Street. Connections to all points in the national Amtrak system can be made at the Back Bay Station, 145 Dartmouth St.; phone (800) 872-7245 for reservations and information.

The Massachusetts Bay Transportation Authority (MBTA) operates commuter rail service from South Station to Framingham, Needham, Franklin and Stoughton, as well as Providence, R.I. MBTA's commuter trains to Fitchburg, Lowell and other northbound and westbound destinations leave from North Station, 135 Causeway St.; phone (800) 392-6100 for schedule and ticket information.

Buses

Greyhound Lines Inc., (800) 231-2222, and Peter Pan Bus Lines, (800) 343-9999, operate from South Station.

Getting Around

Street System

Ralph Waldo Emerson once observed, "We say the cows laid out Boston. Well, there are worse surveyors." Emerson, of course, never had to drive through the city. Downtown—occupying a peninsula surrounded by the Charles River, Boston Inner Harbor and Fort Point Channel—is a challenging place for residents, let alone visitors, to negotiate by vehicle. Furthermore, Boston drivers are legendary for their aggressiveness. Those who must drive in the central part of the city should bring along a navigator or a good map. Fortunately, public transportation options are plentiful and the bewildering tangle of streets is easily traversed on foot.

Boston Common, bordered by Charles, Beacon, Park, Tremont and Boylston streets, is a handy orientation landmark. Beacon Street, the Common's northern border and the southern base of Beacon

Hill, extends east into downtown and west through the Back Bay into Brookline. Commonwealth Avenue runs parallel to Beacon Street as the Back Bay's main thoroughfare. The Back Bay's streets, in fact, do form a logical grid pattern between east-west Boylston Street and limited-access Storrow Memorial Drive, and between north-south Massachusetts Avenue and Arlington Street.

Both Beacon and Commonwealth intersect Massachusetts Avenue, which crosses the Charles River via Harvard Bridge into Cambridge. Harvard Bridge becomes Massachusetts Avenue again on the Cambridge side, passing right through the middle of the MIT campus on its

MBTA / © Amanda Hall / Robert Harding Picture Library / age fotostock

way to Harvard and environs. Cambridge also can be reached from the West End via Cambridge Street, which becomes the Longfellow Bridge (SR 3) crossing the river. It changes to Main Street in Cambridge, running into Massachusetts Avenue several blocks northwest of MIT. The most direct way to get to Harvard from Boston is via the Anderson Memorial Bridge, which becomes John F. Kennedy Street on the Cambridge side.

Back in Boston, Tremont Street branches off Cambridge Street, skirts the southeast side of the Common and runs southwest toward the Roxbury neighborhood. Commercial Street serves as the perimeter of the North End waterfront, becoming Causeway Street on the West End side of the Central Artery and Atlantic Avenue as it turns south to pass the wharves along the waterfront. North Street takes eastbound commuters into the Callahan Tunnel, which crosses Boston Inner Harbor to the airport. Hanover and Salem streets are other major avenues bisecting the North End.

Congress Street is a major downtown and Financial District thoroughfare, crossing Fort Point Channel into the Irish neighborhoods of South Boston. Washington Street runs north through Chinatown and downtown before it becomes the Charlestown Bridge crossing the river into Charlestown.

Visitors will save time and letters by adopting the local practice of dropping the ends of long street names. Massachusetts Avenue, for instance, is always "Mass Ave." Likewise, Commonwealth Avenue and the Massachusetts Turnpike become "Comm Ave." and "Mass Pike." "JFK" is the appropriate shorthand for the city's several John F. Kennedy namesakes.

Unless otherwise posted, the speed limit on most streets is 30 mph. Right turns on red are permitted after a full stop, unless otherwise posted. Avoid rush-hour traffic—particularly in the tunnels and on the bridges—7-9 a.m. and 4-6:30 p.m. Be especially careful in outlying areas when crossing streetcar tracks.

Note: Jaywalking is illegal in Boston; furthermore, city drivers are not known for their kindness to pedestrians, even those who have the right-of-way. Cross only within marked crosswalks, when the light is green or with a flashing "walk" signal.

Parking

On-street city parking is very limited and highly regulated. Posted restrictions vary, from the resident-only parking in Beacon Hill and other city neighborhoods to specific hour restrictions throughout the downtown area. Meters also vary with regard to rates and hours, and the city's meter maids are vigilant.

Parking garages are more convenient, and although rates are not cheap (from $5 per hour to $32 per day) they are worth the expense to avoid meeting with a tow truck. Visitors may also want to inquire about attraction or restaurant validation discounts. Two centrally located garages are hidden underground. The Boston Common Garage is entered from Charles Street; round-trip bus service to the other side of the Common is included in the parking fee. The Prudential Center Garage, 800 Boylston St., has entrances on all sides of the Prudential Tower. Both garages are open daily 24 hours.

Other garages in the vicinity of the Prudential Center and Copley Square include Copley Place Parking, 100 Huntington Ave.; Pilgrim Garage, 50 Dalton St.; and John Hancock Garage, 100 Clarendon St.

The underground garage at Zero Post Office Square used to be above ground; now the square is a public park bounded by Milk, Pearl, Franklin and Congress streets. Garage entrances are on Pearl and Congress. Open 24 hours, it is within walking distance of the New England Aquarium and Faneuil Hall Marketplace. The Government Center Garage, 50 Sudbury St.; Dock Square at Faneuil Hall Marketplace; and Lafayette Place Garage on Chauncy Street offer additional parking near downtown attractions.

Taxis & Limousines

Although time delays due to congestion often increase the fare, taxis are a convenient means of getting around town. Cabs in Boston are metered; the fare is $2.25 for the first 1/8 mile or less and 60c for every 1/8 mile thereafter. Phoning for a pickup or going to a hotel taxi stand is easier than hailing a cab on the street. Local companies include the Independent Taxi Operators Association, (617) 426-8700. Limousine service is available throughout the Boston area for about $60 an hour, normally with a 3-hour minimum.

Public Transportation

MBTA operates the city's trolleys, buses, boats and subway—all of them efficient alternatives to driving. Known everywhere as the "T," Boston's rapid-transit system is the nation's oldest; the first stretch, running between Boylston and Park streets, began operating in 1897.

Four lines—the Red, Blue, Orange and Green—radiate from the four central downtown stations: Downtown Crossing, Park Street, State and Government Center. The Green Line uses trolleys that operate both above and below ground. It also splits into four branches designated by letters: Boston College (B), Cleveland Circle (C), Riverside (D) and Heath Street (E). "T" stations are designated by the letter T within a circle. Subway maps at each station show the lines in color. "Inbound" refers to trains heading toward downtown, "outbound" to trains heading away from downtown. An MBTA information booth is located on Park Street (on the Green Line outbound platform). In addition the Silver Line offers bus rapid-transit service from Dudley Square to downtown and from South Station to the South Boston waterfront; construction of a third phase, which will connect the two existing sections of Silver Line service, is due to begin in 2011 and is expected to be complete by December 2016.

In-city subway fares are $1.70 per ride for passengers who use plastic CharlieCards, the MBTA's reusable and rechargeable fare passes. However, passengers who use CharlieTickets, reusable and rechargeable *paper* fare passes, pay a surcharge, with in-city subway fares $2 per ride. Outbound surface transportation is free; inbound fares from outlying destinations on the Green and Red lines are as much as $2.50. A fare pass or exact change is required. Passes can be purchased from vending machines at the Airport station (Blue Line), Back Bay station (Orange Line), Prudential station (Green Line) and South Station (Red Line). Trains run between 5 a.m. and 12:30 a.m. in most areas; check the timetables posted at the Park Street station to avoid getting stranded.

LinkPasses providing unlimited travel for 1- or 7-day periods are $9 and $15, respectively; under 5 travel free. Passes can be purchased at the North, South and Back Bay train stations; at the Airport, Government Center, Hynes Convention Center and Alewife "T" stations; at the Boston Common Visitor Information Center; and at the BosTix ticket booth at Quincy Market. Free MBTA maps of the public transit system are available at hotels, tourist attractions, and at North and South stations.

Buses and trolleys also offer service crosstown and to the suburbs. Local fares are $1.50; express buses are $3.50 and up. Trolley fares are based on a zone system. A fare pass or exact change is required. For additional MBTA route, schedule and fare information phone (617) 222-5000, (617) 222-3200 for recorded information, (800) 392-6100, or TTY (617) 222-5146.

Commuter boat service operates Monday through Friday and holidays between Rowes Wharf on the downtown Boston waterfront and the Hingham Shipyard dock southeast of the city. One-way fare is $6. Boats depart Rowes Wharf Monday through Friday beginning at 6:50 a.m. for the 35-minute trip; the last boat departs at 8:30 p.m. (no weekend service).

Boats operated by Boston Harbor Cruises travel between Boston's Long Wharf and Pier 4 at the Charlestown Navy Yard. One-way fare is $1.70. Boats depart Long Wharf Mon.-Fri. every 15 minutes 6:30-9 a.m. and 3:30-6:30 p.m., every 30 minutes 9-3:30 and 6:30-8 p.m.; Sat.-Sun. every 30 minutes 10-6. For additional information phone (617) 227-4321 or (877) 733-9425. **Note:** These boat trips are not included in the Boston Visitor Pass package.

What To See

SAVE **5W!TS TOMB,** 186 Brookline Ave., is a 45-minute interactive experience in a re-created Egyptian tomb. Teams of explorers must find their way through a pharaoh's booby-trapped burial chamber by solving hands-on puzzles and overcoming various obstacles.

Time: Allow 45 minutes minimum. **Hours:** Departures require a minimum of two people per team. Open Sun.-Tues. 10-7, Wed.-Thurs. 10-10, Fri.-Sat. 10 a.m.-11 p.m., Memorial Day-Labor Day; Wed.-Thurs. 11-10, Fri.-Sat. 11-11, Sun. 11-7, rest of year. Phone ahead to confirm schedule. **Cost:** $20; $16 (ages 0-12). **Phone:** (617) 375-9487.

ARNOLD ARBORETUM is at 125 Arborway (SR 203) in Jamaica Plain (T: Forest Hills). The 265-acre park, designed by Frederick Law Olmsted in collaboration with Charles Sprague Sargent, contains more than 4,500 kinds of trees, shrubs and vines grouped by family. The Hunnewell Building Visitor Center tells the story about the development of the arboretum. **Tours:** Guided tours are available. **Hours:** Grounds daily dawn-dusk. Visitor center Mon.-Fri. 9-4, Sat. 10-4, Sun. noon-4. Closed major holidays. **Cost:** Donations. **Phone:** (617) 384-5209.

BOSTON ATHENAEUM is at 10 1/2 Beacon St. (T: Park Street). Founded in 1807, the cultural institution and library maintains an impressive collection of manuscripts, maps, archival materials and rare books. More than 600,000 book titles cover such topics as Boston, New England history, English and American literature, and fine and decorative arts.

The organization also holds a number of artworks—including pieces by such painters as Mather

Brown, Annibale Carracci, John Singleton Copley and John Singer Sargent—that are exhibited on a rotating basis. The architecturally stunning building, the athenaeum's fourth home, features a neo-Palladian facade.

Guided tours are available by appointment. **Time:** Allow 1 hour, 30 minutes minimum. **Hours:** Mon.-Fri. 9-5:30 (also Mon. and Wed. 5:30-8), Sat. 9-4, mid-Sept. to late May; Mon.-Fri. 9-5:30 (also Mon. and Wed. 5:30-8), rest of year. Closed major holidays. **Cost:** Donations. **Phone:** (617) 227-0270.

BOSTON CHILDREN'S MUSEUM is on the waterfront at 300 Congress St. (T: Courthouse or South Station). Designed for fun and educational experiences, the museum features hands-on exhibits emphasizing science, culture, the environment, health and fitness, and the arts. Highlights include a three-story climbing structure; a traditional Japanese house; Peep's World; an Arthur & Friends area; and KidStage, a 150-seat children's performance area.

Time: Allow 2 hours minimum. **Hours:** Daily 10-5 (also Fri. 5-9). Closed Thanksgiving and Dec.

25. **Cost:** $12; $9 (ages 1-15 and 65+); $1 (Fri. 5-9 p.m.); free (ages 0-1). **Phone:** (617) 426-6500.

BOSTON COMMON is bounded by Beacon, Charles, Boylston, Tremont and Park sts. (T: Arlington, Boylston Street or Park Street). Various recreational activities, concerts, protests and speeches take place at the public park, which is the oldest in the country. The area was set off in 1634 for common use as a "cow pasture and training field." The Puritans kept stocks and pens for the punishment of those who profaned the Sabbath, and the British gathered in the park before the Battle of Bunker Hill. 🏛

BOSTON HARBOR ISLANDS NATIONAL PARK AREA encompasses 34 islands in Boston Harbor; ferries depart from Long Wharf (T: Aquarium). Totaling 1,200 acres of land within 50 square miles, the national park area includes a state park consisting of 17 islands and offers recreational and educational opportunities as well as spectacular views of the Boston skyline. Such activities as hiking, kayaking, swimming and boating are available, as are ranger-led history tours and nature walks.

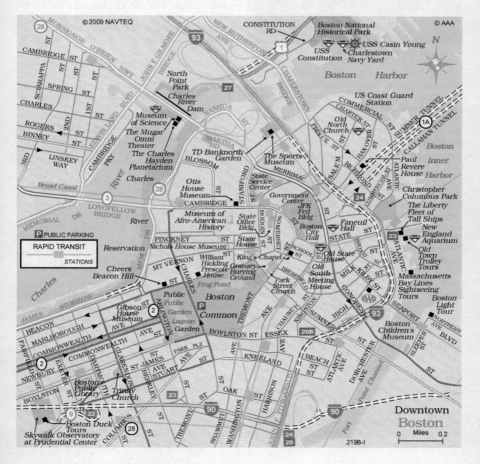

Downtown Boston
0   Miles   0.2

Boston Children's Museum / © Eunice Harris / age fotostock

Ferries traveling to the islands also depart from Hingham, Hull and Quincy; some areas of the park are accessible via automobile. **Hours:** Daily 9-dusk, early May-early Nov. Phone ahead to confirm schedule. **Cost:** Free. Ferry fares vary. **Phone:** (617) 223-8666, or (617) 222-6999 for Harbor Express transportation information. 🎫 ❌ ⬆

Boston Light Tour—*see attraction listing p. 113.*

Fort Warren is on Georges Island *(see Recreation Chart)* and can be reached via ferry from Long Wharf. Built 1834-67, the massive granite fort held Confederate prisoners during the Civil War and later served as a center for laying mines in Boston Harbor during the Spanish-American War and World Wars I and II. Rangers offer historic tours. Ferries to Georges Island also depart from Hingham, Hull and Quincy.

Pets are not permitted. **Hours:** Daily 9-dusk, early May-early Nov. Phone ahead to confirm schedule. **Cost:** Fort free. Ferry fares vary. **Phone:** (617) 223-8666 for information about the fort, or (617) 222-6999 for Harbor Express transportation information. 🍴 🎫

BOSTON PUBLIC LIBRARY is at 700 Boylston St. (T: Copley). Formed in 1848, this is believed to have been the nation's first public library and the first to allow individuals to borrow books and materials. Also functioning as an art and architectural museum, its permanent exhibits include such mural paintings as Edwin Austin Abbey's "The Quest of the Holy Grail" and John Singer Sargent's "Triumph of Religion" as well as the works of other American artists and sculptors.

Hours: Mon.-Sat. 9-5 (also Mon.-Thurs. 5-9), Sun. 1-5, Oct.-May; Mon.-Sat. 9-5 (also Mon.-Thurs. 5-9), rest of year. Closed major holidays. **Cost:** Free. **Phone:** (617) 536-5400. 🍴

BUNKER HILL MONUMENT is in Monument Square on Breed's Hill in Charlestown (T: Community College). Part of the Boston National Historical Park, the monument marks the site of the Battle of Bunker Hill, which took place June 17, 1775. The 221-foot-tall granite obelisk contains a spiral staircase to the top. Educational programs are offered. Leashed pets are permitted on the grounds but not inside the monument. **Hours:** Daily 9-4:30. Closed Jan. 1, Thanksgiving and Dec. 25. **Cost:** Free. **Phone:** (617) 242-5641 or (617) 242-5601.

Battle of Bunker Hill Museum is on the Freedom Trail across the street from Bunker Hill Monument, on Breed's Hill in Charlestown (T: Community College). Housed in the former Charlestown branch library building, the museum contains dioramas and exhibits about The Battle of Bunker Hill, the monument's construction and Charlestown's history. On display are a British drum and such weaponry as cannonballs and a British sword. A 360-degree cyclorama painting depicting the conflict adorns the upstairs.

Time: Allow 45 minutes minimum. **Hours:** Daily 9-6, mid-June through Labor Day; 9-5, rest of year. Closed Jan. 1, Thanksgiving and Dec. 25. **Cost:** Free. **Phone:** (617) 242-5641 or (617) 242-5601.

CHARLES RIVER RESERVATION extends along both sides of the Charles River from the dam at Boston to Newton Upper Falls near SRs 9 and 128 (T: Charles/MGH). Within the 961-acre reservation are bicycle paths, a swimming pool and two wading pools, tennis courts, a playing field and two fitness courses. DCR Hatch Memorial Shell offers free concerts and movies Wednesday through Sunday from mid-April to mid-October. Canoeing, kayaking and sculling are offered May through October. Sailing and windsurfing also can be enjoyed in season.

Hours: Grounds daily dawn-dusk. Hours for recreational facilities may vary; phone ahead. **Cost:** Grounds free. Fees for recreational facilities and equipment rental vary. **Phone:** (617) 626-1250 for information about recreational facilities or concerts, (617) 523-1038 for information about sailing and windsurfing equipment rental and instruction, or (617) 965-5110 for information about canoeing and kayaking equipment rental and instruction. 🎫 ❌

CHARLESTOWN NAVY YARD is off I-93 exit 28 in Charlestown, with a visitor center in Building 5 (T: Community College or North Station). Built in 1800 and today part of Boston National Historical Park, the yard served as a repair and supply depot for 174 years. Such innovations as ship houses and a ropewalk were among the yard's contributions. The visitor center features the exhibit Serving the Navy Fleet and a 10-minute orientation film.

The Navy's first ship of the line, the USS *Independence*, was built and launched here in 1814. Visitors may board the USS *Constitution* and the USS *Cassin Young*. **Tours:** Guided tours are available. **Time:** Allow 2 hours minimum. **Hours:** Visitor center daily 9-6, July 1-Labor Day; 9-5, rest of year. Closed Jan. 1, Thanksgiving and Dec. 25. **Cost:** Donations. **Phone:** (617) 242-5601.

USS *Cassin Young*, at Pier One, just n. of the USS *Constitution*, is named in honor of a navy commander. Restored at the Charlestown Navy Yard in the 1950s, the original destroyer was commissioned in 1943 and served during World War II and the Korean War. The ship is a memorial to the men who served on destroyers and to the vessels they served on. **Tours:** Guided tours are available. **Time:** Allow 30 minutes minimum. **Hours:** Daily 10-5, July 1-Labor Day (weather permitting), with reduced hours in winter; phone ahead for schedule. Closed Jan. 1, Thanksgiving and Dec. 25. **Cost:** Free. **Phone:** (617) 242-5601.

USS *Constitution*, at Pier One, was launched Oct. 21, 1797, at Edmund Hartt's shipyard, a short distance from its present berth, and was the nemesis of French privateers and Barbary Corsairs. It is purportedly the oldest commissioned warship afloat in the world. Engagements with the British in the War of 1812 brought the vessel undying fame and the nickname *Old Ironsides*.

The 44-gun frigate was constructed of seasoned live and white oak and yellow and white pine timbers secured by bolts and copper sheathing made by Paul Revere. Self-guiding tours allow visitors to view the gun deck, featuring 32 24-pound long guns, a galley stove, bilge pumps and the captain's quarters as well as the upper deck, which is known as the spar deck. Guided half-hour tours of the top three decks also are offered.

Note: All visitors are subject to a screening process for security purposes and should allow for an additional half-hour. **Hours:** Tues.-Sun. 10-6, Apr.-Oct.; Thurs.-Sun. 10-4, rest of year. Guided tours are given every 30 minutes 10:30-5:30, Apr.-Oct.; 10:30-3:30 rest of year. Last admission 10 minutes before closing. **Cost:** Free. **Phone:** (617) 242-5670.

USS *Constitution* Museum is at Pier One. Hands-on exhibits let visitors furl a sail, fire a cannon or swing in a hammock. Visitors experience more than 200 years of the ship's history through artifacts, computer simulated re-enactments and a presentation by a historical interpreter about life on board the ship. **Time:** Allow 1 hour minimum. **Hours:** Daily 9-6, Apr.-Oct.; 10-5, rest of year. Closed Jan. 1, Thanksgiving and Dec. 25. **Cost:** Donations. **Phone:** (617) 426-1812.

CHEERS BEACON HILL, 84 Beacon St. (T: Arlington, Charles/MGH or Park Street), is the Boston neighborhood bar that inspired the setting for the popular television show "Cheers." The front entrance of the bar was used for the opening scene on the series that first aired in September 1982 and ran for 11 seasons. This is the place where "everybody knows your name." **Hours:** Open daily at 11. Closing times vary; phone ahead. Closed Dec. 25. **Cost:** Free. **Phone:** (617) 227-9605. ⊓

THE CHRISTIAN SCIENCE PLAZA, 210 Massachusetts Ave. (T: Prudential or Symphony), is home to the world headquarters of the Church of Christ, Scientist. The plaza features architectural and historical standouts such as The Mother Church, as well as a reflecting pool and a fountain. **Time:** Allow 2 hours minimum. **Cost:** Free. **Phone:** (617) 450-2000, or (617) 450-3790 for 24-hour information.

The Mother Church, 210 Massachusetts Ave., houses the First Church of Christ, Scientist. It comprises the 1894 Romanesque Original Church Edifice with a bell tower and stained-glass windows and a large, domed extension completed in 1906 that combines Renaissance and Byzantine architectural concepts. The extension houses one of the world's biggest organs, which has 13,290 pipes.

Hours: Guided 30-minute tours are given Thurs.-Sat. noon-5, Tues. noon-4, Wed. 1-4, Sun. 11-3. Church services in English take place Sun. at 10 and 5. Church services in Spanish take place Sun. at noon. Closed major holidays. Phone ahead to confirm schedule. **Cost:** Free. **Phone:** (617) 450-2000, or (617) 450-3790 for 24-hour information.

DORCHESTER HEIGHTS, just s. of jct. E. Broadway and G St. at Thomas Park in South Boston, is part of the Boston National Historical Park. By fortifying these heights, George Washington drove the British from Boston on March 17, 1776. The Soldiers' Monument, a Georgian Revival tower made of white marble, commemorates the 1776 victory. **Hours:** Daily dawn-dusk. Closed Jan. 1, Thanksgiving and Dec. 25. **Cost:** Donations. **Phone:** (617) 242-5675.

FANEUIL HALL is at Faneuil Hall Square, Merchants Row (T: Government Center or State). The 1742 building was given to the city by Peter Faneuil. It burned in 1761, was rebuilt in 1763 and was enlarged in 1806. National Park Service rangers give historical talks daily.

The upper story served as a meeting hall, the scene of many stirring gatherings during the Revolutionary movement. British officers used the building as a theater during their occupation of the city. On the fourth floor, portraits of past commanders, along with uniforms, firearms, swords and other artifacts, are on display in the Museum of the Ancient and Honorable Artillery Company of Massachusetts; the hall has housed the company's headquarters since 1746.

The Faneuil Hall Marketplace *(see Shopping p. 125)* includes North and South Markets, Faneuil Hall and the adjacent Quincy Market, a renovated 19th-century complex containing more than 125 restaurants, boutiques, produce stands and retail pushcarts. Street performers entertain continuously.

Hours: Faneuil Hall historical talks are given daily every half-hour 9:30-4:30; closed major holidays and when hall meetings are in session. Museum open Mon.-Fri. 9-3. Marketplace open Mon.-Sat. 10-9, Sun. noon-6, with extended hours for food vendors and pubs. Closed Thanksgiving and Dec. 25. **Cost:** Free. **Phone:** (617) 242-5642 for historical information, or (617) 523-1300 for general marketplace information.

FENWAY PARK TOURS departs from the Red Sox Team Store across from the ballpark at 19 Yawkey Way. Visitors discover the history and secrets of the home park of the Boston Red Sox during a 1-hour

narrated tour. Knowledgeable guides discuss Fenway's design as well as the team's most memorable players and owners; highlighted are the red Ted Williams seat, the operation of the stadium's manual scoreboard and a right field foul pole nicknamed the "Pesky Pole."

On occasion, tour patrons are allowed to walk on the warning track, check out the view from the press box and see the State Street Pavilion Club. **Time:** Allow 1 hour minimum. **Hours:** Tours are given on the hour daily 9-4, Mar.-Sept.; 9-3, rest of year (weather permitting). Last tour begins at closing or 4 hours prior to game time, whichever is first. **Cost:** $12; $11 (ages 60+); $10 (ages 3-15 and military with ID). **Phone:** (617) 226-6666.

FRANKLIN PARK ZOO is at One Franklin Park Rd. This 72-acre site is nestled within Boston's historic Franklin Park. The zoo is home to a variety of animals, such as western lowland gorillas, tree kangaroos, Grevy's zebras, Masai giraffes, ring-tailed lemurs, Baird's tapirs and Amur leopards. Highlights of the park include Tropical Forest's indoor gorilla exhibit, Giraffe Savannah and Kalahari Kingdom.

Time: Allow 2 hours minimum. **Hours:** Mon.-Fri. 10-5, Sat.-Sun. 10-6, Apr.-Sept.; 10-4, rest of year (weather permitting). Closed Thanksgiving and Dec. 25. **Cost:** $14; $11 (ages 62+); $8 (ages 2-12). First Sat. of the month 10-noon $7; $5.50 (ages 62+); $4 (ages 2-12). **Phone:** (617) 541-5466. [🅵]

GIBSON HOUSE MUSEUM, 137 Beacon St. (T: Arlington), is an 1859 Boston brownstone with Victorian furnishings. **Hours:** Guided tours are given Wed.-Sun. at 1, 2 and 3. Closed major holidays. **Cost:** $9; $6 (ages 63+ and students with ID); $3 (children). **Phone:** (617) 267-6338.

GOVERNMENT CENTER is bounded by Cambridge, Court, Congress and Sudbury sts. (T: Government Center or State). Government Center is on the site of old Scollay Square, which was named after a prominent local real estate developer in the 1800s. Today the 60-acre urban renewal project encompasses shops; city, state and federal buildings, some of striking contemporary architecture; and a plaza where special events, including summer concerts and holiday festivities, are held. **Phone:** (617) 635-3911 for special events information.

GRANARY BURYING GROUND, at the head of Bromfield St. at jct. Tremont St. (T: Park Street), was established in 1660. Interred on the grounds are three signers of the Declaration of Independence—John Hancock, Samuel Adams and Robert Treat Paine—as well as Paul Revere, Peter Faneuil, Boston Massacre victims and Benjamin Franklin's parents. **Hours:** Daily 9-5. **Cost:** Free.

THE INSTITUTE OF CONTEMPORARY ART, BOSTON is on the waterfront at 100 Northern Ave. (T: Courthouse, South Station or World Trade Center). The institute was founded in 1936 as one of the country's first galleries dedicated solely to contemporary art. Housed in a steel-and-glass building overlooking Boston Harbor, it offers innovative national and international art exhibits, performing arts presentations, films, lectures and new media.

Tours: Guided tours are available. **Time:** Allow 2 hours minimum. **Hours:** Tues.-Sun. 10-5 (also Thurs.-Fri. 5-9). Closed Jan. 1, Thanksgiving and Dec. 25. Phone ahead to confirm schedule. **Cost:** $15; $10 (college students with ID and senior citizens); free (ages 0-17 and to all Thurs. 5-9 p.m.). **Phone:** (617) 478-3100. [fi]

ISABELLA STEWART GARDNER MUSEUM; 280 The Fenway (T: Museum of Fine Arts), exhibits works by such artists as Botticelli, Raphael, Rembrandt and Titian in a 15th-century Venetian-style palazzo surrounding an interior courtyard garden, which blooms year-round. Special exhibitions, concerts and lectures enrich the visit.

Guided tours and self-guiding audio tours are available. **Time:** Allow 1 hour minimum. **Hours:** Tues.-Sun. 11-5. Closed July 4, Thanksgiving and Dec. 25. **Cost:** $12; $10 (ages 65+); $5 (college students with ID); free (ages 0-17). Self-guiding audio tour $4. **Phone:** (617) 566-1401, (617) 278-5156 for the box office, or (617) 278-5147 for tour information. [fi]

JOHN F. KENNEDY PRESIDENTIAL LIBRARY AND MUSEUM is next to the campus of the University of Massachusetts; take [SAVE] I-93N exit 14 or I-93S exit 15 to Morrissey Blvd., following signs (T: JFK/UMASS). Through 25 multimedia exhibits and period settings at the nation's official memorial to President Kennedy, visitors learn about the life and legacy of the 35th president of the United States. The achievements of Jacqueline Kennedy also are described in The First Lady exhibit space.

The museum's collection includes photographs, historical documents, campaign memorabilia, replicas, Kennedy family belongings and other items. An introductory film as well as audio recordings featuring President Kennedy's voice also afford visitors an in-depth perspective of the Kennedy White House.

Designed by architect I.M. Pei, the museum's dramatic structure sits on a 10-acre waterfront site offering panoramic views of the city skyline and the Boston Harbor Islands. **Time:** Allow 2 hours minimum. **Hours:** Daily 9-5. Last film begins 1 hour, 10 minutes before closing. Closed Jan. 1, Thanksgiving and Dec. 25. **Cost:** $12; $10 (ages 62+ and college students with ID); $9 (ages 13-17). **Phone:** (617) 514-1600 or (866) 535-1960. *See color ad p. 107.*

KING'S CHAPEL, Tremont and School sts. (T: Government Center or Park Street), was established in 1686 by the Church of England; the building was completed in 1754. The interior is considered one of the finest examples of Georgian architecture in the United States.

Hours: Self-guiding tours are available Thurs.-Sat. and Mon. 10-4, Tues. and Wed. 10-11:15 and 1:30-4, Sun. 1:30-4, Memorial Day weekend-Labor Day; Sat. 10-4, Sun. 1:30-4, mid-Jan. through day before Memorial Day weekend and day after Labor Day to mid-Dec. Closed Sat.-Sun. following Thanksgiving. Church services take place Wed. at 12:15, Sun. at 11. Family services take place Sun. at 9:45, mid-Sept. to mid-May. Concerts are held Tues. at 12:15. Phone ahead to confirm schedule. **Cost:** Self-guiding tour $2; 50c (children). **Phone:** (617) 227-2155.

King's Chapel Burying Ground is at Tremont and School sts. Established in 1630, this is one of Boston's oldest burying grounds. It contains the graves of Gov. John Winthrop; the Rev. John Cotton; John Davenport, founder of New Haven, Conn.; and William Dawes, who rode with Paul Revere and Samuel Prescott to warn Colonial minutemen of the British advance. **Hours:** Daily 9-5, with reduced hours in winter. **Cost:** Free. **Phone:** (617) 635-4505.

LOUISBURG SQUARE, on Beacon Hill between Mount Vernon and Pinckney sts. (T: Charles/MGH), retains an English courtyard atmosphere.

THE MARY BAKER EDDY LIBRARY is at 200 Massachusetts Ave. (T: Prudential or Symphony). Highlighting the legacies of Mary Baker Eddy, founder of the Church of Christ, Scientist, and *The Christian Science Monitor*, the facility offers two floors of interactive exhibits. Its Mapparium, a three-story painted glass globe, features a sound and light presentation. Galleries celebrate great ideas throughout history, relate the Pulitzer Prize-winning

Isabella Stewart Gardner Museum / © Hemis.fr / SuperStock

journalism of the *Monitor* and explore humanity's search for life's deeper meaning.

Time: Allow 2 hours minimum. **Hours:** Tues.-Sun. 10-4. Hours may vary during special events; phone ahead. Closed Jan. 1, Thanksgiving and Dec.

Boston National Historical Park

Boston National Historical Park consists of seven sites along the Freedom Trail as well as Dorchester Heights' monument in South Boston. Only two of these sites, Bunker Hill Monument and the Charlestown Navy Yard, are owned by the federal government. The others—Faneuil Hall, Old North Church, Old South Meeting House, Old State House and Paul Revere House—are owned privately or managed municipally.

The park's Downtown Visitor Center at 15 State St., next to the Old State House, gives an overview of Boston's Colonial history through audiovisual presentations. Information about the park also is available from the information center at the Charlestown Navy Yard. Both visitor centers are open daily 9-5. Closed Jan. 1, Thanksgiving and Dec. 25.

Rangers conduct free walking tours, talks and programs throughout the park from mid-April through November 30; phone ahead for schedule. For more information phone (617) 242-5601, (617) 242-5642, or TTY (617) 242-5689.

25. **Cost:** $6; $4 (ages 6-17, ages 62+ and students with ID). **Phone:** (617) 450-7000 or (888) 222-3711.

MUSEUM OF AFRICAN AMERICAN HISTORY is at 46 Joy St. The African Meeting House was dedicated in 1806 and is said to be the oldest extant church built by free African-Americans in the United States. The adjacent Abiel Smith School is the nation's first building constructed for the sole purpose of educating African-American children. Permanent and changing exhibits are featured.

Maps detailing a self-guiding tour of the Black Heritage Trail, which links 14 historic sites, are available at the museum. Guided gallery and walking tours are available. **Hours:** Mon.-Sat. 10-4. Closed Jan. 1, Thanksgiving and Dec. 25. **Cost:** Donations. **Phone:** (617) 725-0022.

MUSEUM OF FINE ARTS, BOSTON, Avenue of the Arts, 465 Huntington Ave. (T: Museum of Fine Arts), houses Asiatic, African, Oceanic, European and American works, both ancient and contemporary. The museum first opened in Copley Square in 1876, later relocating to its present location in 1909.

Included in the museum's collection of nearly 450,000 works of art are paintings by Copley, Degas, Gauguin, Monet, Picasso, Rembrandt, Renoir, Sargent and Whistler. Prints, drawings, photographs, textiles and musical instruments also are displayed. The Art of the Ancient World collection features ceramics, coins, jewelry, mummies and sculpture from ancient Egypt, Greece and the Roman Empire. Objects range in date from about 6500 B.C. to A.D. 600.

Guided tours and self-guiding audiotape tours are available. Educational programs are offered. **Hours:** Daily 10-4:45 (also Wed.-Fri. 4:45-9:45). Closed Jan. 1, Patriot's Day, July 4, Thanksgiving and Dec. 25. **Cost:** (valid for 2 days within a 10-day period) $20; $18 (students with ID and senior citizens); $7.50 (ages 7-17 until 3 p.m. on school days, otherwise free). Wed. after 4 p.m. by donation. Audiotape tour $6; $4 (ages 7-17). Under 13 must be with an adult. **Phone:** (617) 267-9300. *See color ad p. 107.*

MUSEUM OF SCIENCE is at Science Park (T: Science Park). With lips agape and eyes wide, young schoolchildren huddle beneath a menacing, lifelike T. Rex as other pint-sized visitors marvel over prehistoric fossils. A few steps away, thunderous claps and dramatic sparks draw crowds into the Theater of Electricity, home to what is said to be the world's largest air-insulated Van de Graaff generator. Similarly entrancing are the winged creatures fluttering about an indoor butterfly garden, where wannabe entomologists can scrutinize such species as swallowtail, viceroy and milkweed.

Three levels of educational adventures await the inquisitive, with gallery themes running the gamut from paleontology to medicine to technology. Stocked full of computer activities, 3-D displays and scientific equipment, the museum encourages a hands-on approach to learning. Understand momentum and harmonic motion by playing in the Science in the Park exhibit space; discover varied ecosystems via sight, sound and touch in New England Habitats; or study each planet's size and composition while stargazing in Welcome to the Universe.

Hours: Daily 9-7 (also Fri. 7-9 p.m.), July 5-Labor Day; 9-5 (also Fri. 5-9), rest of year. Closed Thanksgiving and Dec. 25. **Cost:** $20; $18 (ages 60+); $17 (ages 3-11). **Phone:** (617) 723-2500. *See color ad p. 107.* 🛈

New England Aquarium / © SuperStock

The Charles Hayden Planetarium is at Science Park (T: Science Park). Multimedia shows and interactive astronomy exhibits are offered. Music and laser technology come together within a domed theater. **CLOSURE INFORMATION:** The planetarium closed in January 2010 to begin a yearlong renovation project; phone ahead for updates. **Phone:** (617) 723-2500.

The Mugar Omni Theater is at Science Park (T: Science Park). This IMAX theater shows large-format films on a five-story, domed screen that creates a wraparound effect. **Time:** Allow 1 hour minimum. **Hours:** Films are shown daily. Schedule varies; phone ahead. Closed Thanksgiving and Dec. 25. **Cost:** $9; $8 (ages 60+); $7 (ages 3-11). Reservations are recommended 24 hours in advance. **Phone:** (617) 723-2500.

MUSEUM OF THE NATIONAL CENTER OF AFRO-AMERICAN ARTISTS, off Seaver St. at 300 Walnut Ave., offers changing art exhibits in various media by African-American artists worldwide as well as a permanent display featuring a re-creation of a 25th Dynasty Nubian king's burial chamber. The museum is housed in a neo-Gothic mansion of Roxbury puddingstone and Nova Scotia sandstone. **Time:** Allow 30 minutes minimum. **Hours:** Tues.-Sun. 1-5. **Cost:** $4; $3 (children and senior citizens). **Phone:** (617) 442-8614.

🔺 **NEW ENGLAND AQUARIUM** is on the city's waterfront at Central Wharf off Atlantic Ave. (T: Aquarium). The aquarium is home to more than 40,000 animals representing more than 750 species of fish, invertebrates, mammals, birds, reptiles and amphibians. An outdoor seal exhibit features a raised tank for visitors to view the animals above and below the water's surface.

In the west wing a 5,000-square-foot gallery highlights changing exhibits. Rising from the center of the building is a four-story, circular glass tank containing a re-created Caribbean coral reef community, more than 200,000 gallons of water and hundreds of tropical fish and marine life, including sharks, turtles and moray eels. A colony of penguins

is on the ground level; an exhibit of Australian sea dragons is on the second level. Edge of the Sea lets visitors handle tide pool animals. A Simons IMAX theater also is on-site.

Time: Allow 2 hours minimum. **Hours:** Daily 9-6 (also Fri.-Sat. 6-7 p.m.), July 1-Labor Day; 9-5 (also Sat.-Sun. and holidays 5-6), rest of year. Holiday hours may vary; phone ahead. Closed Thanksgiving and Dec. 25. **Cost:** Aquarium $20.95; $18.95 (ages 60+ and college students with ID); $12.95 (ages 3-11). IMAX theater $9.95; $7.95 (ages 3-11, ages 60+ and college students with ID). Combination ticket $26.95; $24.95 (ages 60+ and college students with ID); $18.95 (ages 3-11). **Phone:** (617) 973-5200. *See color ad p. 107.* 🛈

New England Aquarium Whale Watch—*see attraction listing p. 114.*

NICHOLS HOUSE MUSEUM, 55 Mount Vernon St. (T: Park Street), is a Federal-style house in the heart of Beacon Hill that was the home of Rose Standish Nichols, a prominent Bostonian who was an author, a suffragist and a landscape designer.

The museum preserves the Nichols' 16th- through 19th-century furnishings and presents the typical domestic lifestyle of the Boston Brahmins, a class of New Englanders claiming to be descendents of the founders of the city. **Hours:** Tues.-Sat. 11-4, Apr.-Oct.; Thurs.-Sat. 11-4, rest of year. Closed major holidays. **Cost:** $7; free (ages 0-11). **Phone:** (617) 227-6993.

🔺 **OLD NORTH CHURCH** (Christ Church), 193 Salem St. at the foot of Hull St. (T: Haymarket), was built in 1723 and is the oldest surviving church building in Boston. The first peal of bells on this continent sounded from the church in 1744. On the evening of April 18, 1775, two lanterns were displayed in the steeple to signal that British soldiers were advancing on Lexington by sea and not by land. The steeple has been destroyed and replaced twice following violent storms; the present steeple dates from 1954.

The church has box pews, large windows and the pulpit from which President Ford initiated the celebration of the nation's Bicentennial. Guides regularly offer 7- to 10-minute presentations relating the church's history and its involvement in the American Revolution. Seasonal highlights include the Behind the Scenes Tour, which offers visitors access to normally restricted areas of the building.

Hours: Church open daily 9-6, June-Oct.; daily 9-5, Mar.-May; daily 10-5, Nov.-Dec.; Tues.-Sun. 10-4, rest of year. Behind the Scenes tours are given daily at 10 and on the hour 1-4, June-Oct. Church services take place Sun. at 9 and 11. Closed Thanksgiving and Dec. 25. **Cost:** Church and guided 7- to 10-minute tour by donation. Behind the Scenes tour $8; $6 (students and military with ID and senior citizens). **Phone:** (617) 523-6676.

SAVE **OLD SOUTH MEETING HOUSE,** 310 Washington St. (T: Downtown Crossing or State), was built in 1729 as a Puritan church. It was the site where colonists gathered to protest British rule preceding the Revolutionary War and where Samuel Adams gave the signal that started the Boston Tea Party. Behind the Scaffolding, If These Walls Could Speak and Voices of Protest relate the renovation process and history of the house through photographic exhibits and audio re-enactments.

Time: Allow 30 minutes minimum. **Hours:** Daily 9:30-5, Apr.-Oct.; 10-4, rest of year. Closed Jan. 1, Thanksgiving and Dec. 24-25. **Cost:** $5; $4 (ages 62+ and students with ID); $1 (ages 6-18). **Phone:** (617) 482-6439.

GEM **OLD STATE HOUSE** is at Washington St. at the head of State St. (T: State). The building is on the site of the old 1657 Town House. The present structure, built in 1713, is considered to be Boston's oldest public building.

Paul Revere House © C. Rennie / Robert Harding

Royal governors and provincial representatives presided at the town house before the Revolution. The Boston Massacre occurred at the east front in 1770, and the Declaration of Independence was read to Bostonians on July 18, 1776, from the balcony. In 1780 John Hancock was inaugurated at the state house as first governor of the commonwealth.

The Bostonian Society maintains the building as a museum of Boston history. Exhibition items include tea from the Boston Tea Party, a coat that belonged to John Hancock, a model of the USS *Constitution*, paintings, prints and other artifacts. **Hours:** Daily 9-6, July-Aug.; 9-5, Feb.-June and Sept.-Dec.; 9-4, rest of year. Closed Jan. 1, Thanksgiving and Dec. 25. **Cost:** $7; $6 (ages 62+ and students with ID); $3 (ages 6-18). **Phone:** (617) 720-1713.

OTIS HOUSE MUSEUM, 141 Cambridge St. (T: Bowdoin, Charles/MGH or Government Center), was designed by Charles Bulfinch for Harrison Gray Otis, lawyer, entrepreneur and Boston's third mayor. The 1796 house has been refurbished and decorated to reflect the style of the Federal period of the early 1800s. Additional rooms depict the use of the house as a boarding and medical establishment. It now is headquarters of Historic New England, formerly the Society for the Preservation of New England Antiquities.

Time: Allow 30 minutes minimum. **Hours:** Guided tours are given Wed.-Sun. every half-hour 11-5. Last tour begins 30 minutes before closing. **Cost:** $8; $7 (senior citizens); $4 (students with ID); free (Boston residents); $24 (family). **Phone:** (617) 227-3957, ext. 256, or (617) 227-3956.

PARK STREET CHURCH, Park and Tremont sts. (T: Park Street), was built in 1809 and was the scene of William Lloyd Garrison's first antislavery address in 1829. **Hours:** Tues.-Sat. 9-4, mid-July through Aug. 31; by appointment rest of year. **Cost:** Free. **Phone:** (617) 523-3383.

PAUL REVERE HOUSE, 19 North Square (T: Aquarium, Government Center or Haymarket), was built about 1680 and is the oldest house in downtown Boston. The restored home, which Paul Revere owned 1770-1800, contains 17th- and 18th-century furnishings and Revere memorabilia including silver. A Colonial herb garden and a Revere-made bell are on the grounds.

Guided tours of next-door Pierce/Hichborn House, an 18th-century brick edifice, also are available for a fee. **Hours:** Paul Revere House daily 9:30-5:15, Apr. 15-Oct. 31; daily 9:30-4:15, Apr. 1-14 and Nov.-Dec.; Tues.-Sun. 9:30-4:15, rest of year. Pierce/Hichborn House tour schedule varies; phone ahead. Closed Jan. 1, Thanksgiving and Dec. 25. **Cost:** Paul Revere House $3.50; $3 (ages 62+ and college students with ID); $1 (ages 5-17). A combination ticket with Pierce/Hichborn House is available. **Phone:** (617) 523-2338.

PRUDENTIAL CENTER, between Huntington Ave. and Boylston St. (T: Copley or Prudential), is Boston's first unified business, civic and residential development. The 52-story, 28-acre complex features shops, restaurants, plazas, covered walkways, a hotel and a 3,000-car parking garage.

Skywalk Observatory at Prudential Center, on the 50th floor, offers a panorama of the city and suburbs. The Dreams of Freedom Museum and Wings over Boston, an aerial video tour of the city, are included. **Hours:** Daily 10-10, Apr.-Nov.; 10-8, rest of year (weather permitting). Last elevator to observatory ascends 30 minutes before closing. Closed Dec. 25. **Cost:** $12; $8 (ages 0-11). **Phone:** (617) 859-0648. *See color ad p. 107.*

PUBLIC GARDEN, bounded by Boylston, Charles, Beacon and Arlington sts. (T: Arlington), is landscaped and accented with statuary. Established in 1837, this is believed to have been the first public botanical garden in the country. The swan boats have plied the waters here since 1877.

Time: Allow 30 minutes minimum. **Hours:** Garden daily dawn-dusk. Swan boats operate daily 10-5, late June-Labor Day; daily 10-4, mid-Apr. to late June; Mon.-Fri. noon-4, Sat.-Sun. 10-4, day after Labor Day to mid-Sept. (weather permitting). **Cost:** Garden free. Swan boat fare $2.75; $2 (senior citizens); $1.50 (ages 2-15). **Phone:** (617) 522-1966.

THE SPORTS MUSEUM is on the 5th and 6th floors of the TD Banknorth Garden on Causeway St. (T: North Station). Displays focus on New England sports from the high school level to such professional Boston teams as the Bruins, Celtics, Patriots and Red Sox. Included are artwork, interactive exhibits, memorabilia and multimedia displays. **Hours:** Daily 11-5 on non-game days, 11-3 on game days. Closed major holidays and during Garden events. Phone ahead to confirm schedule. **Cost:** $6; $4 (ages 6-17 and 60+). **Phone:** (617) 624-1234.

STATE HOUSE is on Beacon St. at the head of Park St. (T: Park Street). The original brick front section, designed by Charles Bulfinch and completed in 1798, remains almost unchanged. Statues sculpted by Daniel Chester French, Cyrus Dallin and Thomas Ball are displayed inside, along with historical paintings, stained-glass work and war relics.

Across the street Augustus Saint-Gaudens' Robert Gould Shaw and 54th Regiment Memorial recalls Col. Shaw and the first African-American regiment recruited in the North to serve in the Civil War. **Hours:** State House Mon.-Fri. 9-5. Guided 30- to 45-minute tours are given 10-3:30. Closed major holidays. **Cost:** Free. Reservations are required for guided tours. **Phone:** (617) 727-3676.

TRINITY CHURCH, in Copley Square at 206 Clarendon St. (T: Copley), was consecrated in 1877. Romanesque in style, the church is considered by many to be Henry Hobson Richardson's greatest architectural work. The interior artwork was created by John La Farge.

Hours: Church open Tues.-Sat. 9-6, Sun. 7-7. Self-guiding tours are available Mon.-Fri. 10-3:30,

Sat. 9-4, Sun. 1-5. Guided tours are given Sun. following 11:15 church service; otherwise varies. **Cost:** Church free. Self-guiding or guided tour $6; $4 (students with ID and senior citizens); free (ages 0-15 with adult). Guided tour on Sun. following 11:15 church service free. **Phone:** (617) 536-0944.

 **USS *CONSTITUTION*—**
see Charlestown Navy Yard p. 107.

USS *CONSTITUTION* MUSEUM—
see Charlestown Navy Yard p. 107.

WILLIAM HICKLING PRESCOTT HOUSE is at 55 Beacon St. Built in 1808 by architect Asher Benjamin, the Federal-style townhouse was home to historian William Hickling Prescott 1845-59. Exhibits include Prescott's restored study; an extensive costume collection from the 18th, 19th and 20th centuries; antique furniture; Chinese export porcelain; and English ceramics. **Time:** Allow 30 minutes minimum. **Hours:** Guided tours are given Wed.-Thurs. and Sat. noon-4, May-Oct. Last tour begins 30 minutes before closing. **Cost:** $5; free (ages 0-11). **Phone:** (617) 742-3190.

What To Do
Sightseeing
Boat Tours

Sightseeing cruises of Boston Harbor and Boston Harbor Islands National Park Area *(see attraction listing p. 105)* are offered at Long Wharf throughout the summer by Boston Harbor Cruises; phone (617) 227-4321 or (877) 733-9425. The Salem Ferry docks in Boston at Central Wharf by the New England Aquarium and offers 45-minute excursions to nearby Salem daily. Reservations to sail aboard the 92-foot catamaran are required; phone (978) 741-0220.

BAY STATE CRUISE CO. departs from the w. side of the World Trade Center at 200 Seaport Blvd. A round-trip traditional ferry excursion aboard the *Provincetown II* lasts 3 hours each way and features a 3-hour stop at the preserved 19th-century fishing village of Provincetown *(see Cape Cod p. 174).* The company also offers fast ferry service from Boston to Provincetown.

Hours: Traditional ferry excursions depart Sat. at 9:30 from Boston and at 3:30 from Provincetown, late June-early Sept. Fast ferry trips depart daily at 8:30, 1 and 5:30 from Boston and at 10:30, 3 and 7:30 from Provincetown, mid-May to mid-Oct. Phone ahead to confirm schedule. **Cost:** Round-trip traditional ferry excursion $44; free (ages 0-12). Round-trip fast ferry trip $79; $69 (ages 65+); $58 (ages 3-12). Round-trip bicycle fee for ferry $12. One-way prices also are available. Prices may vary. Reservations are recommended. **Phone:** (617) 748-1428 or (877) 783-3779.

BOSTON LIGHT TOUR departs from Fan Pier at 2 Northern Ave. in South Boston at the Moakley

The Liberty Fleet of Tall Ships / MOTT / Sarah Musumeci

United States Courthouse (T: Courthouse). On the 3.5-hour tour of Little Brewster Island, part of Boston Harbor Islands National Park Area *(see attraction listing p. 105)*, rangers relate the history of the area's lighthouses and maritime traditions. A stop at what is said to be the first lighthouse site in the country is included. Visitors can climb 76 spiraling steps to the top of Boston Light's tower.

Hours: Tours depart Thurs.-Sun. at 10 and 1:30, mid-June to mid-Oct. Phone ahead to confirm schedule. **Cost:** $38; $35 (ages 65+ and military with ID); $19 (ages 3-11). Tours are limited to 48 people. Reservations are recommended. **Parking:** $5-$12. **Phone:** (617) 223-8666.

THE LIBERTY FLEET OF TALL SHIPS sails from the New England Aquarium on the waterfront; a ticket office is at 67 Long Wharf and a ticket booth is in front of the New England Aquarium. Passengers aboard the 125-foot *Liberty Clipper* can hoist sail or simply enjoy the sights of Boston Harbor. Sunday brunch and Boston Tea Party re-enactment cruises also are available. **Time:** Allow 2 hours minimum. **Hours:** Sightseeing cruises depart daily at noon, 3 and 6, June-Sept. **Cost:** Sightseeing cruise $30; $15 (ages 2-12). Reservations are required. **Phone:** (617) 742-0333.

[SAVE] **MASSACHUSETTS BAY LINES WHALE WATCH** departs from 60 Rowes Wharf directly behind the Boston Harbor Hotel. Four-hour whale-watch cruises to Stellwagen Bank National Marine Sanctuary are offered, with marine biologists narrating. **Hours:** Tours depart Mon.-Fri. at 10:30, Sat.-Sun. at 9:30 and 2:30, late May-Labor Day;

Sat. at 10:30, day after Labor Day-last weekend in Sept. **Cost:** $34.95; $29.95 (children and senior citizens). Prices may vary; phone ahead. **Parking:** $12 in Seaport Boulevard lots. **Phone:** (617) 542-8000.

NEW ENGLAND AQUARIUM WHALE WATCH departs from the dock of the aquarium at Central Wharf off Atlantic Ave. (T: Aquarium). Passengers aboard the *Voyager III* enjoy a 3- to 4-hour tour to Stellwagen Bank, a busy whale feeding area. Sightings are guaranteed during the excursion. Passengers are invited to interact with naturalists and view the captain on the bridge.

Hours: Tours depart daily, early Apr.-Oct. 25. Departure times vary; phone ahead. **Cost:** $39.95; $31.95 (ages 0-11). Tour not recommended for children under 30 inches tall. Reservations are recommended. **Phone:** (617) 973-5281.

SPIRIT OF BOSTON, which departs from Commonwealth Pier on Seaport Blvd. at the World Trade Center, offers 2-hour narrated lunch cruises of Boston Harbor and includes live entertainment. Dinner entertainment cruises also are available. **Hours:** All cruises board half-hour prior to sailing. Lunch cruises depart most Wed.-Sun. at noon, May-Sept.; schedule varies rest of year. **Cost:** Lunch cruise $40-$48. Reservations are recommended. **Phone:** (866) 211-3807 for reservations.

Bus and Trolley Tours

Tours encompassing both the city and its environs are available. [SAVE] Gray Line of Boston/Cape Cod, (617) 720-6342 or (800) 343-1328, provides a variety of excursions featuring Boston, Cambridge, Cape Cod, Concord, Lexington, Plymouth and Salem.

BEANTOWN TROLLEY can be boarded at any one of 20 stops. A 2-hour narrated trolley tour shows passengers most of downtown Boston and parts of Cambridge. The trip also includes either admission to the Mapparium at The Mary Baker Eddy Library *(see attraction listing p. 109)* or, from May through October, a 45-minute harbor cruise with stops at the New England Aquarium and the USS *Constitution*.

Time: Allow 3 hours minimum. **Hours:** Daily 9:30-4:30, early Apr.-late Oct.; 9:30-3:30, rest of year. Closed Thanksgiving and Dec. 25. **Cost:** $32; $30 (ages 65+); $11 (ages 5-11). Two-day pass $42; $15 (ages 5-11). **Phone:** (617) 720-6342 or (800) 343-1328.

BOSTON DUCK TOURS departs from the Prudential Center on Huntington Ave. (T: Prudential) and the Museum of Science at Science Park (T: Science Park) as well as evenings from the New England Aquarium (T: Aquarium). Tickets can be purchased at Boston Duck Tours booths at Prudential Center and the Museum of Science as well as from the BosTix booth at Faneuil Hall. Narrated tours of Boston landmarks are inside renovated World War II amphibious landing vehicles, which splash into the Charles River for a waterside view of the city.

Time: Allow 2 hours minimum. **Hours:** Tours are given daily 9 a.m.-30 minutes before dusk, late Mar.-late Nov. **Cost:** $31; $27 (ages 62+ and students and military with ID); $21 (ages 3-11); $6 (ages 0-2). A limited number of tickets is available on a first-come, first-served basis; tickets are sometimes available up to 30 days in advance. **Phone:** (617) 267-3825 for general information.

BOSTON MOVIE TOURS departs from the Boston Common Visitor Information Center on Tremont St. (T: Park Street). The narrated Theater-on-Wheels Bus Tour, which lasts between 2 and 2.5 hours, takes visitors through downtown Boston. Several filming locations are featured during the trip, including sites seen in "The Departed," "Good Will Hunting," "Boston Legal" and "Cheers." The route also highlights many of the city's historic landmarks. A walking tour also is available.

Time: Allow 2 hours, 30 minutes minimum. **Hours:** Theater-on-Wheels Bus Tours are given Wed.-Mon. at 11, June-Aug.; Sat.-Sun. at 11, rest of year. Hours may vary. **Cost:** Theater-on-Wheels Bus Tour $37; $34 (students with ID and senior citizens); $28 (ages 6-12). Reservations are required. **Phone:** (866) 668-4345.

BOSTON TOURS—FROM SUBURBS AND BOSTON, which picks up passengers from suburban and Boston hotels, offers narrated tours of historic Boston, Cambridge and Charlestown. The 6.5-hour tours travel along the Freedom Trail and include Bunker Hill Monument, Victorian Back Bay and Harvard University.

Other visits on the 20-passenger air-conditioned buses include Old North Church, the USS *Constitution,* Faneuil Hall and Charlestown Navy Yard. **Hours:** Tours depart daily, early Apr.-late Nov. Departure times vary. **Cost:** $48; $14 (ages 10-16).

Reservations are required. **Phone:** (781) 899-1454 noon-9:30 p.m. for reservations. *See color ad.*

CITYVIEW TROLLEY TOURS OF HISTORIC BOSTON AND FREEDOM TRAIL can be boarded at any one of eight stops downtown, including Faneuil Hall, the Public Garden and the State House. The narrated trolley tour travels through downtown Boston, bringing visitors closer to distinctive cultural, historic and scenic sections of the city. Several sites along the Freedom Trail are accessible via the tour, including the Boston Common, the Old State House, Paul Revere House and the USS *Constitution.*

One nonstop trip lasts 1-hour, but visitors can hop on and off the trolley at any of the route's stops. The trolley fare also includes either admission to The Sports Museum *(see attraction listing p. 113)* at the TD Banknorth Garden or, from May through October, a 45-minute cruise of Boston Harbor. **Time:** Allow 1 hour minimum. **Hours:** Mon.-Fri. 9:30-5, Sat.-Sun. 9:30-5:30, May-Aug.; 9:30-4:30, Sept.-Nov.; 9:30-4, rest of year. Phone ahead to confirm schedule. **Cost:** $34; $32 (students with ID and senior citizens); $12 (ages 5-12). **Phone:** (617) 363-7899.

OLD TOWN TROLLEY TOURS departs from the Old Town Trolley stop #1 at 200 Atlantic Ave.; it also can be boarded at 16 other stops along the route. The 1-hour, 40-minute narrated tours feature more than 100 points of interest including the Freedom Trail, Faneuil Hall and Old North Church. Tickets include admission to the Old State House *(see attraction listing p. 112)* and all-day unlimited reboarding.

Hours: Tours depart daily 9-5, May-Oct.; 9-4, rest of year. Closed Patriot's Day, Thanksgiving and Dec. 25. Phone ahead to confirm schedule. **Cost:**

Old Town Trolley Tours / MOTT / Kindra Clineff

$36; $33 (ages 60+ and students and active military with ID); $13 (ages 3-12). Prices may vary. Children must be with an adult. **Phone:** (617) 269-7010.

Ghosts & Gravestones departs from the Old Town Trolley stop #1 at 200 Atlantic Ave. The sinister side of Boston comes alive during this 1.5-hour trolley and walking tour. Guides discuss the Salem Witch Trials as well as such serial killers as the Boston Strangler and Fall River's Angel of Death. Stops at two of the city's oldest burial sites—Copp's Hill Burying Ground and Granary Burying Ground—are included.

Hours: Tours depart daily on the hour 6-9, Memorial Day weekend-Oct. 31; Fri.-Sun. on the hour 6-9, mid-Apr. through day before Memorial Day weekend. **Cost:** $37; $24 (ages 3-12). Children must be with an adult. Under 3 are not permitted. Reservations are required. **Phone:** (617) 269-3626.

Industrial Tours

SAMUEL ADAMS BOSTON BREWERY TOUR is off I-93 exit 18; take Melnea Cass Blvd. .8 mi. n.w., SR 28 (Tremont St./Columbus Ave.) 1.7 mi. s., Boylston St. .1 mi. n.w., Brookside Ave. just w., then just s. to 30 Germania St. (T: Stony Brook). Guides relate the story of The Boston Beer Co. and offer visitors a firsthand look at the brewing process. Guests taste the malts and smell the hops used in beer production.

Named after Boston patriot *and* brewer Samuel Adams, the Samuel Adams brand of beer was introduced on Patriot's Day in 1985. At the end of the 1-hour tour, visitors are invited to sample a variety of the company's beers. **Note:** Photo ID is required for beer tastings. **Time:** Allow 1 hour minimum. **Hours:** Tours are given Mon.-Thurs. and Sat. 10-3, Fri. 10-5:30. Last tour begins at closing. Closed Jan. 1, Thanksgiving and Dec. 25. **Cost:** $2. **Phone:** (617) 368-5080.

Guided Walking Tours

From May through October, Boston By Foot offers various walking tours. Allow 1 hour, 30 minutes for each tour except the hour-long children's tour. Tours are given regardless of weather, and reservations are not required. Most tours are $12; $8 (ages 6-12). The Boston Underfoot tour is $14. Phone (617) 367-2345, or (617) 367-3766 for recorded information.

The Beacon Hill tour leaves from the foot of the State House steps, on Beacon Street, Mon.-Fri. at 5:30 p.m., Sat.-Sun. at 2. Tours of Victorian Back Bay depart from the Trinity Church steps, facing Copley Square, Mon. at 5:30 p.m., Fri. at 2, Sun. at 10. The Literary Landmarks tour departs from School and Washington streets Sat. at 10.

Tours starting at the statue of Samuel Adams in front of Faneuil Hall are The Heart of the Freedom Trail tour, given daily at 10 (also Sat.-Sun. at 2); The North End tour, given Fri.-Sun. at 1; Boston Underfoot, given Sun. at 1; and Boston By Little Feet, a children's tour, given Fri.-Sat. at 10, Sun. at 2. Special tours are scheduled once a month.

Conducted tours of the Black Heritage Trail, comprising 14 historic sites, begin at the Robert Gould Shaw and 54th Regiment Memorial on the corner of Park and Beacon streets. Offered by the National Park Service, the tours last 90 minutes and are given Mon.-Sat. at 10, noon and 2, Memorial Day-Labor Day; at 2 by appointment, rest of year. In the off-season tour reservations must be made at least 24 hours in advance. Phone (617) 725-0022 for general information or (617) 742-5415 for guided tour information and off-season tour reservations.

The 90-minute Movie Mile Walking Tour offered by Boston Movie Tours *(see attraction listing p. 115)* takes visitors to more than 30 locations used in film and television; phone (866) 668-4345 for reservations.

OLD BOSTON TOURS departs from 19 North Square and offers a variety of 2-hour guided walking tours through the North End neighborhood. Highlights of The Original Secret Tour include the Old North Church, Copp's Hill Burying Ground and hidden tunnels. Available evenings, The Old Boston Pub Crawl showcases the city's historical pubs and taverns. Also offered are The Sin and Redemption and the Power of Women tours.

Note: Photo ID is required for pub crawls. **Time:** Allow 2 hours minimum. **Hours:** Themed sightseeing tours depart Fri.-Sat. and Wed. at 10 and 3. The Old Boston Pub Crawl departs Fri.-Sat. and Wed. at 6 p.m. **Cost:** $30; $20 (ages 16-21); $15 (ages 8-15). Under 21 are not permitted on pub crawls. Reservations are required. **Phone:** (617) 720-2283.

Self-guiding Tours

A handheld digital audio tour of the Freedom Trail, which leads visitors to 16 historic sites *(see AAA Freedom Trail Walking Tour)*, is available at the Boston Common Visitor Information Center for $15; phone (617) 357-8300.

Walking tour maps of the 1.6-mile-long Black Heritage Trail can be obtained from the Museum of African American History, the Freedom Trail Information Booth and the National Park Service Visitor Center; phone (617) 725-0022 or (617) 742-5415.

Self-guiding tours available from The Boston Women's Heritage Trail relate more than 3 centuries of women's contributions to the city. Points of interest include the Boston Ballet Company, 19 Clarendon St., founded by E. Virginia Williams in 1963; a monument dedicated to African-American abolitionist Harriet Tubman; and "Emancipation," crafted by Harlem-Renaissance sculptor Meta Warrick Fuller. Both the monument and the sculpture are in Harriet Tubman Square at Columbus Avenue and W. Newton Street; phone (617) 522-2872.

AAA Walking Tours

The Freedom Trail

Brush up on your knowledge of history by following Boston's Freedom Trail. The national recreation trail passes many of the city's historic sites. Each stop represents a chapter in American history, with vivid reminders of events that led to American independence. Nowhere else in the city does the shout of "The British are coming! The British are coming!" resonate louder than along the Freedom Trail.

The trail, which begins at Boston Common and ends at Bunker Hill Monument in Charlestown, is simple to follow. Red bricks or granite stones embedded into the sidewalk form a line that guides you from place to place; in some places the red line is painted onto the sidewalk or street.

Here, we divide the trail into two sections, which can be explored in one outing or divided over 2 days. Plan to spend most of the day walking the Boston portion (especially if you tour the attractions)—from Boston Common to Copp's Hill in North End. The Charlestown section may take as long as a half-day if you decide to tour the USS *Constitution* and take in the many sights in the Charlestown Navy Yard.

Names of sites listed in detail in the What To See and Shopping sections are printed in bold type. Even if you choose not to tour a listed site, reading the listing when you reach that point will make the tour more interesting.

Begin the tour at the Visitor Information Center on **Boston Common** ❶ near Tremont Street. The 44-acre park, bounded by Beacon, Charles, Boylston, Tremont and Park streets, once belonged to Boston's first white settler, William Blackstone, who arrived in 1622. When the Puritans disembarked in 1630, they settled in Charlestown but later moved their hamlet across the river due to the presence of a natural spring that provided much-needed drinking water. Originally called *Shawmut*, or "Living Waters," by the American Indians, Puritans renamed the area Boston after a town in England of the same name. The grassy area became common land—"the common"—occupied by grazing cattle and eventually used as a training field for the military.

And now, onward! Follow the red stripe through this pentagon-shaped green oasis that has the reputation of being the country's first public park. Note the absence of bovines. Cows were banished in 1830 after Beacon Hill (north of the park) became a well-to-do neighborhood; affluent residents opposed having farm animals inhabit their front yards.

Continue toward the golden dome of the Massachusetts State House. Once at Beacon Street, you will approach the Robert Gould Shaw and 54th Regiment Memorial ❷. During the Civil War, numerous African-Americans wanted to join the fight, but U.S. Army policy prohibited them from doing so. The rule was modified, but an African-American regiment still required a white commanding officer. The monument, created by Augustus Saint-Gaudens, honors the first regiment of free African-American soldiers recruited in the North and the son of a prominent Boston family who led the troop.

The Massachusetts **State House** ❸ sits across Beacon Street opposite the memorial. Designed by Charles Bulfinch, a Boston native who studied architecture in England, the building's central (original) section features an arched brick portico supporting Corinthian columns. A cornice, balustrade, pediment, stunning golden dome and cupola finish the building, adding an imperial feel. The dome, originally covered in wooden shingles, was adorned with copper from Paul Revere's company in 1802

Boston Common / © Comstock Images / age fotostock

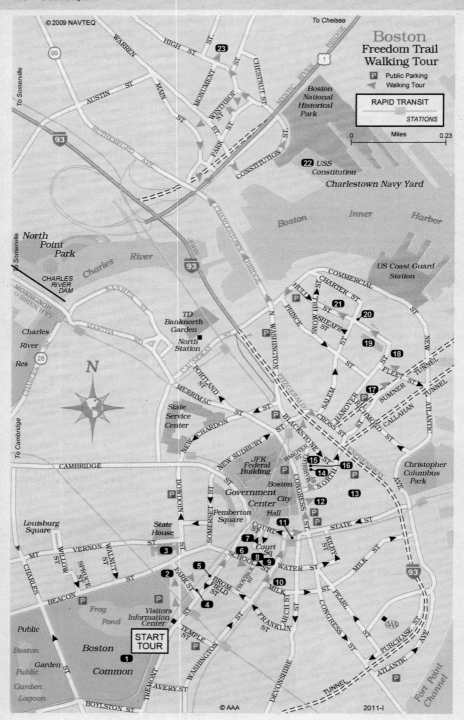

© 2009 NAVTEQ

Boston
Freedom Trail
Walking Tour

P Public Parking
◄ Walking Tour

RAPID TRANSIT
STATIONS

0   Miles   0.23

To Chelsea

Boston
National
Historical
Park

22 USS
Constitution
Charlestown Navy Yard

Boston   Inner   Harbor

US Coast Guard
Station

North
Point
Park

CHARLES
RIVER
DAM

Charles   River

Charles
River
Res

To Cambridge

TD
Banknorth
Garden

North
Station

State
Service
Center

JFK
Federal
Building

Government
Center

Boston
City
Hall

Pemberton
Square

State
House

Louisburg
Square

Frog
Pond

Visitors
Information
Center

**START
TOUR**

*Boston
Common*

Public

Boston

Public
Garden

Garden
Lagoon

Christopher
Columbus
Park

Fort Point
Channel

© AAA   2011-I

and was gilded following the Civil War. The State House holds prominence as a city landmark and is often referred to as the New State House to distinguish it from the Old State House on State Street.

The building sits on Beacon Hill (the tallest of Boston's three hills), land once owned by John Hancock, the colony's richest merchant. Beacon Hill earned its name from a primitive alarm signal that sat atop the hill. In the event the city was attacked, the "beacon" would be lighted as a signal for help. The area remains one of Boston's most well heeled neighborhoods. Elegant Federal-style row houses line Beacon Street and Park Street, once known as Bulfinch Row.

Follow the trail back along Park Street to Tremont Street. Overlooking the Common's northeast corner, also known as "Brimstone Corner," is the stately **Park Street Church 4**. The sobriquet was allegedly assigned as a result of fiery sermons dispensed by street preachers and soapbox orators; a more likely explanation is that brimstone (an ingredient in gunpowder) was stored in the church's crypt during the War of 1812.

The church was built in 1809 on the site of the town granary, which was removed after the State House was completed. Praised by Henry James as "the most interesting mass of brick and mortar in America," this graceful, white-steepled church also is rich in history. William Lloyd Garrison launched his passionate crusade against slavery from the pulpit in 1829, and Samuel Smith's hymn "America" was first sung publicly during the church's 1832 Fourth of July celebration.

Next door, on land that was once part of Boston Common, is the **Granary Burying Ground 5**, where the first body was interred in 1660. This tree-shaded sanctuary is the final resting place for Revolutionary War heroes, nine Massachusetts governors, soldiers and residents of early Boston, some honored with curious epitaphs. Samuel Adams, John Hancock and Robert Treat Paine—all signers of the Declaration of Independence—lie here, as do Paul Revere, Peter Faneuil, Ben Franklin's parents and the five victims of the Boston Massacre.

Extraordinary engravings on some of the headstones attract return visitors. Carvings of skeletons, urns, winged skulls and otherworldly cherubs add a bit of eerie aura to the grounds. Three types of grave markers exist: headstones, most of which have been moved so many times over the years that they no longer correspond to the actual graves; table tombs (appropriately shaped); and vaults, owned by families and usually containing several bodies.

As you wander around the cemetery, note the epitaph on the Franklin obelisk; it was written by their youngest son, Ben. Another interesting stone sits next to the tomb of John Hancock and marks the grave of "Frank, servant to John Hancock, Esqr." The fact that the stone lacks a last name has led some to believe that Frank was Hancock's slave.

Turn left when exiting the graveyard and continue north. Follow Tremont Street to School Street. **King's Chapel 6** is the gray building on the corner. In the late 1600s, King James II ordered that there be an Anglican church built in the colony. Puritans were irate and refused to sell land for its construction; the governor provided an easy remedy in 1687 by seizing a portion of the adjacent burial ground, the city's oldest. Construction of the present granite church began shortly thereafter. Church of England services were held here for British officers and the governor, and, on his visit in 1789, President Washington sat in the Governor's Pew. The

Granary Burying Ground / © Pietro Scozzari / age fotostock

simple exterior hides an elaborate interior. Take note of the columns on the portico—they are actually wood painted to resemble stone.

Sharing space with the church is the **King's Chapel Burying Ground 7**. The first burial is said to have taken place just months after the area was settled, in 1630. This being said, most of those interred are Puritans, who we surmise might not be pleased to have their eternal resting place next door to an Anglican church.

This burial ground is akin to a museum featuring the works of 17th- and 18th-century craftsmen. Gravestones here are notable for their artistry rather than for the names they feature. One such epitaph, arguably the most striking in Boston, marks the grave of Joseph Tapping; etched into the stone is an elaborate depiction of Father Time surrounded by Latin expressions of fatality.

Other headstones to note belong to Mary Chilton, the first Pilgrim to touch Plymouth Rock; William Dawes, who accompanied Paul Revere on his daring midnight ride; and John Winthrop, the first Massachusetts governor. William Paddy's stone is said to be the oldest existing grave marker in Boston. (By the way, the large cage on the front right side of the graveyard is not a tomb but a ventilator shaft for the subway.)

As you walk down School Street, look down (if you haven't been doing so already, following the red stripe) and note the hopscotch-patterned mosaic marking the site of the country's first public school. The Boston Latin School opened its doors in 1635 and was honored by the subsequent naming of this street, which was laid out in 1640. Cotton Mather, Samuel Adams and Benjamin Franklin were educated there. A few steps farther is Old City Hall **8**, constructed in 1864 in the French Empire style. Gracing the courtyard is sculptor Richard Greenough's bronze statue of Benjamin Franklin, the first commemorative statue erected in the city. Bronze tablets depict his many achievements: printer, scientist, inventor, military officer, politician, statesman and signer of the Declaration of Independence. Across the courtyard is a statue of Josiah Quincy, Boston's second mayor.

At the corner of School and Washington streets is the site of the Old Corner Bookstore **9**. The small brick house is a former residence and apothecary shop on land previously owned by William Hutchinson, whose wife, Anne, was banished from Boston in the 1630s by Puritans incensed at her divergent religious teachings. It later served as the headquarters of the estimable publishing firm Ticknor and Fields, becoming Boston's mid-19th century literary center in the process. Ralph Waldo Emerson, Nathaniel Hawthorne, Henry Wadsworth Longfellow and Harriet Beecher Stowe all gathered here; both "The Scarlet Letter" and the words to the "Battle Hymn of the Republic" were printed by this publishing house. When the bookstore moved to larger quarters, the house began a slow decline that lasted until the early 1960s, when it was restored. A jewelry retailer currently occupies the space.

Diagonally across the street at 310 Washington St. is the **Old South Meeting House 10**. Built in 1729, this Georgian-style congregational church was the largest building in Colonial Boston and thus was frequently used as a town meeting site when crowds were too big for Faneuil Hall. Its principal associations are with the heated gatherings of political protestors in the years prior to the Revolution. Enraged citizens met here following the Boston Massacre and also on Dec. 16, 1773, when Bostonians met to consider the new British tax on tea; the Boston Tea Party immediately followed. The church was abused by British troops who occupied the town during the siege on Boston—livestock roamed the church, and its pews and pulpit were used for firewood and building stables. After 1776 the pulpit was recreated and the pews were rebuilt. The Old South Meeting House remained a church until the 1870s and now contains historical exhibits.

Follow the trail north on Washington Street to the **Old State House 11** at the head of State Street. Now surrounded by skyscrapers, the building once was the town's grandest edifice. Located in close proximity to markets and wharves, the building's lower floor originally functioned as a busy merchant's exchange. The Old State House gained its real measure of importance as the setting for stirring speeches and debates between royal officials and American patriots. The center of Colonial government, it was the meeting place of the Massachusetts Assembly, the Court of Suffolk County (later to become the Massachusetts Supreme Judicial Court) and the Boston town government.

Representatives of the Massachusetts Assembly originally met in the second floor rotunda. A visitor's gallery was installed in 1766 in Representatives Hall—the colonists took the opportunity to jeer at those who voted for the royalists.

The trail resumes on the north side of the Old State House. On the building's east gable beneath the clock is a balcony from which royalists made their official decrees to the colonists. On July 18, 1776, however, the tables were turned when the Declaration of Independence was first read publicly in Boston from the same balcony. The Boston Massacre occurred below the balcony in 1770. What began as a dispute over a barber bill led to a riot and left five dead. Patriots used the incident as propaganda to stir up anti-royalist feelings. A circle of stones marks the site. Looking up, you'll note the gilded lion and unicorn—symbols of Great Britain—atop the building. These are replicas, installed in 1882; the originals were torn down and burned in 1776.

The Old State House was eventually outgrown, and government business relocated to the newer Bulfinch-designed Massachusetts State House on Beacon Hill. After being rented to various merchants until the 1830s, the Old State House briefly became Boston's City Hall. When the building was threatened with demolition in 1880, the city of Chicago attempted to purchase it for use as a tourist attraction. A group of citizens were insulted; forming the Bostonian Society in 1881, they determined to preserve the Old State House.

A statue of Samuel Adams, the "organizer of the Revolution," stands in front of the next stop, **Faneuil Hall 12**. Prosperous merchant Peter Faneuil (pronounced "fannel") donated the original building to the city in 1742, when it dominated the Boston waterfront.

Like the Old South Meeting House, it was the scene of tumultuous gatherings held to protest England's tightening control over the colonies. Here, patriots protested the Sugar Act and set forth the principle of "no taxation without representation." It also was the site of the first of the "Tea Meetings" on Nov. 5, 1773. After being fired up by oratory, angry crowds frequently emerged from the "Cradle of Liberty" and engaged in reckless action; the governor's mansion was virtually destroyed by one mob after the 1765 passage of the Stamp Act.

Atop the hall, the gilt grasshopper weather vane is a Boston landmark. In place since 1742, it was a symbol used to screen out spies, for every *true* Bostonian could surely identify the figure crowning Faneuil Hall. The sturdy weather vane has survived an earthquake, a fire and a grasshopper-napping in 1974 (it was thankfully found unharmed). Green glass doorknobs serve as the insect's eyes; inside the stomach are coins and other mementos.

Opposite Faneuil Hall between Clinton and Chatham streets is Faneuil Hall Market, more commonly called **Quincy Market** ⑬. Constructed in 1825, the huge building features a domed central pavilion and Greek porticoes. For nearly 150 years this area served as a retail and wholesale distribution center for meat and produce. Renovated in the 1970s, Quincy Market today consists of three long buildings separated by tree-lined malls. Food stalls, shops, restaurants, a flower market, pushcart vendors, and a gaggle of street entertainers and musicians all add up to a shopping and eating extravaganza. A cigar-smoking likeness of former Boston Celtics coach Red Auerbach rests on one of the South Market benches.

From the marketplace, follow the trail along Union Street. Between Union and Congress streets is a small island known as Carmen Park, the home of The New England Holocaust Memorial, an ethereal monument comprising six etched glass towers dedicated to the Jews who lost their lives in Nazi death camps.

To the right of Union Street is the city's old business district, known as the Blackstone Block, where pigs and chickens as well as people walked the tiny, winding dirt alleys in the 17th and 18th centuries. This part of Boston grew up along the narrow "neck" that once separated the Shawmut Peninsula from the North End. Street names echo previous landscapes and residents: Marsh Lane, Creek Square, Salt Lane and Scott Alley.

Items easily pictured on a sign were often chosen for tavern names (for example, Bell-in-Hand or Boston Stone). Some names have been reincarnated and can be seen marking the entrances of newer establishments—one such watering hole is The Green Dragon Tavern, which takes its name from one of Boston's most famous pubs where secret meetings took place during the Revolution. The Union Oyster House ⑭, built around 1713, is one of the oldest restaurants in the country; it is rumored that Daniel Webster was a regular patron.

Bearing right onto Marshall Street, just past The Green Dragon Tavern, you'll see the Ebenezer Hancock House ⑮, a three-story brick house situated at an angle to the street. Built around 1760, it was occupied by John Hancock's brother, the deputy-paymaster-general of the Continental Army.

Continue to Blackstone Street. On Fridays and Saturdays The Haymarket ⑯ takes place along Blackstone between North and Hanover streets. Vendors no longer sell hay, but the open-air gathering continues—the Boston institution is a swirl of sights, sounds and smells. Savvy shoppers and no-nonsense North End vendors banter over displays of fruits and vegetables. Meat and cheese shops line the street. Saturday is busier, and by the end of the day the area is usually strewn with garbage and leftover produce. First-timers should heed these two pieces of advice: Do not touch the displays, and watch for a "heavy thumb" on the scale.

After passing over Blackstone Street, walk through a portion of the Rose Fitzgerald Kennedy Greenway—several acres of linear urban green space traversing the path of the old elevated Central Artery—toward Cross Street. You're now entering North End, Boston's Italian district. The heart of Boston's first neighborhood, Hanover Street is lined with Italian groceries and little cafés.

Following the Revolution, the North End succumbed to poverty and vice; visiting sailors populated brothels and gambling dens. Richmond Street was known as the "murder district," and North Street was called Ann Street after not-so-ladylike ladies. After 1851, North Street was widened, its name changed, and the brothels were demolished. The district now attracts tourists and is a respectable community.

At the corner of North and Richmond streets, look to the right to see the cupola atop Faneuil Hall. Then proceed on North Street to the **Paul Revere House** ⑰, the two-story clapboard structure on the left overlooking North Square. Revere was a silversmith by trade but also dabbled in engraving, copper plating and working as express rider delivering messages for the patriots. His most famous jaunt took place April 18, 1775; thanks to poet Henry Wadsworth Longfellow, nearly every school-aged child is familiar with his midnight ride.

Built in 1680, the house is a rare example of early Colonial urban architecture and is said to be Boston's oldest building. Puritan ministers Increase Mather and his son Cotton also lived on this site. Behind the house are pretty gardens planted with medicinal herbs and flowers used during Colonial days. Next to the Paul Revere House is the Pierce/Hichborn House. Built about 1711, it is one of the city's earliest surviving brick structures and is an excellent example of early Georgian architecture.

Also on North Square is the brick Mariners' House, which served as a refuge for sailors. Note the anchor on front; it still offers accommodations to seamen. Across the square is the church where Father Edward Taylor once preached to Boston's seamen; it now is an Italian Catholic church.

Following the trail, the next point of interest is St. Stephen's Church ⑱, which is situated at the curve of Hanover Street. This red brick church with a white cupola and golden dome was originally called the "New North Church" to distinguish from the Old North Church (see below). Built in 1804, it is the only Bulfinch-designed church still standing in Boston. Revere's firm, Revere Copper and Brass, cast the bell that was hung in the belfry in 1805; a display inside shows pieces of the Revere copper that originally covered the dome.

Across Hanover Street from St. Stephen's Church are the brick walls of Paul Revere Mall (also called the Prado) ⑲, which lies between Hanover and Unity streets. Laid out in the early 1930s, this restful, tree-shaded enclave features bronze plaques saluting the achievements of various North Enders. Near the Hanover Street boundary is Cyrus Dallin's dashing equestrian statue of Revere.

A gate at the opposite side of the mall leads to a courtyard behind the **Old North Church ⊘**. Ascend the stairs to the church—perhaps Boston's most "revered" landmark. Built in 1723 and officially called Christ Church, it's the oldest church building in Boston (hence the nickname). The Old North Church played a key role in Paul Revere's celebrated midnight ride, the subject of Henry Wadsworth Longfellow's much-recited lyrical poem. The poet described how church sexton Robert Newman hung lanterns in the belfry arch of the Old North Church—"one if by land, two if by sea"—as a signal from Revere that the British were about to march. The lanterns flickered for a short moment, then Newman fled the church (supposedly by climbing out a window), while Revere mounted his horse "And so through the night went his cry of alarm, To every Middlesex village and farm."

The church's exterior, inspired by the London churches designed by British architect Christopher Wren, was constructed using locally-made bricks. Inside, numerous historical treasures can be seen, including brass nameplates that designate family pews—the Reveres occupied No. 54. Along the church's right aisle is the window through which Newman fled the church; bricked over in 1815, it was rediscovered in 1989 during restoration work. Newman also is remembered with a plaque in the small garden on the church's north side. Looking up, you'll see the 191-foot-tall steeple, which was blown over twice by hurricanes but was rebuilt according to original plans; the eight belfry bells were cast in 1744 and range in weight from 620 to 1,545 pounds each. They bear the inscription: "We are the first ring of bells cast for the British Empire in North America."

Heading uphill on Hull Street, turn around to catch a great view of the Old North Church. Copp's Hill Burying Ground ⊘ (sometimes called "Corpse Hill") is on the right, on a promontory overlooking Boston Harbor. Atop North End's highest point, the graveyard is named for a shoemaker who originally owned the land; it was established as a cemetery in 1660 when the King's Chapel Burying Ground became overcrowded.

Copp's Hill holds the graves of Old North Church sexton Robert Newman; Increase Mather, his son Cotton and Cotton's son Samuel, all three Puritan clergymen and educators; and Prince Hall, who led Boston's early free African-American community. During the Revolution, British soldiers camped here. Notice the headstone for Capt. Daniel Malcolm; it is said that damage to this grave marker was incurred when redcoat troops used it for target practice.

There is a pleasant view of the harbor and of Charlestown Navy Yard from this location—look for the distinctive rigging of the USS *Constitution*.

Continue past the cemetery to Commercial Street. At this point, the Freedom Trail travels across the Charlestown Bridge and visits the USS *Constitution* and the Bunker Hill Monument. We recommend stopping here and embarking on the Charlestown portion another day. From this point, it's best to take

the "T" back to Boston Common (Park Street stop) or Faneuil Hall (State Street stop). The closest station is North Station just a few hundred yards away on Causeway Street; to get there from the corner of Commercial and Hull streets, continue south on Commercial Street, which turns into Causeway Street. *See Public Transportation p. 104.*

Begin the Charlestown portion of the tour by crossing the Charlestown Bridge, following the red stripe.

At the foot of the bridge in Charlestown is City Square, the Puritans' point of settlement in 1629. They named the area after King Charles, who issued the colony's charter. Due to the lack of fresh water, most of the original settlers moved to what is now Boston Common, and until the Revolution, Charlestown remained mostly unpopulated grassland.

Once across the bridge, the trail comes to a fork (it circles Charlestown). Since the last guided tour of the USS *Constitution* begins at 3:30 (at 5:30, April through October), we recommend visiting the ship first. To do so, turn right at the first traffic light onto Chelsea Street. Proceed for one block, then turn right onto Warren Street. At the end of Warren, turn left onto Constitution Road, following the path to the **USS *Constitution* ⊘**.

Built at Edmund Hartt's shipyard in the North End—a short distance from its present berth at Pier One—the ship was launched in 1797. Constructed from live oak, red cedar, white oak, pitch pine and locust wood, the 54-gun warship was designed to defeat equal opponents and out-sail stronger ones. Paul Revere provided the original copper sheathing.

The *Constitution* gained undying fame and the nickname "Old Ironsides" (a reaction to the resiliency of the ship's wooden sides) as a result of engagements with the British during the War of 1812. After exploring the Charlestown Navy Yard, continue along the trail to the **Bunker Hill Monument ⊘**. You'll pass charming 19th-century Victorian homes and a delightful park called Winthrop Square, once a military training field. Facing the square on Adams Street are decorative Greek Revival and Italianate townhouses.

The Battle of Bunker Hill, of course, is misnamed; the battle actually took place on neighboring Breed's Hill. Critical to the British occupation of Boston was control of the hills on the Charlestown peninsula; patriots under Col. William Prescott fortified the peninsula by hastily constructing fence-rail shelters and taking up sniper positions at Breed's Hill, which was smaller and closer to the city.

The British advanced. In order to save ammunition and keep a steady barrage capable of breaking the enemy's charge, the American strategy was to withhold fire and use their weapons carefully—a tactic that gave rise to the legendary order not to shoot until they saw "the whites of their eyes." After the command, the patriots fired with first-rate accuracy.

Prescott and his men finally retreated north toward Cambridge, while British forces entrenched themselves as far as Bunker Hill. They had captured the hill and won the battle, but at great cost: Nearly half of the 2,200 redcoats who fought were either killed or wounded. Of an estimated 2,500 to 4,000 colonists engaged, 400 to 600 were casualties. Although a technical victory for the British, the battle provided an important psychological boost to American patriots: They proved they could face the British in traditional field combat.

In 1823 the Bunker Hill Monument Association was formed to purchase the battleground and erect a permanent monument. Solomon Willard's 221-foot-tall obelisk was dedicated June 17, 1843, with a speech by Daniel Webster. A statue of Colonel Prescott stands in front of the granite tower. Inside, a flight of 294 steps leads to the top—the climb is taxing, but the views are impressive.

The monument is the last stop on the tour. To return to downtown Boston, follow the red-striped trail back through Charlestown, cross the bridge and take the "T," following the above directions. A more scenic option is to retrace your steps to the Navy Yard and catch the water shuttle operated by MBTA. The boat, which departs from Pier 4 at the Navy Yard, will take you to Long Wharf on the downtown waterfront, which is a few blocks west of Faneuil Hall. Ferries depart the Navy Yard Mon.-Fri. every 15 minutes 6:45 a.m.-8:15 p.m., Sat.-Sun. every 30 minutes 10:15-6:15. One-way fare is $1.70; 85c (ages 5-11 and senior citizens). Phone (617) 227-4321 for more information.

Spectator Sports

The religious zeal with which Boston was founded has been transformed into a modern-day fanaticism for sports. In few other cities do even the most rarefied academics follow their hometown teams with such enthusiasm. When one considers the city's bragging rights to a number of athletic firsts and bests, its sports obsession seems quite justifiable.

Baseball

The first baseball glove was donned on a Boston field in 1875. A year later, a Harvard student caused a stir by wearing a catcher's mask, another first. The beloved **Boston Red Sox** won the first World Series in 1903 and captured their sixth championship in 2004 after an 86-year drought. Fenway franks, the Green Monster and "The Rocket" are all part of the enduring lore that surrounds the legendary team, which plays April to late September at **Fenway Park** (T: Kenmore). Fenway, one of the game's oldest and most historic stadiums, has been home to the Red Sox since 1912. The park's seats are usually filled for regular season games. Tickets should be purchased well in advance; phone (617) 482-4769 or (877) 733-7699.

Basketball

The **Boston Celtics**, one of the most successful franchises in professional sports history, were National Basketball Association champions for 7 years running between 1959 and 1965—the longest consecutive winning streak of any NBA team. In 2008 the Celtics won their 17th NBA championship after a 22-year-long drought. Hallowed Boston Garden was the Celtics' home until 1995, when the aging facility was replaced by the gleaming **TD Banknorth Garden** on Causeway Street (T: North Station). While faithful fans may forever mourn the Garden's passing, most appreciate the new arena's larger size and more comfortable amenities. Home games are played October through April; phone (866) 423-5849 for tickets.

Followers of college basketball root for the Big East Conference **Boston College Eagles**, **Boston University Terriers** and **Northeastern University Huskies** of the America East Conference, and the Ivy League's **Harvard University Crimson**.

Football

The Oneida Football Club, purportedly the nation's first organized football team, played on the Boston Common between 1862-65. The NFL's **New England Patriots** are one of only two teams to win three Super Bowls in a 4-year span, becoming the seventh franchise to win back-to-back Super Bowls. Zealous spectators watch home games at **Gillette Stadium** in Foxboro, about 45 minutes south of downtown Boston via I-95; phone (800) 543-1776.

Supporters of college football turn out for the **Boston College Eagles**, who play at **Alumni Stadium**, and the **Harvard University Crimson**, who play Ivy League ball at **Harvard Stadium**.

Hockey

The **Boston Bruins** were the first American team to receive a National Hockey League franchise. Historically one of the NHL's most successful teams, the brawling "B's" are five-time Stanley Cup champions. The Bruins face off at the TD Banknorth Garden from October through April. Those interested in seeing the Bruins in action should purchase tickets well in advance; phone (617) 624-2327.

Horse Racing

Thoroughbreds run at **Suffolk Downs Racetrack** in East Boston. Flat races are held from September through June; harness races are simulcast January 1 to mid-December, with some interruptions. Phone (617) 567-3900 for a schedule.

Note: Policies concerning admittance of children to pari-mutuel betting facilities vary. Phone for information.

Recreation

The **Charles River** plays a central role in Boston's sporting life. Miles of jogging and bicycling trails follow the river's course through town. Anglers preserve the centuries-old tradition of fishing on the banks of the Charles. And one of the city's loveliest vistas is the early morning sight of a lone scull gliding on the water.

Bicycling

As a Boston pastime, bicycling hails back to the time ladies gathered their bustles to ride sidesaddle

Charles River / © Amanda Hall / Robert Harding

around Boston Common. Although the city has never been overly conducive to two-wheeled travel, it does have several safe and extremely popular bicycle paths. Visitors can explore them after a stop at **Community Bicycle Supply**, 496 Tremont St., which has mountain bikes and other hybrid bicycles for rent spring through fall (weather permitting); phone (617) 542-8623.

The **Greenbelt Bikeway** originates at the Boston Common and follows the **Emerald Necklace**, a 6-mile chain of parks that includes the Commonwealth Avenue Mall, the Back Bay Fens, and the Riverway, Arborway and Jamaicaway before ending at Franklin Park.

The **Dr. Paul Dudley White Bikeway** is named for President Dwight D. Eisenhower's personal physician, a devoted cyclist and, appropriately enough, a heart surgeon. The approximately 14-mile round-trip follows the north side of the Charles River beginning at the Museum of Science, passing through Cambridge and Newton. At Watertown Square the path crosses the river and heads back toward Boston along its south bank. Several footbridges, particularly the one at the busy intersection of Arlington and Beacon streets (near the Public Garden) minimize interaction with vehicle traffic.

The **Minuteman Bikeway** is an 11-mile path running along an old railroad bed; it begins at the Alewife "T" station (the northern terminus of the Red Line) and passes through the towns of Arlington, Lexington and Bedford.

For information about other area bicycle paths, contact the Division of Urban Parks and Recreation, which operates public recreation facilities throughout the city; phone (617) 626-1250. **Note:** Bicycles are allowed on subway trains only during non-peak hours, and are not permitted on the Green Line at any time.

Fishing

Fishing sustained the Massachusetts Bay Colony in the 17th century, and a maritime foundation supported the Boston economy until well into the 1800s. Today's casual angler can take advantage of several freshwater locations in and around the city. The Charles River, although muddy, is home to catfish, sunfish and crappie. The fishing gets better farther upstream, particularly in the vicinity of Watertown. **Jamaica Pond**, on the Jamaicaway in Jamaica Plain, is stocked with trout and bass. Although numerous joggers trod around the pond, there are enough woodsy spots at the water's edge to make it a peaceful getaway.

Nonresidents must purchase a fishing license. A special 3-day license can be obtained from the Massachusetts Division of Fisheries and Wildlife, 251 Causeway St., Suite 400, Boston, MA 02114-2152; phone (617) 626-1590. Licenses may also be obtained at local town halls, sporting goods stores and retail outlets.

In Gloucester **Charlie's Charters**, 415 Main St., offers daily morning and afternoon fishing charters mid-May to mid-October; phone (978) 281-8992. **Yankee Fishing Fleet**, 75 Essex Ave. in Gloucester, runs chartered deep-sea fishing trips year-round; phone (800) 942-5464. Other charter services are located along Essex Avenue. The pier at man-made **Castle Island**, off William J. Day Boulevard in South Boston, is reputed to be one of the city's best saltwater fishing spots. The *Massachusetts Saltwater Sportfishing Guide* can be obtained from the Division of Marine Fisheries, 251 Causeway St., Boston, MA 02114; phone (617) 626-1520.

Golf

Due to the rigorous winters, golf is not an all-year proposition in Greater Boston. Courses are busy on summer weekends; players should phone in advance to reserve a tee time. Several 18-hole courses are open to the public, including Braintree Municipal Golf Course, 101 Jefferson St. in Braintree, (781) 843-6513; Brookline Golf Public Club at Putterham, 1281 W. Roxbury Pkwy. in Chestnut Hill, (617) 730-2078; Brookmeadow Country Club, 100 Everendon Rd. in Canton, (781) 828-4444; Franklin Park Golf Course, 1 Circuit Dr. in Dorchester, (617) 265-4084; Newton Commonwealth Golf Course, 212 Kenrick St. in Newton, (617) 630-1971; and Sheraton Colonial Golf Club, 1 Audubon Rd. in Wakefield, (781) 876-6031.

Horseback Riding

Some of the longest and most scenic bridle paths are in the **Blue Hills Reservation**, where rates average $50 an hour; phone (617) 698-1802. Check the telephone directory for a complete listing of stables and riding academies in the Boston area.

Jogging and Walking

The banks of the Charles River are the most popular spots for joggers; **Storrow Drive** in Boston and **Memorial Drive** in Cambridge are top routes. Loop runs of varying distances can be tailored by taking advantage of the several bridges that cross the river. Contact the Division of Urban Parks and Recreation for information on other city jogging paths; phone (617) 626-1250.

Walking is, of course, the best way to see Boston. Perhaps the most popular route is the **Freedom Trail**, easily followed via a red line painted on the sidewalk. It conveniently links a number of historic sites. *See Walking Tours p. 117.* Along the **Rose Fitzgerald Kennedy Greenway**, tree-lined parks connect several vibrant districts, including Chinatown and the North End. A byproduct of the Big Dig, the greenbelt follows the former path of the bygone elevated Central Artery.

Tennis

The Division of Urban Parks and Recreation maintains tennis courts throughout the Boston metropolitan area, and nearly all are available on a first-come-first-served basis. There also are courts at **Marine Park** in South Boston. For other locations phone (617) 626-1250.

Water Sports

Boston Harbor is good for more than dumping tea. The **Boston Sailing Center** on Lewis Wharf specializes in sailboat charters or a picnic cruise to the Boston Harbor Islands; phone (617) 227-4198.

The Charles River—christened by Prince Charles of England (later the ruler Charles I) in 1605—has figured prominently in history; Paul Revere rowed across it before taking off on his midnight ride. Later the river was plied by tugboats and freight vessels, and a foul stench from stagnant tidal mud flats often hung in the air. In the early 20th century the Charles River Basin was created, stretching some 9 miles upstream from the harbor.

Today recreational craft rule the Charles, and boathouses and marinas line its banks. **Community Boating**, 21 David G. Mugar Way near the Boston side of the Longfellow Bridge and the Charles/MGH "T" station, offers a 1-day visitor pass with unlimited sailboat use April through October. Sailing lessons also are available; phone (617) 523-1038.

Harvard and other collegiate rowing crews routinely use the river basin for practice sessions. The **Charles River Canoe and Kayak Center**, 2401 Commonwealth Ave. in Newton, has canoes, kayaks, rowboats and rowing shells available for rent from April to early November. Kayaking classes for all levels are offered; phone (617) 965-5110.

Winter Sports

When the weather turns frosty, Bostonians head for the Boston Common's **Frog Pond**, which is transformed from a wading pool to an ice-skating playground November to mid-March. A nearby kiosk houses ice-making equipment, a warming room and skate rental facilities. Ice-skating also is popular on the lagoon at the **Public Garden.** The **Beacon Hill Skate Shop**, 135 S. Charles St., has equipment rentals; phone (617) 482-7400. Public ice-skating rinks are scattered throughout the city; phone (617) 626-1250 for information about locations and hours of operation.

Shopping

Boston carries on the tradition that great cities equal great shopping. Well-heeled couples peruse exclusive Newbury Street boutiques in the Back Bay, the same neighborhood where scruffy college kids often are seen toting bulging Newbury Comics bags. As scrupulous patrons maneuver around polished antiques crowding tiny Beacon Hill stores, tourists weave their way through the ever-hectic Quincy Market, sampling creamy desserts and fresh *chowdah* along the way. Elsewhere in this age-old burg are shrewd bargain hunters pillaging racks for fashion treasure at Filene's Basement, in business since the days of corsets and ascot ties.

As with almost everything else in Boston, shopping has its ties to history. Transformed into a festive commercial showplace in the mid-1970s, **Faneuil Hall Marketplace** (T: Government Center or State) often is cited as Boston's foremost urban attraction. Here you'll come across jugglers, magicians and other entertainers performing before rippling crowds. Young schoolchildren, some perplexed by the unusual spelling of the market's name, gleefully skip about bench-studded pedestrian malls. Besotted pigeons peck at crumbs beneath umbrella-shaded tables, while another, much larger species of natives frequents this locale for more substantial gastronomic delights.

The centerpiece of this shopping extravaganza bounded by North, Congress and State streets is Faneuil Hall *(see attraction listing p. 108),* Colonial Boston's town meeting place. Financed by wealthy merchant Peter Faneuil, the hall opened in 1742 and was modeled after London's mercantile structures. Open fish and produce stalls occupied the lower floor, and the upstairs meeting room soon became a forum for heated gatherings of patriots who had begun to chafe under British rule. Atop the brick building is a whimsical weather vane that has survived an earthquake (1755), a fire (1761) and thievery (stolen and recovered in 1974). This gold-plated grasshopper—a distinctive item an outsider would have difficulty identifying—was used as a means of detecting potential spies during the War of 1812. It now keeps a watchful eye over hordes of modern-day visitors and residents alike.

Opposite the hall is **Quincy Market**—a long, narrow, multistoried structure added in the early 19th century. This copper-domed, Doric-colonnaded, glass-canopied edifice maintains a market-stall layout, although the offerings have expanded beyond basic meats and vegetables. Intoxicating aromas fill the bottom-floor colonnade, where you can savor international and specialty foods—from baklava to raw oysters. Troll the brick and cobblestone alleys along both sides of the building, where pushcarts peddle souvenirs and crafts, scented candles and handmade jewelry.

With the additional North Market and South Market buildings and such nationwide stores as the Gap and Coach, shopping for your own goodies at Faneuil Hall Marketplace is a definite possibility; however, it's easy to see this also is the ideal spot to buy gifts for your friends back home. Decide among such keepsakes as aprons, socks and sleepwear adorned with cartoonish lobsters or delicately sketched swans; bottled miniature model ships; an array of sports-related memorabilia celebrating this town's many beloved teams; and pens, T-shirts and hats embossed with "I ♥ Boston!" or the profusely uttered local phrase *"wicked pissah"* (really great).

A phenomenon that perhaps can be attributed to the city's straight-laced Puritan beginnings is the Boston "look," which, traditionally, has clashed with those flaunted by chic New Yorkers and L.A. jetsetters. Though Bostonians have long clung to conservative, time-honored clothing designs, Hub shoppers certainly have never been left wanting, especially when browsing in the **Back Bay**. Here you'll have no trouble locating the latest Prada clutch, a few key pieces by Mark Jacobs or a hip new pair of Valentino shades.

A number of major retail destinations are scattered about this upscale neighborhood; however, one markedly stands out above the rest. While Big Apple fashionistas haunt Madison Avenue and Hollywood spenders turn up on Rodeo Drive, Boston's own dally along **Newbury Street**. When the weather is agreeable, suburban families, metropolitan socialites, photo-snapping tourists and budget-conscious students cram sidewalks lined by yellow daffodils and moss-covered Victorian brownstones.

Tree-shaded blocks near the Public Garden shelter high-end retailers such as Giorgio Armani and Brooks Brothers. Nearby, well-dressed mannequins front elegant, locally owned boutiques. Both

The Shops at Prudential Center / © Bruno Perousse / age fotostock

window-shoppers and serious collectors will be enchanted by Newbury's posh art galleries, including the family-run Vose Galleries.

Closer to Massachusetts Avenue, the thoroughfare's flavor gets funkier. Here Newbury Street shoppers can explore the flagship store of Life is good, a locally bred enterprise that gained steam in

the mid-1990s. T-shirts emblazoned with a smiling stick figure named Jake were initially sold on street corners by two brothers who beseeched passersby to "Buy a shirt and feed the skinny man!" Today the company's wiry, optimistic mascot adorns a wide variety of goods—from backpacks to beach balls.

For "a wicked good time," visit Newbury Comics. Founded by two MIT students, the flagship store of this New England chain is inundated with hard-to-find CDs and records as well as quirky pop culture gifts, such as talking Darth Vader action figures and zombie survival kits. This enduring Boston institution helped cultivate Newbury Street's appeal in the late 1970s. Since then a multitude of national merchants—H&M, Lucky Brand Jeans and Urban Outfitters are just a few—have set up shop, with the hip accessory stores and independent booksellers that once ruled the scene now fewer and farther between.

The Back Bay, the product of a massive 19th-century land reclamation project, also is home to **Copley Place** (T: Back Bay or Copley), which offers more than 70 stores. Inside this shopping center off Huntington Avenue, manicured hands caress the extravagant purses and knee-high boots lining the walls of Jimmy Choo. Nearby, at sleek Barneys New York, bare feet nervously await a pair of snakeskin heels while another stockinged set model Mary Janes before a full-length mirror. At the mall's core, worn-out shoppers lounge beside a waterfall sculpture in the well-lit atrium, bags from Williams-Sonoma, Neiman Marcus and Ralph Lauren at their feet.

Enclosed bridges link Copley Place to Copley Square's refined Marriott and Westin hotels as well as to **The Shops at Prudential Center** (T: Prudential), where such stores as Ann Taylor Loft, Godiva Chocolatier and L'Occitane entice passersby strolling glass-roofed arcades. Prudential Tower, the second-tallest building in Boston, soars over the busy retail complex. For a break from the clothes racks, head up to the Skywalk Observatory at Prudential Center *(see attraction listing p. 113)* and survey the bustling ant-like creatures below. Or, kick back in the South Garden, a tranquil open-air retreat at the southwest corner of the mall, and take in views of the 750-foot-tall skyscraper mingling with the clouds.

Anchoring The Shops at Prudential Center are Saks Fifth Avenue and Lord & Taylor. The latter also is accessible via an entrance on **Boylston Street**, a busy commercial thoroughfare that is home to a three-story, glass-fronted Apple Store, a dramatic interloper on a block of staid brick and concrete. The Back Bay outlet of off-price retailer Filene's Basement *(see Downtown Crossing below)* is farther east on Boylston as is high-society jeweler

Shreve, Crump & Low. Rub elbows with Massachusetts' upper crust as you peruse emerald-cut diamonds and mabe pearls, 18th- and 19th-century English and American furnishings, silver items and Chinese porcelains. At Boylston's decidedly high-priced **Heritage on the Garden** complex (T: Arlington), affluent patrons stock up on clothing and accessories by such chic European designers as Escada, Hermès and Sonia Rykiel just steps away from the Public Garden *(see attraction listing p. 113).*

On the opposite side of Boston's vibrant botanical park lies the historic **Beacon Hill** neighborhood—a true charmer with its gas-lit lamps, cobblestone passageways and whimsical door knockers. At the base of the hill is Charles Street, an eclectic strip where posh boutiques sell contemporary clothing and home furnishings alongside the crème de la crème of Greater Boston's vast antiquing empire. Connoisseurs stalking fine 18th-century furniture, silver tea sets and decorative porcelain pieces will not be disappointed with the treasures amassed here. Several merchants setting up shop along this lovely brick-faced street offer everything from fine Oriental antiques to bric-a-brac, so even casual shoppers may manage to score a few bargain-priced goodies. Discover some surprisingly affordable items at Upstairs Downstairs, which has the air of a roadside country store, or tackle Eugene Galleries' multitude of old prints, photographs and etchings—many of which depict the near and dear "Hub of the Universe."

Throughout the state, bargain hunters will cherish the absence of sales taxes on single-item clothing purchases of less than $175, and for those on a budget Greater Boston's assortment of discount outlets is heaven-sent. Brand-name markdowns at T.J. Maxx and Marshalls, both founded in nearby Framingham, lure tourists off the Freedom Trail, which edges the bustling Downtown Crossing shopping district in the north and east. For a few sporty souvenirs, poke around the men's section of the stores, where you'll often unearth Boston Celtics and Red Sox T-shirts as well as a hodgepodge of gear emblazoned with the New England Patriots logo.

Wander through **Downtown Crossing** (T: Downtown Crossing) any day of the week and you'll likely encounter energetic street performers and boisterous vendors. Spend an hour or two browsing independent jewelers and camera shops; Windsor Button, in operation here since 1936; numerous sporting goods retailers; and such national chains as Borders, H&M and Macy's. Pedestrian malls—on Washington Street between Winter and Milk streets and on Winter Street between Tremont and Washington streets—attract idlers from the Boston Common (due west) as well as meticulously dressed workers from the Financial District (due east). Packs of lunching men and women effortlessly slurp down overloaded hot dogs as tourists inspect keepsake T-shirts and hoodies neatly plastered on all sides of the ubiquitous Boston pushcart.

Downtown Crossing also is the birthplace of Filene's Basement, one of the country's oldest close-out merchants. The name of the outlet stems from the venerable—but now defunct—Boston-based department store Filene's, which began selling surplus merchandise in this basement-level space in 1909. Each piece of merchandise was automatically and successively marked down in price according to the number of days the item remained unsold; goods not snapped up were given to charity. Fierce crowds reigned at the underground, no-frills shop, where tug-of-war matches sometimes broke out amid clustered bins overflowing with sweaters and lingerie.

The Basement's Downtown Crossing branch is closed until sometime in 2011 as construction workers descend upon the old Filene's department store building. Developers envision a multiuse complex with commercial, residential and educational components. In the meantime Back Bay and suburban outlets of Filene's Basement—tame in comparison to the original, with its communal dressing rooms and frenetic clientele—satiate budget-savvy natives. The "Running of the Brides"—the off-price retailer's notoriously chaotic bridal gown event—continues to take place twice a year in the Hub (it's held annually in other cities). Clothes racks are stripped bare in less than 60 seconds, unabashed brides-to-be try on designer dresses in the aisles, and nerve-racking negotiations transpire over creamy size 8s and 10s.

Just as ardent, though outwardly more reserved, are those scrutinizing shelves in Greater Boston's many used bookstores. Commonwealth Books—crammed with architectural prints, autobiographies, and research materials documenting everything from World War II to Egyptian art—has a shop at the corner of Washington Street and Spring Lane as well as a downtown branch in the basement of the Old South Meeting House *(see attraction listing p. 112).* A few blocks away on West Street, rows of aging paperbacks and hardcovers whisk Brattle Book Shop browsers away to far-off lands. Three stories of collectible postcards, delicate first editions, weathered maps and fanciful novels have tempted buyers since 1825. Rummage through the outdoor area, where a checkerboard mural depicts several Bay State authors, including Dr. Seuss and Nathaniel Hawthorne, who guard over throngs of discounted books.

You're certain to stumble across a few more *al fresco* book sales while window-shopping in nearby **Cambridge** *(see place listing p. 136).* Boston's northerly neighbor also is the ideal hunting ground for those on the lookout for rare and out-of-print texts. The university town boasts several great booksellers, including Harvard Book Store, Grolier Poetry Book Shop, Raven Used Books and Schoenhof's Foreign Books, all of which are located in the Harvard Square vicinity. Weed through travel-related guides and novelties at The Globe Corner Bookstore on Mount Auburn Street; scan titles proffered for a mere $2 apiece by Almost Banned in Harvard Sq. Booksellers on Massachusetts Avenue; or delight young readers with a few gifts from Curious George

Books & Toys, located kitty-corner from the **Harvard Square** "T" station. In the heart of the square you also can pick up a light read for the trip home at the historic Out of Town News kiosk, which carries newspapers and magazines from around the world.

More than 150 stores manage to squeeze into just a few blocks around Harvard Square. The Harvard Cooperative Society, 1400 Massachusetts Ave., is universally known as the Coop (pronounced like the poultry enclosure). Alongside textbooks and dormitory necessities, everything from stationary imprinted with the Harvard insignia to silk ties and caps in crimson (the school's official color) can be bought at the collegiate department store founded by Harvard students in 1882. For a more unique keepsake, search out another collectively owned business, the Cambridge Artists Cooperative Gallery, 59A Church St., and marvel over handmade bracelets and earrings, mosaic frames, and earth-colored plates and jugs.

Although Cambridge residents lament the "invasion" of national chains such as Crate & Barrel, Gap and Urban Outfitters, Harvard Square continues to shelter independent retailers. Funkier, reasonably-priced shops also thrive farther down on **Massachusetts Avenue**, particularly near **Central Square.** Pop into Cheapo Records, 538 Massachusetts Ave., and chat with an erudite cast of characters well-schooled in the ways of classic rock, jazz and blues. To the east lies The Garment District, near **Kendall Square** at 200 Broadway St. Although the secondhand clothes store is quite a hike from both the Central Square and Kendall/MIT "T" stations, a trip here really is like no other. As you enter the colorful warehouse, a colossal mound of clothes lies ahead, with plucky scavengers strewn about the uneven expanse. If diving into this "Dollar-A-Pound" area isn't your style, try on a retro pair of hip-huggers, a vintage Hawaiian shirt or a summery halter dress from the well-organized second floor, where many items are categorized by decade.

Nightlife

While on par with the country's most distinctive metropolises in terms of history, culture and cuisine, Boston falls off the radar with a resounding thud when it comes to nightlife. Most clubs shut down by 1 or 2 a.m., and the "T" complicates late-night planning by stopping service around 12:30 a.m. Even if Boston isn't *exactly* "The City that Never Sleeps," don't start fluffing your pillow once the sun sets over the John Hancock Tower. The "Hub of the Universe" still offers a variety of activities to keep you well-entertained after dark.

A massive guiding light for *bah hoppahs* is the city's landmark CITGO sign. Overlooking **Kenmore Square,** this red, white and blue icon illuminates not only Fenway Park but also Lansdowne Street, which hosts scores of unofficial block parties after a Red Sox game. Although in sports-zealous Boston, it's likely a state law for *all* bars to have at least one flat-screen TV tuned in to the must-see game of the

moment, this district's proximity to the Green Monster obviously dictates a heavy presence of sports bars. Munch on swanky versions of bar classics—pepper jack cheese nachos and sesame chicken tenders—at trendy, retro-stylized amusement facilities such as three-story Jillian's Boston, at Ipswich and Lansdowne streets, and 24,000-square-foot Kings on Dalton Street. Undergraduates and young professionals pack these upscale, though pricey, activity centers, bowling and shooting pool while sipping neon-tinted martinis. Phone (617) 437-0300 for Jillian's Boston or (617) 266-2695 for Kings.

If handcrafted lagers are more your style, pop in to Boston Beer Works, on Brookline Avenue across from **Fenway Park,** for some mako shark skewers marinated in raspberry ale. Basketball and hockey fans regularly head to the brewery's two-level **Canal Street** location (near TD Banknorth Garden, home of the Celtics and the Bruins), which features championship billiard tables and more than a dozen of the obligatory flat-screen TVs. Phone (617) 536-2337 for Boston Beer Works—Fenway or (617) 896-2337 for Boston Beer Works—Canal Street.

For many diehard Sox fans, there's no replacement for the Cask'n Flagon, located on the corner of Brookline Avenue and **Lansdowne Street.** Dig in on The Dugout (their tasty version of a white pizza) while watching the pre-game spectacle unfold outside Fenway's emerald-hued left field wall. Daytime patrons scrutinize the Cask's impressive array of baseball memorabilia, while boisterous twenty-somethings mingle at the neighborhood institution after dark. Thursday through Saturday nights DJs spin a diverse mix, everything from Top 40 hits to hip-hop anthems. Classic rock also reverberates through the old-school hangout, perhaps in tribute to its former existence as a live concert venue (1969-73), when the voices of Jimi Hendrix, Bruce Springsteen and Steven Tyler thundered through the building; phone (617) 536-4840.

Saturated with techno beats, jostling alpha males and body-hugging fashions exhibited by both sexes, Lansdowne Street has long been one of the city's most popular clubbing destinations. New kid on the block House of Blues, (888) 693-2583, opened in 2009. Like its folk art-loving namesakes across the country, the state-of-the-art music hall and restaurant offers varied musical talents most nights. The very first HOB operated in a historic Colonial house in the scholarly city of Cambridge 1992-2003.

Live music venues thrive in Boston, long a haven for talented, creative souls. Everyone knows Aerosmith (a.k.a. "The Bad Boys from Boston") and the big-haired band members of Boston hail from Beantown, but new wave rockers The Cars and the punk-influenced Pixies also practiced their performance skills here before conquering national audiences. In the 1950s and '60s folk great Joan Baez, along with a young Bob Dylan, entertained patrons of Club Passim, 47 Palmer St. in **Cambridge.** In addition past guests of The Paradise, 967 Commonwealth Ave., another longtime haunt, include AC/DC, Elvis

Costello and U2. Phone (617) 492-5300 for Club Passim or (617) 562-8800 for The Paradise.

For indie rock and alternative sounds, head to Cambridge's The Middle East Restaurant & Nightclub. Located in **Central Square** since the early 1970s, this odd assemblage of music halls, eateries and bars along Massachusetts Avenue also welcomes underground hip-hop artists, jazz and blues singers and reggae groups. Adding to the mix are belly dancers—accompanied by a live band on Wednesdays and a DJ on Sunday nights—who entertain diners munching on *falafel* (deep-fried, ground chickpeas) and *tagine* (a slow-cooked North African stew); phone (617) 864-3278.

Jazz and blues jam sessions are the norm at Wally's Café, which, since its establishment in 1947, has evolved into a training ground for students of The Boston Conservatory, the New England Conservatory of Music and, of course, the neighboring Berklee College of Music. Though Wally's was originally located across the street (it moved into an unassuming red-bricked structure at 427 Massachusetts Ave. in 1979), this gritty club is all that remains of a district once buzzing with the beats of several dynamic jazz halls; phone (617) 424-1408.

A relative newcomer to the local jazz scene is the Regattabar, which opened in 1985. The sleek club at The Charles Hotel, 1 Bennett St. in Cambridge, has quickly risen to the top of the charts, securing its status as one of the area's best with sophisticated vibes and top-notch performers. Gifted vocalists, pianists and brass players also wail at the celebrated Scullers Jazz Club in the Doubletree Guest Suites-Boston, 400 Soldiers Field Rd., where you can survey an undulating Charles River and a star-speckled city skyline. Phone (617) 395-7757 for Regattabar or (617) 562-4111 for Scullers Jazz Club.

As night falls, scores of stand-up comics start work in Greater Boston—a locale known as a breeding ground for gifted humorists. Massachusetts natives include late-night TV host Conan O'Brien (born in Brookline), bitingly raw Louis C.K. (raised in Framingham and Newton) and chain-smoking ranter Denis Leary (born in Worcester). Highlighting the region's fresh talent is The Comedy Studio, where you can sip fruity concoctions beside tomorrow's comedic stars. The venue sits atop longtime Harvard Square dive the Hong Kong Restaurant, 1238 Massachusetts Ave. A few Oriental touches adorn the otherwise sparse third-floor comedy club, which offers the same Chinese cuisine that's served downstairs.

Before the show starts, order some spicy Szechuan wontons and chop suey, then wash everything down with a Scorpion Bowl. But beware—one too many slurps from the Hong Kong's trademark, over-the-top cocktail will have you falling off your chair even before the punch lines land. Meant to be shared, the intoxicating drink loaded with extra-long straws also is a fixture at Hong Kong's **Faneuil Hall Marketplace** location. (Unless you're *looking* for a rowdy time, stay clear of next-door Sissy K's,

an obnoxiously loud hangout luring college-age patrons with cheap drinks and not much else.) Phone (617) 661-6507 for The Comedy Studio, (617) 864-5311 for Hong Kong Restaurant at Harvard Square or (617) 227-2226 for Hong Kong Restaurant at Faneuil Hall.

A marketplace by day, Faneuil Hall's historic setting attracts a mixed crowd. Many residents favor The Comedy Connection, which regularly boasts such bigwig comics as Margaret Cho and Jon Stewart in addition to local favorites. At the mock version of the "Cheers" bar in the Quincy Market building, nobody *will* know your name but everybody *will* know you're a tourist. Phone (617) 248-9700 for The Comedy Connection or (617) 227-0150 for Cheers.

For down-home eats and nightly live music, open the stark red door to The Black Rose, 160 State St., a timeless wood-paneled Irish pub on the fringes of Faneuil Hall Marketplace; phone (617) 742-2286. After dinner, be sure to raise your pint glass and toast to new friends at a few more Irish pubs. Peruse the beer selection at Hennessy's of Boston or The Purple Shamrock, both located nearby on Union Street. Or, dance the Irish jig to **Somerville,** a diverse city just north of Cambridge with a happening nightlife scene of its own. If you have two left feet, visit The Burren—a highly acclaimed **Davis Square** pub, restaurant and music hall—on a Monday night, when dancing lessons take place. Phone (617) 742-2121 for Hennessy's of Boston, (617) 227-2060 for The Purple Shamrock or (617) 776-6896 for The Burren.

You'll encounter more warm smiles and foamy beverages at historic taverns throughout the age-old city of Boston, including The Bell-in-Hand, 45-55 Union St., in business locally since the town crier christened the operation back in 1795. Just a few steps away is The Green Dragon Tavern, 11 Marshall St., named after a bygone watering hole where 18th-century Revolutionary leaders often met, likely over a few mugs of ale. Samuel Adams still lingers at many a table, as the patriot's image appears on bottled lagers bearing his name. (While you're in town, sample a few of The Boston Beer Co.'s award-winning beverages after touring their local brewery. *See Industrial Tours p. 116.*) Phone (617) 227-2098 for The Bell-in-Hand Tavern or (617) 367-0055 for The Green Dragon Tavern.

In Boston you'll spot orange and pink Dunkin' Donuts signs on just about every corner (the diet-busting chain was founded in Quincy); however, the area's multitude of college students frequently converge at more bohemian java joints for spoken word poetry and acoustic riffs. While attending Tufts University in Medford, singer-songwriter Tracy Chapman strummed her guitar at Harvard Square's The Nameless Coffeehouse, 3 Church St. in Cambridge, which also welcomed such comedians as Andy Kaufman and Jay Leno early in their careers. The volunteer-run venue typically offers a show the first Saturday of every month; phone (617) 864-1630.

Boston Pops Orchestra / © Stu Rosner

Even if it's an off week for The Nameless Coffee-house, laid-back establishments thrive near Cambridge's Ivy League university, so you'll always find **Harvard Square** ideal for twilight relaxation and reflection. Sip mint tea at Algiers Coffee House in historic Brattle Hall, 40 Brattle St., or savor the flan served up at Café Pamplona, 12 Bow St., a traditional European-style bistro patronized by local intellectuals since 1959. After nibbling on sweet potato fries at the casual Cambridge Common restaurant and bar on Massachusetts Avenue, head downstairs to the lush, dimly lit Lizard Lounge, an intimate showcase for aspiring lyricists and hometown musicians. Alternatively, hard-to-miss Charlie's Kitchen is a beacon on Eliot Street with its mishmash of kitschy neon signs advertising everything from pints of Guinness to "Shish-K-Bab." Phone (617) 492-1557 for Algiers Coffee House, (617) 492-0352 for Café Pamplona, (617) 547-1228 for Cambridge Common, (617) 547-0759 for Lizard Lounge or (617) 492-9646 for Charlie's Kitchen.

Grab a copy of the *Weekly Dig* or *The Boston Phoenix* before heading out for the evening. Both publications offer general bar and club listings as well as detailed information about the latest happenings, including concerts and special events. *The Improper Bostonian* and *Stuff@night* are additional sources documenting trendy and up-and-coming Hub nightspots.

Performing Arts

The performing arts in Boston began in elaborately bedecked theaters, where the likes of Charles Dickens, Ralph Waldo Emerson and Oscar Wilde gave lively readings. Although lingering Puritan prejudice against artistic expression delayed the inception of splashier productions (one 19th-century hall was named the Boston Museum in hopes of camouflaging what went on inside), entertainment here has a long history. The nation's first orchestra, for example, was founded in Boston in the early 19th century; it performed the country's first oratorio in King's Chapel in 1815.

Boston's **Theatre District**, centered along Tremont and Stuart streets just south of the Boston Common, was once well established as a stopover for productions en route to Broadway. Architect Clarence H. Blackall designed several of the extravagant movie palaces that remain standing in the area. Now lavishly restored, these historic theaters provide an elegant backdrop for 21st-century performances. Landmarks include the **Colonial Theatre**, 106 Boylston St., (617) 880-2460; the **Cutler Majestic Theatre**, 219 Tremont St., (617) 824-8000; **The Opera House**, 539 Washington St., (617) 259-3400; and the **Wilbur Theatre**, 246 Tremont St., (617) 423-4008.

Citi Performing Arts Center encompasses **The Shubert Theatre**, 265 Tremont St., as well as one of the city's most versatile facilities, **The Wang Theatre**, 270 Tremont St., a 1920s motion picture house that now hosts large-scale operas, musicals and ballets; phone (617) 482-9393 or (866) 348-9738. The real news in Boston theater, though, is not the touring blockbusters but the proliferation of upstart repertory groups staging vibrant new works, with performing space provided by such facilities as the rehabilitated **Boston Center for the Arts**, 539 Tremont St.; phone (617) 426-5000.

BosTix is Boston's largest ticket agency and a center for entertainment information. Two kiosks—at Faneuil Hall Marketplace and at Copley Square near the corner of Boylston and Dartmouth streets—sell full-price advance tickets as well as half-price tickets for same-day performances, beginning at 11 a.m. (a "daily menu" of available events is posted at each). Credit cards are not accepted; cash and traveler's checks are. The Faneuil Hall booth is open Tues.-Sat. 10-6, Sun. 11-4; the Copley Square booth is open Mon.-Sat. 10-6, Sun. 11-4. Both are closed major holidays. Phone (617) 723-5181 for recorded information.

Calendar, published each Thursday by *The Boston Globe*, carries listings of the city's cultural events for the week. *The Boston Phoenix*, a weekly newspaper, contains movie, theater, gallery and other events listings. Another weekly, *The Improper Bostonian*, also has information about the arts and entertainment.

Dance

The **Boston Ballet Company**, 19 Clarendon St., the city's premier dance company, presents a repertoire of classical and modern works at Citi Performing Arts Center. Tickets are offered by subscription, but they can be obtained for individual performances 1 week prior to the performance; phone (617) 695-6950 or (800) 447-7400. **José Mateo Ballet Theatre**, 400 Harvard St. in Harvard

Square, is an up-and-coming troupe that stages innovative contemporary programs; phone (617)
354-7467.

Film

Most cinemas in downtown Boston show single
features, often on a reserved-seat basis, at an average price of $9. Classic, repertory and foreign films
are offered at universities and neighborhood theaters, usually at a lower admission. The **Brattle
Theatre**, 40 Brattle St., is a landmark film house
that satisfies both classic-movie buffs and fans of
the obscure; phone (617) 876-6837 for the 24-hour
film line. **Loews Cineplex Harvard Square**, 10
Church St., shows films at the artier end of the
mainstream spectrum; phone (617) 864-4581.

The **Harvard Film Archive**, in the Carpenter
Center for the Visual Arts at 24 Quincy St., presents
an excellent mix of classics, documentaries and
little-seen curiosities; phone (617) 495-4700. **Kendall Square Cinema**, One Kendall Square in East
Cambridge, features low-budget independent films
and art house fare; phone (617) 499-1996.

In Boston non-mainstream films are shown at the
Museum of Fine Arts, Boston *(see attraction listing p. 110)*, 465 Huntington Ave.; phone (617)
369-3306. The Art Deco **Coolidge Corner Theatre**,
290 Harvard St. in Brookline, features retrospec-
tives, foreign films, documentaries, kung fu action
spectacles and more; phone (617) 734-2500.

Music

Symphony Hall, 301 Massachusetts Ave., is
home to the **Boston Symphony Orchestra** as well
as the **Boston Pops Orchestra** and is lauded for its
outstanding acoustics. The Boston Symphony Orchestra (BSO) presents more than 250 concerts each
year, with world-class soloists appearing regularly.
The season runs from October through April; in July
and August, the orchestra appears at the **Tanglewood Music Center** in Lenox. Wednesday evening
and Thursday morning rehearsal tickets are considerably less expensive and are sometimes available to
the public; phone (617) 266-1200, or (888)
266-1200 for program information.

Under the direction of maestro Arthur Fiedler, the
Boston Pops Orchestra is often credited with attract-
ing a wider audience to classical music. Fiedler
ended a 50-year reign as conductor in 1979, but the
"Pops" is as popular as ever. Now conducted by
Keith Lockhart, BSO members offer a "light" program of concerts featuring a mix of classical, show
tunes and popular music at Symphony Hall from
early May to early July. The Boston Pops also
makes a week of appearances at the **Hatch Memorial Shell** on the Charles River Esplanade in conjunction with Fourth of July festivities. These free
concerts are among Boston's most delightful summertime events.

CityPass and Go Boston Card

CityPass offers savings to those
planning to visit multiple Boston
attractions. The pass covers the price
of admission to the Museum of Fine
Arts, Boston; Museum of Science;
New England Aquarium; and Skywalk Observatory at Prudential Center as well as admission to either the
Harvard Museum of Natural History
or the John F. Kennedy Presidential
Library and Museum. From March 1,
2010, to Feb. 28, 2011, a pass, valid
for 9 days once the first attraction is
visited, is $46; $29 (ages 3-11). CityPass is available from participating
Boston attractions; phone (208)
787-4300 or (888) 330-5008 for customer service. *See color ad p. 107.*

Go Boston Card is an all-access
pass offering admission to more
than 70 Boston area attractions and
sightseeing options, including Boston Duck Tours, the Museum of Science and Plimoth Plantation. The
card, which is purchased by the day
(1,2,3,5 or 7 consecutive calendar
days), also encompasses a 2-day trolley pass. Priced as low as $28 per
day (based on a 7-day card), Go Boston Card is available at the Boston
Common Visitor Information Center
at 148 Tremont St.; phone (800)
887-9103.

Two noted concert halls are located in museums. The **Isabella Stewart Gardner Museum** *(see attraction listing p. 109)* features soloists and chamber music performances in the Tapestry Room Sat.-Sun. at 1:30 throughout the spring and fall. Phone (617) 278-5150 for schedule information or (617) 278-5156 to purchase tickets. Concerts also take place at the **Museum of Fine Arts, Boston**, 465 Huntington Ave.; phone (617) 267-9300 for information.

The **Boston Camerata** presents vocal and instrumental concerts of medieval, baroque and Renaissance music, plus occasional 19th-century American folk music, at various locations around the city; phone (617) 262-2092.

The presence of the New England Conservatory of Music, the Berklee College of Music and several highly acclaimed university music programs diversifies the Boston music menu. Restored **Jordan Hall**, 30 Gainsborough St. at the New England Conservatory (across the street from Symphony Hall), can accommodate a full orchestra but also is acoustically suited to intimate chamber music performances; phone (617) 585-1260. The hall is home to the **Boston Philharmonic**; phone (617) 236-0999. The **Berklee Performance Center**, 136 Massachusetts Ave., is well known for its jazz programs; phone (617) 747-2261.

Free chamber music and concert performances are given at **Boston University Concert Hall**, in the Tsai Performance Center at 685 Commonwealth Ave. on the Boston University campus; phone (617) 353-8724 for schedule information. MIT *(see attraction listing p. 139)* presents a chapel organ series, and Harvard *(see attraction listing p. 137)* and Radcliffe offer choral and band concerts.

Noontime concerts and recitals are given at **King's Chapel** *(see attraction listing p. 109)*, 58 Tremont St., and at **Trinity Church** *(see attraction listing p. 113)* in Copley Square; phone (617) 227-2155 and (617) 536-0944, respectively. The **Celebrity Series** presents a varied program of events, from orchestras and chamber groups to dance companies and recitals. Performances are given at venues throughout the city, including Symphony Hall, Citi Performing Arts Center and Jordan Hall; phone (617) 482-6661.

Opera

The **Boston Lyric Opera Company** presents three productions each season at The Shubert Theatre of the Citi Performing Arts Center. Both classic and 20th-century works are performed; phone (617) 542-4912 for performance and schedule information. The **Opera Boston** is a professional opera repertory company; phone (617) 451-3388 for ticket and schedule information.

Theater

Although small in stature, Boston's Theatre District brims with lavish period decor. In the 1920s the area around the intersection of Tremont and Stuart streets was a glamorous stopover for Broadway-bound plays testing the waters in the city's grand playhouses. By the 1970s the atmosphere was best described as seedy. Thanks to urban renewal and a resurgence of the performing arts, several of these palaces have found new life.

One of the most intimate is the Wilbur Theatre, which sat through a few dark years before reopening in 1995. The Colonial Theatre is perhaps the city's grandest, a masterpiece of gilded ornamentation, grandiose chandeliers and lavish frescoes incongruously tucked into an office building. Built specifically for legitimate theater and opened in 1900, the Colonial presents a variety of major shows, often musicals straight from their Broadway runs.

The Cutler Majestic Theatre is another ornate reminder of the Theater District's heyday. The 1903 Beaux-Arts building endured a stint as a movie theater in the 1950s before undergoing a substantial renovation under the auspices of Emerson College. Drama, opera and dance productions, both student and professional, are staged here.

The renovated 1910 Shubert Theatre sparkles with brass railings and gold touches in the refurbished lobby. The venue draws major touring productions and is part of the Citi Performing Arts Center, which also encompasses the theater district's most visible landmark: The Wang Theatre. It opened in 1925 as a spectacular motion picture house in the style of Radio City Music Hall (a facility it predated). Also known as the Metropolitan Theater and the Music Hall, it was renamed in the early 1980s for a generous benefactor and renovated to accommodate large-scale performances. The enormous building has a particularly impressive succession of lobbies, all of them appointed in sumptuous style with columns of Italian marble, stained glass, gold leaf decoration and florid ceiling murals.

Smaller theaters and those associated with area colleges and universities also have made a name for themselves. The three stages at the Boston Center for the Arts are devoted to nurturing homegrown talent. The center is known for its often-provocative theater performed in a bare-bones setting. Offbeat productions also appear at the **New Repertory Theatre**, 321 Arsenal St. in Watertown; phone (617) 923-8487. Classics mix with regional premieres at the **Lyric Stage**, 140 Clarendon St. on the second floor of the YWCA building; phone (617) 585-5678.

The **Huntington Theatre Company**, 264 Huntington Ave., is affiliated with Boston University. This resident theater group stages classics as well as new plays; phone (617) 266-0800. The **American Repertory Theatre**, one of the East Coast's most respected repertory companies, performs during the school year at **Harvard's Loeb Drama Center**, 64 Brattle St. in Cambridge; phone (617) 547-8300. Experimental works are produced on the smaller of its two stages; the main stage offers new American plays and freewheeling adaptations of the classics.

Brandeis University's **Spingold Theatre** offers high-caliber productions during the winter theater season; phone (781) 736-3400.

Harvard University's **Hasty Pudding Theatricals** put on one production each spring in the **New College Theatre**, 12 Holyoke St. The student-written musical comedy features an all-male cast whose female characters are played in drag. The troupe also picks the Hasty Pudding Man and Woman of the Year each February. Past honorees include Mel Gibson, Tom Hanks and Julia Roberts; phone (617) 495-5205.

Two area theaters present long-running shows. The **Charles Playhouse**, 74 Warrenton St. (between Charles and Tremont streets), presents the SAVE **Blue Man Group** and "Shear Madness," a comic murder mystery that differs every time it is presented. The elaborate illusions of **Le Grand David and His Own Spectacular Magic Company** unfold on two stages in Beverly: the **Cabot Street Cinema Theater**, 286 Cabot St., and the **Larcom Theater**, 13 Wallis St. Both theaters are about a 30-minute drive northeast of downtown Boston; phone (978) 927-3677 for the Cabot Street Cinema Theater or (978) 922-6313 for the Larcom Theater.

Special Events

Boston bases many of its annual celebrations on past events that shaped the character of the city as well as the nation. **St. Patrick's Day** on March 17 celebrates not only Boston's Irish heritage but also Evacuation Day, when the British troops left the city in 1776. The parade begins at the Broadway "T" station in South Boston. **Patriot's Day**, the third Monday in April, celebrates the American Revolution's beginning with the hanging of lanterns in Old North Church and a re-enactment of Paul Revere's midnight ride to Concord.

The **Battle of Bunker Hill Celebration** is held on the anniversary of that June 17, 1775, battle. **Boston Harborfest**, a weeklong Fourth of July celebration, commemorates the birth of the nation with a turnaround ceremony for the historic USS

Constitution, which is physically turned around in the Charlestown Navy Yard to ensure equal weathering. A Boston Pops Orchestra concert at the Hatch Shell, on the Charles River Esplanade, is complemented by a rousing fireworks display. Other events include the opening ceremonies at Faneuil Hall Marketplace, an Independence Day oration and parade, and a chowderfest on City Hall Plaza. At Old South Meeting House the **Boston Tea Party** is re-enacted by costumed patriots in mid-December.

Boston also is known for sports competition of impressive proportions. The **Boston Marathon**, the city's signature event, attracts top long-distance runners (and wheelchair participants) from around the world. Held the third Monday in April, the race begins in the town of Hopkinton and ends before thousands of spectators at Copley Square. Female runners pound the pavement around downtown Boston during the **Tufts 10K** on Columbus Day. **Head of the Charles Regatta**, an internationally contested sculling event, draws hundreds of thousands of spectators to the banks of the Charles River on the third weekend in October.

The city salutes its ethnic heritage in June along the Charles River with the **Hong Kong Dragon Boat Festival of Boston**, said to be the largest Asian-American celebration in New England. Every weekend from June through August a procession of **Italian Feast Days** takes place in the North End neighborhood. Sponsored by the St. Agrippina, St. Anthony, St. Rocco and St. Joseph societies, these lively fetes include solemn religious services but also high-stepping brass bands, dancing, games and plenty of Italian food.

The **Bells of New England**, a handbell festival, takes place in November at Faneuil Hall. The **Annual Boston Common Lighting** rings in the yuletide season in traditional style with the lighting of a Christmas tree in the heart of downtown. **First Night Boston** ushers in the new year with parades, ice sculpting, and indoor and outdoor concerts, capped off by a spectacular explosion of fireworks over the harbor at midnight.

The Boston Vicinity

ACTON (D-1)

Middlesex West Chamber of Commerce: 77 Great Rd., Suite 214, Acton, MA 01720. **Phone:** (978) 263-0010.

SAVE **THE DISCOVERY MUSEUMS,** 177 Main St., comprises two museums. Geared toward toddlers and pre-kindergartners, the creative exhibits in The Children's Discovery Museum are based on the theory that early childhood learning happens through play. The Science Discovery Museum, for those in kindergarten through eighth grade, houses three floors of hands-on exhibits that encourage children to experiment, problem solve and explore.

Hours: The Children's Discovery Museum daily 9-4:30, in summer; Tues.-Sun. 9-3, during the school year. The Science Discovery Museum daily 10-4:30, in summer; Tues.-Fri. 1-4:30, Sat.-Sun. 10-4:30, during the school year. Schedules vary in Sept.; phone ahead. **Cost:** Single museum $9; $8 (senior citizens). Both museums (same day) $13; $12 (senior citizens). **Phone:** (978) 264-4200 or TTY (978) 264-0030.

AMESBURY (A-6) pop. 12,327, elev. 26'

Settled in the 1640s and incorporated in 1668, Amesbury began as a farming community; however, the town's proximity to the Powow River allowed residents to investigate other trades. The waterway's torrents powered the village's first sawmills; in turn, the success of the local lumber business helped to develop Amesbury into an important shipbuilding center. By the mid-1800s, the city had evolved into an industrial leader, turning out everything from textiles to bricks to machine-made nails. Though Amesbury was then well-known for manufacturing quality carriages, one of its other claims to fame was the Merrimac Hat Co., a major mass producer of trimmed hats and hat bodies.

Reminders of the past are apparent throughout the locale. In the Salisbury Point and Ferry districts, you'll notice a concentration of Georgian and Federal-style dwellings, while Greek Revival and Italianate styles of architecture are apparent in neighborhoods abutting the Powow River falls. If the weather is obliging, rent a boat or a Jet Ski and explore the Merrimack River. Along its banks are the old Merrimac Hat Co. buildings, converted into condominiums in 2000. Though they no longer house soft felt fedoras or brimless beanies, from the outside, the brick structures look much as they did when the plant operated from the mid-1850s to the early 1970s. Fishing and swimming are allowed on the waterway—which starts in Franklin, N.H., and ends in Newburyport *(see place listing p. 151)*— with public boat access and a number of marinas on Merrimack Street.

At the core of the city's industrial heritage, the vital Powow River today boasts the Riverwalk, a multipurpose trail affording picturesque views along the former Boston & Maine Railroad bed. Whether you choose to walk, bicycle or inline skate on the path, be sure to stop and take a look around. The area is frequented by such wildlife as painted turtles, ospreys and minks and is thriving with flora, including lady's slippers, marsh marigolds and black gum trees. Free parking is available at both ends of the scenic corridor, which extends south from downtown Amesbury—where you can stroll a waterfront historic district encompassing many of the community's erstwhile mill sites—to the Carriagetown Marketplace off SR 110.

In 1872 townspeople constructed a dam on the Powow River to exploit the muscle of this natural resource, thereby forming 80-acre Lake Gardner. For Amesbury's modern-day residents, the recreational opportunities afforded by this man-made body of water are key. In summer bring your swimsuit; an automobile entrance to the Lake Gardner beach area is on High Street. Or, drivers can take South Hampton Road to Battis Farm, which is part of the Powow River Conservation Area. Bordering the eastern edge of the lake, the conservation area offers numerous foot trails. From the southern end of Lake Gardner, hike north and traverse a 75-foot-long elevated boardwalk to access the Stage Coach Trail. Paths branching off to the east take you to Powow Hill, the highest point in the county. From this vantage point, to the northeast, you'll see New Hampshire's seacoast region and the southern tip of Maine; face south to sneak a peek at charming Ipswich *(see place listing p. 146)*.

Before a day spent enjoying Amesbury's outdoor retreats, head to nearby Cider Hill Farm on Fern Avenue to pick your own fresh fruits and vegetables. The 145-acre farm is less than a mile north of the junction of South Hampton Road and Market Street (SR 150). Their season begins in early June, when you can nosh on plump strawberries (usually available at the farm through July 4, though the best picking time is in mid-June). Or, sample peaches, plums and nectarines between late July and early October. Of course, if you're visiting Massachusetts in late summer or in the fall, you simply *must* experience the joy of apple picking. More than 50 varieties of the fruit are grown in Cider Hill's orchard. Their apple-picking season starts in mid-August and typically ends sometime in November; phone (978) 388-5525.

Amesbury Chamber of Commerce & Industrial Foundation: 5 Market Sq., Amesbury, MA 01913. **Phone:** (978) 388-3178.

JOHN GREENLEAF WHITTIER HOME, 86 Friend St., was the 1836-92 home of the abolitionist and author, whose works included "Snow-Bound" and "The Barefoot Boy." The house remains almost unchanged and contains original furnishings, portraits, engravings, manuscripts and a large portion of Whittier's library. **Hours:** Wed. and Sat. noon-4 or by appointment, early May-Oct. 31. Last tour begins 30 minutes before closing. Closed July 4. **Cost:** $6; $5 (senior citizens); $3 (ages 7-17). **Phone:** (978) 388-1337 or (978) 388-9826.

RECREATIONAL ACTIVITIES
Tubing

* **Amesbury Sports Park** is at 12 Hunt Rd. **Hours:** Tubing is offered daily, Dec.-Mar. (weather permitting). Hours vary; phone ahead. Other activities are offered year-round. **Phone:** (978) 388-5788.

ANDOVER (A-6) pop. 7,900, elev. 89′

ADDISON GALLERY OF AMERICAN ART, off SR 28 on Chapel Ave. at Phillips Academy, contains a collection of ship models and more than 13,000 pieces of American artwork from the 18th century to the present. Rotating special exhibitions also are displayed. **Note:** The gallery is closed for renovations; reopening is scheduled for spring 2010. Phone ahead for updates and to confirm schedule. **Time:** Allow 30 minutes minimum. **Hours:** Tues.-Sat. 10-5, Sun. 1-5, Sept.-July. Closed major holidays. **Cost:** Free. **Phone:** (978) 749-4015.

ANDOVER HISTORICAL SOCIETY is at 97 Main St. The Amos Blanchard House museum features 19th-century period rooms, changing exhibits about local history, a garden and an 1819 barn. Visitors can delve further into Andover's history in The Caroline M. Underhill Research Center. Guided tours are available by request. **Time:** Allow 1 hour minimum. **Hours:** Research center Tues.-Sat. 10-4. Closed major holidays. **Cost:** Donations. **Phone:** (978) 475-2236.

ROBERT S. PEABODY MUSEUM OF ARCHAEOLOGY, 175 Main St. on the Phillips Academy campus, has changing and permanent exhibits about cultures indigenous to the Americas. **Hours:** Mon.-Fri. 8-5 by appointment. Closed major holidays. **Cost:** Free. **Phone:** (978) 749-4490.

ARLINGTON (E-2) pop. 42,389, elev. 46′

The most significant event in Arlington's history occurred April 19, 1775, when British troops retreating from Concord and Lexington met minutemen from at least 13 towns in several separate skirmishes. By the close of the day the British counted 40 men killed and 80 wounded, while the Americans lost at least 25, with 10 wounded and three captured.

The town's first industry, cotton manufacturing, began in the late 18th century. Wool cards, invented by resident Amos Whittemore, greatly improved the process of textile production. In the 1830s Gage, Hittinger Co. began cutting ice from Spy Pond and selling it to tropical countries, thus establishing a new industry. At the turn of the 20th century, when Boston's trolley line reached Arlington's boundaries, the town became a suburb of Boston.

Jason Russell House and George Abbot Smith History Museum, 7 Jason St., was the scene of fierce hand-to-hand combat between British soldiers and minutemen during the battle of April 19, 1775. The 1740 house contains 17th- and 18th-century furniture and artifacts. The adjacent Smith Museum features an exhibit about Arlington history. The buildings are open on weekends, mid-April through October 31; phone (781) 648-4300.

Old Schwamb Mill, 17 Mill Ln., is a living-history museum exhibiting a working collection of shaft- and pulley belt-driven antique woodworking machinery. Visitors can tour the mill and see demonstrations of elliptical machinery and oval picture frame turning on Tuesdays and Saturdays; phone (781) 643-0554.

Originally an abandoned railroad line, the Minuteman Bikeway is popular with cyclists in summer and cross-country skiers in winter. The 11-mile trail begins in Cambridge at the Alewife "T" station and continues through Arlington, Lexington and Bedford.

Arlington Chamber of Commerce: 1 Whittemore Park, Arlington, MA 02474. **Phone:** (781) 643-4600.

JEFFERSON CUTTER HOUSE, at jct. US 3 and SRs 60 (Pleasant St.) and 2A (Massachusetts Ave.), is a restored 1830 home featuring displays about area history. Five galleries presenting the works of sculptor Cyrus E. Dallin as well as works by local contemporary artists are featured in the Cyrus E. Dallin Art Museum. The chamber of commerce also is on-site. **Hours:** Museum Tues.-Sun. noon-4. Closed major holidays. Phone ahead to confirm schedule. **Cost:** Donations. **Phone:** (781) 641-0747.

BEVERLY (B-7) pop. 39,862, elev. 23′

Founded in 1626 as an extension of Salem, Beverly was named after a town in Yorkshire, England. In 1775 the local schooner *Hannah* was commissioned and armed by Gen. George Washington as the first ship in his Continental Navy. Beverly remained an important port during the first 2 years of the Revolutionary War.

Beverly Chamber of Commerce: 28 Cabot St., Beverly, MA 01915. **Phone:** (978) 232-9559.

BEVERLY HISTORICAL SOCIETY AND MUSEUM, 117 Cabot St., is an umbrella organization managing three local historic homes: Balch House, Cabot House and Hale Farm. **Phone:** (978) 922-1186.

Balch House, 448 Cabot St., stands on part of a land grant given to the "Old Planters" in 1635. Occupied by the Balch family until 1914, this 1677-79 frame house is one of the oldest in the country. Rooms are furnished in period. **Hours:** Guided tours are given Tues.-Sat. noon-4, mid-May to mid-Oct. Closed major holidays. **Cost:** $5; $4 (students with ID and senior citizens); free (ages 0-15). **Phone:** (978) 922-1186.

Cabot House, 117 Cabot St., was built in 1781 for John Cabot, a merchant and Revolutionary War privateer. The brick mansion was home to the Cabot family, said to be the wealthiest in New England in 1780, and later housed a bank. Now home to the Beverly Historical Society, it contains period rooms and exhibits detailing the history of the town, the Beverly Bank and the American Revolution. A research library is available.

Time: Allow 30 minutes minimum. **Hours:** Guided tours are given Thurs.-Sat. and Tues. 10-4, Wed. 1-9. Research library open Tues. and Sat. 10-4, Wed. 1-9. Closed major holidays. **Cost:** House $5; $4 (students with ID and senior citizens); free (ages 0-15). Research library $5 (per hour). **Phone:** (978) 922-1186.

LONG HILL RESERVATION, THE SEDGWICK GARDENS is off SR 128N exit 18, then 1.5 mi. n. on SR 22 to 572 Essex St. This was the summer estate of Ellery and Mabel Sedgwick, who built it in 1925 and modeled it after a Charleston home of the early 1800s. In the house the Sedgwick Gardens Library has an extensive collection of periodicals and books.

Five acres of cultivated grounds and formal gardens have more than 1,000 native species of plants, many of them unusual. Lectures and workshops are offered; phone ahead for schedule and fees. **Tours:** Guided tours are available. **Hours:** Grounds and gardens daily dawn-dusk. Horticultural library by appointment. **Cost:** Free. **Phone:** (978) 921-1944.

BRAINTREE (F-2) pop. 33,698, elev. 90'

GEN. SYLVANUS THAYER BIRTHPLACE is at 31 Tenney Rd. The site includes the 1720 house, furnished in period style, where Gen. Sylvanus Thayer was born in 1785; Thayer is known as "the father of West Point." Displayed within the original saltbox home are period antiques. Also on the property is the Gilbert Bean Museum with three exhibits. **Hours:** House tours are given Wed.-Fri. 1-3, Sat. 10-4. Museum open Thurs.-Sat. 10-4. **Cost:** (includes museum) $5; $3 (ages 0-14). **Phone:** (781) 848-1640.

BROOKLINE (E-2) pop. 57,107, elev. 43'

Brookline Chamber of Commerce: 251 Harvard St., Suite 1, Brookline, MA 02446. **Phone:** (617) 739-1330.

JOHN FITZGERALD KENNEDY NATIONAL HISTORIC SITE, 83 Beals St., preserves the birthplace and boyhood home of the 35th president of the United States. The house, restored to its 1917 appearance by family matriarch Rose Kennedy in 1967, contains original furnishings and family memorabilia. **Hours:** Guided tours of the house are given Wed.-Sun. 10-3, May-Sept. Self-guiding tours (available in several languages) are available 3:30-4:30. Phone ahead to confirm schedule. **Cost:** $3; free (ages 0-17). **Phone:** (617) 566-7937.

[SAVE] **LARZ ANDERSON AUTO MUSEUM** is at 15 Newton St. in Larz Anderson Park overlooking Boston. Located in a historic carriage house, the museum features changing exhibits that focus on the social impact of the automobile. Outdoor car shows are held on some Saturdays and most Sundays May through October. A children's activity room is available. Guided tours are available by appointment. **Hours:** Tues.-Sun. 10-4. Closed Jan. 1, July 4, Thanksgiving and Dec. 25 and 31. **Cost:** $10; $5 (ages 6-12, ages 66+ and students with ID). **Phone:** (617) 522-6547.

CAMBRIDGE (E-2) pop. 101,355, elev. 48'

See map page 138.

Take the short trek from Boston to Cambridge—"Boston's Left Bank"—and you'll notice evidence of a college town before you even arrive. Harvard University's school color, crimson, is reflected in the *Red* Line subway running into the city. As you cross over the Charles River, look for the bright, dutifully maintained markings along the 364.4-smoot-plus-an-ear-long Harvard Bridge; in 1958, 5-foot-7-inch fraternity pledge Oliver R. *Smoot* served as measuring stick. Scholars attracted by educational goliaths Harvard—the country's first college, founded in 1636—and the Massachusetts Institute of Technology also leave their indelible imprints worldwide. Authors Ralph Waldo Emerson and Michael Crichton as well as Presidents Theodore Roosevelt and John F. Kennedy are among Harvard's graduates, while MIT boasts more than 20 Nobel Prize-winning alumni.

Ranging from free-spirited artistic savants to Quadratic formula-loving bookworms, nearly 30,000 people attend school here each year. Leave Cambridge's substantial student population out and you've still got a rather zesty melting pot. In Cambridge you'll likely see punk rockers browsing CDs beside jocks dressed in sneakers and sweats; baby boomers sampling ethnic delicacies at a sidewalk fair; and spectacled, iPod-wearing professors biking to and from the city's many academic campuses.

Like Boston, Cambridge encompasses a variety of individual districts, including Kendall Square, the home of MIT and the hub of the city's technology industry. Visit a few of MIT's museums (*see individual attraction listings*), then head to neighboring Central Square for dinner and take your pick among the Ethiopian, Indian, Italian and Thai restaurants clustered there. Passing through the Cambridgeport, Central Square and Kendall Square neighborhoods every August is the Cambridge Carnival parade. Celebrating African and Caribbean traditions, the flamboyant event also features musical performances and family activities.

In the Alewife district outdoor enthusiasts hike and enjoy bird-watching at Alewife Brook Reservation, a 120-acre urban wilderness. Nearby at the Alewife "T" station, cyclists and inline skaters (and, in winter, cross-country skiers) can access the Minuteman Bikeway, an 11-mile trail stretching through

Cambridge, Arlington, Lexington and Bedford. Recreational activities, including bicycling and jogging, also can be enjoyed along the banks of the Charles River *(see Charles River Reservation p. 106)* and at the Fresh Pond Reservation. Located in northwest Cambridge, Fresh Pond also offers a nine-hole golf course at 691 Huron Ave.; phone (617) 349-6282.

Of course, the epicenter of Cambridge is Harvard Square, crowded with bookstores and hip clothing boutiques *(see Boston Shopping p. 125)*, historic gems, and intimate bistros and lively coffee houses *(see Boston Nightlife p. 128)*. Frequent special events—including MayFair, Bastille Day (in July) and Oktoberfest—add to the hubbub of this popular scene, while street performers entertain crowds of shoppers, tourists and preoccupied undergrads anytime the weather is agreeable. After enjoying the outdoor shows put on by commanding cello players and comical jugglers, take in a production of the American Repertory Theatre, 64 Brattle St., (617) 547-8300, or the José Mateo Ballet Theatre, 400 Harvard St., (617) 354-7467. In addition Harvard's various cultural venues feature everything from opera to Shakespeare; phone (617) 496-2222 for the Office for the Arts at Harvard box office.

Cambridge Office for Tourism: 4 Brattle St., #208, Cambridge, MA 02138. **Phone:** (617) 441-2884 or (800) 862-5678.

Self-guiding tours: Maps of Old Cambridge, which include historic sites in and around Harvard Square, are available for $2.50 from the information booth in Harvard Square. Contact the Cambridge Office for Tourism for more information.

Shopping areas: The CambridgeSide Galleria, 100 CambridgeSide Pl., is anchored by Macy's and Sears. Nearby is Lechmere Canal Park, where shoppers can stroll along a lagoon. Free shuttle buses run to the galleria from the Kendall/MIT "T" station on the Red Line.

CHARLES RIVERBOAT CO. departs from Canal Park at the CambridgeSide Galleria, 100 CambridgeSide Pl. Narrated sightseeing cruises take visitors past historic Boston and Cambridge sites. During the Charles River Tour, the Massachusetts Institute of Technology as well as Harvard and Boston universities can be seen during the 60-minute trip. The Old North Church, USS *Constitution* and Bunker Hill Monument are highlights of the 75-minute Boston Harbor & Locks Tour. A sunset cruise also is offered from June to August.

Time: Allow 1 hour minimum. **Hours:** Charles River Tour cruises depart daily at 11:30, 12:45, 2, 3:15 and 4:30, May-Oct. (weather permitting). Boston Harbor & Locks Tour cruises depart daily at 10, June-Aug. (weather permitting). **Cost:** $14; $11 (senior citizens); $7 (ages 0-9). **Phone:** (617) 621-3001. 🍴

HARVARD UNIVERSITY is at jct. Massachusetts Ave. and Cambridge St.; an information center is on the ground floor of the Holyoke Center at 1350 Massachusetts Ave. (T: Harvard Square). Founded in 1636, Harvard is the oldest institution of higher learning in the country.

In and around the historic "Yard" at Harvard Square, buildings represent the history of architecture in America. They range from Colonial-style Massachusetts Hall, built in 1720; the 19th-century work of Charles Bulfinch; University Hall; Henry Hobson Richardson's late 19th-century Sever Hall; and the contemporary style of Le Corbusier's Carpenter Center for the Visual Arts.

Guided tours of the historic campus depart from the information center. **Hours:** Tours are given Mon.-Sat. at 10, 11:15, 2 and 3:15, late June to mid-Aug.; Mon.-Fri. at 10 and 2, Sat. at 2, mid-Sept. to mid-May. Phone to confirm summer tour times. **Cost:** Free. **Phone:** (617) 495-1573.

Arthur M. Sackler Museum, 485 Broadway at Quincy St., contains Harvard's collections of Asian, Islamic, later Indian and ancient art. Holdings include one of the world's finest collections of ancient Chinese jades, ceramics and bronzes as well as Japanese woodblock prints, Roman sculpture, Greek vases and Indian miniature paintings. Also displayed are highlights of the Fogg Art Museum and the Busch-Reisinger Museum, both of which are closed for renovations until 2013.

Hours: Mon.-Sat. 10-5, Sun. 1-5. Guided tours are given Mon.-Fri. at 12:15 and 2. Closed major holidays. **Cost:** $9; $7 (ages 65+); $6 (college students with ID); free (ages 0-17 and to all Sat. 10-noon). **Phone:** (617) 495-9400.

Carpenter Center for the Visual Arts, 24 Quincy St., is the only building in North America designed by European architect Le Corbusier. The center exhibits contemporary art and video installations in the Main and Sert galleries. Also housed in the building are the Department of Visual and Environmental Studies and the Harvard Film Archive, which has weekly screenings. **Hours:** Main Gallery Mon.-Sat. 9 a.m.-11 p.m., Sun. noon-11. Sert Gallery Tues.-Sun. 1-5. **Cost:** Galleries free. Film archives $8; $6 (students with ID and senior citizens). **Phone:** (617) 495-3251.

Harvard Museum of Natural History, 26 Oxford St., exhibits 12,000 specimens from the university's vast collections. Included are dinosaur fossils, meteorites, gemstones and hundreds of mounted animal displays of species from around the world.

Between 1886 and 1936 father-and-son glass artists Leopold and Rudolph Blaschka created the Ware Collection of Glass Flowers, which showcases 3,000 amazingly realistic models of plants, fruits and flowers. Visitors also can observe live dart frogs in Language of Color. Other museum highlights include a 42-foot-long mounted kronosaurus, a 1,600-pound amethyst geode and three whale skeletons.

Hours: Daily 9-5. Closed Jan. 1, Thanksgiving and Dec. 24-25. **Cost:** (includes Peabody Museum of Archaeology and Ethnology) $9; $7 (ages 65+ and college students with ID); $6 (ages 3-18); free (ages 0-2 and Massachusetts residents Sun. 9-noon). **Phone:** (617) 495-3045. *See color ad p. 107.*

SAVE **Peabody Museum of Archaeology and Ethnology** is at 11 Divinity Ave. The museum is
one of the oldest of its kind in the world. Important
acquisitions of cultural history include North American Indian and Maya arts and artifacts as well as the
Lewis and Clark Indian collection. A small but important selection of paintings, prints, drawings and
more than 500,000 photographs also is housed
within the museum's archives.

Time: Allow 2 hours minimum. **Hours:** Daily
9-5. Closed Jan. 1, Thanksgiving and Dec. 24-25.
Cost: (includes Harvard Museum of Natural History) $9; $7 (ages 65+ and college students with
ID); $6 (ages 3-18); free (ages 0-2 and Massachu-
setts residents Sun. 9-noon). **Phone:** (617)
496-1027.

Semitic Museum is at 6 Divinity Ave. Houses of
Ancient Israel: Domestic, Royal and Divine displays

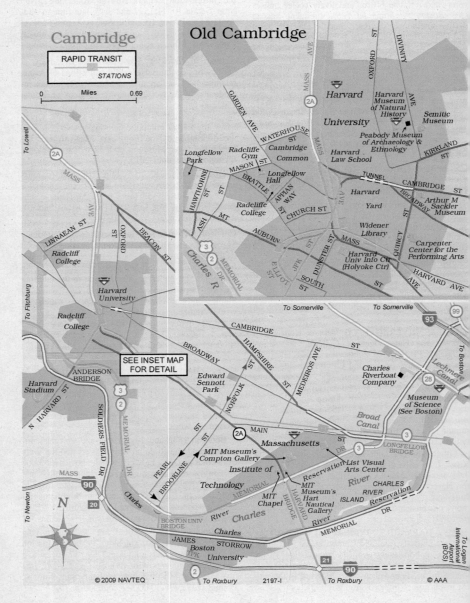

a replica of a 700 B.C.E. Israelite house with artifacts and a view of Solomon's temple. Nuzi and the Hurrians reflects everyday life in a Mesopotamian city around 1350 B.C.E. Coffins, amulets and funerary inscriptions introduce visitors to the Egyptian view of life after death in Ancient Egypt: Magic and the Afterlife. Ancient Cyprus exhibits artifacts from 2500 B.C.E. to 700 C.E. **Time:** Allow 30 minutes minimum. **Hours:** Mon.-Fri. 10-4, Sun. 1-4. Closed major holidays. **Cost:** Free. **Phone:** (617) 495-4631.

MASSACHUSETTS INSTITUTE OF TECHNOLOGY is on the n. shore of the Charles River Basin, with its main building at 77 Massachusetts Ave. (T: Central Square or Kendall/MIT). The institute was founded by William Barton Rogers as a school where students could learn "exactly and thoroughly the fundamental principles of positive science with application to the industrial arts." It was chartered in 1861, but classes did not start until 1865 due to the Civil War. It moved to this site in 1916.

The institute comprises the schools of Architecture and Planning; Engineering; Humanities, Arts and Social Sciences; and Science as well as the Sloan School of Management and the Whitaker College of Health Sciences and Technology. The institute's 135-acre campus extends more than a mile along the Charles River Basin. Ninety-minute guided tours of the campus leave from the Information Center in the lobby of MIT's main building. **Hours:** MIT information center Mon.-Fri. 9-5. Campus tours are given Mon.-Fri. at 11 and 3. Closed major holidays. **Cost:** Free. **Phone:** (617) 253-4795 for the information center.

List Visual Arts Center, in the Wiesner Building at 20 Ames St., presents five to seven shows displaying the works of new and established contemporary artists. Public artworks by such artists as Alexander Calder and Henry Moore are exhibited throughout the MIT campus. **Hours:** Tues.-Sun. noon-6 (also Thurs. 6-8 p.m.). Closed major holidays. **Cost:** Free. **Phone:** (617) 253-4680.

MIT Chapel is on the west campus at 48 Massachusetts Ave. Noted architect Eero Saarinen designed the cylindrical brick structure; the aluminum bell tower is by sculptor Theodore Roszak. A shallow moat surrounds the windowless building, and the bottom of the cylinder is penetrated by irregular arches through which light reflected from the moat plays on the interior walls.

One-hour concerts featuring everything from Renaissance to contemporary music are offered some months. **Hours:** Chapel daily dawn-dusk. Concerts are given Thurs. at noon, Feb.-Mar. and Oct.-Nov. Closed holidays and during spring break. **Cost:** Chapel and concerts free. **Phone:** (617) 253-3913, or (617) 253-2826 for concert information.

MIT Museum is at 265 Massachusetts Ave. The Mark Epstein Innovation Gallery features changing displays about both current and past MIT research. Holography: The Light Fantastic showcases 23 pieces from the museum's extensive hologram collection, which is said to be the world's largest. Through interactive displays, interviews with designers, and robotic relics, Robots and Beyond: Exploring Artificial Intelligence at MIT offers visitors a behind-the-scenes look at the branch of computer science.

Time: Allow 1 hour, 30 minutes minimum. **Hours:** Daily 10-5. Closed major holidays. **Cost:** $7.50: $3 (ages 5-18, ages 61+ and students with ID); free (ages 0-4, MIT ID holders and to all Sun. 10-noon). **Phone:** (617) 253-5927.

MIT Museum's Compton Gallery is in Building 10-150 at 77 Massachusetts Ave. This small, intimate gallery contains changing exhibits that reflect the institute's programs and activities. **Hours:** Daily 10-5. Closed major holidays. **Cost:** Free. **Phone:** (617) 253-5927.

MIT Museum's Hart Nautical Gallery, in Building 5 at 55 Massachusetts Ave., traces the development of naval architecture and marine engineering through exhibits of ship models and marine robotics. **Hours:** Daily 10-5. Closed major holidays. **Cost:** Free. **Phone:** (617) 253-5927.

MOUNT AUBURN CEMETERY, 580 Mount Auburn St., is purportedly the nation's first landscaped cemetery. Founded in 1831, it contains the graves of Mary Baker Eddy, founder of the Church of Christ, Scientist; poets Oliver Wendell Holmes and Henry Wadsworth Longfellow; abolitionist and author Julia Ward Howe; and architect and inventor Buckminster Fuller. It also features an arboretum and outdoor sculptures. Audiotapes describing self-guiding driving and walking tours are available. **Hours:** Daily 8-7, May-Aug.; 8-5, rest of year. Phone ahead to confirm schedule. **Cost:** Free. **Phone:** (617) 547-7105.

OLD CAMBRIDGE encompasses several blocks in and around the perimeter of Harvard Square (T: Harvard Square). The original town plan and many early structures reflect Cambridge's history—Christ Church, built in 1761 and said to be the oldest church building in the city; the 1753 Waterhouse House; and Harvard University, formerly Newtowne College, founded in 1636.

Another major concentration of historic buildings is along Brattle Street, just east of Harvard Square. The most well-known mansion on the street is the Georgian-style Longfellow House, home of poet Henry Wadsworth Longfellow and headquarters for Gen. George Washington, commander in chief of the Continental Army during the Revolutionary War. **Hours:** Visitor information booth Mon.-Fri. 9-5, Sat.-Sun. 9-1. **Phone:** (617) 497-1630.

UNOFFICIAL TOURS: THE ULTIMATE HARVARD EXPERIENCE departs from Harvard Square near the information kiosk (T: Harvard Square). Acting as guides, highly knowledgeable Harvard students take visitors on a tour of the Ivy League university's campus. Historical tidbits, entertaining

Harvard lore and details about student life are revealed during the spirited 70-minute excursions. **Time:** Allow 1 hour, 15 minutes minimum. **Hours:** Tours depart Fri.-Mon. at 10:45, 11:30 and 12:30 (also Sat.-Sun. at 1:30). Hours may vary. **Cost:** Donations. Reservations are required. **Phone:** (617) 674-7788.

CANTON (C-6) elev. 115'

MASS AUDUBON VISUAL ARTS CENTER is at 963 Washington St. Highlighting artwork inspired by nature, the gallery offers changing exhibitions of internationally known painters, photographers and sculptors. Surrounding the arts center, the Mildred Morse Allen Wildlife Sanctuary features a nature trail that leads hikers through a meadow, a forest and a red maple swamp. Red-tailed hawks nest in the sanctuary in spring and summer, while coyotes, deer and foxes make their home here in winter.

Educational programs, including scavenger hunts, are available. **Time:** Allow 1 hour minimum. **Hours:** Arts center Tues.-Sun. 1-5. Trail Tues.-Sun. 9-5. Closed Jan. 1, Thanksgiving and Dec. 25. **Cost:** $4; $3 (ages 3-12 and 67+). **Phone:** (781) 821-8853. 🎫

CAPE ANN (A-8)

At the end of SR 128, Cape Ann consists of Gloucester and Rockport *(see place listings p. 142 and p. 154, respectively).* These communities are separated from the mainland by the tidal Annisquam River. Cape Ann also generally is considered to include the neighboring Essex *(see place listing p. 142)* and Manchester-by-the-Sea. Explored by Norsemen in the 11th century, the area first was settled in 1623 by Englishmen hoping to sell fish to Europe.

DID YOU KNOW

Boston Common is the oldest public park in the country.

CHESTNUT HILL (E-2) elev. 197'

Shopping areas: The Mall at Chestnut Hill, 199 Boylston St., contains Bloomingdale's and numerous specialty shops, including Ann Taylor and Kate Spade.

LONGYEAR MUSEUM, 1125 Boylston St., displays historic artifacts documenting the life of Mary Baker Eddy, discoverer of Christian Science and founder of the Church of Christ, Scientist. Three galleries contain a collection of photographs, documents, artifacts, furniture and portraits. A 12-minute introductory film, audio tours, an interactive computer learning station, a research library and an outdoor exhibit also are included.

Time: Allow 1 hour minimum. **Hours:** Wed.-Sat. and Mon. 10-4, Sun. 1-4. Guided tours with tea are given Mon. at 2. Closed major holidays. **Cost:** Museum free. Guided tour $8. Reservations are required for tours. **Phone:** (617) 278-9000. 🍽

COHASSET (F-3) elev. 24'

Capt. John Smith is said to have landed in Cohasset in 1614. For nearly 2 centuries the town was a fishing and farming community. Many residents now commute to work in Boston, and the town's bayside location attracts summer tourists.

About 2.5 miles offshore is Minot's Light; the 114-foot-tall granite tower was built in 1860 to replace the original iron structure, destroyed in a storm. Moore's Rocks Reservation on Jerusalem Road provides a good view of the bay and light. Elm Street was known as "Ship Cove Lane" because it led to the shipyards and landing sites at Cohasset Harbor. It also was the street on which most of the shipbuilders and sea captains lived.

The Capt. John Wilson House, built in 1810, is restored and furnished in period. Once a ship chandlery, Cohasset Maritime Museum contains model ships, nautical items, navigational equipment, American Indian artifacts and a display depicting the building of Minot's Light. For information about either attraction phone the Cohasset Historical Society at (781) 383-1434.

Cohasset Chamber of Commerce: P.O. Box 336, Cohasset, MA 02025. **Phone:** (781) 383-1010.

CONCORD (E-1) elev. 130'

Concord was a driving force behind Massachusetts' sudden literary renaissance in the 19th century. Ralph Waldo Emerson pursued the soul's relation to the infinite in his essays, poems and journals, and his friend and neighbor, Henry David Thoreau, wrote about the more finite world of nearby Walden Pond. Louisa May Alcott wrote "Little Women" about her childhood in Concord, and her father, Bronson Alcott, conducted his School of Philosophy, bringing together the leaders of American thought.

Joining these local writers was sculptor Daniel Chester French, who created his first, and probably most renowned sculpture—except for the Lincoln Memorial—"The Minute Man." More practical pursuits led Ephraim Bull to cultivate the Concord grape, which was the start of commercial production of table grapes in this country.

Concord maintains a stately New England elegance with its many fine homes and historic sites. As an alternative to a walking tour visitors can rent a canoe from the South Bridge boathouse on the Sudbury River on SR 62. The banks of the river, which feature a canopy of branches and gracious hillside houses, remain much as they were in the 1700s.

Concord is accessible by two scenic highways: SR 119, which travels northwest toward New Hampshire, and Lexington Road (SR 2A), which passes through Minute Man National Historical Park *(see place listing p. 150)* en route to Lexington.

Concord Guides Walking Tours offers 2-hour historical walking tours of Concord. The tours, conducted on weekends mid-April to November 1 (weather permitting), are led by licensed, local guides who discuss the area's American Indian, Colonial and Revolutionary past as well as its literary, natural and social heritage. Reservations are required; phone (978) 287-0897.

Concord Chamber of Commerce: 15 Walden St., Suite 7, Concord, MA 01742. **Phone:** (978) 369-3120.

CONCORD ART ASSOCIATION is at 37 Lexington Rd. The 1760 house features an Underground Railroad entrance, a sculpture garden with a waterfall, and exhibits relating to Concord. **Hours:** Tues.-Sat. 10-4:30, Sun. noon-4. Closed major holidays. **Cost:** Free. **Phone:** (978) 369-2578.

CONCORD MUSEUM, at jct. Cambridge Tpke. and Lexington Rd., contains 13 historical and decorative arts galleries, five period rooms, audio presentations and hands-on activities for adults and children. The introductory film "Exploring Concord" provides a historical overview. Of particular interest are the lantern from Paul Revere's famous ride; the contents of Ralph Waldo Emerson's study, arranged as they were in 1882; and a large collection of Henry David Thoreau's possessions, including the bed, desk and chair from Walden Pond.

Time: Allow 1 hour minimum. **Hours:** Daily 9-5, June-Aug.; Mon.-Sat. 9-5, Sun. noon-5, Apr.-May and Sept.-Dec.; Mon.-Sat. 11-4, Sun. 1-4, rest of year. Closed Easter, Thanksgiving and Dec. 25. **Cost:** $10; $8 (ages 62+ and students with ID); $5 (ages 6-18). An additional fee may be charged during special exhibitions. **Phone:** (978) 369-9763, or (978) 369-9609 for recorded information.

EMERSON HOUSE, 28 Cambridge Tpke., was the home of Ralph Waldo Emerson from 1835 until his death in 1882. The house contains original furnishings and Emerson memorabilia. **Time:** Allow 30 minutes minimum. **Hours:** Guided tours are given Thurs.-Sat. 10-4:30, Sun. 1-4:30, mid-Apr. to late

Oct. **Cost:** $8; $6 (ages 7-17 and 62+). **Phone:** (978) 369-2236.

GREAT MEADOWS NATIONAL WILDLIFE REFUGE has two branches. The Concord Unit is 1.3 mi. e. on SR 62, then n. on Monsen Rd. The Sudbury Unit is on Weir Hill Rd. in Sudbury. The refuge includes nature and interpretive trails along the river, wetland and forested upland. Bird-watching at the Concord Unit is excellent during the spring and fall. **Note:** Dogs and bicycles are not permitted at the refuge. **Hours:** Refuge grounds open daily dawn-dusk. Weir Hill headquarters open Mon.-Fri. 8-4. **Cost:** Free. **Phone:** (978) 443-4661.

LOUISA MAY ALCOTT'S ORCHARD HOUSE, 399 Lexington Rd., was the home of Louisa May Alcott and is where she wrote "Little Women." **Hours:** Mon.-Sat. 10-4:30, Sun. 1-4:30, Apr.-Oct.; Mon.-Fri. 11-3, Sat. 10-4:30, Sun. 1-4:30, rest of year. Closed Jan. 1-15, Easter, Thanksgiving and Dec. 25. **Cost:** $9; $8 (ages 62+ and students with ID); $6 (ages 6-17); $25 (family). **Phone:** (978) 369-4118.

MINUTE MAN NATIONAL HISTORICAL PARK— *see place listing p. 150.*

THE OLD MANSE, 269 Monument St. next to the North Bridge, was built in 1770 by the grandfather of Ralph Waldo Emerson, who spent some of his boyhood at the home. Nathaniel Hawthorne lived here 1842-45 and gave the house its name. His "Mosses from an Old Manse" was written in the study. The home contains the original 18th- and 19th-century American furnishings that belonged to the Emerson-Ripley family.

Hours: Guided tours are given Mon.-Sat. 10-5, Sun. and holidays noon-5, mid-Apr. through Oct. 31. Last tour begins 30 minutes before closing. **Cost:** $8; $7 (ages 63+ and students with ID); $5 (ages 6-12); $25 (family). **Phone:** (978) 369-3909.

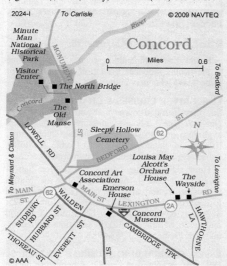

SLEEPY HOLLOW CEMETERY is 1 blk. e. of Monument Square on Bedford St. The cemetery contains the graves of the Alcotts; Ralph Waldo Emerson; Daniel Chester French; Nathaniel Hawthorne, his wife and his daughter; and Henry David Thoreau. **Hours:** Daily 7-dusk. **Cost:** Free. **Phone:** (978) 318-3233.

WALDEN POND STATE RESERVATION, .2 mi. s. on SR 126 at 915 Walden St., consists of 462 acres, including the 102-foot-deep pond of Henry David Thoreau's "Walden." A sign on the north shore marks the site where Thoreau built his cabin in 1845. Fishing, swimming and boating are permitted. *See Recreation Chart.* **Hours:** Grounds daily dawn-dusk. **Cost:** $5 (per private vehicle). **Phone:** (978) 369-3254. 🚻 🚫

DEDHAM (F-2) pop. 23,464, elev. 119′

DEDHAM HISTORICAL SOCIETY, 612 High St., houses a historical and genealogical research library and a history museum that includes Dedham and Chelsea pottery; silver; paintings; artifacts; furniture from the 16th, 17th and 18th centuries; archives; and exhibits. **Hours:** Museum Tues.-Fri. noon-4 and even-dated Sat. 1-4. Library Tues.-Fri. 9-4 and even-dated Sat. 1-4. Archives Tues. and Thurs. noon-4 and even-dated Sat. 1-4. **Cost:** Museum $2; $1 (ages 0-12). Library $5. **Phone:** (781) 326-1385.

FAIRBANKS HOUSE, 511 East St. at Eastern Ave., was built circa 1641 and is said to be the oldest standing timber-frame house in North America. Inhabited by the Fairbanks family until the beginning of the 20th century, the house contains furniture, textiles and other objects that belonged to the family. Guided tours discuss life in New England during the first 3 centuries of European habitation. **Hours:** Guided 45-minute tours are given Tues.-Sat. on the hour 10-5, Sun. 1-5, May-Oct. Last tour begins 1 hour before closing. **Cost:** $5; $2 (ages 6-12). **Phone:** (781) 326-1170.

ESSEX (A-7) pop. 1,426, elev. 26′

Founded as a shipbuilding center, Essex is home to the fishing schooner *Evelina M. Goulart,* one of some 4,000 schooners built in the area.

ESSEX RIVER CRUISES & CHARTERS, 35 Dodge St., offers narrated journeys aboard the *Essex River Queen II.* The 1.5-hour sightseeing excursion offers a glimpse into coastal life, including shipbuilding, fishing and clamming. A 2-hour Coffee & Muffin cruise also is available on Sunday mornings.

Hours: Sightseeing cruises depart Mon.-Sat. at 10:30, 1:30 and 4, May-Oct. Coffee & Muffin cruises depart Sun. at 10:30, May-Oct. Phone ahead to confirm schedule. **Cost:** Sightseeing cruise $25; $22 (ages 65+); $10 (ages 0-12). Coffee & Muffin cruise $26; $12 (ages 0-12). Reservations are recommended. **Phone:** (978) 768-6981.

ESSEX SHIPBUILDING MUSEUM, 66 Main St. (SR 133), is housed in an 1835 schoolhouse on the grounds of the historic A.D. Story shipyard. Featuring antique shipbuilding tools, photographs and documents, the museum also displays artifacts portraying the shipbuilding industry. Tours include a videotape presentation and hands-on activities. **Time:** Allow 1 hour minimum. **Hours:** Wed.-Sun. 10-5, June-Oct.; Sat.-Sun. 10-5, rest of year. Closed major holidays. **Cost:** $7; $6 (ages 61+); $5 (children ages 6+). **Phone:** (978) 768-7541.

FRAMINGHAM (F-1) pop. 66,910, elev. 180′

Settled in 1650, Framingham was named after Gov. Thomas Danforth's English hometown. By 1700 the town had grown to about 70 families. One resident, Crispus Attucks, was killed for inciting a mob against British soldiers March 5, 1770, an incident that later became known as the Boston Massacre. Attucks is considered the first African-American killed in the country's battle for independence.

In 1837 the waterpower of the Sudbury River led to the relocation of a textile company from Lowell to Framingham. Other industries followed. Framingham factories now produce sound systems, electronics, computer software, pharmaceuticals and biomedical products.

MetroWest Chamber of Commerce: 1671 Worcester Rd., Suite 201, Framingham, MA 01701. **Phone:** (508) 879-5600.

[SAVE] **DANFORTH MUSEUM OF ART**, 123 Union Ave., is a fine arts museum with eight galleries, including a children's interactive gallery. Changing exhibits of 19th- and 20th-century American and contemporary art are featured. **Time:** Allow 1 hour minimum. **Hours:** Wed.-Thurs. and Sun. noon-5, Fri.-Sat. 10-5, Sept.-July. Guided tours are offered the first full weekend of the month. Closed major holidays. **Cost:** $10; $8 (ages 65+ and students with ID); free (ages 0-17). **Phone:** (508) 620-0050.

NEW ENGLAND WILD FLOWER SOCIETY— GARDEN IN THE WOODS is 3.7 mi. n. on Union Ave. (becomes Main St. and then Edgell Rd.), .3 mi. e. on Water St., 1 mi. n. on Hemenway Rd. (becomes Eisenhower Rd.), .1 mi. w. on Catherine Rd., then just s. to 180 Hemenway Rd. Garden in the Woods, with the largest landscaped collection of native plants in the region, is an ever-changing 45-acre living museum showcasing more than 1,000 native plant species. Many rare and endangered specimens are displayed throughout the site and also are the highlight of the New England Garden of Rare and Endangered Plants.

Time: Allow 1 hour, 30 minutes minimum. **Hours:** Tues.-Sun. and Mon. holidays 9-5 (also Thurs.-Fri. 5-7, mid-Apr. to early July), mid-Apr. through Oct. 31. Guided tours are given Tues.-Fri. and Mon. holidays at 10, Sat.-Sun. at 2. Last admission 1 hour before closing. **Cost:** $8; $6 (ages 65+ and students with ID); $4 (ages 3-18). **Phone:** (508) 877-7630.

GLOUCESTER (B-7) pop. 30,273, elev. 52′

Gloucester, on Cape Ann, is a summer resort with a rocky coast and safe harbor. The town was settled in 1623 and has remained a fishing center. The harbor also bustles with traffic from sightseeing cruise ships and charter vessels.

Sargent House Museum, 49 Middle St., was built in 1782 for Judith Sargent Murray, who is known for her essays, poems and plays. The collection includes a group of work by John Singer Sargent. The 18th-century Georgian-style home is open by appointment while renovations are under way; phone (978) 281-2432.

Rocky Neck Art Colony *(see attraction listing p. 145)* is said to be the oldest art colony in the country. Within the colony are shops, restaurants and art galleries that feature works from Gloucester, East Gloucester, Rockport, Ipswich and Essex artists.

Cape Ann Chamber of Commerce: 33 Commercial St., Gloucester, MA 01930. **Phone:** (978) 283-1601.

[SAVE] **7 SEAS WHALE WATCH AND CHARTERS** leaves from Seven Seas Wharf on Rogers St. The 3.5- to 4-hour excursion is fully narrated by an area naturalist. Whale sightings are guaranteed; the trip often includes views of humpbacks, finbacks, tuna, dolphins and sharks. Private charters also are available. **Hours:** Trips depart daily at 8:30 and 1:30, late Apr.-late Oct. (weather permitting). Phone ahead to confirm schedule. **Cost:** $45; $39 (ages 62+); $29 (ages 5-15). Reservations are recommended. **Phone:** (978) 283-1776 or (888) 283-1776. *See color ad.* [TI]

BEAUPORT (Sleeper-McCann House) is 2.1 mi. s. of jct. SRs 127 and 128 to 75 Eastern Point Blvd. Built 1907-34 by interior decorator Henry Davis Sleeper, this 40-room house overlooking Gloucester Harbor contains 18th-, 19th- and 20th-century American and European decorative arts and furnishings. Twenty-six rooms are open to the public.

Time: Allow 1 hour minimum. **Hours:** Tours are given Tues.-Sat. on the hour 10-5, June 1-Oct. 15. Last tour begins 1 hour before closing. Closed major holidays. **Cost:** $10; $9 (ages 55+); $5 (ages 6-12 and students with ID); free (ages 0-5 and Gloucester residents). **Phone:** (978) 283-0800.

[GEM] **CAPE ANN HISTORICAL MUSEUM** is at 27 Pleasant St. This combination art and historical museum consists of several galleries that include collections of decorative arts and American antique furniture; exhibits of maritime artifacts and photographs; paintings by Jerome Elwell, Susanna Paine, Gilbert Stuart and Alfred Wiggin; 19th-century toys and dolls; granite quarry artifacts, tools and historic photographs; carved jade; and Paul Revere silver.

The museum is said to house the largest collection of paintings and works on paper by Fitz Hugh Lane, a native of Gloucester, who gained fame as a luminist maritime and landscape painter. The 1804 Captain Elias Davis House affords visitors an opportunity to glimpse into the lifestyle of a sea captain's family in early 19th-century New England. Changing exhibits relating to Cape Ann also are offered throughout the year.

Photography and videotaping are not permitted inside the museum. **Time:** Allow 1 hour minimum. **Hours:** Tues.-Sat. 10-5, Sun. 1-4, Mar.-Jan. Closed major holidays. **Cost:** $8; $6 (ages 66+ and students with ID); free (ages 0-11). **Phone:** (978) 283-0455.

[SAVE] **CAPE ANN WHALE WATCH**, 415 Main St. at Rose's Wharf, offers 3- to 4-hour whale-watch cruises that include narratives by a naturalist from the Whale Conservation Institute. Sightings are guaranteed aboard the *Hurricane II*.

Hours: Cruises depart daily at 8:30 and 1:30, July 1-Labor Day; Mon.-Fri. at 10, Sat.-Sun. at 8:30

and 1:30, May-June; Mon.-Fri. at 1, Sat.-Sun. at 8:30 and 1:30, day after Labor Day-Sept. 30; daily at 10, in Oct.; Sat. at 1:30, in Apr. **Cost:** $45; $40 (ages 60+ and college students and military with ID); $30 (ages 4-15); free (one child under age 4 per paying adult). Reservations are recommended. **Phone:** (978) 283-5110 or (800) 877-5110. *See color ad.*

SAVE **CAPT. BILL & SONS WHALE WATCH** departs from 24 Harbor Loop. Visitors experience whale-watching and learn about the biology and conservation of marine mammals. Sightings are guaranteed during the cruise, which lasts approximately 3.5 hours.

Hours: Cruises depart daily at 9 and 2, July 1-Labor Day; Mon.-Fri. at 10:30, Sat.-Sun. at 9 and 2, May-June; Mon.-Fri. at 11, Sat.-Sun. at 9 and 2, day after Labor Day-Sept. 30; Sun.-Fri. at 10, Sat. at 1, rest of year. **Cost:** $45; $38 (ages 60+); $28 (ages 4-16). Reservations are recommended. **Phone:** (978) 283-6995 or (800) 339-4253. *See color ad.* ⑪

FIRST BAPTIST CHURCH, 38 Gloucester Ave., is a modern structure evocative of a ship and fortress. The interior features a pulpit reminiscent of the Mariner's Chapel in "Moby Dick." An 8-foot-tall cross looms above the congregation. **Time:** Allow 30 minutes minimum. **Hours:** Daily 9-noon. **Cost:** Free. **Phone:** (978) 283-4808.

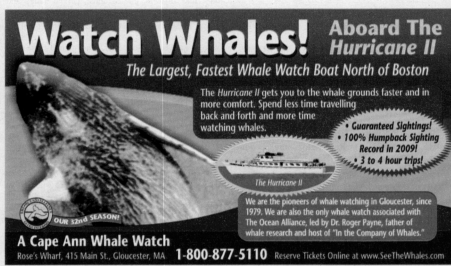

FISHERMEN'S MEMORIAL, on Stacy Blvd. at Western Ave., was erected in 1923, commemorating the 300th anniversary of the founding of the city of Gloucester. The statue is a memorial to the more than 10,000 Gloucester fishermen who have been lost at sea.

HAMMOND CASTLE MUSEUM is on Hesperus Ave. Built by inventor Dr. John Hays Hammond 1926-29, this Medieval Revival-type castle contains furniture and architectural pieces from dwellings and churches abroad as well as Roman, medieval and Renaissance artifacts. **Hours:** Tues.-Sun. 10-4, Memorial Day-Labor Day; Sat.-Sun. 10-4, mid-Sept. to early Oct. Last admission 30 minutes before closing. **Cost:** $10; $8 (ages 65+); $6 (ages 6-12). **Phone:** (978) 283-7673, or (978) 283-2080 for recorded information.

HARBOR TOURS INC., 19 Harbor Loop, offers the 2.5-hour scenic Cape Ann Lighthouse Cruise as well as a 75-minute cruise that includes a demonstration of lobstering.

Hours: Lighthouse cruises depart daily at 2:30, mid-June through Labor Day; Sat.-Sun. at 2:30, early May to mid-June and day after Labor Day-Columbus Day. Lobstering cruises depart daily at 1, mid-June through Labor Day; Sat.-Sun. at 1, early May to mid-June and day after Labor Day-Columbus Day. Hours may vary. **Cost:** Lighthouse cruise $28; $25 (senior citizens); $16 (ages 3-12). Lobstering cruise $16; $8 (ages 3-12). Reservations are required. **Phone:** (978) 283-1979.

NORTH SHORE ARTS ASSOCIATION is at 11 Pirates Ln. Located near one of the earliest artist colonies in America, the association exhibits paintings and sculpture of its artists/members. It also presents workshops, demonstrations and lectures. Four major exhibits are presented yearly. **Time:** Allow 30 minutes minimum. **Hours:** Mon.-Sat. 10-5, Sun. noon-5. **Cost:** Free. **Phone:** (978) 283-1857.

ROCKY NECK ART COLONY is at E. Main St. and Rocky Neck Ave. The colony of artist studios began in the 1850s. The site includes more than 30 galleries. Special programs include Nights on the Neck, offered the first Thursday of the month from May through October. **Time:** Allow 1 hour minimum. **Hours:** Most art galleries open May-Oct.; limited number open rest of year. Individual gallery hours vary; phone ahead. **Cost:** Free. **Phone:** (978) 282-0917 for general information May-Oct., or (978) 283-3598 rest of year. 🕇

SCHOONER *THOMAS E. LANNON* departs from Seven Seas Wharf on Rogers St. The 65-foot-long schooner offers 2-hour sightseeing cruises along Gloucester's historic harbor and rocky shoreline. Passengers can help raise the sails or just sit back and enjoy views of lighthouses, beaches and stately waterfront homes. Music trips also are available June through September.

Hours: Sightseeing cruises depart daily, late June-Labor Day; Sat.-Sun., mid-May to late June

and day after Labor Day to mid-Oct. Departure times vary; phone ahead. **Cost:** Sightseeing cruise $37.50; $32.50 (ages 65+); $25 (ages 0-16). Reservations are recommended. **Phone:** (978) 281-6634.

YANKEE FLEET WHALE WATCH departs from 37 Commercial St. at Gloucester Harbor. The 4-hour cruise is narrated by a research scientist. On-board activities and displays are available. Sightings are guaranteed. **Hours:** Trips depart Mon.-Fri. at 1:30, Sat.-Sun. at 2:30, May-Oct. (weather permitting). Phone ahead to confirm schedule. **Cost:** $41; $34 (ages 63+); $25 (ages 3-16). Prices may vary. Reservations are recommended. **Phone:** (978) 283-0313 or (800) 942-5464. 🕇

HAVERHILL (A-6) pop. 58,969, elev. 35'

Greater Haverhill Chamber of Commerce: 87 Winter St., Haverhill, MA 01830. **Phone:** (978) 373-5663.

THE BUTTONWOODS MUSEUM, 240 Water St., features the 1710 John Ward House, the 1814 Duncan House and Daniel Hunkins' 1850 shoe shop. **Hours:** Museum and visitor center Tues.-Sun. 10-5. **Cost:** $5; $4 (senior citizens); $3 (ages 7-12). **Phone:** (978) 374-4626.

WHITTIER BIRTHPLACE is off I-495 exit 52, then 1 mi. e. on SR 110. This 1688 house is the birthplace and boyhood home of poet John Greenleaf Whittier. Furnished with original pieces, it remains as described in Whittier's poem "Snow-Bound." **Hours:** Wed. and Fri. 11-4, Sat. 10-4, Sun. 1-4 or by appointment, Apr.-Nov. Closed major holidays. **Cost:** $5; $3 (ages 62+ and students 18+ with ID); $2 (ages 7-17). **Phone:** (978) 373-3979.

HINGHAM (F-3) pop. 5,352, elev. 21'

THE OLD ORDINARY, 21 Lincoln St., was built in 1688 and enlarged in 1740 and 1760. The building functioned as a tavern for much of the 18th century; it now houses a collection of historical Hingham artifacts, including period furnishings. **Hours:** Tues.-Sat. 1:30-4:30, mid-June to early Sept. **Cost:** $5; $3 (ages 0-11). **Phone:** (781) 749-7721.

OLD SHIP MEETINGHOUSE, 90 Main St., is one of the oldest continuously used wooden church structures in the country. The frame and walls stand as erected in 1681; the pulpit, pews and galleries date from 1755. **Hours:** Mon.-Fri. 1-4, July-Aug.; by appointment rest of year. **Cost:** Donations. **Phone:** (781) 749-1679.

HULL (E-3) pop. 11,050, elev. 23'

Hull-Nantasket Chamber of Commerce: P.O. Box 140, Hull, MA 02045. **Phone:** (339) 236-1264.

HULL LIFESAVING MUSEUM is at 1117 Nantasket Ave. Built in 1889 as a U.S. Life-Saving Station, the building also served as a Coast Guard station 1915-69. Displays re-create life in a turn-of-the-20th-century lifesaving station and recount the rescue missions of such lifesavers as boatkeeper Joshua James, a lifelong resident of Hull. The museum also includes photographs and stories of notable Boston Harbor shipwrecks and lighthouse artifacts. **Hours:** Sat.-Thurs. 10-4, Fri. 10-1. Closed major holidays. Phone ahead to confirm schedule. **Cost:** $5; $3 (ages 65+); free (ages 0-18). **Phone:** (781) 925-5433.

PARAGON CAROUSEL, opposite Bernie King Pavilion at 205 Nantasket Ave. (SR 228), is a 1928 wooden carousel with 66 horses, two Roman chariots and a Wurlitzer 146-band organ. **Hours:** Open daily, Memorial Day weekend-Labor Day; Sat.-Sun., Easter weekend-day before Memorial Day weekend and day after Labor Day-Oct. 31 (weather permitting). Hours vary; phone ahead. **Cost:** $2.50, or 10 rides for $20. **Phone:** (781) 925-0472.

IPSWICH (A-7) pop. 4,161, elev. 26'

In 1633 Ipswich was settled by a group of 12 colonists, among them several "proper gentlemen" who developed the town into a cultural center. Clothing industries, including shoemaking, lacemaking and machine knitting, later became the town's economic base. Tourism and the digging and marketing of clams are now a major source of income.

Richard T. Crane Jr. Memorial Reservation, 6 miles east on Argilla Road, offers 4 miles of shoreline and beaches on Ipswich Bay. The old Crane residence, called Great House, is open for tours in summer. *See Recreation Chart.*

One-hour guided tours of the 1694 Paine House at Greenwood Farm are offered from May through October. The grounds, which are accessible year-round, encompass pastures, woodlands, a salt marsh, three tidal islands and a 2.5-mile nature path; phone (978) 356-4351.

Ipswich Visitor Information Center: 36 S. Main St., Ipswich, MA 01938. **Phone:** (978) 356-8540.

HEARD HOUSE MUSEUM is at 54 S. Main St. (SR 1A). Completed in 1800, this Federal-style mansion was the elegant homestead of a prominent West Indies and China trade family. The museum contains American and Asian furnishings, decorative objects and a collection of antique carriages and sleighs. On view is a collection of artworks by the important Ipswich artist Arthur Wesley Dow.

Hours: Guided tours are given on the hour Wed.-Thurs. and Sat. 10-3, Fri. noon-3, Sun. 1-3, Memorial Day-day before Columbus Day. Last tour begins at closing. **Cost:** $5; $3 (ages 6-12). Combination ticket with Whipple House Museum $7; $3 (ages 6-12). **Phone:** (978) 356-2811.

WHIPPLE HOUSE MUSEUM is at 1 S. Village Green (SR 1A). Begun in 1677, this timber-frame house was the sumptuous home of a successful Puritan family. The museum contains Colonial furnishings and decorative arts. The housewife's garden in front is planted with herbs known to have been used in the colony in the 17th century.

Hours: Guided tours are given on the hour Wed.-Thurs. and Sat. 10-3, Fri. noon-3, Sun. 1-3, Memorial Day-day before Columbus Day. Last tour begins at closing. **Cost:** $5; $3 (ages 6-12). Combination ticket with Heard House Museum $7; $3 (ages 6-12). **Phone:** (978) 356-2811.

LAWRENCE (A-6) pop. 72,043, elev. 65'

Lawrence was established in 1845 to support the growing number of industries along the Merrimack River. Through the efforts of the Lawrence brothers, Great Stone Dam was built 1845-48 to generate electrical power. Constructed with hand-hewn granite blocks hauled by oxen and laid stone by stone on the river floor, the dam was considered an engineering triumph. The massive dam can be viewed from Falls Bridge.

Merrimack Valley Chamber of Commerce: 264 Essex St., Lawrence, MA 01840. **Phone:** (978) 686-0900.

Self-guiding tours: The Robert Frost Trail is a walking tour that highlights the sites associated with the early years of the poet including where he wrote his first poems and fell in love. A brochure is available from the Lawrence Heritage State Park Visitor Center; phone (978) 794-1655 for more information.

LAWRENCE HERITAGE STATE PARK, 1 Jackson St., commemorates the history of this mill city. Lawrence's mills once produced 800 miles of cloth a day through the labor of thousands of immigrants, who made history during the Bread and Roses Strike of 1912. This strike sparked the American labor movement, bringing about national reforms of laws governing workers' rights. A visitor center and gallery also are on-site. **Hours:** Park open daily dawn-dusk. Visitor center open daily 9-4. **Cost:** Free. **Phone:** (978) 794-1655.

LEXINGTON (E-2)
pop. 30,355, elev. 201′

Lexington is the site of the first conflict of the Revolutionary War, dramatized on the Lexington Battle Green during the Re-enactment of the Battle of Lexington in mid-April. Portions of Battle Road, the route used by British and American soldiers moving from Concord to Boston, now are covered by scenic SR 2A.

Lexington Chamber of Commerce & Visitors Center: 1875 Massachusetts Ave., Lexington, MA 02421. **Phone:** (781) 862-1450.

BUCKMAN TAVERN, 1 Bedford St., was built in 1709 and has furnishings of the Revolutionary War period. It was the headquarters of the Lexington Militia at the beginning of the Revolutionary War. **Hours:** Daily 10-4, Apr.-Oct. Guided tours are given every half-hour. **Cost:** $6; $4 (ages 6-16). Combination ticket with the Hancock-Clarke House and Munroe Tavern $10; $6 (ages 6-16). **Phone:** (781) 862-1703.

HANCOCK-CLARKE HOUSE, 36 Hancock St., was built in 1737. Samuel Adams and John Hancock were at this site when Paul Revere brought the news of the British advance. The house includes period furniture and historical objects. The "First Shot!" orientation film is shown hourly.

Hours: Daily 10-4, mid-June through Oct. 31; Sat.-Sun. 10-4, Apr. 1 to mid-June. Guided tours are given on the hour. **Cost:** $6; $4 (ages 6-16). Combination ticket with Buckman Tavern and Munroe Tavern $10; $6 (ages 6-16). **Phone:** (781) 862-1703.

LEXINGTON BATTLE GREEN, or Common, is at Massachusetts Ave. and Bedford St. The common was the site of the first skirmish of the Revolutionary War, April 19, 1775, between minutemen and Concord-bound British troops. The line where the minutemen stood is marked by a boulder inscribed with Capt. John Parker's courageous words: "Stand your ground; don't fire unless fired upon, but if they mean to have a war, let it begin here."

LIBERTY RIDE departs from the National Heritage Museum at 33 Marrett Rd. During the 90-minute trolley tour, costumed guides offer informative narration about the historical sites of Concord and Lexington. The tour traces Paul Revere's historic ride and the advance and retreat of the British troops.

Visitors can disembark and reboard 90 minutes later at various locations and attractions along the tour route.

Time: Allow 1 hour, 30 minutes minimum. **Hours:** Tours depart daily at 10:30, noon, 1:30 and 3, Memorial Day weekend-Oct. 31. **Cost:** $25; $10 (ages 5-17). Prices may vary; phone ahead. **Phone:** (781) 862-0500, ext. 702, or (339) 223-5623 off-season.

MINUTE MAN NATIONAL HISTORICAL PARK—
see place listing p. 150.

MINUTEMAN STATUE, at the head of Battle Green on Massachusetts Ave., represents Capt. John Parker as he appeared on the morning of April 19, 1775, commanding the minutemen gathered on the green. It faces the line of British approach.

MUNROE TAVERN, 1332 Massachusetts Ave., served as the British headquarters and hospital during the Battle of Lexington. The tour of the circa 1700 building tells the British side of the conflict. **Hours:** Daily noon-4, mid-June through Oct. 31; Sat.-Sun. noon-4, Apr. 1 to mid-June. Guided tours are given on the hour. Last tour begins at closing. **Cost:** $6; $4 (ages 6-16). Combination ticket with Buckman Tavern and Hancock-Clarke House $10; $6 (ages 6-16). **Phone:** (781) 862-1703.

NATIONAL HERITAGE MUSEUM, 33 Marrett Rd., offers a permanent collection related to the history of American freemasonry and fraternalism as well as changing exhibits about American history and popular culture. Decorative arts, documents, artifacts, photographs and fine art are on display. **Hours:** Tues.-Sat. 10-4:30, Sun. noon-4:30. Closed Jan. 1, Easter, Thanksgiving and Dec. 24-25 and 31. **Cost:** Free. **Phone:** (781) 861-6559. [¶]

Lexington

© 2009 NAVTEQ

OLD BELFRY, off Clarke St., is near the Battle Green. It is a reproduction of the original belfry whose bell sounded the alarm that assembled the minutemen. The original was destroyed in 1909.

OLD BURYING GROUND is beyond the Battle Green, next to the Unitarian Church. Among the graves are those of Capt. John Parker, Gov. William Eustis and the Rev. John Hancock. The oldest stone is dated 1690.

REVOLUTIONARY MONUMENT, on the Battle Green, was dedicated in 1799 to the eight men killed in the first battle of the Revolutionary War. It is considered to be the first monument erected commemorating the American Revolution.

LINCOLN (E-1) elev. 208′

Codman House, 36 Codman Rd., is open weekends and represents several architectural styles, including Georgian, Federal, Victorian and Colonial Revival. Gardens are on-site; phone (781) 259-8843.

DeCORDOVA SCULPTURE PARK AND MUSEUM is at jct. Sandy Pond and Trapelo rds. Surrounded by 35 acres of woodlands and lawns, the 1880 castle-like structure is a cultural center for the visual arts. The museum collects and exhibits significant 20th- and 21st-century American art. The park contains 80 sculptures.

Hours: Sculpture park daily dawn-dusk. Museum Tues.-Sun. 10-5. Closed some holidays. **Cost:** Sculpture park and museum $12; $8 (ages 6-12, ages 60+ and students with ID). Sculpture park free outside of museum hours. **Phone:** (781) 259-8355. ⛙

GROPIUS HOUSE, 68 Baker Bridge Rd., was built in 1938 by and for Walter Gropius, director of Germany's Bauhaus School and an innovative and influential architect of the 20th century. Using components ordered from catalogs and building supply stores, he produced a house that blends the Bauhaus principles of function and simplicity with New England traditions. The house has art and furnishings brought from Bauhaus workshops in Germany as well as pieces from the United States.

Hours: Tours are given Wed.-Sun. on the hour 11-4, June 1-Oct. 15; Sat.-Sun. 11-4, rest of year. **Cost:** $10; $9 (ages 65+); $5 (ages 6-12 and students with ID). **Phone:** (781) 259-8098.

MASS AUDUBON'S DRUMLIN FARM WILDLIFE SANCTUARY, on SR 117, .7 mi. e. of SR 126, has 232 acres of pastures, fields, woodlands and ponds. The sanctuary has animals representative of a New England farm including chickens, mules, sheep and pigs as well as various species of such wildlife as deer, owls and hawks. In Drumlin Underground visitors go belowground to see part of the dens or burrows of animals, including those of foxes, woodchucks and skunks. Hayrides are offered April through November.

Time: Allow 1 hour minimum. **Hours:** Tues.-Sun. and some Mon. holidays 9-5, Mar.-Oct.; 9-4, rest of year. Closed Jan. 1, Thanksgiving and Dec. 24-25 and 31. **Cost:** $6; $4 (ages 2-12 and 65+). Hayride $2; $1 (ages 2-12). **Phone:** (781) 259-2200. ⛙

LOWELL (A-6) pop. 105,167, elev. 104′

In 1813, after touring British textile factories, Boston merchant Francis Cabot Lowell supported the development of a power loom that shaped the history of the U.S. textile industry. Looking for a site to set up a factory, a group of investors called "The Boston Associates" discovered Lowell, at the confluence of the Concord and Merrimack rivers. They were impressed by the waterpower potential of the two rivers. Construction of textile mills and a series of power canals began in 1822.

In the following decades the town experienced economic prosperity at the cost of human needs. Reformer Sarah Bagley organized female workers to fight for better conditions. Due to the influx of unskilled immigrants beginning in 1850, protests were often futile. In the early 20th century, just as labor improvements were being realized, the industry began to collapse, forcing residents to leave. High-tech industry is beginning to revitalize the city.

Greater Lowell Chamber of Commerce: 131 Merrimack St., Lowell, MA 01852. **Phone:** (978) 459-8154.

AMERICAN TEXTILE HISTORY MUSEUM is off Lowell Connector exit 5B (Thorndike St.), following signs to 491 Dutton St. The museum chronicles 300 years of American textile production with displays of a large assortment of hand-powered tools and equipment, fabrics and finished clothing. Spinning and weaving demonstrations are given periodically. **Time:** Allow 1 hour, 30 minutes minimum. **Hours:** Wed.-Sun. 10-5. Closed major holidays. **Cost:** $8; $6 (ages 6-16, students with ID and senior citizens). **Phone:** (978) 441-0400.

LOWELL NATIONAL HISTORICAL PARK, off Lowell Connector exit 5B, following signs to the visitor center at 246 Market St., commemorates Lowell's pioneering role in the American Industrial Revolution. The park includes cotton textile mills, workers' housing, a 5.6-mile power canal system and industrial exhibits. The visitor center includes exhibits and a 20-minute video titled "Lowell: The Industrial Revelation."

Guided walking tours are available. Boat and trolley tours along the Pawtucket Canal are offered in summer and fall. Reproductions of 1901 electric trolley cars operate daily early March to late November.

Hours: Visitor center daily 9-5, early Mar.-late Nov.; Mon.-Sat. 9-4:30, Sun. 10-4:30, rest of year. Closed Jan. 1, Thanksgiving and Dec. 24-25. Phone ahead to confirm schedule. **Cost:** Free. Boat and trolley tours $8-$10; $7-$9 (ages 62+); $6-$8 (ages 6-16). Reservations are required for tours. **Phone:** (978) 970-5000 or TTY (978) 970-5002.

Boott Cotton Mills Museum, 115 John St., is housed within the brick walls of a cotton mill built in 1873. Two floors of exhibits chronicle the age of Lowell's textile mills and the Industrial Revolution in general. On the first floor an orientation area gives way to a 1920s weave room containing 88 looms operating with the help of belts, shafts and pulleys.

Exhibits upstairs present Lowell's history from preindustrial days to the present. A slide presentation traces the development of the industrial age, and mill workers present audiovisual histories of their work and times.

Time: Allow 1 hour minimum. **Hours:** Daily 9:30-4:30, early Mar.-late Nov.; Mon.-Fri. 10-2, Sat., federal holidays and school vacation weeks 9:30-4, Sun. 11-4, rest of year. Closed Jan. 1, Thanksgiving and Dec. 24-25. Phone ahead to confirm schedule. **Cost:** $6; $5 (ages 62+); $3 (ages 6-16 and students with ID). Combination ticket with Pawtucket Canal tour $12; $9 (ages 62+); $7 (ages 6-16 and students with ID). **Phone:** (978) 970-5000 or TTY (978) 970-5002.

The Mill Girls and Immigrants Exhibit is in the Patrick J. Mogan Cultural Center at 40 French St. Presented in a former Boott Mill boardinghouse, the exhibit relates the story of the Industrial Revolution by concentrating on Lowell's working people. The histories of the "mill girl" and immigrant work forces are explored.

Hours: Daily 1-5, Memorial Day weekend-Columbus Day; daily 1:30-5, early Mar.-day before Memorial Day weekend and day after Columbus Day-late Nov.; Sat.-Sun., federal holidays and school vacation weeks 1:30-4, rest of year. Closed Jan. 1, Thanksgiving and Dec. 24-25. Phone ahead to confirm schedule. **Cost:** Free. **Phone:** (978) 970-5000 or TTY (978) 970-5002.

NEW ENGLAND QUILT MUSEUM, 18 Shattuck St., presents changing exhibitions of both historic and contemporary quilts. Interpretation of each quilt is provided. **Time:** Allow 30 minutes minimum. **Hours:** Tues.-Sat. 10-4, Sun. noon-4, May-Dec. Closed major holidays and between exhibitions. **Cost:** $7; $5 (students with ID and senior citizens). **Phone:** (978) 452-4207.

WHISTLER HOUSE MUSEUM OF ART, 243 Worthen St., was the 1834 birthplace of James McNeill Whistler. Built in 1823, the house now contains a 19th- and 20th-century New England art collection that includes etchings by Whistler. **Hours:** Wed.-Sat. 11-4. Closed major holidays. **Cost:** $5; $4 (ages 60+ and students with ID); free (ages 0-11). **Phone:** (978) 452-7641.

LYNN (E-3) pop. 89,050, elev. 26'

Founded in 1629, Lynn is one of New England's oldest communities. Once a major shoe manufacturing center, the city is now home to a General Electric plant. Lynn Woods Reservation, a 2,200-acre municipal park, features mineral and glacial traces

and offers hiking, rock climbing, picnicking and cross-country skiing. Spread over several hills, the Victorian-style Pine Grove Cemetery was founded in 1850 and offers a panorama of the area.

The Mary Baker Eddy Home at 12 Broad St. contains furnishings and articles relating to the life of the founder of the Church of Christ, Scientist. Tours are available; phone (781) 593-5634.

Lynn Area Chamber of Commerce: 100 Oxford St., Lynn, MA 01901. **Phone:** (781) 592-2900.

LYNN MUSEUM AND HISTORICAL SOCIETY, 590 Washington Ave., serves as a local visitor center and features exhibits about Lynn and the people who built it. A 10-minute audiovisual presentation provides background information about the community. Permanent displays depict important events in the city's industrial past, from the manufacture of women's shoes to the production of jet engines. **Hours:** Museum and visitor center Tues.-Sat. noon-4 (also Thurs. 4-8). **Cost:** Museum and exhibits $5; free (ages 0-11). Visitor center information free. **Phone:** (781) 581-6200.

MARBLEHEAD (D-3) pop. 20,377, elev. 32'

Founded in 1629, Marblehead flourished as a commercial fishing center and by the mid-18th century was port to hundreds of ships engaged in fishing and overseas trade. Today more than 200 houses built before the American Revolution and nearly 800 constructed during the 1800s still line the town's winding streets. The Powder House, jct. Lattimer St. at 39 Green St., was built in 1755 and is one of the few remaining from the Colonial era. Muskets and powder were stored in this round brick magazine during the French and Indian War, the American Revolution and the War of 1812. The building is not open to the public.

Views of the ocean, islands, harbor and Marblehead shoreline can be enjoyed from Crocker Park, off Front Street downtown, and Chandler Hovey Park, at the end of Harbor and Ocean avenues. The 1896 Marblehead light tower (closed to the public) is on the grounds of Chandler Hovey Park.

Marblehead Chamber of Commerce: 62 Pleasant St., Marblehead, MA 01945. **Phone:** (781) 631-2868.

Self-guiding tours: Maps of a walking tour are available Memorial Day through October 31 from the information booth on Pleasant Street.

ABBOT HALL, 188 Washington St., exhibits the 1684 deed recording the purchase of the peninsula from the Indians and the original "Spirit of '76," painted in 1876 by A.M. Willard. **Hours:** Mon.-Tues. and Thurs.-Fri. 8-5, Wed. 7:30-7:30, June-Oct.; Fri. 8-1, Sat. 10-5, Sun. 11-5, rest of year. Closed Jan. 1, Easter and Dec. 25. Phone ahead to confirm schedule. **Cost:** Donations. **Phone:** (781) 631-0000.

FORT SEWALL, at the n.e. end of Front St., offers views of Marblehead and its harbor as well as Cape Ann and the Atlantic Ocean. Manned during conflicts through the Spanish-American War, the current structure dates from the 1800s and was constructed on the site of the original fort, built in 1644 and enlarged in 1742. **Hours:** Daily dawn-dusk. **Cost:** Free.

JEREMIAH LEE MANSION, 161 Washington St., was the 1768 Georgian home of a wealthy shipowner and patriot who helped secure weapons for the American revolt against King George. Its opulent interiors feature intricate carvings and rare, original hand-painted English wallpaper and 18th- and early 19th-century furnishings, paintings and artifacts. **Time:** Allow 1 hour minimum. **Hours:** Guided tours are given Tues.-Sat. 10-4, June-Oct. **Cost:** $5; $4.50 (ages 65+ and students with ID); free (ages 0-11). **Phone:** (781) 631-1768.

J.O.J. FROST FOLK ART GALLERY, 170 Washington St., displays folk art and paintings of life in Marblehead and at sea by J.O.J. Frost, who began creating scenes of his hometown in the 1920s. Changing exhibitions also are offered. **Time:** Allow 30 minutes minimum. **Hours:** Tues.-Sat. 10-4, June-Oct.; Tues.-Fri. 10-4, rest of year. **Cost:** Donations. **Phone:** (781) 631-1768.

MARBLEHEAD ARTS ASSOCIATION, 8 Hooper St., presents four galleries of changing exhibits every month at the historic King Hooper Mansion. Guided tours are available by appointment. **Time:** Allow 1 hour minimum. **Hours:** Thurs.-Sat. 10-5, Tues.-Wed. and Sun. noon-5, Memorial Day-Labor Day; Tues.-Fri. noon-5, Sun. 1-5, rest of year. Phone ahead to confirm schedule. **Cost:** Donations. **Phone:** (781) 631-2608.

OLD BURIAL HILL, off Orne St., is the resting place of approximately 600 Revolutionary soldiers, as well as fishermen and seamen; some grave markers date from the 1600s and 1700s. Fishermen's Monument commemorates the loss of 65 men and boys in a September 1846 hurricane. The graveyard overlooks Marblehead's historic district, the harbor and the sea.

ST. MICHAEL'S CHURCH, 26 Pleasant St., was built in 1714 and remodeled in 1833 in Gothic Revival style. One of the oldest Episcopal churches in America, it still has an original, elaborate brass chandelier from England. The bell, rung at the news of the Declaration of Independence until it cracked, was recast by Paul Revere and is still used. Guided tours are available by appointment. **Hours:** Mon.-Fri. 8:30-12:30. **Cost:** Free. **Phone:** (781) 631-0657.

MILTON (F-2) pop. 26,062, elev. 24'

BLUE HILLS RESERVATION is off I-93 exit 3; park headquarters is at 695 Hillside St. This is a 7,000-acre state reservation, stretching from Dedham to Quincy and from Milton to Randolph, encompassing terrains from hills and meadows to forests and wetlands. Traversing this park are some 150 miles of hiking, mountain biking and horse trails. Other recreational facilities include tennis courts, a downhill ski area, a beach and a golf course. **Hours:** Daily dawn-dusk. **Cost:** Free. **Phone:** (617) 698-1802. ⊞ ⊠

Mass Audubon's Blue Hills Trailside Museum, off I-93 exit 2B (SR 138N) to 1904 Canton Ave., offers an introduction to the wildlife and history of the Blue Hills. It contains displays about natural sciences, natural history and pioneer and American Indian life. Displays of native wildlife also are featured. An exhibit hall has a wigwam and a viewing tower. Activities include storytelling, live animal programs and seasonal nature talks.

Hours: Fri.-Sun. and Mon. holidays 10-5. Closed Jan. 1 and Dec. 25. Phone ahead to confirm schedule. **Cost:** $3; $2 (ages 65+); $1.50 (ages 3-12). An additional fee may be charged during special events. **Phone:** (617) 333-0690.

MINUTE MAN NATIONAL HISTORICAL PARK (D-1)

The majority of Minute Man National Historical Park is a narrow strip of land on either side of Battle Road (SR 2A), with the Minute Man Visitor Center at one end, just off SR 128, and the North Bridge Visitor Center outside of Concord at the other. Encompassing lands in Concord, Lincoln and Lexington, the park commemorates the opening battles of America's War for Independence. The events of April 19, 1775, were not one but many battles along a 20-mile stretch of hilly road between Boston and Concord.

Gen. Thomas Gage, head of the British forces occupying Boston, chose that day for a demonstration of force, ordering 700 redcoats to march to Concord and seize the rebel supplies of arms and ammunition. Drawing on the tenets of 18th-century warfare, Gage's intention was simply to overawe the Colonials, not to provoke a fight. However, once news of the British mobilization reached the patriots, hundreds of people materialized from the surrounding communities to contest the British march.

After a brief fight on Lexington Green, the British moved to Concord, where the militia drove three companies of redcoats from the North Bridge back to the main force in Concord. After a brief rest, the British began their return march to Boston and were soon met by the militia, who forced the British back to the city under steady gunfire.

A running battle continued back to Boston Harbor. The British sent out flankers to flush out the patriots and protect its column. As the day progressed an increasing number of colonists joined the fight.

Exhausted and near panic, the British column was met at Lexington by a relief force of 1,000 men, swelling the ranks to 1,700. Beyond Lexington the British column met fierce and bloody resistance in the towns of Menotomy, now Arlington, and Charlestown. At 6:30 p.m. the British finally reached the safety of Bunker Hill, which was under the guns of the British warship *Somerset.* In all, the British lost 73 men and the patriots 49; many more were wounded or missing.

MINUTE MAN VISITOR CENTER, on Airport Rd. just n.w. of jct. SR 2A and Massachusetts Ave., serves as a starting point for most visitors. A 25-minute multimedia presentation offers an introduction to the events at Lexington and Concord in 1775. Maps are available for self-guiding tours of the park. **Hours:** Daily 9-5, late Mar.-Nov. 30. **Cost:** Free. **Phone:** (781) 674-1920.

THE NORTH BRIDGE, just w. of Monument St., was the site of "the shot heard 'round the world"— the first major engagement of the Revolution—on April 19, 1775. Just across the bridge stands Daniel Chester French's "The Minute Man" statue, which is engraved with a stanza from Ralph Waldo Emerson's "Concord Hymn." North Bridge Visitor Center is a short walk past the statue and up the hill. Ranger-led educational programs are available daily. **Hours:** Daily dawn-dusk. **Cost:** Free.

NORTH BRIDGE VISITOR CENTER, 174 Liberty St., features uniforms and other relics describing the North Bridge fight. A formal garden overlooks the North Bridge. **Hours:** Daily 9-5, late Mar.-late Oct.; 11-3, rest of year. Phone ahead to confirm schedule. **Cost:** Free. **Phone:** (978) 369-6993.

THE WAYSIDE, 1 mi. e. of Concord on Lexington Rd., was the home of Samuel Whitney, the muster master, or roll caller, of the Concord Minutemen, and later the home of the Bronson Alcott family, the Nathaniel Hawthorne family and Margaret Sidney, an author of children's books during the late 19th century. **Hours:** Wed.-Sun. 9:30-5:30, Memorial Day weekend-Oct. 31. Phone ahead to confirm schedule. **Cost:** $5; free (ages 0-16). **Phone:** (978) 318-7863 or (781) 674-1920.

NATICK (F-1) elev. 158'

Shopping areas: Suburban fashionistas browse racks at the Natick Collection, on SR 9 at 1245 Worcester St. New England's largest shopping mall is home to 200 retailers, including JCPenney, Lord & Taylor, Macy's, Neiman Marcus and Sears.

MASS AUDUBON'S BROADMOOR WILDLIFE SANCTUARY, 280 Eliot St. on SR 16, embraces 623 acres of marsh, ponds and meadows along the Charles River. Wildlife such as wood ducks and great blue herons can be seen from the trails that wind through the sanctuary. The quarter-mile All Persons Trail accommodates wheelchairs and strollers. The visitor center, in a restored barn, incorporates solar and other alternative systems to conserve energy and water.

Hours: Grounds Tues.-Sun. and Mon. holidays dawn-dusk. Visitor center Tues.-Fri. 9-5, Sat.-Sun. and holidays 10-5. Closed Jan. 1, Thanksgiving and Dec. 25. **Cost:** $5; $4 (ages 2-12 and 65+). **Phone:** (508) 655-2296.

NEWBURY (A-7) elev. 20'

Built in the 1650s, Coffin House, at 14 High Rd., reflects the many generations of residency by the Coffin family. Guided tours are given the first and third Saturdays of the month from June to mid-October; phone (978) 462-2634.

SPENCER-PEIRCE-LITTLE FARM is at 5 Littles Ln. The site features a 1690 manor house with interactive exhibits, farm animals and trails. **Hours:** Thurs.-Sun. 11-5, June 1-Oct. 15. **Cost:** $5; $4 (children and senior citizens). **Phone:** (978) 462-2634.
🏕

NEWBURYPORT (A-7) pop. 17,189, elev. 39'

Newburyport lies near the estuary of the Merrimack River, along the waterway's southern bank. A prosperous shipbuilding center by the mid-1700s, the city satiates modern-day seafarers with its wealth of nautical heritage and salt air-inspired recreational pursuits. In addition to such draws as the Custom House Maritime Museum *(see attraction listing),* this port features three lighthouses constructed by the U.S. Coast Guard (which got its start in Newburyport) and a still-lively waterfront with interpretive signs describing early residents' use of the Merrimack.

Several vantage points offer pretty views of the river and mast-filled harbor. Leisurely natives, often joined by plucky nomadic seabirds, regularly dot the seawall at Joppa Park on Water Street. Lovers of the great outdoors also spend time at 16-acre Moseley Woods, on Spofford Street overlooking the Merrimack River, and at Maudslay State Park *(see Recreation Chart),* a 476-acre site nestled on the riverbank. Both parks feature hiking trails; the latter, accessible via Curzon Mill Road, has bridle paths and lovely Victorian gardens as well. In winter cross-country skiers traverse Maudslay's rolling, evergreen-fragrant expanse.

After enjoying the scenery by the water's edge, launch your boat at Cashman Park, off Merrimac Street at Broad Street. Or, cast a line off the shores of Plum Island, separated from the mainland by the Parker River. The 11-mile-long barrier island affords great panoramas of the Merrimack River inlet and is home to the Parker River National Wildlife Refuge *(see attraction listing p. 152)* , which protects more than 800 species of birds, plants and animals. Newburyport often is heralded as one of the country's top bird-watching destinations—a variety of land and water birds migrate to the area in spring, summer, fall and winter. For more information, stop in at the wildlife refuge, or arrange a guided bird-watching tour through the Massachusetts Audubon Society; phone (978) 462-9998.

In addition to luring sailing enthusiasts and wintering flocks of ducks and loons, this region's physical assets have long attracted—and inspired—artists, writers and musicians. The Newburyport Art Association, 65 Water St., (978) 465-8769, displays works by regional artists. At the Firehouse Center for the Arts on Market Square at Waterfront Park,

(978) 462-7336, you can take in a theatrical production or a dance performance. Downtown's Waterfront Park also hosts the Newburyport Riverfront Music Festival the second weekend in July. Other free open-air concerts are typically held throughout the summer, with blanket-toting families crowding many of the city's green spaces for a few tunes amid splendid natural landscapes.

Greater Newburyport Chamber of Commerce & Industry: 38R Merrimac St., Newburyport, MA 01950. **Phone:** (978) 462-6680.

Self-guiding tours: American architecture enthusiasts will appreciate a walking tour of High Street. Styles from the 17th through the 19th centuries, including several notable examples of the Federal period, are represented in the structures.

Shopping areas: Downtown Newburyport boasts several charming brick-lined thoroughfares and historic districts offering chic boutiques, antique stores and art galleries, including Inn Street; Market Square, centered around State, Pleasant and Merrimac streets; and The Tannery, a complex of refurbished leather mill buildings at Federal and Water streets that now shelters eateries and shops.

CUSHING HOUSE MUSEUM AND GARDENS is at 98 High St. Headquarters for the Historical Society of Old Newbury, the 1808 Cushing House is a 21-room, Federal mansion containing period furnishings, portraits, photographs, paperweights, silver, china, needlework and toys. A genealogy library houses volumes of information about the area's first settlers.

A 19th-century French garden, carriage house and garden house also are on the grounds. **Hours:** Guided tours are given Tues.-Fri. 10-4, Sat. noon-4, May-Oct. Last tour begins 1 hour before closing. **Cost:** $7; $2.50 (ages 12-18). **Phone:** (978) 462-2681.

CUSTOM HOUSE MARITIME MUSEUM, 25 Water St., is a classic Greek Revival-style custom house built in 1835 and designed by architect Robert Mills, who also designed the Washington Monument and the U.S. Treasury Building. Exhibits pertain to more than 300 years of maritime history and trade and shipbuilding on the Merrimac River as well as Coast Guard and lifesaving history.

A 15-minute audiovisual program gives visitors an overview of Newburyport. **Hours:** Tues.-Sat. 10-4, Sun. noon-4, mid-May through Dec. 31. **Cost:** $7; $5 (ages 13-18, ages 61+ and students with ID). **Phone:** (978) 462-8681.

MASS AUDUBON'S JOPPA FLATS EDUCATION CENTER is 1 mi. e. on Water St. to 1 Plum Island Tpke. Overlooking the Merrimack River, the 50-acre site offers indoor and outdoor observation areas, walking trails, perennial gardens and interpretive displays. The center highlights the various birds—including bald eagles, snowy owls and warblers—that depend on this locale's salt marshes, mudflats,

rivers, bays and coastal waters. **Time:** Allow 2 hours minimum. **Hours:** Daily 8:30-4. Closed Easter and Dec. 25. **Cost:** Donations. **Phone:** (978) 462-9998. 🛖

PARKER RIVER NATIONAL WILDLIFE REFUGE headquarters is at 6 Plum Island Tpke. (Rolfe's Ln.). The 4,662-acre refuge includes the southern three-fourths of Plum Island and salt marshes west to the mainland and is an excellent bird-watching area. It has a visitor center, hiking trails, observation towers and 6.5 miles of beach.

Surf fishing, nature study, canoeing and kayaking can be enjoyed. Waterfowl hunting is allowed in season. Clamming and limited night surf fishing are available by permit only.

Camping is not permitted. **Hours:** Refuge open daily dawn-dusk (weather permitting); most of the refuge beach is closed Apr.-Aug. to protect nesting shorebirds. Visitor center open daily 11-4. Headquarters open Mon.-Fri. 8-4:30. Phone ahead to confirm schedule. **Cost:** Refuge $5. **Phone:** (978) 465-5753. 🚫

NEWTON (E-2) pop. 83,829, elev. 33'

Originally a part of Cambridge, present-day Newton began to emerge as a separate community in the mid-1630s. Newton residents had to travel to and from the Harvard Square vicinity to conduct business, go to school or attend religious services until a meeting house finally was built within the Newton settlement. Although the building no longer exists, a monument near Centre and Cotton streets marks the site of the early structure.

The American Jewish Historical Society, at 160 Herrick Rd. on the Hebrew College campus, documents the Jewish community's history within Greater Boston through photographs, personal papers and other materials; phone (617) 559-8880.

Newton-Needham Chamber of Commerce: 281 Needham St., Newton, MA 02464. **Phone:** (617) 244-5300.

[SAVE] **HISTORIC NEWTON—JACKSON HOMESTEAD AND MUSEUM,** 527 Washington St., is a Federal-style house constructed in 1809. The homestead serves as a museum housing a collection of historical artifacts and items that interpret Newton's history, including the role of the Jackson Homestead as a stop on the Underground Railroad. Changing exhibits are featured. **Time:** Allow 1 hour minimum. **Hours:** Tues.-Fri. 11-5, Sat.-Sun. noon-5. Closed major holidays. **Cost:** $5; $3 (ages 0-17 and 65+). **Phone:** (617) 796-1450.

NORFOLK (C-6) elev. 218'

STONY BROOK WILDLIFE SANCTUARY/BRISTOL BLAKE STATE RESERVATION is 1 mi. s. on SR 115. A 1-mile self-guiding nature trail, bounded by fields, wetlands and ponds, leads to a boardwalk over a marsh. Other features on the 241-acre site include a butterfly garden and interpretive exhibits in the nature center. **Hours:** Trails daily dawn-dusk.

Nature center Mon.-Sat. 10-5, Sun. 12:30-4, July-Aug.; Tues.-Sat. 10-4, Sun. 12:30-4, rest of year. **Cost:** $4; $3 (ages 3-16 and 66+). **Phone:** (508) 528-3140.

NORTH ANDOVER (A-6) elev. 89′

Settlers arrived in the area during the 1640s; a town called Andover was incorporated in 1646. In 1709 the community split into the North Parish, now known as North Andover, and the South Parish, now known as Andover. North Andover was officially incorporated as a separate entity 146 years later.

Some of North Andover's first residents resided at The Stevens-Coolidge Place, 137 Andover St., now a neo-Georgian Colonial Revival estate. Preservation architect Joseph Everett Chandler redesigned elements of the homestead, including the cultivated gardens, which are open daily to visitors for self-guiding tours. Guided house tours also are available; phone (978) 682-3580.

Just off SR 114 (Salem Turnpike) Harold Parker State Forest offers more than 35 miles of logging roads and trails; 11 ponds; and such recreational opportunities as camping, fishing, hiking, hunting, horseback riding, mountain biking and swimming. *See Recreation Chart and the AAA Northeastern CampBook.*

THE MUSEUM OF PRINTING is at 800 Massachusetts Ave. The history of printing and how it evolved from typesetting in the 1600s to digital in the present is explained and demonstrated throughout a guided tour. Items on display include typesetting and bindery machines. Parking is available adjacent to the museum. **Time:** Allow 1 hour minimum. **Hours:** Fri.-Sat. 10-4. Closed major holidays. **Cost:** $5; $3 (ages 7-16, students with ID and senior citizens). **Phone:** (978) 686-0450.

NORTH WEYMOUTH (F-3) elev. 23′

ABIGAIL ADAMS BIRTHPLACE is at 180 Norton St. Abigail Smith Adams, the wife of John Adams, the second U.S. president, and mother of John Quincy Adams, the sixth U.S. president, was born in the house Nov. 11, 1744. She lived here until her wedding to John Adams, which took place in the home on Oct. 24, 1764. Built in 1685, the home's furnishings depict the 18th-century lifestyle of the Rev. William and Elizabeth Quincy Smith and their four children.

Tours: Guided tours are available. **Hours:** Sat.-Sun. noon-3, July-Aug.; by appointment May-June and Sept.-Oct. Phone ahead to confirm schedule. **Cost:** $5; $1 (ages 0-11). **Phone:** (781) 335-4205.

QUINCY (F-3) pop. 88,025

As the birthplace of the constitution of Massachusetts—as well as of John and John Quincy Adams—Quincy, then part of the town of Braintree, has assured prominence in American history. The city also was the birthplace of John Hancock, the president of the Continental Congress.

The Josiah Quincy House at 20 Muirhead St. was built in 1770 by the prominent lawyer and political leader. In addition to furniture and memorabilia from several generations of Quincy descendants, the house has period wall paneling and fireplaces surrounded by English tiles; phone (617) 227-3956 for tour information.

South Shore Chamber of Commerce: 36 Miller Stile Rd., P.O. Box 690625, Quincy, MA 02269. **Phone:** (617) 479-1111.

ADAMS NATIONAL HISTORICAL PARK is accessible via a visitor center at 1250 Hancock St. Included are the birthplaces of John and John Quincy Adams and The Old House; all three homes are only accessible during a 2-hour guided tour departing from the visitor center. A trolley bus provides transportation to the historic houses from the visitor center, where tours are scheduled and tickets are issued.

Hours: Visitor center daily 9-5, mid-Apr. to early Nov.; Tues.-Fri. 10-4, rest of year. Guided historic house tours are given daily every 30 minutes 9:15-3:15, mid-Apr. to early Nov. Last tour begins 1 hour, 45 minutes before closing. **Cost:** (includes tour fee for all three historic houses) $5; free (ages 0-15). **Phone:** (617) 770-1175.

The John Adams Birthplace is accessible via the Adams National Historical Park visitor center at 1250 Hancock St. Park rangers guide visitors through the 1735 birthplace and boyhood home of the country's second president. The saltbox house was where he wrote his first letters to Abigail Smith, who later became his wife.

Hours: Guided historic house tours are given daily every 30 minutes 9:15-3:15, mid-Apr. to early Nov. Last tour begins 1 hour, 45 minutes before closing. **Cost:** (includes The John Quincy Adams Birthplace and The Old House) $5; free (ages 0-15). **Phone:** (617) 770-1175.

The John Quincy Adams Birthplace is accessible via the Adams National Historical Park visitor center at 1250 Hancock St. Park rangers lead tours through the home in which John and Abigail Adams resided until the end of the Revolution. The house was the 1767 birthplace of their son John Quincy, who became the country's sixth president. Of interest is the law office where the constitution of Massachusetts, which served as a model for the constitutions of other states and the United States, was drafted.

Hours: Guided historic house tours are given daily every 30 minutes 9:15-3:15, mid-Apr. to early Nov. Last tour begins 1 hour, 45 minutes before closing. **Cost:** (includes The John Adams Birthplace and The Old House) $5; free (ages 0-15). **Phone:** (617) 770-1175.

The Old House is accessible via the Adams National Historical Park visitor center at 1250 Hancock St. Park rangers conduct tours of the mansion, home to the Adams family 1788-1927. It features furnishings used by four generations, including two presidents, and a 14,000-volume library with books owned by the family. Outside the 1731 house is an 18th-century-style garden.

Hours: Guided historic house tours are given daily every 30 minutes 9:15-3:15, mid-Apr. to early Nov. Last tour begins 1 hour, 45 minutes before closing. **Cost:** (includes The John Adams Birthplace and The John Quincy Adams Birthplace) $5; free (ages 0-15). **Phone:** (617) 770-1175.

CHURCH OF THE PRESIDENTS is at 1306 Hancock St. Established in 1639, the congregation of the United First Parish Church was an early proponent of religious freedom. The present granite building, designed by noted architect Alexander Parris, was completed in 1828. John Adams donated the land and granite for its construction, and he, his son John Quincy Adams and their wives are buried here.

Time: Allow 30 minutes minimum. **Hours:** Tours are given Mon.-Fri. 9-4:30, Sat.-Sun. noon-4:30, mid-Apr. to mid-Nov. **Cost:** $4; $3 (students with ID and senior citizens). **Phone:** (617) 773-0062.

QUINCY HISTORICAL SOCIETY MUSEUM is at 8 Adams St. The museum features Quincy: of Stone, of Ships, of Minds—a permanent exhibit relating the history of the area. Supplementing this exhibit are items pertaining to the granite stonework and shipbuilding industries that impacted the community and the nation. Also included are displays about the Adams family and John Hancock. A reference and research library is on the premises.

Hours: Museum Mon.-Fri. 9-4. Library Mon. and Wed. 9-noon. **Cost:** $3; $1.50 (children ages 14+ and senior citizens); free (ages 0-13). **Phone:** (617) 773-1144.

USS *SALEM* AND UNITED STATES NAVAL SHIPBUILDING MUSEUM is off I-93 exit 12, then 4.8 mi. s. on SR 3A to the shipyard at the n. end of Fore River Bridge. Visitors may tour the 716-foot ship and investigate the on-board museums, which highlight aspects of military history from the Revolutionary War era to the present.

Several memorial rooms are included aboard the vessel, said to be the world's only preserved heavy cruiser gunship. A considerable weapons collection, books, prints, artwork, photographs, uniforms and helmets are displayed. **Hours:** Daily 10-4, Memorial Day-Labor Day; Sat.-Sun. 10-4, rest of year. Closed non-military holidays. **Cost:** $5; free (ages 0-3 and military with ID). **Phone:** (617) 479-7900.

ROCKPORT (A-8) pop. 5,606, elev. 62′

Rockport is the site of a well-known artists' colony on Cape Ann.

Rockport Chamber of Commerce: 33 Commercial St., P.O. Box 67, Rockport, MA 01966. **Phone:** (978) 546-6575.

JAMES BABSON COOPERAGE SHOP, 1.5 mi. s. on SR 127, is probably the oldest building on Cape Ann. Built in 1658, the shop displays Early American tools and furniture. **Time:** Allow 30 minutes minimum. **Hours:** Tues.-Sun. 2-5, July-Aug. **Cost:** Free. **Phone:** (978) 546-2958 in season.

PAPER HOUSE, .7 mi. off SR 127 via Curtis and Pigeon Hill sts. in Pigeon Cove, is built of 215 thicknesses of newspaper. The furniture, also made of newspaper, includes a desk made of papers concerning Charles Lindbergh's historic flight, a grandfather clock and a piano. **Hours:** Daily 9-5, Apr. 1 to mid-Oct. **Cost:** $1.50; $1 (ages 6-14). **Phone:** (978) 546-2629.

ROCKPORT ART ASSOCIATION, 12 Main St., offers changing exhibits of paintings, photographs, graphics and sculpture. Workshops, artist demonstrations and lectures are scheduled throughout the year. **Hours:** Mon.-Sat. 10-5, Sun. noon-5, June 1-Columbus Day; Tues.-Fri. 10-4, Sat. 10-5, Sun. noon-5, mid-Feb. through May 31 and day after Columbus Day-Dec. 24. Closed major holidays. **Cost:** Free. **Phone:** (978) 546-6604.

SANDY BAY HISTORICAL SOCIETY AND MUSEUM, 40 King St., contains Early American and Victorian rooms, a marine room, children's room, military room, a library of genealogy and local history, fishing relics and full-rigged ship models. Additional items also are displayed. The Old Castle, nearby at Curtis and Granite streets, is a saltbox house built about 1711. Self-guiding tours of the house highlight historical items, including granite quarry tools.

Time: Allow 1 hour minimum. **Hours:** Historical society museum Mon.-Sat. 2-5, mid-June to mid-Sept.; by appointment rest of year. The Old Castle Sat. 2-5, July-Aug. Library Mon. 9-1. Closed major holidays. **Cost:** (includes The Old Castle) $5; free (ages 0-12). **Phone:** (978) 546-9533.

SALEM (D-3) pop. 40,407, elev. 10′

Salem was capital of the Massachusetts Bay Colony from its founding 1626-30. During the witchcraft trials in 1692 the accusations of a group of children and women caused 19 people to be hanged and one to be crushed to death.

By the end of the 18th century Salem was a prosperous shipping center. Ships from this port brought back rare and costly cargoes from around the world. Many handsome old houses are reminiscent of those seafaring days. The *Friendship,* a full-sized replica of a 1797 East Indian merchant ship, is at Central Wharf across from the Custom House on Derby Street. Nathaniel Hawthorne, who wrote "The Scarlet Letter," was born in Salem in 1804. His birthplace may be viewed at The House of the Seven Gables *(see attraction listing p. 156).*

Misery Islands, which can be reached only via private boat, offers visitors a sandy beach for leisurely walks. The 87-acre island also is a wildlife habitat. Offering 45-minute cruises to nearby Boston is The Salem Ferry, which docks off Blaney Street. Reservations to sail aboard the 92-foot catamaran are required; phone (978) 741-0220.

A free 27-minute orientation film detailing the history of Salem and Essex County is presented at the National Park Service Regional Visitor Center, 2 New Liberty St., which also houses exhibits relating the area's heritage. The center is open daily 9-5. Closed Jan. 1, Thanksgiving and Dec. 25. The film "Where Past is Present" is shown daily 9:25-4.

During the month of October, the city embraces its shadowy past with 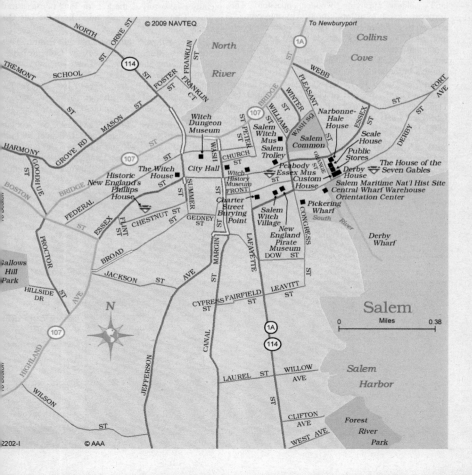 Haunted Happenings. The event features everything from spooky parades and psychic fairs to outlandish costume balls and creepy haunted houses.

Destination Salem: 93 Washington St., P.O. Box 30, Salem, MA 01970. **Phone:** (978) 744-3663.

Self-guiding tours: Maps outlining walking tours are available at the National Park Service Regional Visitor Center; phone (978) 740-1650. *See color ad p. 156*

Shopping areas: Pickering Wharf, between the harbor and Derby Street, houses shops and restaurants in the character of 18th-century wharfside Salem.

CHARTER STREET BURYING POINT, on Charter St., was established 1637 and has the tombs of Gov. Simon Bradstreet, *Mayflower* passenger Richard More, Col. John Hathorne and many other notable Salem citizens. Nearby are the Broad Street and Howard Street burying grounds, which have the tombs of Capt. George Crowninshield and Col. Timothy Pickering.

CITY HALL, 93 Washington St., displays fine portraits and furnishings and contains the Indian deed to the town. The 1838 Greek Revival building is said to be the nation's second-oldest city hall.

Hours: Mon.-Wed. 8-4, Thurs. 8-7, Fri. 8-noon. Closed major holidays. **Cost:** Free. **Phone:** (978) 745-9595.

HISTORIC NEW ENGLAND'S PHILLIPS HOUSE, 34 Chestnut St., was the former home of historic preservationist Stephen Phillips. The Federal-style mansion is filled with five generations of Phillips' family furnishings. Included are fine and decorative arts as well as antique carriages and automobiles. The collection features Fijian throwing clubs, African woodcarvings, Persian carpets, several porcelain items, two Pierce-Arrow vehicles and a Ford Model A.

Time: Allow 30 minutes minimum. **Hours:** Guided tours are given Tues.-Sun. every 30 minutes 11-4, June-Oct.; Sat.-Sun. every 30 minutes 11-4, rest of year. **Cost:** $5; $4 (students with ID and senior citizens); $2.50 (ages 6-12). **Phone:** (978) 744-0440.

THE HOUSE OF THE SEVEN GABLES, 115 Derby St., contains a collection of First-Period buildings, including New England's oldest surviving wooden mansion, The Turner-Ingersoll Mansion (1668). On the grounds are the 1655 Retire Beckett House, Nathaniel Hawthorne's 1804 birthplace, seaside period gardens and a panorama of Salem Harbor. Guided tours of The House of the Seven Gables and Nathaniel Hawthorne's birthplace are included.

Hours: Daily 10-7, July-Oct. (with extended hours in Oct.); 10-5, rest of year. Closed Jan. 1-15, Thanksgiving and Dec. 25. Phone ahead to confirm schedule. **Cost:** $12; $7.25 (ages 5-12). **Phone:** (978) 744-0991. *See color ad.* 🍴

NEW ENGLAND PIRATE MUSEUM, 274 Derby St., features exhibits recounting the history of marauding pirates who once plundered merchant ships off the New England Coast. The museum re-create a colonial seaport, pirate ship and treasure-lade cave. **Time:** Allow 30 minutes minimum. **Hour** Guided tours are given daily 10-5, May-Oct.; Sa Sun. 10-5 in Apr. and Nov. **Cost:** $8; $7 (ages 65+ $6 (ages 4-13). Combination ticket with Witch Du geon Museum and Witch History Museum $19; $1 (ages 65+); $13 (ages 4-13). **Phone:** (97 741-2800.

PEABODY ESSEX MUSEUM, 161 Esse St., offers internationally renowned colle tions of art, architecture and culture encom passing more than 2.4 million works. Co lections include maritime art and history; Americ decorative art, folk art, portraits, furniture and co tumes; art from Japan, China, Korea and India; P cific Islands, American Indian, African and Africa American art; and photography and works of art c paper.

The museum also showcases fine examples Early American architecture. Parks, period garde and 24 historic properties are on the premises. Esp cially noteworthy is the Yin Yu Tang house, a trad tional Chinese merchant's house from the late Qir Dynasty.

Time: Allow 2 hours minimum. **Hours:** Tues Sun. and Mon. holidays 10-5. Closed Jan. Thanksgiving and Dec. 25. **Cost:** (includes fee f historic house tours) $15; $13 (senior citizens); $1 (students with ID); free (ages 0-16). Yin Yu Tar house additional $5. **Phone:** (978) 745-9500 (866) 745-1876. *See color ad.* 🍴

Gardner-Pingree House, 128 Essex St., contai the work of Salem master builder Samuel McIntir Furnished in period, the Federal-style home w built in 1804 for John Gardner, a successful me chant. **Hours:** Daily tour schedule varies; pho

ahead. **Cost:** (includes Peabody Essex Museum and historic house tours) $15; $13 (senior citizens); $11 (students with ID); free (ages 0-16). **Phone:** (978) 745-9500 or (866) 745-1876.

John Ward House is on Brown St. in the Federal Garden area near the Phillips Library. Moved to the museum campus in 1910, the 1684 building originally stood on a 1-acre plot with a kitchen garden, an outhouse and a well. Characterized by its steep gables, large central chimney, diamond-paned windows and second-story overhang, it is one of the earliest structures to be relocated and restored for historic interpretation in the U.S.

Hours: Daily tour schedule varies; phone ahead. **Cost:** (includes Peabody Essex Museum and historic house tours) $15; $13 (senior citizens); $11 (students with ID); free (ages 0-16). **Phone:** (978) 745-9500 or (866) 745-1876.

SALEM MARITIME NATIONAL HISTORIC SITE is on Derby St. on the Old Salem waterfront. Historic buildings of the Port of Salem 1670-1930s are preserved and open to the public, as is *Friendship*, a 342-ton, three-masted tall ship replica. **Time:** Allow 2 hours minimum. **Hours:** Park rangers present a variety of guided tours at the national historic site daily; phone ahead for schedule. **Cost:** Guided tour $5; $3 (ages 6-16 and 62+). **Phone:** (978) 740-1650 or (978) 740-1660.

Central Wharf Warehouse Orientation Center, 193 Derby St. at Salem Maritime National Historic Site, offers exhibits and "To the Farthest Ports of the Rich East," a 17-minute film about Salem's maritime trade following the American Revolution. **Hours:** Daily 9-5. Film is shown daily every half-hour 9:30-4:30. Closed Jan. 1, Thanksgiving and Dec. 25. Phone ahead to confirm schedule. **Cost:** Free. **Phone:** (978) 740-1650 or (978) 740-1660.

Custom House is on the Derby St. waterfront at Salem Maritime National Historic Site. Known by its granite steps and large carved eagle, the structure was built in 1819 and was used to conduct port business and collect tariffs. Nathaniel Hawthorne worked at this site for 3 years while acting as surveyor of the Port of Salem. **Hours:** Park rangers present a variety of guided tours at the national historic site daily; phone ahead for schedule. **Cost:** Guided tour $5; $3 (ages 6-16 and 62+). **Phone:** (978) 740-1650 or (978) 740-1660.

Derby House, on the Derby St. waterfront at Salem Maritime National Historic Site, was built in 1762 by Captain Richard Derby as a wedding gift for his son Elias Hasket Derby, a prominent merchant of the post-Revolutionary War era. The home is furnished in period. **Hours:** Park rangers present a variety of guided tours at the national historic site daily; phone ahead for schedule. **Cost:** Guided tour $5; $3 (ages 6-16 and 62+). **Phone:** (978) 740-1650 or (978) 740-1660.

Derby Wharf lines Salem harbor and is part of Salem Maritime National Historic Site. This was a

base for privateers during the Revolutionary War. Between the Revolutionary War and the War of 1812, when foreign ports were opened to American trade, it was a shipping center. **Hours:** Daily dawn-dusk. **Cost:** Free. **Phone:** (978) 740-1650 or (978) 740-1660.

Narbonne-Hale House, 71 Essex St. at Salem Maritime National Historic Site, was built in 1675. The middle-class home was continuously occupied for nearly 300 years. **Hours:** Park rangers present a variety of guided tours at the national historic site daily; phone ahead for schedule. **Cost:** Guided tour $5; $3 (ages 6-16 and 62+). **Phone:** (978) 740-1650 or (978) 740-1660.

Public Stores, on the Derby St. waterfront at the back of the Custom House at Salem Maritime National Historic Site, was used to store cargoes awaiting re-export or claiming. This 1819 building now displays goods that were imported into Salem in 1829. **Hours:** Daily 9-5. Closed Jan. 1, Thanksgiving and Dec. 25. Phone ahead to confirm schedule. **Cost:** Free. **Phone:** (978) 740-1650 or (978) 740-1660.

Scale House is on the Derby St. waterfront, behind the Custom House at Salem Maritime National Historic Site. Built in 1829, the house stored measuring devices to assess imported cargoes. Equipment is displayed. **Hours:** Daily 9-5. Closed Jan. 1, Thanksgiving and Dec. 25. Phone ahead to confirm schedule. **Cost:** Free. **Phone:** (978) 740-1650 or (978) 740-1660.

West India Goods Store, on the Derby St. waterfront at Salem Maritime National Historic Site, has items including spices, coffee, teas and porcelain from China, India, Africa, the Philippines and other foreign ports that represent Salem's early trade period. **Hours:** Daily 10-5, mid-May to late Oct.; daily 10-4, mid-Apr. to mid-May; Tues.-Sun. noon-4, rest of year. Closed Jan. 1, Thanksgiving and Dec. 25. Phone ahead to confirm schedule. **Cost:** Free. **Phone:** (978) 740-1667.

SALEM TROLLEY departs from the National Park Service Regional Visitor Center at 2 New Liberty St. The 1-hour narrated tours of Salem provide shuttle service to major sites and attractions. Visitors can disembark at any one of 13 stops during the 8-mile journey; all-day, unlimited reboarding is included. **Time:** Allow 1 hour minimum. **Hours:** Tours depart daily (weather permitting) 10-5, Apr.-Oct.; otherwise varies. **Cost:** All-day pass $13; $12 (ages 60+); $5 (ages 6-14). **Phone:** (978) 744-5469.

[SAVE] **SALEM WITCH MUSEUM** is at 19 1/2 Washington Sq. N. opposite Salem Common on SR 1A. An audiovisual presentation about the witch trials of 1692 is offered every half-hour. The exhibit Witches: Evolving Perceptions examines stereotypes, the practice of witchcraft and the phenomenon of witch hunting.

Time: Allow 30 minutes minimum. **Hours:** Daily 10-7, July-Aug.; 10-5, rest of year (with extended hours on Halloween and Fri.-Sat., in Oct.). Closed Jan. 1, Thanksgiving and Dec. 25. **Cost:** $8; $7 (ages 62+); $5.50 (ages 6-14). **Phone:** (978) 744-1692. *See color ad.*

SALEM WITCH VILLAGE, 282 Rear Derby St., features a guided tour through an indoor labyrinth that explains the history of witchcraft and how it has been perceived from medieval times to the present day. **Hours:** Daily 10-9, July-Aug.; 10-6, Mar.-Apr. and Sept.-Oct. (with extended hours in Oct.); 11-4, rest of year. Closed Jan. 1, Thanksgiving and Dec. 25. Phone ahead to confirm schedule. **Cost:** $7; $6 (senior citizens); $5 (ages 6-14). **Phone:** (978) 740-9229.

WITCH DUNGEON MUSEUM, 16 Lynde St., is in a former 19th-century church. A scene from a 1692 witch trial is performed by professional actors. A guided tour of the re-created dungeon is included. **Time:** Allow 30 minutes minimum. **Hours:** Daily 10-5, Apr.-Nov. Closed Easter and Thanksgiving. **Cost:** $8; $7 (ages 62+); $6 (ages 6-14). Combination ticket with New England Pirate Museum and Witch History Museum $19; $16 (ages 65+); $13 (ages 4-13). **Phone:** (978) 741-3570.

WITCH HISTORY MUSEUM is at 197-201 Essex St. An actor dressed in period costume performs a monologue explaining the witch hysteria that gripped the town of Salem in 1692. Guests are led downstairs and through an artificial forest lined with dioramas depicting witch-related events.

Time: Allow 30 minutes minimum. **Hours:** Daily 10-5, Apr.-Nov. Closed Easter and Thanksgiving. **Cost:** $8; $7 (ages 65+); $6 (ages 4-13). Combination ticket with New England Pirate Museum and Witch Dungeon Museum $19; $16 (ages 65+); $13 (ages 4-13). **Phone:** (978) 741-7770.

THE WITCH HOUSE is at 310 1/2 Essex St. The 17th-century home of Judge Jonathan Corwin is furnished in period. Guided tours about 17th-century lifestyles, furniture and architecture, as well as Judge Corwin's role in the 1692 trials, are available. **Time:** Allow 30 minutes minimum. **Hours:** Daily 10-5, early May-early Nov. (with extended hours in Oct.); by appointment rest of year. Phone ahead to confirm schedule. **Cost:** $8.25; $6.25 (ages 62+); $4.25 (ages 6-14). Guided tour $2. **Phone:** (978) 744-8815.

SAUGUS (D-3) pop. 26,078, elev. 20′

The Saugus ironworks began in 1646 with an English investment totaling more than $165,000 by present standards. Its success gave the New World its first sustained production of cast and wrought iron and launched the American iron and steel industry.

Saugus Chamber of Commerce: 394 Lincoln Ave., Saugus, MA 01906. **Phone:** (781) 233-8407.

SAUGUS IRON WORKS NATIONAL HISTORIC SITE, 244 Central St., has a reconstructed blast furnace, working water wheels, a forge and a rolling and slitting mill. This was America's first successfully integrated ironworks. The museum displays artifacts uncovered in excavation, including early ironworks products and a 500-pound hammer used in the original forge.

A video is shown, and blacksmith demonstrations are presented. Iron Works House is a 17th-century house containing Early American furnishings and exhibits. **Tours:** Guided tours are available. **Hours:** Daily 9-5, Apr.-Oct. **Cost:** Free. **Phone:** (781) 233-0050. ⊞

SHARON (C-6) pop. 5,941, elev. 234′

In an area once known as Massapoag, an American Indian word meaning "great waters," Sharon is a residential community. Largemouth bass and pickerel inhabit Lake Massapoag, a popular fishing spot. Rockridge Cemetery contains the grave of and a memorial to Deborah Sampson Gannett, a woman who disguised herself as a man and fought in the Revolutionary War. When her gender was discovered by a physician in 1783, she was given an honorable discharge and a pension for her military service.

MASS AUDUBON'S MOOSE HILL WILDLIFE SANCTUARY is .5 mi. e. of US 1 via SR 27, then 2 mi. s. to 293 Moose Hill St. This is the oldest sanctuary maintained by the Massachusetts Audubon Society. Its 2,000 acres contain woods, meadows, marshes, a butterfly garden, an art gallery and 25 miles of trails. A nature center also is available. **Hours:** Sanctuary daily 7-7. Nature center Mon.-Fri. 9-5, Sat.-Sun. 10-4. Closed Jan. 1, Thanksgiving and Dec. 25. **Cost:** $4; $3 (ages 3-12 and 66+). **Phone:** (781) 784-5691.

STONEHAM (D-2) pop. 22,219, elev. 154′

STONE ZOO is at 149 Pond St. Near the Spot Pond reservoir, the zoo encompasses 26 acres. The facility includes such animals as black bears, North American river otters, white-cheeked gibbons, cougars, hyacinth macaws, jaguars, meerkats, Mexican gray wolves and a snow leopard. Among the exhibits featured are Windows to the Wild, Treasures of the Sierra Madre, Yukon Creek and Touchable Barnyard. **Time:** Allow 2 hours minimum. **Hours:** Daily 10-5 (also Sat.-Sun. 5-6), Apr.-Sept.; 10-4, rest of year. **Cost:** 11; $9 (ages 62+); $7 (ages 2-12). **Phone:** (781) 438-5100. 🚻

STOUGHTON (C-6) elev. 239′

Stoughton was named for William Stoughton, an 18th-century Massachusetts lieutenant governor whose father once had owned the land. The 1868-70 Mary Baker Eddy Historic House, home of the founder of Christian Science, contains period furnishings and an 1840s shoe-making shop; phone (617) 278-9000, ext. 100.

Stoughton Chamber of Commerce: P.O. Box 41, Stoughton, MA 02072. **Phone:** (781) 297-7450.

SUDBURY (E-1) elev. 201′

◤GEM◢ **LONGFELLOW'S WAYSIDE INN OF SUDBURY** is .2 mi. w. off US 20, on Wayside Inn Rd. Made famous by Henry Wadsworth Longfellow's book of poems "Tales of a Wayside Inn," it is one of the country's oldest operating inns. Refurbished by Henry Ford in the 1920s, the inn features period display rooms and an 18th-century tavern. Also on the 120-acre site are the Martha-Mary Chapel; country gardens; a water-powered gristmill; and the 1798 Redstone Schoolhouse, which was made famous by the nursery rhyme "Mary Had A Little Lamb." **Hours:** Inn open daily 9-8; closed July 4 and Dec. 25. Gristmill open Wed.-Sun. 9-5, Apr.-Oct. Schoolhouse open Thurs.-Sun. 11:30-5, May 15-Oct. 15 (weather permitting). Closed July 4 and Dec. 25. **Cost:** Donations. **Phone:** (800) 339-1776. 🚻

SWAMPSCOTT (D-3) pop. 14,412, elev. 38′

On Massachusetts Bay, Swampscott is one of the North Shore's popular summer resorts.

THE MARY BAKER EDDY HISTORIC HOUSE is at 23 Paradise Rd. (SR 1A). While living in the home for a brief period in 1866, Mrs. Eddy experienced the healing that led her to the discovery of Christian Science. The home is equipped with period furnishings, some of which belonged to Eddy. **Time:** Allow 30 minutes minimum. **Hours:**

Wed.-Sat. 10-4, Sun. 1-4, May-Oct.; by appointment rest of year. Closed major holidays. **Cost:** Free. **Phone:** (781) 599-1853, or (800) 277-8943, ext. 100.

TEWKSBURY (B-6) elev. 126′

Wamesit Indian Monument, on Main Street, is a 7-foot-high cast bronze sculpture set on a 9-foot-high granite boulder. It was designed in honor of the peaceful American Indian by Mico Kaufman, a Tewksbury resident and world-class sculptor.

Kaufman also created the Water, Anne Sullivan-Helen Keller Monument, on Main Street, depicting the turning point in Helen Keller's life. A young girl born deaf and blind feels water at the pump, and with three extended fingers understands sign language for the letter W and water. The monument is a tribute to her dedicated teacher Anne Sullivan, a long-time resident of Tewksbury.

TOPSFIELD (A-6) pop. 2,826, elev. 60′

MASS AUDUBON'S IPSWICH RIVER WILDLIFE SANCTUARY is .5 mi. e. of US 1 on SR 97, then s. to 87 Perkins Row. This is the largest of the Massachusetts Audubon Society's sanctuaries, covering 2,267 acres of forests, meadows and wetlands. More than 10 miles of marked trails cross the sanctuary. A backyard bird habitat and a butterfly garden are featured. Pets are not permitted. **Hours:** Trails Tues.-Sun. and Mon. holidays dawn-dusk. Visitor center hours vary; phone ahead. Closed Jan. 1, Thanksgiving and Dec. 24-25. **Cost:** $4; $3 (ages 3-12 and 65+). **Phone:** (978) 887-9264.

WALTHAM (E-2) pop. 59,226, elev. 79′

Waltham was founded in 1636, but was not incorporated into a city until 1884. Beginning in 1854, an Industrial Revolution pioneer operated here; the organization came to be known as the American Waltham Watch Co. Said to be the first to make watches on an assembly line, it produced more than 40 million watches, clocks and other precision instruments until the business closed in the late 1950s. Because of Waltham's association with the company, the city often is referred to as "Watch City."

Stonehurst, The Robert Treat Paine Estate, designed by architect Henry Hobson and landscape architect Frederick Law Olmsted, offers a variety of guided tours and lectures. The innovative home contains original Victorian furnishings, paintings and decorative arts; woodland hiking trails wind through 109 acres of conservation land surrounding the estate. Phone (781) 314-3290.

Waltham West Suburban Chamber of Commerce: 84 South St., Waltham, MA 02453. **Phone:** (781) 894-4700.

SAVE **CHARLES RIVER MUSEUM OF INDUSTRY** is at 154 Moody St. Housed in the 1814 Boston Manufacturing Co. textile mill, this museum features permanent and changing exhibits. Visitors learn about the American Industrial Revolution and era of steam power, the American Waltham Watch Co., and bicycle and automobile manufacturing industries along the Charles River. **Time:** Allow 30 minutes minimum. **Hours:** Thurs.-Sat. 10-5. **Cost:** $5; $3 (children ages 6+, students with ID and senior citizens); free (ages 0-5). **Phone:** (781) 893-5410.

GORE PLACE is at 52 Gore St., on SR 20 at the Waltham-Watertown line. Built in the early 1800s for Gov. Christopher Gore, the mansion is one of the finest examples of Federal domestic architecture in New England. Set in a 40-acre park, the house has been called the "Monticello of the North" and features 22 rooms furnished in period. A small farm with sheep, goats and poultry is on-site.

Hours: Tours are given Mon.-Fri. at 1, Sat. and the second and fourth Sun. of the month at noon, 1, 2 and 3, Sept.-July.; Mon.-Fri. at 1, Sat. at noon, 1, 2 and 3, rest of year. Closed Jan. 1, July 4, Thanksgiving and Dec. 25. Phone ahead to confirm schedule. **Cost:** $10; $5 (ages 5-12). **Phone:** (781) 894-2798.

LYMAN ESTATE GREENHOUSES, .5 mi. n. of jct. US 20 at 185 Lyman St., offers a self-guiding tour through the 19th-century greenhouses containing grapevines, camellia shrubs, orchids, tropical fruit trees and exotic plants. The camellias are in bloom November through April. In June and July, Black Hamburg grape cuttings gathered from the British royal greenhouses at Hampton Court in 1870 ripen. The 1793 mansion (closed to the public) is surrounded by 30 acres of English-style gardens.

Hours: Greenhouses Wed.-Sun. 9:30-4, mid-Dec. to mid-July; Wed.-Sat. 9:30-4, rest of year. Guided greenhouse tours are given the first Wed. of the month 11-2 or by appointment. **Cost:** Self-guiding tour by donation. Guided greenhouse tour $6. **Phone:** (781) 891-4882, ext. 244.

ROSE ART MUSEUM, off South St. on the Brandeis University campus, presents changing exhibits of modern and contemporary art. **Hours:** Wed.-Fri. and Sun. noon-5. Closed university and major holidays. **Cost:** $3; free (ages 0-11, students with ID and senior citizens). **Phone:** (781) 736-3434.

THE WALTHAM MUSEUM INC., 25 Lexington St., focuses on New England's turn-of-the-20th-century manufacturing heritage. Many items produced in Waltham, including automobiles, bicycles and clocks, are on display in the Metz, Waltham Watch, Rudy Currier and Hentzi exhibit rooms. **Time:** Allow 1 hour, 30 minutes minimum. **Hours:** Tues.-Sat. 1-4:30. Closed major holidays. **Cost:** $4; $2 (ages 0-12, ages 56+ and students with ID). **Phone:** (781) 893-9020 or (781) 893-8017.

WATERTOWN (E-2) pop. 32,986, elev. 62'

Watertown-Belmont Chamber of Commerce: 182 Main St., P.O. Box 45, Watertown, MA 02471. **Phone:** (617) 926-1017.

ARMENIAN LIBRARY AND MUSEUM OF AMERICA is .3 mi. s.w. on Church St., then .1 mi. e. to 65 Main St. Said to house the most extensive collection of Armenian artifacts in North America, the museum details the history and culture of Armenians through books, photographs, textiles, documents, coins, folk costumes, musical instruments and artwork.

The Armenian Genocide: In Memoriam exhibit provides information about the World War I extermination of the Armenians by the Turkish government. The library contains oral history tapes and more than 1,000 rare books. **Time:** Allow 1 hour minimum. **Hours:** Museum Fri.-Sun. 1-5, Thurs. 6-9. Library Fri. 1-5. Closed major holidays and Armenian Easter and Christmas. **Cost:** $5; $2 (students with ID); free (ages 0-11). **Phone:** (617) 926-2562.

WELLESLEY (F-1) pop. 26,613, elev. 140'

Wellesley Chamber of Commerce: One Hollis St., Suite 232, Wellesley, MA 02482. **Phone:** (781) 235-2446.

DAVIS MUSEUM AND CULTURAL CENTER, at Wellesley College off SR 135, has a collection of some 10,000 paintings, prints, photographs, drawings and sculptures from classical through contemporary periods. Nationally recognized exhibits are featured. **Hours:** Tues.-Sat. 11-5 (also Wed. 5-8), Sun. noon-4. Closed major holidays. Phone ahead to confirm schedule. **Cost:** Free. **Phone:** (781) 283-2051.

MASSACHUSETTS HORTICULTURAL SOCIETY AT ELM BANK is at 900 Washington St. The 36-acre site on the Charles River includes the New England Trial, Historic Italianate, Bressingham, Goddess and Jim Crockett Memorial gardens. Also on the grounds is the whimsical Weezie's Garden for Children. A library is in the Education Center and contains the society's current collection. **Time:** Allow 30 minutes minimum. **Hours:** Gardens daily 8-dusk. Phone ahead for library hours. **Cost:** Free. **Phone:** (617) 933-4900.

WENHAM (B-7) elev. 51'

Ellery Sedgwick, author and editor of the *Atlantic Monthly* 1909-38, spent many summers just outside Wenham. Long Hill Reservation, The Sedgwick Gardens, his home in Beverly, contains a garden with more than 1,000 native plant species *(see attraction listing p. 136)*.

North Shore Chamber of Commerce: 5 Cherry Hill Dr., Suite 100, Danvers, MA 01923. **Phone:** (978) 774-8565.

WENHAM MUSEUM, on SR 1A at 132 Main St., includes the Claflin-Richards House. Circa 1690, its architecture and furnishings are representative of the 17th, 18th and 19th centuries. The museum has a costume and textile exhibit; a collection of more than 5,000 dolls, dollhouses and toys; changing exhibit galleries; cultural and historical exhibits; and interactive children's exhibits.

A model train room includes a display of railroad relics, antique toy trains and nine running layouts. **Time:** Allow 1 hour minimum. **Hours:** Tues.-Sun. 10-4. Closed major holidays. Phone ahead to confirm schedule. **Cost:** $7; $5 (ages 1-16). **Phone:** (978) 468-2377.

WESTFORD (B-5) elev. 406′

THE BUTTERFLY PLACE, 120 Tyngsboro Rd., features an indoor climate-controlled garden complete with winding paths and flowering plants and shrubs. Caterpillars, chrysalides and hundreds of butterflies from around the world may be seen within the 3,100-square-foot glass atrium.

Note: At press time, The Butterfly Place was closed for renovations and was tentatively scheduled to reopen on Feb. 14, 2010; phone ahead for updates and to confirm schedule. **Time:** Allow 1 hour minimum. **Hours:** Daily 10-5, Feb. 14-Oct. 31. Last admission 30 minutes before closing. Closed Easter.

Cost: $10; $8 (ages 65+); $7 (ages 3-12). **Phone:** (978) 392-0955. 🚗

WESTON (E-1) elev. 165′

SPELLMAN MUSEUM OF STAMPS AND POSTAL HISTORY, .5 mi. n. of jct. SR 30, next to the Regis College campus at 235 Wellesley St., features rare stamps, American and international collections and exhibits describing postal history and famous collectors. A 19th-century post office and intergenerational activities are featured. The Philatelic Research Library also is on-site. **Hours:** Thurs.-Sun. noon-5. Closed most holidays. Phone ahead to confirm schedule. **Cost:** (includes research library) $8; $5 (students with ID and senior citizens); free (ages 0-16). **Phone:** (781) 768-8367.

WEYMOUTH (F-3) pop. 53,988, elev. 30′

ABIGAIL ADAMS BIRTHPLACE—
see North Weymouth p. 153.

Cambridge / © Longfellow House, Old Cambridge

This ends listings for the Boston Vicinity.
The following page resumes the alphabetical listings of cities in Massachusetts.

BOURNE—*see Cape Cod p. 164.*

BOYLSTON (B-5)

TOWER HILL BOTANIC GARDEN is 3.25 mi. n. on Church St. off I-290 exit 24 to 11 French Dr. The 132-acre site includes an heirloom apple orchard; a wildlife refuge pond; secret, vegetable, lawn, cottage, systematic and wildlife gardens; the Orangerie, a greenhouse; and nature trails with views of Mount Wachusett and the Wachusett Reservoir. Special events are held throughout the year.

Time: Allow 1 hour minimum. **Hours:** Tues.-Sun. and Mon. holidays 10-5 (also Wed. 5-8, May-Aug.). Guided tours are given Sun. at 2. Closed Jan. 1, Thanksgiving and Dec. 24-25 and 31. **Cost:** $10; $7 (ages 65+); $5 (ages 6-18). **Phone:** (508) 869-6111. ⓣ

BRAINTREE—*see Boston p. 136.*

BREWSTER—*see Cape Cod p. 164.*

BROCKTON (C-7) pop. 94,304, elev. 128′

Once a major shoe-manufacturing center, Brockton now supports more than 200 other industries.

Named after one of the city's shoe manufacturers, D.W. Field Park, off AMVETS Memorial Highway, offers golfing, picnicking and bicycling in the park's 700 acres of woods, ponds and gardens.

Metro South Chamber of Commerce: 60 School St., Brockton, MA 02301. **Phone:** (508) 586-0500.

Shopping areas: Westgate Mall, SR 24 at CR 27, has Macy's and Sears.

FULLER CRAFT MUSEUM, 455 Oak St., is said to be New England's only contemporary craft museum. Eight galleries display 18 changing exhibits in a variety of media: glass, metal, wood, ceramic and fiber. **Time:** Allow 1 hour minimum. **Hours:** Tues.-Sun. 10-5 (also Wed. 5-9). Guided tours are given Sat. at 2. Closed Jan. 1 and Dec. 25. **Cost:** $8; $5 (ages 65+ and students with ID); free (ages 0-11 and to all Wed. 5-9 p.m.). **Phone:** (508) 588-6000.

BROOKLINE—*see Boston p. 136.*

BUZZARDS BAY—*see Cape Cod p. 165.*

CAMBRIDGE—*see Boston p. 136.*

CANTON—*see Boston p. 140.*

CAPE ANN—*see Boston p. 140.*

Cape Cod

To architects, Cape Cod is a style; to gourmets, a cuisine; and to artists, changing moods and patterns of light, color and space. Summer visitors see the cape as beaches, shops, attractions, entertainment, country clubs and, often, a chance to rub elbows with celebrities. More basic is the Cape Cod of residents. Quiet and individualistic, they view the cape as a haven where life can proceed undisturbed, even by the annual influx of tourists.

US 6 curves northeast along the cape and allows access to the scrub oak-pitch pine covered sand dunes of the Cape Cod National Seashore *(see place listing p. 165)*. Beginning at Sagamore Bridge and ending in Provincetown, the route provides access to many towns on the cape. The cape also is accessible via SR 28, which takes travelers along the southern portion.

Another way to see the island is by traversing the 22-mile-long Cape Cod Rail Trail. The trail offers hikers and bicyclists picturesque scenery and opportunities to explore the natural wonders of the island.

In November 1620 the *Mayflower* Pilgrims landed at the tip of the cape. By the end of the 17th century Cape Cod was a prosperous fishing and whaling center. During the 1800s wealthy sea captains built elaborate homes and furnished them with objects acquired on their world travels. Many homes have been restored as museums.

BARNSTABLE (D-8) pop. 47,821, elev. 72′

Settled in 1636 by pioneers whose livestock thrived in the salty hay marshes, Barnstable developed as a coastal trade center. Fish caught on the Grand Banks and maritime activities were economic mainstays. Sea captains of the village sailed on clipper ships to the Orient. The region now draws summer residents and is a popular seasonal resort.

HYANNIS WHALE WATCHER CRUISES departs from Barnstable Harbor at 269 Millway Rd., .5 mi. n. of jct. SR 6A. Narrated 3.5-hour whale-watching excursions are offered. Clambake cruises are available in summer. **Hours:** Whale-watching excursions depart daily, May-Oct. Departure times vary; phone ahead. **Cost:** Whale-watching excursion $45; $40 (ages 62+); $26 (ages 4-12). Tickets are available on a first-come, first-served basis. **Parking:** $15. **Phone:** (508) 362-6088, or (888) 942-5392 in season. ⑪

TRAYSER MUSEUM GROUP, at the Old Custom House/Post Office on SR 6A, was built in 1856 by the U.S. Department of Treasury. The restored interior features exhibits relating to the Coast Guard and history of lifesaving, publications, photographs, artifacts and video presentations. A village blacksmith shop and old jailhouse also are on-site. **Hours:** Tues.-Sat. 10-3, late June to mid-Oct. **Cost:** $5; $3

Dexter's Grist Mill, Sandwich / Cape Cod Chamber of Commerce

(ages 62+); free (ages 0-9 and active Coast Guard with ID). **Phone:** (508) 362-8521.

BOURNE (E-8) pop. 1,443, elev. 19′

Until 1864, Bourne was a part of Sandwich, one of Cape Cod's oldest towns. After the separation, the new town was named after Jonathan Bourne, the village's most prominent native son, a successful whaling merchant who set up offices in New Bedford. The cape offers travelers only two links to the mainland, one of which—Bourne Bridge—is in town.

The ⌇ Bourne Scallop Festival, held in late September, offers arts and crafts, midway rides, music and, of course, lots of yummy food—from deep-fried scallops to herb-roasted chicken.

APTUCXET TRADING POST MUSEUM is on the s. side of the Bourne Canal Bridge, 1 mi. from jct. US 6 and SR 28 via Shore Rd. The museum is a replica of the trading post built on this site in 1627, perhaps the first such establishment on the continent. Exhibits include 17th-century furnishings and Pilgrim, Dutch and American Indian relics. President Grover Cleveland's private railroad station; the Jefferson Windmill, named for actor Joseph Jefferson; saltworks and an herb garden are on the grounds.

Hours: Guided tours are given Tues.-Sat. 10-4, Sun. 2-5, Memorial Day weekend-Columbus Day. Closed major holidays. **Cost:** $4; $3.50 (ages 61+); $2 (students in grades 1-12). **Phone:** (508) 759-9487. ♿

BREWSTER (D-9) pop. 2,212

Approximately at the geographic center of Cape Cod on SR 6A, Brewster is the setting of stately

early 19th-century homes built by the sea captains who dominated the town's initial economy. The city offers antique shops, art galleries and museums that lure summer visitors to Cape Cod Bay. The Old Gristmill on Stoney Brook Road is one of the country's first gristmills.

Brewster Chamber of Commerce: 2198 Main St., P.O. Box 1241, Brewster, MA 02631. **Phone:** (508) 896-3500.

CAPE COD MUSEUM OF NATURAL HISTORY, 2 mi. w. of SR 124 at 869 SR 6A, has an aquarium, two floors of exhibits, a library, and three nature trails along which native fauna and flora can be seen. Educational programs and nature trips are scheduled year-round. **Time:** Allow 1 hour, 30 minutes minimum. **Hours:** Daily 9:30-4, June-Sept.; Wed.-Sun. 11-3, Apr.-May and Oct.-Dec.; Thurs.-Sun. 11-3, Feb.-Mar. Closed major holidays. **Cost:** $8; $7 (senior citizens); $3.50 (ages 3-12). **Phone:** (508) 896-3867.

BUZZARDS BAY (D-7) pop. 3,549

Cape Cod Canal Region Chamber of Commerce: 70 Main St., Buzzards Bay, MA 02532. **Phone:** (508) 759-6000. *See color ad p. 501.*

CAPE COD CANAL is .2 mi. s. of Main St. on Academy Dr. The 7-mile-long canal is part of a 17.4-mile link between Buzzards Bay and Cape Cod Bay, designed to save an average of 165 miles of coastline travel around the tip of Cape Cod. Recreational facilities include 13.5 miles of paved walking and bicycling paths. Fishing from the shore is permitted; however, swimming is prohibited. Multiple day-use recreation areas are located along both

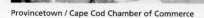
Provincetown / Cape Cod Chamber of Commerce

sides of the canal. A visitor center in Sandwich has films and exhibits about the canal.

Note: Photo ID is required. **Hours:** Daily 8-dusk. Field office Mon.-Fri. 9-4. Closed major holidays. **Phone:** (508) 759-4431, or (508) 833-9678 for the visitor center in Sandwich. 🅰️ 🚫

CAPE COD NATIONAL SEASHORE (C-9)

Occupying 40 miles along Cape Cod's coastline, the 43,608-acre Cape Cod National Seashore offers dunes constantly reshaped by storm and wind, marshland, glacial cliffs and dense forests. Spared the scars of industrial buildup, the beaches, ponds and open fields remain protected in a natural state. The cape also is marked by weathered cottages, villages and lighthouses.

General Information and Activities

The national seashore is open all year. Park headquarters is at the Marconi area in South Wellfleet. Near the headquarters are high cliffs that afford

Destination Cape Cod

*T*o beach or not to beach? On Cape Cod, that is the question. If you choose to beach it, the options seem endless: Find a secluded patch of sand and listen to the waves crash, or people-watch at one of the more popular beaches.

*I*f you'd rather stay in town, opt for some antique hunting, museum hopping or window shopping.

© H. Stanley Johnson / SuperStock

Old Eastham Windmill.
(See listing page 172)

© Garry Black / age fotostock

Sandwich Glass Museum.
(See listing page 176)

*P*laces included in this AAA Destination Area:

Buzzards
Bay
Bourne

Falmouth

Woods
Hole

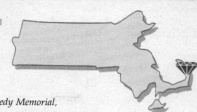

John F. Kennedy Memorial, Hyannis.
(See mention page 173)

© D. Lada / Robertstock

Provincetown
North Truro
Wellfleet
South Wellfleet

Cape Cod

Eastham
Orleans
Brewster
Sagamore
Sandwich
East Sandwich
Dennis
West Barnstable
Yarmouth Port
Barnstable
Harwich
Centerville
Hyannis
West Yarmouth
Chatham
Mashpee
Osterville
Cotuit

© Barry Mason / Alamy

Falmouth Museums on the Green.
(See listing page 172)

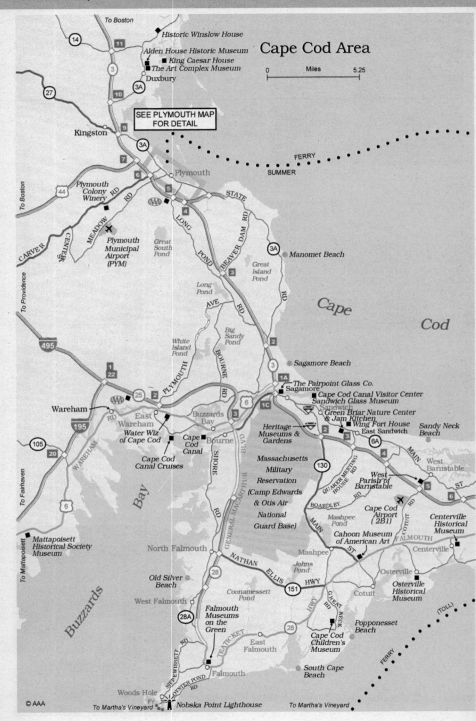

Cape Cod Area

To Boston

Historic Winslow House

Alden House Historic Museum
King Caesar House
The Art Complex Museum
Duxbury

14
11
3
3A
27
10
3A

Kingston
9
3A
7

SEE PLYMOUTH MAP FOR DETAIL

FERRY
SUMMER

To Boston
44

Plymouth Colony Winery

Plymouth
6
5

STATE

Plymouth Municipal Airport (PYM)

Great South Pond

Manomet Beach

To Providence

3A

Cape

Cod

Long Pond

Big Sandy Pond

Great Island Pond

White Island Pond

495

22

Bourne

Sagamore Beach

The Pairpoint Glass Co.
Sagamore
Cape Cod Canal Visitor Center
Sandwich Glass Museum
Green Briar Nature Center & Jam Kitchen
Wing Fort House
East Sandwich

Sandy Neck Beach

Wareham
25
2

East Wareham
Water Wiz of Cape Cod

Buzzards Bay

Bourne

Heritage Museums & Gardens

195
105
20

Cape Cod Canal Cruises

Cape Cod Canal

Massachusetts Military Reservation (Camp Edwards & Otis Air National Guard Base)

130

West Parish of Barnstable

West Barnstable
5

6A
4

To Fairhaven
6

Mattapoisett Historical Society Museum

North Falmouth

Mashpee Pond

Cape Cod Airport (2B1)

Centerville Historical Museum

Cahoon Museum of American Art

Mashpee

Centerville

Osterville

Osterville Historical Museum

To Mattapoisett

Buzzards

Bay

Old Silver Beach

Coonamessett Pond

Johns Pond

151

Cotuit

28

West Falmouth

Falmouth Museums on the Green

28A

East Falmouth

28

Cape Cod Children's Museum

Popponesset Beach

(TOLL)

South Cape Beach

© AAA

Woods Hole
To Martha's Vineyard

Nobska Point Lighthouse

To Martha's Vineyard

FERRY

Miles
0   5.25

© 2009 NAVTEQ

Race Point Beach

Provincetown Municipal
Airport (PVC)

Race
Point
Light

Herring
Cove Beach

Pilgrim Monument &
Provincetown Museum

Wood
End
Light

Long
Point
Light

(TOLL)

ONLY

Provincetown

North Truro

STATE

6

Highland House Museum

Highland Light
(Cape Cod Light)

Cape

Great
Hollow
Beach

OLD COUNTY RD

Truro

ST

Cod

National

ATLANTIC

Seashore

CHEQUESSETT
NECK

Wellfleet Historical
Society Museum

Wellfleet

Wellfleet
Harbor

South
Wellfleet

OCEAN VIEW DR

Cahoon Hollow Beach

Visitor Centers

Mass Audubon's
Wellfleet Bay
Wildlife Sanctuary

STATE

Marconi Beach

Crooks Brook
Beach

Kingsbury Beach

HERRING BROOK RD

NAUSET RD

Nauset Lighthouse

The Old Schoolhouse Museum
Old Eastham Windmill
Eastham
The Swift-Daley House

6

Bay

N

Rock Harbor

Points of Rocks
Beach

Cape Cod
Museum of
Natural
History

Cape Cod
Museum
of Art

6A

Dennis

Brewster

ST

MAIN

RD

13

12

6A

East Orleans
Orleans

ORLEANS

6

OCEAN

Roland C
Nickerson
St Pk

LONG

HARWICH

RD

Upper
Mill
Pond

Long
Pond
RD

28

Beachcomber
Seal Watching

Chatham
Railroad
Museum

Hyannis
Whale
Watcher
Cruises

Barnstable

Trayser
Mus Group

MAIN

SETUCKET

SATUCKET

RD

134

9

10

ORLEANS RD

11

137

East
Harwich

RD

STATION AVE

HIGH BANK

RD

6

8

7

Barnstable
Municipal
Airport
(HYA)

Hyannis

28

West
Dennis

South Dennis
Dennis
Port

Harwich

Brooks
Free
Library

Chatham
Municipal
Airport
(CQX)

Chatham

The
Atwood
House
Museum

Chatham
Lighthouse

West
Yarmouth

South
Yarmouth

LOWER COUNTY RD

Harwich Port

Hyannis
Port

ZooQuarium

Old Bass River
Lighthouse

Cape Cod
Duckmobiles

Cape Cod
Melody
Tent

RD

Sound

FERRY

(TOLL)

Nantucket

Monomoy National
Wildlife Refuge

good views of the beach and ocean, and an inland nature trail traverses a white cedar swamp unusual to the cape. At Pilgrim Heights in North Truro is a spring thought to have been the Pilgrims' first source of fresh water. The spring is reached by a nature trail.

Guided walks and lectures are offered September through October. Interpretive shelters provide historical exhibits. Self-guiding nature trails are open all year; trail leaflets are available at visitor centers and at the head of each trail.

There are four picnic areas, and picnicking is allowed on all beaches; a permit is required to build an open fire. Swimming is permitted on six beaches in the summer and lifeguards are on duty. No license is required for saltwater fishing, but a state license is required for freshwater fishing, and a town license is needed for shellfishing.

Hunting is permitted in season for upland game and migratory waterfowl; federal, state and local laws apply. Camping is prohibited in the seashore, except in privately owned campgrounds.

Three paved bicycle trails, originating near the visitor centers and at the head of the Meadow Beach parking lot, lead to beaches and picnic areas. Trail maps are available at the visitor centers. *See Recreation Chart.*

ADMISSION, charged at the beaches daily late June to early September and on weekends and holidays from Memorial Day to late June and early September through September 30, is $15 (per private vehicle); $3 (per person arriving by other means).

PETS must be physically restricted at all times; leashes are not to exceed 6 feet. Pets are not allowed in public buildings, picnic areas or on trails and are permitted on swimming beaches only during the off-season.

ADDRESS inquiries to the Superintendent, Cape Cod National Seashore, 99 Marconi Site Rd., Wellfleet, MA 02667; phone (508) 771-2144.

VISITOR CENTERS in Provincetown and Eastham provide information on the seashore. Both centers offer evening programs presented in adjacent amphitheaters in the summer; check locally for hours and schedules.

Province Lands Visitor Center, on Race Point Rd. in Provincetown, has an observation platform and offers movies and exhibits. **Hours:** Daily 9-5, early May-Oct. 31. **Phone:** (508) 487-1256.

Salt Pond Visitor Center, on US 6 in Eastham, offers movies and museum exhibits. **Hours:** Daily 9-5, with extended hours in summer. **Phone:** (508) 255-3421.

CENTERVILLE (E-8)

With its maritime location on Nantucket Sound, Centerville was home to wealthy ship captains who built stately homes in the early 1800s. Craigville Beach offers boating, beachcombing and swimming in Nantucket Sound.

[SAVE] **CENTERVILLE HISTORICAL MUSEUM,** 513 Main St., is a 14-room museum housed in an 1854 home to which exhibition wings have been

Highland Light, North Truro / © Jeff Greenberg / age fotostock

added. Exhibits include a Colonial Revival kitchen, Victorian period rooms, gowns and accessories, marine and Civil War artifacts, farm tools, decorative arts and a research library. **Hours:** Tues.-Sat. noon-4, May 1 to mid-Dec. Last tour begins 30 minutes before closing. **Cost:** $6; $5 (students with ID and senior citizens); free (ages 0-8). **Phone:** (508) 775-0331.

CHATHAM (E-9) pop. 1,667, elev. 59′

With Nantucket Sound on one side and the Atlantic Ocean on the other, Chatham is a fine starting place for the saltwater angler in search of bass, bluefish and snapper. Commercial fishing boats unload their catches at the pier on Shore Road every afternoon. Chatham Light, which affords an excellent panorama of the Atlantic, is approximately 2 miles northeast off SR 28.

Chatham Chamber of Commerce: P.O. Box 793, Chatham, MA 02633. **Phone:** (508) 945-5199 or (800) 715-5567.

THE ATWOOD HOUSE MUSEUM, .7 mi. s. at 347 Stage Harbor Rd., was built about 1752 for Joseph C. Atwood, a sea captain, and remained in the Atwood family for nearly 175 years. Fully restored, the two-story house is furnished in several periods. Nine added galleries contain such historical items as portraits and biographies of sea captains, maritime paintings, ship models, antique tools and murals depicting the local residents during the early 20th century.

Time: Allow 1 hour minimum. **Hours:** Tues.-Sat. 10-4, July-Aug.; 1-4 in June and Sept.-Oct.; by appointment rest of year. **Cost:** $5; $3 (children ages 12+ and students with ID); free (ages 0-11). **Phone:** (508) 945-2493.

BEACHCOMBER SEAL WATCHING, which departs from various locations depending on the season, offers views of the playful pinnipeds in their natural habitat as well as a look at Chatham's scenic beaches and harbors. **Hours:** Trips depart daily 9-5, July-Aug. **Cost:** $27; $25 (ages 66+); $23 (ages 3-15). **Phone:** (508) 945-5265.

CHATHAM RAILROAD MUSEUM, on Depot Rd. in the passenger station of the former railroad company, contains artifacts, models of trains, the 1910 New York Central Caboose and a diorama of the Chatham railroad yard. **Hours:** Tues.-Sat. 10-4, mid-June to mid-Sept. **Cost:** Donations. **Phone:** (508) 945-5199.

COTUIT (E-8) elev. 23′

CAHOON MUSEUM OF AMERICAN ART is at 4676 Falmouth Rd. A permanent collection of 19th-, 20th- and 21st-century folk paintings by such artists as Ralph Blakelock, William Bradford, James Buttersworth, Ralph and Martha Cahoon, John J. Enneking and Levi Wells Prentice is on display in a restored 1775 Georgian Colonial house. **Time:** Allow 1 hour minimum. **Hours:** Tues.-Sat. 10-4, Sun. 1-4,

Feb.-Dec. **Cost:** $5; $4 (students with ID and senior citizens); free (ages 0-11). **Phone:** (508) 428-7581.

DENNIS (E-9) pop. 2,798, elev. 24′

Dennis, on SR 6A almost at the midpoint of the north shore of Cape Cod, is the site of graceful old homes, spacious summer residences, artists' studios and the famed Cape Playhouse. The method of cultivating cranberries in bogs originated in Dennis; commercial salt extraction from sea water was initiated in East Dennis in the late 18th century.

Established in 1926, the Cape Playhouse, off SR 6A, continues to offer first-rate theater every summer including plays, comedies, mysteries and musicals; phone (508) 385-3911.

Dennis Chamber of Commerce: 238 Swan River Rd., P.O. Box 1001, West Dennis, MA 02670. **Phone:** (508) 398-3568.

[SAVE] **CAPE COD MUSEUM OF ART** is off SR 6A on the grounds of the Cape Cod Center for the Arts. The museum displays the works of 19th-century to contemporary Cape Cod regional artists and features seven galleries and a sculpture garden. Changing exhibits, films, lectures and special events also are presented.

Time: Allow 1 hour, 30 minutes minimum. **Hours:** Museum Tues.-Wed. and Fri.-Sat. 10-5 (also Mon. 10-5, Memorial Day-Columbus Day), Thurs. 10-8, Sun. noon-5. Guided tours are given Thurs. at 11, Sat. at 11 and 1 (also Sun. at 1, Apr.-Dec.). **Cost:** $8; free (ages 0-18); by donation (Thurs.). **Phone:** (508) 385-4477.

EASTHAM (D-9) elev. 32′

Eastham was settled in 1644 by Plymouth colonists. First Encounter Beach was the spot where Miles Standish and other *Mayflower* forefathers landed during their expedition from Provincetown. Naturalist Henry Beston, enchanted by the area's beauty in 1927, wrote "The Outermost House," a passionate novel about the winds, tides and wildlife of the beach. The hull of the World War II victory ship, the *Gen. James E. Longstreet,* was submerged in the bay for target practice by the Air Force more than 50 years ago. A visitor center for Cape Cod National Seashore *(see place listing p. 165)* is at Salt Pond, off scenic US 6.

Eastham Chamber of Commerce: P.O. Box 1329, Eastham, MA 02642. **Phone:** (508) 240-7211.

Eastham Town Hall: 2500 State Hwy., Eastham, MA 02642. **Phone:** (508) 240-5900.

THE CHESTER RANLETT TOOL MUSEUM, on US 6 behind The Swift-Daley House, displays hundreds of tools and implements from the area, including a wooden crankshaft from the old saltworks, a foot-operated grindstone, cranberry sorters and doorposts from the First Eastham Meeting House. The Dill Beach Shack, which survived the storm of 1978 that ravaged the coast, also is on the grounds. **Time:** Allow 30 minutes minimum. **Hours:** Mon.-Fri.

10-1, July-Aug.; Sat. 10-1, in Sept. Phone ahead to confirm schedule. **Cost:** Free. **Phone:** (508) 240-0871.

OLD EASTHAM WINDMILL, on US 6 opposite the town hall, is the oldest working windmill on Cape Cod. Occasionally corn is ground in the 1680 structure. Built in Plymouth by Thomas Paine, the mill was moved to Eastham in 1793. **Hours:** Mon.-Sat. 10-5, Sun. 1-5, July-Aug. **Cost:** Free. **Phone:** (508) 240-5900.

THE OLD SCHOOLHOUSE MUSEUM, off US 6 at jct. Nauset and Schoolhouse rds., is a one-room schoolhouse built in 1869. Exhibits depict the area's history and include a model schoolroom, farming and household implements, shipwreck treasures, U.S. war memorabilia, old paper currency, a coin collection and a 13-foot jawbone from a 65-foot finback whale. **Time:** Allow 30 minutes minimum. **Hours:** Mon.-Fri. 1-4, July 4-Labor Day weekend. **Cost:** Donations. **Phone:** (508) 255-0788.

THE SWIFT-DALEY HOUSE, on US 6 next to the post office, was built in 1741. Eight furnished rooms feature clothing and artifacts from the Colonial to Victorian periods. **Time:** Allow 1 hour minimum. **Hours:** Mon.-Fri. 10-1, July-Aug.; Sat. 10-1, in Sept. Phone ahead to confirm schedule. **Cost:** Donations. **Phone:** (508) 240-0871.

EAST SANDWICH (E-7) pop. 3,720, elev. 37′

GREEN BRIAR NATURE CENTER & JAM KITCHEN is at 6 Discovery Hill Rd. The nature center promotes author Thornton W. Burgess' interest in nature through natural history exhibits and The Old Briar Patch Trail, a 1-mile, self-guiding nature trail. At the jam kitchen, began in 1903, visitors can watch jams and jellies being made using the same methods as it did at the turn of the 20th century. **Time:** Allow 30 minutes minimum. **Hours:** Mon.-Sat. 10-4, Sun. 1-4, Apr. 15-Dec. 31; Tues.-Sat. 10-4, rest of year. Closed Jan. 1, July 4, Labor Day, Thanksgiving and Dec. 25. **Cost:** Donations. **Phone:** (508) 888-6870.

WING FORT HOUSE is n. of SR 6A at 69 Spring Hill Rd. Built in 1641, the house was occupied continuously by members of the Wing family from 1646 until it became a museum in 1942. Seven rooms are furnished with pieces from various periods. **Tours:** Guided tours are available. **Hours:** Tues.-Sat. 10-4, mid-June to mid-Sept. Closed July 4. **Cost:** $3; $1 (ages 0-11). **Phone:** (508) 833-1540.

FALMOUTH (E-8) pop. 4,115, elev. 44′

Falmouth was settled by Quakers in 1661 and was one of the first New England towns founded on the principles of religious tolerance. Originally a center for whaling, shipbuilding and agriculture, it later supported salt and glass industries. Falmouth is now a picturesque year-round beach resort centered

on a historic village green. It also is a seasonal departure point for passenger-only ferries to Martha's Vineyard *(see place listing p. 186)* and connecting services to Nantucket Island *(see place listing p. 188).*

Falmouth Chamber of Commerce: 20 Academy Ln., Falmouth, MA 02541. **Phone:** (508) 548-8500 or (800) 526-8532.

SAVE **FALMOUTH MUSEUMS ON THE GREEN** is at 55 Palmer Ave. off SR 28 at the Village Green. Two 18th-century houses contain furniture, fine art, toys and textiles; exhibits depicting 19th-century whaling; a colonial kitchen; a display about pre-Civil War medicine; and a room that chronicles the life of Katharine Lee Bates, Falmouth-born poet of "America the Beautiful." The Hallett Barn Visitor Center houses changing exhibits and vintage clothing. Colonial and herb gardens are part of the 2-acre complex.

Tours: Guided tours are available. **Hours:** Tues.-Fri. 10-4, Sat. 10-1, mid-June to mid-Oct. Closed major holidays. **Cost:** Historic house tours $5; free (ages 0-13). Visitor center free. **Phone:** (508) 548-4857.

HARWICH (E-9) elev. 70′

Harwich was named after the English village called "Happy-go-lucky Harwich" by Queen Elizabeth. At the elbow of Cape Cod, it is surrounded by the communities of North, South, East and West Harwich, Harwich Port and Pleasant Lake, all of which are known collectively as the Harwiches. Once a whaling and shipbuilding center, Harwich is now supported by the cranberry and tourism industries.

The town's population triples during the summer, as visitors arrive to enjoy nearby freshwater and saltwater beaches, fishing, scuba diving, sailing and bird-watching. Bicyclists traverse the 22-mile Cape Cod Rail Trail, which winds through woodlands and beaches. Brooks Academy Museum, 80 Parallel St., features historical, maritime and textile displays as well as C.D. Cahoon paintings and sketches, manuscript collections, antique tools, housewares and toys; phone (508) 432-8089.

Harwich Chamber of Commerce: One Schoolhouse Rd., P.O. Box 34, Harwich Port, MA 02646. **Phone:** (508) 432-1165 or (800) 442-7942.

BROOKS FREE LIBRARY, on Main St., contains a collection of figurines by renowned sculptor John Rogers. **Hours:** Tues.-Thurs. 10-7, Fri.-Sat. 10-4. **Cost:** Free. **Phone:** (508) 430-7562.

HYANNIS (E-8) elev. 30′

Hyannis' nearby beaches—particularly Craigville Beach, the largest on the cape—are popular. The town's harbor is deep enough to accommodate ocean-going yachts. A memorial to John F. Kennedy on Ocean Street has a small pool and fountain with a circular fieldstone wall bearing the presidential seal.

The Steamship Authority, a car and passenger ferry, operates daily year-round from Hyannis to Nantucket; for information or reservations phone (508) 477-8600.

Hyannis Area Chamber of Commerce: 397 Main St., P.O. Box 100, Hyannis, MA 02601. **Phone:** (508) 775-2201.

Shopping areas: Cape Cod Mall, on SR 132, has Macy's and Sears. Hyannis Main Street Waterfront District offers more than 200 shops.

CAPE COD CENTRAL RAILROAD departs from 252 Main St. The 2-hour Scenic Excursion Train travels between Hyannis and the Cape Cod Canal, past cranberry bogs, woodlands and marshes. A narrator aboard the train relates the history of the region. Train trips including lunch, dinner or Sunday brunch also are available. **Time:** Allow 2 hours minimum. **Hours:** Scenic Excursion Train departs late May-late Oct. Schedule varies; phone ahead. **Cost:** Scenic Excursion Train $21; $19 (ages 62+); $17 (ages 3-11). **Phone:** (508) 771-3800 or (888) 797-7245. 🍴

CAPE COD DUCKMOBILES departs from 437 Main St. The 45-minute narrated tour offers information about Hyannis. Passengers ride in amphibious vehicles that were used during World War II and the Vietnam War to transport soldiers and supplies from land to sea and back. Approximately 20 minutes of the tour is spent on the water.

Hours: Tours are offered daily every half-hour (weather permitting) 10-5, in summer; at 11:30, 1 and 2:30, in spring and fall. Phone ahead to confirm schedule. **Cost:** $17; $14 (children ages 5+, students with ID and senior citizens); $5 (ages 0-4). **Phone:** (508) 790-2111, or (888) 225-3825 mid-Apr. to mid-Oct.

CAPE COD MELODY TENT, 21 W. Main St., presents intimate theater-in-the-round concerts and comedy shows. **Hours:** Most performances are offered nightly at 8, June 1-Labor Day. Children's shows are offered Wed. at 11 a.m., June 1-Labor Day. **Cost:** Evening performances $30-$100. Children's shows $8-$15. Prices vary depending on show. **Phone:** (508) 775-5630.

HY-LINE CRUISES, at Ocean St. Dock, offers 1-hour narrated tours of Hyannis Harbor and Lewis Bay. A view of the Kennedy family's summer homes is included. Other cruises available include daily ferries to Nantucket Island *(see place listing p. 188)* and Martha's Vineyard *(see place listing p. 186).* **Hours:** Harbor tours depart daily, mid-Apr. to mid-Oct. Departure times vary; phone ahead. **Cost:** Harbor tour $16; $8 (ages 3-11). Prices may vary. **Phone:** (508) 790-0696. *See color ad & p. 485.*

JOHN F. KENNEDY HYANNIS MUSEUM is in the old Town Hall Building at 397 Main St. A statue of

President Kennedy walking on the beach greets visitors at the museum's entrance. Featured are exhibits, photographs and oral histories dedicated to the times that Kennedy spent in the area with his family and friends. A portrait of President Kennedy's son, John Fitzgerald Kennedy Jr., also is on display. An 8-minute videotape, narrated by Walter Cronkite, reflects on the "Summer White House" and place of refuge for the 35th president.

Hours: Mon.-Sat. 9-5, Sun. noon-5, mid-Apr. through Oct. 31; Thurs.-Sat. 10-4, Sun. noon-4, mid-Feb. to mid-Apr. and Nov.-Dec. Holiday hours vary; phone ahead. Last admission 30 minutes before closing. **Cost:** $5; $2.50 (ages 10-17). **Phone:** (508) 790-3077.

MASHPEE (E-8)

Descendants of the Mashpee Indians still gather cranberries from the many bogs in the Mashpee area. Old Indian Meeting House, the second Indian church on the cape, was erected in 1684; it stands in the old burying ground along SR 28 south of town.

Mashpee Chamber of Commerce: 520 Main St., P.O. Box 1245, Mashpee, MA 02649. **Phone:** (508) 477-0792.

CAPE COD CHILDREN'S MUSEUM, 577 Great Neck Rd. S., offers an interactive and educational experience for children. Included are a castle for toddlers, a submarine, a 30-foot pirate ship, a puppet stage, a wooden train, a tree house, a music room and an inflatable planetarium.

Time: Allow 1 hour, 30 minutes minimum. **Hours:** Museum Mon.-Sat. 10-5, Sun. noon-5, Memorial Day weekend-Labor Day and during school vacation weeks; Tues.-Thurs. 10-3, Fri.-Sat. 10-5, Sun. noon-5, rest of year. Planetarium hours vary; phone ahead. Closed Jan. 1, Easter, July 4, Thanksgiving and Dec. 24-25. **Cost:** $6; $5 (ages 60+); free (under 1). Under 15 must be with an adult. **Phone:** (508) 539-8788.

NORTH TRURO (D-8) elev. 20'

HIGHLAND HOUSE MUSEUM is 1 mi. e. off US 6 at Highland Rd., following signs for museum when nearing lighthouse. This museum, circa 1907, is a former hotel and houses paintings and artifacts depicting daily life in Truro from the time of the Pamet Indians to the present. Children's programs also are offered July through August. **Time:** Allow 30 minutes minimum. **Hours:** Mon.-Sat. 10-4:30, Sun. 1-4:30, June-Sept. **Cost:** $4; free (ages 0-12). **Phone:** (508) 487-3397.

HIGHLAND LIGHT is 1 mi. e. off US 6 at Highland Rd., following signs for Cape Cod or Highland Light. Guided tours of Highland Light, also known as Cape Cod Light, afford visitors the opportunity to climb to the top of and walk through the 1857 lighthouse. Its light is visible 20 miles out to sea (weather permitting). A short video presentation shows the lighthouse being moved to save it from

falling into the ocean. **Hours:** Daily 10-5:30, mid-May to mid-Oct. **Cost:** $4. Under 48 inches tall ar not permitted to climb the lighthouse tower. **Phone** (508) 487-1121.

ORLEANS (D-9) pop. 1,716, elev. 64'

Nestled between the beaches of the Atlanti Ocean and the coves and harbors of Cape Cod Bay Orleans has a quaint town center surrounded by pristine shores and forests. The town was incorpo rated in 1797 and named after the Duke of Orleans who visited the area that year while in exile afte the French Revolution.

Orleans residents have always relied heavily o the sea for their livelihoods. During the 19th centur windmill-powered saltworks processed sea wate into salt, deep-sea and shell fishing were major in dustries, and fields fertilized with nutrient-laden sea weed produced hearty crops.

The water is a recreational resource drawing tour ists to beaches and fishing areas on both Cape Co Bay and the ocean. Nauset Beach, on the ocean a Beach Road, has a 1,000-vehicle parking lot, show ers, picnic tables and a snack bar. Skaket Beach, o the bay off Skaket Beach Road, has a 150-car park ing lot, showers, picnic tables and a snack bar. A scenic portion of US 6 runs northward t Provincetown.

Orleans Chamber of Commerce: 44 Main St P.O. Box 153, Orleans, MA 02653. **Phone:** (508 255-1386 or (800) 865-1386.

An information booth is near the corner of SR 6A and Eldredge Parkway.

OSTERVILLE (E-8) elev. 32'

OSTERVILLE HISTORICAL MUSEUM is at 15 W. Bay Rd. The complex contains three building depicting Cape Cod history. The Captain Jonatha Parker House features antiques and original artworl The Cammett House, circa 1750, is a farmhouse fur nished in period reminiscent of the lifestyle of fam lies that lived in Osterville during the late 18 century.

Featuring six wooden boats, tools of the trade an photos, the Boat Shop celebrates the fine craftsman ship of wooden boat building. **Time:** Allow 30 mir utes minimum. **Hours:** Thurs.-Sat. 10-4, June 1 t mid-Oct. Closed July 4. Phone ahead to confir schedule. **Cost:** $5; free (ages 0-11). **Phone:** (508 428-5861.

PROVINCETOWN (C-8) pop. 3,192, elev. 32'

Provincetown was the site of the first landing the Pilgrims. A monument stands on High Pole Hi commemorating the event. Isolated at the tip Cape Cod, the settlement always depended upon th sea for its livelihood. Formerly a whaling port, th town is now an art colony and tourist mecca. Prov incetown is at the northern end of an especially sce nic portion of US 6 that stretches through Cape Co to Orleans.

Miles of beaches line both sides of the peninsula. A bathhouse and parking facilities (fee $15 per vehicle) are at Herring Cove Beach. Along the "Back Shore," from Peaked Hill Bars to Race Point, surf casters catch striped bass from late May to mid-October. Dune tours are conducted daily. Charter boats also are available.

Provincetown Chamber of Commerce: 307 Commercial St., P.O. Box 1017, Provincetown, MA 02657. **Phone:** (508) 487-3424.

ART'S DUNE TOURS departs from 4 Standish St. One-hour day excursions and 2-hour sunset tours allow visitors to explore the sand dunes of Cape Cod National Seashore *(see place listing p. 165)* from enclosed 7- to 9-passenger vans. Along the route, visitors view the remains of the bygone Peaked Hill Lifesaving Station as guides relate the history of the area's lifesaving efforts. Seventeen historic dune shacks once owned by well-known artists and writers, including Harry Kemp and Eugene O'Neill, also can be seen. In addition themed trips highlighting other aspects of the region are offered, as are dinner tours. **Time:** Allow 1 hour, 15 minutes minimum. **Hours:** Departures require a minimum of four adults. Tours depart daily 10-5:30, mid-Apr. through Nov. 1. Hours may vary. **Cost:** Day tour $26; $18 (ages 6-11). Sunset tour $40; $25 (ages 6-11). Rates for themed excursions and sunset tours with dinner vary. Reservations are required. **Phone:** (508) 487-1950 or (800) 894-1951.

DOLPHIN FLEET/*PORTUGUESE PRINCESS* **EXCURSIONS** departs from MacMillan Pier at 307 Commercial St. Three- to 4-hour whale-watching trips are accompanied by a whale expert who conducts scientific research on the whales and environment. Hands-on activities and interactive displays are offered aboard the ship. **Hours:** Trips are offered daily, mid-Apr. through Oct. 31. Departure times vary. **Cost:** $39; $31 (ages 5-12). Prices may vary. Reservations are required. **Phone:** (508) 240-3636 or (800) 826-9300. *See color ad.* ⍟

PILGRIM MONUMENT & PROVINCETOWN MUSEUM, off SR 6 on High Pole Hill, is a 252-foot tower completed in 1910 to honor the first landing of the *Mayflower* Pilgrims. Visitors can climb the monument and explore Provincetown's history in the museum, which displays such items as maritime artifacts, furniture and toys. Building the Pilgrim Monument is an exhibit that relates the monument's 3-year construction 1907-10.

Hours: Daily 9-7, June 1 to mid-Sept.; 9-5, mid-Apr. through May 31 and mid-Sept. through Nov. 30. Last admission 45 minutes before closing. **Cost:** $7; $5 (ages 62+ and students with ID); $3.50 (ages 4-14). **Phone:** (508) 487-1310.

[SAVE] **PROVINCETOWN ART ASSOCIATION AND MUSEUM,** 460 Commercial St., features a collection of more than 2,500 works of American art. **Hours:** Mon.-Fri. 11-8 (also Fri. 8-10 p.m.), Memorial Day-Sept. 30; Thurs.-Sun. noon-5, rest of year. Phone ahead to confirm schedule. **Cost:** $7; free (children). **Phone:** (508) 487-1750.

SAGAMORE (D-8) pop. 3,544

THE PAIRPOINT GLASS CO., on SR 6A next to the Sagamore Bridge, produces glass in the same manner used in 1837, the year the company's predecessor was founded. The glassmakers' art, practiced using a few simple tools, dexterous hands and years of knowledge, can be viewed from a glass wall in the gift shop. **Time:** Allow 30 minutes minimum. **Hours:** Glass-blowing demonstrations are given Mon.-Fri. 9-4, May-Dec.; Mon., Wed. and Fri. 10-3,

rest of year. Closed Jan. 1, July 4, Labor Day, Thanksgiving and Dec. 25. **Cost:** Free. **Phone:** (508) 888-2344 or (800) 899-0953.

SANDWICH (D-8) pop. 3,058, elev. 20′

One of the oldest towns on Cape Cod, Sandwich became the site of one of America's largest glass factories, an industry that flourished during the 19th century. The town also was the home of Thornton W. Burgess, naturalist and author of such children's stories as "Old Mother West Wind" and "Peter Cottontail."

Dexter's Grist Mill, on Main Street, is a restored 1654 gristmill that grinds corn daily. Guides explain the history of the mill and its mechanical operation. The nearby Hoxie House, on Water Street, is a restored 1675 saltbox house. The 1830 First Church of Christ, on SR 130, has a spire designed by noted English architect Christopher Wren.

CAPE COD CANAL VISITOR CENTER is at 60 Ed Moffitt Dr. Housed in a former Coast Guard boathouse, the center features a film about canal history, canal wildlife and wildflowers. Interactive exhibits about the canal's design, history and operation are offered. Highlights include a retired 41-foot-long patrol boat on display, as well as live radar and a virtual boat ride through the canal.

Educational programs are offered. **Time:** Allow 30 minutes minimum. **Hours:** Daily 10-5, late June-late Oct.; Thurs.-Sun. 10-5, mid-May to late June. Phone ahead to confirm schedule. **Cost:** Free. **Phone:** (508) 833-9678. 🅰

HERITAGE MUSEUMS & GARDENS is at Grove and Pine sts. off SR 130. The complex comprises 100 acres of landscaped grounds and several buildings with exhibits pertaining to American art and history. More than 140 varieties of rhododendrons hybridized by the estate's onetime owner Charles O. Dexter, who developed between 5,000 and 10,000 seedlings annually between 1921 and 1943, grace the site.

The best time to view the flowering trees is from early April through Memorial Day. Gardens, nature trails, and a labyrinth made out of native vines also

are on the grounds, as is a 19th-century mill formerly used to grind barley and corn. Special events, workshops, lectures and interpretive programs are offered periodically. **Time:** Allow 2 hours minimum. **Hours:** Daily 10-5, Apr.-Oct. Phone ahead to confirm schedule. **Cost:** (includes all Heritage Museums & Gardens facilities) $12; $11 (ages 65+); $6 (ages 4-12). **Phone:** (508) 888-3300. 🅣 🅰

American History Museum, on the s. end of Heritage Museums & Gardens at 67 Grove St., offers changing exhibitions as well as a collection of military-related miniatures and firearms. The legendary Colt Peacemaker and a weapon used by William F. "Buffalo Bill" Cody are on display. **Hours:** Daily 10-5, Apr.-Oct. **Cost:** (includes all Heritage Museums & Gardens facilities) $12; $11 (ages 65+); $6 (ages 4-12). **Phone:** (508) 888-3300.

Art Museum, on the s. end of Heritage Museums & Gardens at 67 Grove St., houses various examples of folk art and contains a restored, century-old hand-carved carousel made by Charles I.D. Looff. **Hours:** Daily 10-5, Apr.-Oct. **Cost:** (includes all Heritage Museums & Gardens facilities) $12; $11 (ages 65+); $6 (ages 4-12). Carousel ride free. **Phone:** (508) 888-3300.

J.K. Lilly, III Antique Automobile Museum, near the entrance of Heritage Museums & Gardens at 67 Grove St., displays more than 30 vintage vehicles in a two-level replica Shaker barn. Visitors can sit in a 1913 Model T Ford or view one of the first official presidential state cars, which was driven by President William H. Taft. **Hours:** Daily 10-5, Apr.-Oct. **Cost:** (includes all Heritage Museums & Gardens facilities) $12; $11 (ages 65+); $6 (ages 4-12). **Phone:** (508) 888-3300.

SANDWICH GLASS MUSEUM, 129 Main St. (SR 130), preserves and displays more than 5,000 pieces of glass manufactured in Sandwich 1825-88. Exhibits of table lamps, vases, candlesticks and decorative glass are arranged chronologically and include pressed, lacy, colored, enameled, blown, engraved and cut glass. The coloring process of glass as well as glass-making techniques that include blowing, pressing and cutting are

demonstrated. A multimedia presentation, "Sandwich: The First 200 Years," is shown in the theater. Changing exhibits also are offered.

Time: Allow 1 hour minimum. **Hours:** Daily 9:30-5, Apr.-Dec.; Wed.-Sun. 9:30-4, Feb.-Mar. Closed Thanksgiving and Dec. 25. **Cost:** $5; $1.25 (ages 6-14). **Phone:** (508) 888-0251.

THORNTON W. BURGESS MUSEUM, 4 Water St., is a memorial to the well-known children's author and naturalist born in Sandwich in 1874. Housed in the restored 1756 Eldred House, the museum contains a large collection of Burgess' writings, original Harrison Cady illustrations of his animal characters and other mementos of Burgess' life and career. An herb garden is on the grounds. **Hours:** Mon.-Sat. 10-4, Sun. 1-4, Memorial Day-Columbus Day. Closed major holidays. Phone ahead to confirm schedule. **Cost:** Donations. **Phone:** (508) 888-6870.

SOUTH WELLFLEET (D-9)

MASS AUDUBON'S WELLFLEET BAY WILDLIFE SANCTUARY, off US 6, .5 mi. n. of the Eastham/Wellfleet town line, is a 1,100-acre nature preserve. Five miles of hiking trails take visitors through pine woods, while fields lead to salt marsh, creeks, pond, heathland and beach. A nature center with exhibits and a butterfly garden also are on-site. Natural history field walks, cruises and wildlife guided tours are conducted.

Pets are not permitted. **Hours:** Trails daily 8-dusk, with extended hours in summer. Nature center daily 8:30-5, Memorial Day-Columbus Day; Tues.-Sun. 8:30-5, rest of year. **Cost:** $5; $3 (ages 3-12 and 66+). **Phone:** (508) 349-2615.

WELLFLEET (D-9)

An early whaling center, Wellfleet once was the leading oyster-producing port in New England. A town clock in the Congregational Church still strikes ship's time. Situated along the scenic Cape Cod segment of US 6, Wellfleet is a popular yet quiet summer retreat. The Wellfleet Historical Society Museum *(see attraction listing)* offers walking tours of the town. The guided tours depart on Tuesdays and Fridays at 10:15 a.m.; the fee is $3.

Wellfleet Chamber of Commerce: P.O. Box 571, Wellfleet, MA 02667. **Phone:** (508) 349-2510.

WELLFLEET HISTORICAL SOCIETY MUSEUM, 266 Main St., displays such area memorabilia as photographs, china, toys, tools, scrimshaw, American Indian artifacts, lifesaving equipment and Sandwich glass. **Hours:** Wed.-Thurs. and Sat. 1-4, Tues. and Fri. 10-4, late June-early Sept. **Cost:** Donations. **Phone:** (508) 349-9157.

WEST BARNSTABLE (E-8) elev. 43'

WEST PARISH OF BARNSTABLE, 2049 Meetinghouse Way (SR 149), was built in 1717 and is reputedly the oldest Congregational church building in the country. It has a Revere bell cast in 1806 and an

English weathercock dating from 1723. **Hours:** Daily 10-4, Memorial Day-Columbus Day; by appointment rest of year. Church services take place Sun. at 10, year-round. **Cost:** Free. **Phone:** (508) 362-4445.

WEST YARMOUTH (E-9)
pop. 6,460, elev. 20'

Yarmouth Area Chamber of Commerce: 424 SR 28, West Yarmouth, MA 02673. **Phone:** (508) 778-1008 or (800) 732-1008.

[SAVE] **ZOOQUARIUM,** 674 SR 28, is a zoo and an aquarium featuring examples of both land and aquatic animals of the local environment. A petting zoo allows visitors to take a close look at domesticated farm animals, some of which are rare. Discovery Center affords children a hands-on learning experience. Zoorific animal adventure demonstrations are presented regularly throughout the day.

Time: Allow 1 hour minimum. **Hours:** Daily 9:30-5, late June-Labor Day; Thurs.-Mon. 9:30-4, day after Labor Day-Thanksgiving. Schedule varies rest of year; phone ahead. **Cost:** $10; $7 (ages 2-9). **Phone:** (508) 775-8883.

WOODS HOLE (E-7) pop. 935, elev. 19'

On the southwest tip of Cape Cod, Woods Hole is the chief port of the cape and a center for oceanographic research. Ferries to Martha's Vineyard operate year-round. Only limited on-street metered parking is available. A seasonal trolley service, the "WHOOSH," operates between Falmouth and Woods Hole. Guided walking tours of the town are given Mon.-Fri. at 10:30 and 1, July-Aug.; they originate at Woods Hole Historical Museum & Collection *(see attraction listing)*.

MARINE BIOLOGICAL LABORATORY (MBL), on Water St., was established in 1888. The international

---

DID YOU KNOW

The Constitution of Massachusetts is the oldest written document of its kind still in use.

center is devoted to improving the human condition through basic research and education in biology, biomedicine and environmental science. Guided tours include a videotape presentation and a visit to the Marine Resources Center to view marine life used in research. Also highlighted is the Encyclopedia of Life (EOL), in which the MBL is a cornerstone institution. The EOL is an unprecedented effort to create a Web page documenting all 1.8 million named species of animals, plants and other forms of life on Earth.

Parking, which is limited, is on-street and metered. **Time:** Allow 1 hour, 30 minutes minimum. **Hours:** Visitor center Mon.-Sat. 10-4, July-Aug.; Tues.-Sat. 11-4 in June and Sept.; Tues.-Fri. noon-4 in May and Oct.; Wed.-Fri. 11-2, Nov.-Dec. Guided tours are given Mon.-Fri. at 1 and 2, mid-June to mid-Aug. **Cost:** Free. Reservations are recommended. **Phone:** (508) 289-7423.

WOODS HOLE HISTORICAL MUSEUM & COLLECTION, 579 Woods Hole Rd., interprets the history of Woods Hole through photographs, documents, artifacts and works by local artists. A scale model of the town as it was in 1895 is displayed. A boat museum featuring local small craft and a gentleman's workshop of the 1890s also are on the grounds. **Time:** Allow 30 minutes minimum. **Hours:** Tues.-Sat. 10-4, mid-June through Columbus Day. Archives open for research Tues. and Thurs. 10-2 or by appointment, year-round. Phone ahead to confirm archives schedule. **Cost:** Donations. **Phone:** (508) 548-7270.

WOODS HOLE OCEANOGRAPHIC INSTITUTION'S EXHIBIT CENTER, 15 School St., offers displays about the oceanographic research conducted by the institution. Visitors can walk through a full-size model of the interior of the *Alvin,* a research

submersible, and learn about the discovery and exploration of the *Titanic.* Also included are models of remote-operated vehicles and displays about deep-sea exploration and marine mammals. In summer guided tours are offered.

Parking, which is limited, is on-street and metered. Visitors are encouraged to use public transportation from Falmouth. **Time:** Allow 30 minutes minimum. **Hours:** Mon.-Sat. 10-4:30, May-Oct.; Tues.-Fri. 10-4:30, Nov.-Dec. Guided tours geared toward an adult audience are offered Mon.-Fri. at 10:30 and 1, July-Aug. Closed July 4, Thanksgiving and Dec. 25. **Cost:** Donations. Tours are limited to 10 people. Reservations are required for tours. **Phone:** (508) 289-2663, or (508) 289-2252 for tours.

WOODS HOLE SCIENCE AQUARIUM, corner of Water and Albatross sts., is part of a major research center for marine science operated by the National Marine Fisheries Service under the National Oceanic and Atmospheric Administration (NOAA). The aquarium contains a seal pool, a touch tank, a behind-the-scenes area and exhibits about local saltwater species.

Note: Photo ID is required. Because parking in Woods Hole is limited, visitors are encouraged to use public transportation from Falmouth. **Hours:** Tues.-Sat. 11-4, June-Aug.; Mon.-Fri. 11-4, rest of year. Closed major holidays. Phone ahead to confirm schedule. **Cost:** Donations. **Phone:** (508) 495-2001.

YARMOUTH PORT (D-8)
pop. 5,395, elev. 54′

Incorporated in 1639 as part of the Plymouth Bay Colony, Yarmouth Port was chosen by many 19th-century sea captains as the site for their stately

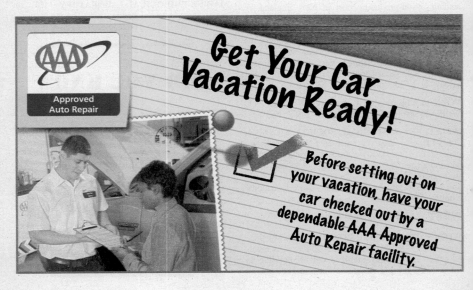

homes. Conservation areas and nature trails in the town spotlight wetlands, salt marshes and some of the Cape's most abundant foliage.

EDWARD GOREY HOUSE is at 8 Strawberry Ln. The former home of acclaimed writer and artist Edward Gorey features everything from original artwork to first edition books and memorabilia. Offbeat author of "The Gashlycrumb Tinies" and "The Doubtful Guest," Gorey also worked on various theater productions, winning awards for his set and costume designs. Still, he is best known for his macabre pen and ink illustrations, which appeared in such publications as *The New Yorker* and *The New York Times* as well as in books by John Updike, Virginia Woolf, H.G. Wells and others.

Time: Allow 1 hour, 30 minutes minimum. **Hours:** Wed.-Sat. 11-4, Sun. noon-4, late June-early Oct.; Thurs.-Sat. 11-4, Sun. noon-4, mid-Apr. to late June; Fri.-Sat. 11-4, Sun. noon-4, early Oct.-late Dec. **Cost:** $5; $3 (students with ID); $2 (ages 6-12). **Phone:** (508) 362-3909.

Heritage Museums & Gardens, Sandwich / © David Lyons / Alamy

This ends listings for Cape Cod.
The following page resumes the alphabetical listings of cities in Massachusetts.

CAPE COD NATIONAL SEASHORE—see Cape Cod p. 165.

CENTERVILLE—see Cape Cod p. 170.

CHARLEMONT (A-2) elev. 584'

RECREATIONAL ACTIVITIES
White-water Rafting
- **Crab Apple Whitewater** is at 2056 Mohawk Tr. **Hours:** Trips are offered May 1 to mid-Oct. Departure days and times vary; phone ahead. **Phone:** (413) 625-2288 or (800) 553-7238.
- **Moxie Outdoor Adventures** is at 1 Thunder Rd. **Hours:** Trips are offered May-Oct. Departure days and times vary; phone ahead. **Phone:** (207) 663-2231 or (800) 866-6943.
- **Zoar Outdoor** is at 7 Main St. **Hours:** Trips are offered Apr.-Oct. Departure days and times vary; phone ahead. **Phone:** (413) 339-4010 or (800) 532-7483.

CHATHAM—see Cape Cod p. 171.

CHESTNUT HILL—see Boston p. 140.

COHASSET—see Boston p. 140.

CONCORD—see Boston p. 140.

COTUIT—see Cape Cod p. 171.

CUMMINGTON (B-2)

BRYANT HOMESTEAD is 1.5 mi. s. off SR 9 on SR 112. Overlooking the Westfield River Valley, this country estate was home to William Cullen Bryant, poet and the editor in chief of the *New York Evening Post* 1829-78. The historic house is furnished with many generations of family antiques and mementoes from Bryant's travels. An exhibit area and a self-guiding nature trail also are featured.

Hours: Grounds daily dawn-dusk. Guided house tours are given Sat.-Sun. (also Labor Day and Columbus Day) 1-5, last Sat. in June to mid-Oct. **Cost:** $6; $3 (ages 6-12). **Phone:** (413) 634-2244.

DALTON (B-2) elev. 1,188'

WAHCONAH FALLS STATE PARK, 3 mi. n. off SR 9, contains a 40-foot waterfall and scenic roads for hiking. Swimming is not permitted. **Hours:** Daily dawn-dusk. **Cost:** Free. **Phone:** (413) 442-8992.

DEDHAM—see Boston p. 142.

DEERFIELD (B-3) elev. 204'

When settled in the 1660s, Deerfield was the northernmost outpost of English colonial civilization. Indian and French attacks on the town included the 1675 Bloody Brook Massacre and the great Deerfield Raid in 1704.

Franklin County Chamber of Commerce: 395 Main St., P.O. Box 898, Greenfield, MA 01302. **Phone:** (413) 773-5463.

HISTORIC DEERFIELD, off US 5 and SR 10, is an outdoor history museum offering interpretive programs and guided and self-guiding house tours. The Flynt Center of Early New England Life features changing exhibitions and items from Historic Deerfield's collection of antiques, decorative arts, furniture and textiles.

Hours: Information center in Hall Tavern daily 9:30-4:30, Apr.-Nov. Flynt Center of Early New England Life daily 9:30-4:30, Apr.-Nov.; Sat.-Sun. 9:30-4:30, rest of year. Guided tours are offered daily 9:30-4:30, Apr.-Nov.; by appointment rest of year. Closed Thanksgiving and Dec. 24-25. **Cost:** (includes all Historic Deerfield facilities) $12; $5 (ages 6-17). **Phone:** (413) 775-7214.

Allen House, on Old Main St., was built in 1734. The story of Henry and Helen Flynt, who founded Historic Deerfield by purchasing old houses then carefully restoring them, is highlighted. Guided tours are offered by appointment. **Hours:** Daily 9:30-4:30, Apr.-Nov. Closed Thanksgiving. **Cost:** (includes all Historic Deerfield facilities) $12; $5 (ages 6-17). **Phone:** (413) 775-7214.

Ashley House, on Old Main St., was built in 1734. It contains a gallery of furniture, ceramics and prints reflecting the tastes of the Connecticut River Valley's elite 1730-80. **Hours:** Guided tours are offered daily 9:30-4:30, Apr.-Nov.; by appointment rest of year. Closed Thanksgiving and Dec. 24-25. **Cost:** (includes all Historic Deerfield facilities) $12; $5 (ages 6-17). **Phone:** (413) 775-7214.

Dwight House, on Old Main St., was built about 1754 in Springfield and moved to Deerfield in 1954. It is home to the Apprentice's Workshop, a historic trades demonstration area and experiential learning space dedicated to the production of textiles (weaving), architectural woodworking and English factory-made ceramics. **Hours:** Daily 9:30-4:30, Apr.-Nov. Closed Thanksgiving. **Cost:** (includes all Historic Deerfield facilities) $12; $5 (ages 6-17). **Phone:** (413) 775-7214.

Frary House, on Old Main St., was built in the mid-1700s and restored in 1890. Displays chronicle Deerfield's role in both the Arts and Crafts and the Colonial Revival movements. **Hours:** Guided tours are offered daily 9:30-4:30, Apr.-Nov.; by appointment rest of year. Closed Thanksgiving and Dec. 24-25. **Cost:** (includes all Historic Deerfield facilities) $12; $5 (ages 6-17). **Phone:** (413) 775-7214.

Henry Needham Flynt Silver and Metalware Collection, on Old Main St., features more than 1,500 pieces of Early American and English silver and pewter, including works by Paul Revere. **Hours:** Daily 9:30-4:30, Apr.-Nov. Closed Thanksgiving. **Cost:** (includes all Historic Deerfield facilities) $12; $5 (ages 6-17). **Phone:** (413) 775-7214.

Hinsdale and Anna Williams House, on Old Main St., has been restored to its 1816-38 appearance using an inventory taken when Hinsdale Williams died. The house features period color wall paint, wallpaper, floor coverings and many objects owned by the Williams family. **Hours:** Guided tours are offered daily 9:30-4:30, Apr.-Nov.; by appointment rest of year. Closed Thanksgiving and Dec. 24-25. **Cost:** (includes all Historic Deerfield facilities) $12; $5 (ages 6-17). **Phone:** (413) 775-7214.

The Sheldon House, on Old Main St., was built in 1755 and reflects the lifestyle of a middle-class farming family 1780-1810. Such themes as the beef trade, housework and illness in the 19th century are explored in a self-guiding tour. **Hours:** Daily 9:30-4:30, Apr.-Nov. Closed Thanksgiving. **Cost:** (includes all Historic Deerfield facilities) $12; $5 (ages 6-17). **Phone:** (413) 775-7214.

The Stebbins House, on Old Main St., was built in 1799 and includes neoclassical furnishings from the period of the New Republic 1799-1820. Visitors on a self-guiding tour view paintings, hand-painted wall decorations, Federal-style furniture and ceramic displays. **Hours:** Daily 9:30-4:30, Apr.-Nov. Closed Thanksgiving. **Cost:** (includes all Historic Deerfield facilities) $12; $5 (ages 6-17). **Phone:** (413) 775-7214.

Wells-Thorn House, on Old Main St., presents a chronological overview of the history of Deerfield 1720-1850. These rooms portray the development of economic life and popular furnishings in the Connecticut River Valley. **Hours:** Guided tours are offered daily 9:30-4:30, Apr.-Nov.; by appointment rest of year. Closed Thanksgiving and Dec. 24-25. **Cost:** (includes all Historic Deerfield facilities) $12; $5 (ages 6-17). **Phone:** (413) 775-7214.

MEMORIAL HALL MUSEUM, on Memorial St., is one of Deerfield's oldest museums. It is housed in a 1799 building that became Deerfield Academy. The museum contains the Sheldon Collection of Colonial, American Indian and military relics; a replica of a period schoolroom; a collection of quilts and needlework; and a pewter display. **Hours:** Daily 11-5, May-Oct. **Cost:** $6; $3 (ages 6-21). **Phone:** (413) 774-3768.

DENNIS—*see Cape Cod p. 171.*

DUXBURY (C-7) pop. 1,426, elev. 31'

Around 1628 Pilgrims settled in Duxbury seeking room for their growing village and grazing lands for their cattle. Well-known residents included Pilgrims John Alden and Miles Standish. Nearby an old burying ground contains some of the pioneers' graves.

[SAVE] **ALDEN HOUSE HISTORIC SITE,** 105 Alden St., was the last home of *Mayflower* Pilgrim John Alden. Built in the mid-1600s, the original two-room house was expanded in the 18th and 19th centuries and was occupied by the Alden family until 1920. Some of its interesting features are the powdered clam-and-oyster-shell ceiling in the

"great" room and the gunstock posts found in the chambers. **Hours:** Mon.-Sat. noon-4, mid-May to mid-Oct.; by appointment rest of year. Last admission 30 minutes before closing. Phone ahead to confirm schedule. **Cost:** $5; $4 (ages 3-17). **Phone:** (781) 934-9092.

THE ART COMPLEX MUSEUM, 189 Alden St., features contemporary art as well as works by Asian, European and American artists, including a collection of Shaker items. Changing exhibits are presented. A Japanese tea ceremony is presented in a tea hut the last Sunday of the month, June through August. Sunday afternoon concerts, workshops and other special events are offered year-round. **Time:** Allow 30 minutes minimum. **Hours:** Wed.-Sun. 1-4. Closed major holidays. **Cost:** Free. **Phone:** (781) 934-6634.

KING CAESAR HOUSE, on King Caesar Rd. at Powder Point, was built in 1809 for shipping magnate Ezra Weston II ("King Caesar"). Represented as it appeared in 1820, the Federal house displays period furnishings and costumes as well as artifacts pertaining to shipbuilding in Duxbury. The Potter Gallery features changing exhibits about local history. **Hours:** Wed.-Sun. 1-4, July-Aug.; Sat.-Sun. 1-4, in Sept. **Cost:** $5; $2 (students with ID and senior citizens). **Phone:** (781) 934-2378.

EASTHAM—*see Cape Cod p. 171.*

EASTHAMPTON (C-2) pop. 15,994, elev. 169'

MASS AUDUBON'S ARCADIA WILDLIFE SANCTUARY is 1 mi. s. of I-91 exit 18 on SR 5, then 1 mi. w. on East St., following signs to 127 Combs Rd. Five miles of marked trails along the Mill River and marshes traverse the 700-acre sanctuary, a haven for native plants and wildlife. A nature center offers trail maps and nature programs. **Time:** Allow 2 hours minimum. **Hours:** Grounds daily dawn-dusk. Nature center Mon.-Fri. 8:30-noon, Sat. 8:30-3:30, Sun. and most holidays noon-3:30. Closed Jan. 1, Thanksgiving and Dec. 25. **Cost:** $4; $3 (ages 3-12 and 66+). **Phone:** (413) 584-3009.

EAST SANDWICH—*see Cape Cod p. 172.*

EAST WAREHAM (E-7) elev. 26'

WATER WIZZ OF CAPE COD is at jct. US 6 and SR 28, 1.5 mi. e. of SR 25. The park has more than 1,000 feet of waterslides, including five serpentine slides, two speed slides, an enclosed free-fall body slide, a 503-foot tube ride and a swimming pool. A lazy river, a wave pool and children's play areas also are featured.

Time: Allow 4 hours minimum. **Hours:** Daily 10-6, mid-June to late Aug.; daily 10-5, late Aug.-Labor Day weekend; Sat.-Sun. 10-5, early to mid-June. Phone ahead to confirm schedule. **Cost:** $30; $15 (ages 65+ and under 48 inches tall); free (ages 0-2). After 4 p.m. $20; $15 (ages 65+ and under 48 inches tall). After 5 p.m. $15. Prices may vary. **Phone:** (508) 295-3255. ⊤ℹ️ ♿

EDGARTOWN—see *Martha's Vineyard p. 186.*

ESSEX—see *Boston p. 142.*

FAIRHAVEN (E-7) elev. 17′

Across the harbor from New Bedford, Fairhaven shares a similar heritage, having developed and prospered from the whaling ships that once lined its docks. Reminders of that era survive in such historic buildings as the Weston-Howland Mansion or the public buildings donated by philanthropist Henry Huttleston Rogers.

Fairhaven Office of Tourism: 43 Center St., Fairhaven, MA 02719. **Phone:** (508) 979-4085.

FALL RIVER (E-6) pop. 91,938, elev. 121′

In the late 19th century America's need for cotton thread and cloth was met in Fall River, where an abundant supply of waterpower made the manufacturing process economical. By 1875 "Spindle City" was the leading textile producer, with more than 120 mills in operation. The Victorian mansions on the heights above the city act as reminders of the wealth made during this boom period. Manufacturers of finished clothing occupy the warehouses and offer bargains in many outlet stores.

In nearby Swansea, Martin House Farm, 22 Stoney Hill Rd., comprises an 18th-century house, two barns and cultivated fields surrounded by dry stone walls and woodlands. Guided tours are offered May through October; phone (508) 379-0376.

Fall River Office of Tourism: One Government Center, Fall River, MA 02722. **Phone:** (508) 324-2028.

Self-guiding tours: A map of the Lizzie Borden Trail, which includes the Fall River Historical Society, the Lizzie Borden Bed & Breakfast and other sites related to the Bordens, is available at the department of tourism and at various locations throughout the town.

Shopping areas: Factory outlets are concentrated on Jefferson, Quequechan and Quarry streets off I-195.

🔻GEM 💾SAVE **BATTLESHIP COVE,** off I-195 exit 5, harbors an impressive collection of historic 20th-century naval ships. The *Hiddensee,* a Soviet-built missile corvette, can be explored. A Bell Huey helicopter that served in Vietnam also is displayed. The cove is the state's official veterans memorial for World War II and the Korean, Vietnam and Persian Gulf wars as well as a memorial for the victims of September 11.

Hours: Daily 9-4:30. Closed Jan. 1, Thanksgiving and Dec. 25. **Cost:** (includes all Battleship Cove attractions) $15; $13 (ages 66+ and veterans with ID); $9 (ages 6-14); $7 (active military with ID); free (ages 0-5 and military in uniform). **Phone:** (508) 678-1100.

PT Boats 796 and 617, off I-195 exit 5 in Battleship Cove, are two fully restored torpedo boats of World War II. **Hours:** Daily 9-4:30. Closed Jan. 1, Thanksgiving and Dec. 25. **Cost:** (includes all Battleship Cove attractions) $15; $13 (ages 66+ and veterans with ID); $9 (ages 6-14); $7 (active military with ID); free (ages 0-5 and military in uniform). **Phone:** (508) 678-1100.

USS *Joseph P. Kennedy Jr.*, off I-195 exit 5 in Battleship Cove, is a destroyer that saw action in Korea, Vietnam and the Cuban Missile Crisis of 1962. **Hours:** Daily 9-4:30. Closed Jan. 1, Thanksgiving and Dec. 25. **Cost:** (includes all Battleship Cove attractions) $15; $13 (ages 66+ and veterans with ID); $9 (ages 6-14); $7 (active military with ID); free (ages 0-5 and military in uniform). **Phone:** (508) 678-1100.

USS *Lionfish*, off I-195 exit 5 in Battleship Cove, is a World War II attack submarine featuring displays and equipment detailing a sailor's day-to-day activities undersea. **Hours:** Daily 9-4:30. Closed Jan. 1, Thanksgiving and Dec. 25. **Cost:** (includes all Battleship Cove attractions) $15; $13 (ages 66+ and veterans with ID); $9 (ages 6-14); $7 (active military with ID); free (ages 0-5 and military in uniform). **Phone:** (508) 678-1100.

USS *Massachusetts* (Big Mamie), off I-195 exit 5 in Battleship Cove, is a 680-foot battleship that survived 35 battles in both the Atlantic and Pacific during World War II. The main deck, gun turrets and bridge as well as the engine room and nine decks of the ship's interior may be visited. A PT boat museum and a scale model aircraft exhibit also are on board.

Hours: Daily 9-4:30. Closed Jan. 1, Thanksgiving and Dec. 25. **Cost:** (includes all Battleship Cove attractions) $15; $13 (ages 66+ and veterans with ID); $9 (ages 6-14); $7 (active military with ID); free (ages 0-5 and military in uniform). **Phone:** (508) 678-1100.

FALL RIVER CAROUSEL is off I-195 exit 5 in Battleship Cove. This is the restored, 1920 Philadelphia Tobaggan Co. Carousel #54 with 48 handpainted, hand-carved horses and two chariots; the carousel is housed in a Victorian-style pavilion. Each ride lasts 3 minutes. **Hours:** Daily 11-5, early June-early Sept.; Sat.-Sun. 11-4:30, Memorial Day weekend-early June and early Sept.-Columbus Day. Phone ahead to confirm schedule. **Cost:** $1, or seven rides for $5. **Phone:** (508) 678-1100.

FALL RIVER HERITAGE STATE PARK, off I-195 exit 5, is next to Battleship Cove. This 8-acre urban park overlooks Battleship Cove. A boardwalk and esplanade follow the waterfront. A visitor center also is on-site. **Hours:** Wed.-Sun. 10-4, July-Aug.; 10-2, Sept.-Oct. Phone ahead to confirm schedule. **Cost:** Free. **Phone:** (508) 675-5759. ♿

FALL RIVER HISTORICAL SOCIETY, 451 Rock St., is a restored 19th-century mill owner's mansion and contains a Lizzie Borden display and memorabilia of Fall River steamships. Victorian Holiday Open House is offered daily late November to late December. **Hours:** Tues.-Fri. 9-4:30, Sat.-Sun. 1-5, June-Sept.; Tues.-Fri. 9-4:30 in May and early Oct. Guided tours are given Tues.-Fri. on the hour 9-11 and 1-3, May 1-early Oct. (also Sat.-Sun. 1-4, June-Sept.). Closed major holidays. **Cost:** $6; $4 (ages 6-14). **Phone:** (508) 679-1071.

SAVE **LIZZIE BORDEN BED & BREAKFAST/MUSEUM** is at 92 Second St. The six-bedroom home, now operated as a bed-and-breakfast and museum, is where on Aug. 4, 1892, Lizzie Borden reputedly killed her parents with an ax. Guided tours include photographs of courtroom evidence, such as the hatchet suspected to have been the murder weapon. Lizzie was acquitted of the murders. **Hours:** Tours are given daily on the hour 11-3. Last tour begins at closing. Closed Thanksgiving and Dec. 25. **Cost:** $12.50; $10 (senior citizens); $5 (ages 7-15). **Phone:** (508) 675-7333.

MARINE MUSEUM, 70 Water St., relates the history of steam transportation through lithographs, paintings, photographs and scale-model ships. The *Titanic* exhibit features a 28-foot-long, 1-ton model of the trans-Atlantic luxury liner. **Hours:** Sat.-Sun. noon-4 (also Sat. 4-5), Fri. 1-5, Jan.-Mar. Phone ahead to confirm schedule. **Cost:** $5; $4 (ages 5-12 and senior citizens). **Phone:** (508) 674-3533 in season.

OLD COLONY AND FALL RIVER RAILROAD MUSEUM is in Battleship Cove at Central and Water sts. Former railroad cars house memorabilia of the Old Colony and Fall River Railroad, among others. Equipment includes a passenger coach with displays, a caboose, a self-propelled diesel coach and a boxcar containing a theater. **Hours:** Fri.-Sun. noon-5, July 1-Sept. 1; Sat.-Sun. noon-4, May-June and Sept. 2 to mid-Oct. **Cost:** $3; $2.50 (ages 65+); $1.50 (ages 5-12). **Phone:** (508) 674-9340.

ST. ANNE'S CHURCH AND SHRINE, opposite St. Anne's Hospital on S. Main St., is a marble Roman Catholic Church built in 1906 by French Canadian immigrants. Features include the shrine of St. Anne (mother of Mary), a series of devotional areas to many saints and a Chapel of Adoration in the lower church. The procession for the Feast of St. Anne is held July 26. **Hours:** Daily 6:30 a.m.-7 p.m. **Cost:** Free. **Phone:** (508) 674-5651.

FALMOUTH—*see Cape Cod p. 172.*

FITCHBURG (A-5) pop. 39,102, elev. 494'

North Central Massachusetts Chamber of Commerce: 860 South St., Fitchburg, MA 01420. **Phone:** (978) 353-7600.

SAVE **FITCHBURG ART MUSEUM** is at 25 Merriam Pkwy. Founded in 1925, the museum's 14 galleries contain permanent collections of American, European and Asian paintings, drawings, prints, ceramics and decorative arts, and antiquities from Mesoamerica, Egypt, Greece and Rome. Changing exhibits also are featured. **Hours:** Wed.-Fri. noon-4 (also first Thurs. of the month 4-8), Sat.-Sun. 11-5. Closed major holidays. **Cost:** $7; $5 (ages 63+ and students with ID); free (ages 0-12 and to all first Thurs. of the month 4-8 p.m.). **Phone:** (978) 345-4207.

FITCHBURG HISTORICAL SOCIETY, 50 Grove St., portrays the city's history through various artifacts. The research library offers a large collection of genealogical and historical material about the people and city of Fitchburg since the 1700s. **Time:** Allow 1 hour minimum. **Hours:** Mon.-Tues. 10-4, Wed. 10-6. **Cost:** Free. **Phone:** (978) 345-1157.

FRAMINGHAM—*see Boston p. 142.*

GLOUCESTER—*see Boston p. 142.*

GREAT BARRINGTON (C-1)
pop. 2,459, elev. 726'

Resort and shopping center of the southern Berkshires, historic Great Barrington was settled about 1726. In August 1774, townspeople openly resisted British judicial rule by seizing the courthouse to prevent the king's court from holding session.

Poet and journalist William Cullen Bryant made his home in Great Barrington 1816-25. Dr. W.E.B. Du Bois, the first African-American to earn a Ph.D. from Harvard, was born in town in 1868.

A garden is named in Du Bois' honor at the Housatonic River Walk. The handiwork of more than 2,000 volunteers, the trail is lined by a variety of plants and trees, including Japanese maples, mountain laurel, sycamores, sumac and American elms. Benches, historical structures and observation areas also are scattered along the .5-mile pedestrian route. The path—designated a National Recreation Trail in 2009—abuts the Housatonic River's west bank between Cottage and Bridge streets downtown. Canoe launches are near Bridge Street and off Brookside Road.

Southern Berkshire Chamber of Commerce: 362 Main St., P.O. Box 810, Great Barrington, MA 01230. **Phone:** (413) 528-1510 or (800) 269-4825.

MONUMENT MOUNTAIN RESERVATION, 4 mi. n. on US 7, covers 503 acres. The 1,642-foot Monument Mountain, memorialized by poet William Cullen Bryant, provides a sweeping view. Nathaniel Hawthorne first met Herman Melville on a hike and picnic on Monument Mountain in 1850. Hiking trails are available. **Hours:** Daily dawn-dusk. **Cost:** Free. **Phone:** (413) 298-3239, ext. 3000. ⛺

MOUNT EVERETT STATE RESERVATION, s.w. off SR 41 near South Egremont off Mount Washington Rd., is a 1,300-acre tract containing 2,624-foot Mount Everett and Guilder Pond. The upper parking area offers a panorama of three states and the Housatonic Valley. **Hours:** Daily dawn-dusk. Closed to vehicles late Nov. to mid-Apr. Phone ahead to confirm schedule. **Cost:** Free. **Phone:** (413) 528-0330.

RECREATIONAL ACTIVITIES
Skiing

- **Butternut Ski Area** is at 380 SR 23 (State Rd.). Other activities are offered. **Hours:** Skiing Mon.-Fri. 9-4, Sat.-Sun. and most holidays 8:15-4, late Nov.-early Apr. (weather permitting). Phone ahead to confirm schedule. **Phone:** (413) 528-2000.

HADLEY (B-3) elev. 125′

HADLEY FARM MUSEUM, next to the town hall at jct. SRs 9 and 47, is housed in a restored 1782 barn. Exhibits include a 15-seat stagecoach, an oxcart, a peddler's wagon, early broom-making machinery and household and farm implements. **Hours:** Fri.-Sat. 11-4, Sun. 1-4, mid-May to mid-Oct.; otherwise by appointment. **Cost:** $5; $3 (students with ID and senior citizens); $1 (ages 0-11). Children must be with an adult. **Phone:** (413) 586-1160.

PORTER-PHELPS-HUNTINGTON   HISTORIC HOUSE MUSEUM is 2 mi. n. on SR 47 to 130 River Dr. The 1752 Georgian-style house, unchanged structurally since 1799, contains the belongings of seven generations of the original owner's extended family. The activities of a wealthy and productive 18th-century household are interpreted through three generations of women. Concerts are presented June through July.

Hours: Guided tours are given Sat.-Wed. 1-4:30 or by appointment, May 15-Oct. 15. **Cost:** $5; $1 (ages 0-12). An additional fee is charged for some concerts. **Phone:** (413) 584-4699.

HANCOCK (B-1)

HANCOCK SHAKER VILLAGE—
see *Pittsfield p. 194.*

RECREATIONAL ACTIVITIES
Skiing

- **Jiminy Peak Mountain Resort** is 1.3 mi. n. on SR 43, .3 mi. e. on Brodie Mountain Rd., then .3 mi. s.e. on Corey Rd. Other activities are offered. **Hours:** Skiing Mon.-Fri. 9 a.m.-10 p.m., Sat.-Sun. and holidays 8:30 a.m.-10 p.m., mid-Nov. to mid-Apr. (weather permitting). **Phone:** (413) 738-5500.

HARVARD (B-5) elev. 286′

The first of two idealistic enterprises to organize in Harvard was a colony of the Shaker Society, founded in 1791; the second was Bronson Alcott's effort to found the settlement of New Eden at Fruitlands.

FRUITLANDS MUSEUMS is .2 mi. s. of SR 2 exit 38A on SR 110 (bear right off the ramp), then 2.25 mi. w. via Old Shirley and Prospect Hill rds. Fruitlands Farmhouse, where Bronson Alcott and leaders of the transcendentalist movement attempted a new social order in 1843, features such items as letters and memorabilia from the leaders. Shaker Museum is housed in an 18th-century building and contains Shaker furniture and artifacts.

Indian Museum displays dioramas and examples of North American Indian art and history. Picture Gallery includes portraits by early 19th-century itinerant artists and landscapes by members of the Hudson River School, the first formally recognized style of American painting. Programs for adults and hands-on children's activities are featured. The grounds offer walking trails.

Guided tours are available by appointment. **Hours:** Grounds daily 10-5, mid-May to mid-Nov.; Sat.-Sun. noon-4, mid-Nov. to late Dec. Museums Mon.-Fri. 11-4, Sat.-Sun. and holidays 11-5, mid-May to mid-Nov. Phone ahead to confirm schedule. **Cost:** Museums $12; $10 (ages 61+ and students with ID); $5 (ages 5-13). Grounds and trails only $6. **Phone:** (978) 456-3924. 🏫 📷

HARWICH—*see Cape Cod p. 172.*

HAVERHILL—*see Boston p. 145.*

HINGHAM—*see Boston p. 145.*

HOLYOKE (C-3) pop. 39,838, elev. 115′

On the Connecticut River, the Pioneer Valley city of Holyoke was the first planned industrial center in the country. Volleyball, first known as mintonette, was invented in 1895 by W.G. Morgan, a physical education instructor at the local YMCA. The Volleyball Hall of Fame *(see Holyoke Heritage State Park),* 444 Dwight St., features a model half-court and interactive exhibits. In March visitors can enjoy the 〰️Holyoke St. Patrick's Day Parade, one of the largest in the country.

Wistariahurst Museum, 238 Cabot St., is a historic house featuring original leather wall coverings, columns and elaborate woodwork as well as a permanent collection of decorative arts, paintings, prints, textiles and manuscripts; phone (413) 322-5660. Dinosaur Footprints, a park off I-91 exit 17A along the west bank of the Connecticut River, boasts fossils and dinosaur footprints preserved in stone.

Greater Holyoke Chamber of Commerce: 177 High St., Holyoke, MA 01040. **Phone:** (413) 534-3376.

Shopping areas: JCPenney, Macy's and Sears have stores in Holyoke Mall at Ingleside, off I-91 exit 15.

CHILDREN'S MUSEUM AT HOLYOKE, in the Heritage State Park Complex at 444 Dwight St., encourages visitors to become actively involved with exhibits. Included are a body playground featuring the two-story Healthy Climber, an interactive building site, a cityscape, a television station, a papermaking exhibit, a science discovery area and a tot lot. Changing displays also are offered.

Performances, workshops and programs also are offered. **Hours:** Wed.-Sat. 10-4, Sun. noon-4. **Cost:** $6; $3 (ages 63+); free (ages 0-1). **Phone:** (413) 536-5437.

HOLYOKE HERITAGE STATE PARK is at 221 Appleton St. The 8-acre park offers cultural and recreational programs. A visitor center offers guided tours and displays about local history. A carousel, a children's museum and The Volleyball Hall of Fame are on-site.

Hours: Park open daily 24 hours. Visitor center open Tues.-Sun. noon-4:30. Carousel open Tues.-Sun. 10:30-4, July-Aug.; Sat.-Sun. noon-4, rest of year. Volleyball hall of fame open Thurs.-Sun. noon-4:30. Closed Jan. 1, Thanksgiving and Dec. 25. **Cost:** Park free. Carousel $1. Hall of fame $3.50; $2.50 (ages 6-17 and 60+). **Phone:** (413) 534-1723 for the visitor center, (413) 538-9838 for the carousel, or (413) 536-0926 for the hall of fame.

MOUNT TOM STATE RESERVATION is off I-91 exit 17A, then 4 mi. n. on US 5. The reservation covers 2,082 acres on the western slope of Mount Tom, which rises 1,214 feet above the Connecticut Valley floor. The park's precipitous ridge is forested with pine, hemlock, hardwoods and spruce. *See Recreation Chart.* **Hours:** Daily 8-8, Memorial Day-Labor Day; 8-6, day after Labor Day-Columbus Day; 8-4, rest of year. **Cost:** Sat.-Sun. and holidays, Memorial Day-Columbus Day, $2 (per private vehicle). **Phone:** (413) 527-4805 or (413) 534-1186.
⏣

HULL—*see Boston p. 145.*

HYANNIS—*see Cape Cod p. 172.*

IPSWICH—*see Boston p. 146.*

LAWRENCE—*see Boston p. 146.*

LENOX (B-1) pop. 1,667, elev. 974′

Founded in 1767, Lenox was the county seat for many years. The town is a Berkshire summer resort and best known for its late 19th-century "cottages"—a whimsical term used by wealthy families of the time to describe their mansions. A representative section of the Berkshires is preserved in Mass Audubon's Pleasant Valley Wildlife Sanctuary, 2 miles north of US 7/20 on W. Dugway Road. Hiking trails traverse the area, and a museum contains exhibits about plants and wildlife; phone (413) 637-0320

Berkshire Scenic Railway Museum, Lenox Station near Housatonic Street and Willow Creek Road, is in a restored 1902 depot that features area railroading exhibits and model train displays. Narrated round-trip train rides also are offered; phone (413) 637-2210.

Shakespeare & Company, 70 Kemble St., whose alumni include Richard Dreyfuss and Sigourney Weaver, performs plays on three stages early May to mid-December; phone (413) 637-1199.

Lenox Chamber of Commerce: 5 Walker St., Lenox, MA 01240. **Phone:** (413) 637-3646.

FRELINGHUYSEN MORRIS HOUSE AND STUDIO is 1 mi. s. on SR 183, .3 mi. s. on Old Stockbridge Rd., then .8 mi. w. to 92 Hawthorne St. The former home of American abstract artists Suzy Frelinghuysen and George L.K. Morris, this Bauhaus-inspired building features paintings by Georges Braque, Juan Gris, Fernand Léger and Pablo Picasso as well as American Cubist art. On the 46-acre wooded grounds are nature trails and the sculpture "The Mountain" by French artist Gaston Lachaise.

Time: Allow 1 hour minimum. **Hours:** Guided 1-hour tours are given Thurs.-Sun. 10-3, late June-Labor Day; Thurs.-Sat. 10-3, day after Labor Day-Columbus Day. **Cost:** $12; $10.50 (ages 65+); $6 (students with ID); free (ages 0-11). **Phone:** (413) 637-0166.

THE MOUNT, EDITH WHARTON'S ESTATE & GARDENS, at 2 Plunkett St. at the s. jct. of US 7 and SR 7A, is a 42-room mansion built in 1902 by writer Edith Wharton, the first woman novelist to win a Pulitzer Prize for fiction and an authority on architecture, interior design and gardens. The estate consists of formal flower gardens, woodland trails, a Georgian Revival stable and a mansion with restored rooms. Wharton's personal 2,600-volume library is on view. Seasonal programs are offered.

Food is available July-Aug. **Time:** Allow 2 hours minimum. **Hours:** Daily 10-5, May-Oct. Last admission 1 hour before closing. **Cost:** $18; $17 (senior citizens); $13 (students with ID); free (ages 0-12). **Phone:** (413) 551-5111.

TANGLEWOOD, 297 West St., is the summer home of the Boston Symphony Orchestra and the home of the Tanglewood Music Center. The 550-acre estate includes Hawthorne Cottage, where Nathaniel Hawthorne wrote several books. Recitals, student concerts, chamber music and larger works are held in the Koussevitzky Music Shed and Seiji Ozawa Hall. **Hours:** The Tanglewood Music Festival takes place late June to early Sept. **Cost:** Concert $19-$105. **Phone:** (617) 266-1492 for festival schedule or (888) 266-1200.

VENTFORT HALL: MANSION AND GILDED AGE MUSEUM is at 104 Walker St. Built in 1893 for Sarah Morgan, the sister of J.P. Morgan, and used as a filming location for the movie "The Cider House Rules," the Elizabethan-style mansion features gables, stained-glass windows, ornate plasterwork and wood carvings, and other architectural elements exemplifying the opulence of the Gilded Age.

In addition to offering tours and exhibits, Ventfort Hall showcases concerts, lectures, plays, children's programs, porch luncheons and Victorian teas. The Les Petites Dames de Mode exhibit highlights 60 exquisite, elegantly dressed 29-inch-tall mannequins depicting Victorian ladies.

Time: Allow 1 hour minimum. **Hours:** Mon.-Fri. 10-5, Sat.-Sun. 10-3. Guided tours daily 10-2, day after Memorial Day-Oct. 31; Sat.-Sun. 10-2, rest of year. Closed Jan. 1, Easter, Thanksgiving and Dec. 25. **Cost:** First floor (includes guided tour and Les Petites Dames de Mode exhibit) $12; $5 (ages 5-16). Second floor $12; $6 (ages 5-16). Combination ticket $20; $11 (ages 5-16). **Phone:** (413) 637-3206.

 **LEXINGTON**—*see Boston p. 147.*

LINCOLN—*see Boston p. 148.*

LOWELL—*see Boston p. 148.*

LYNN—*see Boston p. 149.*

MARBLEHEAD—*see Boston p. 149.*

MARSHFIELD (C-7) pop. 4,246, elev. 24'

HISTORIC WINSLOW HOUSE, at jct. Webster and Careswell sts. (SR 139), was home to the founding family of Marshfield. Considered avant-garde when it was built in 1699, the South Shore mansion was the residence of Judge Issac Winslow, the grandson of *Mayflower* passenger Edward Winslow, who served as a governor of Plymouth Colony.

The house contains 18th-century furniture. On the grounds are the Daniel Webster Law Office, an 18th-century carriage shed and a blacksmith shop. **Hours:** Wed.-Sun. 11-5, Memorial Day-Labor Day. Phone ahead to confirm schedule. **Cost:** $3; $1 (children). **Phone:** (781) 837-5753.

MARTHA'S VINEYARD (F-8)

Martha's Vineyard, like Nantucket, was an early refuge and supply point for the coastal ship traffic that regularly rounded Cape Cod. Vineyard Haven blossomed as a port for such traffic during the 18th and 19th centuries. Edgartown, the island's oldest European settlement, became an important whaling center. Such historic remnants as the Old Whaling Church in Edgartown, Mayhew Chapel and the Indian Burial Ground between West Tisbury and Vineyard Haven, and the Carpenter Gothic cottages of Oak Bluffs are part of Martha's Vineyard's charm.

Its quaint atmosphere, beaches and proximity to Cape Cod and the East Coast make the island—and its six towns—a popular resort area. Edgartown and Vineyard Haven remain the island's principal commercial centers, supplemented in the summer by the bustle of Oak Bluffs' shopping district. The island's fishing heritage continues in the village of Menemsha, near the varicolored clay cliffs of Aquinnah.

Beaches are the island's most obvious recreational asset, providing opportunities for windsurfing and fishing. Four large harbors provide anchorage and departure points for sailing and charter fishing. Bicycling is the most common mode of transportation during the summer; shuttle bus service is available from mid-May to mid-October.

Car and passenger ferries operate daily from Woods Hole *(see Cape Cod p. 177)* to Vineyard Haven year-round and, in summer, to Oak Bluffs. Summer passenger service operates between Oak Bluffs and Falmouth *(see Cape Cod p. 172)* and Hyannis *(see Cape Cod p. 172)* on the south shore of Cape Cod and between Vineyard Haven and New Bedford *(see place listing p. 190).* Seasonal service for passengers only is available from Quonset, R.I., to Oak Bluffs.

Martha's Vineyard Sightseeing provides 2.5-hour tours of the island; phone (508) 627-8687. Vineyard Fast Ferry departs daily late May to mid-October from Quonset Point in North Kingstown, R.I., to Oak Bluffs on Martha's Vineyard; for information or reservations phone (401) 295-4040.

Martha's Vineyard Chamber of Commerce: 24 Beach Rd., P.O. Box 1698, Vineyard Haven, MA 02568. **Phone:** (508) 693-0085 or (800) 505-4815.

Edgartown (F-8) elev. 17 ft

Edgartown is home to several lovely beaches, including East Beach at Cape Poge Wildlife Refuge *(see attraction listing);* South Beach (Katama), 3 miles of barrier beach at the end of Katama Road; and Lighthouse Beach, off North Water Street. Along the harbor, Water Street, which boasts several restored historical structures, is ideal for casual strollers.

CAPE POGE WILDLIFE REFUGE can be reached from the Chappaquiddick ferry landing. Take Chappaquiddick Rd. 2.5 mi. s.e. to Dike Rd., then .5 mi. e. to the parking lots by Dike Bridge; the refuge entrance is over the bridge. The refuge includes a 7-mile-long beach, superb fishing spots, 14 miles of trails and the historic 1801 Cape Poge Lighthouse. Through a variety of guided and self-guiding tours offered on the property, visitors may explore its diverse upland and marine habitats as well as the lighthouse. *See Recreation Chart.*

A free shuttle from the Chappaquiddick ferry landing is available for tour participants; shuttle departs 15 minutes before each tour. **Hours:** Refuge daily 24 hours. Tours are available Memorial Day-Columbus Day weekend (weather permitting). Tour schedules vary; phone ahead.

Cost: $3; free (ages 0-15 and pedestrians mid-Oct. through Memorial Day). Tours $25-$40; $12-$18 (ages 0-14). Reservations are recommended for tours. **Phone:** (508) 627-7689, (508) 627-3599 for tour information and reservations, or (508) 693-7662 for the regional office. 🎟️ 🚫

Mytoi, on Dike Rd., is a 14-acre Japanese-style garden featuring mixed plantings of native and exotic trees and shrubs. A small pond, camellia dell, stone garden, hillside garden, a wooden bridge and winding footpaths also are featured. A rustic shelter offers a panoramic view of the garden. **Time:** Allow 1 hour minimum. **Hours:** Daily dawn-dusk. **Cost:** Donations. **Phone:** (508) 627-7689. ⊞

MARTHA'S VINEYARD MUSEUM is at 59 School St. at Cooke St. The 18th-century Cooke House contains 11 rooms relating Vineyard history. The Pease House Galleries include the Wampanoag Gallery; the Oral History Center, which features the stories of native islanders; and Kid's Space. Also featured are the 1854 Fresnel lens from Gay Head Lighthouse and such vessels and vehicles as a whaleboat and an 1856 fire engine.

The Gale Huntington Library of History also is on-site. It contains reference material relating to Martha's Vineyard that includes books, manuscripts, photographs, maps, oral histories and genealogy information.

Time: Allow 1 hour, 30 minutes minimum. **Hours:** Mon.-Sat. 10-5, mid-June to mid-Oct.; 10-4, rest of year. Library open by appointment. Closed major holidays. Phone ahead to confirm schedule. **Cost:** Museum mid-June to mid-Oct. $7; $6 (senior citizens); $4 (ages 6-15). Museum rest of year $6; $5 (senior citizens); $4 (ages 6-15). Library fees vary. **Phone:** (508) 627-4441.

MASS AUDUBON'S FELIX NECK WILDLIFE SANCTUARY, off Edgartown-Vineyard Haven Rd. on Felix Neck Dr., encompasses 375 acres of beach, marsh, open fields and woodlands that harbor waterfowl. A nature center features a live owl cam, as well as freshwater and saltwater tanks containing local species. Maps available at the center identify wildlife and guide visitors to trails and a turtle pond. **Hours:** Grounds daily dawn-dusk. Phone ahead for nature center hours. **Cost:** $4; $3 (ages 2-12 and 66+). **Phone:** (508) 627-4850.

VINCENT HOUSE MUSEUM, at jct. Main and Church sts., is considered the oldest house on the island. The 1672 residence, moved from its original site in 1977, contains original woodwork, brickwork, glass and hardware. The house's furnishings depict architecture and life on the island throughout the last 4 centuries. Docents conduct tours of the museum and other historic structures.

Hours: Mon.-Fri. 11-3, Memorial Day-Columbus Day. Guided tours are given on the hour. Last tour begins 1 hour before closing. **Cost:** $4; free (ages 0-13). Guided tour $10; free (ages 0-13). **Phone:** (508) 627-4440.

West Tisbury (F-7) elev. 37 ft

LONG POINT WILDLIFE REFUGE is .3 mi. w. on Edgartown-West Tisbury Rd. to Martha's Vineyard airport, 1.3 mi. s. on Waldron's Bottom Rd., e. on Scrubby Neck Rd. (Path), then 1.2 mi. s. on Hughe's Thumb Rd., following signs. The refuge is part of a sand barrens ecosystem that exists in certain areas from New Jersey to Maine.

Home to many rare types of vegetation, such as scrub oak shrublands, sandplain grasslands and coastal heathlands, the refuge contains habitats that

require disturbances for their existence. A beachfront and 2-mile walking trail also are open to visitors. **Time:** Allow 2 hours minimum. **Hours:** Daily 9-5 (also Fri.-Sun. 5-7), June 15-Sept. 15; dawn-dusk, rest of year. **Cost:** $3; free (ages 0-15). **Parking:** $10. **Phone:** (508) 693-7392.

Wildlife Discovery Tour is 1.1 mi. w. on Edgartown-West Tisbury Rd. to Martha's Vineyard airport, 1.5 mi. s. on Deep Bottom Rd. and 1.3 mi. s. on Thumb Point Rd. to off-season parking area. Participants explore the natural wonders of Tisbury Great Pond on this 90-minute guided kayak tour led by naturalists. Basic paddling techniques, local ecology and the history of the refuge also are explained.

Time: Allow 1 hour, 30 minutes minimum. **Hours:** Tours are given daily at 8:30, 11 and 1:30, June 15-Sept. 15. **Cost:** $25; $10 (ages 0-15). Tours are limited to 12 people. Reservations are required. **Phone:** (508) 693-7392.

THE POLLY HILL ARBORETUM is at 809 State Rd. Developed by horticulturalist Polly Hill, the 70-acre site is home to a lovely collection of plants, trees, flowers and other vegetation cultivated by Hill for more than 50 years. Intermingling with such flora as lilacs, dogwood and stewartia are a variety of historic structures. A visitor center and walking trails are offered, and guided tours are available in season.

Time: Allow 45 minutes minimum. **Hours:** Grounds daily dawn-dusk. Visitor center daily 9:30-4, Memorial Day weekend-Columbus Day. Tours are given daily at 2, Memorial Day weekend-Columbus Day. **Cost:** $5; free (ages 0-12). **Phone:** (508) 693-9426. ⊞

MASHPEE—*see Cape Cod p. 174.*

MATTAPOISETT (E-7) elev. 18′

MATTAPOISETT HISTORICAL SOCIETY MUSEUM, 5 Church St., is in a former New England church built in 1821. The museum displays scrimshaw, whaling artifacts, period costumes and antiques. The Carriage House Museum contains carriages, an early fire wagon, tools, an 1890 kitchen, a saltworks model and weaving equipment. **Hours:** Wed.-Sat. 1-4, July-Aug. Closed major holidays. Phone ahead to confirm schedule. **Cost:** $3; $1 (ages 6-15). **Phone:** (508) 758-2844.

MENDON (C-5)

[SAVE] **SOUTHWICK'S ZOO,** 4 mi. s. off SR 16 on Millville St., is one of New England's largest zoos dedicated to the preservation and breeding of rare and endangered species. Children's amusements, including a petting zoo, a deer forest, a playground, rides and shows are offered. Mandrills, large baboons from central Africa, and an African leopard habitat are zoo highlights. Special events are held seasonally.

Educational programs are offered. **Time:** Allow 2 hours minimum. **Hours:** Daily 10-5, mid-Apr. to mid-Oct. **Cost:** Zoo $18.75; $12.75 (ages 3-12 and 62+). Fee for individual rides vary. Combination ticket (includes admission and unlimited mechanical rides) $24. **Phone:** (508) 883-9182 or (800) 258-9182. ⒯ ㋔

MIDDLEBORO (D-7) elev. 100'

ROBBINS MUSEUM OF ARCHAEOLOGY is at 17 Jackson St. The museum houses American Indian artifacts. Exhibits include stone tools; pottery; murals; a diorama of a prehistoric village; and a Walk Through Time, an exhibit showing how culture has changed. **Time:** Allow 30 minutes minimum. **Hours:** Wed. 10-4, Thurs. 10-3, Sat. 10-2, with extended hours some days. Phone ahead to confirm schedule. Closed major holidays. **Cost:** $5; $2 (children). **Phone:** (508) 947-9005.

MILTON—see Boston p. 150.

MINUTE MAN NATIONAL HISTORICAL PARK—see Boston p. 150.

MONTEREY (C-1)

THE BIDWELL HOUSE is n. on Tyringham Rd. from SR 23, then 1 mi. w. on Art School Rd. The 1750 Georgian saltbox is set on 190 acres of woodlands. Built for the first minister of Monterey, it contains 18th- and early 19th-century furniture and decorative arts. Historic woodland trails and summer programs are available.

Tours: Guided tours are available. **Time:** Allow 30 minutes minimum. **Hours:** Thurs.-Mon. 11-4, Memorial Day weekend-Columbus Day. Last tour begins 1 hour before closing. **Cost:** $10; $8 (ages 62+); $5 (students with ID); free (ages 0-6). **Phone:** (413) 528-6888.

NANTUCKET ISLAND (F-9)

Nantucket Island's settlement began in 1659 when a group of colonists seeking economic opportunity and political and religious freedom purchased Nantucket from Thomas Mayhew of Martha's Vineyard for 30 British pounds and two beaver hats. Nantucket soon developed a successful whaling industry. During the 18th century a strong missionary-led Quaker movement took hold on the island.

Much of Nantucket's charm is associated with its cobblestone main street, small lanes, plain Quaker-style homes and handsome houses that date from the whaling days of the early 19th century. Thirty miles off the mainland, Nantucket is reached by air or boat. Daily ferry service is maintained from Hyannis *(see Cape Cod p. 172)* all year and from Martha's Vineyard *(see place listing p. 186)* from early May to late October.

Because streets are narrow, parking in Nantucket is limited. For those who choose not to walk, bicycles and mopeds are preferred modes of transportation. Cars can be parked at Hyannis. However, for those planning to take a car to Nantucket, a car ferry

is available. Reservations for car transport are required; phone (508) 477-8600.

The island supports an art colony; exhibitions are held in Artists' Association Gallery and outdoors throughout the year. Plays and concerts are presented all year.

Sailing and bicycling as well as fishing, particularly for bass and bluefish, are popular. The town maintains four bicycle paths: Milestone, a 6-mile hilly route between Milestone Rotary and Siasconset; Surfside, a 3-mile flat route from Surfside Beach to the junction of Atlantic Avenue and Vesper Lane; Cliff Road, which covers 2.5 rolling miles starting near Derrymore Road; and Madaket, a winding, 5-mile route beginning at the junction of Quaker and Madaket roads.

Nantucket Island Chamber of Commerce: Zero Main St., Nantucket, MA 02554. **Phone:** (508) 228-1700.

A visitor center is at 25 Federal St. A visitor kiosk is at Straight Wharf.

Self-guiding tours: Information about downtown walking tours is available from the Nantucket Historical Association *(see attraction listing).*

MITCHELL HOUSE: BIRTHPLACE OF MARIA MITCHELL, 1 Vestal St., is a typical Quaker-style Nantucket house, built in 1790, that was the birthplace of America's first woman astronomer. Exhibits depict the life of Mitchell, her discoveries and teachings. Vestal Street Observatory, 3 Vestal St., offers 1-hour tours and features an outdoor scale-model of the solar system, a planar sundial, sunspot observations and a permanent astronomy exhibit.

Hours: Mitchell House Mon.-Sat. 10-4, mid-June through Labor Day; Sat.-Sun. 10-4, day after Labor Day to mid-Oct. Observatory tours are given Tues.-Sat. at 11 a.m., mid-June through Labor Day; Sat.-Sun. at noon, rest of year. Phone ahead to confirm schedule. **Cost:** Mitchell House or observatory $5; $4 (children). Combination ticket (includes birthplace house and observatory) with Aquarium and Hinchman House Natural Science Museum $10; $8 (children). **Phone:** (508) 228-2896.

Aquarium, 28 Washington St., displays marine life indigenous to Nantucket's salt marshes, harbors and nearshore waters and features 20 saltwater tanks and two touch tanks. Outdoor excursions also are available. **Time:** Allow 30 minutes minimum. **Hours:** Mon.-Sat. 10-4, early June-Labor Day. Phone ahead to confirm schedule. **Cost:** $6; $5 (children). Combination ticket with Mitchell House: Birthplace of Maria Mitchell, Hinchman House Natural Science Museum and Vestal Street Observatory $10; $8 (children). **Phone:** (508) 228-5387.

Hinchman House Natural Science Museum, 7 Milk St., exhibits native flora and fauna. Live snakes, turtles, frogs, insects and spiders can be seen. Nature and bird-watching walks are offered daily. **Hours:** Mon.-Sat. 10-4, mid-June through Labor Day; Sat.-Sun. 10-4, day after Labor Day to mid-Oct. Phone ahead to confirm schedule. **Cost:** $5; $4 (children). Combination ticket with Aquarium, Mitchell House: Birthplace of Maria Mitchell and Vestal Street Observatory $10; $8 (children). **Phone:** (508) 228-0898.

NANTUCKET HISTORICAL ASSOCIATION is at 15 Broad St. The association maintains 22 historic properties and sites and offers guided walking tours from late May to mid-October. Also on-site is the Whaling Museum, open year-round. **Hours:** Guided walking tours depart from the museum Mon.-Sat. at 11:15 and 2:15, Sun. at 2:15, May 29-June 30 and Sept. 7-Oct. 11; Mon.-Sat. (except July 4) at 4:30, July 1-Sept. 6. **Cost:** Guided walking tour $10; $8 (senior citizens); $4 (ages 6-17). A combination ticket for admission to all historic properties and the Whaling Museum/Peter Foulger Museum is available. **Phone:** (508) 228-1894.

Fire Hose Cart House, 8 Gardner St., is the last example of the old neighborhood fire stations that were built following the Great Fire of 1846. A collection of 19th-century firefighting equipment is displayed. **Time:** Allow 30 minutes minimum. **Hours:** Daily noon-5, May 29-Sept. 6; Thurs.-Mon. noon-4, Sept. 7-Oct. 11 (weather permitting). **Cost:** $6; $5 (senior citizens); $3 (ages 6-17). Combination ticket (includes all Nantucket Historical Association historic sites and Whaling Museum/Peter Foulger Museum) $18; $15 (senior citizens); $9 (ages 6-17). **Phone:** (508) 228-1894.

Hadwen House, 96 Main St., is a Greek Revival-style home built in 1845 by Frederick Brown Coleman for William Hadwen, whale-oil merchant and candlemaker. The mansion's architecture and furnishings reflect the prosperity of Nantucket's whaling era. A garden is on the grounds.

　　Tours: Guided tours are available. **Time:** Allow 30 minutes minimum. **Hours:** Daily noon-5, May 29-Sept. 6; Thurs.-Mon. noon-4, Sept. 7-Oct. 11. **Cost:** $6; $5 (senior citizens); $3 (ages 6-17). Combination ticket (includes all Nantucket Historical Association historic sites and Whaling Museum/Peter Foulger Museum) $18; $15 (senior citizens); $9 (ages 6-17). **Phone:** (508) 228-1894.

Oldest House and Kitchen Garden, on Sunset Hill, was built in the saltbox style in 1686 and also is known as the Jethro Coffin House. This is the only surviving structure from the original 17th-century English settlement. The Kitchen Garden includes 17 raised beds featuring an array of period plants, vegetables and herbs.

　　Hours: Daily noon-5, May 29-Sept. 6; Thurs.-Mon. noon-4, Sept. 7-Oct. 11. **Cost:** $6; $5 (senior citizens); $3 (ages 6-17). Combination ticket (includes all Nantucket Historical Association historic sites and Whaling Museum/Peter Foulger Museum) $18; $15 (senior citizens); $9 (ages 6-17). **Phone:** (508) 228-1894.

Old Gaol, on Vestal St., was built in 1806 and is representative of early New England penal institutions. **Hours:** Daily noon-5, May 29-Sept. 6; Thurs.-Mon. noon-4, Sept. 7-Oct. 11 (weather permitting).

Cost: $6; $5 (senior citizens); $3 (ages 6-17). Combination ticket (includes all Nantucket Historical Association historic sites and Whaling Museum/Peter Foulger Museum) $18; $15 (senior citizens); $9 (ages 6-17). **Phone:** (508) 228-1894.

Old Mill is on Prospect St. Built in 1746, the mill contains its original intricate working machinery. Corn is ground in season (weather permitting). **Hours:** Daily noon-5, May 29-Sept. 6; Thurs.-Mon. noon-4, Sept. 7-Oct. 11 (weather permitting). **Cost:** $6; $5 (senior citizens); $3 (ages 6-17). Combination ticket (includes all Nantucket Historical Association historic sites and Whaling Museum/Peter Foulger Museum) $18; $15 (senior citizens); $9 (ages 6-17). **Phone:** (508) 228-1894.

Quaker Meeting House and Research Library, 7 Fair St., was built in 1838 and was used as a school and a church by the Society of Friends. The society still holds meetings here during the summer months. The Research Library is in the Old Fair Street Museum built in 1904.

　　Time: Allow 30 minutes minimum. **Hours:** Daily noon-5, May 29-Sept. 6; Thurs.-Mon. noon-4, Sept. 7-Oct. 11. **Cost:** Meeting house $6; $5 (senior citizens); $3 (ages 6-17). Combination ticket (includes all Nantucket Historical Association historic sites and Whaling Museum/Peter Foulger Museum) $18; $15 (senior citizens); $9 (ages 6-17). Research library $5. **Phone:** (508) 228-1894.

Whaling Museum/Peter Foulger Museum, 13-15 Broad St., is housed in an 1847 candle factory where whale oil once was refined. The museum depicts the history of Nantucket through exhibitions of furniture, baskets, portraits and other artifacts as well as candle making and decorative arts. Other items on display include ship models, whaling tools, logbooks, a 16-foot-long lens from an island lighthouse, portraits of whaling masters, a 46-foot-long sperm whale skeleton and a large collection of scrimshaw.

　　Time: Allow 2 hours minimum. **Hours:** Daily 10-5, mid-May to early Oct.; Thurs.-Mon. 11-4, late Apr. to mid-May and early Nov.-late Dec.; Sat.-Sun. 11-4, mid-Feb. to late Apr. Phone ahead to confirm schedule. **Cost:** $15; $8 (ages 6-17). Combination ticket with Nantucket Historical Association historic sites $18; $15 (senior citizens); $9 (ages 6-17). **Phone:** (508) 228-1894.

NANTUCKET LIGHTSHIP BASKET MUSEUM is at 49 Union St. Historical and contemporary lightship baskets are exhibited, along with a display detailing how the baskets are made. A large portion of 20th-century basket maker Jose Formoso Reyes' workshop also is on-site. In addition the facility offers demonstrations by basket weavers as well as lectures given by historians and restoration experts. The surrounding 1820 Garden features plants that were commonly found in Nantucket in the early 1800s. **Time:** Allow 30 minutes minimum. **Hours:** Tues.-Sat. 10-4, Memorial Day-Columbus Day.

Cost: $4; $2 (ages 6-17 and senior citizens). Phone: (508) 228-1177. ⓕ

NANTUCKET SHIPWRECK & LIFESAVING MUSEUM is at 158 Polpis Rd. More than 700 shipwrecks have been documented around Nantucket; this museum is dedicated to those who have risked their lives for others. Displayed are lifesaving equipment, surfboats, historic photographs and shipwreck memorabilia. The museum is housed in a building with an exterior replica of the Surfside Lifesaving Station.

Time: Allow 1 hour minimum. Hours: Daily 10-4, mid-May through Columbus Day. Cost: $5; $3 (students with ID); free (ages 0-5). Phone: (508) 228-1885 or (508) 228-2505.

NATICK—see Boston p. 151.

NEW BEDFORD (E-7) pop. 93,768, elev. 52′

New Bedford, due to its position on Buzzards Bay, was once a great whaling port. Fishing and allied industries still contribute one-fifth of the city's income. A passenger ferry operates to Martha's Vineyard; for schedule phone Cape Island Express Lines at (508) 997-1688. Trips to Cuttyhunk Island aboard the MV Alert II depart from Fisherman's Wharf/Pier 3; phone (508) 992-1432.

The New Bedford Public Library was one of the first public libraries in Massachusetts and is housed in a handsome, granite Greek Revival building downtown.

New Bedford Office of Tourism & Marketing: 52 Fisherman's Wharf, Old City Pier #3, New Bedford, MA 02740-7233. Phone: (508) 979-1745 or (800) 508-5353.

ARTWORKS! is at 384 Acushnet Ave. The four-story community arts center features changing exhibits, a ceramic studio and a section designed for teenagers. Workshops and lectures also are presented. Time: Allow 45 minutes minimum. Hours: Tues.-Sat. noon-5 (also second Thurs. of the month 5-9), with extended hours Nov.-Dec. Closed major holidays. Phone ahead to confirm schedule. Cost: Donations. Phone: (508) 984-1588.

BUTTONWOOD PARK ZOO is .4 mi. s. on Chancery St., then .8 mi. w. to 425 Hawthorn St. The zoo's theme, From the Berkshires to the Sea, focuses on the land- and water-based wildlife of Massachusetts. Nearly 200 species are housed in re-created natural habitats. Visitors encounter bald eagles, black bears, bobcats, mountain lions, river otters, seals and farm animals as well as Asian elephants and North American bison. Pony rides and a children's train ride are available.

Time: Allow 2 hours minimum. Hours: Daily 10-5. Last admission 30 minutes before closing. Closed Jan. 1, Thanksgiving and Dec. 25. Cost: $6; $4.50 (ages 12-18 and 66+); $3 (ages 3-12). Phone: (508) 991-6178. ⓕ ⓕ

NEW BEDFORD ART MUSEUM, 608 Pleasant St., presents changing exhibitions throughout the year. Contemporary and historic art as well as local, national and international artists are featured. Time: Allow 1 hour minimum. Hours: Daily 10-5 (also second Thurs. of the month 5-9), Memorial Day-Labor Day; Wed.-Sun. noon-5 (also second Thurs. of the month 5-9), rest of year. Closed major holidays. Cost: $3; $2 (students with ID and senior citizens); free (ages 0-17 with adult and to all second Thurs. of the month 5-9 p.m.). Phone: (508) 961-3072.

NEW BEDFORD FIRE MUSEUM is at 51 Bedford St. in Old Station No. 4, built in 1867. The museum exhibits restored antique fire trucks and pieces of historic fire equipment. Upstairs are helmets, coats and boots for children to try on; a bell to ring; and a 5-foot-long pole to slide down. Time: Allow 30 minutes minimum. Hours: Daily 9-4, July 6-Aug. 31. Cost: $3; $2 (senior citizens); $1 (ages 7-16). Phone: (508) 992-2162.

NEW BEDFORD WHALING NATIONAL HISTORICAL PARK, with a visitor center at 33 William St., is a 13-block, 34-acre district with cobblestone streets, period lighting and preserved buildings, some of which date back to the early 19th century. The visitor center offers maps outlining several self-guiding walking tours, some of which also relate the history of whaling in America. Hours: Visitor center daily 9-5 (also second Thurs. of the month 5-9). Guided tours are available July-Aug.; phone ahead for schedule. Closed Jan. 1, Thanksgiving and Dec. 25. Cost: Free. Phone: (508) 996-4095.

▼ⓖⓔⓜ New Bedford Whaling Museum, 18 Johnny Cake Hill, is one of the largest museums devoted to the history of whales and whaling. The collection includes a changing exhibit gallery and interactive exhibits as well as a fully equipped whaleboat, a humpback whale and rare blue whale skeletons. The park's 22-minute orientation film, "The City That Lit the World," is shown daily in the museum's theater.

Visitors can board a fully rigged, 89-foot, half-scale replica of the whaling bark Lagoda. Hours: Daily 9-5 (also second Thurs. of the month 5-9). Closed Jan. 1, Thanksgiving and Dec. 25. Cost: $10; $9 (ages 59+ and students with ID); $6 (ages 6-14). Phone: (508) 997-0046.

ⓢⒶⓥⒺ Rotch-Jones-Duff House and Garden Museum, 396 County St., is a 23-room Greek Revival mansion designed by Richard Upjohn and built in 1834 for William Rotch Jr., a prominent whaling merchant. Rooms display decorative arts, furniture and personal belongings that chronicle the history of the city over a 150-year period. The grounds encompass a rose parterre garden, a woodland garden and a formal cutting garden. Hours: Mon.-Sat. 10-4, Sun. noon-4. Closed major holidays. Cost: $5; $4 (ages 66+ and students with ID); $2 (ages 3-12). Phone: (508) 997-1401.

Seamen's Bethel is in the historic district at 15 Johnny Cake Hill. Dedicated in 1832 as a nondenominational whalemen's chapel, the building features a ship's bow pulpit and the Old Salt Box meeting room. In the novel "Moby Dick," Herman Melville described its cenotaphs—the stone tablets inscribed with the names of whalemen lost at sea since the 1840s. **Time:** Allow 30 minutes minimum. **Hours:** Mon.-Fri. 10-5, Memorial Day-Columbus Day. **Cost:** Donations. **Phone:** (508) 992-3295.

NEWBURY—*see Boston p. 151.*

NEWBURYPORT—*see Boston p. 151.*

NEWTON—*see Boston p. 152.*

NORFOLK—*see Boston p. 152.*

NORTH ADAMS (A-2) pop. 14,681, elev. 706'

Once a thriving industrial and railroad center, North Adams is now a popular stop-off point along the scenic Mohawk Trail (SR 2), which winds through the Berkshire Mountains and follows the Deerfield River eastward to Greenfield. Commemorating the trail's American Indian origins along the route is the "Hail to the Sunrise" monument in Charlemont. Williamstown *(see place listing p. 205)* is the western terminus of the route. Contact the Mohawk Trail Association for additional information; phone (413) 743-8127.

North Adams Mayor's Office of Tourism & Cultural Development: 6 W. Main St., North Adams, MA 01247. **Phone:** (413) 664-6180.

MASS MoCA (MASSACHUSETTS MUSEUM OF CONTEMPORARY ART) is at jct. SR 2 and Marshall St. Contained within a 13-acre complex consisting of 25 renovated 19th-century factory buildings, changing exhibits feature a tremendous array of contemporary art. Enormous unobstructed space allows for works not previously showcased due to such physical demands as scale or technological complexity. Buildings contain galleries (one as large as a football field), theaters and courtyards for music, dance and film presentations. **Time:** Allow 2 hours minimum. **Hours:** Daily 10-6, July 1-Labor Day; Wed.-Mon. 11-5, rest of year. Guided tours are given daily at 11, 1, 2 and 4 (also Sat.-Sun. at 3), July 1-Labor Day; Mon.-Fri. at 2, Sat.-Sun. at noon and 3, rest of year. Closed Thanksgiving and Dec. 25. **Cost:** $15; $10 (students with ID); $5 (ages 6-16). **Phone:** (413) 662-2111.

MOUNT GREYLOCK STATE RESERVATION is 8.5 mi. s. off SR 2 on Notch Rd. A 12,500-acre park surrounds the commonwealth's highest peak, which offers a panoramic view of five states. At the 3,491-foot summit are the Massachusetts Veterans War Memorial Tower and the rustic Bascom Lodge, built by the Civilian Conservation Corps (CCC). The park features 70 miles of hiking paths and a section of the Appalachian National Scenic Trail; maps are available at the visitor center on Rockwell Road at the park's southern entrance. *See Recreation Chart.*

The Historic Parkway road system is open to vehicles and bicycles from mid-May to early November. The campground and Stony Ledge are accessible by hiking only. **Hours:** Grounds daily dawn-dusk. Visitor center daily 9-5; 9-4:30, rest of year. Closed Jan. 1, Thanksgiving and Dec. 25. **Cost:** Free. **Parking:** $2 at summit. **Phone:** (413) 499-4262. 🍽 🍴 📷 ⛰

NATURAL BRIDGE STATE PARK is .5 mi. n.e. off SR 2 on SR 8 to McCauley Rd. Glacial meltwaters formed this white marble arch and chasm at the end of the last ice age. Nathaniel Hawthorne described it in his "American Notebooks." A visitor center and picnic facilities are near the natural bridge, and a walking trail leads through the chasm and to an abandoned marble quarry. **Time:** Allow 1 hour minimum. **Hours:** Daily 9-5, Memorial Day-Columbus Day. **Cost:** $2 (per private vehicle). **Phone:** (413) 663-6392. 🍴

WESTERN GATEWAY HERITAGE STATE PARK is in the restored freight yard district off SR 8 at 9 Furnace St. bypass. The park features a collection of six renovated buildings containing shops, a restaurant and exhibits.

In the former Boston and Maine Freight House, the visitor center chronicles the cultural history of North Adams; 19th-century railroad and industrial history; and the building of the Hoosac Tunnel 1851-75, an engineering feat that took 196 lives. **Time:** Allow 1 hour, 30 minutes minimum. **Hours:** Visitor center daily 10-5. Closed Jan. 1, Thanksgiving and Dec. 25. **Cost:** Donations. **Phone:** (413) 663-6312.

NORTHAMPTON (C-2)
pop. 28,978, elev. 125'

Settled in 1654, Northampton was an isolated frontier village for its first 150 years. Puritan theologian Jonathan Edwards and President Calvin Coolidge both lived in this city. Northampton's educational center is Smith College, whose attractions include Lyman Plant House and Botanical Gardens.

Greater Northampton Chamber of Commerce: 99 Pleasant St., Northampton, MA 01060. **Phone:** (413) 584-1900.

HISTORIC NORTHAMPTON MUSEUM & EDUCATION CENTER is at 46 Bridge St. (SR 9), just n.e. of jct. US 5. The museum features exhibits relating to Northampton and the Connecticut Valley's history. Included are ceramics, fine art, furniture, photographs and toys as well as a collection of textiles and costumes. **Time:** Allow 30 minutes minimum. **Hours:** Tues.-Sat. 10-5, Sun. noon-5. Closed major holidays. **Cost:** $3; $6 (family). **Phone:** (413) 584-6011.

LOOK MEMORIAL PARK, bordered by Mill River, lies on the Berkshire Trail (SR 9) on the n.w. edge of the city. Within its 200 acres are winding paths, tennis courts, paddleboat facilities, a petting zoo, an amphitheater, a miniature railroad, miniature golf and bumper boats. **Hours:** Park open daily 7-dusk. Facilities open daily 11-7, May-Sept. **Cost:** Mon.-Thurs. $4 (per private vehicle). Fri.-Sun. and holidays $5 (per private vehicle). Fees for recreational facilities vary; phone ahead. **Phone:** (413) 584-5457. 🎟

SMITH COLLEGE MUSEUM OF ART is in the Brown Fine Arts Center at jct. Elm St. and Bedford Terr. on the Smith College campus. Set within a tranquil atmosphere, the museum features many galleries that house a diverse collection of 19th- and early 20th-century American and European paintings. The works of Cezanne, Monet and Picasso are included. Drawings, dramatic sculptures, contemporary pieces created by women, ancient cultural artifacts and changing exhibits also are offered.

Time: Allow 1 hour, 30 minutes minimum. **Hours:** Tues.-Sat. 10-4 (also second Fri. of the month 4-8), Sun. noon-4. Closed major holidays. **Cost:** $5; $4 (ages 65+); $3 (students with ID); $2 (ages 6-12); free (ages 0-5, college students with ID and to all second Fri. of the month 4-8 p.m.). **Phone:** (413) 585-2760.

NORTH ANDOVER—see Boston p. 153.

NORTH EASTON (C-6) elev. 148′

CHILDREN'S MUSEUM IN EASTON is at 9 Sullivan Ave. Interactive art, science and humanities exhibits are housed in a three-story building formerly used as a fire station. Children can work on craft projects, slide down a fire pole, create an off-Broadway production or go on an archeological adventure. Outside, the Wild Place features a butterfly garden and outdoor displays. **Time:** Allow 2 hours minimum. **Hours:** Tues.-Fri. 9-5, Sat.-Sun. noon-5. Closed major holidays. **Cost:** $6; free (under 1). **Phone:** (508) 230-3789. 🎟

NORTHFIELD (A-3) pop. 1,141

NORTHFIELD MOUNTAIN RECREATION AND ENVIRONMENTAL CENTER, 2 mi. n. of SR 2 on SR 63, is an underground, pumped-storage hydroelectric facility topped by a 320-acre reservoir filled by the Connecticut River. During peak electrical demand, water is released from the reservoir through pump turbines to generate electricity.

A free fish-viewing area is open mid-May to mid-June. Hiking, mountain biking, fishing, cross-country skiing and snowshoeing are permitted; fees may be charged. *See Recreation Chart.* **Hours:** Center open Wed.-Sun. 9-5, May-Oct.; Wed.-Sun. 9-4:30 for skiing and snowshoeing, mid-Dec. to mid-Mar. (weather permitting). Closed Easter, Patriot's Day and Dec. 25. **Cost:** Free. **Phone:** (413) 659-3714 or (800) 859-2960. 🎟 🐟 ⊠ ⛰

Quinnetukut II **Interpretive Riverboat Ride** departs from Riverview Picnic Area off SR 63. The 1.5-hour Connecticut River cruise highlights local history and geography. **Hours:** Trips depart Fri.-Sun. at 11, 1:15 and 3, July-Oct. **Cost:** $12; $11 (ages 56+); $6 (ages 0-13). Reservations are recommended. **Phone:** (413) 659-3714.

NORTH GRAFTON (C-5) elev. 331′

WILLARD HOUSE AND CLOCK MUSEUM INC. is off I-90 exit 11, following signs. Built in 1718, this restored saltbox farmhouse is said to be the oldest house in Grafton. The site includes the birthplace and original 1766 workshop of the Willard brothers, America's premier family of 18th-century clockmakers. More than 80 Willard clocks are displayed among period furnishings, Oriental rugs, family portraits and heirlooms.

Hours: Tues.-Sat. 10-4, Sun. 1-4, Apr.-Dec.; Fri.-Sat. 10-4, Sun. 1-4, rest of year. Closed major holidays. **Cost:** $7; $6 (students with ID and senior citizens); $3 (ages 6-12). **Phone:** (508) 839-3500.

NORTH TRURO—see Cape Cod p. 174.

NORTH WEYMOUTH—see Boston p. 153.

NORTON (D-6) elev. 105′

MASSACHUSETTS GOLF MUSEUM is 1.9 mi. n.w. on SR 140 from jct. SRs 123 and 140, then .6 mi. s.w. to 300 Arnold Palmer Blvd. The museum showcases the prominent individuals and moments in Massachusetts golf history through a video, trophies, and interactive and multimedia exhibits. **Time:** Allow 45 minutes minimum. **Hours:** Daily 9-4. Closed major holidays and during special events. Phone ahead to confirm schedule. **Cost:** Free. **Phone:** (774) 430-9100 or (800) 356-2201.

[SAVE] **WINSLOW FARM ANIMAL SANCTUARY** is 2.8 mi. s.e. on Taunton Ave. (SR 140), then .4 mi. w. to 37 Eddy St. The tranquil sanctuary shelters more than 200 previously abandoned or mistreated animals, including cats, goats, miniature horses, rabbits and sheep. An aviary filled with such birds as ducks, peacocks and pheasants; an educational resource center; flowering gardens; a greenhouse; and nature trails are on-site. Such weekend special events as treasure hunts and holiday festivities also are offered.

Tours: Guided tours are available. **Time:** Allow 1 hour, 30 minutes minimum. **Hours:** Wed.-Mon. 11-5 or by appointment. **Cost:** $7; $5 (ages 2-11). An additional fee may be charged during special events. **Phone:** (508) 285-6451.

NORWELL (C-7) elev. 81′

[SAVE] **SOUTH SHORE NATURAL SCIENCE CENTER** is at 48 Jacobs Ln. Nature enthusiasts may explore various trails at a leisurely pace, from the shortest trail at 15 minutes to the longest trail at 50 minutes. Herb and wildflower gardens also are on-site. The Jacobs Pond area has two trails and some of the wildlife that can be seen include turtles, waterfowl and songbirds. The center's indoor museum area—The Ecozone—depicts the ecosystems of southeastern Massachusetts.

Picnicking is permitted in designated areas. **Time:** Allow 30 minutes minimum. **Hours:** Mon.-Sat. 9:30-4:30. Holiday hours vary; phone ahead. **Cost:** $5; $3 (ages 0-15 and 65+). **Phone:** (781) 659-2559.

ONSET (E-7) pop. 1,292, elev. 24'

CAPE COD CANAL CRUISES departs from the Onset Town Pier on Onset Ave. Narrated 2- and 3-hour scenic sightseeing cruises of Cape Cod Canal pass under the Bourne and Sagamore bridges and the vertical-lift railroad bridge. Live entertainment cruises also are offered during summer. **Hours:** Sightseeing trips are offered mid-May to mid-Oct. Departure days and times vary; phone ahead. **Cost:** Three-hour sightseeing trip $16; $8 (ages 5-12). Two-hour sightseeing trip $14; $7 (ages 5-12). Prices may vary. **Phone:** (508) 295-3883.

ORLEANS—see Cape Cod p. 174.

OSTERVILLE—see Cape Cod p. 174.

PITTSFIELD (B-1) pop. 45,793, elev. 1,026'

Pittsfield, the county seat of Berkshire County, began as an agricultural community, but an abundance of natural resources established the city as an industrial center. During the late 19th and early 20th centuries immigrants came to Pittsfield in search of factory jobs, thus creating the diverse ethnic communities found throughout the area.

Cultural offerings in the area include the Berkshire Artisans, a municipal center for the visual arts. The center features a gallery and performance area, workshops, and artist's studios; phone (413) 499-9348. The Albany Berkshire Ballet performs classical and contemporary works year-round. Many of their productions are geared toward young children and their families. For information about performances and venues phone (413) 445-5382.

Recreational opportunities include hiking and camping in Pittsfield State Forest *(see Recreation Chart and the AAA Northeastern CampBook)* and at Onota and Pontoosuc lakes. Of interest is Canoe Meadows Wildlife Sanctuary, 3 miles south on US 7 and 2 miles northeast on Holmes Road, where hiking trails traverse woodlands, fields and marshes.

Pittsfield is credited with the creation of the first agricultural fair. Held on the village green in 1810, the fair was the brainchild of Elkanah Watson, a tireless promoter of agricultural progress and a friend of George Washington.

Self-guiding tours: Maps outlining historic sites, hiking and bicycling routes and tours of the Berkshire region are available. For more information contact the Berkshire Visitors Bureau, 3 Hoosac St., Adams, MA 01220; phone (413) 743-4500 or (800) 237-5747.

ARROWHEAD, 3.5 mi. s. on US 7/20, then 1.5 mi. n.e. on Holmes Rd., is the home of Herman Melville. In 1851, during his 13-year residence, Melville completed "Moby Dick." Original inscriptions from the story "I and My Chimney" are on the fireplace. The house is furnished with 19th-century items, many belonging to the Melvilles. The site also hosts seasonal exhibitions and special events.

Hours: House daily 9:30-4:30, Memorial Day-Columbus Day; by appointment rest of year. Guided tours are given on the hour 10-3, Memorial Day-Columbus Day; by appointment rest of year. Phone ahead to confirm schedule. **Cost:** $12; $8 (ages 6-17); free (ages 0-5). **Phone:** (413) 442-1793.

BERKSHIRE ATHENAEUM, 1 Wendell Ave., is the city's public library. A Herman Melville Memorial Room has works, photographs and personal items of the author. A collection of genealogical records and historical materials with a New England focus is available. **Hours:** Mon.-Fri. 9-5 (also Tues.-Thurs. 5-9), Sat. 10-5, Sept.-June; Mon.-Fri. 9-5 (also Tues. and Thurs. 5-9), Sat. 10-5, rest of year. Closed major holidays. **Cost:** Free. **Phone:** (413) 499-9480.

[SAVE] **BERKSHIRE MUSEUM,** 39 South St., is an art, science and history museum. Featured are interactive science and technology displays and art collections from Egypt, Greece and China as well as a collection of Hudson River School landscapes and American Indian artifacts. An aquarium showcases

marine and freshwater habitats, and a paleontology gallery features an interactive simulated dinosaur excavation site. Films, concerts, children's programs and changing exhibits are presented.

Guided tours are available by appointment. **Time:** Allow 1 hour minimum. **Hours:** Mon.-Sat. 10-5, Sun. noon-5. Closed Jan. 1, Memorial Day, July 4, Labor Day, Thanksgiving and Dec. 25. Phone ahead to confirm schedule. **Cost:** $10; $5 (ages 3-18). An additional fee may be charged during special exhibitions. **Phone:** (413) 443-7171.

HANCOCK SHAKER VILLAGE is 4.2 mi. w. on US 20 (W. Housatonic St.). The 1,200-acre restored Shaker village includes 21 buildings with original Shaker furniture and artifacts, a working farm, and an heirloom herb and vegetable garden. A visitor center features changing exhibitions about Shaker life. The Shakers, dedicated to simplicity, celibacy and equality, founded the village in 1783 and lived here until 1960.

From mid-November to early April interpreters lead visitors through the gardens, an 1830s brick dwelling, the 1826 Round Stone Barn, and a laundry and machine shop. The exterior architecture of the site's other historic structures can be viewed along the guided tours.

Hands-on activities and first-person portrayals are featured from late May to mid-November, with building interiors open for self-guiding tours. Staff demonstrate Shaker woodworking, weaving, oval box making and other 19th-century crafts.

Time: Allow 2 hours, 30 minutes minimum. **Hours:** Daily 10-5, Memorial Day to mid-Oct.; 10-4, mid-Apr. through day before Memorial Day and mid-Oct. to mid-Nov. Guided tours are given Mon.-Fri. at 1, Sat.-Sun. at noon and 2, mid-Nov. to mid-Apr. Closed Jan. 1, Thanksgiving and Dec. 25.

Phone ahead to confirm schedule. **Cost:** Mid-Apr. to mid-Nov. $16.50; $8 (ages 13-17). Rest of year $12.50; $4 (ages 13-17). **Phone:** (413) 443-0188 or (800) 817-1137. *See color ad.*

SOUTH MOUNTAIN CONCERT HALL, 2 mi. s. on US 7, was specifically designed for chamber music. Using timber from an old textile mill, it was constructed in the Colonial style in 1918. Such artists as the Emerson, Juilliard, Guarnieri and Tokyo string quartets have appeared at the 440-seat facility, which features chamber music and recitals during the South Mountain Concerts. **Hours:** Concerts are held Sun. at 3, first weekend in Sept. to mid-Oct. **Cost:** Concert $33-$35. **Phone:** (413) 442-2106.

PLYMOUTH (D-8) pop. 7,658, elev. 38′

It was on Plymouth Rock that the Pilgrims landed in December 1620 to found the second permanent English settlement on the North American continent. During the first winter, half of the 102 people brought by the *Mayflower* died of exposure, cold and hunger. Survivors John Alden, William Bradford, Elder Brewster, Miles Standish and Edward Winslow have been immortalized in poetry and history.

Brewster Gardens on Water Street is the location of the Pilgrims' first gardens, which were called "meersteads." The traditional Thanksgiving Day Celebration is held on Thanksgiving.

The Church of the Pilgrimage, 8 Town Sq., was built in 1840. A Roche pipe organ with three manuals, 55 ranks and 3,000 pipes is showcased; phone (508) 746-3026. The Plymouth Antiquarian Society offers guided tours of a few historic structures, including the Harlow Old Fort House. Located at 119 Sandwich St., it was built by Sgt. William Harlow

in 1677. Displaying exhibits chronicling Colonial life, the house is accessible to visitors in June and August; phone (508) 746-0012.

Plymouth Area Chamber of Commerce: 10 Cordage Park Cir., Suite 231, Plymouth, MA 02360. **Phone:** (508) 830-1620.

Plymouth Information Center: 130 Water St., Plymouth, MA 02360. **Phone:** (508) 747-7525. *See color ad p. 547.*

Self-guiding tours: The Pilgrim Path features more than 20 sites. Brochures featuring a map of the path and descriptions of the sites are available from the information center.

Shopping areas: Main Street Antiques, 46-58 Main St., has more than 200 antique dealers. Featuring clapboard edifices and cobblestone walkways, Village Landing Marketplace, 170 Water St., contains specialty, craft and clothing shops.

ANDY LYNN BOATS, which departs from Town Wharf, offers narrated 4-hour whale-watch cruises. Deep-sea fishing cruises also are available. **Hours:** Whale-watch cruises are offered Apr.-Oct. Departure days and times vary. **Cost:** Whale-watch cruise $40-$75. Prices may vary. Visitors should arrive at the dock 30 minutes before departure. Reservations are required. **Phone:** (508) 746-7776.

BURIAL HILL, at the head of Town Square, is the site of a fort built 1622-23, a watchtower built in 1643 and the burial place of Gov. William Bradford. A replica of the powder house can be seen. On August Fridays, citizens dress in Pilgrim garb and walk from Plymouth Rock to Burial Hill to re-enact the church service attended by the 51 survivors of the winter of 1620-21. **Cost:** Free.

[SAVE] **CAPE COD CRUISES** departs from State Pier. A 1-hour, 35-minute excursion to Provincetown is offered. **Hours:** Cruises depart daily at 10, with return trips leaving Provincetown at 4:30, mid-June through Aug. 30; Sat.-Sun., late May to mid-June; schedule varies in Sept. Phone ahead to confirm schedule. **Cost:** Provincetown and return cruise $40; $35 (ages 62+); $30 (ages 3-11). Prices may vary. Reservations are recommended. **Phone:** (508) 747-2400.

[SAVE] **CAPTAIN JOHN BOATS WHALE-WATCH CRUISES,** 10 Town Wharf, offers 4-hour whale-watching trips with commentary provided by a naturalist guide; sightings are guaranteed. Deep-sea fishing and entertainment cruises also are offered. **Hours:** Trips depart daily at 9, 11 and 2, June-Aug.; daily at noon, Sept.-Oct.; Sat.-Sun. at 9, noon and 2, in May; Sat.-Sun. at noon, in Apr. Phone ahead to confirm schedule. **Cost:** $40; $34 (ages 62+); $28 (ages 3-12). Reservations are recommended. **Phone:** (508) 746-2643. [fork]

COLE'S HILL, on Water St., is the burial place of Pilgrims who died during the first winter as well as

the location of Cyrus Dallin's statue of the American Indian chief Massasoit, who ratified the 1621 peace treaty. **Cost:** Free.

COLONIAL LANTERN TOURS departs from Plymouth Rock (early tours) or from the John Carver Inn at 25 Summer St. (late tour). Participants carry punched-tin lanterns as they traverse the mile-long route on 90-minute guided tours. The Classic History Lantern Tour focuses on Plymouth sites; the Ghosts & Legends Tour reflects on the ghostly lore that colors the town's history.

Hours: Classic tours depart nightly at 7:30, Apr.-Nov.; by appointment rest of year. Ghost tours depart nightly at 7:30 and 9, Apr.-Nov.; by appointment rest of year. Closed July 4. **Cost:** $15; $12

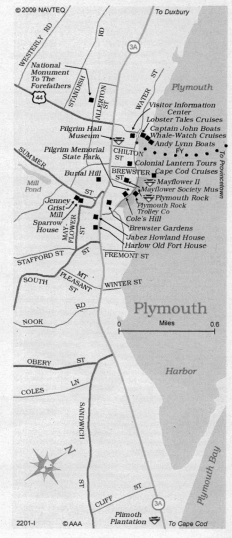

(children and senior citizens). Reservations are recommended. **Phone:** (774) 454-8121, or (774) 454-8126 for reservations.

HEDGE HOUSE MUSEUM, 126 Water St., offers visitors a glimpse into 19th-century life. Built in 1809, the historic house was originally located on Court Street. The structure was moved to its current location overlooking Plymouth Harbor in the early 1900s, when it was saved from demolition by the Plymouth Antiquarian Society.

The building features Federal architecture, octagonal rooms and a carriage house. Antique furnishings, paintings, textiles and toys are on display. Enhancing the charming site are the brick pathways and flowering perennials of the Rose T. Briggs Memorial Garden. **Time:** Allow 45 minutes minimum. **Hours:** Wed.-Sun. 2-6, June-Aug. **Cost:** $5; $2 (ages 5-12). **Phone:** (508) 746-0012.

SAVE **JABEZ HOWLAND HOUSE,** 33 Sandwich St., is the 1667 house that was lived in by *Mayflower* passengers. **Hours:** Tours are given daily 10-4:30, Memorial Day weekend-Columbus Day; Thanksgiving Day and weekend following Thanksgiving 10-3, in Nov. **Cost:** $5; $4 (students with ID and senior citizens). **Phone:** (508) 746-9590.

THE JENNEY GRIST MILL, 6 Spring Ln., is a reconstruction of what is said to be the first mill built in the country. Thirty-minute tours teach visitors about the mill's history and the grinding process. Rebuilt in 1969, the mill is still operational and is used to grind corn into meal. **Time:** Allow 30 minutes minimum. **Hours:** Tours are given every 30 minutes Wed.-Sat. and Mon. 9:30-5, Sun. noon-5, early Apr.-Nov. 30. Last tour begins 30 minutes before closing. Closed Easter and Thanksgiving. **Cost:** $6; free (ages 0-17 with adult). **Phone:** (508) 747-4544. 🍴 👜

LOBSTER TALES CRUISES, departing from Town Wharf at the end of SR 44, offers interactive 1-hour lobster excursions in Plymouth Harbor during which passengers can experience hauling in lobster traps. A 1-hour pirate cruise allows children to battle a pirate ship using water cannons. Passengers can make their own sundaes on a 1.5-hour ice cream cruise.

Hours: Lobster excursions depart daily, Apr.-Oct.; departure times vary. Pirate cruises are offered June-Oct.; departure days and times vary. Ice cream cruises depart Wed. and Fri. at 7 p.m., July-Aug. **Cost:** Pirate cruise $18. Lobster excursion $15; $13 (ages 63+); $11 (ages 0-11). Ice cream cruise $15; $13 (ages 0-11). Reservations are required. **Phone:** (508) 746-5342.

GEM **MAYFLOWER II,** moored at State Pier at Pilgrim Memorial State Park, is a reproduction of the ship that brought English colonists to Plymouth in 1620. An exhibition on the dock relates their story and that of the Wampanoag who lived on the land. On board the vessel modern guides discuss the reproduction ship's construction

and its arrival in Plymouth in 1957. Costumed interpreters talk about the voyage, shipboard life in the 17th century and the colonists' first winter in the New World.

Time: Allow 1 hour minimum. **Hours:** Daily 9-5, late Mar.-late Nov. **Cost:** $10; $9 (ages 62+); $7 (ages 6-12). Combination ticket with Plimoth Plantation $28; $26 (ages 62+); $18 (ages 6-12). **Phone:** (508) 746-1622. *See color ad p. 547.*

MAYFLOWER SOCIETY MUSEUM, 1 blk. w. of Plymouth Harbor at 4 Winslow St., is the headquarters of the General Society of *Mayflower* Descendants. The original home was built in 1754 by Edward Winslow, a Pilgrim descendant and great grandson of Edward Winslow of Massachusetts, third governor of the Plymouth Colony. The estate includes formal gardens and nine rooms with authentic furnishings of the 17th, 18th and 19th centuries.

Videotaping is not permitted. **Time:** Allow 30 minutes minimum. **Hours:** Daily 11-4, mid-June through Sept. 30; Fri.-Sun. 11-4, Memorial Day weekend to mid-June and in Oct. Closed major holidays. Phone ahead to confirm schedule. **Cost:** $5; $4.50 (senior citizens); $2 (ages 6-12). **Phone:** (508) 746-2590.

NATIONAL MONUMENT TO THE FOREFATHERS, 1 blk. n. of US 44 on Allerton St., is a tribute to Plymouth's founding fathers. The 81-foot-tall monument is one of the largest granite statues in the United States. The names of the 102 *Mayflower* passengers are etched on the statue. **Hours:** Daily dawn-dusk, mid-May to mid-Oct. **Cost:** Free.

PILGRIM BELLE CRUISES departs from State Pier. Passengers aboard the *Pilgrim Belle* paddlewheeler enjoy a 75-minute tour of Plymouth Harbor. Guides discuss the area's maritime history, American Indians and the Pilgrims.

The trip offers views of the *Mayflower II (see attraction listing),* Plymouth Beach and Cape Cod Bay. Two historic lighthouses, one of which is said to be the oldest wooden lighthouse in the United States, also can be seen at the entrance to the harbor. **Time:** Allow 1 hour, 30 minutes minimum. **Hours:** Mon.-Fri. 11-8, Sat. 11-9, Sun. 10-8, Apr.-Oct. Phone ahead to confirm schedule. **Cost:** $16; $14 (ages 63+); $11 (ages 3-12). **Phone:** (508) 747-3434.

GEM **PILGRIM HALL MUSEUM,** Court and Chilton sts. (SR 3A), opened in 1824 and is one of the oldest public museums in America. The two-story museum houses a collection of Pilgrim furniture, armor, decorative arts and an Early American painting collection. Highlights include a bible belonging to William Bradford, Plymouth Colony governor and primary drafter of the Mayflower Compact; the cradle of New England's firstborn; and the chair of Pilgrim leader William Brewster. In addition a historical treasure hunt for children is featured.

Hours: Daily 9:30-4:30, Feb.-Dec. Closed Dec. 25. **Cost:** $7; $6 (ages 62+); $4 (ages 5-17); free (ages 0-4 and Plymouth residents); $20 (family, two adults and children). **Phone:** (508) 746-1620. *See color ad p. 547.*

PLIMOTH PLANTATION, 3 mi. s. on SR 3A or off SR 3S exit 4 (Plimoth Plantation Hwy.), is a bicultural living-history museum of 17th-century Plymouth. Costumed interpreters portray settlers in the 1627 English Village, which is complete with homes, barns, gardens and a fort. At the re-created Wampanoag homesite, interpreters teach about the Wampanoag Indian culture. Visitors may interact with and ask questions of residents as they go about their daily routine.

Native artisans and Colonial potters, tailors and furniture makers create goods in the Crafts Center. Exhibits and a short orientation film are presented in the visitor center. **Time:** Allow 2 hours, 30 minutes minimum. **Hours:** Daily 9-5, late Mar.-late Nov. Film shown daily at 2:30. **Cost:** $24; $22 (ages 62+); $14 (ages 6-12). Combination ticket with *Mayflower II* $28; $26 (ages 62+); $18 (ages 6-12). **Phone:** (508) 746-1622. *See color ad p. 547.* [H]

PLYMOUTH ROCK, on Water St. in Pilgrim Memorial State Park, is said to rest on the site where the Pilgrims landed in December 1620. The rock is protected by a neoclassical granite portico erected in 1921 to celebrate the 300th anniversary of the Pilgrims' arrival in Plymouth. A landscaped waterfront park surrounding the portico affords scenic views of Plymouth Harbor. **Hours:** Daily 24 hours. **Cost:** Free. **Phone:** (508) 747-7535. *See color ad p. 547.*

PLYMOUTH ROCK TROLLEY CO., which departs from Pilgrim Memorial State Park on Water St., provides a narrated sightseeing tour past more than 40 historical sites. Tickets include all-day unlimited reboarding, allowing passengers to disembark at any stop. **Time:** Allow 45 minutes minimum. **Hours:** Tours depart daily every hour 10-5, late May-early Oct. **Cost:** $15; $12 (ages 5-12 and 63+). **Phone:** (774) 454-8121.

SPARROW HOUSE, 42 Summer St., was built before 1640 and is considered to be the oldest house in Plymouth. An adjoining craft gallery features American-made crafts. Regular exhibitions showcase the works of local artists. **Hours:** Thurs.-Tues. 10-5. **Cost:** $2; $1 (children). **Phone:** (508) 747-1240.

WINERIES

- **Plymouth Colony Winery** is off SR 3 exit 6B, 3 mi. s.w. on Carver Rd., then .5 mi. s. on Pinewood Rd. **Hours:** Thurs.-Sat. 10-5, Sun. noon-5, May-Dec.; Sat. 10-4, Sun. noon-4, Feb.-Apr. Closed major holidays. **Phone:** (508) 747-3334.

PRINCETON (B-4) elev. 957'

MASS AUDUBON'S WACHUSETT MEADOW WILDLIFE SANCTUARY is .7 mi. w. on SR 62, then 1 mi. n. on Goodnow Rd. The 1,200-acre sanctuary incorporates landscapes ranging from gentle pastures to the rugged foothills of Mount Wachusett. Beaver ponds are home to river otters, wood ducks and herons, and the meadows offer protection to more than 100 species of nesting birds. Twelve miles of hiking trails allow for walks through wetlands, meadows and woodland habitats and to the 1,300-foot summit of Brown Hill.

Pets are not permitted. **Hours:** Trails open daily dawn-dusk. Office open Tues.-Fri. 10-2, Sat. and Mon. holidays 10-4, Sun. 12:30-4. Closed Jan. 1, Thanksgiving and Dec. 24-25. **Cost:** $4; $3 (ages 3-12 and 61+). **Phone:** (978) 464-2712.

RECREATIONAL ACTIVITIES

Skiing and Snowboarding

- [SAVE] **Wachusett Mountain Ski Area** is at 499 Mountain Rd. Other activities are offered. **Hours:** Skiing and snowboarding Mon.-Fri. 9 a.m.-10 p.m., Sat.-Sun. 8 a.m.-10 p.m., late Nov.-early Apr. (weather permitting). Phone ahead to confirm schedule. **Phone:** (978) 464-2300, (978) 464-5101, or (800) 754-1234 in season for snow conditions.

PROVINCETOWN—*see Cape Cod p. 174.*

QUINCY—*see Boston p. 153.*

ROCKPORT—*see Boston p. 154.*

SAGAMORE—*see Cape Cod p. 175.*

SALEM—*see Boston p. 154.*

SANDWICH—*see Cape Cod p. 176.*

SAUGUS—*see Boston p. 158.*

SCITUATE (F-4) pop. 5,069, elev. 46'

Scituate Lighthouse is accessible from SR 3A to the harbor, then via Jericho Road. The 15- and 16-year-old daughters of the lighthouse keeper took fife and drum and frightened away British soldiers who planned to burn the town in the War of 1812.

The Maritime and Irish Mossing Museum, 301 Driftway, is in the former residence of Capt. Benjamin James. The 1739 house features six exhibits relating to the community's maritime history and includes artifacts from Scituate's treasure ship, *Forest Queen*, which wrecked in 1853; phone (781) 545-1083.

Scituate Chamber of Commerce: P.O. Box 401, Scituate, MA 02066-0401. **Phone:** (781) 545-4000.

SHARON—*see Boston p. 158.*

SHEFFIELD (C-1) elev. 666'

[SAVE] **ASHLEY HOUSE** is 1.7 mi. s. on Main St./US 7, .4 mi. s. on Ashley Falls Rd./SR 7A, 1.4 mi. s. on Rannapo Rd., then .2 mi. w. on Cooper Hill Rd. Built in 1735 by Col. John Ashley, the house is viewed via 45-minute guided tours and contains 18th- and early 19th-century furnishings.

The Sheffield Declaration, supporting individual rights and an end to British tyranny, was drafted in the house and published in 1773. In 1781 an enslaved member of the household Elizabeth Freeman, also known as Mum Bett, successfully sued for her freedom. Her court case was instrumental in ending slavery in the state. The Ashley House is a site on the African American Heritage Trail, which passes through 29 Massachusetts and Connecticut towns in the Upper Housatonic Valley.

Parking is limited. Photography is not permitted in the house. **Time:** Allow 1 hour minimum. **Hours:** Grounds daily dawn-dusk. Guided tours are given Sat.-Sun. 10-5, Memorial Day-Columbus Day. Last tour begins 1 hour before closing. **Cost:** $5; $3 (ages 6-12). **Phone:** (413) 298-3239, ext. 3000, Mon.-Fri. 🎦

SHELBURNE FALLS (B-2)
pop. 1,951, elev. 252′

Interesting geological features around Shelburne Falls include some 50 glacial potholes formed several thousand years ago by the Deerfield River.

BRIDGE OF FLOWERS, crossing the Deerfield River between Shelburne Falls and Buckland, is a former trolley bridge. It is now a flower garden that provides displays of annuals and perennials. The bridge is illuminated until 10:30 p.m. in summer. **Time:** Allow 30 minutes minimum. **Hours:** Daily 24 hours, May-Oct. **Cost:** Donations. **Phone:** (413) 625-2544.

SOUTH DARTMOUTH (E-7) elev. 75′

LLOYD CENTER FOR THE ENVIRONMENT is at 430 Potomska Rd. The facility offers several walking trails and sits on 55 acres of oak-hickory forest, freshwater wetlands, salt marsh and estuary. A nature center offers exhibits highlighting the area's marine life. Visitors can handle crabs and sea stars in a touch tank. Bird-watching can be enjoyed from the site's observation deck; harbor seals also can be seen in winter.

Time: Allow 30 minutes minimum. **Hours:** Trails daily dawn-dusk. Nature center Tues.-Sat. 10-4 (also Sun. 10-4, June-Sept.). Closed Jan. 1, Thanksgiving and Dec. 24-25. **Cost:** Donations. **Phone:** (508) 990-0505.

SOUTH DEERFIELD (B-3)
pop. 1,868, elev. 208′

MAGIC WINGS is .2 mi. w. on Elm St., then 2.2 mi. n. to 281 Greenfield Rd. (US 5/SR 10/SR 116). The 8,000-square-foot Francis R. Redmond Conservatory houses more than 4,000 free-flying butterflies from around the world, as well as tropical plants and Japanese carp. Called "flight attendants," employees teach visitors about the butterflies. Park benches and gazebos offer meditation spots; outdoor gardens feature native flora. The facility also presents exhibits and videos about butterflies.

Time: Allow 30 minutes minimum. **Hours:** Daily 9-6, Memorial Day-Labor Day; 9-5, rest of year.

Last admission 30 minutes before closing. Closed Thanksgiving and Dec. 25. **Cost:** $12; $10 (ages 62+); $8 (ages 3-17 and students ages 18-22 with ID). **Phone:** (413) 665-2805. 🍴

MOUNT SUGARLOAF STATE RESERVATION, e. on US 116, is on a forested mountain of red sandstone. A hiking trail and a road lead to the summit, where there is a view of the Connecticut River Valley. **Hours:** Daily 10-6:30. Phone ahead to confirm schedule. **Cost:** Free. **Parking:** Sat.-Sun. and holidays $2. **Phone:** (413) 665-2928 or (413) 586-8706. 🎦

YANKEE CANDLE CO., 25 Greenfield Rd., consists of a factory, candle store, museum and a Bavarian Christmas village. Costumed candlemakers create taper candles. The museum features interactive entertainment, indoor snow and a Santa's workshop. Visitors may dip their own candles; a fee is charged. **Time:** Allow 1 hour minimum. **Hours:** Daily 10-6, with extended hours during holiday season. Closed Thanksgiving and Dec. 25. **Cost:** Free. **Phone:** (413) 665-2929 or (877) 636-7707. 🍴

SOUTH HADLEY (C-3) elev. 126′

JOSEPH ALLEN SKINNER STATE PARK, 4 mi. n. on SR 47, sits atop 954-foot Mount Holyoke, which affords a 70-mile panorama of the Connecticut Valley. Titan's Piazza, a volcanic formation of overhanging rock columns, and Devil's Football, a magnetic boulder, can be seen. The park also features one of the oldest existing summit houses in New England. Special events, offered at the summit house Memorial Day through Columbus Day, include a concert series in July. *See Recreation Chart.*

Hours: Trails daily dawn-dusk. Summit road daily 8-7:45, Memorial Day-Columbus Day (weather permitting). House tours are given Sat.-Sun. and holidays. Concerts are held Thurs. at 7 p.m., in July. Phone ahead to confirm schedule. **Cost:** Sat.-Sun. and holidays $2 (per private vehicle). Mon.-Fri. free. **Phone:** (413) 586-0350. 🎦 🚶

MOUNT HOLYOKE COLLEGE ART MUSEUM is on Lower Lake Rd. on the Mount Holyoke College campus. The grounds comprise historic buildings, lakes, walking trails, botanic gardens and a greenhouse. The museum consists of 10 galleries housing great masterpieces of fine arts. Among its many exhibits the museum also features a collection of more than 14,000 objects ranging from antiquity to the present.

Guided tours are available with special events. **Time:** Allow 1 hour, 30 minutes minimum. **Hours:** Tues.-Fri. 11-5, Sat.-Sun. 1-5. Closed major holidays and last two weeks in Dec. **Cost:** Donations. **Phone:** (413) 538-2245.

SOUTH WELLFLEET—*see Cape Cod p. 177.*

SPENCER (C-4) pop. 6,032

SPENCER STATE FOREST is .5 mi. s. on SR 31. The 965-acre forest commemorates the Howe family. Elias Howe produced his first practical sewing machine in 1845. William Howe, inventor of the truss bridge, and Tyler Howe, inventor of the spring bed, were his uncles. Cross-country skiing, swimming and hiking facilities are available. *See Recreation Chart.* **Phone:** (508) 885-2320 or (508) 886-6333. 🏕 🐾 ⊠

SPRINGFIELD (C-3) pop. 152,082, elev. 101′

On the Connecticut River, Springfield was established as a trading post in 1636. Duryea Motor Wagon Co. of Springfield, one of the first motorcar corporations in the country, was established in 1895. That year in Chicago, a car made in Springfield won what is reputed to be the country's first automobile race.

The game of basketball originated on the Springfield College campus in 1892, a fact commemorated in Springfield at The Naismith Memorial Basketball Hall of Fame *(see attraction listing).*

Beginning the day before Thanksgiving and continuing until early January, 🚗 Bright Nights at Forest Park is said to be New England's largest holiday lighting display. Visitors drive through the park, where more than 600,000 lights adorn a 2.5-mile route.

Greater Springfield Convention and Visitors Bureau: 1441 Main St., Springfield, MA 01103. **Phone:** (413) 787-1548 or (800) 723-1548.

Shopping areas: Macy's, JCPenney Outlet and Sears are at Eastfield Mall on Boston Road (US 20).

FOREST PARK, on SR 83, is a 735-acre municipal park offering baseball fields, tennis courts, lawn bowling, a playground, band concerts, a miniature train ride, an indoor ice rink, a rose garden and The Zoo in Forest Park.

Time: Allow 2 hours minimum. **Hours:** Park open daily 8-dusk. Zoo open daily 10-5, late Mar. to mid-Oct.; Sat.-Sun. 10-3:30, mid-Oct. through Nov. 30 (weather permitting). Last admission 1 hour before closing. **Cost:** Park Mon.-Fri. $4 (per private out-of-state vehicle); $2 (per private in-state vehicle). Park Sat.-Sun. and holidays $5 (per private out-of-state vehicle); $3 (per private in-state vehicle). Zoo $6; $4 (ages 5-12 and 63+); $2 (ages 1-4). Ice rink $4. Train ride $3. **Phone:** (413) 787-6461, or (413) 733-2251 for the zoo. 🏕 ⊠

HATIKVAH HOLOCAUST EDUCATION CENTER is at 1160 Dickinson St. The educational institution is a memorial to holocaust victims and tribute to the survivors. The permanent exhibit is comprised of two sections: A Reason to Remember, which focuses on five Jewish families who lived in Roth, Germany, under Nazi rule; and A Living Memorial,

which offers the history of refugees who settled in the Greater Springfield area.

Time: Allow 30 minutes minimum. **Hours:** Mon.-Fri. 9-2, Sun. by appointment. Closed all Jewish and national holidays. **Cost:** $4; $3 (senior citizens); $2 (students with ID). **Phone:** (413) 734-7700.

⚜ GEM SAVE **THE NAISMITH MEMORIAL BASKETBALL HALL OF FAME,** off I-91 exit 6 at 1000 W. Columbus Ave., is a state-of-the-art museum that features exhibits, basketball memorabilia, interactive videotape monitors, a movie theater and galleries.

The History of the Game Gallery follows the game from its invention in 1891 to today; The Players Gallery affords visitors the opportunity to play virtual hoops against some of the best NBA and WNBA players; The Game Through the Media Gallery re-enacts some of the greatest game moments; The Coaches and Teams Gallery is a locker room setting that allows visitors a look through the "Coach's Playbook;" and The Honors Ring is an interactive timeline of enshrinees from Dr. James Naismith to the present.

Time: Allow 2 hours, 30 minutes minimum. **Hours:** Sun.-Thurs. 10-4, Fri.-Sat. 10-5. Closed Thanksgiving and Dec. 25. **Cost:** $16.99; $13.99 (ages 65+); $11.99 (ages 5-15). **Phone:** (413) 781-6500 or (877) 446-6752. ⓘ

SPRINGFIELD ARMORY NATIONAL HISTORIC SITE, adjoining the Springfield Technical Community College campus on Federal St., was commissioned by Gen. George Washington and was the first of two federal armories in the country. It houses one of the world's most extensive collections of historic military firearms, including the Lyle lifesaving gun. Visitors can read Henry Wadsworth Longfellow's peace poem in front of the Organ of Muskets and learn about the role of female ordnance workers. **Hours:** Daily 9-5. Closed Jan. 1, Thanksgiving and Dec. 25. **Cost:** Free. **Phone:** (413) 734-6478.

⚜ GEM SAVE **SPRINGFIELD MUSEUMS** is at the Quadrangle at 21 Edwards St.; tickets can be purchased at the welcome center on Edwards St. On-site are history, art and science museums as well as the Dr. Seuss National Memorial Sculpture Garden. **Time:** Allow 1 hour minimum per museum. **Hours:** Welcome center daily 10-5. Closed Jan. 1, Easter, July 4, Thanksgiving and Dec. 25. Phone ahead to confirm schedule. **Cost:** (includes admission to all Springfield Museums sites) $12.50; $9 (college students with ID and senior citizens); $6.50 (ages 3-17). Prices may vary. **Phone:** (413) 263-6800 or (800) 625-7738.

Connecticut Valley Historical Museum, at the Quadrangle at 21 Edwards St., highlights various aspects of Connecticut River Valley history since 1636. **CLOSURE INFORMATION:** The museum is closed for reinstallation of exhibits until sometime in late 2010; phone ahead for updates. **Phone:** (413) 263-6800 or (800) 625-7738.

Dr. Seuss National Memorial Sculpture Garden, at the Quadrangle at 21 Edwards St., honors Theodor Seuss Geisel, born in Springfield in 1904 and the creator of the "Dr. Seuss" children's books. The memorial includes bronze, life-size sculptures of Dr. Seuss, the Cat in the Hat, Horton the Elephant, Yertle the Turtle, The Lorax and other characters. **Time:** Allow 1 hour minimum. **Hours:** Daily 9-8, mid-Apr. to mid-Oct.; 9-5, rest of year. **Cost:** Free. **Phone:** (413) 263-6800 or (800) 625-7738. 🅰️

George Walter Vincent Smith Art Museum, at the Quadrangle at 21 Edwards St., contains collections of jade, bronzes, lacquer, porcelains, Middle Eastern rugs, Samurai armor, Chinese cloisonné, American paintings and reproductions of classical and Renaissance sculpture. Changing exhibits are featured. A hands-on Art Discovery Center for children also is available.

Hours: Tues.-Sun. 11-4. Closed Jan. 1, Easter, July 4, Thanksgiving and Dec. 25. Phone ahead to confirm schedule. **Cost:** (includes admission to all Springfield Museums sites) $12.50; $9 (college students with ID and senior citizens); $6.50 (ages 3-17). Prices may vary. **Phone:** (413) 263-6800 or (800) 625-7738.

Michele and Donald D'Amour Museum of Fine Arts, at the Quadrangle at 21 Edwards St., contains numerous galleries of European and American paintings, drawings, prints and sculpture. Included in the exhibits are works by Degas, Homer and Monet. A Currier & Ives gallery also is featured.

Hours: Tues.-Sun. 11-4. Closed Jan. 1, Easter, July 4, Thanksgiving and Dec. 25. Phone ahead to confirm schedule. **Cost:** (includes admission to all Springfield Museums sites) $12.50; $9 (college students with ID and senior citizens); $6.50 (ages 3-17). Prices may vary. **Phone:** (413) 263-6800 or (800) 625-7738.

Museum of Springfield History, at the Quadrangle at 21 Edwards St., exhibits Indian Motocycles and memorabilia, antique Rolls-Royce automobiles, Gee Bee aircraft, Milton Bradley games, Smith & Wesson firearms, and other inventions and products from the city's industrial past. **Hours:** Tues.-Sun. 11-4. Closed Jan. 1, Easter, July 4, Thanksgiving and Dec. 25. Phone ahead to confirm schedule. **Cost:** (includes admission to all Springfield Museums sites) $12.50; $9 (college students with ID and senior citizens); $6.50 (ages 3-17). Prices may vary. **Phone:** (413) 263-6800 or (800) 625-7738.

Springfield Science Museum, at the Quadrangle at 21 Edwards St., features dinosaur and African exhibit halls, an exploration center with hands-on exhibits and a participatory investigation station. Also featured are an aquarium, a mineral hall, American Indian artifacts, interactive life-science exhibits and a planetarium. A highlight is the life-size replica of a Tyrannosaurus rex.

Hours: Museum Tues.-Sat. 10-5, Sun. 11-5. Planetarium hours vary. Closed Jan. 1, Easter, July 4, Thanksgiving and Dec. 25. Phone ahead to confirm

schedule. **Cost:** Museum (includes admission to all Springfield Museums sites) $12.50; $9 (college students with ID and senior citizens); $6.50 (ages 3-17). Planetarium $3; $2 (ages 3-17). Prices may vary. **Phone:** (413) 263-6800 or (800) 625-7738.

STERLING (B-5) elev. 502′

[SAVE] **DAVIS' FARMLAND,** 145 Redstone Hill Rd., features hands-on activities geared toward children under age 9. Pony rides, hayrides, a sanctuary for rare livestock and periodic special events are offered. A zero-depth water play area is included in summer. In fall visitors can pick their own apples in an orchard.

Pets are not permitted. **Time:** Allow 2 hours minimum. **Hours:** Daily 9:30-5, mid-Apr. through Labor Day; Thurs.-Sun. 9:30-5, day after Labor Day to mid-Oct.; Sat.-Sun. 9:30-5, mid- to late Oct. (weather permitting). Last admission 1 hour before closing. Phone ahead to confirm schedule. **Cost:** June 14-Labor Day $16.95; $13.95 (ages 60+); free (ages 0-1). Rest of year $13.95; $10.95 (ages 60+); free (ages 0-1). Prices may vary. Adults are not permitted unless accompanying a child under 13. **Phone:** (978) 422-6666. 🍴

DAVIS' MEGA MAZE, 145 Redstone Hill Rd., is a three-dimensional cornfield labyrinth that includes bridges and several interactive areas. A less challenging courtyard maze also is on-site. Pets are not permitted. **Hours:** Open daily, mid-Aug. to early Nov. (weather permitting). Schedule varies; phone ahead. **Cost:** $16.95; $12.95 (ages 5-12 and 60+). Prices may vary. **Phone:** (978) 422-8888. 🍴

STOCKBRIDGE (C-1) elev. 839′

A Berkshire town, Stockbridge was established as an American Indian mission in 1734. The Rev. John Sergeant taught and preached to the Stockbridge Indians in their language until his death in 1749. His successor, the Rev. Jonathan Edwards, later became the president of Princeton University. Field Chime Tower was erected in 1878 on the site of the mission; the tower's chimes were to be played "from apple blossom time 'til frost."

Guided tours of Stockbridge and Lenox *(see place listing p. 185)* are offered by Berkshire Tour Co. and include visits to the Norman Rockwell Museum *(see attraction listing)*; turn-of-the-century, luxury summer homes known as the "Berkshire Cottages"; and the Village Cemetery, where the first slave to be legally freed in the United States is buried. Phone (781) 438-8620.

Merwin House, 14 Main St., was built around 1825 and enlarged at the end of the century. The house has a collection of European and American furniture and decorative arts that was assembled at the turn of the 20th century; phone (413) 298-4703.

Shopping areas: Main Street and Elm Street have quaint shops offering clothing, crafts and gifts.

SAVE **BERKSHIRE BOTANICAL GARDEN,** at SRs 102 and 183, contains a terraced herb garden, a rock garden, annual and perennial gardens, vegetable and fruit gardens, an arboretum and a pond garden. **Time:** Allow 1 hour minimum. **Hours:** Daily 10-5, May 1-Columbus Day. **Cost:** $10; $7 (ages 60+ and students with ID); free (ages 0-12). **Phone:** (413) 298-3926. 🌐

CHESTERWOOD ESTATE & MUSEUM, off SR 183, 1 mi. s. of SR 102, was the studio and country residence of sculptor Daniel Chester French. Here he fashioned the statue of Abraham Lincoln for the Lincoln Memorial in Washington, D.C. French also created "The Minute Man" statue in Concord (see place listing p. 140). His plaster casts, bronze models, tools, drawings, books and belongings are displayed. An outdoor sculpture show is held every summer.

Time: Allow 1 hour minimum. **Hours:** Daily 10-5, May-Oct. Phone ahead to confirm schedule. **Cost:** $15. Prices may vary. **Phone:** (413) 298-3579.

INDIAN BURIAL GROUND, .5 mi. w. of the town hall on Main St., is a large mound with an obelisk inscribed "The Ancient Burial Place of the Stockbridge Indians, Friends of Our Fathers."

SAVE **MISSION HOUSE,** 19 Main St., was built in 1743 and was the home of John Sergeant, the first missionary to the Stockbridge Mohicans. The house displays a collection of Early American furniture and American Indian artifacts. The Colonial Revival gardens were designed by Fletcher Steele. **Hours:** Daily 10-5, Memorial Day weekend-Columbus Day. Tours are given daily 10:30-4. **Cost:** $6; $3 (ages 6-12). **Phone:** (413) 298-3239, ext. 3000.

SAVE **NAUMKEAG,** on Prospect Hill, is .5 mi. n. of US 7 and SR 102. This was the summer estate of Joseph Choate, an attorney and the ambassador to Britain 1899-1905. Designed by the architectural firm McKim, Mead and White, this Berkshire cottage contains the Choate family's original furnishings. The gardens were designed by Fletcher Steele and Mabel Choate and include a Chinese temple garden. Also featured are Steele's Blue Steps, a chain of fountain pools surrounded by four levels of stairs.

Guided tours of the house and self-guiding tours of the garden are available. **Hours:** Daily 10-5, Memorial Day weekend-Columbus Day. Last tour begins 1 hour before closing. **Cost:** $15; free (ages 0-15). **Phone:** (413) 298-3239, ext. 3000.

GEM **NORMAN ROCKWELL MUSEUM,** 1.4 mi. n.w. on SR 102, then .1 mi. s. on SR 183, features what is said to be the largest collection of original artwork by illustrator Norman Rockwell. The spacious neoclassical building—on 36 acres of rolling lawns and gardens with views of the Housatonic River and the surrounding Berkshire Hills—also houses the Norman Rockwell Archives, a vast repository of the artist's papers and reference photographs.

The museum's collection contains some of Rockwell's most famous works including "Four Freedoms," "Stockbridge Main Street at Christmas" and 323 *Saturday Evening Post* covers. Rockwell's Stockbridge studio has been relocated to the grounds and is open May through October.

The museum also serves as a center devoted to illustration art and features exhibitions showcasing the works of contemporary artists and past masters. Audio tours are available. **Time:** Allow 2 hours minimum. **Hours:** Daily 10-5, May-Oct.; Mon.-Fri. 10-4, Sat.-Sun. and holidays 10-5, rest of year. Closed Jan. 1, Thanksgiving and Dec. 25. **Cost:** $15; $10 (college students with ID); free (ages 0-18 with adult). **Phone:** (413) 298-4100. 🌐

STOCKBRIDGE LIBRARY ASSOCIATION, 46 Main St., houses a museum exhibiting Stockbridge Indian artifacts, inventions by Anson Clark and memorabilia of Cyrus W. Field, financier and promoter of the first trans-Atlantic telegraph cable. A collection of historical books also is included. **Hours:** Library Tues.-Fri. 9-5 (also Tues. and Fri. 5-8), Sat. 9-2. Museum Tues.-Fri. 9-5, Sat. 9-2. **Cost:** Donations. **Phone:** (413) 298-5501.

STONEHAM—see Boston p. 159.

STOUGHTON—see Boston p. 159.

STURBRIDGE (C-4) pop. 2,047

Settled in 1729, Sturbridge became an agricultural community. Orchards and sheep and dairy farms were the main source of income, along with water-powered saw- and gristmills. Textile mills eventually became prominent. The town's focus is now on its re-created village.

Central Mass South Chamber of Commerce: 380 Main St., Sturbridge, MA 01566. **Phone:** (508) 347-2761, (508) 347-7594 or (800) 628-8379.

HYLAND ORCHARD & BREWERY is at 199 Arnold Rd. The 150-acre facility offers seasonal apple- and pumpkin-picking opportunities, a petting zoo and wagon rides. Orchard walking trails are available for exploring. Sweet and hard cider are produced on-site. Maple demonstrations and pancake breakfasts are offered in March. **Time:** Allow 45 minutes minimum. **Hours:** Petting zoo Tues.-Sun. noon-8. Orchard Sat.-Sun. noon-5, Aug.-Oct. Closed major holidays. Phone ahead to confirm schedule. **Cost:** Free. **Phone:** (508) 347-7500.

GEM **OLD STURBRIDGE VILLAGE,** on SR 20W .5 mi. w. of jct. I-84 exit 2 and I-90 exit 9, is a re-created New England rural village of the early 1800s. This 200-acre living-history museum contains more than 40 restored buildings moved from various parts of New England. Throughout the village costumed staff interpret the daily life and work of early New Englanders through four seasons.

Paths lead to a countryside area where three mills are powered by water in season. Nearby is a working historical farm with oxen, cattle, sheep and pigs as well as gardens with heirloom varieties of flowers, vegetables and herbs. Other demonstrations include blacksmithing, hearth cooking, shoemaking and pottery. Displays include collections of antique clocks, firearms and glassware. The visitor center houses Kidstory—a learning gallery where families can explore history. On select evenings in December, Christmas by Candlelight is offered.

Time: Allow 3 hours minimum. **Hours:** Daily 9:30-5, early Apr.-late Oct.; Wed.-Sun. and some Mon. holidays 9:30-4, Jan. 1-early Apr. and late Oct.-Nov. 30; schedule varies in Dec. Closed Dec. 25. Phone ahead to confirm schedule. **Cost:** (valid for 2 days within a 10-day period) $20; $18 (ages 65+); $10 (active military with ID); $7 (ages 3-17). **Phone:** (508) 347-3362, (800) 733-1830 or TTY (508) 347-5383. *See color ad.* 🍴 🎫

SUDBURY—*see Boston p. 159.*

SUTTON (C-5) elev. 346'

PURGATORY CHASM STATE RESERVATION is 1.2 mi. s.e. on Uxbridge Rd., .2 mi. n.e. on Central Tpke., then 1.7 mi. s.e. on Purgatory Rd. The 1,300-acre reservation encompasses Purgatory Chasm, a quarter-mile-long fissure running between granite walls up to 70 feet high. Hiking and rock climbing can be enjoyed. A playground and a visitor center are available. **Hours:** Reservation open daily dawn-dusk. Visitor center open Wed.-Mon. 9-7, Tues. 9-5.

Closed Thanksgiving and Dec. 25. **Cost:** Free. **Phone:** (508) 234-3733. 🎫

SWAMPSCOTT—*see Boston p. 159.*

TAUNTON (D-6) pop. 55,976, elev. 47'

Chartered in 1639, Taunton is a major manufacturing center for clothing, tools, plastics, hardware and ceramic products.

Taunton Area Chamber of Commerce: 12 Taunton Green, Suite 201, Taunton, MA 02780. **Phone:** (508) 824-4068.

Self-guiding tours: A brochure outlining a historical walking tour of Taunton Green and the Church Green is available from the chamber of commerce.

Shopping areas: Silver City Galleria, SRs 24 and 140, houses more than 160 stores including JCPenney, Macy's and Sears.

GERTRUDE M. BOYDEN WILDLIFE REFUGE is w. on US 44, s. on Joseph Warner Blvd., then w. to 1298 Cohannet St. The refuge features many varieties of plants and animals. Noteworthy are the native birds, ranging from the great blue herons of the marsh to the predatory red-tailed hawks. Walking trails and a canoe ramp are available. Fishing also is permitted. **Time:** Allow 1 hour minimum. **Hours:** Daily 9-dusk. **Cost:** Free. **Phone:** (508) 821-1676. 🎫

OLD COLONY HISTORICAL SOCIETY, 66 Church Green, is in a schoolhouse designed by Richard Upjohn and built in 1852. Dedicated to presenting the history of the Taunton area, it contains a museum of American decorative arts as well as a silver collection, a military room and a genealogical library. **Time:** Allow 1 hour minimum. **Hours:** Tues.-Sat. 10-4. Closed holidays and Sat. before Mon. holidays. **Cost:** $4; $2 (ages 12-18 and 65+). Genealogical research $7. **Phone:** (508) 822-1622.

TEWKSBURY—*see Boston p. 159.*

TOPSFIELD—*see Boston p. 159.*

WALES (C-4)

NORCROSS WILDLIFE SANCTUARY is w. off SR 19 or e. off SR at 3230 Peck Rd. This 4,000-acre sanctuary contains rare wildflowers and indigenous flora and fauna. Two natural history museums feature a collection of rocks, seashells, bird carvings and photographs of native plants. A self-guiding trail is on the grounds. **Hours:** Mon.-Sat. 9-4, day after Memorial Day-Thanksgiving; Tues.-Sat. 9-4, rest of year. Closed major holidays. **Cost:** Free. **Phone:** (413) 267-9654.

WALTHAM—*see Boston p. 159.*

WATERTOWN—*see Boston p. 160.*

WELLESLEY—*see Boston p. 160.*

WELLFLEET—*see Cape Cod p. 177.*

WENHAM—*see Boston p. 160.*

WEST BARNSTABLE—*see Cape Cod p. 177.*

WEST BROOKFIELD (C-4)
pop. 1,610, elev. 633′

ROCK HOUSE RESERVATION is on SR 9. The 135-acre reservation has a nature center, a butterfly garden and nature trails. It is named for a rock formation that provided shelter to Indians as early as 8,000 years ago. Other geological formations also are on the grounds. **Time:** Allow 1 hour minimum. **Hours:** Daily dawn-dusk. **Cost:** Free. **Phone:** (978) 840-4446. 🏚

WESTFIELD (C-2) pop. 40,072, elev. 155′

The westernmost town in the Massachusetts colony, Westfield began as an agricultural community but became an industrial center during the Industrial Revolution. Manufacturing, followed by wholesale and retail trade, is now Westfield's largest source of revenue.

Greater Westfield Chamber of Commerce: 53 Court St., Westfield, MA 01085. **Phone:** (413) 568-1618.

Self-guiding tours: Brochures outlining walking and driving tours of the historic area are available from the chamber of commerce.

STANLEY PARK AND CARILLON is at 400 Western Ave. The 275-acre park includes floral, rose, Japanese, herb and perennial gardens; an arboretum; a wildlife sanctuary; and a Colonial pond area with a working mill and a waterwheel. Summer concerts, festivals, garden workshops and children's programs also are offered. **Time:** Allow 2 hours minimum. **Hours:** Daily 7-dusk, first Sat. in May-Mon. after Thanksgiving. **Cost:** Free. **Phone:** (413) 568-9312. 🏚

WESTFIELD ATHENAEUM, at Elm and Court sts., contains the Jasper Rand Art Museum, which displays works by local artists. **Time:** Allow 30 minutes minimum. **Hours:** Athenaeum Mon.-Thurs. 8:30-8, Fri.-Sat. 8:30-5, Sept.-June; Mon.-Thurs. 8:30-8, Fri. 8:30-5, rest of year. Museum Thurs. and Sat. 10-3, Sept.-June; Tues. and Thurs. 10-3, rest of year. Closed major holidays. **Cost:** Free. **Phone:** (413) 568-7833.

WESTFORD—*see Boston p. 161.*

WESTMINSTER (B-4) elev. 1,066′

WACHUSETT BREWING CO. is at 175 State Rd. E. Ten-minute weekday tours and 30- to 45-minute tours on Saturdays explain the brewery's history and the brewing and bottling processes. All guided tours conclude with a tasting. **Hours:** Brewery open Thurs.-Fri. noon-6, Wed. and Sat. noon-5. Tours are given Wed.-Thurs. noon-3, Fri.-Sat. noon-4. Closed major holidays. **Cost:** Donations. **Phone:** (978) 874-9965, ext. 21.

WESTON—*see Boston p. 161.*

WESTPORT (E-6)

WINERIES

• **Westport Rivers Vineyard and Winery** is at 417 Hixbridge Rd. **Hours:** Tues.-Sat. 11-5, Sun.-Mon. 1-5. Tours are given Sat.-Sun. at 1 and 3. Closed major holidays. **Phone:** (508) 636-3423, ext. 2.

WEST SPRINGFIELD (C-2) pop. 27,899

Josiah Day House, 70 Park St., was built in 1754; it was occupied by the Day family until 1902. Thought to be the oldest brick saltbox house in the nation, the dwelling rests on its original foundation. Furnishings depict lifestyles 1700-1900. Guided tours are available by appointment; phone (413) 734-8322.

One of the largest fairs in the Northeast, 🍇 The Big E offers agricultural exhibits, arts and crafts, parades and a circus from mid-September to early October. Also included is the Avenue of States, which features replicas of New England state capitols.

STORROWTON VILLAGE MUSEUM, 1 mi. w. of US 5 on SR 147, is on the exposition grounds. The restored Early American village comprises seven New England buildings dating 1767-1850. They were dismantled, moved and reassembled at Storrowton. Among them are a mansion, farmhouse, smithy, schoolhouse, tavern and church. Craft demonstrations and events also are featured; phone for schedule.

Time: Allow 1 hour, 30 minutes minimum. **Hours:** Guided tours are given Tues.-Sat. 11-3, mid-June to late Aug.; by appointment rest of year. **Cost:** Grounds free. Museum $5; free (ages 0-5). **Phone:** (413) 205-5051. ⓕ

WEST TISBURY—
see Martha's Vineyard p. 187.

WEST YARMOUTH—*see Cape Cod p. 177.*

WEYMOUTH—*see Boston p. 161.*

WILLIAMSTOWN (A-1) pop. 4,754, elev. 603′

Williamstown is the western terminus of a scenic portion of SR 2, which follows sections of the Hoosic and Deerfield rivers and passes through Savoy Mountain State Forest *(see Recreation Chart).*

Williamstown Chamber of Commerce: 7 Denison Park Dr., P.O. Box 357, Williamstown, MA 01267. **Phone:** (413) 458-9077 or (800) 214-3799.

CHAPIN LIBRARY OF RARE BOOKS is .5 mi. e. of US 7 on SR 2 to Hopkins Hall Dr., on the campus of Williams College. The library permanently displays original copies of the Constitution, Bill of Rights, Declaration of Independence and Articles of Confederation. Changing exhibits are featured year-round. **CLOSURE INFORMATION:** The library closed for renovations in September 2008; reopening is scheduled for 2013. In the interim, research services are available at 96 School St.; phone ahead for more information. **Phone:** (413) 597-2462.

STERLING AND FRANCINE CLARK ART INSTITUTE is at 225 South St., near the Williams College campus. Situated on a 140-acre site that includes walking trails and woodlands, the institute is home to a collection of French Impressionist, American, British and old master paintings. Among the paintings are works by Degas, Homer, Monet, Remington, Renoir, Sargent and Turner. The Stone Hill Center houses two exhibition galleries and an art conservation center.

Time: Allow 1 hour minimum. **Hours:** Daily 10-5, July-Aug.; Tues.-Sun. and Mon. holidays 10-5, rest of year. Closed Jan. 1, Thanksgiving and Dec. 25. **Cost:** June-Oct. $12.50; free (ages 0-18 and college students with ID). Rest of year free. Prices may vary; phone ahead. **Phone:** (413) 458-2303. ⓐ

WILLIAMS COLLEGE MUSEUM OF ART, 15 Lawrence Hall Dr., has collections and changing exhibits focusing on American, modern, contemporary and non-Western art. **Hours:** Tues.-Sat. and some Mon. holidays 10-5, Sun. 1-5. Closed Jan. 1, Memorial Day, Thanksgiving and Dec. 25. **Cost:** Free. **Phone:** (413) 597-2429.

WOODS HOLE—*see Cape Cod p. 177.*

WORCESTER (C-4) pop. 172,648, elev. 473′

"The Heart of the Commonwealth" and the third largest city in New England, Worcester, or "The City of Seven Hills," not only is centrally located in the state but also serves as a commercial, industrial and cultural center. The city was known for its 19th-century dramatic, musical and civic events, which influenced educators to found several colleges.

Mechanics Hall, 321 Main St., was built in 1857 and soon became an arena for concerts and other popular social events. A lecture tour of the restored Victorian-style building is offered once a week.

Dr. Robert H. Goddard, the father of U.S. rocketry, was born in Worcester in 1882. Goddard received his doctorate at Clark University and later became a professor. He fired his first rocket in nearby Auburn.

Preservation Worcester offers various walking and bus tours highlighting the city's history and architecture; phone (508) 754-8760 for schedule and prices.

Central Massachusetts Convention & Visitors Bureau: 30 Elm St., Worcester, MA 01609. **Phone:** (508) 755-7400 or (866) 755-7439.

AMERICAN ANTIQUARIAN SOCIETY, 185 Salisbury St. and Park Ave., is a research library of pre-20th-century American history and culture. **Time:** Allow 30 minutes minimum. **Hours:** Mon.-Tues. and Thurs.-Fri. 9-5, Wed. 10-8. Guided 1-hour tours are given Wed. at 3. Closed major holidays. **Cost:** Free. **Phone:** (508) 755-5221.

ⓢⓐⓥⓔ **ECOTARIUM,** e. via SR 9 at 222 Harrington Way, is an indoor/outdoor museum of science and nature offering three floors of interactive exhibits, a digital planetarium, nature trails, animal habitats and a narrow-gauge railroad. From late May to early September visitors can explore the Tree Canopy Walkway, a series of platforms and rope bridges suspended more than 40 feet above an oak and hickory forest floor; a zipline returns guests to ground level.

Time: Allow 2 hours minimum. **Hours:** Museum Tues.-Sat. 10-5, Sun. noon-5. Tree Canopy Walkway program schedule varies; phone ahead. Closed Jan. 1, Easter, Thanksgiving and Dec. 24-25. **Cost:** Museum $10; $8 (ages 3-18, ages 66+ and students with ID). Tree Canopy Walkway $10. Planetarium $5. Explorer Express Train $2.50. Prices may vary. **Phone:** (508) 929-2700.

GODDARD EXHIBITION, on the second floor of Clark University's Goddard Library at Downing and Woodland sts., contains displays of Dr. Robert Goddard's patents, notebooks, manuscripts and memorabilia of early rocketry. **Time:** Allow 30 minutes minimum. **Hours:** Mon.-Thurs. 8 a.m.-midnight, Fri. 8 a.m.-10 p.m., Sat. 10-10, Sun. noon-midnight, when school is in session; otherwise Mon.-Fri. 9-5. Closed major holidays. **Cost:** Free. **Phone:** (508) 793-7572.

HIGGINS ARMORY MUSEUM, 100 Barber Ave., houses weapons and armor from medieval and Renaissance Europe, feudal Japan and ancient Greece and Rome in a Gothic castle setting. Exhibits include helmets, a medieval crossbow and Japanese samurai armor. Arms and armor demonstrations, workshops and audiotape tours are available. **Hours:** Tues.-Sat. 10-4, Sun. noon-4. Closed major holidays. **Cost:** $9; $8 (ages 60+); $7 (ages 6-16). **Phone:** (508) 853-6015.

MASS AUDUBON'S BROAD MEADOW BROOK CONSERVATION CENTER AND WILDLIFE SANCTUARY, 414 Massasoit Rd., features 5 miles of marked trails and wooden walkways, which traverse 400 acres of oak woods, fields, streams and wetlands. The visitor center, which also serves as the visitor information site for the Blackstone River Valley National Heritage Corridor, offers interpretive exhibits that include a 3-D model of the sanctuary.

Hours: Sanctuary daily dawn-dusk. Visitor center Tues.-Sat. 9-4, Sun. 12:30-4. Closed major holidays. **Cost:** $4; $3 (ages 3-12 and 66+). **Phone:** (508) 753-6087.

SALISBURY MANSION, 40 Highland St., was built in 1772 by businessman Stephen Salisbury I. The mansion has been restored to its 1830s appearance. Exhibits include original furnishings and decorative arts from 1740-1835. **Time:** Allow 1 hour minimum. **Hours:** Tues.-Sat. 10-4 (also fourth Thurs. of the month 4-8:30). Closed major holidays. **Cost:** $5;

$4 (students with ID and senior citizens); free (ages 0-17). **Phone:** (508) 753-8278.

WORCESTER ART MUSEUM, 55 Salisbury St., chronicles the history of human creativity spanning 5,000 years through ancient sculpture, mosaics, impressionist paintings and contemporary art. Included are works by Cassatt, Gauguin, de Goya, Monet, Sargent and Whistler.

First opened in 1898, the museum features 35 galleries and houses more than 35,000 works. Paintings spanning the 13th through the 20th centuries are on display, along with decorative arts, sculptures, photographs, prints and drawings. **Hours:** Wed.-Fri. and Sun. 11-5 (also third Thurs. of the month 5-8), Sat. 10-5. Closed major holidays. **Cost:** $10; $8 (ages 65+ and students with ID); free (ages 0-17 and to all Sat. 10-noon). **Phone:** (508) 799-4406.

WORCESTER HISTORICAL MUSEUM is .1 mi. n. on Main St., then .1 mi. w. to 30 Elm St. The museum highlights the city's industrial accomplishments and community history through changing exhibits and programs. On display are textiles, clothing, weapons and artwork. A research library and archives also are featured. **Note:** The facility is not wheelchair accessible. **Time:** Allow 1 hour minimum. **Hours:** Tues.-Sat. 10-4 (also fourth Thurs. of the month 4-8:30). Closed major holidays. **Cost:** $5; $4 (students with ID and senior citizens); free (ages 0-18). **Phone:** (508) 753-8278.

YARMOUTH PORT—*see Cape Cod p. 178.*

Rhode Island

Summers in Newport
Ornate mansions once served as party palaces for those in high society

Fans of Roger Williams
Providence residents revere the man who established Rhode Island's first settlement

Calling Captain and Crew
Sailors swab the decks and hoist the sails in this yachting mecca

Just Beachy
Rhode Island's expansive coastline will put plenty of sand between your toes

A Walk on the Wild Side
Cliff Walk in Newport tiptoes along the rocky bluffs of the Rhode Island Sound

Old Stone Mill, Newport
© Dean Fox / SuperStock

Cliff Walk, Newport / © Barry Winiker / age fotostock

With approximately 400 miles of shoreline, Rhode Island's nautical heritage is as distinct as a brightly colored buoy bobbing in choppy water.

Stark white triangular sails dot the seafoam green waters of Narragansett Bay and Rhode Island Sound. Sea gulls soar from rock to sand to water, squawking maritime hellos.

Anglers unload hulls packed with clams, lobster, shrimp and various fish to be boiled, seared or baked. The delicious aroma of chowder mixes with the sea air to entice hungry bodies into taverns.

Captains spend summer days relaxing at yacht clubs. Children

enjoy orange sunsets in between licks of ice cream, legs dangling off piers. Sailmakers and craftspeople practice their trades in shops along the waterfront.

Chart your inland course carefully. You won't want to miss Touro Synagogue National Historic Site, the oldest Jewish house of worship in the country; Newport's sprawling mansions; a tasting at one of the state's vineyards; and a set or two on the grass courts at the International Tennis Hall of Fame Museum. The state's small size makes it quite navigable.

Bon voyage. It's easy to find a safe harbor in cozy Rhode Island.

Sure, you could call Rhode Island little. It's only 48 miles long and 37 miles wide, ranking the smallest in size of all 50 states.

But don't let its petite presence fool you. The Ocean State is a swell of greatness. Bravely, Rhode Island was the first colony to declare independence from Britain; confidently, it was the last to ratify the Constitution, holding out until the Bill of Rights was added.

Not only does "Little Rhody" have the longest name of any state—"State of Rhode Island and Providence Plantations"—it also has more than 400 miles of shoreline.

And Rhode Island isn't just *one* island: Narragansett Bay takes a big bite into the northeastern corner of the state, leaving 35 islets to explore. Soft green grass grows on bluffs in summer; in winter, brisk breezes lick the jagged cliffs edging sandy beaches.

An Island Oasis

Block Island, once feared by captains and crew for its dense fog and treacherous shoals, now beckons visitors by way of a bright green beam from Southeast Light. It shines the way to Block Island's only town, quaint New Shoreham.

Called Manisses (meaning "Island of the Little God") by the Narragansett Indians, this summer retreat is big on relaxation—just the place for barefoot beach strolling, window shopping and catching some rays.

For grand scenery, head to lush Mohegan Bluffs, a mile from downtown on the island's southeastern shore. From the top of these 200-foot-high cliffs you'll have an up-close view of the brick, Victorian-style Southeast Light, built in 1875. On a clear day you can even see the state's southern coast. Descend a cliff-clinging stairway to the craggy shore and search for seashells. Gazing up, you may feel a bit like a Lilliputian.

A Capital City

Providence, established by minister Roger Williams who was banished from Massachusetts due to his liberal theologies, grew into a major port but never forgot the ideals upon which it was founded. The town is populated with a number of historic churches, including the first Baptist church in America, also founded by Williams.

Aptly named, Providence boasts a powerful economy due to its location on skinny Providence Harbor. The watery band stretches almost 30 miles from downtown Providence to

R hode Island's first known explorer, Giovanni da Verrazano, reaches Narragansett Bay.
1524

Library of Congress

R oger Williams establishes the first permanent settlement on land bought from two Narragansett Indian chiefs.
1636

R hode Island is granted the Charter of Rhode Island and Providence Plantations, which serves as the law of the state for 180 years.
1663

T he state becomes the first to prohibit the importation of slaves.
1774

Rhode Island Historical Timeline

R hode Island preempts other colonies by 2 months in declaring its independence from British rule.
1776

Narragansett Bay, where trading schooners once departed for the West Indies and Africa. Now the port is a major distribution point for oil and coal, and the city serves as the state's seat of government.

Lining Benefit Street are more than 200 restored buildings, which make up what locals call the "Mile of History." These houses, taverns, schools and shops, built by sea captains and shipbuilders, remind us how this and other struggling settlements in Rhode Island relied on ocean commerce for their big break.

Living Large

Newport is a nest for swarms of people who buzz in for summertime fun. In the late 1800s this town on yet another island in Narragansett Bay became *the* place to be for the ultra-rich. But you don't have to be a millionaire to share in its wealth.

Bellevue Avenue and Ocean Drive in Newport give new meaning to the word cottage. When the Astor, Vanderbilt and other families took summer holidays, they vacationed in style. Giant estates—called "cottages" by

their aristocratic owners—overlook the cliffs of Rhode Island Sound.

The Breakers, a 70-room estate modeled after 16th-century *palazzos* in Genoa and Turin, is considered the most ornate of Newport's mansions. Built for Cornelius Vanderbilt II in 1895, one of its luxuries is a tub carved from a single slab of marble; four faucets dispense both rainwater and salt water, hot and cold.

The price tag on the Marble House, another in the Vanderbilt "collection," was $11 million in 1892; $7 million paid for the 500,000 cubic feet of marble used in its construction. The giant ballroom—sumptuous to some, gaudy to others—is swathed in golden decoration from top to bottom.

Home to numerous yacht clubs and the America's Cup Race 1930-83, Newport is synonymous with sailing. Bobbing on the bay's choppy waters are rusty lobster boats, cruisers, colorful sailboats and, of course, enormous yachts. The salty air agrees with Newporters, who stand steady on sea legs.

Try Rhode Island on for size. At first it may seem snug, but it'll grow on you.

The Dorr Rebellion occurs, resulting in a new, more liberal state constitution that takes effect one year later.

1842

Chessie the manatee, tracked with radio and satellite transmitters, breaks manatee travel records by swimming from Florida to Point Judith.

1995

The Newport Bridge across Narragansett Bay is completed, linking Newport and Jamestown.

1969

1794

Extensive production of fashion jewelry begins when Nehemiah Dodge, a Providence goldsmith, develops a process for plating base metal with gold.

1983

Australia II wins the America's Cup, making it the first sailboat outside the United States to do so in 132 years.

1930

The America's Cup race is held in Newport for the first time.

Recreation

From sparkling lakes to sailboat-packed Narragansett Bay to choppy Rhode Island Sound to the steel blue waves that meet the southern coast, water is Rhode Island's best feature.

With so many shores to choose from, **sunbathing, surfing, swimming** and simply **strolling** on the beach are favorite warm-weather pastimes. Surfing lessons are offered at Narragansett Town Beach in Narragansett during the summer. If waves are not your thing, bring a kite and catch some beach breezes.

Fish stories are as plentiful as the catches off Block Island. Tales that begin with "it was *this* big!" may just have merit—this **fishing** spot is said to be one of the best in the world due to the variety and abundance of fish as well as coastal accessibility. In Rhode Island Sound anglers can hook flounder, cod, swordfish, tuna and marlin. Inland waters are stocked with pike and bass. In winter, a cast into Rhode Island's many icy ponds may yield yellow perch, pike, and small- and large-mouth bass.

Like to Bike?

Rhode Island is the place for leisurely beachfront excursions. Try the East Bay Bicycle Path—it's a 14.5-mile-long path that stretches from Providence's India Point to Bristol's Independence Park. **Inline skaters** whoosh and **joggers** tread along this paved stretch. Curving Bellevue and Ocean avenues in Newport also are good places for two wheels; the roads provide splendid views of both the coastline and mansions. Get closer to the edge on Cliff Walk, a rugged **hiking** path that maneuvers along Newport's rocky bluffs.

Load your bike onto a ferry and pedal or **moped** around Block Island to explore its cliff-guarded strands, hidden beaches and lighthouses. In South County, SR 1A from Narragansett to North Kingstown hugs the coast and winds through historic Wickford, where many buildings date from the late 18th century.

Giddyup

Horseback riding along the beach or on trails across the state is another way to see the countryside. In fall, marvel at the colorful natural display from a prickly seat in the back of a hay-filled wagon in West Greenwich or Exeter.

And when snowflakes start falling and icicles form, the options get even cooler. Bundle up and enjoy a ride on a horse-drawn sled. Tighten the laces on some **ice skates** and hit frozen ponds at Goddard or Lincoln Woods state parks. Strap on a helmet and jump on a **snowmobile** to attack the trails at Colt or Lincoln Woods state parks.

Snap on the snow boots and head to Yawgoo Valley in Exeter, Rhode Island's only ski resort. Runs are usually open early December to late March; phone (401) 294-3802. Norman Bird Sanctuary in Middletown isn't just for the birds—**cross-country skiers** also flock to the area's trails.

Don't Forget Your Deck Shoes

You're sure to spot first mates **sailing, boating** or **yachting** on Narragansett Bay. Charters and tours depart from Goat Island and Oldport marinas in the northern cove of Newport Harbor. **Sailboards** and **rowboats** also dot the waters surrounding Block Island.

Kayakers flirt with the waves of Narragansett Bay and Newport Harbor as well as those in New Harbor on Block Island; the season is late May through September. **Canoeists** head for the 45-mile-long Blackstone River, which heads south from the state's northern border to Narragansett Bay; put in at Woonsocket. And don't miss the Wood River in Exeter, Narrow River near Narragansett and Ninigret Pond, in Ninigret Park near Charlestown. When paddling on the pond, don't be surprised to encounter lots of feathered friends—the park is a saltwater refuge for many waterfowl species.

Near the Mohegan Bluffs on Block Island, **hang gliders** can be seen floating through the air. **Parasailing** also is popular on Block Island. Brave souls can **sky dive** in Lincoln, and **climbers** have their choice of clinging to rocks at Lincoln Woods, Snake Den or Fort Wetherill state parks.

Recreational Activities

Throughout the TourBook, you may notice a Recreational Activities heading with bulleted listings of recreation-oriented establishments listed underneath. Similar operations also may be mentioned in Destination City recreation sections. Since normal AAA inspection criteria cannot be applied, these establishments are presented only for information. Age, height and weight restrictions may apply. Reservations often are recommended and sometimes are required. Addresses and/or phone numbers are provided so visitors can contact the attraction for additional information.

Fast Facts

POPULATION: 1,048,319.

AREA: 1,214 square miles; ranks 50th.

CAPITAL: Providence.

HIGHEST POINT: 812 ft., Jerimoth Hill.

LOWEST POINT: Sea level, Atlantic Ocean.

TIME ZONE(S): Eastern. DST.

TEEN DRIVING LAWS: No more than one un-related passenger under age 21 for the first 12 months. Driving is not permitted 1 a.m.-5 a.m. Minimum age for an unrestricted driver's license is 17 years, 6 months. For more information on Rhode Island driver's license regulations contact (401) 462-4368.

SEAT BELT/CHILD RESTRAINT LAWS: Seat belts required for driver and all passengers 18 and older. Children ages 8 until 18, at least 57" and at least 80 lbs. are required to be in a seat belt or child restraint; child restraints required for under age 8, less than 57" and less than 80 lbs. Children under 8 are required to be in the rear seat, if possible.

CELL PHONE RESTRICTIONS: All drivers under 18 are prohibited from using cell phones.

HELMETS FOR MOTORCYCLISTS: Required for all passengers regardless of age, drivers under 21 and all drivers during their first year of licensure.

RADAR DETECTORS: Permitted.

MOVE OVER LAW: Driver is required to slow down and vacate a lane nearest police, fire and rescue vehicles stopped on the side of the road using audible or flashing signals. Law includes tow trucks.

FIREARMS LAWS: Vary by state and/or county. Contact the Bureau of Criminal Identification, Attorney General's Office, 150 S. Main St., Providence, RI 02903; phone (401) 274-4400 ext. 2359.

HOLIDAYS: Jan. 1; Martin Luther King Jr. Day, Jan. (3rd Mon.); Presidents Day, Feb. (3rd Mon.); Memorial Day, May (last Mon.); July 4; Victory Day, Aug. (2nd Mon.); Labor Day, Sept. (1st Mon.); Columbus Day, Oct. (2nd Mon.); Veterans Day, Nov. 11; Thanksgiving, Nov. (4th Thurs.); Christmas, Dec. 25.

TAXES: Rhode Island's statewide sales tax is 7 percent, and there is a 5 percent lodgings tax.

INFORMATION CENTERS: A state welcome center that provides details about attractions, accommodations, historic sites, parks and events is on I-95 in Richmond. It is open daily 8:30-6; closed Jan. 1, Thanksgiving and Dec. 25. Phone (401) 539-3031.

FURTHER INFORMATION FOR VISITORS:

Rhode Island Tourism Division
315 Iron Horse Way, Suite 101
Providence, RI 02908
(800) 556-2484
(800) 250-7384

FISHING AND HUNTING REGULATIONS:

Department of Environmental
Management Division of Fish and
Wildlife
Stedman Government Center
4808 Tower Hill Rd.
Wakefield, RI 02879
(401) 789-3094
(401) 789-0281

NATIONAL FOREST INFORMATION:

Rhode Island Division of Environmental
Management
Stedman Government Center
4808 Tower Hill Rd.
Wakefield, RI 02879
(401) 789-3094
(401) 789-0281

NATIONAL FOREST INFORMATION:

Rhode Island Division of Environmental
Management
Division of Forest Environment
1037 Hartford Pike
North Scituate, RI 02857
(401) 647-3367

© 2009 NAVTEQ

Rhode Island
Orientation

NOT INTENDED FOR DRIVING.
SEE APPROPRIATE AAA SHEET MAP.

Only places listed in the Attractions section appear on this map.
🔻 *See AAA GEM Attractions*
1 *See Chart of Recreation Areas*

0   Miles   14.2

© AAA   4047-I

Rhode Island Temperature Averages
Maximum/Minimum
From the records of The Weather Channel Interactive, Inc.

	JAN	FEB	MAR	APR	MAY	JUNE	JULY	AUG	SEPT	OCT	NOV	DEC
Block Island	39	40	45	53	62	71	77	77	71	62	53	44
	27	28	33	41	49	58	64	64	57	49	41	32
Providence	37	39	48	58	69	77	83	81	73	63	52	42
	20	23	30	39	49	58	64	63	55	43	35	26

Get the lowest rates on hotels at AAA.com/Travel

RECREATION AREAS	MAP LOCATION	CAMPING	PICNICKING	HIKING TRAILS	BOATING	BOAT RAMP	BOAT RENTAL	FISHING	SWIMMING	PETS ON LEASH	BICYCLE TRAILS	WINTER SPORTS	VISITOR CENTER	LODGE/CABINS	FOOD SERVICE
STATE															
Arcadia (D-2) 40,000 acres at Arcadia off SR 165.	❶	•	•	•	•			•			•	•			
Burlingame (E-2) 2,100 acres 5 mi. w. of Charlestown off US 1.	❷	•	•		•	•		•	•						
Charlestown Breachway (E-3) 62 acres 5 mi. s. of Charlestown via US 1 and Charlestown Breach Rd.	❸	•			•	•		•	•						
Colt (C-4) 455 acres 2 mi. w. of Bristol on Narragansett Bay. Historic. Nature program. Horse trails.	❹		•	•	•			•		•	•	•	•		•
East Beach/Ninigret (E-3) 174 acres in Charlestown off US 1.	❺	•	•		•			•	•						
East Matunuck (E-3) 102 acres 3 mi. s.e. of Perryville off US 1.	❻		•					•	•						•
Fort Adams (D-4) 105 acres in w. Newport adjoining Narragansett Bay. Historic. *(See Newport p. 223)*	❼		•		•	•	•	•	•				•		•
George Washington (A-2) 100 acres 2 mi. e. of West Glocester on US 44.	❽	•		•	•			•	•			•			
Goddard Memorial (C-4) 472 acres e. of East Greenwich on Ives Rd. Golf; horse trails. *(See Warwick p. 232)*	❾		•	•	•			•	•	•			•		•
Lincoln Woods (A-4) 627 acres 5 mi. n. of Providence on SR 146. Horse rental, horse trails.	❿		•	•	•	•		•	•	•	•	•			•
Misquamicut Beach (E-2) 57 acres 5 mi. s. of Westerly off SR 1A. Amusements, surfing.	⓫		•						•						•
Pulaski Memorial (A-2) 100 acres 3 mi. n. of West Glocester off US 44. Cross-country skiing.	⓬		•	•				•	•	•		•			
Roger W. Wheeler Beach (E-3) 27 acres e. of Galilee via Sand Hill Cove Rd. Naturalist area, playground.	⓭		•						•						•
Scarborough Beach (E-3) 33 acres 2 mi. n. of Point Judith on Ocean Rd. Surfing.	⓮		•						•						•
World War II Memorial (A-3) 15 acres in Woonsocket off Pond Rd. Tennis.	⓯		•						•				•		
Other															
Block Island Beach (F-3) 18 acres on Block Island. *(See Block Island p. 216)*	⓰		•					•	•						•

Points of Interest

BARRINGTON (C-4) pop. 16,819, elev. 24'

In 1653 the land that is now Barrington was purchased from the Wampanoag Indians and divided among Gov. William Bradford, Capt. Miles Standish and others of the Plymouth colony. One of the first settlers was Rev. John Myles, who in 1649 founded the first Baptist church in the Massachusetts Bay Colony. Many estates are nearby, particularly at Nayatt Point and Rumstick Point on Narragansett Bay.

BARRINGTON TOWN HALL, on SR 114, was built 1887-88. The medieval-style building features a steep-flank gable roof and two circular corner turrets. Glacial rocks and other unusual stones are among the boulders used in the construction of the ground level. The weathervane features a replica of the *Mayflower.* **Time:** Allow 30 minutes minimum. **Hours:** Mon.-Fri. 8:30-4:30. **Cost:** Free. **Phone:** (401) 247-1900.

BLOCK ISLAND (F-3) elev. 22'

Previously called Manisses ("Island of the Little God") by the Narragansett Indians, Luisa by explorer Giovanni da Verrazano, Adriaen's Eylant by Dutch trader Adriaen Block and the Town of New Shoreham by the Rhode Island assembly, Block Island is a popular family vacation resort. The only town, New Shoreham, has the look and feel of vintage New England, with white clapboard Victorian buildings lining its waterfront street.

Sixteen families seeking religious and political freedom bought the 11-square-mile island in 1661 and established it as a democratic settlement.

Block Island features the 18-acre Block Island Beach *(see Recreation Chart)* and many nature, bicycling and hiking trails as well as wildlife sanctuaries. Popular nature trails include the Clayhead Trails, 2 miles north off Corn Neck Road, and the Greenway Trails, a half-mile west off Center Road. There are more than 40 rare and endangered wildlife species on the island; phone Block Island Nature Conservancy at (401) 466-2129.

Mohegan Bluffs, rising to 200 feet along the southeast shore, affords an excellent view of the southern coast of Rhode Island. Southeast Light, a restored lighthouse built in 1875, still stands. Its lantern, 240 feet above sea level, sends light 35 miles out to sea.

Passenger ferries run 2-hour crossings from Newport mid-June through Labor Day; phone (401) 783-4613. A 1-hour crossing aboard an automobile ferry is offered all year from Point Judith; phone (401) 783-4613 in advance for reservations. Island Hi-Speed Ferry offers half-hour crossings between Block Island and Galilee aboard high-speed catamarans mid-May to mid-October; for information or reservations phone (866) 783-7996. Additional ferry service is available from Montauk, Long Island, N.Y. Crossing time is approximately 2 hours; phone (631) 668-5700.

Scheduled air transportation is available from Westerly, while charters are available from other points, including Providence. Phone New England Airlines at (401) 596-2460 or (800) 243-2460.

Block Island Tourism Council: P.O. Box 356, Water Street, Block Island, RI 02807. **Phone:** (401) 466-5200 or (800) 383-2474.

Shopping areas: The New Harbor and the Old Harbor areas contain restaurants, specialty shops and galleries.

THE NORTH LIGHT is 4 mi. from the ferry dock to Settlers' Rock (via taxi, bicycle or moped rental), then a .5-mi. walk n. along a rocky beach. The 1868 granite lighthouse is now a maritime interpretive center. A museum on the first floor features displays about renovation efforts as well as historic photographs and the original French Fresnel light.

Guided tours from the interpretive center are available July through August. Phone 2 days in advance to arrange transportation for the physically impaired. **Time:** Allow 1 hour minimum. **Hours:** Daily 10-4, July 5-Labor Day. **Cost:** $3; free (ages 0-11). **Phone:** (401) 466-3200 or (401) 466-3213.

SETTLERS' ROCK, at Cow Cove, bears the names of the town's first settlers, who landed at the spot in 1661.

RECREATIONAL ACTIVITIES
Horseback Riding

• **Rustic Rides Farm,** West Side Rd. Write P.O. Box 842, Block Island, RI 02807. **Hours:** Daily 9-6. **Phone:** (401) 466-5060.

BRISTOL (C-4) pop. 22,469, elev. 42'

King Philip's War, fought 1675-76 between the Wampanoag Indians and New England settlers, was an attempt by the Indians to resist further encroachment by the English. Wampanoag chieftain King Philip established his stronghold in the swamp at the foot of Mount Hope; he later was killed there.

After the Revolutionary War the triangular trade—the transfer of rum, slaves and molasses among Africa, the Caribbean and New England—made Bristol a popular port for trading vessels and a prosperous community. The result of that wealth still is evident in the fine 18th- and 19th-century homes that grace the town's waterfront, although its harbor now shelters mainly pleasure craft.

Herreshoff Manufacturing Co. designed and built eight defenders of the America's Cup 1893-1934.

The shipyard also built the nation's first torpedo boat in 1876. The tradition of boat building continues in Bristol—local companies have built recent America's Cup contenders and winners.

Bristol Historical and Preservation Society, 48 Court St., chronicles more than 300 years of Bristol history; phone (401) 253-7223. Coggeshall Farm Museum, off SR 114, portrays the lifestyles and work of a 1790s coastal farm; phone (401) 253-9062.

Ferry service, available year-round to Prudence Island and seasonally to Hog Island, departs from the Church Street wharf (weather permitting); phone (401) 253-9808 for schedule and fee information.

SAVE **AUDUBON SOCIETY OF RHODE ISLAND'S ENVIRONMENTAL EDUCATION CENTER** is 4 mi. n. on SR 114 at 1401 Hope St. The state's largest aquarium, the center features a life-size model of a right whale, a tide pool tank containing a rare blue lobster and nature trails on a 29-acre wildlife refuge. Environmental exhibits depict Rhode Island's natural habitats, such as woodlands, wetlands and the shoreline of Narragansett Bay.

Time: Allow 1 hour minimum. **Hours:** Daily 9-5, June-Sept.; Mon.-Sat. 9-5, Sun. noon-5, rest of year. Closed Jan. 1, Easter, July 4, Thanksgiving and Dec. 25. **Cost:** $6; $5 (senior citizens); $4 (ages 4-12). **Phone:** (401) 245-7500. ⊞

◢◣ **BLITHEWOLD MANSION, GARDENS & ARBORETUM,** 1.5 mi. s. via SR 114 at 101 Ferry Rd. overlooking Narragansett Bay, SAVE was the summer residence of Pennsylvania coal magnate Augustus Van Wickle. The 45-room 1908 mansion, styled after a 17th-century English country manor and containing original furnishings, is surrounded by 33 acres of landscaped grounds, gardens and exotic plants.

Of interest are a 100-foot giant sequoia, a bamboo grove, a dozen different gardens growing along the shores of the bay and more than 3,000 trees and shrubs. Signs throughout the gardens recount the estate's history. Christmas at Blithewold is celebrated Wednesday through Sunday beginning the Friday after Thanksgiving and lasting through December; phone for hours and rates. Other events are scheduled year-round.

Time: Allow 2 hours minimum. **Hours:** Mansion and grounds open Wed.-Sun. and most Mon. holidays 10-4, mid-Apr. to Columbus Day. Grounds open daily 10-5. Mansion closed July 4. **Cost:** Mansion and grounds $10; $8 (ages 62+ and full-time students with ID); $2 (ages 6-17); free (ages 0-5). Grounds $5 when mansion is closed. **Phone:** (401) 253-2707.

HERRESHOFF MARINE MUSEUM, SR 114 at jct. Burnside and Hope sts., is home to the America's Cup Hall of Fame as well as 60 original sailing and power yachts designed and built by the Herreshoff Manufacturing Co. 1859-1945, including the 1859 *Sprite* and the 1914 *Aria.* Also displayed are half models, steam engines and photographs chronicling the role of Herreshoff Manufacturing Co.

(1859-1945) during the "Golden Age of Yachting." A videotape presentation depicts shipbuilding, America's Cup races and Herreshoff family history. Dockings and moorings are available for museum visitors.

Time: Allow 1 hour minimum. **Hours:** Daily 10-5, May-Oct.; by appointment rest of year. **Cost:** $8; $7 (ages 65+); $4 (ages 11-17 and students with ID). **Phone:** (401) 253-5000.

LINDEN PLACE, 500 Hope St., is an 1810 Federal mansion built for Gen. George DeWolf. The house later was occupied by the general's descendents, including the prominent Colt family and actress Ethel Barrymore. Numerous dignitaries, among them four U.S. presidents, were entertained at the antique-furnished home. The 1.8-acre site also features a ballroom, carriage barn, summer house, bronze sculptures and rose arbors.

Time: Allow 30 minutes minimum. **Hours:** Mon.-Sat. 10-4, Sun. by appointment, first weekend in May-Columbus Day, in Dec. and by appointment. Closed July 4 and Dec. 24-25. **Cost:** $8; $6 (senior citizens and students with ID); $5 (ages 0-12). **Phone:** (401) 253-0390.

COVENTRY (C-3) elev. 414′

GENERAL NATHANAEL GREENE HOMESTEAD MUSEUM AT SPELL HALL, 50 Taft St., was built overlooking the Pawtuxet River in 1770 by Greene, the Quaker general second in command to George Washington. Each of the two main floors has four rooms, two on either side of a central hall. Every room has a paneled fireplace and large double-hung windows. Period furnishings and Greene family memorabilia complete the ambience.

On the grounds are a veterans' garden and a Revolutionary War field-artillery cannon. **Time:** Allow 30 minutes minimum. **Hours:** Wed. and Sat. 10-5, Sun. 1-5, Apr.-Oct. **Cost:** $5; $3 (ages 5-12). **Phone:** (401) 821-8630.

DID YOU KNOW

The smallest state has the longest name—its official title is *State of Rhode Island and Providence Plantations.*

EAST PROVIDENCE (B-4)
pop. 48,688, elev. 59′

East Providence Area Chamber of Commerce:
1005 Waterman Ave., East Providence, RI 02914.
Phone: (401) 438-1212.

LOOFF CAROUSEL AT CRESCENT PARK is in
Riverside at 700 Bullocks Point Ave. The 1895 carousel, designed by Charles Looff, features 66 hand-carved figures. The park's pavilion has an onion-dome roof and stained-glass windows that project colored lights onto the mirrored carousel frame. Crescent Park overlooks Narragansett Bay.

Food is available during carousel operating hours.
Hours: Thurs.-Sun. noon-8, mid-June through Labor Day; Fri. 4-8, Sat.-Sun. noon-8, day after Labor Day-Columbus Day; Sat.-Sun. noon-6, Easter to mid-June. Also open Mon. holidays. Hours may vary. Phone ahead to confirm schedule. **Cost:** Fare $1; 75c (children on Thurs.). **Phone:** (401) 435-7518 or (401) 433-2828.

JAMESTOWN (D-4) elev. 50′

Historic Jamestown, on Conanicut Island, is accessible by bridges from Newport on the east and from the mainland on the west. Burned by the British in 1775, Jamestown still boasts several old houses.

The original Beavertail Lighthouse at the southern tip of the island was established in 1749; the site is one of the oldest lighthouse locations in the country. A 1938 hurricane uncovered the lighthouse's original base, exposing a fine example of Colonial stonework. The present lighthouse, closed to visitors, was built in 1856. A pictorial display at the assistant lightkeeper's house chronicles the history of lighthouses.

In addition to historic houses and the lighthouse, the island town is represented by attractions of military and agricultural interest. Three U.S. forts guard the entrance to Narragansett Bay.

Jamestown Museum, housed in a 19th-century schoolhouse at 92 Narragansett Ave., displays temporary exhibits and memorabilia from ferries; phone (401) 423-0784.

WATSON FARM is at 455 North Rd. Operating since the late 18th century, this 275-acre working historic seaside farm is home to cattle and sheep. A self-guiding tour goes through the fields and along Narragansett Bay. Pets are not permitted. **Time:** Allow 1 hour minimum. **Hours:** Tues., Thurs. and Sun. 1-5, June 1-Oct. 15. **Cost:** $4; $3 (ages 55+); $2 (students with ID); free (ages 0-6). **Phone:** (401) 423-0005. 🅰

LINCOLN (A-4)

Northern Rhode Island Chamber of Commerce: 6 Blackstone Valley Pl., Suite 301, Lincoln, RI 02865. **Phone:** (401) 334-1000.

GAMBLING ESTABLISHMENTS
- **Twin River Casino** is at 100 Twin River Rd. **Hours:** Mon.-Thurs. 9 a.m.-3 a.m., Fri.-Sun. and holidays 24 hours. **Phone:** (401) 723-3200 or (877) 827-4837.

RECREATIONAL ACTIVITIES
Horseback Riding
- **Sunset Stables** departs from 1 Twin River Rd. Guides lead riders through Lincoln Woods State Park. **Hours:** Daily 9-5. Closed Thanksgiving and Dec. 25. **Phone:** (401) 722-3033.

LITTLE COMPTON (D-5) elev. 104′

Little Compton has several churches and an old burying ground containing the graves of many original settlers. Among the graves is that of Elizabeth Alden Pabodie, daughter of John and Priscilla Alden. In nearby Adamsville a Rhode Island Red hen monument stands to honor the breed developed in Little Compton.

WILBOR HOUSE is on SR 77 at 548 W. Main Rd. The house, built circa 1690 with 1740 and 1860 additions, was home to seven generations of the Wilbor family and exemplifies life in early Little Compton. The museum contains furnishings and artifacts from the 17th, 18th and 19th centuries. Antique farming and household equipment are displayed in an adjoining barn; restored carriages and sleighs are in the Carriage House.

Also on the grounds is a one-room schoolhouse featuring antique books, slates and maps. A Portuguese room displays memorabilia, photographs and documents. Summer exhibits are presented in the archival barn. **Time:** Allow 1 hour minimum. **Hours:** Thurs.-Sun. 1-5, late June-Labor Day; Sat.-Sun. 1-5, day after Labor Day-Columbus Day. **Cost:** $5; $1 (ages 0-11). **Phone:** (401) 635-4035.

WINERIES
- [SAVE] **Sakonnet Vineyards**, 162 W. Main Rd. **Hours:** Daily 10-6, Memorial Day-Columbus Day; 11-5, rest of year. Tastings daily. Tours daily at noon and 3. **Phone:** (401) 635-8486, ext. 119 or (800) 919-4637.

MATUNUCK (E-3) elev. 20′

THEATRE-BY-THE-SEA is at 364 Card's Pond Rd. off Matunuck Beach Rd. Summer theater is presented in a restored, converted 1929 barn. Since the theater opened in 1933, it has presented shows featuring such stars as Marlon Brando, Helen Reddy, Jessica Tandy and Mae West.

Time: Allow 3 hours minimum. **Hours:** Performances are given Tues.-Fri. at 8 p.m. (also Thurs. at 2), Sat. at 5 and 9 p.m., Sun. at 5 p.m., June 3-Sept. 7. Children's theater Fri. at 10 and noon, July-Aug. Hours may vary. Phone ahead to confirm schedule. **Cost:** Tickets $28-$32. Children's theater $7. **Phone:** (401) 782-8587.

MIDDLETOWN (D-4) elev. 34'

During the almost 3 years of British occupation of Newport in the Revolutionary War, Middletown accommodated British Green End Fort and served as the eastern terminus of the British Newport defense lines. A plaque describing the fort's history is all that remains of the site on Vernon Avenue.

Purgatory Chasm, a narrow cleft between the rock ledges of Easton Point off Purgatory Road, has a scenic overlook. Bird's Eye View Helicopters, 211 Airport Rd., provides aerial tours of the Newport mansions, area lighthouses and scenic coastline; for reservations phone (401) 843-8687.

SAVE **NORMAN BIRD SANCTUARY** is at 583 Third Beach Rd. The 325-acre sanctuary features more than 7 miles of trails through grassy fields, swamp woodlands and scenic overlooks. A museum displays mounted birds and other natural history exhibits. Programs, field walks and workshops are scheduled year-round. **Note:** Dogs are not permitted. **Hours:** Daily 9-5. Closed major holidays. **Cost:** $5; $2 (ages 4-13). **Phone:** (401) 846-2577.

PRESCOTT FARM is 2.5 mi. n. of jct. SRs 114 and 138 at 2009 W. Main Rd. The landscape and farm buildings provide a glimpse of 18th-century New England. During the Revolutionary War, Gen. Richard Prescott, commander of the British forces in Rhode Island, was captured here. Visitors can feed ducks and geese at the pond as well as explore a restored 1812 windmill and an 1815 country store with period farm implements. The 1730 guardhouse depicts a soldier's room and Pilgrim furniture from the 1600s. The grounds include a medicinal and culinary herb garden as well as an 18th-century garden. A swan, geese, ducks and rabbits run free on the farm.

Tours: Guided tours are available. **Time:** Allow 30 minutes minimum. **Hours:** Grounds open daily dawn-dusk. Guided tours Tues.-Sat. 10-3, June-Sept. **Cost:** Grounds free. Guided tours $5; free (ages 0-12). **Phone:** (401) 847-6230.

WHITEHALL MUSEUM HOUSE is between SR 138 and Green End Ave. at 311 Berkeley Ave. The house was built in 1729 by Bishop George Berkeley, noted Anglo-Irish cleric, philosopher and educator. An herb garden and 18th-century furnishings complement the house. **Hours:** Tues.-Sun. 10-4, July-Aug.; by appointment rest of year. **Cost:** $5. **Phone:** (401) 846-3116.

WINERIES

• **SAVE** **Newport Vineyards and Winery** is at 909 E. Main Rd. (SR 138). **Hours:** Tastings available Mon.-Sat. 10-5, Sun. noon-5. Tours are given daily at 1 and 3. **Phone:** (401) 848-5161.

NARRAGANSETT (E-3)

Narragansett occupies a narrow strip of land between the Pettaquamscutt River and Narragansett Bay. Its sandy beaches and lush inland woods appealed to wealthy Victorians, who transformed the

area into an exclusive resort by building hotels, Narragansett Pier and the renowned Towers Casino. Built in 1883, the casino has been restored fully and now houses the local chamber of commerce.

Although the 1938 hurricane washed away the pier, locals still refer to the downtown area as "the pier." Area beaches attract many visitors.

Narragansett Chamber of Commerce: 36 Ocean Rd., Box 742, Narragansett, RI 02882. **Phone:** (401) 783-7121.

CANONCHET MEMORIAL, at the corner of Beach St. and Ocean Rd. (SR 1A), opposite the Narragansett town beach at Gazebo Park, is a 6,000-pound limestone sculpture of the historical Narragansett Indian chief. **Hours:** Daily dawn-dusk. **Cost:** Free.

SAVE **FRANCES FLEET WHALE WATCHING** departs from the Port of Galilee at Point Judith, 33 State St. Ocean cruises lasting 4.5 hours provide views of finback, humpback, minke and right whales. Other sightings include sharks, dolphins, sea turtles and various sea birds. Tickets are sold across the street at Capt's Tackle. **Hours:** Trips depart July-Aug. Phone ahead to confirm schedule. **Cost:** Fare $40; $35 (ages 62+); $30 (ages 4-12). Reservations are recommended. **Phone:** (401) 783-4988.

NARRAGANSETT INDIAN MONUMENT, Kingstown Rd. and Strathmore St., is a 23-foot-high sculpture carved from a single Douglas fir tree by artist Peter Toth. The monument honors the American Indian. **Hours:** Daily dawn-dusk. **Cost:** Free.

GEM **SOUTH COUNTY MUSEUM** is entered from Strathmore St. off Kingstown Road/SR 1A at the Narragansett Indian **SAVE** Monument, following signs into Canonchet Farm. This living-history museum features seven buildings with exhibits that allow visitors to experience 19th-century life as it was in towns, on farms and on the sea. The museum includes a living-history farm, letterpress print shop, blacksmith shop, carpenter shop, maritime exhibit and a large collection of horse-drawn farm machinery and carriages.

Tours: Guided tours are available. **Time:** Allow 2 hours minimum. **Hours:** Wed.-Sat. 10-4, July-Aug.; Fri.-Sat. 10-4, May-June and Sept. 1-Oct. 4. Sundays open for special events; call for information. **Cost:** $5; $4 (senior citizens); $2 (ages 6-12). **Phone:** (401) 783-5400.

SOUTHLAND RIVERBOAT CRUISES, at State Pier #3 adjacent to Block Island Ferry, sail on 1.75-hour narrated sightseeing journeys through the Harbor of Refuge, past the historic Point Judith Lighthouse and the 11 islands in Great Salt Pond; passengers also can catch a glimpse of Block Island. Two-hour sunset cruises are available late May to mid-September. Fall foliage cruises take place in October.

Hours: Sightseeing cruise Mon.-Sat. at 11, 1 and 3, Sun. at 1 and 3, mid- to late June and early July-Labor Day; Sat. and Sun. at noon and 2, day after Labor Day-early Oct. Schedule may vary. Phone ahead to confirm schedule. **Cost:** Sightseeing cruise fare $15; $13 (ages 60+); $10 (ages 4-12). **Phone:** (401) 783-2954.

NEWPORT (D-4) pop. 26,475, elev. 6'

Settled in 1639, the small agricultural outpost of Newport had established itself as a shipbuilding center as early as 1646. Said to be among the deepest natural ports in the country, it was one of America's top seaports by the 1760s, rivaling Boston, Charleston and New York.

Newport merchants engaged in the trade and exportation of candles, fish and silver and participated in the triangle trade. Some 150 wharves bustled with activity.

The seaport atmosphere remains. Once the hub of Colonial commerce, cobblestone wharves on the waterfront off Thames Street remain busy. Restored 18th- and 19th-century commercial shops at Bowen's and Bannister's wharves house galleries and restaurants, and the harbor where schooners delivered goods now is packed with elegant yachts and lobster boats.

Notable historical events that shaped the Revolution occurred just a few blocks inland. French general Count de Rochambeau greeted George Washington at the 1739 Old Colony House in Washington Square. The building is said to be the nation's second-oldest capitol; the first Catholic masses celebrated in the state were held here 1780-81. In addition, The Declaration of Independence was read from its balcony, and the Federal Constitution was ratified in the building in 1790. Dwight David Eisenhower, Andrew Jackson, Thomas Jefferson and George Washington were said to have been entertained here.

Trade all but stopped when the British occupied Newport 1776-79, limiting access to the harbor. The French then took over until 1783, leaving the town in near economic despair.

The area was reborn as a resort town when the country's wealthiest citizens recognized its promise as a vacation spot. In the 1800s Newport attracted prosperous planters, coal barons, railroad magnates

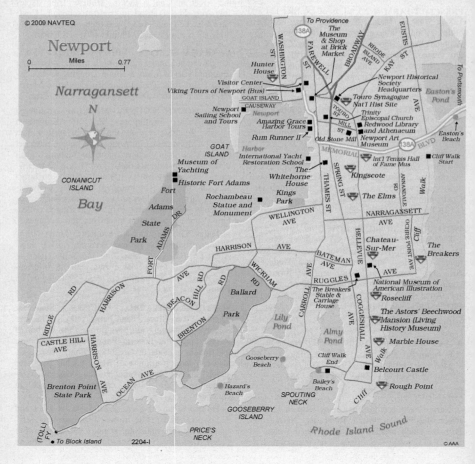

© 2009 NAVTEQ

Newport

Narragansett

Bay

and successful traders and merchants who built extravagant summer homes overlooking the Rhode Island Sound.

Such families as the Astors and Vanderbilts hired noted architect Richard Morris Hunt, venerated for his 19th-century adaptation of the Beaux-Arts style, to design their mansions.

The Cliff Walk, a 3.5-mile walking path, skirts the surrounding bluffs between Easton's Beach and Bailey's Beach. The trail, rough at points, affords beautiful vistas of the rocky coastline and glimpses of the massive "cottages" tucked behind neatly manicured hedges. (Portions of the Cliff Walk are narrow or directly on boulders at the water's edge. Wear good walking shoes and use caution.)

Newport became the hot spot for the elite. Indicative of the snobbery of the "new" Newport, Caroline Astor was credited with creating the "400," a list of families with traceable lineage; it is said to be the first American social register. Presidents Kennedy and Eisenhower later spent vacations in Newport at Hammersmith Farm and Eisenhower Summer House, respectively.

With the rich and the famous came refined recreational pursuits. Newport harbor gained prominence as a yachting center due to its deep water and steady winds. The arrival in the 1930s of the New York Yacht Club, defender of the America's Cup 1851-1983, brought the sport into the local spotlight. Sailing remains a popular pastime—numerous charters are available, and visitors are sure to see handsome craft in the harbor.

Recreational sailing isn't Newport's only claim to maritime fame. Newport was the site of the Naval Academy during the Civil War; the Naval Training Station and the Naval War College were established in the 1880s. In the early 1900s Narragansett Bay was the principal anchorage for the Atlantic Fleet, which was protected by Fort Adams *(see attraction listing p. 223)*, one of the largest bastioned forts in the nation and guardian of the bay until 1945.

The fortifications still can be seen in Fort Adams State Park off Harrison Avenue. A reproduction of the *Providence*, the first authorized ship of the Continental Navy and the first command of John Paul Jones, also is at the park. *See Recreation Chart.*

Newport continues to be a center for U.S. Navy activities with the Naval Underwater Warfare Center and numerous other schools that make up the Naval Education and Training Center.

Two-mile-long Claiborne Pell Bridge connects Newport with Jamestown; there is a $2 charge to cross in either direction. Ferry service to Newport departs the port area on India Street in Providence. Leaving Newport, ferry service continues to Block Island *(see place listing p. 216).* Scenic Ocean Drive passes such public beaches as Gooseberry Beach and Easton's Beach.

Multiple House Tickets

The Preservation Society of Newport County offers both individual admission and multiple house tickets. Included in the Newport Mansions Experience ticket are any five of the preservation society's properties *(see attraction listings beginning on p. 223).* The Breakers Plus package includes admission to The Breakers and any one other Preservation Society house.

The Newport Mansions Experience package is $31; $10 (ages 6-17). The Breakers Plus package is $23; $6 (ages 6-17). Rates are subject to change; please phone ahead. Other packages also are available. Multiple House tickets are available at Preservation Society of Newport County, 424 Bellevue Ave., (401) 847-1000, and at the Newport Visitor Center, 23 America's Cup Ave.

Newport Visitor Information Center: 23 America's Cup Ave., Newport, RI 02840. **Phone:** (401) 845-9123 or (800) 976-5122.

Self-guiding tours: A self-guiding walking tour of Historic Hill includes 26 informative plaques describing historic properties; maps can be obtained from the Newport Historical Society Headquarters, 82 Touro St.; phone (401) 846-0813.

Shopping areas: Brick Market Place, Bowen's Wharf and Bannister's Wharf, along America's Cup Avenue near the harbor front, offer specialty shops in restored buildings. Bellevue Avenue, Franklin Street, Spring Street and Thames Street are prime hunting grounds for antiques.

ACCESS TOURS OF NEWPORT picks up passengers at area accommodations. These in-depth van tours include a scenic overview of Colonial and historic Newport and an up-close look at a mansion's exterior architectural details along with an optional visit inside historic mansions. Tour commentary includes legend, local stories and gossip of the rich and famous who summered in Newport during the Gilded Age. Other tours are available. **Time:** Allow 2 hours, 30 minutes minimum. **Hours:** Tours depart daily at 9:30 and 1:30. **Cost:** Fare (includes pick-up) $49; $25 (ages 2-8). **Phone:** (401) 842-0777 or (877) 868-7774.

AMAZING GRACE **HARBOR TOURS** depart from Oldport Marine on America's Cup Ave. at 9 Sayers Wharf. The *Amazing Grace* offers 1-hour narrated cruises of Newport Harbor and Narragansett Bay, past Newport's mansions, Fort Adams, Brenton Cove, Rose Island Lighthouse, Jamestown and Castle Hill Lighthouse.

Hours: Cruises depart daily every 90 minutes noon-7:30, mid-June through Labor Day; Mon.-Fri.

at 1:30, Sat.-Sun. at noon, 1:30 and 3, mid-May to mid-June and day after Labor Day to mid-Oct. **Cost:** Fare $15; $13 (ages 66+); $9 (ages 0-12). **Phone:** (401) 847-9109.

THE ASTORS' BEECHWOOD MANSION (LIVING HISTORY MUSEUM), 580 Bellevue Ave., was built in 1857 and is one of Newport's oldest "summer cottages." Guided living-history tours feature Beechwood Theater Company actors in period dress representing the Victorian Era. The 45-minute tour covers the first two floors of the home and offers a glimpse of the Astors' lifestyle. The house is decorated for Christmas early November through December; Christmas tours, featuring music in the ballroom, as well as Murder Mystery and Candlelight Musical tours are offered during this period.

Last tour begins at closing. **Tours:** Guided tours are available. **Hours:** Tours depart every 30 minutes daily 10-4, mid-May through Dec. 30; Fri.-Sun. 10-4, early Feb. to mid-May. Candlelight Musical tours are offered mid-Aug. to late Oct. Murder Mystery tours are offered select Fri., in Nov.; select Sat., in Dec. Christmas tours are offered Wed.-Thurs. at 11, noon and 2, Fri.-Sun. at 11, noon, 2 and 3, early Nov.-Dec. 30. Hours may vary. Phone ahead to confirm schedule. **Cost:** Tour $15; $6 (ages 6-17); $40 (family, two adults and up to four children). Christmas tour $20; $8 (ages 6-17); $50 (family, two adults and up to four children). Murder Mystery tour $30; $15 (ages 6-17). Candlelight Musical tour $20; $8 (ages 6-17); $50 (family, two adults and up to four children). Reservations are recommended. **Phone:** (401) 846-3772.

BELCOURT CASTLE, 657 Bellevue Ave., was designed in 1891 by Richard Morris Hunt as the summer residence for Oliver Hazard Perry Belmont and his wife, the former Mrs. William K.

Vanderbilt. The 60-room French Louis XIII-style castle is now home to the Tinney family, whose art collection includes antiques and treasures from 33 countries. Of note are the fine stained-glass collection, European and Asian arms and armor, and the renowned golden coronation coach.

Ghost tour not recommended for children under 7. **Time:** Allow 1 hour minimum. **Hours:** Guided tours daily on the hour 10-4, Apr.-Dec.; call ahead for hours, rest of year. Ghost tours are given Thurs. and Sat. at 5-6:30 p.m. Candlelight tours Fri.-Mon. 6-7 p.m. Last tour begins 1 hour, 30 minutes before closing. Hours may vary. Closed Thanksgiving and Dec. 25. Phone ahead to confirm schedule. **Cost:** Fee $15; $10 (ages 66+ and students with ID); $5 (ages 6-12). Ghost or candlelight tour $18.50. Reservations are required. **Phone:** (401) 846-0669.

THE BREAKERS, 44 Ochre Point Ave., was built in 1895 and is probably the most opulent of Newport's mansions. Though designed by American architect Richard Morris Hunt, this 70-room summer cottage of Cornelius Vanderbilt II appears more the product of the European High Renaissance. Many original furnishings and decorative details were inspired by French and Italian designs of that period.

Vanderbilt's great wealth was reflected in the extensive use of imported French and Italian stone, marble and alabaster as well as the mansion's wooden trim, ceiling paintings, mosaics and gilded plaster. The most spectacular room is the dining room, lavishly decorated with red alabaster, bronze and gilt.

Particularly noteworthy are the 18th-century reception room and the great hall, which is more than two stories high and arrayed with marble columns, pilasters, cornices and plaques.

Last tour begins 1 hour before closing. Self-guiding audio tours are available. **Time:** Allow 1 hour minimum. **Hours:** Daily 9-6, mid-Apr. through Dec. 31; 10-5, rest of year. Closed Thanksgiving and Dec. 25. **Cost:** $18; $4.50 (ages 6-17). Rates are subject to change; please phone ahead. **Phone:** (401) 847-1000.

THE BREAKERS STABLE AND CARRIAGE HOUSE is at Bateman and Coggeshall aves. Just west of The Breakers, the stable was built in 1895 to house Cornelius Vanderbilt's horses, carriages and grooms. Several horse-drawn coaches are exhibited as are Vanderbilt family memorabilia and a model train exhibit. Greenhouses and a 2-acre summer garden are on the grounds.

Time: Allow 30 minutes minimum. **Hours:** Sat.-Sun. and holidays 10-5, late June-Labor Day. **Cost:** $5; $1 (ages 6-17). Free with Newport Mansions Experience ticket. **Phone:** (401) 847-1000.

CHATEAU-SUR-MER, 474 Bellevue Ave., is an ornate Victorian mansion built in 1852 for William S. Wetmore, who made his fortune in China trade. Although it was luxurious

and unusually spacious for its day, the structure was enlarged in 1872 by architect Richard Morris Hunt.

Light streams into the galleried, 45-foot-high, three-story central hall through a stained-glass skylight. The grand staircase is illuminated by stained-glass windows and accented with canvas painted to resemble tapestry.

The huge granite building's library and dining room, by Luigi Frullini of Florence, Italy, are decorated in Renaissance style with leather and lavishly carved walnut. Other notable features include a Turkish sitting room, the French-style ballroom with sliding mirrored doors and a Chinese "moongate" in the wall that surrounds the property.

Time: Allow 1 hour minimum. **Hours:** Daily 10-6, Memorial Day-Columbus Day. Last tour begins 1 hour before closing. **Cost:** $12; $4.50 (ages 6-17). Rates are subject to change; please phone ahead. **Phone:** (401) 847-1000.

THE ELMS, 367 Bellevue Ave., is a neoclassical mansion designed by American architect Horace Trumbauer and built in 1901 as a summer residence for Edward J. Berwind, the king of America's coal industry. The mansion, based on the 18th-century Château d'Asnières near Paris, houses lavish 18th-century French antique furniture and Venetian paintings.

The large proportions of the rooms, especially the entrance hall and ballroom, are awe-inspiring. Noteworthy are the Louis XVI drawing room and the Chinese breakfast room, with lacquered panels that date from the K'ang Hsi period.

Bronze and marble statuary, fountains, terraces and gazebos embellish the well-tended grounds; rare trees and shrubs are labeled. The formal sunken gardens are reminiscent of 18th-century France. Several specialty tours, including the "Rooftop and Behind the Scenes Tour," are available.

Last tour begins 1 hour before closing. Guided tours, as well as self-guiding audio tours, are available. **Hours:** Audio tours daily 10-6, guided tours daily 10-4, Apr.-Dec.; Sat.-Sun. and holidays 10-5, rest of year. Closed Thanksgiving and Dec. 25. **Cost:** $12; $4.50 (ages 6-17). Rooftop and Behind the Scenes Tour admission $15; $4.50 (ages 6-17). Rates are subject to change; please phone ahead. **Phone:** (401) 847-1000.

HISTORIC FORT ADAMS is off Harrison Ave. in Fort Adams State Park. Built 1824-57 and remaining active through World War II, Fort Adams is one of the largest coastal fortifications in the United States. Designed for both land and sea defense, the property provides scenic views of Newport Harbor from atop the walls as well as underground listening tunnels. Tours of the fort feature an exhibit by the Naval War College. *See Recreation Chart.*

Guided tours are given on the hour. Last tour departs at closing. **Time:** Allow 1 hour minimum. **Hours:** Daily 10-4, mid-May to mid-Oct. **Cost:** $10; $5 (ages 6-17); $25 (family). **Phone:** (401) 841-0707.

HUNTER HOUSE, 54 Washington St., was built in 1748 by Jonathan Nichols, a sea merchant and Colonial deputy, and served as the headquarters of the Chevalier de Ternay, admiral over the French naval forces during the American Revolution. The restored house, an outstanding example of Colonial architecture, features fine 18th-century Newport-crafted Goddard-Townsend furniture. Period paintings, paneling and silver as well as a Colonial garden grace the estate.

Time: Allow 1 hour minimum. **Hours:** House open daily 10-6, mid-June through Labor Day. Guided tours depart on the hour daily 10-5, mid-June through Labor Day. **Cost:** $25; $4 (ages 6-17). **Phone:** (401) 847-1000.

INTERNATIONAL TENNIS HALL OF FAME MUSEUM is at 194 Bellevue Ave. The museum is housed in the Newport Casino, a masterpiece of Victorian architecture constructed in 1880 as a social club for Newport society. The casino is known as the birthplace of American lawn tennis because the first U.S. National Lawn Tennis Championships, which evolved into today's U.S. Open, were held here in 1881. Today, the venue hosts the Campbell's Hall of Fame Tennis Championships, which are held annually each July.

The museum chronicles the sport's history from "Court Tennis" of the 13th century to today's professional tours via memorabilia, videos and interactive exhibits portraying the players, the equipment, the rules of the game and the tournaments held around the world. Within the 6-acre complex are the casino's legendary grass courts, which are open to the public May through September.

Guided tours of the museum are available. **Time:** Allow 30 minutes minimum. **Hours:** Daily 9:30-5. Closed Thanksgiving and Dec. 25. **Cost:** $10; $8 (ages 66+, military with ID or students with ID); free (ages 0-16); $25 (family). **Phone:** (401) 849-3990 or (800) 457-1144.

INTERNATIONAL YACHT RESTORATION SCHOOL is at 449 Thames St., in the waterfront district. The school teaches future shipwrights the skills, history and science of restoring and maintaining classic wooden yachts. Visitors can watch students at work restoring the *Coronet*, a 133-foot schooner built in 1885, as well as the school's collection of antique boats. The 2.5-acre waterfront campus offers views of Newport harbor. Water taxi service to the Museum of Yachting is offered.

Time: Allow 1 hour minimum. **Hours:** Daily 10-5, May-Sept.; Mon.-Sat. 10-5, rest of year. Closed major holidays. Phone ahead to confirm schedule. **Cost:** Free. **Phone:** (401) 848-5777.

KINGSCOTE is at 253 Bellevue Ave. The 1841 Gothic Revival-style house, designed for planter George Noble Jones of Savannah, Ga., was the first summer residence to be built in this section of Newport. William Henry King bought the house in 1864 and commissioned architect Stanford White to design additions to it in 1881.

The wooden house, which has interesting towers, gables, eaves and arches, also features a dining room designed by White with a cork ceiling. Although the interior is somber, light spilling through a Tiffany glass wall illuminates the cherry and mahogany dining room. In addition to heavy Victorian furniture, Kingscote contains fine Oriental paintings, rugs and porcelain as well as Goddard-Townsend furniture.

Tours: Guided tours are available. **Time:** Allow 1 hour minimum. **Hours:** Tours are given every half hour daily 10-6, early May-Columbus Day. Last tour begins 1 hour before closing. **Cost:** $12; $4.50 (ages 6-17). Rates are subject to change; please phone ahead. **Phone:** (401) 847-1000.

MARBLE HOUSE, 596 Bellevue Ave., was built in 1892 for William K. Vanderbilt and is one of the most sumptuous of Newport's mansions. The house cost $11 million to build and furnish. Designed by Richard Morris Hunt, the columned white mansion recalls 17th- and 18th-century palaces such as the Petit Trianons of Versailles and the Louvre.

The most elaborate room of this gold-and-marble edifice is the salon, with its carved and gilded woodwork, chandeliers and large ceiling mural. Also of interest are the grand staircase and the Gothic Room. The Harold S. Vanderbilt Memorial Room features yachting trophies and memorabilia. On the grounds is a restored 1914 Chinese teahouse. The house is decorated for the holidays mid-November through January 1. An audio tour is available.

Self-guiding audio tours are available. **Time:** Allow 1 hour minimum. **Hours:** Daily 10-6, Apr.-Dec.; Sat.-Sun. and holidays 10-6, rest of year. Closed Thanksgiving and Dec. 25. **Cost:** $12; $4.50 (ages 6-17). Rates are subject to change; please phone ahead. **Phone:** (401) 847-1000.

THE MUSEUM & SHOP AT BRICK MARKET, 127 Thames St., is housed in the restored 1762 Brick Market building. Featuring items from the collections of the historical society, Newport's history is brought to life through paintings, Colonial silver, furniture and the printing press Ben Franklin's brother brought from England. Exhibits include rare objects of daily life, decorative arts, graphics, artifacts and photographs. The Newport Historical Society and Newport Restoration Foundation offer walking tours of the city that depart from the museum.

Tours: Guided tours are available. **Time:** Allow 1 hour minimum. **Hours:** Museum open daily 10-5. Walking tours are given daily at 11, mid-June through Labor Day. Closed major holidays. **Cost:** Museum $4; $2 (children). Walking tour $12; $8 (ages 8-18). **Phone:** (401) 841-8770.

MUSEUM OF YACHTING is off Fort Adams Rd. in Fort Adams State Park. Located on Newport Harbor, the museum features exhibits including the America's Cup Gallery, the Single-Handed Sailors' Hall of Fame, Hall of Small Boats, a fine arts gallery and an in-the-water classic yacht collection. The museum also has an interactive exhibit area for children.

The museum also may be accessed via the Oldport Water Taxi service in downtown Newport. **Time:** Allow 1 hour minimum. **Hours:** Wed.-Mon. 10-6, May 31-Oct. 31; by appointment rest of year. **Cost:** $5; free (ages 0-17). **Phone:** (401) 847-1018.

MV *MAJESTIC,* 2 Bowen's Ferry Landing adjacent to the Newport Harbor Hotel, offers 1-hour narrated tours on Narragansett Bay and Newport Harbor. **Hours:** Cruises depart daily at 11, 12:30, 2, 3:30, 5 and 6:30, mid-June through Labor Day; at 11, 12:30, 2 and 3:30, May 1 to mid-June and day after Labor Day-Oct. 31. Schedule may vary. Phone ahead to confirm schedule. **Cost:** Fare $15; $14 (ages 63+); $9 (ages 4-12). **Phone:** (401) 849-3575.

NATIONAL MUSEUM OF AMERICAN IL-LUSTRATION is at 492 Bellevue Ave. Situated in Vernon Court, an opulent 1898 mansion surrounded by formal gardens, the museum focuses on artwork created for reproduction in books, periodicals and other print media. Featured artists include Maxfield Parrish, Howard Pyle, Norman Rockwell and NC Wyeth. An 8-minute film introduces visitors to the original works in the collection. Proper dress is required. **Time:** Allow 45 minutes minimum. **Hours:** Museum schedule varies; phone ahead to confirm schedule. Guided tours are offered Fri. at 2 throughout the year. Closed major holidays. **Cost:** $18 (ages 13-64); $16 (65+ and military with ID); $12 (students with ID); $8 (ages 5-12). Reservations are required. **Phone:** (401) 851-8949, 18.

NAVAL WAR COLLEGE MUSEUM is at 686 Cushing Rd. The museum, located within what is said to be the world's oldest naval war college, is dedicated to preserving naval history through hands-on exhibits. Displays include military artifacts, artwork, ship models, uniforms and weaponry. Reservations are required one working day in advance. Visitors must present a valid driver's license or military photo ID, car registration and vehicle proof of insurance at the Naval Station Pass Office. **Time:** Allow 1 hour minimum. **Hours:** Mon.-Fri. 10-4:30, Sat.-Sun. noon-4:30, June-Sept.; Mon.-Fri. 10-4:30, rest of year. **Cost:** Free. **Phone:** (401) 841-2101 or (401) 841-4052.

NEWPORT ART MUSEUM, 76 Bellevue Ave., specializes in the art of southeastern New England. The permanent collection is in the 1864 John N.A. Griswold House, designed in the stick style by architect Richard Morris Hunt. Exhibits are also presented in the 1919 neoclassical Cushing Gallery and at the Coleman Center for Creative Studies. Historical and contemporary works by regional artists and traveling exhibitions also are presented.

Time: Allow 1 hour minimum. **Hours:** Tues.-Sat. 10-5, Sun. noon-5, May-Oct.; Tues.-Sat. 1-4, Sun. noon-4, rest of year. Closed Jan. 1, July 4, Thanksgiving and Dec. 25. **Cost:** $10; $8 (ages 65+); $6

(military and students with ID); free (ages 0-5); by donation (Sat. 10-noon). **Phone:** (401) 848-8200.

NEWPORT HISTORICAL SOCIETY HEADQUAR-TERS, 82 Touro St., has changing exhibits, manuscript archives, a research library and genealogical collections. **Hours:** Tues.-Fri. 9:30-4:30, Sat. 9:30-noon; closed holiday weekends. For research projects, call for appointment. **Cost:** Free. **Phone:** (401) 846-0813.

Seventh Day Baptist Meeting House is part of the headquarters complex of the Newport Historical Society at 82 Touro St. The denomination was founded in Newport in 1671. The modest 1730 structure resembles a house and is laid out in a typical "meeting house plan." Used by the Seventh Day Baptists until 1840, and by other denominations until 1884, the building was moved to Touro Street in 1887. The interior is noted for its complex moldings, raised paneling and hand-carved balusters on the pulpit staircase.

Time: Allow 30 minutes minimum. **Hours:** Tues.-Fri. 9:30-4:30, Sat. 9:30-noon; closed holiday weekends. Hours may vary. Phone ahead to confirm schedule. **Cost:** $5. **Phone:** (401) 846-0813.

NEWPORT SAILING SCHOOL AND TOURS depart from Goat Island Marina, off Washington St. at Dock A5, 5 Marina Plaza, near the Hyatt Hotel. Narrated sailing tours of Newport Harbor and Narragansett Bay are offered. Passengers may take the helm. **Hours:** Daily 10 a.m.-dusk, May-Oct. **Cost:** Fare for 1-hour tour $25. Two-hour tour $40. Reduced rates for seniors 62+ and children ages 0-10. **Phone:** (401) 848-2266.

OCEAN DRIVE is a 10-mile circuit offering panoramas of the rugged Atlantic coastline. Large summer houses border the drive.

OLD STONE MILL, in Touro Park at Bellevue Ave. and Mill St., is a Newport landmark. It is believed by some to have been built by Norsemen long before Columbus' voyage; others claim it dates from the mid-17th century.

REDWOOD LIBRARY AND ATHENAEUM is at 50 Bellevue Ave. Designed by Peter Harrison, the library was built in 1750 and contains many valuable books. It is said to be the oldest U.S. lending library in continuous use. A permanent exhibition of early 18th- and 19th-century portraits includes seven by Gilbert Stuart. **Time:** Allow 30 minutes minimum. **Hours:** Mon.-Sat. 9:30-5:30 (also Tues.-Thurs. 5:30-8), Sun. 1-5. Guided tours are offered Mon.-Fri. at 10:30. Closed major holidays. **Cost:** Donations. **Phone:** (401) 847-0292.

ROCHAMBEAU STATUE AND MONUMENT, in King's Park, commemorates the landing of the French allies in America on July 10, 1780. A fine view can be seen of Newport Harbor and Lime Rock Lighthouse, now the Ida Lewis Yacht Club.

ROSECLIFF, 548 Bellevue Ave., was built in 1902 for Theresa Fair Oelrichs, whose Irish immigrant father discovered the Comstock Silver Lode in Nevada. Designed by Stanford White after Louis XIV's Grand Trianon at Versailles, the terra-cotta mansion replaced a less opulent one. The estate was named for its many rose beds. Sculptor Augustus Saint-Gaudens provided the garden ornamentation.

"The Great Gatsby" was filmed at Rosecliff in 1974; "True Lies" was filmed here in 1994 and "27 Dresses" was filmed in 2007. The mansion boasts a 40-foot by 80-foot ballroom with French doors opening onto terraces; a curving, 18th-century French-style staircase considered one of White's finest works; a Caen Stone carved fireplace; and 18th- and 19th-century sculptures. **Tours:** Guided tours are available. **Time:** Allow 1 hour minimum. **Hours:** Daily 10-6, mid-Apr. to mid-Nov. Last tour begins 1 hour before closing. **Cost:** $12; $4.50 (ages 6-17). Rates are subject to change; please phone ahead. **Phone:** (401) 847-1000.

ROUGH POINT is at 680 Bellevue Ave. The 49-room mansion was the Newport home of tobacco heiress and preservationist Doris Duke. On a promontory overlooking the Atlantic Ocean, the 1891 English Manorial estate sits on grounds designed by Frederick Law Olmsted and purchased in 1922 by James B. Duke, Doris' father. Upon James Duke's death in 1925, Rough Point was part of the fortune left to his only child, 12-year-old Doris.

Rough Point is fully furnished and decorated with Duke's extraordinary collection of fine art, including works by such masters as Gainsborough, Renoir, Rodin and Van Dyck along with pieces of 15th-century Ming Dynasty porcelain, elaborate furniture and Flemish tapestries.

Time: Allow 1 hour minimum. **Hours:** Tues.-Sat. 9:45-3:45, mid-May to early Nov.; Thurs.-Sat. 9:45-1:45, mid-Apr. to mid-May. Phone ahead to confirm schedule. **Cost:** $25 (includes grounds and annual exhibit); free (ages 0-12). **Phone:** (401) 847-8344.

RUM RUNNER II departs from Bannister's Wharf off America's Cup Ave. The *Rum Runner II*, built in 1929, was used to smuggle liquor during the height of Prohibition. Cruises aboard the restored high-speed motor yacht pass by mansions and former speakeasies while guides narrate the history of the boat, Prohibition and Newport.

Time: Allow 1 hour, 30 minutes minimum. **Hours:** Cruises depart daily at 11:30, 1:30, 3:30, 5:30 and 7, mid-June through Labor Day; Mon.-Fri. at 1:30, 3:30 and 5:30, Sat.-Sun. at 11:30, 1:30, 3:30 and 5:30, May 1 to mid-June; daily at 1:30, 3:30 and 5:30, day after Labor Day-Oct. 31. The cruises departing at 5:30 and 7 are cocktail cruises. **Cost:** Fare $18; $15 (ages 66+); $12 (ages 0-12). Cocktail cruise fare $25. **Phone:** (401) 847-0299.

THE WHITEHORNE HOUSE, 416 Thames St., is Newport's only Federal-style mansion open to the public. It houses Doris Duke's collection of 18th-century Newport furniture, including pieces by Goddard and Townsend, as well as silver and pewter by local craftspeople. A period garden is behind the house. **Tours:** Guided tours are available. **Time:** Allow 1 hour minimum. **Hours:** House open Thurs.-Mon. 11-3, May-Oct. Guided tours depart at 10:30 and 3. **Cost:** House $6; free (ages 0-12). Guided tour $12; free (ages 0-12). **Phone:** (401) 847-2448.

TOURO SYNAGOGUE NATIONAL HISTORIC SITE is at 85 Touro St. Built in 1763, the oldest Jewish house of worship in the nation—and the only one to survive from Colonial times—is said to be one of America's most architecturally distinguished buildings of the 18th century. Designed by Peter Harrison, the Georgian structure has a simple, almost austere exterior that contrasts with a graceful interior adorned with massive brass candelabra, hand-carved paneling, balustrades and 12 Ionic and Corinthian columns.

Tours: Guided tours are available. **Hours:** Guided tours depart every 30 minutes Sun.-Fri. noon-2, May-Oct.; Sun. noon-2, mid-Mar. through Apr. 30 and Nov.-Dec. Closed Jewish holidays. Schedules and tour times are subject to change. Phone ahead to confirm schedule. **Cost:** $5; free (ages 0-12). Phone ahead to verify prices. Reservations are required. **Phone:** (401) 847-4794.

TRINITY EPISCOPAL CHURCH, Queen Anne Sq., has been in continuous use since it was built by Richard Munday in 1726. It is inspired by the designs of Christopher Wren. A three-tiered wineglass pulpit, Tiffany windows and a 1733 organ tested by George Frideric Handel grace the interior. The original candle chandeliers hang from the rafters by ropes, Colonial-style.

Time: Allow 30 minutes minimum. **Hours:** Mon.-Fri. 10-4, mid-June to mid-Oct.; Mon.-Fri. 10-1, May 1 to mid-June and mid-Oct. through Oct. 31; also open Sat. 10-4, July 5-Aug. 31; by appointment, rest of year. Closed federal holidays. Services are held Wed. at noon, Sun. at 8 and 10. **Cost:** $4. **Phone:** (401) 846-0660.

VIKING TOURS OF NEWPORT offers narrated trolley tours departing from the convention and visitors bureau information center at 23 America's Cup Ave. The tour covers some 150 points of historical interest, including visits to the Newport mansions.

Hours: Tours depart daily beginning at 10, May-Oct.; Sat. at 11:30, rest of year. **Cost:** Ninety-minute tour $26; $15 (ages 6-17). Three-hour tour $39; $18 (ages 6-17). Four-hour tour $53; $23 (ages 6-17). **Phone:** (401) 847-6921 for exact tour times and reservations.

PAWTUCKET (B-4) pop. 72,958, elev. 86'

Thick forests, rocky land and untamed rivers discouraged Roger Williams from settling the area north of Providence in the 1630s. Called the "place by the waterfall," Pawtucket is where the Blackstone River—designated an American Heritage

River—forms Pawtucket Falls as it tumbles into the Pawtucket River.

With its abundant water power and timber for fuel, Pawtucket soon enticed blacksmiths to set up shop. Despite a setback in 1676 when the town virtually was destroyed in King Philip's War, Pawtucket grew quickly as an innovative manufacturing center, emerging as the birthplace of America's Industrial Revolution. In 1793 Samuel Slater started North America's first successful cotton-manufacturing mill, which was operated by water power.

Pawtucket is part of the Blackstone River Valley, through which the Blackstone River flows for 48 miles. Established by the U.S. Congress in 1986 as a national historic region, the Blackstone River Valley National Heritage Corridor helps preserve the history of the American Industrial Revolution. The area spans nine Rhode Island towns and covers 250,000 acres from Worcester, Mass., to Providence.

A popular recreation area is Slater Memorial Park on Newport Avenue (US 1A). The park offers recreational facilities and attractions, including an 1895 Looff carousel and gardens.

The Pawtucket Red Sox, the AAA International Baseball League affiliate of the Boston Red Sox, play at McCoy Stadium; phone (401) 724-7300 for Pawtucket Red Sox information.

Blackstone Valley Tourism Council and Visitor Center: 175 Main St., Pawtucket, RI 02860. **Phone:** (401) 724-2200 or (800) 454-2882.

Self-guiding tours: Maps and brochures for walking, fall foliage, canoe and driving tours are available at the visitor center.

RHODE ISLAND WATERCOLOR SOCIETY, in a restored historic building at Slater Memorial Park, has changing monthly displays of watercolors. **Hours:** Tues.-Sat. 10-4, Sun. 1-5. Closed major holidays. **Cost:** Free. **Phone:** (401) 726-1876.

SLATER MILL HISTORIC SITE, downtown at 67 Roosevelt Ave., is known as the Birthplace of the American Industrial Revolution. The restored site, on the banks of the Blackstone River, depicts the development of factory production and life in a 19th-century industrial village. Costumed interpreters perform period tasks and craft work. Self-guiding tours include visits to the 1758 Sylvanus Brown House and the 1793 Slater Mill, which houses a working collection of textile machinery.

A 10-ton water wheel powers the 19th-century machine shop within the 1810 Wilkinson Mill. The Apprentice's Alcove allows visitors to run machinery and features a variety of other hands-on exhibits. **Time:** Allow 1 hour, 30 minutes minimum. **Hours:** Tues.-Sun. 10-4, May-Oct.; Sat.-Sun. 11-3, Mar.-Apr. Hours may vary. Phone ahead to confirm schedule. **Cost:** $10; $9 (senior citizens); $8 (ages 6-12). **Phone:** (401) 725-8638.

PORTSMOUTH (D-5) elev. 36′

Portsmouth, once the most populous town in the colony, was settled in 1638. The first settlers, among them free-speech advocate Anne Hutchinson, landed at Founders' Brook on Boyd's Lane. On Pudding Rock is a bronze tablet inscribed with a copy of the Portsmouth Compact. At Butts Hill Fort off Sprague Street, Portsmouth later witnessed Rhode Island's only major land battle of the Revolution.

SAVE **GREEN ANIMALS TOPIARY GARDEN,** .7 mi. w. off SR 114 at 380 Cory's Ln., was the summer estate of Thomas Brayton, who purchased the property in 1872. His Portuguese gardener created the topiaries shortly after the turn of the century. Boxwood-lined ornamental gardens surround more than 80 pieces of topiary, including a lion, a camel and a giraffe, sculpted in privet and yew, as well as boxwood and privet geometric forms and ornamental designs.

Formal, rose, fruit and vegetable gardens are featured. The main house contains period furnishings, Brayton memorabilia and Victorian toy collections. **Time:** Allow 1 hour minimum. **Hours:** Daily 10-6, late May-Columbus Day. **Cost:** $12; $4.50 (ages 6-17). Rates are subject to change; please phone ahead. **Phone:** (401) 847-1000. 🅰

WINERIES

• **Greenvale Vineyards** is at 582 Wapping Rd. **Hours:** Tours and tastings Mon.-Sat. 10-5, Sun. noon-5, Apr.-Dec.; Mon.-Sat. 11-5, Sun. noon-5, rest of year. **Phone:** (401) 847-3777.

PROVIDENCE (B-3) pop. 173,618, elev. 80′

See map page 228.

Providence residents are probably glad that Separatist minister Roger Williams was banished from Plymouth County, Mass., in 1636. His progressive, uncompromising views—that each person had a right to worship without interference or regulation by the state—almost caused his deportation. Fearing arrest, he fled the colony and spent the winter with Wampanoag Indians. Later that year, Narragansett Indians gave him land near a salty cove on which Providence was founded. Williams chose the name in gratitude "for God's merciful providence unto me in my distress."

A monument on Gano Street between Power and Williams streets marks the site where Williams first arrived. Seeking "freedom for the souls of men," he established a haven for religious nonconformists, creating only civil laws. The settlement was laid out along a native footpath running along the Providence River, now present-day Main Street.

Congregations were free to build their own places of worship; Williams himself helped to establish the First Baptist Church on Main Street, the country's first *(see attraction listing)*. Many of the city's church buildings have survived and serve as a reminder of his defense of differing denominations and beliefs.

History also is displayed in colorful, restored residences lining Benefit Street. Commonly called the Mile of History, this concentration of original Colonial homes has fine examples of early Federal, Greek Revival and Italianate architecture. Brick sidewalks with hitching posts border homes and churches displaying historical plaques.

Prospect Terrace, at Congdon and Cushing streets, is a peaceful, grassy plot amid historic homes. A 14-foot-tall granite statue of Roger Williams marks his grave and overlooks downcity (downtown). With an outstretched arm, he blesses the city he founded.

In its early days Providence was a shipping and shipbuilding town. Boats ran the triangular route to Africa, the West Indies and the Colonies to trade rum, slaves and molasses. The passage of the Sugar Act in 1764 began an uprising that culminated at the 1762 Old State House, 150 Benefit St., a brick building where Rhode Island officially declared independence from Great Britain on May 4, 1776.

Nearby at 251 Benefit St. is the Providence Athenaeum, where Edgar Allan Poe once courted Sarah Helen Whitman. Built in 1838, the Greek Revival building is among the nation's oldest libraries and cultural centers.

Sharing space with aged properties are numerous schools that give Providence a noticeable college town feel. An art community in the College Hill-Benefit Street area thrives due to creative endeavors by Rhode Island School of Design students. The 1774 Market House, now an art gallery, was the site of the Providence Tea Party on March 2, 1776. Nearby Brown University *(see attraction listing)* contains a number of early 20th-century structures. Across the Providence River, Johnson & Wales University, Providence College and Rhode Island College also call the city home.

Some of the nation's finest acting companies, including Trinity Square Repertory Players, regularly offer performances at Providence Performing Arts Center, 220 Weybosset St., (401) 421-2787, and Trinity Repertory Theatre, 201 Washington St., (401) 351-4242.

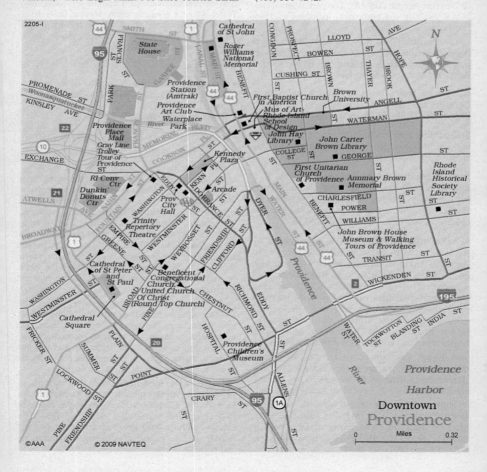

Waterplace Park, on the site of the 1848 Cove Basin, is a 4-acre urban park focused on a 240-foot-diameter basin joining the Providence and Woonasquatucket rivers, which pass through downcity. Activities abound: An amphitheater plays host to performances, and gondola rides are offered May through September by La Gondola, (401) 421-8877.

Joining the park to the east is Providence Riverwalk, with Venetian-style footbridges, more than a mile of cobblestone and brick walkways and 7 acres of parkland.

The petite city is Rhode Island's capital, yet it has not strayed from its founding father's initial goals: Atop the State House stands the Independent Man, a bronze statue reminding citizens of the ideals upon which the city was established.

[SAVE] Gray Line offers various guided bus tours of the Providence area as well as coastal Newport; for schedules and reservations phone (800) 934-8687.

Providence Warwick Convention and Visitors Bureau: 1 W. Exchange St., Providence, RI 02903. **Phone:** (401) 456-0200, or (800) 233-1636 out of R.I.

Shopping areas: Dating from 1828, the Greek Revival Arcade, 65 Weybosset St., is said to be the country's first enclosed shopping mall. It has been updated with specialty stores and restaurants. Renovated commercial buildings on South Main Street, along the Providence River, now house restaurants, offices and shops.

Wayland Square, on the eastern side on the city, offers diverse shops in an early 20th-century neighborhood. Thayer Street, in College Hill, attracts students with shops, bookstores and cafes. Bohemian Wickenden Street is populated with antique and import shops.

Providence Place Mall, overlooking Waterplace Park in the heart of downcity, is hard to miss. It boasts more than 150 stores, including anchors Filene's and Nordstrom.

BENEFICENT CONGREGATIONAL CHURCH, UNITED CHURCH OF CHRIST (ROUND TOP CHURCH) is at 300 Weybosset St. Opened in 1810, the structure is one of the earliest examples of Classical Revival architecture in the country. The New England-style interior houses period fixtures and was the site of many historic events, including the first graduation of Brown University. **Time:** Allow 30 minutes minimum. **Hours:** Mon.-Fri. noon-3, Sun. 9-noon. Worship services Sun. at 10. Closed major holidays. Phone ahead to confirm schedule. **Cost:** Donations. **Phone:** (401) 331-9844.

BROWN UNIVERSITY is on College Hill at jct. College and Prospect sts. Brown, an Ivy League institution, began in 1764 as Rhode Island College in Warren and was relocated to Providence in 1770. The university's Van Wickle gates are at the corner of College and Prospect streets. The admission office, 45 Prospect St., provides information about guided tours. **Tours:** Guided tours are available.

Hours: Admission office open Mon.-Fri. 8:30-5 during the academic year, Mon.-Fri. 8-4 in summer. **Phone:** (401) 863-2378.

Annmary Brown Memorial, 21 Brown St., contains European and American paintings from the Renaissance through the early 20th century along with a collection of centuries-old swords. **Hours:** Mon.-Fri. 1-5, Sept.-May; closed winter and spring school breaks. **Cost:** Free. **Phone:** (401) 863-2405.

John Carter Brown Library, corner of George and Brown sts., is a 1904 Beaux-Arts building considered the classical gem of Brown University. The MacMillan Reading Room contains exhibits. **Hours:** Mon.-Fri. 9-5, Sat. 9-noon. Closed major holidays. **Cost:** Free. **Phone:** (401) 863-2725.

John Hay Library, 20 Prospect St., contains the writings of John Hay, assistant private secretary to President Abraham Lincoln and secretary of state 1898-1905. Also shown are the Harris Collection of American Poetry and Plays, the McLellan Lincoln Collection and the Anne S.K. Brown Military Collection. **Hours:** Mon.-Fri. 9-6, Sun. 1-5 (during academic year). **Cost:** Free. **Phone:** (401) 863-3723.

CATHEDRAL OF ST. JOHN is at 271 N. Main St. Built in 1810, the cathedral is the oldest Episcopal church in the city and one of four original Colonial parishes of Rhode Island. There is an 1851 refurbished Hook organ, and many of Providence's early settlers are buried in an adjoining graveyard. Guided tours of the cathedral are available on request. **Hours:** Mon.-Fri. 11-2. **Cost:** Free. **Phone:** (401) 331-4622.

CATHEDRAL OF ST. PETER AND ST. PAUL, 1 Cathedral Sq., dates from the late 19th century. Renovated in the neo-Gothic style, the Catholic church contains a rare 6,330-pipe Casvant organ, with pipes ranging in size from 6 inches to 32 feet. **Hours:** Mon.-Fri. 8-noon. **Cost:** Free. **Phone:** (401) 331-2434.

[SAVE] **CULINARY ARTS MUSEUM** is at 315 Harborside Blvd. at the Harborside Campus of Johnson & Wales University. Visitors can explore the past, present and future of all things related to cookery at this museum. Within the 25,000-square-foot gallery exhibits include "Diners: Still Cookin' in the 21st Century" and "Country Fair to Culinary Olympics." Changing exhibits also are featured.

Hours: Tues.-Sun. 10-5; closed major holidays and university exam days. **Cost:** $7; $6 (ages 66+); $3 (students with ID); $2 (ages 5-18). **Phone:** (401) 598-2805.

FIRST BAPTIST CHURCH IN AMERICA, 75 N. Main St. at Waterman St., was established by Roger Williams in 1638 and is the oldest Baptist church in America. Faithfully restored, the 1775 structure boasts classical Georgian-style architecture. A Waterford crystal chandelier dating from 1792 hangs in the sanctuary.

Hours: Guided and self-guiding tours available Mon.-Fri. 10-noon and 1-3, Sun. at 11:15, July 1-Labor Day; Mon.-Fri. 10-noon and 1-3, Sun. at 12:15, rest of year. Schedule subject to change. Closed major holidays. Phone ahead to confirm schedule. **Cost:** $2. **Phone:** (401) 454-3418.

FIRST UNITARIAN CHURCH OF PROVIDENCE, Benefit and Benevolent sts., combines elements of classical and Gothic architecture. Built in 1816, it has the largest bell ever cast in the foundry of Paul Revere. **Hours:** Open Mon.-Fri. 9-5. **Cost:** Free. **Phone:** (401) 421-7970.

[SAVE] **GRAY LINE TROLLEY TOURS OF PROVI-DENCE** depart from the trolley booth at the jct. of Fountain and Eddy sts., behind the Biltmore Hotel. One-hour narrated tours showcase the city's historic downtown, including the Brown University area, Federal Hill, Benefit Street and the Providence River. Tickets must be purchased 48 hours in advance and copy of receipt presented at ticket booth. **Time:** Allow 1 hour minimum. **Hours:** Tours are offered Apr.-Nov. Phone ahead for departure times. **Cost:** $18; $16 (college students with ID and 65+); $14 (ages 3-13). **Phone:** (401) 421-3825 or (800) 934-8687.

HAFFENREFFER MUSEUM OF ANTHROPOL-OGY GALLERY is at the corner of Prospect and Waterman sts. on the ground floor of Manning Hall at Brown University. The museum houses anthropological exhibits that interpret a variety of cultures. Brown University students serve as curators for the changing exhibitions. **Time:** Allow 30 minutes minimum. **Hours:** Tues.-Sun. 10-4. Closed major holidays. **Cost:** Free. **Phone:** (401) 863-2065.

JOHN BROWN HOUSE MUSEUM, 52 Power St., was built in 1788 and was the home of wealthy 18th-century merchant and manufacturer John Brown. This restored three-story Georgian-style house is furnished with fine examples of Rhode Island furniture, decorative arts and pewter and silver collections. **Tours:** Guided tours are available. **Hours:** Guided 1-hour tours Tues.-Fri. at 1:30 and 3, Sat. at 10:30, noon, 1:30 and 3, Apr.-Dec.; Fri.-Sat. at 10:30, noon, 1:30 and 3, rest of year. Hours may vary. Phone ahead to confirm schedule. **Cost:** $8; $6 (ages 62+ and students with ID); $4 (ages 7-17). **Phone:** (401) 273-7507.

[GEM] **MUSEUM OF ART—RHODE ISLAND SCHOOL OF DESIGN** is at jct. Benefit and Waterman sts. at 224 Benefit St.; alternate access is via the Chace Center at 20 N. Main St. The museum houses nearly 84,000 works of 'art, ranging from ancient Greek and Roman sculpture to French Impressionist paintings—from Chinese stone and terracotta sculpture to contemporary art in every medium, including textiles, ceramics, glass and furniture. Special exhibitions, lectures, tours, concerts and other programs are offered. Audiotape tours are available.

Hours: Tues.-Sun. 10-5 (also third Thurs. of the month 5-9), Jan.-July and Sept.-Dec.; additional hours second Fri. of the month 5-8, Sept.-June. Closed Jan. 1, July 4, Thanksgiving and Dec. 25. **Cost:** $10; $7 (ages 62+); $3 (college students with ID); $2 (ages 5-18). **Phone:** (401) 454-6500.

PROVIDENCE ART CLUB, 11 Thomas St., is said to be America's second oldest art club. It is in four houses dating from 1786-1885 containing galleries, studios and a clubhouse. Changing exhibitions are featured. **Hours:** Mon.-Fri. noon-4, Sat.-Sun. 2-4. Closed major holidays. **Cost:** Free. **Phone:** (401) 331-1114.

PROVIDENCE CHILDREN'S MUSEUM is at 100 South St. Children ages 1-11 and their families explore a garden planted with plants and trees native to Rhode Island; take a hands-on time-travel adventure; investigate the power of air; and learn about bones, bridges and fountains. Daily programs offer a variety of additional hands-on activities.

Time: Allow 1 hour minimum. **Hours:** Daily 9-6, Apr.-Aug.; Tues.-Sun. and Mon. holidays 9-6, rest of year. Closed Thanksgiving and Dec. 24-25. **Cost:** $7.50; free (ages 0-1, members and to all on select Fri. evenings). **Phone:** (401) 273-5437.

RHODE ISLAND HISTORICAL SOCIETY LI-BRARY, 121 Hope St., has genealogy, graphics and manuscript collections pertaining to Rhode Island history. **Hours:** Wed.-Fri. and second Sat. of month 10-5. **Cost:** $5. **Phone:** (401) 273-8107.

ROGER WILLIAMS NATIONAL MEMORIAL, 282 N. Main St., is located on the common lot of the original 1636 Providence settlement and includes a 4.5-acre landscaped park. A visitor center offers displays and a 5-minute film describing the life of the city's founder. **Hours:** Daily 9-4:30. Closed Jan. 1, Thanksgiving and Dec. 25. **Cost:** Free. **Phone:** (401) 521-7266.

ROGER WILLIAMS PARK can be reached from I-95S exit 17 or I-95N exit 16 to Elmwood Ave., following signs. The 435-acre Victorian era park includes more than 100 acres of lakes as well as several miles of walking paths. The William E. Benedict Memorial to Music amphitheater is a stage for concerts. Also on the grounds are greenhouses and Betsy Williams Cottage, built in 1773. Carousel Village features pony rides, a playground, a replica of a Victorian carousel and other amusements. Boating is offered seasonally.

Hours: Park open daily 7 a.m.-9 p.m. Greenhouses and Carousel Village open daily 10-5 (weather permitting); extended hours in summer. **Cost:** Park admission free. Amusement rides begin at $1.25. Pony rides $2.50. **Phone:** (401) 785-9450 Mon.-Fri. 8:30-4:30.

Roger Williams Park Botanical Center, in Roger Williams Park, is a 12,000-square-foot facility consisting of a pair of greenhouses displaying New England's largest public indoor presentation of botanical gardens. The Conservatory is home to a variety of exotic and tropical plants, large palm trees and two fountains; The Mediterranean Room offers begonia, orchid and carnivorous plant displays, a koi pond, a small desert area and a section of Mediterranean herbs and fruits often used in culinary practices.

Guided tours are available and require a reservation at least one month in advance. **Time:** Allow 1 hour minimum. **Hours:** Tues.-Sun. 11-4 (also Mon. holidays). Last ticket is sold 30 minutes before closing. Phone ahead to verify holiday schedule. **Cost:** $3; $1 (ages 6-12). **Phone:** (401) 785-9450, ext. 250 for guided tour reservations.

Roger Williams Park Museum of Natural History and Planetarium, 1000 Elmwood Ave., features exhibits and educational programs in the sciences. The museum also hosts traveling exhibitions. **Hours:** Museum open daily 10-5. Planetarium shows daily at 2, July-Aug.; Sat.-Sun. at 2, rest of year. **Cost:** $2; $1 (ages 2-7). Planetarium and museum $3; $2 (ages 4-7). Ages 0-3 are not permitted in the planetarium. **Phone:** (401) 785-9457, ext. 221.

[SAVE] **Roger Williams Park Zoo,** 1000 Elmwood Ave., is home to more than 100 species from around the world. Such animals as elephants, giraffes, snow leopards, moon bears, gibbons and kangaroos may be viewed in naturalistic settings. **Hours:** Daily 9-4. Last admission is 30 minutes before closing. Zoo closes at 2 p.m. on the last Sat. in June and is closed Thanksgiving and Dec. 24-25. **Cost:** $12; $8 (ages 62+); $6 (ages 3-12). **Phone:** (401) 785-3510. [T]

STATE HOUSE, on Smith St. between Francis and Gaspee sts., has been the meeting place for the Rhode Island General Assembly since Jan. 1, 1901. Outside the senate chambers is the original parchment Royal Charter of 1663, granted by King Charles II. There also are relics and noteworthy paintings, including a full-length portrait of George Washington by Gilbert Stuart. A large marble dome—said to be the fourth largest unsupported dome in the world—caps the building. A gilded bronze statue, "Independent Man," stands atop the dome.

Guided and self-guiding tours are available. Reservations are recommended for guided tours. **Time:** Allow 1 hour minimum. **Hours:** Mon.-Fri. 9-4. Guided tours are given Mon.-Fri. 9-noon. Closed major holidays. **Cost:** Free. **Phone:** (401) 222-3983.

WALKING TOURS OF PROVIDENCE offers tours departing from the John Brown House at 52 Power St. Offered in summer by the Rhode Island Historical Society, these 90-minute walking tours describe local architecture, culture and history. **Time:** Allow 1 hour, 30 minutes minimum. **Hours:** Tues.-Sat. at 11, June 15-Oct. 15. **Cost:** Fee $12; $10 (ages 62+); $6 (ages 4-12). **Phone:** (401) 331-8575, ext. 45.

SAUNDERSTOWN (D-3) elev. 110'

A Scottish emigrant and his wife established Saunderstown, site of the first snuff mill in the 13 original colonies, on the Mettatuxet River in 1751.

The snuff-grinder's son, Gilbert Stuart, became a renowned portrait painter.

GILBERT STUART BIRTHPLACE AND MUSEUM, 1 mi. e. of US 1 on Gilbert Stuart Rd., dates from 1750. Born in 1755, Stuart was one of America's foremost portrait painters. He was especially noted for his series of paintings of George Washington. Period furnishings, two water wheels, a grist mill, a snuff mill and nature trails are featured. **Tours:** Guided tours are available. **Time:** Allow 30 minutes minimum. **Hours:** Open Thurs.-Mon. 11-3, early May-Sept. 30; limited hours in Oct. Guided tours are given on the hour. Last tour begins at 3. **Cost:** $6; $3 (ages 6-12). **Phone:** (401) 294-3001.

RECREATIONAL ACTIVITIES
Horseback Riding

• **Tower Hill Equestrian Center** is at 2415 Tower Hill Rd. Other activities are offered. **Hours:** Daily 9-4:30. **Phone:** (401) 294-8190.

SMITHFIELD (A-3) elev. 266'

AUDUBON SOCIETY OF RHODE ISLAND, 12 Sanderson Rd., manages more than 9,500 acres of natural wildlife habitats within the state. The headquarters, which includes the Hathaway Library of Natural History, is surrounded by the 75-acre Powder Mill Ledges Wildlife Refuge, with 2.5 miles of nature trails. Other refuges include the George B. Parker Woodland in Coventry, the Fisherville Brook Wildlife Refuge in Exeter and the Environmental Education Center in Bristol. Visitors can snowshoe or cross-country ski on the grounds. Naturalist programs teach about bird feeding, animal survival and vernal pools.

Hours: Office open Mon.-Fri. 9-5, Sat. noon-4; closed holidays. Refuge trails open daily dawn-dusk. **Cost:** Donations. **Phone:** (401) 949-5454.

SOUTH KINGSTOWN (D-3) elev. 58'

Near the observation tower in South Kingstown is a rock that is at the heart of a tragic love story. In 1765 Hannah Robinson, the lovely young daughter of a prominent local citizen, fell in love with her French tutor. Hannah's father disapproved of the courtship, and the couple was forced to meet secretly, often at a large rock more than a mile from her house. They eventually eloped, resulting in Hannah's disinheritance. Her new husband soon deserted her, and Hannah, in declining health, was brought home to die, for the last time passing the rock where she and her beloved had met in happier times.

The University of Rhode Island, established in 1892, is on 1,200 acres in Kingston Village. The village's main street, SR 138, retains its 18th-century charm.

OBSERVATION TOWER AT HANNAH ROBINSON PARK is at jct. US 1 and SR 138, overlooking Bonnet Shores. The 40-foot-high wooden tower, which sits atop a natural, wooded hill overlooking flowering plants and trees, provides a panorama of Narragansett Bay, the Atlantic Ocean and the rocky, uneven shoreline of Rhode Island. **Hours:** Daily dawn-dusk. **Cost:** Free. 🎴

TIVERTON (C-5) pop. 7,282, elev. 50′

A popular resort on the shores of Narragansett Bay and the Sakonnet River, Tiverton was incorporated in 1694 as part of the Massachusetts Bay Colony. A royal decree in 1746 deemed that Tiverton be included within Rhode Island's boundaries, a ruling disregarded by Massachusetts, which reclaimed part of the town in 1862.

Fort Barton, on Highland Road, was a Revolutionary redoubt, where British troops practiced their invasion of Aquidneck Island and Newport. More than 3 miles of nature trails mark the site of the fort overlooking the Sakonnet River.

WARREN (C-4) elev. 49′

RECREATIONAL ACTIVITIES
Canoeing
- **Canoe Passage Outfitters** is s. on Main St./SR 114S, .1 mi. w. on State St., then just s. to 277 Water St. Other activities are offered. **Hours:** Phone ahead to confirm schedule. **Phone:** (401) 529-4878.

WARWICK (C-4) pop. 85,808, elev. 64′

Samuel Gorton, Warwick's founder, was one of early Rhode Island's most colorful characters. An extreme individualist who did not believe in civic or religious authority, Gorton was exiled successively from Plymouth Colony and Portsmouth. Even Roger Williams, also an exile, banished Gorton from Providence. Seeking to avoid persecution, Gorton and several followers purchased lands at Shawomet from the Narragansett Indians in 1643.

Disputing Gorton's claim at Shawomet, the Massachusetts Bay Colony arraigned Gorton and his fellow purchasers before a tribunal, which condemned the men to prison for blasphemy. Upon his release, Gorton went to England to gain protection from Massachusetts. Promised protection by the Earl of Warwick, an important member of Parliament, Gorton confidently returned to Shawomet and renamed it after the earl.

About the beginning of the 19th century, Warwick developed as a confederation of villages built around textile mills along the Pawtuxet River. Now a major retail center and suburban area, Warwick is second in size only to Providence.

Although rapid industrial and commercial expansion erased most vestiges of Warwick's early history, progress has left the 39 miles of coastline along Narragansett and Greenwich bays untouched. Each summer Warwick's beaches and shoreline attract boaters and inland residents.

Warwick City Park on Asylum Road features beach and recreational facilities on 170 acres. Oakland Beach, south from SR 117 on Oakland Beach Avenue, and Conimicut Point, east off SR 117, offer swimming, fishing and scenic views. At low tide, beachcombers search the shore for clams, locally known as quahogs.

Goddard Memorial State Park, which occupies more than 472 acres off SR 1 on Ives Rd., was planted more than 100 years ago with an unusual selection of trees. Considered a fine example of private forestry, the main portion of the park is open from April through September, with limited access the rest of the year. In addition to swimming, hiking, picnicking and a public golf course, the park offers summer concerts in a restored carousel building near the beach. *See Recreation Chart.*

Several annual events are held early May through mid-June as part of Warwick's 🚩 Gaspee Days Celebration, including arts and crafts fairs, a parade, fireworks displays and colonial encampments. The celebration commemorates the 1772 burning of an armed British schooner, the HMS *Gaspee,* by prominent Rhode Island colonists protesting oppressive British taxes and trade laws. Phone (401) 781-1772.

Regional art is featured year-round at Warwick Museum of Art in Kentish Artillery Armory, 3259 Post Rd.; phone (401) 737-0010.

Warwick Department of Economic Development Tourism Office: 3275 Post Rd., Warwick, RI 02886. **Phone:** (401) 738-2000, ext. 6402, (800) 492-7942 or TTY (401) 739-9150.

Shopping areas: Major malls include Rhode Island Mall, I-295 exit 1 at the junction of SRs 2 and 113, which features Sears and Kohl's; and Warwick Mall, I-295 exit 2 at the junction of SRs 2 and 5, which is anchored by Filene's, JCPenney and Macy's.

WESTERLY (E-2) pop. 17,682, elev. 34′

The first permanent European settlers of Westerly, so named for its westerly position in the state, supposedly were John and Mary Babcock, who eloped in 1648. They were joined more than a decade later by residents from Newport, Providence and Warwick, who bought shares from a Newport company that claimed title to the Misquamicut tract, as this region was called.

Border disputes between Connecticut and Rhode Island plagued the region for more than 50 years until the boundary line officially was drawn in 1728. Throughout the Revolutionary War the coast around Westerly was besieged by marauding British expeditions. Nearby Watch Hill, now a quiet resort town, was established as a lookout for British privateers. Shipbuilding, agriculture and trade sustained the village throughout the 18th century.

Prosperity reigned in the late 19th century, a result of textile manufacturing and granite quarrying. Westerly is a supply center for nearby seaside resorts. There are many public beaches with bathhouse facilities between Weekapaug and Watch Hill, including Misquamicut State Beach *(see Recreation Chart).* Wilcox Park, on Broad Street, is a 14-acre

Victorian strolling park that includes collections of day lilies and dwarf conifers, a library and a display about the granite industry; phone (401) 596-2877.

The Greater Westerly-Pawcatuck Chamber of Commerce: 1 Chamber Way, Westerly, RI 02891. **Phone:** (401) 596-7761 or (800) 732-7636.

FLYING HORSE CAROUSEL, Watch Hill Beach at Bay St., was built in 1867. Each horse is hand-carved and has a real horsehair tail and mane and a leather saddle. **Time:** Allow 30 minutes minimum. **Hours:** Daily 11-9, July 1-Labor Day; Sat.-Sun. noon-5, day after Labor Day-Columbus Day. **Cost:** Fare $1.50. Open only to children ages 2-12. **Phone:** (401) 348-6007.

WEST GREENWICH (C-2) elev. 327′

RECREATIONAL ACTIVITIES

Horseback Riding

• **Stepping Stone Ranch**, 201 Escoheag Hill Rd., West Greenwich, RI 02817. **Hours:** Daily 9-4:30, May-Oct.; Sat.-Sun. 10-3:30, rest of year. Closed some holidays. Reservations are required. **Phone:** (401) 397-3725.

WICKFORD (D-4) elev. 5′

Settled in 1707, Wickford was a key port for shipping produce from the rich plantations of South County to the bustling markets of Newport. Commerce came to a halt during the Revolutionary War, but Wickford's economy rebounded with a shipping boom 1780-1830. Many houses from this period still stand.

Nearby in North Kingstown, the Quonset Air Museum, 488 Eccleston Ave., chronicles Rhode Island's aviation history while allowing visitors to observe aircraft from World War II to the post-Vietnam War era being restored; phone (401) 294-9540.

Martha's Vineyard Fast Ferry operates from Quonset Point at 1347 Roger Williams Way in North Kingstown to Oak Bluffs, Martha's Vineyard, with daily departures late May to mid-October; for information or reservations phone (401) 295-4040.

OLD NARRAGANSETT CHURCH, Church Ln. off Main St., was built in 1707 and was moved to its present site in 1800. Among the oldest Episcopal churches in the country, the church is one of the state's four original Colonial parishes. Of interest are the box pews, wineglass pulpit and slave gallery. The church organ dates from 1660. Communion silver donated by Queen Anne still is used for services the first Sunday in August, designated Queen Anne Sunday. **Tours:** Guided tours are available. **Hours:** Guided tours are given Thurs.-Mon. 11-4, July-Aug. **Cost:** Free. **Phone:** (401) 294-4357.

SMITH'S CASTLE, 1.5 mi. n. on US 1 to 55 Richard Smith Dr., is a historic house museum built in 1678 by Richard Smith Jr. Members of the prominent Updike family, which later laid out Wickford, lent prestige to the plantation when they inherited much of the property in 1692. The house has been a trading post, a slaveholding plantation and a successful dairy farm. Docents in period costumes interpret 4 centuries of life within the house.

Tours: Guided tours are available. **Hours:** Guided tours are given Thurs.-Sun. at noon, 1, 2 and 3, June-Aug.; Fri.-Sun. at noon, 1, 2 and 3 in May and Sept.-Oct.; phone for appointment rest of year. Grounds open daily. **Cost:** Guided tour $5; $1 (ages 6-12). Grounds free. **Phone:** (401) 294-3521.

WOONSOCKET (A-3) pop. 43,224, elev. 162′

MUSEUM OF WORK AND CULTURE is off SR 146, 2 mi. n. on SR 104/Providence St./S. Main St. to 42 S. Main St. Exhibits housed in a former textile mill tell the stories of French Canadian immigrants who left their farms to work in local mills prior to the Great Depression. Displays trace difficulties due to low-paying jobs; grim factory conditions; the establishment of organized labor; and ultimate successes as the workers acclimated to American life. Hands-on displays, films and walk-through sets are included.

The renovated Rhode Island box car of the Merci Train is on display. The 49-car train arrived in the United States in 1949 filled with gifts from French citizens who were grateful for American relief aid they had received after World War II.

Hours: Tues.-Fri. 9:30-4, Sat. 10-5, Sun. 1-4. Closed major holidays. **Cost:** $7; $5 (ages 62+ and students with ID); free (ages 0-9). **Phone:** (401) 769-9675.

America on the Move is made possible by generous support from General Motors Corporation, AAA, State Farm Companies Foundation, The History Channel, United States Congress, U.S. Department of Transportation, Exxon Mobil, American Public Transportation Association, American Road & Transportation Builders Association, Association of American Railroads, National Asphalt Pavement Association, The UPS Foundation.

No matter the Disney destination, the smiles are always the same.

Let a AAA/CAA Travel professional help you get there.

A Disney vacation can take you to the world's greatest Theme Parks, *Walt Disney World* Resort in Florida and *Disneyland* Resort in California, and much, much more. Chart a course for magic on *Disney Cruise Line*, featuring fun for every member of the family. Or immerse your family in the stories of some of the world's greatest destinations with *Adventures by Disney*. A brand-new way for you to travel the globe.

Whatever you choose, make sure you book through your AAA/CAA Travel professional to receive exclusive benefits.

DISNEY PARKS
Where dreams come true

238

Save First, Then Travel
with the lowest hotel rates on AAA.com

- **AAA.com**pare:
67% of the time, the lowest rate on standard double occupancy rooms at partner hotels can be found at AAA.com*

- **AAA.com**plete:
Mapping, Diamond Ratings, reviews and destination information

- **AAA.com**fort:
Booking and service from the travel name you trust

Visit your nearest AAA office, click on AAA.com or call 1-866-AAA-SAVE (222-7283).

67% AAA.com
16% AARP℠ · 15% Travelocity · 11% Orbitz · 10% Expedia

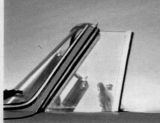

Show Your Card & Save

Connecticut

Old Lighthouse Museum,
Stonington
© Ric Ergenbright
Danita Delimont Stock
Photography

AVON—See Hartford p. 268.

BERLIN—See Hartford p. 269.

BETHEL pop. 9,137

BEST WESTERN BERKSHIRE INN   *Book great rates at AAA.com*   **Phone:** (203)744-3200

Hotel
$109-$139 All Year

Address: 11 Stony Hill Rd (US 6) 06801 **Location:** I-84, exit 8, just e. **Facility:** 69 one-bedroom standard units. 3 stories, interior corridors. **Parking:** on-site. **Amenities:** high-speed Internet, voice mail, irons, hair dryers. **Guest Services:** valet laundry, wireless Internet. **Business Services:** business center. **Free Special Amenities: expanded continental breakfast and room upgrade (subject to availability with advance reservations).**

AAA Benefit:
Members save up to 20%, plus 10% bonus points with rewards program.

MICROTEL INN & SUITES   *Book at AAA.com*   **Phone:** (203)748-8318

Hotel
$79-$99 All Year

Address: 80 Benedict Rd 06801 **Location:** I-84, exit 8, 1 mi e on US 6. **Facility:** 78 one-bedroom standard units. 2 stories (no elevator), interior corridors. *Bath:* combo or shower only. **Parking:** on-site. **Amenities:** high-speed Internet, voice mail, irons, hair dryers. *Some:* dual phone lines. **Guest Services:** valet laundry, wireless Internet. **Business Services:** meeting rooms, business center.

STONY HILL INN   *Book great rates at AAA.com*   **Phone:** (203)743-5533

Motel
$75-$120 All Year

Address: 50 Stony Hill Rd (US 6) 06801 **Location:** I-84, exit 8, 0.8 mi e. **Facility:** 36 one-bedroom standard units. 1 story, exterior corridors. *Bath:* combo or shower only. **Parking:** on-site. **Amenities:** voice mail, irons, hair dryers. *Some:* high-speed Internet. **Pool(s):** outdoor. **Leisure Activities:** *Fee:* driving range. **Guest Services:** coin laundry, wireless Internet. **Business Services:** meeting rooms. **Free Special Amenities: continental breakfast and local telephone calls.**

------ WHERE TO DINE ------

SYCAMORE DRIVE IN   **Phone:** 203/748-2716

American
$2-$11

A diner theme weaves through the upbeat and nostalgic 1950s drive-in restaurant, which displays Elvis and James Dean photographs and has black-and-white-checkered flooring and a working jukebox. Drivers blink their car lights to get curbside service. French-style burgers made with 100 percent U.S. Choice ground round steak are ground daily on site. Also on the menu are franks, club sandwiches and homemade root beer, the recipe for which was handed down from the original owners. Casual dress. **Reservations:** not accepted. **Hours:** 7 am-9 pm. Closed major holidays. **Address:** 282 Greenwood Ave 06801 **Location:** Jct SR 53, just e on SR 302. **Parking:** on-site.

BOZRAH

FITCH CLAREMONT VINEYARD B&B   **Phone:** 860/889-0260

Historic Bed
& Breakfast
$159-$189 All Year

Address: 83 Fitchville Rd 06334 **Location:** SR 2, exit 24 westbound, 0.4 mi e; exit 23 eastbound, just n, then 1.7 mi e. Located in a quiet area. **Facility:** Built in 1790 nestled in a working vineyard, the inn offers individually decorated rooms with gas fireplaces and a sunroom overlooking the vineyard. Smoke free premises. 4 one-bedroom standard units, some with whirlpools. 2 stories (no elevator), interior corridors. **Parking:** on-site. **Terms:** office hours 10 am-10 pm, 2 night minimum stay - weekends, 14 day cancellation notice-fee imposed. **Amenities:** hair dryers. **Guest Services:** wireless Internet. **Business Services:** fax.

BRANFORD pop. 28,683   (See map and index starting on p. 300)

AMERICAS BEST VALUE INN   *Book great rates at AAA.com*   **Phone:** (203)488-4381   **22**

Motel
$55-$90 5/1-10/31
$55-$85 11/1-4/30

Address: 565 E Main St 06405 **Location:** I-95, exit 56, 0.4 mi w on US 1. **Facility:** 22 one-bedroom standard units. 1 story, exterior corridors. **Parking:** on-site. **Terms:** cancellation fee imposed. **Amenities:** hair dryers. *Some:* irons. **Guest Services:** wireless Internet.

BAYMONT INN & SUITES   *Book great rates at AAA.com*   **Phone:** (203)488-4991   **23**

Hotel
$99-$179 5/1-10/31
$59-$109 11/1-4/30

Address: 3 Business Park Dr 06405 **Location:** I-95, exit 56, just n. **Facility:** 85 one-bedroom standard units. 2 stories (no elevator), interior corridors. **Parking:** on-site, winter plug-ins (fee). **Amenities:** voice mail, irons, hair dryers. **Pool(s):** heated indoor. **Leisure Activities:** saunas, whirlpool, exercise room. **Guest Services:** coin laundry, wireless Internet. **Business Services:** meeting rooms. **Free Special Amenities: expanded continental breakfast and high-speed Internet.**

(See map and index starting on p. 300)

HOLIDAY INN EXPRESS *Book great rates at AAA.com*

Phone: (203)488-4035 **25**

Hotel
$110-$130 All Year

Address: 309 E Main St 06405 **Location:** I-95, exit 55, 0.4 mi w. **Facility:** 96 one-bedroom standard units. 3 stories, interior corridors. *Bath:* combo or shower only. **Parking:** on-site. **Terms:** check-in 4 pm. **Amenities:** high-speed Internet, voice mail, irons, hair dryers. **Pool(s):** heated indoor. **Leisure Activities:** whirlpool, exercise room. **Guest Services:** valet and coin laundry, wireless Internet. **Business Services:** meeting rooms, business center. **Free Special Amenities:** expanded continental breakfast and high-speed Internet.

RODEWAY INN & SUITES *Book great rates at AAA.com*

Phone: (203)481-4528 **24**

Motel
$69-$95 All Year

Address: 81 Leetes Island Rd 06405 **Location:** I-95, exit 56, just s. **Facility:** 32 one-bedroom standard units. 2 stories (no elevator), exterior corridors. **Parking:** on-site. **Terms:** 7 day cancellation notice. **Amenities:** voice mail, irons, hair dryers. *Some:* safes. **Leisure Activities:** picnic tables, outdoor gas grills, horseshoes. **Guest Services:** coin laundry, airport transportation-Tweed New Haven Regional Airport, wireless Internet. **Free Special Amenities: continental breakfast and high-speed Internet.**

---- **WHERE TO DINE** ----

PASTA COSI

Phone: 203/483-9397 **30**

Italian
$13-$26

Typically when the chef owns the restaurant you can expect some surprisingly ambitious food creations, and that observation is true here. Their specialties of ravioli, fresh-made pasta and sauce, steak Marsala, lobster a la vodka and others prove this point. Casual dress. **Bar:** Beer & wine. **Reservations:** suggested. **Hours:** 5 pm-10 pm, Sun from 4 pm. Closed major holidays; also Mon. **Address:** 1018 Main St 06405 **Location:** Between Park Pl and Harrison Ave; center. **Parking:** on-site.

USS CHOWDER POT III

Phone: 203/481-2356 **29**

Seafood
$7-$29

Locals and tourists alike rave about the good food, attentive service and creative nautical decor. A long-time favorite is the lobster bisque—a thick, creamy concoction full of lobster chunks. Prime rib is also featured. Buffet is served 5 pm-6:30 pm. Casual dress. Entertainment. **Bar:** Full bar. **Reservations:** not accepted. **Hours:** 11:30 am-9 pm, Fri & Sat-10 pm, Sun noon-9 pm; hours vary in summer. Closed: 11/25, 12/25. **Address:** 560 E Main St 06405 **Location:** I-95, exit 56, just n on US 1. **Parking:** on-site.

BRIDGEPORT pop. 139,529

BRIDGEPORT HOLIDAY INN & CONVENTION CENTER *Book at AAA.com*

Phone: (203)334-1234

Hotel
$119-$159 All Year

Address: 1070 Main St 06604 **Location:** SR 8, exit 2 northbound, 0.7 mi se; exit southbound, just s, then just e. **Facility:** 209 units. 202 one-bedroom standard units. 7 one-bedroom suites. 9 stories, interior corridors. *Bath:* combo or shower only. **Parking:** on-site (fee). **Amenities:** dual phone lines, voice mail, irons, hair dryers. *Some:* high-speed Internet. **Pool(s):** heated indoor/outdoor. **Leisure Activities:** exercise room. **Guest Services:** valet and coin laundry, area transportation, wireless Internet. **Business Services:** conference facilities, business center.

BRISTOL—See Hartford p. 269.

BROOKFIELD

THE NEWBURY INN *Book at AAA.com*

Phone: (203)775-0220

Motel
$89-$99 All Year

Address: 1030 Federal Rd 06804 **Location:** Jct SR 25, 0.9 mi nw. **Facility:** 46 one-bedroom standard units, some with efficiencies and/or whirlpools. 2 stories (no elevator), interior/exterior corridors. *Bath:* combo or shower only. **Parking:** on-site. **Amenities:** voice mail, irons, hair dryers. *Some:* DVD players. **Guest Services:** wireless Internet. **Business Services:** meeting rooms, business center.

---- **WHERE TO DINE** ----

OSAKA JAPANESE RESTAURANT

Phone: 203/740-7790

Japanese
$8-$20

The casual Japanese restaurant offers good value in its soups, salads, entrees and bento box lunches. Included in the good selection of sushi rolls are California rolls. Casual dress. **Bar:** Full bar. **Reservations:** accepted. **Hours:** noon-3 & 5-10 pm, Fri-11 pm, Sat 5 pm-11 pm, Sun 5 pm-10 pm. Closed: 11/25. **Address:** 777 Federal Rd, #5 06804 **Location:** Jct US 202, 0.6 mi n on US 7. **Parking:** on-site.

BROOKLYN

AMERICAS BEST VALUE INN *Book great rates at AAA.com*

Phone: (860)774-9644

Motel
$70-$110 All Year

Address: 479 Providence Rd (Rt 6) 06234 **Location:** I-395, exit 91, 2 mi w. **Facility:** 22 one-bedroom standard units. 1 story, exterior corridors. **Parking:** on-site. **Terms:** 3 day cancellation notice-fee imposed. **Amenities:** hair dryers. *Some:* irons. **Guest Services:** wireless Internet. **Free Special Amenities: continental breakfast and early check-in/late check-out.**

CENTERBROOK

—— WHERE TO DINE ——

GABRIELLE'S

New American
$12-$28

Phone: 860/767-2440

The simple but elegant dining room offers fine contemporary American preparations of fresh seafood and pasta. All menu items, including the fabulous desserts, are made in-house. Dressy casual. **Bar:** Full bar. **Reservations:** suggested. **Hours:** 11:30 am-2:30 & 5-9:30 pm, Sun 11 am-3 & 5-9:30 pm. Closed: 11/25, 12/25. **Address:** 78 Main St 06409 **Location:** I-9, exit 4 southbound, 0.8 mi w on SR 154 S; exit 3 northbound, 0.9 mi w on SR 154 S. **Parking:** on-site.

CHESHIRE pop. 5,789 (See map and index starting on p. 300)

CHESHIRE RED CARPET INN & SUITES *Book great rates at AAA.com* **Phone: (203)272-3244** **8**

AAA SAVE

Motel
$80-$125 All Year

Address: 1106 S Main St 06410 **Location:** On SR 10, 0.5 mi s of jct SR 42 W. **Facility:** 25 one-bedroom standard units, some with efficiencies (no utensils) and/or whirlpools. 2 stories (no elevator), exterior corridors. **Parking:** on-site. **Terms:** cancellation fee imposed. **Amenities:** high-speed Internet, voice mail, irons, hair dryers. **Guest Services:** coin laundry, wireless Internet.

CHESTER

—— WHERE TO DINE ——

RIVER TAVERN

New American
$8-$32

Phone: 860/526-9417

The tavern entices tourists who can sit by the back window and look out at the river or sit up front to see the activity around the many boutique shops on Main Street. The modern dining room displays colorful art on yellow walls and has retro-style chairs at tables and at the bar. The talented chef uses fresh local ingredients whenever possible in seasonally changing dishes such as hand-made tagliatelle pasta with a spicy bacon, asparagus and Parmesan cream sauce. Casual dress. **Bar:** Full bar. **Reservations:** suggested. **Hours:** 11:30 am-2:30 & 5:30-9:30 pm, Fri & Sat-10:30 pm, Sun 11 am-2:30 & 4:30-9 pm. Closed: 1/1, 12/25. **Address:** 23 Main St 06412 **Location:** SR 9, exit 6 1.2 mi ne on SR 148. **Parking:** street.

CLINTON pop. 3,516

CLINTON MOTEL

AAA SAVE

Motel
$62-$98 5/1-10/31
$52-$82 11/1-4/30

Phone: 860/669-8850

Address: 163 E Main St 06413 **Location:** I-95, exit 64, 1.9 mi s; jct US 1 and SR 145. **Facility:** 15 one-bedroom standard units. 1 story, exterior corridors. **Parking:** on-site. **Amenities:** irons, hair dryers. **Pool(s):** outdoor. **Guest Services:** wireless Internet. **Free Special Amenities:** local telephone calls and high-speed Internet.

COVENTRY

SPECIAL JOYS BED & BREAKFAST

Bed & Breakfast
$75 All Year

Phone: (860)742-6359

Address: 41 N River Rd 06238 **Location:** US 44, 1.1 mi s on SR 31, just e. **Facility:** English-style gardens, an antique doll shop and a sunroom enhance the B&B, which offers a full breakfast daily. Smoke free premises. 2 one-bedroom standard units. 2 stories (no elevator), interior corridors. *Bath:* shower only. **Parking:** on-site. **Terms:** age restrictions may apply, 3 day cancellation notice. ASK

CROMWELL—See Hartford p. 269.

DANBURY pop. 74,848

COMFORT SUITES *Book great rates at AAA.com* **Phone: (203)205-0800**

AAA SAVE

Hotel
$99-$179 All Year

Address: 89 Mill Plain Rd 06811 **Location:** I-84, exit 2 eastbound; exit 2B westbound, just n, then just e. **Facility:** Smoke free premises. 76 one-bedroom standard units, some with whirlpools. 4 stories, interior corridors. **Parking:** on-site. **Amenities:** video games (fee), high-speed Internet, dual phone lines, voice mail, safes, irons, hair dryers. **Pool(s):** heated outdoor. **Leisure Activities:** exercise room. **Guest Services:** valet and coin laundry, wireless Internet. **Business Services:** meeting rooms, business center. **Free Special Amenities:** expanded continental breakfast and high-speed Internet. *(See color ad p 243)*

COURTYARD DANBURY — *Book great rates at AAA.com*

Phone: (203)730-2228

Hotel
$161-$197 All Year

Address: 3 Eagle Rd 06810 **Location:** I-84, exit 8 (Newtown Rd), 0.5 mi w. **Facility:** Smoke free premises. 125 units. 121 one-bedroom standard units, some with whirlpools. 4 one-bedroom suites. 4 stories, interior corridors. *Bath:* combo or shower only. **Parking:** on-site. **Terms:** cancellation fee imposed. **Amenities:** high-speed Internet, dual phone lines, voice mail, irons, hair dryers. **Pool(s):** heated indoor. **Leisure Activities:** whirlpool, exercise room. **Guest Services:** valet and coin laundry, wireless Internet. **Business Services:** meeting rooms, business center.

AAA Benefit:
Members save a minimum 5% off the best available rate.

DANBURY PLAZA HOTEL & CONFERENCE CENTER — *Book at AAA.com*

Phone: (203)794-0600

Hotel
$89-$149 All Year

Address: 18 Old Ridgebury Rd 06810 **Location:** I-84, exit 2 eastbound; exit 2A westbound. **Facility:** 242 one-bedroom standard units. 10 stories, interior corridors. *Bath:* combo or shower only. **Parking:** on-site. **Terms:** cancellation fee imposed. **Amenities:** dual phone lines, voice mail, hair dryers. *Fee:* video games, high-speed Internet. *Some:* fax. **Pool(s):** heated indoor. **Leisure Activities:** exercise room. **Guest Services:** valet and coin laundry, area transportation, wireless Internet. **Business Services:** conference facilities, business center.

ETHAN ALLEN HOTEL — *Book at AAA.com*

Phone: (203)744-1776

Hotel
$95-$144 All Year

Address: 21 Lake Ave Ext 06811 **Location:** I-84, exit 4, 0.3 mi w on US 6 and 202. Located in a commercial area. **Facility:** Smoke free premises. 193 units. 189 one-bedroom standard units. 4 one-bedroom suites. 2-6 stories, interior corridors. **Parking:** on-site. **Terms:** cancellation fee imposed. **Amenities:** video games (fee), voice mail, irons, hair dryers. *Some:* DVD players (fee). **Pool(s):** outdoor. **Leisure Activities:** exercise room. **Guest Services:** complimentary and valet laundry, area transportation, wireless Internet. **Business Services:** conference facilities, business center.

HAMPTON INN DANBURY-BETHEL — *Book great rates at AAA.com*

Phone: (203)748-6677

Hotel
$81-$144 All Year

Address: 81 Newtown Rd 06810 **Location:** I-84, exit 8 (Newtown Rd), just s. **Facility:** 116 one-bedroom standard units. 4 stories, interior corridors. *Bath:* combo or shower only. **Parking:** on-site. **Terms:** 1-7 night minimum stay, cancellation fee imposed. **Amenities:** video games (fee), voice mail, irons, hair dryers. **Pool(s):** heated indoor. **Leisure Activities:** whirlpool, exercise room. **Guest Services:** valet and coin laundry, wireless Internet. **Business Services:** meeting rooms, business center.

AAA Benefit:
Members save up to 10% everyday!

HILTON GARDEN INN DANBURY — *Book great rates at AAA.com*

Phone: (203)205-2000

Hotel
$99-$209 All Year

Address: 119 Mill Plain Rd 06811 **Location:** I-84, exit 1 eastbound, just n, then just e; exit 2B westbound, just n, then just w. **Facility:** 158 one-bedroom standard units. 4 stories, interior corridors. *Bath:* combo or shower only. **Parking:** on-site. **Terms:** 1-7 night minimum stay, cancellation fee imposed. **Amenities:** video games (fee), high-speed Internet, dual phone lines, voice mail, irons, hair dryers. **Pool(s):** heated indoor. **Leisure Activities:** whirlpool, exercise room. **Guest Services:** valet and coin laundry, area transportation-within 5 mi, wireless Internet. **Business Services:** meeting rooms, business center. **Free Special Amenities:** high-speed Internet.

AAA Benefit:
Members save 5% or more everyday!

▼ See AAA listing p 242 ▼

HOLIDAY INN *Book at AAA.com*

Phone: (203)792-4000

Hotel
$94-$159 5/1-10/31
$89-$149 11/1-4/30

Address: 80 Newtown Rd 06810 **Location:** I-84, exit 8 (Newtown Rd), 0.5 mi s on US 6 W. Located in a commercial area. **Facility:** 114 one-bedroom standard units. 4 stories, interior corridors. *Bath:* combo or shower only. **Parking:** on-site. **Amenities:** voice mail, irons, hair dryers. *Some:* high-speed Internet. **Pool(s):** outdoor. **Leisure Activities:** exercise room. **Guest Services:** valet and coin laundry, area transportation, wireless Internet. **Business Services:** meeting rooms, business center.

 / SOME UNITS FEE FEE FEE

MARON HOTEL & SUITES *Book great rates at AAA.com*

Phone: (203)791-2200

Hotel
$89-$189 All Year

Address: 42 Lake Ave Extension 06811 **Location:** I-84, exit 4, 0.5 mi w on US 6 and 202. **Facility:** 87 units. 24 one-bedroom standard units, some with efficiencies and/or whirlpools. 63 one-bedroom suites, some with efficiencies and/or whirlpools. 3 stories, interior corridors. *Bath:* combo or shower only. **Parking:** on-site. **Amenities:** video games (fee), dual phone lines, voice mail, irons, hair dryers. **Leisure Activities:** exercise room. **Guest Services:** valet laundry, wireless Internet. **Business Services:** meeting rooms, business center. **Free Special Amenities: continental breakfast and high-speed Internet.**

 CALL / SOME UNITS FEE

QUALITY INN & SUITES *Book great rates at AAA.com*

Phone: (203)743-6701

Hotel
$81-$129 5/1-10/31
$75-$109 11/1-4/30

Address: 78 Federal Rd 06810 **Location:** I-84, exit 7 (US 7 N), 0.5 mi n to exit 11 (Federal Rd), 0.8 mi s on White Turkey Rd, then just w. **Facility:** 72 one-bedroom standard units. 3 stories, interior corridors. *Bath:* combo or shower only. **Parking:** on-site. **Amenities:** voice mail, safes (fee), irons, hair dryers. *Some:* DVD players (fee), dual phone lines. **Pool(s):** heated indoor. **Leisure Activities:** exercise room. **Guest Services:** valet and coin laundry, wireless Internet. **Business Services:** meeting rooms, business center. **Free Special Amenities: expanded continental breakfast and high-speed Internet.**

 / SOME UNITS

RESIDENCE INN DANBURY *Book great rates at AAA.com*

Phone: (203)797-1256

Extended Stay
Hotel
$161-$197 All Year

Address: 22 Segar St 06810 **Location:** I-84, exit 4 eastbound, just n; exit westbound, just e on Lake Ave Extension, then just s. **Facility:** Smoke free premises. 78 units. 31 one-bedroom standard units, some with efficiencies, kitchens and/or whirlpools. 40 one- and 7 two-bedroom suites, some with kitchens. 4 stories, interior corridors. *Bath:* combo or shower only. **Parking:** on-site. **Terms:** cancellation fee imposed. **Amenities:** high-speed Internet, dual phone lines, voice mail, irons, hair dryers. **Pool(s):** heated indoor. **Leisure Activities:** whirlpool, exercise room. **Guest Services:** valet and coin laundry, area transportation, wireless Internet. **Business Services:** meeting rooms, business center.

 / SOME UNITS FEE

AAA Benefit:
Members save a minimum 5% off the best available rate.

SPRINGHILL SUITES DANBURY *Book great rates at AAA.com*

Phone: (203)744-7333

Hotel
$152-$186 All Year

Address: 30 Old Ridgebury Rd 06810 **Location:** I-84, exit 2 eastbound; exit 2A westbound. **Facility:** Smoke free premises. 106 one-bedroom standard units, some with whirlpools. 4 stories, interior corridors. *Bath:* combo or shower only. **Parking:** on-site. **Terms:** cancellation fee imposed. **Amenities:** video games (fee), high-speed Internet, dual phone lines, voice mail, irons, hair dryers. **Pool(s):** heated indoor. **Leisure Activities:** whirlpool, exercise room. **Guest Services:** valet and coin laundry. **Business Services:** meeting rooms, business center.

CALL

AAA Benefit:
Members save a minimum 5% off the best available rate.

—— WHERE TO DINE ——

CHUCK'S STEAK HOUSE

Phone: 203/792-5555

Steak
$7-$30

Ask for a table near the fireplace or in the solarium at this sprawling roadside family restaurant with a rustic decor. Fresh fish, hearty steak and a crispy vegetable salad bar are featured highlights. Casual dress. **Bar:** Full bar. **Reservations:** not accepted. **Hours:** 11:30 am-2:30 & 4:30-10 pm, Fri & Sat-10:30 pm, Sun 4 pm-10 pm. Closed: 11/25, 12/25. **Address:** 20 Segar St 06810 **Location:** I-84, exit 4. **Parking:** on-site.

CALL

ICHIRO

Phone: 203/792-8881

Japanese
$8-$28

This place is known for hibachi grills where guests enjoy a show from their chef as their food is prepared in front of them. Hibachi dinners include clear broth onion soup, green salad with ginger dressing, hibachi noodles, vegetables and shrimp. The sushi bar, steak dishes and lunch box specials are a great value. Casual dress. **Bar:** Full bar. **Reservations:** accepted. **Hours:** 11 am-3 & 4:30-10 pm, Fri & Sat-11 pm, Sun noon-10 pm. **Address:** 69 Newtown Rd 06810 **Location:** I-84, exit 8 (Newtown Rd), 0.6 mi sw. **Parking:** on-site. CALL

DAYVILLE

COMFORT INN & SUITES *Book at AAA.com*

Phone: (860)779-3200

Hotel
$120-$130 5/1-10/31
$110-$120 11/1-4/30

Address: 16 Tracy Rd 06241 **Location:** I-395, exit 94, just w. **Facility:** 78 one-bedroom standard units. 3 stories, interior corridors. *Bath:* combo or shower only. **Parking:** on-site. **Terms:** cancellation fee imposed. **Amenities:** video games (fee), dual phone lines, voice mail, irons, hair dryers. *Some:* high-speed Internet. **Pool(s):** heated indoor. **Leisure Activities:** exercise room. **Guest Services:** coin laundry, wireless Internet. **Business Services:** meeting rooms, business center.

 CALL / SOME UNITS

EAST HARTFORD—See Hartford p. 270.

EAST HAVEN pop. 28,189   (See map and index starting on p. 300)

QUALITY INN   *Book great rates at AAA.com*   Phone: (203)469-5321

Hotel
$85-$180 5/1-10/15
$69-$84 10/16-4/30

Address: 30 Frontage Rd 06512 **Location:** I-95, exit 51 eastbound, 0.5 mi e; exit westbound, 0.8 mi w on N Frontage Rd to overpass, then 0.8 mi e. **Facility:** 81 one-bedroom standard units, some with whirlpools. 2 stories (no elevator), interior/exterior corridors. *Bath:* combo or shower only. **Parking:** on-site. **Terms:** cancellation fee imposed. **Amenities:** dual phone lines, voice mail, irons, hair dryers. **Pool(s):** outdoor. **Leisure Activities:** exercise room. **Guest Services:** wireless Internet. **Business Services:** PC. **Free Special Amenities:** expanded continental breakfast and high-speed Internet.

EAST WINDSOR—See Hartford p. 270.

ENFIELD—See Hartford p. 271.

Three generations and they all have the same ears.

There's so much in life worth celebrating. But often, our "day to day" has to come before those things that truly last. This is the year to gather with all the people who make you the happiest and celebrate at the place where dreams come true.

Enjoy EXCLUSIVE benefits when you book your *AAA Vacations® Disneyland®* Resort package at your local AAA Travel office, or online at **AAA.com**.

What will you celebrate?

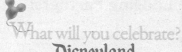

ESSEX pop. 2,573

GRISWOLD INN

Classic Historic
Country Inn
$110-$350 All Year

Phone: 860-767-1776

Address: 36 Main St 06426 **Location:** SR 9, exit 3, 1.3 mi e. **Facility:** Find varied room types at this restored Colonial inn; open since 1776, it's one of the oldest continuously operating inns in the country. Smoke free premises. 31 units. 23 one-bedroom standard units. 8 one-bedroom suites. 3 stories, interior/exterior corridors. *Bath:* combo or shower only. **Parking:** on-site. **Terms:** cancellation fee imposed. **Amenities:** irons, hair dryers. **Dining:** restaurant, see separate listing. **Guest Services:** TV in common area. **Business Services:** meeting rooms. 🍴 ✉ 🅦 / SOME UNITS 🛏

—— **WHERE TO DINE** ——

THE BLACK SEAL SEAFOOD GRILLE

American
$7-$24

Phone: 860-767-0233

In the heart of Essex village, this is a great stop in the midst of browsing the quaint gift shops. Enhancing the casual nautical feel are wood floors and plenty of ship memorabilia. A starter of French onion soup or a group-friendly nacho platter sets the stage for an entree of baked sea scallop casserole with leeks, shiitake mushrooms and tomato in sherry-cream sauce with a Parmesan Ritz cracker crumb crust. Casual dress. **Bar:** Full bar. **Reservations:** not accepted. **Hours:** 11:30 am-10 pm. Closed: 11/25, 12/25. **Address:** 15 Main St 06426 **Location:** Between Nott Ln and Cross St; center. **Parking:** street.

GRISWOLD INN

American
$9-$35

Phone: 860-767-1776

The epitome of New England ambience, this nautical themed eatery serves classic fare in a historic inn near the waterfront. Feast-worthy menu choices include prime rib, country ham and fresh fish. Traditional entertainment is offered nightly in the 250-year-old Tap Room lounge. Casual dress. **Entertainment. Bar:** Full bar. **Reservations:** suggested. **Hours:** 11:30 am-2:30 & 5:30-9 pm, Fri-10 pm, Sat 5 pm-10 pm, Sun 10 am-2 & 5-9 pm; hours vary off season. Closed: 12/25; also for dinner 12/24. **Address:** 36 Main St 06426 **Location:** SR 9, exit 3, 1.3 mi e; in Griswold Inn. **Parking:** on-site. **Classic Historic**

FAIRFIELD

BEST WESTERN BLACK ROCK INN   *Book great rates at AAA.com*

AAA SAVE

Hotel
$119-$209 5/1-10/31
$99-$169 11/1-4/30

Phone: (203)659-2200

Address: 100 Kings Hwy Cutoff 06824 **Location:** I-95, exit 24, just sw. **Facility:** Smoke free premises. 60 units. 56 one-bedroom standard units. 4 one-bedroom suites. 2 stories, interior corridors. *Bath:* combo or shower only. **Parking:** on-site. **Amenities:** video games (fee), high-speed Internet, dual phone lines, voice mail, irons, hair dryers. **Leisure Activities:** exercise room. **Guest Services:** valet laundry, wireless Internet. **Business Services:** business center. **Free Special Amenities:** continental breakfast and newspaper. 🍴 CALL 🅼 ✉ 🎬 🛏 🖥 / SOME UNITS FEE 🐾

AAA Benefit:
Members save up to 20%, plus 10% bonus points with rewards program.

—— **WHERE TO DINE** ——

JOE'S AMERICAN BAR & GRILL

American
$9-$24

Phone: 203/319-1600

If it's Americana you want, you'll get all that and more at Joe's, where the bill of fare includes all-American favorites like hearty burgers, fresh-from-the-oven chicken pot pies, Maryland lump crab cakes, and Joe's classic meatloaf. Pizzas, pastas, steaks and salads round out the extensive menu, giving diners the freedom to choose from a vast selection of offerings. There's nothing more American than that, except, of course, for apple pie, so save some room. Casual dress. **Bar:** Full bar. **Reservations:** not accepted. **Hours:** 11:30 am-10 pm, Fri & Sat-11 pm. Closed: 12/25. **Address:** 750 Post Rd (US 1) 06824 **Location:** I-95, exit 21 eastbound, just se, then 0.9 mi ne; exit 23 westbound, 0.7 mi se. **Parking:** on-site. CALL 🅼

FARMINGTON—See Hartford p. 272.

GLASTONBURY—See Hartford p. 273.

GRANBY—See Hartford p. 273.

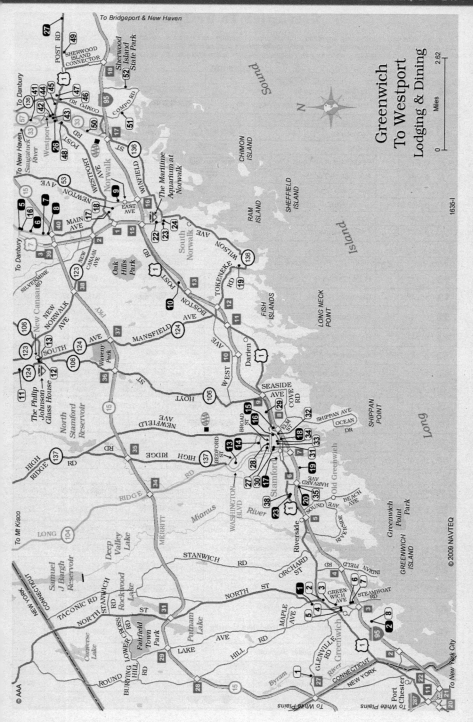

Greenwich
To Westport
Lodging & Dining

1635-I

© 2009 NAVTEQ

© AAA

Greenwich To Westport

This index helps you "spot" where approved lodgings and restaurants are located on the corresponding detailed maps. Lodging daily rate range is for comparison only and show the property's high season. Restaurant rate range is a combination of lunch and/or dinner. Turn to the listing page for more detailed rate information and consult display ads for special promotions.

GREENWICH

Map Page	OA	Lodgings	Diamond Rated	High Season	Page
❶ / p. 247		The Stanton House Inn	◇◇◇	$159-$239	250
❷ / p. 247		Homestead Inn - Thomas Henkelmann	◇◇◇◇	$250-$495	250

Map Page	OA	Restaurants	Diamond Rated	Cuisine	Meal Range	Page
① / p. 247		Rebecca's	◇◇◇	New American	$25-$45	250
② / p. 247		Asiana Cafe	◇◇	Asian	$6-$21	250
③ / p. 247		Restaurant Jean-Louis	◇◇◇	French	$19-$69	250
④ / p. 247		Aux Delices Foods	◇	Breads/Pastries	$7-$13	250
⑤ / p. 247		Elm Street Oyster House	◇◇	Seafood	$18-$35	250
⑥ / p. 247		Riina's Fresco Café	◇◇	Italian	$9-$19	251
⑦ / p. 247		Abis	◇◇	Japanese	$8-$26	250
⑧ / p. 247		Thomas Henkelmann	◇◇◇◇	French	$24-$50	251

NORWALK

Map Page	OA	Lodgings	Diamond Rated	High Season	Page
❺ / p. 247		Hilton Garden Inn Norwalk	◇◇◇	$89-$289	310
❻ / p. 247		Courtyard Norwalk	◇◇◇	$188-$230	309
❼ / p. 247	AAA	**Four Points by Sheraton Norwalk**	◇◇◇	Rates not provided SAVE	310
❽ / p. 247		Homestead Studio Suites-Norwalk-Stamford	◇◇	$105-$149	310
❾ / p. 247	AAA	**Norwalk Inn & Conference Center**	◇◇	$89-$139 SAVE	310
❿ / p. 247	AAA	**Doubletree Hotel-Norwalk**	◇◇◇	$89-$239 SAVE	309

Map Page	OA	Restaurants	Diamond Rated	Cuisine	Meal Range	Page
⑯ / p. 247		Tuscan Oven Trattoria	◇◇◇	Northern Italian	$12-$28	310
⑰ / p. 247		La Paella	◇◇◇	Spanish	$15-$35	310
⑱ / p. 247		Meigas	◇◇◇	Spanish	$15-$38	310
⑲ / p. 247		River Cat Grill	◇◇◇	American	$11-$34	310

STAMFORD

Map Page	OA	Lodgings	Diamond Rated	High Season	Page
⓭ / p. 247	AAA	**Stamford Plaza Hotel and Conference Center** - see color ad p 320	◇◇◇	$119-$349 SAVE	321
⓮ / p. 247		Stamford Suites Hotel	◇◇	$149-$199	321
⓯ / p. 247	AAA	**Amsterdam Hotel - Greenwich/Stamford**	◇◇	$90-$170 SAVE	318
⓰ / p. 247	AAA	**Holiday Inn Stamford Downtown** - see color ad p 319	◇◇◇	$99-$259 SAVE	319
⓱ / p. 247		Hampton Inn & Suites	◇◇◇	$62-$269	318
⓲ / p. 247	AAA	**Stamford Marriott Hotel & Spa** - see color ad p 320	◇◇◇	$209-$239 SAVE	319
⓳ / p. 247	AAA	**Hilton Stamford Hotel & Executive Meeting Center** - see color ad p 318	◇◇◇	$89-$289 SAVE	318
⓴ / p. 247		La Quinta Inn & Suites Stamford	◇◇	$79-$199	319

Map Page	OA	Restaurants	Diamond Rated	Cuisine	Meal Range	Page
㉗ / p. 247		Bennett's Steak & Fish House	◇◇◇	Steak	$13-$39	321
㉘ / p. 247		Telluride	◇◇◇	American	$16-$48	322

Map Page	OA	Restaurants (cont'd)	Diamond Rated	Cuisine	Meal Range	Page
29 / p. 247	AAA	**Brasitas**	◆◆	Latin American	$8-$26	321
30 / p. 247		Il Falco	◆◆◆	Northern Italian	$16-$36	321
31 / p. 247		SBC Downtown	◆◆	American	$7-$22	322
32 / p. 247		Morton's The Steakhouse	◆◆◆	Steak	$26-$42	321
33 / p. 247		Kona Grill	◆◆◆	New American	$9-$30	321
34 / p. 247		P.F. Chang's China Bistro	◆◆◆	Chinese	$7-$20	322
35 / p. 247		City Limits Diner	◆◆	American	$15-$22	321

OLD GREENWICH

Map Page	OA	Lodging	Diamond Rated	High Season	Page
23 / p. 247	AAA	**Hyatt Regency Greenwich**	◆◆◆	$99-$319 (SAVE)	311

Map Page	OA	Restaurant	Diamond Rated	Cuisine	Meal Range	Page
38 / p. 247		Winfield's	◆◆◆	American	$11-$45	312

WESTPORT

Map Page	OA	Lodgings	Diamond Rated	High Season	Page
26 / p. 247		The Inn at National Hall	◆◆◆◆	$355-$895	330
27 / p. 247		The Westport Inn	◆◆◆	$119-$300	331

Map Page	OA	Restaurants	Diamond Rated	Cuisine	Meal Range	Page
41 / p. 247		Coffee An' Donut Shop	◆	Breads/Pastries	$5-$10	331
42 / p. 247		Tavern On Main	◆◆	New England	$10-$32	333
43 / p. 247		ACQUA	◆◆◆	Italian	$10-$38	331
44 / p. 247		Manolo	◆◆◆	Mediterranean	$20-$40	332
45 / p. 247		Dressing Room - A Homegrown Restaurant	◆◆◆	American	$12-$30	331
46 / p. 247		Taipan	◆◆◆	Asian	$8-$24	333
47 / p. 247		The Little Kitchen	◆◆◆	Chinese	$6-$30	331
48 / p. 247		Da Pietro's Restaurant	◆◆	Italian	$13-$36	331
49 / p. 247		Angelina's	◆	Pizza	$6-$15	331
50 / p. 247		River House Tavern	◆◆◆	American	$12-$29	333
51 / p. 247		Splash	◆◆◆	Pacific Rim	$13-$32	333
52 / p. 247		Positano's	◆◆◆	Southern Italian	$17-$32	332

NEW CANAAN

Map Page	OA	Restaurants	Diamond Rated	Cuisine	Meal Range	Page
11 / p. 247		The Roger Sherman Inn	◆◆◆	Continental	$13-$44	299
12 / p. 247		Sole'	◆◆◆	Italian	$14-$38	299
13 / p. 247		Le Pain Quotidien	◆◆	Natural/Organic	$9-$14	298

SOUTH NORWALK

Map Page	OA	Restaurants	Diamond Rated	Cuisine	Meal Range	Page
22 / p. 247		Barcelona Restaurant & Wine Bar	◆◆◆	Mediterranean	$6-$26	317
23 / p. 247		Wasabi Chi	◆◆◆	Japanese	$11-$55	317
24 / p. 247		Match	◆◆◆	New American	$21-$38	317

GREENWICH (See map and index starting on p. 247)

HOMESTEAD INN - THOMAS HENKELMANN   *Book at AAA.com*   Phone: (203)869-7500   2

Historic Boutique
Country Inn
$250-$495 All Year

Address: 420 Field Point Rd 06830 **Location:** I-95, exit 3, just n on Arch St, immediately on Horseneck Ln, then 0.4 mi s. **Facility:** Staff at this elegant country inn go above and beyond by providing attentive service; rooms feature Bulgari amenities, Frette linens and bathrobes. 18 units. 11 one-bedroom standard units. 7 one-bedroom suites. 3 stories (no elevator), interior/exterior corridors. *Bath:* combo or shower only. **Parking:** on-site and valet. **Terms:** age restrictions may apply, 7 day cancellation notice. **Amenities:** high-speed Internet, voice mail, hair dryers. *Some:* DVD players. **Dining:** Thomas Henkelmann, see separate listing. **Guest Services:** valet laundry, wireless Internet. **Business Services:** meeting rooms. 🍴 🍸 🎥

THE STANTON HOUSE INN   Phone: 203/869-2110   1

Historic Bed
& Breakfast
$159-$239 All Year

Address: 76 Maple Ave 06830 **Location:** Just n of US 1; center. **Facility:** A restored inn featuring individually decorated rooms with a country flair; located near fine shops and gourmet restaurants. Smoke free premises. 20 units. 18 one-bedroom standard units. 2 one-bedroom suites. 3 stories (no elevator), interior/exterior corridors. *Bath:* combo or shower only. **Parking:** on-site. **Terms:** office hours 7 am-10 pm, age restrictions may apply, 7 day cancellation notice-fee imposed. **Amenities:** voice mail, irons, hair dryers. *Some:* DVD players, safes. **Pool(s):** outdoor. **Leisure Activities:** horseshoes. **Guest Services:** valet laundry, wireless Internet. **Business Services:** meeting rooms.
🔊 ✕ / SOME UNITS FEE 🛒 ▮

——— WHERE TO DINE ———

ABIS   Phone: 203/862-9100   7

Japanese
$8-$26

Patrons have the choice of sitting in the hibachi room or the traditional Japanese cuisine room. In the hibachi room, guests sit before the chef and are entertained as their meals are whipped up in amusing fashion. The Japanese room features a koi pond and a section with a tatami room in which guests remove their shoes and sit at a table that is low to the floor. Among selections is a wide choice of fresh sushi, sashimi and tempura. Casual dress. **Bar:** Full bar. **Reservations:** accepted. **Hours:** 11:30 am-2:30 & 5:30-9:30 pm, Fri-10:30 pm, Sat noon-2:30 & 5-10:30 pm, Sun 11:30 am-2:30 & 5-9:30 pm. Closed major holidays. **Address:** 381 Greenwich Ave 06830 **Location:** I-95, exit 3, just ne on Arch St, then just s. **Parking:** street.

ASIANA CAFE   Phone: 203/622-6833   2

Asian
$6-$21

The Asia-inspired restaurant serves many classic and contemporary Thai and Vietnamese dishes. Offerings range from sesame chicken and Mandarin beef to pan-seared bass and miso-glazed salmon. The hip, modern decor emphasizes natural elements, wood and metal. Casual dress. **Bar:** Full bar. **Reservations:** suggested. **Hours:** 11 am-10 pm, Fri & Sat-11 pm, Sun noon-10 pm. Closed major holidays. **Address:** 130 E Putnam Ave (US 1) 06830 **Location:** I-95, exit 3 northbound, just n on Arch St, just ne on Field Point Rd, then 0.5 mi ne; exit 4 southbound, 0.6 mi n on Indian Field Rd, then 0.9 mi w. **Parking:** street.

AUX DELICES FOODS   Phone: 203/622-6644   4

Breads/Pastries
$7-$13

This small restaurant appeals to guests looking for a quick yet hearty bite to eat. Most meals are already prepared and displayed in glass cases. A long marble-topped communal table in the middle offers seating, as do outside cafe-style tables. The menu comprises excellent made-from-scratch desserts, salads, sandwiches and some dinner items, such as chicken francaise, eggplant parmigiana and crab cakes. Beverages include many specialty teas, coffees, espressos and cappuccinos. Casual dress. **Reservations:** not accepted. **Hours:** 7:30 am-6:30 pm, Sun-5 pm. Closed major holidays. **Address:** 3 W Elm St 06830 **Location:** I-95, exit 3, just n on Arch St, just nw on Sound View Dr, just ne on Field Point Rd, then just e. **Parking:** street.

ELM STREET OYSTER HOUSE   Phone: 203/629-5795   5

Seafood
$18-$35

Bright and lively decor is a great backdrop for excellent seafood selections along the lines of seared tuna in wasabi and sesame crust; lobster paella with littlenecks, mussels, shrimp and andouille sausage; and pan-fried lump crab cakes with cognac-peppercorn mayonnaise. Casual dress. **Bar:** Full bar. **Reservations:** accepted, for lunch. **Hours:** 11:30 am-10 pm, Fri & Sat-11 pm, Sun 5 pm-9 pm. Closed: 11/25, 12/25. **Address:** 11 W Elm St 06830 **Location:** I-95, exit 3, just n on Arch St, just nw on Sound View Dr, just ne on Field Point Rd, then just e. **Parking:** street.

REBECCA'S   Phone: 203/532-9270   1

New American
$25-$45

Attentive service and carefully prepared dishes can be expected at this minimalist hot spot. Light wood flooring and white-washed walls adorned with calming artwork all play well together. Those interested in watching the chef prepare creations up close can ask to dine at the counter, which overlooks the distinctive glass-enclosed kitchen. The menu changes seasonally but normally incorporates fresh seafood, high-quality meats and chicken. Dressy casual. **Bar:** Full bar. **Reservations:** suggested. **Hours:** Open 5/1-8/28 & 9/7-4/30; 11:30 am-2:30 & 5:30-9:30 pm, Fri-10:30 pm, Sat 5:30 pm-10:30 pm. Closed major holidays; also Sun & Mon. **Address:** 265 Glenville Rd 06831 **Location:** I-95, exit 3, just n on Arch St, just nw on Sound View Dr, just ne on Field Point Rd, 0.6 mi nw on Brookside Dr, then 1.6 mi w. **Parking:** street.

RESTAURANT JEAN-LOUIS   Phone: 203/622-8450   3

French
$19-$69

Since opening in 1985, this refined yet intimate restaurant has been serving some of the best French cuisine in the area. The daily changing five-course degustation menu affords a great way to sample the chef's innovations. Some enticing choices may include caviar, escargots, sea scallops, medallions of beef, filet mignon or braised leg of rabbit. Semi-formal attire. **Bar:** Full bar. **Reservations:** suggested. **Hours:** noon-2 & 6-9 pm. Closed major holidays; also Sat & Sun. **Address:** 61 Lewis St 06830 **Location:** I-95, exit 3, just n on Arch St, just nw on Sound View Dr, just n on Field Point Rd, just ne on W Putnam Ave, just se on Benedict Pl, then just e. **Parking:** street.

(See map and index starting on p. 247)

RIINA'S FRESCO CAFÉ

Italian
$9-$19

Phone: 203/869-6200 ⑥

This small but charming Italian cafe has fresh floral arrangements, contemporary lighting and warm painted walls. A glass bakery case showcase houses desserts that pair well with cappuccino or espresso. The menu features creative twists on panini, pizza and pasta dishes, such as pizza made with fresh arugula, goat cheese, red onion, cannellini beans and tomato with oil and vinegar. Cavatelli rapini with sauteed broccoli rabe, crumbled sausage, caramelized garlic and pecorino cheese delights. Casual dress. **Hours:** 7 am-10 pm, Mon-3 pm. Closed major holidays. **Address:** 375 Greenwich Ave 06830 **Location:** I-95, exit 3, 0.4 mi n on Arch St, then just se. **Parking:** street. CALL 🅜

THOMAS HENKELMANN

French
$24-$50

Phone: 203/869-7500 ⑧

In a historic Victorian home surrounded by gardens and finely manicured lawns, the contemporary country dining room is elegantly decorated with original artwork displayed on the barn board walls. The five-course degustation menu is a great way to taste many of the chef's creative dishes. The changing menu may include lobster bisque, yellowfin tuna, moulard duck and a Grand Marnier souffle to top it all off. Semi-formal attire. **Bar:** Full bar. **Reservations:** suggested. **Hours:** Open 5/1-2/28 & 3/14-4/30; noon-2:30 & 6-9:30 pm, Sat & Sun from 6 pm; hours vary 3/14-3/31. Closed major holidays; also Mon & Sun 1/1-11/30. **Address:** 420 Field Point Rd 06830 **Location:** I-95, exit 3, just n on Arch St, immediately on Horseneck Ln, then 0.4 mi s; in Homestead Inn - Thomas Henkelmann. **Parking:** on-site and valet. **Historic** CALL 🅜

GRISWOLD

AMERICINN LODGE & SUITES OF GRISWOLD *Book great rates at AAA.com*

 (AAA) (SAVE)

Hotel
$90-$270 All Year

Phone: (860)376-3200

Address: 375 Voluntown Rd 06351 **Location:** I-395, exit 85, w on SR 138. **Facility:** 76 units. 70 one-bedroom standard units, some with whirlpools. 6 one-bedroom suites, some with efficiencies and/or whirlpools. 4 stories, interior corridors. *Bath:* combo or shower only. **Parking:** on-site. **Terms:** cancellation fee imposed. **Amenities:** high-speed Internet, voice mail, safes (fee), irons, hair dryers. **Pool(s):** heated indoor. **Leisure Activities:** whirlpool, limited exercise equipment. **Guest Services:** coin laundry, area transportation-casinos, wireless Internet. **Business Services:** meeting rooms, business center. **Free Special Amenities:** expanded continental breakfast and early check-in/late check-out. CALL 🅜 🏊 📷 💻 / SOME UNITS ✕ FEE 🍴 FEE 🍴

GROTON pop. 10,010

BEST WESTERN OLYMPIC INN *Book great rates at AAA.com*

 (AAA) (SAVE)

Hotel
$110-$190 5/1-10/31
$100-$170 11/1-4/30

Phone: (860)445-8000

Address: 360 Rt 12 06340 **Location:** I-95, exit 86, 0.6 mi n. **Facility:** 140 units. 139 one-bedroom standard units, some with whirlpools. 1 one-bedroom suite. 4 stories, interior corridors. **Parking:** on-site. **Amenities:** high-speed Internet, irons, hair dryers. **Dining:** Flanagan's, see separate listing. **Pool(s):** heated indoor. **Leisure Activities:** saunas, whirlpool, exercise room. **Guest Services:** valet and coin laundry, airport transportation-Groton-New London Airport, area transportation-Mohegan Sun casino, bus & train stations, wireless Internet. **Business Services:** meeting rooms, business center. **Free Special Amenities:** full breakfast and high-speed Internet.

✈ 🍴 CALL 🅜 🏊 ✕ 🐾 🍴 🍴 💻 / SOME UNITS ✕

AAA Benefit:
Members save up to 20%, plus 10% bonus points with rewards program.

GROTON INN & SUITES *Book great rates at AAA.com*

(AAA) (SAVE)

Hotel
$129-$219 5/1-10/23
$119-$169 10/24-4/30

Phone: (860)445-9784

Address: 99 Gold Star Hwy 06340 **Location:** I-95, exit 86, 0.3 mi ne on SR 184. **Facility:** 112 units. 69 one-bedroom standard units, some with kitchens. 23 one- and 20 two-bedroom suites with kitchens. 2 stories (no elevator), interior/exterior corridors. **Parking:** on-site. **Terms:** 2 night minimum stay - seasonal and/or weekends. **Amenities:** CD players, irons, hair dryers. *Some:* DVD players (fee), high-speed Internet. **Leisure Activities:** grills, picnic tables, horseshoes. **Guest Services:** valet and coin laundry, wireless Internet. **Business Services:** conference facilities, business center. **Free Special Amenities:** full breakfast and room upgrade (subject to availability with advance reservations).

🍴 🍸 🛁 🐾 🍴 🍴 💻 / SOME UNITS ✕

HAMPTON INN GROTON/MYSTIC/NEW LONDON *Book great rates at AAA.com*

Hotel
Rates not provided

Phone: 860/405-1585

Address: 300 Long Hill Rd/Rt 1 06340 **Location:** I-95, exit 85 northbound; exit 86 southbound, just s on US 1. **Facility:** 80 units. 76 one-bedroom standard units. 4 one-bedroom suites. 4 stories, interior corridors. *Bath:* combo or shower only. **Parking:** on-site. **Amenities:** video games (fee), high-speed Internet, dual phone lines, voice mail, irons, hair dryers. **Pool(s):** heated indoor. **Leisure Activities:** exercise room. **Guest Services:** valet and coin laundry, wireless Internet. **Business Services:** meeting rooms, business center. 🏊 🐾 🍴 🍴 💻 / SOME UNITS ✕

AAA Benefit:
Members save up to 10% everyday!

HILTON GARDEN INN MYSTIC/GROTON

Book great rates at AAA.com   **Phone:** (860)445-6800

Hotel
$99-$219 All Year

Address: 224 Gold Star Hwy 06340 **Location:** I-95, exit 86 northbound, 0.5 mi ne; exit southbound, just n on US 1, then 0.4 mi ne on SR 184. **Facility:** 128 one-bedroom standard units, some with whirlpools. 4 stories, interior corridors. *Bath:* combo or shower only. **Parking:** on-site. **Terms:** 1-7 night minimum stay, cancellation fee imposed. **Amenities:** high-speed Internet, voice mail, irons, hair dryers. **Pool(s):** heated indoor. **Leisure Activities:** whirlpool, exercise room. **Guest Services:** valet and coin laundry, wireless Internet. **Business Services:** meeting rooms, business center.

⊞ Hilton **Garden Inn**

AAA Benefit:
Members save 5% or more everyday!

🍴 🍸 CALL 🛗M 🏊 🐾 🔒 📷 💻 / SOME UNITS ✕

MYSTIC MARRIOTT HOTEL & SPA

Book great rates at AAA.com   **Phone:** (860)446-2600

(AAA) [SAVE]

Hotel
$199-$289 All Year

Address: 625 North Rd (SR 117) 06340 **Location:** I-95, exit 88, just ne. **Facility:** An upscale elegance is found throughout this classic, modern hotel; the two-story lobby features fresh flower arrangements and a Starbucks. Smoke free premises. 285 units. 283 one-bedroom standard units, some with whirlpools. 2 one-bedroom suites with whirlpools. 6 stories, interior corridors. *Bath:* combo or shower only. **Parking:** on-site and valet. **Terms:** check-in 4 pm, cancellation fee imposed. **Amenities:** CD players, dual phone lines, voice mail, safes, irons, hair dryers. *Fee:* video games, high-speed Internet. *Some:* DVD players. **Dining:** Octagon, see separate listing. **Pool(s):** heated indoor. **Leisure Activities:** whirlpool, exercise room, spa. *Fee:* steamroom. **Guest Services:** valet and coin laundry, wireless Internet. **Business Services:** conference facilities, business center. *(See color ad p 295)*

Marriott
HOTELS & RESORTS

AAA Benefit:
Members save a minimum 5% off the best available rate.

🍴 CALL 🛗M 🏊 ✕ ✕ 🔒 💻 / SOME UNITS 🔒

FREE newspaper

QUALITY INN

Book great rates at AAA.com   **Phone:** (860)445-8141

(AAA) [SAVE]

Motel
$70-$170 All Year

Address: 404 Bridge St 06340 **Location:** I-95, exit 87 northbound, 0.8 mi se; exit southbound, 0.5 mi s. **Facility:** 110 one-bedroom standard units, some with whirlpools. 2 stories (no elevator), exterior corridors. **Parking:** on-site. **Terms:** check-in 4 pm. **Amenities:** irons, hair dryers. **Pool(s):** heated indoor. **Leisure Activities:** exercise room. **Guest Services:** valet and coin laundry, wireless Internet. **Business Services:** meeting rooms, PC. **Free Special Amenities:** expanded continental breakfast and high-speed Internet. 🏊 🔒 💻 / SOME UNITS ✕ 🔒 📷

——— WHERE TO DINE ———

FLANAGAN'S

Phone: 860/445-6511

(AAA)

American
$5-$17

Classic dishes are made with fresh ingredients. The pub nurtures a laid-back atmosphere. Casual dress. **Bar:** Full bar. **Reservations:** accepted. **Hours:** 6 am-10 pm, Fri-11 pm, Sat 7 am-11 pm, Sun 7 am-10 pm. Closed: 4/4, 11/25, 12/25. **Address:** 360 Rt 12 06340 **Location:** I-95, exit 86, 0.6 mi n; in Best Western Olympic Inn. **Parking:** on-site.

OCTAGON

Menu on AAA.com   **Phone:** 860/326-0360

(AAA)

Steak
$18-$30

Amid crisp decor is an eight-sided open grill, where artfully presented and multi-dimensional choices— including fresh, local seafood and the highest-caliber beef—are prepared. Service is sharp. Dressy casual. **Bar:** Full bar. **Reservations:** suggested, weekends. **Hours:** 5:30 pm-9 pm; Fri & Sat-10 pm. **Address:** 625 North Rd (SR 117) 06340 **Location:** I-95, exit 88, just ne; in Mystic Marriott Hotel & Spa. **Parking:** on-site and valet. CALL 🛗M

GUILFORD

COMFORT INN

Book at AAA.com   **Phone:** (203)453-5600

Hotel
$69-$189 All Year

Address: 300 Boston Post Rd 06437 **Location:** I-95, exit 59, just s, then 0.3 mi se on US 1. **Facility:** 45 one-bedroom standard units. 2 stories, interior corridors. **Parking:** on-site. **Terms:** 2 night minimum stay - seasonal and/or weekends, 7 day cancellation notice-fee imposed. **Amenities:** high-speed Internet, voice mail, safes, irons, hair dryers. **Guest Services:** wireless Internet. **Business Services:** meeting rooms, business center. (ASK) 🛗 🔒 📷 💻 / SOME UNITS ✕

TOWER INN & SUITES

Book at AAA.com   **Phone:** (203)453-9069

Motel
$60-$160 All Year

Address: 320 Boston Post Rd 06437 **Location:** I-95, exit 59, just s, then just se on US 1. **Facility:** 19 units. 7 one-bedroom standard units. 12 one-bedroom suites. 1-2 stories, exterior corridors. **Parking:** on-site. **Terms:** 2 night minimum stay - seasonal and/or weekends, 7 day cancellation notice-fee imposed. **Amenities:** high-speed Internet, irons, hair dryers. **Guest Services:** wireless Internet.

(ASK) 🔒 📷 💻 / SOME UNITS ✕

—— **WHERE TO DINE** ——

THE PLACE

Seafood
$10-$16

Phone: 203/453-9276

Dining experiences are memorable at the outdoor clambake. Since 1971, patrons have sat on tree-stump chairs to watch cooks prepare their meals over the fire pit. The menu is limited to shellfish, lobster, chicken, steak and corn on the cob. The owners encourage guests to bring their own drinks and other dinner accompaniments, such as salad or beans. A large, red-and-white canopy protects diners from the elements in case of bad weather. Casual dress. **Hours:** Open 5/1-10/31; 5 pm-9 pm, Fri-10 pm, Sat 1 pm-10 pm, Sun noon-9 pm. **Address:** 901 Boston Post Rd (US 1) 06437 **Location:** I-95, exit 58 northbound, 0.4 mi s on SR 77, then just e; exit 59 southbound, 0.3 mi n on Goose Ln, then 0.7 mi w. **Parking:** on-site. 🗐

SHORELINE DINER & VEGETARIAN ENCLAVE

American
$5-$13

Phone: 203/458-7380

Large selections of vegetarian meals, breakfast items, Greek specialties and American favorites—such as nachos and bacon cheeseburgers—are served by friendly staff. Casual dress. **Reservations:** not accepted. **Hours:** 7 am-11 pm. Closed: 12/25. **Address:** 345 Boston Post Rd (US 1) 06437 **Location:** I-95, exit 59, just se on Goose Ln, then just e. **Parking:** on-site.

THE STONE HOUSE RESTAURANT

Seafood
$9-$28

Phone: 203/458-3700

Just steps from the restaurant's front door, fresh lobster and fish arrive by boat. Here they are expertly prepared and served along with other favorites such as stuffed clams oreganato, roasted rack of lamb with garlic popover and white bean Provencal. Also worth consideration are warm oysters, Maryland crab cakes, seared diver scallops, grilled swordfish and grilled aged sirloin. The pub serves lighter fare. Dressy casual. **Bar:** Full bar. **Reservations:** suggested. **Hours:** 11:30 am-3 & 5-10 pm, Sun noon-3 & 5-9 pm. Closed: 12/24, 12/25; also Mon. **Address:** 506 Whitfield St 06437 **Location:** I-95, exit 58, 2 mi se via SR 77. **Parking:** on-site.

HAMDEN   (See map and index starting on p. 300)

CLARION HOTEL & SUITES HAMDEN-NEW HAVEN   *Book at AAA.com*

Motel
$129-$139 All Year

Phone: (203)288-3831   **16**

Address: 2260 Whitney Ave 06518 **Location:** Just n off SR 15, exit 61. **Facility:** 103 units. 87 one-bedroom standard units. 16 one-bedroom suites, some with whirlpools. 2-4 stories, interior corridors. *Bath:* combo or shower only. **Parking:** on-site. **Terms:** check-in 4 pm. **Amenities:** high-speed Internet, dual phone lines, voice mail, irons, hair dryers. **Pool(s):** heated indoor. **Leisure Activities:** whirlpool, exercise room. **Guest Services:** valet laundry, wireless Internet. **Business Services:** meeting rooms, business center. [ASK] [🍴] CALL [&M] 🏊 ✕ 🎦 💻 / SOME UNITS 🐾 🛗 🖨

—— **WHERE TO DINE** ——

KUMO

Japanese
$7-$32

Phone: 203/281-3166   **26**

Simple yet attractive Asian decor infuses some tatami seating areas, the sushi counter and hibachi grills where guests watch as chefs prepare meals in front of them. Choices include a wide variety of fresh sushi, sashimi and tempura. Casual dress. **Bar:** Full bar. **Reservations:** accepted. **Hours:** 11 am-3 & 4:30-10:30 pm, Fri & Sat-11 pm, Sun noon-10 pm. Closed: 11/25. **Address:** 218 Skiff St 06514 **Location:** I-91, exit 6, 0.8 mi nw on Willow St, 3.4 mi n on Whitney Ave, then just nw. **Parking:** on-site.

RISTORANTE LUCE

International
$11-$29

Phone: 203/230-0228   **25**

Elegant art deco appointments and excellent service make this restaurant a local favorite for a special evening out. Fresh fish, pasta and certified Angus beef are wonderful suggestions. The wine list, which includes more than 1,000 selections, spans five decades. Dressy casual. **Bar:** Full bar. **Reservations:** suggested. **Hours:** 11:30 am-2:30 & 5-9:30 pm, Sat from 5 pm, Sun 2 pm-8 pm. Closed major holidays. **Address:** 2987 Whitney Ave 06518 **Location:** SR 40 N, exit SR 10, just n. **Parking:** on-site.

Destination Hartford
pop. 121,578

Capitol Avenue, Hartford.

Richard Cummins
Lonely Planet Images

*A*n appreciation and reverence for history and a sense of purpose for the future come together in an appealing blend in Hartford.

*V*estiges of its Colonial New England past can be seen in homes and gardens restored to their 18th- and 19th-century splendor. The arts are enjoyed in museums and concerts that feature classic as well as contemporary works. Downtown parks are abloom with roses and tempt visitors with an old-fashioned carousel and riverfront walkways—all enticements difficult to resist.

Bushnell Park, Hartford.
(See listing page 45)

© Gibson Stock Photography

MASSACHUSETTS
CONNECTICUT

See Vicinity
map page 256

Farmington
Plainville
Bristol
Southington

*P*laces included in this AAA Destination City:

New England Air Museum, Windsor Locks.
(See listing page 61)

© James Schwabel / Alamy

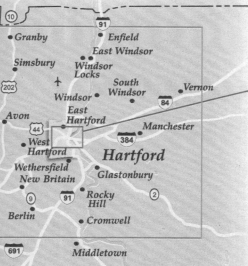

See Downtown
map page 256

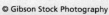

© Gibson Stock Photography

Hill-Stead Museum, Farmington.
(See listing page 56)

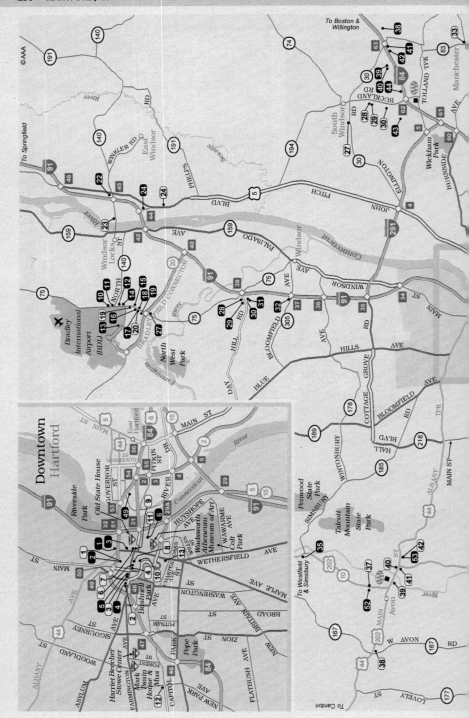

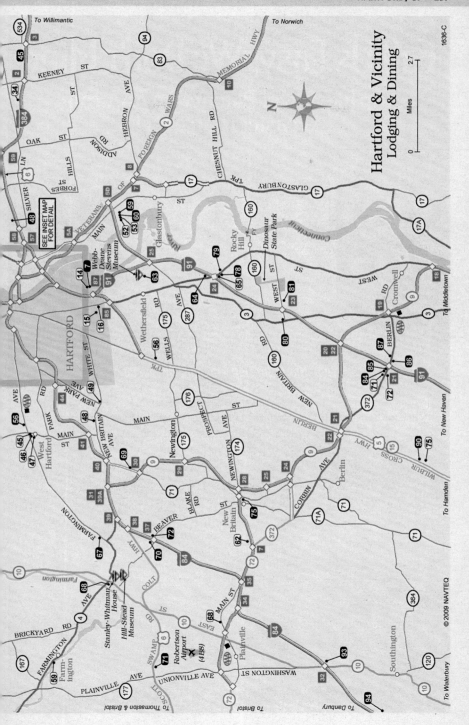

Hartford & Vicinity
Lodging & Dining

1636-C

N

Miles
0   2.7

© 2009 NAVTEQ

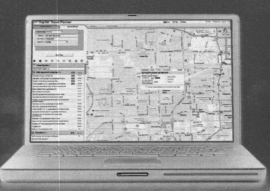

✈ Airport Accommodations

Map Page	OA	BRADLEY INTERNATIONAL	Diamond Rated	High Season	Page
27 / p. 256		Hampton Inn Hartford/Airport, 1.5 mi e of airport	▽▽▽	$89-$179	281
12 / p. 256	AAA	**Days Inn Bradley International Airport, 1 mi e of airport**	▽▽	Rates not provided SAVE	282
17 / p. 256	AAA	**Doubletree Hotel Bradley International Airport, 1.5 mi e of airport**	▽▽	$90-$210 SAVE	282
15 / p. 256		Fairfield Inn Hartford-Airport, 1 mi e of airport	[fyi]	$129-$139	282
10 / p. 256		Holiday Inn Express Bradley Airport, 1.1 mi se of airport	▽▽▽	Rates not provided	283
18 / p. 256		Homewood Suites by Hilton, 1.3 mi e of airport	▽▽▽	$109-$179	283
16 / p. 256		La Quinta Inn Hartford-Airport, 1.3 mi e of airport	▽▽	$65-$129	283
19 / p. 256		Ramada Inn Bradley International Airport, 1.5 mi e of airport	▽▽	$89-$99	283
13 / p. 256	AAA	**Sheraton Hotel At Bradley International Airport, inside airport**	▽▽▽	$109-$299 SAVE	283

Hartford and Vicinity

This index helps you "spot" where approved lodgings and restaurants are located on the corresponding detailed maps. Lodging daily rate range is for comparison only and show the property's high season. Restaurant rate range is a combination of lunch and/or dinner. Turn to the listing page for more detailed rate information and consult display ads for special promotions.

HARTFORD

Map Page	OA	Lodgings	Diamond Rated	High Season	Page
1 / p. 256		Crowne Plaza Hartford Downtown	▽▽▽	$99-$199	264
2 / p. 256	AAA	**The Hilton Hartford Hotel**	▽▽▽	$109-$259 SAVE	264
3 / p. 256		Residence Inn by Marriott Downtown Hartford	▽▽▽	$220-$268	265
4 / p. 256	AAA	**Holiday Inn Express Downtown Hartford**	▽▽▽	$99-$189 SAVE	264
5 / p. 256		Homewood Suites by Hilton Hartford Downtown	▽▽▽	$139-$219	265
6 / p. 256	AAA	**Marriott Hartford Downtown**	▽▽▽▽	$287-$351 SAVE	265
7 / p. 256		Holiday Inn Express Hotel & Suites Hartford	▽▽▽	$100-$145	264

Map Page	OA	Restaurants	Diamond Rated	Cuisine	Meal Range	Page
1 / p. 256		M & M Coffee Shop	▽▽	New American	$5-$26	266
2 / p. 256		Hot Tomato's	▽▽	Northern Italian	$9-$32	266
3 / p. 256		Black Eyed Sally's	▽▽	Barbecue	$8-$21	265
4 / p. 256		The Asylum Cafe	▽▽	Italian	$8-$25	265
6 / p. 256		Max Downtown	▽▽▽	Steak	$8-$38	267
7 / p. 256		Morton's The Steakhouse	▽▽▽	Steak	$32-$58	267
8 / p. 256		Trumbull Kitchen	▽▽▽	American	$7-$25	267
9 / p. 256		Spris	▽▽▽	Northern Italian	$15-$35	267
10 / p. 256		Vito's By The Park	▽▽	Italian	$10-$29	267
11 / p. 256		Vivo	▽▽▽	Northern Italian	$12-$39	267

Map Page	OA	Restaurants (cont'd)	Diamond Rated	Cuisine	Meal Range	Page
⑫ / p. 256		Wood-N-Tap Bar & Grill	◆◆	American	$7-$25	267
⑬ / p. 256		Peppercorn's Grill	◆◆◆	Italian	$9-$35	267
⑭ / p. 256		U.S.S. Chowder Pot IV	◆◆	Seafood	$7-$29	267
⑮ / p. 256		Carbone's Restaurant	◆◆◆	Italian	$11-$30	265
⑯ / p. 256		Costa Del Sol Restaurant	◆◆◆	Spanish	$9-$26	265

WINDSOR LOCKS

Map Page	OA	Lodgings	Diamond Rated	High Season	Page
⑩ / p. 256		Holiday Inn Express Bradley Airport	◆◆◆	Rates not provided	283
⑪ / p. 256		SpringHill Suites Hartford Airport/Windsor Locks	◆◆◆	$143-$175	284
⑫ / p. 256	AAA	**Days Inn Bradley International Airport**	◆◆	Rates not provided [SAVE]	282
⑬ / p. 256	AAA	**Sheraton Hotel At Bradley International Airport**	◆◆◆	$109-$299 [SAVE]	283
⑭ / p. 256		Candlewood Suites	◆◆◆	$79-$149	282
⑮ / p. 256		Fairfield Inn Hartford-Airport	[fyi]	$129-$139	282
⑯ / p. 256		La Quinta Inn Hartford-Airport	◆◆	$65-$129	283
⑰ / p. 256	AAA	**Doubletree Hotel Bradley International Airport**	◆◆◆	$90-$210 [SAVE]	282
⑱ / p. 256		Homewood Suites by Hilton	◆◆◆	$109-$179	283
⑲ / p. 256		Ramada Inn Bradley International Airport	◆◆	$89-$99	283

Map Page	OA	Restaurants	Diamond Rated	Cuisine	Meal Range	Page
⑲ / p. 256		Skyline Restaurant	◆◆	Italian	$7-$25	284
⑳ / p. 256		Skooter's	◆	American	$3-$13	284

EAST WINDSOR

Map Page	OA	Lodgings	Diamond Rated	High Season	Page
㉒ / p. 256	AAA	**Comfort Inn**	◆◆◆	$85-$105 [SAVE]	270
㉓ / p. 256	AAA	**Clarion Inn & Suites**	◆◆◆	$73-$86 [SAVE]	270
㉔ / p. 256	AAA	**Holiday Inn Express East Windsor - Airport**	◆◆◆	$70-$110 [SAVE]	271

Map Page	OA	Restaurants	Diamond Rated	Cuisine	Meal Range	Page
㉓ / p. 256		Maine Fish Market	◆◆	Seafood	$7-$25	271
㉔ / p. 256		Jonathan Pasco's	◆◆	Italian	$18-$31	271

WINDSOR

Map Page	OA	Lodgings	Diamond Rated	High Season	Page
㉗ / p. 256		Hampton Inn Hartford/Airport	◆◆◆	$89-$179	281
㉘ / p. 256	AAA	**Courtyard Hartford Windsor**	◆◆◆	$148-$180 [SAVE]	281
㉙ / p. 256		Hartford/Windsor Marriott Airport	◆◆◆	$197-$241	281
㉚ / p. 256		Hilton Garden Inn Hartford North Bradley International Airport	◆◆◆	$89-$199	281
㉛ / p. 256	AAA	**Hyatt Summerfield Suites Hartford North/ Windsor**	◆◆◆	$99-$399 [SAVE]	282
㉜ / p. 256		The Residence Inn by Marriott Hartford-Windsor	◆◆◆	$152-$186	282

SIMSBURY

Map Page	OA	Lodging	Diamond Rated	High Season	Page
35 / p. 256		Simsbury Inn	▽▽▽	$169-$500	277

MANCHESTER

Map Page	OA	Lodgings	Diamond Rated	High Season	Page
38 / p. 256	AAA	**Manchester Super 8 and Conference Center**	▽▽	$65-$150 SAVE	274
39 / p. 256		Residence Inn Hartford/Manchester	▽▽▽	$152-$186	275
40 / p. 256		Courtyard Hartford Manchester	▽▽▽	$140-$171	274
41 / p. 256		Extended StayAmerica Hartford-Manchester	▽▽	$79-$129	274
42 / p. 256	AAA	**Americas Best Value Inn**	▽	$60-$75 SAVE	274
43 / p. 256		Hampton Inn & Suites Hartford-Manchester	▽▽▽	$139-$159	274
44 / p. 256		Fairfield Inn & Suites Hartford Manchester	▽▽▽	$135-$165	274
45 / p. 256	AAA	**The Mansion Inn Bed and Breakfast**	▽▽▽	$105-$180 SAVE	275

Map Page	OA	Restaurants	Diamond Rated	Cuisine	Meal Range	Page
33 / p. 256		Cavey's Restaurant-Italian	▽▽▽	Northern Italian	$16-$30	275
34 / p. 256		Nulli's Restaurant	▽▽	Italian	$6-$17	275

EAST HARTFORD

Map Page	OA	Lodgings	Diamond Rated	High Season	Page
48 / p. 256		Holiday Inn	▽▽▽	$90-$169	270
49 / p. 256	AAA	**Sheraton Hartford Hotel**	▽▽▽	$89-$229 SAVE	270

AVON

Map Page	OA	Lodgings	Diamond Rated	High Season	Page
52 / p. 256		Residence Inn by Marriott Hartford-Avon	▽▽▽	$170-$208	268
53 / p. 256		Avon Old Farms Hotel	▽▽▽	$109-$229	268

Map Page	OA	Restaurants	Diamond Rated	Cuisine	Meal Range	Page
37 / p. 256		Toshi Japanese Restaurant	▽▽	Japanese	$8-$25	268
38 / p. 256		Amici Italian Grill	▽▽▽	Italian	$5-$24	268
39 / p. 256		Carmen Anthony	▽▽▽	Seafood	$11-$50	268
40 / p. 256		Max A Mia Ristorante	▽▽	Italian	$8-$30	268
41 / p. 256		Avon Old Farms Inn	▽▽▽	New American	$7-$25	268
42 / p. 256		Seasons Restaurant	▽▽▽	Continental	$9-$40	268

WEST HARTFORD

Map Page	OA	Lodging	Diamond Rated	High Season	Page
56 / p. 256	AAA	**West Hartford Inn**	▽	$88-$128 SAVE	279

Map Page	OA	Restaurants	Diamond Rated	Cuisine	Meal Range	Page
45 / p. 256		Arugula	▽▽▽	Mediterranean	$10-$33	279
46 / p. 256		Grant's	▽▽▽	American	$8-$38	280
47 / p. 256		Restaurant Bricco	▽▽▽	American	$8-$28	280
48 / p. 256		Tapas	▽▽	Mediterranean	$6-$15	280
49 / p. 256		The Corner Pug	▽▽	English	$8-$26	280

GLASTONBURY

Map Page	OA	Lodgings	Diamond Rated	High Season	Page
59 / p. 256	AAA	**Homewood Suites by Hilton Hartford South-Glastonbury**	▽▽▽	$110-$209 SAVE	273

GLASTONBURY (cont'd)

Map Page	OA	Lodgings (cont'd)	Diamond Rated	High Season	Page
60 / p. 256	AAA	**Hilton Garden Inn Hartford South/Glastonbury**	◆◆◆	$169-$215 SAVE	273

Map Page	OA	Restaurants	Diamond Rated	Cuisine	Meal Range	Page
52 / p. 256		Max Fish	◆◆◆	Seafood	$11-$30	273
53 / p. 256		Max Amore	◆◆◆	Northern Italian	$8-$25	273

WETHERSFIELD

Map Page	OA	Lodgings	Diamond Rated	High Season	Page
63 / p. 256		Chester Bulkley House	◆◆◆	$95-$145	280
64 / p. 256	AAA	**Comfort Inn**	◆◆◆	$99-$179 SAVE	280

Map Page	OA	Restaurant	Diamond Rated	Cuisine	Meal Range	Page
56 / p. 256		Carmen Anthony	◆◆◆	Seafood	$7-$49	281

FARMINGTON

Map Page	OA	Lodgings	Diamond Rated	High Season	Page
67 / p. 256		Homewood Suites by Hilton	◆◆◆	$109-$169	272
68 / p. 256		The Farmington Inn	◆◆◆	$109-$179	272
69 / p. 256		Courtyard by Marriott Hartford-Farmington	◆◆◆	$161-$197	272
70 / p. 256		Marriott Hotel-Farmington	◆◆◆	$180-$220	272
71 / p. 256	AAA	**Centennial Inn Suites**	◆◆	$141-$181 SAVE	272
72 / p. 256		Extended StayAmerica Deluxe Hartford-Farmington	◆◆	$89-$129	272

Map Page	OA	Restaurant	Diamond Rated	Cuisine	Meal Range	Page
59 / p. 256		Apricots	◆◆◆	Continental	$8-$35	273

NEW BRITAIN

Map Page	OA	Lodging	Diamond Rated	High Season	Page
75 / p. 256		La Quinta Inn & Suites New Britain/South Hartford	◆◆◆	$59-$109	276

Map Page	OA	Restaurant	Diamond Rated	Cuisine	Meal Range	Page
62 / p. 256		Great Taste Chinese Restaurant	◆◆◆	Chinese	$7-$35	276

ROCKY HILL

Map Page	OA	Lodgings	Diamond Rated	High Season	Page
78 / p. 256		Hampton Inn-Hartford/Rocky Hill	◆◆◆	$89-$169	276
79 / p. 256	AAA	**Howard Johnson Express Inn**	◆◆	$70-$120 SAVE	277
80 / p. 256		Residence Inn by Marriott Hartford-Rocky Hill	◆◆◆	$180-$190	277
81 / p. 256	AAA	**Hartford Marriott Rocky Hill**	◆◆◆	$170-$208 SAVE	277

Map Page	OA	Restaurant	Diamond Rated	Cuisine	Meal Range	Page
65 / p. 256		Dakota of Rocky Hill	◆◆	American	$8-$26	277

CROMWELL

Map Page	OA	Lodgings	Diamond Rated	High Season	Page
84 / p. 256		Courtyard Hartford Cromwell	◆◆◆	$149-$182	269
85 / p. 256		Super 8	◆	$65-$85	269
86 / p. 256	AAA	**Comfort Inn**	◆◆	$69-$160 SAVE	269
87 / p. 256	AAA	**Crowne Plaza Cromwell**	◆◆◆	$69-$179 SAVE	269

Map Page	OA	Restaurants	Diamond Rated	Cuisine	Meal Range	Page
(71) / p. 256		Oyama Japanese Cuisine	🔷🔷	Japanese	$9-$38	270
(72) / p. 256		Cromwell Diner	🔷	American	$4-$15	270

BERLIN

Map Page	OA	Lodging	Diamond Rated	High Season	Page
(90) / p. 256	🔺🔺🔺	**Best Western New England Inn & Suites**	🔷🔷🔷	$90-$100 SAVE	269

Map Page	OA	Restaurant	Diamond Rated	Cuisine	Meal Range	Page
(75) / p. 256		Hawthorne Inn	🔷🔷🔷	American	$8-$27	269

SOUTHINGTON

Map Page	OA	Lodgings	Diamond Rated	High Season	Page
(93) / p. 256		Holiday Inn Express	🔷🔷🔷	$109-$129	278
(94) / p. 256		Residence Inn Southington	🔷🔷🔷	$152-$186	278

SOUTH WINDSOR

Map Page	OA	Restaurants	Diamond Rated	Cuisine	Meal Range	Page
(27) / p. 256	🔺🔺🔺	**The Mill on the River**	🔷🔷🔷	American	$9-$29	278
(28) / p. 256		Sakura Garden Japanese Steak House	🔷🔷🔷	Japanese	$9-$29	279
(29) / p. 256		Bellini's	🔷🔷🔷	Italian	$7-$25	278
(30) / p. 256		Burtons Grill	🔷🔷🔷	American	$11-$33	278

PLAINVILLE

Map Page	OA	Restaurant	Diamond Rated	Cuisine	Meal Range	Page
(68) / p. 256		J Timothy's Taverne	🔷🔷	American	$8-$29	276

HARTFORD pop. 121,578 (See map and index starting on p. 256)

CROWNE PLAZA HARTFORD DOWNTOWN *Book at AAA.com* **Phone:** (860)549-2400 **1**

Hotel
$99-$199 All Year

Address: 50 Morgan St 06120 **Location:** I-91, exit 32B; I-84, exit 50 eastbound; exit 52 westbound. **Facility:** 350 units. 346 one-bedroom standard units. 4 one-bedroom suites with whirlpools. 18 stories, interior corridors. *Bath:* combo or shower only. **Parking:** on-site (fee). **Amenities:** video games (fee), CD players, high-speed Internet, voice mail, safes, irons, hair dryers. *Some:* dual phone lines. **Pool(s):** outdoor. **Leisure Activities:** exercise room. **Guest Services:** valet and coin laundry, area transportation, wireless Internet. **Business Services:** conference facilities, business center.

THE HILTON HARTFORD HOTEL *Book great rates at AAA.com* **Phone:** (860)728-5151 **2**

(AAA) (SAVE)

Hotel
$109-$259 All Year

Address: 315 Trumbull St 06103 **Location:** Downtown. Located at Civic Center Plaza; next to shopping mall. **Facility:** 393 units. 382 one-bedroom standard units. 7 one-, 3 two- and 1 three-bedroom suites. 22 stories, interior corridors. *Bath:* combo or shower only. **Parking:** on-site (fee). **Terms:** 1-7 night minimum stay, cancellation fee imposed. **Amenities:** dual phone lines, voice mail, irons, hair dryers. **Fee:** video games, high-speed Internet. *Some:* CD players. **Dining:** M & M Coffee Shop, see separate listing. **Pool(s):** heated indoor. **Leisure Activities:** saunas, whirlpool, steamroom, exercise room. **Guest Services:** valet and coin laundry, wireless Internet. **Business Services:** conference facilities, business center. **Free Special Amenities:** newspaper and high-speed Internet.

(H)
Hilton
AAA Benefit:
Members save 5% or
more everyday!

HOLIDAY INN EXPRESS DOWNTOWN HARTFORD *Book great rates at AAA.com* **Phone:** (860)246-9900 **4**

(AAA) (SAVE)

Hotel
$99-$189 All Year

Address: 440 Asylum St 06103 **Location:** I-84, exit 48, just se via Spring St. **Facility:** 96 one-bedroom standard units. 9 stories, interior corridors. *Bath:* combo or shower only. **Parking:** on-site (fee). **Terms:** cancellation fee imposed. **Amenities:** high-speed Internet, dual phone lines, voice mail, irons, hair dryers. **Leisure Activities:** exercise room. **Guest Services:** valet and coin laundry, wireless Internet. **Business Services:** meeting rooms, business center. **Free Special Amenities:** expanded continental breakfast and high-speed Internet.

HOLIDAY INN EXPRESS HOTEL & SUITES HARTFORD *Book at AAA.com* **Phone:** (860)525-1000 **7**

Hotel
$100-$145 All Year

Address: 185 Brainard Rd 06114 **Location:** I-91, exit 27, just e, then just s. **Facility:** 129 units. 128 one-bedroom standard units. 1 one-bedroom suite. 3 stories, interior corridors. *Bath:* combo or shower only. **Parking:** on-site. **Terms:** cancellation fee imposed. **Amenities:** video games (fee), high-speed Internet, dual phone lines, voice mail, irons, hair dryers. **Pool(s):** heated outdoor. **Leisure Activities:** whirlpool, exercise room. **Guest Services:** valet and coin laundry, area transportation, wireless Internet. **Business Services:** meeting rooms, business center.

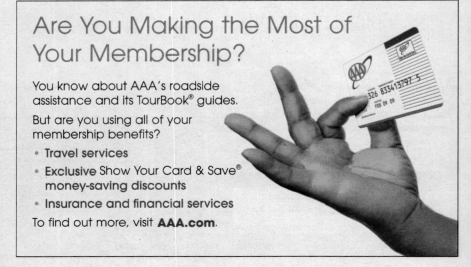

(See map and index starting on p. 256)

HOMEWOOD SUITES BY HILTON HARTFORD DOWNTOWN   *Book great rates at AAA.com*

Phone: (860)524-0223 **5**

Extended Stay Hotel
$139-$219 All Year

Address: 338 Asylum St 06103 **Location:** Between Ann and High sts; downtown. **Facility:** 116 units. 52 one-bedroom standard units with efficiencies. 56 one- and 8 two-bedroom suites with efficiencies. 12 stories, interior corridors. *Bath:* combo or shower only. **Parking:** on-site (fee). **Terms:** 1-7 night minimum stay, cancellation fee imposed. **Amenities:** high-speed Internet, voice mail, irons, hair dryers. *Some:* DVD players. **Leisure Activities:** exercise room. **Guest Services:** valet and coin laundry, wireless Internet. **Business Services:** meeting rooms, business center.

 CALL 🅜 📷 🖥 📠 🖨 / SOME UNITS FEE 🐾 ✕

AAA Benefit:
Members save 5% or more everyday!

MARRIOTT HARTFORD DOWNTOWN   *Book great rates at AAA.com*

Phone: (860)249-8000 **6**

(AAA) SAVE
▼▼▼
Hotel
$287-$351 All Year

Address: 200 Columbus Blvd 06103 **Location:** I-91, exit 29A, just w, exit Columbus Blvd, then just n; downtown. Adjacent to convention center. **Facility:** The lobby offers many areas to relax and socialize; a pool, whirlpool and fitness center provide nice views on the penthouse floor. Smoke free premises. 409 units. 403 one-bedroom standard units. 6 one-bedroom suites. 22 stories, interior corridors. *Bath:* combo or shower only. **Parking:** on-site (fee) and valet. **Terms:** check-in 4 pm, cancellation fee imposed. **Amenities:** CD players, dual phone lines, voice mail, safes, irons, hair dryers. *Fee:* video games, high-speed Internet. **Dining:** Vivo, see separate listing, nightclub. **Pool(s):** heated indoor. **Leisure Activities:** whirlpool, spa. **Guest Services:** valet laundry, area transportation-within 5 mi, wireless Internet. **Business Services:** conference facilities, business center. **Free Special Amenities:** newspaper.

🍽 🍸 CALL 🅜 🏊 ⚕ ✕ 🎬 🖨 / SOME UNITS 🖥

Marriott
HOTELS & RESORTS

AAA Benefit:
Members save a minimum 5% off the best available rate.

RESIDENCE INN BY MARRIOTT DOWNTOWN HARTFORD   *Book great rates at AAA.com*

Phone: (860)524-5550 **3**

▼▼▼
Extended Stay Hotel
$220-$268 All Year

Address: 942 Main St 06103 **Location:** I-91, exit 29A northbound; exit 31 southbound. **Facility:** Smoke free premises. 120 units. 88 one-bedroom standard units, some with efficiencies or kitchens. 18 one- and 14 two-bedroom suites with kitchens. 8 stories, interior corridors. *Bath:* combo or shower only. **Parking:** on-site (fee). **Terms:** cancellation fee imposed. **Amenities:** high-speed Internet, dual phone lines, voice mail, irons, hair dryers. **Leisure Activities:** exercise room. **Guest Services:** valet and coin laundry, wireless Internet. **Business Services:** meeting rooms, business center.

 ✕ 🎬 🖥 📠 🖨 / SOME UNITS FEE 🐾

Residence Inn

AAA Benefit:
Members save a minimum 5% off the best available rate.

WHERE TO DINE

THE ASYLUM CAFE

Phone: 860/524-8651 **4**

Italian
$8-$25

A local favorite for late-night pizzas, calzones and sandwiches, this eatery in the heart of the city occupies a narrow room with a long bar that's open to the dining area. Large plasma-screen TVs can be seen from every seat. Service is always friendly. Casual dress. **Bar:** Full bar. **Reservations:** not accepted. **Hours:** 1 pm-11 pm, Fri & Sat-midnight. Closed major holidays. **Address:** 253 Asylum St 06103 **Location:** Between Ann and Haynes sts; downtown. **Parking:** street. CALL 🅜

BLACK EYED SALLY'S

Phone: 860/278-7427 **3**

▼▼▼
Barbecue
$8-$21

A fun, lively and in-your-face atmosphere shares the stage with great Cajun and Creole barbecue choices. Live blues can be heard four nights a week. Casual dress. **Bar:** Full bar. **Reservations:** suggested. **Hours:** 11:30 am-10 pm, Fri-11 pm, Sat 5 pm-11 pm. Closed major holidays; also Sun. **Address:** 350 Asylum St 06103 **Location:** Between Ann and High sts; downtown. **Parking:** on-site (fee) and street.

CARBONE'S RESTAURANT

Phone: 860/296-9646 **15**

▼▼▼
Italian
$11-$30

Where else but in "Little Italy" would you expect to find such tasty treats as wild mushroom and rice soup, pasta with roasted garlic and sauteed escarole with tender portobellos? Here they are prepared with abundant flavor and fresh ingredients. Dressy casual. **Bar:** Full bar. **Reservations:** suggested. **Hours:** 11:30 am-9:30 pm, Sat 5 pm-10 pm. Closed major holidays; also Sun. **Address:** 588 Franklin Ave 06114 **Location:** I-91, exit 27, 0.6 mi w on Airport Rd and Brown St, then 0.4 mi s. **Parking:** on-site.

COSTA DEL SOL RESTAURANT

Phone: 860/296-1714 **16**

▼▼▼
Spanish
$9-$26

As noteworthy for its attractive decor and pleasant background music as for its food, this restaurant entices with excellent Spanish seafood dishes and paella. Everything about this eatery sings the praises of Spain, including the signature house specialty, flan. Dressy casual. **Bar:** Full bar. **Reservations:** suggested. **Hours:** 11:30 am-2 & 5:30-10 pm, Sat from 5 pm, Sun 4 pm-8 pm. Closed major holidays; also Mon. **Address:** 901 Wethersfield Ave 06114 **Location:** I-91, exit 27, 0.5 mi w on Airport Rd, then 0.5 mi s. **Parking:** on-site. CALL 🅜

(See map and index starting on p. 256)

HOT TOMATO'S   **Phone:** 860/249-5100   ②

Northern Italian
$9-$32

Representative of the restaurant's distinctive dishes are preparations of homemade pasta and tempting desserts. Casual dress. **Bar:** Full bar. **Reservations:** accepted. **Hours:** 11:30 am-3 & 4-10 pm, Thurs-11 pm, Fri-midnight, Sat 4 pm-midnight, Sun 4 pm-9 pm. Closed: 11/25, 12/25. **Address:** 1 Union Pl 06103 **Location:** I-84, exit 48, just s on Asylum St. **Parking:** street.

M & M COFFEE SHOP   **Phone:** 860/240-7222   ①

New American
$5-$26

This restaurant's hip style, which incorporates shades of bright blue and orange, is hard to miss. Extraordinary booths have light that shines out from within. Patrons can sip espresso with a sandwich or fill up on baby back ribs or Cajun rib-eye with tobacco onions. Casual dress. **Bar:** Full bar. **Reservations:** accepted. **Hours:** 6:30 am-9:30 & 5:30-9:30 pm, Sat 7 am-11 & 6-9:30 pm, Sun 7 am-10 & 5:30-9:30 pm. **Address:** 315 Trumbull St 06103 **Location:** Downtown; in The Hilton Hartford Hotel. **Parking:** on-site. CALL ♿Ⓜ

(See map and index starting on p. 256)

MAX DOWNTOWN

Steak
$8-$38

Phone: 860/522-2530

In the center of the bustling business district, the hip, modern restaurant has vaulted ceilings, artisan chandeliers and a vibrant color scheme with large murals. The innovative cuisine includes Pacific Rim-inspired dishes and other regional fare. A superb selection of traditional chop house classics, which are served with such sauces as cognac-peppercorn cream sauce and Richard's bearnaise, complements choices that reflect a global emphasis. Dressy casual. **Bar:** Full bar. **Reservations:** suggested. **Hours:** 11:30 am-2:30 & 5-10 pm, Sat 5 pm-11 pm, Sun 4:30 pm-9:30 pm. Closed: 1/1, 11/25, 12/24, 12/25. **Address:** 185 Asylum St 06103 **Location:** Downtown; across from civic center. **Parking:** on-site and valet.

MORTON'S THE STEAKHOUSE

Steak
$32-$58

Phone: 860/724-0044

Patrons should make sure to reserve ahead for the popular, well-known steakhouse. Large portions, including huge cuts of fine beef and plentiful seafood, are the norm. Even the vegetables are oversized, with baked potatoes big enough for sharing. Dressy casual. **Bar:** Full bar. **Reservations:** suggested. **Hours:** 5 pm-11 pm, Sun-10 pm. Closed major holidays. **Address:** 852 Main St 06103 **Location:** Downtown; in State House Square. **Parking:** on-site.

PEPPERCORN'S GRILL

Italian
$9-$35

Phone: 860/547-1714

The two-level dining room features a colorful Tuscany-inspired painted mural. Although homemade pasta dishes are the main draw, there are some nice chicken and steak dishes as well. As the name might suggest, freshly ground pepper is an important flavor and is offered with every course except dessert. Dressy casual. **Bar:** Full bar. **Reservations:** suggested. **Hours:** 11:30 am-10 pm, Thurs-11 pm, Fri & Sat-midnight. Closed major holidays; also Sun. **Address:** 357 Main St 06105 **Location:** Between Capitol Ave and Buckingham St; downtown. **Parking:** street.

SPRIS

Northern Italian
$15-$35

Phone: 860/247-7747

Menu highlights include Northern Italian pasta, beef, chicken and seafood dishes. The restaurant is one of downtown's most popular hot spots. Dressy casual. **Bar:** Full bar. **Reservations:** suggested. **Hours:** 11:30 am-2 & 5-10 pm, Fri-11 pm, Sat 5 pm-11 pm. Closed: 1/1, 11/25, 12/25; also Sun. **Address:** 10 Constitution Plaza 06103 **Location:** Corner of Columbus Blvd and Charter Oak Ave; downtown. **Parking:** on-site (fee) and valet.

TRUMBULL KITCHEN

American
$7-$25

Phone: 860/493-7417

Enjoy both an eclectic menu and a fusion dining experience in stylish trappings. Casual dress. **Bar:** Full bar. **Reservations:** suggested. **Hours:** 11:30 am-11 pm, Thurs & Fri-midnight, Sat noon-midnight, Sun 4 pm-10 pm. Closed major holidays. **Address:** 150 Trumbull St 06103 **Location:** I-91, exit 32B; I-84, exit 50 eastbound; exit 52 westbound; downtown. **Parking:** on-site (fee).

U.S.S. CHOWDER POT IV

Seafood
$7-$29

Phone: 860/244-3311

Locals and tourists alike rave about the good food, attentive service and creative nautical decor. A longtime favorite is the lobster bisque—a thick, creamy concoction full of lobster chunks. Prime rib is also featured. Casual dress. **Bar:** Full bar. **Reservations:** not accepted. **Hours:** 11:30 am-10 pm, Fri & Sat-11 pm, Sun noon-9 pm. Closed: 11/25, 12/25. **Address:** 165 Brainard Rd 06114 **Location:** I-91, exit 27, just e on Airport Rd, then just s. **Parking:** on-site.

VITO'S BY THE PARK

Italian
$10-$29

Phone: 860/244-2200

Patrons can take in nice views of nearby Bushnell Park while enjoying one of many distinctive pizzas, which range from Hawaiian with fresh pineapple slices to clams casino, topped with baby clams, bacon and onions. Great Italian pasta dishes also are available. Dressy casual. **Bar:** Full bar. **Reservations:** suggested. **Hours:** 11:30 am-10 pm, Thurs & Fri-11 pm, Sat noon-4 & 5-11 pm, Sun 4 pm-9 pm. Closed major holidays. **Address:** 26 Trumbull St 06103 **Location:** Between Jewel and Gold sts; downtown. **Parking:** street.

VIVO

Northern Italian
$12-$39

Phone: 860/249-8000

Inspired by Tuscany, the contemporary trattoria has an open-kitchen design, vaulted wood-beamed ceilings and long windows overlooking a bustling downtown street. Some Napa Valley interpretations enhance the menu. When available, the crudo platter—which features seasonal vegetables, marinated olives, sliced cured meats and hand-carved cheeses—is worth trying. Dressy casual. **Bar:** Full bar. **Reservations:** suggested. **Hours:** 6:30 am-11 & 11:30-10 pm, Sat & Sun 7 am-noon & 5-10 pm. **Address:** 200 Columbus Blvd 06103 **Location:** I-91, exit 29A, just w, exit Columbus Blvd, then just n; downtown; in Marriott Hartford Downtown. **Parking:** on-site (fee) and valet.

WOOD-N-TAP BAR & GRILL

American
$7-$25

Phone: 860/232-8277

In the city's West End, the restaurant nicely merges traditional pub fare with quick, smart service. Dressy casual. **Bar:** Full bar. **Reservations:** not accepted. **Hours:** 11:30 am-1 am, Fri & Sat-2 am. Closed: 11/25, 12/25. **Address:** 99 Sisson Ave 06106 **Location:** I-84, exit 46, just s. **Parking:** on-site and street.

The Hartford Vicinity

AVON (See map and index starting on p. 256)

AVON OLD FARMS HOTEL   *Book at AAA.com*   Phone: (860)677-1651 [53]

▼▼▼

Hotel
$109-$229 All Year

Address: 279 Avon Mountain Rd 06001 **Location:** Jct US 44 and SR 10. **Facility:** 157 units. 154 one-bedroom standard units. 1 one- and 2 two-bedroom suites. 2-3 stories, interior/exterior corridors. **Parking:** on-site, winter plug-ins. **Amenities:** voice mail, irons, hair dryers. *Some:* dual phone lines. **Dining:** Seasons Restaurant, see separate listing. **Pool(s):** outdoor. **Leisure Activities:** sauna, exercise room, horseshoes. **Guest Services:** valet laundry, wireless Internet. **Business Services:** meeting rooms, business center. [ASK] [🍴] [🏊] [✕] [▣] / SOME UNITS [🐕] [✕] [📶] [🖥]

RESIDENCE INN BY MARRIOTT HARTFORD-AVON   *Book great rates at AAA.com*   Phone: (860)678-1666 [52]

▼▼▼

Extended Stay
Hotel
$170-$208 All Year

Address: 55 Simsbury Rd (SR 202 & SR 10) 06001 **Location:** Jct US 44, just n. **Facility:** Smoke free premises. 100 units. 36 one-bedroom standard units with efficiencies. 45 one- and 19 two-bedroom suites, some with efficiencies or kitchens. 3 stories, interior corridors. *Bath:* combo or shower only. **Parking:** on-site. **Terms:** cancellation fee imposed. **Amenities:** high-speed Internet, voice mail, irons, hair dryers. *Some:* DVD players. **Pool(s):** heated outdoor. **Leisure Activities:** whirlpool, exercise room, sports court. **Guest Services:** valet and coin laundry, wireless Internet. **Business Services:** meeting rooms, business center.

[CALL] [♿M] [🏊] [✕] [✕] [🎥] [📶] [🖥] [▣] / SOME UNITS FEE [🐕]

> **AAA Benefit:**
> Members save a
> minimum 5% off the
> best available rate.

―――― WHERE TO DINE ――――

AMICI ITALIAN GRILL   Phone: 860/677-7089 [38]

▼▼▼

Italian
$5-$24

Upscale and casual decor come together at this hot spot. Pasta dishes are homemade and come with a complimentary house salad. Fried calamari primes the palate for an entree of lasagna or panini, followed by luscious tiramisu. Dressy casual. **Bar:** Full bar. **Reservations:** suggested. **Hours:** 11 am-10 pm, Fri & Sat-11 pm. Closed: 11/25, 12/25. **Address:** 401 W Main St 06001 **Location:** Jct SR 10, 1.8 mi w on US 44. **Parking:** on-site. CALL [♿M]

AVON OLD FARMS INN   Phone: 860/677-2818 [41]

▼▼▼

New American
$7-$25

The foyer, lobby and private dining rooms are original to this 1757 former home of Nathaniel North. Among the inn's classic dinners is veal Sentino topped with mushrooms, white asparagus and fontina cheese. Other menu standouts include tender steaks and baked stuffed shrimp with walnut bread stuffing. Dressy casual. **Bar:** Full bar. **Reservations:** suggested. **Hours:** 11:30 am-9 pm, Fri & Sat-10 pm, Sun 10 am-4 pm. Closed: 12/25. **Address:** 1 Nod Rd 06001 **Location:** Jct US 44 and SR 10. **Parking:** on-site.

CARMEN ANTHONY   Phone: 860/677-7788 [39]

▼▼▼

Seafood
$11-$50

Award-winning crab cakes and New England clam chowder are two of the best ways to start the meal. An elegant dining experience features attentive service in an intimate setting. Dressy casual. **Bar:** Full bar. **Reservations:** accepted. **Hours:** 11 am-4 & 5-10 pm, Fri & Sat-11 pm, Sun noon-9 pm. Closed: 12/25. **Address:** 51 E Main St 06001 **Location:** Jct Simsbury Rd, just e on US 44; in The Shops at River Park. **Parking:** on-site. CALL [♿M]

DAKOTA   Phone: 860/677-4311 [36]

▼▼

American
$12-$29

The restaurant presents a warm, inviting atmosphere with a touch of Southwest feel and Aboriginal artifacts. The steak is served juicy, hot and sizzling, and the fish and seafood are ocean fresh. Casual dress. **Bar:** Full bar. **Reservations:** suggested. **Hours:** 4:30 pm-9 pm, Fri & Sat-10 pm. **Address:** 225 W Main St (US 44) 06001 **Location:** Jct US 202 and SR 10, 1.1 mi w. **Parking:** on-site. CALL [♿M]

MAX A MIA RISTORANTE   Phone: 860/677-6299 [40]

▼▼

Italian
$8-$30

The popular restaurant was designed to resemble a vineyard farmhouse. Rustic wood-trimmed ceilings, large light fixtures and colorful abstract paintings of vegetables and other foods painted on the walls add to the country appeal. Another highlight is the open kitchen, which offers a view of the large brick oven. Selections on the broad menu offer a creative twist on Italian favorites, pizza and seafood. Casual dress. **Bar:** Full bar. **Reservations:** accepted. **Hours:** 11:30 am-10 pm, Fri & Sat-11 pm, Sun 11 am-9 pm. Closed: 11/25, 12/24, 12/25. **Address:** 70 E Main St (SR 44) 06001 **Location:** Just w of jct SR 10. **Parking:** on-site.

SEASONS RESTAURANT   Phone: 860/269-0240 [42]

▼▼▼

Continental
$9-$40

This elegant dining room overlooks a tree-lined stream. The diverse Continental menu features a few regional specialties such as crispy Long Island duck and pan-seared sea bass. Casual dining available in The Pub. Dressy casual. Entertainment. **Bar:** Full bar. **Reservations:** suggested. **Hours:** 6:30-10 am, 11:30-2 & 5-9 pm, Sat 7 am-11 & 5-9 pm, Sun 7 am-1 pm. Closed: 11/25, 12/25. **Address:** 279 Avon Mountain Rd 06001 **Location:** Jct US 44 and SR 10; in Avon Old Farms Hotel. **Parking:** on-site.

TOSHI JAPANESE RESTAURANT   Phone: 860/677-8242 [37]

▼▼

Japanese
$8-$25

The Japanese restaurant prepares a wide variety of sushi, sashimi and tempura. The decor is contemporary and natural, with clean white walls, light wood and a gray slate-like tiled floor. Casual dress. **Bar:** Full bar. **Reservations:** suggested, weekends. **Hours:** 11:30 am-2:30 & 5-10 pm, Fri & Sat-10:30 pm, Sun-9 pm. Closed: 7/4, 11/25, 12/25. **Address:** 136 Simsbury Rd (SR 10), Bldg #4 06001 **Location:** 0.6 mi n of jct US 44; in Riverdale Farms Shopping Plaza. **Parking:** on-site.

BERLIN   (See map and index starting on p. 256)

BEST WESTERN NEW ENGLAND INN & SUITES   *Book great rates at AAA.com*   Phone: (860)828-3000

 AAA SAVE
◆◆◆◆◆
Hotel
$90-$100 All Year

Address: 2253 Berlin Tpke 06037 **Location:** I-91, exit 17 northbound, 4.9 mi n on SR 15 (Berlin Tpke); exit 22N southbound, 2.5 mi n on SR 9 to exit 22, follow signs to US 5 and SR 15 S (Berlin Tpke) for 2.8 mi. **Facility:** 53 one-bedroom standard units, some with kitchens and/or whirlpools. 2 stories, interior corridors. *Bath:* combo or shower only. **Parking:** on-site. **Amenities:** high-speed Internet, dual phone lines, voice mail, irons, hair dryers. **Pool(s):** heated indoor. **Leisure Activities:** exercise room. **Guest Services:** valet and coin laundry, wireless Internet. **Business Services:** meeting rooms, business center. **Free Special Amenities: full breakfast and high-speed Internet.**

AAA Benefit:
Members save up to 20%, plus 10% bonus points with rewards program.

CALL ☐M 🏊 🎮 🖥 📺 📠 / SOME UNITS ✕

——— **WHERE TO DINE** ———

HAWTHORNE INN   Phone: 860/828-3571   75

◆◆◆
American
$8-$27

Friendly service characterizes the area favorite, which has built its reputation on prime rib and seafood. Casual dress. **Bar:** Full bar. **Reservations:** accepted. **Hours:** 11:30 am-8:30 pm, Tues-Thurs to 9 pm, Fri & Sat-9:30 pm, Sun 11 am-2 pm. Closed: 12/24, 12/25; also Sun 7/1-8/31. **Address:** 2421 Berlin Tpke 06037 **Location:** I-91, exit 17 northbound, 4.7 mi n on SR 15 (Berlin Tpke); exit 22N southbound, 2.5 mi n on SR 9 to exit 22, follow signs to US 5 and SR 15 (Berlin Tpke), then 3 mi s; in Hawthorne Inn. **Parking:** on-site.

CALL ☐M

BRISTOL pop. 60,032

CLARION HOTEL BRISTOL   *Book at AAA.com*   Phone: (860)589-7766

◆◆◆
Hotel
$97-$126 All Year

Address: 42 Century Dr 06010 **Location:** I-84, exit 31, 3.2 mi n on SR 229. Located in Technology Park. **Facility:** Smoke free premises. 120 one-bedroom standard units. 6 stories, interior corridors. **Parking:** on-site. **Amenities:** video games (fee), dual phone lines, voice mail, irons, hair dryers. **Pool(s):** heated indoor. **Leisure Activities:** sauna, exercise room. **Guest Services:** valet and coin laundry, wireless Internet. **Business Services:** meeting rooms, business center.

ASK 🍴 🍸 CALL ☐M 🏊 ✕ 🎮 📠 / SOME UNITS FEE 🖥

CROMWELL   (See map and index starting on p. 256)

COMFORT INN   *Book great rates at AAA.com*   Phone: (860)635-4100   86

AAA SAVE
◆◆
Hotel
$69-$160 All Year

Address: 111 Berlin Rd 06416 **Location:** I-91, exit 21, just e on SR 372. **Facility:** 76 one-bedroom standard units. 4 stories, interior corridors. **Parking:** on-site. **Amenities:** high-speed Internet, voice mail, irons, hair dryers. **Leisure Activities:** exercise room. **Guest Services:** valet laundry, wireless Internet. **Business Services:** business center. **Free Special Amenities: expanded continental breakfast and high-speed Internet.** 🍴 🎮 📠 / SOME UNITS FEE 🐕 ✕ 🖥 🏊

COURTYARD HARTFORD CROMWELL   *Book great rates at AAA.com*   Phone: (860)635-1001   84

◆◆◆
Hotel
$149-$182 All Year

Address: 4 Sebethe Dr 06416 **Location:** I-91, exit 21, just w. **Facility:** Smoke free premises. 145 units. 143 one-bedroom standard units, some with whirlpools. 2 one-bedroom suites with whirlpools. 3 stories, interior corridors. *Bath:* combo or shower only. **Parking:** on-site. **Terms:** cancellation fee imposed. **Amenities:** high-speed Internet, dual phone lines, voice mail, irons, hair dryers. **Pool(s):** heated indoor. **Leisure Activities:** saunas, exercise room. **Guest Services:** valet and coin laundry, wireless Internet. **Business Services:** meeting rooms, business center.

AAA Benefit:
Members save a minimum 5% off the best available rate.

🍴 🍸 CALL ☐M 🏊 ✕ 🎮 🖥 📠 / SOME UNITS 🖥

CROWNE PLAZA CROMWELL   *Book great rates at AAA.com*   Phone: (860)635-2000   87

AAA SAVE
◆◆◆◆
Hotel
$69-$179 All Year

Address: 100 Berlin Rd 06416 **Location:** I-91, exit 21, just e on SR 372. **Facility:** Smoke free premises. 215 one-bedroom standard units. 2-4 stories, interior corridors. **Parking:** on-site, winter plug-ins. **Amenities:** video games (fee), CD players, voice mail, irons, hair dryers. **Pool(s):** heated indoor. **Leisure Activities:** saunas, whirlpool, exercise room. **Guest Services:** valet laundry, wireless Internet. **Business Services:** conference facilities, business center. **Free Special Amenities: newspaper and high-speed Internet.**

🍴 🍸 CALL ☐M 🏊 ✕ ✕ 📠 / SOME UNITS FEE 🖥 FEE 🖥

SUPER 8   *Book at AAA.com*   Phone: (860)632-8888   85

◆
Hotel
$65-$85 All Year

Address: 1 Industrial Park Rd 06416 **Location:** I-91, exit 21, just w on SR 372. **Facility:** 112 one-bedroom standard units. 3 stories, interior corridors. **Parking:** on-site. **Amenities:** hair dryers. *Some:* irons. **Guest Services:** wireless Internet. **Business Services:** meeting rooms.

ASK 🍴 CALL ☐M 🎮 📠 / SOME UNITS ✕ FEE 🖥

—— WHERE TO DINE ——

CROMWELL DINER   Phone: 860/635-7112   72

American
$4-$15

Patrons can try made-to-order omelets with tasty fried potatoes or any of the diner's breakfast items served all day in its bright, modern setting. The attentive, neighborly service staff also serves Greek, Italian and Jewish dishes. Casual dress. **Bar:** Full bar. **Reservations:** accepted. **Hours:** 24 hours. **Address:** 135 Berlin Rd 06416 **Location:** I-91, exit 21, just w on SR 372. **Parking:** on-site.

OYAMA JAPANESE CUISINE   Phone: 860/632-2324   71

Japanese
$9-$38

Oyama is a consistent favorite among locals and lunching professionals. The large restaurant has high ceilings and a few hibachi tables. The minimalist decor features a modest collection of Asia-themed art. The menu lists sushi, noodles and classic Japanese fare. Favorites include the romance roll, which is filled with avocado, cucumber and mango and topped with chunks of crabmeat, and the affordable and filling lunch bento boxes. Hibachi chefs entertain while the service staff is attentive. Casual dress. **Bar:** Full bar. **Reservations:** accepted. **Hours:** 11:30 am-3 & 5-10 pm, Fri & Sat-11 pm, Sun noon-10 pm. Closed: 11/25, 12/25. **Address:** 136-150 Berlin Rd 06416 **Location:** I-91, exit 21, just w. **Parking:** on-site. CALL &M

EAST HARTFORD pop. 49,575   (See map and index starting on p. 256)

HOLIDAY INN   *Book at AAA.com*   Phone: (860)528-9611   48

Hotel
$90-$169 All Year

Address: 363 Roberts St 06108 **Location:** I-84, exit 58, just w. **Facility:** 130 one-bedroom standard units. 5 stories, interior corridors. *Bath:* combo or shower only. **Parking:** on-site. **Terms:** cancellation fee imposed. **Amenities:** dual phone lines, voice mail, irons, hair dryers. **Pool(s):** heated indoor. **Leisure Activities:** exercise room. **Guest Services:** valet and coin laundry, wireless Internet. **Business Services:** meeting rooms, business center.

(ASK) 🍴 🍸 🏊 📹 📠 / SOME UNITS FEE 🐾 ✕ 🛗 🖥️

SHERATON HARTFORD HOTEL   *Book great rates at AAA.com*   Phone: (860)528-9703   49

(AAA) (SAVE)

Hotel
$89-$229 All Year

Address: 100 E River Dr 06108 **Location:** I-84, exit 53 eastbound, just s; exit 54 westbound to exit 3 (Darlin St), just n. **Facility:** Smoke free premises. 215 units. 214 one-bedroom standard units. 1 one-bedroom suite. 8 stories, interior corridors. *Bath:* combo or shower only. **Parking:** on-site. **Terms:** cancellation fee imposed. **Amenities:** dual phone lines, voice mail, irons, hair dryers. **Fee:** video games, high-speed Internet. **Pool(s):** heated indoor. **Leisure Activities:** exercise room, volleyball. **Guest Services:** valet laundry, area transportation-within 10 mi, wireless Internet. **Business Services:** conference facilities, business center. **Free Special Amenities:** newspaper.

| (S) **Sheraton** |
| HOTELS & RESORTS |
| **AAA Benefit:** |
| Members get up to 15% off, plus Starwood Preferred Guest® bonuses. |

🍴 🍸 CALL &M 🏊 ✕ 📹 📠 / SOME UNITS 🐾 🛗 FEE 🖥️

—— WHERE TO DINE ——

MARGARITAS MEXICAN RESTAURANT   Phone: 860/289-7212

Mexican
$6-$16

Diners will feel as though they have just stepped south of the border at this fun Mexican cantina. Traditional music fills the air while warm terracotta colored walls accented by painted pottery and unique jeweled star lanterns surround you. Sip on a large margarita while enjoying the freshly prepared fajitas, burritos, enchiladas, or quesadilla's. Casual dress. **Bar:** Full bar. **Hours:** 11:30 am-10 pm, Fri & Sat-11 pm. Closed: 4/4, 11/25, 12/25. **Address:** 350 Roberts St 06108 **Location:** I-84, exit 58, just ne. **Parking:** on-site.
CALL &M

EAST WINDSOR   (See map and index starting on p. 256)

COMFORT INN   *Book great rates at AAA.com*   Phone: (860)254-5383   22

(AAA) (SAVE)

Hotel
$85-$105 All Year

Address: 141 Prospect Hill Rd 06088 **Location:** I-91, exit 45, just e on SR 140, then just n. **Facility:** 58 units. 53 one-bedroom standard units. 5 one-bedroom suites, some with whirlpools. 4 stories, interior corridors. *Bath:* combo or shower only. **Parking:** on-site. **Amenities:** high-speed Internet, voice mail, irons, hair dryers. **Pool(s):** heated indoor. **Leisure Activities:** exercise room. **Guest Services:** valet and coin laundry, wireless Internet. **Business Services:** meeting rooms, business center. **Free Special Amenities:** expanded continental breakfast and newspaper.

🍴 CALL &M 🏊 📹 🛗 🖥️ 📠 / SOME UNITS ✕

HOLIDAY INN EXPRESS EAST WINDSOR - AIRPORT

Book great rates at AAA.com

Phone: (860)627-6585   24

AAA [SAVE]

♦♦♦

Hotel

$70-$110 All Year

Address: 260 Main St (US 5) 06088 **Location:** I-91, exit 44, just s. **Facility:** 116 one-bedroom standard units. 2 stories (no elevator), interior corridors. *Bath:* combo or shower only. **Parking:** on-site. **Terms:** cancellation fee imposed. **Amenities:** voice mail, irons, hair dryers. *Fee:* video games, safes. **Leisure Activities:** exercise room. **Guest Services:** valet laundry, airport transportation-Bradley International Airport, area transportation-within 5 mi & Six Flags New England, wireless Internet. **Business Services:** meeting rooms, business center.

[icons] CALL ⟨M⟩ 📺 💻 / SOME UNITS FEE 🐾 ✕ 🔒

FREE expanded continental breakfast and high-speed Internet

—— **WHERE TO DINE** ——

JONATHAN PASCO'S

Phone: 860/627-7709   24

♦♦ ♦♦

Italian

$18-$31

Guests can appreciate original New England colonial architecture while sitting in the refurbished home, which was built in 1784. The friendly staff is happy to tell stories or answer questions about the home. Dressy casual. **Bar:** Full bar. **Reservations:** suggested. **Hours:** 5 pm-10 pm, Sun 11 am-2 & 3-9 pm. Closed: 1/1, 11/25, 12/25. **Address:** 31 S Main St 06088 **Location:** I-91, exit 44, 0.6 mi s on US 5. **Parking:** on-site.

MAINE FISH MARKET

Phone: 860/623-2281   23

♦♦ ♦♦

Seafood

$7-$25

This fish house serves seafood any which way, but mainly broiled, boiled or fried, and there are combination platters for those who want some variety. Portions are large and the casual nature makes it great for families. Casual dress. **Bar:** Full bar. **Reservations:** not accepted. **Hours:** 10:30 am-9 pm, Fri & Sat-10 pm, Sun noon-9 pm. Closed major holidays. **Address:** 60 Bridge St 06088 **Location:** I-91, exit 45, 1.5 mi w. **Parking:** on-site.

ENFIELD

CROWNE PLAZA HOTEL ENFIELD-SPRINGFIELD

Book at AAA.com

Phone: 860/741-2211

♦♦♦♦

Hotel

Rates not provided

Address: 1 Bright Meadow Blvd 06082 **Location:** I-91, exit 49, just e on service road. **Facility:** 174 units. 171 one-bedroom standard units. 3 one-bedroom suites. 6 stories, interior corridors. *Bath:* combo or shower only. **Parking:** on-site. **Amenities:** CD players, high-speed Internet, dual phone lines, voice mail, safes, irons, hair dryers. **Pool(s):** outdoor, heated indoor. **Leisure Activities:** sauna, whirlpool, 2 lighted tennis courts, exercise room, basketball, horseshoes, shuffleboard, volleyball. *Fee:* game room. **Guest Services:** valet laundry, area transportation, wireless Internet. **Business Services:** conference facilities, business center.

[icons] CALL ⟨M⟩ ⛱ ✕ 📺 💻 / SOME UNITS ✕ FEE 🔒 FEE 📷

HAMPTON INN & SUITES ENFIELD

Book great rates at AAA.com

Phone: 860/741-3111

♦♦♦♦

Hotel

Rates not provided

Address: 20 Phoenix Ave 06082 **Location:** I-91, exit 47E, just se. **Facility:** 108 one-bedroom standard units. 5 stories, interior corridors. *Bath:* combo or shower only. **Parking:** on-site. **Amenities:** voice mail, irons, hair dryers. **Pool(s):** heated indoor. **Leisure Activities:** whirlpool, exercise room. **Guest Services:** valet and coin laundry, wireless Internet. **Business Services:** meeting rooms, business center.

[icons] CALL ⟨M⟩ ⛱ 📺 💻 / SOME UNITS ✕ 🔒 📷

AAA Benefit:

Members save up to 10% everyday!

RED ROOF INN # 7105

Book at AAA.com

Phone: (860)741-2571

♦♦ ♦♦

Motel

$61-$109 5/1-10/31

$56-$109 11/1-4/30

Address: 5 Hazard Ave 06082 **Location:** I-91, exit 47E. **Facility:** 108 one-bedroom standard units. 2 stories (no elevator), exterior corridors. *Bath:* combo or shower only. **Parking:** on-site. **Amenities:** video games (fee), voice mail. **Guest Services:** wireless Internet.

[ASK] [icons] CALL ⟨M⟩ 📺 / SOME UNITS 🐾 ✕ FEE 🔒 FEE 📷

—— **WHERE TO DINE** ——

FIGARO RESTAURANT

Phone: 860/745-2414

♦♦ ♦♦

Italian

$7-$30

Experienced staffers tend to the favorite eatery, which infuses its traditional seafood, steak, chicken and pasta dishes with an Italian flair. Casual dress. **Bar:** Full bar. **Reservations:** not accepted. **Hours:** 11:30 am-10 pm, Sun noon-9 pm. Closed: 12/25. **Address:** 90 Elm St 06082 **Location:** I-91, exit 48, just e. **Parking:** on-site.

HAZARD GRILLE

Phone: 860/239-0004

American
$7-$28

The distinctive restaurant might make patrons feel as though they are dining outdoors. Inside are barn walls, pressed-tin storm shutters and hanging lanterns. Excellent sandwiches and pasta dishes line the menu. Casual dress. **Bar:** Full bar. **Hours:** 11:30 am-9 pm, Fri & Sat-10 pm, Sun noon-9 pm. Closed: 12/25. **Address:** 39 Hazard Ave 06082 **Location:** I-91, exit 47E, 0.8 mi e. **Parking:** on-site.

FARMINGTON (See map and index starting on p. 256)

CENTENNIAL INN SUITES   *Book great rates at AAA.com*

Phone: (860)677-4647   **71**

Condominium
$141-$181 11/1-4/30
$121-$161 5/1-10/31

Address: 5 Spring Ln 06032 **Location:** US 6, 0.3 mi e of jct SR 177. **Facility:** 96 units. 30 one-bedroom standard units. 56 one- and 10 two-bedroom suites. 2 stories (no elevator), interior/exterior corridors. *Bath:* combo or shower only. **Parking:** on-site. **Terms:** cancellation fee imposed. **Amenities:** DVD players, high-speed Internet, voice mail, irons, hair dryers. *Fee:* video library, safes. **Pool(s):** outdoor. **Leisure Activities:** grills, exercise room, sports court. **Guest Services:** valet and coin laundry, wireless Internet. **Business Services:** meeting rooms, business center. **Free Special Amenities: expanded continental breakfast and high-speed Internet.**

COURTYARD BY MARRIOTT HARTFORD-FARMINGTON   *Book great rates at AAA.com*

Phone: (860)521-7100   **69**

Hotel
$161-$197 All Year

Address: 1583 Southeast Rd 06032 **Location:** SR 9, exit 30, just ne on SR 71. **Facility:** Smoke free premises. 119 units. 117 one-bedroom standard units, some with whirlpools. 2 one-bedroom suites. 4 stories, interior corridors. *Bath:* combo or shower only. **Parking:** on-site. **Terms:** cancellation fee imposed. **Amenities:** video games (fee), high-speed Internet, voice mail, irons, hair dryers. *Some:* DVD players (fee). **Pool(s):** heated indoor. **Leisure Activities:** whirlpool, exercise room. **Guest Services:** valet and coin laundry, wireless Internet. **Business Services:** meeting rooms, business center.

AAA Benefit:
Members save a minimum 5% off the best available rate.

EXTENDED STAYAMERICA DELUXE HARTFORD-FARMINGTON   *Book at AAA.com*

Phone: (860)676-2790   **72**

Extended Stay
Hotel
$89-$129 All Year

Address: 1 Batterson Park Rd 06032 **Location:** I-84, exit 37, just ne. **Facility:** 91 units. 90 one-bedroom standard units with kitchens. 1 one-bedroom suite with kitchen. 3 stories, interior corridors. *Bath:* combo or shower only. **Parking:** on-site. **Terms:** office hours 7 am-11 pm, cancellation fee imposed. **Amenities:** DVD players, voice mail, irons, hair dryers. **Leisure Activities:** exercise room. **Guest Services:** coin laundry, wireless Internet.

THE FARMINGTON INN   *Book at AAA.com*

Phone: (860)269-3401   **68**

Hotel
$109-$179 All Year

Address: 827 Farmington Ave 06032 **Location:** I-84, exit 39, 1.8 mi w on SR 4. **Facility:** Smoke free premises. 72 one-bedroom standard units. 2 stories, interior corridors. **Parking:** on-site. **Amenities:** voice mail, irons, hair dryers. *Some:* DVD players. **Leisure Activities:** spa. **Guest Services:** valet laundry, wireless Internet. **Business Services:** business center.

HOMEWOOD SUITES BY HILTON   *Book great rates at AAA.com*

Phone: (860)321-0000   **67**

Extended Stay
Hotel
$109-$169 All Year

Address: 2 Farm Glen Blvd 06032 **Location:** I-84, exit 39, 0.6 mi e on SR 4. **Facility:** 121 units. 116 one- and 5 two-bedroom suites with efficiencies. 3 stories, interior corridors. *Bath:* combo or shower only. **Parking:** on-site. **Terms:** 1-7 night minimum stay, cancellation fee imposed. **Amenities:** high-speed Internet, dual phone lines, voice mail, irons, hair dryers. *Fee:* video library, video games. **Pool(s):** heated indoor. **Leisure Activities:** exercise room. **Guest Services:** valet and coin laundry, area transportation. **Business Services:** meeting rooms, business center.

AAA Benefit:
Members save 5% or more everyday!

MARRIOTT HOTEL-FARMINGTON   *Book great rates at AAA.com*

Phone: (860)678-1000   **70**

Hotel
$180-$220 All Year

Address: 15 Farm Springs Rd 06032 **Location:** I-84, exit 37, just n. Located in an industrial park. **Facility:** Smoke free premises. 381 units. 377 one-bedroom standard units. 4 one-bedroom suites. 4 stories, interior corridors. *Bath:* combo or shower only. **Parking:** on-site. **Terms:** check-in 4 pm, cancellation fee imposed. **Amenities:** voice mail, irons, hair dryers. *Fee:* video games, high-speed Internet. **Pool(s):** heated indoor. **Leisure Activities:** whirlpool, jogging, exercise room. **Guest Services:** valet and coin laundry, wireless Internet. **Business Services:** conference facilities, business center.

AAA Benefit:
Members save a minimum 5% off the best available rate.

─── **WHERE TO DINE** ───

APRICOTS

Phone: 860/673-5405 ⑤⑨

Continental
$8-$35

For eclectic dining with a river view, try Apricots. While the menu emphasizes seafood, Angus beef, New Zealand lamb and Long Island duck are notable entrees. Patio dining 11:30 am-4 pm in season. Dressy casual. **Bar:** Full bar. **Reservations:** suggested. **Hours:** 11:30 am-10 pm, Sun-9 pm. Closed: 1/1, 12/25. **Address:** 1593 Farmington Ave 06032 **Location:** SR 4, 3 mi w. **Parking:** on-site.

GLASTONBURY pop. 7,157 (See map and index starting on p. 256)

HILTON GARDEN INN HARTFORD SOUTH/GLASTONBURY   *Book great rates at AAA.com*

Phone: (860)659-1025 ⑥⓪

Hotel
$169-$215 All Year

Address: 85 Glastonbury Blvd 06033 **Location:** SR 3, exit Main St, just se. **Facility:** 150 units. 144 one-bedroom standard units. 6 one-bedroom suites with whirlpools. 6 stories, interior corridors. *Bath:* combo or shower only. **Parking:** on-site. **Terms:** 1-7 night minimum stay, cancellation fee imposed. **Amenities:** video games (fee), high-speed Internet, dual phone lines, voice mail, irons, hair dryers. **Pool(s):** heated indoor. **Leisure Activities:** whirlpool, sun deck, exercise room. **Guest Services:** valet and coin laundry, wireless Internet. **Business Services:** meeting rooms, business center. **Free Special Amenities:** high-speed Internet.

Hilton Garden Inn

AAA Benefit:
Members save 5% or more everyday!

HOMEWOOD SUITES BY HILTON HARTFORD SOUTH-GLASTONBURY   *Book great rates at AAA.com*

Phone: (860)652-8111 ⑤⑨

Extended Stay Hotel
$110-$209 All Year

Address: 65 Glastonbury Blvd 06033 **Location:** SR 3, exit Main St, just se. **Facility:** 136 units. 56 one-bedroom standard units with efficiencies, some with whirlpools. 75 one- and 5 two-bedroom suites with efficiencies. 6 stories, interior corridors. *Bath:* combo or shower only. **Parking:** on-site. **Terms:** 1-7 night minimum stay, cancellation fee imposed. **Amenities:** video games (fee), high-speed Internet, dual phone lines, voice mail, irons, hair dryers. **Pool(s):** heated outdoor. **Leisure Activities:** billiards, table tennis, exercise room, sports court. **Guest Services:** valet and coin laundry, wireless Internet. **Business Services:** meeting rooms, business center. **Free Special Amenities:** full breakfast and high-speed Internet.

HOMEWOOD SUITES Hilton

AAA Benefit:
Members save 5% or more everyday!

─── **WHERE TO DINE** ───

MAX AMORE

Phone: 860/659-2819 ⑤③

Northern Italian
$8-$25

The open kitchen sends aromas of roasted garlic and oak-grilled seafood into a stylish dining room and heightens your appetite for this delicious food with a European flair. The bistro atmosphere and cordial service are a plus. Dressy casual. **Bar:** Full bar. **Reservations:** suggested. **Hours:** 11:30 am-2:30 & 5-10 pm, Fri-11 pm, Sat 11 am-3 & 4-11 pm, Sun 11 am-3 & 4-9 pm. Closed: 11/25, 12/25. **Address:** 140 Glastonbury Blvd 06033 **Location:** SR 3, exit Main St; in Shops at Somerset Square. **Parking:** on-site.

MAX FISH

Phone: 860/652-3474 ⑤②

Seafood
$11-$30

Fresh high-quality seafood takes the marquee at this restaurant, where diners might start with East and West Coast raw oysters, then choose a flown-in fish, such as Costa Rican mahi mahi or Alaskan wild-caught halibut. A favorite preparation method is "la plancha," in which the fish is served on a metal plate with rio rice, haricots verts and a mustard seed beurre blanc sauce. The creamy pumpkin cheesecake dessert, when it's in season, is simply sublime. Dressy casual. **Bar:** Full bar. **Reservations:** suggested. **Hours:** 11:30 am-11 pm, Thurs-Sat to midnight, Sun 4 pm-10 pm. Closed: 11/25, 12/25. **Address:** 110 Glastonbury Blvd 06033 **Location:** SR 3, exit Main St; in Shops at Somerset Square. **Parking:** on-site.

GRANBY

─── **WHERE TO DINE** ───

GUADALAJARA GRILL

Phone: 860/844-0066

Mexican
$6-$20

Yes, guests will find the usual staples of burritos, enchiladas and fajitas, but there also are dozens of distinct dishes. Service is welcoming. Casual dress. **Bar:** Full bar. **Reservations:** not accepted. **Hours:** 11 am-10 pm, Fri & Sat-11 pm. **Address:** 9 Bank St 06035 **Location:** Jct SR 20 and US 202/SR 10, just e; in shopping plaza. **Parking:** on-site.

MANCHESTER   (See map and index starting on p. 256)

AMERICAS BEST VALUE INN

Phone: 860/643-1555   **42**

AAA SAVE

Motel
$60-$75 All Year

Address: 400 Tolland Tpke 06042 **Location:** I-84, exit 63, 0.3 mi w. **Facility:** 31 one-bedroom standard units. 1 story, exterior corridors. *Bath:* combo or shower only. **Parking:** on-site. **Amenities:** high-speed Internet, hair dryers. *Some:* irons.

FREE room upgrade (subject to availability with advance reservations) and high-speed Internet

---

COURTYARD HARTFORD MANCHESTER   *Book great rates at AAA.com*

Phone: (860)533-8484   **40**

Hotel
$140-$171 All Year

Address: 225 Slater St 06040 **Location:** I-84, exit 63, 0.5 mi nw, then 0.6 mi sw. **Facility:** Smoke free premises. 90 units. 87 one-bedroom standard units, some with whirlpools. 3 one-bedroom suites. 3 stories, interior corridors. *Bath:* combo or shower only. **Parking:** on-site. **Terms:** cancellation fee imposed. **Amenities:** high-speed Internet, dual phone lines, voice mail, irons, hair dryers. **Pool(s):** heated indoor. **Leisure Activities:** whirlpool, exercise room. **Guest Services:** valet and coin laundry, wireless Internet. **Business Services:** meeting rooms, business center.

AAA Benefit:
Members save a minimum 5% off the best available rate.

EXTENDED STAYAMERICA HARTFORD-MANCHESTER   *Book at AAA.com*

Phone: (860)643-5140   **41**

Extended Stay
Hotel
$79-$129 All Year

Address: 340 Tolland Tpke 06040 **Location:** I-84, exit 63, 0.3 mi se on SR 30, then just sw. **Facility:** 104 one-bedroom standard units with efficiencies. 3 stories, interior corridors. *Bath:* combo or shower only. **Parking:** on-site. **Terms:** office hours 7 am-11 pm, cancellation fee imposed. **Amenities:** dual phone lines, voice mail, irons. *Some:* hair dryers. **Guest Services:** coin laundry, wireless Internet.

FAIRFIELD INN & SUITES HARTFORD MANCHESTER   *Book great rates at AAA.com*

Phone: (860)648-9796   **44**

Hotel
$135-$165 All Year

Address: 121 Pavilions Dr 06040 **Location:** I-84, exit 62 eastbound, just n on Buckland St, then 0.3 mi e; exit 62 westbound, just ne on Pleasant Valley Rd, just s on Buckland St, then 0.3 mi e. Adjacent to Buckland Hills Mall. **Facility:** Smoke free premises. 93 units. 71 one-bedroom standard units. 22 one-bedroom suites. 3 stories, interior corridors. *Bath:* combo or shower only. **Parking:** on-site. **Terms:** cancellation fee imposed. **Amenities:** voice mail, irons, hair dryers. *Some:* CD players. **Pool(s):** heated indoor. **Leisure Activities:** whirlpool, exercise room. **Guest Services:** valet and coin laundry, wireless Internet. **Business Services:** meeting rooms, business center.

AAA Benefit:
Members save a minimum 5% off the best available rate.

HAMPTON INN & SUITES HARTFORD-MANCHESTER   *Book great rates at AAA.com*

Phone: (860)644-1736   **43**

Hotel
$139-$159 All Year

Address: 1432 Pleasant Valley Rd 06042 **Location:** I-84, exit 62, 0.4 mi n on Buckland St, then 0.5 mi w. **Facility:** Smoke free premises. 107 one-bedroom standard units. 3 stories, interior corridors. *Bath:* combo or shower only. **Parking:** on-site. **Terms:** 1-7 night minimum stay, cancellation fee imposed. **Amenities:** high-speed Internet, voice mail, irons, hair dryers. **Pool(s):** heated indoor. **Leisure Activities:** exercise room. **Guest Services:** valet and coin laundry, wireless Internet. **Business Services:** meeting rooms, business center.

AAA Benefit:
Members save up to 10% everyday!

MANCHESTER SUPER 8 AND CONFERENCE CENTER   *Book great rates at AAA.com*

Phone: (860)643-1864   **38**

AAA SAVE

Hotel
$65-$150 5/1-9/30
$55-$150 10/1-4/30

Address: 20 Taylor St 06040 **Location:** I-84, exit 63 eastbound, just ne on SR 30; exit westbound, 0.7 mi e on SR 30. **Facility:** Smoke free premises. 76 one-bedroom standard units, some with whirlpools. 3 stories, interior corridors. **Parking:** on-site. **Terms:** check-in 4 pm. **Amenities:** video library (fee), high-speed Internet, voice mail, safes, irons, hair dryers. *Some:* DVD players. **Leisure Activities:** picnic tables, exercise room. *Fee:* game room. **Guest Services:** coin laundry, wireless Internet. **Business Services:** meeting rooms, business center. **Free Special Amenities:** expanded continental breakfast and early check-in/late check-out.

THE MANSION INN BED AND BREAKFAST

Bed & Breakfast
$105-$180 All Year

Phone: 860/646-0453   **45**

Address: 139 Hartford Rd 06040 **Location:** I-384, exit 3, then w. **Facility:** One can fully enjoy any of the guest rooms here which have been restored with imagination and flower garden colors. Smoke free premises. 5 one-bedroom standard units. 2 stories (no elevator), interior corridors. **Parking:** on-site. **Terms:** office hours 9 am-8 pm, check-in 4 pm, 14 day cancellation notice-fee imposed. **Amenities:** irons, hair dryers. **Guest Services:** wireless Internet. **Business Services:** fax. **Free Special Amenities:** full breakfast.

RESIDENCE INN HARTFORD/MANCHESTER   *Book great rates at AAA.com*

Extended Stay
Hotel
$152-$186 All Year

Phone: (860)432-4242   **39**

Address: 201 Hale Rd 06042 **Location:** I-84, exit 63, 0.5 mi nw, then 0.6 mi sw. **Facility:** Smoke free premises. 96 units. 39 one-bedroom standard units, some with efficiencies or kitchens. 36 one- and 21 two-bedroom suites, some with efficiencies or kitchens. 3 stories, interior corridors. **Bath:** combo or shower only. **Parking:** on-site. **Terms:** cancellation fee imposed. **Amenities:** high-speed Internet, dual phone lines, voice mail, irons, hair dryers. **Pool(s):** outdoor. **Leisure Activities:** whirlpool, exercise room, sports court, basketball. **Guest Services:** valet and coin laundry, wireless Internet. **Business Services:** meeting rooms, business center.

AAA Benefit:
Members save a
minimum 5% off the
best available rate.

 CALL 🛗M 🏊 ✉ ✕ 🐾 🍴 📺 💻 / SOME UNITS FEE 🐕

------ **WHERE TO DINE** ------

CAVEY'S RESTAURANT-ITALIAN

Northern Italian
$16-$30

Phone: 860/643-2751   **33**

This is the adventurous diner's paradise. Savory choices abound, but dessert offerings are phenomenal. Standouts include the Covey sampler and chocolate planet, a torte with caramel, cardamom sauce and sorbet in an exquisite arrangement. Smoking is permitted in the lounge. Dressy casual. **Bar:** Full bar. **Reservations:** suggested. **Hours:** 5:30 pm-9:30 pm, Fri & Sat-10 pm. Closed major holidays; also Sun & Mon. **Address:** 45 E Center St 06040 **Location:** On US 6 and 44, just e of jct SR 83; downtown. **Parking:** on-site.

JOHN HARVARD'S BREWHOUSE

American
$9-$20

Phone: 860/644-2739

Known for their onsite micro-brewery, diners may enjoy one of the 8 freshly brewed lagers or ales as they view the production of the beer through a glass wall in the dining room. The recipe for the beer is believed to have originated from William Shakespeare and brought to America in 1637 by John Harvard, after whom Harvard University is named. The menu offers chicken sandwiches and burgers as well as some home-style favorites such as grilled meatloaf and chicken pot pie. Casual dress. **Bar:** Full bar. **Hours:** 11:30 am-midnight, Fri & Sat-1 am, Sun-11 pm. Closed: 11/25, 12/25. **Address:** 1487 Pleasant Valley Rd 06040 **Location:** I-84, exit 62 eastbound, 0.4 mi nw on Buckland St, then just sw; exit westbound, just sw. **Parking:** on-site. CALL 🛗M

NULLI'S RESTAURANT

Italian
$6-$17

Phone: 860/647-1500   **34**

The casual, locally popular eatery schedules live entertainment Thursday through Saturday. Varied menu selections include veal, chicken, seafood and vegetarian dishes. Guests can relax after dinner with a cappuccino. Casual dress. **Bar:** Full bar. **Reservations:** accepted. **Hours:** 11 am-9 pm, Fri & Sat-10 pm. Closed major holidays; also Sun & Mon. **Address:** 706 Hartford Rd 06040 **Location:** I-384, exit 2, just n on Keeney St, then 0.5 mi w. **Parking:** on-site.

SHADY GLEN DAIRY STORES

American
$5-$9

Phone: 860/649-4245

The roadside diner is a local favorite for its value-priced soups, salads, sandwiches and burgers. After dinner, guests often splurge on a banana split made with one of the many ice cream flavors. Casual dress. **Hours:** 7 am-10 pm, Sun from 10:30 am. Closed: 4/4, 11/25, 12/25. **Address:** 840 E Middle Tpke 06040 **Location:** On US 6 and 44, 1 mi w of jct SR 85. **Parking:** on-site.

MIDDLETOWN pop. 43,167

INN AT MIDDLETOWN   *Book at AAA.com*

Historic
Hotel
$139-$209 All Year

Phone: (860)854-6300

Address: 70 Main St 06457 **Location:** SR 9, exit 15, just sw on Dr. Martin Luther King Jr Way, then 0.4 mi se. **Facility:** A National Guard Armory has been transformed into this intimate, New England-style inn; rooms feature Colonial-style decor and modern amenities. Smoke free premises. 100 units. 88 one-bedroom standard units. 12 one-bedroom suites. 5 stories, interior corridors. **Bath:** combo or shower only. **Parking:** on-site and valet. **Terms:** cancellation fee imposed. **Amenities:** high-speed Internet, dual phone lines, voice mail, irons, hair dryers. **Dining:** Tavern at the Armory, see separate listing. **Pool(s):** heated indoor. **Leisure Activities:** whirlpool, exercise room. **Guest Services:** valet laundry, wireless Internet. **Business Services:** meeting rooms, business center.

(ASK) 🍴 🍸 CALL 🛗M 🏊 ✕ 🐾 💻 / SOME UNITS 🍴 🖥

------ **WHERE TO DINE** ------

AMICI ITALIAN GRILL

Italian
$5-$20

Phone: 860/346-0075

Upscale and casual decor come together at this Riverview Center location where you will find values throughout the menu. Casual dress. **Bar:** Full bar. **Reservations:** accepted. **Hours:** 11 am-10 pm, Fri & Sat-11 pm. Closed: 11/25, 12/25. **Address:** 280 Main St 06457 **Location:** SR 9, exit 15, just w on Washington St. **Parking:** street.

FIRST & LAST TAVERN

American
$6-$20

Phone: 860/347-2220

The striking brick exterior carries over to the inside, where specialties include brick-oven pizzas. Casual dress. **Bar:** Full bar. **Reservations:** not accepted. **Hours:** 11:30 am-9 pm, Wed & Thurs-10 pm, Fri & Sat-11 pm. Closed major holidays. **Address:** 220 Main St 06457 **Location:** SR 9, exit 15, just w on Washington St, then just s. **Parking:** on-site (fee) and street.

FORBIDDEN CITY BISTRO Phone: 860/343-8288

Chinese
$9-$25

The trendy Manhattan-style restaurant is tops for healthful China-inspired dishes. Upscale square dishes and thin-lipped stemware enhance dish presentation and wines from the extensive list. Dark wood tables are topped with modern placemats and candles. Knowledgeable staffers gladly assist with wine pairings. Many lunch specials include a choice of soup. Orchard crispy shrimp with melon and fruit glaze is a memorable entree. Desserts include lavender creme brulee and the Asian Key lime tart. Dressy casual. **Bar:** Full bar. **Reservations:** suggested. **Hours:** 11:30 am-9:30 pm, Fri & Sat-10:30 pm, Sun noon-9:30 pm. Closed 11/25, 12/25. **Address:** 335 Main St 06457 **Location:** Jct SR 9, just sw on SR 66, then just s. **Parking:** street. CALL &M

IT'S ONLY NATURAL RESTAURANT Phone: 860/346-9210

Vegetarian
$8-$22

Bright colors and warm plates welcome diners to the restaurant. Soybean tempeh cakes and sweet potato fries are two tempting choices. Family artwork and cultural sounds add to the experience. During warmer months, this place offers seating on the deck. Dressy casual. **Bar:** Full bar. **Reservations:** accepted. **Hours:** 11 am-9 pm, Fri & Sat-10 pm. Closed major holidays. **Address:** 386 Main St 06457 **Location:** SR 9, exit 15, just w on Washington St, then s on Melilli Plaza St; in rear of Main Street Market. **Parking:** on-site.

TAVERN AT THE ARMORY *Menu on AAA.com* Phone: 860/854-6323

New England
$8-$29

Located within the historic town armory, the upscale colonial tavern features an array of menu choices, from sandwiches and burgers to fresh seafood and steak. For a romantic evening, request a table by the fireplace. Casual dress. **Bar:** Full bar. **Reservations:** accepted. **Hours:** 7 am-9 pm, Fri-10 pm, Sat 7 am-noon & 5-10 pm, Sun 7 am-noon & 5-9 pm. **Address:** 70 Main St 06457 **Location:** SR 9, exit 15, just sw on Dr. Martin Luther King Jr Way, then 0.4 mi se; in Inn at Middletown. **Parking:** valet and street. **Historic** CALL &M

NEW BRITAIN pop. 71,538 (See map and index starting on p. 256)

LA QUINTA INN & SUITES NEW BRITAIN/SOUTH HARTFORD *Book at AAA.com* Phone: (860)348-1463 **75**

Hotel
$59-$109 All Year

Address: 65 Columbus Blvd 06051 **Location:** SR 9, exit 26 northbound; exit 27 southbound, then just nw. **Facility:** 135 one-bedroom standard units. 6 stories, interior corridors. *Bath:* combo or shower only. **Parking:** on-site. **Amenities:** video games (fee), voice mail, irons, hair dryers. **Leisure Activities:** exercise room. **Guest Services:** valet and coin laundry, wireless Internet. **Business Services:** meeting rooms, business center. ASK CALL &M 📶 ▣ / SOME UNITS ✕ ▯ ▱

—— WHERE TO DINE ——

GREAT TASTE CHINESE RESTAURANT Phone: 860/229-7373 **62**

Chinese
$7-$35

The setting is one of casual yet simple elegance; service is cordial but unobtrusive. The excellent variety on the menu includes fresh seafood, meat and authentic multi-regional Chinese cuisine, with the noted specialty being Peking duck. Dressy casual. **Bar:** Full bar. **Reservations:** suggested. **Hours:** 11 am-10 pm, Fri & Sat-11 pm, Sun noon-10 pm. Closed: 11/25. **Address:** 597 W Main St 06053 **Location:** SR 72, exit 7, just w on SR 372, then just e. **Parking:** on-site.

PLAINVILLE (See map and index starting on p. 256)

—— WHERE TO DINE ——

J TIMOTHY'S TAVERNE Phone: 860/747-6813 **68**

American
$8-$29

The 1789 tavern sports a comfortable, relaxed atmosphere and some of the best "dirty" chicken wings in the area. Also of note are a delicious stuffed filet Gorgonzola, French onion soup and a tasty caramel turtle pie. Casual dress. **Bar:** Full bar. **Reservations:** not accepted. **Hours:** 11:30 am-10 pm, Fri & Sat-midnight. Closed major holidays; also 5/30. **Address:** 143 New Britain Ave 06062 **Location:** I-84, exit 34 eastbound, 0.4 mi n on Crooked St, then 0.6 mi nw of SR 372; exit 34 westbound, 0.6 mi nw on Crooked St, then 0.6 mi nw on SR 372. **Parking:** on-site.

ROCKY HILL (See map and index starting on p. 256)

HAMPTON INN-HARTFORD/ROCKY HILL *Book great rates at AAA.com* Phone: (860)563-7877 **78**

Hotel
$89-$169 All Year

Address: 20 Waterchase Dr 06067 **Location:** I-91, exit 24, just s. **Facility:** 99 one-bedroom standard units. 4 stories, interior corridors. *Bath:* combo or shower only. **Parking:** on-site. **Terms:** 1-7 night minimum stay, cancellation fee imposed. **Amenities:** video games (fee), voice mail, irons, hair dryers. **Pool(s):** outdoor. **Leisure Activities:** exercise room. **Guest Services:** valet and coin laundry, wireless Internet. **Business Services:** business center. 🛏⊹ CALL &M 🏊 📶 ▯ ▣ ▣ / SOME UNITS ✕

HARTFORD MARRIOTT ROCKY HILL   *Book great rates at AAA.com*   Phone: (860)257-6000 **81**

AAA (SAVE)
▼▼▼▼
Hotel
$170-$208 All Year

Address: 100 Capital Blvd 06067 **Location:** I-91, exit 23, just e. **Facility:** Smoke free premises. 251 units. 247 one-bedroom standard units. 4 one-bedroom suites. 4 stories, interior corridors. **Parking:** on-site. **Terms:** check-in 4 pm, cancellation fee imposed. **Amenities:** voice mail, irons, hair dryers. *Fee:* video games, high-speed Internet. *Some:* dual phone lines. **Pool(s):** heated indoor. **Leisure Activities:** whirlpool, exercise room. **Guest Services:** valet laundry, wireless Internet. **Business Services:** meeting rooms, business center. **Free Special Amenities:** newspaper.

Marriott
HOTELS & RESORTS

AAA Benefit:
Members save a
minimum 5% off the
best available rate.

HOWARD JOHNSON EXPRESS INN   *Book great rates at AAA.com*   Phone: (860)529-3341 **79**

AAA (SAVE)
▼▼▼
Motel
$70-$120 All Year

Address: 1760 Silas Deane Hwy 06067 **Location:** I-91, exit 24, just e on SR 99. **Facility:** 32 one-bedroom standard units, some with whirlpools. 2 stories (no elevator), exterior corridors. **Parking:** on-site. **Terms:** 7 day cancellation notice-fee imposed. **Amenities:** high-speed Internet, safes, irons, hair dryers. **Free Special Amenities: continental breakfast and high-speed Internet.**

RESIDENCE INN BY MARRIOTT HARTFORD-ROCKY HILL   *Book great rates at AAA.com*   Phone: (860)257-7500 **80**

▼▼▼
Extended Stay
Hotel
$180-$190 All Year

Address: 680 Cromwell Ave 06067 **Location:** I-91, exit 23, 0.4 mi w on West St, then just n. **Facility:** Smoke free premises. 96 units. 38 one-bedroom standard units, some with efficiencies or kitchens. 37 one- and 21 two-bedroom suites, some with efficiencies or kitchens. 3 stories, interior corridors. **Bath:** combo or shower only. **Parking:** on-site. **Terms:** cancellation fee imposed. **Amenities:** high-speed Internet, voice mail, irons, hair dryers. **Pool(s):** heated indoor. **Leisure Activities:** whirlpool, exercise room, sports court. **Guest Services:** valet and coin laundry, wireless Internet. **Business Services:** meeting rooms, business center.

AAA Benefit:
Members save a
minimum 5% off the
best available rate.

---- **WHERE TO DINE** ----

DAKOTA OF ROCKY HILL   Phone: 860/257-7752 **65**

▼▼▼
American
$8-$26

The restaurant presents a warm, inviting atmosphere with a touch of Southwest feel and aboriginal artifacts. The steak is served juicy, hot and sizzling, and the fish and seafood are ocean fresh. Casual dress. **Bar:** Full bar. **Hours:** 11:30 am-2:30 & 5-10 pm, Fri-10:30 pm, Sat 11:30 am-10:30 pm, Sun 10 am-2 & 4-9:30 pm; Sunday brunch. Closed: 11/25, 12/25. **Address:** 1489 Silas Deane Hwy 06067 **Location:** I-91, exit 24, just s. **Parking:** on-site.

SIMSBURY (See map and index starting on p. 256)

SIMSBURY 1820 HOUSE   *Book at AAA.com*   Phone: (860)658-7658

▼▼▼
Historic
Country Inn
$129-$229 All Year

Address: 731 Hopmeadow St 06070 **Location:** US 202/SR 10, 2 mi n of jct SR 185; center. **Facility:** Graciously restored country manor and carriage house. 32 units. 30 one-bedroom standard units. 2 one-bedroom suites, some with whirlpools. 3-4 stories (no elevator), interior/exterior corridors. **Parking:** on-site. **Amenities:** video library, dual phone lines, voice mail, irons, hair dryers. *Some:* DVD players. **Leisure Activities:** *Fee:* massage, in room spa services. **Guest Services:** valet laundry, area transportation, wireless Internet. **Business Services:** meeting rooms, business center.

SIMSBURY INN   *Book at AAA.com*   Phone: (860)651-5700 **35**

▼▼▼
Hotel
$169-$500 All Year

Address: 397 Hopmeadow St 06070 **Location:** On US 202/SR 10, 0.4 mi n of jct SR 185. **Facility:** Smoke free premises. 97 one-bedroom standard units. 4 stories, interior corridors. **Parking:** on-site. **Amenities:** dual phone lines, voice mail, irons, hair dryers. *Some:* DVD players, high-speed Internet. **Dining:** Evergreens Restaurant, see separate listing. **Pool(s):** heated indoor. **Leisure Activities:** saunas, whirlpool, tennis court, jogging, exercise room. *Fee:* massage, in room spa services. **Guest Services:** complimentary and valet laundry, area transportation, wireless Internet. **Business Services:** conference facilities, business center.

---- **WHERE TO DINE** ----

ANTONIO'S   Phone: 860/651-3333

▼▼
American
$6-$17

Established in 1964, the family-run restaurant prepares many traditional favorites. The walls are covered with knickknacks, and a large fish tank is in the center of the dining area. Casual dress. **Bar:** Full bar. **Reservations:** accepted. **Hours:** 11:30 am-9 pm, Fri-10 pm, Sat noon-10 pm, Sun noon-9 pm. Closed: 12/25. **Address:** 1185 Hopmeadow St 06070 **Location:** Jct SR 315, just n on US 202/SR 10. **Parking:** on-site.

EVERGREENS RESTAURANT   Phone: 860/651-5700

▼▼▼▼
Continental
$6-$29

Grand glass windows in the sophisticated dining room overlook the country hills nearby. American/Continental fare lines a seasonal menu that may include corn and crab bisque, which is filled with lump crabmeat, bacon and chives; porcini mushroom ravioli; and the grilled double-cut pork chop served in a tangy brown-sugar glaze and sweet mango chutney. Casual dress. **Bar:** Full bar. **Reservations:** suggested **Hours:** 11:30 am-2:30 & 5:30-9 pm, Fri & Sat 5:30 pm-10 pm; Sunday brunch seatings at 11 am & 1 pm Closed: 12/25; also Mon. **Address:** 397 Hopmeadow St 06070 **Location:** On US 202/SR 10, 0.4 mi n of jct SR 185; in Simsbury Inn. **Parking:** on-site. CALL 🐾M

METRO BIS   Phone: 860/651-1908

▼▼▼
American
$7-$24

Among the chef-owned bistro's imaginative dishes are Gorgonzola-crusted steak, mixed greens with candied walnuts and Prosperi balsamic salad dressing, yellowfin tuna carpaccio, seared sea scallops with lobster whipped potatoes and crispy marinated calamari. Contributing to the intimate atmosphere are soft lighting, fleur-de-lis stenciling, Parisian subway artifacts and an open-concept kitchen. Dressy casual. **Bar:** Full bar. **Reservations:** suggested. **Hours:** 11:30 am-2:30 & 5:30-9:30 pm. Closed: 4/4, 11/25, 12/25; also Sun. **Address:** 928 Hopmeadow St 06070 **Location:** Center; in Simsburytown Shops. **Parking:** on-site. CALL 🐾M

SAKIMURA   Phone: 860/651-7929

▼▼▼
Japanese
$8-$25

The extensive, accommodating menu ranges from health-conscious delicacies to deep-fried items, light-fried seafood, broiled beef, fish or teriyaki-style chicken. Trusting diners are sure to enjoy the sushi and sashimi platters. Casual dress. **Bar:** Beer & wine. **Reservations:** suggested. **Hours:** 11:30 am-2:30 & 5-9:30 pm, Fri & Sat-10 pm, Sun noon-9:30 pm. Closed: 11/25. **Address:** 10 Wilcox St 06070 **Location:** Just e of US 202/SR 10; center. **Parking:** on-site.

SOUTHINGTON   (See map and index starting on p. 256)

HOLIDAY INN EXPRESS   *Book at AAA.com*   Phone: (860)276-0736   **93**

▼▼▼
Hotel
$109-$129 All Year

Address: 120 Laning St 06489 **Location:** I-84, exit 32, just s on SR 10, then just e. **Facility:** 122 one-bedroom standard units, some with whirlpools. 3 stories, interior corridors. *Bath:* combo or shower only. **Parking:** on-site. **Terms:** cancellation fee imposed. **Amenities:** video games (fee), high-speed Internet, dual phone lines, voice mail, irons, hair dryers. **Pool(s):** outdoor. **Leisure Activities:** exercise room. **Guest Services:** valet and coin laundry, wireless Internet. **Business Services:** meeting rooms, business center. (ASK) 📶↕ CALL 🐾M 🏊 📹 💻 / SOME UNITS ✖ FEE 🛏 FEE 🖨

RESIDENCE INN SOUTHINGTON   *Book great rates at AAA.com*   Phone: (860)621-4440   **94**

▼▼▼
Hotel
$152-$186 All Year

Address: 778 West St 06489 **Location:** I-84, exit 31, just s. **Facility:** Smoke free premises. 94 units. 41 one-bedroom standard units, some with efficiencies or kitchens. 41 one- and 12 two-bedroom suites, some with efficiencies or kitchens. 4 stories, interior corridors. *Bath:* combo or shower only. **Parking:** on-site. **Terms:** cancellation fee imposed. **Amenities:** video games (fee), high-speed Internet, dual phone lines, voice mail, irons, hair dryers. **Pool(s):** heated indoor. **Leisure Activities:** whirlpool, exercise room, sports court. **Guest Services:** valet and coin laundry, area transportation, wireless Internet. **Business Services:** meeting rooms, business center. 📶↕ CALL 🐾M 🏊 ✖ ✖ 📹 🛏 🖨 💻 / SOME UNITS FEE 🐾

AAA Benefit:
Members save a minimum 5% off the best available rate.

SOUTH WINDSOR   (See map and index starting on p. 256)

—— WHERE TO DINE ——

BELLINI'S   Phone: 860/432-3461   **29**

▼▼▼
Italian
$7-$25

Diners appreciate this restaurant for its freshly prepared dishes at affordable prices. On the menu are thin-crust pizzas, steaks, oversize salads and classic Italian dishes, such as a delicious sweet sausage and cavatelli dish made with fresh spinach, tomato, garlic and roasted pepperonata. Among tantalizing made-from-scratch desserts is the sinfully rich chocolate cake layered with ganache and hazelnut mousse. A beautiful mahogany bar and tables play into the simple yet refined atmosphere. Casual dress. **Bar:** Full bar. **Reservations:** suggested. **Hours:** 11:30 am-10 pm, Fri & Sat-11 pm, Sun noon-9 pm. Closed: 11/25, 12/25. **Address:** 501 Evergreen Way, Suite 538 06074 **Location:** Center; at The Shops at Evergreen Walk. **Parking:** street. CALL 🐾M

BURTONS GRILL   Phone: 860/432-4575   **30**

▼▼▼
American
$11-$33

This always bustling restaurant, which sports sophisticated contemporary decor, is in an upscale outdoor shopping area and has a patio that opens during warmer months. Guests might start with sesame-crusted tuna served chilled and rare with spicy cucumber salad, wasabi and ginger; then move on to a 14-ounce aged Angus rib-eye beef that's seasoned, grilled and served with caramelized onion sage butter; and end with delicious made-in-house Key lime pie. Casual dress. **Bar:** Full bar. **Reservations:** suggested. **Hours:** 11:30 am-10 pm, Fri & Sat-11 pm, Sun-9 pm. Closed: 4/4, 11/25, 12/25. **Address:** 100 Evergreen Way 06074 **Location:** Center; at The Shops at Evergreen Walk. **Parking:** on-site. CALL 🐾M

THE MILL ON THE RIVER   Phone: 860/289-7929   **27**

AAA
▼▼▼
American
$9-$29

Dining is a real pleasure at this restored mill in a romantic park setting, with a fountain and overlooking a river with a dam and waterfall. This restaurant features a vast array of creative cuisine as well as traditional specialties. Patio dining is available seasonally. Casual dress. **Bar:** Full bar. **Reservations:** suggested **Hours:** 11:30 am-2 & 5-9:30 pm, Fri-10 pm, Sat 5 pm-10 pm, Sun 11 am-2 & 3-8:30 pm. **Address:** 989 Ellington Rd 06074 **Location:** I-291, exit 4, 2.5 mi ne on SR 30. **Parking:** on-site.

TourBookMark

Lodging Listing Symbols

Member Values

AAA or **CAA** or **SAVE** offers members a rate guarantee and up to two special amenities as part of their Official Appointment partnership with AAA.

- **ASK** May offer discount
- **fyi** Informational listing only
- **ECO** Certified by eco-certification organizations

Member Services

- ✈ Airport transportation
- 🛏 Pets allowed (call property for restrictions and fees)
- 🍴 Restaurant on premises
- 🍴+ Restaurant off premises (walking distance)
- 24🍴 24-hour room service
- 🍸 Full bar
- 👶 Child care
- ♿M Accessibility features (call property for available services and amenities)

Leisure Activities

- 🎰 Full-service casino
- 🏊 Pool
- 💪 Health club on premises
- 💪→ Health club off premises (walking distance)
- ✖ Recreational activities

In-Room Amenities

- ✕ Designated non-smoking rooms
- 📽 Movies
- 🍱 Refrigerator
- 📟 Microwave
- 💻 Coffee maker
- 🎬 No air conditioning
- 📺 No TV
- 📺 No cable TV
- ☎ No telephones

Safety Features
(Mexico and Caribbean only)

- **S** Sprinklers
- **D** Smoke detectors

Call property for detailed information about fees & restrictions relating to the lodging listing symbols.

CHOICE HOTELS INTERNATIONAL ®

Book today at choicehotels.com or 800.228.1222

SAKURA GARDEN JAPANESE STEAK HOUSE

Japanese
$9-$29

Phone: 860/648-9888 (28)

In an upscale outdoor shopping village, this restaurant is a visual standout from its striking entry to its small koi pond bridge to its stylish and awe-inspiring dining room. A curved pebble stone wall hugs the sushi bar, and guests almost always pack the large granite-topped bar. Cowboy-dressed chefs entertain guests at the hibachi tables while others enjoy the fresh sushi, sashimi and other Japanese dishes. Servers dressed in all black are knowledgeable and attentive. Dressy casual. **Bar:** Full bar. **Reservations:** accepted. **Hours:** 11:30 am-10 pm, Fri & Sat-11 pm, Sun-9 pm. Closed: 11/25, 12/25. **Address:** 800 Evergreen Way 06074 **Location:** At the Shops at Evergreen Walk; center. **Parking:** on-site. CALL 🔲Ⓜ

VERNON

COMFORT INN

AAA SAVE

Hotel
Rates not provided

Book great rates at AAA.com

Phone: 860/871-2432

Address: 425 Hartford Tpke (SR 30) 06066 **Location:** I-84, exit 65, just n. Adjacent to shopping area. **Facility:** 67 one-bedroom standard units. 2 stories (no elevator), interior corridors. **Parking:** on-site. **Amenities:** high-speed Internet, dual phone lines, voice mail, irons, hair dryers. **Leisure Activities:** exercise room. **Guest Services:** valet and coin laundry, wireless Internet. **Business Services:** business center. **Free Special Amenities:** continental breakfast and high-speed Internet.

🍽 🐾 🛏 📶 🖥 / SOME UNITS ✉

HOLIDAY INN EXPRESS HARTFORD-VERNON

Hotel
$99-$129 5/1-11/16
$79-$110 11/17-4/30

Book at AAA.com

Phone: (860)648-2000

Address: 346 Kelly Rd 06066 **Location:** I-84, exit 64, 0.4 mi w. **Facility:** 63 one-bedroom standard units, some with efficiencies and/or whirlpools. 2 stories, interior corridors. *Bath:* combo or shower only. **Parking:** on-site. **Terms:** cancellation fee imposed. **Amenities:** high-speed Internet, dual phone lines, voice mail, irons, hair dryers. **Leisure Activities:** exercise room. **Guest Services:** valet laundry, wireless Internet. **Business Services:** business center.

ASK 🍽 CALL 🔲Ⓜ 🐾 🖥 / SOME UNITS ✉ 🛏 📶

——— **WHERE TO DINE** ———

ANGELLINO'S

Italian
$7-$20

Phone: 860/644-7702

A pleasant place for a quick lunch or family dinner, this hometown favorite includes many pasta dishes that can be made with sauces ranging from Gorgonzola cream to fra diavolo to basil pesto. Focaccia sandwiches, oversized salads and seafood preparations include bay scallops fritto, which are breaded with a crisp coating and tossed with capers in a fresh lemon and butter sauce and served over linguine. Casual dress. **Bar:** Full bar. **Reservations:** not accepted. **Hours:** 11 am-9:30 pm, Fri & Sat-10:30 pm. Closed: 11/25, 12/25. **Address:** 346 Kelly Rd 06066 **Location:** I-84, exit 64, 0.4 mi w. **Parking:** on-site. CALL 🔲Ⓜ

REIN'S NEW YORK STYLE DELI-RESTAURANT

Deli
$3-$12

Phone: 860/875-1344

For more than 25 years, the traditional New York-style Jewish delicatessen has served food that feeds the soul and warms the heart. Corned beef, pastrami, smoked fish and pickles, as well as on-site bakery treats including cheesecake, are staples here. Casual dress. **Bar:** Full bar. **Reservations:** not accepted. **Hours:** 7 am-midnight. Closed: 11/25, 12/25; also for dinner 11/25 & 1/1. **Address:** 435A Hartford Tpke (SR 30) 06066 **Location:** I-84, exit 65, just n. **Parking:** on-site.

WOOD-N-TAP

American
$9-$22

Phone: 860/872-6700

This neighborhood gathering place features a fun and lively bar area with 12 large flat-panel high-definition TVs, plus another in the bathroom so patrons won't miss a minute of their favorite sports game. Friendly staffers in casual T-shirts provide attentive service. The large menu offers eight varieties of burgers, including bison, in addition to pizza, a few pasta selections, grilled items such as Atlantic salmon and swordfish, and the highly popular firehouse wings and baby back ribs. Casual dress. **Bar:** Full bar. **Reservations:** not accepted. **Hours:** 11:30 am-1 am, Fri & Sat-2 am. Closed: 11/25, 12/25. **Address:** 236 Hartford Tpke 06066 **Location:** I-84, exit 64 eastbound, just s on SR 83, then just e; exit 65 westbound, 0.6 mi sw. **Parking:** on-site. CALL 🔲Ⓜ

WEST HARTFORD pop. 63,589 (See map and index starting on p. 256)

WEST HARTFORD INN

AAA SAVE

Hotel
$88-$128 All Year

Book great rates at AAA.com

Phone: (860)236-3221 (56)

Address: 900 Farmington Ave 06119 **Location:** I-84, exit 41, 2 mi n on Main St, then just e. **Facility:** 52 one-bedroom standard units. 5 stories, interior corridors. *Bath:* combo or shower only. **Parking:** on-site. **Terms:** cancellation fee imposed. **Amenities:** video library, voice mail, irons, hair dryers. *Some:* DVD players, CD players. **Leisure Activities:** exercise room. **Guest Services:** valet laundry, wireless Internet. **Free Special Amenities:** continental breakfast and high-speed Internet.

CALL 🔲Ⓜ 🐾 🖥 / SOME UNITS ✉ FEE 🛏 FEE 📶

——— **WHERE TO DINE** ———

ARUGULA

Mediterranean
$10-$33

Phone: 860/561-4888 (45)

Terra cotta sponge-painted walls, rustic dark hardwood flooring, blue sconces and colorful framed artwork contribute to the dining room's quaint Mediterranean feel. Boutiques surround the nice location. Large appetizers are meant to be shared, and entrees include many types of flatbread pizzas, as well as pasta and chicken dishes. Those who don't opt for one of the fine wine selections might try any of more than 50 tea varieties, such as some rare white and red Rooibos teas from South Africa. Dressy casual. **Bar:** Full bar. **Reservations:** suggested. **Hours:** 11:30 am-2:30 & 5:30-close, Mon from 5:30 pm. Closed major holidays; also Sun except 5/1-5/31 & 10/1-12/31. **Address:** 953 Farmington Ave 06107 **Location:** I-84, exit 41 eastbound, 2 mi n on S Main St, then just w; exit 43 westbound, just e on Park Ave, 0.5 mi n on Trout Brook Dr, then just w. **Parking:** street.

THE CORNER PUG

English
$8-$26

Phone: 860/231-0241   **49**

Guests might be fooled by the cute name. Inside is an upscale pub offering meals made from tempting ingredients. It is said that a wrinkly faced little pooch founded this place. Casual dress. **Bar:** Full bar. **Reservations:** not accepted. **Hours:** 11:30 am-10 pm, Fri & Sat-11 pm, Sun 11 am-10 pm. Closed: 7/4, 11/25, 12/25. **Address:** 1046 New Britain Ave 06110 **Location:** I-84, exit 41, 0.3 mi s on SR 173, then 0.9 mi e. **Parking:** on-site.

GRANT'S

American
$8-$38

Phone: 860/236-1930   **46**

The dining room is a perfect setting for romance or entertaining. Truffle frites can be characterized as a personal indulgence. The patisserie prepares a sweet selection of treats. Dressy casual. **Bar:** Full bar. **Reservations:** suggested. **Hours:** 11:30 am-3 & 5-10 pm, Fri & Sat-11 pm, Sun 11 am-3 & 4-9 pm. Closed: 11/25, 12/25. **Address:** 977 Farmington Ave 06107 **Location:** I-84, exit 41, 2 mi n on Main St, then just w on SR 4. **Parking:** on-site (fee) and street.

RESTAURANT BRICCO

American
$8-$28

Phone: 860/233-0220   **47**

The open kitchen has an open brick oven where wood-fired stone pie pizzas are finished. There are also plenty of rich and sweet dessert choices. Dressy casual. **Bar:** Full bar. **Reservations:** not accepted. **Hours:** 11:30 am-3 & 5-10 pm, Fri & Sat-11 pm, Sun 4 pm-9 pm. Closed: 11/25, 12/24, 12/25. **Address:** 78 LaSalle Rd 06107 **Location:** I-84, exit 41, 2 mi n on Main St, just w on SR 4, then just s. **Parking:** on-site (fee) and street.

TAPAS

Mediterranean
$6-$15

Phone: 860/521-4609   **48**

Sumptuous dishes are prepared with fresh, creative ingredients. Greek and Middle Eastern flavors fill the menu, and daily blackboard specials let diners easily sample numerous courses. Casual dress. **Bar:** Beer & wine. **Reservations:** not accepted. **Hours:** 11 am-9 pm, Fri & Sat-10 pm, Sun noon-9 pm. Closed major holidays. **Address:** 1150 New Britain Ave 06110 **Location:** I-84, exit 41, just s on SR 173, then 0.5 mi e on SR 71. **Parking:** on-site.

WETHERSFIELD pop. 26,271   (See map and index starting on p. 256)

CHESTER BULKLEY HOUSE

Historic Bed
& Breakfast
$95-$145 All Year

Phone: 860/563-4236   **63**

Address: 184 Main St 06109 **Location:** Center of The Old Village. Located in a historic district. **Facility:** Located in the historic district, this restored 1830 house boasts beautiful antiques in the common areas. Smoke free premises. 5 one-bedroom standard units. 2 stories (no elevator), interior corridors. *Bath:* some shared or private, combo or shower only. **Parking:** on-site. **Terms:** check-in 4 pm, 14 day cancellation notice. **Amenities:** *Some:* hair dryers. **Guest Services:** TV in common area.

ASK ⊞→ ✕ ⺠

COMFORT INN   *Book great rates at AAA.com*

Hotel
·$99-$179 5/1-10/31
$89-$159 11/1-4/30

Phone: (860)563-2311   **64**

Address: 1330 Silas Deane Hwy 06109 **Location:** I-91, exit 24, 0.4 mi n. **Facility:** 107 one-bedroom standard units. 4 stories, interior corridors. **Parking:** on-site. **Terms:** cancellation fee imposed. **Amenities:** video games (fee), voice mail, irons, hair dryers. *Some:* high-speed Internet, dual phone lines. **Pool(s):** heated indoor. **Leisure Activities:** sauna, whirlpool, exercise room. **Guest Services:** valet and coin laundry, wireless Internet. **Business Services:** meeting rooms, business center. Free **Special Amenities:** expanded continental breakfast and high-speed Internet.

⊞→ CALL ⒼM 🚗 ✕ 📷 📺 / SOME UNITS ✕ 🛏 🍽

------ **WHERE TO DINE** ------

CARMEN ANTHONY   Phase: 860/529-7557

Seafood
$7-$49

Regulars know the award-winning crab cakes and New England clam chowder are two of the best ways to start off an elegant dining experience in this intimate setting. Attentive service is a plus. Dressy casual. **Bar:** Full bar. **Reservations:** accepted. **Hours:** 11 am-4 & 5-10 pm, Sat from 5 pm, Sun 4 pm-9 pm. Closed: 12/25. **Address:** 1770 Berlin Tpke 06109 **Location:** Northbound side of US 5 and SR 15. **Parking:** on-site.

CALL

WINDSOR   (See map and index starting on p. 256)

COURTYARD HARTFORD WINDSOR   *Book great rates at AAA.com*   **Phone: (860)683-0022**   **28**

Hotel
$148-$180 All Year

Address: 1 Day Hill Rd 06095 **Location:** I-91, exit 38 northbound; exit 38B southbound. **Facility:** Smoke free premises. 149 units. 137 one-bedroom standard units. 12 one-bedroom suites. 2-3 stories, interior corridors. *Bath:* combo or shower only. **Parking:** on-site. **Terms:** cancellation fee imposed. **Amenities:** high-speed Internet, dual phone lines, voice mail, irons, hair dryers. *Some:* DVD players. **Pool(s):** heated indoor. **Leisure Activities:** whirlpool, exercise room. **Guest Services:** valet and coin laundry, airport transportation-Bradley International Airport, wireless Internet. **Business Services:** meeting rooms, business center. **Free Special Amenities:** newspaper and early check-in/late check-out.

AAA Benefit:
Members save a minimum 5% off the best available rate.

HAMPTON INN HARTFORD/AIRPORT   *Book great rates at AAA.com*   **Phone: (860)683-1118**   **27**

Hotel
$89-$179 All Year

Address: 2168 Poquonock Ave 06095 **Location:** On SR 75, jct SR 20. **Facility:** 110 one-bedroom standard units, some with whirlpools. 2 stories, interior corridors. *Bath:* combo or shower only. **Parking:** on-site. **Terms:** 1-7 night minimum stay, cancellation fee imposed. **Amenities:** high-speed Internet, dual phone lines, voice mail, irons, hair dryers. **Pool(s):** heated indoor. **Leisure Activities:** whirlpool, exercise room. **Guest Services:** valet and coin laundry, area transportation, wireless Internet. **Business Services:** meeting rooms, business center.

AAA Benefit:
Members save up to 10% everyday!

HARTFORD/WINDSOR MARRIOTT AIRPORT   *Book great rates at AAA.com*   **Phone: (860)688-7500**   **29**

Hotel
$197-$241 All Year

Address: 28 Day Hill Rd 06095 **Location:** I-91, exit 38 northbound; exit 38B southbound. **Facility:** Smoke free premises. 295 units. 291 one-bedroom standard units. 8 suites. 8 stories, interior corridors. *Bath:* combo or shower only. **Parking:** on-site. **Terms:** cancellation fee imposed. **Amenities:** dual phone lines, voice mail, irons, hair dryers. **Pool(s):** heated indoor. **Leisure Activities:** exercise room. **Guest Services:** valet and coin laundry, wireless Internet. **Business Services:** conference facilities, business center.

   CALL

Marriott
HOTELS & RESORTS
AAA Benefit:
Members save a minimum 5% off the best available rate.

HILTON GARDEN INN HARTFORD NORTH
BRADLEY INTERNATIONAL AIRPORT   *Book great rates at AAA.com*   **Phone: (860)688-6400**   **30**

Hotel
$89-$199 All Year

Address: 555 Corporate Dr 06095 **Location:** I-91, exit 38 northbound; exit 38B southbound. **Facility:** 157 units. 156 one-bedroom standard units. 1 one-bedroom suite. 6 stories, interior corridors. *Bath:* combo or shower only. **Parking:** on-site. **Terms:** 1-7 night minimum stay, cancellation fee imposed. **Amenities:** high-speed Internet, dual phone lines, voice mail, irons, hair dryers. **Pool(s):** heated indoor. **Leisure Activities:** whirlpool, exercise room. **Guest Services:** valet and coin laundry, wireless Internet. **Business Services:** meeting rooms, business center.

Hilton
Garden Inn
AAA Benefit:
Members save 5% or more everyday!

HYATT SUMMERFIELD SUITES HARTFORD NORTH/WINDSOR   *Book great rates at AAA.com*

Phone: (860)298-8000   **31**

Hotel
$99-$399 All Year

Address: 200 Corporate Dr 06095 **Location:** I-91, exit 38 northbound; exit 38B southbound. **Facility:** Smoke free premises. 132 units. 61 one-bedroom standard units with kitchens. 65 one- and 6 two-bedroom suites. 7 stories, interior corridors. *Bath:* combo or shower only. **Parking:** on-site. **Terms:** cancellation fee imposed. **Amenities:** video library, DVD players, high-speed Internet, dual phone lines, voice mail, irons, hair dryers. **Pool(s):** heated indoor. **Leisure Activities:** whirlpool, gas grills, exercise room. **Guest Services:** valet and coin laundry, airport transportation-Bradley International Airport, area transportation-within 5mi, wireless Internet. **Business Services:** meeting rooms, business center. **Free Special Amenities: full breakfast and high-speed Internet.**

HYATT
HOTELS & RESORTS
AAA Benefit:
Ask for the AAA rate and save 10%.

THE RESIDENCE INN BY MARRIOTT HARTFORD-WINDSOR   *Book great rates at AAA.com*

Phone: (860)688-7474   **32**

Hotel
$152-$186 All Year

Address: 100 Dunfey Ln 06095 **Location:** I-91, exit 37, just w on SR 305 to Dunfey Ln, then 0.3 mi n. **Facility:** Smoke free premises. 96 units. 72 one-bedroom standard units with kitchens. 24 two-bedroom suites with kitchens. 2 stories (no elevator), exterior corridors. **Parking:** on-site. **Terms:** cancellation fee imposed. **Amenities:** CD players, voice mail, irons, hair dryers. **Pool(s):** outdoor. **Leisure Activities:** whirlpool, sports court, basketball. **Guest Services:** valet and coin laundry, wireless Internet. **Business Services:** meeting rooms, business center.

Residence Inn
Marriott
AAA Benefit:
Members save a minimum 5% off the best available rate.

WINDSOR LOCKS pop. 12,043   (See map and index starting on p. 256)

CANDLEWOOD SUITES   *Book at AAA.com*

Phone: (860)623-2000   **14**

Extended Stay
Hotel
$79-$149 All Year

Address: 149 Ella T Grasso Tpke 06096 **Location:** I-91, exit 40, 2.5 mi w on SR 20, then 0.6 mi n on SR 75. **Facility:** 120 units. 100 one-bedroom standard units with efficiencies. 20 one-bedroom suites with efficiencies. 3 stories, interior corridors. *Bath:* combo or shower only. **Parking:** on-site. **Terms:** cancellation fee imposed. **Amenities:** video library, DVD players, high-speed Internet, voice mail, irons, hair dryers. **Pool(s):** heated indoor. **Leisure Activities:** exercise room. **Guest Services:** complimentary and valet laundry, area transportation, wireless Internet. **Business Services:** meeting rooms, business center.

DAYS INN BRADLEY INTERNATIONAL AIRPORT   *Book great rates at AAA.com*

Phone: 860/623-9417   **12**

Motel
Rates not provided

Address: 185 Ella T Grasso Tpke 06096 **Location:** On SR 75, 1 mi n of SR 20. **Facility:** 100 one-bedroom standard units. 2 stories (no elevator), interior corridors. **Parking:** on-site. **Amenities:** voice mail, irons, hair dryers. *Some:* CD players. **Leisure Activities:** exercise room. **Guest Services:** valet laundry, airport transportation-Bradley International Airport, wireless Internet. **Business Services:** meeting rooms, business center. **Free Special Amenities: expanded continental breakfast and high-speed Internet.**

DOUBLETREE HOTEL BRADLEY INTERNATIONAL AIRPORT   *Book great rates at AAA.com*

Phone: (860)627-5171   **17**

Hotel
$90-$210 All Year

Address: 16 Ella T Grasso Tpke 06096 **Location:** I-91, exit 40, 2.5 mi w on SR 20, then just n on SR 75. **Facility:** 200 units. 198 one-bedroom standard units. 2 one-bedroom suites. 5 stories, interior corridors. *Bath:* combo or shower only. **Parking:** on-site. **Terms:** 1-7 night minimum stay, cancellation fee imposed. **Amenities:** dual phone lines, voice mail, irons, hair dryers. **Pool(s):** heated indoor. **Leisure Activities:** exercise room. **Guest Services:** valet and coin laundry, airport transportation-Bradley International Airport, area transportation-within 5 mi, wireless Internet. **Business Services:** meeting rooms, business center.

DOUBLETREE
HOTELS • SUITES • RESORTS • CLUBS
AAA Benefit:
Members save 5% or more everyday!

FAIRFIELD INN HARTFORD-AIRPORT   *Book great rates at AAA.com*

Phone: (860)627-9333   **15**

(fyi)
Motel
$129-$139 All Year

Under major renovation, scheduled to be completed April 2009. **Last rated:** ◇◇ **Address:** 2 Loten Dr 06096 **Location:** I-91, exit 40, 2.5 mi w on SR 20, then just n on SR 75. **Facility:** Smoke free premises. 134 one-bedroom standard units. 3 stories, interior/exterior corridors. **Parking:** on-site. **Terms:** cancellation fee imposed. **Amenities:** high-speed Internet, voice mail, irons, hair dryers. **Leisure Activities:** exercise room. **Guest Services:** valet laundry, wireless Internet. **Business Services:** business center.

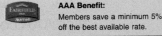
FAIRFIELD INN
Marriott
AAA Benefit:
Members save a minimum 5% off the best available rate.

HOLIDAY INN EXPRESS BRADLEY AIRPORT *Book at AAA.com*

Phone: 860/386-6300 **10**

Hotel
Rates not provided

Address: 600 Spring St 06096 **Location:** I-91, exit 40, 2.5 mi w on SR 20, 1.1 mi n on SR 75, then just e. Located in a commercial area. **Facility:** Smoke free premises. 107 one-bedroom standard units. 3 stories, interior corridors. *Bath:* combo or shower only. **Parking:** on-site. **Amenities:** high-speed Internet, dual phone lines, voice mail, irons, hair dryers. **Pool(s):** heated indoor. **Leisure Activities:** exercise room. **Guest Services:** valet and coin laundry, wireless Internet. **Business Services:** meeting rooms, business center.

HOMEWOOD SUITES BY HILTON *Book great rates at AAA.com*

Phone: (860)627-8463 **18**

Extended Stay Hotel
$109-$179 All Year

Address: 65 Ella T Grasso Tpke 06096 **Location:** I-91, exit 40, 2.5 mi w on SR 20, then just n on SR 75. **Facility:** 132 units. 124 one- and 8 two-bedroom suites with efficiencies. 3 stories, interior/exterior corridors. **Parking:** on-site. **Terms:** 1-7 night minimum stay, cancellation fee imposed. **Amenities:** high-speed Internet, dual phone lines, voice mail, irons, hair dryers. **Pool(s):** outdoor. **Leisure Activities:** whirlpool, exercise room, sports court, basketball. **Guest Services:** valet and coin laundry, area transportation, wireless Internet. **Business Services:** meeting rooms, business center.

AAA Benefit:
Members save 5% or more everyday!

LA QUINTA INN HARTFORD-AIRPORT *Book at AAA.com*

Phone: (860)623-3336 **16**

Hotel
$65-$129 All Year

Address: 64 Ella T Grasso Tpke 06096 **Location:** I-91, exit 40, 2.5 mi w on SR 20, then just n on SR 75. Located in a commercial area. **Facility:** 102 one-bedroom standard units. 4 stories, interior corridors. **Parking:** on-site. **Amenities:** video games (fee), voice mail, irons, hair dryers. *Some:* high-speed Internet. **Guest Services:** valet and coin laundry, wireless Internet. **Business Services:** meeting rooms, business center.

RAMADA INN BRADLEY INTERNATIONAL AIRPORT *Book at AAA.com*

Phone: (860)623-9494 **19**

Hotel
$89-$99 All Year

Address: 5 Ella T Grasso Tpke 06096 **Location:** I-91, exit 40, 2.5 mi w on SR 20, then just n on SR 75. **Facility:** 148 units. 147 one-bedroom standard units. 1 one-bedroom suite with whirlpool. 2 stories, interior corridors. **Parking:** on-site. **Amenities:** video games (fee), high-speed Internet, voice mail, irons, hair dryers. **Pool(s):** heated indoor/outdoor. **Leisure Activities:** exercise room. **Guest Services:** valet and coin laundry, area transportation, wireless Internet. **Business Services:** meeting rooms.

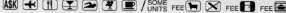

SHERATON HOTEL AT BRADLEY INTERNATIONAL AIRPORT *Book great rates at AAA.com*

Phone: (860)627-5311 **13**

Hotel
$109-$299 All Year

Address: 1 Bradley International Airport 06096 **Location:** At Bradley International Airport terminal. **Facility:** Smoke free premises. 237 units. 236 one-bedroom standard units. 1 one-bedroom suite. 8 stories, interior corridors. **Parking:** on-site (fee). **Terms:** check-in 4 pm, 3 day cancellation notice-fee imposed. **Amenities:** high-speed Internet, dual phone lines, voice mail, irons, hair dryers. *Some: Fee:* DVD players. **Pool(s):** heated indoor. **Leisure Activities:** exercise room. **Guest Services:** valet laundry, wireless Internet. **Business Services:** meeting rooms, business center. **Free Special Amenities:** newspaper and high-speed Internet.

AAA Benefit:
Members get up to 15% off, plus Starwood Preferred Guest® bonuses.

SPRINGHILL SUITES HARTFORD
AIRPORT/WINDSOR LOCKS

Phone: (860)758-7000   **11**

▼▼▼▼
Hotel
$143-$175 All Year

Address: 225 Ella T Grasso Tpke 06096 **Location:** I-91, exit 40, 2.4 mi nw on SR 20, then 1 mi n on SR 75. **Facility:** Smoke free premises. 119 one-bedroom standard units. 4 stories, interior corridors. *Bath:* shower only. **Parking:** on-site. **Terms:** cancellation fee imposed. **Amenities:** high-speed Internet, dual phone lines, voice mail, irons, hair dryers. *Some:* DVD players. **Pool(s):** heated indoor. **Leisure Activities:** exercise room. **Guest Services:** valet and coin laundry, area transportation, wireless Internet. **Business Services:** meeting rooms, business center.

AAA Benefit:
Members save a
minimum 5% off the
best available rate.

🖼 🍴 CALL 🅟Ⓜ 🏊 ✖ 📷 🖪 🖨 🖵

─────── **WHERE TO DINE** ───────

SKOOTER'S

Phone: 860/623-6100   **20**

◆
American
$3-$13

Guests can savor a great breakfast or sandwich while the jukebox spins oldies at the 1950s-style diner. Casual dress. **Reservations:** not accepted. **Hours:** 6 am-10:30 pm. Closed: 1/1, 11/25, 12/25. **Address:** 50 Ella T Grasso Tpke 06096 **Location:** I-91, exit 40, 2.5 mi w on SR 20, then just n on SR 75. **Parking:** on-site.

SKYLINE RESTAURANT

Phone: 860/623-9296   **19**

◆ ◆
Italian
$7-$25

Adjacent to the airport, the restaurant has some tables that offer views of the runway. On the menu is a large selection of hearty Italian dishes and sandwiches. Casual dress. **Bar:** Full bar. **Reservations:** accepted. **Hours:** 10:30 am-midnight, Sun 11 am-9 pm. Closed major holidays. **Address:** 106 Ella T Grasso Tpke 06096 **Location:** I-91, exit 40, 2.5 mi w on SR 20, then 0.4 mi n on SR 75. **Parking:** on-site.

Bushnell Park / Ed Homonylo / Getty Images

This ends listings for the Hartford Vicinity.
The following page resumes the alphabetical listings of cities in Connecticut.

HARWINTON

—— WHERE TO DINE ——

LANDING ZONE GRILLE

International
$9-$30

Phone: 860/485-2733

Unexpected gourmet dishes are created on the wood-fired open grill at this hidden gem on a grass patch next to a small plane landing area. Once the airport's check-in area, the restaurant features flying memorabilia and walls of signatures of pilots who once flew to this location. The overall look is basic and mismatched, but it's still a fun place to be. Casual dress. **Bar:** Full bar. **Reservations:** not accepted. **Hours:** 10:30 am-9:30 pm. Closed major holidays; also Mon & Tues. **Address:** 525 Burlington Rd 06791 **Location:** Jct SR 72, just e on SR 4. **Parking:** on-site.

IVORYTON

THE COPPER BEECH INN

Country Inn
$225-$400 All Year

Phone: 860/767-0330

Address: 46 Main St 06442 **Location:** SR 9, exit 3, 1.7 mi w. **Facility:** The 1880s home of an ivory importer, this restored property features renovated accommodations including two carriage houses. Smoke free premises. 22 one-bedroom standard units, some with whirlpools. 2 stories (no elevator), interior corridors. *Bath:* combo or shower only. **Parking:** on-site. **Terms:** 2 night minimum stay - weekends, 14 day cancellation notice-fee imposed. **Amenities:** CD players, irons, hair dryers. *Some:* DVD players, honor bars. **Dining:** restaurant, see separate listing. **Guest Services:** valet laundry, wireless Internet. **Business Services:** meeting rooms. [ASK] [❚❙] [✕] [▣] / SOME UNITS FEE [🐾]

—— WHERE TO DINE ——

COPPER BEECH INN RESTAURANT

New American
$25-$36

Phone: 860/767-0330

In a country inn, the formal dining room is an elegant setting for an innovative New French and American meal. Food preparations draw on an international flair. The well-trained staff pampers guests throughout the delightful experience and offers wine recommendations from a vast list of quality global choices. Dressy casual. **Bar:** Full bar. **Reservations:** suggested. **Hours:** 5:30 pm-9 pm, Fri & Sat-9:30 pm. Closed: 12/25. **Address:** 46 Main St 06442 **Location:** SR 9, exit 3, 1.7 mi w; in The Copper Beech Inn. **Parking:** on-site.

KENT pop. 2,858

—— WHERE TO DINE ——

BULL'S BRIDGE INN

New England
$12-$25

Phone: 860/927-1000

Seated near the cozy fireplace or on the quaint porch, you will enjoy a variety of fine offerings including steak and fresh seafood. Try the grilled salmon with salsa; tempting creme brulee is just one of many mouthwatering desserts served here. Casual dress. **Bar:** Full bar. **Reservations:** not accepted. **Hours:** 5 pm-9:30 pm, Fri & Sat-10 pm, Sun 4 pm-9 pm. Closed: 11/25, 12/25. **Address:** 333 Kent Rd 06757 **Location:** 4 mi s on US 7. **Parking:** on-site.

LAKEVILLE

INTERLAKEN INN RESORT AND CONFERENCE CENTER *Book great rates at AAA.com*

Resort
Hotel
$169-$259 All Year

Phone: (860)435-9878

Address: 74 Interlaken Rd 06039 **Location:** On SR 112, 0.5 mi w of jct SR 41. **Facility:** Near a lake, the complex offers different types of rooms, from contemporary to quaint, B&B-style. Smoke free premises. 86 one-bedroom standard units, some with kitchens and/or whirlpools. 2 stories (no elevator), interior/exterior corridors. *Bath:* combo or shower only. **Parking:** on-site. **Terms:** 2 night minimum stay - seasonal and/or weekends, 7 day cancellation notice-fee imposed. **Amenities:** video library, voice mail, irons. *Some:* DVD players, hair dryers. **Pool(s):** heated outdoor. **Leisure Activities:** saunas, boating, canoeing, paddleboats, boat dock, fishing, pitch & chip, 2 tennis courts, pavilion, hiking trails, spa. **Guest Services:** valet laundry, wireless Internet. **Business Services:** meeting rooms, business center. **Free Special Amenities:** local telephone calls and high-speed Internet. [❚❙] [Y] [🏊] [✦] [✕] [✕] / SOME UNITS FEE [🐾] FEE [📶] FEE [▦] [▢]

—— WHERE TO DINE ——

THE BOATHOUSE

American
$9-$30

Phone: 860/435-2111

A fun mix of creative American dishes as well as an extensive sushi bar makes this a very unique spot. The overall relaxed, warm ambiance is enhanced by beautiful boats hung from the ceiling, numerous fireplaces and banquette seating with comfy pillows to lay back and unwind. Casual dress. **Bar:** Full bar. **Reservations:** accepted. **Hours:** noon-9 pm, Fri & Sat-10 pm; closing hours vary in summer. Closed: 11/25, 12/25. **Address:** 349 Main St 06039 **Location:** Jct US 44 and SR 41. **Parking:** on-site.

LEDYARD

ALMOST IN MYSTIC/MARES INN

Bed & Breakfast
$125-$225 All Year

Phone: 860/572-7556

Address: 333 Colonel Ledyard Hwy 06339 **Location:** I-95, exit 89, 1 mi ne to Gold Star Hwy, 0.6 mi w, then 0.7 mi n. Located in a quiet rural area. **Facility:** Smoke free premises. 4 one-bedroom standard units, some with kitchens. 2 stories (no elevator), interior corridors. *Bath:* combo or shower only. **Parking:** on-site. **Terms:** age restrictions may apply, 14 day cancellation notice-fee imposed. **Amenities:** video library. **Leisure Activities:** *Fee:* massage. **Guest Services:** wireless Internet. **Business Services:** fax. [✕] [☎] / SOME UNITS [🐾] [📶] [▦] [▢]

GRAND PEQUOT TOWER AT FOXWOODS RESORT

CASINO *Book great rates at AAA.com*

Phone: (860)312-3000

(AAA) (SAVE)

▽▽▽ ▽▽▽

Hotel
$205-$395 5/1-11/29
$185-$395 11/30-4/30

Address: SR 2 06339 **Location:** Jct SR 214. **Facility:** This luxury hotel is attached to Foxwoods Casino, which includes food and retail outlets, entertainment facilities and a spa. 806 units. 696 one-bedroom standard units. 92 one- and 18 two-bedroom suites, some with whirlpools. 19 stories, interior corridors. *Bath:* combo or shower only. **Parking:** on-site and valet. **Terms:** check-in 4 pm, cancellation fee imposed. **Amenities:** high-speed Internet, dual phone lines, voice mail, safes, irons, hair dryers. *Some:* CD players. **Dining:** 17 restaurants, also, Paragon, see separate listing, nightclub, name entertainment. **Pool(s):** heated indoor. **Leisure Activities:** saunas, whirlpools, steamrooms, walking trails, hiking trails, spa. *Fee:* golf-18 holes, game room. **Guest Services:** valet laundry, wireless Internet, beauty salon. **Business Services:** meeting rooms, business center.
(See color ad inside front cover)

GREAT CEDAR HOTEL AT FOXWOODS RESORT

CASINO *Book great rates at AAA.com*

Phone: (860)312-3000

(AAA) (SAVE)

▽▽▽ ▽▽▽

Hotel
$165-$585 All Year

Address: SR 2 06339 **Location:** Jct SR 214. **Facility:** This traditional resort is decorated with American Indian artifacts and is attached to Foxwoods Casino. 312 units. 264 one-bedroom standard units. 37 one- and 11 two-bedroom suites, some with whirlpools. 8 stories, interior corridors. *Bath:* combo or shower only. **Parking:** on-site and valet. **Terms:** check-in 4 pm, cancellation fee imposed. **Amenities:** high-speed Internet, dual phone lines, voice mail, safes, irons, hair dryers. **Dining:** 17 restaurants, nightclub, name entertainment. **Pool(s):** heated indoor. **Leisure Activities:** saunas, whirlpools, walking trails, hiking trails. *Fee:* golf-18 holes. **Guest Services:** valet laundry. **Business Services:** meeting rooms, fax (fee). **Free Special Amenities:** newspaper and high-speed Internet.
(See color ad inside front cover)

MGM GRAND AT FOXWOODS

Book great rates at AAA.com

Phone: (860)312-6464

(AAA) (SAVE)

▽▽▽ ▽▽▽

Contemporary
Hotel
$99-$499 All Year

Address: 240 MGM Grand Dr 06338 **Location:** Jct SR 214 and SR 2. **Facility:** This 30-story high-rise features modern rooms with spacious showers. Four large pillars frame a central water feature in the striking lobby. 825 units. 769 one-bedroom standard units. 56 one-bedroom suites. 26 stories, interior corridors. *Bath:* combo or shower only. **Parking:** on-site and valet. **Terms:** check-in 4 pm, cancellation fee imposed. **Amenities:** voice mail, safes, honor bars, irons, hair dryers. **Dining:** 3 restaurants, also, Alta Strada, Craftsteak, Junior's, see separate listings, nightclub, name entertainment. **Pool(s):** heated outdoor, heated indoor. **Leisure Activities:** whirlpools, performing arts theatre, walking trails, hiking trails, spa. *Fee:* saunas, steamrooms, golf-18 holes. **Guest Services:** valet laundry, wireless Internet. **Business Services:** conference facilities, business center. **Free Special Amenities:** local telephone calls and high-speed Internet. *(See color ad inside front cover)*

TWO TREES INN AT FOXWOODS RESORT CASINO

Book great rates at AAA.com

Phone: (860)312-3000

(AAA) (SAVE)

▽▽▽ ▽▽▽

Hotel
$155-$245 5/1-8/31
$130-$225 9/1-4/30

Address: 240 Indiantown Rd 06339 **Location:** On SR 214, just sw of jct SR 2. Adjacent to Foxwoods Resort Casino. **Facility:** 280 units. 220 one-bedroom standard units. 60 one-bedroom suites. 3 stories, interior corridors. *Bath:* combo or shower only. **Parking:** on-site. **Terms:** check-in 4 pm, cancellation fee imposed. **Amenities:** dual phone lines, voice mail, irons, hair dryers. **Pool(s):** heated indoor. **Leisure Activities:** whirlpool, hiking trails, exercise room. *Fee:* golf-18 holes. **Guest Services:** valet laundry, area transportation, wireless Internet. **Business Services:** meeting rooms, fax (fee).
(See color ad inside front cover)

—— WHERE TO DINE ——

ALTA STRADA

Phone: 860/312-2582

▽▽▽

Italian
$28-$45

This upscale Italian eatery features more than 1,000 bottles of wine from hanging glass walls. Guests sit at comfortable circular booths at tables dressed with fine white linens. There is also a Mediterranean grill outdoors for alfresco dining. Among homemade pasta dishes are maltagliatta pasta with corn, chanterelle mushrooms, and pancetta or beef tenderloin with truffled potatoes and grilled red onions. Dressy casual. **Bar:** Full bar. **Reservations:** suggested. **Hours:** 5 pm-10 pm, Fri-11 pm, Sat 10 am-2 & 5-11 pm, Sun 10 am-2 & 5-10 pm. **Address:** 240 MGM Grand Dr 06338 **Location:** Jct SR 214 and SR 2; in MGM Grand at Foxwoods. **Parking:** on-site and valet.

CRAFTSTEAK

Phone: 860/312-7272

(AAA)

▽▽▽ ▽▽▽

Steak
$50-$100

The latest restaurant by the popular "Top Chef" TV show judge, Chef Tom Colicchio, this place uses top-quality seasonal ingredients from artisanal farms and the world's top ranchers. Diners salivate over the wide selection of steaks including corn-fed and grass-fed beef, as well as varied cuts of Wagyu beef. The raw bar offers a selection of mouthwatering oysters. Servers know a lot about the "craft" that goes into the preparation of the food. Dressy casual. **Bar:** Full bar. **Reservations:** suggested. **Hours:** 5 pm-10 pm, Fri & Sat-11 pm. **Address:** 39 Norwich-Westerly Rd 06338 **Location:** Jct SR 214 and 2; in MGM Grand at Foxwoods. **Parking:** on-site and valet.

Seasonal cuisine featuring superb steaks & seafood

HARD ROCK CAFE

Phone: 860/312-7625

(SAVE)

▽▽ ▽▽

American
$12-$24

Rock 'n' roll memorabilia decorates the walls of the popular theme restaurant. Live music on the weekends contributes to the bustling atmosphere. On the menu is a wide variety of American cuisine—from burgers and sandwiches to seafood, steaks and pasta. Casual dress. **Bar:** Full bar. **Reservations:** accepted. **Hours:** 11 am-midnight, Fri & Sat-1 am. **Address:** 39 Norwich-Westerly Rd 06338 **Location:** Jct SR 214; adjacent to Foxwoods Resort Casino. **Parking:** on-site.

JUNIOR'S

American
$10-$25

Phone: 860/312-2253

The small chain originally began in 1950 in Brooklyn, N.Y., and is widely known for serving outstanding cheesecakes, including classic strawberry, decadent chocolate mousse and red velvet varieties. Inside the MGM Grand, this location also offers overstuffed deli sandwiches, 10-ounce steak burgers and sides of pickled beets with onions, coleslaw and pickles. The dining room features three-story ceilings with colorful Brooklyn-inspired props, including the bridge and pictures of Coney Island. Casual dress. **Bar:** Beer only. **Reservations:** accepted. **Hours:** 7 am-11 pm, Fri & Sat-2 am. **Address:** 240 MGM Dr 06338 **Location:** Jct SR 214 and 2; in MGM Grand Hotel at Foxwoods Resort Casino. **Parking:** on-site. CALL 🅼

PARAGON *Menu on AAA.com*

🔺

🔻🔻🔻🔻

Northern
Continental
$32-$85

Phone: 860/312-3000

On the 24th floor of the Grand Pequot Tower, the restaurant has some tables that offer excellent views of Connecticut woodlands. A classical pianist often handles the music throughout the night. This elegant spot's Continental cuisine includes many French- and Asian-inspired dishes and tableside preparations. Dressy casual. **Bar:** Full bar. **Reservations:** suggested. **Hours:** 5 pm-10 pm, Fri & Sat-10:30 pm. Closed: Mon-Wed. **Address:** Rt 2 06339 **Location:** Jct SR 214; in Grand Pequot Tower at Foxwoods Resort Casino. **Parking:** on-site and valet. CALL 🅼

LITCHFIELD pop. 1,328

LITCHFIELD INN

🔺 SAVE

🔻🔻🔻

Country Inn
$228-$336 5/1-12/31
$200-$300 1/1-4/30

Phone: 860/567-4503

Address: 432 Bantam Rd 06759 **Location:** 1.5 mi w on US 202. **Facility:** Smoke free premises. 32 one-bedroom standard units. 2 stories, interior corridors. **Parking:** on-site. **Terms:** 3 day cancellation notice-fee imposed. **Amenities:** irons, hair dryers. **Guest Services:** valet laundry, wireless Internet. **Business Services:** meeting rooms, business center. **Free Special Amenities: continental breakfast and high-speed Internet.** / SOME UNITS 🐕 🔒

─── WHERE TO DINE ───

ASPEN GARDEN RESTAURANT

🔻🔻🔻

American
$6-$17

Phone: 860/567-9477

The popular corner spot offers seasonal outdoor seating. Guests can sample generous portions of Greek specialties, pasta, chicken, shrimp and pizzas. Casual dress. **Bar:** Full bar. **Reservations:** accepted. **Hours:** 11 am-9 pm, Fri-10 pm, Sat 7 am-10 pm, Sun 7 am-9 pm; Fri & Sat-11 pm in summer. Closed: 4/4, 11/25, 12/25. **Address:** 51 West St 06759 **Location:** Jct SR 63, just w on US 202; access town green.

WEST STREET GRILL

🔻🔻🔻

New American
$9-$34

Phone: 860/567-3885

The restaurant mixes Colonial and modern decor elements to match its modern American cuisine. Making the intimate room look larger are framed mirrors, which accent the exposed brick walls, and French doors. Original Thomas McKnight artwork is displayed. Excellent selections include caramelized diver scallops with butternut squash dumplings in orange-scallion sauce and such Asia-inspired dishes as rock shrimp with green tea soba noodles in sweet and spicy garlic-chili sauce. Dressy casual. **Bar:** Full bar. **Reservations:** suggested. **Hours:** 11:30 am-2:30 & 5:30-9 pm; Saturday & Sunday brunch. Closed: 12/25; also Mon & Tues. **Address:** 43 West St 06759 **Location:** On SR 118, just w of jct SR 63. **Parking:** on-site. **Parking:** street.

MADISON

———— WHERE TO DINE ————

CAFE ALLEGRE

Italian
$10-$22

Phone: 203/245-7773

Traditional Italian dishes and an elegant atmosphere make this an experience worth savoring. Casual dress. **Bar:** Full bar. **Reservations:** suggested. **Hours:** 11:30 am-2:30 & 5:30-10 pm, Fri-10:30 pm, Sat 5:30 pm-10:30 pm, Sun 1 pm-9 pm. Closed: 12/25; also Mon. **Address:** 725 Boston Post Rd 06443 **Location:** I-95, exit 61, 0.7 mi s on SR 79, then e on US 1. **Parking:** on-site.

MANCHESTER—See Hartford p. 274.

MANSFIELD CENTER pop. 973

BEST WESTERN REGENT INN　*Book great rates at AAA.com*

Phone: 860/423-8451

Hotel
Rates not provided

Address: 123 Storrs Rd 06250 **Location:** On SR 195, just n of jct US 6. **Facility:** 87 one-bedroom standard units. 2 stories (no elevator), interior corridors. **Parking:** on-site. **Amenities:** voice mail, irons, hair dryers. *Some:* high-speed Internet. **Pool(s):** heated indoor. **Leisure Activities:** whirlpool, limited exercise equipment. **Guest Services:** coin laundry, wireless Internet, beauty salon. **Business Services:** meeting rooms, business center. **Free Special Amenities: continental breakfast and high-speed Internet.**

AAA Benefit:
Members save up to 20%, plus 10% bonus points with rewards program.

MERIDEN pop. 58,244

EXTENDED STAYAMERICA HARTFORD-MERIDEN　*Book at AAA.com*

Extended Stay Hotel
$74-$129　All Year

Phone: (203)630-1927

Address: 366 Bee St 06450 **Location:** I-91, exit 17 northbound, just e on E Main St, then 0.7 mi n; exit 19 southbound, 0.5 mi w on Baldwin Ave, then 0.6 mi s. **Facility:** 104 one-bedroom standard units with efficiencies. 3 stories, interior corridors. *Bath:* combo or shower only. **Parking:** on-site. **Terms:** office hours 7 am-11 pm, cancellation fee imposed. **Amenities:** voice mail, irons. *Some:* hair dryers. **Guest Services:** coin laundry, wireless Internet.

FOUR POINTS BY SHERATON MERIDEN　*Book great rates at AAA.com*

Hotel
Rates not provided

Phone: 203-238-2380

Address: 275 Research Pkwy 06450 **Location:** I-91, exit 17 southbound; exit 16 northbound, 0.5 mi e, then 0.5 mi s. **Facility:** Smoke free premises. 150 units. 140 one-bedroom standard units. 10 one-bedroom suites. 6 stories, interior corridors. *Bath:* combo or shower only. **Parking:** on-site. **Amenities:** video games (fee), dual phone lines, voice mail, irons, hair dryers. **Pool(s):** heated indoor. **Leisure Activities:** sun deck with grill, library, exercise room. **Guest Services:** valet and coin laundry, area transportation-within 5 mi, wireless Internet. **Business Services:** conference facilities, business center. **Free Special Amenities: newspaper and high-speed Internet.**

FOUR POINTS BY SHERATON
AAA Benefit:
Members get up to 15% off, plus Starwood Preferred Guest® bonuses.

HAMPTON INN　*Book great rates at AAA.com*

Hotel
Rates not provided

Phone: 203-235-5154

Address: 10 Bee St 06450 **Location:** I-91, exit 17 southbound; exit 16 northbound, just n. **Facility:** 124 one-bedroom standard units. 4 stories, interior corridors. *Bath:* combo or shower only. **Parking:** on-site. **Amenities:** video games (fee), voice mail, irons, hair dryers. **Leisure Activities:** exercise room. **Guest Services:** valet laundry, wireless Internet. **Business Services:** meeting rooms, PC. **Free Special Amenities: expanded continental breakfast and high-speed Internet.**

AAA Benefit:
Members save up to 10% everyday!

HOLIDAY INN EXPRESS & SUITES　*Book great rates at AAA.com*

Hotel
$99　All Year

Phone: (203)443-5700

Address: 2104 N Broad St 06450 **Location:** I-91, exit 17 northbound, 3.6 mi n on SR 15 (Berlin Tpke); exit 22N southbound, 2.5 mi n on SR 9 to exit 22, follow signs to US 5 and SR 15 S (Berlin Tpke) for 2.6 mi. **Facility:** 91 one-bedroom standard units. 3 stories, interior corridors. *Bath:* combo or shower only. **Parking:** on-site. **Amenities:** high-speed Internet, voice mail, irons, hair dryers. **Pool(s):** heated indoor. **Leisure Activities:** exercise room. **Guest Services:** valet and coin laundry, wireless Internet. **Free Special Amenities: expanded continental breakfast and high-speed Internet.**

QUALITY INN & SUITES   *Book at AAA.com*

Phone: (203)440-9770

Hotel
$75-$199 5/1-12/31
$69-$159 1/1-4/30

Address: 2090 N Broad St 06450 **Location:** I-91, exit 17 northbound, 3.6 mi n on SR 15 (Berlin Tpke); exit 22N southbound, 2.5 mi n on SR 9 to exit 22, follow signs to US 5 and SR 15 S (Berlin Tpke) for 2.6 mi. **Facility:** 34 one-bedroom standard units, some with whirlpools. 3 stories, interior corridors. *Bath:* combo or shower only. **Parking:** on-site. **Amenities:** voice mail, irons, hair dryers. **Leisure Activities:** exercise room. **Guest Services:** wireless Internet. **Business Services:** meeting rooms, PC.

RESIDENCE INN MERIDEN   *Book great rates at AAA.com*

Phone: (203)634-7770

Extended Stay
Hotel
$134-$164 All Year

Address: 390 Bee St 06450 **Location:** I-91, exit 16 northbound, just e on E Main St, then 0.7 mi n; exit 19 southbound, 0.5 mi w on Baldwin Ave, then 0.5 mi s. **Facility:** Smoke free premises. 106 units. 81 one- and 25 two-bedroom suites with efficiencies. 2-3 stories, interior/exterior corridors. *Bath:* combo or shower only. **Parking:** on-site. **Terms:** cancellation fee imposed. **Amenities:** high-speed Internet, voice mail, irons, hair dryers. **Pool(s):** heated outdoor. **Leisure Activities:** whirlpool, exercise room, sports court. **Guest Services:** valet and coin laundry, wireless Internet. **Business Services:** meeting rooms, business center.

AAA Benefit:
Members save a minimum 5% off the best available rate.

—— **WHERE TO DINE** ——

AMERICAN STEAKHOUSE

Phone: 203/634-9994

Steak
$4-$11

This is an ideal stop for the budget-conscious traveler, offering cafeteria-style family dining with value-priced a la carte items such as burgers or grilled chicken sandwiches. Guests can spend a few more dollars for access to the salad bar, which has a few hot items. Casual dress. **Reservations:** not accepted. **Hours:** 11 am-9 pm, Fri-Sun to 10 pm. Closed: 11/25, 12/25. **Address:** 1170 E Main St 06450 **Location:** I-91, exit 17 southbound; exit 16 northbound, 0.3 mi e. **Parking:** on-site.

MIDDLETOWN—See Hartford p. 275.

MILFORD pop. 52,305   (See map and index starting on p. 300)

FAIRFIELD INN BY MARRIOTT-MILFORD   *Book great rates at AAA.com*

Phone: (203)877-8588 **43**

Hotel
$129-$134 All Year

Address: 111 Schoolhouse Rd 06460 **Location:** I-95, exit 35, just se. **Facility:** Smoke free premises. 104 one-bedroom standard units. 4 stories, interior corridors. *Bath:* combo or shower only. **Parking:** on-site. **Terms:** cancellation fee imposed. **Amenities:** video games (fee), voice mail, irons, hair dryers. **Pool(s):** outdoor. **Leisure Activities:** exercise room. **Guest Services:** valet and coin laundry, wireless Internet. **Business Services:** business center.

AAA Benefit:
Members save a minimum 5% off the best available rate.

HAMPTON INN   *Book great rates at AAA.com*

Phone: 203/874-4400 **42**

Hotel
Rates not provided

Address: 129 Plains Rd 06460 **Location:** I-95, exit 36. **Facility:** 148 units. 147 one-bedroom standard units. 1 one-bedroom suite. 3 stories, interior corridors. **Parking:** on-site. **Amenities:** video games (fee), voice mail, irons, hair dryers. **Leisure Activities:** exercise room. **Guest Services:** valet and coin laundry, wireless Internet. **Business Services:** meeting rooms, business center.

AAA Benefit:
Members save up to 10% everyday!

HILTON GARDEN INN MILFORD   *Book great rates at AAA.com*

Phone: (203)783-9988 **39**

Hotel
$99-$179 All Year

Address: 291 Old Gate Ln 06460 **Location:** I-95, exit 40, just s. **Facility:** 120 units. 116 one-bedroom standard units. 4 one-bedroom suites. 4 stories, interior corridors. *Bath:* combo or shower only. **Parking:** on-site. **Terms:** 1-7 night minimum stay, cancellation fee imposed. **Amenities:** high-speed Internet, voice mail, irons, hair dryers. **Pool(s):** heated indoor. **Leisure Activities:** whirlpool, exercise room. **Guest Services:** valet and coin laundry, area transportation, wireless Internet. **Business Services:** meeting rooms, business center.

AAA Benefit:
Members save 5% or more everyday!

HYATT PLACE MILFORD
Book great rates at AAA.com
Phone: (203)877-9800 **40**

Hotel
$99-$209 All Year

Address: 190 Old Gate Ln 06460 **Location:** I-95, exit 40, 0.4 mi s.
Facility: 86 one-bedroom standard units. 6 stories, interior corridors. *Bath:* combo or shower only. **Parking:** on-site. **Terms:** cancellation fee imposed. **Amenities:** high-speed Internet, voice mail, irons, hair dryers. **Leisure Activities:** whirlpool, exercise room. **Guest Services:** valet laundry, wireless Internet. **Business Services:** meeting rooms, business center. **Free Special Amenities: continental breakfast and high-speed Internet.**

HYATT PLACE

AAA Benefit:
Ask for the AAA rate
and save 10%.

RESIDENCE INN MILFORD
Book great rates at AAA.com
Phone: (203)283-2100 **45**

Extended Stay
Hotel
$159-$174 All Year

Address: 62 Rowe Ave 06460 **Location:** I-95, exit 35, just nw. **Facility:** Smoke free premises. 74 units. 30 one-bedroom standard units, some with efficiencies or kitchens. 33 one- and 11 two-bedroom suites with kitchens. 3 stories, interior corridors. *Bath:* combo or shower only. **Parking:** on-site. **Terms:** cancellation fee imposed. **Amenities:** high-speed Internet, voice mail, irons, hair dryers. **Pool(s):** heated outdoor. **Leisure Activities:** exercise room. **Guest Services:** valet and coin laundry, wireless Internet. **Business Services:** meeting rooms, business center.

Residence Inn

AAA Benefit:
Members save a
minimum 5% off the
best available rate.

SPRINGHILL SUITES MILFORD
Book great rates at AAA.com
Phone: (203)283-0200 **44**

Hotel
$139-$149 All Year

Address: 50 Rowe Ave 06460 **Location:** I-95, exit 35, just nw. **Facility:** Smoke free premises. 124 one-bedroom standard units, some with whirlpools. 3 stories, interior corridors. *Bath:* combo or shower only. **Parking:** on-site. **Terms:** cancellation fee imposed. **Amenities:** high-speed Internet, dual phone lines, voice mail, irons, hair dryers. **Pool(s):** heated indoor. **Leisure Activities:** whirlpool, exercise room. **Guest Services:** valet and coin laundry, wireless Internet. **Business Services:** business center.

SPRINGHILL SUITES

AAA Benefit:
Members save a
minimum 5% off the
best available rate.

SUPER 8
Book great rates at AAA.com
Phone: 203/878-3575 **41**

Motel
Rates not provided

Address: 1015 Boston Post Rd 06460 **Location:** I-95, exit 39A, just s. **Facility:** 50 one-bedroom standard units. 2-3 stories, exterior corridors. *Bath:* combo or shower only. **Parking:** on-site. **Amenities:** voice mail, hair dryers. *Some:* irons. **Guest Services:** wireless Internet. *(See color ad p 303)*

FREE continental breakfast and high-speed Internet

------ WHERE TO DINE ------

GUSTO RESTAURANT
Menu on AAA.com
Phone: 203/876-7464 **38**

Italian
$9-$26

Guests might start with a complimentary order of fresh focaccia bread with roasted garlic and flavored oil, then try panzanella (a Tuscan salad). The lively atmosphere and creative Italian cuisine make this restaurant a popular spot. Outside seating is also available. Casual dress. **Bar:** Full bar. **Reservations:** suggested. **Hours:** 11:30 am-10 pm, Sat from 4 pm, Sun 4 pm-8:30 pm. Closed major holidays. **Address:** 255 Boston Post Rd 06460 **Location:** I-95, exit 36, just s on Plains Rd. **Parking:** on-site.

SCRIBNER'S
Phone: 203/878-7019 **36**

Seafood
$16-$50

Fresh fish and shellfish are prepared in the classic New England style. Favorites include swordfish Gorgonzola, catfish, lobster piccata, Maine lobster and steak. The extensive wine list features more than 150 bottles. Casual dress. **Bar:** Full bar. **Reservations:** suggested. **Hours:** 5 pm-9:30 pm; hours vary in season. Closed major holidays. **Address:** 31 Village Rd 06460 **Location:** I-95, exit 41, 2.3 mi s via e on Marsh Hill Rd, s on Merwin Ave, e on Chapel St, then just s on Kings Row. **Parking:** on-site.

STONEBRIDGE RESTAURANT
Phone: 203/874-7947 **37**

American
$8-$27

The dining room is casual yet refined with polished wood tabletops. Views of the Wepawaug River waterfall are wonderful from the more casual glass-enclosed patio. The menu is filled with fresh seafood, choice cuts of beef, poultry and pasta dishes. Guests can put together a meal with a starter of lobster bisque, an entree of grilled vegetable pizza with feta cheese and kalamata olives or chicken francaise over capellini pasta with spinach, and a dessert, such as the triple chocolate mousse cake. Casual dress. **Bar:** Full bar. **Reservations:** accepted. **Hours:** 11:30 am-9 pm, Fri & Sat-10 pm, Sun-8 pm; seasonal hours may vary. Closed: 1/1, 12/25. **Address:** 50 Daniel St 06460 **Location:** Jct US 1, 1.3 mi ne on SR 162. **Parking:** on-site.

MORRIS

WINVIAN *Book at AAA.com*

Boutique Resort Hotel

$750-$2300 All Year

Phone: (860)567-9600

Address: 155 Alain White Rd 06763 **Location:** Jct SR 109, 1 mi n. **Facility:** Inspired architects designed each of the individually themed cottages to provide an overall whimsical, yet wholly lush, experience for guests. Smoke free premises. 19 units. 1 one-bedroom suite. 18 cottages. 1-3 stories (no elevator), interior/exterior corridors. **Parking:** on-site and valet. **Terms:** 2 night minimum stay - weekends, age restrictions may apply, 60 day cancellation notice-fee imposed. **Amenities:** video library, DVD players, CD players, high-speed Internet, dual phone lines, voice mail, safes, honor bars, irons, hair dryers. **Dining:** restaurant, see separate listing. **Leisure Activities:** fishing, cross country skiing, bicycles, hiking trails, exercise room, spa, horseshoes, game room. **Guest Services:** valet laundry, area transportation, wireless Internet. **Business Services:** conference facilities, business center. FEE ⬛⬛⬛⬛⬛⬛⬛ / SOME UNITS ⬛⬛

------ WHERE TO DINE ------

WINVIAN

French

$85-$100

Phone: 860/567-9600

An incredible wooden staircase leads to the upper-level restaurant, where original oil paintings reflect on the property's history. The often-changing three-course menu offers creative choices along the lines of white asparagus, fig and prosciutto salad with quail egg and balsamic vinaigrette or pan-seared skate with lobster over corn and red pepper salsa. Fine meal enders include European cheeses or the dessert trio of mini chocolate souffle, rhubarb soup and banana parfait. Semi-formal attire. **Bar:** Full bar. **Reservations:** required. **Hours:** 12:30 pm-2:30 & 7-9:30 pm. Closed: Mon & Tues. **Address:** 155 Alain White Rd 06763 **Location:** Jct SR 109, 1 mi n; in Winvian. **Parking:** on-site and valet.

MYSTIC pop. 4,001

THE ADAMS HOUSE

Historic Bed & Breakfast

$95-$175 All Year

Phone: 860/572-9551

Address: 382 Cow Hill Rd 06355 **Location:** I-95, exit 89, 0.5 mi n. **Facility:** Knickknacks and period pieces furnish this restored 1749 Colonial home. Smoke free premises. 2 one-bedroom standard units. 1 story, exterior corridors. *Bath:* combo or shower only. **Parking:** on-site. **Terms:** office hours 8 am-10 pm, 2 night minimum stay - seasonal and/or weekends, 7 day cancellation notice-fee imposed. **Amenities:** hair dryers. ⬛ / SOME UNITS ⬛⬛⬛

BEST WESTERN MYSTIC (NOW KNOWN AS RAMADA MYSTIC)

⬛⬛ SAVE

⬛⬛⬛⬛

Hotel

$69-$199 All Year

Phone: (860)536-4281

Address: 9 Whitehall Ave 06355 **Location:** I-95, exit 90, just n on SR 27. **Facility:** Smoke free premises. 150 one-bedroom standard units, some with whirlpools. 2 stories (no elevator), interior corridors. **Parking:** on-site. **Amenities:** video games (fee), irons, hair dryers. **Pool(s):** heated indoor. **Leisure Activities:** sauna, playground, exercise room. *Fee:* game room. **Guest Services:** valet laundry, area transportation-casinos, wireless Internet. **Business Services:** meeting rooms, business center. **Free Special Amenities: continental breakfast and local telephone calls.**
⬛⬛⬛⬛⬛⬛⬛⬛⬛

COMFORT INN OF MYSTIC *Book great rates at AAA.com*

⬛⬛ SAVE

⬛⬛⬛

Hotel

$71-$180 All Year

Phone: (860)572-8531

Address: 48 Whitehall Ave 06355 **Location:** I-95, exit 90, just n on SR 27. **Facility:** 120 one-bedroom standard units, some with whirlpools. 2 stories, interior corridors. **Parking:** on-site. **Terms:** cancellation fee imposed. **Amenities:** voice mail, irons, hair dryers. *Some:* high-speed Internet. **Pool(s):** outdoor. **Leisure Activities:** exercise room. **Guest Services:** valet laundry, area transportation (fee)-Mohegan Sun Casino, wireless Internet. **Business Services:** meeting rooms, business center. **Free Special Amenities: expanded continental breakfast and high-speed Internet.**
⬛⬛ CALL ⬛⬛⬛⬛ / SOME UNITS FEE ⬛⬛⬛⬛

HAMPTON INN & SUITES/MYSTIC *Book great rates at AAA.com*

⬛⬛⬛

Hotel

$109-$229 All Year

Phone: (860)536-2536

Address: 6 Hendel Dr 06355 **Location:** I-95, exit 90. **Facility:** Smoke free premises. 92 one-bedroom standard units. 3 stories, interior corridors. *Bath:* combo or shower only. **Parking:** on-site. **Terms:** 1-7 night minimum stay, cancellation fee imposed. **Amenities:** high-speed Internet, voice mail, irons, hair dryers. **Pool(s):** heated indoor. **Leisure Activities:** exercise room. **Guest Services:** valet laundry, wireless Internet. **Business Services:** meeting rooms, business center.
⬛⬛ CALL ⬛⬛⬛⬛⬛ / SOME UNITS ⬛⬛

AAA Benefit:
Members save up to 10% everyday!

AAA.com/TravelGuide ... Destination Information and Ideas.

HILTON MYSTIC

Book great rates at AAA.com

Phone: (860)572-0731

(AAA) (SAVE)
▽▽▽
Hotel
$209-$259 All Year

Address: 20 Coogan Blvd 06355 **Location:** I-95, exit 90, 0.5 mi s, then e. Opposite Marinelife Aquarium. **Facility:** Smoke free premises. 182 one-bedroom standard units, some with whirlpools. 4 stories, interior corridors. *Bath:* combo or shower only. **Parking:** on-site. **Terms:** check-in 4 pm, 1-7 night minimum stay, cancellation fee imposed. **Amenities:** dual phone lines, voice mail, irons, hair dryers. **Pool(s):** heated indoor. **Leisure Activities:** exercise room. **Guest Services:** valet laundry, area transportation-within 5 mi, wireless Internet. **Business Services:** conference facilities, business center. *(See color ad p 293)*

Hilton

AAA Benefit:
Members save 5% or more everyday!

(icons) / SOME UNITS FEE 🛏 FEE 🍴

FREE local telephone calls and high-speed Internet

HOLIDAY INN EXPRESS

Book great rates at AAA.com

Phone: (860)572-9065

(AAA) (SAVE)
▽▽▽
Hotel
$99-$269 All Year

Address: 6 Coogan Blvd 06355 **Location:** I-95, exit 90, just s on SR 27, then just e. **Facility:** Smoke free premises. 77 units. 75 one-bedroom standard units, some with whirlpools. 2 one-bedroom suites. 2-3 stories, interior corridors. *Bath:* combo or shower only. **Parking:** on-site. **Amenities:** high-speed Internet, irons, hair dryers. **Pool(s):** heated indoor. **Leisure Activities:** whirlpool, exercise room. **Guest Services:** valet and coin laundry, wireless Internet. **Business Services:** business center. **Free Special Amenities: continental breakfast and high-speed Internet.**

(icons) CALL

HOWARD JOHNSON INN

Book great rates at AAA.com

Phone: (860)536-2654

(AAA) (SAVE)
▽▽▽
Hotel
$79-$179 5/1-10/31
$69-$159 11/1-4/30

Address: 253 Greenmanville Ave 06355 **Location:** I-95, exit 90, just se. **Facility:** 77 one-bedroom standard units, some with whirlpools. 2 stories (no elevator), interior corridors. **Parking:** on-site. **Terms:** check-in 4 pm. **Amenities:** voice mail, safes, irons, hair dryers. **Pool(s):** heated indoor. **Leisure Activities:** sun deck. **Guest Services:** wireless Internet. **Business Services:** business center. **Free Special Amenities: newspaper and high-speed Internet.**

(icons) / SOME UNITS

Your Journey Begins
18,000 Years Ago
AT THE MASHANTUCKET PEQUOT MUSEUM

MASHANTUCKET
PEQUOT
MUSEUM
& RESEARCH CENTER

- Life-size 16th c. Indian village
- 4 acres of interactive exhibits
- 18-story observation tower
- Gift shop, restaurant

www.pequotmuseum.org
Smithsonian Affiliate   AAA

110 Pequot Trail, Mashantucket CT 06338 • (800) 411-9671 • I-95, Exit 92

HYATT PLACE MYSTIC

Book great rates at AAA.com

Phone: (860)536-9997

(AAA) (SAVE)
▽▽▽▽

Hotel
$99-$299 All Year

Address: 224 Greenmanville Ave 06355 **Location:** I-95, exit 90, just se. **Facility:** Smoke free premises. 79 one-bedroom standard units. 3 stories, interior corridors. *Bath:* combo or shower only. **Parking:** on-site. **Terms:** cancellation fee imposed. **Amenities:** dual phone lines, voice mail, safes, irons, hair dryers. *Some:* high-speed Internet. **Pool(s):** heated outdoor. **Leisure Activities:** exercise room. **Guest Services:** valet laundry, wireless Internet. **Business Services:** meeting rooms, business center. **Free Special Amenities: continental breakfast and high-speed Internet.**

CALL ⌐M ⇒ ✕ ☺ ◻ ⊡

HYATT PLACE

AAA Benefit:
Ask for the AAA rate
and save 10%.

INN AT MYSTIC

Phone: (860)536-9604

(AAA) (SAVE)
▽▽▽▽

Motel
$95-$315 All Year

Address: 3 Williams Ave 06355 **Location:** On US 1 at SR 27. **Facility:** Smoke free premises. 67 one-bedroom standard units, some with whirlpools. 1-2 stories (no elevator), interior/exterior corridors. **Parking:** on-site. **Terms:** 2 night minimum stay - seasonal and/or weekends, cancellation fee imposed. **Amenities:** hair dryers. *Some:* dual phone lines, irons. **Dining:** Flood Tide Restaurant, see separate listing. **Pool(s):** heated outdoor. **Leisure Activities:** boating, canoeing, sailboats, fishing, kayaks, putting green, tennis court, walking trail. **Guest Services:** wireless Internet. **Business Services:** meeting rooms.

🍴 ⇒ ✚ ✕ ✕ ☺ / SOME UNITS FEE 🐾 ◻ ⊡

FREE full breakfast and high-speed Internet

RESIDENCE INN MYSTIC GROTON   *Book great rates at AAA.com*

Phone: (860)536-5150

▽▽▽▽

Extended Stay
Hotel
$149-$199 All Year

Address: 40 Whitehall Ave 06355 **Location:** I-95, exit 90, just n on SR 27. **Facility:** Smoke free premises. 128 units. 62 one-bedroom standard units with efficiencies, some with whirlpools. 48 one- and 18 two-bedroom suites, some with efficiencies or kitchens. 3 stories, interior corridors. *Bath:* combo or shower only. **Parking:** on-site. **Terms:** cancellation fee imposed. **Amenities:** video games (fee), high-speed Internet, dual phone lines, voice mail, safes, irons, hair dryers. **Pool(s):** heated indoor. **Leisure Activities:** whirlpool, exercise room, sports court. **Guest Services:** valet and coin laundry, wireless Internet. **Business Services:** meeting rooms, PC.

⇒ ✕ ✕ ☺ ◻ ▦ ⊡ / SOME UNITS FEE 🐾

AAA Benefit:
Members save a
minimum 5% off the
best available rate.

▼ See AAA listing p 252 ▼

STEAMBOAT INN

Bed & Breakfast
$170-$300 5/1-10/31
$135-$265 11/1-4/30

Phone: (860)536-8300

Address: 73 Steamboat Wharf 06355 **Location:** On US 1; center. **Facility:** Located alongside the Mystic River, this inn offers charming and spacious rooms, most with water views and fireplaces. Smoke free premises. 11 one-bedroom standard units, some with whirlpools. 2 stories (no elevator), interior/exterior corridors. *Bath:* combo or shower only. **Parking:** on-site. **Terms:** office hours 8 am-9 pm, 2 night minimum stay - weekends, 5 day cancellation notice-fee imposed. **Amenities:** video library, DVD players, CD players, hair dryers. *Some:* irons. **Leisure Activities:** fishing, bicycles. **Guest Services:** wireless Internet. **Business Services:** meeting rooms.

TABER INNE & SUITES

Motel
$149-$255 5/1-11/30
$119-$235 12/1-4/30

Phone: 860/536-4904

Address: 66 Williams Ave 06355 **Location:** On US 1, 0.4 mi e of jct SR 27. **Facility:** Smoke free premises. 32 units. 29 one-bedroom standard units, some with whirlpools. 3 two-bedroom suites. 1-2 stories (no elevator), exterior corridors. **Parking:** on-site. **Terms:** 2 night minimum stay - seasonal and/or weekends, 5 day cancellation notice-fee imposed. **Amenities:** irons, hair dryers. **Pool(s):** heated indoor. **Leisure Activities:** exercise room. **Guest Services:** wireless Internet. **Business Services:** meeting rooms. **Free Special Amenities:** continental breakfast and high-speed Internet.

WHALER'S INN

Motel
$109-$259 All Year

Phone: (860)536-1506

Address: 20 E Main St 06355 **Location:** On US 1, 0.5 mi w of jct SR 27. **Facility:** Smoke free premises. 49 one-bedroom standard units, some with whirlpools. 2-3 stories (no elevator), interior/exterior corridors. *Bath:* combo or shower only. **Parking:** on-site. **Terms:** 2 night minimum stay - seasonal and/or weekends, 4 day cancellation notice-fee imposed. **Amenities:** high-speed Internet, voice mail, irons, hair dryers. *Some:* DVD players. **Dining:** Bravo Bravo, see separate listing. **Leisure Activities:** bicycles, exercise room. *Fee:* massage. **Guest Services:** valet laundry, wireless Internet. **Business Services:** meeting rooms, business center.

WHITEHALL MANSION

Historic Bed
& Breakfast
$89-$199 5/1-10/31
$79-$189 11/1-4/30

Phone: (860)572-7280

Address: 42 Whitehall Ave 06355 **Location:** I-95, exit 90, just n on SR 27. Located in a commercial area. **Facility:** The 1771 Whitehall Mansion offers rooms with period furnishings, Colonial decor, fireplaces and modern baths. Check-in is at the Residence Inn. Smoke free premises. 5 one-bedroom standard units with whirlpools. 2 stories (no elevator), interior corridors. **Parking:** on-site. **Terms:** check-in 4 pm, cancellation fee imposed. **Amenities:** irons, hair dryers. **Guest Services:** wireless Internet.

——— WHERE TO DINE ———

ANCIENT MARINER

Seafood
$7-$24

Phone: 860/536-5200

Renovated with a warm, casual New England nautical atmosphere, the restaurant sits along the main strip. Among classic Japan-influenced dishes are clams casino, chicken pot pie and wasabi pea-crusted tuna salad. For dessert, homemade banana bread pudding satisfies. Casual dress. **Bar:** Full bar. **Reservations:** accepted. **Hours:** 11 am-10 pm. Closed: 11/25, 12/24, 12/25. **Address:** 21 W Main St 06355 **Location:** Jct SR 215, just e on US 1. **Parking:** street.

ANTHONY J'S BISTRO

New Italian
$7-$24

Phone: 860/536-0448

This contemporary Italian restaurant earns high marks for its homemade stone pizza pies and "hot rocks" entrees, which guests cook over heated imported stones from Italy. Choices include steak teriyaki, spiced chicken and seafood scampi with Atlantic sea scallops, fresh fish, jumbo shrimp, calamari, Maine lobster meat, garlic and olive oil. Flower boxes and taupe paint decorate the exterior, which leads into a cavernous dining room with exposed stone, brick walls and low mood lighting. Dressy casual. **Bar:** Full bar. **Reservations:** not accepted. **Hours:** 11 am-10 pm. Closed major holidays. **Address:** 6 Holmes St 06355 **Location:** I-95, exit 90, 1.1 mi s on SR 27, then just w. **Parking:** street.

AZU RESTAURANT & BAR

Small Plates
$10-$35

Phone: 860/536-6336

The contemporary restaurant and bar serves a mix of American classics and ethnic classics such as dim sum, satays, fajitas, pasta dishes, hamburgers, steaks and crab cakes. Particularly worth trying are azutini made with mango puree and miniature pulled-pork sandwiches with pommes frites. Understated decor includes white walls and ceilings and black floor tiles. Service is casual and friendly. Dressy casual. **Bar:** Full bar. **Reservations:** suggested, weekends. **Hours:** 11:30 am-9 pm, Fri-10 pm, Sat 7 am-10 pm, Sun 7 am-9 pm. Closed: 1/1, 11/25, 12/25. **Address:** 32 W Main St 06355 **Location:** Between Pearl and Gravel sts; downtown. **Parking:** street.

BARTLEBY'S CAFE

Coffee/Tea
$5-$10

Phone: 860/245-0017

Black and white tile floors accent the cozy cafe, which displays original artwork for sale. Many guests appreciate the chess boards, old books and free wireless Internet. Specialty coffees pair with sandwiches such as the large Reuben or BLT. Also offered are large salads, wraps and homemade soups that change daily but may include a creamy cup of chicken with a splash of tequila that provides a hint of heat. Desserts, most prepared by a local baker, line glass cases. Casual dress. **Reservations:** not accepted. **Hours:** 7 am-9 pm. **Address:** 46 W Main St 06355 **Location:** On US 1; center. **Parking:** street.

BRAVO BRAVO

New Italian
$8-$28

Phone: 860/536-3228

The chef produces some truly creative and flavorful fare: lobster bisque, chicken and broccoli ravioli with tender sun-dried tomatoes in a superb cream sauce and banana chip creme brulee. Outside terrace dining is available in season. Dressy casual. **Bar:** Full bar. **Reservations:** suggested. **Hours:** 11:30 am-2:30 & 5-9 pm, Fri & Sat-10 pm, Sun 5 pm-9 pm. Closed major holidays; also Mon. **Address:** 20 E Main St 06355 **Location:** On US 1, 0.5 mi w of jct SR 27; in Whaler's Inn. **Parking:** street.

CAPTAIN DANIEL PACKER INNE

American
$9-$30

Phone: 860/536-3555

This restored 1754 inn, which incorporates a pub, small dining room and bar, can be busy at times. The hardwood charcoal grill is perfectly suited for the exceptional variety of fresh seafood, prime and choice meats and the chef's daily specials. Casual dress. Entertainment. **Bar:** Full bar. **Reservations:** suggested. **Hours:** 11 am-4 & 5-10 pm. Closed: 12/25. **Address:** 32 Water St 06355 **Location:** I-95, exit 89, 1.4 mi s on Allyn St, then 0.5 mi e on US 1. **Parking:** on-site.

FLOOD TIDE RESTAURANT   *Menu on AAA.com*

Continental
$8-$36

Phone: 860/536-8140

Views of the Mystic River lend tranquility to the surroundings inside this sea captain-style home, complete with a wood-burning fireplace. Solid choices include split pea soup with pureed red peppers and Maine crab cakes, not to mention the memorable bananas Foster. Dressy casual. Entertainment. **Bar:** Full bar. **Reservations:** suggested. **Hours:** Open 5/1-12/31 & 2/1-4/30; 5:30 pm-9:30 pm, Fri & Sat-10 pm; Sunday brunch 11 am-2 pm; seasonal hours may vary. Closed: 12/24. **Address:** 3 Williams Ave 06355 **Location:** On US 1 at SR 27; in Inn at Mystic. **Parking:** on-site.

GO FISH

Seafood
$18-$37

Phone: 860/536-2662

In the Olde Mistick Shopping Village, the restaurant is a great place to stop and enjoy tasty seafood as well as a selection of raw bar and sushi offerings. Choices from an extensive wine list pair with landlubber favorites, such as pan-roasted breast of chicken with mushroom bolognese sauce, garlic spinach and buttered egg noodles. The large contemporary dining room features a large bar in the center and a collection of colorful paintings, glassware and distinctive sculptures. Casual dress. **Bar:** Full bar. **Reservations:** not accepted. **Hours:** 11:30 am-2:30 & 4:30-9 pm, Fri & Sat-9:30 pm, Sun noon-9 pm. Closed: 11/25, 12/25. **Address:** Olde Mistick Village 06355 **Location:** I-95, exit 90, just s on Greenmanville Ave, then just e. **Parking:** on-site.

JAMMS RESTAURANT

American
$5-$24

Phone: 860/536-2683

Within walking distance of the seaport museum and marine aquarium, this casual eatery serves steak, fresh seafood and pasta. The menu lists tossed salads, grilled salmon with red potatoes, chocolate-raspberry cake and other flavorful choices. A separate lounge provides an alternative to the large dining room. Casual dress. **Bar:** Full bar. **Hours:** 11:30 am-10 pm, Fri & Sat-midnight, Sun 10 am-10 pm. Closed: 11/25, 12/24, 12/25. **Address:** 8 Coogan Blvd 06355 **Location:** I-95, exit 90, just s on SR 27; opposite Mystic Aquarium; next to Seaport Motor Inn. **Parking:** on-site.

MYSTIC DRAWBRIDGE ICE CREAM

Desserts
$2-$5

Phone: 860/572-7978

The ice cream parlor has been serving ice cream continually at the same location under various owners since the 1800s. Patrons can moor their boats at the parlor then walk up the steps to indulge in ice cream made on the premises from premium ingredients. Outside seats are right on the river. Service is casual and friendly. Casual dress. **Reservations:** not accepted. **Hours:** 11 am-10 pm, Fri & Sat-11 pm. Closed major holidays. **Address:** 2 W Main St 06355 **Location:** On US 1, just e of jct SR 215; at foot of drawbridge. **Parking:** street.

MYSTIC MARKET
Deli
$6-$8

Phone: 860/572-7992

This gourmet grocery market also offers an espresso bar and a number of made-to-order sandwiches, paninis, wraps and salads. Pre-made dinners are available for take out or to be heated and eaten at a cafe-style tables inside. Scrumptious desserts and breads are baked in house. Flavorful gelato varieties offer a refreshing summer treat. Friendly staff members take orders from behind counters. Casual dress. **Reservations:** not accepted. **Hours:** 7 am-7 pm, Sun 8 am-5 pm. Closed: 11/25, 12/25. **Address:** 63 Williams Ave 06355 **Location:** On US 1, 0.4 mi e of jct SR 27. **Parking:** on-site.

MYSTIC PIZZA

Pizza
$5-$18

Phone: 860/536-3700

The original pizza shop where the famous movie was filmed, Mystic Pizza lets patrons get their own "slice of heaven" as they reminisce over the photos on the walls. Casual dress. **Bar:** Beer & wine. **Reservations:** not accepted. **Hours:** 10:30 am-10 pm. Closed major holidays. **Address:** 56 W Main St 06355 **Location:** Jct SR 215, just w on US 1. **Parking:** street.

RICE SPICE NOODLES

Thai
$10-$18

Phone: 860/572-8488

A favorite haunt for good Thai food, this place turns out tom kha gai soup (chicken in coconut soup with galangal) and delicious pad thai noodles with shrimp, chicken, tofu, egg, bean sprouts and peanuts. Mango sticky rice makes for a tasty dessert. The small dining room is attractive with a simplistic modern feel. A red accent wall and vinyl floors add a pop of color. Servers are knowledgeable and attentive. Guests can bring their own bottles for a $3 per person opening fee. Casual dress. **Reservations:** accepted. **Hours:** 11:30 am-2:45 & 5-9:30 pm, Fri-10 pm, Sat 11:30 am-10 pm, Sun 11:30 am-9:30 pm. Closed: 11/25, 12/25. **Address:** 4 Roosevelt Ave 06355 **Location:** SR 27, just w on US 1. **Parking:** on-site. CALL ⑤M

S & P OYSTER CO

Seafood
$9-$30

Phone: 860/536-2674

Noted as having the city's best view, the restaurant affords a striking look out over the gorgeous river, historic homes, legendary drawbridge and distant lighthouse from its floor-to-ceiling windows. Guests can start with the signature oyster stew; follow with certified Angus strip steak or seafood ambrosia with shrimp, Stonington sea scallops, crab and cod topped with seafood stuffing; and finish with a decadent house dessert, such as creme brulee with raspberry coulis. Casual dress. **Bar:** Full bar. **Reservations:** accepted. **Hours:** 11:30 am-9 pm, Fri & Sat-10 pm; hours vary in summer. Closed: 11/25, 12/24, 12/25. **Address:** 1 Holmes St 06355 **Location:** Corner of US 1; center. **Parking:** on-site. CALL ⑤M

SEAMEN'S INNE RESTAURANT AND PUB

Regional American
$8-$26

Phone: 860/572-5303

Built as a replica of a sea captain's home, the restaurant is a nice spot for pleasant dining and reliable New England fare. Specialties include baked stuffed lobster and fresh seafood pot pie. Casual dress. **Bar:** Full bar. **Reservations:** suggested. **Hours:** 11:30 am-8:30 pm, Fri & Sat-9 pm; extended hours in summer. Closed: 12/24, 12/25; also Mon in winter. **Address:** 105 Greenmanville Ave 06355 **Location:** I-95, exit 90, 0.8 mi s on SR 27. **Parking:** on-site.

STEAK LOFT

American
$8-$32

Phone: 860/536-2661

Surrounded by antiques, farm tools and quilts in this New England replica farmhouse, guests dine on Angus beef, fresh seafood and a full dessert selection. Flavorful mushroom Florentine soup and Maryland crab cakes are notable treats. Casual dress. **Bar:** Full bar. **Hours:** 11:30 am-2:30 & 4:30-9:30 pm, Fri-10:30 pm, Sat 4:30 pm-10:30 pm, Sun 11:30 am-9:30 pm. Closed: 11/25, 12/24, 12/25. **Address:** Olde Mistick Village 06355 **Location:** I-95, exit 90, just s. **Parking:** on-site. CALL ⑤M

NAUGATUCK pop. 30,989

COMFORT INN NAUGATUCK *Book great rates at AAA.com*

Hotel
$75-$95 All Year

Phone: (203)723-9356

Address: 716 New Haven Rd 06770 **Location:** Jct SR 63 and 8, 0.8 mi s. **Facility:** 50 one-bedroom standard units. 3 stories, interior corridors. *Bath:* combo or shower only. **Parking:** on-site. **Amenities:** high-speed Internet, voice mail, irons, hair dryers. **Leisure Activities:** exercise room. **Guest Services:** valet and coin laundry, wireless Internet. **Business Services:** meeting rooms, business center. **Free Special Amenities: expanded continental breakfast and high-speed Internet.** CALL ⑤M 🐾 🖥 🖨 / SOME UNITS ✕

------ **WHERE TO DINE** ------

NARDELLI'S GRINDER SHOPPE

Sandwiches
$5-$8

Phone: 203/729-9470

Soft loaves of bread are topped with imported Italian Pruzitini ham, capicola, salami, provolone cheese, mayo, lettuce, tomato, olives, hot sauce and the "classic mix," a well-kept secret blend of onions and green peppers. Among other cold and hot grinders are chicken parmigiana, sausage and peppers, and the turkey club. Owned and operated by a third-generation Nardelli family member, this place employs staffers who pride themselves on serving guests with a smile. Casual dress. **Reservations:** not accepted. **Hours:** 9 am-9 pm. Closed major holidays; also Sun. **Address:** 87 Maple St 06770 **Location:** SR 8, exit 26 (northbound), 0.4 mi n on S Main St, then just w; exit 27 (southbound), then just w. **Parking:** on-site. CALL ⑤M

NEW BRITAIN—See Hartford p. 276.

NEW CANAAN (See map and index starting on p. 247)

------ **WHERE TO DINE** ------

LE PAIN QUOTIDIEN

Natural/Organic
$9-$14

Phone: 203/920-4143 ⑬

In the heart of an upscale shopping district, this eatery is part of a chain that began in Brussels. This location shares the original's farmhouse feel. All organic ingredients go into healthful choices such as vegan soups; roast beef tartines with caper mayo, diced tomatoes and scallions; or made-in-house quiches. The mixed berry tart features strawberries, blueberries and raspberries. The "to go" area has glass counters displaying baked goods as well as a gourmet coffee station. Casual dress. **Reservations:** not accepted. **Hours:** 7:30 am-9 pm, Fri-10 pm, Sat 8 am-10 pm, Sun 8 am-8 pm. Closed major holidays. **Address:** 81 Elm St 06840 **Location:** SR 15, exit 37, 2.1 mi n on SR 124, then just w. **Parking:** street. CALL ⑤M

THE ROGER SHERMAN INN

Phone: 203/966-4541   ⑪

Continental
$13-$44

In a historic 1700s inn named for a famous Connecticut patriot who signed all four key documents of the Revolutionary period, the restaurant serves familiar food in low-key elegance and comfort. Seafood and meat are the menu staples. Dressy casual. **Bar:** Full bar. **Reservations:** suggested. **Hours:** noon-2:30 & 5:30-9 pm, Sat from 5:30 pm. Closed: 7/4, 12/25; also Mon. **Address:** 195 Oenoke Ridge 06840 **Location:** Merritt Pkwy, exit 37, 3 mi n on SR 124. **Parking:** on-site. **Historic.**

SOLE'

Phone: 203/972-8887   ⑫

Italian
$14-$38

In the center of town, the restaurant is a great place for dinner before or after a movie at the theater next door. Tables in the front offer great views of the upscale boutique shops lining the main street. The wood-burning oven turns out tasty pizzas, while homemade pasta dishes are full of flavor and desserts, including authentic tiramisu, are superb. The beautiful sky-painted ceiling, crisp linen tablecloths and stone wall accents add to the chic atmosphere. Dressy casual. **Bar:** Full bar. **Reservations:** suggested. **Hours:** noon-3 & 5-10 pm, Fri-10:30 pm, Sat noon-3 & 5:30-10:30 pm, Sun 5 pm-9 pm. Closed: 1/1, 11/25, 12/25; also Super Bowl Sun. **Address:** 105 Elm St 06840 **Location:** Between Park St and South Ave; downtown. **Parking:** on-site.

NEW HARTFORD

——— WHERE TO DINE ———

CHATTERLEY'S CAFE

Phone: 860/379-2428

American
$8-$25

Whether for lunch or dinner, patrons of the corner eatery find only fresh and creative ingredients served with a tempting flair. Casual dress. **Bar:** Full bar. **Reservations:** accepted. **Hours:** 11:30 am-4:30 & 5-9:30 pm, Fri-10:30 pm, Sat 11:30 am-5 & 5:30-10:30 pm, Sun 11:30 am-5 & 5:30-9:30 pm. Closed: 12/25. **Address:** 2 Bridge St 06057 **Location:** Jct SR 219, just w on US 44. **Parking:** on-site.

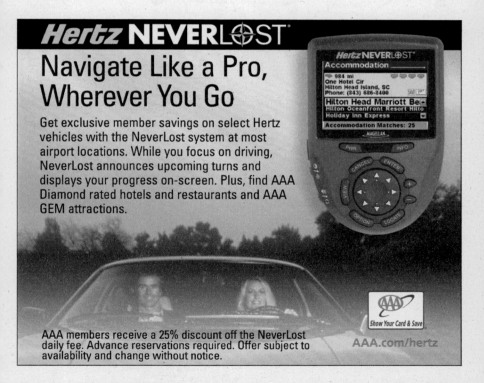
Get a Fresh Perspective on AAATravelViews.com

- Blogs from our experts on popular and unique destinations
- The latest in helpful travel advice and news
- Photos, videos, maps and special member offers
- Comments and Q&A with AAA experts

Share travel at
AAATravelViews.com

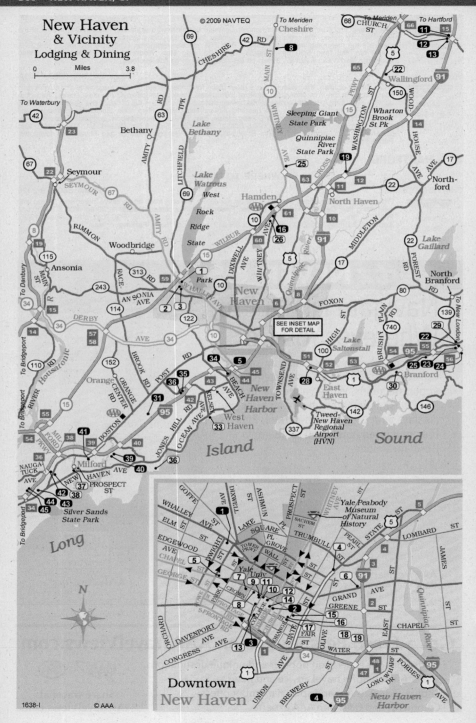

New Haven
& Vicinity
Lodging & Dining

© 2009 NAVTEQ

Miles
0   3.8

To Meriden
Cheshire

To Meriden
CHURCH ST
To Hartford

To Waterbury

Bethany

Lake
Bethany

Seymour

Lake
Watrous
West
Rock
Ridge
State

Hamden

Sleeping Giant
State Park

Quinnipiac
River
State Park

Wallingford

Wharton
Brook
St Pk

North Haven

North-
ford

Woodbridge

Park

New
Haven

Lake
Gaillard

North
Branford

Ansonia

To Danbury

ANSONIA AVE

DERBY

SEE INSET MAP
FOR DETAIL

FOXON ST

Lake
Saltonstall

To New London

To Bridgeport

Orange

New
Haven
Harbor

East
Haven

Branford

West
Haven

Tweed-
New Haven
Regional
Airport
(HVN)

Island

Sound

Milford

NEW
HAVEN
PROSPECT
ST

Silver Sands
State Park

To Bridgeport

Long

N

Downtown
New Haven

GOFFE

WHALLEY

ELM ST

EDGEWOOD
AVE

CHAPEL

GEORGE

ORCHARD

DAVENPORT
AVE

CONGRESS

DIXWELL

ASHMUN ST

PROSPECT ST

WHITNEY ST

SACHEM ST

Yale Peabody
Museum
of Natural
History

LAKE

SQUARE

TOWER PKWY

WALL ST

PL
GROVE

TRUMBULL

PEARL ST

STATE ST

LOMBARD ST

JAMES ST

Yale
Univ

CROWN

COLLEGE ST

PRINCE

S FRONTAGE RD

GRAND AVE

GREENE

OLIVE ST

WATER ST

EAST ST

CHAPEL ST

Quinnipiac River

UNION AVE

BREWERY

FORBES AVE

NEW HAVEN AVE

New Haven
Harbor

1638-I   © AAA

New Haven and Vicinity

This index helps you to "spot" where approved lodgings and restaurants are located on the corresponding detailed maps. Lodging daily rate range is for comparison only and show the property's high season. Restaurant rate range is a combination of lunch and/or dinner. Turn to the listing page for more detailed rate information and consult display ads for special promotions.

NEW HAVEN

Map Page	OA	Lodgings	Diamond Rated	High Season	Page
❶ / p. 300	AAA	**Courtyard New Haven Downtown at Yale**	◆◆◆	$170-$208 SAVE	303
❷ / p. 300		Omni New Haven Hotel at Yale	◆◆◆	$159-$289	303
❸ / p. 300	AAA	**New Haven Hotel**	[fyi]	$59-$399 SAVE	303
❹ / p. 300		La Quinta Inn & Suites	◆◆	$99-$199	303
❺ / p. 300		Premiere Hotel & Suites	◆◆◆	$149-$239	303

Map Page	OA	Restaurants	Diamond Rated	Cuisine	Meal Range	Page
① / p. 300		Carmine's Tuscan Grill Ristorante	◆◆◆	Italian	$8-$28	305
② / p. 300		Akasaka	◆◆	Japanese	$8-$20	304
③ / p. 300		Athenian Diner Restaurant	◆	American	$3-$20	304
④ / p. 300		Carmen Anthony	◆◆◆	Steak	$7-$35	305
⑤ / p. 300		India Palace	◆◆	Indian	$8-$20	305
⑥ / p. 300		Adriana's	◆◆	Italian	$8-$17	304
⑦ / p. 300		Scoozzi Trattoria & Wine Bar	◆◆◆	Northern Italian	$10-$28	306
⑧ / p. 300		Atticus Bookstore Cafe	◆	American	$8-$10	305
⑨ / p. 300		Union League Cafe	◆◆◆	French	$9-$34	306
⑩ / p. 300		Claire's Corner Copia	◆	Vegetarian	$7-$11	305
⑪ / p. 300		Bespoke	◆◆◆	New American	$26-$29	305
⑫ / p. 300		Zinc	◆◆◆	American	$13-$28	306
⑬ / p. 300		Pacifico	◆◆◆	New Latin American	$16-$43	306
⑭ / p. 300		John Davenport's at the Top of the Park	◆◆◆	Seafood	$10-$33	306
⑮ / p. 300	AAA	**Central Steakhouse**	◆◆◆	Steak	$15-$28	305
⑯ / p. 300	AAA	**Bentara Malaysian Restaurant**	◆◆◆	Asian	$8-$30	305
⑰ / p. 300		Foster's	◆◆◆	New American	$8-$28	305
⑱ / p. 300		Frank Pepe Pizzeria Napoletana	◆	Pizza	$6-$22	305
⑲ / p. 300		Tre Scalini Ristorante	◆◆◆	Italian	$10-$23	306

CHESHIRE

Map Page	OA	Lodging	Diamond Rated	High Season	Page
❽ / p. 300	AAA	**Cheshire Red Carpet Inn & Suites**	◆◆	$80-$125 SAVE	242

WALLINGFORD

Map Page	OA	Lodgings	Diamond Rated	High Season	Page
⓫ / p. 300	AAA	**Courtyard New Haven Wallingford**	◆◆◆	$125-$153 SAVE	325
⓬ / p. 300		Fairfield Inn New Haven Wallingford	◆◆	$89-$119	325
⓭ / p. 300		Homewood Suites by Hilton New Haven/Wallingford	◆◆◆	$89-$189	325

Map Page	OA	Restaurant	Diamond Rated	Cuisine	Meal Range	Page
㉒ / p. 300		Sabbatic Al's Cafe	◆◆	American	$5-$16	325

HAMDEN

Map Page	OA	Lodging	Diamond Rated	High Season	Page
16 / p. 300		Clarion Hotel & Suites Hamden-New Haven	◆◆◆	$129-$139	253

Map Page	OA	Restaurants	Diamond Rated	Cuisine	Meal Range	Page
25 / p. 300		Ristorante Luce	◆◆◆	International	$11-$29	253
26 / p. 300		Kumo	◆◆	Japanese	$7-$32	253

NORTH HAVEN

Map Page	OA	Lodging	Diamond Rated	High Season	Page
19 / p. 300		Holiday Inn	◆◆◆	$117-$170	309

BRANFORD

Map Page	OA	Lodgings	Diamond Rated	High Season	Page
22 / p. 300	AAA	**Americas Best Value Inn**	◆	$55-$90 [SAVE]	240
23 / p. 300	AAA	**Baymont Inn & Suites**	◆◆	$99-$179 [SAVE]	240
24 / p. 300	AAA	**Rodeway Inn & Suites**	◆	$69-$95 [SAVE]	241
25 / p. 300	AAA	**Holiday Inn Express**	◆◆◆	$110-$130 [SAVE]	241

Map Page	OA	Restaurants	Diamond Rated	Cuisine	Meal Range	Page
29 / p. 300		USS Chowder Pot III	◆◆	Seafood	$7-$29	241
30 / p. 300		Pasta Cosi	◆◆	Italian	$13-$26	241

EAST HAVEN

Map Page	OA	Lodging	Diamond Rated	High Season	Page
28 / p. 300	AAA	**Quality Inn**	◆◆	$85-$180 [SAVE]	245

ORANGE

Map Page	OA	Lodging	Diamond Rated	High Season	Page
31 / p. 300		Courtyard New Haven Orange	◆◆◆	$170-$208	314

WEST HAVEN

Map Page	OA	Lodgings	Diamond Rated	High Season	Page
34 / p. 300	AAA	**Super 8**	◆	$70-$90 [SAVE]	330
35 / p. 300	AAA	**Best Western Executive Hotel**	◆◆	$69-$180 [SAVE]	330
36 / p. 300	AAA	**Hampton Inn & Suites-West Haven**	◆◆◆	$99-$169 [SAVE]	330

Map Page	OA	Restaurant	Diamond Rated	Cuisine	Meal Range	Page
33 / p. 300		Jimmies	◆◆	Seafood	$5-$25	330

MILFORD

Map Page	OA	Lodgings	Diamond Rated	High Season	Page
39 / p. 300		Hilton Garden Inn Milford	◆◆◆	$99-$179	289
40 / p. 300	AAA	**Hyatt Place Milford**	◆◆◆	$99-$209 [SAVE]	290
41 / p. 300	AAA	**Super 8** - see color ad p 303	◆◆	Rates not provided [SAVE]	290
42 / p. 300	AAA	**Hampton Inn**	◆◆	Rates not provided [SAVE]	289
43 / p. 300		Fairfield Inn by Marriott-Milford	◆◆	$129-$134	289
44 / p. 300		SpringHill Suites Milford	◆◆◆	$139-$149	290
45 / p. 300		Residence Inn Milford	◆◆◆	$159-$174	290

Map Page	OA	Restaurants	Diamond Rated	Cuisine	Meal Range	Page
36 / p. 300	AAA	**Scribner's**	◆◆	Seafood	$16-$50	290
37 / p. 300		Stonebridge Restaurant	◆◆	American	$8-$27	290
38 / p. 300	AAA	**Gusto Restaurant**	◆◆	Italian	$9-$26	290

NEW HAVEN pop. 123,626 (See map and index starting on p. 300)

COURTYARD NEW HAVEN DOWNTOWN AT YALE
Book great rates at AAA.com   Phone: (203)777-6221

AAA SAVE
Hotel
$170-$208 All Year

Address: 30 Whalley Ave 06511 **Location:** SR 34, exit 2, 0.5 mi w on N Frontage Rd, then 0.8 mi n on Howe St; I-95, exit 47; I-91, exit 1; downtown. **Facility:** Smoke free premises. 207 units. 206 one-bedroom standard units. 1 one-bedroom suite. 8 stories, interior corridors. *Bath:* combo or shower only. **Parking:** on-site (fee). **Terms:** cancellation fee imposed. **Amenities:** video games (fee), CD players, high-speed Internet, dual phone lines, voice mail, safes, irons, hair dryers. **Leisure Activities:** exercise room. **Guest Services:** valet and coin laundry, wireless Internet. **Business Services:** meeting rooms, business center.

AAA Benefit:
Members save a minimum 5% off the best available rate.

LA QUINTA INN & SUITES
Book at AAA.com   Phone: (203)562-1111 4

Hotel
$99-$199 All Year

Address: 400 Sargent Dr 06511 **Location:** I-95, exit 46. **Facility:** 152 one-bedroom standard units. 8 stories, interior corridors. *Bath:* combo or shower only. **Parking:** on-site. **Amenities:** video games (fee), voice mail, irons, hair dryers. **Pool(s):** outdoor. **Leisure Activities:** exercise room. **Guest Services:** valet and coin laundry, area transportation, wireless Internet. **Business Services:** business center.

NEW HAVEN HOTEL
Book great rates at AAA.com   Phone: (203)498-3100 3

AAA SAVE
[fyi]
Hotel
$59-$399 All Year

Under major renovation, scheduled to be completed June 2010. Last rated:
Address: 229 George St 06510 **Location:** SR 34, exit 2, 0.3 mi w on N Frontage Rd, just n on York St, then just e; I-95, exit 47; I-91, exit 1; downtown. **Facility:** Smoke free premises. 92 units. 88 one-bedroom standard units. 4 one-bedroom suites. 7 stories, interior corridors. *Bath:* shower only. **Parking:** on-site (fee). **Terms:** cancellation fee imposed. **Amenities:** voice mail, irons, hair dryers. **Leisure Activities:** exercise room. **Guest Services:** valet laundry, wireless Internet. **Business Services:** meeting rooms, business center.

OMNI NEW HAVEN HOTEL AT YALE
Book at AAA.com   Phone: (203)772-6664 2

Hotel
$159-$289 All Year

Address: 155 Temple St 06510 **Location:** Center of downtown. Adjacent to Yale Green. **Facility:** 306 units. 298 one-bedroom standard units. 8 one-bedroom suites. 19 stories, interior corridors. *Bath:* combo or shower only. **Parking:** on-site (fee) and valet. **Terms:** cancellation fee imposed. **Amenities:** high-speed Internet, dual phone lines, voice mail, honor bars, irons, hair dryers. *Some: Fee:* DVD players. **Dining:** John Davenport's at the Top of the Park, see separate listing. *Bath:* shower only. **Leisure Activities:** exercise room, spa. **Guest Services:** valet laundry, wireless Internet. **Business Services:** conference facilities, business center.

PREMIERE HOTEL & SUITES
Book at AAA.com   Phone: (203)777-5337 5

Extended Stay Hotel
$149-$239 All Year

Address: 3 Long Wharf Dr 06511 **Location:** I-95, exit 46, 0.6 mi nw. **Facility:** Smoke free premises. 112 one-bedroom standard units with kitchens. 2 stories (no elevator), exterior corridors. **Parking:** on-site. **Amenities:** high-speed Internet, voice mail, irons, hair dryers. **Pool(s):** outdoor. **Leisure Activities:** whirlpool, exercise room, sports court. **Guest Services:** valet and coin laundry, area transportation, wireless Internet. **Business Services:** meeting rooms, business center.

▼ See AAA listing p 290 ▼

(See map and index starting on p. 300)

──────── *The following lodging was either not evaluated or did not* ────────
meet AAA rating requirements but is listed for your information only.

THE STUDY AT YALE   **Phone:** 203/503-3900

[fyi]   Not evaluated. **Address:** 1157 Chapel St 06511 **Location:** SR 34, exit 2, 0.3 mi w on N Frontage Rd, 0.4 mi n on York St, then just w; I-95, exit 47; I-91, exit 1; downtown. Facilities, services, and decor characterize a mid-scale property.

──────── **WHERE TO DINE** ────────

ADRIANA'S   **Phone:** 203/865-6474   **⑥**

▼▼ ▼▼
Italian
$8-$17

Classic Northern and Southern Italian cuisine is prepared with locally fresh and imported ingredients from Italy. Veal preparations stand out on a menu that also lists many pasta and seafood dishes. Homemade dishes are full of flavor and reasonably priced. Dressy casual. **Bar:** Full bar. **Reservations:** accepted. **Hours:** 11:30 am-10 pm, Sat from 5 pm; hours may vary in season. Closed: 4/4, 12/25. **Address:** 771 Grand Ave 06511 **Location:** I-91, exit 2, just n on Hamilton St, then just w. **Parking:** on-site.

AKASAKA   **Phone:** 203/387-4898   **②**

▼▼ ▼▼
Japanese
$8-$20

In a small shopping plaza, the restaurant is accented by Japanese artwork and a wood-paneled ceiling. The excellent sushi bar offers not only a wide variety of fresh sushi but also sashimi and tempura selections. Friendly yet casual aspects of the service include a warm cloth for washing hands before the meal and a complimentary pickled cucumber and carrot bowl. Casual dress. **Bar:** Full bar. **Reservations:** accepted, weekends. **Hours:** 11 am-3 & 4:30-10 pm, Fri & Sat-11 pm, Sun 3 pm-10 pm. Closed: 11/25. **Address:** 1450 Whalley Ave 06515 **Location:** SR 15, exit 59, just s on SR 69. **Parking:** on-site.

ARCHIE MOORE'S BAR & RESTAURANT   **Phone:** 203/773-9870

▼
American
$7-$22

The restaurant is known for its Buffalo wings, but its sandwiches, burgers and soups also are great choices. Casual dress. **Bar:** Full bar. **Hours:** 11:30 am-midnight, Fri & Sat-1 am. **Address:** 188 1/2 Willow St 06511 **Location:** I-91, exit 6, 0.4 mi nw. **Parking:** on-site.

ATHENIAN DINER RESTAURANT   **Phone:** 203/397-1556   **③**

▼
American
$3-$20

Patrons can nosh on traditional hamburgers, sandwiches, seafood and a large selection of desserts at the popular eatery, recognized year after year as one of the city's best diners. Casual dress. **Bar:** Full bar. **Reservations:** not accepted. **Hours:** 24 hours. Closed: 12/25. **Address:** 1426 Whalley Ave 06515 **Location:** SR 15, exit 59, just s on SR 69 at jct SR 63. **Parking:** on-site.

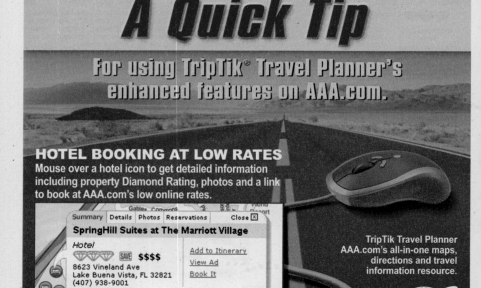

(See map and index starting on p. 300)

ATTICUS BOOKSTORE CAFE
Phone: 203/776-4040

American
$8-$10

The currant scone is a great breakfast choice, while a lunch favorite is the vegetable sandwich with black bean soup. Other choices at this distinctive cafe include delicious desserts and pastries. Casual dress. **Reservations:** not accepted. **Hours:** 7 am-10 pm, Sun 8 am-9 pm. Closed: 1/1, 7/4, 12/25. **Address:** 1082 Chapel St 06510 **Location:** Just sw of Yale Green; downtown. **Parking:** street.

BENTARA MALAYSIAN RESTAURANT
Phone: 203/562-2511 16

Asian
$8-$30

The eclectic restaurant presents a menu of excellent Malaysia-influenced cuisine, as well as a 27-page international wine list. Casual dress. **Bar:** Full bar. **Reservations:** suggested. **Hours:** 11:30 am-2:30 & 5-9:30 pm, Fri & Sat-10:30 pm. Closed major holidays; also for lunch Sat & Sun in summer. **Address:** 76 Orange St 06510 **Location:** Corner of Orange and Center sts; downtown. **Parking:** on-site and street.

BESPOKE
Phone: 203/562-4644 11

New American
$26-$29

The expert chef consistently prepares memorable meals using organic ingredients from local markets whenever possible. A perfect meal may begin with goat cheese and roasted beet salad with red and yellow baby beets, marcona almonds, orange segments, goat cheese tempura and microgreens; progress to porcini-dusted mahi mahi with asparagus puree, lobster-corn emulsion and roasted fingerling potatoes; and end with semifrozen banana and chocolate mousse topped with dolce de leche gelato. Dressy casual. **Bar:** Full bar. **Reservations:** suggested. **Hours:** 5 pm-9 pm, Fri & Sat-10:30 pm, Sun 1 pm-7 pm. **Address:** 266 College St 06510 **Location:** Between Chapel and Crown sts; downtown. **Parking:** street.

CARMEN ANTHONY
Phone: 203/773-1444 4

Steak
$7-$35

Popular with the business lunch crowd, the restaurant's mouthwatering and zestfully prepared steaks share menu space with preparations of fine, fresh seafood. Dressy casual. **Bar:** Full bar. **Reservations:** accepted. **Hours:** 11:30 am-4 & 5-10 pm, Fri & Sat-11 pm, Sun 4 pm-9 pm. Closed: 7/4, 9/6, 12/25. **Address:** 660 State St 06511 **Location:** Corner of Audubon St; downtown. **Parking:** street. CALL 🅼

CARMINE'S TUSCAN GRILL RISTORANTE
Phone: 203/389-2805 1

Italian
$8-$28

Patrons can escape into the Old World amid murals of Venice and garden courtyard decor. Tasty menu choices include pasta, chicken and seafood dishes, as well as Angus beef specialties. Casual dress. **Bar:** Full bar. **Reservations:** accepted. **Hours:** 11:30 am-3 & 4:30-10 pm, Fri-11 pm, Sat noon-3 & 4:30-11 pm, Sun 1 pm-8 pm. **Address:** 1500 Whalley Ave 06515 **Location:** SR 15, exit 59, just s on SR 69. **Parking:** on-site. CALL 🅼

CENTRAL STEAKHOUSE
Phone: 203/787-7885 15

Steak
$15-$28

The sophisticated yet trendy downtown restaurant lets diners watch a plasma-screen TV linked to a video camera tracking activity in the open kitchen. Although the place is known for its steaks, it also prepares excellent New Zealand rack of lamb, pan-roasted filet of red snapper and grilled veal porterhouse. It's hard not to find a perfectly suited glass or bottle of wine from the extensive list. Dressy casual. **Bar:** Full bar. **Reservations:** suggested. **Hours:** 5 pm-9 pm, Fri & Sat-10 pm. Closed: major holidays, 12/24; also Sun & Mon. **Address:** 99 Orange St 06510 **Location:** Between Center and Chapel sts; downtown. **Parking:** street.

CLAIRE'S CORNER COPIA
Phone: 203/562-3888 10

Vegetarian
$7-$11

The gourmet vegetarian restaurant has been serving New Haven since 1975 with an all-day breakfast, bakery items and many distinctive and tasty kosher, Italian and Mexican creations, such as pizzette, soup, quiche of the day and pita sandwiches. Most ingredients are organic. Casual dress. **Hours:** 8 am-9 pm, Fri-10 pm, Sat 9 am-10 pm, Sun 9 am-9 pm. Closed major holidays. **Address:** 1000 Chapel St 06510 **Location:** Corner of College St; center of downtown. **Parking:** on-site (fee) and street.

FOSTER'S
Phone: 203/859-6666 17

New American
$8-$28

A newer member to the city dining scene, the restaurant occupies a historic building in the trendy 9th Square district. The modern space features many Asian accents, including bamboo flooring and a gray stone block wall. A menu that the chef calls "eccentric American" lists choices such as goat cheese and apple tart with caramelized onion over mixed greens or steak with porcini mushrooms and potato risotto. Early diners can opt for the budget-friendly three-course tasting menu. Dressy casual. **Bar:** Full bar. **Reservations:** suggested. **Hours:** 11:30 am-2:30 & 5-10 pm, Fri & Sat-11 pm. Closed: 1/1, 11/25, 12/25. **Address:** 56-62 Orange St 06510 **Location:** Between Center and Crown sts; downtown. **Parking:** street. CALL 🅼

FRANK PEPE PIZZERIA NAPOLETANA
Phone: 203/865-5762 18

Pizza
$6-$22

Established in 1925, the popular eatery is famous for coal-fired thin crust pizzas topped with fresh mozzarella and a secret sauce. Expect long lines but the wait is worthwhile. If you're lucky, you'll get seated at one of the many tables that offer views of the open kitchen. Casual dress. **Bar:** Beer & wine. **Reservations:** not accepted. **Hours:** 11:30 am-10 pm. Closed major holidays. **Address:** 157 Wooster St 06511 **Location:** Between Chestnut St and DePalma Ct; downtown. **Parking:** on-site.

INDIA PALACE
Phone: 203/776-9010 5

Indian
$8-$20

North Indian cuisine is served in a casual setting. Aromatic dishes of the subcontinent range from tandoori, curry, korma and vindaloo choices to several vegetarian specialties. The lunch buffet is another option. Parking is in the rear. Casual dress. **Bar:** Beer & wine. **Reservations:** accepted. **Hours:** 11:30 am-10:30 pm. Closed: 11/25, 12/25. **Address:** 65 Howe St 06511 **Location:** SR 34, exit 3, w on N Frontage Rd, then n. **Parking:** on-site.

(See map and index starting on p. 300)

JOHN DAVENPORT'S AT THE TOP OF THE PARK
Phone: 203/772-6664   14

Seafood
$10-$33

Patrons take in panoramic views of downtown New Haven, the Town Green and Long Island Sound while dining. The menu offers a variety of beef, seafood and chicken dishes. Entertainment is offered in the lounge on weekends. Dressy casual. **Bar:** Full bar. **Reservations:** suggested. **Hours:** 6-11 am, 11:30-2 & 5:30-10 pm. **Address:** 155 Temple St 06510 **Location:** Center of downtown; in Omni New Haven Hotel at Yale. **Parking:** on-site (fee).

PACIFICO
Phone: 203/772-4002   13

New Latin
American
$16-$43

Near Yale University, this contemporary and colorful hot spot resides in a two-story building with eclectic decor, including wood floors, shades of bright red and orange, a neon blue ceiling and fish accents in the art and on the booth fabric. The lower-level has an open kitchen with some seating around the bar, while upstairs diners who sit by one of the many windows with have a view of the bustling street below. The house soup with mussels, shrimp and clams in a tomato broth is delicious. Dressy casual. **Bar:** Full bar. **Reservations:** suggested. **Hours:** 11:30 am-2:30 & 5-9 pm, Fri & Sat-1 am, Sun noon-4 & 5-10 pm. **Address:** 220 College St 06510 **Location:** Corner of Crowne St; downtown. **Parking:** street.

SCOOZZI TRATTORIA & WINE BAR
Phone: 203/776-8268   7

Northern Italian
$10-$28

Just below street level, this sanctuary from the hustle above serves traditional and contemporary dishes, along with the largest variety of Italian wines around. Dressy casual. **Bar:** Full bar. **Reservations:** suggested. **Hours:** noon-2:30 & 5-9 pm, Fri-9:30 pm, Sat noon-9:30 pm, Sun noon-3 & 5-8:30 pm; Sunday brunch. Closed: 1/1, 11/25, 12/24, 12/25; also Mon. **Address:** 1104 Chapel St 06510 **Location:** Between High and York sts; downtown. **Parking:** on-site (fee) and street.

TRE SCALINI RISTORANTE
Phone: 203/777-3373   19

Italian
$10-$23

In the city's historic Little Italy district, the restaurant prepares reliably good food. Dressy casual. **Bar:** Full bar. **Reservations:** suggested, weekends. **Hours:** 11:30 am-2:30 & 5-9 pm, Fri-9:30 pm, Sat 5 pm-10 pm, Sun 4 pm-8 pm. Closed: 1/1, 12/25. **Address:** 100 Wooster St 06511 **Location:** Between Water and Chapel sts; corner of Franklin and Wooster sts; downtown. **Parking:** valet and street.

UNION LEAGUE CAFE
Phone: 203/562-4299   9

French
$9-$34

The elegant "old-time" steakhouse is steeped in traditional decor: wood floors, carved mahogany walls and ceilings, decorative sconces and chandeliers. Amid the bustling activity of Yale University and local shops, this fine French bistro is a favorite, and reservations are encouraged. The wait staff, garbed in crisp black and white, put forth a plethora of knowledge. Casual dress. **Bar:** Full bar. **Reservations:** suggested. **Hours:** 11:30 am-2:30 & 5:30-9:30 pm, Fri-10 pm, Sat 5:30 pm-10 pm. Closed major holidays; also Sun. **Address:** 1032 Chapel St 06510 **Location:** Center of downtown. **Parking:** street.

ZINC
Phone: 203/624-0507   12

American
$13-$28

This modern, sleek restaurant offers an intriguing and exotic menu of Asia-influenced dishes, including offerings of excellent-quality steak, lamb, diver scallops and fresh fish. Among the fabulous and hard-to-resist desserts are chocolate hazelnut mousse cake and the trio of homemade sorbets. Dressy casual. **Bar:** Full bar. **Reservations:** accepted. **Hours:** noon-2:30 & 5-9:30 pm, Fri & Sat-10 pm, Sun 4:30 pm-8:30 pm. Closed: major holidays, 12/24; also Mon 7/5-9/4. **Address:** 964 Chapel St 06510 **Location:** I-95, exit 47, on SR 34 W, exit 1, just ne on Church St, then just nw; across from New Haven Green. **Parking:** street.

─────────── *The following restaurant has not been evaluated by AAA* ───────────
but is listed for your information only.

DOWNTOWN AT THE TAFT
Phone: 203/624-6331

fyi

Not evaluated. Representative of distinctive dishes are homemade pastas and desserts. The owner's insightful commentary is offered on the wine list. The historic site's original architecture has been preserved. **Address:** 261 College St 06510 **Location:** Just w of Yale Green; downtown.

NEW LONDON pop. 25,671

HOLIDAY INN

Phone: (860)442-0631

Hotel
$129-$189 5/1-10/31
$119-$179 11/1-4/30

Address: 269 N Frontage Rd 06320 **Location:** I-95, exit 82A northbound, 0.8 mi s, just w on Colman St, then 0.6 mi s; exit 83 southbound, 0.6 mi s. **Facility:** 136 one-bedroom standard units. 2 stories (no elevator), interior corridors. **Bath:** combo or shower only. **Parking:** on-site. **Terms:** 2 night minimum stay - seasonal and/or weekends, cancellation fee imposed. **Amenities:** dual phone lines, voice mail, irons, hair dryers. *Some:* high-speed Internet. **Pool(s):** heated indoor. **Leisure Activities:** whirlpool, exercise room. **Guest Services:** valet and coin laundry, wireless Internet. **Business Services:** meeting rooms, business center.

ASK 🍴 ▼ 🛥 🎥 💻 / SOME UNITS ✕ 🚪 🖥

RADISSON HOTEL
Book at AAA.com

Phone: (860)443-7000

Hotel
$89-$199 All Year

Address: 35 Governor Winthrop Blvd 06320 **Location:** I-95, exit 83 northbound, 0.6 mi s on US 1, then w; exit 84 southbound, 0.8 mi s on Eugene O'Neill Dr, then w. **Facility:** 120 one-bedroom standard units. 5 stories, interior corridors. **Parking:** on-site. **Terms:** 2 night minimum stay - seasonal and/or weekends, 3 day cancellation notice. **Amenities:** video games (fee), dual phone lines, voice mail, irons, hair dryers. **Pool(s):** heated indoor. **Leisure Activities:** exercise room. **Guest Services:** valet laundry, wireless Internet. **Business Services:** conference facilities, business center.

ASK 🍴 ▼ 🛥 💻 / SOME UNITS ✕ FEE 🚪 FEE 🖥

RED ROOF INN #7145
Book at AAA.com

Phone: (860)444-0001

Motel
$55-$100 All Year

Address: 707 Colman St 06320 **Location:** I-95, exit 82A northbound, 0.4 mi e, then just n; exit 83 southbound, 0.6 mi s. **Facility:** 108 one-bedroom standard units. 2 stories (no elevator), exterior corridors. **Bath:** combo or shower only. **Parking:** on-site. **Amenities:** video games (fee), voice mail. *Some:* irons, hair dryers. **Guest Services:** wireless Internet. **Business Services:** fax (fee).

ASK 🐾 / SOME UNITS 🐕 ✕ 🚪 🖥

—— WHERE TO DINE ——

GRIDLOCK GRILLE
Phone: 860/442-7146

American
$4-$15

Serving breakfast, lunch and dinner, the restaurant specializes in USDA choice prime rib, large salads and fresh seafood, particularly lobsters up to 9 pounds from the lobster tank. Basic preparations satisfy weary travelers who venture in from the interstate nearby. Casual dress. **Bar:** Full bar. **Reservations:** accepted. **Hours:** 7 am-10 pm, Fri & Sat-10:30 pm. Closed: 12/25. **Address:** 566 Colman St 06320 **Location:** I-95, exit 82A northbound; exit 83 southbound, 0.3 mi s on US 1. **Parking:** on-site.

NEW MILFORD pop. 6,633

THE HOMESTEAD INN   *Book at AAA.com*
Phone: (860)354-4080

Historic Bed
& Breakfast
$105-$220 All Year

Address: 5 Elm St 06776 **Location:** Just e of village green off Main St; center. **Facility:** This 1850s Victorian is beside the village green near the town's center; simpler bungalows, detached from the main house, also are offered. Smoke free premises. 15 units. 14 one-bedroom standard units. 1 one-bedroom suite. 2 stories, interior/exterior corridors. *Bath:* combo or shower only. **Parking:** on-site. **Terms:** office hours 7 am-9 pm, 2 night minimum stay - seasonal and/or weekends. **Amenities:** video library, DVD players, irons, hair dryers. **Guest Services:** wireless Internet.

ASK ⊠ / SOME UNITS FEE 🐾 🛗 🖥

ROCKY RIVER INN & SUITES
Phone: 860/355-3208

AAA SAVE

Motel
$50-$300 All Year

Address: 236 Kent Rd 06776 **Location:** Jct US 7 and 202, 1.5 mi n on US 7. **Facility:** 36 units. 31 one-bedroom standard units, some with efficiencies and/or whirlpools. 3 one- and 2 two-bedroom suites, some with whirlpools. 1-2 stories, exterior corridors. *Bath:* combo or shower only. **Parking:** on-site. **Terms:** 7 day cancellation notice-fee imposed. **Amenities:** irons, hair dryers. **Guest Services:** wireless Internet. **Free Special Amenities: local telephone calls and high-speed Internet.**

 🍴 🎥 🛗 🖥 🖥 / SOME UNITS ⊠ 🐾 📶 ☎

—— WHERE TO DINE ——

ADRIENNE-FINE AMERICAN DINING   *Menu on AAA.com*
Phone: 860/354-6001

AAA
American
$17-$27

This charming, country classic eatery is housed in a 19th-century home with fireplaces and plank floors. The chef/owner prepares sophisticated dishes of beef, game, seafood and duck with each of her seasonal menus. Dessert hounds should try the bittersweet chocolate terrine. Casual dress. **Bar:** Full bar. **Reservations:** suggested. **Hours:** Open 5/1-2/28 & 3/14-4/30; 5:30 pm-9 pm, Fri & Sat-9:30 pm, Sun 11:30 am-3:30 pm. Closed: 1/1, 12/25; also Mon. **Address:** 218 Kent Rd 06776 **Location:** Jct US 7 and 202, 1.3 mi n on US 7. **Parking:** on-site.

THE COOKHOUSE
Phone: 860/355-4111

Barbecue
$8-$29

Authentic sweet smoked barbecue chicken, pork, ribs, brisket, burgers, steak and seafood are served in the country-style surroundings of a three-story open interior barn with wood and rafters. Pasta and daily fish specials are also available. Casual dress. **Bar:** Full bar. **Reservations:** not accepted. **Hours:** 11:30 am-10 pm, Fri & Sat-11 pm, Sun-9 pm. Closed: 11/25, 12/25. **Address:** 31 Danbury Rd 06776 **Location:** Just s on US 7 and 202. **Parking:** on-site.

JOEY'S SEAFOOD RESTAURANT
Phone: 860/355-2255

Seafood
$17-$24

A nondescript slope-roofed home gives way to the quaint and cozy stucco-walled dining room dotted with original art for sale. Fresh fish and other seafood is prepared simply for uncomplicated but fresh flavor. Lemon rum cake or pecan pie bring up the end of the meal. Casual dress. **Bar:** Full bar. **Reservations:** suggested. **Hours:** 5 pm-9 pm, Fri & Sat-10 pm. Closed: 11/25, 12/25; also Mon. **Address:** 188 Danbury Rd (US 7) 06776 **Location:** Jct US 7 and 202, 1.8 mi s. **Parking:** on-site.

NEWTOWN pop. 1,843

—— WHERE TO DINE ——

THE INN AT NEWTOWN
Phone: 203/270-1876

American
$9-$30

In a historic Colonial home in the quaint village of Newtown, the restaurant serves excellent seafood, steak and chicken dishes. Menu standouts include sea scallops with jumbo sweet pea ravioli in a Chardonnay cream sauce and the housemade pecan pie. For a romantic evening, request a table in the formal dining room. The more casual tap room offers a view of Main Street. Casual dress. **Bar:** Full bar. **Reservations:** suggested. **Hours:** 11:30 am-9:30 pm, Fri & Sat-10 pm, Sun 11 am-9 pm. Closed: 1/1, 9/6, 12/25. **Address:** 19 Main St 06470 **Location:** I-84, exit 10, 1 mi sw on US 6, then just se on SR 25. **Parking:** on-site.

NIANTIC pop. 3,085

HILLTOP INN   *Book great rates at AAA.com*

Hotel
$50-$230 All Year

Phone: (860)739-3951

Address: 239 Flanders Rd 06357 **Location:** I-95, exit 74, 0.5 mi se on SR 161. **Facility:** 90 one-bedroom standard units. 2 stories (no elevator), interior corridors. **Parking:** on-site. **Terms:** cancellation fee imposed. **Amenities:** video library (fee), voice mail, irons, hair dryers. *Some:* high-speed Internet. **Pool(s):** outdoor. **Leisure Activities:** exercise room. **Guest Services:** coin laundry, wireless Internet. **Business Services:** meeting rooms, PC. *(See color ad p 293)*

FREE full breakfast and high-speed Internet

INN AT HARBOR HILL MARINA

Bed & Breakfast
$210-$265 5/1-10/31
$135-$185 11/1-4/30

Phone: 860/739-0331

Address: 60 Grand St 06357 **Location:** I-95, exit 74, 3 mi s on SR 161. **Facility:** Overlooking the marina docks and a picturesque river, this inn offers views of the water from all rooms. Smoke free premises. 9 one-bedroom standard units. 3 stories (no elevator), interior corridors. *Bath:* shower only. **Parking:** office hours 7 am-9 pm, 2 night minimum stay - weekends, age restrictions may apply, 10 day cancellation notice-fee imposed. **Amenities:** video library, CD players, hair dryers. *Some:* DVD players, irons. **Leisure Activities:** marina, fishing. **Guest Services:** wireless Internet. **Business Services:** meeting rooms.

MOTEL 6 - 1063   *Book at AAA.com*

Motel
$55-$65 All Year

Phone: (860)739-6991

Address: 269 Flanders Rd 06357 **Location:** I-95, exit 74, just s. **Facility:** 96 one-bedroom standard units. 2 stories (no elevator), exterior corridors. *Bath:* combo or shower only. **Parking:** on-site. **Pool(s):** outdoor. **Guest Services:** coin laundry, wireless Internet.

 FEE

SLEEP INN & SUITES   *Book great rates at AAA.com*

Hotel
$70-$220 All Year

Phone: (860)739-1994

Address: 5 King Arthur Dr 06357 **Location:** I-95, exit 74, just s. **Facility:** 73 one-bedroom standard units, some with whirlpools. 3 stories, interior corridors. *Bath:* shower or tub only. **Parking:** on-site. **Terms:** check-in 4 pm. **Amenities:** high-speed Internet, dual phone lines, voice mail, irons, hair dryers. **Pool(s):** heated indoor. **Leisure Activities:** exercise room. **Guest Services:** coin laundry, wireless Internet. **Business Services:** meeting rooms, PC. **Free Special Amenities:** continental breakfast and local telephone calls.

CALL FEE   FEE

------ WHERE TO DINE ------

CONSTANTINE'S RESTAURANT

Seafood
$5-$24

Phone: 860/739-2848

Since 1929 this family-oriented, popular eatery has served diners in search of traditional New England fare. Fresh seafood, lobster, clam broth chowder and prime rib rule the roost. Extended summer hours make it convenient for those visiting the nearby children's museum. Casual dress. **Bar:** Full bar. **Reservations:** not accepted. **Hours:** 11:30 am-10 pm, Sun noon-9 pm; 11:30 am-9 pm off season. Closed: 11/25, 12/25; also Mon. **Address:** 252 Main St 06357 **Location:** SR 156, just w of jct SR 161. **Parking:** on-site.

NOANK pop. 1,830

------ WHERE TO DINE ------

ABBOTT'S LOBSTER IN THE ROUGH

Seafood
$4-$20

Phone: 860/536-7719

This restaurant has served coastal fare every summer season for more than 50 years. Steamed lobster from 2 to 10 pounds is the trademark, along with steamers, mussels and corn on the cob. The cooking process ensures a tender outcome no matter which size is chosen. Land-fare lovers can order a hot dog or oven-roasted chicken. The indoor/outdoor Noank Harbor location inspires informality. Casual dress. **Hours:** Open 5/1-10/11; noon-7 pm; to 9 pm 6/1-8/29. Closed: Mon-Thurs 5/1-5/31 & 8/30-10/11. **Address:** 117 Pearl St 06340 **Location:** 0.3 mi e of center from Main St; on the waterfront. **Parking:** on-site.

NORFOLK

MANOR HOUSE

Historic Bed
& Breakfast
Rates not provided

Phone: 860/542-5690

Address: 69 Maple Ave 06058 **Location:** Jct SR 272, just e on US 44, then 0.3 mi n. **Facility:** The property is an 1898 Victorian Tudor-style estate and includes a spacious common room and sun porch. Smoke free premises. 9 units. 8 one-bedroom standard units, some with whirlpools. 1 one-bedroom suite. 3 stories (no elevator), interior corridors. *Bath:* combo or shower only. **Parking:** on-site. **Terms:** age restrictions may apply. **Amenities:** hair dryers. **Guest Services:** TV in common area.

NORTH HAVEN pop. 23,035   (See map and index starting on p. 300)

HOLIDAY INN   *Book at AAA.com*   Phone: (203)239-6700   **19**

Hotel
$117-$170 5/1-10/31
$112-$122 11/1-4/30

Address: 201 Washington Ave 06473 **Location:** I-91, exit 12 on US 5. **Facility:** 143 units. 139 one-bedroom standard units, some with whirlpools. 4 one-bedroom suites. 2 stories, interior corridors. *Bath:* combo or shower only. **Parking:** on-site. **Amenities:** high-speed Internet, voice mail, irons, hair dryers. **Pool(s):** heated indoor. **Leisure Activities:** saunas, exercise room. **Guest Services:** valet and coin laundry, wireless Internet. **Business Services:** conference facilities, business center.

NORTH STONINGTON —See also Stonington.

ANTIQUES AND ACCOMMODATIONS   Phone: 860/535-1736

Historic Bed
& Breakfast
Rates not provided

Address: 32 Main St 06359 **Location:** I-95, exit 92, 2.5 mi nw on SR 2, then 0.3 mi n. **Facility:** Candlelit breakfasts are a specialty at this property set on manicured grounds in a historic village. Smoke free premises. 3 one-bedroom standard units. 2 stories (no elevator), interior corridors. *Bath:* combo or shower only. **Parking:** on-site. **Terms:** office hours 9 am-9 pm, age restrictions may apply. **Amenities:** hair dryers. **Guest Services:** wireless Internet.

HILLTOP INN & SUITES   *Book at AAA.com*   Phone: 860/535-0500

Motel
Rates not provided

Address: 373 Norwich Westerly Rd 06359 **Location:** I-95, exit 92, 3.4 mi n on SR 2. **Facility:** 138 one-bedroom standard units, some with whirlpools. 2 stories (no elevator), interior/exterior corridors. *Bath:* combo or shower only. **Parking:** on-site, winter plug-ins. **Amenities:** voice mail, safes (fee), hair dryers. *Some:* irons. **Leisure Activities:** exercise room. **Guest Services:** valet laundry, area transportation, wireless Internet. **Business Services:** meeting rooms.

THE INN AT LOWER FARM B & B   Phone: 860/535-9075

Historic Bed
& Breakfast
$125-$185 5/1-10/31
$105-$158 11/1-4/30

Address: 119 Mystic Rd 06359 **Location:** I-95, exit 90, 1.5 mi n on SR 27, 1.4 mi e on SR 184, then 3.4 mi n on SR 201. **Facility:** Step back in time at this 18th-century Colonial farmhouse on nearly five acres of rural lawns, gardens and marsh; most rooms have a working fireplace. Smoke free premises. 4 one-bedroom standard units, some with whirlpools. 2 stories (no elevator), interior corridors. *Bath:* combo or shower only. **Parking:** on-site. **Terms:** 2 night minimum stay - seasonal and/or weekends, age restrictions may apply, 7 day cancellation notice-fee imposed. **Amenities:** CD players, hair dryers. **Guest Services:** TV in common area, wireless Internet. **Business Services:** fax.

NORWALK pop. 82,951   (See map and index starting on p. 247)

COURTYARD NORWALK   *Book great rates at AAA.com*   Phone: (203)849-9111   **6**

Hotel
$188-$230 All Year

Address: 474 Main Ave 06851 **Location:** I-95, exit 15, 3.5 mi n, just e, then just s; from SR 15 (Merritt Pkwy), exit 40B, 0.6 mi n. **Facility:** Smoke free premises. 145 units. 133 one-bedroom standard units. 12 one-bedroom suites. 4 stories, interior corridors. *Bath:* combo or shower only. **Parking:** on-site. **Terms:** cancellation fee imposed. **Amenities:** high-speed Internet, voice mail, irons, hair dryers. **Pool(s):** heated indoor. **Leisure Activities:** whirlpool, exercise room. **Guest Services:** valet and coin laundry, area transportation, wireless Internet. **Business Services:** meeting rooms, business center.

AAA Benefit:
Members save a
minimum 5% off the
best available rate.

DOUBLETREE HOTEL-NORWALK   *Book great rates at AAA.com*   Phone: (203)853-3477   **10**

Hotel
$89-$239 All Year

Address: 789 Connecticut Ave (US 1) 06854 **Location:** I-95, exit 13, just e. **Facility:** 265 units. 263 one-bedroom standard units. 2 one-bedroom suites. 8 stories, interior corridors. *Bath:* combo or shower only. **Parking:** on-site. **Terms:** 1-7 night minimum stay, cancellation fee imposed. **Amenities:** video games (fee), voice mail, irons, hair dryers. **Pool(s):** heated indoor. **Leisure Activities:** sun deck, exercise room. **Guest Services:** valet and coin laundry, wireless Internet. **Business Services:** conference facilities, business center. **Free Special Amenities:** newspaper and high-speed Internet.

DOUBLETREE
HOTELS·SUITES·RESORTS·CLUBS
AAA Benefit:
Members save 5% or
more everyday!

(See map and index starting on p. 247)

FOUR POINTS BY SHERATON NORWALK
Book great rates at AAA.com Phone: 203/849-9828 [7]

AAA (SAVE)

Hotel
Rates not provided

Address: 426 Main Ave 06851 **Location:** I-95, exit 15, 3.5 mi n via US 7, just e, then 0.7 mi s. **Facility:** 127 units. 125 one-bedroom standard units. 2 one-bedroom suites. 4 stories, interior corridors. *Bath:* combo or shower only. **Parking:** on-site. **Amenities:** video games (fee), CD players, dual phone lines, voice mail, irons, hair dryers. *Some:* DVD players, high-speed Internet. **Leisure Activities:** exercise room. **Guest Services:** valet and coin laundry, area transportation-within 10 mi, wireless Internet. **Business Services:** meeting rooms. **Free Special Amenities: newspaper and high-speed Internet.**

FOUR POINTS
BY SHERATON

AAA Benefit:
Members get up to 15% off, plus Starwood Preferred Guest® bonuses.

HILTON GARDEN INN NORWALK
Book great rates at AAA.com Phone: (203)523-4000 [5]

Hotel
$89-$289 All Year

Address: 560 Main Ave 06851 **Location:** I-95, exit 15, 3.5 mi n via US 7, then just n. **Facility:** Smoke free premises. 170 one-bedroom standard units. 3 stories, interior corridors. *Bath:* combo or shower only. **Parking:** on-site. **Terms:** 1-7 night minimum stay, cancellation fee imposed. **Amenities:** video games (fee), high-speed Internet, dual phone lines, voice mail, irons, hair dryers. *Some:* DVD players. **Pool(s):** heated indoor. **Leisure Activities:** whirlpool, exercise room. **Guest Services:** valet and coin laundry, area transportation, wireless Internet. **Business Services:** meeting rooms, business center.

Hilton
Garden Inn

AAA Benefit:
Members save 5% or more everyday!

HOMESTEAD STUDIO SUITES-NORWALK-STAMFORD
Book at AAA.com Phone: (203)847-6888 [8]

Extended Stay Hotel
$105-$149 All Year

Address: 400 Main Ave 06851 **Location:** I-95, exit 15, 3.5 mi n via US 7, just e, then 1 mi s. **Facility:** 131 units. 122 one-bedroom standard units with efficiencies. 9 one-bedroom suites with efficiencies. 3 stories, interior corridors. *Bath:* combo or shower only. **Parking:** on-site. **Terms:** cancellation fee imposed. **Amenities:** voice mail, irons, hair dryers. *Some:* dual phone lines. **Leisure Activities:** exercise room. **Guest Services:** valet and coin laundry, wireless Internet.

NORWALK INN & CONFERENCE CENTER
Book great rates at AAA.com Phone: (203)838-2000 [9]

AAA (SAVE)

Hotel
$89-$139 All Year

Address: 99 East Ave 06851 **Location:** I-95, exit 16, 0.5 mi n. **Facility:** 71 one-bedroom standard units, some with whirlpools. 2 stories (no elevator), interior corridors. **Parking:** on-site. **Terms:** cancellation fee imposed. **Amenities:** high-speed Internet, voice mail, irons, hair dryers. *Some: Fee:* DVD players. **Pool(s):** outdoor. **Leisure Activities:** sauna, steamroom, exercise room. **Guest Services:** valet and coin laundry, wireless Internet. **Business Services:** meeting rooms, business center. **Free Special Amenities: full breakfast and high-speed Internet.**

—— WHERE TO DINE ——

LA PAELLA
Phone: 203/831-8636 [17]

Spanish
$15-$35

Spanish cuisine makes up the menu at this contemporary yet classically styled restaurant. The intimate dining room is painted in a vibrant terra cotta color and has beautifully framed paintings on its walls. Attentive service adds to the pleasant atmosphere. Menu selections may include Argentinean beef tenderloin, grilled Chilean sea bass and paella Valenciana, which is made with chicken, Spanish sausage and seafood and served with saffron rice. Dressy casual. **Bar:** Full bar. **Reservations:** suggested. **Hours:** noon-2:30 & 5:30-10 pm, Sat 5:30 pm-11 pm, Sun 5 pm-9 pm. Closed major holidays; also Mon. **Address:** 44 Main St 06851 **Location:** Just n of jct Main and Wall sts. **Parking:** street.

MEIGAS
Phone: 203/866-8800 [18]

Spanish
$15-$38

On the lower level of an office building that was once an old brick trolley building, the space is accented with brightly painted yellow walls and terra cotta floor tiles. Tables are nicely covered and set with fresh flowers, and cobalt blue and yellow dishware accents the exposed brick walls. Entrees include an array of authentic Spanish dishes including a salt-cured, slow-cooked cod fish with black olives, sun-dried tomatoes and parsley aioli. Dressy casual. **Bar:** Full bar. **Reservations:** suggested. **Hours:** 11:30 am-3 & 5-9:30 pm, Fri-10:30 pm, Sat 5 pm-10:30 pm, Sun 11:30 am-3 & 5-9:30 pm; Sunday brunch. Closed major holidays; also Mon. **Address:** 10 Wall St 06850 **Location:** Between Main and Brook sts; center. **Parking:** street.

RIVER CAT GRILL
Phone: 203/854-0860 [19]

American
$11-$34

Near the shore in the charming Rowayton section of town, the grill offers some of its best seating at tables by the brick fireplace or in comfy banquettes (with additional throw pillows) by the window. In warmer months, the outdoor cafe-style patio is the place to be. On the menu are thin pizzas, pasta and preparations of fresh seafood. Casual dress. **Bar:** Full bar. **Reservations:** accepted. **Hours:** 11:30 am-4 & 5:30-10 pm, Fri & Sat-10:30 pm, Sun 5:30 pm-9:30 pm. Closed: Mon in winter. **Address:** 148 Rowayton Ave 06853 **Location:** I-95, exit 12, 1.4 mi se on SR 136. **Parking:** on-site.

TUSCAN OVEN TRATTORIA
Phone: 203/846-4600 [16]

Northern Italian
$12-$28

Tuscany comes to life for those who drive through the stonewall entrance. Although the restaurant is in a commercial area, diners are likely to feel miles away due to the rustic Italian design and exquisite decor. Creative preparations of fresh seafood, steak and poultry pair with choices from an extensive wine list. Casual dress. **Bar:** Full bar. **Reservations:** accepted. **Hours:** 11:30 am-10 pm, Sun 11 am-9 pm. Closed: 7/4, 11/25, 12/25. **Address:** 544 Main Ave 06851 **Location:** I-95, exit 15, 3.9 mi n on US 7. **Parking:** on-site.

NORWICH pop. 36,117

COMFORT SUITES

Hotel
$120-$180 5/1-11/1
$90-$150 11/2-4/30

Book great rates at AAA.com   Phone: (860)892-9292

Address: 275 Otrobando Ave 06360 **Location:** SR 2, exit 27, just w. **Facility:** Smoke free premises. 119 units. 111 one-bedroom standard units. 8 one-bedroom suites with whirlpools. 5 stories, interior corridors. *Bath:* combo or shower only. **Parking:** on-site. **Amenities:** video games (fee), voice mail, irons, hair dryers. **Pool(s):** heated indoor. **Leisure Activities:** sauna, whirlpool, exercise room. *Fee:* game room. **Guest Services:** valet and coin laundry, area transportation-Mohegan Sun Casino, wireless Internet. **Business Services:** meeting rooms, business center. **Free Special Amenities: full breakfast and high-speed Internet.**

COURTYARD NORWICH

Hotel
$121-$147 All Year

Book great rates at AAA.com   Phone: (860)886-2600

Address: 181 W Town St 06360 **Location:** I-395, exit 82, just w. **Facility:** Smoke free premises. 120 units. 115 one-bedroom standard units, some with whirlpools. 5 one-bedroom suites. 5 stories, interior corridors. *Bath:* combo or shower only. **Parking:** on-site. **Terms:** cancellation fee imposed. **Amenities:** video games (fee), high-speed Internet, voice mail, irons, hair dryers. **Pool(s):** heated indoor. **Leisure Activities:** whirlpool, exercise room. **Guest Services:** valet and coin laundry, area transportation, wireless Internet. **Business Services:** meeting rooms, business center.

AAA Benefit:
Members save a minimum 5% off the best available rate.

HOLIDAY INN NORWICH

Hotel
$129-$269 All Year

Book great rates at AAA.com   Phone: (860)889-5201

Address: 10 Laura Blvd 06360 **Location:** I-395, exit 80, just sw of SR 82. **Facility:** 134 one-bedroom standard units. 6 stories, interior corridors. *Bath:* combo or shower only. **Terms:** cancellation fee imposed. **Amenities:** video games (fee), voice mail, irons, hair dryers. **Pool(s):** heated indoor. **Leisure Activities:** sun deck, exercise room. **Guest Services:** valet and coin laundry, area transportation-Mohegan Sun Casino, wireless Internet. **Business Services:** meeting rooms, business center. **Free Special Amenities: high-speed Internet.**

THE SPA AT NORWICH INN

Historic
Hotel
$175-$350 All Year

Book at AAA.com   Phone: (860)886-2401

Address: 607 W Thames St 06360 **Location:** I-395, exit 79A, 0.5 mi e on SR 2A, then 1.3 mi n on SR 32. **Facility:** Gracious 1930s hotel, modern duplex and suite villas overlooking Norwich Golf Course. All villas with fireplace. 100 units. 46 one-bedroom standard units. 54 one-bedroom suites, some with kitchens and/or whirlpools. 1-4 stories, interior/exterior corridors. **Parking:** on-site and valet. **Terms:** check-in 4 pm. **Amenities:** CD players, voice mail, safes, irons, hair dryers. *Some:* DVD players, high-speed Internet, dual phone lines. **Dining:** Kensington's, see separate listing. **Pool(s):** outdoor, heated outdoor, heated indoor. **Leisure Activities:** saunas, whirlpools, steamrooms, 2 lighted tennis courts, jogging, exercise room, spa. *Fee:* golf-18 holes. **Guest Services:** valet laundry, wireless Internet. **Business Services:** conference facilities, business center.

—— WHERE TO DINE ——

KENSINGTON'S

Regional American
$12-$42

Phone: 860/886-2401

Inside, you will discover vivid colors, rich tapestries, original-style artwork and crystal chandeliers that create an elegant and comfortable atmosphere. The chef takes great pride in serving such items as mahi mahi chowder, cream of spinach soup, fresh seasonal fruit salads, crisp green salads, perfectly seasoned and prepared pork and smoked chicken with sprouts. Terrace dining is available, weather permitting. Dressy casual. **Bar:** Full bar. **Reservations:** suggested. **Hours:** 7-10 am, 11:30-2:30 & 6-9 pm, Fri-10 pm, Sat 7 am-11, 11:30-12:30 & 5:30-10 pm, Sun 7 am-2:30 & 6-9 pm; closing hours extended in summer. **Address:** 607 W Thames St 06360 **Location:** I-395, exit 79A, 0.5 mi e on SR 2A, then 1.3 mi n on SR 32; in The Spa at Norwich Inn. **Parking:** on-site and valet.

OLD GREENWICH (See map and index starting on p. 247)

HYATT REGENCY GREENWICH

Hotel
$99-$319 All Year

Book great rates at AAA.com   Phone: (203)637-1234

Address: 1800 E Putnam Ave 06870 **Location:** I-95, exit 5, 0.5 mi n on US 1. **Facility:** 373 units. 361 one-bedroom standard units, some with whirlpools. 12 one-bedroom suites. 4 stories, interior corridors. *Bath:* combo or shower only. **Parking:** on-site (fee) and valet. **Terms:** cancellation fee imposed. **Amenities:** dual phone lines, voice mail, irons, hair dryers. *Fee:* video games, high-speed Internet. *Some:* DVD players. **Dining:** Winfield's, see separate listing. **Pool(s):** heated indoor. **Leisure Activities:** sauna, whirlpool, steamroom. **Guest Services:** valet laundry, area transportation-within 5 mi, wireless Internet, beauty salon. **Business Services:** conference facilities, business center. **Free Special Amenities: early check-in/late check-out and preferred room (subject to availability with advance reservations).**

AAA Benefit:
Ask for the AAA rate and save 10%.

(See map and index starting on p. 247)

------ **WHERE TO DINE** ------

WINFIELD'S

American
$11-$45

Phone: 203/637-1234   (38)

Beautiful, exotic trees and vine-covered pillars surround those who dine under the large glass atrium. A taster's lunch menu, complete with dessert, often is available. One of the most popular dishes is braised short ribs with cauliflower horseradish mash. Dressy casual. **Bar:** Full bar. **Reservations:** accepted. **Hours:** 6:30 am-10:30 & 11:30-2:30 pm, Fri & Sat also 5 pm-10 pm. **Address:** 1800 E Putnam Ave 06870 **Location:** I-95, exit 5, 0.5 mi n on US 1; in Hyatt Regency Greenwich. **Parking:** on-site and valet.

OLD LYME

BEE & THISTLE INN & SPA

Historic
Country Inn
$150-$275 All Year

Phone: 860/434-1667

Address: 100 Lyme St 06371 **Location:** I-95, exit 70 southbound, just n on US 1; exit northbound, just w on SR 156, then 1.2 mi n on US 1. Located in a historic district. **Facility:** Entered via a stately, circular, brick driveway, this clapboard Dutch Colonial was built in 1756 and sits on the shores of the Lieutenant River. Smoke free premises. 9 one-bedroom standard units. 3 stories (no elevator), interior corridors. *Bath:* combo or shower only. **Parking:** on-site. **Terms:** office hours 8 am-10 pm, 2 night minimum stay - weekends, 10 day cancellation notice-fee imposed. **Amenities:** hair dryers. *Some:* irons. **Dining:** restaurant, see separate listing. **Leisure Activities:** exercise room, spa. **Guest Services:** wireless Internet. **Business Services:** meeting rooms. ⊞ ⊠ 𝕎

------ **WHERE TO DINE** ------

BEE & THISTLE INN

American
$12-$65

Phone: 860/434-1667

The restaurant is known for consistently creative cuisine that changes seasonally to take advantage of prevailing fresh ingredients. The charming country inn setting boasts garden views. A dress code and age restrictions may apply. Dressy casual. **Bar:** Full bar. **Reservations:** suggested. **Hours:** Open 5/1-12/31 & 2/1-4/30; 5:30 pm-9 pm. Closed: 1/1, 12/24, 12/25; also Mon & Tues. **Address:** 100 Lyme St 06371 **Location:** I-95, exit 70 southbound, just n on US 1; exit northbound, just w on SR 156, then 1.2 mi n on US 1; in Bee & Thistle Inn. **Parking:** on-site.

OLD LYME INN

American
$9-$34

Phone: 860/434-2600

Elegantly decorated dining rooms await guests at this restaurant in the historic section of the village. A variety of prime steak choices and seafood options are highlights. More casual lunches also are served. Dressy casual. **Bar:** Full bar. **Reservations:** suggested. **Hours:** 11:30 am-2 & 4:30-9 pm, Sun 11 am-3 & 5-8 pm. **Address:** 85 Lyme St 06371 **Location:** I-95, exit 70 northbound, just n on SR 156, then 0.5 mi e on US 1; exit southbound, just n; in Old Lyme Inn. **Parking:** on-site.

OLD MYSTIC pop. 3,205

THE OLD MYSTIC INN

Historic Bed
& Breakfast
$165-$215 5/1-11/30
$135-$175 12/1-4/30

Phone: 860/572-9422

Address: 52 Main St 06372-0634 **Location:** I-95, exit 90, 1.3 mi n. **Facility:** Fireplaces are featured in some guest rooms at this country-style home and carriage house dating from 1784; dining options are available upon request. Smoke free premises. 8 one-bedroom standard units, some with whirlpools. 2 stories (no elevator), interior/exterior corridors. **Parking:** on-site. **Terms:** office hours 8 am-4 pm, 2 night minimum stay - seasonal and/or weekends, 3 day cancellation notice-fee imposed. **Amenities:** hair dryers. **Guest Services:** TV in common area, wireless Internet. (ASK) ⊠ 𝕎 ☎

OLD SAYBROOK pop. 1,962

COMFORT INN OLD SAYBROOK   *Book great rates at AAA.com*

Hotel
$79-$179 5/1-10/31
$69-$120 11/1-4/30

Phone: (860)395-1414

Address: 100 Essex Rd 06475 **Location:** SR 9, exit 1 northbound, just e; exit 2 southbound, just n on SR 154, then 0.9 mi se. **Facility:** 120 one-bedroom standard units. 3 stories, interior corridors. **Parking:** on-site. **Terms:** 2 night minimum stay - seasonal and/or weekends, cancellation fee imposed. **Amenities:** irons, hair dryers. *Some:* high-speed Internet. **Pool(s):** heated indoor. **Leisure Activities:** saunas, exercise room. **Guest Services:** valet and coin laundry, wireless Internet. **Free Special Amenities:** expanded continental breakfast and high-speed Internet.

⊞ ⊟ ⊞ ⊞ / SOME UNITS ⊠ ⊟ ⊞

DAYS INN   *Book at AAA.com*

Motel
Rates not provided

Phone: 860/388-3453

Address: 1430 Boston Post Rd 06475 **Location:** I-95, exit 66, 0.3 mi s on SR 166, then 0.5 mi e on US 1 N. **Facility:** 50 one-bedroom standard units, some with whirlpools. 2 stories (no elevator), exterior corridors. **Parking:** on-site. **Amenities:** irons, hair dryers. *Some: Fee:* DVD players, video games. **Guest Services:** wireless Internet. **Business Services:** PC.

⊞ ⊟ ⊞ / SOME UNITS FEE ⊞ ⊠ ⊞

HERITAGE MOTOR INN

Motel
$99-$149 5/22-11/1
$76-$106 5/1-5/21

Phone: 860/388-3743

Address: 1500 Boston Post Rd 06475 **Location:** I-95, exit 66, 0.4 mi s on SR 166, then 0.4 mi ne on US 1. **Facility:** Smoke free premises. 13 units. 12 one-bedroom standard units. 1 one-bedroom suite. 1 story, exterior corridors. *Bath:* combo or shower only. **Parking:** on-site. **Terms:** open 5/1-11/1, office hours 9 am-9 pm, 2 night minimum stay - weekends, 14 day cancellation notice.

(ASK) ⊠ ☎ ⊟ / SOME UNITS ⊞

SAYBROOK POINT INN & SPA
Book great rates at AAA.com

Phone: (860)395-2000

Hotel
$199-$899 5/1-10/31
$199-$799 11/1-4/30

Address: 2 Bridge St 06475 **Location:** On SR 154, 2.2 mi s of jct US 1; at Saybrook Point. **Facility:** Large guest rooms, many with a balcony and fireplace, are offered at this resort overlooking the river and sound. Smoke free premises. 82 units. 78 one-bedroom standard units, some with whirlpools. 4 one-bedroom suites with whirlpools. 3 stories, interior corridors. **Parking:** on-site. **Terms:** check-in 4 pm, 2 night minimum stay - seasonal and/or weekends, 3 day cancellation notice. **Amenities:** video library, voice mail, irons, hair dryers. *Some:* DVD players. **Dining:** Terra Mar, see separate listing. **Pool(s):** heated outdoor, heated indoor. **Leisure Activities:** sauna, whirlpool, steamroom, tennis & country club privileges, bicycles, spa. *Fee:* marina, beach pass, mopeds. **Guest Services:** valet and coin laundry, area transportation-train station & downtown, wireless Internet. **Business Services:** conference facilities, business center. *(See color ad p 296)*

FREE local telephone calls and high-speed Internet

LIBERTY INN
Phone: 860/388-1777

Motel
$58-$130 All Year

Address: 55 Spring Brook Rd 06475 **Location:** I-95, exit 68 southbound; exit 67 northbound, 0.9 mi n on US 1, then w. **Facility:** 22 one-bedroom standard units. 2 stories (no elevator), exterior corridors. **Parking:** on-site. **Amenities:** irons, hair dryers. **Guest Services:** wireless Internet.

———— WHERE TO DINE ————

ALFORNO BRICK OVEN PIZZA & RISTORANTE
Phone: 860/399-2346

Italian
$6-$25

Guests can try a specialty brick-oven grilled pizza or any of many pasta and chicken dishes at the Tuscan trattoria. All sauces and desserts are homemade. Contributing to the contemporary feel are decorative fabric hung from the ceiling and colorful lighting fixtures that dangle above tables. Casual dress. **Bar:** Full bar. **Reservations:** not accepted. **Hours:** noon-3 & 4-9 pm, Fri & Sat-10 pm. Closed: 4/4, 11/25, 12/24, 12/25. **Address:** 1654 Boston Post Rd 06475 **Location:** I-95, exit 66, just se on SR 166, then just e; in shopping plaza. **Parking:** on-site.

ASPEN
Phone: 860/395-5888

New American
$10-$25

The open dining room features a large double-sided fireplace, floor-to-ceiling arched windows and an earthy color palate. The contemporary granite-topped bar with flat-screen TVs is open to the dining room, while the lower-level lounge is a cool place for martinis and live music on weekend nights. Lunch options include sandwiches and large salads, and the menu goes more sophisticated at dinner with choices such as seared yellowfin tuna or charred all-natural flat-iron steak. Dressy casual. **Bar:** Full bar. **Reservations:** accepted. **Hours:** 11:30 am-2 & 5:30-10 pm, Fri & Sat-11 pm, Mon 5:30 pm-10 pm. **Address:** 2 Main St 06475 **Location:** I-95, exit 67 northbound, 0.5 mi s; exit 68 southbound, 0.9 mi sw on US 1, then 0.4 mi s on SR 154; in Shops at Saybrook Country Barn. **Parking:** on-site.

THE DOCK & DINE
Phone: 860/388-4665

Seafood
$7-$25

Who could resist such innovative fare as white bean, andouille sausage and escargot soup? Or the stunning riverfront views overlooking Long Island Sound and the harbor, where boat slips house everything from small Boston whalers to luxurious yachts? If that's not convincing enough, entertainment is offered on weekends, in season. Examples of the casual, family-friendly restaurant's traditional New England fare include baked scrod, fried clams, roast turkey and New York strip. Casual dress. **Bar:** Full bar. **Reservations:** suggested. **Hours:** 11:30 am-10 pm; to 9 pm off season. Closed: 11/25, 12/24, 12/25; also Mon & Tues 10/9-4/8. **Address:** 145 College St 06475 **Location:** 2 mi s of US 1 on SR 154, via Main St. **Parking:** on-site.

PAPERBACK CAFE
Phone: 860/388-9718

American
$4-$20

Offerings include fine baked goods, excellent soups, salads, wraps and healthy sandwiches usually served with carrot sticks and garlic-ranch dressing. Gourmet coffees, espresso, cappuccino and desserts are fitting meal-enders. The eclectic dining area has large bookshelves filled with magazines and other literature guests can read while eating. Jazz musicians perform on weekends, and the Main Street patio is great for seasonal people-watching. Guests who want alcohol should bring their own. Casual dress. **Hours:** 7 am-4 pm, Fri & Sat-10 pm. Closed: 4/4, 11/25, 12/25. **Address:** 210 Main St 06475 **Location:** I-95, exit 67 northbound, 0.8 mi s on SR 154; exit 68 southbound, 0.6 mi sw on US 1, then 0.7 mi s. **Parking:** on-site.

PENNY LANE PUB & RESTAURANT
Phone: 860/388-9646

American
$7-$22

Nestled between quaint shops, the two-story British Victorian pub and restaurant is the perfect stop for lunch or dinner. Home-style shepherd's pie, classic fish and chips and grilled bratwurst with sauerkraut are some of the many menu choices. Casual dress. **Bar:** Full bar. **Reservations:** accepted. **Hours:** 11:30 am-9 pm, Fri & Sat-10 pm, Sun-8 pm. Closed: 11/25, 12/25. **Address:** 150 Main St 06475 **Location:** I-95, exit 67, 1 mi se on Elm St, then just s. **Parking:** street.

TERRA MAR
Menu on AAA.com

Phone: 860/388-1111

New American
$10-$40

Guests who relax in the intimate dining room, which overlooks Long Island Sound, can select from an innovative menu of seafood and meat entrees. Elegant subtle decor does not detract from the spectacular views of sunsets, sailboats and maritime life around the active marina, which are a delight to observe, especially from a table by the window. The chef prepares delectable and memorable dishes: fresh salmon and swordfish, prime cuts of beef and made-from-scratch pastries and desserts. Dressy casual. **Bar:** Full bar. **Reservations:** suggested. **Hours:** 7-10 am, 11:30-2:15 & 5:30-9 pm, Fri & Sat-9:30 pm; Sunday brunch. **Address:** 2 Bridge St 06475 **Location:** On SR 154, 2.2 mi s of jct US 1; at Saybrook Point; in Saybrook Point Inn & Spa. **Parking:** on-site.

ORANGE pop. 13,233   (See map and index starting on p. 300)

COURTYARD NEW HAVEN ORANGE   *Book great rates at AAA.com*   Phone: (203)799-2200   **31**

Hotel
$170-$208 All Year

Address: 136 Marsh Hill Rd 06477 **Location:** I-95, exit 41, just n. **Facility:** Smoke free premises. 121 units. 115 one-bedroom standard units. 6 one-bedroom suites. 3 stories, interior corridors. *Bath:* combo or shower only. **Parking:** on-site. **Terms:** cancellation fee imposed. **Amenities:** dual phone lines, voice mail, irons, hair dryers. **Pool(s):** heated outdoor. **Leisure Activities:** exercise room. **Guest Services:** valet and coin laundry, wireless Internet. **Business Services:** meeting rooms, business center.

AAA Benefit:
Members save a
minimum 5% off the
best available rate.

PLAINFIELD pop. 2,638

HOLIDAY INN EXPRESS HOTEL &
SUITES-PLAINFIELD   *Book at AAA.com*   Phone: (860)564-1010

Hotel
$69-$109 5/1-10/31
$59-$79 11/1-4/30

Address: 18 Pratt Rd 06374 **Location:** I-395, exit 87, just se. **Facility:** 66 units. 65 one-bedroom standard units, some with whirlpools. 1 one-bedroom suite with kitchen. 3 stories, interior corridors. *Bath:* combo or shower only. **Parking:** on-site. **Amenities:** high-speed Internet, dual phone lines, voice mail, irons, hair dryers. **Pool(s):** heated indoor. **Leisure Activities:** whirlpool, exercise room. **Guest Services:** coin laundry, wireless Internet. **Business Services:** meeting rooms, business center.

QUALITY INN   *Book at AAA.com*   Phone: (860)564-4021

Hotel
$66-$100 All Year

Address: 55 Lathrop Rd 06374 **Location:** I-395, exit 87, just se. **Facility:** 49 one-bedroom standard units. 2 stories, interior corridors. **Parking:** on-site. **Amenities:** irons, hair dryers. *Some:* high-speed Internet. **Pool(s):** heated outdoor. **Leisure Activities:** exercise room. **Guest Services:** coin laundry, wireless Internet. **Business Services:** meeting rooms, business center.

PLAINVILLE—See Hartford p. 276.

PUTNAM pop. 6,746

—— **WHERE TO DINE** ——

THE COURTHOUSE BAR & GRILLE   Phone: 860/963-0074

American
$7-$25

Patrons plead guilty pleasures as they deliberate and reach a decision from among offerings of traditional but whimsical pub fare. Casual dress. **Bar:** Full bar. **Hours:** 11:30 am-9:30 pm, Thurs-10 pm, Fri & Sat-11 pm. Closed: 11/25, 12/25. **Address:** 121 Main St 06260 **Location:** I-395, exit 97, 1.6 mi w on US 44, then just n. **Parking:** street.

J.D. COOPER'S   Phone: 860/928-0501

American
$7-$32

Chicken, pasta, seafood and some of the area's best steaks are served in a casual but intimate setting. Casual dress. **Bar:** Full bar. **Reservations:** accepted. **Hours:** 11:30 am-8:30 pm, Thurs-Sat to 9 pm. Closed: 7/4, 12/25. **Address:** 146 Park Rd 06260 **Location:** I-395, exit 95, 0.8 mi se. **Parking:** on-site.

RIDGEFIELD pop. 7,212

WEST LANE INN   Phone: 203/438-7323

Historic Bed
& Breakfast
$170-$425 All Year

Address: 22 West Ln 06877 **Location:** I-684, exit 6, 12 mi e on SR 35, w of jct SR 33. **Facility:** Built in 1849, this charming country manor offers many modern-day conveniences; some intimate rooms with fireplaces are available. Smoke free premises. 18 one-bedroom standard units. 2-3 stories (no elevator), interior corridors. **Parking:** on-site. **Terms:** 2 night minimum stay - seasonal, 10 day cancellation notice. **Amenities:** video library, voice mail, irons, hair dryers. *Some:* DVD players. **Guest Services:** valet laundry, wireless Internet. **Business Services:** meeting rooms.

—— **WHERE TO DINE** ——

BERNARD'S   Phone: 203/438-8282

French
$9-$36

Elegant, formal lunches and dinners set the base for sublime dessert creations, such as a rich and silky chocolate mousse kissed by Grand Marnier and served in a pool of vanilla cream. A pianist performs on weekends. Dressy casual. **Bar:** Full bar. **Hours:** noon-2:30 & 6-9 pm, Fri & Sat 10 pm, Sun noon-2:30 & 5-8 pm. Closed: 1/1, 5/31, 12/25; also Mon & 2 1/2 weeks in Aug. **Address:** 20 West Ln 06877 **Location:** Jct SR 33 and 35. **Parking:** on-site and valet.

THE ELMS RESTAURANT

American
$17-$30

Phone: 203/438-9206

Housed in an 18th-century clapboard inn, this restaurant and tavern has crackling fireplaces and wood floors that echo with centuries of history. Under elm trees and away from bustling Main Street, the covered terrace is a relaxing retreat. Chef Brendan Walsh is known for his creative reinventions of Yankee cuisine classics such as chowders, stews, roasts and spoon breads. The menu changes seasonally to incorporate fresh ingredients. Dressy casual. **Bar:** Full bar. **Reservations:** suggested. **Hours:** 11:30 am-2:30 & 5:30-9:30 pm, Sun 11:30 am-8:30 pm; closing hours may vary. Closed: 4/4, 12/25; also Mon & Tues. **Address:** 500 Main St 06877 **Location:** Jct SR 116 and 35, just s on SR 33. **Parking:** on-site. **Historic**

STONEHENGE INN

New American
$18-$28

Phone: 203/438-6511

This charming country sophisticate beside a picturesque pond offers not only interesting dishes filled with compatible flavors, but also a lovely setting in which to enjoy good company and the excellent food. Jackets are appropriate, especially weekends. Dressy casual. **Bar:** Full bar. **Reservations:** suggested. **Hours:** 6 pm-8:30 pm, Fri & Sat-9 pm. Closed: 1/1; also Sun. **Address:** 35 Stonehenge Rd (Rt 7) 06877 **Location:** US 7, 1 mi s of jct SR 35; in Stonehenge Inn. **Parking:** on-site and valet.

RIVERTON

OLD RIVERTON INN

Historic
Country Inn
$99-$225 All Year

Phone: 860/379-8678

Address: 436 E River Rd (SR 20) 06065 **Location:** Center. **Facility:** Built in 1796 as a stagecoach stop, the inn offers rooms which vary in style and size. Smoke free premises. 12 one-bedroom standard units. 3 stories (no elevator), interior corridors. *Bath:* combo or shower only. **Parking:** on-site. **Terms:** 10 day cancellation notice-fee imposed. **Dining:** restaurant, see separate listing. **Guest Services:** wireless Internet. **Business Services:** meeting rooms.

———— **WHERE TO DINE** ————

OLD RIVERTON INN

American
$18-$25

Phone: 860/379-8678

Once a stop on the Hartford-Albany stage route, the circa 1796 inn now functions as charming Colonial dining room where guests dine on hearty, home-cooked meals, including homemade dessert, pastry and fresh bread. Casual dress. **Bar:** Full bar. **Reservations:** suggested. **Hours:** 5 pm-8:30 pm, Sun noon-4 pm. Closed: 12/25; also Mon-Thurs. **Address:** 436 E River Rd (SR 20) 06065 **Location:** Center; in Old Riverton Inn. **Parking:** on-site. **Historic**

SWEET PEA'S

American
$8-$31

Phone: 860/379-7020

The charming Victorian home is suitable for romantic candlelit dinners. Surrounded by antiques, lace and curios of the past, diners can peruse a refreshing and eclectic menu. Dishes are complemented by fresh bread and cookies. Casual dress. **Bar:** Full bar. **Reservations:** suggested. **Hours:** 11:30 am-2:30 & 5-8 pm, Fri & Sat-9 pm, Sun 11:30 am-8 pm. Closed: 1/1, 12/25; also Mon. **Address:** 6 Riverton Rd (SR 20) 06065 **Location:** Jct SR 8, 2.2 mi ne on SR 20. **Parking:** on-site.

ROCKY HILL—See Hartford p. 276.

SHELTON pop. 38,101

COURTYARD BY MARRIOTT SHELTON   *Book great rates at AAA.com*

Hotel
$170-$208 All Year

Phone: (203)929-1500

AAA Benefit:
Members save a minimum 5% off the best available rate.

Address: 780 Bridgeport Ave 06484 **Location:** SR 8, exit 12, 0.3 mi w. **Facility:** Smoke free premises. 161 units. 149 one-bedroom standard units. 12 one-bedroom suites. 7 stories, interior corridors. *Bath:* combo or shower only. **Parking:** on-site. **Terms:** cancellation fee imposed. **Amenities:** video games (fee), voice mail, irons, hair dryers. *Some:* high-speed Internet. **Pool(s):** heated indoor. **Leisure Activities:** exercise room. **Guest Services:** valet and coin laundry, wireless Internet. **Business Services:** conference facilities, business center.

HILTON GARDEN INN SHELTON   *Book great rates at AAA.com*

Hotel
$89-$219 All Year

Phone: (203)447-1000

Hilton Garden Inn

AAA Benefit:
Members save 5% or more everyday!

Address: 25 Old Stratford Rd 06484 **Location:** SR 8, exit 12, just w. **Facility:** Smoke free premises. 142 units. 139 one-bedroom standard units. 3 one-bedroom suites with whirlpools. 6 stories, interior corridors. *Bath:* combo or shower only. **Parking:** on-site. **Terms:** 1-7 night minimum stay, cancellation fee imposed. **Amenities:** dual phone lines, voice mail, irons, hair dryers. *Some:* DVD players (fee), high-speed Internet. **Pool(s):** heated indoor. **Leisure Activities:** whirlpool, exercise room. **Guest Services:** valet and coin laundry, area transportation, wireless Internet. **Business Services:** meeting rooms, business center.

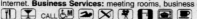

HOLIDAY INN EXPRESS HOTEL & SUITES *Book at AAA.com* **Phone:** (203)925-5900

WWW
Hotel
$129-$179 All Year

Address: 695 Bridgeport Ave 06484 **Location:** SR 8, exit 12, 0.3 mi w, then just s. **Facility:** 128 one-bedroom standard units. 6 stories, interior corridors. *Bath:* combo or shower only. **Parking:** on-site. **Terms:** cancellation fee imposed. **Amenities:** video games (fee), high-speed Internet, dual phone lines, voice mail, irons, hair dryers. **Pool(s):** heated indoor. **Leisure Activities:** exercise room. **Guest Services:** valet and coin laundry, area transportation, wireless Internet. **Business Services:** meeting rooms, business center. ASK 📶 CALL 🅜 🏊 🎥 🖥 📷 🖨 / SOME UNITS ✕

HOMESTEAD STUDIO SUITES-SHELTON-FAIRFIELD COUNTY *Book at AAA.com* **Phone:** (203)926-6868

WWW
Hotel
$105-$149 All Year

Address: 945 Bridgeport Ave 06484 **Location:** SR 8, exit 11, 0.5 mi w. **Facility:** 140 one-bedroom standard units with efficiencies. 3 stories, interior corridors. *Bath:* combo or shower only. **Parking:** on-site. **Terms:** cancellation fee imposed. **Amenities:** voice mail, irons, hair dryers. **Guest Services:** valet and coin laundry, wireless Internet.
ASK CALL 🅜 🐾 🎥 🖥 📷 🖨 / SOME UNITS 🐕 ✕

RESIDENCE INN SHELTON FAIRFIELD COUNTY *Book great rates at AAA.com* **Phone:** (203)926-9000

WWW
Hotel
$152-$186 All Year

Address: 1001 Bridgeport Ave 06484 **Location:** SR 8, exit 11, 0.3 mi w. **Facility:** Smoke free premises. 96 units. 72 one- and 24 two-bedroom standard units with kitchens. 2 stories (no elevator), exterior corridors. *Bath:* combo or shower only. **Parking:** on-site. **Terms:** cancellation fee imposed. **Amenities:** CD players, voice mail, irons, hair dryers. **Pool(s):** outdoor. **Leisure Activities:** whirlpool, sports court. **Guest Services:** valet and coin laundry, area transportation, wireless Internet. **Business Services:** business center.
CALL 🅜 🏊 🐾 ✕ 🎥 🖥 📷 🖨 / SOME UNITS FEE 🐕

AAA Benefit:
Members save a minimum 5% off the best available rate.

—— WHERE TO DINE ——

THE METRO GRILLE & BAR **Phone:** 203/929-1000

WWW
American
$8-$26

The strip-mall restaurant has an upscale, trendy atmosphere and a spacious, attractive dining area. Dishes are loaded with flavor and fresh ingredients. A small menu sampling includes fresh salads, Asian pasta with scallops, shrimp spiced with curry, delicately seasoned New York strip and blueberry cheesecake. At times the restaurant may be noisy, but this reflects its fun and lively atmosphere. Dressy casual. **Bar:** Full bar. **Reservations:** suggested. **Hours:** 11:30 am-10 pm, Fri & Sat-11 pm, Sun 4 pm-8 pm. Closed major holidays. **Address:** 882 Bridgeport Ave 06484 **Location:** SR 8, exit 11, 0.5 mi w. **Parking:** on-site.
CALL 🅜

SHERMAN

—— WHERE TO DINE ——

AMERICAN PIE COMPANY, INC **Phone:** 860/350-0662

WW
American
$6-$16

The bakery/restaurant presents a menu filled with homestyle favorites, such as shepherd's pie, chicken pot pie and meatloaf. Also among choices are sandwich wraps, salads and burgers. Diners shouldn't miss the tempting homemade cakes, pies or cheesecake. The seasonal outdoor seating area is between the white picket fence and flower beds. Casual dress. **Bar:** Beer & wine. **Reservations:** not accepted. **Hours:** 7 am-8 pm, Fri & Sat-9 pm, Mon-3 pm. Closed: 4/4, 11/25, 12/25. **Address:** 29 Rt 37 Center 06784 **Location:** Jct SR 39. **Parking:** on-site.

SIMSBURY—See Hartford p. 277.

SOUTHBURY

CORNUCOPIA AT OLDFIELD BED AND BREAKFAST **Phone:** 203/267-6772

WWW
Historic Bed
& Breakfast
$150-$250 All Year

Address: 782 Main St N 06488 **Location:** I-84, exit 15, 1.5 mi n. **Facility:** This circa-1818 home sits on 2.5 acres of rolling lawn and extensive gardens. Rooms are comfortable and nicely decorated; there is also a large flagstone patio with bistro tables overlooking the stream that crosses the yard. Smoke free premises. 4 one-bedroom standard units. 3 stories (no elevator), interior corridors. **Parking:** on-site. **Terms:** check-in 4 pm, 14 day cancellation notice-fee imposed. **Amenities:** video library, DVD players, CD players, hair dryers. **Pool(s):** outdoor. **Leisure Activities:** horseshoes. **Guest Services:** wireless Internet. **Business Services:** meeting rooms.
ASK 🏊 ✕ 🎥 📷 / SOME UNITS FEE 🐕

CROWNE PLAZA SOUTHBURY *Book great rates at AAA.com* **Phone:** (203)598-7600

AAA SAVE

WWW
Hotel
$109-$159 All Year

Address: 1284 Strongtown Rd 06488 **Location:** I-84, exit 16, just n on SR 188. **Facility:** 197 units. 189 one-bedroom standard units. 4 one- and 4 two-bedroom suites. 3 stories, interior corridors. *Bath:* combo or shower only. **Parking:** on-site. **Amenities:** dual phone lines, voice mail, irons, hair dryers. *Some:* high-speed Internet. **Pool(s):** heated indoor. **Leisure Activities:** sauna, whirlpool, exercise room. *Fee:* massage. **Guest Services:** valet laundry, area transportation-within 5 mi, wireless Internet. **Business Services:** conference facilities, business center.
 🍴 🍸 CALL 🅜 🏊 ✕ 🎥 🖨 / SOME UNITS FEE 🐕 ✕ 🖥 📷

HERITAGE HOTEL

Hotel
$99-$179 All Year

Book at AAA.com

Phone: (203)264-8200

Address: 522 Heritage Rd 06488 **Location:** I-84, exit 15, 0.4 mi n on SR 67, then 1 mi w. **Facility:** Smoke free premises. 163 units. 158 one-bedroom standard units. 5 one-bedroom suites, some with whirlpools. 3 stories, interior corridors. *Bath:* combo or shower only. **Parking:** on-site. **Terms:** check-in 4 pm, cancellation fee imposed. **Amenities:** video games (fee), dual phone lines, voice mail, irons, hair dryers. *Some:* honor bars. **Dining:** Eight Mile Brook, see separate listing. **Pool(s):** heated outdoor, heated indoor. **Leisure Activities:** saunas, whirlpools, steamrooms, 2 lighted tennis courts, racquetball courts, recreation programs, spa, basketball, volleyball. *Fee:* golf-9 holes. **Guest Services:** valet laundry, area transportation, wireless Internet. **Business Services:** conference facilities, business center.

—— WHERE TO DINE ——

EIGHT MILE BROOK

American
$6-$25

Phone: 203/264-8200

Beautiful woodwork, cathedral ceilings and a massive stone fireplace lend to the dining room's lodge-like feel. Some tables near the floor-to-ceiling windows overlook the hotel's grounds. A buffet lunch is available, but patrons also may order from the menu of sandwiches, steaks and seafood. Casual dress. **Bar:** Full bar. **Reservations:** suggested, weekends. **Hours:** 7-9:30 am, 11:30-2 & 6-9 pm, Fri & Sat-10 pm, Sun 11:30 am-2 & 6-9 pm. **Address:** 522 Heritage Rd 06488 **Location:** I-84, exit 15, 0.4 mi n on SR 67, then 1 mi w; in Heritage Hotel. **Parking:** on-site.

LEO'S

American
$5-$16

Phone: 203/264-9190

"Food fit for a king" is sure to please those looking for a good breakfast place or dinner value. Freshly squeezed orange juice complements the challah bread French toast with peach compote. Among great dinner choices are chicken francaise sauteed in white wine, lemon and butter or beef tips sauteed in shallots, Burgundy wine and brown sauce with mushrooms. Casual dress. **Bar:** Full bar. **Reservations:** not accepted. **Hours:** 8 am-8:30 pm. Closed: 4/4, 11/25, 12/25. **Address:** 7 Poverty Rd 06488 **Location:** Corner of Main St S, in Bennett Square; center. **Parking:** on-site.

SOUTHINGTON—See Hartford p. 278.

SOUTH NORWALK   (See map and index starting on p. 247)

—— WHERE TO DINE ——

BARCELONA RESTAURANT & WINE BAR

Mediterranean
$6-$26

Phone: 203/899-0088   (22)

This trendy and lively dinner stop impresses with a spicy lineup of hot and cold tapas. Casual dress. Entertainment. **Bar:** Full bar. **Reservations:** suggested. **Hours:** 5 pm-1 am, Fri & Sat-2 am. Closed: 5/31, 12/25. **Address:** 63-65 N Main St 06854 **Location:** I-95, exit 15, 0.5 mi s on West Ave, then just se. **Parking:** on-site and street.

MATCH

New American
$21-$38

Phone: 203/852-1088   (24)

This eclectic restaurant is in the heart of the SoNo dining and shopping district. The vibrantly decorated room features an imported stainless steel Italian wood-burning oven, distinctive orange banquettes, Bomanite floors and an exposed brick wall. The changing menu may feature creamy corn and shucked lobster ravioli, grilled veal porterhouse or crispy fillet of Alaskan halibut. Dressy casual. **Bar:** Full bar. **Reservations:** suggested. **Hours:** 5 pm-10 pm, Fri & Sat-11 pm. Closed: 11/25, 12/25. **Address:** 98 Washington St 06854 **Location:** I-95, exit 14 northbound, 0.3 mi nw on Fairfield Ave, then just e; exit 16 southbound, 0.4 mi se on East Ave, then 0.7 mi w via SR 136. **Parking:** on-site (fee) and street.

WASABI CHI

Japanese
$11-$55

Phone: 203/286-0181   (23)

This highly stylish Japanese restaurant impresses with its lime green walls, decorative Buddha and dragon statues and hanging paper lanterns. Excellent dishes include spicy beef teriyaki served with mashed potatoes and bok choy, brochette of shrimp with spicy lemon garlic reduction and the large and attractive sushi "love boat." Desserts of green tea mascarpone cheesecake or Asian sticky black rice pudding thrill the palate. Dressy casual. **Bar:** Full bar. **Reservations:** suggested. **Hours:** noon-2:30 & 5-10 pm, Fri-11 pm, Sat 5 pm-11 pm, Sun 4 pm-9:30 pm. Closed: 1/1, 12/25; also Mon. **Address:** 2 S Main St 06854 **Location:** Corner of SR 136; downtown. **Parking:** street.

SOUTHPORT

—— WHERE TO DINE ——

SOUTHPORT BREWING COMPANY

American
$8-$24

Phone: 203/256-2337

Patrons can choose from an ever-changing sample of distinctive brews on tap to complement delicious and artistically presented pub food. The setting is contemporary. Full menu choices also are served between lunch and dinner in the bar. Casual dress. **Bar:** Full bar. **Reservations:** not accepted. **Hours:** 11:30 am-3 & 5-10 pm, Fri-11 pm, Sat 11:30 am-11 pm, Sun 11:30 am-9 pm. Closed: 11/25, 12/25. **Address:** 2600 Post Rd 06490 **Location:** I-95, exit 19, 0.5 mi ne on US 1. **Parking:** on-site.

Plan. Map. Go.
TripTik® Travel Planner on AAA.com

SOUTH WINDSOR—See Hartford p. 278.

STAMFORD pop. 117,083 (See map and index starting on p. 247)

AMSTERDAM HOTEL - GREENWICH/STAMFORD *Book great rates at AAA.com* Phone: (203)327-4300 **15**

Hotel
$90-$170 All Year

Address: 19 Clarks Hill Ave 06902 **Location:** I-95, exit 8 northbound, just n on Atlantic St, 0.6 mi ne on Tresser Blvd, then just s; exit southbound, just nw on Elm St, ne on Main St, then just s. **Facility:** 86 one-bedroom standard units. 6 stories, interior corridors. **Parking:** on-site. **Amenities:** irons, hair dryers. *Some:* DVD players. **Leisure Activities:** exercise room. **Guest Services:** area transportation-within 3 mi & train station, wireless Internet. **Business Services:** meeting rooms, business center. **Free Special Amenities:** continental breakfast and high-speed Internet.

HAMPTON INN & SUITES *Book great rates at AAA.com* Phone: (203)353-9855 **17**

Hotel
$62-$269 All Year

Address: 26 Mill River St 06902 **Location:** I-95, exit 7 northbound, 0.3 mi n on Elm St; exit 6 southbound, just nw via W Main St; exit southbound, just n on Canal St, 0.5 mi w on Tresser Blvd, then just n via W Main St. **Facility:** 99 units. 98 one-bedroom standard units. 1 one-bedroom suite. 5 stories, interior corridors. *Bath:* combo or shower only. **Parking:** on-site. **Terms:** 1-7 night minimum stay, cancellation fee imposed. **Amenities:** video games (fee), voice mail, irons, hair dryers. **Leisure Activities:** exercise room. **Guest Services:** valet and coin laundry, area transportation, wireless Internet. **Business Services:** meeting rooms, business center.

AAA Benefit:
Members save up to
10% everyday!

HILTON STAMFORD HOTEL & EXECUTIVE MEETING CENTER *Book great rates at AAA.com* Phone: (203)967-2222 **19**

Hotel
$89-$289 All Year

Address: 1 First Stamford Pl 06902 **Location:** I-95, exit 7 northbound, just s on Greenwich Ave, then just w; exit 6 southbound, just s on West Ave, 0.3 mi w on Baxter Ave, just n on Fairfield Ave, then just e. **Facility:** 484 units. 475 one-bedroom standard units. 9 one-bedroom suites. 10 stories, interior corridors. **Parking:** on-site (fee) and valet. **Terms:** 1-7 night minimum stay, cancellation fee imposed. **Amenities:** high-speed Internet (fee), dual phone lines, voice mail, safes, irons, hair dryers. **Pool(s):** heated indoor. **Leisure Activities:** whirlpool, tennis court, sun deck. **Guest Services:** valet laundry, area transportation-within 5 mi, wireless Internet. **Business Services:** conference facilities, business center. *(See color ad below)*

Hilton
AAA Benefit:
Members save 5%
or more everyday!

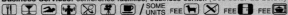

FREE newspaper

▼ See AAA listing above ▼

The Newly Renovated Hilton Stamford Is Ready to Welcome You

Whether you're traveling for business or looking for a relaxing retreat, the Hilton Stamford Hotel & Executive Meeting Center offers the ideal combination of convenience, comfort and personalized service. The Hilton Stamford is conveniently located close to Stamford's lively business, shopping and entertainment district and directly off Interstate 95.

1 First Stamford Place, Stamford, CT 06902
203-967-2222 | www.hiltonstamfordhotel.com

AAA
Approved

HHONORS
HILTON WORLDWIDE

Hilton
Stamford
Hotel & Executive Meeting Center

(See map and index starting on p. 247)

HOLIDAY INN STAMFORD DOWNTOWN *Book great rates at AAA.com* **Phone:** (203)358-8400 **16**

 AAA SAVE
▼▼▼▼
Historic Retro Resort Hotel
$99-$259 All Year

Address: 700 E Main St 06901 **Location:** I-95, exit 8 southbound, just n on Elm; exit northbound, .n on Atlantic St, 0.3 mi e on Tresser Blvd, then just n on Elm; downtown. **Facility:** This pet-friendly hotel offers a spacious atrium and multi-level lobby. Guest rooms are contemporary. Smoke free premises. 383 units. 377 one-bedroom standard units. 6 one-bedroom suites. 10 stories, interior corridors. *Bath:* combo or shower only. **Parking:** on-site (fee). **Amenities:** video games (fee), voice mail, irons, hair dryers. *Some:* high-speed Internet, dual phone lines, safes. **Pool(s):** heated indoor. **Leisure Activities:** exercise room. **Guest Services:** valet and coin laundry, area transportation-within 5 mi, wireless Internet. **Business Services:** conference facilities, business center. *(See color ad below)*

🍴 🍸 🏊 ✕ 🎮 🖥 / SOME UNITS FEE 🐕 📶 🖨

FREE high-speed Internet

LA QUINTA INN & SUITES STAMFORD *Book at AAA.com* **Phone:** (203)357-7100 **20**

▼▼▼
Hotel
$79-$199 All Year

Address: 135 Harvard Ave 06902 **Location:** I-95, exit 6 northbound, just s; exit southbound, just w on Grenhart Rd, then just s. **Facility:** 158 one-bedroom standard units. 8 stories, interior corridors. *Bath:* combo or shower only. **Parking:** on-site. **Amenities:** video games (fee), voice mail, irons, hair dryers. **Pool(s):** heated indoor. **Leisure Activities:** exercise room. **Guest Services:** valet and coin laundry, wireless Internet. **Business Services:** business center.

ASK 🍴 🍸 CALL 📶 🏊 🎮 🖥 / SOME UNITS 🐕 ✕ 📶 🖨

STAMFORD MARRIOTT HOTEL & SPA *Book great rates at AAA.com* **Phone:** (203)357-9555 **18**

AAA SAVE
▼▼▼▼
Hotel
$209-$239 All Year

Address: 243 Tresser Blvd 06901 **Location:** I-95, exit 8, just n under viaduct, then n. **Facility:** Smoke free premises. 506 units. 500 one-bedroom standard units. 6 one-bedroom suites. 17 stories, interior corridors. *Bath:* combo or shower only. **Terms:** cancellation fee imposed. **Amenities:** high-speed Internet (fee), dual phone lines, voice mail, irons, hair dryers. *Some:* CD players. *Fee:* DVD players. **Dining:** 2 restaurants. **Pool(s):** heated indoor/outdoor.

Marriott
HOTELS & RESORTS

AAA Benefit:
Members save a minimum 5% off the best available rate.

Leisure Activities: saunas, whirlpool, spa. **Guest Services:** valet and coin laundry, area transportation-within city limits, wireless Internet. **Business Services:** conference facilities, business center. *(See color ad p 320)*

🍴 🍸 CALL 📶 🏊 ✚ ✕ 🎮 📶 🖥 / SOME UNITS FEE 🐕 FEE 🖨

FREE newspaper and early check-in/late check-out

───── ▼ *See AAA listing above* ▼ ─────

It's a new day.
It's a new Holiday Inn.

$20.7 Million dollar renovation now completed! Vibrant colors and a Manhattan feel, this Holiday Inn is ideal for every traveler.

Holiday Inn Stamford Downtown
700 E. Main St.
Stamford, CT
203-358-8400
www.histamford.com

Holiday Inn

©2010 InterContinental® Hotels Group. All rights reserved. Most hotels are independently owned and/or operated.

▼ See AAA listing p 319 ▼

DIRECTLY ACROSS THE STREET FROM THE STAMFORD TOWN CENTER MALL

Hotel Features Include:
- Pet Friendly Rooms
- Indoor/Outdoor Pool
- The luxurious Agora Spa located on the 2nd floor

For information or to make reservations, call 800.228.9290 or visit www.stamfordmarriott.com.

STAMFORD MARRIOTT HOTEL & SPA
243 Tresser Blvd
Stamford, CT 06901
Phone 203.357.9555
www.stamfordmarriott.com

Marriott.
STAMFORD HOTEL & SPA

© 2009 Marriott International, Inc.

Approved

▼ See AAA listing p 321 ▼

Stamford Plaza

HOTEL & CONFERENCE CENTER

Experience luxurious accommodations and amenities, along with premier service and meticulous attention to detail. Comfort, relaxation in an ideal location...

- 448 Luxurious Guest Rooms and Suites
- Oversized Comfortable Beds
- In-room Workstations with High-Speed Internet access
- 37 Meeting Rooms • Business Center
- Heated Indoor Pool • Full Service Health Club
- Casual Dining at our Terrace Restaurant

Approved

2701 Summer Street
Stamford, Connecticut 06905
203-359-1300

S
Stamford Plaza
HOTEL & CONFERENCE CENTER

877-604-6072 www.stamfordplazahotel.com

RELAX

AAA SAVES YOU
5-15% with AAA's Preferred Lodging Partners!

Visit Over 1,100 AAA Offices Click AAA.com Call 1-866-222-7283

(See map and index starting on p. 247)

STAMFORD PLAZA HOTEL AND CONFERENCE CENTER   *Book great rates at AAA.com*

Phone: (203)359-1300 **13**

(AAA) [SAVE]
▼▼▼
Hotel
$119-$349 All Year

Address: 2701 Summer St 06905 **Location:** I-95, exit 8 northbound, 1.7 mi w on Atlantic and Bedford sts; exit 7 southbound, n on Atlantic and Bedford sts. **Facility:** Smoke free premises. 448 units. 416 one-bedroom standard units. 18 one- and 14 two-bedroom suites. 5 stories, interior corridors. *Bath:* combo or shower only. **Parking:** on-site (fee). **Terms:** cancellation fee imposed. **Amenities:** dual phone lines, voice mail, irons, hair dryers. *Fee:* video games, high-speed Internet. **Pool(s):** heated indoor. **Leisure Activities:** sauna, whirlpool, steamroom. **Guest Services:** valet laundry, wireless Internet. **Business Services:** conference facilities, business center. *(See color ad p 320)*

🍽 🍸 ⊇ ⊕ ⊠ ✖ 📹 💻
/ SOME UNITS 🛏 FEE 📶 FEE 🖥

FREE newspaper and early check-in/late check-out

STAMFORD SUITES HOTEL   *Book at AAA.com*

Phone: (203)359-7300 **14**

▼▼
Extended Stay Hotel
$149-$199 All Year

Address: 720 Bedford St 06901 **Location:** I-95, exit 8 northbound, 0.8 mi n on Atlantic St; exit southbound, just nw on Elm St, just w on Broad St, then just n. **Facility:** 45 one-bedroom suites with kitchens and whirlpools. 7 stories, interior corridors. **Parking:** on-site. **Terms:** cancellation fee imposed. **Amenities:** dual phone lines, voice mail, irons, hair dryers. **Guest Services:** valet laundry, wireless Internet. **Business Services:** business center.

[ASK] 🍽 ⊕ 📹 📶 🖥 💻 / SOME UNITS ✖

—— WHERE TO DINE ——

BENNETT'S STEAK & FISH HOUSE

Phone: 203/978-7995 **27**

▼▼▼
Steak
$13-$39

A favorite among locals, the restaurant features some excellent seafood and steak preparations. The upscale atmosphere has a traditional Italian feel, with white-washed walls and a large painted mural of rolling meadows and a farmhouse. Attentive servers are dressed professionally in black suspenders and red bow ties. Dressy casual. **Bar:** Full bar. **Reservations:** suggested. **Hours:** noon-3 & 5-10 pm, Thurs-Sat 5 pm-11 pm, Sun 5 pm-9 pm. Closed: 12/25. **Address:** 24-26 Spring St 06901 **Location:** Between Summer and Bedford sts; downtown. **Parking:** on-site.

BRASITAS

Phone: 203/323-3176 **29**

(AAA)
▼▼
Latin American
$8-$26

The casual restaurant prepares Latino dishes, including Mexican, Chilean, Colombian, Ecuadorian, Argentinean, South American and West Indian cuisine. Dressy casual. **Reservations:** accepted. **Hours:** 11 am-10 pm, Fri & Sat-11 pm, Sun 12:30 pm-10 pm. **Address:** 954 E Main St 06902 **Location:** I-95, exit 9, just w. **Parking:** on-site and valet.

CITY LIMITS DINER

Phone: 203/348-7000 **35**

▼▼
American
$15-$22

This art deco eatery was designed to combine the luxury of fine dining with the comforts of a diner. Breakfast is served all day, as are freshly squeezed juices. The dinner menu features a number of great burgers, sandwiches and oversized salads, as well as all-natural hanger steaks and delicious Maryland-style lump crab cakes. Glass display cases tempt with made-in-house desserts, pies and cakes. Casual dress. **Bar:** Full bar. **Reservations:** not accepted. **Hours:** 7 am-11 pm, Fri & Sat-midnight. Closed: 11/25, 12/25. **Address:** 135 Harvard Ave 06902 **Location:** I-95, exit 6 northbound, just s; exit 6 southbound, just w on Grenhart Rd, then just s. **Parking:** on-site. CALL 🔊M

IL FALCO

Phone: 203/327-0002 **30**

▼▼▼
Northern Italian
$16-$36

Subdued elegance characterizes this intimate Italian bistro, which is perfect for an adults' night out. It's difficult to go wrong with any of the creative and attractively presented dishes. The dessert cart tempts before the meal even begins. Dressy casual. **Bar:** Full bar. **Reservations:** suggested. **Hours:** noon-3 & 5:30-10:30 pm, Fri-11 pm, Sat 5:30 pm-11 pm. Closed major holidays; also Sun. **Address:** 59 Broad St 06901 **Location:** Between Summer St and Washington Blvd; downtown. **Parking:** on-site.

KONA GRILL

Phone: 203/324-5700 **33**

▼▼▼
New American
$9-$30

The eclectic menu reflects Pacific influences. In addition to noodle dishes and sushi, it lists specialties of macadamia nut chicken and lemon grass-encrusted swordfish. The dining room has a large aquarium, a private area and a sushi bar. The patio opens during warm weather. Casual dress. **Bar:** Full bar. **Reservations:** accepted. **Hours:** 11 am-11 pm. Closed: 11/25, 12/25. **Address:** 230 Tresser Blvd 06901 **Location:** I-95, exit 8 northbound, just n on Atlantic St, then just e; exit 7 southbound, just n on Canal St, then just w; at Stamford Town Center Mall. **Parking:** on-site. CALL 🔊M

MORTON'S THE STEAKHOUSE

Phone: 203/324-3939 **32**

▼▼▼
Steak
$26-$42

Patrons should make sure to reserve ahead for the popular, well-known steakhouse. Large portions, including huge cuts of fine beef and plentiful seafood, are the norm. Even the vegetables are oversized, with baked potatoes big enough for sharing. Dressy casual. **Bar:** Full bar. **Reservations:** suggested. **Hours:** 5 pm-10 pm, Fri & Sat-11 pm. Closed: 1/1, 11/25, 12/25. **Address:** 377 N State St 06901 **Location:** I-95, exit 8 southbound, just w; exit northbound, 0.5 mi w on S State St, just s on Elm St, then just w. **Parking:** on-site (fee) and valet.

(See map and index starting on p. 247)

P.F. CHANG'S CHINA BISTRO

Phone: 203/363-0434 **34**

Chinese
$7-$20

Trendy, upscale decor provides a pleasant backdrop for New Age Chinese dining. Appetizers, soups and salads are a meal by themselves. Vegetarian plates and sides, noodles, meins, chicken and meat dishes are created from exotic, fresh ingredients. Casual dress. **Bar:** Full bar. **Reservations:** accepted. **Hours:** 11 am-11 pm, Fri & Sat-midnight. Closed: 11/25, 12/25. **Address:** 230 Tresser Blvd 06901 **Location:** At the Stamford Town Center. **Parking:** on-site (fee) and valet. CALL 〔符〕M

SBC DOWNTOWN

Phone: 203/327-2337 **31**

American
$7-$22

Patrons can choose from an ever-changing sample of distinctive brews on tap to complement delicious and artistically presented pub food. Full menu choices also are served between lunch and dinner in the bar. Casual dress. **Bar:** Full bar. **Reservations:** not accepted. **Hours:** 11:30 am-10 pm, Fri & Sat-11 pm, Sun 2 pm-9:30 pm. Closed: 4/4, 11/25, 12/25. **Address:** 131 Summer St 06901 **Location:** Between Main and Broad sts; downtown. **Parking:** on-site (fee).

TELLURIDE

Phone: 203/357-7679 **28**

American
$16-$48

The crowds come for cuisine spiced up with chilies and herbs. The bright flavors of lime, cilantro, poblano chilies, avocado and fruits infuse the feisty appetizers, huge salads, sandwiches and entrees. Cornmeal-crusted trout, ancho-dusted prawn and lobster gazpacho salads, butternut squash ravioli, pancetta-wrapped pork and traditional Chilean pot pie are a few of the possibilities. The service is friendly, relaxed and unobtrusive. Casual dress. **Bar:** Full bar. **Reservations:** suggested. **Hours:** 11:30 am-10 pm, Sat from 5 pm, Sun 5 pm-9 pm. Closed: 1/1, 11/25, 12/25. **Address:** 245 Bedford St 06901 **Location:** I-95, exit 8, 0.6 mi n on Atlantic and Bedford sts. **Parking:** on-site (fee).

STONINGTON pop. 1,032—See also North Stonington.

ANOTHER SECOND PENNY INN

Phone: (860)535-1710

Historic Bed & Breakfast
$119-$215 5/1-10/31
$99-$179 11/1-4/30

Address: 870 Pequot Tr 06378 **Location:** I-95, exit 91, 0.8 mi s on SR 234. **Facility:** Set amid fields and a forest, this 1710 Colonial home has rooms with contemporary amenities and such home-like touches as bathrobes and picnic baskets. Smoke free premises. 3 one-bedroom standard units. 3 stories (no elevator), interior corridors. **Parking:** on-site. **Terms:** office hours 9 am-9 pm, check-in 4 pm, 2 night minimum stay - seasonal and/or weekends, age restrictions may apply, 7 day cancellation notice-fee imposed. **Amenities:** video library, DVD players, CD players, voice mail, irons, hair dryers. **Leisure Activities:** badminton, croquet. *Fee:* hearth cooking classes. **Guest Services:** valet laundry, wireless Internet. **Business Services:** meeting rooms. **Free Special Amenities: full breakfast and high-speed Internet.** 〔✕〕 〔📞〕 / SOME UNITS FEE 〔🐾〕

------ **WHERE TO DINE** ------

WATER STREET CAFE

Phone: 860/535-2122

New American
$6-$26

Nestled amid antique shops, the eclectic restaurant displays original oil paintings illuminated by distinctive track lighting. Mostly fresh seafood is prepared with many Asian and Middle Eastern ingredients and flavor-enhancing spices. The raw bar is filled with local oysters and clams. Casual dress. **Bar:** Full bar. **Hours:** 11:30 am-2:30 & 5-10 pm, Fri & Sat-11 pm. Closed major holidays. **Address:** 142 Water St 06378 **Location:** Between Pearl and Grand sts; downtown. **Parking:** street.

STORRS pop. 10,996

NATHAN HALE INN & CONFERENCE CENTER   *Book at AAA.com*

Phone: (860)427-7888

Hotel
$174-$239 All Year

Address: 855 Bolton Rd 06268 **Location:** Off SR 195. Located on the University of Connecticut campus. **Facility:** Smoke free premises. 100 one-bedroom standard units. 5 stories, interior corridors. *Bath:* combo or shower only. **Parking:** on-site. **Terms:** cancellation fee imposed. **Amenities:** video games (fee), dual phone lines, voice mail, irons, hair dryers. *Some:* high-speed Internet. **Pool(s):** heated indoor. **Leisure Activities:** whirlpool, exercise room. **Guest Services:** wireless Internet. **Business Services:** meeting rooms, business center.
〔ASK〕 〔🍴〕 〔📶〕 CALL 〔符〕M 〔🏊〕 〔✕〕 〔📷〕 〔💻〕 / SOME UNITS 〔📞〕 〔📺〕

------ **WHERE TO DINE** ------

ALTNAVEIGH INN

Phone: 860/429-4490

American
$5-$30

Named for its hilltop location, the local landmark treats guests to an intimate dining experience. Traditional entrees are served with tempting accompaniments. Dressy casual. **Bar:** Full bar. **Reservations:** accepted. **Hours:** 11:30 am-2:30 & 5:30-9 pm, Fri-10 pm, Sat 5:30 pm-10 pm. Closed: 5/31, 7/4, 12/24, 12/25; also Sun & Mon. **Address:** 957 Storrs Rd 06268 **Location:** I-84, exit 68, 9.6 mi s on SR 195. **Parking:** on-site.

STRATFORD pop. 49,976

COMFORT SUITES   *Book great rates at AAA.com*

Phone: (203)375-9528

Hotel
$90-$99 6/1-4/30
$80-$90 5/1-5/31

Address: 1500 South Ave 06615 **Location:** I-95, exit 31, just se. **Facility:** Smoke free premises. 82 one-bedroom standard units, some with whirlpools. 3 stories, interior corridors. *Bath:* combo or shower only. **Parking:** on-site. **Amenities:** high-speed Internet, voice mail, irons, hair dryers. **Pool(s):** heated indoor. **Leisure Activities:** exercise room. **Guest Services:** valet and coin laundry, wireless Internet. **Business Services:** meeting rooms, business center. **Free Special Amenities: full breakfast and local telephone calls.** CALL 〔符〕M 〔🏊〕 〔✕〕 〔📷〕 〔📞〕 〔📺〕 〔💻〕

HOMEWOOD SUITES BY HILTON   *Book great rates at AAA.com*

Extended Stay
Hotel
$119-$189 All Year

Address: 6905 Main St 06614 **Location:** SR 15, exit 53, just n. **Facility:** 135 units. 52 one-bedroom standard units with efficiencies. 53 one- and 30 two-bedroom suites with efficiencies. 3 stories, interior corridors. *Bath:* combo or shower only. **Parking:** on-site. **Terms:** 1-7 night minimum stay, cancellation fee imposed. **Amenities:** video library, DVD players, high-speed Internet, dual phone lines, voice mail, irons, hair dryers. **Pool(s):** heated indoor. **Leisure Activities:** whirlpool, exercise room. **Guest Services:** valet and coin laundry, wireless Internet. **Business Services:** meeting rooms, business center.

Phone: (203)377-3322

AAA Benefit:
Members save 5% or
more everyday!

CALL / SOME UNITS

——— WHERE TO DINE ———

KNAPP'S LANDING RESTAURANT

Seafood
$6-$23

To get to this hidden gem, diners have to drive through an industrial area and pass by a small airfield. Seating is offered in the main dining room or on the patio. The view of the Housatonic River as it flows into Long Island Sound is spectacular. Service is casual and friendly. Food is simple and delicious, and this place is known for its lobster roll (a whole lobster!) and delicious made-on-the-premises desserts. The crust on the Key lime pie is scrumptious. Casual dress. **Bar:** Full bar. **Reservations:** accepted. **Hours:** 11:30 am-2:30 & 4:30-9 pm, Fri-9:30 pm, Sat noon-3 & 4:30-9:30 pm, Sun noon-8 pm. Closed major holidays; also Mon. **Address:** 520 Sniffens Ln 06614 **Location:** Jct SR 113, just ne; across from Sikorsky Memorial Airport. **Parking:** on-site.

Phone: 203/378-5999

CALL

TOLLAND

THE TOLLAND INN

Historic Bed
& Breakfast
$99-$239 All Year

Address: 63 Tolland Green 06084 **Location:** I-84, exit 68, 0.8 mi nw on SR 195 and 74. **Facility:** A gravel, circular drive invites you into this restored 1800 Colonial house, which is located across from the town's green. Smoke free premises. 7 units. 4 one-bedroom standard units, some with whirlpools. 3 one-bedroom suites with whirlpools. 3 stories (no elevator), interior corridors. *Bath:* combo or shower only. **Parking:** on-site. **Terms:** check-in 4 pm, age restrictions may apply, 14 day cancellation notice-fee imposed. **Amenities:** *Some:* DVD players, hair dryers. **Guest Services:** wireless Internet.

Phone: 860/872-0800

/ SOME UNITS

TRUMBULL pop. 34,243

MARRIOTT TRUMBULL MERRITT PKWY   *Book great rates at AAA.com*

Hotel
$219-$229 All Year

Address: 180 Hawley Ln 06611 **Location:** Jct SR 108 and 8, exit 8, 0.7 mi e. **Facility:** Smoke free premises. 323 units. 320 one-bedroom standard units. 3 one-bedroom suites. 5 stories, interior corridors. *Bath:* combo or shower only. **Parking:** on-site. **Terms:** check-in 4 pm, cancellation fee imposed. **Amenities:** voice mail, safes, irons, hair dryers. *Fee:* video games, high-speed Internet. *Some:* dual phone lines. **Pool(s):** heated outdoor, heated indoor. **Leisure Activities:** whirlpool, exercise room. **Guest Services:** valet laundry, area transportation-Bridgeport train, wireless Internet. **Business Services:** conference facilities, business center. **Free Special Amenities:** newspaper.

Phone: (203)378-1400

Marriott
HOTELS & RESORTS
AAA Benefit:
Members save a
minimum 5% off the
best available rate.

CALL / SOME UNITS

UNCASVILLE

BEST WESTERN CRISTATA INN   *Book great rates at AAA.com*

Hotel
$79-$389 All Year

Address: 2255 Rt 32 06382 **Location:** SR 2A, exit 1, just n. **Facility:** 105 units. 98 one-bedroom standard units. 7 one-bedroom suites with whirlpools. 4 stories, interior corridors. *Bath:* combo or shower only. **Parking:** on-site. **Amenities:** voice mail, safes, irons, hair dryers. *Some:* high-speed Internet. **Pool(s):** heated indoor. **Leisure Activities:** exercise room. **Guest Services:** valet and coin laundry, area transportation-Mohegan Sun Casino, wireless Internet. **Business Services:** meeting rooms, PC. **Free Special Amenities:** expanded continental breakfast and high-speed Internet.

Phone: (860)848-0660

Best Western
AAA Benefit:
Members save up to
20%, plus 10%
bonus points with
rewards program.

CALL / SOME UNITS

MICROTEL INN & SUITES   *Book great rates at AAA.com*

Hotel
Rates not provided

Address: 1954 Norwich New London Tpke 06382 **Location:** I-395, exit 79A, just e on SR 2A, then just s on SR 32. **Facility:** 120 one-bedroom standard units. 3 stories, interior corridors. *Bath:* combo or shower only. **Parking:** on-site. **Amenities:** voice mail, irons, hair dryers. *Some:* dual phone lines. **Guest Services:** valet and coin laundry, area transportation-Mohegan Sun Casino, wireless Internet. **Free Special Amenities:** expanded continental breakfast and local telephone calls.

Phone: 860/367-0880

CALL / SOME UNITS

MOHEGAN SUN

Book great rates at AAA.com

Phone: (860)862-3375

Hotel
$199-$599 All Year

Address: 1 Mohegan Sun Blvd 06382 **Location:** I-395, exit 79A, 1 mi e. **Facility:** This self-contained casino offers luxury level guestrooms, hospitable staff, a shopping mall and enticing restaurants. 1176 units. 990 one-bedroom standard units. 160 one- and 26 two-bedroom suites, some with whirlpools. 33 stories, interior corridors. *Bath:* combo or shower only. **Parking:** on-site and valet. **Terms:** check-in 4 pm, cancellation fee imposed. **Amenities:** video games (fee), high-speed Internet, dual phone lines, voice mail, safes, honor bars, irons, hair dryers. *Some:* DVD players (fee), CD players. **Dining:** 24 restaurants, also, Big Bubba's BBQ, Jasper's White Summer Shack, Jimmy Buffett's Margaritaville, Michael Jordan's Steakhouse, Todd English's Tuscany, see separate listings, entertainment. **Pool(s):** heated indoor. **Leisure Activities:** whirlpool, steamrooms, spa. *Fee:* saunas, golf-18 holes, kids quest. **Guest Services:** valet laundry, wireless Internet. **Business Services:** conference facilities, business center.

—— WHERE TO DINE ——

BIG BUBBA'S BBQ

Phone: 860/862-9800

Barbecue
$10-$30

Diners nosh on Southern home-style barbecue, such as wood-smoked ribs, beef, chicken and pork, in a lively atmosphere. Casual dress. **Bar:** Full bar. **Reservations:** accepted. **Hours:** 11:30 am-10 pm, Fri & Sat-midnight. **Address:** 1 Mohegan Sun Blvd 06382 **Location:** I-395, exit 79A, 1 mi e; in Mohegan Sun. **Parking:** on-site and valet.

JASPER'S WHITE SUMMER SHACK

Phone: 860/862-9500

Seafood
$6-$28

This casual eatery is a fun and lively place that serves the freshest of fish and shellfish. Dishes are creative and flavorful. Casual dress. **Bar:** Full bar. **Reservations:** not accepted. **Hours:** 11:30 am-11 pm. **Address:** 1 Mohegan Sun Blvd 06382 **Location:** I-395, exit 79A, 1 mi e; in Mohegan Sun. **Parking:** on-site and valet.

JIMMY BUFFETT'S MARGARITAVILLE

Phone: 860/862-2626

American
$10-$22

Caribbean-inspired twists infuse bar classics, such as the cheeseburger in paradise and Cuban meatloaf survival sandwich. Also on the menu are ribs, steak, chicken and fish. Accents amid the lively tropical decor include a larger-than-life margarita machine hanging from the ceiling, tables within faux boats, flat-panel TVs playing Jimmy Buffett videos and a live stage for entertainment on some nights. Those seeking a quieter escape should head to the second-floor patio overlooking the river. Casual dress. **Bar:** Full bar. **Reservations:** not accepted. **Hours:** 11 am-1 am. **Address:** 1 Mohegan Sun Blvd 06382 **Location:** I-395, exit 79A, 1 mi e; in Mohegan Sun. **Parking:** on-site.

MICHAEL JORDAN'S STEAKHOUSE

Phone: 860/862-8600

Steak
$25-$37

Owned by and named after the basketball legend, this modern American steakhouse was created with the same drive for excellence that Michael Jordan displayed on the court. House favorites include MJ's Prime Delmonico steak with balsamic-ginger broth and portobello mushrooms, and the "cowboy," a Prime bone-in rib-eye steak with horseradish crust and Mexican chocolate. A parent or guardian must accompany guests younger than 21. Dressy casual. **Bar:** Full bar. **Reservations:** suggested. **Hours:** 5 pm-11 pm, Fri-midnight, Sat 4 pm-midnight, Sun 4 pm-11 pm. **Address:** 1 Mohegan Sun Blvd 06382 **Location:** I-395, exit 79A, 1 mi e; in Mohegan Sun. **Parking:** on-site and valet.

TODD ENGLISH'S TUSCANY

Phone: 860/862-3238

Northern Italian
$16-$47

Beneath the Mohegan Sun indoor waterfall, the restaurant entices diners with a wonderful selection of authentic Italian cuisine. Menu items include freshly prepared antipasti, homemade fettuccine bolognese and delicious pastries and desserts. The lunch buffet is a bit more casual. Casual dress. **Bar:** Full bar. **Reservations:** suggested. **Hours:** 6 am-11 & 5-10 pm, Fri-11 pm, Sat 6 am-1 & 5-11 pm, Sun 6 am-1 & 4-10 pm. **Address:** 1 Mohegan Sun Blvd 06382 **Location:** I-395, exit 79A, 1 mi e; in Mohegan Sun. **Parking:** on-site and valet.

UNION

—— WHERE TO DINE ——

TRAVELER'S FOOD & BOOKS

Phone: 860/684-4920

American
$6-$17

This traveler's reprieve serves wholesome food in a family atmosphere. Bibliophiles are delighted by the presentation of a free book with each meal. Casual dress. **Bar:** Full bar. **Hours:** 7 am-8 pm. Closed: 11/25, 12/25. **Address:** 1257 Buckley Hwy 06076 **Location:** I-84, exit 74, just e. **Parking:** on-site.

Read, Share, Ask, Plan. Join the travel
conversation at AAATravelViews.com

VERNON—See Hartford p. 279.

WALLINGFORD pop. 17,509   (See map and index starting on p. 300)

COURTYARD NEW HAVEN WALLINGFORD   *Book great rates at AAA.com*   Phone: (203)284-9400   ⓫

Hotel
$125-$153 All Year

Address: 600 Northrop Rd 06492 **Location:** I-91, exit 15, just w on SR 68. **Facility:** Smoke free premises. 149 units. 137 one-bedroom standard units. 12 one-bedroom suites. 3 stories, interior corridors. *Bath:* combo or shower only. **Parking:** on-site. **Terms:** cancellation fee imposed. **Amenities:** high-speed Internet, voice mail, irons, hair dryers. **Pool(s):** heated indoor. **Leisure Activities:** whirlpool, exercise room. **Guest Services:** valet and coin laundry, area transportation-within 3 mi, wireless Internet. **Business Services:** meeting rooms, business center. **Free Special Amenities: high-speed Internet.**

AAA Benefit:
Members save a minimum 5% off the best available rate.

🍴 CALL 🔊ᴹ 🏊 ✕ 📽 🖥 / SOME UNITS 🔒 🖥

FAIRFIELD INN NEW HAVEN WALLINGFORD   *Book great rates at AAA.com*   Phone: (203)284-0001   ⓬

Hotel
$89-$119 All Year

Address: 100 Miles Dr 06492 **Location:** I-91, exit 15, just w on SR 68. **Facility:** Smoke free premises. 119 one-bedroom standard units. 4 stories, interior corridors. *Bath:* combo or shower only. **Terms:** cancellation fee imposed. **Amenities:** video games (fee), voice mail, irons, hair dryers. **Pool(s):** outdoor. **Guest Services:** valet and coin laundry, wireless Internet. **Business Services:** business center.

AAA Benefit:
Members save a minimum 5% off the best available rate.

CALL 🔊ᴹ 🏊 FEE➕ ✕ 📽 🖥 / SOME UNITS 🔒 🖥

HOMEWOOD SUITES BY HILTON NEW HAVEN/WALLINGFORD   *Book great rates at AAA.com*   Phone: (203)284-2600   ⓭

Extended Stay Hotel
$89-$189 All Year

Address: 90 Miles Dr 06492 **Location:** I-91, exit 15, nw on SR 68, then just s. **Facility:** 104 units. 54 one-bedroom standard units with kitchens. 43 one- and 7 two-bedroom suites with efficiencies. 4 stories, interior corridors. *Bath:* combo or shower only. **Parking:** on-site. **Terms:** 1-7 night minimum stay, cancellation fee imposed. **Amenities:** video games (fee), high-speed Internet, voice mail, irons, hair dryers. *Some:* DVD players. **Pool(s):** heated indoor. **Leisure Activities:** whirlpool, exercise room, sports court. **Guest Services:** valet and coin laundry, wireless Internet. **Business Services:** meeting rooms, business center.

AAA Benefit:
Members save 5% or more everyday!

CALL 🔊ᴹ 🏊 ✕ 📽 🔒 🖥 🖥 / SOME UNITS FEE🐕 ✕

─── **WHERE TO DINE** ───

SABBATIC AL'S CAFE   Phone: 203/679-0574   ㉒

American
$5-$16

The neighborhood favorite serves sandwiches and steaks with tempting accompaniments in a pub atmosphere. Casual dress. **Bar:** Full bar. **Reservations:** accepted. **Hours:** 11 am-1 am, Fri & Sat-2 am, Sun-11 pm. Closed: 4/4, 11/25, 12/25. **Address:** 181 N Colony Rd 06492 **Location:** SR 15, exit 66, 2.4 mi s on US 5. **Parking:** on-site.

WASHINGTON

THE MAYFLOWER INN & SPA   *Book great rates at AAA.com*   Phone: (860)868-9466

Boutique Country Inn
$540-$1600 All Year

Address: 118 Woodbury Rd 06793 **Location:** 0.3 mi s on SR 47. **Facility:** Rolling hills, stately maple trees, streams and formal gardens accent the inn's 28 secluded acres; accommodations are impeccably appointed. Smoke free premises. 30 units. 20 one-bedroom standard units. 10 one-bedroom suites. 2-3 stories, interior corridors. **Parking:** on-site and valet. **Terms:** 2 night minimum stay - weekends, 21 day cancellation notice. **Amenities:** video library, DVD players, CD players, dual phone lines, voice mail, safes, honor bars, hair dryers. **Dining:** restaurant, see separate listing. **Pool(s):** heated outdoor, heated indoor. **Leisure Activities:** saunas, whirlpool, steamroom, putting green, golf club privileges, tennis court, cross country skiing, kayaks, snowshoeing, hammocks, hiking trails, jogging, exercise room, spa. **Guest Services:** valet laundry, wireless Internet. **Business Services:** meeting rooms, administrative services, PC.

🍴 24🕐 🍸 🏊 🗙 ✕ 📽

—— WHERE TO DINE ——

THE MAYFLOWER INN DINING ROOM

Regional
American
$11-$40

Phone: 860/868-9466

Although the dining room is formal, guests are encouraged to be comfortable while gazing over the Shakespeare garden, dining al fresco and enjoying lighter but no less flavorful dishes inspired by fresh seasonal produce. The extremely attentive servers cater to guests' every whim. Dressy casual. **Bar:** Full bar. **Reservations:** suggested. **Hours:** 7:30 am-10, noon-2 & 6-9 pm. **Address:** 118 Woodbury Rd 06793 **Location:** 0.3 mi s on SR 47; in The Mayflower Inn & Spa. **Parking:** on-site and valet.

WASHINGTON DEPOT

—— WHERE TO DINE ——

G.W. TAVERN

American
$10-$32

Phone: 860/868-6633

Named after George Washington, the restaurant honors the former president's passage through this small town at the foothills of the Berkshire Mountains. Built circa 1850, the once Colonial home is nicely decorated with many Washington-inspired sculptures and art pieces. The seasonal patio overlooks the river below. Casual dress. **Bar:** Full bar. **Reservations:** suggested. **Hours:** 11:30 am-2:30 & 5:30-10 pm, Fri & Sat-11 pm, Sun 11:30 am-3 & 5-9:30 pm; Sunday brunch. Closed: 7/4, 11/25, 12/25. **Address:** 20 Bee Brook Rd 06794 **Location:** On SR 47, 2.9 mi s of jct US 202. **Parking:** on-site. **Historic**

WATERBURY pop. 107,271

COURTYARD WATERBURY DOWNTOWN   *Book great rates at AAA.com*

Hotel
$109-$119 All Year

Phone: (203)596-1000

Address: 63 Grand St 06702 **Location:** I-84, exit 22, just n; downtown. **Facility:** Smoke free premises. 199 units. 192 one-bedroom standard units, some with efficiencies. 7 one-bedroom suites with efficiencies. 11 stories, interior corridors. **Parking:** on-site. **Terms:** cancellation fee imposed. **Amenities:** high-speed Internet, voice mail, irons, hair dryers. *Some:* dual phone lines. **Dining:** Diorio, see separate listing. **Pool(s):** heated indoor. **Leisure Activities:** whirlpool, exercise room. **Guest Services:** valet and coin laundry, wireless Internet. **Business Services:** conference facilities, business center.

HAMPTON INN-WATERBURY   *Book great rates at AAA.com*

Hotel
Rates not provided

Phone: 203/753-1777

Address: 777 Chase Pkwy 06708 **Location:** I-84, exit 17 westbound, 0.5 mi e; exit 18 eastbound, 0.5 mi w. Located across from Naugatuck Valley Community Technical College. **Facility:** 91 one-bedroom standard units, some with whirlpools. 4 stories, interior corridors. *Bath:* combo or shower only. **Parking:** on-site. **Amenities:** video games (fee), high-speed Internet, voice mail, irons, hair dryers. **Pool(s):** heated indoor. **Leisure Activities:** exercise room. **Guest Services:** valet and coin laundry, wireless Internet. **Business Services:** meeting rooms, business center.

CALL

HOLIDAY INN & COCO KEY WATER RESORT   *Book great rates at AAA.com*

Hotel
$89-$149 All Year

Phone: (203)706-1000

Address: 3580 E Main St 06705 **Location:** I-84, exit 25A eastbound, just ne on Austin Rd, then just e; exit 26 westbound, just ne via Waterbury Rd. **Facility:** Smoke free premises. 282 units. 280 one-bedroom standard units. 2 one-bedroom suites. 4 stories, interior corridors. *Bath:* combo or shower only. **Parking:** on-site. **Terms:** check-in 4 pm. **Amenities:** voice mail, irons, hair dryers. **Pool(s):** heated indoor. **Leisure Activities:** whirlpool, racquetball court, exercise room. **Fee:** indoor water park, game room. **Guest Services:** valet and coin laundry, wireless Internet. **Business Services:** conference facilities, business center. **Free Special Amenities:** full breakfast and newspaper.

HOLIDAY INN EXPRESS   *Book at AAA.com*   Phone: (203)575-1500

Hotel
$109-$189 All Year

Address: 88 Union St 06706 **Location:** I-84, exit 22 westbound, 0.5 mi w; exit eastbound, just n on S Main St, then just e. **Facility:** 111 units. 109 one-bedroom standard units. 2 one-bedroom suites. 8 stories, interior corridors. *Bath:* combo or shower only. **Parking:** on-site. **Terms:** cancellation fee imposed. **Amenities:** video games (fee), high-speed Internet, dual phone lines, voice mail, irons, hair dryers. **Pool(s):** outdoor. **Leisure Activities:** exercise room. **Guest Services:** coin laundry, wireless Internet. **Business Services:** meeting rooms, business center.

------ **WHERE TO DINE** ------

AMERICAN STEAKHOUSE   Phone: 203/756-7529

Steak
$4-$15

Diners mingle in the large, open dining room of this simple, cafeteria-style restaurant, which specializes in steak and seafood entrees. The salad bar lines up hot and cold items. The style is primarily self-service. Casual dress. **Bar:** Beer & wine. **Reservations:** not accepted. **Hours:** 11:30 am-9 pm, Fri & Sat-10 pm. Closed: 11/25, 12/25. **Address:** 1011 Wolcott St 06705 **Location:** I-84, exit 23, 2.5 mi n on SR 69. **Parking:** on-site.

BACCO'S RESTAURANT   Phone: 203/755-0635

Italian
$6-$26

The restaurant provides a comfortable setting in which families can enjoy a special meal. Although flavorful pizza is a house favorite, the daily specials don't pale in comparison. Dinner is prix fixe Tuesday through Thursday and on Sunday. Casual dress. **Bar:** Full bar. **Reservations:** suggested. **Hours:** 11:30 am-10 pm, Fri-10:45 pm, Sat noon-10:45 pm, Sun noon-9 pm. Closed: 1/1, 12/25; also Mon. **Address:** 1230 Thomaston Ave 06704 **Location:** SR 8, exit 36, 0.3 mi e on Huntingdon Ave, then just s. **Parking:** on-site.

CARMEN ANTHONY   Phone: 203/757-3040

Steak
$9-$50

Mouthwatering and zestfully prepared steaks share menu space with preparations of fine, fresh seafood. Dressy casual. **Bar:** Full bar. **Reservations:** accepted. **Hours:** 11 am-4 & 5-9 pm, Thurs & Fri-10 pm, Sat 5 pm-10 pm, Sun 4 pm-8:30 pm. Closed: 12/25. **Address:** 496 Chase Ave 06704 **Location:** SR 8, exit 36, 1 mi e on Colonial, Huntingdon, Homer and Chase aves. **Parking:** on-site. CALL

DIORIO   Phone: 203/754-5111

Northern Italian
$11-$36

This historic restaurant, opened 1927, prides itself on fresh pasta and creative daily specials that jockey for space on the varied menu of assorted grilled entrees and homemade desserts. The waitstaff is polite and accommodating. Valet parking is available Thursday-Saturday evening. Dressy casual. **Bar:** Full bar. **Reservations:** accepted, weekends. **Hours:** 11:30 am-2:30 & 5:30-10 pm, Sat from 5:30 pm. Closed major holidays; also Sun, except Mother's Day. **Address:** 231 Bank St 06702 **Location:** I-84, exit 22, just n; downtown; adjacent to Courtyard by Marriott. **Parking:** valet and street.

NARDELLI'S GRINDER SHOPPE   Phone: 203/754-5600

Sandwiches
$5-$8

More than 4,000 Italian grinders are sold each week at this popular eatery, which covers the walls with the many awards it has won. Soft loaves of bread are topped with imported Italian pruzitini ham, capicola, salami, provolone cheese, mayo, lettuce, tomato, olives, hot sauce and the "classic mix," a secret blend of onions, cucumbers and green peppers. Other cold or hot grinders include chicken parmigiana, sausage and peppers, and the turkey club. Casual dress. **Reservations:** not accepted. **Hours:** 9 am-9 pm. Closed major holidays; also Sun. **Address:** 540 Plank Rd 06705 **Location:** I-84, exit 25 eastbound, 0.9 mi e on Reidville Dr, just nw on Scott Rd, then just sw; exit westbound, 0.5 mi sw. **Parking:** on-site. CALL

NARDELLI'S GRINDER SHOPPE   Phone: 203/753-7400

Sandwiches
$5-$8

More than 4,000 Italian grinders are sold each week at this popular eatery, the first franchised location since the original two stores opened. Soft loaves of bread are topped with imported Italian pruzitini ham, capicola, salami, provolone cheese, mayo, lettuce, tomato, olives, hot sauce and the "classic mix," a secret blend of onions, cucumbers and green peppers. Other cold and hot grinders include chicken parmigiana, sausage and peppers, and the turkey club. Casual dress. **Reservations:** not accepted. **Hours:** 9 am-9 pm. Closed major holidays; also Sun. **Address:** 515 Watertown Ave 06708 **Location:** SR 8, exit 35, just sw on E Aurora St, then just s. **Parking:** on-site. CALL

TEQUILA'S   Phone: 203/755-4806

Mexican
$7-$20

Mexican flair punctuates the creative cuisine and standard fare that Tequila's does well. Twenty-three flavors of margaritas complement enchiladas, fajitas and paella, not to mention the crisp chips and salsa that start the meal. Casual dress. **Bar:** Full bar. **Reservations:** not accepted. **Hours:** 11 am-11 pm, Fri & Sat-midnight. Closed: 7/4, 11/25, 12/25. **Address:** 733 Lakewood Rd 06704 **Location:** Jct Wolcott St, just nw. **Parking:** on-site. CALL

WATERFORD

OAKDELL MOTEL   *Book great rates at AAA.com*   Phone: (860)442-9446

Motel
$60-$150 5/1-10/31
$65-$95 11/1-4/30

Address: 983 Hartford Tpke 06385 **Location:** I-95, exit 82, 2 mi n on SR 85. **Facility:** 22 one-bedroom standard units. 2 stories (no elevator), interior/exterior corridors. *Bath:* combo or shower only. **Parking:** on-site. **Pool(s):** outdoor. **Guest Services:** wireless Internet. **Free Special Amenities:** continental breakfast and local telephone calls.

RODEWAY INN AT CROSSROAD   *Book at AAA.com*   Phone: (860)442-7227

Motel
$60-$150 All Year

Address: 211 Parkway N 06385 **Location:** I-95, exit 81 northbound, just nw; exit southbound, 0.6 mi w. **Facility:** 38 one-bedroom standard units, some with efficiencies (no utensils). 2 stories (no elevator), exterior corridors. **Parking:** on-site. **Terms:** cancellation fee imposed. **Amenities:** hair dryers. **Pool(s):** outdoor. **Leisure Activities:** limited exercise equipment. **Guest Services:** coin laundry, wireless Internet. (ASK) ⬛ ⬛ ⬛ / SOME UNITS FEE ⬛ ⬛

SPRINGHILL SUITES MYSTIC WATERFORD   *Book great rates at AAA.com*   Phone: (860)439-0151

Hotel
$149-$169 All Year

Address: 401 N Frontage Rd 06385 **Location:** I-95, exit 82A northbound, 0.8 mi n, just w, then 0.8 mi s; exit 83 southbound, 0.9 mi s. **Facility:** Smoke free premises. 80 one-bedroom standard units. 3 stories, interior corridors. **Bath:** combo or shower only. **Parking:** on-site. **Terms:** cancellation fee imposed. **Amenities:** high-speed Internet, dual phone lines, voice mail, irons, hair dryers. **Pool(s):** heated indoor. **Leisure Activities:** whirlpool, exercise room. **Guest Services:** valet and coin laundry, wireless Internet. **Business Services:** business center.

⬛ CALL ⬛ ⬛ ⬛ ⬛ ⬛ ⬛ ⬛ ⬛

AAA Benefit:
Members save a minimum 5% off the best available rate.

—— WHERE TO DINE ——

CHARLEY'S   Phone: 860/447-3320

American
$8-$18

Decorated to resemble the original saloon dining experience in Boston's Back Bay district, the mall restaurant offers just the break shoppers need. Favorite choices include the well-known New England clam chowder with large pieces of whole clams, boned chicken with cornmeal stuffing and any of the dinner salads. Casual dress. **Bar:** Full bar. **Hours:** 11 am-10 pm, Fri & Sat-11 pm, Sun-9 pm. Closed: 12/25. **Address:** 850 Hartford Tpke 06385 **Location:** On SR 85; in Crystal Mall. **Parking:** on-site. CALL ⬛

UNK'S ON THE BAY   Phone: 860/443-2717

Seafood
$5-$22

Family owned and operated since 1963, the restaurant offers an array of fresh local seafood, steak, poultry and pasta. Friendly service and a nice view of the Niantic River await guests. Outside deck dining is available in season. Casual dress. **Bar:** Full bar. **Hours:** 11:30 am-9 pm, Sun noon-8 pm; seasonal hours may vary. Closed: 11/25, 12/25; also Mon. **Address:** 361 Rope Ferry Rd 06385 **Location:** At Mago Point on SR 156, under Niantic River Bridge. **Parking:** on-site.

WESTBROOK pop. 2,238

—— WHERE TO DINE ——

BILL'S SEAFOOD   Phone: 860/399-7224

Seafood
$3-$24

This popular riverfront restaurant is near the Singing Bridge and offers picturesque views from the large deck and large glass windows on one side of the dining area. A band plays cheerful music five days a week. The atmosphere is casual and fun, with dishes served mostly on paper plates. Preparations of mostly fresh seafood include lobster, crab cakes, shrimp and local steamer and littleneck clams. Casual dress. **Bar:** Full bar. **Reservations:** not accepted. **Hours:** 11 am-9:30 pm. Closed: 11/25, 12/25. **Address:** 548 Boston Post Rd 06498 **Location:** I-95, exit 65, 0.5 mi s on SR 153, then 1.1 mi sw on US 1. **Parking:** on-site.

CAFE ROUTIER   Phone: 860/399-8700

French
$22-$29

This trendy restaurant is in a renovated historic home with deep red walls accented with black-and-white modern city pictures. Contemporary music plays over the speakers. The delicious trio of oysters starter features a pair with bacon, leek and thyme butter sauce, a pair served raw with mignonette sauce and a pair marinated with mint, cilantro and white balsamic vinegar. Traditional and exotic entrees might center on venison or boar chops, and the in-house pastry chef creates fine desserts. Dressy casual. **Bar:** Full bar. **Reservations:** suggested. **Hours:** 5:30 pm-10 pm. Closed major holidays. **Address:** 1353 Boston Post Rd 06498 **Location:** I-95, exit 65, 0.4 mi sw on SR 153, then just 0.3 mi se on US 1. **Parking:** on-site.

CREATIVE COOKING RESTAURANT   Phone: 860/399-7872

Cajun
$7-$25

The chef's own homemade blends spice up Cajun dishes that also reflect Southern French influences. Casual dress. **Bar:** Full bar. **Reservations:** accepted. **Hours:** 11 am-9 pm, Fri & Sat-10 pm, Sun 10 am-9 pm. Closed major holidays. **Address:** 1835 Boston Post Rd 06498 **Location:** I-95, exit 65 northbound, 0.4 mi s on SR 153, then 1.3 mi ne on US 1; exit 66 southbound, 0.4 mi s on SR 166, then 0.8 mi sw on US 1. **Parking:** on-site.

THE RESTAURANT AT WATER'S EDGE RESORT & SPA   Phone: 860/399-5901

Continental
$10-$38

Under cathedral-height ceilings, large windows provide amazing views of the resort grounds and Long Island Sound. Old World charm infuses the dining room, which has linen-covered tables, floral print carpeting and fabric chairs. Servers are young and friendly. The experienced chef creates popular dishes such as forest mushroom risotto with black pepper leek ragout and goat cheese foam; homemade stuffed ravioli with three cheeses and rock shrimp; and Hawaiian ahi tuna with lobster miso broth. Dressy casual. **Bar:** Full bar. **Reservations:** suggested. **Hours:** 7-11 am, 11:30-2:30 & 5:30-9 pm, Fri & Sat-10 pm, Sun 7 am-8:45 & 5:30-9 pm. **Address:** 1525 Boston Post Rd 06498 **Location:** I-95, exit 65, 0.6 mi s on SR 153, then 0.7 mi se on US 1. **Parking:** on-site. CALL ⬛

There's *so much* in life *worth celebrating*

Birthdays. Anniversaries. Personal triumphs. Reunions. Promising new beginnings. *Walt Disney World* ® Resort will make it easier for you to magnify these moments in wonderful Disney style! This is the year to gather all the people who make you the happiest and celebrate at the place where dreams come true.

And with *AAA Vacations*®, you'll enjoy special benefits and great values. Ask your AAA/CAA Travel professional today!

©Disney

WEST HARTFORD—See Hartford p. 279.

WEST HAVEN pop. 52,360 (See map and index starting on p. 300)

BEST WESTERN EXECUTIVE HOTEL   *Book great rates at AAA.com*   Phone: (203)933-0344   35

Hotel
$69-$180 All Year

Address: 490 Sawmill Rd 06516 **Location:** I-95, exit 42, 0.3 mi w on SR 162. **Facility:** Smoke free premises. 100 one-bedroom standard units, some with whirlpools. 7 stories, interior corridors. **Parking:** on-site. **Amenities:** video library, high-speed Internet, dual phone lines, voice mail, safes (fee), irons, hair dryers. **Pool(s):** heated indoor. **Leisure Activities:** exercise room. **Guest Services:** valet and coin laundry, wireless Internet. **Business Services:** meeting rooms, business center. **Free Special Amenities: continental breakfast and high-speed Internet.**

AAA Benefit:
Members save up to 20%, plus 10% bonus points with rewards program.

HAMPTON INN & SUITES-WEST HAVEN   *Book great rates at AAA.com*   Phone: (203)932-0404   36

Hotel
$99-$169 All Year

Address: 510 Saw Mill Rd 06516 **Location:** I-95, exit 42, 0.5 mi w on SR 162. **Facility:** Smoke free premises. 98 one-bedroom standard units. 4 stories, interior corridors. *Bath:* combo or shower only. **Parking:** on-site. **Terms:** 1-7 night minimum stay, cancellation fee imposed. **Amenities:** video games (fee), high-speed Internet, voice mail, irons, hair dryers. **Pool(s):** heated indoor. **Leisure Activities:** exercise room. **Guest Services:** valet and coin laundry, wireless Internet. **Business Services:** meeting rooms, business center.

AAA Benefit:
Members save up to 10% everyday!

SUPER 8   *Book great rates at AAA.com*   Phone: (203)932-9000   34

Hotel
$70-$90 All Year

Address: 7 Kimberly Ave 06516 **Location:** I-95, exit 44, just s over bridge. **Facility:** 82 one-bedroom standard units. 2 stories (no elevator), interior corridors. **Parking:** on-site. **Terms:** 7 day cancellation notice-fee imposed. **Amenities:** hair dryers. **Guest Services:** coin laundry, wireless Internet. **Free Special Amenities: continental breakfast and high-speed Internet.**

——— WHERE TO DINE ———

JIMMIES   Phone: 203/934-3212   33

Seafood
$5-$25

The bright, airy and informal setting blends well with the two-mile-long stretch of boardwalk overlooking Long Island Sound. With a view of the beach by your side, you'll dine on fresh seafood, steak, lobster, prime rib, sandwiches, soups and salads. Casual dress. **Bar:** Full bar. **Hours:** 11 am-9:30 pm, Fri & Sat-11 pm. Closed: 11/25, 12/25. **Address:** 5 Rock St 06516 **Location:** I-95, exit 42, 2 mi e on Sawmill Rd and Kelsey Ave; at Savin Rock. **Parking:** on-site.

WESTON

——— WHERE TO DINE ———

COBB'S MILL INN, BY THE WATERFALL   Phone: 203/227-7221

Continental
$10-$38

This charming restaurant, housed in a converted pre-Revolutionary War mill, prepares Continental fare. A bank of windows faces a lush forest and waterfall just across the way. Early birds will find dinner specials Monday-Thursday, 5 pm-6:30 pm. Casual dress. **Bar:** Full bar. **Reservations:** suggested. **Hours:** 11 am-close, Sat from 4 pm, Sun 11 am-2 & 4-close; Sunday brunch. Closed: 12/25. **Address:** 12 Old Mill Rd 06883 **Location:** Merritt Pkwy, exit 42, 4 mi n, then just w. **Parking:** on-site. **Historic**

WESTPORT pop. 25,749 (See map and index starting on p. 247)

THE INN AT NATIONAL HALL   *Book at AAA.com*   Phone: (203)221-1351   26

Historic
Hotel
$355-$895 All Year

Address: Two Post Rd W 06880 **Location:** I-95, exit 17, 1.5 mi n on SR 33. **Facility:** This historic riverfront property offers luxurious, individually themed rooms furnished with fine antiques. Smoke free premises. 16 units. 8 one-bedroom standard units, some with whirlpools. 7 one- and 1 two-bedroom suites, some with kitchens and/or whirlpools. 3 stories, interior corridors. **Parking:** on-site and valet. **Terms:** 2 night minimum stay - seasonal and/or weekends, 14 day cancellation notice-fee imposed. **Amenities:** video library, DVD players, CD players, dual phone lines, voice mail, safes, hair dryers. *Some:* irons. **Guest Services:** valet laundry, wireless Internet. **Business Services:** meeting rooms, PC.

(See map and index starting on p. 247)

THE WESTPORT INN   *Book at AAA.com*   Phone: (203)259-5236   **27**

Motel
$119-$300 All Year

Address: 1595 Post Rd E 06880 **Location:** I-95, exit 18 northbound, n to US 1, then 1.5 mi e; exit 19 southbound, 1 mi w. **Facility:** Smoke free premises. 115 units. 113 one-bedroom standard units. 1 one- and 1 two-bedroom suites with whirlpools. 2 stories, interior/exterior corridors. **Parking:** on-site. **Amenities:** DVD players, voice mail, irons, hair dryers. **Pool(s):** heated indoor. **Leisure Activities:** saunas, exercise room. **Guest Services:** valet laundry, wireless Internet. **Business Services:** meeting rooms, business center.

WHERE TO DINE

ACQUA   Phone: 203/222-8899   **43**

Italian
$10-$38

The restaurant's loft setting features window tables with views of the Saugatuck River. Food is prepared with a Mediterranean flair. The ravioli dish, which changes daily, is a solid menu choice. Casual dress. **Bar:** Full bar. **Reservations:** accepted. **Hours:** noon-2:30 & 5:30-9:30 pm, Fri & Sat-10:30 pm. Closed major holidays; also Sun. **Address:** 43 Main St 06880 **Location:** SR 15, exit 41, 1.8 mi s on SR 33, then just e on Post Rd E. **Parking:** street.

ANGELINA'S   Phone: 203/227-0865   **49**

Pizza
$6-$15

Included in the restaurant's large variety of delicious pizzas, are a Hawaiian with ham and pineapple; clams casino with clams, garlic and bacon; and the classic pepperoni and cheese. Those in the mood for something else will find Italian-American favorites, such as baked ziti, eggplant parmigiana, chicken and veal dishes. Casual dress. **Bar:** Beer & wine. **Reservations:** not accepted. **Hours:** 11 am-10 pm. Closed: 4/4, 11/25, 12/25. **Address:** 1092 Post Rd E (US 1) 06880 **Location:** I-95, exit 18, 1.1 mi n on SR 476, then 0.4 mi e. **Parking:** on-site.

COFFEE AN' DONUT SHOP   Phone: 203/227-3808   **41**

Breads/Pastries
$5-$10

President Bill Clinton put this place on the map when he declared the homemade doughnuts here the "best on earth." He was so enamored with the family's secret recipe that he even had the treats sent to the White House, which is probably why the walls display many pictures of him amid other prominent politicians. Guests can enjoy breakfast or lunch at the counter or at a small table. Luscious doughnut varieties include chocolate glazed, coconut or powdered sugar. Casual dress. **Reservations:** not accepted. **Hours:** 7 am-3 pm, Sun 8 am-1 pm. **Address:** 343 Main St 06880 **Location:** SR 15, exit 42, 0.9 mi sw on SR 57. **Parking:** on-site.

DA PIETRO'S RESTAURANT   Phone: 203/454-1213   **48**

Italian
$13-$36

Since opening in 1988, this intimate 22-seat restaurant has earned a reputation for excellent Northern Italian and Southern French dishes that incorporate homemade pastas, seafood and high-quality steaks. Tables are draped in elegant cloths and accented with fine china and silverware. Dressy dress. **Bar:** Full bar. **Reservations:** suggested, weekends. **Hours:** noon-2 & 5-10 pm, Sat & Mon from 5 pm. Closed major holidays; also Sun. **Address:** 36 Riverside Ave (SR 33) 06880 **Location:** I-95, exit 17 northbound, 0.4 mi n on SR 136, then 1.1 mi ne; exit southbound, 1.3 mi ne. **Parking:** street.

DRESSING ROOM - A HOMEGROWN RESTAURANT   Phone: 203/226-1114   **45**

American
$12-$30

The first restaurant venture co-owned by the late Paul Newman is much like his products in that it features "organic and locally grown ingredients." The dining room occupies an old barn. Guests can reserve a table by the large stone fireplace or enjoy a drink at the bar. Artisan cheeses from Connecticut farms are great starters to a meal of pan-seared Atlantic Cod with early tomatoes, heirloom beans, garlic and anchovies. Hazelnut cake with homemade coffee ice cream is worth the splurge. Dressy casual. **Bar:** Full bar. **Reservations:** suggested. **Hours:** 11:30 am-2 & 5:30-11 pm, Fri & Sat-11:30 pm, Sun-9 pm. Closed: 1/1, 11/25, 12/25; also for lunch Mon & Tues. **Address:** 27 Powers Ct 06880 **Location:** Jct SR 33, 0.5 mi e on US 1; adjacent to Westport Country Playhouse. **Parking:** on-site.

THE LITTLE KITCHEN   Phone: 203/454-5540   **47**

Chinese
$6-$30

This contemporary, Asian-style restaurant enchants with its dramatic red color scheme. Most of the dishes are creatively prepared and presented with fresh fruit. Many Indonesian recipes are available. Dressy casual. **Bar:** Full bar. **Reservations:** suggested, for dinner. **Hours:** 11:30 am-10 pm, Fri & Sat-11 pm, Sun noon-10 pm. Closed: 11/25. **Address:** 423 Post Rd E 06880 **Location:** I-95, exit 18 southbound, 1 mi n on SR 476 N, then 0.8 mi w; exit 17 northbound, 1.6 mi n on SR 33, then 0.7 mi e. **Parking:** on-site.
CALL

(See map and index starting on p. 247)

MANOLO

Mediterranean
$20-$40

Phone: 203/227-0703 **44**

One of the best chefs in this gourmet dining town carefully crafts his menu using only the freshest ingredients from area farms. The difference is evident in dishes ranging from arugula salad with fresh figs and prosciutto de parma in balsamic glaze or roasted chicken with forest mushrooms. The underground restaurant is minimalistic in style, with white tea candles topping each table and a subdued neutral color scheme with light wood planks used to create an artsy ceiling. Dressy casual. **Bar:** Full bar. **Reservations:** suggested. **Hours:** 5:30 pm-9 pm, Fri & Sat-10 pm. Closed: 11/25, 12/25; also Sun. **Address:** 8 Church Ln 06880 **Location:** Corner of US 1 (Post Rd); center. **Parking:** street.

POSITANO'S

Southern Italian
$17-$32

Phone: 203/454-4922 **52**

Similar to the Italian town for which it is named, this restaurant occupies a bright yellow stucco building directly on a sandy beach. Guests are treated to stunning views of the coastline and Long Island Sound. Professionally dressed wait staff are attentive, and dishes are memorable. A notable example is clams oreganate, which are stuffed and baked, but other seafood, fresh pasta and veal dishes also satisfy. Dressy casual. **Bar:** Full bar. **Reservations:** accepted. **Hours:** noon-10 pm. Closed major holidays. **Address:** 233 Hills Point Rd 06880 **Location:** Jct US 1, 1.7 mi s. **Parking:** on-site.

See map and index starting on p. 247)

RIVER HOUSE TAVERN   Phone: 203/226-5532   (50)

▼▼▼▼
American
$12-$29

Guests can relax by the stone fireplace or watch fisherman and boaters on the Saugatuck River right outside the floor-to-ceiling windows. Roasted candy and golden beet salad with baby arugula, goat cheese, candied pecans and blood orange vinaigrette is a tempting starter. Entrees include Long Island duck or truffle-scented roasted half chicken with lemon-thyme jus, hand-cut steak fries and baby carrots. Homemade desserts include molten flourless chocolate cake with cherry sorbet. Casual dress. **Bar:** Full bar. **Reservations:** suggested. **Hours:** 11:30 am-3 & 5-9 pm. Closed: 12/25. **Address:** 299 Riverside Ave 06880 **Location:** Jct US 1, 0.9 mi s on SR 33. **Parking:** on-site.

SPLASH   Phone: 203/454-7798   (51)

▼▼▼▼
Pacific Rim
$13-$32

Whether it is the expansive view of the Long Island Sound, the spacious outdoor deck or the imaginative Pacific Rim cuisine that draws diners in, all are in store for a wonderful, lively night out. Casual dress. **Bar:** Full bar. **Reservations:** accepted. **Hours:** noon-2:30 & 5:30-10 pm, Fri & Sat-11 pm, Sun 11 am-3 & 5-9 pm; 5:30 pm-10 pm, Fri & Sat-11 pm, Sun 11 am-3 & 5-9 in winter. Closed: 1/1, 11/25, 12/25; also Mon in winter. **Address:** 260 Compo Rd S 06880 **Location:** I-95, exit 17 northbound; exit 18 southbound, 0.5 mi s, then just sw on Julian Brodie Rd; at Westport Longshore Golf Course. **Parking:** on-site.

TAIPAN   Phone: 203/227-7400   (46)

▼▼▼▼
Asian
$8-$24

Located in an unassuming shopping plaza, this Southeast Asian jewel brings the tropics to life with a dining room featuring banana trees, birdcages and a waterfall cascading into a koi pond beneath the floor. Dressy casual. **Bar:** Full bar. **Reservations:** accepted. **Hours:** 11:30 am-10 pm, Fri & Sat-11 pm, Sun noon-10 pm. Closed: 11/25, 12/25. **Address:** 376 Post Rd E 06880 **Location:** Jct SR 476, 0.9 mi w. **Parking:** on-site.
 CALL

TAVERN ON MAIN   Phone: 203/221-7222   (42)

▼▼▼ ▼▼▼
New England
$10-$32

In a historic Colonial home built circa 1810, the restaurant has three brick fireplaces, low beamed ceilings, wide plank floors and Early American ironwork. This place prides itself on serving regional New England cuisine, such as baby lamb chops with Parmesan-herb crust and minted couscous; potato-wrapped sea bass on a bed of Swiss chard with Cabernet sauce; and New England lobster stew, which features lobster meat with carrots and leeks in a rich lobster broth with a hint of cream. Dressy casual. **Bar:** Full bar. **Reservations:** accepted, for dinner. **Hours:** 11:30 am-10 pm, Fri & Sat-11 pm. Closed: 1/1, 12/24, 12/25; also Super Bowl Sun. **Address:** 146 Main St 06880 **Location:** I-95, exit 17 eastbound, 0.4 mi ne on SR 136, continue 1.2 mi ne on SR 33, just w on US 1, then just n; exit 18 westbound, 1 mi n on SR 476, 1.3 mi w on US 1, then just n. **Parking:** street. **Historic**

WETHERSFIELD—See Hartford p. 280.

WINDSOR—See Hartford p. 281.

WINDSOR LOCKS—See Hartford p. 282.

WOODBURY pop. 1,298

—— WHERE TO DINE ——

CARMEN ANTHONY   Phone: 203/266-0011

▼▼▼▼
Seafood
$7-$49

This eatery offers a delightful selection of fresh fish from around the globe. Sea bass calabrese is a signature Italian fish dish on a menu that also lists classic steak and other seafood entrees. **Bar:** Full bar. **Reservations:** suggested. **Hours:** 11:30 am-4 & 5-10 pm, Fri-11 pm, Sat 11 am-3 & 5-11 pm, Sun noon-9 pm. Closed: 12/25. **Address:** 757 Main St S (US 6) 06798 **Location:** I-84, exit 15, 3.5 mi n; center. **Parking:** on-site. CALL

CURTIS HOUSE   Phone: 203/263-2101

▼▼▼ ▼▼▼
American
$10-$35

Seafood, steak and chops are examples of regional American preparations served in the spacious dining room. Servings are dished up generously. Casual dress. **Bar:** Full bar. **Hours:** noon-2 & 5-8:30 pm, Fri-9 pm, Sat noon-2:30 & 5-9 pm, Sun noon-8 pm, Mon 5 pm-8:30 pm. Closed: 5/31, 9/6, 12/25. **Address:** 506 Main St S (SR 6) 06798 **Location:** I-84, exit 15, 5 mi n. **Parking:** on-site.

GOOD NEWS CAFE   Phone: 203/266-4663

▼▼▼▼
American
$8-$30

A touch of whimsy and playfulness welcomes patrons to the dining room. The bright yellow walls are lined with colorful original art, small statuary is here and there, and dressed up dinner tables are reassuring. The creative menu makes very good use of unusual international ingredients. Flavors shine bright. And the ever-changing dessert menu is no less exciting. Semi-formal attire. **Bar:** Full bar. **Reservations:** suggested. **Hours:** 11:30 am-10 pm, Sun from noon. Closed major holidays; also Tues. **Address:** 694 Main St S (US 6) 06798 **Location:** Jct SR 64. **Parking:** on-site. CALL

JOHN'S CAFE   Phone: 203/263-0188

▼▼▼▼
American
$8-$30

This quaint yet modern restaurant has three large French doors that open to the outdoor patio in warmer months. Guests enjoy many homemade pasta dishes, including one made with fresh whole clams in white wine sauce, as well as roasted chicken with homemade chutney, filet mignon and specialty grilled pizza. Dressy casual. **Bar:** Full bar. **Reservations:** suggested. **Hours:** 11:30 am-2:30 & 5:30-9 pm, Sun from 4:30. Closed major holidays. **Address:** 693 Main St 06798 **Location:** I-84, exit 15, 3.7 mi n on US 6. **Parking:** on-site.

WOODSTOCK

INN AT WOODSTOCK HILL   *Book at AAA.com*   **Phone:** (860)928-052

Historic
Country Inn
$135-$250 All Year

Address: 94 Plaine Hill Rd 06281 **Location:** 0.8 mi n on SR 169. **Facility:** Some guest rooms at th early-19th-century, Christopher Wren-style country estate feature fireplaces. Smoke free premises. 2 one-bedroom standard units. 3 stories (no elevator), interior corridors. *Bath:* combo or shower only **Parking:** on-site. **Terms:** 3 day cancellation notice. **Amenities:** video library, DVD players, dual phon lines, voice mail, irons, hair dryers. **Dining:** restaurant, see separate listing. **Guest Services:** wireless Internet. **Business Services:** meeting rooms.

—— WHERE TO DINE ——

INN AT WOODSTOCK HILL   *Menu on AAA.com*   **Phone:** 860/928-052

Continental
$11-$49

Guests can dine in an elegant and romantic country setting with that special someone or a group of friend and family. Representative of fine Continental cuisine are dishes including butternut squash soup ar flounder del Ray stuffed with crabmeat. The friendly and knowledgeable staff aims to please. Dressy casua **Bar:** Full bar. **Reservations:** suggested. **Hours:** 5 pm-8 pm, Sun-7 pm; also 11 am-2 pm Thurs-Sat 5/ 12/31. **Address:** 94 Plaine Hill Rd 06281 **Location:** 0.8 mi n on SR 169; in Inn at Woodstock Hill. **Parking** on-site. **Historic**

Massachusetts

ACTON—See Boston p. 390.

AMESBURY—See Boston p. 391.

AMHERST

ALLEN HOUSE VICTORIAN BED & BREAKFAST INN

Phone: 413/253-500(

▼▼▼

Historic Bed
& Breakfast

$85-$195 All Year

Address: 599 Main St 01002 **Location:** 0.8 mi e; center of downtown. **Facility:** The 1886 Queer Anne stick-style home boasts antiques, Oriental rugs, an antique-style radio/clock, down comforters and pillows and English toiletries. Smoke free premises. 6 one-bedroom standard units. 2 stories (nc elevator), interior corridors. *Bath:* shower only. **Parking:** on-site. **Terms:** office hours 7 am-11 pm, 2-3 night minimum stay - seasonal and/or weekends, 14 day cancellation notice-fee imposed **Amenities:** hair dryers. **Leisure Activities:** *Fee:* massage. **Guest Services:** TV in common area wireless Internet. **Business Services:** fax. FEE

AMHERST INN BED & BREAKFAST

Phone: 413/253-500(

▼▼▼

Historic Bed
& Breakfast

$85-$195 All Year

Address: 257 Main St 01002 **Location:** 0.3 mi e; center. **Facility:** An easy walk to town, the 185(Victorian-style B&B's rooms represent famous designers; find antique-style radios and alarm clocks and down bedding. Smoke free premises. 8 one-bedroom standard units. 2 stories (no elevator) interior corridors. *Bath:* shower only. **Parking:** on-site. **Terms:** office hours 7 am-11 pm, 2-3 nigh minimum stay - seasonal and/or weekends, 14 day cancellation notice-fee imposed. **Amenities:** hai dryers. **Leisure Activities:** *Fee:* massage. **Guest Services:** TV in common area, wireless Internet.

FEE

UNIVERSITY LODGE

Book at AAA.com

Phone: (413)256-8111

▼

Motel

$59-$159 All Year

Address: 345 N Pleasant St 01002 **Location:** 0.6 mi n. **Facility:** 20 one-bedroom standard units. : stories (no elevator), exterior corridors. **Parking:** on-site. **Terms:** office hours 8 am-9 pm, 2 nigh minimum stay - seasonal and/or weekends, cancellation fee imposed. **Amenities:** irons.

ASK / SOME UNITS FEE

—— WHERE TO DINE ——

CHEZ ALBERT

Phone: 413/253-3811

▼▼

French

$9-$26

This intimate, 15-table French bistro features marble tile flooring and copper-top tables. Crispy oyster served with fennel and creme fraiche lead into entrees such as mushroom en croute, which feature trumpet mushrooms baked in a savory pasty puff. Creme brulee strikes the finishing note. Casual dress **Bar:** Full bar. **Reservations:** suggested. **Hours:** 11:30 am-2 & 5-9 pm, Thurs-Sat to 10 pm, Sun 5 pm-9 pm Closed: 12/24, 12/25; also Mon. **Address:** 27 S Pleasant St 01002 **Location:** Just n of jct SR 9 and 116 center. **Parking:** street.

JUDIE'S

Phone: 413/253-349

▼▼

American

$9-$20

Known for its giant popovers, which can be served alone with homemade apple butter or stuffed with varie(tasty selections, the restaurant also prepares gumbo, shrimp scampi, sirloin tips, a vegetarian medley an other dishes. Casual dress. **Bar:** Full bar. **Hours:** 11:30 am-10 pm, Fri & Sat-11 pm. Closed: 11/25, 12/25 **Address:** 51 N Pleasant St 01002 **Location:** Between Main St and Kellogg Ave; downtown. **Parking** street.

THE LOOSE GOOSE CAFE

Phone: 413/549-466

▼

American

$5-$8

The small cafe serves patrons a variety of delicatessen sandwiches and coffees. The homemade cookie and muffins merit strong consideration. Casual dress. **Reservations:** not accepted. **Hours:** 7 am-8 pm, Sa 8 am-6 pm, Sun 11 am-6 pm; seasonal hours may vary. Closed major holidays. **Address:** 1 E Pleasant S 01002 **Location:** Center. **Parking:** on-site.

ANDOVER—See Boston p. 391.

ARLINGTON—See Boston p. 393.

AUBURN

COMFORT INN

Book at AAA.com

Phone: (508)832-830(

▼▼▼

Hotel

$79-$139 5/1-10/31
$69-$119 11/1-4/30

Address: 426 Southbridge St 01501 **Location:** I-90, exit 10, 1 mi n on SR 12; I-290, exit 9 to SR 12 Located across from a shopping mall. **Facility:** 71 one-bedroom standard units, some with whirlpools 3 stories, interior corridors. **Parking:** on-site. **Terms:** cancellation fee imposed. **Amenities:** voice ma safes (fee), irons, hair dryers. **Leisure Activities:** limited exercise equipment. **Guest Services:** vale and coin laundry, wireless Internet. **Business Services:** meeting rooms, business center.

ASK CALL / SOME UNITS FEE

FAIRFIELD INN & SUITES WORCESTER AUBURN   *Book great rates at AAA.com*   Phone: (508)832-9500

Hotel
$109-$133 All Year

Address: 718 A Southbridge St 01501 **Location:** I-290, exit 8, 1 mi s on SR 12. **Facility:** Smoke free premises. 82 units. 78 one-bedroom standard units, some with whirlpools. 4 one-bedroom suites. 3 stories, interior corridors. *Bath:* combo or shower only. **Parking:** on-site. **Terms:** cancellation fee imposed. **Amenities:** high-speed Internet, voice mail, irons, hair dryers. *Some:* DVD players (fee), CD players. **Pool(s):** heated indoor. **Leisure Activities:** whirlpool, limited exercise equipment. **Guest Services:** valet and coin laundry, wireless Internet. **Business Services:** meeting rooms, business center.

CALL 🛎️M 🛬 ✕ 🎇 📺 / SOME UNITS 🛗 📺

AAA Benefit:
Members save a minimum 5% off the best available rate.

HAMPTON INN   *Book great rates at AAA.com*   Phone: (508)832-5531

Hotel
$115-$123 All Year

Address: 736 Southbridge St 01501 **Location:** I-290, exit 8, 1 mi s on SR 12; I-90, exit 10, 2.4 mi s on SR 12. **Facility:** 82 one-bedroom standard units. 3 stories, interior corridors. *Bath:* combo or shower only. **Parking:** on-site. **Terms:** 1-7 night minimum stay, cancellation fee imposed. **Amenities:** video games (fee), high-speed Internet, dual phone lines, voice mail, irons, hair dryers. **Pool(s):** heated indoor. **Leisure Activities:** whirlpool, exercise room. **Guest Services:** valet and coin laundry, wireless Internet. **Business Services:** meeting rooms, business center.

CALL 🛎️M 🛬 🎇 🛗 📺 📺 / SOME UNITS ✕

AAA Benefit:
Members save up to 10% everyday!

HOLIDAY INN EXPRESS HOTEL & SUITES   *Book at AAA.com*   Phone: (508)832-2500

Hotel
$139-$169 All Year

Address: 10 Johnson St 01501 **Location:** I-290, exit 8, just n on SR 12. **Facility:** 113 one-bedroom standard units. 4 stories, interior corridors. *Bath:* combo or shower only. **Parking:** on-site. **Terms:** cancellation fee imposed. **Amenities:** high-speed Internet, voice mail, irons, hair dryers. **Leisure Activities:** whirlpool, exercise room. **Guest Services:** valet and coin laundry, wireless Internet. **Business Services:** business center. ASK CALL 🛎️M 🎇 🛗 📺 📺 / SOME UNITS ✕

LA QUINTA INN   *Book at AAA.com*   Phone: (508)832-7000

Hotel
$65-$129 All Year

Address: 446 Southbridge St 01501 **Location:** I-90, exit 10, 1.2 mi n on SR 12. **Facility:** 99 units. 96 one-bedroom standard units. 3 one-bedroom suites. 3 stories, interior corridors. **Parking:** on-site. **Amenities:** video games (fee), voice mail, irons, hair dryers. **Guest Services:** wireless Internet.

ASK 🍴 🎇 📺 / SOME UNITS 🛗 ✕ 🛗 📺

─── **WHERE TO DINE** ───

PERIWINKLES BAR & GRILLE   Phone: 508/832-9705

American
$6-$20

A great salad bar complements the restaurant mix of Italian, seafood and American dishes, including chicken cacciatore, the fixings-loaded super burger and the fried seafood combination with scallops, haddock and shrimp. Among appetizers are mozzarella sticks, cheese nachos and an onion blossom. Knotty pine walls and TVs with keno lend to the simple decor. Casual dress. **Bar:** Full bar. **Reservations:** not accepted. **Hours:** 11:30 am-11 pm, Fri & Sat-1 am, Sun noon-9 pm. **Closed:** 11/25, 12/25. **Address:** 917 Southbridge St 01501 **Location:** I-90, exit 10, 1.2 mi sw on SR 12. **Parking:** on-site.

PICCADILLY PUB   Phone: 508/832-4762

American
$8-$15

Patrons at the informal, folksy restaurant range from families to neatly pressed professionals. Fish and chips, clam chowder in a bread bowl, burgers, sandwiches, and special dinners, such as Yankee pot roast and homemade meatloaf, are well-complemented by a selection of microbrews. Portions are ample, and the service is efficient. Casual dress. **Bar:** Full bar. **Reservations:** not accepted. **Hours:** 11:30 am-10 pm, Thurs-Sat to 11 pm, Sun noon-9 pm. **Closed:** 11/25, 12/25. **Address:** 602 Southbridge St 01501 **Location:** I-90, exit 10, just s on SR 12; I-290, exit 8 to SR 12 S. **Parking:** on-site.

BARNSTABLE—See Cape Cod p. 467.

BARRE pop. 1,150

JENKINS INN   Phone: 978/355-6444

Historic Country Inn
$180-$260 All Year

Address: 7 West St 01005 **Location:** On SR 122 and 32. Located on town center. **Facility:** English gardens and a gift shop enhance this 1834 house, where rooms boast pillow-top mattresses, a duvet bedding package and extra pillows. Smoke free premises. 4 units. 3 one-bedroom standard units. 1 one-bedroom suite. 2 stories (no elevator), interior corridors. *Bath:* combo or shower only. **Parking:** on-site. **Terms:** check-in 4 pm, 2 night minimum stay - seasonal and/or weekends, 7 day cancellation notice-fee imposed. **Amenities:** video library, DVD players, CD players, irons, hair dryers. **Guest Services:** wireless Internet. **Business Services:** PC.

🍴 ✕ 🎇 🛗 📺 / SOME UNITS FEE 🐾 📺

BEDFORD—See Boston p. 394.

BEVERLY—See Boston p. 394.

BILLERICA—See Boston p. 395.

Destination Boston
pop. 589,141

Boston Harbor.

*T*he first thing Bostonians probably think of when they hear "Samuel Adams" is a frosty beer, not a revolutionary colonist; hearing "John Hancock" conjures up images of the insurance company housed in New England's tallest building; and the Celtics refer to a basketball team, not a group of Irish immigrants.

*H*ere the present and past meld in a curious manner. Explore both.

George Washington Statue in Public Garden, Boston. (See listing page 113)

Massachusetts Office of Travel and Tourism

*P*laces included in this AAA Destination City:

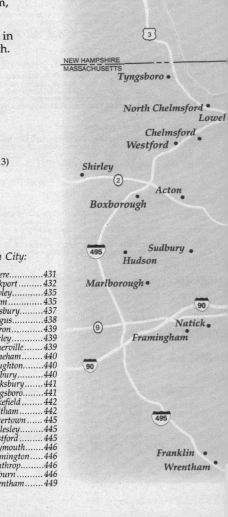

NEW HAMPSHIRE
MASSACHUSETTS

Tyngsboro •

North Chelmsford •
Lowel

Chelmsford •
Westford •

Shirley •

Acton •

Boxborough •

Sudbury •
Hudson •

Marlborough •

Natick •

Framingham •

Franklin •
Wrentham •

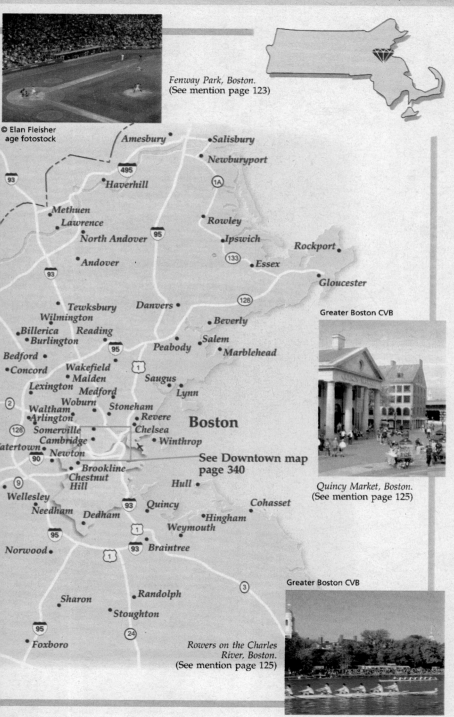

© Elan Fleisher
age fotostock

Fenway Park, Boston.
(See mention page 123)

Greater Boston CVB

Quincy Market, Boston.
(See mention page 125)

Greater Boston CVB

Rowers on the Charles
River, Boston.
(See mention page 125)

See Downtown map
page 340

Boston

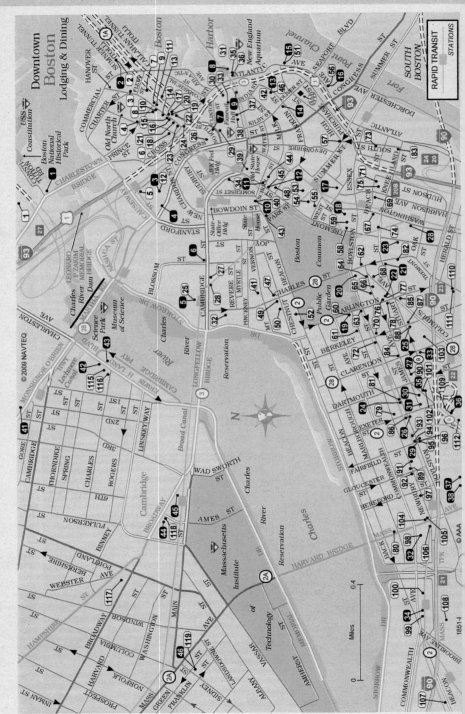

Downtown
Boston
Lodging & Dining

RAPID TRANSIT
STATIONS

Downtown Boston

This index helps you "spot" where approved lodgings and restaurants are located on the corresponding detailed maps. Lodging daily rate range is for comparison only and show the property's high season. Restaurant rate range is a combination of lunch and/or dinner. Turn to the listing page for more detailed rate information and consult display ads for special promotions.

DOWNTOWN BOSTON

Map Page	OA	Lodgings	Diamond Rated	High Season	Page
1 / p. 340	AAA	Residence Inn by Marriott Boston Harbor on Tudor Wharf	◆◆◆	$229-$349 SAVE	364
2 / p. 340	AAA	Fairmont Battery Wharf - see color ad p 357	◆◆◆	$209-$579 SAVE	356
3 / p. 340	AAA	Onyx Hotel	◆◆◆	$179-$719 SAVE	363
4 / p. 340		Bulfinch Hotel	◆◆◆	$199-$359	355
5 / p. 340	AAA	The Liberty Hotel - see color ad p 362	◆◆◆◆	$295-$650 SAVE	361
6 / p. 340		Holiday Inn-Boston at Beacon Hill	◆◆◆	$229-$329	358
7 / p. 340		Millennium Bostonian Hotel	◆◆◆	$189-$389	363
8 / p. 340	AAA	Boston Marriott Long Wharf Hotel	◆◆◆	$269-$399 SAVE	354
9 / p. 340		Harborside Inn of Boston	◆◆◆	$139-$325	357
10 / p. 340		Fifteen Beacon	◆◆◆◆	$250-$1400	357
11 / p. 340	AAA	Boston Omni Parker House Hotel	◆◆◆	$179-$599 SAVE	354
12 / p. 340	AAA	Nine Zero Hotel	◆◆◆	$249-$599 SAVE	363
13 / p. 340	AAA	Hilton Boston Financial District	◆◆◆	$119-$479 SAVE	358
14 / p. 340	AAA	The Langham, Boston	◆◆◆	$195-$535 SAVE	360
15 / p. 340	AAA	Boston Harbor Hotel - see color ad p 353	◆◆◆	$290-$645 SAVE	353
16 / p. 340	AAA	InterContinental Boston - see color ad p 361	◆◆◆	$319-$599 SAVE	360
17 / p. 340	AAA	Hyatt Regency Boston	◆◆◆	$159-$599 SAVE	360
18 / p. 340		The Ritz-Carlton, Boston Common	◆◆◆◆	$495-$795	365
19 / p. 340	AAA	Taj Boston	◆◆◆	Rates not provided SAVE	366
20 / p. 340	AAA	Four Seasons Hotel Boston	◆◆◆◆	$450-$700 SAVE	357
21 / p. 340	AAA	Radisson Hotel Boston	◆◆◆	$159-$429 SAVE	363
22 / p. 340	AAA	The Boston Park Plaza Hotel & Towers - see color ad p 354	◆◆◆	$129-$369 SAVE	354
23 / p. 340	AAA	Courtyard Boston Downtown/Tremont	◆◆◆	$124-$269 SAVE	355
24 / p. 340		Charlesmark Hotel	◆◆◆	$169-$249	355
25 / p. 340		The Back Bay Hotel	◆◆◆◆	$185-$505	353
26 / p. 340	AAA	The Lenox Hotel	◆◆◆	$195-$465 SAVE	361
27 / p. 340	AAA	The Fairmont Copley Plaza Boston - see color ad p 358	◆◆◆◆	$209-$579 SAVE	356
28 / p. 340		Doubletree Hotel Boston Downtown	◆◆◆	$99-$379	355
29 / p. 340	AAA	Mandarin Oriental, Boston	◆◆◆◆◆	$345-$995 SAVE	362
30 / p. 340	AAA	Copley Square Hotel	◆◆◆	$199-$599 SAVE	355
31 / p. 340		Courtyard by Marriott Boston, Copley Square	◆◆◆	$159-$269	355
32 / p. 340	AAA	The Eliot Hotel	◆◆◆◆	$355-$645 SAVE	355
33 / p. 340	AAA	Hotel 140	◆◆	$139-$389	360
34 / p. 340	AAA	Hotel Commonwealth	◆◆◆◆	$269-$498 SAVE	360
35 / p. 340	AAA	The Westin Copley Place Boston	◆◆◆◆	$179-$569 SAVE	366
36 / p. 340	AAA	Boston Marriott Copley Place	◆◆◆	$229-$349 SAVE	353
37 / p. 340	AAA	Sheraton Boston	◆◆◆	$169-$599 SAVE	365
38 / p. 340	AAA	Hilton Boston Back Bay	◆◆◆	$179-$639 SAVE	358

Map Page	OA	Restaurants	Diamond Rated	Cuisine	Meal Range	Page
1 / p. 340		Olives	◆◆◆	Mediterranean	$19-$39	374
2 / p. 340	AAA	Sensing	◆◆◆◆	International	$12-$42	376

Map Page	OA	Restaurants (cont'd)	Diamond Rated	Cuisine	Meal Range	Page
③ / p. 340		Ristorante Lucia	◆◆◆	Italian	$10-$26	375
④ / p. 340		Sage	◆◆◆	Italian	$21-$34	376
⑤ / p. 340		The Fours	◆◆	American	$8-$20	370
⑥ / p. 340		Joe Tecce's Ristorante & Cafe	◆◆	Italian	$8-$25	370
⑦ / p. 340		Prezza	◆◆◆	Italian	$25-$42	375
⑧ / p. 340		Mike's Pastry	◆	Breads/Pastries	$3-$7	373
⑨ / p. 340		Florentine Cafe	◆◆◆	Italian	$10-$32	370
⑩ / p. 340		Caffe Vittoria	◆	Coffee/Tea	$3-$5	368
⑪ / p. 340		The Daily Catch	◆◆	Seafood	$7-$24	369
⑫ / p. 340	⌘	**Ruby Room**	◆◆◆	American	$11-$20	376
⑬ / p. 340		Mamma Maria	◆◆◆◆	Regional Italian	$26-$38	372
⑭ / p. 340		Trattoria Il Panino	◆◆	Italian	$14-$30	377
⑮ / p. 340		Ristorante Fiore	◆◆◆	Italian	$13-$36	375
⑯ / p. 340		Cantina Italiana	◆◆	Italian	$11-$30	368
⑰ / p. 340		Piccola Venezia	◆◆	Italian	$6-$24	375
⑱ / p. 340		Ristorante "Saraceno"	◆◆	Italian	$11-$29	375
⑲ / p. 340		Modern Pastry	◆	Breads/Pastries	$3-$9	373
⑳ / p. 340		Villa Francesca Ristorante and Caffe	◆◆◆	Italian	$9-$32	378
㉑ / p. 340		Lucca Restaurant	◆◆◆	Northern Italian	$10-$37	372
㉒ / p. 340		Bricco	◆◆◆	Italian	$24-$42	367
㉓ / p. 340		Taranta	◆◆◆	Italian	$19-$36	377
㉔ / p. 340		Mother Anna's	◆◆	Italian	$10-$25	373
㉕ / p. 340		Scampo	◆◆◆	Italian	$15-$42	376
㉖ / p. 340		Union Oyster House	◆◆	Regional Seafood	$10-$33	377
㉗ / p. 340		Antonio's Cucina Italiana	◆◆	Italian	$6-$17	366
㉘ / p. 340		Harvard Gardens	◆◆	American	$9-$24	370
㉙ / p. 340		McCormick & Schmick's	◆◆◆	Seafood	$7-$26	372
㉚ / p. 340	⌘	**Durgin Park**	◆	Regional American	$6-$25	369
㉛ / p. 340		Chart House	◆◆◆	Seafood	$30-$45 [SAVE]	368
㉜ / p. 340		Panificio	◆	Breads/Pastries	$7-$22	374
㉝ / p. 340		Kingfish Hall	◆◆	Regional Seafood	$12-$30	371
㉞ / p. 340		The Kinsale	◆◆	Irish	$9-$22	371
㉟ / p. 340		Legal Sea Foods	◆◆	Seafood	$9-$42	371
㊱ / p. 340		Sel de la Terre	◆◆	Southern French	$10-$32	376
㊲ / p. 340		Ned Devine's Irish Pub	◆◆	Irish	$11-$20	373
㊳ / p. 340		Cheers Faneuil Hall	◆◆	American	$7-$20	368
㊴ / p. 340		Oceanaire	◆◆◆	Seafood	$7-$40	374
㊵ / p. 340		Mooo...	◆◆◆◆	Regional Steak	$16-$48	373
㊶ / p. 340		Lala Rokh	◆◆◆	Iranian	$9-$20	371
㊷ / p. 340		Sultan's Kitchen	◆	Turkish	$6-$9	377
㊸ / p. 340		No. 9 Park	◆◆◆◆	French	$39-$96	374
㊹ / p. 340		Parker's Restaurant	◆◆◆	American	$13-$38	374
㊺ / p. 340		KO Prime	◆◆◆◆	Southern Continental	$24-$43	371
㊻ / p. 340		Caliterra	◆◆◆	American	$15-$36	368
㊼ / p. 340		Toscano	◆◆	Italian	$9-$35	377
㊽ / p. 340		Silvertone Bar & Grill	◆◆	American	$10-$20	376

Map Page	OA	Restaurants (cont'd)	Diamond Rated	Cuisine	Meal Range	Page
49 / p. 340		Figs	◆◆	Italian	$8-$19	369
50 / p. 340		75 Chestnut	◆◆◆	American	$8-$20	366
51 / p. 340		Meritage	◆◆◆◆	Regional American	$16-$34	373
52 / p. 340		Cheers Beacon Hill	◆◆	American	$7-$20	368
53 / p. 340		Locke-Ober	◆◆◆	Steak	$13-$62	372
54 / p. 340		Mantra	◆◆◆	International	$10-$39	372
55 / p. 340		Fajitas & Ritas	◆◆	Mexican	$7-$15	369
56 / p. 340		Miel	◆◆◆◆	French	$14-$34	373
57 / p. 340		Radius	◆◆◆◆	French	$17-$135	375
58 / p. 340		Teatro	◆◆◆	Northern Italian	$13-$31	377
59 / p. 340		blu	◆◆◆	French	$13-$34	367
60 / p. 340		The Cafe	◆◆◆	Continental	$15-$50	368
61 / p. 340		29 Newbury	◆◆	American	$9-$33	366
62 / p. 340		P.F. Chang's China Bistro	◆◆	Chinese	$10-$24	375
63 / p. 340		Parish Cafe	◆◆	Deli	$9-$16	374
64 / p. 340		Finale	◆◆◆	Breads/Pastries	$6-$18	369
65 / p. 340		Via Matta	◆◆◆	Italian	$14-$39	378
66 / p. 340		Legal Sea Foods	◆◆◆	Seafood	$9-$42	371
67 / p. 340		Penang	◆◆	Pacific Rim	$7-$23	375
68 / p. 340		Maggiano's Little Italy	◆◆◆	Italian	$11-$38	372
69 / p. 340		East Ocean City	◆◆	Chinese	$6-$25	369
70 / p. 340		Rattlesnake Bar & Grill	◆◆	American	$8-$18	375
71 / p. 340		Peach Farm	◆◆	Chinese	$8-$34	374
72 / p. 340		Cottonwood Cafe	◆◆	Southwestern	$8-$26	369
73 / p. 340		Les Zygomates	◆◆◆	French	$11-$36	372
74 / p. 340		Montien Thai Restaurant & Lounge	◆◆	Thai	$9-$22	373
75 / p. 340		China Pearl	◆◆	Chinese	$4-$20	368
76 / p. 340		Bonfire	◆◆◆	Steak	$18-$44	367
77 / p. 340		McCormick & Schmick's	◆◆◆	Seafood	$7-$26	373
78 / p. 340		Davio's Northern Italian Steakhouse	◆◆◆	Northern Italian	$9-$49	369
79 / p. 340		Stephanie's on Newbury	◆◆	American	$12-$30	377
80 / p. 340		The Wine Cellar	◆◆◆	Fondue	$28-$50	378
81 / p. 340		Bangkok Blue Thai Restaurant	◆◆	Thai	$7-$18	367
82 / p. 340		Pigalle	◆◆◆◆	French	$35-$115	375
83 / p. 340		South Street Diner	◆	American	$5-$15	376
84 / p. 340		Skipjack's	◆◆	Seafood	$9-$31	376
85 / p. 340		Smith & Wollensky	◆◆◆	Steak	$9-$44	376
86 / p. 340		Morton's The Steakhouse	◆◆◆	Steak	$28-$51	373
87 / p. 340		Grill 23 & Bar	◆◆◆	Steak	$25-$59	370
88 / p. 340		Stanhope Grille	◆◆◆	New American	$11-$34	377
89 / p. 340		Kashmir Indian Restaurant	◆◆	Regional Indian	$9-$21	371
90 / p. 340		The Oak Room	◆◆◆	Steak	$10-$55	374
91 / p. 340		Tapeo Restaurant & Tapas Bar	◆◆	Spanish	$8-$25	377
92 / p. 340	AAA	**L'Espalier**	◆◆◆◆◆	French	$25-$175	372
93 / p. 340		Atlantic Fish	◆◆◆	Seafood	$10-$36	367
94 / p. 340		Abe & Louie's	◆◆◆	Steak	$14-$50	366
95 / p. 340		Top of the Hub	◆◆◆	American	$22-$70	377

Map Page	OA	Restaurants (cont'd)	Diamond Rated	Cuisine	Meal Range	Page
96 / p. 340		Legal Sea Foods	▽▽▽	Seafood	$9-$42	371
97 / p. 340		Sonsie	▽▽	American	$9-$29	376
98 / p. 340		Clio	▽▽▽▽	French	$28-$45	369
99 / p. 340		Eastern Standard Kitchen and Drinks	▽▽	American	$9-$28	369
100 / p. 340		Petit Robert Bistro & Pastry Bar	▽▽▽	French	$7-$20	375
101 / p. 340		Turner Fisheries Restaurant & Bar	▽▽▽	Regional Seafood	$24-$36	377
102 / p. 340		The Palm Restaurant	▽▽▽	Steak	$13-$52	374
103 / p. 340	◉	**33 Restaurant & Lounge**	▽▽▽	American	$23-$51	366
104 / p. 340		Match Burgers & Martinis	▽▽	American	$6-$23	372
105 / p. 340		The Capital Grille	▽▽▽	Steak	$26-$45	368
106 / p. 340		Bhindi Bazaar Indian Cafe	▽▽	Indian	$11-$16	367
107 / p. 340		Audubon Circle Restaurant Bar	▽▽	American	$8-$17	367
108 / p. 340		House of Blues	▽▽	Southern	$9-$22	370
109 / p. 340		Legal Sea Foods	▽▽▽	Seafood	$9-$42	371
110 / p. 340		Masa	▽▽▽	Southwestern	$18-$29	372
111 / p. 340		Icarus	▽▽▽	American	$28-$36	370
112 / p. 340		Brasserie Jo	▽▽▽	French	$11-$35	367

CAMBRIDGE

Map Page	OA	Lodgings	Diamond Rated	High Season	Page
41 / p. 340		Hampton Inn Boston/Cambridge	▽▽▽	$129-$499	400
42 / p. 340	◉	**Hotel Marlowe**	▽▽▽▽	$209-$1800 SAVE	401
43 / p. 340	◉	**Royal Sonesta Hotel Boston** - see color ad p 402	▽▽▽▽	$209-$609 SAVE	403
44 / p. 340		Residence Inn Boston Cambridge Center	▽▽▽	$219-$349	402
45 / p. 340	◉	**Boston Marriott Cambridge**	▽▽▽	$229-$399 SAVE	399
46 / p. 340	◉	**Le Meridien Cambridge**	▽▽▽▽	$139-$499 SAVE	402

Map Page	OA	Restaurants	Diamond Rated	Cuisine	Meal Range	Page
115 / p. 340	◉	**Bambara**	▽▽▽	American	$5-$28	403
116 / p. 340		The Cheesecake Factory	▽▽▽	American	$9-$32	403
117 / p. 340		Cambridge Brewing Co	▽▽	American	$8-$22	403
118 / p. 340		Legal Sea Foods	▽▽▽	Seafood	$11-$26	404
119 / p. 340		Sidney's	▽▽▽	American	$12-$30	405

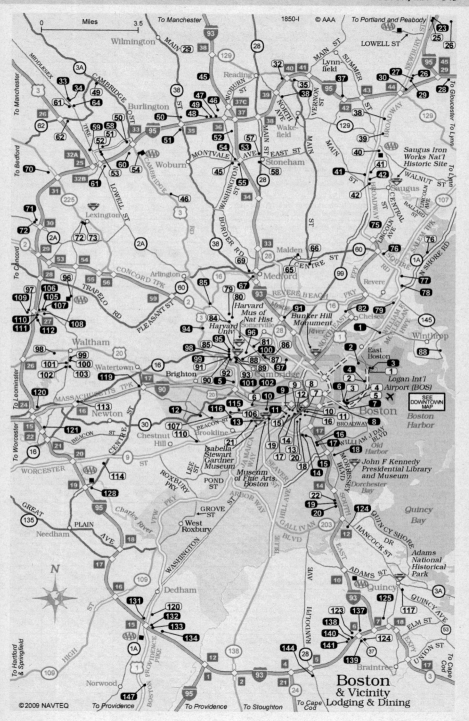

Boston & Vicinity
Lodging & Dining

©2009 NAVTEQ

✈ Airport Accommodations

Map Page	OA	BOSTON LOGAN INTERNATIONAL AIRPORT	Diamond Rated	High Season	Page
15 / p. 345	AAA	Best Western Roundhouse Suites, 4 mi w of terminal	◇◇◇	$159-$239 SAVE	379
1 / p. 345		Courtyard Boston Logan Airport, 1.5 mi n of terminal	◇◇◇	$149-$259	382
16 / p. 345		Doubletree Club Hotel Boston-Bayside, 3.5 mi sw of terminal	◇◇◇	$79-$299	383
2 / p. 345	AAA	Embassy Suites Boston at Logan Airport, just w of terminal	◇◇◇	$129-$469 SAVE	384
14 / p. 345		Hampton Inn & Suites Boston Crosstown Center, 3.5 mi sw of terminal	◇◇◇	$109-$349 SAVE	384
3 / p. 345	AAA	Hilton Boston Logan Airport, at the terminal	◇◇◇◇	$169-$639 SAVE	385
4 / p. 345	AAA	Hyatt Harborside at Boston's Logan International Airport, at the terminal	◇◇◇	$129-$559 SAVE	386
82 / p. 345	AAA	Wyndham Boston/Chelsea, 2.7 mi nw of terminal	◇◇◇	$149-$299 SAVE	406
78 / p. 345		Comfort Inn & Suites Boston Airport, 3 mi n of terminal	◇◇◇	$100-$220	431
75 / p. 345		Fairfield Inn & Suites Boston North, 7 mi ne of terminal	◇◇◇	$69-$159	431
76 / p. 345	AAA	Four Points by Sheraton Boston Logan, 3.5 mi n of terminal	◇◇◇	$109-$220 SAVE	431
79 / p. 345		Hampton Inn Boston Logan Airport, 1.9 mi n of terminal	◇◇◇	$80-$330	431
77 / p. 345	AAA	Rodeway Inn, 5 mi n of terminal	◇◇	$69-$189 SAVE	432
41 / p. 345		Holiday Inn Express Boston Logan Airport, 8 mi ne of terminal	◇◇◇	$99-$169	438
83 / p. 345		Suburban Extended Stay Logan Airport, 2 mi ne of terminal	◇◇	$119-$135	446

Boston and Vicinity

This index helps you "spot" where approved lodgings and restaurants are located on the corresponding detailed maps. Lodging daily rate range is for comparison only and show the property's high season. Restaurant rate range is a combination of lunch and/or dinner. Turn to the listing page for more detailed rate information and consult display ads for special promotions.

BOSTON

Map Page	OA	Lodgings	Diamond Rated	High Season	Page
1 / p. 345		Courtyard Boston Logan Airport	◇◇◇	$149-$259	382
2 / p. 345	AAA	Embassy Suites Boston at Logan Airport - see color ad p 356	◇◇◇	$129-$469 SAVE	384
3 / p. 345	AAA	Hilton Boston Logan Airport	◇◇◇◇	$169-$639 SAVE	385
4 / p. 345	AAA	Hyatt Harborside at Boston's Logan International Airport	◇◇◇	$129-$559 SAVE	386
5 / p. 345	AAA	Doubletree Guest Suites-Boston/Cambridge	◇◇◇	$109-$409 SAVE	383
6 / p. 345	AAA	The Seaport Hotel and Seaport World Trade Center	◇◇◇◇	$179-$499 SAVE	386
7 / p. 345	AAA	Renaissance Boston Waterfront Hotel	◇◇◇	$249-$369 SAVE	386
8 / p. 345	AAA	Westin Boston Waterfront - see color ad p 365	◇◇◇◇	$169-$599 SAVE	387
9 / p. 345		The Colonnade Hotel Boston	◇◇◇	$199-$429	381
10 / p. 345		Howard Johnson Hotel Fenway	◇	$109-$239	385
11 / p. 345	AAA	The Midtown Hotel	◇◇	$149-$309 SAVE	386

BOSTON (cont'd)

Map Page	OA	Lodgings (cont'd)	Diamond Rated	High Season	Page
12 / p. 345	AAA	**Best Western Terrace Inn**	◆◆	$99-$239 [SAVE]	381
13 / p. 345	AAA	**Best Western Boston-The Inn at Longwood Medical** - see color ad p 379	◆◆◆	$199-$309 [SAVE]	379
14 / p. 345	AAA	**Hampton Inn & Suites Boston Crosstown Center**	◆◆◆	$109-$349 [SAVE]	384
15 / p. 345	AAA	**Best Western Roundhouse Suites**	◆◆◆	$159-$239 [SAVE]	379
16 / p. 345		Holiday Inn Express	◆◆◆	Rates not provided	385
17 / p. 345		Courtyard by Marriott South Boston	◆◆◆	$189-$279	382
18 / p. 345		Doubletree Club Hotel Boston-Bayside	◆◆◆	$79-$299	383
19 / p. 345		Ramada Boston - see color ad p 382	◆◆	$129-$189	386
20 / p. 345		Comfort Inn Boston - see color ad p 382	◆◆◆	$109-$179	381

Map Page	OA	Restaurants	Diamond Rated	Cuisine	Meal Range	Page
1 / p. 345		Connolly's Pub	◆◆	American	$12-$24	388
2 / p. 345		Harborside Grill	◆◆◆	American	$15-$38	388
3 / p. 345	AAA	**Aura**	◆◆◆◆	Regional Seafood	$14-$48	387
4 / p. 345		No Name Restaurant	◆	Regional Seafood	$8-$18	389
5 / p. 345		LTK Bar & Kitchen	◆◆◆	Seafood	$10-$29	388
6 / p. 345		The Elephant Walk-Boston	◆◆◆	French	$7-$28	388
7 / p. 345		Sibling Rivalry	◆◆◆◆	Regional American	$12-$32	389
8 / p. 345	AAA	**Hamersley's Bistro**	◆◆◆	French	$25-$40	388
9 / p. 345		Giacomo's	◆◆	Italian	$12-$25	388
10 / p. 345		The Butcher Shop	◆◆◆	Specialty	$14-$32	387
11 / p. 345		B&G Oysters Ltd	◆◆◆	Seafood	$16-$28	387
12 / p. 345		Aquitaine Bar a Vin Bistrot	◆◆◆	French	$9-$29	387
13 / p. 345		Metropolis Cafe	◆◆◆	Mediterranean	$16-$20	389
14 / p. 345		Tremont 647	◆◆	American	$13-$26	389
15 / p. 345		Betty's Wok and Noodle Diner	◆◆	Asian	$7-$22	387
16 / p. 345		Union Bar and Grille	◆◆◆	Steak	$16-$33	389
17 / p. 345		House of Siam	◆◆	Thai	$9-$18	388
18 / p. 345		Stella Restaurant & Bar	◆◆◆	Italian	$16-$30	389
19 / p. 345		Bravo Restaurant	◆◆◆	American	$15-$25	387
20 / p. 345		Flour Bakery & Cafe	◆	Breads/Pastries	$5-$15	388
21 / p. 345		Longwood Grille & Bar	◆◆	American	$9-$19	388
22 / p. 345	AAA	**Freeport Tavern**	◆◆◆	American	$9-$24	388

DANVERS

Map Page	OA	Lodging	Diamond Rated	High Season	Page
23 / p. 345		Residence Inn Boston-North Shore/Danvers	◆◆◆	$125-$149	408

Map Page	OA	Restaurants	Diamond Rated	Cuisine	Meal Range	Page
25 / p. 345	AAA	**The Hardcover**	◈◈	American	$15-$36	409
26 / p. 345		Spero's Sports Pub & Grill	◈◈	American	$8-S18	409

PEABODY

Map Page	OA	Lodgings	Diamond Rated	High Season	Page
26 / p. 345		Hampton Inn Boston-Peabody	◈◈◈	$79-$119	428
27 / p. 345		Homewood Suites by Hilton	◈◈◈	$89-$209	429
28 / p. 345		Homestead Studio Suites Hotel-Boston/Peabody	◈◈	$70-$115	429
29 / p. 345		SpringHill Suites Boston/Peabody	◈◈◈	$99-$134	429
30 / p. 345		Holiday Inn Hotel & Suites	◈◈	$89-$119	429

BILLERICA

Map Page	OA	Lodgings	Diamond Rated	High Season	Page
33 / p. 345		Hampton Inn Bedford/Burlington	◈◈◈	$79-$179	395
34 / p. 345		Homewood Suites by Hilton	◈◈◈	$109-$199	395

WAKEFIELD

Map Page	OA	Lodgings	Diamond Rated	High Season	Page
37 / p. 345	AAA	**Sheraton Colonial Hotel Boston North & Conference Center**	◈◈◈	$95-$235 SAVE	442
38 / p. 345	AAA	**Lord Wakefield Hotel**	◈◈	$70-$140 SAVE	442

Map Page	OA	Restaurant	Diamond Rated	Cuisine	Meal Range	Page
35 / p. 345		Bellino's Trattoria	◈◈	Italian	$7-S19	442

SAUGUS

Map Page	OA	Lodgings	Diamond Rated	High Season	Page
41 / p. 345		Holiday Inn Express Boston Logan Airport	◈◈◈	$99-$169	438
42 / p. 345	AAA	**Red Roof Inn #7305**	◈◈	$95-$110 SAVE	438

Map Page	OA	Restaurants	Diamond Rated	Cuisine	Meal Range	Page
38 / p. 345		Ristorante Donatello	◈◈	Regional Italian	$11-$32	438
39 / p. 345		Jimmy's Steer House	◈◈	Steak	$7-S17	438
40 / p. 345	AAA	**The Continental Restaurant**	◈◈	American	$7-$28	438
41 / p. 345		Sake	◈◈	Japanese	$8-$29	439
42 / p. 345		Kowloon Restaurant	◈◈	Chinese	$7-S24	438

WOBURN

Map Page	OA	Lodgings	Diamond Rated	High Season	Page
45 / p. 345	AAA	**Residence Inn by Marriott-Boston/Woburn**	◈◈◈	$199-$219 SAVE	448
46 / p. 345	AAA	**Red Roof Inn Woburn #238**	◈◈	$79-$130 SAVE	448
47 / p. 345		Hampton Inn Boston-Woburn	◈◈◈	$109-$159	447
48 / p. 345		Courtyard Boston Woburn	◈◈◈	$154-$169	447
49 / p. 345		Fairfield Inn by Marriott-Boston/Woburn	◈◈◈	$99-$129	447
50 / p. 345		Extended Stay Deluxe Boston-Woburn	◈◈	$75-$110	447
51 / p. 345	AAA	**Holiday Inn Select**	◈◈◈	$109-$199 SAVE	448
52 / p. 345		Hilton Boston/Woburn	◈◈◈	$99-$239	447
53 / p. 345		Courtyard by Marriott Woburn/Boston North	◈◈◈	$164-$189	447
54 / p. 345	AAA	**Best Western New Englander**	◈◈◈	$99-$109 SAVE	446

WOBURN (cont'd)

Map Page	OA	Lodgings (cont'd)	Diamond Rated	High Season	Page
55 / p. 345	AAA	**Comfort Inn Boston/Woburn**	◈◈◈	$70-$240 SAVE	446

Map Page	OA	Restaurants	Diamond Rated	Cuisine	Meal Range	Page
45 / p. 345		Polcari's	◈◈	Italian	$6-$21	449
46 / p. 345		Masa	◈◈◈	Southwestern	$9-$29	448

BURLINGTON

Map Page	OA	Lodgings	Diamond Rated	High Season	Page
58 / p. 345	AAA	**Boston Marriott Burlington**	◈◈◈	$189-$229 SAVE	398
59 / p. 345		Candlewood Suites Boston-Burlington	◈◈	$59-$90	398
60 / p. 345	AAA	**Hyatt Summerfield Suites Boston/Burlington**	◈◈◈	$89-$249	398
61 / p. 345		Hilton Garden Inn Boston/Burlington	◈◈◈	$79-$199	398

Map Page	OA	Restaurants	Diamond Rated	Cuisine	Meal Range	Page
49 / p. 345		Lester's Roadside Bar-B-Q	◈	Barbecue	$7-$14	399
50 / p. 345		Fitzwilliam's Irish Pub	◈◈	Irish	$7-$14	398
51 / p. 345		The Dandelion Green	◈◈	American	$9-$35	398
52 / p. 345		Summer Winter	◈◈◈	American	$10-$26	399
53 / p. 345		Legal Sea Foods	◈◈◈	Seafood	$10-$42	399
54 / p. 345		Cafe Escadrille	◈◈◈	Continental	$10-$40	398

BEDFORD

Map Page	OA	Lodging	Diamond Rated	High Season	Page
64 / p. 345	AAA	**Doubletree Hotel Bedford Glen - see color ad p 384**	◈◈◈	$99-$239 SAVE	394

Map Page	OA	Restaurants	Diamond Rated	Cuisine	Meal Range	Page
61 / p. 345		Bistro 44	◈◈◈	American	$12-$37	394
62 / p. 345		Bamboo	◈◈◈	Asian	$8-$21	394

MEDFORD

Map Page	OA	Lodging	Diamond Rated	High Season	Page
67 / p. 345	AAA	**Hyatt Place Boston/Medford**	◈◈◈	$89-$299 SAVE	422

Map Page	OA	Restaurant	Diamond Rated	Cuisine	Meal Range	Page
69 / p. 345		Modern Pastry	◈	Breads/Pastries	$3-$9	422

LEXINGTON

Map Page	OA	Lodgings	Diamond Rated	High Season	Page
70 / p. 345	AAA	**Quality Inn & Suites**	◈◈	$63-$90 SAVE	419
71 / p. 345	AAA	**element Lexington**	◈◈◈	$109-$429 SAVE	418
72 / p. 345	AAA	**aloft Lexington**	◈◈◈	$89-$399 SAVE	418

Map Page	OA	Restaurants	Diamond Rated	Cuisine	Meal Range	Page
72 / p. 345		Khushboo	◈◈	Indian	$10-$22	419
73 / p. 345		Lemon Grass Thai Cuisine	◈◈	Thai	$8-$18	419

REVERE

Map Page	OA	Lodgings	Diamond Rated	High Season	Page
75 / p. 345		Fairfield Inn & Suites Boston North	◈◈◈	$69-$159	431
76 / p. 345	AAA	**Four Points by Sheraton Boston Logan**	◈◈◈	$109-$220 SAVE	431
77 / p. 345	AAA	**Rodeway Inn**	◈◈	$69-$189 SAVE	432
78 / p. 345		Comfort Inn & Suites Boston Airport	◈◈◈	$100-$220	431

REVERE (cont'd)

Map Page	OA	Lodgings (cont'd)	Diamond Rated	High Season	Page
79 / p. 345		Hampton Inn Boston Logan Airport	◆◆◆	$80-$330	431

Map Page	OA	Restaurant	Diamond Rated	Cuisine	Meal Range	Page
76 / p. 345		Mount Vernon at the Wharf	◆◆	American	$7-$30	432

CHELSEA

Map Page	OA	Lodging	Diamond Rated	High Season	Page
82 / p. 345	AAA	**Wyndham Boston/Chelsea** - see color ad p 364	◆◆◆	$149-$299 SAVE	406

ARLINGTON

Map Page	OA	Lodging	Diamond Rated	High Season	Page
85 / p. 345	AAA	**Homewood Suites by Hilton-Cambridge/Arlington** - see color ad p 401	◆◆◆	$199-$299 SAVE	393

WINTHROP

Map Page	OA	Lodging	Diamond Rated	High Season	Page
88 / p. 345		Suburban Extended Stay Logan Airport	◆◆	$119-$135	446

SOMERVILLE

Map Page	OA	Lodging	Diamond Rated	High Season	Page
91 / p. 345		La Quinta Inn & Suites Boston/Somerville	◆◆◆	$89-$219	439

Map Page	OA	Restaurants	Diamond Rated	Cuisine	Meal Range	Page
79 / p. 345		Diva Indian Bistro	◆◆	Regional Indian	$10-$20	439
80 / p. 345		Rosebud Diner	◆◆	American	$6-$14	439
81 / p. 345		Dali Restaurant & Tapas Bar	◆◆	Regional Spanish	$5-$25	439

CAMBRIDGE

Map Page	OA	Lodgings	Diamond Rated	High Season	Page
94 / p. 345	AAA	**Best Western Hotel Tria**	◆◆◆	$159-$299 SAVE	399
95 / p. 345	AAA	**Sheraton Commander Hotel**	◆◆◆	$129-$479 SAVE	403
96 / p. 345		Irving House at Harvard	◆	$180-$325	402
97 / p. 345	AAA	**Holiday Inn Express Hotel & Suites**	◆◆◆	$109-$169 SAVE	401
98 / p. 345	AAA	**Harvard Square Hotel**	◆◆	$119-$299 SAVE	401
99 / p. 345	AAA	**The Charles Hotel, Harvard Square** - see color ad p 400	◆◆◆◆	$199-$750 SAVE	400
100 / p. 345	AAA	**The Inn at Harvard**	◆◆◆	$139-$399 SAVE	402
101 / p. 345		Courtyard by Marriott Boston Cambridge	◆◆◆	$159-$269	400
102 / p. 345	AAA	**Hyatt Regency Cambridge**	◆◆◆	$99-$529 SAVE	401

Map Page	OA	Restaurants	Diamond Rated	Cuisine	Meal Range	Page
84 / p. 345		The Elephant Walk-Cambridge	◆◆◆	French	$12-$20	403
85 / p. 345		Harvest	◆◆◆	New American	$14-$38	404
86 / p. 345		East Coast Grill & Raw Bar	◆◆	Barbecue	$16-$26	403
87 / p. 345		Haveli	◆◆	Indian	$8-$16	404
88 / p. 345		Oggi Gourmet	◆	Pizza	$5-$15	405
89 / p. 345		Sandrine's Bistro	◆◆◆	French	$8-$35	405
90 / p. 345		Rialto - see color ad p 400	◆◆◆◆	Regional Continental	$21-$42	405
91 / p. 345		Henrietta's Table - see color ad p 400	◆◆◆	Regional American	$8-$28	404
92 / p. 345		Bombay Club	◆◆	Regional Indian	$8-$18	403

Map Page	OA	Restaurants (cont'd)	Diamond Rated	Cuisine	Meal Range	Page
93 / p. 345		Spice Thai Cuisine	◆◆	Provincial Thai	$7-$17	405

WALTHAM

Map Page	OA	Lodgings	Diamond Rated	High Season	Page
105 / p. 345		Holiday Inn Express Boston/Waltham	◆◆◆	$84-$158	443
106 / p. 345		Courtyard by Marriott Boston-Waltham	◆◆◆	$170-$208	442
107 / p. 345	AAA	**Best Western TLC Hotel** - see color ad p 380	◆◆	$80-$160 SAVE	442
108 / p. 345	AAA	**Hilton Garden Inn Boston/Waltham**	◆◆◆	$99-$259 SAVE	443
109 / p. 345		Doubletree Guest Suites Boston/Waltham	◆◆◆	$99-$239	443
110 / p. 345	AAA	**The Westin Waltham-Boston**	◆◆◆	$109-$369 SAVE	443
111 / p. 345		Extended Stay Deluxe Boston-Waltham	◆◆	$79-$99	443
112 / p. 345	AAA	**Hyatt Summerfield Suites Boston/Waltham**	◆◆◆	$99-$289 SAVE	443

Map Page	OA	Restaurants	Diamond Rated	Cuisine	Meal Range	Page
96 / p. 345		Grassfield's Food & Spirits	◆◆	American	$6-$17	444
97 / p. 345		Green Papaya Thai Cuisine	◆◆	Thai	$6-$15	444
98 / p. 345		Il Capriccio	◆◆◆	Northern Italian	$23-$36	444
99 / p. 345		Jake's Dixie Roadhouse	◆◆	American	$8-$21	444
100 / p. 345		Watch City Brewing Company	◆◆	American	$13-$18	444
101 / p. 345		Tuscan Grill	◆◆◆	Regional Italian	$16-$26	444
102 / p. 345		Erawan of Siam	◆◆	Thai	$6-$16	444
103 / p. 345		Tempo	◆◆◆	American	$16-$32	444

BROOKLINE

Map Page	OA	Lodgings	Diamond Rated	High Season	Page
115 / p. 345		Holiday Inn Boston-Brookline	◆◆◆	$159-$239	397
116 / p. 345	AAA	**Courtyard Boston Brookline**	◆◆◆	$129-$229 SAVE	397

Map Page	OA	Restaurants	Diamond Rated	Cuisine	Meal Range	Page
106 / p. 345		Paris Creperie	◆	French	$4-$8	397
107 / p. 345		The Fireplace	◆◆◆	American	$8-$33	397

NEWTON

Map Page	OA	Lodgings	Diamond Rated	High Season	Page
119 / p. 345	AAA	**Crowne Plaza Boston/Newton**	◆◆◆	$99-$229 SAVE	426
120 / p. 345	AAA	**Boston Marriott Newton**	◆◆◆	$219-$249 SAVE	426
121 / p. 345	AAA	**Hotel Indigo Boston-Newton Riverside** - see color ad p 385	◆◆◆	$119-$259 SAVE	426

Map Page	OA	Restaurants	Diamond Rated	Cuisine	Meal Range	Page
113 / p. 345		Blue Ribbon Bar-B-Q	◆	Barbecue	$6-$16	426
114 / p. 345		Skipjack's	◆◆	Seafood	$8-$35	426

QUINCY

Map Page	OA	Lodgings	Diamond Rated	High Season	Page
124 / p. 345	AAA	**Best Western Adams Inn**	◆◆	$129-$159 SAVE	430
125 / p. 345	AAA	**Boston Marriott Quincy**	◆◆◆	$209-$229 SAVE	430

Map Page	OA	Restaurant	Diamond Rated	Cuisine	Meal Range	Page
117 / p. 345		The Fours Restaurant & Sports Bar	◆◆	American	$8-$19	430

NEEDHAM

Map Page	OA	Lodging	Diamond Rated	High Season	Page
128 / p. 345	AAA	**Sheraton Needham Hotel**	◈◈◈	$99-$349 SAVE	424

DEDHAM

Map Page	OA	Lodgings	Diamond Rated	High Season	Page
131 / p. 345		Holiday Inn Boston/Dedham Hotel & Conference Center	◈◈◈	$99-$219	410
132 / p. 345		Residence Inn Boston Dedham	◈◈◈	$159-$189	410
133 / p. 345		Fairfield Inn by Marriott-Boston/Dedham	◈◈◈	$116-$142	409
134 / p. 345		Hilton Boston Dedham	◈◈◈	$109-$269	409

Map Page	OA	Restaurant	Diamond Rated	Cuisine	Meal Range	Page
120 / p. 345		50's Diner	◈	American	$4-$9	410

BRAINTREE

Map Page	OA	Lodgings	Diamond Rated	High Season	Page
137 / p. 345		Extended StayAmerica Boston-Braintree	◈◈	$70-$104	396
138 / p. 345	AAA	**Holiday Inn Express-Braintree**	◈◈◈	$99-$179 SAVE	396
139 / p. 345		Sheraton Braintree Hotel	◈◈◈	$79-$389	396
140 / p. 345	AAA	**Hampton Inn Braintree**	◈◈◈	$109-$209 SAVE	396
141 / p. 345		Candlewood Suites Boston - Braintree	◈◈	$89-$129	396

Map Page	OA	Restaurants	Diamond Rated	Cuisine	Meal Range	Page
123 / p. 345		Ascari	◈◈	American	$7-$18	396
124 / p. 345		Legal Sea Foods	◈◈◈	Seafood	$9-$42	396

RANDOLPH

Map Page	OA	Lodging	Diamond Rated	High Season	Page
144 / p. 345		Comfort Inn	◈◈◈	$89-$150	430

NORWOOD

Map Page	OA	Lodging	Diamond Rated	High Season	Page
147 / p. 345		Hampton Inn	◈◈◈	$99-$169	427

WILMINGTON

Map Page	OA	Restaurant	Diamond Rated	Cuisine	Meal Range	Page
29 / p. 345		Ninety Nine	◈◈	American	$7-$14	446

READING

Map Page	OA	Restaurant	Diamond Rated	Cuisine	Meal Range	Page
32 / p. 345		Mandarin Reading	◈◈	Chinese	$6-$16	431

STONEHAM

Map Page	OA	Restaurants	Diamond Rated	Cuisine	Meal Range	Page
57 / p. 345		Gaetano's Ristorante	◈◈	Italian	$7-$22	440
58 / p. 345		Felicia's	◈◈	Italian	$6-$20	440

MALDEN

Map Page	OA	Restaurants	Diamond Rated	Cuisine	Meal Range	Page
65 / p. 345		Pearl Street Station	◈◈	American	$6-$18	420
66 / p. 345		Dockside Restaurant	◈◈	American	$7-$16	420

CHESTNUT HILL

Map Page	OA	Restaurant	Diamond Rated	Cuisine	Meal Range	Page
110 / p. 345		Legal Sea Foods	◈◈◈	Seafood	$9-$36	406

DOWNTOWN BOSTON   (See map and index starting on p. 340)

THE BACK BAY HOTEL   *Book at AAA.com*   **Phone:** (617)266-7200 🔲25

Boutique
Hotel
$185-$505 All Year

Address: 350 Stuart St 02116 **Location:** At Berkley. **Facility:** Located in South End, this 1925 structure was once a police station and is now an upscale, boutique hotel with a contemporary design. Smoke free premises. 225 units. 222 one-bedroom standard units. 3 one-bedroom suites. 10 stories, interior corridors. *Bath:* combo or shower only. **Parking:** valet. **Amenities:** CD players, high-speed Internet, dual phone lines, voice mail, safes, irons, hair dryers. *Some:* DVD players. **Dining:** Stanhope Grille, see separate listing. **Leisure Activities:** exercise room. **Guest Services:** valet laundry, wireless Internet. **Business Services:** meeting rooms, business center.

BOSTON HARBOR HOTEL   *Book great rates at AAA.com*   **Phone:** (617)439-7000 🔲15

Hotel
$290-$645 5/1-11/11
$285-$490 11/12-4/30

Address: 70 Rowes Wharf 02110 **Location:** At Rowes Wharf. **Facility:** At Rowes Wharf, gracious hospitality is prevalent at this luxury hotel which overlooks Boston Harbor. 230 units. 204 one-bedroom standard units. 25 one- and 2 two-bedroom suites, some with whirlpools. 16 stories, interior corridors. *Bath:* combo or shower only. **Parking:** on-site (fee) and valet. **Terms:** cancellation fee imposed. **Amenities:** DVD players, CD players, high-speed Internet (fee), dual phone lines, voice mail, safes, honor bars, irons, hair dryers. **Dining:** Meritage, see separate listing. **Pool(s):** heated indoor. **Leisure Activities:** saunas, whirlpool, steamrooms, spa. *Fee:* boat dock. **Guest Services:** valet laundry, airport transportation-Boston Logan International Airport, area transportation-within 10 mi, wireless Internet. **Business Services:** conference facilities, business center. Affiliated with A Preferred Hotel.
(See color ad below)

FREE newspaper

BOSTON MARRIOTT COPLEY PLACE   *Book great rates at AAA.com*   **Phone:** (617)236-5800 🔲36

Hotel
$229-$349 All Year

Address: 110 Huntington Ave 02116 **Location:** Just s of Copley Place. Located between Copley Place and Prudential Center. **Facility:** Smoke free premises. 1148 units. 1101 one-bedroom standard units. 47 one-bedroom suites. 38 stories, interior corridors. *Bath:* combo or shower only. **Parking:** on-site (fee) and valet. **Terms:** check-in 4 pm, cancellation fee imposed. **Amenities:** video games (fee), voice mail, safes, irons, hair dryers. **Dining:** 2 restaurants, entertainment. **Pool(s):** heated indoor. **Leisure Activities:** whirlpool. *Fee:* massage. **Guest Services:** valet laundry. **Business Services:** conference facilities, business center. **Free Special Amenities:** newspaper.

▼ *See AAA listing above* ▼

(See map and index starting on p. 340)

BOSTON MARRIOTT LONG WHARF HOTEL *Book great rates at AAA.com* Phone: (617)227-0800

Hotel
$269-$399 All Year

Address: 296 State St 02109 **Location:** On historic Long Wharf. Located across from New England Aquarium. **Facility:** Smoke free premises. 412 one-bedroom standard units. 7 stories, interior corridors. *Bath:* combo or shower only. **Parking:** valet. **Terms:** check-in 4 pm, cancellation fee imposed. **Amenities:** high-speed Internet (fee), dual phone lines, voice mail, safes, irons, hair dryers. **Dining:** 2 restaurants. **Pool(s):** heated indoor. **Leisure Activities:** saunas, whirlpool, sun deck. *Fee:* game room. **Guest Services:** valet and coin laundry, wireless Internet, tanning facilities. **Business Services:** conference facilities, business center. **Free Special Amenities:** newspaper.

Marriott
HOTELS & RESORTS
AAA Benefit:
Members save a minimum 5% off the best available rate.

BOSTON OMNI PARKER HOUSE HOTEL *Book great rates at AAA.com* Phone: (617)227-8600

Historic Hotel
$179-$599 5/1-11/12
$159-$499 11/13-4/30

Address: 60 School St 02108 **Location:** Corner of Tremont and School sts; northeast corner of Boston Common. **Facility:** Parker House, built in 1855 by Harvey Parker, is reputed to be Boston's oldest continuous service hotel. Its opulent lobby exudes elegance and grace. Smoke free premises. 551 units. 530 one-bedroom standard units. 21 one-bedroom suites. 14 stories, interior corridors. *Bath:* combo or shower only. **Parking:** valet. **Terms:** cancellation fee imposed. **Amenities:** dual phone lines, voice mail, safes, irons, hair dryers. *Fee:* video games, high-speed Internet. *Some:* honor bars. **Dining:** 2 restaurants, also, Parker's Restaurant, see separate listing. **Leisure Activities:** exercise room. **Guest Services:** valet laundry, wireless Internet. **Business Services:** conference facilities, business center.

THE BOSTON PARK PLAZA HOTEL & TOWERS *Book great rates at AAA.com* Phone: (617)426-2000

Classic Historic Hotel
$129-$369 All Year

Address: 50 Park Plaza at Arlington St 02116 **Location:** Just s of Boston Common and Public Gardens. **Facility:** This historic property boasts a spacious, open lobby. Smoke free premises. 941 units. 919 one-bedroom standard units. 20 one- and 2 three-bedroom suites. 15 stories, interior corridors. *Bath:* combo or shower only. **Parking:** on-site (fee) and valet. **Terms:** cancellation fee imposed. **Amenities:** high-speed Internet (fee), voice mail, safes, irons, hair dryers. **Dining:** 5 restaurants, also, Bonfire, Finale, McCormick & Schmick's, Smith & Wollensky, see separate listings, nightclub. **Leisure Activities:** exercise room. **Guest Services:** valet laundry, wireless Internet, beauty salon. **Business Services:** conference facilities, business center. *(See color ad below)*

▼ See AAA listing above ▼

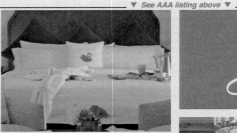

(See map and index starting on p. 340)

BULFINCH HOTEL *Book at AAA.com* Phone: (617)624-0202

Hotel
$199-$359 5/1-11/30
$159-$229 12/1-4/30

Address: 107 Merrimac St 02114 **Location:** At Lancaster St. Located at Bulfinch Triangle. **Facility:** Smoke free premises. 79 one-bedroom standard units. 9 stories, interior corridors. *Bath:* combo or shower only. **Parking:** valet. **Amenities:** CD players, high-speed Internet, voice mail, irons, hair dryers. **Dining:** Flat Iron Tapas Bar & Lounge, see separate listing. **Leisure Activities:** limited exercise equipment. **Guest Services:** valet laundry. **Business Services:** fax (fee).

CHARLESMARK HOTEL *Book at AAA.com* Phone: (617)247-1212 24

Boutique Contemporary Retro Hotel
$169-$249 5/1-10/31
$129-$219 11/1-4/30

Address: 655 Boylston St 02116 **Location:** I-90, exit 22, at Copley Square; between Dartmouth and Exeter sts. Located in historic Back Bay. **Facility:** Smoke free premises. 40 one-bedroom standard units. 6 stories, interior corridors. *Bath:* combo or shower only. **Parking:** no self-parking. **Terms:** 2-3 night minimum stay - seasonal, cancellation fee imposed. **Amenities:** DVD players, CD players, voice mail, irons, hair dryers. **Guest Services:** valet laundry, wireless Internet. **Business Services:** PC.

COPLEY SQUARE HOTEL *Book great rates at AAA.com* Phone: (617)536-9000 30

Historic Hotel
$199-$599 All Year

Address: 47 Huntington Ave 02116 **Location:** I-90, exit 22, just n. **Facility:** Said to be Boston's oldest continuously operating hotel, the recently renovated boutique-style property offers intimate-size guest rooms. Smoke free premises. 143 units. 139 one- and 3 two-bedroom standard units. 1 one-bedroom suite. 7 stories, interior corridors. *Bath:* combo or shower only. **Parking:** valet. **Terms:** cancellation fee imposed. **Amenities:** voice mail, safes, irons, hair dryers. **Leisure Activities:** exercise room. **Guest Services:** valet laundry, wireless Internet. **Free Special Amenities: newspaper and high-speed Internet.**

COURTYARD BOSTON DOWNTOWN/TREMONT *Book great rates at AAA.com* Phone: (617)426-1400 23

Hotel
$124-$269 All Year

Address: 275 Tremont St 02116 **Location:** Between Stuart and Oak sts; in Theater District. Adjacent to Shubert Theatre. **Facility:** Smoke free premises. 315 units. 307 one-bedroom standard units. 8 one-bedroom suites, some with whirlpools. 15 stories, interior corridors. *Bath:* combo or shower only. **Parking:** valet. **Terms:** cancellation fee imposed. **Amenities:** high-speed Internet, dual phone lines, voice mail, irons, hair dryers. **Dining:** nightclub. **Leisure Activities:** exercise room. **Guest Services:** valet and coin laundry. **Business Services:** conference facilities, business center. **Free Special Amenities: local telephone calls and high-speed Internet.**

AAA Benefit:
Members save a minimum 5% off the best available rate.

COURTYARD BY MARRIOTT BOSTON, COPLEY SQUARE *Book great rates at AAA.com* Phone: (617)437-9300 31

Hotel
$159-$269 All Year

Address: 88 Exeter St 02116 **Location:** I-90, exit 22, just n; between Huntington Ave and Boylston St. **Facility:** Smoke free premises. 81 units. 76 one-bedroom standard units. 5 one-bedroom suites. 10 stories, interior corridors. *Bath:* combo or shower only. **Parking:** valet. **Terms:** cancellation fee imposed. **Amenities:** video games (fee), high-speed Internet, dual phone lines, voice mail, irons, hair dryers. **Leisure Activities:** exercise room. **Guest Services:** valet and coin laundry. **Business Services:** business center.

AAA Benefit:
Members save a minimum 5% off the best available rate.

DOUBLETREE HOTEL BOSTON DOWNTOWN *Book great rates at AAA.com* Phone: (617)956-7900 28

Hotel
$99-$379 All Year

Address: 821 Washington St 02111 **Location:** I-93, exit 20 northbound, exit 22 southbound. Opposite New England Medical Center, Theater District. **Facility:** Smoke free premises. 267 units. 256 one-bedroom standard units. 11 one-bedroom suites. 6 stories, interior corridors. *Bath:* combo or shower only. **Parking:** valet. **Terms:** 1-7 night minimum stay, cancellation fee imposed. **Amenities:** dual phone lines, voice mail, irons, hair dryers. *Some:* CD players. **Guest Services:** valet laundry, wireless Internet. **Business Services:** meeting rooms, business center.

DOUBLETREE
HOTELS·SUITES·RESORTS·CLUBS
AAA Benefit:
Members save 5% or more everyday!

THE ELIOT HOTEL *Book great rates at AAA.com* Phone: (617)267-1607 32

Historic Hotel
$355-$645 All Year

Address: 370 Commonwealth Ave 02215 **Location:** At Massachusetts Ave. Located in historic Back Bay area. **Facility:** The extensive use of Italian marble brings a European-style elegance to the service-oriented hotel, which was built in 1925; staff are attentive. Smoke free premises. 95 units. 16 one-bedroom standard units. 79 one-bedroom suites. 9 stories, interior corridors. *Bath:* combo or shower only. **Parking:** valet. **Terms:** cancellation fee imposed. **Amenities:** dual phone lines, voice mail, honor bars, irons, hair dryers. *Some:* DVD players. **Dining:** Clio, see separate listing. **Leisure Activities:** *Fee:* massage. **Guest Services:** valet laundry, wireless Internet, shoeshine. **Business Services:** meeting rooms, PC. **Free Special Amenities: newspaper and room upgrade (subject to availability with advance reservations).**

(See map and index starting on p. 340)

FAIRMONT BATTERY WHARF
Book great rates at AAA.com   Phone: (617)994-9000

Hotel
$209-$579 All Year

Address: Three Battery Wharf 02109 **Location:** At Battery Wharf, e of north end. **Facility:** Although it's in a remote setting, the hotel is within walking distance of North End and Faneuil Hall Marketplace. Smoke free premises. 150 units. 128 one-bedroom standard units. 22 one-bedroom suites, some with whirlpools. 5 stories, interior corridors. **Parking:** valet. **Terms:** cancellation fee imposed. **Amenities:** DVD players, CD players, high-speed Internet (fee), dual phone lines, voice mail, honor bars, irons, hair dryers. **Dining:** Sensing, see separate listing. **Leisure Activities:** exercise room. **Guest Services:** valet laundry, airport transportation-Boston Logan International Airport, area transportation-Back Bay, financial district & water taxi, wireless Internet. **Business Services:** conference facilities, business center. *(See color ad p 357)*

FREE newspaper and room upgrade (subject to availability with advance reservations)

THE FAIRMONT COPLEY PLAZA BOSTON
Book great rates at AAA.com   Phone: (617)267-5300

Classic Historic
Hotel
$209-$579 All Year

Address: 138 St. James Ave 02116 **Location:** At Copley Square. **Facility:** Huge ballrooms and crystal chandeliers set the tone for this elegant, historic hotel set in a pedestrian-friendly area close to an open-air mall. 383 units. 366 one-bedroom standard units. 17 one-bedroom suites, some with whirlpools. 6 stories, interior corridors. *Bath:* combo or shower only. **Parking:** valet. **Terms:** cancellation fee imposed. **Amenities:** video library, high-speed Internet (fee), dual phone lines, voice mail, safes, honor bars, irons, hair dryers. *Some:* DVD players, CD players. **Dining:** The Oak Room, see separate listing, entertainment. **Leisure Activities:** exercise room. **Guest Services:** valet laundry, wireless Internet. **Business Services:** conference facilities, business center. *(See color ad p 358)*

Read, Share, Ask, Plan. Join the travel
conversation at AAATravelViews.com

(See map and index starting on p. 340)

FIFTEEN BEACON *Book at AAA.com* **Phone:** (617)670-1500 **10**

▼▼▼ ▼▼▼

Hotel
$250-$1400 All Year

Address: 15 Beacon St 02108 **Location:** Just e of State House; just ne of Boston Common; center. **Facility:** Conveniently located near the State House, Boston Common and other historical attractions, the upscale hotel is distinguished by high-end amenities. Smoke free premises. 60 units. 57 one-bedroom standard units, some with whirlpools. 3 one-bedroom suites with whirlpools. 10 stories, interior corridors. *Bath:* combo or shower only. **Parking:** valet. **Terms:** cancellation fee imposed. **Amenities:** DVD players, CD players, high-speed Internet, dual phone lines, voice mail, fax, safes, honor bars, hair dryers. **Dining:** Mooo..., see separate listing. **Guest Services:** valet laundry, area transportation, wireless Internet. **Business Services:** meeting rooms, PC.

ASK FEE 🛬 🍴 24🛎 🍸 FEE 🏋 ⊗ 🎥 / SOME UNITS FEE 🐾

FOUR SEASONS HOTEL BOSTON *Book great rates at AAA.com* **Phone:** (617)338-4400 **20**

(AAA) (SAVE)

▼▼▼ ▼▼▼

Hotel
$450-$700 All Year

Address: 200 Boylston St 02116 **Location:** Between Arlington and Charles sts. Opposite Public Gardens. **Facility:** Attention to service characterizes this luxury hotel; guest rooms overlook a manicured roof-garden or Boston's Public Garden. Smoke free premises. 273 units. 196 one-bedroom standard units. 77 one-bedroom suites. 16 stories, interior corridors. *Bath:* combo or shower only. **Parking:** valet. **Terms:** cancellation fee imposed. **Amenities:** video library, DVD players, CD players, high-speed Internet (fee), dual phone lines, voice mail, safes, honor bars, irons, hair dryers. *Some:* fax. **Dining:** entertainment. **Pool(s):** heated indoor. **Leisure Activities:** saunas, whirlpool, steamrooms, spa. **Guest Services:** valet laundry, airport transportation (fee)-Boston Logan International Airport, area transportation-within 3 mi, wireless Internet. **Business Services:** conference facilities, business center. **Free Special Amenities:** newspaper.

FEE 🛬 🍴 24🛎 🍸 🏋 CALL 🄜 🏊 🏋 ⊗ ⊗ 🎥 / SOME UNITS 🐾

HARBORSIDE INN OF BOSTON *Book at AAA.com* **Phone:** (617)723-7500 **9**

▼▼▼

Boutique Contemporary Retro Hotel
$139-$325 All Year

Address: 185 State St 02109 **Location:** Jct Atlantic Ave. **Facility:** Smoke free premises. 98 one-bedroom standard units. 8 stories, interior corridors. *Bath:* combo or shower only. **Parking:** no self-parking. **Terms:** cancellation fee imposed. **Amenities:** DVD players, CD players, voice mail, irons, hair dryers. **Guest Services:** valet laundry, wireless Internet. **Business Services:** PC. ⊗ 🎥

▼ See AAA listing p 356 ▼

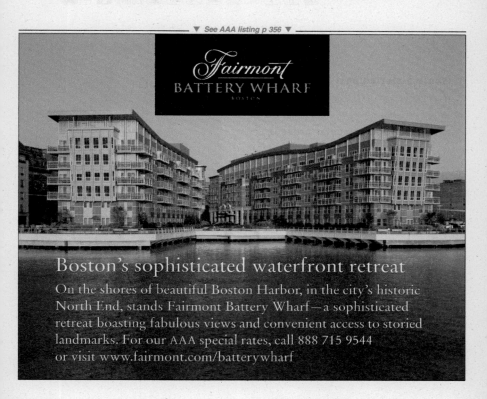

Fairmont
BATTERY WHARF
BOSTON

Boston's sophisticated waterfront retreat

On the shores of beautiful Boston Harbor, in the city's historic North End, stands Fairmont Battery Wharf—a sophisticated retreat boasting fabulous views and convenient access to storied landmarks. For our AAA special rates, call 888 715 9544 or visit www.fairmont.com/batterywharf

(See map and index starting on p. 340)

HILTON BOSTON BACK BAY *Book great rates at AAA.com* Phone: (617)867-6000

AAA SAVE

Hotel
$179-$639 All Year

Address: 40 Dalton St 02115 **Location:** At Dalton and Belvidere sts. Adjacent to Prudential Center. **Facility:** Smoke free premises. 390 units. 389 one-bedroom standard units. 1 two-bedroom suite. 26 stories, interior corridors. *Bath:* combo or shower only. **Parking:** on-site (fee). **Terms:** 1-7 night minimum stay, cancellation fee imposed. **Amenities:** video games (fee), dual phone lines, voice mail, safes, irons, hair dryers. **Dining:** 2 restaurants, nightclub. **Pool(s):** heated indoor. **Leisure Activities:** whirlpool, exercise room. **Guest Services:** valet laundry, wireless Internet. **Business Services:** conference facilities, business center.

Hilton

AAA Benefit:
Members save 5% or more everyday!

HILTON BOSTON FINANCIAL DISTRICT *Book great rates at AAA.com* Phone: (617)556-0006

AAA SAVE

Historic
Hotel
$119-$479 All Year

Address: 89 Broad St 02110 **Location:** Corner of Broad and Franklin sts. Located in financial district. **Facility:** A full complement of amenities enhance the stylishly-appointed guest rooms at this luxury hotel; about 12 rooms are cozier than may be expected. Smoke free premises. 362 units. 296 one-bedroom standard units. 66 one-bedroom suites. 14 stories, interior corridors. *Bath:* combo or shower only. **Parking:** valet. **Terms:** 1-7 night minimum stay, cancellation fee imposed. **Amenities:** dual phone lines, voice mail, honor bars, irons, hair dryers, high-speed Internet. **Dining:** Caliterra, see separate listing. **Leisure Activities:** exercise room. **Guest Services:** valet laundry, wireless Internet. **Business Services:** conference facilities, business center.

Hilton

AAA Benefit:
Members save 5% or more everyday!

HOLIDAY INN-BOSTON AT BEACON HILL *Book at AAA.com* Phone: (617)742-7630 6

Hotel
$229-$329 5/1-11/13
$189-$259 11/14-4/30

Address: 5 Blossom St 02114 **Location:** At Cambridge and Blossom sts; center. Located in Beacon Hill District. **Facility:** Smoke free premises. 303 units. 301 one-bedroom standard units. 2 one-bedroom suites. 14 stories, interior corridors. *Bath:* combo or shower only. **Parking:** valet. **Terms:** check-in 4 pm, cancellation fee imposed. **Amenities:** video games (fee), voice mail, irons, hair dryers. *Some:* high-speed Internet. **Pool(s):** heated indoor. **Leisure Activities:** lifeguard on duty, exercise room. **Guest Services:** valet and coin laundry, wireless Internet. **Business Services:** meeting rooms, business center.

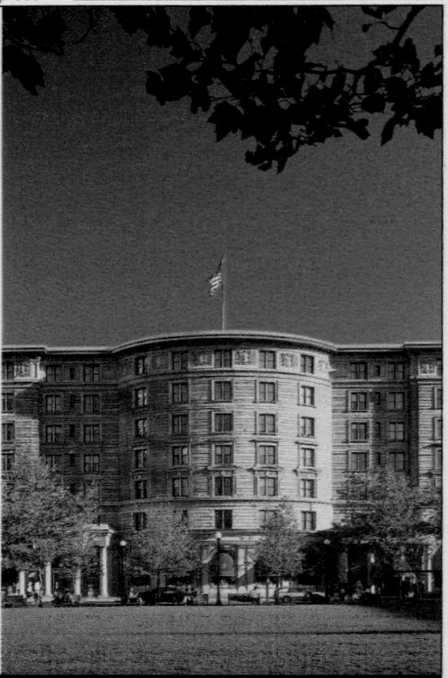

▼ See AAA listing p 356 ▼

(See map and index starting on p. 340)

HOTEL 140   *Book great rates at AAA.com*   Phone: (617)585-5600   33

AAA SAVE
◇◇◇
· Hotel
$139-$389 5/1-10/31
$109-$169 11/1-4/30

Address: 140 Clarendon St 02116 **Location:** At Stuart St; borders Back Bay and south end. **Facility:** Smoke free premises. 60 units. 57 one-bedroom standard units, some with kitchens. 3 two-bedroom suites, some with kitchens. 14 stories, interior corridors. *Bath:* combo or shower only. **Parking:** on-site (fee). **Terms:** 3 day cancellation notice-fee imposed. **Amenities:** high-speed Internet, voice mail, irons, hair dryers. *Some:* DVD players. **Leisure Activities:** limited exercise equipment. **Guest Services:** coin laundry, wireless Internet. **Business Services:** meeting rooms, business center. **Free Special Amenities:** continental breakfast and high-speed Internet.

[icons] / SOME UNITS FEE

HOTEL COMMONWEALTH   *Book great rates at AAA.com*   Phone: (617)933-5000   34

AAA SAVE
◇◇◇
Hotel
$269-$498 5/1-11/30
$209-$339 12/1-4/30

Address: 500 Commonwealth Ave 02215 **Location:** On SR 2; at Beacon St and Brookline Ave. Located in Kenmore Square. **Facility:** This beautiful hotel has luxurious decor and details making it a lovely destination for both business and leisure travelers. Smoke free premises. 149 one-bedroom standard units. 5 stories, interior corridors. *Bath:* combo or shower only. **Parking:** valet. **Terms:** cancellation fee imposed. **Amenities:** video library, DVD players, CD players, high-speed Internet, dual phone lines, voice mail, safes, honor bars, irons, hair dryers. *Some:* video games. **Dining:** Eastern Standard Kitchen and Drinks, see separate listing. **Leisure Activities:** exercise room. *Fee:* massage. **Guest Services:** valet laundry, wireless Internet. **Business Services:** conference facilities, business center. [icons] / SOME UNITS FEE

HYATT REGENCY BOSTON   *Book great rates at AAA.com*   Phone: (617)912-1234   17

AAA SAVE
◇◇◇
Hotel
$159-$599 All Year

Address: 1 Ave De Lafayette 02111 **Location:** Just e of Boston Common at Lafayette Pl. **Facility:** Guest rooms on several floors of this heart-of-town hotel look out onto a central, atrium-like common area; convenient to the theater district. Smoke free premises. 498 units. 479 one-bedroom standard units. 19 one-bedroom suites, some with whirlpools. 21 stories, interior corridors. *Bath:* combo or shower only. **Parking:** valet. **Terms:** check-in 4 pm, cancellation fee imposed. **Amenities:** video games (fee), voice mail, honor bars, irons, hair dryers. *Some:* high-speed Internet (fee). **Pool(s):** heated indoor. **Leisure Activities:** saunas, steamroom, exercise room. *Fee:* massage. **Guest Services:** valet laundry, wireless Internet. **Business Services:** conference facilities, business center.

[icons] / SOME UNITS

INTERCONTINENTAL BOSTON   *Book great rates at AAA.com*   Phone: (617)747-1000   16

AAA SAVE
◇◇◇
Hotel
$319-$599 5/1-10/31
$249-$499 11/1-4/30

Address: 510 Atlantic Ave 02210 **Location:** I-93, exit 23 southbound; exit 20 northbound; at Pearl St. **Facility:** A luxury, residential appeal is found throughout the property; units on the top floors provide views of the city or water. Smoke free premises. 424 units. 398 one-bedroom standard units. 26 one-bedroom suites. 21 stories, interior corridors. **Parking:** on-site (fee) and valet. **Amenities:** high-speed Internet (fee), dual phone lines, voice mail, safes, honor bars, irons, hair dryers. **Dining:** 2 restaurants, also, Miel, see separate listing. **Pool(s):** heated indoor. **Leisure Activities:** steamrooms, exercise room, spa. **Guest Services:** valet laundry, wireless Internet. **Business Services:** conference facilities, business center. *(See color ad p 361)*

[icons] / SOME UNITS FEE

FREE newspaper

THE LANGHAM, BOSTON   *Book great rates at AAA.com*   Phone: (617)451-1900   14

AAA SAVE
◇◇◇
Hotel
$195-$535 All Year

Address: 250 Franklin St 02110 **Location:** On Post Office Square; center. Located in financial district across from park. **Facility:** A designated landmark, this Renaissance Revival-style building was constructed in 1922 as the Federal Reserve Bank. Smoke free premises. 318 units. 300 one-bedroom standard units. 18 one-bedroom suites, some with whirlpools. 9 stories, interior corridors. *Bath:* combo or shower only. **Parking:** valet. **Terms:** cancellation fee imposed. **Amenities:** dual phone lines, voice mail, safes, honor bars, irons, hair dryers. *Fee:* video games, high-speed Internet. *Some:* DVD players, CD players. **Dining:** entertainment. **Pool(s):** heated indoor. **Leisure Activities:** saunas, whirlpool, spa. **Guest Services:** valet laundry, wireless Internet. **Business Services:** meeting rooms, business center.

[icons] / SOME UNITS FEE

FREE local telephone calls and newspaper

(See map and index starting on p. 340)

THE LENOX HOTEL *Book great rates at AAA.com* **Phone:** (617)536-5300 26

Classic Historic
Hotel
$195-$465 All Year

Address: 61 Exeter St 02116 **Location:** I-90, exit 22, just n at Boylston. Adjacent to library and Prudential Center. **Facility:** Richly decorated accommodations and common areas are characteristic of this hotel; some guest rooms include a fireplace. Smoke free premises. 214 units. 210 one-bedroom standard units. 4 one-bedroom suites, some with whirlpools. 11 stories, interior corridors. **Parking:** valet. **Terms:** cancellation fee imposed. **Amenities:** CD players, dual phone lines, voice mail, safes, irons, hair dryers. *Some:* DVD players. **Dining:** 2 restaurants. **Leisure Activities:** exercise room. **Guest Services:** valet laundry, wireless Internet. **Business Services:** meeting rooms, business center. **Free Special Amenities:** local telephone calls and high-speed Internet.

🍽 24 🛬 ✉ 🎥 🖨 / SOME UNITS FEE 🛏

THE LIBERTY HOTEL *Book great rates at AAA.com* **Phone:** (617)224-4000 5

Hotel
$295-$650 All Year

Address: 215 Charles St 02114 **Location:** I-93, exit 26 (Storrow Dr). **Facility:** Situated in the iconic 1851 Charles Street Jail, the property's modern decor and upscale accommodations create a memorable stay. Smoke free premises. 298 units. 288 one-bedroom standard units. 10 one-bedroom suites. 5-16 stories, interior corridors. *Bath:* combo or shower only. **Parking:** valet. **Terms:** cancellation fee imposed. **Amenities:** high-speed Internet, dual phone lines, voice mail, safes, honor bars, irons, hair dryers. **Dining:** 2 restaurants, also, Scampo, see separate listing. **Leisure Activities:** exercise room. **Guest Services:** valet laundry, wireless Internet. **Business Services:** conference facilities, business center. *(See color ad p 362)*

🍽 24 CALL 🖳M ✉ 🎥 / SOME UNITS 🛏

FREE newspaper and high-speed Internet

▼ See AAA listing p 360 ▼

REST ASSURED, OUR BEDS ARE AMONG
THE MOST COMFORTABLE IN BOSTON

Do you live an InterContinental life?

INTERCONTINENTAL.
BOSTON

510 Atlantic Avenue • 617.747.1000   intercontinentalboston.com

(See map and index starting on p. 340)

MANDARIN ORIENTAL, BOSTON   *Book great rates at AAA.com*   Phone: (617)535-8888   29

Hotel
$345-$995 All Year

Address: 776 Boylston St 02199 **Location:** At Prudential Center. **Facility:** The luxury hotel's staff is in tune with guests' needs and wants. The bedding is particularly memorable, as is the state-of-the-art full-service spa. Smoke free premises. 148 units. 136 one-bedroom standard units. 12 one-bedroom suites, some with whirlpools. 15 stories, interior corridors. **Parking:** valet. **Terms:** cancellation fee imposed. **Amenities:** high-speed Internet (fee), dual phone lines, voice mail, safes, honor bars, irons, hair dryers. *Some:* DVD players, CD players. **Dining:** 3 restaurants. **Leisure Activities:** spa. **Guest Services:** valet laundry, area transportation-within 2 mi, wireless Internet. **Business Services:** conference facilities, business center. **Free Special Amenities:** newspaper.

CALL / SOME UNITS

▼ *See AAA listing p 361* ▼

(See map and index starting on p. 340)

MILLENNIUM BOSTONIAN HOTEL   *Book at AAA.com*   Phone: (617)523-3600   **7**

Hotel
$189-$389 All Year

Address: 26 North St 02109 Location: West end of Faneuil Hall Marketplace. Facility: Smoke free premises. 201 units. 196 one-bedroom standard units. 5 one-bedroom suites. 8 stories, interior corridors. Bath: combo or shower only. Parking: valet. Terms: cancellation fee imposed. Amenities: high-speed Internet (fee), dual phone lines, voice mail, safes, honor bars, irons, hair dryers. Leisure Activities: exercise room. Guest Services: valet laundry, wireless Internet. Business Services: meeting rooms, business center.

NINE ZERO HOTEL   *Book great rates at AAA.com*   Phone: (617)772-5800   **12**

Boutique Hotel
$249-$599 5/1-11/20
$229-$599 11/21-4/30

Address: 90 Tremont St 02108 Location: Just ne of Boston Common; motor entrance on Bosworth. Facility: This sleek, modern boutique-style hotel offers extensive in-room business amenities including a printer/copier; headboards resemble a wingback chair. Smoke free premises. 190 units. 185 one-bedroom standard units. 5 one-bedroom suites, some with whirlpools. 19 stories, interior corridors. Bath: combo or shower only. Parking: valet. Terms: cancellation fee imposed. Amenities: video games (fee), CD players, high-speed Internet, dual phone lines, voice mail, safes, honor bars, irons, hair dryers. Some: DVD players. Dining: KO Prime, see separate listing. Leisure Activities: exercise room. Guest Services: valet laundry, wireless Internet. Business Services: meeting rooms, business center.

ONYX HOTEL   *Book great rates at AAA.com*   Phone: (617)557-9955   **3**

Boutique Hotel
$179-$719 5/1-11/19
$159-$559 11/20-4/30

Address: 155 Portland St 02114 Location: Just n of corner of Merrimac and Traverse sts; 3 blks s of TD Bank North Garden. Facility: The trendy, boutique hotel is a bit off-the-beaten-path but convenient to the Fleet Center and Quincy Market-Faneuil Hall. Smoke free premises. 112 units. 110 one-bedroom standard units. 2 one-bedroom suites. 10 stories, interior corridors. Bath: combo or shower only. Parking: valet. Terms: cancellation fee imposed. Amenities: video games (fee), dual phone lines, voice mail, safes, honor bars, irons, hair dryers. Dining: Ruby Room, see separate listing. Leisure Activities: exercise room. Guest Services: valet laundry, wireless Internet. Business Services: meeting rooms. Fee: PC, fax.

RADISSON HOTEL BOSTON   *Book great rates at AAA.com*   Phone: (617)482-1800   **21**

Hotel
$159-$429 All Year

Address: 200 Stuart St 02116 Location: At Park Square and Charles St. Facility: Smoke free premises. 356 one-bedroom standard units. 24 stories, interior corridors. Bath: combo or shower only. Parking: on-site (fee) and valet. Terms: cancellation fee imposed. Amenities: video games (fee), high-speed Internet, voice mail, safes, irons, hair dryers. Pool(s): heated indoor. Leisure Activities: sun deck, exercise room. Fee: driving range. Guest Services: valet laundry, wireless Internet. Business Services: conference facilities, PC (fee). Free Special Amenities: newspaper and high-speed Internet.

(See map and index starting on p. 340)

**RESIDENCE INN BY MARRIOTT BOSTON HARBOR
ON TUDOR WHARF**   *Book great rates at AAA.com*   Phone: (617)242-9000

AAA SAVE
▽▽▽▽

Hotel
$229-$349 All Year

Address: 34-44 Charles River Ave 02129 **Location:** Just se of SR 99 at Charlestown Bridge. Located on Tudor Wharf. **Facility:** Smoke free premises. 168 units. 60 one-bedroom standard units with efficiencies. 100 one- and 8 two-bedroom suites with efficiencies. 8 stories, interior corridors. *Bath:* combo or shower only. **Parking:** valet. **Terms:** cancellation fee imposed. **Amenities:** video games (fee), high-speed Internet, dual phone lines, voice mail, irons, hair dryers. **Pool(s):** heated indoor. **Leisure Activities:** whirlpool, exercise room. **Guest Services:** valet and coin laundry, wireless Internet. **Business Services:** meeting rooms, business center. **Free Special Amenities: full breakfast and newspaper.**

🍴 CALL 🛗M 🏊 ✖ 🎥 🛎 🖨 🖥 / SOME UNITS FEE 🐾

▼ *See AAA listing p 406* ▼

(See map and index starting on p. 340)

THE RITZ-CARLTON, BOSTON COMMON *Book great rates at AAA.com* **Phone:** (617)574-7100 **18**

Hotel

$495-$795 5/1-11/30

$395-$695 12/1-4/30

Address: 10 Avery St 02111 **Location:** At Washington and Avery sts; 1 blk e of Boston Common. **Facility:** Hip and sleek meet elegance in this luxury hotel, which occupies the 9th through 12th floors; sandwiched between the financial and theater districts. Smoke free premises. 193 units. 148 one-bedroom standard units. 31 one- and 14 two-bedroom suites, some with whirlpools. 12 stories, interior corridors. **Parking:** valet. **Terms:** cancellation fee imposed. **Amenities:** CD players, dual phone lines, voice mail, safes, honor bars, irons, hair dryers. *Fee:* video games, high-speed Internet. *Some:* DVD players. **Pool(s):** heated indoor. **Leisure Activities:** spa, basketball. *Fee:* saunas, whirlpools, steamrooms, racquetball courts. **Guest Services:** valet laundry, area transportation, wireless Internet. **Business Services:** conference facilities, business center.

FEE 🚭 🍽 24 CALL 🄼 🏊 FEE 🛎 🗙 🗴 🎥 / SOME UNITS FEE 🐕 💻

SHERATON BOSTON *Book great rates at AAA.com* **Phone:** (617)236-2000 **37**

Hotel

$169-$599 All Year

Address: 39 Dalton St 02199 **Location:** I-90, exit 22. Located at Prudential Center. **Facility:** Smoke free premises. 1216 units. 1066 one-bedroom standard units. 150 one-bedroom suites. 29 stories, interior corridors. *Bath:* combo or shower only. **Parking:** on-site (fee) and valet. **Terms:** cancellation fee imposed. **Amenities:** dual phone lines, voice mail, irons, hair dryers. *Fee:* video games, high-speed Internet. **Dining:** 3 restaurants. **Pool(s):** heated indoor/outdoor. **Leisure Activities:** sauna, whirlpool, sun deck. **Guest Services:** valet laundry. **Business Services:** conference facilities, business center.

ECO 🍽 24 🛎 CALL 🄼 🏊 📶 🗙 🗴 🎥 💻 / SOME UNITS 🐕

▼ *See AAA listing p 387* ▼

Travel Basics: Keep a AAA Atlas in every vehicle in the household.

(See map and index starting on p. 340)

TAJ BOSTON   *Book great rates at AAA.com*   Phone: 617/536-5700   **19**

Historic
Hotel
Rates not provided

Address: 15 Arlington St 02117 **Location:** At Arlington and Newbury sts; overlooks the Public Gardens. **Facility:** Old-World charm merges with graciousness, elegance and history at this 1920s Boston landmark; service is friendly and appreciative. 273 units. 228 one-bedroom standard units. 45 one-bedroom suites, some with whirlpools. 17 stories, interior corridors. *Bath:* combo or shower only. **Parking:** on-site (fee) and valet. **Amenities:** video library, CD players, dual phone lines, voice mail, safes, honor bars, irons, hair dryers. *Fee:* video games, high-speed Internet. *Some:* DVD players. **Dining:** The Cafe, see separate listing. **Leisure Activities:** exercise room. *Fee:* massage. **Guest Services:** valet laundry, airport transportation (fee)-General Edward Lawrence Logan International Airport, area transportation-downtown, wireless Internet. **Business Services:** conference facilities, business center. **Free Special Amenities:** newspaper and early check-in/late check-out.

THE WESTIN COPLEY PLACE BOSTON   *Book great rates at AAA.com*   Phone: (617)262-9600   **35**

Hotel
$179-$569 All Year

Address: 10 Huntington Ave 02116 **Location:** I-90, exit 22, at Copley Square. **Facility:** Overstuffed seating in earth tones, soft lighting and a welcoming staff contribute to a cozy, comfortable stay at this contemporary hotel. Smoke free premises. 803 units. 798 one-bedroom standard units. 5 one-bedroom suites. 36 stories, interior corridors. *Bath:* combo or shower only. **Parking:** valet. **Terms:** cancellation fee imposed. **Amenities:** dual phone lines, voice mail, safes, honor bars, irons, hair dryers. *Fee:* video games, high-speed Internet. *Some:* DVD players, CD players. **Dining:** 4 restaurants, also, Turner Fisheries Restaurant & Bar, see separate listing. **Pool(s):** heated indoor. **Leisure Activities:** whirlpool, spa. **Guest Services:** valet laundry, wireless Internet. **Business Services:** conference facilities, business center.

WESTIN
HOTELS & RESORTS

AAA Benefit:
Enjoy up to 15% off
your next stay, plus
Starwood Preferred
Guest® bonuses.

—— **WHERE TO DINE** ——

29 NEWBURY   Phone: 617/536-0290   **61**

American
$9-$33

The eclectic menu has hints of Asian and American cuisine. A cozy bar and dining area make for a fun dinner or lunch. Casual dress. **Bar:** Full bar. **Reservations:** accepted. **Hours:** 11:30 am-close, Sun from 10 am. Closed: 11/25, 12/25. **Address:** 29 Newbury St 02116 **Location:** Between Berkeley and Arlington sts. **Parking:** street.

33 RESTAURANT & LOUNGE   Phone: 617/572-3311   **103**

American
$23-$51

Ultra hip design elements—including dramatic lighting, brick archways and maple-paneled ceilings—set the scene for a cool and serene dining experience, while world beats lend an exotic air to the clubby atmosphere. The contemporary American menu attracts a mixed crowd of devotees hungry for truffled corn vichyssoise, pappardelle with braised short ribs and ahi tuna with yuzu syrup. If available, the homemade lemon-olive oil ice cream is different and dynamite. Dressy casual. **Bar:** Full bar. **Reservations:** suggested. **Hours:** 5 pm-11 pm. Closed: 11/25, 12/25; also Sun & Mon. **Address:** 33 Stanhope St 02116 **Location:** Between Berkeley and Clarendon sts. **Parking:** valet and street.

75 CHESTNUT   Phone: 617/227-2175   **50**

American
$8-$20

The cozy restaurant, tucked among the brownstones of Beacon Hill, is just off the Public Gardens and Boston Common. Padded tables covered with linens, a painted-tin ceiling and artwork in ornate frames complement innovative offerings along the lines of grilled figs, clam and shrimp chowder, salmon steamed in lettuce leaves and truffled macaroni and cheese. A lighter menu is presented in the bar. Patrons can have nearby parking validated. Dressy casual. **Bar:** Full bar. **Reservations:** suggested. **Hours:** 5 pm-10 pm; Saturday & Sunday brunch 11:30 am-2:30 pm 9/1-6/30. Closed: 12/25. **Address:** 75 Chestnut St 02108 **Location:** 1 blk n of Public Gardens, just w of Charles St. **Parking:** no self-parking.

ABE & LOUIE'S   Phone: 617/536-6300   **94**

Steak
$14-$50

Across from the Prudential building and Hines Convention Center in Back Bay is one of the city's newer steakhouses. In the dining room, dark wood-paneled walls rise to meet an arched gold-leaf-covered ceiling. While the forte is dry-aged, prime steaks and chops, guests also can savor swordfish, salmon, tuna, lobster, shrimp or chicken. Side dishes such as creamed spinach or blue cheese mashed potatoes are sized to share. Service is crisp and quick, especially at lunch. Dressy casual. **Bar:** Full bar. **Reservations:** suggested, for dinner. **Hours:** 11:30 am-11 pm, Fri & Sat-midnight. Closed: 12/25. **Address:** 793 Boylston St 02116 **Location:** At Fairfield St. **Parking:** no self-parking.

ANTONIO'S CUCINA ITALIANA   Phone: 617/367-3310   **27**

Italian
$6-$17

A local favorite near Massachusetts General Hospital, the restaurant sometimes has guests outside eager to be seated in the small, often-crowded dining room. The kitchen prepares a nice selection of pasta dishes, including the house favorite lobster ravioli, as well as veal, chicken and seafood. In addition to beer and wine, it offers after-dinner drinks. Casual dress. **Bar:** Beer & wine. **Reservations:** accepted. **Hours:** 11 am-10 pm, Fri & Sat-10:30 pm. Closed: 11/25, 12/25; also Sun. **Address:** 288 Cambridge St 02114 **Location:** Between Grove and Anderson sts; 1 blk from Massachusetts General Hospital. **Parking:** no self-parking.

ARTU   Phone: 617/742-4336

Italian
$10-$28

Service is friendly, and the staff welcomes every patron like family. Both the menu variety and portion sizes are large. The menu consists of freshly made Italian dishes from traditional riso con fagioli soup to mouthwatering pasta dishes to several signature dishes. Casual dress. **Bar:** Full bar. **Reservations:** suggested. **Hours:** 11 am-11 pm. Closed: 12/25. **Address:** 6 Prince St 02113 **Location:** Just e of Hanover St. **Parking:** street.

(See map and index starting on p. 340)

ARTU

Italian
$10-$28

Phone: 617/227-9023

Service is friendly, and the staff welcomes every patron like family. Both the menu variety and portion sizes are large. The menu consists of freshly made Italian dishes from traditional riso con fagioli soup to mouthwatering pasta dishes to several signature dishes. Casual dress. **Bar:** Beer & wine. **Reservations:** not accepted. **Hours:** 11 am-11 pm, Sun-Tues from 5 pm. Closed major holidays. **Address:** 89 Charles St 02114 **Location:** Just s of Mt Vernon St. **Parking:** street.

ATLANTIC FISH

Seafood
$10-$36

Phone: 617/267-4000   93

A nautical feel prevails at this contemporary spot where the fresh seafood options include raw-bar items, homemade chowders and many baked and fried favorites. The unrestrained use of plank wood on the curved ceiling, walls and floors lends to the at-sea atmosphere. A hand-painted seascape mural lines one set of tables, while model ships encased in glass add to the décor in other areas. Dressy casual. **Bar:** Full bar. **Reservations:** suggested. **Hours:** 11 am-11 pm, Fri & Sat-midnight. Closed: 12/25. **Address:** 761 Boylston St 02116 **Location:** Between Fairfield and Exeter sts. **Parking:** street.

AUDUBON CIRCLE RESTAURANT BAR

American
$8-$17

Phone: 617/421-1910   107

At the Audubon Circle in Kenmore Square, the minimalist restaurant is a popular spot for nightlife. Grilled sandwiches and steaks are dinner favorites. Casual dress. **Bar:** Full bar. **Reservations:** not accepted. **Hours:** 11:30 am-1 am, Sun from 11 am. Closed: 7/4, 11/25, 12/24, 12/25. **Address:** 838 Beacon St 02215 **Location:** Kenmore Square at Audubon Cir. **Parking:** street.

BANGKOK BLUE THAI RESTAURANT

Thai
$7-$18

Phone: 617/266-1010   81

The quaint restaurant prepares a nice selection of Thai dishes. Menu offerings range from vegetarian, curry and noodle dishes to seafood, beef and duck selections. Seasonal sidewalk dining is popular from April through October. Casual dress. **Bar:** Beer & wine. **Reservations:** accepted. **Hours:** 11:30 am-3 & 5-10 pm, Sat & Sun noon-10 pm. Closed major holidays. **Address:** 651 Boylston St 02116 **Location:** Between Exeter and Dartmouth sts. **Parking:** no self-parking.

BEER WORKS

American
$8-$19

Phone: 617/896-2337

Of the 50 microbrews created at the brewery, 16 are on tap at any given time. Food favorites from the "bold American" menu include beer-basted barbecue steak tips, sugarcane-seared salmon, sour cream and chive fries and the Big Dig brownie. The second level has 15 billiard tables. Two overhead glass garage doors open onto seating for about 40 on the sidewalk. Service is friendly and efficient. Parking is validated except during Fleet Center events. Casual dress. **Bar:** Beer & wine. **Reservations:** not accepted. **Hours:** 11:30 am-midnight. Closed: 11/25, 12/25. **Address:** 112 Canal St 02114 **Location:** Just s of Fleet Center and North Station. **Parking:** no self-parking.

BHINDI BAZAAR INDIAN CAFE

Indian
$11-$16

Phone: 617/450-0660   106

The small cafe provides a simple, comfortable setting for enjoying Indian food. The kitchen prepares dishes from the northern, southern, eastern, central and coastal regions of India. A lunch buffet is set up daily. Casual dress. **Bar:** Beer & wine. **Reservations:** accepted. **Hours:** 11:30 am-3 & 5-11 pm, Sat noon-4 & 5-11 pm, Sun noon-4 & 5-10 pm. **Address:** 95 Massachusetts Ave 02115 **Location:** Between Newbury St and Commonwealth Ave. **Parking:** no self-parking.

BLU

French
$13-$34

Phone: 617/375-8550   59

Off the lobby, the restaurant is made up of two distinct sections: an informal cafeteria and a "tablecloth" full-service outlet. Corn bisque or something from the raw bar paves the way for interesting main courses such as lacquered quail and Delmonico steak with Gorgonzola and roasted fig. Tempting desserts hit the right finishing note. Service is right on, but the floor-to-ceiling windows and openness contribute to a high noise level. Dressy casual. **Bar:** Full bar. **Reservations:** suggested. **Hours:** 11:30 am-2 & 5:30-10 pm, Fri-11 pm, Sat 5:30 pm-11 pm. Closed major holidays; also Sun. **Address:** 4 Avery St 02111 **Location:** Between Tremont and Washington sts; southeast corner of Boston Common; in Sports Club LA, 4th floor. **Parking:** on-site (fee).

BONFIRE

Steak
$18-$44

Phone: 617/262-3473   76

Todd English is responsible for this trendy steakhouse, which resides in a historic hotel. Some of the high-quality cuts of meat are skewered and roasted or grilled. Prime steaks are cooked over maple and apple wood. Valet parking is available. Dressy casual. **Bar:** Full bar. **Reservations:** suggested. **Hours:** 5 pm-close. Closed major holidays; also Sun. **Address:** 50 Park Plaza 02116 **Location:** Just s of Boston Common and the Public Gardens; in The Boston Park Plaza Hotel & Towers. **Parking:** street.

BRASSERIE JO

French
$11-$35

Phone: 617/425-3240   112

Home-style Alsatian food is served in the 1940 Parisian-style bistro. Semi-formal attire. **Bar:** Full bar. **Reservations:** accepted. **Hours:** 6:30 am-1 am. **Address:** 120 Huntington Ave 02116 **Location:** Just s of Copley Square; in The Colonnade Boston. **Parking:** on-site (fee) and valet.

BRICCO

Italian
$24-$42

Phone: 617/248-6800   22

The restaurant serves innovative and classic Italian dishes. A richly appointed bar shares the ground floor with a dining room with crisp white table linens, and those seated in the dining room can look through a window wall onto Hanover Street or into the show kitchen. In good weather, the windows open to allow the sounds and sights of the North End to enter. Service is correct and friendly. Dressy casual. **Bar:** Full bar. **Reservations:** suggested. **Hours:** 5 pm-11 pm. Closed major holidays. **Address:** 241 Hanover St 02113 **Location:** Between Richmond and Cross sts; in North End. **Parking:** valet.

(See map and index starting on p. 340)

THE CAFE
Phone: 617/536-5700   **60**

Continental
$15-$50

Overlooking tony Newbury Street, this upscale eatery has plush and comfortable decor within a window-filled dining room. The team of chefs takes great care in preparing top-notch fare of fresh fish and grilled meats with a strong international influence. Dressy casual. **Bar:** Full bar. **Reservations:** suggested. **Hours:** 6:30 am-10 pm; Saturday & Sunday brunch. **Address:** 15 Arlington St 02116 **Location:** At Arlington and Newbury sts; overlooks the Public Gardens; in Taj Boston. **Parking:** valet. CALL &M

CAFFE VITTORIA
Phone: 617/227-7606   **10**

Coffee/Tea
$3-$5

Established in 1929 as the city's first Italian cafe, this place sustains an Old World atmosphere accented by vintage pictures, a display of many antique chrome espresso machines and marble-topped round cafe tables that match the marble tile flooring. The menu is limited to pastries, homemade gelato, cakes and other desserts, in addition to a nice selection of specialty coffees such as cafe mocha, cappuccino and espresso. Casual dress. **Bar:** Full bar. **Hours:** 7 am-midnight, Fri & Sat-12:30 am. **Address:** 296 Hanover St 02113 **Location:** Between Parmenter and Prince sts; in North End. **Parking:** street.

CALITERRA
Phone: 617/348-1234   **46**

American
$15-$36

On the ground floor of a historic hotel, the comfortable restaurant has terrazzo floors and rich woods on the walls. Murals feature the wine country. This place is great for power lunches and relaxing dinners. The seasonally changing, California-influenced menu features one ingredient, such as fresh spring asparagus or figs, for a whole season. Among other choices are pasta dishes, pizza, roast salmon and lamb loin. Service is expedient. Dressy casual. **Bar:** Full bar. **Reservations:** accepted. **Hours:** 6:30 am-11 pm, Sat & Sun from 7 am. **Address:** 89 Broad St 02110 **Location:** Corner of Broad and Franklin sts; in Hilton Boston Financial District. **Parking:** valet. CALL &M

CANTINA ITALIANA
Phone: 617/723-4577   **16**

Italian
$11-$30

An institution since 1931, the restaurant is believed to be the oldest Italian eatery in the North End. Traditional preparations are wonderfully flavorful, the local staff is friendly and knowledgeable, and the prices are reasonable. This is a terrific spot for a night out. Casual dress. **Bar:** Beer & wine. **Reservations:** suggested. **Hours:** 11:30 am-11 pm, Sun noon-10:30 pm. Closed: 11/25, 12/24, 12/25. **Address:** 346 Hanover St 02113 **Location:** Between Tileston and N Bennet sts; in North End. **Parking:** no self-parking.

THE CAPITAL GRILLE
Phone: 617/262-8900   **105**

Steak
$26-$45

Cherry wood and red leather assist in making this "clubby" dining room a beautiful spot to dine on excellent cuts of dry-aged beef. The staff is highly attentive and knowledgeable. Dressy casual. **Bar:** Full bar. **Reservations:** suggested. **Hours:** 5 pm-10 pm, Thurs-Sat to 11 pm, Sun 4 pm-10 pm. Closed: 7/4, 11/25, 12/25; also Super Bowl Sun. **Address:** 359 Newbury St 02115 **Location:** Between Hereford and Massachusetts aves; in Back Bay. **Parking:** valet and street.

CHARLEY'S
Phone: 617/266-3000

American
$9-$24

An institution for many years, the casual eatery on Newbury and Gloucester serves a wide selection of traditional American fare. The lively and fun spot is good for families during lunch and early dinners. Casual dress. **Bar:** Full bar. **Hours:** 11:30 am-midnight, Sat from 9 am, Sun 9 am-11 pm. Closed: 11/25, 12/25. **Address:** 284 Newbury St 02115 **Location:** At Gloucester St. **Parking:** street.

CHART HOUSE
Phone: 617/227-1576   **31**

[SAVE]

Seafood
$30-$45

Directly on the water, the restaurant offers a great view of the waterway and its many yachts. Examples of the fabulous food include prime rib, filet mignon, tomato-basil chicken and varied fresh fish and seafood dishes. Casual dress. **Bar:** Full bar. **Reservations:** accepted. **Hours:** 5 pm-10 pm, Sat 4 pm-10:30 pm, Sun 4 pm-10 pm. Closed: 12/25. **Address:** 60 Long Wharf 02110 **Location:** On Long Wharf. **Parking:** valet.

CHEERS BEACON HILL
Phone: 617/227-9605   **52**

American
$7-$20

Originally the Bull & Finch Pub and inspiration for the "Cheers" TV series, this place is packed during peak tourist seasons. The menu is divided into sections named after the show's characters—such as Sam's starters and "eNormous" burgers—and contains good wholesome pub food and some Boston standards: baked beans, clam chowder, scrod and cream pie. The staff is friendly and upbeat. Casual dress. **Bar:** Full bar. **Reservations:** not accepted. **Hours:** 11:30 am-11:45 pm. Closed: 12/25. **Address:** 84 Beacon St 02108 **Location:** Opposite North End of Public Gardens. **Parking:** no self-parking.

CHEERS FANEUIL HALL
Phone: 617/227-0150   **38**

American
$7-$20

In the heart of the Faneuil Hall complex, the eatery has a bar that replicates the set from the "Cheers" TV series. This place is packed during peak tourist seasons. The menu is divided into sections named after the show's characters—such as Sam's starters and "eNormous" burgers—and contains good wholesome pub food and some Boston standards: baked beans, clam chowder, scrod and cream pie. The staff is friendly and upbeat. Casual dress. **Bar:** Full bar. **Reservations:** not accepted. **Hours:** 11:30 am-11:45 pm. Closed: 12/25. **Address:** 2 Faneuil Hall Market Pl 02109 **Location:** Center; west end of central building in complex. **Parking:** street.

CHINA PEARL
Phone: 617/426-4338   **75**

Chinese
$4-$20

A local favorite, the restaurant offers a great variety of small dishes, such as steamed shrimp dumplings, spare ribs with black bean sauce or deep-fried shrimp rolls, just to mention a few of the tasty dim sum offerings. Additionally, an extensive menu of a la carte items lists choices ranging from seafood, squab and duck to chicken, beef and pork dishes. The atmosphere is family-friendly and bustling, with dim sum carts rolled around the dining rooms and colorful Chinese artwork. Casual dress. **Bar:** Full bar. **Reservations:** accepted. **Hours:** 8:30 am-11 pm. **Address:** 9 Tyler St 02111 **Location:** Jct Essex St; in Chinatown, on 2nd Floor. **Parking:** no self-parking.

(See map and index starting on p. 340)

CLIO

French
$28-$45

Phone: 617/536-7200   98

The restaurant enables diners to peek into the kitchen from a street-side window to watch the chefs prepare works of culinary art, with each plate selected to complement the course it contains. The atmosphere is relaxed, with subdued décor, muted natural woods and a distinguished, leopard-pattern carpet. Chef Kenneth Oringer received the James Beard Award as New England's best chef in 2001. Semi-formal attire. **Bar:** Full bar. **Reservations:** suggested. **Hours:** 6:30 am-10:30 & 5:30-10 pm, Sat 7 am-11 & 5:30-10:30 pm, Sun 7 am-noon & 5:30-10:30 pm. Closed: 1/1. **Address:** 370 Commonwealth Ave 02215 **Location:** Corner of Commonwealth and Massachusetts aves; in The Eliot Hotel. **Parking:** valet.

COTTONWOOD CAFE

Southwestern
$8-$26

Phone: 617/247-2225   72

The delightful find serves an appetizing selection of Southwestern cuisine, from enchiladas to a nicely marinated and prepared mixed grill. The respectable appetizer menu includes spicy Absolut heat wings, ultimate nachos and hot snake bites. Servers are knowledgeable about ingredients and preparations. Casual dress. **Bar:** Full bar. **Reservations:** accepted. **Hours:** 11:30 am-9 pm, Fri & Sat-10 pm; Saturday & Sunday brunch. Closed major holidays. **Address:** 222 Berkeley St 02116 **Location:** At St. James St; in Back Bay area. **Parking:** no self-parking.

THE DAILY CATCH

Seafood
$7-$24

Phone: 617/523-8567   11

The landmark restaurant has been serving fresh seafood specialties since 1973. Be sure to try New England clam chowder. Casual dress. **Bar:** Beer & wine. **Hours:** 11 am-10 pm, Fri & Sat-11 pm. Closed: 11/25, 12/25. **Address:** 323 Hanover St 02113 **Location:** Between Prince and Parmenter sts. **Parking:** no self-parking.

DAVIO'S NORTHERN ITALIAN STEAKHOUSE

Northern Italian
$9-$49

Phone: 617/357-4810   78

The restaurant occupies the former Mohr & McPherson furniture showroom, just a couple of blocks off the southeast corner of the Public Gardens. Spinach salad with roasted peppers, portobello mushrooms, goat cheese and garlic represents the offerings. On the bistro-like upper level, tables inlaid with granite surround the small center bar. Dressy casual. **Bar:** Full bar. **Reservations:** suggested. **Hours:** 11:30 am-11 pm, Sat from 5 pm, Sun 5 pm-10 pm. Closed: 12/25. **Address:** 75 Arlington St 02116 **Location:** Between Stuart and St. James sts. **Parking:** on-site (fee).

DURGIN PARK

Regional American
$6-$25

Phone: 617/227-2038   30

Generous portions of traditional New England fare, including fresh seafood, pot roast and homemade desserts, are served at family-style tables in the long-lived restaurant's second-floor dining room. Service is informal. Casual dress. **Bar:** Full bar. **Hours:** 11:30 am-10 pm, Sun-9 pm. Closed: 12/25. **Address:** 340 Faneuil Hall Marketplace 02109 **Location:** In North Market Building. **Parking:** no self-parking.

EASTERN STANDARD KITCHEN AND DRINKS

American
$9-$28

Phone: 617/532-9100   99

In Kenmore Square and within walking distance of Fenway Park, the casual, comfortable and fun restaurant serves meals in a lively dining room. An accomplished cooking team and well-informed staff enhance the experience. Casual dress. **Bar:** Full bar. **Reservations:** accepted. **Hours:** 7 am-2 am. **Address:** 528 Commonwealth Ave 02215 **Location:** On SR 2 at Beacon St and Brookline Ave; in Hotel Commonwealth. **Parking:** valet.

EAST OCEAN CITY

Chinese
$6-$25

Phone: 617/542-2504   69

The freshest spices accent freshly caught seafood delivered by the bucket. The result is flavorful Asian food. Diners also can choose a meal from an aquarium. This place has been in business for more than a decade. Casual dress. **Bar:** Full bar. **Reservations:** accepted. **Hours:** 11 am-10 pm, Fri & Sat-11 pm, Sun noon-10 pm. Closed: Chinese New Year. **Address:** 27 Beach St 02111 **Location:** In leather district. **Parking:** street.

FAJITAS & RITAS

Mexican
$7-$15

Phone: 617/426-1222   55

Just like the name of the restaurant their specialty is the fajitas. A wide variety of ingredients and plenty of margaritas will keep your party busy. Casual dress. **Bar:** Full bar. **Hours:** 11:30 am-9 pm, Wed & Thurs-10 pm, Fri & Sat-11 pm, Sun noon-8 pm. Closed: 12/25. **Address:** 25 West St 02111 **Location:** Between Tremont and Washington sts. **Parking:** street.

FIGS

Italian
$8-$19

Phone: 617/742-3447   49

A sophisticated and expensive free-form variety of pizza is the specialty at this place, which has locations here and in Charlestown, Wellesley and Chestnut Hill. Casual dress. **Bar:** Beer & wine. **Hours:** 5:30 pm-10 pm, Sat from noon, Sun noon-9 pm. Closed: 11/25, 12/25. **Address:** 42 Charles St 02114 **Location:** Between Chestnut and Lime sts; 1 blk n of Public Gardens. **Parking:** street.

FINALE

Breads/Pastries
$6-$18

Phone: 617/423-3184   64

Finale, indeed, pays tribute to the finale of a meal: dessert. Molten chocolate cake with coffee ice cream and chocolate sauce and vanilla creme brulee garnished with orange butter cookies and fresh fruit are available all year, and a multitude of other desserts cycle with the seasons. Also on the menu are pastries, soups, salads and limited entrees and some dessert wines and beers to complement them. The atmosphere is informal. Casual dress. **Bar:** Beer & wine. **Reservations:** not accepted. **Hours:** 11:30 am-11:30 pm, Fri-midnight, Sat 5 pm-midnight, Sun 4 pm-11 pm, Mon 11:30 am-11 pm. Closed major holidays. **Address:** 1 Columbus Ave 02116 **Location:** Just s of Boston Common and Public Gardens; in The Boston Park Plaza Hotel & Towers. **Parking:** street. CALL M

(See map and index starting on p. 340)

FLORENTINE CAFE Phone: 617/227-1777

Italian
$10-$32

The cafe offers not only a nouveau Italian menu but also great views of Little Italy. Casual dress. **Bar:** Full bar. **Reservations:** required. **Hours:** noon-4 & 5-11 pm. Closed: 12/25. **Address:** 333 Hanover St 02113 **Location:** Between Prince and Cross sts; in North End. **Parking:** street.

THE FOURS Phone: 617/720-4455

American
$8-$20

Originally named for the number worn by hockey great Bobby Orr, this trendy, sports-themed restaurant and bar serves up generous portions of salad, burgers, pasta, seafood and steak amid a warm decor peppered with Boston-area team memorabilia. Casual dress. **Bar:** Full bar. **Reservations:** not accepted. **Hours:** 11 am-midnight. Closed: 11/25, 12/25. **Address:** 166 Canal St 02114 **Location:** Just s to Bank North Garden and North Station. **Parking:** no self-parking. CALL

GRILL 23 & BAR Phone: 617/542-2255

Steak
$25-$59

First and foremost, this is a specialty steakhouse with cuts ranging in size from 10 to 18 ounces and a reputation for desserts. Also on the menu are salmon, lobster, tuna, scallops and sea bass, as well as some combinations. Filet mignon and swordfish are particularly good. Six massive marble columns support the ceiling of the dining room, which is on the original trading floor of the 1923 Salada Tea Building, hence the restaurant's name. Dressy casual. **Bar:** Full bar. **Reservations:** suggested. **Hours:** 5:30 pm-10:30 pm, Fri & Sat-11 pm, Sun-10 pm. Closed: 1/1, 7/4, 12/25. **Address:** 161 Berkeley St 02116 **Location:** Corner of Berkeley and Stuart sts. **Parking:** valet.

HARVARD GARDENS Phone: 617/523-2727

American
$9-$24

Upscale comfort food is on the extensive menu at the laid-back eatery near Beacon Hill and Mass General Hospital. At night the ambience takes on a more romantic note with candlelight. The staff is friendly and helpful. Casual dress. **Bar:** Full bar. **Reservations:** accepted. **Hours:** 11:30 am-10 pm, Thurs & Fri-11 pm, Sat 11 am-3 & 5-11 pm, Sun 11 am-3 & 5-10 pm. **Address:** 316 Cambridge St 02114 **Location:** At Grove St; in Back Bay; near Massachusetts General Hospital. **Parking:** street.

HOUSE OF BLUES Phone: 888/693-2583

Southern
$9-$22

Across the street from Fenway Park, this is a popular spot before and after games. Guests enjoy the Southern blues theme, especially in colorful wall murals and artwork depicting blues legends. Bands play on selected dates in the restaurant and next door in the large concert venue. The menu features sandwiches, burgers, salads and Southern entrees such as Cajun meatloaf, baby back barbecue ribs and Creole jambalaya with shrimp, chicken, andouille sausage, tasso ham and roasted green onions. Casual dress. **Bar:** Full bar. **Reservations:** not accepted. **Hours:** 11 am-9 pm, Fri & Sat-10 pm. Closed: 1/1, 11/25, 12/25. **Address:** 15 Lansdowne St 02215 **Location:** Between Brookline Ave and Ipswich St; opposite Fenway Park. **Parking:** on-site (fee).

ICARUS Phone: 617/426-1790

American
$28-$36

In South End, the restaurant presents a menu of creative, seasonally changing American cuisine. Guests might start with grilled shrimp with mango and jalapeno sorbet, then sink their teeth into pepper-crusted venison with cranberries and wild rice. Duck, beef, seafood and vegetarian dishes—such as autumn squash risotto with sage, apples and Parmesan—also are offered. Brass and clean lines lend a modernist backdrop to antique oak tables and chairs. Live jazz is featured Friday night. Casual dress. **Bar:** Full bar. **Reservations:** suggested. **Hours:** 6 pm-9:30 pm, Fri-10 pm, Sat 5:30 pm-10 pm, Sun 5:30 pm-9 pm. Closed major holidays; also Sun & Mon 1/1-1/31. **Address:** 3 Appleton St 02116 **Location:** Just w of Tremont St. **Parking:** valet.

JASPER'S WHITE SUMMER SHACK Phone: 617/867-9955

Regional Seafood
$5-$27

Created to resemble an old-fashioned fish house with barnboard floors and overhung tin eaves, the eatery plays lively music for patrons who savor its fresh fish and shellfish preparations. Dishes vary from traditional fried seafood to a boiled lobster feast to even a few landlubber favorites. Casual dress. **Bar:** Full bar. **Reservations:** not accepted. **Hours:** 11:30 am-10 pm, Fri & Sat-11 pm; seasonal hours may vary. Closed major holidays. **Address:** 50 Dalton St 02115 **Location:** Just w of Hynes Convention Center. **Parking:** no self-parking.

JOE'S AMERICAN BAR & GRILL Phone: 617/536-4200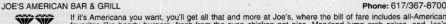

American
$10-$29

If it's Americana you want, you'll get all that and more at Joe's, where the bill of fare includes all-American favorites like hearty burgers, fresh-from-the-oven chicken pot pies, Maryland lump crab cakes, and Joe's classic meatloaf. Pizzas, pastas, steaks and salads round out the extensive menu, giving diners the freedom to choose from a vast selection of offerings. There's nothing more American than that, except, of course, for apple pie, so save some room. Casual dress. **Bar:** Full bar. **Hours:** 11:30 am-11 pm. Closed: 12/25. **Address:** 279 Dartmouth St 02116 **Location:** Jct Newbury St; in Back Bay. **Parking:** no self-parking.

JOE'S AMERICAN BAR & GRILL Phone: 617/367-8700

American
$9-$29

If it's Americana you want, you'll get all that and more at Joe's, where the bill of fare includes all-American favorites like hearty burgers, fresh-from-the-oven chicken pot pies, Maryland lump crab cakes, and Joe's classic meatloaf. Pizzas, pastas, steaks and salads round out the extensive menu, giving diners the freedom to choose from a vast selection of offerings. There's nothing more American than that, except, of course, for apple pie, so save some room. Casual dress. **Bar:** Full bar. **Hours:** 11:30 am-11 pm. Closed: 12/25. **Address:** 100 Atlantic Ave 02110 **Location:** At Commercial Wharf. **Parking:** valet.

JOE TECCE'S RISTORANTE & CAFE Phone: 617/742-6210

Italian
$8-$25

Founded in 1948 and located here since 1966, the family-operated restaurant prepares Neapolitan cuisine from generations-old recipes. Family members tend to every facet of the operation. Distinctive dining rooms capture the flavor of old neighborhoods. Red and white table linens soften the stone floors and walls, while mahogany and brass add richness. Some walls are decorated with patterns of seashells. Portions are generous enough for sharing. Casual dress. **Bar:** Full bar. **Reservations:** accepted. **Hours:** 11:30 am-1 am. Closed: 1/1, 11/25, 12/25. **Address:** 61 N Washington St 02114 **Location:** Just under interstate from jct New Chardon St; in North End. **Parking:** valet.

(See map and index starting on p. 340)

KASHMIR INDIAN RESTAURANT

Regional Indian
$9-$21

Phone: 617/536-1695   (89)

Among other restaurants and upscale shops on Newbury Street, the basement restaurant is graced with white linens, carved chairs and Indian art. Lamb vindaloo, keema mutter and chicken curry are good bets, as are the numerous vegetarian selections. Traditional desserts such as kheer, a rice pudding of sorts, and badami kulfi, an ice cream made with saffron and nuts, are a good way to finish. Daily lunch buffets are laid out. Casual dress. **Bar:** Beer & wine. **Reservations:** accepted. **Hours:** 11:30 am-11 pm. **Address:** 279 Newbury St 02116 **Location:** Corner of Gloucester and Newbury sts; in Back Bay. **Parking:** valet and street.

KINGFISH HALL

Regional Seafood
$12-$30

Phone: 617/523-8862   (33)

The terrific eatery prepares fresh seafood both traditionally and creatively. An enticing meal might start with a bowl of Kingfish Hall clam chowder or seafood gumbo and then progress to the New England lobster boil of lobster, steamers, corn on the cob and red bliss potatoes. Also on the menu are other seafood choices, landlubber favorites and not-to-be-missed desserts. Casual dress. **Bar:** Full bar. **Reservations:** suggested. **Hours:** 11:30 am-10 pm, Fri & Sat-11 pm, Sun noon-9:30 pm. Closed: 11/25, 12/25. **Address:** 188 Faneuil Hall Market Pl 02109 **Location:** At Faneuil Hall South Market building. **Parking:** street.

THE KINSALE

Irish
$9-$22

Phone: 617/742-5577   (34)

On the street level of the Government Center complex, the authentic pub was built in Ireland and reconstructed here. The eclectic menu leans toward traditional Irish fare, such as Irish stew, shepherd's pie, bangers and mash, boiled dinner and fish and chips. An upbeat and noisy after-work crowd patronizes the lounge, but the dining areas are quieter. Parking is validated for four hours in the complex's garage. Casual dress. Entertainment. **Bar:** Full bar. **Hours:** 11 am-2 am, Sat from 10 am, Sun 10 am-12:30 am, Mon & Tues 11 am-12:30 am. Closed: 11/25, 12/25. **Address:** 2 Center Plaza Government Center 02108 **Location:** At Government Center. **Parking:** on-site (fee). CALL 🅰️🅼

KO PRIME

Southern
Continental
$24-$43

Phone: 617/772-0202   (45)

The contemporary decor includes bamboo floors and cylindrical backlit tray ceilings. The atmosphere is upbeat and, at times, loud. A shimmering veil separates the dining room from the kitchen. Cuisine is California-influenced French Provencal. Roast chicken crepinette is highly touted, as are luscious desserts such as lemon creme brulee with lavender biscotti and molten chocolate banana cake. Dressy casual. **Bar:** Full bar. **Reservations:** suggested. **Hours:** 6:30 am-10:30 & 5-10 pm, Sat 8 am-noon & 5-10 pm. Closed major holidays; also Sun & Mon. **Address:** 90 Tremont St 02108 **Location:** Just ne of Boston Common; motor entrance on Bosworth; in Nine Zero Hotel. **Parking:** valet. CALL 🅰️🅼

LALA ROKH

Iranian
$9-$20

Phone: 617/720-5511   (41)

On the lower level of a brownstone only a couple of blocks from Boston Common, the restaurant presents a menu of classic Persian dishes, which are served by well-informed and cordial staff members who patiently explain the intricacies of each choice. Persian family artwork, as well as pictures and maps dating from 1620, decorate the casual dining rooms. Dressy casual. **Bar:** Beer & wine. **Reservations:** accepted. **Hours:** noon-3 & 5:30-10 pm, Sat & Sun from 5:30 pm. Closed: 1/1, 11/25, 12/24, 12/25. **Address:** 97 Mt. Vernon St 02108 **Location:** Just e of Charles St; in Beacon Hill. **Parking:** on-site (fee).

LEGAL SEA FOODS

Seafood
$9-$42

Phone: 617/742-5300   (35)

Legal prides itself on a reputation for freshness and consistency. More than 40 varieties of seafood can be grilled, broiled, fried or prepared Cajun style. Try the clam chowder that has been served at every presidential inauguration since 1981. The nautically inspired dining room is upscale and attractive with its rich cherry wood paneling and intricately detailed model ships. Casual dress. **Bar:** Full bar. **Reservations:** accepted. **Hours:** 11 am-11 pm, Fri & Sat-midnight. Closed: 12/25. **Address:** 255 State St 02110 **Location:** On historic Long Wharf; adjacent to New England Aquarium. **Parking:** street. CALL 🅰️🅼

LEGAL SEA FOODS

Seafood
$9-$42

Phone: 617/266-6800   (96)

Legal prides itself on a reputation for freshness and consistency. More than 40 varieties of seafood can be grilled, broiled, fried or prepared Cajun style. Try the clam chowder that has been served at every presidential inauguration since 1981. The nautically inspired dining room is upscale and attractive with its rich cherry wood paneling and intricately detailed model ships. Casual dress. **Bar:** Full bar. **Reservations:** accepted. **Hours:** 11 am-10:30 pm, Fri & Sat-11:30 pm, Sun noon-10 pm. Closed: 12/25. **Address:** 800 Boylston St 02199 **Location:** At Prudential Center; in historic Back Bay area. **Parking:** on-site (fee). CALL 🅰️🅼

LEGAL SEA FOODS

Seafood
$9-$42

Phone: 617/266-7775   (109)

Legal prides itself on a reputation for freshness and consistency. More than 40 varieties of seafood can be grilled, broiled, fried or prepared Cajun style. Try the clam chowder that has been served at every presidential inauguration since 1981. The nautically inspired dining room is upscale and attractive with its rich cherry wood paneling and intricately detailed model ships. Casual dress. **Bar:** Full bar. **Reservations:** accepted. **Hours:** 11 am-10 pm, Fri & Sat-10:30 pm, Sun noon-9 pm. Closed: 11/25, 12/25. **Address:** 100 Huntington Ave 02116 **Location:** Near Dartmouth St entrance; in Copley Place Galleries. **Parking:** on-site (fee).

LEGAL SEA FOODS

Seafood
$9-$42

Phone: 617/426-4444   (66)

Legal prides itself on a reputation for freshness and consistency. More than 40 varieties of seafood can be grilled, broiled, fried or prepared Cajun style. Try the clam chowder that has been served at every presidential inauguration since 1981. The nautically inspired dining room is upscale and attractive with its rich cherry wood paneling and intricately detailed model ships. Casual dress. **Bar:** Full bar. **Reservations:** accepted. **Hours:** 11:30 am-11 pm, Fri & Sat-midnight, Sun noon-11 pm. Closed: 12/25. **Address:** 26 Park Square 02116 **Location:** Just s of Boston Common and Public Gardens. **Parking:** street. CALL 🅰️🅼

(See map and index starting on p. 340)

L'ESPALIER
Menu on AAA.com   Phone: 617/262-3023   92

French
$25-$175

Located in the newly built Mandarin Oriental in tony Back Bay, this is one of Boston's premier "special occasion" restaurants. The intimate and sophisticated atmosphere complements the culinary service and delivery of exceptional and innovative modern French cuisine. Three-course prix-fixe or seven-course degustation menus change seasonally. In addition to a standard meat and fish menu, there are caviar and vegetarian degustation menus. Semi-formal attire. **Bar:** Full bar. **Reservations:** required. **Hours:** 11:30 am-2 & 5:30-10 pm, Sat & Sun from noon. Closed: 9/6, 12/25. **Address:** 774 Boylston St 02199 **Location:** Back Bay area at Fairfield St; within Mandarin Oriental. **Parking:** no self-parking.

LES ZYGOMATES
Phone: 617/542-5108   73

French
$11-$36

Many France-inspired items are created with care from high-quality ingredients and accented with delicate, flavorful sauces. Free jazz entertainment enhances the ambience six nights a week. Wine tastings take place on Tuesday. Dressy casual. **Bar:** Full bar. **Reservations:** suggested. **Hours:** 11:30 am-10 pm, Sat from 6 pm. Closed major holidays; also Sun. **Address:** 129 South St 02111 **Location:** Between Tufts and Beach sts; in Leather District. **Parking:** street.

LOCKE-OBER
Phone: 617/542-1340   53

Steak
$13-$62

At the end of an alley and between the Financial District and the State House is one of Boston's longtime fixtures, now reopened under the eye of one of the city's premiere chefs. White table linens accent the ornate back bar along the wall of one of the dining rooms. Chafing dishes, with covers supported by a system of cables and counterweights, line that bar. Diners can sample traditional "power" fare and rub shoulders with some of the wielders. Semi-formal attire. **Bar:** Full bar. **Reservations:** suggested. **Hours:** 11:30 am-2:30 & 5:30-10 pm, Fri-11 pm, Sat 5:30 pm-11 pm. Closed major holidays; also Sun. **Address:** 3 Winter Pl 02108 **Location:** At Tremont and Winter sts; center. **Parking:** valet and street.

LUCCA RESTAURANT
Phone: 617/742-9200   21

Northern Italian
$10-$37

The menu comprises Northern Italian preparations of seafood, beef, veal and chicken. No matter what dish is chosen, a wine from the extensive list will complement well. Dressy casual. **Bar:** Full bar. **Reservations:** suggested. **Hours:** 5 pm-12:15 am, Sat & Sun from noon. Closed: 11/25, 12/25. **Address:** 226 Hanover St 02113 **Location:** Between Parmenter and Cross sts; in North End. **Parking:** valet and street.

MAGGIANO'S LITTLE ITALY
Phone: 617/542-3456   68

Italian
$11-$38

Diners savor scrumptious, traditional favorites served in a bustling atmosphere reminiscent of Little Italy. The dining area projects an early-20th-century feel; loud conversations bouncing off high ceilings evoke a sense of the Roaring '20s. Casual dress. **Bar:** Full bar. **Reservations:** suggested. **Hours:** 11:30 am-2:30 & 5-10 pm, Fri-11 pm, Sat 11:30 am-11 pm, Sun 11:30 am-10 pm. Closed: 12/25. **Address:** 4 Columbus Ave 02116 **Location:** Just s of Boston Common and Public Gardens. **Parking:** street. CALL 🅛🅜

MAMMA MARIA
Phone: 617/523-0077   13

Regional Italian
$26-$38

Locals frequent this upscale restaurant, which occupies a converted town house overlooking North Square. Regional Italian cuisine is the focus of the menu, but other dishes appear as well. The chef focuses on using fresh local and regional ingredients in his memorable creations. Casual dress. **Bar:** Full bar. **Reservations:** suggested. **Hours:** 5 pm-10 pm, Fri & Sat-11 pm. Closed major holidays; also Super Bowl Sun. **Address:** 3 North Square 02113 **Location:** Corner of Prince and Garden cts; in North End. **Parking:** valet.

MANTRA
Phone: 617/542-8111   54

International
$10-$39

This contemporary yet sophisticated, Ladder District restaurant is located in an old bank, which still features unique elements such as marble walls and flooring as well as a large vault door on the lower level. Design features in the restrooms include see-through mirrored doors on the ladies' bathroom stalls; no one can see into the stalls, only out. Dressy casual. **Bar:** Full bar. **Reservations:** suggested. **Hours:** 11:30 am-2 & 5:30-10:30 pm, Sat from 5:30 pm. Closed: 12/25; also Sun. **Address:** 52 Temple Pl 02111 **Location:** Between Cambridge and Derne sts, just w of Government Center; in Ladder District. **Parking:** valet.

MASA
Phone: 617/338-8884   110

Southwestern
$18-$29

Menu items are prepared in Southwestern style and explode with taste. This fun favorite of the after-work crowd also presents wonderful desserts, including an outstanding pumpkin cheesecake with lime. Dressy casual. **Bar:** Full bar. **Reservations:** accepted. **Hours:** 5 pm-10 pm, Fri & Sat-11 pm. Closed: 11/25, 12/25. **Address:** 439 Tremont St 02116 **Location:** Between Arlington and E Berkeley sts. **Parking:** street.

MATCH BURGERS & MARTINIS
Phone: 617/247-9922   104

American
$6-$23

A sleek gas fireplace set into a long wall accents this hip and retro eatery, where tasty dishes vary from lighter fare of specialty mini-burgers and grilled pizza to heartier entrees. Pan-seared cookie dough with ice cream is a must. The young professional crowd frequents this welcome and sometimes noisy spot. Casual dress. **Bar:** Full bar. **Reservations:** accepted. **Hours:** 5 pm-10 pm, Thurs-Sat to 11 pm. Closed major holidays. **Address:** 94 Massachusetts Ave 02116 **Location:** Between Commonwealth Ave and Newbury St; in Back Bay area. **Parking:** no self-parking.

MCCORMICK & SCHMICK'S
Phone: 617/720-5522   29

Seafood
$7-$26

This place is all about seafood, which is imported from all over the world. Among good choices are Washington state oysters, Maine clams, delicate Hawaiian escolar and tuna from Ecuador. The clublike decor is cozy, and expert staff provide able assistance. Casual dress. **Bar:** Full bar. **Reservations:** suggested. **Hours:** 11:30 am-11 pm, Sun-10 pm. Closed major holidays. **Address:** North Market Bldg 02109 **Location:** Just s of Boston Common and Public Gardens; in The Boston Park Plaza Hotel & Towers. **Parking:** street.

(See map and index starting on p. 340)

MCCORMICK & SCHMICK'S
Phone: 617/482-3999   (77)

Seafood
$7-$26

This place is all about seafood, which is imported from all over the world. Among good choices are Washington state oysters, Maine clams, delicate Hawaiian escolar and tuna from Ecuador. The clublike decor is cozy, and expert staff provide able assistance. Casual dress. **Bar:** Full bar. **Reservations:** suggested, for dinner. **Hours:** 11:30 am-11 pm. **Address:** 34 Columbus Ave 02116 **Location:** Just s of Boston Common and Public Gardens; in Faneuil Hall Marketplace. **Parking:** on-site (fee). CALL

MERITAGE
Phone: 617/439-3995   (51)

Regional American
$16-$34

Chic, upbeat décor sets the tone for this new concept in dining, where the wine is chosen first, then the food to match. Arranged by characteristics of wine suitable for pairing, the seasonally changing menu lists small starter-sized portions or large plates. Examples of typical dishes include rack of lamb, braised pork cheeks, ostrich fan fillet, quail, duck, rabbit and fresh seafood. Presentations are truly artistic. A knowledgeable staff provides attentive, unobtrusive service. Dressy casual. **Bar:** Full bar. **Reservations:** suggested. **Hours:** 5:30 pm-10:30 pm; Sunday brunch 10:30 am-2:30 pm. Closed: Mon. **Address:** 70 Rowes Wharf 02110 **Location:** At Rowes Wharf; in Boston Harbor Hotel, 2nd floor. **Parking:** on-site (fee) and valet. CALL

MIEL
Phone: 617/217-5151   (56)

French
$14-$34

Accomplished chef Jacques Chibois creates memorable blends such as lobster vinaigrette with tarragon mustard or tuna tartare-lemon marinade with basil creme fraiche ice cream and cucumber coulis. The ever-changing menu always amazes. The spacious dining room's warm appeal is felt in the somewhat circular window-filled room with water views, soothing modern decor and comfortable toile-upholstered chairs. The knowledgeable staff is well versed in preparations, ingredients and even wine pairings. Dressy casual. **Bar:** Full bar. **Reservations:** accepted. **Hours:** 7 am-11 pm. **Address:** 510 Atlantic Ave 02210 **Location:** I-93, exit 23 southbound; exit 20 northbound; at Pearl St, in InterContinental Boston. **Parking:** on-site (fee) and valet.

MIKE'S PASTRY
Phone: 617/742-3050   (8)

Breads/Pastries
$3-$7

A landmark in the North End since "nearly forever," the popular bakery always has long lines, but it's well worth the wait. To say it bustles is an understatement. Seating options are limited. The pastries are homemade and unbelievably fresh. Those who can't make it into this place can order online. Casual dress. **Hours:** 8 am-9 pm, Tues 9 am-8 pm, Fri 8 am-10:30 pm, Sat 8 am-11 pm, Sun 8 am-9:30 pm. **Address:** 300 Hanover St 02113 **Location:** Between Wesley Pl and Prince St; in North End. **Parking:** street.

MODERN PASTRY
Phone: 617/523-3783   (19)

Breads/Pastries
$3-$9

In the heart of the North End, this local institution creates amazing fresh and from-scratch pastries that can't be missed. Crowd pleasers include giant lobster tails: homemade pastry shells filled at the time guests order with a luscious, creamy concoction. Among the additional delights are Italian cookies, Boston cream pie and ricotta pie. Casual dress. **Hours:** 7 am-10 pm. Closed: 12/25. **Address:** 257 Hanover St 02113 **Location:** In North End. **Parking:** no self-parking.

MONTIEN THAI RESTAURANT & LOUNGE
Phone: 617/338-5600   (74)

Thai
$9-$22

Curries, noodles, fresh fish, crispy duck and delicious pad thai are some of the numerous delectable mainstays at the popular, cozy restaurant. Casual dress. **Bar:** Full bar. **Reservations:** accepted, weekends. **Hours:** 11:30 am-10:30 pm, Sun 4 pm-10 pm. Closed major holidays. **Address:** 63 Stuart St 02116 **Location:** At Tremont St; in Theater District. **Parking:** street.

MOOO...
Phone: 617/670-2515   (40)

Regional Steak
$16-$48

The upscale, clubby restaurant is less than a block from the State House. Crisp white linens and a vase of three red roses on each table are a sharp contrast to the dark walls. Table spacing is a bit tight and some noise intrudes from the bar, but food and service don't disappoint. A seasonally changing menu includes baked stuffed lobster, pan-roasted salmon, Dover sole, beef Wellington, rack of lamb, duck and chops. There is also a tasting menu, with or without matching wines. Dressy casual. **Bar:** Full bar. **Reservations:** suggested. **Hours:** 7 am-11 pm, Sat & Sun from 8 am. **Address:** 15 Beacon St 02108 **Location:** Just e of State House; just ne of Boston Common; in Fifteen Beacon center. **Parking:** valet.

MORTON'S THE STEAKHOUSE
Phone: 617/266-5858   (86)

Steak
$28-$51

Patrons should make sure to reserve ahead for the popular, well-known steakhouse. Large portions, including huge cuts of fine beef and plentiful seafood, are the norm. Even the vegetables are oversized, with baked potatoes big enough for sharing. Dressy casual. **Bar:** Full bar. **Reservations:** accepted. **Hours:** 5:30 pm-11 pm, Fri & Sat from 5 pm, Sun 5 pm-10 pm. Closed major holidays. **Address:** 1 Exeter St 02116 **Location:** Corner of Exeter and Boylston sts. **Parking:** valet. CALL

MOTHER ANNA'S
Phone: 617/523-8496   (24)

Italian
$10-$25

Family operated for four generations, the friendly North End staple serves classic home-style Italian cooking. The family-oriented spot is one of the oldest restaurants in Little Italy. During his time as a congressman, John F. Kennedy dined here often. Casual dress. **Bar:** Full bar. **Reservations:** not accepted. **Hours:** 11:30 am-10 pm. Closed: 12/25. **Address:** 211 Hanover St 02113 **Location:** Between Richmond and Cross sts; in North End. **Parking:** no self-parking.

NED DEVINE'S IRISH PUB
Phone: 617/248-8800   (37)

Irish
$11-$20

On two levels at one end of Quincy Market, the Irish pub-style eatery nurtures a lively mood. The staff is friendly, and menu and ale selections are vast. Casual dress. **Bar:** Full bar. **Hours:** 11:30 am-11 pm. Closed: 11/25, 12/25. **Address:** 250 Faneuil Hall Marketplace 02109 **Location:** Within Quincy Market and Faneuil Hall. **Parking:** street.

(See map and index starting on p. 340)

NO. 9 PARK
French
$39-$96

Phone: 617/742-9991   [43]

The New American bistro serves refined European country fare heavily influenced by the cuisine of Southern France and, to a lesser extent, Italy. Prune-stuffed gnocchi has become a much-requested favorite on the seasonally changing menu. Seven- and nine-course prix fixe menus are offered with and without wine pairings. The cafe, between two dining areas and part of the bar, serves a lighter menu for an additional hour nightly. Valet parking is available during dinner only. Dressy casual. **Bar:** Full bar. **Reservations:** suggested. **Hours:** 5:30 pm-11 pm. Closed major holidays; also Sun & Columbus Day. **Address:** 9 Park St 02108 **Location:** Back Bay; corner of Park and Beacon sts; northeast corner of Boston Common; opposite State House. **Parking:** valet and street.

THE OAK ROOM
Steak
$10-$55

Phone: 617/267-5300   [90]

Opposite Copley Place, the elegant, sophisticated restaurant-with its oak-lined walls, ornate ceilings and crisp white linens-specializes in prime steaks dry-aged to 21 days, as well as chops, pasta and fresh seafood. Dish presentations are large and straightforward. Tuxedoed waiters and white-jacketed runners team to offer service that's neither too leisurely, nor too rushed, nor at all stuffy. Semi-formal attire. **Bar:** Full bar. **Reservations:** suggested. **Hours:** 6:30 am-10:30 pm, Fri & Sat-11 pm. **Address:** 138 St. James Ave 02116 **Location:** At Copley Square; in The Fairmont Copley Plaza Boston. **Parking:** valet.

OCEANAIRE
Seafood
$7-$40

Phone: 617/742-2277   [39]

Fresh fish and shellfish are flown in daily from around the globe. The sleek, handsomely designed dining room has a raw bar and is tastefully appointed in an art deco/nautical theme. The menu notes the seafood available daily and the varied preparation styles, such as broiled, grilled and blackened. Dressy casual. **Bar:** Full bar. **Reservations:** suggested. **Hours:** 11:30 am-10 pm, Fri & Sat-11 pm, Sun 5 pm-9 pm. Closed: 7/4, 11/25, 12/25. **Address:** 40 Court St 02108 **Location:** Between Tremont and Washington sts; in Financial District. **Parking:** no self-parking.

OLIVES
Mediterranean
$19-$39

Phone: 617/242-1999   [1]

This is the original location to showcase chef Todd English's rustic, creative, Mediterranean-inspired fare. The menu evolves seasonally but always offers handmade pasta selections, organic produce and excellent seafood and meat. Dressy casual. **Bar:** Full bar. **Reservations:** required. **Hours:** 5:30 pm-10 pm, Sat 5 pm-10:30 pm, Sun 5 pm-9 pm, Mon 5:30 pm-9:30 pm. Closed: 11/25, 12/25. **Address:** 10 City Square 02129 **Location:** On City Square; in Charlestown. **Parking:** valet.

THE PALM RESTAURANT
Steak
$13-$52

Phone: 617/867-9292   [102]

This bustling restaurant is noted for prime, dry-aged steaks and Nova Scotia lobsters, huge portions are delivered by an attentive staff in an atmosphere that is fun and lively. At the end of the meal, servers present tempting pastries tableside. Caricature-lined walls lend to the feeling that patrons are dining in an art gallery. Even if you bring a big appetite you still may leave with a doggy bag. Casual dress. **Bar:** Full bar. **Reservations:** suggested. **Hours:** 11:30 am-10 pm, Sat 5 pm-11 pm, Sun 5 pm-9 pm. Closed major holidays. **Address:** 200 Dartmouth St 02116 **Location:** I-90, exit 22, at Copley Square; at Westin Copley Square. **Parking:** on-site (fee).

PANIFICIO
Breads/Pastries
$7-$22

Phone: 617/227-4340   [32]

At the city's South End, the small restaurant often gets busy. The steamed mussels appetizer comes highly recommended, as do any of the entrees. Lovers of French cuisine enjoy this spot. Casual dress. **Bar:** Beer & wine. **Reservations:** not accepted. **Hours:** 7 am-9:30 pm, Sun-9 pm. Closed major holidays. **Address:** 144 Charles St 02114 **Location:** Between Revere and Pinckney sts; on Beacon Hill. **Parking:** on-site.

PAPA RAZZI
Italian
$10-$26

Phone: 617/536-9200

Italy has changed and so has authentic Italian food. It's lighter, fresher, more exciting Italian, and it's just what you'll find amid the elegant yet comfortable atmosphere that is Papa Razzi. If the steamy bowls of pasta don't tempt you, one of the aromatic pizzas or a warm panini sandwich definitely will. In addition there is a fine wine list, an array of salads, chicken, and fish options to choose from. Dressy casual. **Bar:** Full bar. **Reservations:** suggested. **Hours:** 11:30 am-11 pm, Thurs-Sat to midnight. Closed: 12/25. **Address:** 271 Dartmouth St 02116 **Location:** Between Boylston and Newbury sts. **Parking:** no self-parking.

PARISH CAFE
Deli
$9-$16

Phone: 617/247-4777   [63]

Sandwiches designed by other chefs are the main attraction here. Gourmet ingredients and hearty portions keep guests returning. Casual dress. **Hours:** 11:30 am-2 am. Closed: 12/25. **Address:** 361 Boylston St 02116 **Location:** Between Arlington and Berkeley sts. **Parking:** street.

PARKER'S RESTAURANT
American
$13-$38

Phone: 617/227-8600   [44]

One of the oldest restaurants in the city, this place has a history that staff members are eager to share. The kitchen originated the Parker House roll and Boston scrod, which was interpreted as the "freshest white fish of the day." A delightful Old World feel permeates the dining room. Good New England fare is the menu's focus. Casual dress. **Bar:** Full bar. **Reservations:** accepted. **Hours:** 6:30 am-2 & 5:30-10 pm, Sat from 7 am, Sun 7 am-noon. **Address:** 60 School St 02108 **Location:** Corner of Tremont and School sts; northeast corner of Boston Common; in Boston Omni Parker House Hotel. **Parking:** on-site (fee) and valet. **Historic**

PEACH FARM
Chinese
$8-$34

Phone: 617/482-3332   [71]

This past winner of a "Best of Boston" award was known to be a favorite haunt of the city's most famed gastronome, Julia Child. The decor may be Spartan, but the Hong Kong-style food is anything but. Guests can order from the fish tank or ask the servers to translate the specials posted on the walls. Not to be missed are clams in black bean sauce or lobster with ginger and scallions. Landlubbers will find bliss in Hong Kong-style sirloin steak and spicy, salted pork ribs. Casual dress. **Bar:** Beer & wine. **Reservations:** not accepted. **Hours:** 11 am-3 am. **Address:** 4 Tyler St 02111 **Location:** Between Kneeland and Main sts. **Parking:** no self-parking.

(See map and index starting on p. 340)

PENANG   Phone: 617/451-6373   67

Pacific Rim
$7-$23

A setting similar to a bamboo hut provides a tropical backdrop for Malaysian, Chinese, Middle Eastern, Thai and Indian food. Exotic spices, from mild to spicy, accent each dish, including many vegetarian choices. Casual dress. **Bar:** Beer & wine. **Hours:** 11:30 am-11:30 pm, Fri & Sat-midnight. **Address:** 685-691 Washington St 02111 **Location:** At LaGrange St. **Parking:** on-site (fee).

PETIT ROBERT BISTRO & PASTRY BAR   Phone: 617/375-0699   100

French
$7-$20

In the two lower levels of an old Kenmore Square brownstone, the chef-owned bistro creates memorable and authentic French cuisine. A miniature Eiffel Tower marks the entrance. Casual dress. **Bar:** Full bar. **Reservations:** accepted. **Hours:** 11 am-11 pm. Closed major holidays. **Address:** 468 Commonwealth Ave 02215 **Location:** Kenmore Square. **Parking:** street.

P.F. CHANG'S CHINA BISTRO   Phone: 617/573-0821   62

Chinese
$10-$24

Trendy, upscale decor provides a pleasant backdrop for New Age Chinese dining. Appetizers, soups and salads are a meal by themselves. Vegetarian plates and sides, noodles, meins, chicken and meat dishes are created from exotic, fresh ingredients. Casual dress. **Hours:** 11 am-11 pm, Fri & Sat-midnight. Closed: 11/25, 12/25. **Address:** 8 Park Plaza, Suite D6 02116 **Location:** Just s of Boston Common and Public Gardens. **Parking:** on-site (fee).

PICCOLA VENEZIA   Phone: 617/523-3888   17

Italian
$6-$24

In the heart of Little Italy, the traditional, family-oriented eatery displays Old World touches. The menu offers a nice variety. Casual dress. **Bar:** Full bar. **Hours:** 11:30 am-9:30 pm, Fri & Sat-10:30 pm. Closed: 11/25, 12/25. **Address:** 263 Hanover St 02113 **Location:** In North End. **Parking:** street.

PIGALLE   Phone: 617/423-4944   82

French
$35-$115

The intimate and sophisticated spot has a warm, romantic feel. French fare is modern and creative. Examples of chef specialties include crispy phyllo tuna rolls, steak tartare with toasted brioche, duck livers with Parmesan risotto and more seasonal offerings. Dressy casual. **Bar:** Full bar. **Reservations:** suggested. **Hours:** 5:30 pm-10 pm, Fri & Sat-10:30 pm, Sun 5 pm-9:30 pm. Closed major holidays; also Mon. **Address:** 75 Charles St S 02116 **Location:** Jct Stuart St; in theater district. **Parking:** on-site (fee).

 CALL

PREZZA   Phone: 617/227-1577   7

Italian
$25-$42

Amid the narrow North End streets, the restaurant is named after a town in the Abruzzo region of Italy that is known for dishes that rely on pork and polenta. Although there are other menu choices, this place doesn't stray from its rustic roots. Dishes made from hand-made pasta, including a lush gnocchi bolognese, are wonderful, as are hearty dishes cooked on the wood-fired grill, such as the double-thick pork loin. The seasonal menu lists luxurious desserts and a selection of cheeses too. Dressy casual. **Bar:** Full bar. **Reservations:** suggested, weekends. **Hours:** 5:30 pm-10 pm, Fri & Sat 5 pm-10:30 pm. Closed major holidays. **Address:** 24 Fleet St 02113 **Location:** At Hanover St; in North End. **Parking:** valet and street.

RADIUS   Phone: 617/426-1234   57

French
$17-$135

In a former financial-district bank building near South Station, the sleek, modern, upscale restaurant serves new French cuisine. The range of offerings is wide, with snapper, pork, veal, lamb, duck, pheasant, beef, scallops, cod and vegetables populating the main-course section. Six- and nine-course prix fixe menus, with or without wine pairings, are also offered at dinner. On the lower level, the former vault serves as the wine cellar. Valet parking is available only at dinnertime. Dressy casual. **Bar:** Full bar. **Reservations:** suggested. **Hours:** 11:30 am-2:30 & 5:30-10 pm, Fri-11 pm, Sat 5:30 pm-11 pm. Closed major holidays; also Sun. **Address:** 8 High St 02110 **Location:** At Summer St. **Parking:** street.

RATTLESNAKE BAR & GRILL   Phone: 617/859-8555   70

American
$8-$18

A lively atmosphere infuses the restaurant's fun setting, which incorporates painted wall murals and a roof deck. Selections of the chef's Latin-style cooking range from salads and sandwiches served with Latin fries to entrees such as pepita-crusted salmon or slow-braised barbecue beef brisket. Casual dress. **Bar:** Full bar. **Reservations:** accepted. **Hours:** 11:30 am-1 am. **Address:** 384 Boylston St 02116 **Location:** Between Berkeley and Arlington sts; in Back Bay area. **Parking:** no self-parking. CALL

RISTORANTE FIORE   Phone: 617/371-1176   15

Italian
$13-$36

Guests relax in a quiet and romantic setting over plates of enjoyable Italian cuisine and great wine. The staff is knowledgeable. Casual dress. **Bar:** Full bar. **Reservations:** suggested, weekends. **Hours:** 11:30 am-11 pm, Sun from noon. Closed: 12/25. **Address:** 250 Hanover St 02113 **Location:** Between Parmenter and Richmond sts; in North End. **Parking:** valet and street.

RISTORANTE LUCIA   Phone: 617/367-2353   3

Italian
$10-$26

The old-school Italian restaurant serves food in large portions. Contributing to the atmosphere are great background music and wonderful and colorful wall and ceiling murals. Casual dress. **Bar:** Full bar. **Reservations:** suggested, weekends. **Hours:** 11:30 am-10 pm, Fri-Sun to 11 pm. Closed: 11/25, 12/25. **Address:** 415 Hanover St 02113 **Location:** Between Prince and Cross sts; in North End. **Parking:** street.

RISTORANTE "SARACENO"   Phone: 617/227-5888   18

Italian
$11-$29

Another terrific area eatery, the restaurant offers upstairs and downstairs seating in a casual setting. Representative of traditional Italian fare are cheesy lasagna, plentiful antipasti and flavorful veal saltimbocca. Casual dress. **Bar:** Beer & wine. **Reservations:** accepted. **Hours:** noon-10:30 pm. Closed major holidays. **Address:** 286 Hanover St 02113 **Location:** Between Parmenter and Prince sts; in North End. **Parking:** street.

(See map and index starting on p. 340)

RUBY ROOM

Phone: 617/557-9955 ⑫

American
$11-$20

Thoroughly contemporary and cozy at the same time, the restaurant employs a casual approach to service and a creative approach to its food. Dishes range from an oversized cheeseburger to Asian-style spring rolls to expertly grilled steak and salmon. A nice selection of specialty martinis and a wine list are available. Casual dress. **Bar:** Full bar. **Hours:** 7 am-10 & 4-11 pm, Sat & Sun 8 am-11 & 4-11 pm. **Address:** 155 Portland St 02114 **Location:** Just n of corner of Merrimac and Traverse sts; 3 blks s of TD Bank North Garden; in Onyx Hotel. **Parking:** valet.

SAGE

Phone: 617/248-8814 ④

Italian
$21-$34

The size of the entrees makes up for the size of the dining room, which consists of just 10 tables draped in white linen. The chef uses fresh herbs and spices to add a tasty flavor to New American dishes. Dressy casual. **Bar:** Beer & wine. **Reservations:** suggested. **Hours:** 5:30 pm-10 pm. Closed major holidays. **Address:** 1395 Washington St 02118 **Location:** Corner of Salem St; in North End. **Parking:** street.

SCAMPO

Phone: 617/536-2100 ㉕

Italian
$15-$42

An upscale restaurant with a lively bar, this place satisfies guests with great small plates for sharing, including made-in-house mozzarella cheese appetizers, pizzas, seafood and homemade pastas. The best seat in the house lets patrons watch the chefs create delectable menu items using the freshest of ingredients. Dressy casual. **Bar:** Full bar. **Reservations:** accepted. **Hours:** 11:30 am-2:30 & 5:30-10 pm, Thurs-Sat to 11 pm. **Address:** 215 Charles St 02114 **Location:** I-93, exit 26 (Storrow Dr); in The Liberty Hotel. **Parking:** valet.

SEL DE LA TERRE

Phone: 617/720-1300 ㊱

Southern French
$10-$32

In a ground-floor corner-storefront spot near New England Aquarium, the restaurant offers casual, country dining influenced by the cuisine of Southern France. Freshness is ensured in dishes that combine only what is available daily. Main courses vary from roasted free-range chicken to grilled Angus beef to garlic- and mustard-crusted lamb. Desserts such as mango sorbet or buttermilk ice cream with fresh raspberries are excellent. Casual dress. **Bar:** Full bar. **Reservations:** required. **Hours:** 11 am-12:30 am. Closed: 1/1, 12/25. **Address:** 255 State St 02109 **Location:** State St and Atlantic Ave; at Long Wharf. **Parking:** on-site (fee) and valet. CALL [&M]

SENSING

Phone: 617/994-9000 ②

International
$12-$42

One of Boston's newest restaurants, this place showcases a young chef who is one to watch. To describe his creations is nearly impossible; suffice it to say that he blends the freshest available ingredients, both local and global, using international influences. The decor reflects a modern, trendy style that combines comfort and chic appointments. Casual dress. **Bar:** Full bar. **Reservations:** accepted. **Hours:** 6 am-2 & 6-10 pm. **Address:** Three Battery Wharf 02109 **Location:** At Battery Wharf, e of north end; in Fairmont Battery Wharf. **Parking:** valet. CALL [&M]

SILVERTONE BAR & GRILL

Phone: 617/338-7887 ㊽

American
$10-$20

A great place to meet friends after work and into the night, the restaurant has a contemporary and retro look to it. Casual dress. **Bar:** Full bar. **Hours:** 11:30 am-11 pm, Sat from 6 pm. Closed: 11/25, 12/25; also Sun. **Address:** 69 Bromfield St 02108 **Location:** Between Park and Beacon sts. **Parking:** street.

SKIPJACK'S

Phone: 617/536-3500 ㊼

Seafood
$9-$31

Just off Copley Square behind Trinity Church, the restaurant offers a wide variety of fresh fish from around the world at reasonable prices. The wine list emphasizes budget-friendly French and American vintages. While the dessert list is limited, the choices, such as warm chocolate bread pudding smothered in whipped cream, are wonderful. Two hours of validated parking in a local lot is available all day weekends and after 5 pm on weekdays. Service is friendly and professional. Casual dress. **Bar:** Full bar. **Reservations:** suggested. **Hours:** 11:30 am-10:30 pm, Fri & Sat 11 am-midnight. Closed: 11/25, 12/25. **Address:** 199 Clarendon St 02116 **Location:** Corner of St. James and Clarendon sts. **Parking:** no self-parking. CALL [&M]

SMITH & WOLLENSKY

Phone: 617/423-1112 ㊄

Steak
$9-$44

Patrons savor the flavors of New Orleans at the elegant, well-known steakhouse. A tempting menu awaits, as does the clublike atmosphere, which incorporates rich, dark woods and soft lighting. Service is professional and capable. Casual dress. **Bar:** Full bar. **Reservations:** accepted. **Hours:** 11:30 am-3 & 5-10 pm, Fri-11 pm, Sat 4:30 pm-11 pm, Sun 4:30 pm-10 pm. **Address:** 101 Arlington St 02116 **Location:** Just s of Boston Common and Public Gardens; in The Boston Park Plaza Hotel & Towers. **Parking:** valet.

SONSIE

Phone: 617/351-2500 ㊶

American
$9-$29

Internationally varied food, from Thai starters to American burgers and brick-oven specialty pizzas, is served in a bustling, trendy and artsy bistro atmosphere. In good weather, French doors that line one end of the restaurant open to make a sidewalk cafe. A limited cafe menu is available between lunch and dinner and in the late evening. Casual dress. **Bar:** Full bar. **Reservations:** suggested. **Hours:** 11:30 am-2:30 & 6-11 pm, Sat & Sun 11:30 am-3 & 6-11 pm. Closed: 12/25. **Address:** 327 Newbury St 02115 **Location:** Just s of Massachusetts Ave. **Parking:** no self-parking.

SOUTH STREET DINER

Phone: 617/350-0028 ㊸

American
$5-$15

Exemplifying what a 1950s diner should look like, the greasy spoon is near the South Station train station. Such choices as griddled pancakes, any-style eggs, sandwiches, wraps and greasy burgers with fries represent classic diner fare to a T. The patio opens during warmer months. Casual dress. **Bar:** Beer & wine. **Hours:** 5 pm-5 am, Fri-Sun 24 hours. Closed major holidays. **Address:** 178 Kneeland St 02111 **Location:** At South St. **Parking:** street.

(See map and index starting on p. 340)

STANHOPE GRILLE   Phone: 617/266-7200

New American
$11-$34

Seasonal menus offer the freshest options for discriminating diners. Ever popular are the rack of lamb with honey Guinness sauce or wild mushrooms and asparagus with tawny port sauce in puff pastry. Dressy casual. **Bar:** Full bar. **Reservations:** suggested. **Hours:** 11:30 am-2 & 5:30-10 pm, Fri & Sat-11 pm, Sun-10 pm. **Address:** 350 Stuart St 02116 **Location:** At Berkeley St; in Back Bay Hotel. **Parking:** valet and street.

STEPHANIE'S ON NEWBURY   Phone: 617/236-0990   79

American
$12-$30

The inviting foyer has a cozy seating area by the crackling fireplace and bar. The three main dining spaces are two first-floor rooms and a second-story sky-lit area, and sidewalk cafe seating is a seasonal addition. Creativity infuses some comfort food classics, such as macaroni and cheese, shepherd's pie, meatloaf and chicken pot pie. Dressy casual. **Bar:** Full bar. **Reservations:** accepted. **Hours:** 11:30 am-11 pm, Sun 10 am-10 pm; Sunday brunch. Closed: 11/25, 12/24, 12/25. **Address:** 190 Newbury St 02116 **Location:** Corner of Exeter St. **Parking:** street.

SULTAN'S KITCHEN   Phone: 617/570-9009   42

Turkish
$6-$9

Turkish cuisine relies heavily on fresh citrus fruits, vegetables, garlic, grains and olive oil. Popular with the lunch crowd because of the value it offers, this place keeps things simple with counter service, Styrofoam containers, plastic utensils and self-seating in the second-floor dining room. Casual dress. **Hours:** 11 am-5:30 pm. Closed major holidays; also Sun. **Address:** 116 State St 02109 **Location:** At Broad St; in financial district. **Parking:** street.

TAPEO RESTAURANT & TAPAS BAR   Phone: 617/267-4799   91

Spanish
$8-$25

Tasty, memorable dishes are prepared thoughtfully at the lively eatery, which has a dining room upstairs overlooking bustling Newbury Street. Casual dress. **Bar:** Full bar. **Reservations:** accepted. **Hours:** 5:30 pm-10 pm, Thurs & Fri-11 pm, Sat noon-11 pm, Sun noon-10 pm. Closed major holidays. **Address:** 266 Newbury St 02116 **Location:** Between Fairfield and Gloucester sts, just s of US 20. **Parking:** street.

TARANTA   Phone: 617/720-0052   23

Italian
$19-$36

A distinctive fusion of Southern Italian and Peruvian flavors influences the creative choices at the popular North End spot. A cozy, rustic and romantic ease infuses the three floors of space. Casual dress. **Bar:** Full bar. **Reservations:** suggested. **Hours:** 5:30 pm-10 pm. Closed major holidays. **Address:** 210 Hanover St 02113 **Location:** Jct Cross St; in North End. **Parking:** street.

TEATRO   Phone: 617/778-6841   58

Northern Italian
$13-$31

In the heart of the theater district, the restaurant has dramatic and ornate high ceilings. Delightful Northern Italian dishes are appealingly presented. Casual dress. **Bar:** Full bar. **Reservations:** suggested, weekends. **Hours:** 5 pm-10:30 pm, Fri & Sat-11:30 pm, Sun 4 pm-10 pm. Closed: 1/1, 12/25; also Mon. **Address:** 177 Tremont St 02111 **Location:** Between Avery and Essex sts; just ne of Boston Common. **Parking:** street.

TOP OF THE HUB   Phone: 617/536-1775   95

American
$22-$70

The restaurant affords spectacular panoramic views of the city and the Charles River. Creativity marks the varied menu of native seafood, aged meat, poultry and vegetarian entrées. The chef also presents five- and seven-course tasting menus of seasonal items. The pastries are a work of art. A regular schedule of live jazz is offered in the lounge. Dressy casual. **Entertainment. Bar:** Full bar. **Reservations:** suggested. **Hours:** 11:30 am-1 am, Fri & Sat-2 am, Sun 11 am-1 am. Closed: 12/25. **Address:** 800 Boylston St 02199 **Location:** On 52nd floor of Prudential Tower. **Parking:** on-site (fee) and valet.

TOSCANO   Phone: 617/723-4090   47

Italian
$9-$35

This busy Italian restaurant caters to the Beacon Hill residents. The dining room is warm with a rustic theme of brick walls, cream colors and some historic maps. The staff is friendly and they carry on conversations that make anyone feel like their part of the family. Casual dress. **Bar:** Full bar. **Reservations:** suggested. **Hours:** 11:30 am-2:30 & 5:30-10 pm, Sun from 5:30 pm. Closed major holidays. **Address:** 47 Charles St 02114 **Location:** At Mt. Vernon St; in Beacon Hill. **Parking:** valet and street.

TRATTORIA IL PANINO   Phone: 617/720-1336   14

Italian
$14-$30

This small, charming restaurant serves excellent Italian-American veal, chicken and seafood pasta dishes. Although the atmosphere is on the plain side, it incorporates rustic wood tabletops, Tuscany-inspired vines running the length of the ceiling and plenty of framed pictures of the owner with well-known celebrities, some of whom have dined here. Casual dress. **Bar:** Full bar. **Hours:** 11 am-10 pm, Fri & Sat-11 pm, Sun noon-11 pm. Closed major holidays. **Address:** 11 Parmenter St 02113 **Location:** Between Hanover and Salem sts; in North End. **Parking:** street.

TURNER FISHERIES RESTAURANT & BAR   Phone: 617/424-7425   101

Regional Seafood
$24-$36

The "hall-of-fame" clam chowder stands out on a diverse menu of creative fresh fish dishes, including herb-crusted cod, braised monkfish, pan-roasted haddock and more. Preparations are rich and flavorful. Casual dress. **Bar:** Full bar. **Reservations:** accepted. **Hours:** 5 pm-10 pm. Closed: 12/25; also Sun. **Address:** 10 Huntington Ave 02116 **Location:** I-90, exit 22, at Copley Square; in The Westin Copley Place Boston. **Parking:** valet and street.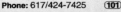

UNION OYSTER HOUSE   Phone: 617/227-2750   26

Regional Seafood
$10-$33

Considered to be the oldest continually run restaurant in the country, the oyster house opened its doors in 1826. To this day, it serves fresh seafood and New England favorites. The emphasis is on the lively and historical atmosphere. Casual dress. **Bar:** Full bar. **Reservations:** accepted. **Hours:** 11 am-9:30 pm, Fri & Sat-10 pm. Closed major holidays. **Address:** 41 Union St 02108 **Location:** At Quincy Market. **Parking:** street. **Historic**

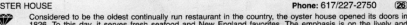

(See map and index starting on p. 340)

VIA MATTA   Phone: 617/422-0008   (65)

Italian
$14-$39

The frequently changing menu features creative Italy-inspired specialties that combine the freshest seasonal ingredients. Outdoor dining is an option when the weather permits. Valet parking is available in the evening. Casual dress. **Bar:** Full bar. **Reservations:** accepted. **Hours:** 11:30 am-2:30 & 5:30-10 pm, Fri & Sat-11 pm. Closed: 1/1, 11/25, 12/25; also Sun. **Address:** 79 Park Plaza 02116 **Location:** Corner of Arlington St; 1 blk s of the Public Gardens; 'T' stop-Arlington via Greenline. **Parking:** valet and street.

VILLA FRANCESCA RISTORANTE AND CAFFE   Phone: 617/367-2948   (20)

Italian
$9-$32

A must-stop for tourists strolling through the North End, the bistro prepares wonderful Italian interpretations of veal, fish, chicken and pork. Homemade desserts are elegantly presented. Cannoli shells are piped with delicious ricotta cream at the table. Casual dress. **Bar:** Full bar. **Reservations:** accepted. **Hours:** 11:30 am-12:30 am, Sun-11:30 pm, Mon 5 pm-12:30 am. Closed: 11/25, 12/25. **Address:** 150 Richmond St 02109 **Location:** In North End. **Parking:** valet and street.

THE WINE CELLAR   Phone: 617/236-0080   (80)

Fondue
$28-$50

The wonderful fondue eatery has patrons cook meats and shellfish in a piping-hot broth rather than peanut oil, providing a tasty and healthier alternative. Individual entrées, including rack of lamb, steak frites and seafood ravioli, are another option. Valet parking is available on Friday and Saturday evenings. Casual dress. **Bar:** Beer & wine. **Reservations:** accepted. **Hours:** 5:30 pm-10:30 pm. Closed major holidays. **Address:** 30 Massachusetts Ave 02115 **Location:** At Beacon St. **Parking:** no self-parking.

——— *The following restaurant has not been evaluated by AAA* ———
but is listed for your information only.

FLAT IRON TAPAS BAR & LOUNGE   Phone: 617/778-2900

Not evaluated. An extension of the original Flat Iron Tapas Bar & Lounge in Montreal, this second restaurant benefits from a terrific locale in the Bulfinch Triangle area, which is convenient to Government Center, Faneuil Hall and TD Banknorth Gardens. The menu lists a respectable selection of well-prepared Flat Iron Tapas Bar & Lounge. **Address:** 107 Merrimac St 02114 **Location:** At Lancaster St; in Bulfinch Hotel.

BOSTON pop. 589,141 (See map and index starting on p. 345)

BEST WESTERN BOSTON-THE INN AT LONGWOOD MEDICAL

Book great rates at AAA.com

Hotel

$199-$309 5/1-10/31
$189-$299 11/1-4/30

Phone: (617)731-4700 **13**

Address: 342 Longwood Ave 02115 **Location:** Adjoining Children's Hospital at Brookline Ave. Attached to the Galleria and food court, Longwood Medical Area. **Facility:** Smoke free premises. 155 one-bedroom standard units, some with efficiencies. 8 stories, interior corridors. *Bath:* combo or shower only. **Parking:** on-site (fee). **Amenities:** video games (fee), high-speed Internet, voice mail, irons, hair dryers. **Dining:** Longwood Grille & Bar, see separate listing. **Guest Services:** valet laundry, wireless Internet. **Business Services:** meeting rooms, PC, fax (fee). *(See color ad below)*

AAA Benefit:
Members save up to 20%, plus 10% bonus points with rewards program.

🍴 🍸 FEE➕ ✖ 🎮 💻 / SOME UNITS FEE 🛎 🖥

FREE local telephone calls and high-speed Internet

BEST WESTERN ROUNDHOUSE SUITES

Book great rates at AAA.com

Hotel

$159-$239 5/1-10/31
$139-$199 11/1-4/30

Phone: (617)989-1000 **15**

Address: 891 Massachusetts Ave 02118 **Location:** I-93, exit 18, just sw; just n of Newmarket Square. Located in South Boston. **Facility:** Smoke free premises. 92 units. 46 one-bedroom standard units. 46 one-bedroom suites. 6 stories, interior corridors. *Bath:* combo or shower only. **Parking:** on-site. **Amenities:** video games (fee), dual phone lines, voice mail, safes, irons, hair dryers. **Leisure Activities:** limited exercise equipment. **Guest Services:** valet laundry, area transportation-within 2 mi, wireless Internet. **Business Services:** meeting rooms, business center. **Free Special Amenities: continental breakfast and high-speed Internet.**

AAA Benefit:
Members save up to 20%, plus 10% bonus points with rewards program.

🍴 CALL ♿Ⓜ ✖ 🎮 🛎 🖥 💻 / SOME UNITS FEE 🐾

Visit AAA.com for one-stop travel planning and reservations.

▼ See AAA listing p 518 ▼

A REFRESHING BREAK FROM YOUR BUSINESS ROUTINE

Central MA hotel has luxurious bedding, spacious work desk and free Internet

Close to Wachusett Mountain Ski Area, area colleges & universities, recreational activities indoor pool, whirlpool, fitness room, restaurant and phenomenal meeting facilities.

10% to 15%*

Courtyard by Marriott*
Courtyard by Marriott Fitchburg
150 Royal Plaza Dr Fitchburg, MA 01420
T 978.342.7100 F 978.343.7376
courtyardfitchburg.com

Approved

*15% off weekday and 10% off lowest available rate on weekends. Single/Double occupancy

The World's Largest Hotel Chain

TLC Hotel

• Conveniently located off route 95/128 minutes from Boston, Cambridge, Lexington & Concord • Free continental breakfast – kids stay free under 17 • Piccadilly Pub Restaurant on premises • Complimentary parking, public transportation to train at driveway entrance • Boston tours leaving daily with advance reservations • Rooms feature 25" TV, premium movie channels, Nintendo 64, coffee, iron/board • Hairdryer, complimentary Internet, USA Today • Indoor pool & fitness center • Business center

TLCwaltham.com
380 Winter Street • Waltham, MA 02451
Phone 781-890-7800 • Fax 781-890-4937
Toll Free: 877-852-4683

Approved

Royal Plaza Hotel & Trade Center

• Convenient location off I-495 & minutes from the Mass Pike • Continental or Full Breakfast Available • Complimentary High - Speed Internet • Zachary's Restaurant & All-Star Bar and Grill located on site • Heated Indoor Pool with Deck • Meeting/Banquet/Conference Facilities up to 1,100 • Rooms feature 25" TV, Pay-Per-View, Nintendo 64, dataports, Coffee, Iron/Board,Hairdryer & USA Today

www.rplazahotels.com
181 Boston Post Road West
Marlborough, MA 01752
Phone 508-460-0700
Fax 508-480-8218
Toll Free: 888-543-9500

AAA.com/TravelGuide ... Destination Information and Ideas.

(See map and index starting on p. 345)

BEST WESTERN TERRACE INN   *Book great rates at AAA.com*   Phone: (617)566-6260   **12**

AAA SAVE

Motel
$99-$239 All Year

Address: 1650 Commonwealth Ave 02135 **Location:** Just s of SR 30, then just w of jct Washington St at Mt. Hood Rd. Located in a residential area. **Facility:** Smoke free premises. 74 units. 68 one-bedroom standard units, some with efficiencies. 6 one-bedroom suites with efficiencies. 2 stories (no elevator), exterior corridors. *Bath:* combo or shower only. **Parking:** on-site. **Amenities:** irons, hair dryers. **Guest Services:** wireless Internet. **Business Services:** PC. **Free Special Amenities:** continental breakfast and high-speed Internet.

AAA Benefit:
Members save up to 20%, plus 10% bonus points with rewards program.

THE COLONNADE HOTEL BOSTON   *Book at AAA.com*   Phone: (617)424-7000   **9**

Hotel
$199-$429 5/1-11/6
$189-$399 11/7-4/30

Address: 120 Huntington Ave 02116 **Location:** Just s of Copley Square. **Facility:** Smoke free premises. 285 units. 280 one-bedroom standard units. 5 one-bedroom suites. Interior corridors. *Bath:* combo or shower only. **Parking:** on-site (fee) and valet. **Terms:** cancellation fee imposed. **Amenities:** DVD players, CD players, high-speed Internet (fee), dual phone lines, voice mail, safes, honor bars, irons, hair dryers. **Dining:** Brasserie Jo, see separate listing. **Pool(s):** heated outdoor. **Leisure Activities:** exercise room. **Guest Services:** valet laundry, wireless Internet. **Business Services:** conference facilities, business center. Affiliated with A Preferred Hotel.

ASK

COMFORT INN BOSTON   *Book at AAA.com*   Phone: (617)287-9200   **20**

Hotel
$109-$179 7/2-4/30
$99-$159 5/1-7/1

Address: 900 William T Morrissey Blvd 02122 **Location:** I-93, exit 13 northbound, 0.5 mi sw; exit 12 southbound, follow signs. **Facility:** Smoke free premises. 132 units. 130 one-bedroom standard units. 2 one-bedroom suites. 5 stories, interior corridors. *Bath:* combo or shower only. **Parking:** on-site. **Amenities:** dual phone lines, voice mail, safes, irons, hair dryers. **Leisure Activities:** exercise room. **Guest Services:** valet and coin laundry, area transportation, wireless Internet. **Business Services:** PC (fee). *(See color ad p 382)* ASK

▼ See AAA listing p 417 ▼

(See map and index starting on p. 345)

COURTYARD BOSTON LOGAN AIRPORT *Book great rates at AAA.com* Phone: (617)569-5250

Hotel
$149-$259 All Year

Address: 225 McClellan Hwy (Rt 1AN) 02128 **Location:** I-90, exit 20, on SR 1A; 1.5 mi n of Boston Logan International Airport Terminal. **Facility:** Smoke free premises. 351 units. 346 one-bedroom standard units. 5 one-bedroom suites. 12 stories, interior corridors. *Bath:* combo or shower only. **Parking:** on-site. **Terms:** cancellation fee imposed. **Amenities:** dual phone lines, voice mail, irons, hair dryers. *Some:* high-speed Internet. **Pool(s):** outdoor. **Leisure Activities:** exercise room. **Guest Services:** valet and coin laundry, wireless Internet. **Business Services:** meeting rooms, business center.

AAA Benefit:
Members save a minimum 5% off the best available rate.

COURTYARD BY MARRIOTT SOUTH BOSTON *Book great rates at AAA.com* Phone: (617)436-8200

Hotel
$189-$279 All Year

Address: 63 R Boston St 02125 **Location:** I-93, exit 18 southbound, follow signs for Andrews Square; exit 16 northbound. **Facility:** Smoke free premises. 164 units. 161 one-bedroom standard units, some with whirlpools. 3 one-bedroom suites. 6 stories, interior corridors. *Bath:* combo or shower only. **Parking:** on-site. **Terms:** cancellation fee imposed. **Amenities:** high-speed Internet, dual phone lines, voice mail, irons, hair dryers. **Pool(s):** heated indoor. **Leisure Activities:** whirlpool, exercise room. **Guest Services:** valet and coin laundry, wireless Internet. **Business Services:** meeting rooms, business center.

AAA Benefit:
Members save a minimum 5% off the best available rate.

(See map and index starting on p. 345)

DOUBLETREE CLUB HOTEL BOSTON-BAYSIDE   *Book great rates at AAA.com*   Phone: (617)822-3600

Hotel
$79-$299 All Year

Address: 240 Mt. Vernon St 02125 **Location:** I-93, exit 15, 0.3 mi se. Adjacent to Bayside Expo Center. **Facility:** Smoke free premises. 197 units. 195 one-bedroom standard units. 2 one-bedroom suites. 6 stories, interior corridors. *Bath:* combo or shower only. **Parking:** on-site (fee). **Terms:** 1-7 night minimum stay, cancellation fee imposed. **Amenities:** video games (fee), dual phone lines, voice mail, irons, hair dryers. **Leisure Activities:** exercise room. **Guest Services:** valet laundry, area transportation, wireless Internet. **Business Services:** meeting rooms, business center.

AAA Benefit:
Members save 5% or more everyday!

DOUBLETREE GUEST
SUITES-BOSTON/CAMBRIDGE   *Book great rates at AAA.com*   Phone: (617)783-0090   ⑤

Hotel
$109-$409 All Year

Address: 400 Soldiers Field Rd 02134 **Location:** I-90, exit 20 westbound; exit 18 eastbound. **Facility:** 308 units. 8 one-bedroom standard units. 300 one-bedroom suites. 15 stories, interior corridors. *Bath:* combo or shower only. **Parking:** on-site (fee) and valet. **Terms:** 1-7 night minimum stay, cancellation fee imposed. **Amenities:** dual phone lines, voice mail, irons, hair dryers. **Fee:** video games, high-speed Internet. **Dining:** nightclub, entertainment. **Pool(s):** heated indoor. **Leisure Activities:** whirlpool, exercise room. **Guest Services:** valet and coin laundry, area transportation-Copley Square, Harvard Square, Boston Common, New England Aquarium, wireless Internet. **Business Services:** meeting rooms, business center.

AAA Benefit:
Members save 5% or more everyday!

▼ See AAA listing p 407 ▼

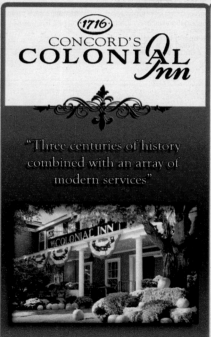
Create complete trip routings and custom place maps
with the TripTik® Travel Planner on AAA.com

(See map and index starting on p. 345)

EMBASSY SUITES BOSTON AT LOGAN AIRPORT

Book great rates at AAA.com **Phone:** (617)567-5000 **2**

AAA SAVE

Hotel
$129-$469 All Year

Address: 207 Porter St 02128 **Location:** I-90, exit 20, at General Edward Lawrence Logan International Airport. **Facility:** Smoke free premises. 273 one-bedroom suites. 5-10 stories, interior corridors. *Bath:* combo or shower only. **Parking:** valet. **Terms:** 1-7 night minimum stay, cancellation fee imposed. **Amenities:** video games (fee), high-speed Internet, dual phone lines, voice mail, irons, hair dryers. **Pool(s):** heated indoor. **Leisure Activities:** whirlpool, exercise room. **Guest Services:** valet and coin laundry, airport transportation-Boston Logan International Airport, area transportation-water taxi & subway, wireless Internet. **Business Services:** conference facilities, business center. *(See color ad p 356)*

AAA Benefit:
Members save 5% or more everyday!

FREE full breakfast and preferred room (subject to availability with advance reservations)

HAMPTON INN & SUITES BOSTON CROSSTOWN CENTER
Book great rates at AAA.com

Phone: (617)445-6400 **14**

AAA SAVE

Hotel
$109-$349 All Year

Address: 811 Massachusetts Ave 02118 **Location:** I-93, exit 18, just e; entrance off Melnea Cass Blvd. South Boston area. **Facility:** Smoke free premises. 175 one-bedroom standard units. 9 stories, interior corridors. *Bath:* combo or shower only. **Parking:** on-site (fee). **Terms:** 1-7 night minimum stay, cancellation fee imposed. **Amenities:** video games (fee), voice mail, irons, hair dryers. **Pool(s):** heated indoor. **Leisure Activities:** exercise room. **Guest Services:** valet laundry, airport transportation-Boston Logan International Airport, area transportation-within 5 mi, wireless Internet. **Business Services:** meeting rooms, business center. **Free Special Amenities:** full breakfast and high-speed Internet.

AAA Benefit:
Members save up to 10% everyday!

▼ See AAA listing p 394 ▼

(See map and index starting on p. 345)

HILTON BOSTON LOGAN AIRPORT   *Book great rates at AAA.com*   Phone: (617)568-6700

Hotel
$169-$639 All Year

Address: 1 Hotel Dr 02128 **Location:** At General Edward Lawrence Logan International Airport. **Facility:** Richly decorated guest rooms feature plush "Beds by Hilton," and guests have direct access to Logan's terminals A and E via walkways and bridges. Smoke free premises. 599 units. 595 one-bedroom standard units. 4 two-bedroom suites. 10 stories, interior corridors. *Bath:* combo or shower only. **Parking:** on-site (fee) and valet. **Terms:** 1-7 night minimum stay, cancellation fee imposed. **Amenities:** video games (fee), dual phone lines, voice mail, safes, irons, hair dryers. *Some:* CD players. **Dining:** 2 restaurants, also, Connolly's Pub, see separate listing. **Pool(s):** heated indoor. **Leisure Activities:** saunas, whirlpool, steamrooms, jogging, exercise room. **Guest Services:** valet laundry, wireless Internet. **Business Services:** conference facilities, business center. **Free Special Amenities:** newspaper and early check-in/late check-out.

Hilton
AAA Benefit:
Members save 5% or more everyday!

HOLIDAY INN EXPRESS   *Book at AAA.com*   Phone: 617/288-3030   16

Hotel
Rates not provided

Address: 69 Boston St 02125 **Location:** I-93, exit 18 southbound, exit 16 northbound, follow signs for Andrews Square. **Facility:** Smoke free premises. 118 units. 114 one-bedroom standard units. 4 one-bedroom suites with whirlpools. 6 stories, interior corridors. *Bath:* combo or shower only. **Parking:** on-site. **Amenities:** video games (fee), dual phone lines, voice mail, irons, hair dryers. **Leisure Activities:** exercise room. **Guest Services:** valet and coin laundry, area transportation (fee), wireless Internet. **Business Services:** meeting rooms, business center.

HOWARD JOHNSON HOTEL FENWAY   *Book at AAA.com*   Phone: (617)267-8300   10

Motel
$109-$239 5/1-11/1
$89-$169 11/2-4/30

Address: 1271 Boylston St 02215 **Location:** I-90, exit Brookline Ave S, backing onto Fenway Park. **Facility:** Smoke free premises. 94 one-bedroom standard units. 2 stories (no elevator), interior corridors. **Terms:** check-in 4 pm. **Amenities:** voice mail, safes, irons, hair dryers. **Pool(s):** outdoor. **Guest Services:** wireless Internet.

(See map and index starting on p. 345)

HYATT HARBORSIDE AT BOSTON'S LOGAN
INTERNATIONAL AIRPORT   *Book great rates at AAA.com*   Phone: (617)568-1234   **4**

AAA SAVE

Hotel
$129-$559 All Year

Address: 101 Harborside Dr 02128 **Location:** I-90, exit 20, follow Hotel Dr to Harborside Dr. Located on Boston harborfront. **Facility:** Smoke free premises. 270 units. 269 one-bedroom standard units. 1 one-bedroom suite with whirlpool. 14 stories, interior corridors. *Bath:* combo or shower only. **Parking:** on-site (fee) and valet. **Terms:** cancellation fee imposed. **Amenities:** high-speed Internet (fee), voice mail, irons, hair dryers. **Dining:** Harborside Grill, see separate listing. **Pool(s):** heated indoor. **Leisure Activities:** sauna, whirlpool, jogging, exercise room. **Guest Services:** valet laundry, airport transportation-Boston Logan International Airport, area transportation (fee)-water taxi to downtown, wireless Internet. **Business Services:** conference facilities, business center.

HYATT
HOTELS & RESORTS

AAA Benefit:
Ask for the AAA rate
and save 10%.

THE MIDTOWN HOTEL   *Book great rates at AAA.com*   Phone: (617)262-1000   **11**

AAA SAVE

Hotel
$149-$309 5/1-10/31
$99-$309 11/1-4/30

Address: 220 Huntington Ave 02115 **Location:** 3 blks sw of Copley Pl; just n of Symphony Hall and Massachusetts Ave. Opposite Prudential Center. **Facility:** Smoke free premises. 159 one-bedroom standard units. 2 stories, interior corridors. **Parking:** on-site (fee). **Amenities:** high-speed Internet (fee), voice mail, irons, hair dryers. *Some:* dual phone lines. **Pool(s):** heated outdoor. **Guest Services:** valet laundry, wireless Internet, beauty salon. **Business Services:** meeting rooms, PC (fee).

RAMADA BOSTON   *Book great rates at AAA.com*   Phone: (617)287-9100   **19**

Hotel
$129-$189 5/1-11/15
$109-$189 11/16-4/30

Address: 800 William T Morrissey Blvd 02122 **Location:** I-93, exit 13 northbound, 0.5 mi sw; exit 12 southbound, follow signs. **Facility:** Smoke free premises. 174 units. 173 one-bedroom standard units. 1 one-bedroom suite with efficiency and whirlpool. 2-3 stories, interior corridors. *Bath:* combo or shower only. **Parking:** on-site. **Amenities:** voice mail, safes, irons, hair dryers. **Pool(s):** outdoor. **Leisure Activities:** *Fee:* game room. **Guest Services:** valet and coin laundry, area transportation, wireless Internet. **Business Services:** meeting rooms, PC (fee). *(See color ad p 382)*

RENAISSANCE BOSTON WATERFRONT HOTEL   *Book great rates at AAA.com*   Phone: (617)338-4111   **7**

AAA SAVE

Hotel
$249-$369 All Year

Address: 606 Congress St 02210 **Location:** At D St. **Facility:** Smoke free premises. 471 units. 459 one-bedroom standard units. 12 one-bedroom suites, some with whirlpools. 21 stories, interior corridors. *Bath:* combo or shower only. **Parking:** valet. **Terms:** check-in 4 pm, cancellation fee imposed. **Amenities:** high-speed Internet, voice mail, safes, irons, hair dryers. **Pool(s):** heated indoor. **Leisure Activities:** sauna, whirlpool, exercise room. *Fee:* massage. **Guest Services:** valet laundry, wireless Internet. **Business Services:** conference facilities, business center. **Free Special Amenities:** newspaper.

RENAISSANCE
HOTELS & RESORTS

AAA Benefit:
Members save a
minimum 5% off the
best available rate.

THE SEAPORT HOTEL AND SEAPORT WORLD
TRADE CENTER   *Book great rates at AAA.com*   Phone: (617)385-4000   **6**

AAA SAVE

Hotel
$179-$499 All Year

Address: 1 Seaport Ln 02210 **Location:** MBTA-Silverline, World Trade Center Shop. **Facility:** Located near the Seaport World Trade Center Boston, rooms at the no-tipping, non-smoking hotel overlook either the airport or downtown Boston. Smoke free premises. 427 units. 400 one-bedroom standard units. 27 one-bedroom suites. 18 stories, interior corridors. *Bath:* combo or shower only. **Parking:** on-site (fee) and valet. **Amenities:** high-speed Internet, voice mail, safes, irons, hair dryers. **Dining:** Aura, see separate listing. **Pool(s):** heated indoor. **Leisure Activities:** steamrooms, spa. **Guest Services:** valet laundry, area transportation-limited areas within city, wireless Internet. **Business Services:** conference facilities, business center. **Free Special Amenities:** newspaper and high-speed Internet. Affiliated with A Preferred Hotel.

W BOSTON

fyi
Hotel
$179-$579 All Year

Too new to rate. **Address:** 100 Stuart St 02116 **Location:** In Theater District. **Amenities:** 235 units.

Phone: 617/261-8700

W
HOTELS

AAA Benefit:
Special member room rates,
plus Starwood Preferred
Guest® bonuses.

(See map and index starting on p. 345)

———— WHERE TO DINE ————

AQUITAINE BAR A VIN BISTROT **Phone:** 617/424-8577 **12**

French
$9-$29

Inspired by Parisian neighborhood bistros, the restaurant, with its high ceilings, open kitchen and French-inspired art, creates a warm and inviting atmosphere in which to sample sophisticated, classic fare. The menu offers stellar steak frites with black truffle vinaigrette, buttery sea scallops with bacon and mushrooms and simple yet satisfying roasted salmon with braised cabbage and parsnip puree. Servers will help with the wine list, which comprises French and Californian selections. Casual dress. **Bar:** Full bar. **Reservations:** suggested, weekends. **Hours:** 11:30 am-3 & 5:30-10 pm, Thurs & Fri-11 pm, Sat 10 am-3 & 5:30-11 pm, Sun 10 am-3 & 5:30-10 pm. Closed: 11/25, 12/25. **Address:** 569 Tremont Ave 02118 **Location:** Jct Union Park St; between Clarendon and Dartmouth sts. **Parking:** street.

AURA **Phone:** 617/385-4300 **3**

Regional Seafood
$14-$48

Located on Boston's Fish Pier, the restaurant invites patrons to dine in casual refinement amid soothing natural wood, green plants and crisp white table linens. The wait staff is attentive without being intrusive. Regional New England fare is raised to a different level. Desserts are artistic and wonderful. Parking is validated for up to three hours. Dressy casual. **Bar:** Full bar. **Reservations:** suggested. **Hours:** 6:30 am-10 pm. **Address:** 1 Seaport Ln 02210 **Location:** At Seaport World Trade Center; in The Seaport Hotel and Seaport World Trade Center. **Parking:** on-site (fee) and valet. CALL 👍 M

BEER WORKS **Phone:** 617/536-2337

American
$8-$19

The brewery creates 50 microbrews, 16 of which are on tap at any given time. Favorites from the "bold American" menu include beer-basted barbecue steak tips, sugarcane-seared salmon, sour cream and chive fries and the Big Dig brownie. Sports fans can keep up with the action on large- and small-screen TVs hanging throughout the dining area. Service is friendly and efficient. Casual dress. **Bar:** Beer & wine. **Hours:** 11:30 am-1 am. Closed: 11/25, 12/25. **Address:** 61 Brookline Ave 02215 **Location:** Opposite Fenway Park. **Parking:** no self-parking.

BETTY'S WOK AND NOODLE DINER **Phone:** 617/424-1950 **15**

Asian
$7-$22

Although the restaurant looks like an old-style diner, the food surprisingly doesn't reflect it at all. Instead, the menu mixes Asian and Latin dishes. The food is good, and desserts are homemade. Casual dress. **Bar:** Beer & wine. **Reservations:** accepted. **Hours:** noon-9:30 pm, Fri & Sat-11 pm. Closed major holidays. **Address:** 250 Huntington Ave 02139 **Location:** Just w of Massachusetts Ave. **Parking:** street.

B&G OYSTERS LTD **Phone:** 617/423-0550 **11**

Seafood
$16-$28

Seats fill quickly at the tiny fish house, which is known for its extensive selection of local oysters, magnificent chowders, fabulous fried clams and a knock-out lobster roll served with homemade pickles and fabulous fries. Service is casual, knowledgeable and efficient and, together with the food, contributes to a memorable dining experience. Casual dress. **Bar:** Beer & wine. **Hours:** 11:30 am-11 pm, Sat noon-11 pm, Sun noon-10 pm. Closed major holidays. **Address:** 550 Tremont Ave 02118 **Location:** At Waltham St. **Parking:** street.

BRAVO RESTAURANT **Phone:** 617/369-3474 **19**

American
$15-$25

The restaurant's terrace overlooks the Calderwood Courtyard and the west wing of the museum. The eclectic menu changes monthly and offers local ingredients, including seafood wherever possible. Museum pieces are rotated into the dining room frequently. Casual dress. **Bar:** Full bar. **Reservations:** accepted. **Hours:** 11:30 am-3 pm, Wed-Fri also 5:30 pm-8:30 pm; Saturday & Sunday brunch. Closed major holidays; also Patriots Day. **Address:** 465 Huntington Ave 02115 **Location:** At Museum of Fine Arts, Upper Level Galleria, West Wing. **Parking:** on-site (fee).

THE BUTCHER SHOP **Phone:** 617/423-4800 **10**

Specialty
$14-$32

Guests can order their favorite cuts of meat, as well as homemade sausages and pates, and food also can be sampled from the wine bar. Favorite options include the charcuterie and artisan cheese platters, roast chicken, steak tartare and the butcher's daily special. Casual dress. **Bar:** Beer & wine. **Reservations:** suggested. **Hours:** 11:30 am-3:30 & 4:30-11 pm, Sun & Mon-10 pm. Closed major holidays. **Address:** 552 Tremont St 02118 **Location:** Jct Waltham St; in South End. **Parking:** valet.

(See map and index starting on p. 345)

CONNOLLY'S PUB
Phone: 617/568-6700   ①

American
$12-$24

The convenient and casual spot employs friendly staffers. The nicely varied menu appeals to nearly everyone. Casual dress. **Bar:** Full bar. **Hours:** 11 am-12:30 am. **Address:** One Hotel Dr 02128 **Location:** At General Edward Lawrence Logan International Airport; in Hilton Boston Logan Airport. **Parking:** on-site (fee) and valet. CALL

THE ELEPHANT WALK-BOSTON
Phone: 617/247-1500   ⑥

French
$7-$28

In a gold-domed, cupola-topped Colonial brick building on the border of Boston and Brookline, the restaurant is marked by a parade of gold elephants on the facade. The food is a combination of French and Southeast Asian, predominantly Cambodian, cuisines. Casual dress. **Bar:** Full bar. **Reservations:** suggested, Fri & Sat. **Hours:** 11:30 am-2:30 & 5-10 pm, Fri-11 pm, Sat 5 pm-11 pm, Sun 11:30 am-2:30 & 5-10 pm; Sunday brunch. Closed: 7/4, 11/25, 12/24, 12/25. **Address:** 900 Beacon St 02215 **Location:** On Brookline/Boston line at Park Dr. **Parking:** on-site (fee) and valet.

FLOUR BAKERY & CAFE
Phone: 617/267-4300   ⑳

Breads/Pastries
$5-$15

The South End cafe prepares wonderful baked goods for those with a sweet tooth, in addition to gourmet sandwiches that reflect French and American influences. The setting is casual, with additional sidewalk seating, weather permitting. Casual dress. **Reservations:** not accepted. **Hours:** 7 am-9 pm, Sat 8 am-6 pm, Sun 9 am-5 pm. Closed: 11/25, 12/25, 12/26; also 11/26. **Address:** 1595 Washington St 02118 **Location:** Jct Rutland St. **Parking:** street.

FREEPORT TAVERN
Phone: 617/282-7700   ㉒

American
$9-$24

In addition to many seafood selections, the comprehensive menu lists some beef, pork, chicken, lamb and vegetarian dishes. Although the atmosphere is intended to be casual, the fresh flowers, style of dress and upscale, hunt-club décor lend a more formal feel. Piano bar entertainment is offered Wednesday through Saturday. Casual dress. **Bar:** Full bar. **Reservations:** suggested, weekends. **Hours:** 4 pm-11 pm; Sunday brunch 10:30 am-2:30 pm. Closed: 12/25. **Address:** 780 William T Morrissey Blvd 02122 **Location:** I-93, exit 13 northbound, 0.5 mi sw; exit 12 southbound, follow signs. **Parking:** on-site. CALL

GIACOMO'S
Phone: 617/536-5723   ⑨

Italian
$12-$25

A sibling to another location in the North End, this South End restaurant remains a local favorite for its casual decor, friendly staff and fresh Italian food. Pastas, sauces, desserts and everything else on the menu are created in house. Casual dress. **Bar:** Beer & wine. **Reservations:** accepted. **Hours:** 5 pm-10 pm, Fri & Sat-11 pm, Sun-9:30 pm. Closed major holidays. **Address:** 431 Columbus Ave 02116 **Location:** At Pembroke St; in South End. **Parking:** valet.

HAMERSLEY'S BISTRO
Phone: 617/423-2700   ⑧

French
$25-$40

In a former South End piano factory, Hamersley's Bistro is something of a Boston tradition. Representative of exceptional French-American cuisine are choices such as duck confit and seared scallops with glazed sweetbreads. Guests should be sure to try one of the pastry chef's divine and unusual desserts. Dressy casual. **Bar:** Full bar. **Reservations:** suggested. **Hours:** 5:30 pm-9:30 pm, Fri & Sat-10 pm, Sun 11 am-2 & 5:30-9:30 pm; Sunday brunch. Closed major holidays; also 1/2-1/7. **Address:** 553 Tremont St 02116 **Location:** At Clarendon St. **Parking:** valet.

HARBORSIDE GRILL
Phone: 617/568-6060   ②

American
$15-$38

The panoramic view of the Boston Harbor and the downtown skyline makes for a memorable dining experience. Staff prepare an array of New England seafood specialties and grilled entrées in an open kitchen. A water shuttle is available from downtown. Casual dress. **Bar:** Full bar. **Reservations:** suggested, for dinner. **Hours:** 6 am-10 pm. **Address:** 101 Harborside Dr 02128 **Location:** I-90, exit 20, follow Hotel Dr to Harborside Dr; in Hyatt Harborside at Boston's Logan International Airport. **Parking:** street.

HOUSE OF SIAM
Phone: 617/267-1755   ⑰

Thai
$9-$18

About two blocks from the T's Orange Line's Massachusetts Ave stop in the historic South End, the restaurant resides under a green awning on a corner brownstone. Dusty rose walls mark the split-level dining room decorated with traditional Thai statues and artwork. A Thai staff lends authenticity. Starters ranging from Siam rolls to shrimp satay lead to seafood, curry, noodle and vegetarian dishes. The more than 30 specialties include Bangkok duck, barbecue pork and lemongrass chicken. Casual dress. **Bar:** Beer & wine. **Reservations:** suggested, weekends. **Hours:** 11:30 am-10 pm, Fri-11 pm, Sat noon-11 pm, Sun noon-10 pm. **Address:** 542 Columbus Ave 02116 **Location:** Between Worcester and W Springfield sts; in South End. **Parking:** street. CALL

LONGWOOD GRILLE & BAR
Phone: 617/731-4700   ㉑

American
$9-$19

On the menu are homemade soups, creative sandwiches and several heartier entrees. The location is in the Longwood Medical area, convenient to the entire facility. Casual dress. **Bar:** Full bar. **Reservations:** accepted. **Hours:** 7 am-midnight, Sun from 8 am. **Address:** 342 Longwood Ave 02115 **Location:** Adjoining Children's Hospital at Brookline Ave; in Best Western Boston-The Inn at Longwood Medical. **Parking:** on-site (fee). CALL

LTK BAR & KITCHEN
Phone: 617/330-7430   ⑤

Seafood
$10-$29

A fun new restaurant concept incorporates a modern, upbeat atmosphere and plenty of high-tech gadgetry. Creative menu ideas come straight from the test kitchen of Legal Seafood, and the excellent-quality fresh seafood comes right off the boat at this waterfront location. Dressy casual. **Bar:** Full bar. **Reservations:** accepted. **Hours:** 11:30 am-1 am, Thurs-Sat to 2 am. Closed: 12/25. **Address:** 225 Northern Ave 02210 **Location:** At D St. **Parking:** no self-parking.

(See map and index starting on p. 345)

METROPOLIS CAFE
Phone: 617/247-2931

Mediterranean
$16-$20

The cafe offers patrons a charming, intimate atmosphere with delightful food. Tables are a bit close together but that certainly doesn't detract from the overall dining experience. Casual dress. **Bar:** Full bar. **Reservations:** not accepted. **Hours:** 5:30 pm-10 pm, Thurs-Sat to 11 pm, Sun 9 am-3 & 5:30-10 pm; Sunday brunch. Closed: 1/1, 11/25, 12/25. **Address:** 584 Tremont St 02118 **Location:** Between Upton and Union Park sts; in South End. **Parking:** on-site and valet.

NO NAME RESTAURANT
Phone: 617/338-7539

Regional Seafood
$8-$18

This restaurant has been in the same family since the 1920s when it was originally built for fishermen. Diners have a good view of the harbor from the second-floor dining room, which has dark woodwork and a nautical theme. Fish entrees come broiled or fried and in ample portions. Casual dress. **Bar:** Beer & wine. **Reservations:** accepted. **Hours:** 11 am-10 pm, Sun-9 pm. Closed: 11/25, 12/25. **Address:** 15 1/2 Fish Pier 02127 **Location:** Harborfront on fishing pier; just e of World Trade Center. **Parking:** on-site.

SIBLING RIVALRY
Phone: 617/338-5338 ⑦

Regional American
$12-$32

Sibling chefs David and Bob Kinkead go head to head in their joint-venture restaurant. In the center row of the terrific and distinctive menu is a list of ingredients, and each chef takes one or two common ingredients and creates something of his own. The results are exciting and flavorful. On busy Tremont Street in the South End, the dining room is appointed in trendy decor and tended by skilled servers. Valet parking is available in the evening. Casual dress. **Bar:** Full bar. **Reservations:** suggested. **Hours:** 5:30 pm-9:45 pm, Sat 5 pm-10:45 pm, Sun 4 pm-8:45 pm. Closed major holidays. **Address:** 525 Tremont St 02116 **Location:** At Berkeley. **Parking:** valet.

STELLA RESTAURANT & BAR
Phone: 617/247-7747 ⑱

Italian
$16-$30

The South End restaurant offers a fun, cosmopolitan atmosphere in which the friendly and helpful staff serves good Italian fare, including salads, pizza, pasta and full dinners. The full menu is available until 11 pm, and the late night menu goes to 1:30 am. Casual dress. **Bar:** Full bar. **Reservations:** suggested. **Hours:** 5:30 pm-11 pm; Sunday brunch 10 am-3 pm. Closed: 1/1, 11/25, 12/25. **Address:** 1525 Washington St 02118 **Location:** Jct W Brookline St; in South End. **Parking:** street. CALL Ⓢ Ⓜ

TREMONT 647
Phone: 617/266-4600 ⑭

American
$13-$26

Chefs prepare meals before guests' eyes in the hip, intimate restaurant's open kitchen. Menu choices may include wood-grilled beef sirloin, barbecue chicken pizza, pumpkin and ricotta ravioli and the signature Chilean sea bass. It's a good idea to ask about hours for special Saturday pajama brunches. Dressy casual. **Bar:** Full bar. **Reservations:** accepted. **Hours:** 5:30 pm-10 pm, Fri-10:30 pm, Sat 10:30 am-2 & 5:30-10:30 pm, Sun 10:30 am-3 & 5:30-10 pm; Saturday & Sunday brunch. Closed: 11/25, 12/24, 12/25. **Address:** 647 Tremont St 02118 **Location:** Corner of W Brookline St; in South End. **Parking:** street.

UNION BAR AND GRILLE
Phone: 617/423-0555 ⑯

Steak
$16-$33

In the city's South End, this is one more restaurant of a growing number in this locale. Great food makes up the Sunday brunches and nightly dinners at this popular mingling spot for neighbors. Reservations are strongly suggested. Casual dress. **Bar:** Full bar. **Reservations:** suggested. **Hours:** 5:30 pm-11 pm, Thurs & Fri-midnight, Sat 10 am-3 & 5:30-midnight, Sun 10 am-3 & 5:30-11 pm. Closed major holidays. **Address:** 1357 Washington St 02118 **Location:** At Union Park; in South End. **Parking:** valet and street.

─────── *The following restaurant has not been evaluated by AAA* ───────
but is listed for your information only.

THE PARAMOUNT
Phone: 617/720-1152

fyi

Not evaluated. Guests order moderately priced dishes at the counter of this quaint diner-style spot and then look around to see if one of the limited tables is open. Locals frequent this place. **Address:** 44 Charles St 02114

The Boston Vicinity

ACTON

―――― WHERE TO DINE ――――

CROSSROADS CAFE   **Phone:** 978/263-9733

American
$9-$19

This neighborhood pub and eatery is at the end of a collection of stores, only a mile from the access road to Nashoba Valley ski area. Dark, high-backed, almost private booths provide seating, and walls lined with old prints of Boston sights, the Boston Red Sox and the New York Yankees add local flavor. The menu is eclectic with items such as Boston crab cakes, baked scrod, au poivre burger, tenderloin tips, shrimp scampi and fajitas. Reservations are not taken at this popular spot. Casual dress. **Bar:** Full bar. **Hours:** 11:30 am-10 pm, Fri-11 pm, Sat noon-11 pm, Sun 11 am-9 pm. Closed major holidays. **Address:** 405 Nagog Square 01720 **Location:** I-495, exit 31, 3 mi se on SR 2A and 119, 2 mi w of SR 27; in Nagog Park Shopping Center. **Parking:** on-site. CALL ⟨ḃM⟩

NOT YOUR AVERAGE JOE'S   **Phone:** 978/635-0101

American
$9-$18

The restaurant exemplifies the "in-trend" style of contemporary design through vibrant color schemes, comfortable banquettes and stools, and smartly dressed staff. However, the high point is the food. Chefs whip up gourmet comfort foods of homemade meatloaf with a flavorful twist, creative handmade pizzas, sandwiches, salads and more. Casual dress. **Bar:** Full bar. **Hours:** 11:30 am-10 pm, Fri & Sat-11 pm, Sun noon-9 pm. Closed: 11/25, 12/25. **Address:** 305 Main St 01720 **Location:** Just w of SR 2. **Parking:** street.

SCUPPERJACK'S   **Phone:** 978/263-8327

American
$9-$25

A rustic, nautical ambience, with the dining room and lounge overlooking scenic Nagog Pond, appeals to families and busy professionals. The salad bar or clam chowder start off the meal, which then moves on to prime rib, the house specialty for almost 30 years. Alternatives include lobster, baked scrod, fish and chips, lobster pie, lamb chops, chicken and a selection of steaks, including steak au poivre and filet mignon. Desserts are homemade. Bright foliage enhances the setting during autumn. Casual dress. **Bar:** Full bar. **Reservations:** suggested. **Hours:** 11:30 am-2:30 & 4:30-9 pm, Fri-9:30 pm, Sat 4 pm-9:30 pm, Sun 1 pm-8 pm; Sun 4 pm-9 pm in summer. Closed: 12/25; also Mon 1/1-4/15. **Address:** 3 Nagog Park 01720 **Location:** I-495, exit 31, 3 mi se on SR 2A and 119; 2 mi w of SR 27; in Nagog Park Shopping Center. **Parking:** on-site.

――――― *The following restaurants have not been evaluated by AAA* ―――――
but are listed for your information only.

SORRENTO'S BRICK OVEN PIZZERIA   **Phone:** 978/264-9006

[fyi]   Not evaluated. The casual pizzeria prepares all the expected favorites. **Address:** 251 Main St 01720

SPRIGS   **Phone:** 978/263-3325

[fyi]   Not evaluated. Both the chef and general manager own this lovely eatery and serve an array of items, including creative pastas with mushroom varieties, grilled rack of lamb, fresh haddock and several vegetarian items. **Address:** 5 Strawberry Hill Rd 01720 **Location:** Just off SR 2A (Great Rd).

▼ See AAA listing p 416 ▼

AMESBURY pop. 12,327

FAIRFIELD INN BY MARRIOTT-AMESBURY   *Book great rates at AAA.com*   Phone: (978)388-3400

Hotel
$109-$139 All Year

Address: 35 Clarks Rd 01913 **Location:** I-95, exit 58 southbound; exit 58B northbound; I-495, exit 55 northbound, 0.5 mi e. **Facility:** Smoke free premises. 105 one-bedroom standard units. 4 stories, interior corridors. *Bath:* combo or shower only. **Parking:** on-site. **Terms:** cancellation fee imposed. **Amenities:** video games (fee), voice mail, irons, hair dryers. **Pool(s):** outdoor. **Guest Services:** valet and coin laundry, wireless Internet. **Business Services:** business center.

AAA Benefit:
Members save a minimum 5% off the best available rate.

── **WHERE TO DINE** ──

ACAPULCOS FAMILY RESTAURANT & CANTINA   Phone: 978/834-0000

Mexican
$7-$17

The Mexican cantina serves wonderful fresh dishes and creative margaritas. Among traditional offerings are fajitas, enchiladas and burritos. Casual dress. **Bar:** Full bar. **Hours:** 11 am-10 pm, Fri & Sat-11 pm. Closed major holidays. **Address:** 100 Macy St 01913 **Location:** I-495, exit 55, just e. **Parking:** on-site.

──── *The following restaurant has not been evaluated by AAA* ────
but is listed for your information only.

MAD RIVER TAVERN   Phone: 978/834-0020

[fyi]

Not evaluated. This storefront restaurant backs up to a waterfall-like sluiceway. The dining room has high ceilings, hardwood floors and cherry furniture. A huge gold-gilded mirror, flickering oil lamps, and cozy table spacing give this small room an intimate feel, while large, ornate framed landscapes and still-life oils help to make the room feel larger than it is. A deli-like area in the rear has small tables and a three-seat bar facing the open kitchen. The menu focuses largely on fresh seafood. **Address:** 37 Main St 01913 **Location:** I-495, exit 54, 1.4 mi n on SR 150, 1 mi n of jct SR 110; in historic downtown.

ANDOVER pop. 7,900

COURTYARD BOSTON ANDOVER   *Book great rates at AAA.com*   Phone: (978)794-0700

Hotel
$154-$164 All Year

Address: 10 Campanelli Dr 01810 **Location:** I-93, exit 45, just e on River Rd; 2 mi n of jct I-495/93. Located in Riverbend Business Park. **Facility:** Smoke free premises. 146 units. 134 one-bedroom standard units. 12 one-bedroom suites. 3 stories, interior corridors. *Bath:* combo or shower only. **Parking:** on-site. **Terms:** cancellation fee imposed. **Amenities:** video games (fee), high-speed Internet, dual phone lines, voice mail, irons, hair dryers. **Pool(s):** heated indoor. **Leisure Activities:** whirlpool, exercise room. **Guest Services:** valet and coin laundry. **Business Services:** meeting rooms, business center.

AAA Benefit:
Members save a minimum 5% off the best available rate.

HOMEWOOD SUITES BY HILTON   Phone: 978/475-6000

Hotel
$99-$399 5/1-11/13
$79-$299 11/14-4/30

Address: 4 Riverside Dr 01810 **Location:** I-93, exit 45, 0.5 mi e. Located in Andover Research Park. **Facility:** Smoke free premises. 82 units. 24 one-bedroom standard units with efficiencies. 55 one- and 3 two-bedroom suites, some with efficiencies or kitchens. 3 stories, interior corridors. **Parking:** on-site. **Terms:** cancellation fee imposed. **Amenities:** video games (fee), dual phone lines, voice mail, irons, hair dryers. **Pool(s):** heated outdoor. **Leisure Activities:** whirlpool, barbecue & picnic area, exercise room, sports court. **Guest Services:** valet and coin laundry, wireless Internet. **Business Services:** meeting rooms, business center.

AAA Benefit:
Members save 5% or more everyday!

FREE full breakfast and high-speed Internet

LA QUINTA INN & SUITES   *Book at AAA.com*   Phone: (978)685-6200

Hotel
$79-$119 All Year

Address: 131 River Rd 01810 **Location:** I-93, exit 45, just w; I-495, exit 40B, 2 mi n. **Facility:** 168 units. 161 one-bedroom standard units. 7 one-bedroom suites. 3 stories, interior corridors. *Bath:* combo or shower only. **Parking:** on-site. **Amenities:** video games (fee), voice mail, irons, hair dryers. **Pool(s):** heated indoor. **Leisure Activities:** whirlpool, exercise room. **Guest Services:** valet and coin laundry, wireless Internet. **Business Services:** meeting rooms, PC.

RESIDENCE INN BY MARRIOTT BOSTON-ANDOVER   *Book great rates at AAA.com*   Phone: (978)683-0382

Extended Stay
Hotel
$139-$159 All Year

Address: 500 Minuteman Rd 01810 **Location:** I-93, exit 45, 0.3 mi w, then 0.5 mi n. **Facility:** Smoke free premises. 120 units. 48 one-bedroom standard units, some with efficiencies or kitchens. 47 one- and 25 two-bedroom suites, some with efficiencies or kitchens. 3 stories, interior corridors. *Bath:* combo or shower only. **Parking:** on-site. **Terms:** check-in 4 pm, cancellation fee imposed. **Amenities:** high-speed Internet, dual phone lines, voice mail, irons, hair dryers. **Pool(s):** heated outdoor. **Leisure Activities:** whirlpool, exercise room, sports court. **Guest Services:** valet and coin laundry. **Business Services:** meeting rooms, business center.

CALL

AAA Benefit:
Members save a
minimum 5% off the
best available rate.

SPRINGHILL SUITES BOSTON/ANDOVER   *Book great rates at AAA.com*   Phone: (978)688-8200

Hotel
$94-$149 All Year

Address: 550 Minuteman Rd 01810 **Location:** I-93, exit 45, 0.3 mi w, then 0.6 mi n. **Facility:** Smoke free premises. 136 one-bedroom standard units. 4 stories, interior corridors. *Bath:* combo or shower only. **Parking:** on-site. **Terms:** cancellation fee imposed. **Amenities:** high-speed Internet, dual phone lines, voice mail, irons, hair dryers. **Pool(s):** heated indoor. **Leisure Activities:** whirlpool, exercise room. **Guest Services:** valet and coin laundry. **Business Services:** meeting rooms, business center.

CALL

AAA Benefit:
Members save a
minimum 5% off the
best available rate.

STAYBRIDGE SUITES BOSTON/ANDOVER   *Book at AAA.com*   Phone: (978)686-2000

Extended Stay
Hotel
$110-$140 All Year

Address: 4 Tech Dr 01810 **Location:** I-93, exit 45, just sw via Shattuck Rd. Located in Andover Technical Park. **Facility:** 133 units. 55 one-bedroom standard units with efficiencies. 51 one- and 27 two-bedroom suites with efficiencies. 3 stories, interior corridors. *Bath:* combo or shower only. **Parking:** on-site. **Terms:** cancellation fee imposed. **Amenities:** DVD players, high-speed Internet, dual phone lines, voice mail, irons, hair dryers. **Pool(s):** heated outdoor. **Leisure Activities:** exercise room, sports court. **Guest Services:** complimentary and valet laundry, wireless Internet. **Business Services:** meeting rooms, business center.

ASK CALL

WYNDHAM BOSTON/ANDOVER HOTEL   *Book great rates at AAA.com*   Phone: (978)975-3600

Hotel
$109-$199 All Year

Address: 123 Old River Rd 01810 **Location:** I-93, exit 45, just e on River Rd. Located behind an office park. **Facility:** 293 units. 287 one-bedroom standard units. 6 one-bedroom suites. 5 stories, interior corridors. *Bath:* combo or shower only. **Parking:** on-site. **Terms:** cancellation fee imposed. **Amenities:** video games (fee), dual phone lines, voice mail, irons, hair dryers. **Pool(s):** heated indoor. **Leisure Activities:** whirlpool, exercise room. **Guest Services:** valet laundry, wireless Internet. **Business Services:** conference facilities. **Fee:** PC, fax. **Free Special Amenities:** local telephone calls and high-speed Internet.

▼ See AAA listing p 418 ▼

—— **WHERE TO DINE** ——

THE CHATEAU ITALIAN FAMILY DINING   Phone: 978/687-2442

Italian
$8-$23

The tradition began in 1933 and continues under the ownership and operation of the Nocera family. Extensive menu offerings are sure to please nearly all appetites. The terrific eatery for family and friends even offers function areas. Casual dress. **Bar:** Full bar. **Hours:** 11:15 am-10 pm, Fri & Sat-11 pm, Sun 10 am-9:30 pm. Closed: 11/25, 12/25. **Address:** 131 River Rd 01810 **Location:** I-93, exit 45, just w. **Parking:** on-site. CALL

GRASSFIELDS FOOD & SPIRITS   Phone: 978/475-7996

American
$6-$18

This freestanding, family-friendly restaurant is convenient both to downtown and the interstate. A half-wall topped with a brass railing separates the dining room's two tiers. The food is good, simple New England fare, with seafood, steaks, chops and chicken prepared broiled, baked, grilled or fried. To answer an often-asked question: strawberry shortcake is made with real biscuits. This place is popular, so expect to wait during peak times. Casual dress. **Bar:** Full bar. **Hours:** 11:15 am-9:30 pm, Fri & Sat-10 pm, Sun-9 pm. Closed: 11/25, 12/25. **Address:** 207 N Main St 01810 **Location:** I-495, exit 41, 1 mi s on SR 28; in Shawsheen Plaza. **Parking:** on-site. CALL

NINETY NINE RESTAURANT   Phone: 978/475-8033

American
$7-$18

This popular pub is committed to serving large portions of great food at reasonable prices. Guest favorites include hot wings, burgers, seafood, barbecue ribs and chicken. While reservations are not taken, call-ahead seating is offered. A children's menu is also available. Casual dress. **Bar:** Full bar. **Hours:** 11:30 am-10:30 pm, Thurs-Sat to 11 pm, Sun-10 pm. Closed: 11/25, 12/25. **Address:** 464 Lowell St 01810 **Location:** On SR 133. **Parking:** on-site.

THAI SWEET BASIL   Phone: 978/470-8098

Thai
$7-$15

Convenient to both the downtown area and the interstate, you will find this small store-front restaurant. The atmosphere is informal and enhanced by the Thai nationals as servers and the Thai tapestries that hang on the walls. You might start with basil rolls or the chicken coconut soup. A wide variety of noodle, rice and curry dishes is offered, some vegetarian, others with chicken, duck, beef, pork, lamb and seafood. Casual dress. **Bar:** Beer & wine. **Reservations:** not accepted. **Hours:** 11:30 am-3 & 4-9:30 pm, Sat 11:30 am-10 pm, Sun noon-9 pm. Closed: 7/4, 11/25, 12/25. **Address:** 209 N Main St 01810 **Location:** I-495, exit 41, 1 mi s on SR 28; in Shawsheen Plaza. **Parking:** on-site.

ARLINGTON pop. 42,389   (See map and index starting on p. 345)

—— **WHERE TO DINE** ——

NOT YOUR AVERAGE JOE'S   Phone: 781/643-1666

American
$9-$24

Contemporary art, vibrant colors, comfortable banquettes and stools, and smartly dressed staff, this restaurant presents an in-trend atmosphere. The high point is the food; the chefs whip up gourmet comfort foods of homemade meatloaf with a flavorful twist, creative handmade pizzas, sandwiches, salads and more. Casual dress. **Bar:** Full bar. **Hours:** 11:30 am-10 pm, Fri & Sat-11 pm, Sun noon-10 pm. Closed: 11/25, 12/25. **Address:** 645 Massachusetts Ave 02476 **Location:** Just w of SR 60; downtown. **Parking:** street. CALL

BEDFORD   (See map and index starting on p. 345)

------ WHERE TO DINE ------

BAMBOO   **Phone:** 781/275-5888   62

Asian
$8-$21

The upscale Asian theme incorporates minimalist-modern decor, mustard-painted walls, dark woods, bamboo plants and classical-Asian instrumental background music. Flavorful dishes combine fresh crispy vegetables and high-quality meats and seafood. Casual dress. **Bar:** Full bar. **Hours:** 11:30 am-9:45 pm, Fri & Sat-10:45 pm. Closed major holidays. **Address:** 213 Burlington Rd 01730 **Location:** On SR 62, just e of US 3. **Parking:** on-site.

BISTRO 44   **Phone:** 781/275-5500   61

American
$12-$37

Off the lobby or by way of a separate entrance marked by a striking black awning, the restaurant boasts a stylish décor with such interesting touches as leaded art glass that trims the doors. The menu is regional American with an emphasis on New England foods. Seared scallops and red-pepper fettuccine with grilled vegetables are among the offerings, as are sandwiches for lighter eaters. The reasonable wine list includes several selections from New England vineyards. Dressy casual. **Bar:** Full bar. **Reservations:** suggested. **Hours:** 6:30 am-10 pm. Closed: 12/25. **Address:** 44 Middlesex Tpke 01730 **Location:** I-95, exit 32B, 2.5 mi n; in Doubletree Hotel Bedford Glen. **Parking:** on-site.

DALYA'S RESTAURANT   *Menu on AAA.com*   **Phone:** 781/275-0700

American
$9-$36

American and Mediterranean cuisine is served in a European farmhouse atmosphere with a cozy fireplace, lace curtains and antique tables with double tablecloths. The seasonally changing menu might include such delights as Mediterranean pot roast, baked scrod, beef tenderloin, vegetarian lasagna, lobster ravioli, duck, lamb and bouillabaisse. This is a popular spot for meeting a friend or for a casual business lunch. Staff members in long-sleeved shirts, ties and long aprons provide service. Dressy casual. **Bar:** Full bar. **Reservations:** suggested. **Hours:** 11:30 am-2 & 5:30-9 pm, Sat from 5:30 pm. Closed major holidays; also Sun. **Address:** 20 North Rd 01730 **Location:** SR 4 and 225, just n of jct SR 62 W; at Bedford Farms. **Parking:** on-site.

BEVERLY   pop. 39,862

------ WHERE TO DINE ------

THE BEVERLY DEPOT   **Phone:** 978/927-5402

American
$15-$36

Located in a beautifully converted 1890s train station on a still-active commuter rail line, The Beverly Depot provides a variety of steaks and seafood and an excellent salad bar. This landmark has forty foot ceilings and three working fireplaces. The restaurant remains popular, the service efficient, and the food dependably good. Casual dress. **Bar:** Full bar. **Reservations:** accepted. **Hours:** 4 pm-10 pm, Fri & Sat-10:30 pm, Sun 3 pm-9 pm. Closed: 7/4, 12/24, 12/25; also Super Bowl Sun. **Address:** 10 Park St 01915 **Location:** SR 1A, just w, facing Post Office, 0.5 mi s of jct SR 62; at railroad station. **Parking:** on-site.

NOT YOUR AVERAGE JOE'S   Phone: 978/927-8950

American
$9-$18

The restaurant exemplifies the "in-trend" style of high-art contemporary design through vibrant color schemes, comfortable banquettes and stools, and smartly dressed staff. However, the high point is the food. Chefs whip up gourmet comfort foods of homemade meatloaf with a flavorful twist, creative hand-made pizzas, sandwiches, salads and more. Casual dress. **Bar:** Full bar. **Hours:** 11:30 am-10 pm, Fri & Sat-11 pm, Sun noon-10 pm. Closed: 11/25, 12/25. **Address:** 45 Enon St 01915 **Location:** SR 128, exit 20A, 0.8 mi n on SR 1A. **Parking:** street.

BILLERICA   (See map and index starting on p. 345)

COURTYARD BY MARRIOTT BILLERICA/BEDFORD   *Book great rates at AAA.com*   Phone: (978)670-7500

Hotel
$169-$189 All Year

Address: 270 Concord Rd 01821 **Location:** US 3, exit 27, just w. **Facility:** Smoke free premises. 210 units. 196 one-bedroom standard units. 14 one-bedroom suites. 8 stories, interior corridors. *Bath:* combo or shower only. **Parking:** on-site. **Terms:** cancellation fee imposed. **Amenities:** high-speed Internet, dual phone lines, voice mail, irons, hair dryers. **Pool(s):** heated indoor. **Leisure Activities:** exercise room. **Guest Services:** valet and coin laundry, area transportation, wireless Internet. **Business Services:** conference facilities, business center.

AAA Benefit:
Members save a minimum 5% off the best available rate.

HAMPTON INN BEDFORD/BURLINGTON   *Book great rates at AAA.com*   Phone: (978)262-9977   **33**

Hotel
$79-$179 All Year

Address: 25 Middlesex Tpke 01821 **Location:** I-95, exit 32B, 2.5 mi n. **Facility:** 129 one-bedroom standard units. 4 stories, interior corridors. *Bath:* combo or shower only. **Parking:** on-site. **Terms:** 1-7 night minimum stay, cancellation fee imposed. **Amenities:** high-speed Internet, dual phone lines, voice mail, irons, hair dryers. **Pool(s):** heated outdoor. **Leisure Activities:** exercise room. **Guest Services:** valet and coin laundry, area transportation, wireless Internet. **Business Services:** meeting rooms, business center.

AAA Benefit:
Members save up to 10% everyday!

HOMEWOOD SUITES BY HILTON   *Book great rates at AAA.com*   Phone: (978)670-7111   **34**

Extended Stay
Hotel
$109-$199 All Year

Address: 35 Middlesex Tpke 01821 **Location:** I-95, exit 32B, 2.5 mi n. **Facility:** 147 units. 140 one- and 7 two-bedroom suites with efficiencies. 4 stories, interior corridors. *Bath:* combo or shower only. **Parking:** on-site. **Terms:** 1-7 night minimum stay, cancellation fee imposed. **Amenities:** video games (fee), high-speed Internet, dual phone lines, voice mail, irons, hair dryers. *Some:* DVD players. **Pool(s):** heated indoor. **Leisure Activities:** whirlpool, exercise room. **Guest Services:** valet and coin laundry, area transportation. **Business Services:** meeting rooms, business center.

HOMEWOOD SUITES Hilton

AAA Benefit:
Members save 5% or more everyday!

—————— **WHERE TO DINE** ——————

NAKED FISH   Phone: 978/663-6500

Seafood
$9-$28

The restaurant presents a selection of unadorned "naked" seafood, beef and chicken, as well as some Cuban and "not-so-naked" choices. Naked seafood is grilled over an open wood fire after being dressed only with lemon and olive oil. Interesting sides, such as coconut steamed rice, make the choice of only one difficult. Although limited in number, the desserts are excellent, particularly the banana flan. The modern, Impressionist, Caribbean-influenced dining room can be bustling and noisy. Casual dress. **Bar:** Full bar. **Reservations:** suggested. **Hours:** 11:30 am-10 pm, Sat 3 pm-11 pm, Sun 3 pm-9 pm. **Address:** 15 Middlesex Tpke 01821 **Location:** I-95, exit 34B, 2.5 mi n. **Parking:** on-site.

BOXBOROUGH

HOLIDAY INN BOXBOROUGH WOODS   *Book at AAA.com*   Phone: (978)263-8701

Hotel
$99-$169 All Year

Address: 242 Adams Pl 01719 **Location:** I-495, exit 28, just e on SR 111. **Facility:** Smoke free premises. 143 units. 136 one-bedroom standard units. 7 one-bedroom suites. 3 stories, interior corridors. **Parking:** on-site. **Terms:** cancellation fee imposed. **Amenities:** video games (fee), high-speed Internet, dual phone lines, voice mail, irons, hair dryers. **Dining:** The Minuteman Grille, see separate listing. **Pool(s):** heated indoor. **Leisure Activities:** exercise room. **Guest Services:** valet and coin laundry. **Business Services:** conference facilities, PC.

—————— **WHERE TO DINE** ——————

THE MINUTEMAN GRILLE   Phone: 978/263-8701

American
$12-$22

The restaurant presents a menu of traditional steaks, burgers, soups, salads and pasta and chicken dishes. Casual dress. **Bar:** Full bar. **Reservations:** accepted. **Hours:** 6:30 am-10 pm, Fri-11 pm, Sat 7 am-11 pm. Closed: 1/1, 12/25. **Address:** 242 Adams Pl 01719 **Location:** I-495, exit 28, just e on SR 111; in Holiday Inn Boxborough Woods. **Parking:** on-site.

BRAINTREE pop. 33,698   (See map and index starting on p. 345)

CANDLEWOOD SUITES BOSTON - BRAINTREE   *Book at AAA.com*   Phone: (781)849-7450   141

▼▼▼ ▼▼▼
Extended Stay Hotel
$89-$129 All Year

Address: 235 Wood Rd 02184 **Location:** I-93, exit 6, just n on SR 37, then 0.5 mi w. **Facility:** 133 units. 101 one-bedroom standard units with efficiencies. 32 one-bedroom suites with efficiencies. 4 stories, interior corridors. *Bath:* combo or shower only. **Parking:** on-site. **Terms:** cancellation fee imposed. **Amenities:** video library, DVD players, high-speed Internet, voice mail, irons, hair dryers **Leisure Activities:** exercise room. **Guest Services:** complimentary and valet laundry.

ASK ⊠ 🖥 🖼 📺 / SOME UNITS FEE 🐕 ✕

EXTENDED STAYAMERICA BOSTON-BRAINTREE   *Book at AAA.com*   Phone: (781)356-8333   137

▼▼▼ ▼▼▼
Extended Stay Hotel
$70-$104 All Year

Address: 20 Rockdale St 02184 **Location:** I-93, exit 6, just se. **Facility:** 103 units. 102 one-bedroom standard units with efficiencies. 1 one-bedroom suite with efficiencies. 3 stories, interior corridors. *Bath:* combo or shower only. **Parking:** on-site. **Terms:** office hours 7 am-11 pm, cancellation fee imposed. **Amenities:** voice mail, irons. **Guest Services:** coin laundry, wireless Internet.

ASK CALL 🕭M ⊠ 🖥 🖼 📺 / SOME UNITS FEE 🐕 ✕

HAMPTON INN BRAINTREE   *Book great rates at AAA.com*   Phone: (781)380-3300   140

AAA SAVE
▼▼▼ ▼▼▼
Hotel
$109-$209 All Year

Address: 215 Wood Rd 02184 **Location:** I-93, exit 6, just n on SR 37, then 0.5 mi w. **Facility:** 103 one-bedroom standard units. 4 stories, interior corridors. *Bath:* combo or shower only. **Parking:** on-site. **Terms:** 1-7 night minimum stay, cancellation fee imposed. **Amenities:** video games (fee), dual phone lines, voice mail, irons, hair dryers. **Pool(s):** heated indoor. **Leisure Activities:** whirlpool, exercise room. **Guest Services:** valet and coin laundry, area transportation-within 4 mi, wireless Internet. **Business Services:** meeting rooms, business center. **Free Special Amenities: expanded continental breakfast and newspaper.**

🍴+ CALL 🕭M 🏊 ⊠ 📺 / SOME UNITS 🐕 ✕ 🖥 🖼

Hampton Inn
AAA Benefit:
Members save up to 10% everyday!

HOLIDAY INN EXPRESS-BRAINTREE   *Book great rates at AAA.com*   Phone: (781)848-1260   138

AAA SAVE
▼▼▼ ▼▼▼
Hotel
$99-$179 5/1-10/31
$99-$139 11/1-4/30

Address: 190 Wood Rd 02184 **Location:** I-93, exit 6, just n on SR 37, then 0.4 mi w. **Facility:** 103 one-bedroom standard units. 3 stories, interior corridors. *Bath:* combo or shower only. **Parking:** on-site. **Amenities:** video games (fee), dual phone lines, voice mail, irons, hair dryers. **Leisure Activities:** limited exercise equipment. **Guest Services:** valet and coin laundry, wireless Internet. **Business Services:** business center. **Free Special Amenities: expanded continental breakfast and high-speed Internet.**

🍴+ ⊠ 📺 / SOME UNITS ✕ 🖥 🖼

SHERATON BRAINTREE HOTEL   Phone: 781/848-0600   139

▼▼▼ ▼▼▼
Hotel
$79-$389 All Year

Address: 37 Forbes Rd 02184 **Location:** I-93, exit 6, just s on SR 37, then just w. Located across from a shopping mall. **Facility:** Smoke free premises. 374 units. 370 one-bedroom standard units, some with whirlpools. 4 one-bedroom suites with whirlpools. 2-6 stories, interior corridors. *Bath:* combo or shower only. **Parking:** on-site. **Amenities:** dual phone lines, voice mail, irons, hair dryers. *Fee:* video games, high-speed Internet. **Pool(s):** outdoor, heated indoor. **Leisure Activities:** whirlpool. **Guest Services:** valet laundry, area transportation. **Business Services:** conference facilities, business center.

🍴 🍷 🏊 FEE 🏋 ✕ 🏸 📺 / SOME UNITS 🐕 FEE 🖥

Sheraton
HOTELS & RESORTS
AAA Benefit:
Members get up to 15% off, plus Starwood Preferred Guest® bonuses.

―――― **WHERE TO DINE** ――――

ASCARI   Phone: 781/228-2020   123

▼▼ ▼▼
American
$7-$18

Well-prepared American fare incorporates fine-quality ingredients. Friendly and accommodating servers circulate through a distinctive setting marked by sports photographs and racing memorabilia, in addition to many TVs airing sporting events. The dining room and lounge overlook two European indoor racetracks. The facility is a hot spot for team building, reunions and friendly gatherings with a competitive edge. Casual dress. **Bar:** Full bar. **Reservations:** accepted. **Hours:** 11:30 am-9 pm, Fri-Sun to 10 pm. Closed major holidays. **Address:** 290 Wood Rd 02184 **Location:** I-93, exit 6, just n on SR 35, then 0.7 mi w; at F1 Boston. **Parking:** on-site. CALL 🕭M

LEGAL SEA FOODS   Phone: 781/356-3070   124

▼▼▼ ▼▼
Seafood
$9-$42

Legal prides itself on a reputation for freshness and consistency. More than 40 varieties of seafood can be grilled, broiled, fried or prepared Cajun style. Try the clam chowder that has been served at every presidential inauguration since 1981. The nautically inspired dining room is upscale and attractive with its rich cherry wood paneling and intricately detailed model ships. Casual dress. **Bar:** Full bar. **Reservations:** accepted. **Hours:** 11 am-10 pm, Fri & Sat-11 pm, Sun noon-9 pm. Closed: 11/25, 12/25. **Address:** 250 Granite St 02184 **Location:** I-93, exit 6, just s; in South Shore Plaza. **Parking:** on-site.
CALL 🕭M

BROOKLINE pop. 57,107   (See map and index starting on p. 345)

COURTYARD BOSTON BROOKLINE   *Book great rates at AAA.com*   Phone: (617)734-1393   116

Hotel
$129-$229 All Year

Address: 40 Webster St 02446 **Location:** 1.3 mi sw of Kenmore Square, just s of Beacon St, then just w of Harvard St. **Facility:** Smoke free premises. 188 units. 187 one-bedroom standard units, some with whirlpools. 1 one-bedroom suite. 8 stories, interior corridors. *Bath:* combo or shower only. **Parking:** on-site (fee). **Terms:** cancellation fee imposed. **Amenities:** high-speed Internet, dual phone lines, voice mail, irons, hair dryers. **Pool(s):** heated indoor. **Leisure Activities:** whirlpool, exercise room. **Guest Services:** valet and coin laundry, area transportation-Longwood Medical area, wireless Internet. **Business Services:** meeting rooms, business center. **Free Special Amenities: high-speed Internet.**

AAA Benefit:
Members save a minimum 5% off the best available rate.

HOLIDAY INN BOSTON-BROOKLINE   *Book at AAA.com*   Phone: (617)277-1200   115

Hotel
$159-$239 All Year

Address: 1200 Beacon St 02446 **Location:** 1 mi sw of Kenmore Square; at Beacon and St. Paul sts. **Facility:** Smoke free premises. 225 units. 213 one-bedroom standard units. 12 one-bedroom suites. 2-6 stories, interior corridors. *Bath:* combo or shower only. **Parking:** on-site (fee). **Terms:** check-in 4 pm, cancellation fee imposed. **Amenities:** video games (fee), dual phone lines, voice mail, irons, hair dryers. **Pool(s):** heated indoor. **Leisure Activities:** whirlpool, exercise room. **Guest Services:** valet and coin laundry, area transportation, wireless Internet. **Business Services:** meeting rooms, PC.

─── **WHERE TO DINE** ───

THE FIREPLACE   Phone: 617/975-1900   107

American
$8-$33

The memorable dishes created by the chef and his team are the result of excellent skills and culinary training. A menu offering might blend pomegranate seeds and dried cranberries with parchment-baked fish. An impressive selection of artisan cheese is offered. The attractive and cozy décor incorporates colorful painted walls and artwork, copper-topped tables and a roaring wood fireplace. Dressy casual. **Bar:** Full bar. **Reservations:** accepted. **Hours:** 11 am-2:30 & 5-10 pm, Thurs-Sat to 11 pm; Saturday & Sunday brunch. Closed major holidays. **Address:** 1634 Beacon St 02446 **Location:** In Washington Square. **Parking:** street.

PARIS CREPERIE   Phone: 617/232-1770   106

French
$4-$8

Even folks who are not usually crepe lovers should give this place a try. Made-to-order crepes are stuffed with varied fresh sweet or savory ingredients, including Peking duck, steak and cheese, marmalade, fresh fruits and veggies, Nutella and even s'mores. All are neatly folded, wrapped in paper and served on a pizza tray. Soups, coffee, teas and fresh smoothies also are available. Delicious treats include frozen hot chocolate or the Jimmy Carter smoothie made with bananas and peanut butter. Casual dress. **Reservations:** not accepted. **Hours:** 10 am-10 pm, Fri-11 pm, Sat 8 am-11 pm, Sun 8 am-10 pm. Closed: 11/25, 12/25. **Address:** 278 Harvard St 02446 **Location:** Just nw of Beacon St; at Green St. **Parking:** no self-parking.

BURLINGTON pop. 22,876   (See map and index starting on p. 345)

BOSTON MARRIOTT BURLINGTON   *Book great rates at AAA.com*   Phone: (781)229-6565   5

Hotel
$189-$229 All Year

Address: 1 Mall Rd 01803 **Location:** I-95, exit 33B, jct SR 3A. **Facility:** Smoke free premises. 419 units. 417 one-bedroom standard units. 2 one-bedroom suites. 9 stories, interior corridors. *Bath:* combo or shower only. **Parking:** on-site. **Terms:** check-in 4 pm, cancellation fee imposed. **Amenities:** dual phone lines, voice mail, irons, hair dryers. *Fee:* video games, high-speed Internet. **Dining:** Fitzwilliam's Irish Pub, Summer Winter, see separate listings. **Pool(s):** heated outdoor, heated indoor. **Leisure Activities:** sauna, whirlpool. **Guest Services:** complimentary and valet laundry, area transportation-within 2 mi, wireless Internet. **Business Services:** conference facilities, business center.

Marriott
HOTELS & RESORTS

AAA Benefit:
Members save a
minimum 5% off the
best available rate.

CANDLEWOOD SUITES BOSTON-BURLINGTON   *Book at AAA.com*   Phone: (781)229-4300   5

Extended Stay
Hotel
$59-$90 All Year

Address: 130 Middlesex Tpke 01803 **Location:** I-95, exit 32B, just n. **Facility:** 139 units. 104 one-bedroom standard units with efficiencies. 35 one-bedroom suites with efficiencies. 4 stories, interior corridors. *Bath:* combo or shower only. **Parking:** on-site. **Terms:** cancellation fee imposed. **Amenities:** video library, DVD players, CD players, high-speed Internet, dual phone lines, voice mail, irons, hair dryers. **Leisure Activities:** exercise room. **Guest Services:** complimentary and valet laundry, area transportation. **Business Services:** fax.

HILTON GARDEN INN BOSTON/BURLINGTON   *Book great rates at AAA.com*   Phone: (781)272-8800   6

Hotel
$79-$199 All Year

Address: 5 Wheeler Rd 01803 **Location:** I-95, exit 32B, just s on Middlesex Tpke. **Facility:** 179 units. 178 one-bedroom standard units. 1 one-bedroom suite. 4 stories, interior corridors. *Bath:* combo or shower only. **Parking:** on-site. **Terms:** 1-7 night minimum stay, cancellation fee imposed. **Amenities:** video games (fee), high-speed Internet, voice mail, irons, hair dryers. **Pool(s):** heated indoor. **Leisure Activities:** exercise room. **Guest Services:** valet and coin laundry, area transportation, wireless Internet. **Business Services:** meeting rooms, business center.

Hilton
Garden Inn

AAA Benefit:
Members save 5% or
more everyday!

**HYATT SUMMERFIELD SUITES
BOSTON/BURLINGTON**   *Book great rates at AAA.com*   Phone: (781)270-0800   6

Extended Stay
Hotel
$89-$249 All Year

Address: 2 Van de Graaff Dr 01803 **Location:** I-95, exit 33A, just s on US 3, then 0.5 mi w on Wayside Rd. **Facility:** Smoke free premises. 150 units. 111 one- and 39 two-bedroom suites, some with efficiencies or kitchens. 3 stories, interior corridors. *Bath:* combo or shower only. **Parking:** on-site. **Terms:** check-in 4 pm, cancellation fee imposed. **Amenities:** video library (fee), DVD players, high-speed Internet, dual phone lines, voice mail, irons, hair dryers. **Pool(s):** heated outdoor. **Leisure Activities:** whirlpool, gas grills, picnic area, exercise room, sports court. **Guest Services:** valet and coin laundry, area transportation-within 5 mi, wireless Internet. **Business Services:** meeting rooms, business center. **Free Special Amenities:** full breakfast and high-speed Internet.

HYATT
SUMMERFIELD
SUITES™

AAA Benefit:
Ask for the AAA rate
and save 10%.

—— WHERE TO DINE ——

CAFE ESCADRILLE   Phone: 781/273-1916   5

Continental
$10-$40

Family-operated since 1974, the cafe prepares creative gourmet entrées, such as steak au poivre and duck a l'orange. The elegant, candlelit atmosphere is reminiscent of the early days of World War I in Europe. Diners are urged to save room for a delicious dessert. Dressy casual. **Bar:** Full bar. **Reservations:** accepted, except Sat. **Hours:** 11:30 am-midnight. Closed major holidays; also Sun except Easter & Mother's Day. **Address:** 26 Cambridge St 01803 **Location:** On SR 3A, 0.3 mi s of I-95/SR 128, exit 33A. **Parking:** on-site.

THE DANDELION GREEN   Phone: 781/273-1616   5

American
$9-$35

Abundant greenery and natural wood accents complement lively, candlelit dining in a contemporary setting. Steak, chops and seafood reign. The pub menu lists lighter fare. The lounge is open Saturday at noon for lunch. In winter, the restaurant also serves lunch beginning at noon on the weekends; call for specific dates. Casual dress. **Bar:** Full bar. **Reservations:** suggested. **Hours:** 11:30 am-2:30 & 4-10 pm, Sat from 4 pm, Sun noon-8 pm; Sun 3 pm-9 pm 7/1-9/6. Closed: 12/24, 12/25. **Address:** 90 Burlington Mall Rd 01803 **Location:** I-95, exit 33B southbound, 1 mi w; exit 32B northbound, 0.5 mi e, past Burlington Mall; in Marketplace Shopping Center. **Parking:** on-site.

FITZWILLIAM'S IRISH PUB   Phone: 781/221-6643   5

Irish
$7-$14

Off the main lobby, this pub was built on site by Irish artisans who journeyed here for that task. Several "snugs" make for an almost totally private eating experience. Among selections are shepherd's pie, Guinness beef stew and fish and chips, along with numerous sandwiches and soups, including Irish potato and bacon soup and, of course, New England clam chowder. Portions are generous. Casual dress. **Bar:** Full bar. **Reservations:** not accepted. **Hours:** 11:30 am-11 pm, Sun noon-10 pm. **Address:** 1 Mall Rd 01803 **Location:** I-95, exit 33B, jct SR 3A; in Boston Marriott Burlington. **Parking:** on-site.

(See map and index starting on p. 345)

LEGAL SEA FOODS

Phone: 781/270-9700   (53)

Seafood
$10-$42

Legal prides itself on a reputation for freshness and consistency. More than 40 varieties of seafood can be grilled, broiled, fried or prepared Cajun style. Try the clam chowder that has been served at every presidential inauguration since 1981. The nautically inspired dining room is upscale and attractive with its rich cherry wood paneling and intricately detailed model ships. Casual dress. **Bar:** Full bar. **Hours:** 11 am-10 pm, Fri & Sat-10:30 pm, Sun noon-9 pm. Closed: 12/25. **Address:** 75 Middlesex Tpke 01803 **Location:** I-95, exit 32B; in Burlington Mall. **Parking:** on-site. CALL ⚫M

LESTER'S ROADSIDE BAR-B-Q

Phone: 781/221-7427   (49)

Barbecue
$7-$14

The quick-serve restaurant lets patrons get a bite of Southern barbecue for a speedy on-site meal or for take-out. The owner-chef prepares the real thing from homemade marinades and sauces, smoked meats and a nice selection of not-to-be-missed accompaniments, especially macaroni and cheese. Casual dress. **Hours:** 11 am-8:30 pm, Fri & Sat-9 pm. Sun noon-8 pm. Closed major holidays. **Address:** 367A Cambridge St 01803 **Location:** Just w of SR 62. **Parking:** on-site.

NOT YOUR AVERAGE JOE'S

Phone: 781/505-1303

American
$9-$18

This eatery exemplifies the "in-trend" style of high-art contemporary design through vibrant color schemes, comfortable seating and smartly dressed staff. However, the high point is the food. The cooking team whips up gourmet comfort foods of homemade meatloaf with a flavorful twist, creative hand-made pizzas, sandwiches, salads and more. Casual dress. **Bar:** Full bar. **Hours:** 11:30 am-10 pm, Fri & Sat-11 pm, Sun noon-10 pm. Closed: 11/25, 12/25. **Address:** 4C Wayside Rd 01803 **Location:** On US 3. **Parking:** on-site.

SUMMER WINTER

Phone: 781/221-6643   (52)

American
$10-$26

This elegant, upscale dining experience is a creative blend of international and New England inspirations. Local fish and shellfish might be paired with Asian herbs. Other menu possibilities are barbecue duck in a Singapore pancake, Asian salad with dipping sauce, traditional Maine steamed lobster and cassoulet with duck confit. Warm wood tones and natural fibers lend a contemporary but comfortable feel. The staff is well-versed in both the dish preparations and wine recommendations. Dressy casual. **Bar:** Full bar. **Reservations:** accepted. **Hours:** 11:30 am-2:30 & 5:30-10 pm. Closed major holidays. **Address:** 1 Mall Rd 01803 **Location:** I-95, exit 33B, jct SR 3A; in Boston Marriott Burlington. **Parking:** on-site. CALL ⚫M

CAMBRIDGE pop. 101,355   (See maps and indexes starting on p. 340, 345)

BEST WESTERN HOTEL TRIA

Book great rates at AAA.com

Phone: (617)491-8000   (94)

AAA SAVE

Hotel
$159-$299 5/1-10/31
$129-$259 11/1-4/30

Address: 220 Alewife Brook Pkwy 02138 **Location:** Jct SR 2, 16 and US 3; in North Cambridge; I-90 (Massachusetts Tpke), exit Cambridge/Allston to SR 2 W (Fresh Pond Pkwy). **Facility:** 121 one-bedroom standard units. 4 stories, interior corridors. *Bath:* combo or shower only. **Parking:** on-site. **Amenities:** high-speed Internet, dual phone lines, voice mail, irons, hair dryers. **Pool(s):** heated indoor. **Leisure Activities:** whirlpool, exercise room. **Guest Services:** valet laundry, area transportation-within 5 mi, wireless Internet. **Business Services:** business center. **Free Special Amenities:** full breakfast and high-speed Internet.

AAA Benefit:
Members save up to 20%, plus 10% bonus points with rewards program.

🍽 ✈ 🎥 📞 💻 / SOME UNITS FEE 🐕 ✕

BOSTON MARRIOTT CAMBRIDGE

Book great rates at AAA.com

Phone: (617)494-6600   (45)

AAA SAVE

Hotel
$229-$399 All Year

Address: 2 Cambridge Center 02142 **Location:** Corner of Broadway and Third St. **Facility:** Smoke free premises. 431 units. 419 one-bedroom standard units. 12 one-bedroom suites. 26 stories, interior corridors. *Bath:* combo or shower only. **Parking:** valet. **Terms:** check-in 4 pm, cancellation fee imposed. **Amenities:** voice mail, irons, hair dryers. *Fee:* video games, high-speed Internet. *Some:* safes. **Dining:** 2 restaurants. **Pool(s):** heated indoor. **Leisure Activities:** sauna, whirlpool, exercise room. **Guest Services:** complimentary and valet laundry, wireless Internet. **Business Services:** conference facilities, business center.

Marriott
HOTELS & RESORTS

AAA Benefit:
Members save a minimum 5% off the best available rate.

🍽 🍸 CALL ⚫M ✈ ✕ ✕ 🎥 💻 / SOME UNITS 📶

(See maps and indexes starting on p. 340, 345)

THE CHARLES HOTEL, HARVARD SQUARE   *Book great rates at AAA.com*   Phone: (617)864-1200

Hotel
$199-$750 All Year

Address: One Bennett St 02138 **Location:** Just s of Harvard Square, at Eliot St. **Facility:** Superlative service with numerous, high-end amenities make for a delightful stay at this hotel near many shops, restaurants and the Charles River. Smoke free premises. 294 units. 250 one-bedroom standard units. 44 one-bedroom suites. 10 stories, interior corridors. *Bath:* combo or shower only. **Parking:** on-site (fee) and valet. **Terms:** cancellation fee imposed. **Amenities:** DVD players, CD players, high-speed Internet, dual phone lines, voice mail, safes, honor bars, irons, hair dryers. **Dining:** 2 restaurants, also, Henrietta's Table, Rialto; see separate listings, nightclub. **Pool(s):** heated indoor. **Leisure Activities:** saunas, whirlpool, steamrooms, spa. **Guest Services:** valet laundry, wireless Internet. **Business Services:** meeting rooms, business center.
(See color ad below)

FREE newspaper and high-speed Internet

COURTYARD BY MARRIOTT BOSTON CAMBRIDGE   *Book great rates at AAA.com*   Phone: (617)492-7777

Hotel
$159-$269 All Year

Address: 777 Memorial Dr 02139 **Location:** On US 3 and SR 2. **Facility:** Smoke free premises. 203 units. 197 one-bedroom standard units. 6 one-bedroom suites. 16 stories, interior corridors. *Bath:* combo or shower only. **Parking:** on-site (fee). **Terms:** cancellation fee imposed. **Amenities:** voice mail, irons, hair dryers. **Pool(s):** heated indoor. **Leisure Activities:** exercise room. **Guest Services:** valet and coin laundry, wireless Internet. **Business Services:** meeting rooms, business center.

AAA Benefit:
Members save a minimum 5% off the best available rate.

HAMPTON INN BOSTON/CAMBRIDGE   *Book great rates at AAA.com*   Phone: (617)494-5300

Hotel
$129-$499 All Year

Address: 191 Monsignor O'Brien Hwy 02141 **Location:** I-93, exit 26, 0.3 mi n on SR 28. **Facility:** 114 one-bedroom standard units. 7 stories, interior corridors. *Bath:* combo or shower only. **Parking:** on-site. **Terms:** 1-7 night minimum stay, cancellation fee imposed. **Amenities:** video games (fee), high-speed Internet, dual phone lines, voice mail, safes, irons, hair dryers. **Leisure Activities:** exercise room. **Guest Services:** valet and coin laundry. **Business Services:** meeting rooms, PC.

AAA Benefit:
Members save up to 10% everyday!

▼ *See AAA listing above* ▼

(See maps and indexes starting on p. 340, 345)

HARVARD SQUARE HOTEL   *Book great rates at AAA.com*   Phone: (617)864-5200   98

Hotel
$119-$299 All Year

Address: 110 Mt Auburn St 02138 **Location:** At Mt Auburn and Eliot sts. Located in Harvard Square. **Facility:** Smoke free premises. 73 one-bedroom standard units. 5 stories, interior corridors. *Bath:* combo or shower only. **Parking:** on-site (fee). **Terms:** cancellation fee imposed. **Amenities:** voice mail, irons, hair dryers. **Guest Services:** valet laundry, wireless Internet. **Business Services:** PC (fee). **Free Special Amenities: newspaper and preferred room (subject to availability with advance reservations).**

HOLIDAY INN EXPRESS HOTEL & SUITES   *Book great rates at AAA.com*   Phone: (617)577-7600   97

Hotel
$109-$169 All Year

Address: 250 Monsignor O'Brien Hwy 02141 **Location:** I-93, exit 26, 0.5 mi n on SR 28. **Facility:** 112 units. 98 one-bedroom standard units. 14 one-bedroom suites. 8 stories, interior corridors. *Bath:* combo or shower only. **Parking:** on-site. **Amenities:** dual phone lines, voice mail, irons, hair dryers. **Guest Services:** valet laundry, wireless Internet. **Business Services:** PC. **Free Special Amenities: full breakfast and high-speed Internet.** / SOME UNITS

HOTEL MARLOWE   *Book great rates at AAA.com*   Phone: (617)868-8000   42

Boutique
Contemporary Retro
Hotel
$209-$1800 9/8-4/30
$169-$1200 5/1-9/7

Address: 25 Edwin H Land Blvd 02141 **Location:** Just sw of jct SR 28. Adjacent to and northeast of Cambridge Galleria Mall. **Facility:** The hip, upbeat, cutting-edge and whimsical property is part of the Galleria shopping mall and within walking distance of the Museum of Science. Smoke free premises. 236 units. 227 one-bedroom standard units. 9 one-bedroom suites with whirlpools. 8 stories, interior corridors. *Bath:* combo or shower only. **Parking:** on-site (fee) and valet. **Terms:** cancellation fee imposed. **Amenities:** high-speed Internet, dual phone lines, voice mail, safes, honor bars, irons, hair dryers. *Some:* DVD players. **Dining:** Bambara, see separate listing. **Leisure Activities:** kayaks, bicycles, exercise room. **Guest Services:** valet laundry, wireless Internet. **Business Services:** meeting rooms, business center. CALL / SOME UNITS

HYATT REGENCY CAMBRIDGE   *Book great rates at AAA.com*   Phone: (617)492-1234   102

Hotel
$99-$529 All Year

Address: 575 Memorial Dr 02139 **Location:** On US 3 and SR 2. **Facility:** 469 units. 459 one-bedroom standard units. 10 one-bedroom suites, some with whirlpools. 16 stories, interior corridors. *Bath:* combo or shower only. **Parking:** on-site (fee) and valet. **Terms:** check-in 4 pm, cancellation fee imposed. **Amenities:** dual phone lines, voice mail, safes, irons, hair dryers. *Fee:* video games, high-speed Internet. *Some:* CD players. **Pool(s):** heated indoor. **Leisure Activities:** saunas, steamrooms, rental bicycles. *Fee:* massage. **Guest Services:** valet laundry, area transportation-within 2 mi, wireless Internet. **Business Services:** conference facilities, business center.

CALL / SOME UNITS FEE

HYATT
HOTELS & RESORTS

AAA Benefit:
Ask for the AAA rate
and save 10%.

▼ *See AAA listing p 393* ▼

(See maps and indexes starting on p. 340, 345)

THE INN AT HARVARD *Book great rates at AAA.com* Phone: (617)491-2222 **100**

Hotel
$139-$399 All Year

Address: 1201 Massachusetts Ave 02138 **Location:** Jct Quincy, Bow and Harvard sts. Opposite Harvard Yard. **Facility:** Smoke free premises. 111 one-bedroom standard units. 4 stories, interior corridors. *Bath:* combo or shower only. **Parking:** valet. **Terms:** cancellation fee imposed. **Amenities:** voice mail, irons, hair dryers. **Leisure Activities:** exercise room. **Guest Services:** valet laundry, wireless Internet. **Business Services:** meeting rooms, PC (fee). **Free Special Amenities:** newspaper.

IRVING HOUSE AT HARVARD *Book at AAA.com* Phone: (617)547-4600 **96**

Motel
$180-$325 5/1-11/16
$175-$325 11/17-4/30

Address: 24 Irving St 02138 **Location:** Between Kirkland and Cambridge sts. Located on campus. **Facility:** Smoke free premises. 44 one-bedroom standard units. 4 stories (no elevator), interior corridors. *Bath:* some shared or private, combo or shower only. **Parking:** on-site. **Guest Services:** coin laundry, wireless Internet. **Business Services:** PC.

LE MERIDIEN CAMBRIDGE *Book great rates at AAA.com* Phone: (617)577-0200 **46**

Hotel
$139-$499 All Year

Address: 20 Sidney St 02139 **Location:** On SR 2A, 1 mi n of river. **Facility:** A short walk from Harvard Square, the newly renovated property features plush linens, soothing colors and state-of-the-art technological amenities. Smoke free premises. 210 units. 196 one-bedroom standard units. 14 one-bedroom suites, some with whirlpools. 8 stories, interior corridors. *Bath:* combo or shower only. **Parking:** on-site (fee) and valet. **Terms:** 3 day cancellation notice-fee imposed. **Amenities:** high-speed Internet, dual phone lines, voice mail, safes, honor bars, irons, hair dryers. **Dining:** Sidney's, see separate listing. **Leisure Activities:** exercise room. *Fee:* pool privileges. **Guest Services:** valet laundry, area transportation-within 1 mi, wireless Internet. **Business Services:** conference facilities, business center. **Free Special Amenities: newspaper and high-speed Internet.**

Le **MERIDIEN**

AAA Benefit:
Members get up to 15% off, plus Starwood Preferred Guest® bonuses.

RESIDENCE INN BOSTON CAMBRIDGE CENTER *Book great rates at AAA.com* Phone: (617)349-0700 **44**

Hotel
$219-$349 All Year

Address: 6 Cambridge Center 02142 **Location:** Corner of Ames St and Broadway. **Facility:** Smoke free premises. 221 units. 110 one-bedroom standard units with efficiencies. 90 one- and 21 two-bedroom suites, some with efficiencies or kitchens. 16 stories, interior corridors. *Bath:* combo or shower only. **Parking:** on-site (fee). **Terms:** check-in 4 pm, cancellation fee imposed. **Amenities:** high-speed Internet, dual phone lines, voice mail, irons, hair dryers. *Some:* DVD players (fee). **Pool(s):** heated indoor. **Leisure Activities:** whirlpool, exercise room. **Guest Services:** valet and coin laundry, wireless Internet. **Business Services:** meeting rooms, business center.

AAA Benefit:
Members save a minimum 5% off the best available rate.

▼ See AAA listing p 403 ▼

ROYAL SONESTA HOTEL
BOSTON

• Charles Riverfront location with skyline views
• 3 miles from Logan Airport
• Elegant on-site dining
• Complimentary in-room high speed Internet
• Kids 12 and under stay and eat free
  (restrictions apply)

617.806.4200
800.Sonesta Sonesta.com

40 Edwin Land Boulevard • Cambridge, MA 02412

Now That's *Refreshing*

Take the surprise out of hotel and restaurant visits. Let the simple, reliable AAA/CAA Diamond Ratings guide your decisions.

(See maps and indexes starting on p. 340, 345)

ROYAL SONESTA HOTEL BOSTON   *Book great rates at AAA.com*   Phone: (617)806-4200   **43**

Hotel
$209-$609 All Year

Address: 40 Edwin H Land Blvd 02142-1299 **Location:** Just sw of SR 28. **Facility:** The hotel's stylish lobby and pre-function areas have the ambience of a modern-art gallery. Smoke free premises. 400 one-bedroom standard units, some with whirlpools. 10 stories, interior corridors. *Bath:* combo or shower only. **Parking:** on-site (fee) and valet. **Terms:** cancellation fee imposed. **Amenities:** video games (fee), high-speed Internet, dual phone lines, voice mail, safes, honor bars, irons, hair dryers. **Dining:** 2 restaurants. **Pool(s):** heated indoor. **Leisure Activities:** saunas, whirlpool, sun deck, exercise room. *Fee:* massage. **Guest Services:** valet laundry, area transportation-Quincy Market, Copley, Prudential & Kendell Squares, wireless Internet. **Business Services:** conference facilities, business center. **Free Special Amenities: high-speed Internet.** *(See color ad p 402)*

SHERATON COMMANDER HOTEL   *Book great rates at AAA.com*   Phone: (617)547-4800   **95**

Hotel
$129-$479 All Year

Address: 16 Garden St 02138 **Location:** Just n of Harvard Square. Located on Cambridge Common. **Facility:** Smoke free premises. 176 units. 162 one-bedroom standard units, some with whirlpools. 14 one-bedroom suites. 7 stories, interior corridors. *Bath:* combo or shower only. **Parking:** valet. **Amenities:** video games, high-speed Internet (fee), dual phone lines, voice mail, irons, hair dryers. *Some:* fax, safes. **Leisure Activities:** sun deck, exercise room. **Guest Services:** valet laundry, wireless Internet. **Business Services:** conference facilities, business center.   / SOME UNITS

(S) **Sheraton**
HOTELS & RESORTS

AAA Benefit:
Members get up to
15% off, plus
Starwood Preferred
Guest® bonuses.

WHERE TO DINE

BAMBARA   Phone: 617/868-4444   **115**

American
$5-$28

In the Hotel Marlowe and the Cambridge Galleria Mall, this restaurant puts forth a wonderful and varied menu inspired by local delicacies such as Maine lobster, mussels, Chatham cod and fresh produce, in addition to duck, veal shank and a tasty grilled rib-eye. Casual dress. **Bar:** Full bar. **Reservations:** accepted. **Hours:** 6:30-10 am, 11:30-2:30 & 5:30-10 pm, Fri-11 pm, Sat 8 am-2 & 5:30-11 pm, Sun 8 am-2 & 5:30-10 pm. **Address:** 25 Edwin H Land Blvd 02141 **Location:** Just sw of jct SR 28; in Hotel Marlowe. **Parking:** valet. CALL

BOMBAY CLUB   Phone: 617/661-8100   **92**

Regional Indian
$8-$18

This second-floor restaurant presents a menu of cuisine representing many of India's regions and states, such as aloo tikki from Delhi, sali boti from Bombay and karahi paneer from Punjab. Many dishes are vegetarian. Yogurt and cheese are made and spices ground here daily. No monosodium glutamate is used. Parking is partially validated only at University Place and Charles Hotel garages. Lunch buffets are set up daily. Casual dress. **Bar:** Full bar. **Reservations:** accepted. **Hours:** 11:30 am-11 pm. Closed: 11/25, 12/25. **Address:** 57 JF Kennedy St (Harvard Square) 02138 **Location:** Just s of Harvard Square; in Galleria Mall. **Parking:** street.

CAMBRIDGE BREWING CO   Phone: 617/494-1994   **117**

American
$8-$22

Opening in 1989, the restaurant was one of the country's first brewery restaurants. In addition to developing new beer styles, this place serves creative pizzas, great burgers, fresh seafood and an eclectic mix of new American cuisine. Worth trying is a meal of vegetarian chili; baby spinach with pears, pecans and Gorgonzola; and braised lamb shank or sesame seared salmon. Some of the brick patio is beneath an awning. Casual dress. **Bar:** Beer & wine. **Reservations:** accepted. **Hours:** 11:30 am-10 pm, Sat noon-11 pm, Sun 3 pm-10 pm. Closed major holidays. **Address:** 1 Kendall Square, Bldg 100 02139 **Location:** Between Broadway and Hampshire St; at Kendall Square. **Parking:** street. CALL

THE CHEESECAKE FACTORY   Phone: 617/252-3810   **116**

American
$9-$32

A display case of mouthwatering cheesecakes is the first thing visitors see as they walk through the door. The extensive menu incorporates many types of cuisine, including Asian, Italian, Greek and Spanish. Casual dress. **Bar:** Full bar. **Hours:** 11 am-11 pm, Fri & Sat-12:30 am. Closed: 11/25, 12/25. **Address:** 100 Cambridgeside Pl 02141 **Location:** Just sw of jct SR 28; in Cambridgeside Galleria. **Parking:** on-site (fee). CALL

EAST COAST GRILL & RAW BAR   Phone: 617/491-6568   **86**

Barbecue
$16-$26

Fresh seafood, spicy barbecue and grilled entrees are served in the restaurant's bustling dining room. Casual dress. **Bar:** Full bar. **Reservations:** not accepted. **Hours:** 5:30 pm-10 pm, Sun 11 am-2:30 & 5:30-10 pm. Closed major holidays. **Address:** 1271 Cambridge St 02139 **Location:** Between Prospect and Oakland sts. **Parking:** street.

THE ELEPHANT WALK-CAMBRIDGE   Phone: 617/492-6900   **84**

French
$12-$20

The lengthy menu has a split personality-one Cambodian, the other French-and a fusion of the two is evident. Offerings range from bistro fare to classic French dishes. Preparations of sea bass, steak, chicken, lamb, duck, shrimp and catfish populate both sides of the menu. Many Cambodian dishes can be prepared for vegetarians, and one featured offering is entirely vegetarian. The wine list is extensive. Casual dress. **Bar:** Full bar. **Reservations:** suggested, Fri & Sat. **Hours:** 11 am-10 pm, Sat from 5 pm, Sun 11:30 am-2:30 & 5-10 pm; Sunday brunch. Closed: 7/4, 11/25, 12/24, 12/25. **Address:** 2067 Massachusetts Ave 02140 **Location:** On SR 2A, 0.3 mi n of Porter Square. **Parking:** on-site.

(See maps and indexes starting on p. 340, 345)

HARVEST

New American
$14-$38

Phone: 617/868-2255 [85]

The restaurant, a short walk from Harvard Square, invites patrons to dine on the planter-enclosed patio or in one of two rooms decorated in a "sophisticated-agrarian" style that incorporates woven-wicker show plates, white table linens and large landscape pictures. The menu is adjusted seasonally and may feature steaks and chops. An open kitchen and server workstations are adjacent to the small bar area at one end of the restaurant. Dressy casual. **Bar:** Full bar. **Reservations:** suggested. **Hours:** noon-10 pm, Fri & Sat-11 pm, Sun 11:30 am-10 pm. Closed: 1/1, 7/4, 12/25. **Address:** 44 Brattle St 02138 **Location:** Just off Harvard Square; center. **Parking:** street. CALL 🔊Ⓜ

HAVELI

Indian
$8-$16

Phone: 617/497-6548 [87]

The restaurant offers a lunch buffet daily until 3 pm, as well as a la carte menu selections that include a nice selection of vegetarian, chicken, lamb and shrimp dishes. Tandoori chicken, lamb and fish dishes are marinated then cooked in a clay oven. Casual dress. **Bar:** Full bar. **Reservations:** accepted. **Hours:** 11:45 am-3 & 5-11 pm. Closed: 11/25. **Address:** 1248-50 Cambridge St 02139 **Location:** Jct Prospect St. **Parking:** street.

HENRIETTA'S TABLE

Regional American
$8-$28

Phone: 617/661-5005 [91]

Near Harvard Square, the wonderful bistro is worth the trip for such choices as Yankee pot roast, baked Gloucester scrod, free-range duck and vegetarian fare. Chef Peter Davis describes the from-scratch cooking as "fresh and honest," and it is. This place prides itself on using the best ingredients while supporting local and regional farmers and purveyors. Casual dress. **Bar:** Full bar. **Reservations:** accepted. **Hours:** 6:30 am-11, noon-3 & 5:30-10 pm, Sat 7 am-11 & noon-3 pm, Sun noon-3 pm. **Address:** One Bennett St 02138 **Location:** Just s of Harvard Square, at Eliot St; in The Charles Hotel, Harvard Square. **Parking:** on-site (fee) and valet. *(See color ad p 400)* CALL 🔊Ⓜ

JASPER'S WHITE SUMMER SHACK

Seafood
$7-$36

Phone: 617/520-9500

Reputed to serve the freshest fish and shellfish, the casual eatery offers a fun and lively dining experience. Dishes vary from traditional fried seafood to a boiled lobster feast to even a few landlubber favorites. Casual dress. **Bar:** Full bar. **Hours:** 11:30 am-10 pm, Fri-11 pm, Sat noon-11 pm, Sun noon-9 pm. Closed major holidays. **Address:** 149 Alewife Brook Pkwy 02140 **Location:** On SR 2; adjacent to Alewife 'T' stop on Redline. **Parking:** on-site.

JOHN HARVARD'S BREWHOUSE

American
$9-$20

Phone: 617/868-3585

Known for their onsite micro-brewery, diners may enjoy one of the 8 freshly brewed lagers or ales as they view the production of the beer through a glass wall in the dining room. The recipe for the beer is believed to have originated from William Shakespeare and brought to America in 1637 by John Harvard, after whom Harvard University is named. The menu offers chicken sandwiches and burgers as well as some home-style favorites such as grilled meatloaf and chicken pot pie. Casual dress. **Bar:** Full bar. **Reservations:** accepted. **Hours:** 11:30 am-9:30 pm. Closed: 11/25, 12/25. **Address:** 33 Dunster St 02138 **Location:** Between Harvard (SR 2A) and Mt Auburn sts. **Parking:** street.

LEGAL SEA FOODS

Seafood
$11-$26

Phone: 617/864-3400 [118]

Legal prides itself on a reputation for freshness and consistency. More than 40 varieties of seafood can be grilled, broiled, fried or prepared Cajun style. Try the clam chowder that has been served at every presidential inauguration since 1981. The nautically inspired dining room is upscale and attractive with its rich cherry wood paneling and intricately detailed model ships. Casual dress. **Bar:** Full bar. **Reservations:** accepted. **Hours:** 11 am-10 pm, Fri & Sat-11 pm, Sun noon-10 pm. **Address:** 5 Cambridge Center 02139 **Location:** At Kendall Square; adjacent to Residence Inn by Marriott Cambridge. **Parking:** on-site (fee). CALL 🔊Ⓜ

(See maps and indexes starting on p. 340, 345)

OGGI GOURMET

Phone: 617/492-6444   88

Pizza
$5-$15

At Harvard Square, the restaurant specializes in gourmet pizza, sandwiches and salads. Web surfers will appreciate wireless Internet service. Casual dress. **Reservations:** not accepted. **Hours:** 7 am-8 pm, Sat & Sun noon-7 pm. Closed major holidays. **Address:** 1350 Massachusetts Ave 02138 **Location:** At Harvard Square; in Holyoke Center Arcade. **Parking:** street.

RIALTO

Phone: 617/661-5050   90

Regional
Continental
$21-$42

The menu leans toward fresh seafood but also lists lamb, duck, beef, pork and chicken. The ingredients say New England, but the style of preparation borrows from countries around the Mediterranean. Presentation is elegant, yet not overdone. Desserts include something for the chocolate lover, as well as those who prefer a simple cheese plate. Service in the casually elegant, high-energy dining room is friendly and attentive. Dressy casual. **Bar:** Full bar. **Reservations:** required. **Hours:** 5:30 pm-10 pm, Fri & Sat-11 pm. Closed: 1/1, 12/25. **Address:** One Bennett St 02138 **Location:** At Eliot St, just s of Harvard Square; in The Charles Hotel Harvard Square. **Parking:** valet. *(See color ad p 400)* CALL ⬛M

SANDRINE'S BISTRO

Phone: 617/497-5300   89

French
$8-$35

The casual bistro prepares authentic and creative Alsatian cuisine, such as pan-seared frog legs and foie gras starters and entrées of wild-mushroom ravioli, poussin with whole roasted garlic, and grilled sourdough with ratatouille, tofu and grilled mushrooms. As desserts go, it's hard to beat crème brûlée or chocolate Kougelhopf. The finest, freshest ingredients also factor into lunch sandwiches and meal-sized salads. Tablecloths covered with butcher paper distinguish the dining area. Casual dress. **Bar:** Beer & wine. **Reservations:** suggested. **Hours:** 11:30 am-2:30 & 5:30-10:30 pm, Sun from 5:30 pm. Closed: 12/25. **Address:** 8 Holyoke St 02138 **Location:** In Harvard Square; adjacent to Holyoke Center. **Parking:** street.

SIDNEY'S

Phone: 617/494-0011   119

American
$12-$30

On the second floor of the hotel, the restaurant exudes contemporary style and comfort. Diners may view the open kitchen, where the chef orchestrates the staff to create memorable dishes of upscale American grill food prepared with a Mediterranean twist. Outdoor seating is an option during the warmer months. Dressy casual. **Bar:** Full bar. **Reservations:** suggested. **Hours:** 6:30 am-10 pm, Sat & Sun 7 am-10 pm. **Address:** 20 Sidney St 02139 **Location:** On SR 2A, 1 mi n of river; in Le Meridien Cambridge. **Parking:** valet. CALL ⬛M

SPICE THAI CUISINE

Phone: 617/868-9560   93

Provincial Thai
$7-$17

Off Harvard Square on a side street, this restaurant is popular with students. The expected Thai dishes, including reasonably priced curries, satays and pad thai, are found along with soups and salads. Ice creams are refreshing finishes. Unpretentious and cozy, crowded to some, the dining room is narrow with banquettes lining the perimeter and a mirror along one wall. Colorfully set tables are placed closely enough to allow previewing the menu on a neighbor's table if the timing is right. Casual dress. **Reservations:** suggested. **Hours:** 11:30 am-3 & 5-10 pm, Fri-10:30 pm, Sat & Sun noon-10:30 pm. Closed: 7/4, 11/25, 12/25. **Address:** 24 Holyoke St 02138 **Location:** In Harvard Square; adjacent to Holyoke Center. **Parking:** street. CALL ⬛M

CHELMSFORD

CHELSEA pop. 35,080   (See map and index starting on p. 345)

WYNDHAM BOSTON/CHELSEA   *Book great rates at AAA.com*   Phone: (617)884-2900   82

AAA SAVE
▽▽▽▽
Hotel
$149-$299 5/1-11/15
$89-$199 11/16-4/30

Address: 201 Everett Ave 02150 **Location:** 0.3 mi se of SR 16. **Facility:** Smoke free premises. 180 one-bedroom standard units. 7 stories, interior corridors. *Bath:* combo or shower only. **Parking:** on-site. **Terms:** cancellation fee imposed. **Amenities:** high-speed Internet, dual phone lines, voice mail, irons, hair dryers. **Pool(s):** heated indoor. **Leisure Activities:** whirlpool, exercise room. **Guest Services:** valet laundry, airport transportation-General Edward Lawrence Logan International Airport, area transportation-within 3 mi, wireless Internet. **Business Services:** meeting rooms, business center. *(See color ad p 364)*

✈ 🍴 🍸 CALL 🆓M ➤ ✕ 🛏 🖥 🖵

FREE newspaper and high-speed Internet

CHESTNUT HILL   (See map and index starting on p. 345)

------ **WHERE TO DINE** ------

LEGAL SEA FOODS   Phone: 617/277-7300   110

▽▽▽▽
Seafood
$9-$36

Legal prides itself on a reputation for freshness and consistency. More than 40 varieties of seafood can be grilled, broiled, fried or prepared Cajun style. Try the clam chowder that has been served at every presidential inauguration since 1981. The nautically inspired dining room is upscale and attractive with its rich cherry wood paneling and intricately detailed model ships. Casual dress. **Bar:** Full bar. **Reservations:** accepted. **Hours:** 11 am-10 pm, Fri & Sat-11 pm, Sun noon-10 pm. **Address:** 43 Boylston St 02467 **Location:** I-95, exit 20, 3.3 mi e on SR 9; in Chestnut Hill Shopping Center. **Parking:** on-site.

CALL 🆓M

COHASSET

------ **WHERE TO DINE** ------

RED LION INN AND RESORT   Phone: 781/383-1704

▽▽▽▽
Regional American
$9-$29

In a seaside inn dating to 1704, the restaurant features a row of banquettes and close tables and offers cozy dining. Memorable dishes such as pan-seared sole, steamed mussels and herb-crusted lamb share menu space with lighter fare of burgers, salads and soups. Casual dress. **Bar:** Full bar. **Reservations:** accepted. **Hours:** 4 pm-1 pm, Fri-Sun from noon. Closed: Mon & Tues. **Address:** 71 S Main St 02025 **Location:** Just e of SR 3A. **Parking:** on-site.

CONCORD

BEST WESTERN AT HISTORIC CONCORD   *Book great rates at AAA.com*

Phone: (978)369-6100

Hotel
$129-$179 5/1-11/30
$119-$159 12/1-4/30

Address: 740 Elm St 01742 **Location:** 1.8 mi w, just off SR 2 and 2A. **Facility:** Smoke free premises. 106 one-bedroom standard units. 2 stories (no elevator), interior corridors. **Parking:** on-site. **Amenities:** irons, hair dryers. *Some:* high-speed Internet. **Pool(s):** outdoor. **Leisure Activities:** exercise room. **Guest Services:** coin laundry, wireless Internet. **Business Services:** meeting rooms, PC. **Free Special Amenities: expanded continental breakfast and high-speed Internet.**

AAA Benefit:
Members save up to 20%, plus 10% bonus points with rewards program.

CONCORD'S COLONIAL INN   *Book great rates at AAA.com*

Phone: (978)369-9200

Historic
Country Inn
$109-$229 All Year

Address: 48 Monument Square 01742 **Location:** On the green; between SR 2A and 62. **Facility:** On the town square, this country inn includes an original section built in the early 1700s. Smoke free premises. 56 units. 46 one-bedroom standard units. 8 one-, 1 two- and 1 three-bedroom suites with efficiencies, some with whirlpools. 3 stories (no elevator), interior/exterior corridors. *Bath:* combo or shower only. **Parking:** on-site. **Terms:** cancellation fee imposed. **Amenities:** voice mail, irons, hair dryers. *Some:* DVD players. **Dining:** The Colonial Inn Restaurants, see separate listing. **Guest Services:** valet laundry, wireless Internet. **Business Services:** conference facilities, PC, fax (fee). *(See color ad p 383)*

FREE early check-in/late check-out and high-speed Internet

THE HAWTHORNE INN

Phone: (978)369-5610

Bed & Breakfast
$145-$325 All Year

Address: 462 Lexington Rd 01742 **Location:** 0.8 mi e of town square. Located in historic zone. **Facility:** Antiques and the owner's private art collection are featured in guest rooms at this 1870 Colonial-style home. Smoke free premises. 7 one-bedroom standard units. 2 stories (no elevator), interior corridors. *Bath:* combo or shower only. **Parking:** on-site. **Terms:** office hours 8 am-8 pm, 14 day cancellation notice-fee imposed. **Amenities:** video library, DVD players, CD players, voice mail, irons, hair dryers. **Guest Services:** area transportation, wireless Internet.

── WHERE TO DINE ──

THE COLONIAL INN RESTAURANTS

Phone: 978/369-2373

Regional American
$8-$28

The dining room provides updated versions of some of the established New England favorites like the most popular colonial chicken pot pie. Fresh local seafood is central to the menu. Finish with the Indian pudding and ice cream. Crisp white table linens contrast with polished mahogany and flickering simulated oil lamps, yet combine to provide a glimpse into the Colonial heritage of this long-lived inn. Dressy casual. Entertainment. **Bar:** Full bar. **Reservations:** suggested. **Hours:** 7 am-10 pm, Sun 7:30 am-9 pm. **Address:** 48 Monument Square 01742 **Location:** On the green; between SR 2A and 62; in Concord's Colonial Inn. **Parking:** on-site.

PAPA RAZZI

Phone: 978/371-0030

Northern Italian
$10-$26

Italy has changed and so has authentic Italian food. It's lighter, fresher, more exciting Italian, and it's just what you'll find amid the elegant yet comfortable atmosphere that is Papa Razzi. If the steamy bowls of pasta don't tempt you, one of the aromatic pizzas or a warm panini sandwich definitely will. In addition there is a fine wine list, an array of salads, chicken, and fish options to choose from. Dressy casual. **Bar:** Full bar. **Reservations:** accepted. **Hours:** 11:30 am-10 pm. Closed: 11/25, 12/25. **Address:** 768 Elm St (SR 2) 01742 **Location:** 1.8 mi w, just off SR 2 and 2A. **Parking:** on-site.

DANVERS pop. 25,212   (See map and index starting on p. 345)

COMFORT INN NORTH SHORE   *Book great rates at AAA.com*

Phone: (978)777-1700

Hotel
$79-$199 5/1-10/31
$69-$129 11/1-4/30

Address: 50 Dayton St 01923 **Location:** Just w of US 1; 0.8 mi n of jct SR 114, exit Center St northbound, w under US 1; exit Dayton St southbound. **Facility:** 140 one-bedroom standard units. 5 stories, interior corridors. *Bath:* combo or shower only. **Parking:** on-site. **Terms:** check-in 4 pm. **Amenities:** video games (fee), high-speed Internet, voice mail, irons, hair dryers. **Pool(s):** heated outdoor, heated indoor. **Leisure Activities:** exercise room. **Guest Services:** valet and coin laundry, wireless Internet. **Business Services:** meeting rooms, business center. *(See color ad p 436)*

FREE expanded continental breakfast and early check-in/late check-out

(See map and index starting on p. 345)

COURTYARD BOSTON DANVERS   *Book great rates at AAA.com*
   Phone: (978)777-8630

Hotel
$119-$149 All Year

Address: 275 Independence Way 01923 Location: SR 128, exit 24. Located behind Liberty Tree Mall. Facility: Smoke free premises. 121 units. 119 one-bedroom standard units. 2 one-bedroom suites. 3 stories, interior corridors. Bath: combo or shower only. Parking: on-site. Terms: cancellation fee imposed. Amenities: high-speed Internet, dual phone lines, voice mail, irons, hair dryers. Pool(s): heated outdoor. Leisure Activities: exercise room. Guest Services: valet and coin laundry. Business Services: meeting rooms, business center.

AAA Benefit: Members save a minimum 5% off the best available rate.

CROWN PLAZA BOSTON NORTH SHORE AND COCO KEY WATER RESORT   *Book great rates at AAA.com*
Phone: 978/777-2500

Hotel
Rates not provided

Address: 50 Ferncroft Rd 01923 Location: I-95, exit 50, follow signs for US 1 S to Ferncroft Village. Facility: Smoke free premises. 366 units. 363 one-bedroom standard units. 3 one-bedroom suites. 8 stories, interior corridors. Bath: combo or shower only. Parking: on-site. Terms: check-in 4 pm. Amenities: dual phone lines, voice mail, irons, hair dryers. Dining: 4 restaurants. Pool(s): heated indoor. Leisure Activities: sauna, whirlpool, steamrooms, indoor water park, spa. Guest Services: valet laundry, area transportation-within 7 mi, wireless Internet. Business Services: conference facilities, business center.

EXTENDED STAYAMERICA BOSTON-DANVERS   *Book at AAA.com*
Phone: (978)762-7414

Hotel
$55-$75 All Year

Address: 102 Newbury St 01923 Location: On US 1 southbound. Facility: 104 one-bedroom standard units with efficiencies. 3 stories, interior corridors. Bath: combo or shower only. Parking: on-site. Terms: cancellation fee imposed. Amenities: voice mail, irons. Guest Services: coin laundry, wireless Internet.

RESIDENCE INN BOSTON-NORTH SHORE/DANVERS   *Book great rates at AAA.com*
Phone: (978)777-7171 23

Extended Stay Hotel
$125-$149 All Year

Address: 51 Newbury St 01923 Location: US 1 N, just s of jct SR 114. Located in a commercial area. Facility: Smoke free premises. 96 one-bedroom standard units. 2 stories (no elevator), exterior corridors. Bath: combo or shower only. Parking: on-site. Terms: cancellation fee imposed. Amenities: high-speed Internet, voice mail, irons, hair dryers. Pool(s): heated outdoor. Leisure Activities: whirlpool, exercise room, sports court. Guest Services: valet and coin laundry. Business Services: PC.

AAA Benefit: Members save a minimum 5% off the best available rate.

(See map and index starting on p. 345)

TOWNEPLACE SUITES BOSTON-NORTH
  SHORE/DANVERS   *Book great rates at AAA.com*

Phone: (978)777-6222

Hotel
$104-$124 All Year

Address: 238 Andover St 01923 **Location:** Southwest corner of jct US 1 and SR 114; SR 114 eastbound, enter just w of US 1 (no westbound entrance); US 1 southbound, enter through shopping center. Located in a commercial area. **Facility:** Smoke free premises. 127 units. 97 one-bedroom standard units with efficiencies. 30 two-bedroom suites with kitchens. 4 stories, interior corridors. *Bath:* combo or shower only. **Parking:** on-site. **Terms:** cancellation fee imposed. **Amenities:** dual phone lines, voice mail, irons, hair dryers. **Pool(s):** heated outdoor. **Leisure Activities:** limited exercise equipment. **Guest Services:** valet and coin laundry, wireless Internet. **Business Services:** PC.

AAA Benefit:
Members save a minimum 5% off the best available rate.

CALL 🖕M 🏊 ✕ 🎥 🖥 🖨 💾 / SOME UNITS FEE 🐾

──── **WHERE TO DINE** ────

CALITRI'S

Phone: 978/777-1266

Italian
$8-$18

Conveniently located, the eatery is appealing to families offering a nice selection of fare: pizza, pasta and more; ample parking is available. Casual dress. **Bar:** Full bar. **Hours:** 11 am-midnight. Closed: 4/4, 11/25, 12/25. **Address:** 126 Newbury St 01923 **Location:** On US 1 S, just n of SR 114. **Parking:** on-site.

THE HARDCOVER

Phone: 978/774-1223   (25)

American
$15-$36

There's no need to suffer the anxiety of sneaking food into the library. Here, hardcover classics surround guests in the pleasant, cozy setting. The energetic wait staff works in teams to keep diners satisfied, well fed and always coming back for more. Casual dress. **Bar:** Full bar. **Hours:** 4 pm-10 pm, Fri & Sat-10:30 pm, Sun 3 pm-9 pm. Closed: 12/24, 12/25; also Super Bowl Sun. **Address:** 15A Newbury St 01923 **Location:** US 1 N, just s of jct SR 114; I-95, exit 44 (no access from US 1 S), 2.2 mi n. **Parking:** on-site.

PONTE VECCHIO

Phone: 978/777-9188

Italian
$9-$13

In a small mall just off the interstate on the road to the fairgrounds, the classic Italian restaurant sports both a formal dining room and a trattoria, separated by the lounge. The formal dining room is open only for dinner. Casual dress. **Bar:** Full bar. **Hours:** 11:30 am-3 & 5-10:30 pm, Sun 4 pm-9 pm. Closed major holidays. **Address:** 435 Newbury St 01923 **Location:** I-95, exit 50, just n on US 1; in Hawthorne North Shopping Center. **Parking:** on-site.

SPERO'S SPORTS PUB & GRILL

Phone: 978/774-5200   (26)

American
$8-$18

The family-run restaurant is near the interstate and a short distance from the North Shore and Liberty Tree malls. The dining room has ornate banquettes, mirrored wall hangings and white tablecloths. The menu mixes Greek, American and Italian items, such as dolmadakia (grape leaves), octapodia, fried calamari, pork chops, lamb, chicken, fresh seafood, veal piccata or scaloppine, baklava and tiramisu. Service is friendly and attentive. Casual dress. **Bar:** Full bar. **Reservations:** not accepted. **Hours:** 4 pm-12:30 am, Fri-Sun from 11:30 am. Closed major holidays. **Address:** 101 Andover St 01923 **Location:** I-95, exit 47, 0.5 mi e on SR 114. **Parking:** on-site.

DEDHAM pop. 23,464   (See map and index starting on p. 345)

FAIRFIELD INN BY MARRIOTT-BOSTON/DEDHAM   *Book great rates at AAA.com*   Phone: (781)326-6700   [133]

Hotel
$116-$142 All Year

Address: 235 Elm St 02026 **Location:** I-95, exit 15A, just n, then 0.3 mi e. **Facility:** Smoke free premises. 150 units. 141 one-bedroom standard units. 9 one-bedroom suites. 3 stories, interior/exterior corridors. *Bath:* combo or shower only. **Parking:** on-site. **Terms:** cancellation fee imposed. **Amenities:** high-speed Internet, voice mail, irons, hair dryers. **Pool(s):** heated outdoor. **Leisure Activities:** exercise room. **Guest Services:** valet and coin laundry, wireless Internet. **Business Services:** business center.

AAA Benefit:
Members save a minimum 5% off the best available rate.

🍽⁺ CALL 🖕M 🏊 ✕ 🎥 🖥 / SOME UNITS 🖥 🖨

HILTON BOSTON DEDHAM   *Book great rates at AAA.com*

Phone: (781)329-7900   [134]

Hotel
$109-$269 All Year

Address: 25 Allied Dr 02026 **Location:** I-95, exit 14, just e. Located next to a conservation area. **Facility:** 256 units. 255 one-bedroom standard units. 1 one-bedroom suite with whirlpool. 4 stories, interior corridors. **Parking:** on-site. **Terms:** 1-7 night minimum stay, cancellation fee imposed. **Amenities:** video games (fee), dual phone lines, voice mail, irons, hair dryers. **Pool(s):** heated indoor. **Leisure Activities:** whirlpool, 2 tennis courts, racquetball courts, jogging. **Guest Services:** valet laundry, area transportation, wireless Internet. **Business Services:** meeting rooms, business center.

Hilton
AAA Benefit:
Members save 5% or more everyday!

🍽 🍸 🏊 🛅 ✕ 🎥 🖥 / SOME UNITS FEE 🐾 ✕ FEE 🖥 FEE 🖨

(See map and index starting on p. 345)

HOLIDAY INN BOSTON/DEDHAM HOTEL & CONFERENCE CENTER   *Book at AAA.com*

Phone: (781)329-1000   131

Hotel
$99-$219 All Year

Address: 55 Ariadne Rd 02026 **Location:** I-95, exit 15A on US 1. **Facility:** Smoke free premises. 202 one-bedroom standard units. 2-8 stories, interior corridors. **Parking:** on-site. **Terms:** cancellation fee imposed. **Amenities:** dual phone lines, voice mail, irons, hair dryers. **Pool(s):** heated indoor. **Leisure Activities:** exercise room. **Guest Services:** valet and coin laundry, area transportation, wireless Internet. **Business Services:** meeting rooms, business center.

ASK ❙❙ ⊻ CALL 🅼 🌊 ✕ 🐾 💻 / SOME UNITS FEE 🛄 FEE 🖥

RESIDENCE INN BOSTON DEDHAM   *Book great rates at AAA.com*

Phone: (781)407-0999   132

Extended Stay Hotel
$159-$189 All Year

Address: 259 Elm St 02026 **Location:** I-95, exit 15A, just n, then 0.4 mi e. **Facility:** Smoke free premises. 81 units. 18 one-bedroom standard units with efficiencies. 57 one- and 6 two-bedroom suites, some with efficiencies or kitchens. 3 stories, interior corridors. *Bath:* combo or shower only. **Parking:** on-site. **Terms:** cancellation fee imposed. **Amenities:** dual phone lines, voice mail, irons, hair dryers. **Pool(s):** heated indoor. **Leisure Activities:** whirlpool, exercise room, sports court. **Guest Services:** valet and coin laundry, wireless Internet. **Business Services:** business center.

❙❙ 🌊 ✕ ✕ 🐾 🛄 💻 / SOME UNITS FEE 🐕

AAA Benefit:
Members save a minimum 5% off the best available rate.

WHERE TO DINE

50'S DINER

Phone: 781/326-1955   120

American
$4-$9

The diner is tucked in among commercial buildings. Lines out the door attest to its popularity. Breakfast is available all day. Other offerings include soups, salads, sandwiches, wraps, grilled sandwiches, fountain drinks and homemade desserts. Parking tends to be limited. Casual dress. **Hours:** 7 am-3 pm. Closed major holidays. **Address:** 5 Commercial Cir 02026 **Location:** I-95, exit 15A, 0.5 mi n, then just e via Enterprise Dr. **Parking:** on-site.

JOE'S AMERICAN BAR & GRILL

Phone: 781/329-0800

American
$9-$30

If it's Americana you want, you'll get all that and more at Joe's, where the bill of fare includes all-American favorites like hearty burgers, fresh-from-the-oven chicken pot pies, Maryland lump crab cakes, and Joe's classic meatloaf. Pizzas, pastas, steaks and salads round out the extensive menu, giving diners the freedom to choose from a vast selection of offerings. There's nothing more American than that, except, of course, for apple pie, so save some room. Casual dress. **Bar:** Full bar. **Hours:** 11 am-11 pm, Fri & Sat-midnight. Closed: 12/25. **Address:** 985 Providence Hwy 02026 **Location:** I-95, exit 15A on US 1. **Parking:** on-site.

VINNY T'S OF BOSTON

Phone: 781/320-8999

Italian
$7-$25

The Old World-themed family restaurant is decorated with elegant chandeliers, rich wood floors, Roman sculptures and an abundance of framed photos and artwork set in Italy. Meals, which are freshly prepared on site, might include chicken Marsala, lasagna and mussels fra diavolo. Casual dress. **Bar:** Full bar. **Reservations:** accepted. **Hours:** 11 am-10 pm, Fri & Sat-11 pm, Sun 11:30 am-10 pm. Closed: 11/25, 12/25. **Address:** 233 Elm St 02026 **Location:** I-95, exit 15A, 0.3 mi n on US 1, then 0.3 mi e. **Parking:** on-site. CALL 🅼

ESSEX pop. 1,426

WHERE TO DINE

WINDWARD GRILLE

Phone: 978/768-0050

American
$10-$24

The restaurant is located in a circa 1680 farmhouse only a mile or so from the center of Essex and its antique shops, picturesque harbor and the Essex Ship Building Museum. Classic presentations of popular New England fare, mostly fresh seafood, occupy the menu. Alternatively, beef, veal and chicken items are available. Starters range from an excellent clam chowder to oysters or cherrystones on the half shell to fried smelt. You might finish with one of the traditional homemade desserts. Casual dress. **Bar:** Full bar. **Reservations:** not accepted. **Hours:** 11:30 am-9 pm; Sunday brunch. Closed: 11/25, 12/25. **Address:** 109 Eastern Ave 01929 **Location:** SR 128, exit 14, 2.2 mi nw on SR 133. **Parking:** on-site. **Historic**

WOODMAN'S OF ESSEX

Phone: 978/768-6057

Seafood
$6-$24

This popular landmark restaurant is reported to be the place where fried clams were first served in 1916. The classic, expanded clam bar sports no-frills wooden tables and booths and a self-service, walk-up counter with separate lines for food and drinks. Casual dress. **Bar:** Full bar. **Hours:** 11 am-8 pm, Fri & Sat-9 pm; 11 am-9 pm, Fri & Sat-10 pm 7/1-9/30. Closed: 11/25, 12/25. **Address:** 121 Main St 01929 **Location:** On SR 133; center. **Parking:** on-site. 🎴 ⬛

FOXBORO pop. 5,509

COMFORT INN FOXBORO   *Book at AAA.com*

Phone: (508)543-1000

Hotel
$79-$229 All Year

Address: 4 Fisher St 02035 **Location:** I-95, exit 7A, just e. **Facility:** 128 units. 127 one-bedroom standard units. 1 one-bedroom suite with whirlpool. 3 stories, interior/exterior corridors. **Parking:** on-site. **Terms:** cancellation fee imposed. **Amenities:** voice mail, safes (fee), irons, hair dryers. **Leisure Activities:** exercise room. **Guest Services:** valet and coin laundry, wireless Internet. **Business Services:** meeting rooms, PC, fax (fee). ASK ❙❙ 🐾 💻 / SOME UNITS ✕ 🛄 🖥

FOXBOROUGH COURTYARD BY MARRIOTT   *Book great rates at AAA.com*   Phone: (508)543-5222

Hotel
$159-$175 All Year

Address: 35 Foxborough Blvd 02035 **Location:** I-95, exit 7A, 0.5 mi s; I-495, exit 12, 1.3 mi n, just off SR 140. Located in Foxborough Business Park. **Facility:** Smoke free premises. 149 units. 137 one-bedroom standard units. 12 one-bedroom suites. 3 stories, interior corridors. *Bath:* combo or shower only. **Parking:** on-site. **Terms:** cancellation fee imposed. **Amenities:** high-speed Internet, dual phone lines, voice mail, irons, hair dryers. **Pool(s):** heated indoor. **Leisure Activities:** whirlpool, exercise room. **Guest Services:** valet and coin laundry. **Business Services:** meeting rooms, PC, fax.

AAA Benefit:
Members save a
minimum 5% off the
best available rate.

FOXBOROUGH RESIDENCE INN BY MARRIOTT   *Book great rates at AAA.com*   Phone: (508)698-2800

Extended Stay
Hotel
$165-$169 All Year

Address: 250 Foxborough Blvd 02035 **Location:** I-95, exit 7A, 0.6 mi s on SR 140, 0.7 mi e, then just n. Located in Foxborough Business Center. **Facility:** Smoke free premises. 108 units. 52 one-bedroom standard units with efficiencies. 35 one- and 21 two-bedroom suites with kitchens. 3 stories, interior corridors. *Bath:* combo or shower only. **Parking:** on-site. **Terms:** cancellation fee imposed. **Amenities:** video games (fee), dual phone lines, voice mail, irons, hair dryers. **Pool(s):** heated outdoor. **Leisure Activities:** whirlpool, exercise room, sports court. **Guest Services:** valet and coin laundry, area transportation, wireless Internet. **Business Services:** meeting rooms, business center.

RENAISSANCE BOSTON HOTEL AND SPA AT
PATRIOT PLACE   *Book great rates at AAA.com*   Phone: (508)543-5500

Hotel
$260-$318 All Year

Address: 28 Patriot Pl 02035 **Location:** I-495, exit 14A, 5 mi ne via US 1. **Facility:** Smoke free premises. 150 units. 146 one-bedroom standard units. 4 one-bedroom suites. 5 stories, interior corridors. *Bath:* combo or shower only. **Parking:** valet. **Terms:** cancellation fee imposed. **Amenities:** high-speed Internet (fee), voice mail, safes, irons, hair dryers. **Dining:** Twenty8 Food & Spirits, see separate listing. **Pool(s):** heated indoor. **Leisure Activities:** exercise room, spa. **Guest Services:** valet laundry, wireless Internet. **Business Services:** meeting rooms, business center.

AAA Benefit:
Members save a
minimum 5% off the
best available rate.

----- **WHERE TO DINE** -----

DAVIO'S   Phone: 508/339-4810

Northern Italian
$10-$42

The Philly cheese steak spring rolls appetizer, served with spicy homemade ketchup and spicy mayo, sets up a meal of homemade pasta such as al dente angel hair pasta with fresh basil in pomodoro sauce or lobster mascarpone ravioli with asparagus, vine-ripe tomatoes and brandy cream. The tempting dessert tray includes molten chocolate cake served with vanilla ice cream. Diners also love the gourmet pizzas, steaks and dipping sauces and olives served with bread at the start of their meals. Dressy casual. **Bar:** Full bar. **Reservations:** suggested. **Hours:** 11:30 am-3 & 5-10 pm, Fri & Sat-11 pm. Closed: 12/25. **Address:** Patriot Place 02035 **Location:** I-495, exit 14A, 4.5 mi n on US 1; adjacent to Gillette Stadium. **Parking:** on-site.

LAFAYETTE HOUSE   Phone: 508/543-5344

Continental
$8-$35

This colonial restaurant, where Generals Washington and Lafayette and Ben Franklin were once guests, was built in 1784 and functioned as a tavern in the early 1800s. Now it's a place to rest and enjoy family and friends in a casual dining atmosphere. The restaurant is made up of spacious separate rooms with period decor suitable for group functions or individual dining. Traditional preparations of veal, lamb, native seafood, pasta and chicken populate the menu. Dressy casual. **Bar:** Full bar. **Reservations:** suggested. **Hours:** 11:45 am-3 & 5-10 pm, Sun 11:30 am-10 pm. Closed major holidays. **Address:** 109 Washington St (Rt 1) 02035 **Location:** US 1, 0.5 mi n of jct SR 140. **Parking:** on-site. **Historic**

NINETY NINE RESTAURANT   Phone: 508/543-1199

American
$7-$18

This popular pub is committed to serving large portions of great food at reasonable prices. Guest favorites include hot wings, burgers, seafood, barbecue ribs and chicken. While reservations are not taken, call-ahead seating is offered. A children's menu is also available. Casual dress. **Bar:** Full bar. **Hours:** 11 am-10:30 pm, Thurs-Sat to 11:30 pm, Sun-10 pm. Closed: 11/25, 12/25. **Address:** 4 Fisher St 02035 **Location:** I-95, exit 7A, just e. **Parking:** on-site.

PICCADILLY PUB   Phone: 508/543-0535

American
$8-$15

Patrons at the informal, folksy restaurant range from families to neatly pressed professionals. Fish and chips, clam chowder in a bread bowl, burgers, sandwiches, and special dinners, such as Yankee pot roast and homemade meatloaf, are well-complemented by a selection of microbrews. Portions are ample, and the service is efficient. Casual dress. **Bar:** Full bar. **Reservations:** not accepted. **Hours:** 11:30 am-10 pm, Thurs-Sat to 11 pm, Sun noon-9 pm. Closed: 11/25, 12/25. **Address:** 25 Foxboro Blvd 02035 **Location:** I-95, exit 7A, 0.5 mi s; I-495, exit 12, 1.3 mi n, just off SR 140; in Foxboro Office Park. **Parking:** on-site.

TWENTY8 FOOD & SPIRITS   Phone: 508/543-5500

American
$11-$26

Contemporary decor marks a dining area with high ceilings and floor-length windows that overlook Patriot Stadium. Football fans enjoy having pre- or post-game meals here. Regional and sustainable modern American cuisine makes up a menu that includes flatbreads and appetizers from the stone hearth. Particularly worth a try are chicken spring rolls with served with hoisin, barbecue and mango dipping sauces or the wedge salad with Vermont blue cheese, crumbled bacon and chopped tomatoes. Casual dress. **Bar:** Full bar. **Reservations:** accepted. **Hours:** 6:30 am-11 pm. **Address:** 28 Patriot Pl 02035 **Location:** I-495, exit 14A, 5 mi ne via US 1; in Renaissance Boston Hotel and Spa at Patriot Place. **Parking:** on-site.

CALL 🅰🅼

FRAMINGHAM pop. 66,910

BEST WESTERN FRAMINGHAM   *Book great rates at AAA.com*   Phone: (508)872-8811

AAA SAVE
♦♦♦♦

Hotel
$100-$130 5/1-10/31
$90-$120 11/1-4/30

Address: 130 Worcester Rd 01702 **Location:** I-90, exit 13, 0.5 mi s to SR 9; 1 mi w of Speen St; just w of Shopper's World Mall. **Facility:** 184 units. 181 one-bedroom standard units. 3 one-bedroom suites, some with efficiencies. 2-6 stories, interior corridors. **Parking:** on-site. **Amenities:** voice mail, irons, hair dryers. **Pool(s):** heated indoor. **Leisure Activities:** sauna. **Guest Services:** valet and coin laundry, wireless Internet. **Business Services:** meeting rooms, PC, fax (fee). **Free Special Amenities: expanded continental breakfast and high-speed Internet.**

🛏 🍸 🛎 🎥 💻 / SOME UNITS 🐕 ✕ FEE 🔌 FEE 🖨

AAA Benefit:
Members save up to 20%, plus 10% bonus points with rewards program.

RED ROOF INN #7068   *Book great rates at AAA.com*   Phone: (508)872-4499

AAA SAVE
♦♦ ♦♦

Motel
$65-$109 5/1-10/31
$59-$79 11/1-4/30

Address: 650 Cochituate Rd 01701 **Location:** I-90, exit 13, follow SR 30 E. **Facility:** 170 one-bedroom standard units. 2 stories (no elevator), exterior corridors. **Bath:** combo or shower only. **Parking:** on-site. **Amenities:** video games (fee), voice mail. **Some:** irons, hair dryers. **Guest Services:** wireless Internet. **Free Special Amenities: local telephone calls.**

🛏➔ 🐾 / SOME UNITS 🐕 ✕ 🔌 🖨 🖨

RESIDENCE INN BOSTON/FRAMINGHAM   *Book great rates at AAA.com*   Phone: (508)370-0001

AAA SAVE
♦♦♦

Extended Stay
Hotel
$189-$209 All Year

Address: 400 Staples Dr 01702 **Location:** SR 9 W to Crossing Blvd, then s. **Facility:** Smoke free premises. 125 units. 24 one-bedroom standard units with efficiencies. 82 one- and 19 two-bedroom suites, some with efficiencies or kitchens. 5 stories, interior corridors. **Bath:** combo or shower only. **Parking:** on-site. **Terms:** cancellation fee imposed. **Amenities:** high-speed Internet, dual phone lines, voice mail, irons, hair dryers. **Pool(s):** heated indoor. **Leisure Activities:** whirlpool, exercise room. **Guest Services:** valet and coin laundry, wireless Internet. **Business Services:** meeting rooms, PC. **Free Special Amenities: full breakfast and high-speed Internet.**

CALL 🅰🅼 🍳 ✕ 🔌 🖨 💻 / SOME UNITS FEE 🐕

AAA Benefit:
Members save a minimum 5% off the best available rate.

SHERATON FRAMINGHAM HOTEL & CONFERENCE CENTER   *Book great rates at AAA.com*   Phone: (508)879-7200

AAA SAVE
♦♦♦

Hotel
$89-$235 All Year

Address: 1657 Worcester Rd 01701 **Location:** I-90, exit 12, follow signs to SR 9 W. **Facility:** Smoke free premises. 375 one-bedroom standard units. 6 stories, interior corridors. **Bath:** combo or shower only. **Parking:** on-site. **Amenities:** dual phone lines, voice mail, irons, hair dryers. **Fee:** video games, high-speed Internet. **Pool(s):** outdoor, heated indoor. **Leisure Activities:** sauna, steamroom. **Guest Services:** valet laundry, area transportation-within 5 mi. **Business Services:** conference facilities, business center. **Free Special Amenities: newspaper and early check-in/late check-out.**

🍽 🍸 🍳 🛎 ✕ 🎥 💻 / SOME UNITS 🐕 FEE 🔌

AAA Benefit:
Members get up to 15% off, plus Starwood Preferred Guest® bonuses.

———— **WHERE TO DINE** ————

GOLD STAR   Phone: 508/370-3535

Indian
$7-$15

Traditional curry, korma and vindaloo preparations, including several complete specialty dinners, are offered. A luncheon buffet is set up daily. Service is friendly in the unassuming restaurant, which is almost hidden among other restaurants on the side of a strip mall. Casual dress. **Bar:** Beer & wine. **Reservations:** accepted. **Hours:** 11:30 am-10 pm, Fri & Sat-11 pm. **Address:** 341 Cochituate Rd 01701 **Location:** Between SR 9 and 30; just w of Shopper's World Mall and Wal-Mart. **Parking:** on-site.

CALL 🅰🅼

Plan. Map. Go.
TripTik® Travel Planner on AAA.com

AAA

JOHN HARVARD'S BREWHOUSE

American
$9-$20

Phone: 508/875-2337

Known for their onsite micro-brewery, diners may enjoy one of the 8 freshly brewed lagers or ales as they view the production of the beer through a glass wall in the dining room. The recipe for the beer is believed to have originated from William Shakespeare and brought to America in 1637 by John Harvard, after whom Harvard University is named. The menu offers chicken sandwiches and burgers as well as some home-style favorites such as grilled meatloaf and chicken pot pie. Casual dress. **Bar:** Full bar. **Reservations:** suggested. **Hours:** 11:30 am-9:30 pm. Closed: 11/25, 12/25. **Address:** 1 Worcester Rd 01701 **Location:** On SR 9; in rear corner of Shopper's World Mall, between AC Moore and Marshall. **Parking:** on-site. CALL

KEN'S STEAK HOUSE

Steak
$5-$32

Phone: 508/875-4455

Providing for its guests since 1941, the popular suburban restaurant focuses on steaks, such as sirloin, filet mignon and London broil, but also serves fish, chicken, veal, roast beef and lamb dishes, as well as hamburgers and sandwiches, amid pleasant surroundings accented by wood, a fireplace, stained-glass windows, flowers and plants. Choices include chicken saltimbocca, Block Island swordfish, Norwegian salmon and baked stuffed lobster. Proper business attire is requested at dinner. Dressy casual. **Bar:** Full bar. **Reservations:** accepted. **Hours:** 11:30 am-9 pm, Fri & Sat-10 pm, Sun 1 pm-9 pm. Closed: 7/4, 12/25. **Address:** 95 Worcester Rd 01701 **Location:** I-90, exit 13, 1 mi w, then 1.5 mi e of SR 9. **Parking:** on-site. CALL

LEGAL SEA FOODS

Seafood
$9-$42

Phone: 508/766-0600

Legal prides itself on a reputation for freshness and consistency. More than 40 varieties of seafood can be grilled, broiled, fried or prepared Cajun style. Try the clam chowder that has been served at every presidential inauguration since 1981. The nautically inspired dining room is upscale and attractive with its rich cherry wood paneling and intricately detailed model ships. Casual dress. **Bar:** Full bar. **Reservations:** accepted. **Hours:** 11 am-10 pm, Fri & Sat-11 pm, Sun noon-10 pm. Closed: 12/25. **Address:** 50-60 Worcester Rd 01701 **Location:** I-90, exit 13, 1.2 mi w on SR 9; opposite Shopper's World Mall. **Parking:** on-site. CALL

NAKED FISH

Seafood
$9-$28

Phone: 508/820-9494

The restaurant presents a selection of unadorned "naked" seafood, beef and chicken, as well as some Cuban and "not-so-naked" choices. Naked seafood is grilled over an open wood fire after being dressed only with lemon and olive oil. Interesting sides, such as coconut steamed rice, make the choice of only one difficult. Although limited in number, the desserts are excellent, particularly the banana flan. The modern, Impressionist, Caribbean-influenced dining room can be bustling and noisy. Casual dress. **Bar:** Full bar. **Reservations:** accepted. **Hours:** 11:30 am-10 pm, Sat noon-11 pm, Sun noon-9 pm. Closed: 11/25, 12/24, 12/25. **Address:** 725 Cochituate Rd (SR 30) 01701 **Location:** I-95, exit 22, just e. **Parking:** on-site. CALL

TENNESSEE'S REAL BBQ REAL FAST

American
$7-$15

Phone: 508/626-7140

In a strip shopping center near several area malls, the popular barbecue joint has patrons order at the counter and then wait for their order to be called. Plastic utensils, brown paper towels torn from a roll as napkins and corrugated metal used as part of the decor set the tone. The entry doors are made to resemble wooden screened doors. Food is provided hot, quick and in ample portions. Lots of booths and a few single spots at the counter allow for seating. Casual dress. **Bar:** Beer only. **Reservations:** not accepted. **Hours:** 11 am-10 pm, Sun-9 pm. Closed: 4/4, 11/25, 12/25. **Address:** 341 Cochituate Rd 01701 **Location:** Between SR 9 and 30; just w of Shopper's World Mall and Wal-Mart. **Parking:** no self-parking. CALL

FRANKLIN pop. 29,560

HAMPTON INN   *Book great rates at AAA.com*

Hotel
$109-$179 All Year

Phone: (508)520-2999

Address: 735 Union St 02038 **Location:** I-495, exit 16, just ne. **Facility:** 94 one-bedroom standard units, some with whirlpools. 3 stories, interior corridors. *Bath:* combo or shower only. **Parking:** on-site. **Terms:** 1-7 night minimum stay, cancellation fee imposed. **Amenities:** dual phone lines, voice mail, irons, hair dryers. **Pool(s):** outdoor. **Leisure Activities:** exercise room. **Guest Services:** valet laundry, wireless Internet. **Business Services:** meeting rooms, business center.

AAA Benefit:
Members save up to 10% everyday!

HAWTHORN SUITES   *Book great rates at AAA.com*

Phone: (508)553-3500

Address: 835 Upper Union St 02038 **Location:** I-495, exit 16, just s, then 0.3 mi e. **Facility:** Smoke free premises. 100 units. 54 one-bedroom standard units, some with kitchens. 46 one-bedroom suites, some with efficiencies, kitchens and/or whirlpools. 3 stories, interior corridors. *Bath:* combo or shower only. **Parking:** on-site. **Amenities:** DVD players, dual phone lines, voice mail, irons, hair dryers. **Pool(s):** heated indoor. **Leisure Activities:** whirlpool, exercise room, sports court. **Guest Services:** valet and coin laundry, wireless Internet. **Business Services:** meeting rooms, business center. **Free Special Amenities:** high-speed Internet. CALL    FEE

RESIDENCE INN BOSTON FRANKLIN   *Book great rates at AAA.com*   Phone: (508)541-8188

Extended Stay Hotel
$160-$179 All Year

Address: 4 Forge Pkwy 02038 **Location:** I-495, exit 17, 0.7 mi nw off SR 140 N. Located in Forge Park Office Complex. **Facility:** Smoke free premises. 108 units. 38 one-bedroom standard units, some with efficiencies or kitchens. 48 one- and 22 two-bedroom suites, some with efficiencies or kitchens. 3 stories, interior corridors. *Bath:* combo or shower only. **Parking:** on-site. **Terms:** cancellation fee imposed. **Amenities:** dual phone lines, voice mail, irons, hair dryers. **Pool(s):** heated indoor. **Leisure Activities:** whirlpool, exercise room, sports court. **Guest Services:** valet and coin laundry, wireless Internet. **Business Services:** meeting rooms, business center.

AAA Benefit:
Members save a minimum 5% off the best available rate.

CALL 🔊📶 ➰ ⊠ ☒ 🎦 🔲 🖥 🖥 / SOME UNITS FEE 🐾

——— WHERE TO DINE ———

JOE'S AMERICAN BAR & GRILL   Phone: 508/553-9313

American
$9-$30

If it's Americana you want, you'll get all that and more at Joe's, where the bill of fare includes all-American favorites like hearty burgers, fresh-from-the-oven chicken pot pies, Maryland lump crab cakes, and Joe's classic meatloaf. Pizzas, pastas, steaks and salads round out the extensive menu, giving diners the freedom to choose from a vast selection of offerings. There's nothing more American than that, except, of course, for apple pie, so save some room. Casual dress. **Bar:** Full bar. **Reservations:** accepted. **Hours:** 11:30 am-11 pm. Closed: 12/25. **Address:** 466 King St 02038 **Location:** I-495, exit 16, just ne. **Parking:** on-site. CALL 🔊📶

PEPPER TERRACE THAI CUISINE   Phone: 508/528-1216

Thai
$8-$17

Just off the interstate in the same complex as the local AAA office, the cozy restaurant is tucked away on one side of a large shopping center. White table linens under glass, ornate Thai carvings, flights of brightly colored birds and lots of greenery in brass planters make for a cheery setting. Patrons find all of the standards, plus such dishes as coo chee salmon, mango curry, several vegetarian dishes and duck ginger, basil or tamarind. Spicy soups and salads also share menu space. Casual dress. **Bar:** Beer & wine. **Reservations:** accepted. **Hours:** 11:30 am-3:30 & 5-9 pm, Sun 3 pm-9 pm. Closed: 11/25; also week of 7/4. **Address:** 400 Franklin Village Dr 02038 **Location:** I-495, exit 17, just e; in Franklin Village Shopping Plaza. **Parking:** on-site. CALL 🔊📶

GLOUCESTER pop. 30,273

BASS ROCKS OCEAN INN   *Book great rates at AAA.com*   Phone: (978)283-7600

Motel
$170-$450 5/1-11/1

Address: 107 Atlantic Rd 01930 **Location:** At terminus SR 128, 0.5 mi n on Bass Ave, then 0.8 mi s. **Facility:** Smoke free premises. 51 one-bedroom standard units, some with whirlpools. 2 stories (no elevator), exterior corridors. **Parking:** on-site. **Terms:** open 5/1-11/1, office hours 7 am-11 pm, 2-4 night minimum stay - weekends, 7 day cancellation notice. **Amenities:** video library, DVD players, irons, hair dryers. **Pool(s):** heated outdoor. **Leisure Activities:** billiards, bocci, boardgames, bicycles, horseshoes. *Fee:* golf & tennis privileges. **Guest Services:** wireless Internet. **Business Services:** PC. **Free Special Amenities:** expanded continental breakfast and high-speed Internet.

➰ ⊠ ☒ 🔲 🖥 / SOME UNITS 🖥

CAPE ANN MOTOR INN   Phone: 978/281-2900

Motel
$100-$185 5/1-10/17
$85-$100 10/18-4/30

Address: 33 Rockport Rd 01930 **Location:** 2 mi n of terminus of SR 128 via SR 127A. **Facility:** Designated smoking area. 31 units. 30 one-bedroom standard units, some with efficiencies. 1 one-bedroom suite with kitchen and whirlpool. 3 stories (no elevator), exterior corridors. **Parking:** on-site. **Terms:** office hours 7:30 am-9 pm, 2 night minimum stay - seasonal and/or weekends, 7 day cancellation notice-fee imposed. **Leisure Activities:** limited beach access. **Guest Services:** wireless Internet. **Business Services:** PC. ☒ 🎵 🔲 / SOME UNITS 🐾 🖥

——— WHERE TO DINE ———

AMELIA'S SUBS & SEAFOOD   Phone: 978/281-8855

American
$5-$20

In a residential area opposite a salt marsh and the entrance to a beach lot is a lavishly landscaped gray clapboard building. The large deck is furnished with picnic tables and bright red and white umbrellas. Inside, tables are accented with cheery yellow and white silk flowers. Guests order food at the counter, and servers bring food to the tables. Generous portions of fried seafood, hot and cold subs and other sandwiches, pasta dinners and seafood chowder are served in disposable containers. Casual dress. **Hours:** 10 am-8 pm; to 10 pm 5/26-10/31. Closed: 1/1, 11/25, 12/25. **Address:** 78 Thatcher Rd 01930 **Location:** 1.2 mi n of terminus of SR 128 via SR 127A; corner of Witham. **Parking:** on-site. CALL 🔊📶

THE GLOUCESTER HOUSE RESTAURANT   *Menu on AAA.com*   Phone: 978/283-1812

Regional Seafood
$9-$27

The complex comprises the main casual restaurant, an informal coffee shop and a cafe where the atmosphere is laid-back and the food is served without fanfare. Fresh fish, lobster, scallops and shrimp are the forte. Many tables overlook the docks, where fishing and tour boats come and go. A collection of antique anchors adds to the decor. Casual dress. **Bar:** Full bar. **Reservations:** suggested. **Hours:** 11:30 am-9 pm, Sat & Sun-10 pm. Closed: 11/25, 12/25. **Address:** 63 Rogers St 01930 **Location:** SR 127, 0.8 mi s of SR 128, exit 10; at Seven Seas Wharf. **Parking:** on-site. CALL 🔊📶

HORIZON CHINESE RESTAURANT

Chinese
$4-$22

Phone: 978/283-8815

On the ground floor of an office building facing the harbor, the small storefront restaurant is decorated with large, oak-framed, rice-paper prints and maple-colored paneled walls accented with brass. Specialties include sesame chicken, crispy garlic shrimp, savory squid and Peking roast duck. Combination platters are served for both lunch and dinner. Limited off-street parking is available. Casual dress. **Hours:** 11 am-10 pm, Fri & Sat-11 pm, Sun noon-10 pm. Closed: 11/25. **Address:** 4 Rogers St 01930 **Location:** Jct Washington, Main and Rogers sts; center. **Parking:** street. CALL ⓛⓂ

PASSPORTS

American
$8-$23

Phone: 978/281-3680

Tucked into an oversized storefront on the corner of Center Street, the down-home restaurant reflects an international flair. On the menu are dishes prepared with a bit of license, such as clam chowder with corn and sweet potatoes. Also tempting are generous portions of Southwestern pasta, Asian-crusted tuna, mango salmon, grilled duck, crispy Mandarin shrimp, Mandarin scallops and lobster ravioli. Service is attentive and friendly. Casual dress. **Bar:** Beer & wine. **Reservations:** suggested. **Hours:** 11:30 am-9 pm. Closed: 11/25, 12/25. **Address:** 110 Main St 01930 **Location:** Corner of Main and Center sts; center. **Parking:** street. CALL ⓛⓂ

TWO SISTERS COFFEE SHOP

American
$4-$8

Phone: 978/281-3378

Just a couple of blocks off the waterfront, the small storefront cafe specializes in breakfast. The menu includes omelets, pancakes and home fries, as well as homemade soups and sandwiches that make for hearty lunches. Almost 15 varieties of breads, 10 of which are made here, can be used for toast or sandwiches. Service is folksy and efficient and the restaurant is squeaky clean. Parking meters are limited to 30 minutes, so visitors should stay aware. Casual dress. **Hours:** 6 am-1:30 pm, Sat & Sun-1 pm. Closed: 11/25, 12/25. **Address:** 27 Washington St 01930 **Location:** 0.7 mi s of SR 128 from rotary; 2 blks n of waterfront; just n of Legion Memorial Building. **Parking:** street.

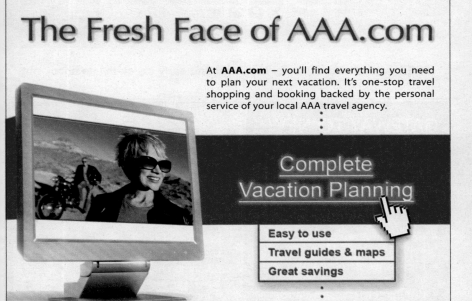

HAVERHILL pop. 58,969

BEST WESTERN MERRIMACK VALLEY   *Book great rates at AAA.com*   Phone: (978)373-1511

Hotel
$74-$189 All Year

Address: 401 Lowell Ave 01832 **Location:** I-495, exit 49 (SR 110). **Facility:** Smoke free premises. 126 one-bedroom standard units. 2-3 stories, interior corridors. *Bath:* combo or shower only. **Parking:** on-site. **Amenities:** voice mail, irons, hair dryers. *Fee:* video games, safes. *Some:* CD players, dual phone lines. **Pool(s):** heated indoor. **Leisure Activities:** whirlpool, exercise room. **Guest Services:** valet and coin laundry, wireless Internet. **Business Services:** meeting rooms, PC.
(See color ad below)

AAA Benefit:
Members save up to 20%, plus 10% bonus points with rewards program.

FREE expanded continental breakfast and high-speed Internet

COMFORT SUITES   *Book great rates at AAA.com*   Phone: (978)374-7755

Hotel
$70-$150 5/1-10/31
$60-$100 11/1-4/30

Address: 106 Bank Rd 01832 **Location:** I-495, exit 49 (SR 110), 0.5 mi s. **Facility:** Smoke free premises. 131 one-bedroom standard units. 4 stories, interior corridors. **Parking:** on-site. **Amenities:** high-speed Internet, voice mail, irons, hair dryers. *Some:* dual phone lines. **Leisure Activities:** exercise room. **Guest Services:** valet and coin laundry, wireless Internet. **Business Services:** meeting rooms, PC.
(See color ad p 390)

FREE expanded continental breakfast and early check-in/late check-out

---

▼ See AAA listing above ▼

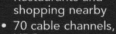

—— **WHERE TO DINE** ——

JOSEPH'S TRATTORIA BAKERY CAFE　　　　　　　　Phone: 978/374-8288

Italian
$9-$34

Everything is made fresh daily at the upbeat, sometimes bustling, location. Among bakery offerings are mouthwatering pastries and breads, including delicious Tuscan bread baked in a stone hearth oven. Fresh pasta, some dishes of which are available in half orders, and stone-baked pizzas are favorite offerings. The bakery opens at 7 am. Casual dress. **Bar:** Full bar. **Hours:** 11:30 am-9 pm, Fri & Sat-10 pm, Sun 12:30 pm-8 pm. Closed major holidays. **Address:** 145 Oxford Ave 01835 **Location:** I-495, exit 48, 1 mi e to SR 125, then just s. **Parking:** on-site. CALL &M

ORIENTAL GARDEN　　　　　　　　Phone: 978/373-5626

Chinese
$5-$20

Traditional Chinese fare shares menu space with a nice selection of Thai dishes. The restaurant is in the Westgate Shopping Center, a small strip mall. The food is well-prepared. Casual dress. **Bar:** Full bar. **Reservations:** accepted. **Hours:** 11:30 am-12:30 am, Fri & Sat-1:30 am, Sun noon-12:30 am. Closed: 11/25. **Address:** 400 Lowell Ave, #13 01832 **Location:** I-495, exit 49 (SR 110). **Parking:** on-site.

HINGHAM pop. 5,352

—— **WHERE TO DINE** ——

NINO'S STEAK AND CHOP HOUSE　　　　　　　　Phone: 781/340-7300

Italian
$9-$19

From the sunken, rock-walled bar to the large, open-beamed dining room—which overlooks the quarry from which the stone came to build the structure—a strong feeling of warmth and style emanates from the cozy restaurant. From 1917 to 1935, the front three rooms were the showroom and offices for the quarry, which has a pond ranging in depth from 15 to 50 feet. Steaks and chops are the specialty, but pasta, chicken, veal and seafood alternatives abound. The dessert menu is verbal and tempting. Casual dress. **Bar:** Full bar. **Reservations:** not accepted. **Hours:** 5 pm-9 pm, Fri & Sat-10 pm, Sun 4 pm-8 pm. Closed major holidays; also Mon & Super Bowl Sun. **Address:** 415 Whiting St 02043 **Location:** SR 53, 1.3 mi n of jct SR 228; SR 3, exit 15, 2 mi ne via Cushing St. **Parking:** on-site.

TOSCA　　　　　　　　Phone: 781/740-0080

Regional Italian
$22-$30

Most offerings, including beef, pork, lamb and chicken dishes, are grilled over an open wood fire, and the aromas grab guests as they enter town. The menu changes seasonally, and when possible, includes items from local farmers and producers. Artistic, interesting desserts are well worth the calories. The Granary Marketplace location is only a block from the water. White table linens and white-frocked servers counter the rustic brick walls and rough-hewn ceiling beams. Casual dress. **Bar:** Full bar. **Reservations:** suggested. **Hours:** 5 pm-10 pm, Fri & Sat-11 pm, Sun 4 pm-9 pm. Closed: 12/24, 12/25; also Mon. **Address:** 14 North St 02043 **Location:** Just w of SR 3A; just n of rotary. **Parking:** on-site. CALL &M

HUDSON pop. 14,388

HOLIDAY INN EXPRESS HOTEL & SUITES　　*Book at AAA.com*　　　　Phone: (978)562-1001

Hotel
$99-$149 5/1-10/31
$89-$129 11/1-4/30

Address: 121 Coolidge St 01749 **Location:** I-495, exit 26, 0.3 mi e on SR 62. **Facility:** Smoke free premises. 69 one-bedroom standard units, some with whirlpools. 3 stories, interior corridors. *Bath:* combo or shower only. **Parking:** on-site. **Amenities:** high-speed Internet, dual phone lines, voice mail, irons, hair dryers. **Leisure Activities:** exercise room. **Guest Services:** valet and coin laundry, wireless Internet. **Business Services:** meeting rooms, PC. ASK CALL &M

HULL pop. 11,050

CLARION NANTASKET BEACH RESORT HOTEL & SPA　　*Book great rates at AAA.com*　　　　Phone: (781)925-4500

AAA SAVE

Hotel
$128-$264 5/1-9/25
$128-$184 9/26-4/30

Address: 45 Hull Shore Dr 02045 **Location:** SR 3, exit 14, 9.4 mi n via SR 228. **Facility:** 105 units. 97 one-bedroom standard units, some with whirlpools. 8 one-bedroom suites with efficiencies or kitchens. 3 stories, interior corridors. *Bath:* combo or shower only. **Parking:** on-site. **Terms:** 3 day cancellation notice. **Amenities:** high-speed Internet, dual phone lines, voice mail, safes (fee), irons, hair dryers. **Dining:** Raffael's at Nantasket, see separate listing. **Pool(s):** heated indoor/outdoor. **Leisure Activities:** whirlpool, spa. **Guest Services:** valet and coin laundry, area transportation (fee)-commuter line & boat, wireless Internet. **Business Services:** meeting rooms, business center. *(See color ad p 381)*

CALL &M / SOME UNITS

FREE early check-in/late check-out and high-speed Internet

—— **WHERE TO DINE** ——

RAFFAEL'S AT NANTASKET　　　　　　　　Phone: 781/925-4515

AAA

Italian
$8-$22

On the menu is traditional American-Italian food, including a nice selection of pasta, parmigiana and Marsala preparations, as well as such fresh fish as the native catch. Ocean views make the location unbeatable. If the weather cooperates, outdoor seating is a good choice. Casual dress. **Bar:** Full bar. **Reservations:** accepted. **Hours:** 6:30 am-10:30 & 11:30-9:30 pm, Sun 10 am-9 pm. Closed: 12/25. **Address:** 45 Hull Shore Dr 02045 **Location:** SR 3, exit 14, 9.4 mi n via SR 228; in Clarion Nantasket Beach Hotel & Spa. **Parking:** on-site.

IPSWICH pop. 4,161

KAEDE BED & BREAKFAST

Bed & Breakfast
$110-$165 5/1-10/21
$95-$135 10/22-4/30

Phone: 978/356-800(

Address: 16 N Main St 01938 **Location:** Just ne of SR 133 and 1A; center. Located in historic district **Facility:** Smoke free premises. 9 units. 8 one-bedroom standard units. 1 one-bedroom suite. 2 storie (no elevator), interior corridors. *Bath:* combo or shower only. **Parking:** on-site. **Terms:** 14 da cancellation notice-fee imposed. **Guest Services:** TV in common area, wireless Internet. **Busines Services:** PC. [ASK] [✚] [✕] [🍳] [☎] / SOME UNITS [🅆]

-------- WHERE TO DINE --------

ITHAKI

Mediterranean
$9-$37

Phone: 978/356-009(

The restaurant takes its name from the smallest of the Ionian Islands and Odysseus' home. Fine linens o granite tables and walls textured to look like ancient sandstone lend to a relaxing atmosphere. A 10-sea stool bar leads to the first of two dining rooms. Among traditional favorites are true Greek salad, grap leaves, moussaka and the specialty lamb, either roasted or on shish kebab. Revani, a honey-soaked cak common all over Greece, is a great choice to finish. Dressy casual. **Bar:** Full bar. **Reservations:** suggeste weekends. **Hours:** 11:30 am-2 & 5-9 pm, Fri & Sat-9:30 pm, Sun 4:30 pm-8:30 pm. Closed: 11/25, 12/25 also Mon. **Address:** 25 Hammatt St 01938 **Location:** From town square, just sw on Market St, then just n at Depot Square. **Parking:** on-site. CALL [&M]

LAWRENCE pop. 72,043

HOLIDAY INN EXPRESS   *Book great rates at AAA.com*

Phone: (978)975-4050

[AAA] [SAVE]

Hotel
$69-$129 All Year

Address: 224 Winthrop Ave 01843 **Location:** I-495, exit 42A, just s on SR 114. **Facility:** Smoke free premises. 126 one-bedroom standard units. 5 stories, interior corridors. *Bath:* combo or shower only. **Parking:** on-site. **Terms:** 30 day cancellation notice. **Amenities:** video games, high-speed Internet, voice mail, irons, hair dryers. **Leisure Activities:** limited exercise equipment. **Guest Services:** valet laundry, wireless Internet. **Business Services:** business center. *(See color ad p 392)*

[✚] CALL [&M] [✕] [🍳] [💻] / SOME UNITS FEE [🐾] [🍴] [📶]

FREE expanded continental breakfast and high-speed Internet

LEXINGTON pop. 30,355   (See map and index starting on p. 345)

ALOFT LEXINGTON   *Book great rates at AAA.com*

Phone: (781)761-1700 [72]

[AAA] [SAVE]

Contemporary
Hotel
$89-$399 All Year

Address: 727 Marrett Rd - A 02173 **Location:** I-95, exit 30B, just w. **Facility:** Smoke free premises. 136 one-bedroom standard units. 4 stories, interior corridors. *Bath:* shower only. **Parking:** on-site. **Terms:** cancellation fee imposed. **Amenities:** high-speed Internet, dual phone lines, voice mail, safes, irons, hair dryers. **Pool(s):** heated indoor. **Leisure Activities:** exercise room. **Guest Services:** valet and coin laundry, airport transportation-Hanscom Air Force Base/Bedford Civil Airport, area transportation-within 3 mi, wireless Internet. **Business Services:** meeting rooms, business center. **Free Special Amenities: local telephone calls and high-speed Internet.**

[✈] [🏊] [✕] [🍳] [🍴] [💻] / SOME UNITS [🐾]

aloft
A VISION OF W HOTELS

AAA Benefit:
Enjoy the new twist, get up to 15% off Starwood Preferred Guest® bonuses.

ELEMENT LEXINGTON

Phone: 781/761-1750 [71]

[AAA] [SAVE]

Hotel
$109-$429 All Year

Address: 727 Marrett Rd 02173 **Location:** I-95, exit 30B. **Facility:** Smoke free premises. 120 units. 117 one-bedroom standard units with efficiencies. 3 one-bedroom suites. 3 stories, interior corridors. **Parking:** on-site. **Terms:** cancellation fee imposed. **Amenities:** high-speed Internet (fee), dual phone lines, voice mail, irons, hair dryers. **Pool(s):** heated indoor. **Leisure Activities:** exercise room. **Guest Services:** valet and coin laundry, airport transportation-Hanscom Air Force Base/Bedford Civil Airport, area transportation-within 3 mi. **Business Services:** meeting rooms, business center. **Free Special Amenities: expanded continental breakfast and high-speed Internet.**

[✈] CALL [&M] [🏊] [✕] [🍴] [🍳] [💻] / SOME UNITS FEE [🐾]

element

AAA Benefit:
Experience element, get up to 15% off Starwood Preferred Guest® bonuses.

(See map and index starting on p. 345)

QUALITY INN & SUITES   *Book great rates at AAA.com*   Phone: (781)861-0850   **70**

Hotel

$63-$90 5/1-10/31
$63-$72 11/1-4/30

Address: 440 Bedford St 02420 **Location:** I-95, exit 31B, just n on SR 4 and 225, continue n and use jug handle to reverse direction. **Facility:** 204 units. 176 one-bedroom standard units. 28 one-bedroom suites with efficiencies. 2 stories (no elevator), exterior corridors. **Parking:** on-site. **Amenities:** voice mail, irons, hair dryers. **Pool(s):** heated outdoor. **Leisure Activities:** whirlpool. **Guest Services:** valet and coin laundry, airport transportation-Hanscom Air Force Base/Bedford Civil Airport, area transportation-within 3 mi, wireless Internet. **Business Services:** PC. **Free Special Amenities: continental breakfast and high-speed Internet.**

——— **WHERE TO DINE** ———

KHUSHBOO   Phone: 781/863-2900   **72**

Indian
$10-$22

Khushboo, which means "aroma," is on the second floor of a downtown building overlooking Main Street. Among offerings of Southern Indian cuisine are many vegetarian dishes, as well as wonderful tandoori preparations and appropriately spicy vindaloos and curries. Lassi drinks, made from yogurt, help quench the fire. Guests might finish with one of the traditionally prepared desserts or ice creams. Casual dress. **Bar:** Full bar. **Reservations:** accepted. **Hours:** 11 am-10 pm, Fri & Sat-11 pm. Closed: 11/25. **Address:** 1709 Massachusetts Ave 02420 **Location:** Center. **Parking:** on-site.

LEMON GRASS THAI CUISINE   Phone: 781/862-3530   **73**

Thai
$8-$18

In a storefront location in the center of town, the restaurant prepares a wide range of traditional Thai offerings. Favorites include the golden bags starter and excellent chicken coconut soup. Seafood, beef and pork are prepared with curry, garlic or ginger sauces. Also on the menu are noodle, rice and vegetarian dishes. Among tempting desserts are unusual ginger and coconut ice creams and Thai custard. The simple but not plain decor incorporates large pictures and brass statues. Casual dress. **Bar:** Full bar. **Hours:** 11:30 am-9 pm, Sat noon-10 pm, Sun noon-9 pm, Mon 11:30 am-9 pm. Closed: 7/4, 11/25, 12/25. **Address:** 1710 Massachusetts Ave 02420 **Location:** I-95, exit 31A, 2 mi s on SR 4 and 225; center. **Parking:** on-site.

NOT YOUR AVERAGE JOE'S   Phone: 781/674-2828

American
$9-$18

The restaurant represents the trendy style of contemporary design with vibrant color schemes, comfortable banquettes and stools and smartly dressed staff. The high point is the food, including creative hand-made pizza, sandwiches and salads. Chefs whip up gourmet comfort foods, such as homemade meatloaf, with a flavorful twist. Casual dress. **Bar:** Full bar. **Hours:** 11:30 am-10 pm, Fri & Sat-11 pm, Sun noon-9 pm. Closed: 11/25, 12/25. **Address:** 1727 Massachusetts Ave 02173 **Location:** On SR 225; downtown. **Parking:** on-site. CALL

LOWELL pop. 105,167

COURTYARD BOSTON LOWELL/CHELMSFORD   *Book great rates at AAA.com*   Phone: (978)458-7575

Hotel
$144-$174 All Year

Address: 30 Industrial Ave E 01852 **Location:** I-495, exit 35C to Lowell connector, then exit 3. Located in a commercial area. **Facility:** Smoke free premises. 120 units. 118 one-bedroom standard units. 2 one-bedroom suites. 3 stories, interior corridors. *Bath:* combo or shower only. **Parking:** on-site. **Terms:** cancellation fee imposed. **Amenities:** high-speed Internet, dual phone lines, voice mail, irons, hair dryers. **Pool(s):** outdoor. **Leisure Activities:** exercise room. **Guest Services:** valet and coin laundry, area transportation. **Business Services:** meeting rooms, PC.

AAA Benefit:
Members save a
minimum 5% off the
best available rate.

DOUBLETREE RIVERFRONT HOTEL   Phone: 978/452-1200

Hotel
Rates not provided

Address: 50 Warren St 01852 **Location:** I-495, exit 35C, via Gorham and Church sts, follow signs; 0.5 mi from end of Lowell connector; center. **Facility:** 252 units. 251 one-bedroom standard units. 1 one-bedroom suite. 9 stories, interior corridors. *Bath:* combo or shower only. **Parking:** on-site. **Amenities:** video games (fee), voice mail, irons, hair dryers. **Pool(s):** heated indoor. **Leisure Activities:** sauna, whirlpool, exercise room. **Guest Services:** valet and coin laundry, area transportation, wireless Internet. **Business Services:** meeting rooms, business center.

DoubleTree
HOTELS•SUITES•RESORTS•CLUBS

AAA Benefit:
Members save 5% or
more everyday!

LYNN pop. 89,050

DIAMOND DISTRICT INN   Phone: 781/595-2200

Historic Bed
& Breakfast
$145-$290 All Year

Address: 142 Ocean St 01902 **Location:** 0.8 mi s of SR 129; eastern terminus of SR 129A via Wolcott St. **Facility:** Some units at the 1911 Georgian-style house, originally built for shoemaker P.J. Harney, feature a fireplace; a beach is within walking distance. Smoke free premises. 10 units. 8 one-bedroom standard units, some with whirlpools. 2 one-bedroom suites, some with whirlpools. 3 stories (no elevator), interior/exterior corridors. *Bath:* combo or shower only. **Parking:** on-site. **Terms:** office hours 9 am-9 pm, 2-3 night minimum stay - weekends, 14 day cancellation notice-fee imposed. **Amenities:** video library, voice mail. *Some:* CD players. **Leisure Activities:** whirlpool.

MALDEN pop. 56,340   (See map and index starting on p. 345)

——— WHERE TO DINE ———

DOCKSIDE RESTAURANT   Phone: 781/321-3000   66

American
$7-$16

Traditional American fare—burgers, soups, sandwiches and more—makes up the menu. The convenient location offers lots of nearby parking and shopping in the mall. Casual dress. **Bar:** Full bar. **Reservations:** accepted. **Hours:** 11:30 am-2 am, Sun noon-midnight. **Address:** 229 Centre St 02148 **Location:** On US 1 S. **Parking:** on-site.

PEARL STREET STATION   Phone: 781/322-6410   65

American
$6-$18

In what was the Boston and Maine Railroad Station at the turn of the 19th century, the restaurant prepares good, ordinary and affordable comfort foods. Casual dress. **Bar:** Full bar. **Hours:** 11:30 am-2 am, Sun 1 pm-midnight. Closed major holidays. **Address:** 53 Summer St 02148 **Location:** At Hamden Rd. **Parking:** on-site.

MARBLEHEAD pop. 20,377

THE HARBOR LIGHT INN   *Book at AAA.com*   Phone: (781)631-2186

Historic Bed
& Breakfast
$155-$345 All Year

Address: 58 Washington St 01945 **Location:** Center. **Facility:** Located in the historic, old town district; buildings dating to 1729 comprise the refined, elegantly decorated inn. Some rooms feature a canopy bed. Smoke free premises. 20 units. 19 one-bedroom standard units, some with whirlpools. 1 one-bedroom suite with whirlpool. 3 stories (no elevator), interior corridors. *Bath:* combo or shower only. **Parking:** on-site. **Terms:** office hours 8 am-10 pm, 2-3 night minimum stay - seasonal and/or weekends, 14 day cancellation notice-fee imposed. **Amenities:** video library, DVD players, CD players, irons, hair dryers. **Pool(s):** heated outdoor. **Guest Services:** wireless Internet. **Business Services:** PC.

THE MARBLEHEAD INN   Phone: (781)639-9999

Bed & Breakfast
$99-$250 All Year

Address: 264 Pleasant St 01945 **Location:** On SR 114. **Facility:** Built in 1872, the Victorian home offers elegantly-decorated rooms furnished with period antiques; located near Marblehead's historic district. Smoke free premises. 10 units. 1 one-bedroom standard unit. 9 one-bedroom suites with efficiencies, some with whirlpools. 3 stories (no elevator), interior corridors. *Bath:* combo or shower only. **Parking:** on-site. **Terms:** 14 day cancellation notice-fee imposed. **Amenities:** hair dryers. **Guest Services:** wireless Internet.

——— WHERE TO DINE ———

BARNACLE RESTAURANT   Phone: 781/631-4236

Regional Seafood
$5-$30

Representative of an "old" New England fish house, the terrific waterside spot serves fresh fried seafood. Marblehead's parking situation can be challenging, but it's worth the effort to find a spot. Casual dress. **Bar:** Full bar. **Hours:** 11:30 am-10 pm. Closed major holidays; also Tues 11/15-3/31. **Address:** 141 Front St 01945 **Location:** On Harbor. **Parking:** street.

THE LANDING RESTAURANT AND PUB

Phone: 781/639-1266

American
$8-$29

Whether patrons choose the lighter menu in the informal pub, with its epoxy-encased charts for tabletops; the fine-dining menu in the two-level dining room with table linens; or the outdoor deck on the water, they can expect food that satisfies both the eye and palate. Clam chowder with grilled corn is a must. Entrées include such dishes as scrod three ways, salmon, veal Oscar, steak au poivre, pork porterhouse and pasta primavera. Dressy casual. **Bar:** Full bar. **Reservations:** accepted. **Hours:** 11:30 am-10 pm; Sunday brunch; hours vary off season. Closed: 11/25, 12/25. **Address:** 81 Front St 01945 **Location:** Corner of State St; on waterfront in historic area. **Parking:** street.

MARLBOROUGH pop. 36,255

BEST WESTERN ROYAL PLAZA HOTEL & TRADE CENTER   *Book great rates at AAA.com*

Phone: (508)460-0700

Hotel
$100-$140 All Year

Address: 181 Boston Post Rd W 01752 **Location:** I-495, exit 24B, 1 mi w on US 20. **Facility:** 431 one-bedroom standard units. 6 stories, interior corridors. **Parking:** on-site. **Amenities:** video games (fee), voice mail, irons, hair dryers. **Dining:** 2 restaurants. **Pool(s):** heated indoor. **Leisure Activities:** exercise room. *Fee:* game room. **Guest Services:** valet laundry, wireless Internet. **Business Services:** conference facilities, business center. **Free Special Amenities: full breakfast and high-speed Internet.** *(See color ad p 380)*

AAA Benefit:
Members save up to 20%, plus 10% bonus points with rewards program.

COMFORT INN   *Book great rates at AAA.com*

Phone: (508)460-1000

Hotel
$72-$82 All Year

Address: 880 Donald J Lynch Blvd 01752 **Location:** I-290, exit 25B, just ne off mall access road. **Facility:** 65 one-bedroom standard units. 2 stories (no elevator), interior corridors. **Parking:** on-site. **Amenities:** irons, hair dryers. **Leisure Activities:** limited exercise equipment. **Guest Services:** coin laundry, wireless Internet. **Free Special Amenities: continental breakfast and high-speed Internet.**

COURTYARD BOSTON MARLBOROUGH   *Book great rates at AAA.com*

Phone: (508)480-0015

Hotel
$170-$208 All Year

Address: 75 Felton St 01752 **Location:** I-495, exit 24B, just w; just off US 20. **Facility:** Smoke free premises. 202 one-bedroom standard units. 5 stories, interior corridors. *Bath:* combo or shower only. **Parking:** on-site. **Terms:** cancellation fee imposed. **Amenities:** video games (fee), dual phone lines, voice mail, irons, hair dryers. **Pool(s):** heated indoor. **Leisure Activities:** exercise room. **Guest Services:** valet and coin laundry, area transportation, wireless Internet. **Business Services:** meeting rooms, business center.

AAA Benefit:
Members save a minimum 5% off the best available rate.

EMBASSY SUITES HOTEL-BOSTON MARLBOROUGH   *Book great rates at AAA.com*

Phone: (508)485-5900

Hotel
$109-$199 All Year

Address: 123 Boston Post Rd W 01752 **Location:** I-495, exit 24B, 0.5 mi w; just off US 20. **Facility:** 229 units. 226 one- and 3 two-bedroom suites, some with kitchens. 6 stories, interior corridors. *Bath:* combo or shower only. **Parking:** on-site. **Terms:** 1-7 night minimum stay, cancellation fee imposed. **Amenities:** video games (fee), high-speed Internet, dual phone lines, irons, hair dryers. *Some:* CD players. **Pool(s):** heated indoor. **Leisure Activities:** whirlpool, exercise room. *Fee:* game room. **Guest Services:** valet and coin laundry, area transportation, wireless Internet. **Business Services:** meeting rooms, business center.

AAA Benefit:
Members save 5% or more everyday!

HAMPTON INN   *Book great rates at AAA.com*

Phone: (508)787-9888

Hotel
$99-$149 All Year

Address: 277 Boston Post Rd W 01752 **Location:** I-495, exit 24B, 1.1 mi w on US 20. **Facility:** 144 one-bedroom standard units, some with whirlpools. 5 stories, interior corridors. *Bath:* combo or shower only. **Parking:** on-site. **Terms:** 1-7 night minimum stay, cancellation fee imposed. **Amenities:** video games (fee), high-speed Internet, dual phone lines, voice mail, irons, hair dryers. **Pool(s):** heated indoor. **Leisure Activities:** whirlpool, exercise room. **Guest Services:** valet and coin laundry, area transportation, wireless Internet. **Business Services:** meeting rooms, business center.

AAA Benefit:
Members save up to 10% everyday!

RESIDENCE INN BY MARRIOTT BOSTON MARLBOROUGH *Book great rates at AAA.com*

Phone: (508)481-1500

Extended Stay Hotel
$170-$208 All Year

Address: 112 Donald Lynch Blvd 01752 **Location:** I-290, exit 25B, 3 mi ne. **Facility:** Smoke free premises. 112 units. 52 one-bedroom standard units, some with efficiencies or kitchens. 39 one- and 21 two-bedroom suites, some with efficiencies or kitchens. 4 stories, interior corridors. *Bath:* combo or shower only. **Parking:** on-site. **Terms:** cancellation fee imposed. **Amenities:** high-speed Internet, dual phone lines, irons, hair dryers. **Pool(s):** heated indoor. **Leisure Activities:** whirlpool, putting green, exercise room, sports court. **Guest Services:** valet and coin laundry, area transportation, wireless Internet. **Business Services:** meeting rooms, business center.

AAA Benefit:
Members save a minimum 5% off the best available rate.

CALL / SOME UNITS FEE

——— WHERE TO DINE ———

CHINA TASTE RESTAURANT

Phone: 508-229-2882

Regional Chinese
$5-$17

Mandarin and Hunan dishes are the focus at the almost-hidden restaurant, next to a supermarket in a strip shopping mall. A luncheon buffet and 32 specials are offered Monday through Saturday. Those who arrive at the peak of lunch hour should expect to wait. Casual dress. **Bar:** Full bar. **Hours:** 11:30 am-10 pm, Sat-11 pm, Sun & holidays noon-10 pm. Closed: 11/25. **Address:** 197A Boston Post Rd W 01752 **Location:** I-495, exit 24B, 0.7 mi w. **Parking:** on-site. CALL

LINGUINE'S

Phone: 508/481-9747

Italian
$6-$15

The informal eatery has counter service at lunch and table service after 5 pm and on weekends. The portions, from sandwiches, calzones and pizza to pasta, with or without protein enhancements, are large and the sauces fresh. A line of area office workers is out the door at lunch. Casual dress. **Bar:** Beer & wine. **Reservations:** not accepted. **Hours:** 11:30 am-9 pm, Sat noon-10 pm, Sun 3 pm-9 pm. Closed major holidays. **Address:** 350 Boston Post Rd W 01752 **Location:** I-495, exit 24B, 1.2 mi w on US 20. **Parking:** on-site.

PICCADILLY PUB

Phone: 508/485-4416

American
$7-$16

Patrons at the informal, folksy restaurant range from families to neatly pressed professionals. Fish and chips, clam chowder in a bread bowl, burgers, sandwiches, and special dinners, such as Yankee pot roast and homemade meatloaf, are well-complemented by a selection of microbrews. Portions are ample, and the service is efficient. Casual dress. **Bar:** Full bar. **Reservations:** accepted. **Hours:** 11 am-10 pm, Thurs-Sat to 11 pm, Sun noon-9 pm. Closed: 11/25, 12/25. **Address:** 587 Bolton St 01752 **Location:** I-495, exit 25A, 1.5 mi e to SR 85, then 1 mi s; exit 24A, 1.8 mi e on US 20, then 1.4 mi n on SR 85. **Parking:** on-site.

CALL

TANDOORI GRILL

Phone: 508/357-6551

Indian
$11-$22

In a strip mall, the informal restaurant serves Northern Indian dishes, including tandoori chicken, lamb, seafood, biryani and vegetarian specialties. Lamb vindaloo is particularly good. Leavened and unleavened breads are baked, stuffed, grilled or fried. Traditional desserts and beverages complete the authentic experience. Guests can explore the daily buffet at lunch and dinner. Small framed tapestries on the walls and earthen vessels on a shelf above one wall add a measure of authenticity. Casual dress. **Bar:** Beer only. **Hours:** 11:30 am-3 & 5-10 pm. Closed major holidays. **Address:** 197 H Boston Post Rd 01752 **Location:** I-495, exit 24B, 0.7 mi w; just off US 20. **Parking:** on-site. CALL

MEDFORD pop. 55,765   (See map and index starting on p. 345)

HYATT PLACE BOSTON/MEDFORD *Book great rates at AAA.com*

Phone: (781)395-8500   **67**

Hotel
$89-$299 All Year

Address: 116 Riverside Ave NE 02155 **Location:** I-93, exit 32, just sw via SR 60 and River St. **Facility:** Smoke free premises. 157 one-bedroom standard units. 8 stories, interior corridors. *Bath:* combo or shower only. **Parking:** on-site. **Terms:** cancellation fee imposed. **Amenities:** voice mail, irons, hair dryers. *Some:* high-speed Internet. **Pool(s):** heated indoor. **Leisure Activities:** exercise room. **Guest Services:** valet laundry, area transportation-within 3 mi, wireless Internet. **Business Services:** meeting rooms, PC. **Free Special Amenities: continental breakfast and high-speed Internet.**

HYATT PLACE

AAA Benefit:
Ask for the AAA rate and save 10%.

CALL

——— WHERE TO DINE ———

MODERN PASTRY

Phone: 781/396-3618   **69**

Breads/Pastries
$3-$9

The amazing pastries at this must stop for fresh and from-scratch delicacies are not to be missed. Crowd-pleasers include the giant lobster tails, homemade pastry shells filled, at the time you order, with what might be a blend of mascarpone and ricotta cheeses. The ingredients are uncertain but the taste is undeniably good. Additional delights are Italian cookies, Boston cream pie and ricotta pie. The sole hiccup: Parking is a challenge, but it's worth the effort to make do. Casual dress. **Hours:** 9 am-7 pm, Sat 8 am-6 pm, Sun 8 am-2 pm, Mon 9 am-6 pm. Closed: 12/25. **Address:** 20 Salem St 02155 **Location:** On SR 60. **Parking:** no self-parking.

(See map and index starting on p. 345)

NOT YOUR AVERAGE JOE'S   Phone: 781/393-9681

♦♦♦ ♦♦♦

American
$9-$18

This eatery exemplifies the "in-trend" style of high-art contemporary design through vibrant color schemes, comfortable seating and smartly dressed staff. However, the high point is the food. The cooking team whips up gourmet comfort foods of homemade meatloaf with a flavorful twist, creative hand-made pizzas, sandwiches, salads and more. Casual dress. **Bar:** Full bar. **Hours:** 11:30 am-10 pm, Fri & Sat-11 pm, Sun noon-10 pm. Closed: 11/25, 12/25. **Address:** 501 Middlesex Fells Pkwy 02155 **Location:** On SR 28, just s of SR 16. **Parking:** street.

METHUEN pop. 43,789

—— WHERE TO DINE ——

CAPELLINI'S ITALIAN RESTAURANT   Phone: 978/837-3334

♦♦♦ ♦♦♦

Italian
$7-$19

Just off the highway, the family-friendly restaurant welcomes guests into a warm, friendly dining room. Starters such as toasted ravioli and fried calamari warm up the palate for an array of pasta, seafood, veal and chicken dishes. An interesting choice is capellini with artichoke hearts, black olives, mushrooms and pasta in a garlic and wine sauce. Bread with spiced olive oil for dipping is excellent. Casual dress. **Bar:** Beer & wine. **Hours:** 11:30 am-9 pm, Fri & Sat-10 pm, Sun 2 pm-9 pm. Closed major holidays. **Address:** 126 Merrimack St 01844 **Location:** I-495, exit 46, just ne on SR 110. **Parking:** on-site.

CALL

FIRESIDE RESTAURANT & PUB   Phone: 978/683-2945

♦♦♦

American
$7-$19

An obvious favorite among locals and employees of area businesses, the restaurant always seems busy. Well-prepared comfort foods incorporate good ingredients. Casual dress. **Bar:** Full bar. **Hours:** 11 am-10 pm, Mon & Tues-9 pm, Sun noon-9 pm. Closed major holidays. **Address:** 171 Pelham St 01844 **Location:** I-93, exit 47, just w. **Parking:** on-site.

JACKSON'S RESTAURANT   Phone: 978/688-5021

♦♦♦ ♦♦♦

American
$9-$23

Originally an old-fashioned diner in the 1940s, the restaurant has gone through several transformations and additions and is now a family restaurant along the Merrimack River. Traditional American fare, including a great selection of comfort foods, is well prepared and tasty. **Bar:** Full bar. **Reservations:** not accepted. **Hours:** 11 am-close, Sun from noon. Closed: 12/25; also Mon. **Address:** 478 Lowell St 01844 **Location:** I-495, exit 46, 0.4 mi sw. **Parking:** on-site. CALL

NOT YOUR AVERAGE JOE'S   Phone: 978/974-0015

♦♦♦ ♦♦♦

American
$9-$19

In a mall known as "The Loop," the restaurant represents the trendy style of contemporary design with vibrant color schemes, comfortable banquettes and stools and smartly dressed staff. The high point is the food, including creative hand-made pizza, sandwiches and salads. Chefs whip up gourmet comfort foods, such as homemade meatloaf, with a flavorful twist. Casual dress. **Bar:** Full bar. **Hours:** 11:30 am-10 pm, Fri & Sat-11 pm, Sun noon-9 pm. Closed: 11/25, 12/25. **Address:** 90 Pleasant Valley St 01844 **Location:** At the loop. **Parking:** on-site. CALL ⟨🚹M⟩

NATICK

COURTYARD BOSTON NATICK   *Book great rates at AAA.com*

Hotel
$209-$229 All Year

Phone: (508)655-6100

Address: 342 Speen St 01760 **Location:** I-90, exit 13, e on SR 9, then 0.5 mi n. Located behind Natick Mall. **Facility:** Smoke free premises. 181 units. 176 one-bedroom standard units, some with whirlpools. 5 one-bedroom suites. 6 stories, interior corridors. *Bath:* combo or shower only. **Parking:** on-site. **Terms:** cancellation fee imposed. **Amenities:** video games (fee), high-speed Internet, dual phone lines, voice mail, irons, hair dryers. **Pool(s):** heated indoor. **Leisure Activities:** whirlpool, exercise room. **Guest Services:** valet and coin laundry, area transportation, wireless Internet. **Business Services:** meeting rooms, business center.

AAA Benefit:
Members save a minimum 5% off the best available rate.

CROWNE PLAZA BOSTON-NATICK   *Book at AAA.com*

Hotel
$99-$209 All Year

Phone: (508)653-8800

Address: 1360 Worcester St 01760 **Location:** I-90, exit 12, 5 mi e; SR 9, 4 mi e of Framingham Center. Opposite Natick Mall. **Facility:** Smoke free premises. 251 units. 250 one-bedroom standard units. 1 one-bedroom suite. 7 stories, interior corridors. **Parking:** on-site. **Amenities:** CD players, voice mail, irons, hair dryers. *Some:* DVD players. **Leisure Activities:** exercise room. **Guest Services:** valet laundry, area transportation, wireless Internet. **Business Services:** conference facilities, business center.

HAMPTON INN BOSTON-NATICK   *Book great rates at AAA.com*

Hotel
$109-$279 All Year

Phone: (508)653-5000

Address: 319 Speen St 01760 **Location:** I-90, exit 13, 0.5 mi se on SR 9. Adjacent to a shopping mall. **Facility:** Smoke free premises. 185 units. 185 one-bedroom standard units. 3 one-bedroom suites, some with efficiencies (no utensils). 7 stories, interior corridors. *Bath:* combo or shower only. **Parking:** on-site. **Terms:** 1-7 night minimum stay, cancellation fee imposed. **Amenities:** voice mail, irons, hair dryers. **Leisure Activities:** exercise room. **Guest Services:** valet and coin laundry, wireless Internet. **Business Services:** meeting rooms, business center.

AAA Benefit:
Members save up to 10% everyday!

------ **WHERE TO DINE** ------

KELLY'S ROAST BEEF

American
$5-$17

Phone: 508/872-4900

Family owned and operated since 1951, the restaurant offers upscale fast food-style service and ample portions. Signature items include roast beef sandwiches, clam chowder and lobster rolls. Colorful decor features carousel horses, large aquariums and pictures of yesteryear Revere Beach. The restaurant sits atop a hill overlooking Natick's malls and is attached to a unique furniture store. Casual dress. **Hours:** 10 am-10 pm, Fri & Sat-11 pm, Sun 11 am-9 pm. Closed: 4/4, 11/25, 12/25. **Address:** 2 Under Price Way 01760 **Location:** Just s of SR 9; opposite Natick Mall; next to Jordan's Furniture. **Parking:** on-site.

SKIPJACK'S

Seafood
$9-$27

Phone: 508/628-9900

The fish house is convenient to several major shopping areas. The menu outlines the source of the fresh fish—for example, Gulf of Maine salmon and Pacific sea bass—which can be grilled, broiled or prepared "SkipJack's style." Other offerings include great buttered rolls, selections from a good wine list, raw bar items and several beef and chicken dishes for those not in the mood for seafood. Dressy casual. **Bar:** Full bar. **Reservations:** accepted. **Hours:** 5 pm-10 pm, Fri & Sat 4 pm-11 pm, Sun 4 pm-9 pm. Closed: 11/25, 12/25. **Address:** 1400 Worcester St (Rt 9) 01760 **Location:** I-90 (Massachusetts Tpke), exit 13, 1 mi w on SR 9; in Milton's Shopping Plaza, west end. **Parking:** on-site.

NEEDHAM pop. 28,911   (See map and index starting on p. 345)

SHERATON NEEDHAM HOTEL   *Book great rates at AAA.com*

Hotel
$99-$349 All Year

Phone: (781)444-1110   128

Address: 100 Cabot St 02494 **Location:** I-95, exit 19A, just e. **Facility:** Smoke free premises. 247 units. 226 one-bedroom standard units. 21 one-bedroom suites. 5 stories, interior corridors. *Bath:* combo or shower only. **Parking:** on-site (fee). **Terms:** cancellation fee imposed. **Amenities:** dual phone lines, voice mail, irons, hair dryers. *Fee:* video games, high-speed Internet. **Pool(s):** heated indoor. **Leisure Activities:** whirlpool, exercise room. **Guest Services:** valet laundry, area transportation-within 5 mi. **Business Services:** conference facilities, business center. **Free Special Amenities:** newspaper and preferred room (subject to availability with advance reservations).

Sheraton
HOTELS & RESORTS
AAA Benefit:
Members get up to 15% off, plus Starwood Preferred Guest® bonuses.

------ **WHERE TO DINE** ------

NOT YOUR AVERAGE JOE'S

American
$9-$18

Phone: 781/453-9300

This trendy, yet very contemporary restaurant is packed with vibrant color schemes, comfortable banquettes and stools, and smart-dressed staff. The high point is the food, where chefs whip up gourmet foods of homemade meatloaf with a flavorful twist, creative handmade pizzas, sandwiches, salads and more. Casual dress. **Bar:** Full bar. **Hours:** 11:30 am-10 pm, Fri & Sat-11 pm, Sun noon-10 pm. Closed: 11/25, 12/25. **Address:** 109 Chapel St 02492 **Location:** I-95, exit 19B, 1.5 mi sw via Highland Ave, then just w. **Parking:** street.

NEWBURYPORT pop. 17,189

HARRISON INN

Historic
Hotel
$170-$320 All Year

Phone: 978/499-8500

Address: 11 Brown Square 01950 **Location:** I-95, exit 57, 2.6 mi e on SR 1A, just n on Green St, just w on Pleasant St, then just s. **Facility:** In a building dating from 1809, the hotel offers modern accommodations. Smoke free premises. 24 units. 18 one- and 2 two-bedroom standard units. 2 one- and 1 two-bedroom suites. 4 stories, interior corridors. **Parking:** on-site. **Terms:** check-in 4 pm, 3 day cancellation notice-fee imposed. **Amenities:** voice mail, irons, hair dryers. **Guest Services:** wireless Internet. / SOME UNITS FEE

WHERE TO DINE

THE BLACK COW TAP & GRILL

Steak
$17-$32

Phone: 978/499-8811

Known for its fresh grilled fish and steaks, the waterfront restaurant lets guests sit on the deck in the summer and around the cozy fireplace during cooler seasons. In addition to such choices as baked haddock and filet mignon, the menu lists braised lamb shank, hoisin-glazed sea scallops and vegetarian penne pasta with artichoke hearts and feta cheese. Casual dress. **Bar:** Full bar. **Reservations:** suggested. **Hours:** 11:30 am-3 & 5-9:30 pm, Fri & Sat-11 pm. Closed: 11/25, 12/25. **Address:** 54 R Merrimac St 01950 **Location:** 2.6 mi e on SR 113 and 1A, n on Green St to the end. **Parking:** on-site. CALL

THE JEWEL IN THE CROWN

Indian
$6-$16

Phone: 978/463-0956

A nice selection of Indian cuisine includes ample curried dishes, thin crepes known as dosa and wonderful Indian breads called naan. Appropriate background music lends to the comfortably casual atmosphere. Dressy casual. **Bar:** Full bar. **Hours:** 11:30 am-10:30 pm, Thurs-Sun to 11 pm. Closed major holidays. **Address:** 23 Pleasant St 01950 **Location:** Between State and Green sts; center; in historic district. **Parking:** street.

NOT YOUR AVERAGE JOE'S

American
$9-$18

Phone: 978/462-3808

The restaurant exemplifies the "in-trend" style of high-art contemporary design through vibrant color schemes, comfortable banquettes and stools, and smartly dressed staff. However, the high point is the food. Chefs whip up gourmet comfort foods of homemade meatloaf with a flavorful twist, creative hand-made pizzas, sandwiches, salads and more. Casual dress. **Bar:** Full bar. **Hours:** 11:30 am-10 pm, Fri & Sat-11 pm, Sun noon-10 pm. Closed: 11/25, 12/25. **Address:** 1 Market Square 01950 **Location:** Downtown; in Firehouse Center. **Parking:** on-site.

SZECHUAN TASTE & THAI CAFE
Asian
$6-$15

Phone: 978/463-0686

A delightful mix of Thai and regional Chinese fare can be ordered for takeout or eaten in. Duck, seafood and game hen preparations, as well as vegetarian items, are available. Monosodium glutamate is strictly avoided. An aquarium and ornate, inlaid chairs and love seats lend visual interest, as do interesting carved tables that depart from the norm. A lounge and sushi bar occupy the basement. Servers in black vests and bow ties project a level of formality above what is delivered. Casual dress. **Bar:** Full bar. **Hours:** 11:30 am-10 pm, Fri & Sat 11 am-11 pm. Closed: 11/25. **Address:** 19 Pleasant St 01950 **Location:** Center; in historic area. **Parking:** street.

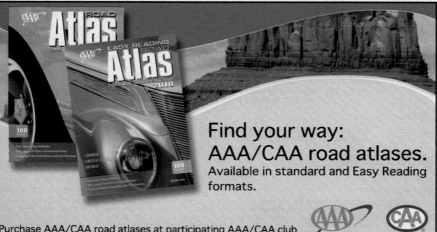

NEWTON pop. 83,829 (See map and index starting on p. 345)

BOSTON MARRIOTT NEWTON   *Book great rates at AAA.com*   Phone: (617)969-1000

(AAA) (SAVE)
▽▽▽▽
Hotel
$219-$249 All Year

Address: 2345 Commonwealth Ave 02466 **Location:** I-95, exit 24, just e; I-90, exit 14 eastbound; exit 15 westbound. **Facility:** Smoke free premises. 430 units. 424 one-bedroom standard units. 6 one-bedroom suites. 7 stories, interior/exterior corridors. *Bath:* combo or shower only. **Parking:** on-site (fee). **Terms:** cancellation fee imposed. **Amenities:** high-speed Internet (fee), voice mail, irons, hair dryers. **Dining:** 2 restaurants. **Pool(s):** heated indoor. **Leisure Activities:** whirlpool. **Guest Services:** valet and coin laundry, area transportation-Riverside T Station. **Business Services:** conference facilities, business center.

Marriott
HOTELS & RESORTS

AAA Benefit:
Members save a minimum 5% off the best available rate.

🍴 🍸 CALL 🚹 🏊 ⚕ ✕ ⚒ 🖥 / SOME UNITS 🛗

CROWNE PLAZA BOSTON/NEWTON   *Book great rates at AAA.com*   Phone: (617)969-3010

(AAA) (SAVE)
▽▽▽▽
Hotel
$99-$229 All Year

Address: 320 Washington St 02458 **Location:** I-90, exit 17. **Facility:** Smoke free premises. 270 c bedroom standard units, some with whirlpools. 12 stories, interior corridors. *Bath:* combo or sho only. **Parking:** on-site (fee). **Terms:** cancellation fee imposed. **Amenities:** video games (fee), h speed Internet, dual phone lines, voice mail, irons, hair dryers. **Pool(s):** heated indoor. **Leis Activities:** exercise room. **Guest Services:** valet laundry, area transportation-within 5 mi. **Busin Services:** conference facilities, business center. **Free Special Amenities: continental breakfast** a **high-speed Internet.** 🍴 🏊 ✕ ⚒ 🖥 / SOME UNITS 🐾 FEE 🛗 FEE 🖨

HOTEL INDIGO BOSTON-NEWTON RIVERSIDE   *Book great rates at AAA.com*   Phone: (617)969-5300

(AAA) (SAVE)
▽▽▽▽
Boutique
Contemporary Retro
Hotel
$119-$259 All Year

Address: 399 Grove St 02462 **Location:** I-95, exit 22, just e. **Facility:** Smoke free premises. 191 units. 190 one-bedroom standard units. 1 one-bedroom suite. 7 stories, interior corridors. *Bath:* combo or shower only. **Parking:** on-site. **Terms:** cancellation fee imposed. **Amenities:** high-speed Internet, voice mail, safes, irons, hair dryers. **Dining:** 2 restaurants. **Pool(s):** heated outdoor. **Leisure Activities:** exercise room. **Guest Services:** valet laundry, wireless Internet. **Business Services:** meeting rooms, business center. *(See color ad p 385)*

🍴 🍸 🏊 ✕ ⚒ 🖥 / SOME UNITS FEE 🐾 FEE 🛗

FREE local telephone calls and high-speed Internet

—— WHERE TO DINE ——

BLUE RIBBON BAR-B-Q   Phone: 617/332-2583

▽
Barbecue
$6-$16

Generous portions of New York-style barbecue is served here or for takeout. Casual dress. **Hours:** 11 a pm, Sun-8 pm. Closed major holidays. **Address:** 1375 Washington St 02465 **Location:** I-90, exit 17 16). **Parking:** street.

SKIPJACK'S   Phone: 617/964-4244

▽▽
Seafood
$8-$35

In a busy commercial area, this fish house is still convenient to the interstate. Hardwood floors, a whole of signal flags and pictures of the sea set the stage. Interesting specialty preparations include items suc Jamaican jerked mahi mahi, giant sea scallop ravioli and broiled salmon au poivre. Casual dress. **Bar:** bar. **Hours:** 11:30 am-10 pm, Fri & Sat noon-11 pm, Sun 11:30 am-9 pm. Closed: 11/25, 12 **Address:** 55 Needham St 02461 **Location:** I-95, exit 19A, 1.1 mi ne. **Parking:** on-site. CALL 🚹

—— The following restaurant has not been evaluated by AAA —— but is listed for your information only.

KAROUN   Phone: 617/964-34

[fyi]

Not evaluated. Karoun has American-Middle Eastern fare and belly dancing Friday and Satur **Address:** 839 Washington St 02160

NORTH ANDOVER

—— WHERE TO DINE ——

BOLLYWOOD GRILL   Phone: 978/689-7

(AAA)
▽▽
Indian
$7-$21

Just off the interstate, the restaurant is in a shopping mall that is coming back to life. The name comes f the movie-making area of India in Bombay. Stills of Indian and American artists line the walls. From pakc and curries to saag, vindaloo and kebabs, the menu incorporates all the Indian favorites. When the m says the vindaloo is spicy, believe it. Traditional desserts such as kheer and kulfi and drinks such as la round out the offerings. Casual dress. **Bar:** Full bar. **Reservations:** required, weekends. **Hours:** 11:30 a & 5-10:30 pm. Closed: 12/25. **Address:** 350 Winthrop Ave 01845 **Location:** I-495, exit 42, 0.6 mi s on 114; in North Andover Mall. **Parking:** on-site. CALL 🚹

HINA BLOSSOM RESTAURANT

Chinese
$7-$18

Phone: 978/682-2242

Generous portions of Cantonese, Hunan and Szechuan dishes are served at the relaxed restaurant, which is just opposite Lawrence Municipal Airport. Patrons can pick and choose from the extensive lunch and dinner buffets or make selections from the full menu. Pu pu platters, egg rolls and crab rangoon make good starters for a meal of beef, chicken or pork in kung pao, orange, yu hsiang, sweet-and-sour or lobster sauce varieties. The comedy club offers entertainment Friday and Saturday at 9:30 pm. Casual dress. **Bar:** Full bar. **Reservations:** not accepted. **Hours:** 11:30 am-9:30 pm, Sun from noon. Closed: 11/25. **Address:** 946 Osgood St 01845 **Location:** SR 125 and 133, 4 mi ne of jct SR 114; opposite Lawrence Airport. **Parking:** on-site.

OE FISH

Seafood
$8-$25

Phone: 978/685-3663

Those who want fresh fish but don't want to dress up to get it can head to the casual restaurant. From the raw bar to simple meals such as baked salmon to the widely touted Singapore shrimp, the seafood is fresh. Clam chowder is excellent. Limited beef and chicken selections are also available. The open kitchen resembles a beachside fish shack. Guests can relax in one of the beadboard banquettes or at a table in front of the fireplace. Servers are friendly and efficient. Casual dress. **Bar:** Full bar. **Reservations:** suggested, weekends. **Hours:** 11:30 am-10 pm, Fri-10:30 pm, Sat noon-10:30 pm, Sun noon-9 pm. Closed major holidays. **Address:** 1120 Osgood St 01845 **Location:** On SR 125; just n of jct SR 133 E; opposite Butcher Boy Marketplace. **Parking:** on-site. CALL ⬛M

ORTH CHELMSFORD

AWTHORN SUITES BY WYNDHAM   *Book great rates at AAA.com*

Hotel
$90-$99 All Year

Phone: (978)256-5151

Address: 25 Research Pl 01863 **Location:** US 3, exit 32, 0.3 mi ne on SR 4. Located in a technology park. **Facility:** 105 units. 45 one-bedroom standard units with efficiencies. 60 one-bedroom suites with efficiencies. 3 stories, interior corridors. *Bath:* combo or shower only. **Parking:** on-site. **Terms:** cancellation fee imposed. **Amenities:** DVD players, video games (fee), high-speed Internet, dual phone lines, voice mail, irons, hair dryers. **Leisure Activities:** exercise room. **Guest Services:** valet and coin laundry, wireless Internet. **Business Services:** meeting rooms, business center. **Free Special Amenities: full breakfast and high-speed Internet.**

CALL ⬛M 📺 🔲 📠 💻 / SOME UNITS FEE 🐾 ✕

NORWOOD pop. 28,587   (See map and index starting on p. 345)

OURTYARD BOSTON NORWOOD   *Book great rates at AAA.com*

Hotel
$129-$155 All Year

Phone: (781)762-4700

Address: 300 River Ridge Dr 02062 **Location:** I-95, exit 9 northbound, 4.3 mi n on US 1; exit 10 southbound, 0.4 mi nw on Coney St, then 1.7 mi ne on US 1. Located in River Ridge Office Park. **Facility:** Smoke free premises. 148 units. 138 one-bedroom standard units. 10 one-bedroom suites. 2-3 stories, interior corridors. *Bath:* combo or shower only. **Parking:** on-site. **Terms:** cancellation fee imposed. **Amenities:** high-speed Internet, voice mail, irons, hair dryers. **Pool(s):** heated indoor. **Leisure Activities:** whirlpool, exercise room. **Guest Services:** valet and coin laundry. **Business Services:** meeting rooms, business center. **Free Special Amenities: local telephone calls and high-speed Internet.**

🍴 CALL ⬛M 🏊 ✕ 📺 💻 / SOME UNITS 🔲 📠

COURTYARD Marriott

AAA Benefit:
Members save a minimum 5% off the best available rate.

OUR POINTS BY SHERATON NORWOOD HOTEL & CONFERENCE CENTER   *Book great rates at AAA.com*

Hotel
$125-$235 All Year

Phone: (781)769-7900

Address: 1125 Boston-Providence Tpke 02062 **Location:** I-95, exit 9 northbound, 4.1 mi ne on US 1; exit 11B southbound, 0.5 mi nw on Neponset St, 0.6 mi w on Dean St, then 0.3 mi s on US 1. **Facility:** Smoke free premises. 230 units. 227 one-bedroom standard units. 3 one-bedroom suites. 5 stories, interior corridors. *Bath:* combo or shower only. **Parking:** on-site. **Terms:** 2-3 night minimum stay - seasonal and/or weekends, cancellation fee imposed. **Amenities:** video games (fee), high-speed Internet, dual phone lines, voice mail, irons, hair dryers. **Dining:** One Bistro, see separate listing. **Pool(s):** heated indoor. **Leisure Activities:** whirlpool, exercise room. **Guest Services:** valet laundry, area transportation-within 5 mi. **Business Services:** meeting rooms, business center. **Free Special Amenities: newspaper and high-speed Internet.**

🍴 🍽 🏊 ✕ 📺 💻 / SOME UNITS FEE 🔲

FOUR ᛝ POINTS
BY SHERATON

AAA Benefit:
Members get up to 15% off, plus Starwood Preferred Guest® bonuses.

AMPTON INN   *Book great rates at AAA.com*

Hotel
$99-$169 All Year

Phone: (781)769-7000   [147]

Address: 434 Providence Hwy 02062 **Location:** I-95, exit 9 northbound, 5.9 mi ne on US 1; exit 11B southbound, 1.3 mi nw on Neponset St, then 0.4 mi n on US 1. **Facility:** Smoke free premises. 139 units. 138 one-bedroom standard units. 1 one-bedroom suite. 6 stories, interior corridors. *Bath:* combo or shower only. **Parking:** on-site. **Terms:** 1-7 night minimum stay, cancellation fee imposed. **Amenities:** video games (fee), high-speed Internet, dual phone lines, voice mail, irons, hair dryers. **Pool(s):** heated indoor. **Leisure Activities:** whirlpool, exercise room. **Guest Services:** valet and coin laundry, area transportation, wireless Internet. **Business Services:** meeting rooms, business center.

🍴 CALL ⬛M 🏊 ✕ 📺 💻 / SOME UNITS FEE 🐾 🔲 📠

Hampton Inn

AAA Benefit:
Members save up to 10% everyday!

(See map and index starting on p. 345)

RESIDENCE INN BOSTON-NORWOOD   *Book great rates at AAA.com*   Phone: (781)278-9595

(AAA) (SAVE)

▼▼▼

Extended Stay Hotel
$169-$209 All Year

Address: 275 Norwood Park S 02062 **Location:** I-95, exit 9 northbound, 3.7 mi n on US 1; exit 11B southbound, 0.5 mi nw on Neponset St, 0.6 mi w on Dean St, then 0.8 mi s on US 1. **Facility:** Smoke free premises. 96 units. 53 one-bedroom standard units with efficiencies. 24 one- and 19 two-bedroom suites, some with efficiencies or kitchens. 4 stories, interior corridors. *Bath:* combo or shower only. **Parking:** on-site. **Terms:** cancellation fee imposed. **Amenities:** high-speed Internet, voice mail, irons, hair dryers. **Pool(s):** heated indoor. **Leisure Activities:** whirlpool, exercise room, sports court. **Guest Services:** valet and coin laundry, wireless Internet. **Business Services:** meeting rooms, business center. **Free Special Amenities: full breakfast and high-speed Internet.**

CALL 🅼 ➋ ✕ ✕ 📷 🖥 🖼 🖵 / SOME UNITS FEE 🐕

AAA Benefit:
Members save a minimum 5% off the best available rate.

——— WHERE TO DINE ———

THE CHATEAU ITALIAN FAMILY DINING   Phone: 781/762-5335

▼▼ ▼▼▼

Italian
$8-$20

The tradition began in 1933, and this place remains under the ownership and operation of the Nocera family. The dining room overlooks the links at Norwood Country Club and is well suited for dining with families and friends, as well as for group functions. The extensive menu satisfies many tastes. Casual dress. **Bar:** Full bar. **Reservations:** accepted. **Hours:** 11:15 am-10 pm, Sun noon-9 pm. Closed: 7/4, 11/25, 12/25. **Address:** 404 Providence Hwy 02062 **Location:** I-95, exit 9 northbound, 6 mi ne on US 1; exit 11B southbound, 1.3 mi nw on Neponset St, then 0.5 mi n on US 1. **Parking:** on-site. CALL 🅼

ONE BISTRO   Phone: 781/255-3117

▼▼▼▼▼

American
$8-$30

Yellow and milk-chocolate awnings mark the location of the upscale bistro. An interior of rich oak and white table linens projects a formality beyond the casually friendly atmosphere. Food is artistically presented in filling proportions. Guests will find pizzas, a raw bar, salads and starters that include crab cakes, chicken satay, blue cheese and pear salad. Main courses range from roast salmon, lobster and seared tuna to steaks, chicken, pork chops, veal and lamb. Desserts are made to order. Dressy casual. **Bar:** Full bar. **Reservations:** suggested. **Hours:** 11:30 am-midnight; Sunday brunch. Closed: 12/25. **Address:** 1125 Boston-Providence Tpke 02062 **Location:** I-95, exit 9 northbound, 4.1 mi ne on US 1; exit 11B southbound, 0.5 mi nw on Neponset St, 0.6 mi w on Dean St, then 0.3 mi s on US 1; in Four Points by Sheraton Norwood Hotel & Conference Center. **Parking:** on-site. CALL 🅼

SKY RESTAURANT   Phone: 781/255-8888

▼▼▼

American
$9-$38

Mahogany paneling, lamp sculptures, a waterfall wall and other cranberry walls with sky pictures merge in a more formal setting than the contemporary American menu might suggest. International twists characterize dishes such as grilled Jamaican chicken, maple-glazed roast pork chop, braised lamb shank, steaks, roast scrod and Asian salmon. If a burger or barbecue chicken pizza catches the diner's eye, he should indulge. Service is professional and friendly. Dressy casual. **Bar:** Full bar. **Hours:** 11:30 am-10 pm, Thurs-Sat to 11 pm, Sun 10 am-9 pm. **Address:** 1369 Boston-Providence Tpke 02062 **Location:** I-95 and SR 128, exit 15B, 4.5 mi s on US 1. **Parking:** on-site. CALL 🅼

PEABODY pop. 48,129   (See map and index starting on p. 345)

BOSTON MARRIOTT PEABODY   *Book great rates at AAA.com*   Phone: (978)977-9700

(AAA) (SAVE)

▼▼▼▼

Hotel
$139-$169 All Year

Address: 8A Centennial Dr 01960 **Location:** SR 128, exit 28, then s. Located in the Centennial Office Park. **Facility:** Smoke free premises. 256 units. 253 one-bedroom standard units. 3 one-bedroom suites. 6 stories, interior corridors. **Parking:** on-site. **Terms:** check-in 4 pm, cancellation fee imposed. **Amenities:** dual phone lines, voice mail, irons, hair dryers. *Fee:* video games, high-speed Internet. **Pool(s):** heated indoor. **Leisure Activities:** whirlpool, exercise room. **Guest Services:** valet and coin laundry. **Business Services:** conference facilities, business center. **Free Special Amenities: newspaper.**

🍴 🍸 ➋ ✕ 📷 🖵 / SOME UNITS 🖥

Marriott
HOTELS & RESORTS

AAA Benefit:
Members save a minimum 5% off the best available rate.

HAMPTON INN BOSTON-PEABODY   *Book great rates at AAA.com*   Phone: (978)536-2020

▼▼▼

Hotel
$79-$119 All Year

Address: 59 Newbury St 01960 **Location:** On US 1 northbound. **Facility:** 120 one-bedroom standard units. 6 stories, interior corridors. *Bath:* combo or shower only. **Parking:** on-site. **Terms:** 1-7 night minimum stay, cancellation fee imposed. **Amenities:** voice mail, irons, hair dryers. **Pool(s):** heated indoor. **Guest Services:** valet laundry, area transportation, wireless Internet. **Business Services:** business center.

🍴➕ CALL 🅼 ➋ FEE 🐕 📷 🖵 / SOME UNITS ✕ 🖥

Hampton Inn

AAA Benefit:
Members save up to 10% everyday!

(See map and index starting on p. 345)

HOLIDAY INN HOTEL & SUITES   *Book at AAA.com*   Phone: (978)535-4600   30

▼▼ ▼▼
Hotel
$89-$119 9/12-4/30
$79-$99 5/1-9/11

Address: 1 Newbury St 01960 **Location:** I-95, exit 44 A northbound, U-turn before lights to US 1 N; exit 44 southbound, just s on US 1, then U-turn to US 1 N. **Facility:** Smoke free premises. 184 units. 163 one-bedroom standard units. 21 one-bedroom suites with efficiencies. 4 stories, interior corridors. *Bath:* combo or shower only. **Parking:** on-site. **Terms:** cancellation fee imposed. **Amenities:** voice mail, irons, hair dryers. *Some:* safes. **Pool(s):** heated indoor. **Leisure Activities:** exercise room. **Guest Services:** valet and coin laundry, wireless Internet. **Business Services:** meeting rooms, business center. (ASK) 🍴 ▼ 🛏 ✕ 📹 🖥 / SOME UNITS 🔲 🖼

HOMESTEAD STUDIO SUITES HOTEL-BOSTON/PEABODY   *Book at AAA.com*   Phone: (978)531-6632   28

▼▼ ▼▼
Hotel
$70-$115 All Year

Address: 200 Jubilee Dr 01960 **Location:** SR 128, exit 28, just s to Centennial Dr, w to the end, n to Jubilee Dr, then 1.1 mi e. **Facility:** 94 units. 69 one-bedroom standard units with efficiencies. 25 one-bedroom suites with efficiencies. 3 stories, interior corridors. *Bath:* combo or shower only. **Parking:** on-site. **Terms:** cancellation fee imposed. **Amenities:** dual phone lines, voice mail, irons, hair dryers. **Pool(s):** heated indoor. **Leisure Activities:** limited exercise equipment. **Guest Services:** coin laundry, wireless Internet. (ASK) 🛏 📹 🔲 🖼 🖥 / SOME UNITS FEE 🐕 ✕

HOMEWOOD SUITES BY HILTON   *Book great rates at AAA.com*   Phone: (978)536-5050   27

▼▼▼▼
Extended Stay Hotel
$89-$209 All Year

Address: 57 Newbury St 01960 **Location:** On US 1 northbound. **Facility:** 85 one-bedroom suites with efficiencies. 6 stories, interior corridors. *Bath:* combo or shower only. **Parking:** on-site. **Terms:** check-in 4 pm, 1-7 night minimum stay, cancellation fee imposed. **Amenities:** dual phone lines, voice mail, irons, hair dryers. **Pool(s):** heated indoor. **Leisure Activities:** exercise room. **Guest Services:** valet and coin laundry, area transportation, wireless Internet. **Business Services:** meeting rooms, business center.

🍴 CALL 🕎M 🛏 📹 🔲 🖼 🖥 / SOME UNITS FEE 🐕 ✕

AAA Benefit:
Members save 5% or more everyday!

SPRINGHILL SUITES BOSTON/PEABODY   *Book great rates at AAA.com*   Phone: (978)535-5000   29

▼▼ ▼▼
Hotel
$99-$134 All Year

Address: 43 Newbury St 01960 **Location:** On US 1 northbound. **Facility:** Smoke free premises. 164 one-bedroom standard units. 6 stories, interior corridors. *Bath:* combo or shower only. **Parking:** on-site. **Terms:** cancellation fee imposed. **Amenities:** dual phone lines, voice mail, irons, hair dryers. **Pool(s):** heated indoor. **Leisure Activities:** whirlpool, exercise room. **Guest Services:** valet and coin laundry, wireless Internet. **Business Services:** meeting rooms, business center.

CALL 🕎M 🛏 ✕ 📹 🔲 🖼 🖥

AAA Benefit:
Members save a minimum 5% off the best available rate.

—— WHERE TO DINE ——

CENTURY HOUSE RESTAURANT AND EPICUREAN SHOPPE   Phone: 978/531-1410

▼▼ ▼▼
American
$7-$28

Along a busy commercial strip of shopping centers and car dealers, the restaurant is roughly equidistant from I-95 and US 1 on the west and SR 128 on the east. It has been in the same family of operators since 1957. The Epicurean Shoppe, which provides oven-ready take-out dishes, was added in 1983. Popular among diners of all ages, this place provides good portions of wholesome food at a fair price. Service is friendly. Casual dress. **Bar:** Full bar. **Reservations:** suggested. **Hours:** 7 am-10 pm, Sun 7 am-11 & noon-10 pm. Closed: 12/25. **Address:** 235 Andover St 01960 **Location:** On SR 114; 0.9 mi w of SR 128, exit 25B. **Parking:** on-site.

LEGAL SEA FOODS   Phone: 978/532-4500

Seafood
$8-$41

Legal prides itself on a reputation for freshness and consistency. More than 40 varieties of seafood can be grilled, broiled, fried or prepared Cajun style. Try the clam chowder that has been served at every presidential inauguration since 1981. The nautically inspired dining room is upscale and attractive with its rich cherry wood paneling and intricately detailed model ships. Casual dress. **Bar:** Full bar. **Reservations:** accepted. **Hours:** 11 am-10 pm, Fri & Sat-10:30 pm, Sun-9 pm. **Address:** 210 Andover St 01960 **Location:** SR 128, exit 25B, 0.3 mi w; at main entrance of North Shore Mall. **Parking:** on-site.

CALL 🕎M

SU CHANG'S   Phone: 978/531-3366

Chinese
$6-$14

The restaurant occupies what resembles a two-story residence on a corner lot convenient to both the main highway and major shopping areas. White tablecloths and waiters in black and white give a picture of more formality than is encouraged. A sampling of regional favorites includes Peking duck, Hunan-style pork, lamb with scallions, lemon shrimp that is almost like dessert and starters such as scallion pie and beef teriyaki. Spicy dishes are not overly so. Service is efficient and friendly. Casual dress. **Bar:** Full bar. **Reservations:** suggested, weekends. **Hours:** 11:30 am-10 pm, Fri & Sat-11 pm. Closed: 11/25. **Address:** 373 Lowell St 01960 **Location:** SR 128, exit 26, just w to jct Prospect St. **Parking:** on-site.

(See map and index starting on p. 345)

SYLVAN STREET GRILLE
Phone: 978/774-1724

▼▼▼ ▼▼▼
American
$8-$19

On a busy corner near several malls and theater complexes, the grill serves regional favorites such as fried clams and baked Boston scrod, in addition to preparations of steak, chicken, ribs and pasta. Sandwiches, burgers and quiche are available at lunch. The dining room evokes the mood of a nostalgic, upscale pub. A small patio with a waterfall is open in good weather. Casual dress. **Bar:** Full bar. **Hours:** 11:30 am-11:30 pm. Closed: 11/25, 12/25. **Address:** 12 Sylvan St 01960 **Location:** SR 128, exit 24 (Endicott St), 0.4 mi w. **Parking:** on-site. CALL Ⓛ Ⓜ

QUINCY pop. 88,025 (See map and index starting on p. 345)

BEST WESTERN ADAMS INN *Book great rates at AAA.com*
Phone: (617)328-1500 **124**

(AAA) (SAVE)
▼▼▼ ▼▼▼
Hotel
$129-$159 5/1-10/31
$114-$154 11/1-4/30

Address: 29 Hancock St 02171 **Location:** I-93, exit 12 southbound; exit 11 northbound, SR 203 to SR 3A, just over the bridge, follow signs. **Facility:** 105 one-bedroom standard units. 3 stories, interior corridors. *Bath:* combo or shower only. **Parking:** on-site. **Amenities:** high-speed Internet, voice mail, irons, hair dryers. **Pool(s):** outdoor. **Guest Services:** valet and coin laundry, airport transportation-Boston Logan International Airport, area transportation-Falcon Pier & South Station, wireless Internet. **Business Services:** conference facilities, business center. **Free Special Amenities: continental breakfast and high-speed Internet.**

AAA Benefit:
Members save up to 20%, plus 10% bonus points with rewards program.

🛫 🍽 🍸 🏊 ✈ 🎥 💻 / SOME UNITS ✕ 🛢 🖨

BOSTON MARRIOTT QUINCY *Book great rates at AAA.com*
Phone: (617)472-1000 **125**

(AAA) (SAVE)
▼▼▼ ▼▼▼
Hotel
$209-$229 All Year

Address: 1000 Marriott Dr 02169 **Location:** I-93, exit 7; SR 3, exit 18/19 southbound; exit 19 northbound; in Crown Colony Office Development. **Facility:** Smoke free premises. 464 units. 456 one-bedroom standard units. 8 one-bedroom suites. 9 stories, interior corridors. *Bath:* combo or shower only. **Parking:** on-site. **Terms:** check-in 4 pm, cancellation fee imposed. **Amenities:** high-speed Internet (fee), dual phone lines, voice mail, irons, hair dryers. **Dining:** 3 restaurants. **Pool(s):** heated indoor. **Leisure Activities:** sauna, whirlpool, exercise room. **Guest Services:** valet and coin laundry, area transportation-South Shore Plaza, Logan Express, Quincy Adams 'T', Royal Street Office Park, wireless Internet. **Business Services:** conference facilities, business center. **Free Special Amenities: newspaper.**

Marriott
HOTELS & RESORTS

AAA Benefit:
Members save a minimum 5% off the best available rate.

ECO 🍽 🍸 CALL Ⓛ Ⓜ 🏊 ✕ ✕ 🎥 💻 / SOME UNITS FEE 🛢

————— WHERE TO DINE —————

THE FOURS RESTAURANT & SPORTS BAR
Phone: 617/471-4447 **117**

▼▼▼ ▼▼▼
American
$8-$19

Originally named for the number worn by hockey great Bobby Orr, this trendy, sports-themed restaurant and bar serves up generous portions of salad, burgers, pasta, seafood and steak amid a warm decor peppered with Boston-area team memorabilia. In addition to pub favorites, the menu lists New England clam chowder, chicken Diane, fettuccine Alfredo and veal parmigiana. Service is casual and friendly. Casual dress. **Bar:** Full bar. **Hours:** 11 am-1 am. Closed: 11/25, 12/25. **Address:** 15 Cottage Ave 02169 **Location:** Center; opposite Norfolk County Courthouse. **Parking:** on-site. CALL Ⓛ Ⓜ

RANDOLPH pop. 30,963 (See map and index starting on p. 345)

COMFORT INN *Book at AAA.com*
Phone: (781)961-1000 **144**

▼▼▼ ▼▼▼
Hotel
$89-$150 5/1-10/31
$89-$130 11/1-4/30

Address: 1374 N Main St 02368 **Location:** I-93, exit 5A, just s. **Facility:** 158 one-bedroom standard units. 4 stories, interior corridors. *Bath:* combo or shower only. **Parking:** on-site. **Terms:** cancellation fee imposed. **Amenities:** video games (fee), dual phone lines, voice mail, irons, hair dryers. **Pool(s):** outdoor. **Leisure Activities:** exercise room. **Guest Services:** valet and coin laundry, area transportation, wireless Internet. **Business Services:** meeting rooms, business center.

(ASK) 🍽 🍸 🏊 🎥 💻 / SOME UNITS ✕ 🛢 🖨

————— WHERE TO DINE —————

CAFFE BELLA
Phone: 781/961-7729

▼▼▼ ▼▼▼
Mediterranean
$15-$28

Steaks, chops, pork, fresh fish and thin pizzas, all grilled over hardwood, are favorites at this Italian restaurant where the menu changes often. Homemade bread and unusual desserts are delicious meal complements. Portions are generous. In a small shopping mall, this place has simple wooden furniture that lends to a rustic, almost wine cellar-like, appearance. Reservations are not taken. Casual dress. **Bar:** Full bar. **Hours:** 5 pm-10 pm. Closed major holidays; also Sun. **Address:** 19 Warren St 02368 **Location:** SR 24, exit 20A, 1.5 mi e on SR 139; in Randolph Village Shopping Plaza. **Parking:** on-site.

NOT YOUR AVERAGE JOE'S
Phone: 781/961-7200

▼▼▼ ▼▼▼
American
$9-$18

The restaurant exemplifies the "in-trend" style of high-art contemporary design through vibrant color schemes, comfortable banquettes and stools, and smartly dressed staff. However, the high point is the food. Chefs whip up gourmet comfort foods of homemade meatloaf with a flavorful twist, creative hand-made pizzas, sandwiches, salads and more. Casual dress. **Bar:** Full bar. **Hours:** 11:30 am-10 pm, Fri & Sat-11 pm, Sun noon-9 pm. Closed: 11/25, 12/25. **Address:** 16 Mazzeo Dr 02368 **Location:** On SR 139. **Parking:** street.

(See map and index starting on p. 345)

RICK'S CAFE

Phone: 781/961-3339

American
$6-$20

Fashioned after a rural roadhouse in line with the legend about this place's birth in a garage back room, the restaurant counts travel posters, maps, gas stations, stainless steel bath vanities and wrenches for cabinet handles into its decor. The eclectic menu lists coconut shrimp, nachos, several salads, burgers, sandwiches, seafood, beef, pasta and pizza. Lobster roll and seafood casserole are signature specialties. Service is friendly. Casual dress. **Bar:** Full bar. **Reservations:** suggested, weekends. **Hours:** 11 am-11 pm. Closed: 11/25, 12/25. **Address:** 63 Mazzeo Dr 02368 **Location:** SR 24, exit 20A, 0.6 mi e on SR 139. **Parking:** on-site. CALL ♿M

READING pop. 23,708 (See map and index starting on p. 345)

—— WHERE TO DINE ——

MANDARIN READING

Phone: 781/942-8200 (32)

Chinese
$6-$16

Just off the rotary and the interstate, a two-story, hexagonal clapboard "tower" topped in skylights marks the restaurant's entrance. The multilevel, multiroom restaurant is accented with Oriental art and brass railings. The menu mixes traditional Chinese and Japanese cuisine, and the well-stocked daily lunch and Sunday dinner buffets are popular among locals. There is also a six-seat sushi bar. The screened patio opens during good weather. Casual dress. **Bar:** Full bar. **Reservations:** accepted. **Hours:** 11:30 am-10 pm, Fri & Sat-11 pm, Sun noon-10 pm. Closed: 11/25. **Address:** 296 Salem St 01867 **Location:** I-95, exit 40, just n on SR 129 from rotary. **Parking:** on-site. CALL ♿M

REVERE pop. 47,283 (See map and index starting on p. 345)

COMFORT INN & SUITES BOSTON AIRPORT   *Book at AAA.com*   **Phone:** (781)485-3600 (78)

Hotel
$100-$220 5/1-11/15
$79-$220 11/16-4/30

Address: 85 American Legion Hwy 02151 **Location:** Jct SR 1A and 60, 3 mi n of Boston Logan International Airport. **Facility:** Smoke free premises. 208 one-bedroom standard units. 8 stories, interior corridors. *Bath:* combo or shower only. **Parking:** on-site. **Amenities:** high-speed Internet, dual phone lines, voice mail, irons, hair dryers. **Dining:** Margaritas Mexican Restaurant, see separate listing. **Pool(s):** heated indoor. **Leisure Activities:** exercise room. **Guest Services:** valet and coin laundry, area transportation, wireless Internet. **Business Services:** meeting rooms, business center.

FAIRFIELD INN & SUITES BOSTON NORTH   *Book great rates at AAA.com*   **Phone:** (781)324-1900 (75)

Hotel
$69-$159 All Year

Address: 100 Morris St 02151 **Location:** On US 1, 1.5 mi n of jct SR 60. **Facility:** Smoke free premises. 154 units. 148 one-bedroom standard units. 6 one-bedroom suites. 5 stories, interior corridors. *Bath:* combo or shower only. **Parking:** on-site. **Terms:** cancellation fee imposed. **Amenities:** voice mail, irons, hair dryers. **Pool(s):** heated indoor. **Leisure Activities:** whirlpool, exercise room. **Guest Services:** valet and coin laundry, wireless Internet. **Business Services:** meeting rooms, business center.

AAA Benefit:
Members save a minimum 5% off the best available rate.

FOUR POINTS BY SHERATON BOSTON LOGAN   *Book great rates at AAA.com*   **Phone:** (781)284-7200 (76)

Hotel
$109-$220 All Year

Address: 407 Squire Rd 02151 **Location:** On US 1 and SR 60. **Facility:** Smoke free premises. 180 one-bedroom standard units. 2-7 stories, interior corridors. *Bath:* combo or shower only. **Parking:** on-site. **Terms:** cancellation fee imposed. **Amenities:** video games (fee), dual phone lines, voice mail, irons, hair dryers. **Dining:** 2 restaurants. **Pool(s):** heated indoor. **Leisure Activities:** exercise room. **Guest Services:** valet laundry, airport transportation-Boston Logan International Airport, area transportation-Airport 'T' station, wireless Internet. **Business Services:** meeting rooms, business center. **Free Special Amenities:** continental breakfast and high-speed Internet.

FOUR POINTS BY SHERATON

AAA Benefit:
Members get up to 15% off, plus Starwood Preferred Guest® bonuses.

HAMPTON INN BOSTON LOGAN AIRPORT   *Book great rates at AAA.com*   **Phone:** (781)286-5665 (79)

Hotel
$80-$330 All Year

Address: 230 Lee Burbank Hwy 02151 **Location:** On SR 1A, 1.9 mi n of Boston Logan International Airport, then 0.6 mi s of terminus SR 60. **Facility:** 227 units. 202 one-bedroom standard units. 25 one-bedroom suites. 7 stories, interior corridors. *Bath:* combo or shower only. **Parking:** on-site. **Terms:** 1-7 night minimum stay, cancellation fee imposed. **Amenities:** dual phone lines, voice mail, irons, hair dryers. **Pool(s):** heated indoor. **Leisure Activities:** whirlpool, exercise room. **Guest Services:** valet and coin laundry, area transportation, wireless Internet. **Business Services:** meeting rooms, business center.

AAA Benefit:
Members save up to 10% everyday!

(See map and index starting on p. 345)

RODEWAY INN   *Book great rates at AAA.com*   Phone: (781)284-3663   77

AAA SAVE

▽▽▽ ▽▽▽
Hotel
$69-$189 All Year

Address: 309 American Legion Hwy 02151 **Location:** Jct SR 107 and 60, just w. **Facility:** Smoke free premises. 34 one-bedroom standard units. 3 stories (no elevator), interior corridors. *Bath:* shower only. **Parking:** on-site. **Amenities:** voice mail, safes, irons, hair dryers. **Guest Services:** airport transportation-Boston Logan International Airport, area transportation-'T' station, wireless Internet. **Free Special Amenities: local telephone calls and newspaper.** ☒ ⬆ ☒ ☒

──── WHERE TO DINE ────

KELLY'S ROAST BEEF   Phone: 781/284-9129

▽▽▽
American
$6-$17

Since 1951, the restaurant has been serving from this original waterfront location. Piled-high quality roast beef sandwiches, burgers and seafood specialties include a delicious grilled lobster roll. Traditional New England-style clam chowder is a favorite. Casual dress. **Reservations:** not accepted. **Hours:** 5 am-2:30 am, Fri & Sat-3 am. Closed: 11/25, 12/25. **Address:** 410 Revere Beach Blvd 02151 **Location:** Just e of SR 1A. **Parking:** street.

MARGARITAS MEXICAN RESTAURANT   Phone: 781/289-8249

▽▽▽ ▽▽▽
Mexican
$8-$18

Diners will feel as though they have just stepped south of the border at this fun Mexican cantina. Traditional music fills the air while warm terracotta colored walls accented by painted pottery and unique jeweled star lanterns surround you. Sip on a large margarita while enjoying the freshly prepared fajitas, burritos, enchiladas, or quesadilla's. Casual dress. **Bar:** Full bar. **Hours:** 4 pm-11 pm. Closed: 4/4, 11/25, 12/25. **Address:** 85 American Legion Hwy 02151 **Location:** Jct SR 1A and 60, 3 mi n of Boston Logan International Airport ; in Comfort Inn & Suites Boston Airport. **Parking:** on-site.

MOUNT VERNON AT THE WHARF   Phone: 781/286-3830   76

▽▽▽ ▽▽▽
American
$7-$30

The Henry family has been in the restaurant business since 1935. This restaurant presents a menu of seafood, steak and some Italian entrees. Bonuses here include friendly service and great wharf views from the seasonal deck. Casual dress. **Bar:** Full bar. **Reservations:** accepted. **Hours:** 11 am-11 pm. Closed: 12/25. **Address:** 543 N Shore Rd (SR 1A) 02151 **Location:** 0.3 mi e of jct SR 1A, SR 60 and US 1, then 1.1 mi n. **Parking:** on-site.

ROCKPORT pop. 5,606

ADDISON CHOATE INN   Phone: 978/546-7543

AAA SAVE

▽▽▽ ▽▽▽
Historic Bed
& Breakfast
$145-$199 5/1-10/31
$115-$130 11/1-4/30

Address: 49 Broadway 01966 **Location:** 0.3 mi w on SR 127A. Located in a semi-residential area. **Facility:** This in-town, 1851 Greek Revival inn is within walking distance of shops, restaurants and the waterfront; breakfast is served daily. Smoke free premises. 8 units. 5 one-bedroom standard units. 1 one-bedroom suite. 2 cottages. 2-3 stories (no elevator), interior/exterior corridors. *Bath:* combo or shower only. **Parking:** on-site. **Terms:** office hours 7 am-10 pm, 2-3 night minimum stay - seasonal and/or weekends, age restrictions may apply, 10 day cancellation notice-fee imposed. **Amenities:** video library, CD players, hair dryers. *Some:* DVD players. **Guest Services:** wireless Internet. **Business Services:** PC. **Free Special Amenities: expanded continental breakfast and high-speed Internet.** ⬆ ☒ ☎ / SOME UNITS ☒ 🍴 🍽 🖥

EMERSON INN BY THE SEA   *Book great rates at AAA.com*   Phone: (978)546-6321

AAA SAVE

▽▽▽ ▽▽ ▽▽
Historic
Country Inn
$139-$379 5/1-10/31
$89-$279 11/1-4/30

Address: 1 Cathedral Ave 01966 **Location:** Just e of SR 127. **Facility:** Constructed in 1846, the inn was moved in 1912 to its present location; wide porches and a fourth-floor sun deck overlook the ocean. Smoke free premises. 38 units. 34 one-bedroom standard units, some with whirlpools. 2 one-bedroom suites. 2 houses. 4 stories (no elevator), interior corridors. *Bath:* combo or shower only. **Parking:** on-site. **Terms:** office hours 7 am-10:30 pm, check-in 4 pm, 2-3 night minimum stay - seasonal and/or weekends, 14 day cancellation notice-fee imposed. **Amenities:** irons, hair dryers. **Dining:** The Grand Cafe at the Emerson Inn by the Sea, see separate listing. **Pool(s):** heated outdoor. **Leisure Activities:** sauna, badminton, croquet, horseshoes, volleyball. **Guest Services:** wireless Internet. **Business Services:** meeting rooms, business center. *(See color ad p 433)* 🍴 🏊 ☒ ☒ / SOME UNITS 🍴 🍽

FREE expanded continental breakfast and high-speed Internet

INN ON COVE HILL/CALEB NORWOOD JR GUEST HOUSE   Phone: (978)546-2701

▽▽ ▽▽ ▽▽
Historic Bed
& Breakfast
$130-$175 All Year

Address: 37 Mt. Pleasant St 01966 **Location:** Just s on SR 127A. **Facility:** This restored 1791 Federal-style home is one of the oldest in town; guest rooms are comfortable with lovely decor. Smoke free premises. 7 units. 6 one-bedroom standard units. 1 one-bedroom suite. 3 stories (no elevator), interior/exterior corridors. *Bath:* combo or shower only. **Parking:** on-site. **Terms:** office hours 7 am-7 pm, 2 night minimum stay - seasonal and/or weekends, 10 day cancellation notice. ⓘASK ⬆ ☒ ☎

LINDEN TREE INN

Bed & Breakfast
Rates not provided

Phone: 978/546-2494

Address: 26 King St 01966 **Location:** Just e of SR 127. Located in a residential area. **Facility:** The inn is located within walking distance of a beach and Main Street; a delicious home-baked breakfast is served each morning. Smoke free premises. 16 units. 15 one-bedroom standard units, some with efficiencies. 1 one-bedroom suite. 3 stories (no elevator), interior/exterior corridors. *Bath:* combo or shower only. **Parking:** on-site. **Terms:** office hours 10 am-9 pm. **Amenities:** *Some:* CD players. **Guest Services:** wireless Internet.

OLD FARM INN AT HALIBUT POINT

Bed & Breakfast
Rates not provided

Phone: 978/546-3237

Address: 291 Granite St 01966 **Location:** 2 mi nw on SR 127. Adjacent to Halibut State Park. **Facility:** Smoke free premises. 8 units. 6 one-bedroom standard units, some with kitchens. 1 one- and 1 two-bedroom suites. 2 stories (no elevator), interior/exterior corridors. *Bath:* combo or shower only. **Parking:** on-site. **Terms:** office hours 8 am-8 pm, age restrictions may apply. **Amenities:** irons, hair dryers. **Guest Services:** wireless Internet.

ROCKPORT INN & SUITES *Book great rates at AAA.com*

Hotel
$109-$229 5/1-10/1
$79-$159 10/2-4/30

Phone: (978)546-3300

Address: 183 Main St 01966 **Location:** On SR 127. **Facility:** Smoke free premises. 79 units. 73 one-bedroom standard units. 6 one-bedroom suites. 2 stories (no elevator), exterior corridors. **Parking:** on-site. **Terms:** 2-3 night minimum stay - seasonal and/or weekends, 3 day cancellation notice-fee imposed. **Amenities:** voice mail, irons, hair dryers. **Pool(s):** heated indoor. **Leisure Activities:** whirlpool, 2 tennis courts, limited exercise equipment. **Guest Services:** coin laundry, wireless Internet. **Business Services:** meeting rooms, PC. *(See color ad p 434)*

CALL

FREE expanded continental breakfast and high-speed Internet

THE SALLY WEBSTER INN

Bed & Breakfast
$115-$145 5/1-10/31
$100-$125 11/1-4/30

Phone: 978/546-9251

Address: 34 Mt. Pleasant St 01966 **Location:** Just s on SR 127A. **Facility:** This circa 1832 Colonial home is now a cozy B&B consisting of well-appointed, individually decorated guest rooms. Smoke free premises. 8 one-bedroom standard units. 3 stories (no elevator), interior corridors. *Bath:* combo or shower only. **Parking:** on-site. **Terms:** office hours 7 am-9 pm, 2 night minimum stay - seasonal, 10 day cancellation notice-fee imposed. **Guest Services:** wireless Internet. **Business Services:** PC.

▼ See AAA listing p 432 ▼

THE TUCK INN B&B

AAA SAVE

Bed & Breakfast
$119-$175 5/1-10/31
$94-$155 11/1-4/30

Phone: 978/546-7260

Address: 17 High St 01966 **Location:** 2 blks s off Central Square via Mt. Pleasant and High sts. **Facility:** Guests at this circa 1790 Colonial-style home start each day with a Continental breakfast consisting of fresh muffins and baked goods. Smoke free premises. 13 units. 11 one- and 1 two-bedroom standard units. 1 one-bedroom suite with kitchen. 1-2 stories (no elevator), interior/exterior corridors. *Bath:* combo or shower only. **Parking:** on-site. **Terms:** office hours 9 am-9 pm, 2 night minimum stay - seasonal and/or weekends, 10 day cancellation notice. **Amenities:** hair dryers. **Pool(s):** outdoor. **Guest Services:** wireless Internet. **Business Services:** PC. **Free Special Amenities: expanded continental breakfast and high-speed Internet.**

The following lodging was either not evaluated or did not meet AAA rating requirements but is listed for your information only.

CAPE HEDGE INN

fyi

Phone: 978/546-3436

Not evaluated. **Address:** 151 South St 01966 **Location:** 1.8 mi s on SR 127A. Facilities, services, and decor characterize a mid-scale property.

WHERE TO DINE

ELLEN'S HARBORSIDE

American
$5-$23

Phone: 978/546-2512

A nautical motif punctuates the dining rooms, one of which overlooks the picturesque harbor. The restaurant, a family operation for three generations, is a favorite among the locals for its value. Fresh seafood, barbecue and numerous sandwiches and salads fill the menu. Casual dress. **Hours:** Open 5/3-10/31; 11:30 am-9 pm. Closed: Mon 5/3-5/31. **Address:** 1 T Wharf 01966 **Location:** Center. **Parking:** street.

THE FISH SHACK

Regional Seafood
$9-$16

Phone: 978/546-6667

Overlooking the harbor, the cozy restaurant serves mostly seafood in a casual friendly atmosphere. In season, take the public shuttle instead of attempting parking. Casual dress. **Bar:** Full bar. **Hours:** Open 5/13-12/31 & 3/15-3/31; 11 am-9 pm; Thurs-Sun to 8 pm 3/15-3/31 & 9/2-12/31. Closed major holidays. **Address:** 21 Dock Square 01966 **Location:** Center. **Parking:** street.

▼ See AAA listing p 433 ▼

Stay. Play. Dine. Save.
Visit AAA.com/Travel for Information To Go!

THE GRAND CAFE AT THE EMERSON INN BY THE SEA   *Menu on AAA.com*

Phone: 978/546-9500

Regional
American
$19-$31

Off the lobby of the inn, the dining room abuts a partially screened veranda from which views of the grounds, pool and Atlantic Ocean beyond can be enjoyed. Casual dress. **Bar:** Full bar. **Reservations:** suggested. **Hours:** 8 am-10 & 6-9 pm; hours vary off season. **Address:** 1 Cathedral Ave 01966 **Location:** Just e of SR 127; in Emerson Inn by the Sea. **Parking:** on-site.

THE GREENERY

Phone: 978/546-9593

American
$6-$22

From the dining room, guests look out over the inner harbor and Motif 1, one of the most photographed and painted scenes around. A meal might begin with chilled gazpacho, clam chowder, crab cakes or littlenecks in garlic sauce, then move on to a main course of mostly grilled or poached seafood, although other choices include roast duck and grilled sirloin. Wild blueberry gingerbread and ice cream profiterole are among desserts. The front part of the restaurant is a cafe with a blackboard menu. Casual dress. **Reservations:** accepted. **Hours:** 7 am-9 pm; to 4 pm 12/1-3/31. Closed: 12/25. **Address:** 15 Dock Square 01966 **Location:** Center. **Parking:** street.

THE LOBSTER POOL RESTAURANT

Phone: 978/546-7808

Regional Seafood
$6-$25

Patrons can drink in spectacular sunsets over Folly Cove and Ipswich Bay while savoring New England classics such as lobster, fried clams, burgers, sandwiches, clam chowder and homemade desserts. Counter service, disposable plates and indoor and outdoor picnic seating contribute to the laid-back atmosphere. Guests may bring their own drink. Casual dress. **Hours:** Open 5/1-11/30 & 3/1-4/30; 11:30 am-9 pm. **Address:** 329 Granite St 01966 **Location:** 2.4 mi nw on SR 127; 5.5 mi n of SR 128, exit 11 (Grant traffic circle). **Parking:** on-site and street.

ROWLEY pop. 1,434

COUNTRY GARDEN INN & SPA

Phone: 978/948-7773

Motel
$119-$329 5/1-10/31
$89-$299 11/1-4/30

Address: 101 Main St 01969 **Location:** On SR 1A. **Facility:** Smoke free premises. 23 units. 22 one-bedroom standard units, some with efficiencies and/or whirlpools. 1 one-bedroom suite. 1-2 stories (no elevator), exterior corridors. *Bath:* combo or shower only. **Parking:** on-site. **Terms:** office hours 9 am-11 pm, check-in 4 pm, 2 night minimum stay - seasonal and/or weekends, 10 day cancellation notice-fee imposed. **Amenities:** video library, irons, hair dryers. *Some:* DVD players. **Pool(s):** heated outdoor. **Leisure Activities:** exercise room. **Guest Services:** area transportation-Rowley 'T' Commuter Rail, wireless Internet. **Business Services:** PC. **Free Special Amenities:** local telephone calls and high-speed Internet.

—— WHERE TO DINE ——

AGAWAM DINER

Phone: 978/948-7780

American
$5-$10

While cruising the North Shore looking at antiques, folks can stop at the diner, built in 1954 by Fodero Dining Car Co. The same family has been operating this ship-shape eatery in this location since 1967. Portions are large, particularly of meatloaf and stuffed peppers. Wonderful coconut cream pie is among the many homemade desserts. Service is folksy. Casual dress. **Hours:** 5 am-11 pm, Sun-10 pm. Closed: 12/25. **Address:** 166 Newburyport Tpke 01969 **Location:** I-95, exit 54, 3 mi e, jct US 1 and SR 133. **Parking:** on-site.

PUD'S RESTAURANT & PUB

Phone: 978/948-7551

American
$7-$19

This friendly pub and eatery is the perfect place for families to enjoy generous portions of consistently quality food. Menu offerings are varied from seafood and pasta to a few chicken, steak and chop selections. Burgers and sandwiches are available anytime. A price-busters menu with smaller portions at a lower cost is also popular. Large TV screens in the lounge normally emphasize sports programming. Casual dress. **Bar:** Full bar. **Reservations:** accepted. **Hours:** 11 am-10 pm. Closed: 7/4, 11/25, 12/25. **Address:** 255 Newburyport Tpke 01969 **Location:** I-95, exit 54, 3 mi e on SR 133, then 0.3 mi n on US 1. **Parking:** on-site. CALL

SALEM pop. 40,407

HAWTHORNE HOTEL   *Book at AAA.com*

Phone: (978)744-4080

Classic Historic
Hotel
$139-$224 5/1-11/18
$114-$202 11/19-4/30

Address: 18 Washington Square W 01970 **Location:** On SR 1A. Adjoins historic district, faces Salem Witch Museum. **Facility:** Dating from 1925, this hotel faces Salem Common and is walking distance to the center of the historic and notable town of Salem. 93 units. 86 one-bedroom standard units. 7 one-bedroom suites. 3-6 stories, interior corridors. *Bath:* combo or shower only. **Parking:** on-site. **Terms:** 2 night minimum stay - seasonal and/or weekends, 3 day cancellation notice-fee imposed. **Amenities:** dual phone lines, voice mail, irons, hair dryers. **Dining:** Nathaniel's, see separate listing. **Leisure Activities:** limited exercise equipment. **Guest Services:** valet laundry, wireless Internet. **Business Services:** meeting rooms, business center.

THE SALEM INN   *Book at AAA.com*

Historic Bed
& Breakfast

$169-$350 5/1-11/3
$119-$229 11/4-4/30

Address: 7 Summer St 01970 **Location:** On SR 114 at Essex St; SR 128, exit 25A, 3 mi e
Facility: The three buildings making up the inn were added over a 40-year period from 1834 to 1874
some units include a working fireplace. Smoke free premises. 40 units. 32 one-bedroom standar
units, some with whirlpools. 8 one-bedroom suites. 3-4 stories (no elevator), interior corridors. Batr
combo or shower only. **Parking:** on-site. **Terms:** office hours 8 am-10 pm, 2 night minimum stay
seasonal and/or weekends, 7 day cancellation notice-fee imposed. **Amenities:** irons, hair dryers
Guest Services: wireless Internet. **Business Services:** PC.

Phone: (978)741-068

▼ *See AAA listing p 407* ▼

▼ *See AAA listing p 437* ▼

Get the lowest rates on hotels at AAA.com/Travel

--- **WHERE TO DINE** ---

BEER WORKS   Phone: 978/745-2337

American
$8-$19

The brewery creates 50 microbrews, 16 of which are on tap at any given time. Favorites from the "bold American" menu include beer-basted barbecue steak tips, sugarcane-seared salmon, sour cream and chive fries and the Big Dig brownie. Sports fans can keep up with the action on large- and small-screen TVs hanging throughout the dining area. Service is friendly and efficient. Casual dress. **Bar:** Beer & wine. **Reservations:** not accepted. **Hours:** 11:30 am-midnight. Closed: 11/25, 12/25. **Address:** 278 Derby St 01970 **Location:** S of SR 1A; center. **Parking:** street.

CAPT.'S WATERFRONT GRILL   Phone: 978/741-0555

Seafood
$9-$26

The waterfront location of this lively restaurant enhances its overall appeal. The creative menu features fresh regional seafood. Casual dress. **Bar:** Full bar. **Hours:** 11:30 am-9 pm, Fri & Sat-10 pm. **Address:** 94 Wharf St 01970 **Location:** On Pickering Wharf. **Parking:** street.

FINZ SEAFOOD & GRILL   Phone: 978/744-8485

Regional
Seafood
$6-$25

Windows on three sides of the dining room overlook the marina, and a waterside deck is open in good weather. Rich, creamy clam chowder or something from the raw bar gets things started. Entrees emphasize seafood, but the menu also lists the likes of braised lamb shanks, filet mignon, Southwestern chicken and a vegetarian plate. The dining area is light and bright, with light oak floors, undraped windows and glass bricks serving as room dividers and divider tops. Service is casual and friendly. Casual dress. **Bar:** Full bar. **Reservations:** suggested. **Hours:** 11:30 am-12:30 am. Closed: 11/25, 12/25. **Address:** 76 Wharf St 01970 **Location:** Center; at Pickering Wharf. **Parking:** street. CALL

LYCEUM BAR & GRILL   Phone: 978/745-7665

American
$8-$32

Close to the courthouse and among other legal offices, the restaurant is named appropriately after the place where Aristotle established a school. Arched ceilings overlaid with oak lattice and beams supported by Greek pillars fit the setting. Dishes such as fish chowder, salmon, cod, baked stuffed lobster, barbecue chicken and Black Angus steaks emphasize fresh, mostly local or regional ingredients. Dressy casual. **Bar:** Full bar. **Reservations:** required, Sat. **Hours:** 11:30 am-3 & 5:30-10 pm, Sat from 5:30 pm, Sun 11 am-3 & 5:30-9 pm. Closed: 7/4, 11/25, 12/25. **Address:** 43 Church St 01970 **Location:** Center. **Parking:** street.
CALL

NATHANIEL'S   Phone: 978/825-4311

American
$17-$32

This little gem offers menu items such as skillet-roasted lobster, wild-mushroom ravioli, seared sea scallops and seafood chowder. The restaurant is a nice spot for casually elegant dining in a traditional atmosphere. A large portrait of Nathaniel occupies one end of the dining room, and framed histories occupy much of the rest of the wall space not given to the windows and six sets of French doors. Servers are pleasant, attentive and, for the most part, informal. Dressy casual. **Bar:** Full bar. **Reservations:** suggested. **Hours:** 6 am-11 & 5-10 pm. **Address:** 18 Washington Square W 01970 **Location:** On SR 1A; in Hawthorne Hotel. **Parking:** on-site.

VICTORIA STATION   Phone: 978/745-3400

American
$10-$28

Popular with families for more than 25 years, Victoria Station specializes in prime rib and daily fresh seafood specials, all of which are served in ample portions by the casual, efficient and friendly staff. Deck dining overlooking the water is available in summer. English station names are found throughout the restaurant, and the railroad theme is carried to the point of using rails and spikes to make footrests at the bar. The salad bar remains well stocked. Casual dress. **Bar:** Full bar. **Reservations:** suggested. **Hours:** 11:30 am-10 pm, Thurs-Sat to 11 pm; to 9 pm, Fri & Sat-10 pm 11/1-5/1. Closed: 12/25. **Address:** 86 Wharf St 01970 **Location:** Center; at Pickering Wharf. **Parking:** street.

SALISBURY pop. 4,484

--- **WHERE TO DINE** ---

SYLVAN ST GRILLE   Phone: 978/462-7919

American
$6-$19

Just off the interstate and almost adjacent to a theater complex, the grill serves regional favorites such as fried clams and baked Boston scrod, in addition to preparations of steaks, chicken, ribs and pasta. Sandwiches, burgers and quiche are available at lunch. The dining room evokes the mood of a nostalgic, upscale pub. Antique posters and signs and sporting memorabilia hang from the walls, and potted plants abound. One section has an open beam ceiling. Casual dress. **Bar:** Full bar. **Hours:** 11:30 am-10:30 pm, Fri & Sat-11:30 pm. Closed: 11/25, 12/25. **Address:** 195 Elm St 01952 **Location:** I-95, exit 58, 0.3 mi e on SR 110. **Parking:** on-site. CALL

SAUGUS pop. 26,078 (See map and index starting on p. 345)

HOLIDAY INN EXPRESS BOSTON LOGAN AIRPORT *Book at AAA.com* Phone: (781)233-1800 41

Hotel
$99-$169 5/1-11/1
$79-$129 11/2-4/30

Address: 999 Broadway 01906 **Location:** On US 1, 3.4 mi s of jct SR 128. **Facility:** 145 one-bedroom standard units. 4 stories, interior corridors. *Bath:* combo or shower only. **Parking:** on-site. **Terms:** cancellation fee imposed. **Amenities:** voice mail, irons, hair dryers. **Pool(s):** indoor. **Leisure Activities:** exercise room. **Guest Services:** valet and coin laundry, wireless Internet. **Business Services:** meeting rooms, business center.

(ASK) (+) (T+) CALL (&M) / SOME UNITS

RED ROOF INN #7305 *Book great rates at AAA.com* Phone: (781)941-1400 42

Hotel
$95-$110 5/1-10/31
$85-$100 11/1-4/30

Address: 920 Broadway 01906 **Location:** I-95, exit 44 northbound, 3.2 mi s on US 1; exit Main St/Saugus southbound to U-turn. Located in a commercial area. **Facility:** 117 units. 113 one-bedroom standard units. 4 one-bedroom suites. 3 stories, interior corridors. *Bath:* combo or shower only. **Parking:** on-site. **Amenities:** video games (fee), voice mail. **Guest Services:** wireless Internet. **Business Services:** fax (fee). **Free Special Amenities:** local telephone calls.

(T+) CALL (&M) / SOME UNITS

───── WHERE TO DINE ─────

BORDER CAFE Phone: 781/233-5308

Mexican
$6-$15

This casual, family-friendly restaurant is cheerful and noisy with the feel of walking onto a plaza fiesta. Items served in generous portions include both spicy Mexican and Cajun specialties. Casual dress. **Bar:** Full bar. **Hours:** 11:30 am-11 pm, Fri & Sat-midnight. **Address:** 356 Broadway 01906 **Location:** On US 1 southbound. **Parking:** on-site.

THE CONTINENTAL RESTAURANT Phone: 781/233-2587 40

American
$7-$28

Generous portions of traditional New England fare can be expected at the established, still popular restaurant. Rows of overstuffed banquettes separated by leaded-glass and dark-wood partitions provide an atmosphere in sharp contrast to the busy world just outside the massive oak doors. Fresh seafood, steaks, chops, duck and lamb are all offered. Meals start with signature cottage cheese dip with crackers and end with homemade desserts. A second generation has taken on day-to-day operation. Semi-formal attire. **Bar:** Full bar. **Reservations:** suggested. **Hours:** 11:30 am-10 pm, Fri & Sat-11 pm, Sun noon-10 pm. Closed: 12/25. **Address:** 266 Broadway 01906 **Location:** US 1, 2.3 mi s of jct SR 128. **Parking:** on-site. CALL (&M)

JIMMY'S STEER HOUSE Phone: 781/233-8600 39

Steak
$7-$17

In a strip mall with several other eateries, the restaurant sports gold, black, red and green awnings to let guests know this is the right place. The casual atmosphere shows hints of the arts and crafts period in the style of booths, lamps and framed posters on the wall. The menu mixes salads, seafood, chicken and steaks, and portions provide good value. Guests can expect to wait during prime dining hours, particularly on weekends. Casual dress. **Bar:** Full bar. **Reservations:** not accepted. **Hours:** 4:30 pm-10 pm, Fri & Sat 11:30 am-10:30 pm, Sun noon-9 pm. Closed: 11/25, 12/25. **Address:** 114 Broadway 01906 **Location:** I-95, exit 44A, 1.7 mi s on US 1, northbound; 0.3 mi n of SR 129 W. **Parking:** on-site. CALL (&M)

KELLY'S ROAST BEEF Phone: 781/233-5000

American
$5-$20

Family owned and operated since 1951, the restaurant offers upscale fast food-style service and ample portions. Signature items include roast beef sandwiches, clam chowder and lobster rolls. Colorful decor features carousel horses, a mural of the original Kelly's location and two large aquariums: one that separates the counter area and dining room and another that's part of the glass walls that separate a party room from the rest of the restaurant. Walk-up counter service moves smoothly. Casual dress. **Hours:** 10 am-1 am. Closed: 11/25, 12/25. **Address:** 595 Broadway 01906 **Location:** I-95, exit 44, 2.7 mi s on US 1. **Parking:** on-site. CALL (&M)

KOWLOON RESTAURANT Phone: 781/233-0077 42

Chinese
$7-$24

A landmark since the 1950s, the pagoda-style restaurant has been run by the same family for all those years. The food remains traditional with all the favorites, and a Thai grill offers additional variety. Dressy casual. **Bar:** Full bar. **Reservations:** accepted. **Hours:** 11:30 am-2 am. Closed major holidays. **Address:** 948 Broadway (US 1 N) 01906 **Location:** 4 mi s of SR 128. **Parking:** on-site.

ORZO CAFE TRATTORIA Phone: 781/233-6815

Italian
$6-$23

In a small mall area on the northbound side of a busy highway, the restaurant displays an extensive use of dark woods, plant-topped dividers, a large mural on one of the dark pink walls and an open kitchen. The feel is relaxed and almost homey. Veal is always a good choice among offerings of sandwiches, pizza, calzones, pasta, steaks, pork chops, chicken and seafood prepared Marsala, parmigiana, piccata, cacciatore and fra diavolo. Service is friendly and efficient. Casual dress. **Bar:** Full bar. **Hours:** 11:30 am-10 pm, Fri & Sat 10:30 pm, Sun 1 pm-8 pm. Closed: 7/4, 11/25, 12/25. **Address:** 114 Broadway 01906 **Location:** I-95, exit 44A, 1.7 mi s on US 1, northbound; 0.3 mi n of SR 129 W. **Parking:** on-site. CALL (&M)

RISTORANTE DONATELLO Phone: 781/233-9975 38

Regional Italian
$11-$32

Patrons choose from a wide selection of wood-grilled items and finely prepared entrees, including pasta, seafood and meat dishes, not to mention antipasti, salads, pizza and a variety of sides. Because parking is limited, complimentary valet parking is offered at dinner. A wood-fired brick oven and pizza station occupies one of the rear corners of the bright, modern and informal space. Servers work in teams to provide a personal level of service that is friendly and yet efficient. Casual dress. **Bar:** Full bar. **Reservations:** required, weekends. **Hours:** 11:30 am-3:30 & 4-10:30 pm. Closed major holidays. **Address:** 44 Broadway 01906 **Location:** On US 1 northbound; SR 128, exit 44, 2 mi s. **Parking:** on-site. CALL (&M)

(See map and index starting on p. 345)

SAKE

Japanese
$8-$29

Phone: 781/233-3858 (41)

On the northbound side of US 1, the Japanese eatery serves terrific sushi, tempura battered items and much more. Diners who want Western utensils will need to request them. A separate dining room has traditional low-level tables and overstuffed pillows for seats. Casual dress. **Bar:** Full bar. **Hours:** 11:30 am-10:30 pm, Sun noon-9:30 pm. Closed: 7/4, 11/25. **Address:** 670 Broadway 01906 **Location:** On US 1 northbound. **Parking:** on-site.

SPUD'S RESTAURANT & PUB

American
$7-$19

Phone: 781/233-2757

This friendly pub and eatery is the perfect place for families to enjoy generous portions of consistently quality food. Menu offerings are varied from seafood and pasta to a few chicken, steak and chop selections. Burgers and sandwiches are available anytime. A price-busters menu with smaller portions at a lower cost is also popular. Large TV screens in the lounge normally emphasize sports programming. Casual dress. **Bar:** Full bar. **Hours:** 11 am-10 pm. Closed: 7/4, 11/25, 12/25. **Address:** 22 Lincoln Ave 01906 **Location:** US 1, exit Essex St, 1 mi e to rotary, then 1.5 mi n. **Parking:** on-site. CALL 🚹🅜

SHARON pop. 5,941

HOLIDAY INN EXPRESS *Book at AAA.com*

Hotel
$100-$129 All Year

Phone: (781)784-1000

Address: 395 Old Post Rd 02067 **Location:** I-95, exit 9, 0.5 mi s on US 1. **Facility:** 95 one-bedroom standard units. 2 stories (no elevator), interior corridors. **Parking:** on-site. **Amenities:** dual phone lines, voice mail, safes (fee), irons, hair dryers. **Leisure Activities:** exercise room. **Guest Services:** valet laundry, wireless Internet. **Business Services:** PC.

ASK 🚹📺 🍴 🎬 📶 📼 💻 / SOME UNITS ✕

SHIRLEY pop. 1,427

—— WHERE TO DINE ——

BULL RUN RESTAURANT

American
$5-$20

Phone: 978/425-4311

Steak, stuffed swordfish, cheese tortellini and shrimp scampi are noteworthy meal mentions in this family-operated 1740 Colonial tavern. Attentive servers ply their trade amid whiskey-barrel tables, pine wood floors and two fireplaces. Casual dress. **Bar:** Full bar. **Reservations:** suggested. **Hours:** 11 am-10 pm. Closed: Mon & Tues. **Address:** 215 Great Rd 01464 **Location:** Jct SR 13, 6 mi e on SR 2A. **Parking:** on-site. **Historic**

SOMERVILLE pop. 77,478 (See map and index starting on p. 345)

LA QUINTA INN & SUITES BOSTON/SOMERVILLE *Book at AAA.com*

Hotel
$89-$219 All Year

Phone: (617)625-5300 (91)

Address: 23 Cummings St 02143 **Location:** I-93, exit 29 northbound, just ne on SR 28, then just s on Middlesex Ave; exit 31 southbound, 1 mi e on SR 16, then 0.5 mi s on SR 28 to Middlesex Ave. **Facility:** 147 units. 123 one-bedroom standard units. 24 one-bedroom suites. 7 stories, interior corridors. *Bath:* combo or shower only. **Parking:** on-site. **Amenities:** video games (fee), high-speed Internet, dual phone lines, voice mail, irons, hair dryers. **Leisure Activities:** limited exercise equipment. **Guest Services:** complimentary and valet laundry, area transportation. **Business Services:** meeting rooms, business center.

ASK ✈ 🍴 CALL 🅜 🎬 🍴 💻 / SOME UNITS 🐕 ✕ 📼

—— WHERE TO DINE ——

DALI RESTAURANT & TAPAS BAR

Regional Spanish
$5-$25

Phone: 617/661-3254 (81)

Patrons experience a fun and sometimes loud dining experience in this bustling eatery, which offers fare from many regions of Spain. Choices include more than 40 tapas items (appetizer-style selections) and eight to 10 main courses. The signature dish is pescado a la sal: fresh fish baked in coarse salt. Some guests enjoy grilling their own meat, seafood and vegetables on a stone from the Canary Islands. Parking is only on the street. It is wise to heed the parking signs. Casual dress. **Bar:** Beer & wine. **Hours:** 5:30 pm-11 pm, Sun noon-11 pm. Closed: 1/1, 11/25, 12/24, 12/25. **Address:** 415 Washington St 02143 **Location:** Corner of Beacon and Washington sts; on Somerville-Cambridge line. **Parking:** street.

DIVA INDIAN BISTRO

Regional Indian
$10-$20

Phone: 617/629-4963 (79)

A short walk from the Davis T-stop on the Red Line, the restaurant makes the round, windowed tandoor kitchen the focal point of its dining room. The front wall opens to make a streetside cafe in summer. Dishes from Bangalore, Jadras and Bombay are featured. Lamb vindaloo, keema mutter and chicken curry are good bets, as are the numerous vegetarian selections. A daily lunch buffet is set up. Non-alcoholic beer and wine, as well as bottled water, are served. Casual dress. **Bar:** Full bar. **Reservations:** accepted. **Hours:** 11:30 am-11 pm. **Address:** 246 Elm St 02144 **Location:** Corner of Elm and Chester sts; center; in Davis Square. **Parking:** street.

ROSEBUD DINER

American
$6-$14

Phone: 617/666-6015 (80)

Not far from Tufts University, the 1941 Worcester dining car has seven booths and about a dozen stools at the counter. The menu centers on good old American comfort food, such as chicken pot pie and burgers. Servers are folksy and efficient. Casual dress. **Bar:** Full bar. **Reservations:** not accepted. **Hours:** 8 am-11 pm, Fri & Sat-midnight. Closed: 11/25, 12/25. **Address:** 381 Summer St 02145 **Location:** Corner of Summer and Elm sts; center; at Davis Square. **Parking:** street.

STONEHAM pop. 22,219 (See map and index starting on p. 345)

—— WHERE TO DINE ——

FELICIA'S

Italian
$6-$20

Phone: 781/438-9399 (58)

The family-run eatery has served traditional Italian fare for more than 50 years and under the reign of three generations of the same family. Casual dress. **Bar:** Full bar. **Reservations:** accepted. **Hours:** 11:30 am-10 pm, Fri & Sat-10:30 pm, Sun noon-9 pm. Closed: 4/4, 11/25. **Address:** 423 Main St 02180 **Location:** On SR 28, at Franklin St. **Parking:** street.

GAETANO'S RISTORANTE

Italian
$7-$22

Phone: 781/279-0100 (57)

The casual yet lively Italian bistro has a large and loyal local following. Among traditional dishes are parmigiana preparations, pizzas and pastas. Casual dress. **Bar:** Full bar. **Reservations:** accepted. **Hours:** 11:30 am-9 pm, Fri & Sat-10 pm, Sun 4 pm-9 pm. Closed major holidays. **Address:** 271 Main St 02180 **Location:** On SR 28, between Flint Ave and Lindenwood Rd. **Parking:** on-site and street.

STOUGHTON

COURTYARD BOSTON STOUGHTON   *Book great rates at AAA.com*

Hotel
$169-$179 All Year

Phone: (781)297-7000

Address: 200 Technology Center Dr 02072 **Location:** On SR 139, at Randolph town line; SR 24, exit 20A, just e. **Facility:** Smoke free premises. 152 units. 140 one-bedroom standard units. 12 one-bedroom suites. 4 stories, interior corridors. *Bath:* combo or shower only. **Parking:** on-site. **Terms:** cancellation fee imposed. **Amenities:** video games (fee), high-speed Internet, voice mail, irons, hair dryers. **Pool(s):** heated indoor. **Leisure Activities:** whirlpool, exercise room. **Guest Services:** valet and coin laundry, wireless Internet. **Business Services:** meeting rooms, business center.

AAA Benefit:
Members save a minimum 5% off the best available rate.

—— WHERE TO DINE ——

NOCERA'S ITALIAN FAMILY DINING

Italian
$9-$19

Phone: 781/341-2503

The family-operated restaurant is geared toward families. Each dining room is decorated in light woods with brass accents; one is tiered. Traditional dishes incorporate veal, chicken and seafood, and house specialties include toasted ravioli, lasagna, calamari and tripe in tomato sauce. Also on the menu are pizza, sandwiches and numerous salads. Service is friendly. Casual dress. **Bar:** Full bar. **Hours:** 11:15 am-9 pm, Fri & Sat-10 pm, Sun 10 am-8:30 pm. Closed: 11/25, 12/25. **Address:** 1165 Park St, Rt 27 02072 **Location:** SR 24, exit 18B, 1 mi n on SR 27. **Parking:** on-site.

SUDBURY

LONGFELLOW'S WAYSIDE INN

Country Inn
Rates not provided

Phone: 978/443-1776

Address: 72 Wayside Inn Rd 01776 **Location:** I-495, exit 24A, 6.5 mi e, 5.6 mi w of SR 27, off US 20, follow signs. Located in a quiet rural area. **Facility:** A tree-lined country road leads to this inn, which has been in operation since 1716. The property is closed July 3-4 and December 24-25. Smoke free premises. 10 one-bedroom standard units. 2 stories, interior corridors. *Bath:* combo or shower only. **Parking:** on-site. **Amenities:** hair dryers. **Dining:** restaurant, see separate listing. **Guest Services:** TV in common area, wireless Internet. **Business Services:** meeting rooms.

—— WHERE TO DINE ——

LONGFELLOW'S WAYSIDE INN

Regional American
$9-$33

Phone: 978/443-1776

Visitors can join family, friends or business associates for a trip back in time at this 17th-century inn, where staff in Colonial costumes epitomize fine hospitality. A working gristmill provides flour for homemade bread, and equal attention is paid to other Yankee New England menu items. Of the dining areas, the tap room—with its original open beams and wide plank floors—is a favorite; to ensure seating in it, reservations are a must. Dressy casual. **Bar:** Full bar. **Reservations:** suggested. **Hours:** 11:30 am-3 & 5-9 pm, Sun from noon; closing hours vary in winter. Closed: 7/4, 12/25; also for dinner 12/24. **Address:** 72 Wayside Inn Rd 01776 **Location:** I-495, exit 24A, 6.5 mi e, 5.6 mi w of SR 27, off US 20, follow signs; in Longfellow's Wayside Inn. **Parking:** on-site. **Historic**

SKY RESTAURANT

American
$9-$29

Phone: 978/440-8855

Guests are as likely to see construction workers in jeans as business people in suits in this semi-rural setting. International twists characterize the contemporary American dishes, such as grilled Jamaican chicken, maple-glazed roast pork chop, braised lamb shank, steaks, roast scrod and Asian salmon. The burgers and barbecue chicken pizza also are worth the indulgence. Service is professional and friendly. Casual dress. **Bar:** Full bar. **Hours:** 11:30 am-9 pm, Thurs-Sat to 10 pm, Sun noon-9 pm. Closed: 7/4, 11/25, 12/25. **Address:** 120 Boston Post Rd 01776 **Location:** 1.5 mi e on US 20. **Parking:** on-site.

TEWKSBURY

EXTENDED STAYAMERICA BOSTON-TEWKSBURY   *Book at AAA.com*   Phone: (978)863-9888

Extended Stay
Hotel
$57-$75 All Year

Address: 1910 Andover St 01876 **Location:** I-93, exit 43B, just w; I-495, exit 39, just e. **Facility:** 92 one-bedroom standard units with efficiencies. 3 stories, interior corridors. *Bath:* combo or shower only. **Parking:** on-site. **Terms:** cancellation fee imposed. **Amenities:** dual phone lines, voice mail, irons. **Guest Services:** coin laundry, wireless Internet.

ASK 🎥 📞 📠 💻 / SOME UNITS FEE 🐕 ✕

FAIRFIELD INN BY MARRIOTT-BOSTON/ANDOVER/TEWKSBURY   *Book great rates at AAA.com*   Phone: (978)640-0700

Hotel
$84-$114 All Year

Address: 1695 Andover St 01876 **Location:** I-495, exit 39, 0.3 mi w on SR 133. Located in a quiet area. **Facility:** Smoke free premises. 133 one-bedroom standard units. 5 stories, interior corridors. *Bath:* combo or shower only. **Parking:** on-site. **Terms:** cancellation fee imposed. **Amenities:** voice mail, irons, hair dryers. **Guest Services:** valet and coin laundry, wireless Internet. **Business Services:** PC.

🛗 ♿ 🏊 👨‍🦽 ✕ 🎥 💻 / SOME UNITS 📞 📠

> **FAIRFIELD INN**
>
> **AAA Benefit:**
> Members save a
> minimum 5% off the
> best available rate.

HOLIDAY INN TEWKSBURY-ANDOVER   *Book at AAA.com*   Phone: (978)640-9000

Hotel
$89-$179 All Year

Address: 4 Highwood Dr 01876-1138 **Location:** I-495, exit 39, just w on SR 133. Located in Highwood Office Park. **Facility:** 227 units. 217 one-bedroom standard units. 10 one-bedroom suites. 5 stories, interior corridors. *Bath:* combo or shower only. **Parking:** on-site. **Amenities:** voice mail, irons, hair dryers. *Some:* high-speed Internet. **Pool(s):** heated indoor. **Leisure Activities:** saunas, whirlpool, exercise room. **Guest Services:** valet laundry, area transportation, wireless Internet. **Business Services:** meeting rooms, PC.

ASK 🛗 🍸 🏊 ✕ 🎥 💻 / SOME UNITS FEE 🐕 ✕ 📞 📠

RESIDENCE INN BY MARRIOTT BOSTON-TEWKSBURY-ANDOVER   *Book great rates at AAA.com*   Phone: (978)640-1003

Extended Stay
Hotel
$179-$189 All Year

Address: 1775 Andover St 01876 **Location:** I-495, exit 39, 0.3 mi w on SR 133. Located in a quiet rural area. **Facility:** Smoke free premises. 130 units. 96 one- and 34 two-bedroom suites with efficiencies. 3 stories, exterior corridors. *Bath:* combo or shower only. **Parking:** on-site. **Terms:** cancellation fee imposed. **Amenities:** high-speed Internet, voice mail, irons, hair dryers. **Pool(s):** heated outdoor. **Leisure Activities:** whirlpool, exercise room, sports court. **Guest Services:** valet and coin laundry, area transportation, wireless Internet. **Business Services:** PC.

🛗 CALL ♿M 🏊 ✕ ✕ 🎥 📞 📠 💻 / SOME UNITS FEE 🐕

> **Residence Inn Marriott**
>
> **AAA Benefit:**
> Members save a
> minimum 5% off the
> best available rate.

TOWNEPLACE SUITES BOSTON TEWKSBURY   *Book great rates at AAA.com*   Phone: (978)863-9800

Extended Stay
Hotel
$99-$139 All Year

Address: 20 International Pl 01876 **Location:** I-495, exit 39, 0.3 mi nw. **Facility:** Smoke free premises. 95 units. 69 one-bedroom standard units with kitchens. 4 one- and 22 two-bedroom suites with kitchens. 3 stories, interior corridors. *Bath:* combo or shower only. **Parking:** on-site. **Terms:** cancellation fee imposed. **Amenities:** high-speed Internet, dual phone lines, voice mail, irons, hair dryers. **Pool(s):** heated outdoor. **Leisure Activities:** exercise room. **Guest Services:** valet and coin laundry. **Business Services:** PC.

🛗 CALL ♿M 🏊 ✕ 🎥 📞 📠 💻 / SOME UNITS FEE 🐕

> **TownePlace Suites Marriott**
>
> **AAA Benefit:**
> Members save a
> minimum 5% off the
> best available rate.

TYNGSBORO pop. 8,600

STONEHEDGE INN & SPA   *Book great rates at AAA.com*   Phone: (978)649-4400

Country Inn
$235-$320 All Year

Address: 160 Pawtucket Blvd 01879 **Location:** On SR 113, 2 mi se of jct SR 3A. **Facility:** Amenities such as guest robes and heated towel racks give this 38-acre country estate a retreat-like ambience. Smoke free premises. 30 one-bedroom standard units, some with whirlpools. 2 stories, interior corridors. **Parking:** on-site. **Terms:** 3 day cancellation notice-fee imposed. **Amenities:** high-speed Internet, voice mail, honor bars, irons, hair dryers. **Dining:** Left Bank, see separate listing. **Pool(s):** heated indoor. **Leisure Activities:** sauna, whirlpool, steamroom, tennis court, exercise room, spa. **Guest Services:** valet laundry, wireless Internet. **Business Services:** meeting rooms, fax (fee). **Free Special Amenities:** continental breakfast and high-speed Internet.

🍽 24🛗 🏊 ✕ ✕

——— WHERE TO DINE ———

LEFT BANK

Phone: 978/649-4400

Regional
American
$12-$36

On 38 acres of spacious and beautifully landscaped grounds, the restaurant occupies an intimate country manor marked by an equestrian theme and elegant décor. Although two chef's menus are offered, guests also can order a la carte. Provençal French cuisine is served in spectacular presentations with a broad selection of wines. With the largest wine cellar in New England, the restaurant offers a monthly six-course wine-dinner program. Semi-formal attire. **Bar:** Full bar. **Reservations:** suggested. **Hours:** 7-10 am, 11:30-3 & 5:30-9 pm, Fri-10 pm, Sat 7-11 am, 11:30-3 & 5:30-10 pm, Sun 7 am-2 & 5:30-8:30 pm; Sunday brunch. **Address:** 160 Pawtucket Blvd 01879 **Location:** On SR 113, 2 mi se of jct SR 3A; in Stonehedge Inn & Spa. **Parking:** on-site.

WAKEFIELD pop. 24,804   (See map and index starting on p. 345)

LORD WAKEFIELD HOTEL

Phone: 781/245-6100   38

Hotel
$70-$140 All Year

Address: 595 North Ave 01880 **Location:** I-95, exit 39, jct SR 128. **Facility:** 85 one-bedroom standard units. 2 stories (no elevator), interior corridors. **Parking:** on-site. **Terms:** cancellation fee imposed. **Amenities:** voice mail, irons, hair dryers. **Pool(s):** outdoor. **Guest Services:** valet laundry, wireless Internet. **Business Services:** meeting rooms, PC. **Free Special Amenities:** continental breakfast and high-speed Internet.

SHERATON COLONIAL HOTEL BOSTON NORTH & CONFERENCE CENTER   *Book great rates at AAA.com*

Phone: (781)245-9300   37

Hotel
$95-$235 All Year

Address: 1 Audubon Rd 01880 **Location:** I-95, exit 42, just n. Located in a quiet area. **Facility:** Smoke free premises. 280 one-bedroom standard units. 2-11 stories, interior corridors. *Bath:* combo or shower only. **Parking:** on-site. **Terms:** cancellation fee imposed. **Amenities:** dual phone lines, voice mail, irons, hair dryers. *Fee:* video games, high-speed Internet. **Pool(s):** heated indoor. **Leisure Activities:** saunas, whirlpool, tennis facilities. *Fee:* 4 indoor tennis courts, massage. **Guest Services:** valet laundry, area transportation-within 5 mi. **Business Services:** conference facilities, business center.

(S) Sheraton
HOTELS & RESORTS

AAA Benefit:
Members get up to 15% off, plus Starwood Preferred Guest® bonuses.

——— WHERE TO DINE ———

BELLINO'S TRATTORIA

Phone: 781/246-7666   35

Italian
$7-$19

Just off the highway at one end of a small shopping center, the bustling bistro features soups, salads, hot and cold sandwiches, pizzas, calzones and a range of specialty pastas and main courses. Among choices are tuna topped with sage, roasted garlic and capers, homemade fusilli and cheese ravioli in homemade meat sauce. Alcoholic beverages are not served, but guests can bring their own wine for a $5 corkage fee. Casual dress. **Bar:** Beer & wine. **Hours:** 11 am-9 pm, Fri & Sat-10 pm, Sun 4 pm-9 pm. Closed: 11/25, 12/25; also Mon. **Address:** 146 Lowell St 01880 **Location:** I-95, exit 40, just s on SR 129, immediately off the traffic circle. **Parking:** on-site.

WALTHAM pop. 59,226   (See map and index starting on p. 345)

BEST WESTERN TLC HOTEL   *Book great rates at AAA.com*

Phone: (781)890-7800   107

Hotel
$80-$160 All Year

Address: 380 Winter St 02451 **Location:** I-95, exit 27B northbound; exit 27A southbound, just ne. **Facility:** 100 one-bedroom standard units. 6 stories, interior corridors. **Parking:** on-site. **Amenities:** video games (fee), irons, hair dryers. **Pool(s):** heated indoor. **Leisure Activities:** limited exercise equipment. **Guest Services:** wireless Internet. **Business Services:** meeting rooms, PC. **Free Special Amenities:** expanded continental breakfast and high-speed Internet. *(See color ad p 380)*

Best
Western

AAA Benefit:
Members save up to 20%, plus 10% bonus points with rewards program.

COURTYARD BY MARRIOTT BOSTON-WALTHAM   *Book great rates at AAA.com*

Phone: (781)419-0900   106

Hotel
$170-$208 All Year

Address: 387 Winter St 02451 **Location:** I-95, exit 27B northbound; exit 27A southbound, on northeast corner. **Facility:** Smoke free premises. 117 units. 114 one-bedroom standard units. 3 one-bedroom suites. 5 stories, interior corridors. *Bath:* combo or shower only. **Parking:** on-site. **Terms:** cancellation fee imposed. **Amenities:** video games (fee), high-speed Internet, dual phone lines, voice mail, irons, hair dryers. **Pool(s):** heated indoor. **Leisure Activities:** whirlpool, exercise room. **Guest Services:** valet and coin laundry, area transportation, wireless Internet. **Business Services:** meeting rooms, business center.

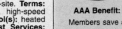

COURTYARD
Marriott

AAA Benefit:
Members save a minimum 5% off the best available rate.

(See map and index starting on p. 345)

DOUBLETREE GUEST SUITES BOSTON/WALTHAM

Book great rates at AAA.com **Phone:** (781)890-6767   `109`

Hotel
$99–$239 All Year

Address: 550 Winter St 02451 **Location:** I-95, exit 27B, just w. **Facility:** 275 one-bedroom suites, some with whirlpools. 8 stories, interior corridors. **Parking:** on-site. **Terms:** 1-7 night minimum stay, cancellation fee imposed. **Amenities:** video games (fee), dual phone lines, voice mail, irons, hair dryers. **Pool(s):** heated indoor. **Leisure Activities:** sauna, whirlpool, exercise room. **Guest Services:** valet and coin laundry, area transportation, wireless Internet. **Business Services:** conference facilities, business center.

AAA Benefit:
Members save 5% or more everyday!

EXTENDED STAY DELUXE BOSTON-WALTHAM

Book at AAA.com   **Phone:** (781)622-1900   `111`

Extended Stay Hotel
$79–$99 All Year

Address: 32 4th Ave 02451 **Location:** I-95, exit 27A, just se. **Facility:** 136 one-bedroom standard units with efficiencies. 3 stories, interior corridors. *Bath:* combo or shower only. **Parking:** on-site. **Terms:** cancellation fee imposed. **Amenities:** DVD players, dual phone lines, voice mail, irons, hair dryers. **Pool(s):** heated outdoor. **Leisure Activities:** exercise room. **Guest Services:** valet and coin laundry, area transportation, wireless Internet.

HILTON GARDEN INN BOSTON/WALTHAM

Book great rates at AAA.com   **Phone:** (781)890-0100   `108`

Hotel
$99–$259 All Year

Address: 420 Totten Pond Rd 02451 **Location:** I-95, exit 27A, just e. **Facility:** 148 one-bedroom standard units. 6 stories, interior corridors. *Bath:* combo or shower only. **Parking:** on-site. **Terms:** 1-7 night minimum stay, cancellation fee imposed. **Amenities:** video games (fee), dual phone lines, voice mail, irons, hair dryers. **Pool(s):** heated indoor. **Leisure Activities:** exercise room. **Guest Services:** valet and coin laundry, area transportation-within 5 mi, wireless Internet. **Business Services:** meeting rooms, business center. **Free Special Amenities: room upgrade (subject to availability with advance reservations) and high-speed Internet.**

AAA Benefit:
Members save 5% or more everyday!

HOLIDAY INN EXPRESS BOSTON/WALTHAM

Book at AAA.com   **Phone:** (781)890-2800   `105`

Hotel
$84–$158 All Year

Address: 385 Winter St 02451 **Location:** I-95, exit 27B northbound; exit 27A southbound, just ne. **Facility:** Smoke free premises. 108 units. 107 one-bedroom standard units. 1 one-bedroom suite. 2-6 stories, interior corridors. *Bath:* combo or shower only. **Parking:** on-site. **Terms:** cancellation fee imposed. **Amenities:** voice mail, irons, hair dryers. **Leisure Activities:** exercise room. **Guest Services:** valet and coin laundry, area transportation, wireless Internet. **Business Services:** business center.

HYATT SUMMERFIELD SUITES BOSTON/WALTHAM

Book great rates at AAA.com **Phone:** (781)290-0026   `112`

Extended Stay Hotel
$99–$289 All Year

Address: 54 4th Ave 02451 **Location:** I-95, exit 27A, just e; behind The Westin, Waltham-Boston. **Facility:** Smoke free premises. 135 units. 84 one- and 51 two-bedroom suites with kitchens. 3 stories, interior corridors. *Bath:* combo or shower only. **Parking:** on-site. **Terms:** cancellation fee imposed. **Amenities:** DVD players, CD players, dual phone lines, voice mail, irons, hair dryers. *Some:* high-speed Internet. **Pool(s):** heated outdoor. **Leisure Activities:** whirlpool, grills, exercise room. **Guest Services:** valet and coin laundry, area transportation-within 6 mi, wireless Internet. **Business Services:** meeting rooms, business center. **Free Special Amenities: full breakfast and high-speed Internet.**

AAA Benefit:
Ask for the AAA rate and save 10%.

THE WESTIN WALTHAM-BOSTON

Book great rates at AAA.com   **Phone:** (781)290-5600   `110`

Hotel
$109–$369 All Year

Address: 70 3rd Ave 02451 **Location:** I-95, exit 27A, just se. **Facility:** Cloaked in blue reflective glass, this impressive hotel is nestled on a hillside overlooking the reservoir. Smoke free premises. 346 units. 316 one-bedroom standard units. 30 one-bedroom suites, some with whirlpools. 8 stories, interior corridors. *Bath:* combo or shower only. **Parking:** on-site (fee) and valet. **Terms:** cancellation fee imposed. **Amenities:** dual phone lines, voice mail, safes, honor bars, irons, hair dryers. *Fee:* video games, high-speed Internet. *Some:* DVD players, CD players. **Pool(s):** heated indoor. **Leisure Activities:** sauna, whirlpool, exercise room. **Guest Services:** valet laundry, area transportation-within 5 mi, wireless Internet. **Business Services:** conference facilities, business center.

WESTIN
HOTELS & RESORTS
AAA Benefit:
Enjoy up to 15% off your next stay, plus Starwood Preferred Guest® bonuses.

────── **WHERE TO DINE** ──────

THE CHATEAU ITALIAN FAMILY DINING

Phone: 781/894-3339

Italian
$8–$25

The tradition began in 1933 under the ownership and operation of the Nocera family, which still is the case today. Families, friends and groups frequent the restaurant for its extensive menu of good food. Casual dress. **Bar:** Full bar. **Hours:** 11:15 am-10 pm, Sun 11:30 am-9 pm. Closed: 7/4, 11/25, 12/25. **Address:** 195 School St 02451 **Location:** Just n of US 20, at Exchange St. **Parking:** on-site.

(See map and index starting on p. 345)

ERAWAN OF SIAM
Phone: 781/899-3399   102

Thai
$6-$16

Elaborate wall hangings, either carved from wood in relief or on sequined fabric, depict Thai life in the classy dining room. An indoor oak breezeway supported by six sets of columns ends in a decoratively roofed shrine with khundoke, a traditional sit-on-the-floor area. Cuisine relies on fresh vegetables, meat, fowl and seafood and assorted spices, from curries and ginger to jasmine and cardamom. Dishes are as colorful as they are good. Service is attentive and friendly. Casual dress. **Bar:** Full bar. **Reservations:** accepted. **Hours:** 11:30 am-3 & 4:30-10 pm, Fri-10:30 pm, Sat 4:30 pm-10:30 pm, Sun 4:30 pm-10 pm. Closed: 1/1, 7/4, 11/25. **Address:** 469 Moody St 02453 **Location:** 0.5 mi s of jct US 20; downtown. **Parking:** on-site.

GRASSFIELD'S FOOD & SPIRITS
Phone: 781/647-0844   96

American
$6-$17

A half-wall topped with a brass railing separates the dining room's two tiers in this casual, family-friendly restaurant. Many matted and framed pictures of sailing vessels, interspersed with large, framed mirrors, occupy the wall above the light-wood wainscoting. The food is good, simple New England fare, with seafood, steaks, chops and chicken prepared broiled, baked, grilled or fried. To answer an often-asked question: Strawberry shortcake is made with real biscuits. Service is folksy. Casual dress. **Bar:** Full bar. **Hours:** 11:30 am-9:30 pm, Fri & Sat-10 pm, Sun noon-9 pm. Closed: 11/25, 12/25. **Address:** 880 Lexington St 02451 **Location:** I-95, exit 27A, 1.2 mi e, then 1 mi n; in Wal-Lex Shopping Center. **Parking:** on-site.

GREEN PAPAYA THAI CUISINE
Phone: 781/487-9988   97

Thai
$6-$15

At the end of a small shopping plaza just off the interstate, the restaurant prepares the expected range of curries, noodles and fried rice, along with marinated grilled salmon, beef macadamia, squid sauteed in spices and a selection of vegetarian dishes. Ginger or coconut ice cream or lychees in syrup over ice end the meal on a delicious note. Thai iced tea is always refreshing. At lunch, the small joint parking lot fills with the vehicles of nearby office workers. Casual dress. **Bar:** Beer & wine. **Hours:** 11:30 am-3 & 5-9:30 pm, Fri & Sat-10 pm, Sun 5 pm-9:30 pm. Closed: 7/4, 11/25; 12/25; also for lunch 9/6. **Address:** 475 Winter St 02451 **Location:** I-95, exit 27B, just w; in Reservoir Plaza. **Parking:** on-site. CALL

IL CAPRICCIO
Phone: 781/894-2234   98

Northern Italian
$23-$36

The seasonally adjusted menu features innovative Northern Italian dishes that emphasize simple preparation and maximum taste. There is nothing ordinary about the food here. Antipasti, as pistachio-stuffed rabbit loin, lead to lasagna or other primi. Friendly, professional and attentive servers circulate through the dining room, which can become loud. Dressy casual. **Bar:** Full bar. **Reservations:** suggested. **Hours:** 5 pm-10 pm. Closed major holidays; also Sun. **Address:** 888 Main St 02453 **Location:** I-95, exit 26, 1.1 mi e on US 20. **Parking:** on-site.

JAKE'S DIXIE ROADHOUSE
Phone: 781/894-4227   99

American
$8-$21

In a storefront just south of the bridge at the beginning of Moody Street, the city's "restaurant row," the restaurant employs servers in jeans and T-shirts. Platter names such as the Bubba, Delta double, Memphis ribs and Tennessee triple speak to their regional genesis. Chili is full of pulled pork, and sandwiches overflow the buns. All is available in bulk for take-home, too. Between tap and bottle, more than 20 brews are available. City parking is close by. Casual dress. **Bar:** Full bar. **Reservations:** suggested, Fri & Sat. **Hours:** 5 pm-10 pm, Thurs & Fri 11:30 am-11:30 pm. Closed: 4/4, 11/25, 12/25. **Address:** 220 Moody St 02453 **Location:** Just s of US 20; downtown. **Parking:** on-site. CALL

NAKED FISH
Phone: 781/684-0500

Seafood
$9-$28

The restaurant presents a selection of unadorned "naked" seafood, beef and chicken, as well as some Cuban and "not-so-naked" choices. Naked seafood is grilled over an open wood fire after being dressed only with lemon and olive oil. Interesting sides, such as coconut steamed rice, make the choice of only one difficult. Although limited in number, the desserts are excellent, particularly the banana flan. The modern, Impressionist, Caribbean-influenced dining room can be bustling and noisy. Casual dress. **Bar:** Full bar. **Reservations:** suggested. **Hours:** 11:30 am-10 pm, Sat from 4 pm, Sun 4 pm-9 pm. Closed: 11/25, 12/24, 12/25. **Address:** 455 Totten Pond Rd 02451 **Location:** I-95, exit 27A, just s; in Home Suites Inn of Boston-Waltham. **Parking:** on-site. CALL

TEMPO
Phone: 781/891-9000   103

American
$16-$32

On the city's main street, the attractive, warm setting incorporates dark tones and soft lighting. A large kitchen-viewing window lets patrons watch the preparation of an ever-changing selection of dishes, such as baked brie in puff pastry, flash-fried calamari or tasty homemade bread with hummus. Among the creative entrées are pistachio-crusted lamb, pan-roasted organic salmon and naturally raised rib-eye steak. Irresistible desserts include lemon-zest cheesecake with blueberries. Casual dress. **Bar:** Full bar. **Reservations:** accepted. **Hours:** 5 pm-10 pm, Thurs-Sat to 11 pm. Closed major holidays. **Address:** 474 Moody St 02453 **Location:** Downtown. **Parking:** street.

TUSCAN GRILL
Phone: 781/891-5486   101

Regional Italian
$16-$26

With intimately spaced tables, the lively, bustling and popular trattoria provides wholesome country fare and homemade pasta from Tuscany. Most items are grilled or cooked on the rotisserie. From a limited number of seats at the service counter, guests can watch the chef at work. Casually uniformed servers are friendly, knowledgeable and work efficiently as a team. Casual dress. **Bar:** Full bar. **Reservations:** suggested. **Hours:** 5:30 pm-9:30 pm, Wed-Sat to 10 pm, Sun 5 pm-9 pm. Closed: major holidays, 12/24; also Mon. **Address:** 361 Moody St 02453 **Location:** 0.5 mi s of jct US 20; downtown. **Parking:** on-site.

WATCH CITY BREWING COMPANY
Phone: 781/647-4000   100

American
$13-$18

Wraparound windows at the front of the dining area enable patrons to look down Moody Street, the city's "restaurant row." The luncheon menu of pub fare expands at dinner to include dishes such as lasagna, seared scallops with ravioli, braised pork loin, Brie-stuffed chicken, grilled salmon and biscuit-crusted meatloaf. All of the beers are brewed on site. The dining area surrounds the bar and, because of hard surfaces on floors and walls, can become loud. Service is friendly. Casual dress. **Bar:** Beer & wine. **Hours:** 11:30 am-10 pm, Thurs-10:30 pm, Fri & Sat-11 pm, Sun-9 pm. Closed major holidays. **Address:** 256 Moody St 02453 **Location:** 0.3 mi s of jct US 20; downtown. **Parking:** street. CALL

WATERTOWN pop. 32,986

―――― **WHERE TO DINE** ――――

NOT YOUR AVERAGE JOE'S
Phone: 617/926-9229

American
$9-$18

The restaurant exemplifies the "in-trend" style of high-art contemporary design through vibrant color schemes, comfortable banquettes and stools, and smartly dressed staff. However, the high point is the food. Chefs whip up gourmet comfort foods of homemade meatloaf with a flavorful twist, creative hand-made pizzas, sandwiches, salads and more. Casual dress. **Bar:** Full bar. **Hours:** 11:30 am-10 pm, Fri & Sat-11 pm, Sun noon-10 pm. Closed: 11/25, 12/25. **Address:** 55 Main St 02472 **Location:** On US 20. **Parking:** street.

WELLESLEY pop. 26,613

―――― **WHERE TO DINE** ――――

AMARIN OF THAILAND
Phone: 781/239-1350

Thai
$6-$17

Traditional Asian spices, mostly Thai, complement the regionally eclectic fare. The number of peppers beside a menu item is a reliable guide to the level of spiciness. Satays or spring rolls are good lead-ins to the numerous chicken, beef, pork or seafood dishes. Rattan furniture adds additional warmth. Casual dress. **Bar:** Beer & wine. **Reservations:** suggested, weekends. **Hours:** 11:30 am-3 & 5-9:45 pm, Fri & Sat-10:30 pm, Sun 4 pm-9:30 pm. Closed: 7/4, 11/25, 12/25. **Address:** 27 Grove St 02482 **Location:** Just w of SR 135 and 61, just s of square. **Parking:** street.

BLUE GINGER, AN EAST-WEST BISTRO
Phone: 781/283-5790

Pacific Rim
$14-$38

While the content of the menu remains fairly constant, chef/owner Ming Tsai's preparations vary with the seasonal availability of ingredients. Pacific Rim cuisine-mostly Chinese, Japanese and Thai-is blended with French flavors and techniques to provide food in which East truly meets West. Tasty desserts include an excellent Tahitian crème brûlée and an assortment of Blue Ginger cookies. Overstuffed sofas in small conversational groupings serve as a combination lounge and waiting area. Dressy casual. **Bar:** Full bar. **Reservations:** suggested, for dinner. **Hours:** 11:30 am-2 & 5:30-9:30 pm, Fri-10 pm, Sat 5 pm-10 pm, Sun 5 pm-9 pm. Closed major holidays. **Address:** 583 Washington St 02482 **Location:** SR 16, just se of SR 135. **Parking:** on-site. CALL &M

WESTFORD

HAMPTON INN & SUITES
WESTFORD-CHELMSFORD   *Book great rates at AAA.com*
Phone: (978)392-1555

Hotel
$99-$139 All Year

Address: 9 Nixon Rd 01886 **Location:** I-495, exit 32. **Facility:** 110 one-bedroom standard units. 4 stories, interior corridors. *Bath:* combo or shower only. **Parking:** on-site. **Terms:** 1-7 night minimum stay, cancellation fee imposed. **Amenities:** high-speed Internet, voice mail, irons, hair dryers. **Pool(s):** heated indoor. **Leisure Activities:** exercise room. **Guest Services:** valet and coin laundry, wireless Internet. **Business Services:** meeting rooms, business center.

CALL &M ≋ 📷 💻 / SOME UNITS ⊠ 🔋 🖨

AAA Benefit:
Members save up to
10% everyday!

If your visit to a listed property doesn't meet your expectations, now you can tell us about it immediately, instead of waiting until you're home.

Visit **AAA.com/TourBookComments** to complete an easy online form.

RESIDENCE INN BOSTON WESTFORD

Book great rates at AAA.com

Phone: (978)392-1407

Extended Stay
Hotel
$152-$186 All Year

Address: 7 Lan Dr 01886 **Location:** I-495, exit 32, just s, then 0.5 w on SR 110. Located in Primrose Park. **Facility:** Smoke free premises. 108 units. 44 one-bedroom standard units, some with efficiencies or kitchens. 43 one- and 21 two-bedroom suites, some with efficiencies or kitchens. 3 stories, interior corridors. *Bath:* combo or shower only. **Parking:** on-site. **Terms:** cancellation fee imposed. **Amenities:** dual phone lines, voice mail, irons, hair dryers. **Pool(s):** heated indoor. **Leisure Activities:** whirlpool, exercise room, sports court. **Guest Services:** valet and coin laundry, wireless Internet. **Business Services:** business center.

AAA Benefit:
Members save a
minimum 5% off the
best available rate.

------- WHERE TO DINE -------

WESTFORD GRILLE

Phone: 978/392-0708

American
$7-$24

The popular restaurant and brewery caters to travelers, businesspeople, sports enthusiasts and children. Although the menu centers on American food, Italian and Mexican dishes also are prepared. Casual dress. **Bar:** Full bar. **Reservations:** accepted. **Hours:** 11:30 am-9 pm, Fri-10 pm, Sat 4 pm-10 pm. Closed major holidays; also Sun. **Address:** 142 Littleton Rd 01886 **Location:** I-495, exit 32, just se to SR 110, then just ne. **Parking:** on-site.

WEYMOUTH pop. 53,988

------- WHERE TO DINE -------

HEARTH 'N KETTLE RESTAURANT

Phone: 781/331-7007

American
$5-$15

Traditional Cape Cod cooking is served in an informal, family-friendly atmosphere. The diverse menu has the standards, from bacon, eggs and omelets for breakfast and sandwiches, chowders and salads for lunch to old favorites such as meatloaf and chicken pot pie for dinner. Fresh seafood is the forte. Finish the meal with one of the traditional New England desserts, such as Indian pudding or a distinctive treatment of strawberry shortcake. A few vegetarian selections are offered. Casual dress. **Bar:** Full bar. **Reservations:** not accepted. **Hours:** 7 am-close. Closed: 12/25. **Address:** 151 Main St 02188 **Location:** SR 18, exit 16A, 0.5 mi n of SR 3. **Parking:** on-site.

WILMINGTON pop. 21,363 (See map and index starting on p. 345)

------- WHERE TO DINE -------

NINETY NINE

Phone: 978/657-9694 (29)

American
$7-$14

This popular pub is committed to serving large portions of great food at reasonable prices. Guest favorites include hot wings, burgers, seafood, barbecue ribs and chicken. While reservations are not taken, call-ahead seating is offered. A children's menu is also available. Casual dress. **Bar:** Full bar. **Hours:** 11:15 am-11:30 pm, Sun-10 pm. Closed: 11/25, 12/25. **Address:** 144 Lowell St 01887 **Location:** On SR 129. **Parking:** on-site.

WINTHROP pop. 18,303 (See map and index starting on p. 345)

SUBURBAN EXTENDED STAY LOGAN AIRPORT

Book at AAA.com

Phone: (617)539-9466 (88)

Hotel
$119-$135 6/15-4/30
$100-$110 5/1-6/14

Address: 312 Shirley St 02152 **Location:** On SR 145 at Pearl Ave. **Facility:** Smoke free premises. 30 units. 13 one-bedroom standard units with efficiencies. 17 one-bedroom suites with efficiencies. 3 stories, interior corridors. **Parking:** on-site. **Terms:** cancellation fee imposed. **Amenities:** voice mail, hair dryers. **Guest Services:** valet laundry, wireless Internet.

WOBURN pop. 37,258 (See map and index starting on p. 345)

BEST WESTERN NEW ENGLANDER

Book great rates at AAA.com

Phone: (781)935-8160 (54)

Hotel
$99-$109 5/1-10/31
$89-$99 11/1-4/30

Address: 1 Rainin Rd 01801 **Location:** I-93, exit 36, just e. **Facility:** 99 one-bedroom standard units. 5 stories, interior corridors. *Bath:* combo or shower only. **Parking:** on-site. **Amenities:** high-speed Internet, dual phone lines, voice mail, safes (fee), irons, hair dryers. **Pool(s):** heated indoor. **Leisure Activities:** exercise room. **Guest Services:** valet laundry, area transportation-within 3 mi, wireless Internet. **Business Services:** meeting rooms, PC. **Free Special Amenities:** expanded continental breakfast and high-speed Internet.

AAA Benefit:
Members save up to
20%, plus 10%
bonus points with
rewards program.

COMFORT INN BOSTON/WOBURN

Book great rates at AAA.com

Phone: (781)933-5363 (55)

Hotel
$70-$240 All Year

Address: 14 Hill St 01801 **Location:** I-93, exit 36, just sw. **Facility:** 65 units. 61 one- and 4 two-bedroom standard units. 5 stories, interior corridors. *Bath:* combo or shower only. **Parking:** on-site. **Amenities:** high-speed Internet, dual phone lines, voice mail, safes, irons, hair dryers. **Leisure Activities:** limited exercise equipment. **Guest Services:** valet and coin laundry, wireless Internet. **Business Services:** PC. **Free Special Amenities:** continental breakfast and high-speed Internet.

(See map and index starting on p. 345)

COURTYARD BOSTON WOBURN   *Book great rates at AAA.com*

Phone: (781)932-3200   **48**

Hotel
$154-$169 All Year

Address: 240 Mishawum Rd 01801 **Location:** I-95, exit 36 southbound, 0.3 mi w; northbound, just n, then 0.5 mi w. **Facility:** Smoke free premises. 120 units. 118 one-bedroom standard units. 2 one-bedroom suites. 3 stories, interior corridors. *Bath:* combo or shower only. **Parking:** on-site. **Terms:** cancellation fee imposed. **Amenities:** high-speed Internet, dual phone lines, voice mail, irons, hair dryers. **Pool(s):** heated outdoor. **Leisure Activities:** exercise room. **Guest Services:** valet and coin laundry. **Business Services:** meeting rooms, business center.

AAA Benefit:
Members save a minimum 5% off the best available rate.

COURTYARD BY MARRIOTT WOBURN/BOSTON NORTH   *Book great rates at AAA.com*

Phone: (781)938-9001   **53**

Hotel
$164-$189 All Year

Address: 700 Unicorn Park 01801 **Location:** I-93, exit 36, just e, then 0.6 mi n. Located in the Unicorn Park office complex. **Facility:** Smoke free premises. 186 units. 180 one-bedroom standard units, some with whirlpools. 6 one-bedroom suites. 6 stories, interior corridors. *Bath:* combo or shower only. **Parking:** on-site. **Terms:** cancellation fee imposed. **Amenities:** video games (fee), high-speed Internet, dual phone lines, voice mail, irons, hair dryers. **Pool(s):** heated indoor. **Leisure Activities:** whirlpool, exercise room. **Guest Services:** valet and coin laundry, area transportation, wireless Internet. **Business Services:** meeting rooms, business center.

AAA Benefit:
Members save a minimum 5% off the best available rate.

EXTENDED STAY DELUXE BOSTON-WOBURN   *Book at AAA.com*

Phone: (781)938-3737   **50**

Extended Stay
Hotel
$75-$110 All Year

Address: 831 Main St 01801 **Location:** I-95, exit 35, just n on SR 38. **Facility:** 100 one-bedroom standard units with efficiencies. 3 stories, interior corridors. *Bath:* combo or shower only. **Parking:** on-site. **Terms:** cancellation fee imposed. **Amenities:** DVD players, dual phone lines, voice mail, irons, hair dryers. **Pool(s):** heated outdoor. **Leisure Activities:** exercise room. **Guest Services:** valet and coin laundry, wireless Internet.

FAIRFIELD INN BY MARRIOTT-BOSTON/WOBURN   *Book great rates at AAA.com*   Phone: (781)938-7575   **49**

Hotel
$99-$129 All Year

Address: 285 Mishawum Rd 01801 **Location:** I-95, exit 36, 0.3 mi w, just n, then 0.5 mi w. **Facility:** Smoke free premises. 129 one-bedroom standard units. 5 stories, interior corridors. *Bath:* combo or shower only. **Parking:** on-site. **Terms:** cancellation fee imposed. **Amenities:** voice mail, irons, hair dryers. **Pool(s):** outdoor. **Guest Services:** valet laundry, wireless Internet. **Business Services:** PC.

AAA Benefit:
Members save a minimum 5% off the best available rate.

HAMPTON INN BOSTON-WOBURN   *Book great rates at AAA.com*

Phone: (781)935-7666   **47**

Hotel
$109-$159 All Year

Address: 315 Mishawum Rd 01801 **Location:** I-95, exit 36, just n, then just w. Opposite Woburn Mall. **Facility:** Smoke free premises. 98 one-bedroom standard units. 5 stories, interior corridors. *Bath:* combo or shower only. **Parking:** on-site. **Terms:** 1-7 night minimum stay, cancellation fee imposed. **Amenities:** dual phone lines, voice mail, irons, hair dryers. **Dining:** Joe's American Bar & Grill, see separate listing. **Leisure Activities:** limited exercise equipment. **Guest Services:** valet laundry, wireless Internet. **Business Services:** PC.

AAA Benefit:
Members save up to 10% everyday!

HILTON BOSTON/WOBURN   *Book great rates at AAA.com*

Phone: (781)932-0999   **52**

Hotel
$99-$239 All Year

Address: 2 Forbes Rd 01801 **Location:** I-95, exit 36, 0.5 mi s via Washington St, then just e at Lukoil; jct Cedar St. **Facility:** 344 one-bedroom standard units. 7 stories, interior corridors. *Bath:* combo or shower only. **Parking:** on-site. **Terms:** 1-7 night minimum stay, cancellation fee imposed. **Amenities:** high-speed Internet (fee), voice mail, irons, hair dryers. **Pool(s):** heated indoor. **Leisure Activities:** exercise room. **Guest Services:** valet laundry, area transportation. **Business Services:** conference facilities, business center.

Hilton
AAA Benefit:
Members save 5% or more everyday!

(See map and index starting on p. 345)

HOLIDAY INN SELECT
Book great rates at AAA.com   **Phone:** (781)935-8760   **51**

Hotel
$109-$199 5/1-10/31
$99-$199 11/1-4/30

Address: 15 Middlesex Canal Park Rd 01801 **Location:** I-95, exit 35, s via SR 38. **Facility:** 195 units. 193 one-bedroom standard units. 2 one-bedroom suites. 4 stories, interior corridors. *Bath:* combo or shower only. **Parking:** on-site. **Amenities:** dual phone lines, voice mail, irons, hair dryers. **Pool(s):** heated indoor. **Leisure Activities:** exercise room. **Guest Services:** valet laundry, area transportation-within 5 mi, wireless Internet. **Business Services:** meeting rooms, business center.

RED ROOF INN WOBURN #238
Book great rates at AAA.com   **Phone:** (781)935-7110   **46**

Hotel
$79-$130 5/1-10/31
$59-$130 11/1-4/30

Address: 19 Commerce Way 01801 **Location:** I-95, exit 36, just n, then just w on Mishawum Rd. **Facility:** 159 one-bedroom standard units. 5 stories, interior corridors. *Bath:* combo or shower only. **Parking:** on-site. **Amenities:** video games (fee), voice mail, irons. **Pool(s):** heated indoor. **Guest Services:** coin laundry, wireless Internet. **Business Services:** meeting rooms. **Free Special Amenities: local telephone calls.**

RESIDENCE INN BY MARRIOTT-BOSTON/WOBURN
Book great rates at AAA.com   **Phone:** (781)376-4000   **45**

Extended Stay Hotel
$199-$219 All Year

Address: 300 Presidential Way 01801 **Location:** I-93, exit 37C, just nw. Located in Metro North Office Park. **Facility:** Smoke free premises. 149 units. 67 one-bedroom standard units, some with efficiencies or kitchens. 62 one- and 20 two-bedroom suites, some with efficiencies or kitchens. 7 stories, interior corridors. *Bath:* combo or shower only. **Parking:** on-site. **Terms:** cancellation fee imposed. **Amenities:** video games (fee), high-speed Internet, dual phone lines, voice mail, irons, hair dryers. **Pool(s):** heated indoor. **Leisure Activities:** whirlpool, exercise room. **Guest Services:** valet and coin laundry, area transportation-within 5 mi. **Business Services:** meeting rooms, business center. **Free Special Amenities: full breakfast and high-speed Internet.**

AAA Benefit:
Members save a minimum 5% off the best available rate.

------ WHERE TO DINE ------

JOE'S AMERICAN BAR & GRILL
Phone: 781/935-7200

American
$9-$24

If it's Americana you want, you'll get all that and more at Joe's, where the bill of fare includes all-American favorites like hearty burgers, fresh-from-the-oven chicken pot pies, Maryland lump crab cakes, and Joe's classic meatloaf. Pizzas, pastas, steaks and salads round out the extensive menu, giving diners the freedom to choose from a vast selection of offerings. There's nothing more American than that, except, of course, for apple pie, so save some room. Casual dress. **Bar:** Full bar. **Reservations:** suggested. **Hours:** 11:30 am-11 pm. Closed: 12/25. **Address:** 311 Mishawum Rd 01801 **Location:** I-95, exit 36, just n, then just w; in Hampton Inn Boston-Woburn. **Parking:** on-site.

MASA
Phone: 781/938-8886   **46**

Southwestern
$9-$29

The terrific bistro has an airy, contemporary feel with a large, attractive bar on one side and plush banquette seating on the other. Creative homemade dishes may include lamb spring rolls, plantain tostones, empanadas, pan-seared mahi mahi or grilled pork tenderloins. The weekend brunch is not to be missed. Casual dress. **Bar:** Full bar. **Reservations:** required. **Hours:** 11:30 am-3 & 4:30-10 pm, Sat & Sun from 10 am. Closed major holidays. **Address:** 350 Cambridge Rd 01801 **Location:** On US 3; in Horn Pond Plaza. **Parking:** on-site.

(See map and index starting on p. 345)

POLCARI'S Phone: 781/938-1900 ㊺

Italian
$6-$21

The menu centers on traditional American-Italian fare: tasty pasta, pizzas, parmigiana dishes and Italian pastries. The location is convenient to the interstate. Casual dress. **Bar:** Full bar. **Reservations:** accepted. **Hours:** 11:30 am-10:30 pm, Fri & Sat-11:30 pm. Closed: 11/25, 12/25. **Address:** 309 Montvale Ave 01801 **Location:** I-93, exit 36, just w. **Parking:** on-site.

SPUD'S RESTAURANT & PUB   Phone: 781/937-0304

American
$7-$19

This friendly pub and eatery is the perfect place for families to enjoy generous portions of consistently quality food. Menu offerings are varied from seafood and pasta to a few chicken, steak and chop selections. Burgers and sandwiches are available anytime. A price-busters menu with smaller portions at a lower cost is also popular. Large TV screens in the lounge normally emphasize sports programming. Casual dress. **Bar:** Full bar. **Hours:** 11 am-10 pm. Closed: 7/4, 11/25, 12/25. **Address:** 1 Rainin Rd 01801 **Location:** I-93, exit 36, just e. **Parking:** on-site.

WRENTHAM

—— WHERE TO DINE ——

LUCIANO'S   Phone: 508/384-3050

Northern Italian
$9-$39

The traditional Northern Italian menu features freshly made pasta and quality chicken, veal, beef, chops and seafood. Celebrity guest pictures hang behind the reception desk in the lobby. Dressy casual. **Bar:** Full bar. **Reservations:** required, weekends. **Hours:** 11:30 am-3 & 4-9 pm, Sat 11:30 am-2:30 & 4:30-10 pm, Sun 11 am-3 & 4-8 pm. Closed: 1/1, 12/25. **Address:** 800 Washington St 02093 **Location:** I-495, exit 14A, 0.6 mi n on US 1. **Parking:** on-site and valet. CALL ♿M

Cambridge / © Longfellow House, Old Cambridge

This ends listings for the Boston Vicinity.
The following page resumes the alphabetical listings of cities in Massachusetts.

BOURNE—See Cape Cod p. 467.

BOXBOROUGH—See Boston p. 395.

BRAINTREE—See Boston p. 396.

BREWSTER—See Cape Cod p. 467.

BROCKTON pop. 94,304

COUNTRY INN & SUITES BY CARLSON   *Book at AAA.com*   Phone: 508/559-0099

Hotel
Rates not provided

Address: 50 Christy's Dr 02301 **Location:** SR 24, exit 18A, just e. **Facility:** 63 units. 17 one-bedroom standard units, some with whirlpools. 46 one-bedroom suites. 3 stories, interior corridors. *Bath:* combo or shower only. **Parking:** on-site. **Amenities:** high-speed Internet, voice mail, irons, hair dryers. **Pool(s):** heated indoor. **Leisure Activities:** whirlpool, exercise room. **Guest Services:** coin laundry, wireless Internet. **Business Services:** meeting rooms, business center.

HOLIDAY INN BOSTON-BROCKTON   *Book at AAA.com*   Phone: (508)588-6300

Hotel
$99-$139 All Year

Address: 195 Westgate Dr 02401 **Location:** SR 24, exit 18A, 0.3 mi e on SR 27. Located next to Westgate Mall. **Facility:** 189 units. 186 one-bedroom standard units. 3 one-bedroom suites. 3 stories, interior corridors. *Bath:* combo or shower only. **Parking:** on-site. **Amenities:** video games (fee), dual phone lines, voice mail, irons, hair dryers. **Pool(s):** heated indoor. **Leisure Activities:** whirlpool, exercise room. **Guest Services:** valet and coin laundry, wireless Internet. **Business Services:** conference facilities, PC.

QUALITY INN   *Book at AAA.com*   Phone: (508)588-3333

Hotel
$63-$109 All Year

Address: 1005 Belmont St 02301 **Location:** SR 24, exit 17A, just e on SR 123. **Facility:** 64 one-bedroom standard units, some with whirlpools. 3 one-bedroom suites. 3 stories (no elevator), interior corridors. **Parking:** on-site. **Amenities:** high-speed Internet, voice mail, irons, hair dryers. **Pool(s):** outdoor. **Guest Services:** wireless Internet. **Business Services:** meeting rooms.

RESIDENCE INN BOSTON BROCKTON   *Book great rates at AAA.com*   Phone: (508)583-3600

Extended Stay
Hotel
$139-$159 All Year

Address: 124 Liberty St 02301 **Location:** SR 24, exit 17B, just w, just s on Pearl St, then 0.3 mi se via Mill St connector. **Facility:** Smoke free premises. 88 units. 36 one-bedroom standard units with efficiencies. 38 one- and 14 two-bedroom suites, some with efficiencies or kitchens. 4 stories, interior corridors. *Bath:* combo or shower only. **Parking:** on-site. **Terms:** cancellation fee imposed. **Amenities:** video games (fee), high-speed Internet, dual phone lines, voice mail, irons, hair dryers. **Pool(s):** heated indoor. **Leisure Activities:** whirlpool, exercise room, sports court. **Guest Services:** valet and coin laundry, wireless Internet. **Business Services:** meeting rooms, PC.

AAA Benefit:
Members save a minimum 5% off the best available rate.

SUPER 8-BROCKTON   *Book at AAA.com*   Phone: (508)588-8887

Hotel
$69-$99 All Year

Address: 385 Westgate Dr 02301 **Location:** SR 24, exit 18A, 0.3 mi e on SR 27. Located next to Westgate Mall. **Facility:** 57 one-bedroom standard units, some with whirlpools. 2 stories, interior corridors. **Parking:** on-site. **Terms:** cancellation fee imposed. **Amenities:** voice mail, irons, hair dryers. **Guest Services:** wireless Internet.

—— WHERE TO DINE ——

CHRISTO'S RESTAURANT   **Phone:** 508/588-4200

Greek
$6-$15

The casual, family-oriented Greek restaurant serves steak, chops, fresh seafood, chicken, lamb and pizza. Greek salads are a favorite, as are the daily lunch specials. Homemade desserts are excellent. The food is a good value, making a visit here worth the drive. Casual dress. **Bar:** Full bar. **Hours:** 11 am-11 pm, Sun noon-10 pm. Closed: 11/25, 12/25. **Address:** 782 Crescent St 02302 **Location:** SR 24, exit 18A, 4 mi se, then 1.4 mi se on SR 27. **Parking:** on-site.

BROOKLINE—See Boston p. 397.

BURLINGTON—See Boston p. 398.

BUZZARDS BAY—See Cape Cod p. 469.

CAMBRIDGE—See Boston p. 399.

Destination Cape Cod

*T*he best things in Cape Cod are natural.

*S*pying through binoculars, you may catch a glimpse of tern on Monomoy Island. On two wheels you can cruise by white sand dunes topped with sea oats. A pair of hiking shoes can take you into the great outdoors along numerous nature trails, and water sports abound in the surrounding sea.

© Steve Vidler / eStock Photo

Shopping in Provincetown.

MOTT / Kindra Clineff

Beaches, Cape Cod

*P*laces included in this AAA Destination Area:

③

㉕

⑥

Buzzards Bay •

Bourne •

㉘

North Falmouth •

West Falmouth •

Falmouth •

Woods • **Hole**

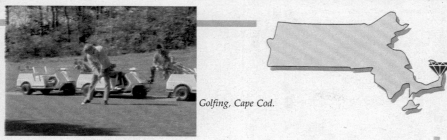

Golfing, Cape Cod.

Cape Cod Chamber of Commerce

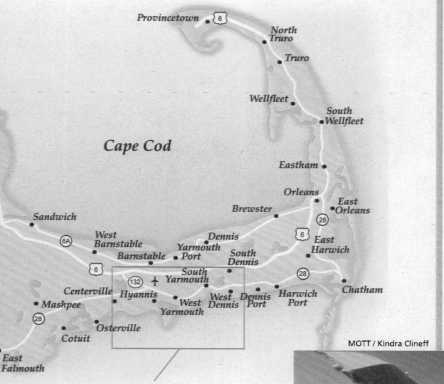

Provincetown 6

North
Truro

Truro

Wellfleet

South
Wellfleet

Cape Cod

Eastham

Orleans

Brewster

East
Orleans

Sandwich

28

6A

West
Barnstable

Dennis

Yarmouth
Port

South
Dennis

6 East
Harwich

Barnstable

6

132

South
Yarmouth

28

Centerville

Hyannis

West
Yarmouth

West
Dennis

Dennis
Port

Harwich
Port

Chatham

Mashpee

28

Osterville

Cotuit

East
Falmouth

**See Vicinity
map page 454**

MOTT / Kindra Clineff

*Spending time outdoors,
Cape Cod.*

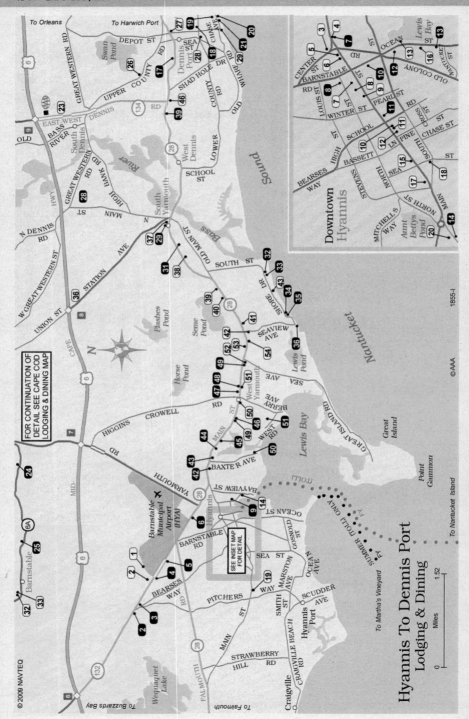

Hyannis To Dennis Port
Lodging & Dining

Downtown Hyannis

For Continuation Of Detail See Cape Cod Lodging & Dining Map

See Inset Map For Detail

© 2009 NAVTEQ

©AAA

1855-I

Hyannis To Dennis Port

This index helps you "spot" where approved lodgings and restaurants are located on the corresponding detailed maps. Lodging daily rate range is for comparison only and show the property's high season. Restaurant rate range is a combination of lunch and/or dinner. Turn to the listing page for more detailed rate information and consult display ads for special promotions.

HYANNIS

Map Page	OA	Lodgings	Diamond Rated	High Season	Page
2 / p. 454		Cape Codder Resort & Spa - see color ad p 482	◆◆◆	$119-$239	482
3 / p. 454	AAA	**Holiday Inn Hyannis**	◆◆◆	$119-$209 SAVE	484
4 / p. 454	AAA	**Days Inn -** see color ad p 484	◆◆	$75-$225 SAVE	483
5 / p. 454		Courtyard Hyannis	◆◆◆	$109-$189	483
6 / p. 454	AAA	**Radisson Hotel Hyannis**	◆◆◆	$109-$209 SAVE	485
7 / p. 454		Heritage House Hotel	◆◆◆	$79-$299	483
8 / p. 454	AAA	**Hyannis Travel Inn -** see color ad p 486	◆◆	$69-$149 SAVE	485
9 / p. 454	AAA	**Anchor-In Distinctive Waterfront Lodging -** see color ad p 481	◆◆◆	$99-$279 SAVE	481
10 / p. 454	AAA	**SeaCoast Inn**	◆◆	$69-$149 SAVE	485
11 / p. 454	AAA	**Hyannis Inn Motel**	◆◆	$50-$175 SAVE	484
12 / p. 454		Cape Cod Harbor House Inn	◆◆	Rates not provided	482
13 / p. 454	AAA	**Hyannis Harbor Hotel -** see color ad p 485	◆◆◆	$79-$299 SAVE	484
14 / p. 454		Resort and Conference Center at Hyannis	◆◆◆	$160-$300	485

Map Page	OA	Restaurants	Diamond Rated	Cuisine	Meal Range	Page
1 / p. 454		Barbyann's Restaurant	◆◆	American	$7-$30	489
2 / p. 454		Naked Oyster Bistro & Raw Bar	◆◆◆	Seafood	$12-$34	490
3 / p. 454		Ying's	◆◆	Asian	$8-$26	491
4 / p. 454		Persy's Place	◆◆	American	$4-$15	490
5 / p. 454		Fazio's Trattoria	◆◆	Italian	$10-$22	490
6 / p. 454		Thai House Restaurant	◆	Thai	$8-$16	491
7 / p. 454	AAA	**Alberto's Ristorante**	◆◆◆	Northern Italian	$7-$20	489
8 / p. 454		Schooners	◆◆	American	$7-$20	491
9 / p. 454		The British Beer Company	◆◆	British	$7-$22	489
10 / p. 454		Pavilion Indian Cuisine	◆◆	Indian	$12-$22	490
11 / p. 454		The Original Gourmet Brunch	◆	American	$7-$9	490
12 / p. 454		The Egg & I	◆	American	$5-$8	489
13 / p. 454		Spanky's Clam Shack	◆◆	Seafood	$10-$27	491
14 / p. 454		Tugboats	◆◆	Seafood	$8-$28	491
15 / p. 454		Dragon Lite Restaurant	◆◆	Chinese	$6-$17	489
16 / p. 454		The Black Cat	◆◆	American	$9-$35	489
17 / p. 454		Brazilian Grill	◆◆	Brazilian	$8-$26	489
18 / p. 454		Roadhouse Cafe	◆◆◆	Steak	$16-$37	490

Map Page	OA	Restaurants (cont'd)	Diamond Rated	Cuisine	Meal Range	Page
(19) / p. 454		Il Maestro Ristorante	◆◆	Italian	$16-$28	490
(20) / p. 454	⬭	**The Paddock**	◆◆◆	American	$8-$43	490

DENNIS PORT

Map Page	OA	Lodgings	Diamond Rated	High Season	Page
(17) / p. 454	⬭	**Holiday Hill Motor Inn**	◆◆	$59-$129 [SAVE]	475
(18) / p. 454		Colonial Village Motel & Cottages	◆◆	Rates not provided	475
(19) / p. 454		An English Garden B&B	◆◆◆	$99-$165	474
(20) / p. 454	⬭	**'By The Sea' Guests Bed & Breakfast & Suites**	◆◆◆	$125-$460 [SAVE]	474
(21) / p. 454	⬭	**Corsair & Cross Rip Oceanfront** - see color ad p 475	◆◆	$125-$375 [SAVE]	475

Map Page	OA	Restaurants	Diamond Rated	Cuisine	Meal Range	Page
(26) / p. 454		Clancy's	◆◆	American	$8-$24	476
(27) / p. 454		The Egg & I	◆	American	$5-$9	476
(28) / p. 454		Sundae School	◆	Desserts	$3-$7	476
(29) / p. 454		Ocean House	◆◆◆	American	$20-$34	476

BARNSTABLE

Map Page	OA	Lodgings	Diamond Rated	High Season	Page
(24) / p. 454		The Acworth Inn	◆◆◆	$155-$250	467
(25) / p. 454		Ashley Manor Inn	◆◆◆	$185-$245	467

Map Page	OA	Restaurants	Diamond Rated	Cuisine	Meal Range	Page
(32) / p. 454		Barnstable Restaurant & Tavern	◆◆	American	$8-$26	467
(33) / p. 454		Dolphin Restaurant	◆◆	American	$8-$26	467

SOUTH YARMOUTH

Map Page	OA	Lodgings	Diamond Rated	High Season	Page
(28) / p. 454	⬭	**Blue Rock Golf Resort**	◆◆	$95-$215 [SAVE]	505
(29) / p. 454	⬭	**Ambassador Inn & Suites**	◆◆	$60-$190 [SAVE]	505
(31) / p. 454	⬭	**Clarion Inn** - see color ad p 506	◆◆◆	$79-$249 [SAVE]	506
(32) / p. 454	⬭	**Riviera Beach Resort**	◆◆◆	$135-$550 [SAVE]	507
(33) / p. 454	⬭	**Blue Water on The Ocean**	◆◆	$90-$199 [SAVE]	505
(34) / p. 454		Surfcomber on the Ocean	◆◆	Rates not provided	507
(35) / p. 454		Ocean Mist Resort	◆◆	Rates not provided	506
(36) / p. 454	⬭	**Red Jacket Beach**	◆◆◆	$125-$430 [SAVE]	507

Map Page	OA	Restaurants	Diamond Rated	Cuisine	Meal Range	Page
(36) / p. 454		Ardeo	◆◆	Mediterranean	$7-$23	507
(37) / p. 454		Riverway Lobster House	◆◆	Seafood	$9-$25	508
(38) / p. 454		Piccadilly Deli & Cafe	◆	American	$5-$12	507
(39) / p. 454	⬭	**The Pancake Man**	◆	American	$6-$12	507

Map Page	OA	Restaurants (cont'd)	Diamond Rated	Cuisine	Meal Range	Page
(40) / p. 454		Gerardi's Cafe	◈◈◈	Italian	$12-$22	507
(41) / p. 454		Christopher's Ribs and Seafood	◈◈	Seafood	$9-$22	507
(42) / p. 454		Skippy's Pier 1 Restaurant	◈◈	American	$8-$27	508
(43) / p. 454		The Skipper Restaurant & Chowder House	◈◈	Seafood	$7-$28	508

WEST DENNIS

Map Page	OA	Lodging	Diamond Rated	High Season	Page
(39) / p. 454		Inn at Swan River	◈◈	$110-$259	509

Map Page	OA	Restaurant	Diamond Rated	Cuisine	Meal Range	Page
(46) / p. 454		Kream' N Kone	◈	Seafood	$5-$16	509

WEST YARMOUTH

Map Page	OA	Lodgings	Diamond Rated	High Season	Page
(42) / p. 454		Hampton Inn & Suites Cape Cod	◈◈◈	$109-$289	511
(43) / p. 454	AAA	**Tidewater Inn** - see color ad p 488	◈◈	$69-$159 SAVE	511
(44) / p. 454	AAA	**The Cove at Yarmouth**	◈◈◈	$200 SAVE	510
(45) / p. 454	AAA	**Bayside Resort Hotel** - see color ad p 483	◈◈◈	$80-$180 SAVE	510
(46) / p. 454		The Yarmouth Resort	◈◈	Rates not provided	512
(47) / p. 454	AAA	**Town 'N Country Motor Lodge** - see color ad p 487	◈◈	$34-$178 SAVE	511
(48) / p. 454	AAA	**The Cape Point Hotel** - see color ad p 487	◈◈◈	$60-$170 SAVE	510
(49) / p. 454	AAA	**The Mariner Motor Lodge** - see color ad p 487	◈◈	$40-$140 SAVE	511
(50) / p. 454	AAA	**Green Harbor on the Ocean**	◈◈◈	$95-$800 SAVE	510
(51) / p. 454	AAA	**Inn at Lewis Bay**	◈◈◈	$128-$158 SAVE	511

Map Page	OA	Restaurants	Diamond Rated	Cuisine	Meal Range	Page
(49) / p. 454	AAA	**Yarmouth House Restaurant**	◈◈	American	$6-$27	513
(50) / p. 454		Keltic Kitchen	◈	American	$3-$10	512
(51) / p. 454		Ann & Fran's Kitchen	◈	American	$4-$9	512
(52) / p. 454		Molly's Restaurant & Pub	◈◈	Irish	$9-$25	512
(53) / p. 454	AAA	**Captain Parker's Pub & Restaurant**	◈◈	Seafood	$5-$20	512
(54) / p. 454		Lobster Boat	◈	Seafood	$7-$29	512

SOUTH DENNIS

Map Page	OA	Restaurant	Diamond Rated	Cuisine	Meal Range	Page
(23) / p. 454		Bangkok Thai Cuisine II	◈◈	Thai	$7-$17	504

© AAA

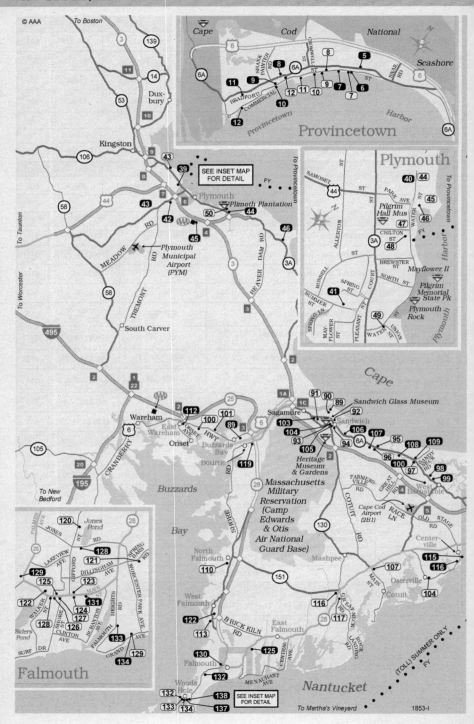

To Boston

Cape Cod National Seashore

Provincetown

Plymouth

To Provincetown

Plimoth Plantation

Plymouth Municipal Airport (PYM)

Pilgrim Hall Mus

Mayflower II

Pilgrim Memorial State Pk

Plymouth Rock

Cape

Sandwich Glass Museum

Sandwich

Heritage Museum & Gardens

Massachusetts Military Reservation (Camp Edwards & Otis Air National Guard Base)

Cape Cod Airport (2B1)

West Barnstable

Centerville

Osterville

Cotuit

Mashpee

North Falmouth

West Falmouth

East Falmouth

Woods Hole

Falmouth

Buzzards Bay

Wareham

East Wareham

Onset

Bourne

Sagamore

Nantucket

To Martha's Vineyard

To New Bedford

To Taunton

To Worcester

Kingston

Duxbury

South Carver

Jones Pond

Siders Pond

1853-I

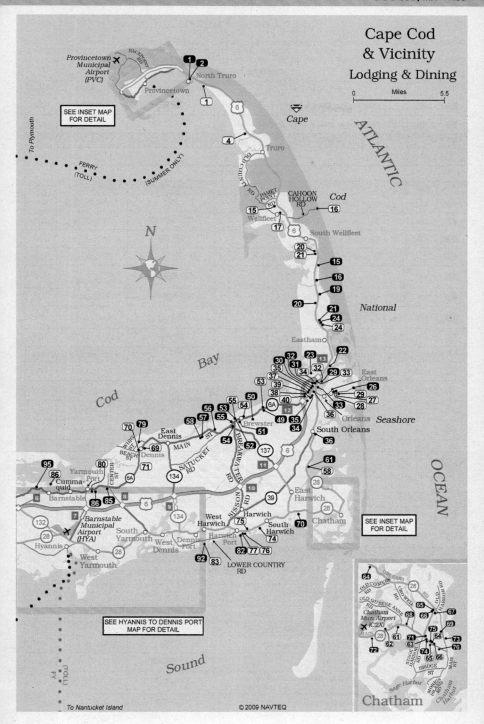

Cape Cod
& Vicinity
Lodging & Dining

Miles
0   5.5

ATLANTIC

Cape

Cod

National

Seashore

OCEAN

Bay

Cod

Sound

Provincetown
Municipal
Airport
(PVC)

SEE INSET MAP
FOR DETAIL

To Plymouth

FERRY
(TOLL)

(SUMMER ONLY)

N

North Truro

Provincetown

RACE POINT RD

Truro

OLD COUNTY RD

PAMET POINT RD

CAHOON
HOLLOW
RD

Wellfleet

South Wellfleet

Eastham

East
Orleans

Orleans

South Orleans

East
Dennis

Dennis

Yarmouth
Port

Cumma-
quid

Barnstable

Barnstable
Municipal
Airport
(HYA)

Hyannis

West
Yarmouth

South
Yarmouth

West
Dennis

Dennis
Port

Harwich
Port

West
Harwich

Harwich

South
Harwich

East
Harwich

Chatham

Brewster

LOWER COUNTRY
RD

SEE INSET MAP
FOR DETAIL

SEE HYANNIS TO DENNIS PORT
MAP FOR DETAIL

To Nantucket Island

© 2009 NAVTEQ

Chatham

Chatham
Mun Airport
(C2X)

Sage Harbor

Chatham Harbor

Cape Cod & Vicinity

This index helps you "spot" where approved lodgings and restaurants are located on the corresponding detailed maps. Lodging daily rate range is for comparison only and show the property's high season. Restaurant rate range is a combination of lunch and/or dinner. Turn to the listing page for more detailed rate information and consult display ads for special promotions.

NORTH TRURO

Map Page	OA	Lodgings	Diamond Rated	High Season	Page
❶ / p. 458		East Harbour Motel & Cottages	♦♦	$90-$230	492
❷ / p. 458	AAA	**Crows Nest Resort** - see color ad p 498	♦♦♦	$79-$389 SAVE	492

Map Page	OA	Restaurant	Diamond Rated	Cuisine	Meal Range	Page
① / p. 458		Adrian's	♦♦	Regional Italian	$12-$30	493

PROVINCETOWN

Map Page	OA	Lodgings	Diamond Rated	High Season	Page
❺ / p. 458	AAA	**Cape Colony Inn**	♦	$119-$269 SAVE	499
❻ / p. 458		Surfside Hotel & Suites	♦♦♦	$139-$329	500
❼ / p. 458		Bayshore & Chandler	♦♦	$105-$325	498
❽ / p. 458	AAA	**Crowne Pointe Historic Inn & Spa**	♦♦♦♦	$129-$499 SAVE	500
❾ / p. 458		White Wind Inn	♦♦♦	Rates not provided	500
❿ / p. 458		Anchor Inn Beach House	♦♦♦	$150-$400	498
⓫ / p. 458	AAA	**Chateau Provincetown** - see color ad p 499	♦♦	$99-$269 SAVE	499
⓬ / p. 458	AAA	**The Masthead**	♦♦	$137-$517 SAVE	500

Map Page	OA	Restaurants	Diamond Rated	Cuisine	Meal Range	Page
⑦ / p. 458	AAA	**Fanizzi's by the Sea**	♦♦	American	$6-$24	501
⑧ / p. 458		Ciro & Sal's Restaurant	♦♦	Italian	$15-$35	500
⑨ / p. 458		The Mews	♦♦	Continental	$18-$34	501
⑩ / p. 458		Devon's	♦♦♦	New American	$9-$30	501
⑪ / p. 458		The Lobster Pot	♦♦	Seafood	$6-$24	501
⑫ / p. 458		Front Street Restaurant	♦♦♦	New Continental	$19-$32	501

SOUTH WELLFLEET

Map Page	OA	Lodgings	Diamond Rated	High Season	Page
⓯ / p. 458	AAA	**The Even'tide Motel & Cottages**	♦♦	$75-$310 SAVE	504
⓰ / p. 458	AAA	**Wellfleet Motel and Lodge** - see color ad p 508	♦♦	$75-$220 SAVE	505

Map Page	OA	Restaurants	Diamond Rated	Cuisine	Meal Range	Page
⑳ / p. 458	AAA	**Van Rensselaer's Restaurant & Raw Bar**	♦♦	American	$14-$32	505
㉑ / p. 458	AAA	**Catch of the Day Restaurant & Seafood Market**	♦	Seafood	$9-$20	505

EASTHAM

Map Page	OA	Lodgings	Diamond Rated	High Season	Page
⓳ / p. 458	AAA	**Midway Motel and Cottages, Inc**	♦♦	$76-$144 SAVE	476
⑳ / p. 458		Penny House Inn	♦♦♦	$205-$449	477
㉑ / p. 458	AAA	**Four Points by Sheraton Eastham Cape Cod**	♦♦♦	$205-$350 SAVE	476
㉒ / p. 458		Eagle Wing Guest Motel	♦♦	$70-$170	476

EASTHAM (cont'd)

Map Page	OA	Lodgings (cont'd)	Diamond Rated	High Season	Page
23 / p. 458		Whalewalk Inn & Spa	◆◆◆	· $220-$420	477
24 / p. 458		Town Crier Motel	◆◆	$129-$199	477

Map Page	OA	Restaurant	Diamond Rated	Cuisine	Meal Range	Page
24 / p. 458	◬	**Arnold's Lobster & Clam Bar**	◆	Regional Seafood	$4-$30	477

EAST ORLEANS

Map Page	OA	Lodging	Diamond Rated	High Season	Page
26 / p. 458		Nauset Knoll Motor Lodge	◆	$120-$185	478

Map Page	OA	Restaurants	Diamond Rated	Cuisine	Meal Range	Page
27 / p. 458		Nauset Beach Club Restaurant	◆◆◆	Northern Italian	$12-$34	478
28 / p. 458		Sundae School	◆	Desserts	$3-$7	478
29 / p. 458		Joe's Beach Road Bar & Grill @ The Barley Neck Inn	◆◆	American	$15-$26	478

ORLEANS

Map Page	OA	Lodgings	Diamond Rated	High Season	Page
29 / p. 458		Orleans Inn	◆◆	$250-$450	494
30 / p. 458	◬	**Seashore Park Inn**	◆	$99-$179 SAVE	495
31 / p. 458	◬	**Rodeway Inn**	◆	$59-$275 SAVE	495
32 / p. 458		Governor Prence Inn	◆◆	$99-$169	493
33 / p. 458		The Cove - see color ad p 493	◆◆	$69-$224	493
34 / p. 458	◬	**Olde Tavern Motel & Inn** - see color ad p 494	◆◆	$59-$189 SAVE	494
35 / p. 458	◬	**Skaket Beach Motel** - see color ad p 496	◆◆	$65-$175 SAVE	495
36 / p. 458		Ridgewood Motel & Cottages - see color ad p 495	◆	$60-$97	494

Map Page	OA	Restaurants	Diamond Rated	Cuisine	Meal Range	Page
32 / p. 458		Orleans Inn Restaurant	◆◆	Seafood	$9-$20	498
33 / p. 458	◬	**The Lobster Claw**	◆◆	Seafood	$8-$30	497
34 / p. 458		Cooke's Seafood	◆	Seafood	$5-$17	497
35 / p. 458		Mahoney's Atlantic Bar & Grill	◆◆	American	$16-$27	497
36 / p. 458		Land-Ho Restaurant	◆◆	American	$6-$22	497
37 / p. 458	◬	**Capt'n Elmer's Restaurant & Fish Market**	◆	Seafood	$8-$25	497
38 / p. 458		ABBA	◆◆◆	Mediterranean	$18-$35	497
39 / p. 458		Lobster Pound	◆	Seafood	$8-$23	497
40 / p. 458		Old Jailhouse Tavern	◆◆	American	$7-$26	497

PLYMOUTH

Map Page	OA	Lodgings	Diamond Rated	High Season	Page
39 / p. 458	◬	**Best Western Cold Spring** - see color ad p 547	◆◆◆	$99-$199 SAVE	545
40 / p. 458	◬	**Radisson Hotel Plymouth Harbor** - see color ad p 547	◆◆◆	$144-$414 SAVE	548
41 / p. 458		John Carver Inn & Spa - see color ad p 547	◆◆◆	$99-$329	548
42 / p. 458	◬	**Comfort Inn**	◆◆◆	Rates not provided SAVE	548

PLYMOUTH (cont'd)

Map Page	OA	Lodgings (cont'd)	Diamond Rated	High Season	Page
43 / p. 458		Hampton Inn & Suites - Plymouth Kingston - see color ad p 547	▽▽▽	$99-$159	548
44 / p. 458		Pilgrim Sands on Long Beach - see color ad p 547	▽▽	$84-$195	548
45 / p. 458		Hilton Garden Inn Plymouth	▽▽▽	$99-$199	548
46 / p. 458		Blue Spruce Motel & Townhouses	▽▽	$89-$149	545

Map Page	OA	Restaurants	Diamond Rated	Cuisine	Meal Range	Page
43 / p. 458		The RooBar	▽▽▽	American	$12-$30	550
44 / p. 458		East Bay Grille	▽▽	Seafood	$9-$28	548
45 / p. 458		Lobster Hut	▽	Seafood	$7-$20	549
46 / p. 458		Wood's Seafood	▽	Seafood	$5-$30	550
47 / p. 458		Mamma Mia's Restaurant on the Waterfront	▽▽	Italian	$5-$19	549
48 / p. 458		Isaac's on the Waterfront	▽▽	Seafood	$7-$23	549
49 / p. 458		Water Street Cafe	▽	American	$6-$9	550
50 / p. 458		Stoneforge Plymouth	▽▽	American	$7-$29	550

BREWSTER

Map Page	OA	Lodgings	Diamond Rated	High Season	Page
49 / p. 458		Ocean Edge Resort & Golf Club	▽▽▽	$125-$595	468
50 / p. 458	ⒶⒶⒶ	**Old Sea Pines Inn**	▽▽▽	$85-$165 SAVE	468
51 / p. 458		Pepper House Inn	▽▽▽	$135-$225	469
52 / p. 458		The Bramble Inn	▽▽	$158-$188	467
53 / p. 458		The Captain Freeman Inn	▽▽▽	Rates not provided	468
54 / p. 458		The Candleberry Inn on Cape Cod	▽▽▽	$145-$225	468
55 / p. 458		Old Manse Inn	▽▽▽	$145-$275	468
56 / p. 458		Isaiah Clark House B & B Inn	▽▽▽	$145-$195	468
57 / p. 458		Brewster By The Sea Inn & Spa	▽▽▽	$235-$350	468
58 / p. 458		Michael's Cottages and Bed & Breakfast	▽▽	$100-$200	468

Map Page	OA	Restaurants	Diamond Rated	Cuisine	Meal Range	Page
53 / p. 458		Ocean Grille	▽▽▽	Steak	$11-$42	469
54 / p. 458		Brewster Fish House	▽▽	Seafood	$10-$35	469
55 / p. 458		Bramble Inn & Restaurant	▽▽▽	Continental	$18-$74	469

EAST HARWICH

Map Page	OA	Lodging	Diamond Rated	High Season	Page
61 / p. 458	ⒶⒶⒶ	**Wequassett Resort and Golf Club** - see color ad p 472	▽▽▽▽	$185-$1375 SAVE	477

Map Page	OA	Restaurant	Diamond Rated	Cuisine	Meal Range	Page
58 / p. 458	ⒶⒶⒶ	**twenty-eight Atlantic**	▽▽▽▽	Regional American	$22-$50	477

CHATHAM

Map Page	OA	Lodgings	Diamond Rated	High Season	Page
64 / p. 458		Pleasant Bay Village - see color ad p 472	▽▽▽	$155-$525	473
65 / p. 458		Carriage House Inn	▽▽▽	$169-$289	471
66 / p. 458	ⒶⒶⒶ	**Captain's House Inn of Chatham**	▽▽▽▽	$185-$475 SAVE	470
67 / p. 458		Moses Nickerson House Inn	▽▽▽	$119-$259	472

CHATHAM (cont'd)

Map Page	OA	Lodgings (cont'd)	Diamond Rated	High Season	Page
68 / p. 458		Chatham Highlander	◆◆	$79-$219	471
69 / p. 458	AAA	**Chatham Bars Inn**	◆◆◆◆	$295-$2750 SAVE	471
70 / p. 458		Chatham Seafarer	◆◆	$105-$215	471
71 / p. 458	AAA	**The Old Harbor Inn**	◆◆◆	$129-$329 SAVE	473
72 / p. 458		Chatham Motel	◆◆	$85-$225	471
73 / p. 458		Hawthorne Motel	◆◆	$230-$320	471
74 / p. 458		The Bradford Inn of Chatham	◆◆◆	$115-$550	470
75 / p. 458		Chatham Wayside Inn	◆◆◆	$130-$545	471
76 / p. 458		The Cranberry Inn of Chatham	◆◆◆	$150-$310	471

Map Page	OA	Restaurants	Diamond Rated	Cuisine	Meal Range	Page
61 / p. 458	AAA	**Marley's Restaurant**	◆◆	American	$14-$25	473
62 / p. 458		Pate's	◆◆	American	$14-$26	473
63 / p. 458		Vining's Bistro	◆◆	International	$17-$30	473
64 / p. 458		The Wild Goose Tavern	◆◆	American	$9-$28	473
65 / p. 458		Celestino's Cafe & Bakery	◆◆	Breads/Pastries	$8-$42	473
66 / p. 458		The Impudent Oyster	◆◆	Seafood	$8-$27	473

DENNIS

Map Page	OA	Lodging	Diamond Rated	High Season	Page
79 / p. 458		Isaiah Hall B & B Inn	◆◆◆	$125-$375	474

Map Page	OA	Restaurants	Diamond Rated	Cuisine	Meal Range	Page
69 / p. 458		Scargo Cafe	◆◆	American	$10-$30	474
70 / p. 458		Ice Cream Smuggler	◆	Desserts	$3-$5	474
71 / p. 458		Captain Frosty's	◆	Regional Seafood	$5-$18	474

HARWICH PORT

Map Page	OA	Lodging	Diamond Rated	High Season	Page
82 / p. 458		Alyce's Dunscroft By-The-Sea	◆◆◆	$155-$455	480

Map Page	OA	Restaurants	Diamond Rated	Cuisine	Meal Range	Page
74 / p. 458		L'Alouette Bistro	◆◆◆	French	$22-$32	480
75 / p. 458		Sundae School	◆	Desserts	$3-$7	481
76 / p. 458		The Port	◆◆◆	American	$19-$31	481
77 / p. 458		Hot Stove Saloon	◆	American	$7-$12	480

YARMOUTH PORT

Map Page	OA	Lodgings	Diamond Rated	High Season	Page
85 / p. 458		One Centre Street Inn	◆◆◆	$145-$250	513
86 / p. 458		Inn at Cape Cod	◆◆◆	$195-$345	513

Map Page	OA	Restaurant	Diamond Rated	Cuisine	Meal Range	Page
80 / p. 458		Inaho Japanese Restaurant	◆◆	Japanese	$14-$27	514

BUZZARDS BAY

Map Page	OA	Lodging	Diamond Rated	High Season	Page
89 / p. 458	AAA	**Bay Motor Inn**	◆	$62-$139 SAVE	469

DENNIS PORT

Map Page	OA	Lodging	Diamond Rated	High Season	Page
92 / p. 458		Edgewater Beach Resort	▼▼▼	Rates not provided	475

Map Page	OA	Restaurant	Diamond Rated	Cuisine	Meal Range	Page
83 / p. 458		The Ebb Tide Restaurant	▼▼	Seafood	$17-$32	476

BARNSTABLE

Map Page	OA	Lodging	Diamond Rated	High Season	Page
95 / p. 458		Beechwood Inn	▼▼▼	$140-$210	467

Map Page	OA	Restaurant	Diamond Rated	Cuisine	Meal Range	Page
86 / p. 458		Mattakeese Wharf	▼▼	Seafood	$9-$40	467

WEST BARNSTABLE

Map Page	OA	Lodgings	Diamond Rated	High Season	Page
98 / p. 458		Honeysuckle Hill Bed & Breakfast	▼▼▼	$167-$294	509
99 / p. 458		Bursley Manor	▼▼▼	$195	509
100 / p. 458	AAA	**The Maple Street Inn**	▼▼▼	$135-$249 SAVE	509

SANDWICH

Map Page	OA	Lodgings	Diamond Rated	High Season	Page
103 / p. 458		Shady Nook Inn & Motel	▼	Rates not provided	503
104 / p. 458		The Dan'l Webster Inn & Spa - see color ad p 482	▼▼▼	$179-$399	502
105 / p. 458		Isaiah Jones Homestead	▼▼▼	$190-$300	502
106 / p. 458	AAA	**Country Acres Motel**	▼▼	$74-$129 SAVE	501
107 / p. 458	AAA	**The Earl of Sandwich Motel - see color ad p 502**	▼▼	$75-$129 SAVE	502
108 / p. 458		Spring Garden Inn	▼▼	$79-$130	503
109 / p. 458		Sandy Neck Motel	▼▼	$65-$129	502

Map Page	OA	Restaurants	Diamond Rated	Cuisine	Meal Range	Page
89 / p. 458		Seafood Sam's	▼	Seafood	$7-$18	504
90 / p. 458	AAA	**Aqua Grille**	▼▼▼	American	$9-$25	503
91 / p. 458		The British Beer Company Restaurant & Pub	▼▼	British	$6-$19	503
92 / p. 458		Marshland Restaurant	▼	American	$5-$17	504
93 / p. 458		The Dan'l Webster Inn	▼▼▼	American	$7-$33	504
95 / p. 458		6A Cafe	▼	American	$5-$12	503
96 / p. 458		The Bee-Hive Tavern	▼▼	American	$6-$22	503
97 / p. 458		Amari Bar & Ristorante	▼▼▼	Italian	$11-$31	503

EAST WAREHAM

Map Page	OA	Lodging	Diamond Rated	High Season	Page
112 / p. 458	AAA	**Atlantic Motel**	▼	$90-$200 SAVE	516

Map Page	OA	Restaurants	Diamond Rated	Cuisine	Meal Range	Page
100 / p. 458		Charlie's Place A Family Restaurant	▼	American	$8-$17	516
101 / p. 458	AAA	**Lindsey's Family Restaurant**	▼▼	American	$6-$25	517

CENTERVILLE

Map Page	OA	Lodgings	Diamond Rated	High Season	Page
115 / p. 458		Captain David Kelley House	▼▼▼	$108-$190	470

CENTERVILLE (cont'd)

Map Page	OA	Lodgings (cont'd)	Diamond Rated	High Season	Page
116 / p. 458		Long Dell Inn	◈◈	$145-$185	470

BOURNE

Map Page	OA	Lodging	Diamond Rated	High Season	Page
119 / p. 458		Quality Inn	◈◈	$150-$210	467

WEST FALMOUTH

Map Page	OA	Lodging	Diamond Rated	High Season	Page
122 / p. 458		Chapoquoit Inn Bed & Breakfast	◈◈	$225-$275	509

Map Page	OA	Restaurant	Diamond Rated	Cuisine	Meal Range	Page
113 / p. 458		Chapoquoit Grill	◈◈	American	$10-$23	510

EAST FALMOUTH

Map Page	OA	Lodging	Diamond Rated	High Season	Page
125 / p. 458		Capewind Waterfront Resort	◈◈	$68-$254	476

FALMOUTH

Map Page	OA	Lodgings	Diamond Rated	High Season	Page
128 / p. 458		Holiday Inn Cape Cod/Falmouth	◈◈◈	$159-$289	478
129 / p. 458	AAA	**Inn on the Square**	◈◈◈	$89-$299 SAVE	478
130 / p. 458		Captain Tom Lawrence House Inn	◈◈◈	$140-$270	478
131 / p. 458	AAA	**Mariner Motel**	◈◈	$69-$189 SAVE	479
132 / p. 458		Woods Hole Passage Bed & Breakfast Inn	◈◈◈	$125-$195	479
133 / p. 458	AAA	**Falmouth Heights Motor Lodge**	◈◈	$69-$269 SAVE	478
134 / p. 458	AAA	**Seaside Inn**	◈◈	$79-$319 SAVE	479

Map Page	OA	Restaurants	Diamond Rated	Cuisine	Meal Range	Page
120 / p. 458		Coonamessett Inn Cahoon Dining Room	◈◈◈	Regional American	$9-$32	479
121 / p. 458		Margo's	◈	American	$6-$19	480
122 / p. 458		Quarterdeck Restaurant	◈◈	American	$5-$26	480
123 / p. 458		Peking Palace	◈◈	Asian	$9-$17	480
124 / p. 458		Betsy's Diner	◈	American	$4-$11	479
125 / p. 458		Roo Bar of Falmouth	◈◈	American	$11-$30	480
126 / p. 458		Fire Fly Woodfire Grill & Bar	◈◈	American	$8-$29	479
127 / p. 458		The Golden Swan Fine Indian Cuisine	◈◈	Indian	$6-$20	479
128 / p. 458		La Cucina Sul mare	◈◈	Northern Italian	$6-$20	480
129 / p. 458		British Beer Company Restaurant	◈◈	British	$6-$18	479

WOODS HOLE

Map Page	OA	Lodgings	Diamond Rated	High Season	Page
137 / p. 458	AAA	**Sands of Time Motor Inn**	◈◈	$95-$225 SAVE	513
138 / p. 458	AAA	**Sleepy Hollow Motor Inn**	◈◈	$90-$225 SAVE	513

Map Page	OA	Restaurants	Diamond Rated	Cuisine	Meal Range	Page
132 / p. 458		Phusion Grille	◈◈◈	International	$18-$28	513
133 / p. 458		Fishmonger's Cafe	◈◈	Seafood	$7-$25	513
134 / p. 458		Pie in the Sky Bakery & Internet Cafe	◈	American	$5-$8	513

TRURO

Map Page	OA	Restaurant	Diamond Rated	Cuisine	Meal Range	Page
(4) / p. 458		The Whitman House Restaurant	▽▽	American	$7-$26	508

WELLFLEET

Map Page	OA	Restaurants	Diamond Rated	Cuisine	Meal Range	Page
(15) / p. 458	AAA	**Moby Dick's Family Restaurant**	▽	Seafood	$6-$22	509
(16) / p. 458		Beachcomber	▽	Seafood	$4-$20	508
(17) / p. 458	AAA	**Winslow's Tavern**	▽▽	Mediterranean	$9-$27	509

OSTERVILLE

Map Page	OA	Restaurant	Diamond Rated	Cuisine	Meal Range	Page
(104) / p. 458		Wimpy's Seafood Cafe	▽▽	American	$9-$26	498

COTUIT

Map Page	OA	Restaurant	Diamond Rated	Cuisine	Meal Range	Page
(107) / p. 458	AAA	**The Regatta of Cotuit at the Crocker House**	▽▽▽▽	American	$12-$38	474

NORTH FALMOUTH

Map Page	OA	Restaurant	Diamond Rated	Cuisine	Meal Range	Page
(110) / p. 458	AAA	**Silver Lounge Restaurant**	▽▽	American	$4-$25	492

MASHPEE

Map Page	OA	Restaurants	Diamond Rated	Cuisine	Meal Range	Page
(116) / p. 458		Bleu	▽▽▽	American	$9-$30	491
(117) / p. 458		Simmer	▽▽▽	New American	$19-$32	492

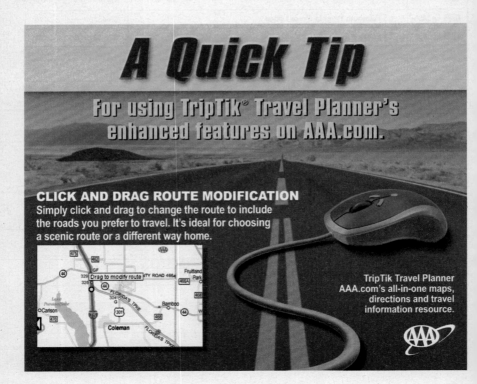

BARNSTABLE pop. 47,821   (See maps and indexes starting on p. 454, 458)

THE ACWORTH INN
▼◆▼◆▼
Historic Bed
& Breakfast
$155-$250 5/1-10/31
$110-$200 11/1-4/30

Phone: (508)362-3330   24

Address: 4352 Main St 02637 **Location:** US 6, exit 7, 0.5 mi w of jct Willow St. **Facility:** The B&B is a comfortable and charming 19th-century house with airy, country decor set among majestic shade trees in an unspoiled area. Smoke free premises. 5 one-bedroom standard units, some with whirlpools. 2 stories (no elevator), interior corridors. *Bath:* combo or shower only. **Parking:** on-site. **Terms:** office hours 10 am-8 pm, 2 night minimum stay - seasonal, 14 day cancellation notice-fee imposed. **Amenities:** CD players, irons, hair dryers. *Some:* DVD players. **Guest Services:** wireless Internet.
ASK ⊠ ☎ / SOME UNITS 📺 🛏

ASHLEY MANOR INN
▼◆▼◆▼
Historic Bed
& Breakfast
$185-$245 5/1-10/31
$160-$185 11/1-4/30

Phone: 508/362-8044   25

Address: 3660 Main St 02630 **Location:** On US 6A, 0.6 mi e. **Facility:** Boxwood hedges, mature trees and manicured lawns lend a gracious ambiance to the inn's two-acre grounds; all but one unit have a fireplace. Smoke free premises. 6 units. 5 one- and 1 two-bedroom standard units, some with whirlpools. 2 stories (no elevator), interior corridors. **Parking:** on-site. **Terms:** office hours 8 am-10 pm, 2 night minimum stay, age restrictions may apply, 14 day cancellation notice-fee imposed. **Amenities:** DVD players, voice mail, hair dryers. *Some:* irons. **Leisure Activities:** tennis court. **Guest Services:** wireless Internet. ⊠ 🖥 / SOME UNITS 🛏

BEECHWOOD INN
▼◆▼◆▼
Historic Bed
& Breakfast
$140-$210 All Year

Phone: (508)362-6618   95

Address: 2839 Main St (SR 6A) 02630 **Location:** US 6A, 0.8 mi w. **Facility:** Guest rooms, three of which have a fireplace, at this restored Queen Anne-style home are furnished with lovely antiques. Smoke free premises. 6 one-bedroom standard units. 3 stories (no elevator), interior/exterior corridors. *Bath:* combo or shower only. **Parking:** on-site. **Terms:** office hours 7 am-9 pm, 2-3 night minimum stay - seasonal and/or weekends, age restrictions may apply, 15 day cancellation notice-fee imposed. **Amenities:** hair dryers. *Some:* DVD players, irons. **Guest Services:** wireless Internet.
🍴+ ⊠ ☎ 🛏

—— WHERE TO DINE ——

BARNSTABLE RESTAURANT & TAVERN
▼◆▼◆▼
American
$8-$26

Phone: 508/362-2355   32

This restaurant, located opposite the courthouse, has been a tavern since the late 1700s. Passionate cooking and friendly service will be found here, with a large menu featuring Cape Cod American cuisine created by Chef Bob Calderone. Dining on the patio under large umbrellas and weekend evening entertainment are seasonal, weather-permitting, occurrences. Casual dress. **Bar:** Full bar. **Reservations:** accepted. **Hours:** 11:30 am-9 pm; seasonal hours vary. Closed: 12/25. **Address:** 3176 Main St 02630 **Location:** On SR 6A; center. **Parking:** on-site.

DOLPHIN RESTAURANT
▼◆▼◆
American
$8-$26

Phone: 508/362-6610   33

Patrons can experience traditional New England fare with an updated twist at the popular, third-generation family eatery. Lighter dishes, salads and entrees feature largely fresh, local seafood, chicken, beef, veal and lamb. Most desserts and sauces are made on the premises. A white picket fence and flower gardens line the brick sidewalk in front of this single-story clapboard and cedar shake building. Light pine-paneled walls are hung with original art. Service is casual and folksy. Casual dress. **Bar:** Full bar. **Reservations:** accepted. **Hours:** 11:30 am-3 & 5-9:30 pm, Fri & Sat-10 pm, Sun 5 pm-9:30 pm. Closed: 11/25, 12/25. **Address:** 3250 Main St 02630 **Location:** On US 6A; center. **Parking:** on-site.

MATTAKEESE WHARF
▼◆▼◆
Seafood
$9-$40

Phone: 508/362-4511   86

Open-walled perimeter decks surround a nautically themed dining room and lounge, a local landmark for 35 years. Fresh local seafood is a specialty, but steak, chops and pasta are also offered. Patrons can expect a wait to sit on the deck to watch the sunset; plenty of others like to do the same. Casual dress. Entertainment. **Bar:** Full bar. **Reservations:** accepted, for dinner. **Hours:** Open 5/1-10/31; 11:30 am-9 pm. **Address:** 271 Mill Way 02630 **Location:** 0.5 mi n of US 6A; overlooking Barnstable Harbor. **Parking:** on-site. 🎵

BOURNE pop. 1,443   (See map and index starting on p. 458)

QUALITY INN   *Book at AAA.com*
▼◆▼◆▼
Hotel
$150-$210 7/1-4/30
$120-$170 5/1-6/30

Phone: (508)759-0800   119

Address: 100 Trowbridge Rd 02532 **Location:** Just w of rotary on Cape Cod side of bridge on SR 28. **Facility:** Smoke free premises. 43 one-bedroom standard units, some with whirlpools. 2 stories (no elevator), interior corridors. **Parking:** on-site. **Terms:** 2 night minimum stay - seasonal and/or weekends, 3 day cancellation notice-fee imposed. **Amenities:** voice mail, irons, hair dryers. **Pool(s):** heated indoor. **Leisure Activities:** whirlpool. **Guest Services:** wireless Internet. **Business Services:** PC. ASK 🍴 🍸 🏊 ⊠ 🛏 🖥 🖥

BREWSTER pop. 2,212   (See map and index starting on p. 458)

THE BRAMBLE INN
▼◆▼◆ ▼◆▼◆
Country Inn
$158-$188 5/1-12/31 &
4/15-4/30

Phone: 508/896-7644   52

Address: 2019 Main St 02631 **Location:** On SR 6A, just e of jct SR 124. **Facility:** Smoke free premises. 5 one-bedroom standard units. 2 stories (no elevator), interior corridors. *Bath:* combo or shower only. **Parking:** on-site. **Terms:** open 5/1-12/31 & 4/15-4/30, office hours 9 am-9 pm, 2 night minimum stay - weekends, 14 day cancellation notice-fee imposed. **Amenities:** irons, hair dryers. **Dining:** restaurant, see separate listing. **Guest Services:** wireless Internet. **Business Services:** fax.
 ASK 🍴 ⊠ ☎

(See map and index starting on p. 458)

BREWSTER BY THE SEA INN & SPA
Phone: 508/896-3910　[57]

▼▼▼▼▼
Bed & Breakfast
$235-$350 5/1-11/30
$135-$175 12/1-4/30

Address: 716 Main St 02631 **Location:** 2.2 mi w on SR 6A of jct SR 124. **Facility:** Built in 1850, the former farmhouse has a handsome decor; a landscaped deck and pool area offers guests a peaceful spot to relax. Smoke free premises. 8 units. 6 one-bedroom standard units, some with whirlpools. 2 one-bedroom suites. 2 stories (no elevator), interior corridors. *Bath:* combo or shower only. **Parking:** on-site. **Terms:** office hours 7 am-9 pm, 2-3 night minimum stay - seasonal and/or weekends, 14 day cancellation notice-fee imposed. **Amenities:** DVD players, irons, hair dryers. **Pool(s):** heated outdoor. **Leisure Activities:** whirlpool. **Guest Services:** wireless Internet. **Business Services:** PC, fax (fee).

ASK ⬤ ✕ ♿ / SOME UNITS 🖥 💻

THE CANDLEBERRY INN ON CAPE COD
Phone: 508/896-3300　[54]

▼▼▼▼▼
Historic Bed & Breakfast
$145-$225 5/1-10/31
$125-$195 11/1-4/30

Address: 1882 Main St 02631 **Location:** On SR 6A, 0.3 mi w of jct SR 124. **Facility:** The 1800s Federal-style home features attractive guest rooms furnished with antiques; some rooms have a fireplace; a full breakfast is served daily. Smoke free premises. 8 units. 7 one-bedroom standard units. 1 one-bedroom suite. 2 stories (no elevator), interior corridors. *Bath:* combo or shower only. **Parking:** on-site. **Terms:** office hours 8 am-8 pm, 2 night minimum stay - seasonal and/or weekends, 14 day cancellation notice-fee imposed. **Amenities:** video library, DVD players, irons, hair dryers. *Some:* CD players. **Guest Services:** wireless Internet.　📶 ✕ ☎ / SOME UNITS 🖥

THE CAPTAIN FREEMAN INN
Phone: 508/896-7481　[53]

▼▼▼▼▼
Historic Bed & Breakfast
Rates not provided

Address: 15 Breakwater Rd 02631 **Location:** On SR 6A, just e of jct SR 124. Located in a residential area. **Facility:** Believed to have been built in 1860 for an aristocratic shipmaster, the inn features guest rooms with antique furnishings. Smoke free premises. 12 one-bedroom standard units, some with whirlpools. 3 stories (no elevator), interior corridors. **Parking:** on-site. **Terms:** office hours 8 am-7 pm, age restrictions may apply. **Amenities:** video library, hair dryers. **Pool(s):** heated outdoor. **Leisure Activities:** bicycles.　📶 🍽 ⬤ ✕ / SOME UNITS 📶 ☎ 🖥

ISAIAH CLARK HOUSE B & B INN
Phone: 508/896-2223　[56]

▼▼▼▼▼
Historic Bed & Breakfast
$145-$195 5/1-11/7

Address: 1187 Main St 02631 **Location:** On SR 6A, 1.5 mi w of SR 124. **Facility:** The former sea captain's home, less than a mile from the beach, offers modern comforts with a Colonial motif; an impressive breakfast is served daily. Smoke free premises. 7 one-bedroom standard units. 2 stories (no elevator), interior corridors. **Parking:** on-site. **Terms:** open 5/1-11/7, office hours 10 am-7 pm, 2 night minimum stay - seasonal and/or weekends, age restrictions may apply, 14 day cancellation notice-fee imposed. **Amenities:** hair dryers. **Guest Services:** wireless Internet. **Business Services:** fax.　ASK ✕ ☎

MICHAEL'S COTTAGES AND BED & BREAKFAST
Phone: 508/896-4025　[58]

▼▼▼ ▼▼▼
Cottage
$100-$200 All Year

Address: 618 Main St 02631 **Location:** On SR 6A, 2.3 mi w of SR 124. **Facility:** Smoke free premises. 7 units. 2 one-bedroom standard units. 1 house and 4 cottages. 1-2 stories (no elevator), exterior corridors. *Bath:* combo or shower only. **Parking:** on-site. **Terms:** office hours 8 am-11 pm, 2 night minimum stay - seasonal and/or weekends, 14 day cancellation notice-fee imposed. **Amenities:** hair dryers. *Some:* DVD players, irons. **Guest Services:** wireless Internet.

ASK ✕ / SOME UNITS 🖥 📺 💻

OCEAN EDGE RESORT & GOLF CLUB　*Book at AAA.com*
Phone: (508)896-9000　[49]

▼▼▼▼▼
Resort
Hotel
$125-$595 5/1-10/31
$99-$295 11/1-4/30

Address: 2907 Main St 02631 **Location:** On SR 6A, 2.3 mi e of SR 124. **Facility:** Set on 1,200 acres, the resort offers some units with Cape Cod Bay views; guest may select from hotel-style rooms and one-, two- and three-bedroom villas. Smoke free premises. 335 units. 291 one-bedroom standard units. 2 one-, 17 two- and 25 three-bedroom suites, some with whirlpools. 2 stories (no elevator), interior/exterior corridors. **Parking:** on-site. **Terms:** check-in 4 pm, 14 day cancellation notice-fee imposed. **Amenities:** voice mail, irons, hair dryers. *Some:* DVD players (fee), safes. **Dining:** Ocean Grille, see separate listing. **Pool(s):** 3 outdoor, heated outdoor, 2 heated indoor. **Leisure Activities:** saunas, whirlpools, limited beach access, playground, exercise room, basketball, volleyball. *Fee:* golf-18 holes, 11 tennis courts, bicycles. **Guest Services:** valet laundry, area transportation, wireless Internet. **Business Services:** conference facilities, business center.

ASK 🍽 🍴 ⬤ ✕ ✕ 💻 / SOME UNITS 🖥

OLD MANSE INN
Phone: (508)896-3149　[55]

▼▼▼▼▼
Historic Bed & Breakfast
$145-$275 5/1-10/15
$125-$250 10/16-4/30

Address: 1861 Main St 02631 **Location:** On SR 6A, 0.3 mi w of jct SR 124. **Facility:** Dating from 1807, the inn's guest rooms feature distinct decor with a New England nautical theme; some units include antiques and a flat-panel HDTV. Smoke free premises. 12 one-bedroom standard units, some with whirlpools. 3 stories (no elevator), interior corridors. *Bath:* combo or shower only. **Parking:** on-site. **Terms:** office hours 9 am-9 pm, 2-3 night minimum stay - seasonal and/or weekends, age restrictions may apply, 14 day cancellation notice-fee imposed. **Amenities:** DVD players, hair dryers. *Some:* CD players. **Leisure Activities:** bicycles. **Guest Services:** wireless Internet.　ASK ✕ ☎

OLD SEA PINES INN
Phone: (508)896-6114　[50]

🔺🔺🔺 SAVE
▼▼▼▼▼
Historic Bed & Breakfast
$85-$165 All Year

Address: 2553 Main St 02631 **Location:** On SR 6A, 1.3 mi e of jct SR 124. **Facility:** Formerly a girls-only finishing school, the inn has the atmosphere of a 1930s summer home; some guest rooms are situated in outlying buildings. Smoke free premises. 24 units. 21 one- and 2 two-bedroom standard units. 1 one-bedroom suite with efficiency. 3 stories (no elevator), interior/exterior corridors. *Bath:* some shared or private, combo or shower only. **Parking:** on-site. **Terms:** office hours 8 am-10 pm, 2-3 night minimum stay - seasonal and/or weekends, 14 day cancellation notice-fee imposed. **Amenities:** irons, hair dryers. *Some:* DVD players. **Leisure Activities:** croquet. **Guest Services:** wireless Internet. **Business Services:** meeting rooms, PC. **Free Special Amenities:** full breakfast and high-speed Internet.　✕ ☎ / SOME UNITS 📶 🖥 📺

(See map and index starting on p. 458)

PEPPER HOUSE INN

Historic Bed
& Breakfast
$135-$225 All Year

Phone: (508)896-2062   **51**

Address: 2062 Main St 02631 **Location:** On SR 6A, just e of SR 124. **Facility:** The circa-1793 Colonial home features many original aspects, such as the wood floors and woodwork; a full breakfast is served daily 8 to 9:30 am. Smoke free premises. 4 one-bedroom standard units. 2 stories (no elevator), interior corridors. *Bath:* combo or shower only. **Parking:** on-site. **Terms:** office hours 8 am-9 pm, 2 night minimum stay - seasonal and/or weekends, 14 day cancellation notice-fee imposed. **Amenities:** hair dryers. **Guest Services:** wireless Internet. [ASK] [📶] [✕] [🅿] / SOME UNITS [🛏]

—— WHERE TO DINE ——

BRAMBLE INN & RESTAURANT

Continental
$18-$74

Phone: 508/896-7644   **55**

A professional, attentive wait staff caters to guests in the cozy surroundings of a restored 1861 house. The four-course menu offers creatively prepared appetizers and entrées. Daily selections feature varied fare with an emphasis on fresh seafood. Dressy casual. **Bar:** Full bar. **Reservations:** suggested. **Hours:** Open 5/1-12/31 & 4/1-4/30; 5:30 pm-9 pm, Fri & Sat-9:30 pm; seasonal hours vary. Closed: 12/24, 12/25. **Address:** 2019 Main St 02631 **Location:** On SR 6A, just e of jct SR 124; in The Bramble Inn. **Parking:** on-site. **Historic**

BREWSTER FISH HOUSE

Seafood
$10-$35

Phone: 508/896-7867   **54**

You're in for quite a treat: shrimp and linguine with sun-dried tomatoes and a huge house salad. Fresh seafood is the specialty, but there is also a great selection of pasta to choose from while prompt and efficient staffers cater to your needs. Very popular restaurant; due to limited seating, you can expect a wait. Casual dress. **Bar:** Full bar. **Hours:** 11:30 am-3 & 5-9:30 pm, Sun from noon; seasonal hours may vary. Closed: 1/1, 11/25, 12/24, 12/25. **Address:** 2208 Main St 02631 **Location:** On SR 6A, 0.5 mi e of jct SR 124. **Parking:** on-site.

OCEAN GRILLE

Steak
$11-$42

Phone: 508/896-9000   **53**

Lending to the dining room's nautical theme are model sailboats along the walls and large windows overlooking the grounds. The menu lists steak and seafood prepared with a decorative flair. Casual dress. **Bar:** Full bar. **Reservations:** suggested. **Hours:** 7 am-11 & 5-9 pm; seasonal hours vary. **Address:** 2907 Main St 02631 **Location:** On SR 6A, 2.3 mi e of SR 124; in Ocean Edge Resort & Golf Club. **Parking:** on-site and valet.

BUZZARDS BAY pop. 3,549   (See map and index starting on p. 458)

BAY MOTOR INN

Cottage
$62-$139 5/1-10/25 &
4/1-4/30

Phone: (508)759-3989   **89**

Address: 223 Main St 02532 **Location:** SR 25, 0.5 mi w of Bourne rotary, exit 3. **Facility:** 17 units. 8 one-bedroom standard units, some with efficiencies. 9 cottages. 1 story, exterior corridors. *Bath:* combo or shower only. **Parking:** on-site. **Terms:** open 5/1-10/25 & 4/1-4/30, office hours 7 am-11 pm, 2 night minimum stay - weekends, 7 day cancellation notice-fee imposed. **Pool(s):** outdoor. **Free Special Amenities: local telephone calls and preferred room (subject to availability with advance reservations).** [📶] [🏊] [🐾] [🛏] / SOME UNITS FEE [🐾] [✕] [🖥] [📺]

CENTERVILLE (See maps and indexes starting on p. 454, 458)

CAPTAIN DAVID KELLEY HOUSE

▼◇▼◇▼
Bed & Breakfast
$108-$190 All Year

Phone: 508/775-4707 **115**

Address: 539 Main St 02632 **Location:** 0.9 mi s of SR 28. **Facility:** This Greek-Revival home was originally built in 1835 for Captain David Kelley; a full breakfast, including homemade scones, is served each morning. Smoke free premises. 6 units. 5 one- and 1 two-bedroom standard units. 2 stories (no elevator), interior corridors. *Bath:* combo or shower only. **Parking:** on-site. **Terms:** office hours 7 am-9 pm, 2 night minimum stay - seasonal and/or weekends, age restrictions may apply, 15 day cancellation notice-fee imposed. **Amenities:** CD players, irons, hair dryers. *Some:* DVD players. **Guest Services:** wireless Internet. (ASK) (¶⁺) (✕) (☎) (▭)

LONG DELL INN

▼◇▼◇▼
Bed & Breakfast
$145-$185 5/1-12/15

Phone: 508/775-2750 **116**

Address: 436 S Main St 02632 **Location:** SR 28, 1.5 mi s, just w. **Facility:** Smoke free premises. 6 one-bedroom standard units. 2 stories (no elevator), interior/exterior corridors. *Bath:* combo or shower only. **Parking:** on-site. **Terms:** open 5/1-12/15, office hours 8 am-10 pm, 2 night minimum stay - seasonal and/or weekends, 14 day cancellation notice-fee imposed. **Amenities:** irons, hair dryers. **Guest Services:** wireless Internet. **Business Services:** PC. (ASK) (✕) (☎)

CHATHAM pop. 1,667 (See map and index starting on p. 458)

THE BRADFORD INN OF CHATHAM *Book at AAA.com*

▼◇▼◇▼
Hotel
$115-$550 5/1-10/16
$115-$340 10/17-4/30

Phone: (508)945-1030 **74**

Address: 26 Cross St 02633 **Location:** Just e of rotary, just off Main St; downtown. **Facility:** Smoke free premises. 42 units. 34 one-bedroom standard units, some with whirlpools. 8 one-bedroom suites, some with whirlpools. 1-2 stories (no elevator), interior corridors. *Bath:* combo or shower only. **Parking:** on-site. **Terms:** office hours 8 am-10 pm, check-in 4 pm, 1-3 night minimum stay - seasonal and/or weekends, age restrictions may apply, 21 day cancellation notice-fee imposed. **Amenities:** video library, DVD players, CD players, irons, hair dryers. **Pool(s):** heated outdoor. **Leisure Activities:** exercise room. **Guest Services:** wireless Internet. **Business Services:** PC. (¶⁺) CALL (🛗) (🏊) (✕)

CAPTAIN'S HOUSE INN OF CHATHAM *Book great rates at AAA.com*

(AAA) (SAVE)
▼◇▼◇▼ ▼◇▼◇▼
Bed & Breakfast
$185-$475 All Year

Phone: (508)945-0127 **66**

Address: 369 Old Harbor Rd 02633 **Location:** 0.8 mi n of rotary on SR 28. **Facility:** Fine antiques and elegantly furnished rooms, many with fireplaces, characterize this inn dating from 1839. Smoke free premises. 16 units. 12 one-bedroom standard units, some with whirlpools. 4 one-bedroom suites, some with whirlpools. 2 stories (no elevator), interior/exterior corridors. *Bath:* combo or shower only. **Parking:** on-site. **Terms:** office hours 7 am-11 pm, 2-4 night minimum stay - seasonal and/or weekends, age restrictions may apply, 14 day cancellation notice-fee imposed. **Amenities:** video library, DVD players, CD players, voice mail, irons, hair dryers. **Pool(s):** heated outdoor. **Leisure Activities:** lawn games. **Guest Services:** wireless Internet. **Business Services:** PC. Free Special Amenities: full breakfast and high-speed Internet. (🏊) FEE (✚) (✕) / SOME UNITS (🗄) (▭)

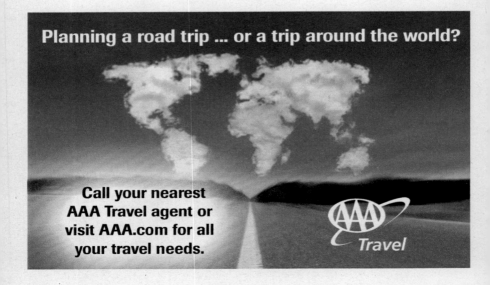

(See map and index starting on p. 458)

CARRIAGE HOUSE INN

Bed & Breakfast
$169-$289 5/1-10/31
$139-$209 11/1-4/30

Phone: 508/945-4688 65

Address: 407 Old Harbor Rd 02633 **Location:** 1 mi n of rotary on SR 28 S; entrance off Orleans Rd. **Facility:** This 1860 inn is furnished with antiques and reproductions; two guest rooms have canopy beds. Smoke free premises. 6 one-bedroom standard units. 2 stories (no elevator), interior/exterior corridors. *Bath:* shower only. **Parking:** on-site. **Terms:** office hours 9 am-8 pm, 2-3 night minimum stay - seasonal and/or weekends, age restrictions may apply, 21 day cancellation notice-fee imposed. **Amenities:** video library, DVD players, CD players, irons, hair dryers. **Leisure Activities:** *Fee:* massage. **Guest Services:** wireless Internet. **Business Services:** PC. [icons]

CHATHAM BARS INN   *Book great rates at AAA.com*

AAA SAVE

Resort Hotel
$295-$2750 5/1-11/28
$195-$1235 11/29-4/30

Phone: (508)945-0096 69

Address: 297 Shore Rd 02633 **Location:** Oceanfront. 0.8 mi e of rotary on Main St, 0.8 mi n. **Facility:** As evident in the attentive staff, architectural style and attention to detail, the inn is a destination resort with an Old World charm. Smoke free premises. 217 units. 171 one-bedroom standard units, some with whirlpools. 45 one- and 1 two-bedroom suites, some with whirlpools. 2-3 stories (no elevator), interior/exterior corridors. *Bath:* combo or shower only. **Parking:** on-site and valet. **Terms:** check-in 4 pm, 2-7 night minimum stay - seasonal and/or weekends, 60 day cancellation notice-fee imposed. **Amenities:** CD players, voice mail, safes, honor bars, irons, hair dryers. *Some:* DVD players. **Dining:** 2 restaurants. **Pool(s):** heated outdoor. **Leisure Activities:** limited beach access, 3 tennis courts, recreation programs in season, lawn games,, rental bicycles, exercise room, spa. *Fee:* charter fishing, hydrotherapy pool, harbor tour. **Guest Services:** valet laundry, area transportation-within 5 mi, wireless Internet. **Business Services:** conference facilities, business center. **Free Special Amenities: local telephone calls and high-speed Internet.**
[icons]

CHATHAM HIGHLANDER

[icons]

Motel
$79-$219 5/1-10/31
$79-$129 11/1-4/30

Phone: (508)945-9038 68

Address: 946 Main St 02633 **Location:** 0.5 mi w of rotary on SR 28. **Facility:** Smoke free premises. 28 units. 26 one- and 1 two-bedroom standard units, some with efficiencies. 1 one-bedroom suite with kitchen. 1 story, exterior corridors. *Bath:* combo or shower only. **Parking:** on-site. **Terms:** office hours 8 am-10 pm, 2-3 night minimum stay - seasonal and/or weekends, 14 day cancellation notice-fee imposed. **Pool(s):** 2 heated outdoor. **Leisure Activities:** shuffleboard. **Guest Services:** wireless Internet. [icons] / SOME UNITS [icon]

CHATHAM MOTEL

[icons]

Motel
$85-$225 5/1-10/31

Phone: 508/945-2630 72

Address: 1487 Main St 02633 **Location:** 1.8 mi w of rotary on SR 28 N. **Facility:** Smoke free premises. 32 one-bedroom standard units, some with kitchens. 1-2 stories (no elevator), interior/exterior corridors. **Parking:** on-site. **Terms:** open 5/1-10/31, office hours 8:30 am-10 pm, 2 night minimum stay - weekends, 14 day cancellation notice-fee imposed. **Pool(s):** outdoor. **Guest Services:** wireless Internet. [ASK] [icons] / SOME UNITS [icon]

CHATHAM SEAFARER   *Book at AAA.com*

Motel
$105-$215 6/15-12/1
$105-$155 5/1-6/14

Phone: (508)432-1739 70

Address: 2079 Main St 02633 **Location:** 2.8 mi w of rotary on SR 28. **Facility:** Smoke free premises. 20 one-bedroom standard units, some with efficiencies. 1 story, exterior corridors. **Parking:** on-site. **Terms:** open 5/1-12/1, office hours 8 am-10 pm, 3 night minimum stay - seasonal and/or weekends, 15 day cancellation notice-fee imposed. **Amenities:** hair dryers. *Some:* irons. **Pool(s):** heated outdoor. **Guest Services:** wireless Internet. [icons] / SOME UNITS [icon]

CHATHAM WAYSIDE INN   *Book at AAA.com*

[icons]

Hotel
$130-$545 All Year

Phone: (508)945-5550 75

Address: 512 Main St 02633 **Location:** 0.3 mi e of rotary; downtown. **Facility:** Smoke free premises. 56 units. 55 one-bedroom standard units, some with whirlpools. 1 one-bedroom suite with whirlpool. 3 stories, interior corridors. *Bath:* combo or shower only. **Parking:** on-site. **Terms:** check-in 4 pm, 2-3 night minimum stay - seasonal and/or weekends, 21 day cancellation notice-fee imposed. **Amenities:** video library, DVD players, CD players, voice mail, irons, hair dryers. **Dining:** The Wild Goose Tavern, see separate listing. **Pool(s):** heated outdoor. **Leisure Activities:** exercise room. **Guest Services:** wireless Internet. **Business Services:** meeting rooms, PC. [icons] CALL [icons]

THE CRANBERRY INN OF CHATHAM

[icons]

Bed & Breakfast
$150-$310 5/1-10/25
$120-$190 10/26-4/30

Phone: 508/945-9232 76

Address: 359 Main St 02633 **Location:** 0.5 mi e of rotary. **Facility:** Originally built in 1830, this restored inn features some premier rooms with a working fireplace; a complimentary beverage is served each afternoon. Smoke free premises. 18 units. 15 one- and 1 two-bedroom standard units. 1 one- and 1 two-bedroom suites. 2 stories (no elevator), interior corridors. *Bath:* combo or shower only. **Parking:** on-site. **Terms:** office hours 8 am-9 pm, 2-3 night minimum stay - seasonal and/or weekends, 30 day cancellation notice-fee imposed. **Amenities:** hair dryers. **Guest Services:** wireless Internet. [icons] / SOME UNITS [icon]

HAWTHORNE MOTEL

Motel
$230-$320 6/20-10/15
$175-$255 5/15-6/19

Phone: 508/945-0372 73

Address: 196 Shore Rd 02633 **Location:** Oceanfront. 0.8 mi e of rotary via Main St, 0.5 mi n. **Facility:** Smoke free premises. 27 units. 26 one-bedroom standard units, some with efficiencies. 1 cottage. 1 story, exterior corridors. **Parking:** on-site. **Terms:** open 5/15-10/15, office hours 6 am-8 pm, 4 night minimum stay - seasonal and/or weekends, 30 day cancellation notice-fee imposed. **Amenities:** hair dryers. **Leisure Activities:** limited beach access. **Guest Services:** wireless Internet. **Business Services:** PC. [icons] / SOME UNITS [icon]

(See map and index starting on p. 458)

MOSES NICKERSON HOUSE INN

Bed & Breakfast
$119-$259 All Year

Phone: 508/945-5859   67

Address: 364 Old Harbor Rd 02633 **Location:** 0.8 mi n of rotary on SR 28 S. **Facility:** Wide pine-plank floors, many fireplaces, antique furnishings and colorful gardens distinguish this inn built in 1839. Smoke free premises. 7 one-bedroom standard units. 2 stories (no elevator), interior corridors. *Bath:* combo or shower only. **Parking:** on-site. **Terms:** office hours 9 am-9 pm, 2-3 night minimum stay - seasonal and/or weekends, age restrictions may apply, 14 day cancellation notice-fee imposed. **Amenities:** irons, hair dryers. *Some:* DVD players, CD players. **Guest Services:** wireless Internet. **Business Services:** PC. ☒

▼ See AAA listing p 473 ▼

▼ See AAA listing p 477 ▼

AAA.com/TravelGuide ... Destination
Information and Ideas.

(See map and index starting on p. 458)

THE OLD HARBOR INN

Bed & Breakfast
$129-$329 All Year

Phone: (508)945-4434 **71**

Address: 22 Old Harbor Rd 02633 **Location:** On SR 28, just n of rotary. Located in a residential area. **Facility:** Nestled in a quiet residential area, this English country-style inn features two guest rooms with a gas fireplace offering a warm, romantic ambiance. Smoke free premises. 9 units. 8 one-bedroom standard units. 1 one-bedroom suite with whirlpool. 2 stories (no elevator), interior/exterior corridors. **Parking:** on-site. **Terms:** office hours 8 am-9 pm, 2-4 night minimum stay - seasonal and/or weekends, 14 day cancellation notice-fee imposed. **Amenities:** video library, CD players, hair dryers. *Some:* DVD players. **Leisure Activities:** exercise room. **Guest Services:** wireless Internet. **Business Services:** fax (fee). **Free Special Amenities: full breakfast and high-speed Internet.**

 / SOME UNITS

PLEASANT BAY VILLAGE

Hotel
$155-$525 5/1-10/26

Phone: (508)945-1133 **64**

Address: 1191 Orleans Rd 02633 **Location:** From rotary, just n on Old Harbor Rd, 2 mi ne on SR 28. Amidst extensive Oriental-style gardens. Smoke free premises. 58 units. 48 one-bedroom standard units, some with efficiencies and/or whirlpools. 2 one-bedroom suites with kitchens and whirlpools. 8 cottages. 1 story, exterior corridors. *Bath:* combo or shower only. **Parking:** on-site. **Terms:** open 5/1-10/26, office hours 8 am-11 pm, 2-3 night minimum stay - seasonal and/or weekends, 30 day cancellation notice-fee imposed. **Amenities:** voice mail, irons, hair dryers. *Some:* DVD players. **Pool(s):** heated outdoor. **Leisure Activities:** whirlpool, playground, shuffleboard, game room. **Guest Services:** coin laundry, wireless Internet. **Business Services:** PC. **(See color ad p 472)**

—— WHERE TO DINE ——

CELESTINO'S CAFE & BAKERY

Breads/Pastries
$8-$42

Phone: 508/945-9700 **65**

This French bakery-themed restaurant serves organic free-trade coffee, soups, salads and sandwiches. Some house-baked desserts, including popular cupcakes, are on display in glass cases near the takeout area. Those hoping to dine inside shouldn't be taken aback by the elegant suede upholstered chairs and cloth-covered table service, as this place is casual and the service makes guests feel at home. Comfortable resort clothes are entirely appropriate. Numerous crepes and gourmet omelets are available for breakfast, while lunch offerings include the twin Indonesian lump crab cakes atop baby arugula with spicy tomato remoulade or roasted Cuban pork sandwich with smoked ham, Swiss cheese, yellow mustard and pickled cucumbers served on a ciabatta roll. Casual dress. **Bar:** Beer & wine. **Reservations:** accepted. **Hours:** Open 5/1-11/20 & 2/1-4/30; 8 am-8 pm, Thurs-Sat to 10 pm. Closed major holidays. **Address:** 513 Main St 02633 **Location:** 0.3 mi e of rotary. **Parking:** on-site. CALL

THE IMPUDENT OYSTER

Seafood
$8-$27

Phone: 508/945-3545 **66**

Locals find the American cuisine served here a shining star. Distinctively prepared local seafood and other fare boast international influences. Attentive service and casual surroundings make this place a popular stop. Casual dress. **Bar:** Full bar. **Reservations:** suggested, for dinner. **Hours:** 11:30 am-3 & 5-10 pm, Sun from noon; closing hours may vary Sun-Thurs. Closed: 11/25, 12/25; also for dinner 12/24. **Address:** 15 Chatham Bars Ave 02633 **Location:** Off Main St, 0.3 mi e of rotary. **Parking:** street.

MARLEY'S RESTAURANT

American
$14-$25

Phone: 508/945-1700 **61**

Named for the family cat, the family-friendly, family-operated eatery lets patrons enjoy seafood fried, broiled or Cajun-style. Steaks are chargrilled, and prime rib is slow-roasted. Also on the menu are steamed lobster and a vegetarian selection. Not that hungry? Try one of the many sandwiches or salads. Table linens, fresh flowers, lots of natural wood and greenery give this place a warm, inviting look. The patio is open in good weather. Service is upbeat and friendly. Casual dress. **Bar:** Full bar. **Reservations:** not accepted. **Hours:** Open 5/1-12/24; 5 pm-close. Closed: 11/25. **Address:** 1077 Main St 02633 **Location:** 0.7 mi w of rotary on SR 28. **Parking:** on-site. CALL

PATE'S

American
$14-$26

Phone: 508/945-9777 **62**

The menu offers a variety of simply prepared but decidedly fresh entrees which includes fresh local seafood, fish, steak and poultry. The good food, casual setting and efficient, friendly wait staff are very popular with locals and tourists alike. 2 lb lobsters are a favorite-boiled and baked. Casual dress. **Bar:** Full bar. **Hours:** Open 5/1-1/15 & 4/1-4/30; 5:30 pm-9:30 pm; Sun-Thurs to 9 pm 9/7-1/15. Closed: 11/25, 12/24, 12/25. **Address:** 1260 Main St 02633 **Location:** 1.3 mi w of rotary on SR 28. **Parking:** on-site.

VINING'S BISTRO

International
$17-$30

Phone: 508/945-5033 **63**

In the upstairs section of a shopping building, this intimate bistro serves expertly prepared cuisine in a tavern-like atmosphere. House-made mozzarella with heirloom tomatoes and stuffed peppers over arugula are tasty starters to whet the appetite. Entrees include Kobe beef short ribs, Tuscan chicken and Portuguese-style Chatham scrod served in a sizzling cast-iron skillet. Casual dress. **Bar:** Full bar. **Reservations:** suggested. **Hours:** Open 5/1-12/31 & 4/1-4/30; 5:30 pm-9 pm, Fri & Sat-10 pm; seasonal hours may vary. **Address:** 595 Main St 02633 **Location:** Corner of Main and Seaview sts; downtown; in the Gallery Building upstairs. **Parking:** street.

THE WILD GOOSE TAVERN

American
$9-$28

Phone: 508/945-5550 **64**

A great spot for a quick bite for lunch, dinner or with drinks, the tavern is inside Chatham Wayside Inn and is convenient to shops. Casual dress. **Bar:** Full bar. **Reservations:** accepted. **Hours:** Open 5/1-12/31 & 2/1-4/30; 8 am-9 pm; hours vary off season. **Address:** 512 Main St 02633 **Location:** 0.3 mi e of rotary; in Chatham Wayside Inn. **Parking:** on-site. CALL

COTUIT   (See map and index starting on p. 458)

------ WHERE TO DINE ------

THE REGATTA OF COTUIT AT THE CROCKER HOUSE

Phone: 508/428-5715   107

American
$12-$38

In a 200-plus-year-old dark-red Victorian that was once a stagecoach inn, the restaurant offers diners an extensive menu of New American cuisine prepared with Asian and Continental influences. Farm-raised buffalo tenderloin is one of the more distinctive selections. Eight intimate, candlelit dining rooms are appointed with antiques, Limoges and crystal. Service is upbeat and attentive. Dressy casual. **Bar:** Full bar. **Reservations:** suggested. **Hours:** 5 pm-9 pm. Closed: 1/1, 12/25; also Mon 9/14-6/15 & Sun 11/1-5/15. **Address:** 4631 Falmouth Rd 02635 **Location:** On SR 28, just e of jct SR 130. **Parking:** on-site. **Historic**

DENNIS pop. 2,798   (See map and index starting on p. 458)

ISAIAH HALL B & B INN

Phone: 508/385-9928   79

Historic Bed & Breakfast
$125-$375 5/1-11/1
$110-$189 11/2-4/30

Address: 152 Whig St 02638 **Location:** 0.5 mi ne of SR 6A via Hope Ln; center. Located in a residential area. **Facility:** This 1857 farmhouse is on a quiet, tree-lined street in the heart of Cape Cod and features rooms with lace canopy, four-poster beds with handmade quilts. Smoke free premises. 12 units. 10 one-bedroom standard units. 2 one-bedroom suites. 2 stories (no elevator), interior corridors. *Bath:* combo or shower only. **Parking:** on-site. **Terms:** office hours 7 am-9 pm, 2-3 night minimum stay - weekends, age restrictions may apply, 14 day cancellation notice-fee imposed. **Amenities:** video library, DVD players, irons, hair dryers. **Guest Services:** wireless Internet.

------ WHERE TO DINE ------

CAPTAIN FROSTY'S

Phone: 508/385-8548   71

Regional Seafood
$5-$18

Old posts made of driftwood support the sign of this seasonal clam shack. For more than 30 years, this owner-operated spot has served sublime lobster rolls and fried clams. Lobster is plentiful and packed into a grilled roll with a hint of mayonnaise, and lightly breaded clams are deep-fried to a crisp golden brown. The batter is neither heavy nor floury. Diners read from a board above the counter, then order and pay the cashier. The staff is pleasant, but service is limited. Casual dress. **Hours:** 11 am-9 pm; hours may vary off season. **Address:** 219 Rt 6A 02638 **Location:** On SR 6A. **Parking:** on-site.

ICE CREAM SMUGGLER

Phone: 508/385-5307   70

Desserts
$3-$5

From humble beginnings in 1979, the ice cream shop now produces and serves on the order of 60 to 75 gallons of homemade ice creams and specialty desserts, such as fudge bottom pies. A favorite flavor is the excellent mocha chip. The squeaky-clean shop employs an extensively trained staff. Casual dress. **Reservations:** not accepted. **Hours:** Open 5/1-10/17 & 4/15-4/30; noon-9 pm, Fri & Sat-10 pm; 11 am-10:30 pm in summer. **Address:** 716 Main St 02638 **Location:** On SR 6A, just w of the Playhouse. **Parking:** on-site.

SCARGO CAFE

Phone: 508/385-8200   69

American
$10-$30

In a two-story cedar shake building just east of the town square and opposite Cape Cod Playhouse, the restaurant serves American fare with some ethnic twists. Dishes such as "down under" beef filets from Australia and Tuscan veal saltimbocca sit alongside seafood dishes, such as salmon Siam, baked scrod and grilled swordfish. Lighter options include soups, salads and sandwiches. The house specialty dessert is grapenut custard. Friendly, efficient service shows the owners really care. Casual dress. **Bar:** Full bar. **Hours:** 11 am-3 & 4:30-10 pm, Sat & Sun 11 am-10 pm; to 11 pm 6/15-9/15. Closed: 11/25, 12/25. **Address:** 799 Main St 02638 **Location:** On SR 6A, 1.8 mi w of SR 134; in Dennis Center. **Parking:** on-site.

CALL

DENNIS PORT pop. 3,612   (See maps and indexes starting on p. 454, 458)

AN ENGLISH GARDEN B&B   *Book at AAA.com*

Phone: (508)398-2915   19

Bed & Breakfast
$99-$165 5/1-10/27

Address: 32 Inman Rd 02639 **Location:** SR 28, 0.6 mi s on Depot St to Lower County Rd, just e to Inman Rd, then just s. **Facility:** The 1922 inn, 150 yards from the beach, is surrounded by a white picket fence and a garden with English roses, hydrangeas and tulips. Smoke free premises. 11 units. 9 one-bedroom standard units, some with whirlpools. 2 one-bedroom suites with kitchens. 2-3 stories (no elevator), interior/exterior corridors. *Bath:* combo or shower only. **Parking:** on-site. **Terms:** open 5/1-10/27, office hours 10 am-7 pm, 2 night minimum stay - weekends, age restrictions may apply, 7 day cancellation notice. **Amenities:** hair dryers. *Some:* irons. **Guest Services:** wireless Internet. **Business Services:** PC. ASK CALL / SOME UNITS

'BY THE SEA' GUESTS BED & BREAKFAST & SUITES

Phone: (508)398-8685   20

 SAVE

Bed & Breakfast
$125-$460 5/1-12/31

Address: 57 Chase Ave & Inman Rd Ext 02639 **Location:** Oceanfront. 1.2 mi se of SR 28 via Depot St. Located on the ocean. **Facility:** This seaside property includes a century-old, 12-room inn with a wrap-around veranda; breakfast is not included in the room rate. Smoke free premises. 17 units. 12 one-bedroom standard units. 3 one- and 2 two-bedroom suites with kitchens. 2-3 stories (no elevator), interior corridors. *Bath:* combo or shower only. **Parking:** on-site. **Terms:** open 5/1-12/31, office hours 8 am-8 pm, 2-3 night minimum stay - seasonal and/or weekends, 14 day cancellation notice-fee imposed. **Amenities:** high-speed Internet, voice mail. *Some:* DVD players, CD players, irons. **Leisure Activities:** limited beach access, beach towels, umbrellas, chairs. **Guest Services:** coin laundry. **Business Services:** fax (fee). **Free Special Amenities:** full breakfast and high-speed Internet.

(See maps and indexes starting on p. 454, 458)

COLONIAL VILLAGE MOTEL & COTTAGES

Motel
Rates not provided

Phone: 508/398-2071   **18**

Address: 426 Lower County Rd 02639 **Location:** SR 28, 0.5 mi s on Depot St, then just e. **Facility:** Smoke free premises. 59 units. 48 one-bedroom standard units, some with efficiencies. 1 two-bedroom suite with efficiency. 10 cottages. 1-2 stories (no elevator), exterior corridors. *Bath:* combo or shower only. **Parking:** on-site. **Terms:** open 5/20-10/1, office hours 7 am-11 pm. **Pool(s):** outdoor, heated indoor. **Leisure Activities:** sauna, whirlpool. **Business Services:** fax (fee).

CORSAIR & CROSS RIP OCEANFRONT   *Book great rates at AAA.com*

Motel
$125-$375 5/1-10/18
$125-$275 4/16-4/30

Phone: (508)398-6600   **21**

Address: 41 Chase Ave 02639 **Location:** 1 mi se of SR 28 via Depot St. **Facility:** Smoke free premises. 47 units. 46 one-bedroom standard units, some with efficiencies and/or whirlpools. 1 one-bedroom suite with kitchen. 2 stories (no elevator), exterior corridors. **Parking:** on-site. **Terms:** open 5/1-10/18 & 4/16-4/30, office hours 9 am-9 pm, 2 night minimum stay - weekends, 15 day cancellation notice-fee imposed. **Amenities:** voice mail, hair dryers. *Some:* CD players, irons. **Pool(s):** outdoor, heated outdoor, heated indoor. **Leisure Activities:** whirlpools, beach chairs, recreational room, table tennis, air hockey, playground. **Guest Services:** coin laundry, wireless Internet. **Business Services:** meeting rooms, PC, fax (fee). *(See color ad below)*

FREE local telephone calls and newspaper

EDGEWATER BEACH RESORT   *Book at AAA.com*

Condominium
Rates not provided

Phone: 508/398-6922   **92**

Address: 95 Chase Ave 02639 **Location:** 1.3 mi s of SR 28 via Belmont Ave. **Facility:** This beachfront property offers many rooms with a balcony and a private outdoor jacuzzi. 76 units. 14 one-bedroom standard units with efficiencies and whirlpools. 49 one- and 13 two-bedroom suites with efficiencies and whirlpools. 2 stories (no elevator), exterior corridors. *Bath:* combo or shower only. **Parking:** on-site. **Terms:** office hours 7:30 am-9:30 pm, check-in 4 pm. **Amenities:** DVD players, voice mail, irons, hair dryers. **Pool(s):** heated indoor/outdoor. **Leisure Activities:** whirlpool, limited beach access, putting green, exercise room. **Guest Services:** wireless Internet. **Business Services:** fax (fee).

HOLIDAY HILL MOTOR INN   *Book great rates at AAA.com*

Motel
$59-$129 5/8-10/12

Phone: (508)394-5577   **17**

Address: 352 Main St (SR 28) 02639 **Location:** 0.8 mi e of jct SR 134. **Facility:** 56 one-bedroom standard units. 2 stories (no elevator), exterior corridors. **Parking:** on-site. **Terms:** open 5/8-10/12, office hours 7 am-midnight, 7 day cancellation notice-fee imposed. **Amenities:** irons, hair dryers. **Pool(s):** heated outdoor. **Leisure Activities:** *Fee:* miniature golf, amusement center, game room. **Guest Services:** wireless Internet.

(See maps and indexes starting on p. 454, 458)

—— WHERE TO DINE ——

CLANCY'S
Phone: 508/394-6661   26

▼▼ ▼▼
American
$8-$24

Natural wood, brass and etched glass highlight the dining room where generous portions of beef, seafood and pasta are served. The dining area and open-air deck afford a peaceful view of the marsh and river. Casual dress. **Bar:** Full bar. **Reservations:** not accepted. **Hours:** 11:30 am-10 pm, Sun from 11 am; hours may vary in winter. Closed: 11/25, 12/25. **Address:** 8 Upper County Rd 02639 **Location:** SR 28, 0.8 mi n, just n on Depot St, then 0.7 mi nw. **Parking:** on-site.

THE EBB TIDE RESTAURANT
Phone: 508/398-8733   83

▼▼ ▼▼
Seafood
$17-$32

Since 1959 this seaside restaurant has been an institution and the local folks anticipate its reopening each season. The decor has a wonderfully classic style of ocean-blue Naugahyde armchairs where guests settle in comfortably and peruse the menu, which offers an excellent selection of fresh seafood, shellfish and many landlubber favorites. Casual dress. **Bar:** Full bar. **Reservations:** not accepted. **Hours:** 4:30 pm-9 pm; hours vary in season. Closed major holidays. **Address:** 94 Chase St 02639 **Location:** 1.3 mi s of SR 28 via Depot St. **Parking:** on-site.

THE EGG & I
Phone: 508/394-8912   27

▼
American
$5-$9

The basic, full-service restaurant specializes in wholesome, straightforward breakfast offerings. On the weekends and every day during the high season, patrons can take advantage of a brunch buffet. Casual dress. **Reservations:** not accepted. **Hours:** 7 am-1 pm, Sat & Sun-2 pm. **Address:** 605 Main St 02639 **Location:** On SR 28. **Parking:** on-site.

OCEAN HOUSE
Phone: 508/394-0700   29

▼▼ ▼▼
American
$20-$34

The terrific oceanside location offers panoramic views of Nantucket Sound. The dishes are primarily seafood and are nicely prepared. Dressy casual. **Bar:** Full bar. **Reservations:** suggested. **Hours:** Open 5/1-12/30 & 3/30-4/30; 5 pm-10 pm; seasonal hours may vary. Closed: 12/25. **Address:** 421 Old Wharf Rd 02639 **Location:** 0.5 mi s of SR 39. **Parking:** on-site.

SUNDAE SCHOOL
Phone: 508/394-9122   28

▼
Desserts
$3-$7

The family-owned creamery opened its first location in 1976 and now operates three locations on the Cape. The three dozen flavors of homemade ice cream are wonderful. Hand-packed containers are readily available, as are homemade chocolate fudge, frappes and sundaes. Guests can sit indoors or out. Casual dress. **Reservations:** not accepted. **Hours:** Open 5/1-10/15 & 4/20-4/30; 11 am-11 pm; seasonal hours may vary. **Address:** 381 Lower County Rd 02639 **Location:** Just e of SR 28. **Parking:** on-site.

EAST FALMOUTH pop. 6,615   (See map and index starting on p. 458)

CAPEWIND WATERFRONT RESORT
Phone: 508/548-3400   125

▼▼ ▼▼
Motel
$68-$254 All Year

Address: 34 Maravista Ext 02536 **Location:** 2.2 mi e via SR 28, then just s, follow signs. Located in a secluded area. **Facility:** Smoke free premises. 31 one-bedroom standard units, some with kitchens. 1 story, exterior corridors. **Parking:** on-site. **Terms:** office hours 9 am-5 pm, 30 day cancellation notice-fee imposed. **Amenities:** irons, hair dryers. *Some:* DVD players. **Pool(s):** heated outdoor. **Leisure Activities:** boating, paddleboats, boat dock, horseshoes, volleyball. **Guest Services:** wireless Internet. **Business Services:** PC. (ASK) 🚭 ⊠ ✕ 🛏 🖥 🖥 / SOME UNITS FEE 🛒

EASTHAM   (See map and index starting on p. 458)

EAGLE WING GUEST MOTEL
Phone: 508/240-5656   22

▼▼ ▼▼
Motel
$70-$170 5/1-10/11

Address: 960 State Hwy 02642 **Location:** 0.8 mi n of Eastham/Orleans rotary. **Facility:** Smoke free premises. 19 one-bedroom standard units. 1 story, exterior corridors. **Parking:** on-site. **Terms:** open 5/1-10/11, office hours 8 am-10 pm, 2 night minimum stay - seasonal and/or weekends, age restrictions may apply, 14 day cancellation notice-fee imposed. **Amenities:** hair dryers. *Some:* irons. **Pool(s):** outdoor. **Guest Services:** wireless Internet. 🚭 FEE 🏃 ✕ 🛏

FOUR POINTS BY SHERATON EASTHAM CAPE COD   *Book great rates at AAA.com*
Phone: (508)255-5000   21

(AAA) (SAVE)

▼▼ ▼▼
Hotel
$205-$350 All Year

Address: 3800 US 6 02642 **Location:** On US 6; 1 mi n of National Seashore Visitor's Center. **Facility:** Designated smoking area. 107 units. 105 one-bedroom standard units. 2 one-bedroom suites. 2 stories (no elevator), interior corridors. *Bath:* combo or shower only. **Parking:** on-site. **Terms:** 2-3 night minimum stay - seasonal and/or weekends. **Amenities:** video games (fee), irons, hair dryers. **Pool(s):** outdoor, heated indoor. **Leisure Activities:** saunas, whirlpool, 2 lighted tennis courts, exercise room, basketball. *Fee:* game room. **Guest Services:** wireless Internet. **Business Services:** meeting rooms, PC. **Free Special Amenities:** high-speed Internet.

🍴 🍷 🚭 ⊠ ✕ 🎦 🛏 🖥

FOUR ✕ POINTS
BY SHERATON

AAA Benefit:
Members get up to 15% off, plus Starwood Preferred Guest® bonuses.

MIDWAY MOTEL AND COTTAGES, INC
Phone: 508/255-3117   19

(AAA) (SAVE)

▼▼ ▼▼
Motel
$76-$144 5/1-10/17
$82 3/1-4/30

Address: 5460 State Hwy 02651 **Location:** On US 6, 2.5 mi n of National Seashore Visitor's Center. **Facility:** Smoke free premises. 11 units. 8 one- and 1 two-bedroom standard units, some with kitchens. 2 cottages. 1 story, exterior corridors. **Parking:** on-site. **Terms:** open 5/1-10/17 & 3/1-4/30, office hours 7 am-10 pm, 2 night minimum stay - seasonal, 10 day cancellation notice, 30 day for cottage. **Amenities:** video library, hair dryers. *Some:* DVD players, irons. **Leisure Activities:** badminton, recreation room, playground, horseshoes, shuffleboard. **Guest Services:** wireless Internet. **Free Special Amenities:** preferred room (subject to availability with advance reservations).

⊠ ✕ 🎦 🅿 🛏 🖥 🖥

(See map and index starting on p. 458)

PENNY HOUSE INN

WWW

Historic Bed
& Breakfast

$205-$449 5/1-10/19
$185-$350 10/20-4/30

Phone: 508/255-6632   20

Address: 4885 State Hwy 6 02642 **Location:** 1.9 mi n of National Seashore Visitor's Center. **Facility:** Dating from 1751, this charming inn is a former sea captain's home. Smoke free premises. 12 units. 9 one-bedroom standard units, some with whirlpools. 3 one-bedroom suites with whirlpools. 2 stories (no elevator), interior corridors. *Bath:* combo or shower only. **Parking:** on-site. **Terms:** office hours 8 am-9 pm, 2 night minimum stay - seasonal, age restrictions may apply, 20 day cancellation notice-fee imposed. **Amenities:** video library, DVD players, CD players, irons, hair dryers. **Pool(s):** heated outdoor. **Leisure Activities:** *Fee:* massage. **Guest Services:** wireless Internet.

ASK ⊠ / SOME UNITS ▯ ▭

TOWN CRIER MOTEL   *Book at AAA.com*

WW

Motel

$129-$199 6/25-4/30
$69-$109 5/1-6/24

Phone: (508)255-4000   24

Address: 3620 State Hwy 02642 **Location:** On US 6; 0.8 mi n of National Seashore Visitor's Center. **Facility:** Smoke free premises. 36 one-bedroom standard units. 1 story, exterior corridors. **Parking:** on-site. **Terms:** office hours 9 am-9 pm, 2 night minimum stay - seasonal and/or weekends, 7 day cancellation notice-fee imposed. **Amenities:** hair dryers. **Pool(s):** heated indoor/outdoor. **Leisure Activities:** limited exercise equipment. **Guest Services:** wireless Internet.

▯ ⊠ ▯ ▯ ▭ ▭

WHALEWALK INN & SPA

WWW

Historic Bed
& Breakfast

$220-$420 5/1-1/1 &
4/1-4/30

Phone: (508)255-0617   23

Address: 220 Bridge Rd 02642 **Location:** US 6, rotary exit Eastham/Orleans, exit Rock Harbor Rd, then just s. Located in a quiet area. **Facility:** A converted 1830s home, the inn offers elegantly-appointed guest rooms, some with a working fireplace; a full gourmet breakfast is served daily. Smoke free premises. 16 units. 10 one-bedroom standard units, some with whirlpools. 5 one-bedroom suites, some with kitchens and/or whirlpools. 1 cottage. 1-2 stories (no elevator), interior/exterior corridors. *Bath:* combo or shower only. **Parking:** on-site. **Terms:** open 5/1-1/1 & 4/1-4/30, office hours 7 am-9 pm, 2 night minimum stay - seasonal and/or weekends, age restrictions may apply, 14 day cancellation notice-fee imposed. **Amenities:** video library, DVD players, CD players, irons, hair dryers. **Pool(s):** heated indoor. **Leisure Activities:** sauna, whirlpool, exercise room, spa. **Guest Services:** wireless Internet. ⊠ ⊠ ⊠ ▯ / SOME UNITS ▯ ▭

—— **WHERE TO DINE** ——

ARNOLD'S LOBSTER & CLAM BAR   *Menu on AAA.com*

AAA

WW

Regional
Seafood

$4-$30

Phone: 508/255-2575   24

Fresh Cape lobster, steamers, oysters, mussels, fried and baked entrees and some burgers and sandwiches are served very informally in the old Cape Cod tradition with paper plates and plastic utensils in this spot very popular with tourists and locals. Casual dress. **Bar:** Full bar. **Hours:** Open 5/15-9/6; 11:30 am-9:30 pm; to 8 pm 5/15-6/18. **Address:** 3580 US 6 02651 **Location:** 0.7 mi n of National Seashore Visitor's Center. **Parking:** on-site. ▧

EAST HARWICH pop. 4,744   (See map and index starting on p. 458)

WEQUASSETT RESORT AND GOLF CLUB

AAA SAVE

WWW WWW

Resort
Hotel

$185-$1375 5/1-11/30

Phone: (508)432-5400   61

Address: 2173 Route 28 02645 **Location:** US 6, exit 11, first left to Pleasant Bay Rd, then 2.5 mi e. **Facility:** On 25 wooded acres overlooking the harbor, the inn offers luxurious cottage units in the New England tradition. Smoke free premises. 120 units. 100 one-bedroom standard units, some with whirlpools. 19 one-bedroom suites, some with whirlpools. 1 cottage. 1-2 stories (no elevator), exterior corridors. *Bath:* combo or shower only. **Parking:** on-site. **Terms:** open 5/1-11/30, 3-5 night minimum stay - seasonal and/or weekends, 30 day cancellation notice-fee imposed. **Amenities:** video library, high-speed Internet, dual phone lines, voice mail, safes, honor bars, irons, hair dryers. *Some:* DVD players. **Dining:** 2 restaurants, also, twenty-eight Atlantic, see separate listing. **Pool(s):** 2 heated outdoor. **Leisure Activities:** whirlpools, rental boats, boat dock, 4 tennis courts (1 lighted), bocci, croquet, launch to Outer Beach, firepit, exercise room. *Fee:* sailboats, poolside cabanas, boardwalk, children's aquatic splash pad, golf-18 holes, tennis instruction, massage. **Guest Services:** valet laundry, area transportation-within 8 mi, wireless Internet, personal trainer. **Business Services:** meeting rooms, business center. *(See color ad p 472)*

▯ ▯ ▯ ▯ ⊠ ⊠ ⊠ ▭ / SOME UNITS ▯

FREE room upgrade (subject to availability with advance reservations)

—— **WHERE TO DINE** ——

TWENTY-EIGHT ATLANTIC

AAA

WWW WWW

Regional
American

$22-$50

Phone: 508/430-3000   58

Upscale fine dining is what patrons expect in the 19th-century sea captain's mansion, which affords breathtaking views of Pleasant Bay. The menu lists innovative preparations of fresh seafood, beef, poultry and lamb, as well as a vegetarian sampler. The wine selection is ample. Service is attentive, and the atmosphere is rich but not stuffy. From May through September, lunch is served in The Outer Bar & Grille. Dressy casual. Entertainment. **Bar:** Full bar. **Reservations:** suggested. **Hours:** Open 5/1-12/12 & 4/4-4/30; 7 am-11 & 6-10 pm; seasonal hours vary. Closed: for lunch 7/1-9/1. **Address:** 2173 Route 28 02645 **Location:** US 6, exit 11, first left to Pleasant Bay Rd, then 2.5 mi e; in Wequassett Resort and Golf Club. **Parking:** on-site. CALL ▧

EAST ORLEANS   (See map and index starting on p. 458)

NAUSET KNOLL MOTOR LODGE
Phone: 508/255-2364   **26**

Motel
$120-$185 5/1-10/18
$120 4/17-4/30

Address: 237 Beach Rd 02643 **Location:** US 6, exit 13 (Orleans rotary), 1 mi w on SR 6A, then 3 mi se on Main St to Nauset Beach. **Facility:** Smoke free premises. 12 one-bedroom standard units. 1 story, exterior corridors. *Bath:* combo or shower only. **Parking:** on-site. **Terms:** open 5/1-10/18 & 4/17-4/30, office hours 8 am-8 pm, 7 day cancellation notice. **Leisure Activities:** beach access.

——— WHERE TO DINE ———

JOE'S BEACH ROAD BAR & GRILL @ THE BARLEY NECK INN
Phone: 508/255-0212   **29**

American
$15-$26

This converted 1857 sea captain's house serves contemporary French cuisine with an Asian influence. The atmosphere is intimate and casually elegant. A brasserie menu is served in a casual grille. Casual dress. Entertainment. **Bar:** Full bar. **Reservations:** suggested. **Hours:** 5 pm-10 pm. Closed: 12/25. **Address:** 5 Beach Rd 02643 **Location:** US 6, rotary exit Eastham/Orleans, 1 mi w on SR 6A, then 1.5 mi e on Main St. **Parking:** on-site. CALL

NAUSET BEACH CLUB RESTAURANT
Phone: 508/255-8547   **27**

Northern Italian
$12-$34

Fresh and innovative Italian cuisine includes preparations of chicken, eggplant, lamb, seafood and beef. A good wine list complements the menu. Casual dress. **Bar:** Full bar. **Reservations:** suggested. **Hours:** 5 pm-10 pm. Closed: 11/25, 12/25. **Address:** 222 Main St 02643 **Location:** 1.5 mi e of SR 6A. **Parking:** on-site.

SUNDAE SCHOOL
Phone: 508/255-5473   **28**

Desserts
$3-$7

The family-owned creamery opened its first location in 1976 and now operates three locations on the Cape. The three dozen flavors of homemade ice cream are wonderful. Hand-packed containers are readily available, as are homemade chocolate fudge, frappes and sundaes. Guests can sit only outdoors. Casual dress. **Reservations:** not accepted. **Hours:** Open 6/1-9/15; noon-8 pm. **Address:** 210 Main St 02643 **Location:** 0.5 mi e of SR 39. **Parking:** on-site.

FALMOUTH pop. 4,115   (See map and index starting on p. 458)

CAPTAIN TOM LAWRENCE HOUSE INN
Phone: 508/548-9178   **130**

Historic Bed
& Breakfast
$140-$270 5/1-10/31
$115-$200 11/1-4/30

Address: 75 Locust St 02540 **Location:** 0.3 mi s of SR 28 on road to Woods Hole. Located in a residential area. **Facility:** This cozy sea captain's Civil War era home is located on the National Register of Historic Places and offers guests inviting rooms with canopied four-poster beds and central air conditioning. Smoke free premises. 7 one-bedroom standard units, some with efficiencies. 2 stories (no elevator), interior corridors. *Bath:* shower only. **Parking:** on-site. **Terms:** office hours 9 am-9 pm, 2-3 night minimum stay - weekends, 14 day cancellation notice-fee imposed. **Amenities:** hair dryers. **Guest Services:** wireless Internet.

FALMOUTH HEIGHTS MOTOR LODGE
Phone: (508)548-3623   **133**

(AAA) [SAVE]

Motel
$69-$269 5/1-11/2

Address: 146 Falmouth Heights Rd 02540 **Location:** 0.8 mi e on SR 28, then 0.5 mi s. **Facility:** Smoke free premises. 27 one-bedroom standard units, some with efficiencies. 1-2 stories (no elevator), interior/exterior corridors. *Bath:* combo or shower only. **Parking:** on-site. **Terms:** open 5/1-11/2, office hours 8 am-10 pm, 14 day cancellation notice-fee imposed. **Amenities:** irons, hair dryers. **Pool(s):** outdoor. **Leisure Activities:** beach chairs, gas grills, glider swings, picnic grove, bike storage, playground. **Guest Services:** wireless Internet. **Free Special Amenities: continental breakfast and high-speed Internet.**

HOLIDAY INN CAPE COD/FALMOUTH   *Book at AAA.com*
Phone: (508)540-2000   **128**

Hotel
$159-$289 5/1-10/15
$99-$199 10/16-4/30

Address: 291 Jones Rd 02540 **Location:** 0.5 mi e of SR 28, just e of jct Gifford St. **Facility:** Smoke free premises. 98 one-bedroom standard units, some with whirlpools. 3 stories (no elevator), interior corridors. *Bath:* combo or shower only. **Parking:** on-site. **Amenities:** video games (fee), voice mail, irons, hair dryers. **Pool(s):** heated indoor. **Leisure Activities:** exercise room. *Fee:* game room. **Guest Services:** valet and coin laundry, wireless Internet. **Business Services:** meeting rooms, PC.

(See map and index starting on p. 458)

MARINER MOTEL

Phone: 508/548-1331 [131]

Motel
$69-$189 5/1-10/31
$69-$89 11/1-4/30

Address: 555 Main St 02540 **Location:** 0.5 mi e on SR 28. **Facility:** Smoke free premises. 30 one-bedroom standard units. 1 story, exterior corridors. *Bath:* combo or shower only. **Parking:** on-site. **Terms:** office hours 7:30 am-11 pm, 14 day cancellation notice-fee imposed. **Pool(s):** heated outdoor. **Leisure Activities:** picnic tables, playground. **Guest Services:** wireless Internet. **Free Special Amenities:** local telephone calls and high-speed Internet.

⁜▸ 🏊 ⊠ 🛢 / SOME UNITS FEE 🐾

SEASIDE INN

Phone: (508)540-4120 [134]

Hotel
$79-$319 5/1-9/5
$59-$199 9/6-4/30

Address: 263 Grand Ave 02540 **Location:** Jct SR 28, 1.3 mi s via Falmouth Heights Rd. **Facility:** Smoke free premises. 23 units. 21 one-bedroom standard units, some with efficiencies and/or whirlpools. 2 one-bedroom suites with efficiencies. 2-3 stories (no elevator), interior/exterior corridors. *Bath:* combo or shower only. **Parking:** on-site. **Terms:** office hours 8:30 am-9 pm, 2 night minimum stay - seasonal and/or weekends, 10 day cancellation notice-fee imposed. **Amenities:** voice mail, irons, hair dryers. **Leisure Activities:** beach access. **Guest Services:** wireless Internet. **Free Special Amenities:** newspaper and high-speed Internet. ⁜▸ ⊠ 🖥 / SOME UNITS 🛢 🗄

WOODS HOLE PASSAGE BED & BREAKFAST INN

Phone: 508/548-9575 [132]

Bed & Breakfast
$125-$195 5/1-10/31
$100-$140 11/1-4/30

Address: 186 Woods Hole Rd 02540 **Location:** 1.5 mi s. Located in a residential area. **Facility:** The 1880 barn-red, cedar-shake-clad inn is nestled on spacious grounds, well-hidden off the road; the four carriage-house rooms are a recent addition. Smoke free premises. 5 one-bedroom standard units. 2 stories (no elevator), interior corridors. *Bath:* shower only. **Parking:** on-site. **Terms:** office hours 8 am-8 pm, 2-3 night minimum stay, 14 day cancellation notice-fee imposed. **Amenities:** hair dryers. **Leisure Activities:** bicycles, horseshoes. **Guest Services:** TV in common area, wireless Internet.

⊠ 🅦 🅩

The following lodging was either not evaluated or did not meet AAA rating requirements but is listed for your information only.

RED HORSE INN

Phone: 508/548-0053

[fyi]

Not evaluated. **Address:** 28 Falmouth Heights Rd 02540 **Location:** 0.8 mi e on SR 28, then just s. Facilities, services, and decor characterize a mid-scale property.

--- **WHERE TO DINE** ---

BETSY'S DINER

Phone: 508/540-0060 [124]

American
$4-$11

Betsy's, located toward the west end of Main Street, is an original 1957 diner. Breakfast all day, burgers, sandwiches and an assortment of dinner plates like meatloaf, franks and beans, broiled scrod and grilled chicken livers complement the house specialty, roast turkey dinner. The service is friendly and the portions large. Casual dress. **Reservations:** not accepted. **Hours:** 6 am-8 pm, Fri & Sat-9 pm, Sun-2 pm. Closed: 4/4, 11/25, 12/25; also 5/11. **Address:** 457 Main St 02540 **Location:** 0.3 mi e of center. **Parking:** on-site. CALL 👓M

BRITISH BEER COMPANY RESTAURANT

Phone: 508/540-9600 [129]

British
$6-$18

Tables in the traditional pub's front dining room look out over the harbor to Martha's Vineyard beyond. Roughly 20 draft beers and more than 50 bottled brews come from around the world. On the menu is a wide selection of hot and cold sandwiches, half-pound burgers and traditional British fare, such as fish and chips and shepherd's pie. Casual dress. Entertainment. **Bar:** Full bar. **Reservations:** accepted. **Hours:** 11:30 am-10 pm, Sun from noon. Closed: 11/25, 12/25. **Address:** 263 Grand Ave 02540 **Location:** 1.3 mi se via Falmouth Heights Rd. **Parking:** street. CALL 👓M

COONAMESSETT INN CAHOON DINING ROOM

Phone: 508/548-2300 [120]

Regional American
$9-$32

The manicured grounds of the white-trimmed, red-shingled traditional New England country inn issue an invitation to relax and enjoy elegant fine dining with gracious hospitality. Fresh seafood, produce grown on the Coonamessett farm and fine meats are prepared with flair. Service is attentive, efficient and friendly. Dressy casual. **Bar:** Full bar. **Reservations:** accepted. **Hours:** 11:30 am-9 pm; Sunday brunch. Closed: 12/25. **Address:** 311 Gifford St 02540 **Location:** 0.8 mi n of SR 28. **Parking:** on-site and valet. CALL 👓M

FIRE FLY WOODFIRE GRILL & BAR

Phone: 508/548-7953 [126]

American
$8-$29

In the bustling section of Falmouth shops, the restaurant employs a friendly and accommodating staff. The creative menu includes a delectable selection of New England cuisine. Casual dress. **Bar:** Full bar. **Reservations:** accepted. **Hours:** 11:30 am-10 pm, Fri & Sat-11:30 pm; 5 pm-10 pm 1/1-3/31. Closed: 12/25; also Sun & Mon 1/1-3/31. **Address:** 271 Main St 02540 **Location:** Between Cahoon Ct and Elm Arch Way; downtown. **Parking:** on-site.

THE GOLDEN SWAN FINE INDIAN CUISINE

Phone: 508/540-6580 [127]

Indian
$6-$20

Both the early-bird and the regular menus are extensive and varied with an emphasis on traditional preparations of seafood, veal, chicken and pork. The cozy, relaxed atmosphere displays certain decor touches that bespeak its European heritage. Casual dress. **Bar:** Full bar. **Reservations:** suggested. **Hours:** 11:30 am-2:30 & 5-10 pm. Closed: 11/25, 12/25. **Address:** 323 Main St 02540 **Location:** SR 28; center. **Parking:** street.

(See map and index starting on p. 458)

LA CUCINA SUL MARE   Phone: 508/548-5600   (128)

Northern Italian
$6-$20

Under a green awning in center of town are benches that serve as the waiting area for this cozy, popular, emerging restaurant. Bare wood tables at lunch give way to white tablecloths accented with fresh flowers and candles in glass holders at dinner. Stucco walls with shutter-framed paintings of the sea give life to the "kitchen by the sea" name. The menu goes beyond Northern Italian in its extensive use of fresh seafood, such as salmon with almonds on a bed of fresh spinach sauteed with garlic. Casual dress. **Bar:** Full bar. **Reservations:** not accepted. **Hours:** 11:30 am-2 & 5-10 pm, Mon from 5 pm. Closed: 11/25, 12/25; also for dinner 12/24. **Address:** 237 Main St 02540 **Location:** Center. **Parking:** on-site and street. CALL 🔊M

MARGO'S   Phone: 508/548-0590   (121)

American
$6-$19

Next to the Falmouth Mall is a casual pub-style eatery offering sandwiches and luncheon specials for hungry shoppers, tourists and locals. Casual dress. **Bar:** Full bar. **Reservations:** not accepted. **Hours:** 11:30 am-9 pm, Sun from noon. Closed: 11/25, 12/25. **Address:** 97 Spring Bars Rd 02540 **Location:** 0.5 mi e of SR 28; in Falmouth Trade Center. **Parking:** on-site.

PEKING PALACE   Phone: 508/540-8204   (123)

Asian
$9-$17

The new restaurant has attractive, comfortable and inviting Asian decor and a large sushi bar as the focal point. On the Japanese side of the vast menu are sushi, sashimi, tempura and teriyaki offerings, while the Chinese side lists a bountiful selection of beef, chicken, duck, pork and vegetarian dishes. Chow mein, egg foo yong and noodle dishes are perennial favorites. More than 10 soups and 30-plus appetizers mean plenty of options. The pu pu platter is ideal for sharing. Casual dress. **Bar:** Full bar. **Reservations:** accepted. **Hours:** 11:30 am-midnight. **Address:** 452 Main St 02540 **Location:** Center of village. **Parking:** on-site.

QUARTERDECK RESTAURANT   Phone: 508/548-9900   (122)

American
$5-$26

A good part of the family-oriented restaurant's interior planking and paneling, some dating to the 1600s, was salvaged from a local boatyard. Stained-glass windows came from a church in Maine. Most days, guests can find Tommy Leonard, the originator of the Falmouth Road Race, behind the bar. Typical New England fare—from chowder and kale soup to shrimp, scrod, salmon and lobster—can be found on the largely seafood menu. Prime rib, sirloin steak and chicken parmigiana also put in an appearance. Casual dress. **Bar:** Full bar. **Reservations:** not accepted. **Hours:** 11:30 am-10 pm. Closed: 4/4, 11/25, 12/25. **Address:** 164 Main St 02540 **Location:** Center. **Parking:** on-site and street. CALL 🔊M

ROO BAR OF FALMOUTH   Phone: 508/548-8600   (125)

American
$11-$30

The storefront eatery sits in the center of town. Works by local artists provide the whimsical basis for the decor and are offset by white table linens covered with butcher paper. The atmosphere is upbeat, almost loud. The back bar has a ladder on wheels to access top-shelf libations. Creative American cuisine with international accents—such as pan-seared salmon with Thai curry sauce, pork tenderloin with Mongolian glaze and seafood Provencal—is prepared in the open kitchen. Casual dress. **Bar:** Full bar. **Hours:** 5 pm-10 pm, Fri-Sun from 11:30 am. Closed: 11/25, 12/25; also Tues in winter. **Address:** 285 Main St 02540 **Location:** Center. **Parking:** street. CALL 🔊M

——— *The following restaurant has not been evaluated by AAA* ———
but is listed for your information only.

BEN & BILL'S CHOCOLATE EMPORIUM   Phone: 508/548-7878

[fyi]

Not evaluated. On Main Street in the middle of town, the popular confectionery makes hand-prepared candies and gourmet ice cream from generations-old family recipes. Limited seating is available at sidewalk tables. This spot is one of four locations in Massachusetts and Maine. **Address:** 209 Main St 02540 **Location:** Center.

HARWICH PORT pop. 1,809   (See map and index starting on p. 458)

ALYCE'S DUNSCROFT BY-THE-SEA   Phone: 508/432-0810   (82)

Bed & Breakfast
$155-$455 5/1-10/31 &
4/1-4/30

Address: 24 Pilgrim Rd 02646 **Location:** 0.3 mi s of SR 28. Located in a residential area. **Facility:** Quiet and charming, the inn sits only a few feet from the coastline; a full breakfast is served each morning. Smoke free premises. 8 units. 7 one-bedroom standard units, some with whirlpools. 1 cottage. 1-2 stories (no elevator), interior/exterior corridors. *Bath:* combo or shower only. **Parking:** on-site. **Terms:** open 5/1-10/31 & 4/1-4/30, office hours 8 am-8 pm, 1-3 night minimum stay, 21 day cancellation notice-fee imposed. **Amenities:** irons, hair dryers. **Leisure Activities:** beach access. **Guest Services:** wireless Internet. **Business Services:** fax (fee).
🛎️ ⊠ / SOME UNITS 📶 📺 📼

——— **WHERE TO DINE** ———

HOT STOVE SALOON   Phone: 508/432-9911   (77)

American
$7-$12

The new town addition serves good pizza, burgers and salads. Sports lovers can keep up with the action on high-definition and plasma televisions skirting the perimeter of the bar. Casual dress. **Bar:** Full bar. **Reservations:** not accepted. **Hours:** 11:30 am-9 pm. Closed: major holidays, 12/24. **Address:** 551 Main St 02646 **Location:** On SR 28; center. **Parking:** on-site.

L'ALOUETTE BISTRO   Phone: 508/430-0405   (74)

French
$22-$32

New proprietors continue a longstanding tradition of serving superb French cuisine. Meticulously prepared delicacies may include crispy duck with a creative blend of fruits and spices, warm Wellfleet oysters and Bouillabaisse are only but a few of the items that may be on the menu. Casual dress. **Bar:** Full bar. **Reservations:** suggested. **Hours:** 5 pm-9 pm, Fri & Sat-10 pm; call to verify hours. Closed: 12/25; also Mon off season. **Address:** 787 Main St 02646 **Location:** 1 mi e on SR 28. **Parking:** on-site.

(See map and index starting on p. 458)

THE PORT

American
$19-$31

Phone: 508/430-5410   76

The chef-owner prepares eye-appealing, flavorful and creative dishes, such as fried calamari served with hot banana peppers and red sauce; pasta fiore (sautéed shrimp, scallops and lobster over angel hair in a rich sherried Parmesan-cream sauce with shiitake mushrooms and scallions); and swordfish garnished with homemade guacamole and served over baby spring greens. Modern and upscale best describe the décor. Casual dress. **Bar:** Full bar. **Reservations:** accepted. **Hours:** Open 5/1-12/15 & 4/15-4/30; 5 pm-10 pm. **Address:** 541 SR 28 02646 **Location:** Center. **Parking:** on-site.

SUNDAE SCHOOL

Desserts
$3-$7

Phone: 508/430-2444   75

The family-owned creamery opened its first location in 1976 and now operates three locations on the Cape. The three dozen flavors of homemade ice cream are wonderful. Hand-packed containers are readily available, as are homemade chocolate fudge, frappes and sundaes. Guests can sit indoors or out. Casual dress. **Hours:** Open 5/20-9/15; noon-10 pm; seasonal hours may vary. **Address:** 606 Main St 02646 **Location:** On SR 28. **Parking:** on-site.

HYANNIS   (See map and index starting on p. 454)

ANCHOR-IN DISTINCTIVE WATERFRONT LODGING   *Book great rates at AAA.com*

Phone: (508)775-0357   9

Hotel
$99-$279 5/1-10/23
$69-$129 10/24-4/30

Address: 1 South St 02601 **Location:** 0.5 mi se; overlooking Lewis Bay. **Facility:** Smoke free premises. 42 one-bedroom standard units, some with efficiencies and/or whirlpools. 2 stories (no elevator), interior/exterior corridors. *Bath:* combo or shower only. **Parking:** on-site. **Terms:** office hours 6:30 am-11 pm, 2 night minimum stay - seasonal and/or weekends, 7 day cancellation notice-fee imposed. **Amenities:** voice mail, irons, hair dryers. *Some:* DVD players. **Pool(s):** heated outdoor. **Leisure Activities:** shuffleboard. **Guest Services:** wireless Internet. *(See color ad below)*

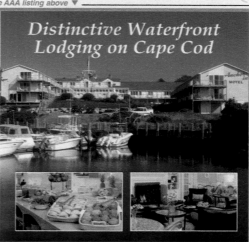

FREE expanded continental breakfast and high-speed Internet

(See map and index starting on p. 454)

CAPE CODDER RESORT & SPA   *Book great rates at AAA.com*   Phone: (508)771-3000   **2**

Hotel

$119-$239 5/1-10/11
$109-$199 10/12-4/30

Address: 1225 Iyannough Rd 02601 **Location:** US 6, exit 6, 1.5 mi se on SR 132. **Facility:** Smoke free premises. 287 units. 265 one-bedroom standard units. 16 one- and 6 two-bedroom suites with whirlpools. 2-3 stories (no elevator), interior corridors. *Bath:* combo or shower only. **Parking:** on-site. **Terms:** 2 night minimum stay - seasonal and/or weekends, 4 day cancellation notice-fee imposed. **Amenities:** voice mail, irons, hair dryers. *Some:* DVD players, CD players, safes. **Dining:** Hearth 'n Kettle Restaurant, see separate listing. **Pool(s):** heated indoor. **Leisure Activities:** sauna, whirlpool, tennis court, playground, spa, volleyball. **Guest Services:** valet laundry, wireless Internet. **Business Services:** conference facilities, business center. *(See color ad below)*

CAPE COD HARBOR HOUSE INN   Phone: 508/771-1880   **12**

Motel

Rates not provided

Address: 119 Ocean St 02601 **Location:** Opposite ferry docks. **Facility:** Smoke free premises. 19 units. 18 one-bedroom standard units with kitchens. 1 one-bedroom suite with kitchen and whirlpool. 2 stories (no elevator), exterior corridors. **Parking:** on-site. **Terms:** open 5/1-10/29, office hours 8 am-9 pm. **Amenities:** video library, DVD players, CD players, irons, hair dryers. **Guest Services:** area transportation, wireless Internet.

(See map and index starting on p. 454)

COURTYARD HYANNIS   *Book great rates at AAA.com*   Phone: (508)775-6600   **5**

▼♦♦♦▼
Hotel
$109-$189 All Year

Address: 707 Iyannough Rd 02601 **Location:** On SR 132, 0.3 mi nw of jct SR 28. Adjacent to a mall. **Facility:** Smoke free premises. 119 one-bedroom standard units. 2 stories, interior corridors. **Bath:** combo or shower only. **Parking:** on-site. **Terms:** 3 day cancellation notice-fee imposed. **Amenities:** high-speed Internet, dual phone lines, voice mail, irons, hair dryers. **Pool(s):** heated indoor. **Leisure Activities:** exercise room. **Guest Services:** valet and coin laundry, wireless Internet. **Business Services:** meeting rooms, PC.

🍴→ CALL 🔊ᴹ 🏊 ❌ 📷 🖥 🖳

AAA Benefit:
Members save a
minimum 5% off the
best available rate.

DAYS INN   *Book great rates at AAA.com*   Phone: (508)771-6100   **4**

AAA SAVE
▼♦♦♦▼ ♦♦ ♦♦
Hotel
$75-$225 5/1-10/20
$65-$195 10/21-4/30

Address: 867 Iyannough Rd 02601 **Location:** US 6, exit 6, 2.3 mi se on SR 132. Adjacent to Cape Cod Mall. **Facility:** 99 one-bedroom standard units. 2 stories (no elevator), interior corridors. **Parking:** on-site. **Amenities:** irons, hair dryers. *Some:* safes. **Pool(s):** outdoor, heated indoor. **Leisure Activities:** whirlpool, exercise room. **Guest Services:** valet laundry, wireless Internet. **Business Services:** PC.
(See color ad p 484)

🍴→ 🏊 📷 🖳 / SOME UNITS ❌ 🖥 🖳

FREE early check-in/late check-out and room upgrade (subject to availability with advance reservations)

HERITAGE HOUSE HOTEL   *Book at AAA.com*   Phone: (508)775-7000   **7**

▼♦♦♦▼
Hotel
$79-$299 5/1-10/31
$69-$109 11/1-4/30

Address: 259 Main St 02601 **Location:** Center. **Facility:** 143 one-bedroom standard units. 2-3 stories, interior corridors. **Parking:** on-site. **Terms:** check-in 4 pm, 7 day cancellation notice-fee imposed. **Amenities:** irons, hair dryers. **Pool(s):** outdoor, heated indoor. **Leisure Activities:** saunas, whirlpool. **Guest Services:** wireless Internet. **Business Services:** meeting rooms.

ASK 🍴 🍸 🏊 📷 🖥 🖳 / SOME UNITS ❌

▼ See AAA listing p 510 ▼

AAA.com ... #1 Destination for Vacation
Information and Navigation

(See map and index starting on p. 454)

HOLIDAY INN HYANNIS   *Book great rates at AAA.com*   Phone: (508)775-1153   **3**

AAA SAVE
▽▽▽
Hotel
$119-$209 5/1-10/18
$89-$159 10/19-4/30

Address: 1127 Iyannough Rd 02601 **Location:** US 6, exit 6, 2.3 mi se on SR 132. **Facility:** 196 units. 176 one-bedroom standard units, some with whirlpools. 20 one-bedroom suites with whirlpools. 2 stories, interior corridors. *Bath:* combo or shower only. **Parking:** on-site. **Terms:** 2 night minimum stay - seasonal and/or weekends, 3 day cancellation notice. **Amenities:** video games (fee), voice mail, safes, irons, hair dryers. **Pool(s):** heated indoor. **Leisure Activities:** whirlpool, exercise room. **Guest Services:** valet laundry, wireless Internet. **Business Services:** meeting rooms, business center. **Free Special Amenities:** newspaper and high-speed Internet.

🍽 🏊 📷 💻 / SOME UNITS ✕ 🖥

HYANNIS HARBOR HOTEL   *Book great rates at AAA.com*   Phone: (508)775-4420   **13**

AAA SAVE
▽▽▽
Motel
$79-$299 5/1-10/29
$69-$179 4/19-4/30

Address: 213 Ocean St 02601 **Location:** 0.9 mi s. Located across from ferry dock. **Facility:** Smoke free premises. 136 units. 133 one-bedroom standard units, some with whirlpools. 3 two-bedroom suites. 2 stories (no elevator), exterior corridors. *Bath:* combo or shower only. **Parking:** on-site. **Terms:** open 5/1-10/29 & 4/19-4/30, 2 night minimum stay - seasonal and/or weekends, 3 day cancellation notice-fee imposed. **Amenities:** video library, DVD players, CD players, safes, irons, hair dryers. **Pool(s):** heated outdoor, heated indoor. **Leisure Activities:** whirlpools. **Guest Services:** coin laundry, wireless Internet. **Business Services:** meeting rooms, PC. *(See color ad p 485)*

🍽 🏊 ✕ 🖥 💻

HYANNIS INN MOTEL   Phone: (508)775-0255   **11**

AAA SAVE
▽▽▽
Motel
$50-$175 All Year

Address: 473 Main St 02601 **Location:** Center. **Facility:** Smoke free premises. 77 one-bedroom standard units, some with whirlpools. 2 stories (no elevator), exterior corridors. *Bath:* combo or shower only. **Parking:** on-site. **Terms:** 7 day cancellation notice-fee imposed. **Amenities:** voice mail, irons, hair dryers. **Pool(s):** heated indoor. **Leisure Activities:** saunas. **Guest Services:** wireless Internet. **Free Special Amenities:** local telephone calls and high-speed Internet.

🍽 🍸 🏊 ✕ / SOME UNITS 🖥

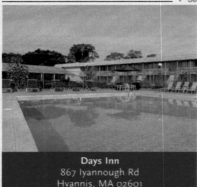

(See map and index starting on p. 454)

HYANNIS TRAVEL INN *Book great rates at AAA.com*   Phone: (508)775-8200

Motel
$69-$149 5/1-11/30
$69-$135 2/10-4/30

Address: 18 North St 02601 **Location:** Just n of Main St. **Facility:** Smoke free premises. 83 one-bedroom standard units. 3 stories (no elevator), interior corridors. *Bath:* combo or shower only. **Parking:** on-site. **Terms:** open 5/1-11/30 & 2/10-4/30, office hours 7:30 am-11 pm, 3 day cancellation notice. **Amenities:** irons, hair dryers. **Pool(s):** outdoor, heated indoor. **Leisure Activities:** whirlpool. **Guest Services:** wireless Internet. *(See color ad p 486)*

RADISSON HOTEL HYANNIS *Book great rates at AAA.com*   Phone: (508)771-1700

Hotel
$109-$209 5/1-10/18
$89-$139 10/19-4/30

Address: 287 Iyannough Rd 02601 **Location:** On SR 28, 0.3 mi se of jct SR 132. **Facility:** Smoke free premises. 160 one-bedroom standard units, some with whirlpools. 2 stories, interior corridors. **Parking:** on-site. **Terms:** 2 night minimum stay - seasonal and/or weekends, 3 day cancellation notice. **Amenities:** video games (fee), dual phone lines, voice mail, safes, irons, hair dryers. **Pool(s):** heated indoor. **Leisure Activities:** sauna, steamroom, exercise room. **Business Services:** conference facilities. **Free Special Amenities:** newspaper and high-speed Internet.

RESORT AND CONFERENCE CENTER AT HYANNIS *Book at AAA.com*   Phone: (508)775-7775

Hotel
$160-$300 5/1-9/5
$110-$225 9/6-4/30

Address: 35 Scudder Ave 02601 **Location:** Just sw of W Main St Rotary. **Facility:** Smoke free premises. 232 units. 224 one-bedroom standard units. 8 one-bedroom suites. 2 stories, interior corridors. *Bath:* combo or shower only. **Parking:** on-site. **Terms:** 2-3 night minimum stay - seasonal and/or weekends, 14 day cancellation notice-fee imposed. **Amenities:** voice mail, irons, hair dryers. **Pool(s):** heated outdoor, heated indoor. **Leisure Activities:** sauna, whirlpool, steamrooms, playground, exercise room, spa. *Fee:* golf-18 holes, game room. **Guest Services:** wireless Internet. **Business Services:** conference facilities, business center.

SEACOAST INN   Phone: 508/775-3828

Hotel
$69-$149 5/1-10/31

Address: 33 Ocean St 02601 **Location:** Just s of Main St; corner of Ocean and South sts. **Facility:** Smoke free premises. 26 one-bedroom standard units, some with efficiencies. 2 stories (no elevator), interior corridors. **Parking:** on-site. **Terms:** open 5/1-10/31, office hours 7:30 am-9 pm, 3 day cancellation notice. **Guest Services:** wireless Internet. **Business Services:** PC. **Free Special Amenities: continental breakfast and high-speed Internet.**

▼ See AAA listing p 484 ▼

▼ See AAA listing p 485 ▼

(See map and index starting on p. 454)
——— **WHERE TO DINE** ———

ALBERTO'S RISTORANTE   *Menu on AAA.com*   Phase: 508/778-1770   ⑦

Northern Italian
$7-$20

This romantic, pretty restaurant is draped in white, and a corner fireplace adds a cozy touch. Vegetables and spicy herbs outnumber the noodles in the delightful and refreshing minestrone soup. The grilled pork tenderloin with grilled vegetables is generously plated. Lemon gelato rolled in white chocolate with raspberry sauce is just right for a finish. A selection of "sunset dinners" is available 3-6 pm Monday through Saturday and noon-6 pm on Sunday. Casual dress. **Bar:** Full bar. **Reservations:** accepted, in season. **Hours:** 11:30 am-close. Closed: 11/25, 12/24, 12/25. **Address:** 360 Main St 02601 **Location:** Just w of jct Barnstable Rd; downtown. **Parking:** on-site.

BARBYANN'S RESTAURANT   Phone: 508/775-9795   ①

American
$7-$30

Sirloin tips, pizza, swordfish and burgers are staples at the bustling family restaurant. Although a bit off the beaten path, it's only a couple of miles from the beach, airport and Cape Cod Mall. Servers show a fine ability to keep up during busy times. Contributing to the country decor are pictures of Cape Cod life. A large fireplace is the focus of the lounge. Casual dress. **Bar:** Full bar. **Reservations:** accepted. **Hours:** 11:30 am-10 pm, Sun 11 am-9 pm; Sunday brunch. Closed: 11/25, 12/24, 12/25. **Address:** 120 Airport Rd 02601 **Location:** 0.5 mi n of jct SR 28 and 132, just n of SR 132. **Parking:** on-site.

THE BLACK CAT   Phone: 508/778-1233   ⑯

American
$9-$35

Mahogany-paneled walls and brass light fixtures enhance the nautical club feel of the cozy restaurant, which displays crew-racing memorabilia such as a two-man scull suspended from the ceiling. Silk flowers and cut-glass oil lamps grace each table. Seasonal offerings include seating on vinyl furniture on the patio, which is shaded by black-and-white awnings, and valet parking. Servers are friendly and efficient. Lighter fare is served in the tavern after 3 pm. Casual dress. Entertainment. **Bar:** Full bar. **Reservations:** accepted. **Hours:** Open 5/1-12/31 & 2/14-4/30; 11:30 am-9 pm, Fri & Sat-10 pm; hours may vary in winter. Closed: 12/25. **Address:** 165 Ocean St 02601 **Location:** 0.8 mi s; opposite ferry dock. **Parking:** on-site.

BOBBY BYRNE'S RESTAURANT AND PUB   Phone: 508/775-1425

American
$8-$20

The popular pub provides dependably good food—from light salads and soups to sandwiches and burgers, as well as more substantial main courses—in a congenial atmosphere. Plenty of parking in this shopping center location makes the restaurant an easy stop for lunch or dinner. Casual dress. **Bar:** Full bar. **Hours:** 11 am-11 pm, Fri & Sat-midnight. Closed: 11/25, 12/25. **Address:** 489 Bearses Way 02601 **Location:** On SR 28, 0.7 mi w of jct SR 132. **Parking:** on-site.

BRAZILIAN GRILL   Phone: 508/771-0109   ⑰

Brazilian
$8-$26

Rough-hewn timbers and walls adorned with cowboy paraphernalia from the ranch lands of Brazil provide a setting that is unusual on Cape Cod. Guests order a la carte or churrascaria de rodizio, in which meats are carved at the table from skewers taken fresh from the fire by a churresqueiro—a style of service popular in the South. The menu lists vegetarian dishes, pasta and seafood. The salad bar is extensive, and all desserts are made in the kitchen. Casual dress. **Bar:** Full bar. **Reservations:** suggested. **Hours:** 11:30 am-10 pm, Fri & Sat-10:30 pm, Sun noon-10 pm. Closed: 12/25. **Address:** 680 Main St 02601 **Location:** At west end of Main St; center. **Parking:** on-site and street.

THE BRITISH BEER COMPANY   Phone: 508/771-1776   ⑨

British
$7-$22

The pub has an ornate back bar, lots of rich dark wood, a center section of high tables and some perimeter booths. Roughly 20 draft beers and more than 50 bottled brews come from around the world. On the menu is a wide selection of hot and cold sandwiches, half-pound burgers and traditional British fare, such as fish and chips and shepherd's pie. Casual dress. Entertainment. **Bar:** Full bar. **Reservations:** accepted. **Hours:** 11 am-11 pm. Closed: 11/25, 12/24, 12/25. **Address:** 412 Main St 02601 **Location:** Center. **Parking:** on-site and street. CALL Ⓛ Ⓜ

COOKE'S SEAFOOD   Phone: 508/775-0450

Seafood
$5-$16

The counter-service establishment specializes in fried, broiled and baked seafood. Casual dress. **Bar:** Beer & wine. **Reservations:** not accepted. **Hours:** Open 5/1-11/26 & 3/1-4/30; 11:30 am-9 pm. Closed: 11/25. **Address:** 1120 Rt 132 02601 **Location:** US 6, exit 6, 2.3 mi se. **Parking:** on-site.

DRAGON LITE RESTAURANT   Phone: 508/775-9494   ⑮

Chinese
$6-$17

Savor authentic Chinese recipes in Szechuan, Mandarin, Cantonese and Hunan cuisine styles in the tidy, inviting dining room. Generous lunch and dinner combinations are served by an efficient and prompt wait staff. Casual dress. **Bar:** Full bar. **Reservations:** accepted. **Hours:** 11:30 am-10 pm, Fri & Sat-10:30 pm, Sun 1 pm-10 pm. **Address:** 620 Main St 02601 **Location:** Corner of Main and Sea sts; downtown. **Parking:** on-site.

THE EGG & I   Phone: 508/771-1596   ⑫

American
$5-$8

Tasty specialty versions of eggs Benedict, create-your-own omelets, real home fries, cinnamon French toast, Belgian waffles, traditional and Swedish pancakes and a few sandwiches make up the homestyle cooking prevalent at The Egg & I, a landmark 1971 restaurant near JFK Hyannis Museum. Fruits, homemade muffins, baked beans and Vermont maple syrup are available a la carte. A friendly wait staff and country decor lend to a warm experience for those who sit at tables or in the few counter seats. Casual dress. **Hours:** 6 am-3 pm. **Address:** 521 Main St 02601 **Location:** Between High School Rd and Pine St; downtown. **Parking:** street. **Historic**

(See map and index starting on p. 454)

FAZIO'S TRATTORIA
Phone: 508/775-9400   5

Italian
$10-$22

Generous portions of homestyle Italian fare are prepared with grilled vegetables, veal, chicken, shellfish and fresh pasta and served in this unpretentious, storefront restaurant. Other specialties include brick-oven pizzas, bread served with olive oil and large, colorful salads. Daily blackboard specials rarely disappoint. A few tables at the front line the windows. Recorded music from a former pop era provides a suitable background. Casual dress. **Bar:** Beer & wine. **Reservations:** accepted. **Hours:** 11:30 am-2:30 & 5-close, Sat & Sun from 5 pm. Closed: 4/4, 11/25, 12/25. **Address:** 294 Main St 02601 **Location:** Just e of Center St and Old Colony Rd. **Parking:** street.

HEARTH 'N KETTLE RESTAURANT
Phone: 508/771-3000

American
$7-$20

Traditional Cape Cod cooking is served in an informal, family-friendly atmosphere. The diverse menu has the standards, from bacon, eggs and omelets for breakfast and sandwiches, chowders and salads for lunch to old favorites such as meatloaf and chicken pot pie for dinner. Fresh seafood is the forte. Finish the meal with one of the traditional New England desserts, such as Indian pudding or a distinctive treatment of strawberry shortcake. A few vegetarian selections are offered. Casual dress. **Bar:** Full bar. **Hours:** 7 am-close. Closed: 12/25. **Address:** 1225 Iyannough Rd 02601 **Location:** US 6, exit 6, 1.5 mi se on SR 132; in Cape Codder Resort & Spa. **Parking:** on-site. *(See color ad p 482)*

IL MAESTRO RISTORANTE
Phone: 508/775-1168   19

Italian
$16-$28

The cozy, family-operated restaurant is at the end of a small strip mall and is a short walk to the Melody Tent. Starters range from antipasti, stuffed mushrooms and traditional Caesar salad to homemade soups such as stracciatella en brode to calamari. Rounding out the menu are homemade ravioli, grilled steaks, native seafood and chicken and veal prepared various ways. Service is friendly. Casual dress. **Bar:** Full bar. **Reservations:** suggested. **Hours:** 4:30 pm-10 pm; hours vary off season. Closed: 11/25, 12/24, 12/25. **Address:** 187C W Main St 02601 **Location:** 0.4 mi w of west end rotary. **Parking:** on-site.

NAKED OYSTER BISTRO & RAW BAR
Phone: 508/778-6500   2

Seafood
$12-$34

This restaurant, located in a business park just south of the airport, prides itself on serving locally bought produce and seafood. A mirrored glass wall lists the farm sources. The menu features well-prepared raw-bar items in addition to entrées such as filet mignon, pan-seared scallops and cedar-planked salmon. An extensive wine list is offered. The contemporary décor incorporates dark-wood wall moldings, light-wood floors, and cream- and dark-brown booths and window treatments. Casual dress. **Bar:** Full bar. **Reservations:** accepted. **Hours:** 11:30 am-3 & 4-9 pm, Sat & Sun from 4 pm. Closed major holidays; also Sun 9/5-5/29. **Address:** 20 Independence Dr 02601 **Location:** Just n of SR 132. **Parking:** on-site.

NOT YOUR AVERAGE JOE'S
Phone: 508/778-1424

American
$9-$18

The restaurant represents the trendy style of contemporary design with vibrant color schemes, comfortable banquettes and stools and smartly dressed staff. The high point is the food, including creative hand-made pizza, sandwiches and salads. Chefs whip up gourmet comfort foods, such as homemade meatloaf, with a flavorful twist. Casual dress. **Bar:** Full bar. **Reservations:** accepted. **Hours:** 11:30 am-10 pm, Fri & Sat-11 pm, Sun noon-9 pm. Closed: 11/25, 12/25. **Address:** 793 Iyannough Rd 02601 **Location:** On SR 132; in Cape Cod Mall. **Parking:** on-site. CALL 🐾Ⓜ

THE ORIGINAL GOURMET BRUNCH
Phone: 508/771-2558   11

American
$7-$9

Toward the west end of Main Street and set back from the street a bit, this popular, unpretentious eatery lines up celebrity guests on the picture-lined walls. It is evident breakfast is king, from the specialty brunch to the Latin-influenced conquistador scramble to standards such as quiche Lorraine, eggs Benedict and omelets. If it feels too late for breakfast, clam chowder, chili or onion soup followed by a burger or specialty sandwich might be just the thing. Service is folksy and attentive. Casual dress. **Bar:** Beer & wine. **Hours:** 7 am-2 pm. Closed: 11/25, 12/25. **Address:** 517 Main St 02601 **Location:** Set back s of Main St, just w of High School Rd; center. **Parking:** street.

THE PADDOCK   *Menu on AAA.com*
Phone: 508/775-7677   20

American
$8-$43

This restaurant, themed around horse racing, offers elegant, candlelit ambiance in its Victorian main dining room. The bright, cheery garden room, with its inlaid marble floor and vaulted, hexagonal-beamed ceiling, is the setting for lunch and, at times, dinner. This is a busy local favorite that has been operated by the same family since 1969. Casual dress. Entertainment. **Bar:** Full bar. **Reservations:** suggested. **Hours:** Open 5/1-11/8 & 4/1-4/30; 11:30 am-2:30 & 5-10 pm, Sun noon-9 pm. **Address:** 20 Scudder Ave 02601 **Location:** 1 mi w at Main St rotary. **Parking:** on-site and valet. CALL 🐾Ⓜ

PAVILION INDIAN CUISINE
Phone: 508/790-0985   10

Indian
$12-$22

Chicken, lamb, beef, seafood and vegetarian dishes are prepared vindaloo, korma, curry and tandoori style and accompanied by basmati (a popular Indian long-grained, thin rice). Of note is the spiced lamb vindaloo. Casual dress. **Bar:** Beer & wine. **Reservations:** accepted. **Hours:** 11 am-2:30 & 4:30-11 pm. **Address:** 511 Main St 02601 **Location:** Between High School Rd and Pine St; downtown. **Parking:** on-site.

PERSY'S PLACE
Phone: 508/790-8200   4

American
$4-$15

The full-service breakfast and lunch stop offers a large breakfast menu with traditional New England favorites and new creations such as a Thanksgiving omelet and apple-walnut buttermilk pancakes. Although breakfast is served all day, the menu also lists chowders, sandwiches and New England specialty plates. Casual dress. **Reservations:** not accepted. **Hours:** 7 am-3 pm. **Address:** 247 Main St 02601 **Location:** Center. **Parking:** on-site.

ROADHOUSE CAFE
Phone: 508/775-2386   18

Steak
$16-$37

The bright yellow clapboard exterior accented with black awnings indicates this is the place. The atmosphere has been described as "clubby" with rich woods, antiques and posters in the dining rooms. Crisp linens add a touch of formality. The menu begins with soups, chowders and more than 20 appetizers, which are followed by such native seafood as broiled scrod, baked scallops and grilled salmon, as well as steak, chicken, veal and pasta, as main courses. Homemade desserts change seasonally. Casual dress. Entertainment. **Bar:** Full bar. **Reservations:** suggested. **Hours:** 4 pm-10 pm, Fri & Sat-midnight. Closed: 1/1, 12/24, 12/25. **Address:** 488 South St 02601 **Location:** Just s of Main St, jct Sea St; downtown. **Parking:** valet. CALL 🐾Ⓜ

(See map and index starting on p. 454)

SAM DIEGO'S MEXICAN COOKERY AND BAR — Phone: 508/771-8816

Mexican
$7-$18

The lively, bi-level dining room's stylized Mexican roadhouse and Southwestern decor incorporates lots of neon, plants, cacti and a large, three-dimensional sun. Good food is served in generous portions. In warm weather, seating expands to a large patio. The dining room is smoke-free. Casual dress. **Bar:** Full bar. **Reservations:** not accepted. **Hours:** 11:30 am-midnight. Closed: 11/25, 12/24, 12/25. **Address:** 950 Iyannough Rd 02601 **Location:** On SR 132. **Parking:** on-site. CALL (&M)

SCHOONERS — Phone: 508/778-7588 〔8〕

American
$7-$20

Rich dark woods accented with brass, models of schooners, nautical art and table linens add up to a comfortable backdrop for the eclectic menu, which lists such items as roast duck, grilled lamb chops, veal Parmesan and asparagus affumicata. Chicken tandoori is a popular choice. Service varies a bit but is friendly. In the center of the space is a small stool bar. Pizza and take-out are available until 1 am. A patio at the rear provides the only area for smoking. Casual dress. Entertainment. **Bar:** Full bar. **Reservations:** suggested, weekends & in summer. **Hours:** 11:30 am-10:30 pm. Closed: 12/25. **Address:** 372 Main St 02601 **Location:** Center. **Parking:** on-site. CALL (&M)

SPANKY'S CLAM SHACK — Phone: 508/771-2770 〔13〕

Seafood
$10-$27

On Hyannis Harbor adjacent to the Hy-Line cruise terminal, the restaurant lets patrons get a quick meal at the fast-serve, to-go counter; a more leisurely counter in the dining room overlooking the docks; or a casual experience on the open deck. As might be expected, the specialty is seafood. Fried clams are so light they seem almost baked. Parking is available in the adjacent metered lot. Casual dress. **Bar:** Full bar. **Reservations:** not accepted. **Hours:** Open 5/1-10/31 & 4/15-4/30; 6 am-11 pm, Fri-midnight, Sat-1 am. **Address:** 138 Ocean St 02601 **Location:** 0.9 mi s; adjacent to ferry docks. **Parking:** on-site and street.

THAI HOUSE RESTAURANT — Phone: 508/862-1616 〔6〕

Thai
$8-$16

Close to the east end of Main Street and within walking distance of the ferry docks is an informal storefront chef-operated Thai restaurant. Begin with chicken sate and coconut soup, then choose from an assortment of authentic rice and noodle dishes, curries or house beef, duck, chicken and seafood specialties. Nearly 20 dishes appeal to vegetarians. Food is prepared without monosodium glutamate. Thai pictures, wall hangings and art decorate the dining room. Casual dress. **Bar:** Beer & wine. **Reservations:** not accepted. **Hours:** 11 am-10 pm, Sun 4 pm-9:30 pm. Closed: 11/25, 12/25. **Address:** 304-306 Main St 02601 **Location:** Center. **Parking:** street. CALL (&M)

TUGBOATS — Phone: 508/775-6433 〔14〕

Seafood
$8-$28

Formerly a sail loft, the 1989-established second-floor eatery overlooks Hyannis Harbor and marina and is popular for outdoor dining. At lunch, beachgoers in swimsuit cover-ups sit alongside professionals in starched shirts and ties. Fresh seafood preparations, such as clam chowder, charbroiled swordfish tips, Cajun blackened shrimp and broiled scrod, are tasty. Two heated, awning-covered decks with roll-down vinyl sides flank the glass-walled lounge and small main dining room. Casual dress. **Bar:** Full bar. **Reservations:** accepted, off season. **Hours:** Open 5/1-10/25 & 4/15-4/30; noon-10 pm. Closed: Mon 4/15-5/25. **Address:** 21 Arlington St 02601 **Location:** At Hyannis Marina. **Parking:** on-site.

YING'S — Phone: 508/790-2432 〔3〕

Asian
$8-$26

The Asian eatery dabbles in Thai, Korean and Japanese cuisine, including specialties from the sushi bar. The large menu focuses on tasty preparations. Casual dress. **Bar:** Full bar. **Reservations:** not accepted. **Hours:** 11:30 am-10 pm, Fri & Sat-11 pm. Closed: 11/25, 12/25. **Address:** 59 Center St 02601 **Location:** Just se off Barnstable Rd, nw off Main St. **Parking:** on-site.

MASHPEE (See map and index starting on p. 458)

——— *The following lodging was either not evaluated or did not* ———
meet AAA rating requirements but is listed for your information only.

THE RESORT AT NEW SEABURY — Phone: 508/477-9111

〔fyi〕

Not evaluated. **Address:** 20 Red Brook Rd 02649 **Location:** Jct SR 151 and 28, 2.6 mi s via Great Neck Rd. Facilities, services, and decor characterize a mid-scale property.

——— **WHERE TO DINE** ———

BLEU — Phone: 508/539-7907 〔116〕

American
$9-$30

Unusual presentations distinguish this elegant restaurant's creative dishes. The chef uses fresh ingredients to design his menu and provide the ultimate in eye appeal and taste. Large overhead lantern lights provide for a more relaxed feel to the upscale atmosphere. Casual dress. **Bar:** Full bar. **Reservations:** suggested. **Hours:** 11:30 am-4 & 5-10 pm. Closed: 11/25, 12/25. **Address:** 10 Market St 02649 **Location:** At Mashpee Commons. **Parking:** on-site.

BOBBY BYRNE'S RESTAURANT AND PUB — Phone: 508/477-0600

American
$7-$17

The popular pub serves dependably good food—from light salads and soups to sandwiches and burgers and more substantial main courses—in a congenial atmosphere. Plenty of parking and a shopping complex location make this an easy spot to break for lunch or dinner. Heaters on the sidewalk cafe extend the outdoor dining "season." Entertainment is slated Friday and Saturday nights. Casual dress. **Bar:** Full bar. **Reservations:** not accepted. **Hours:** 11 am-11 pm, Fri & Sat-midnight. Closed: 11/25, 12/25. **Address:** 6 Central Square 02649 **Location:** Jct SR 28 and 151; in Mashpee Commons. **Parking:** on-site. CALL (&M)

(See map and index starting on p. 458)

COOKE'S SEAFOOD
Phone: 508/477-9595

Seafood
$6-$20

The largely self-serve restaurant specializes in preparations of fish and shellfish. Casual dress. **Bar:** Beer only. **Reservations:** not accepted. **Hours:** Open 5/1-10/29 & 3/1-4/30; 11:30 am-9 pm, Fri & Sat-9:30 pm; to 8:30 pm off season. Closed: 11/25. **Address:** 7 Ryan's Way 02649 **Location:** Just n of SR 28, off Mashpee traffic circle, on Great Neck North Rd. **Parking:** on-site.

SIMMER
Phone: 508/539-0025   (117)

New American
$19-$32

This trendy spot is the perfect place for those looking for a sophisticated dining experience that provides an excuse for dressing up. Diners also enjoy the three-course early prix fixe menu that's perfect before a trip to the nearby cinema. The menu changes seasonally but may include scallop and corn chowder with smoked bacon and sweet potato hay or a barbecue Painted Hill skirt steak with fingerling potatoes and Swiss chard. Dressy casual. **Bar:** Full bar. **Reservations:** accepted. **Hours:** 4:30 pm-11:30 pm. Closed: 1/1, 11/25, 12/25. **Address:** 20 Joy St 02649 **Location:** Jct SR 151, 1.7 mi n via SR 28 N; in Roche Brothers Shopping Center. **Parking:** on-site. CALL ⑤M

NORTH FALMOUTH pop. 3,355   (See map and index starting on p. 458)

——— WHERE TO DINE ———

SILVER LOUNGE RESTAURANT
Phone: 508/563-2410   (110)

American
$4-$25

This popular eatery features a wide selection of traditional favorites and sandwiches. The rustic-style pub proudly displays marine items, model ships and fishing nets, as well as a restored railroad caboose. Casual dress. **Bar:** Full bar. **Hours:** 11:30 am-midnight. Closed: 11/25, 12/25. **Address:** 412 Rt 28A 02556 **Location:** 0.5 mi s of jct SR 151. **Parking:** on-site.

NORTH TRURO   (See map and index starting on p. 458)

CROWS NEST RESORT
Phone: 508/487-9031   **2**

Motel
$79-$389 5/1-11/30
$72-$389 4/1-4/30

Address: 496 Shore Rd 02652 **Location:** Oceanfront. US 6, exit SR 6A/Shore Rd, 3.4 mi n. **Facility:** Smoke free premises. 21 units. 4 one-bedroom standard units with kitchens and whirlpools. 8 one-, 8 two- and 1 three-bedroom suites with kitchens and whirlpools. 2 stories (no elevator), exterior corridors. **Parking:** on-site. **Terms:** open 5/1-11/30 & 4/1-4/30, office hours 8 am-9 pm, 2-7 night minimum stay - seasonal and/or weekends, 90 day cancellation notice-fee imposed. **Amenities:** DVD players, high-speed Internet (fee), voice mail, irons, hair dryers. **Leisure Activities:** limited beach access, fishing. **Guest Services:** complimentary laundry, wireless Internet. **Business Services:** fax. (See color ad p 498) ⊠ ▤ ▤ ▤ ▤

FREE local telephone calls and high-speed Internet

EAST HARBOUR MOTEL & COTTAGES
Phone: 508/487-0505   **1**

Motel
$90-$230 5/1-10/21

Address: 618 Shore Rd 02652 **Location:** Oceanfront. US 6, exit SR 6A/Shore Rd, 4 mi n. **Facility:** Smoke free premises. 17 units. 9 one-bedroom standard units. 1 one-bedroom suite with kitchen. 7 cottages. 1 story, exterior corridors. *Bath:* combo or shower only. **Parking:** on-site. **Terms:** open 5/1-10/21, office hours 9 am-9 pm, 2 night minimum stay - weekends, 30 day cancellation notice-fee imposed. **Amenities:** DVD players, irons. **Leisure Activities:** limited beach access. **Guest Services:** coin laundry, wireless Internet. ⊠ ▤ ▤ ▤ / SOME UNITS ▨

(See map and index starting on p. 458)

──── **WHERE TO DINE** ────

ADRIAN'S

Regional Italian
$12-$30

Phone: 508/487-4360   ①

Adrian's open, airy and casual decor allows for a comfortable meal out. The menu centers on regional Italian dishes and an array of pizzas and pasta dishes, not to mention gourmet breakfast. Guests can dine on the deck in season. Casual dress. **Bar:** Full bar. **Reservations:** accepted. **Hours:** Open 5/15-10/11; 8 am-noon & 5:30-9 pm; hours may vary off season. **Address:** 535 Rt 6 02666 **Location:** 5.3 mi ne of Truro Center. **Parking:** on-site.

ORLEANS pop. 1,716   (See map and index starting on p. 458)

THE COVE

Motel
$69-$224 All Year

Phone: (508)255-1203   ㉝

Address: 13 S Orleans Rd (SR 28) 02653 **Location:** US 6, rotary exit Eastham/Orleans, just w on SR 6A, then just n. **Facility:** Smoke free premises. 47 units. 40 one-bedroom standard units. 7 one-bedroom suites, some with efficiencies or kitchens. 2 stories (no elevator), interior/exterior corridors. *Bath:* combo or shower only. **Parking:** on-site. **Terms:** office hours 8 am-9 pm, 2-3 night minimum stay - seasonal, 10 day cancellation notice-fee imposed. **Amenities:** DVD players, voice mail, irons, hair dryers. **Pool(s):** heated outdoor. **Leisure Activities:** shuffleboard. **Guest Services:** wireless Internet. **Business Services:** PC, fax. *(See color ad below)*

GOVERNOR PRENCE INN   *Book at AAA.com*
Motel
$99-$169 5/15-10/12

Phone: (508)255-1216   ㉜

Address: 66 SR 6A 02653 **Location:** 0.5 mi w of rotary. **Facility:** Smoke free premises. 56 one-bedroom standard units. 1-2 stories (no elevator), exterior corridors. **Parking:** on-site. **Terms:** open 5/15-10/12, office hours 8 am-9 pm, 2 night minimum stay - seasonal and/or weekends, 10 day cancellation notice-fee imposed. **Pool(s):** outdoor. **Guest Services:** wireless Internet.

──── ▼ See AAA listing above ▼ ────

Read, Share, Ask, Plan. Join the travel conversation at AAATravelViews.com

(See map and index starting on p. 458)

ORLEANS INN **Phone:** (508)255-2222 29

 Historic
Country Inn
$250-$450 All Year

Address: 21 SR 6A 02653 **Location:** On SR 28 and 6A, exit rotary, just w. **Facility:** This 1875 sea captain's mansion was home to a direct descendant of a passenger on the Mayflower. Smoke free premises. 11 units. 10 one-bedroom standard units. 1 one-bedroom suite. 2 stories (no elevator), interior corridors. *Bath:* combo or shower only. **Parking:** on-site. **Terms:** cancellation fee imposed. **Amenities:** high-speed Internet, voice mail, irons, hair dryers. *Some:* DVD players. **Dining:** restaurant, see separate listing. **Guest Services:** wireless Internet. **Business Services:** meeting rooms, PC, fax.

RIDGEWOOD MOTEL & COTTAGES **Phone:** 508/255-0473 36

Motel
$60-$97 5/1-10/17

Address: 10 Quanset Rd 02662 **Location:** Jct SR 28 and 39; US 6, exit 11, left onto SR 137 S, then first left onto Pleasant Bay Rd for 1 mi, then 1.5 mi n on SR 39. **Facility:** Smoke free premises. 17 units. 12 one-bedroom standard units. 5 cottages. 1 story, exterior corridors. *Bath:* shower only. **Parking:** on-site. **Terms:** open 5/1-10/17, office hours 8 am-10 pm, 2 night minimum stay, 7 day cancellation notice, 28 day for cottages-fee imposed. **Pool(s):** outdoor. **Leisure Activities:** playground, horseshoes, volleyball. *(See color ad p 495)*

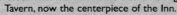

(See map and index starting on p. 458)

RODEWAY INN   *Book great rates at AAA.com*   **Phone:** (508)255-1514   **31**

Hotel
$59-$275 All Year

Address: 48 Cranberry Hwy 02653 **Location:** Jct SR 6A and 28. **Facility:** Smoke free premises. 43 units. 39 one- and 4 two-bedroom standard units. 2 stories (no elevator), exterior corridors. *Bath:* combo or shower only. **Parking:** on-site. **Terms:** office hours 7 am-11 am, 3 night minimum stay - seasonal, 4 day cancellation notice-fee imposed. **Amenities:** voice mail, irons, hair dryers. **Pool(s):** heated outdoor. **Guest Services:** coin laundry, wireless Internet. **Free Special Amenities:** continental breakfast and high-speed Internet.

SEASHORE PARK INN   *Book great rates at AAA.com*   **Phone:** (508)255-2500   **30**

Motel
$99-$179 5/1-10/19 &
4/17-4/30

Address: 24 Canal Rd 02653 **Location:** US 6, rotary exit Eastham/Orleans, just w on SR 6A. **Facility:** Smoke free premises. 62 one-bedroom standard units, some with efficiencies. 2 stories (no elevator), exterior corridors. **Parking:** on-site. **Terms:** open 5/1-10/19 & 4/17-4/30, office hours 8 am-9 pm, 2 night minimum stay - seasonal and/or weekends, 10 day cancellation notice-fee imposed. **Amenities:** *Some:* hair dryers. **Pool(s):** outdoor, heated indoor. **Leisure Activities:** sauna, whirlpool, pool table. *Fee:* game room. **Guest Services:** wireless Internet. **Free Special Amenities: continental breakfast and local telephone calls.**

SKAKET BEACH MOTEL   *Book great rates at AAA.com*   **Phone:** (508)255-1020   **35**

Motel
$65-$175 4/1-4/30
$65-$170 5/1-11/28

Address: 203 Cranberry Hwy (Rt 6A) 02653 **Location:** US 6, exit 12, just e. **Facility:** 46 units. 45 one-bedroom standard units, some with efficiencies. 1 one-bedroom suite with kitchen. 1-2 stories (no elevator), exterior corridors. *Bath:* combo or shower only. **Parking:** on-site. **Terms:** open 5/1-11/28 & 4/1-4/30, office hours 8 am-8 pm, 2-3 night minimum stay - seasonal and/or weekends, 10 day cancellation notice-fee imposed. **Amenities:** irons, hair dryers. **Pool(s):** heated outdoor. **Leisure Activities:** croquet, bocci, picnic areas, charcoal grills, horseshoes. **Guest Services:** coin laundry, wireless Internet. *(See color ad p 496)*

FREE continental breakfast and high-speed Internet

▼ See AAA listing p 494 ▼

Stay. Play. Dine. Save.
Visit AAA.com/Travel for Information To Go!

▼ See AAA listing p 495 ▼

SKAKET BEACH MOTEL
203 Cranberry Highway, Route 6A
Orleans, MA 02653

For Reservations, please call
(508) 255-1020 or 1-800-835-0298
www.skaketbeachmotel.com

Charming hospitality, unique location, distinctive amenities, and undivided attention to detail. Minutes from our door you will find beautiful beaches, boating, golf, shops and many restaurants. Freshly baked cranberry and blueberry muffins each morning, make the Skaket Beach Motel a great choice.

(See map and index starting on p. 458)

------ **WHERE TO DINE** ------

ABBA

Mediterranean
$18-$35

Phone: 508/255-8144   (38)

The chef-owned bistro is a bit out of the way but is quite the find. Creative Mediterranean dishes reflect Israeli and Thai influences. This place is an absolute must for Cape Cod visitors. Outdoor seating is an option during the warmer months. Dressy casual. **Bar:** Full bar. **Reservations:** suggested. **Hours:** 5 pm-10 pm. Closed: 11/25, 12/25; also Mon in winter. **Address:** 89 Old Colony Way 02653 **Location:** At West Rd and Old Colony Way. **Parking:** on-site.

CAPT'N ELMER'S RESTAURANT & FISH MARKET

Seafood
$8-$25

Phone: 508/255-3350   (37)

Established in 1976, this combination eatery and adjacent fish market uses traditional recipes to drive its menu, which includes baked stuffed sole, fish and chips, a steamer dinner and varied pasta dishes. For starters, many enjoy the fried calamari for sharing or stuffed quahogs—a real local favorite. Deliberate and familiar service prevails. Casual dress. **Bar:** Full bar. **Reservations:** not accepted. **Hours:** Open 5/1-11/30; 11 am-9:30 pm. **Address:** 18 Old Colony Way 02653 **Location:** Center of village; just w of jct Main St and SR 6A (Cranberry Hwy) Old Kings Hwy. **Parking:** on-site.

COOKE'S SEAFOOD
Seafood
$5-$17

Phone: 508/255-5518   (34)

This locally popular, largely self-serve restaurant specializes in preparations of fish and shellfish. Casual dress. **Bar:** Beer & wine. **Hours:** 11:30 am-8 pm; seasonal hours vary. Closed: major holidays, 12/24. **Address:** 1 S Orleans Rd 02653 **Location:** On SR 28 at jct SR 6A; 0.5 mi w of rotary. **Parking:** on-site.

HEARTH 'N KETTLE RESTAURANT

American
$5-$15

Phone: 508/240-0111

Traditional Cape Cod cooking is served in an informal, family-friendly atmosphere. The diverse menu has the standards, from bacon, eggs and omelets for breakfast and sandwiches, chowders and salads for lunch to old favorites such as meatloaf and chicken pot pie for dinner. Fresh seafood is the forte. Finish the meal with one of the traditional New England desserts, such as Indian pudding or a distinctive treatment of strawberry shortcake. A few vegetarian selections are offered. Casual dress. **Bar:** Full bar. **Hours:** 7 am-close. Closed: 12/25. **Address:** 9 West Rd 02653 **Location:** US 6, exit 12, just e on SR 6A. **Parking:** on-site. CALL 🛗M

LAND-HO RESTAURANT

American
$6-$22

Phone: 508/255-5165   (36)

Where SR 6A crosses Main Street is this restaurant of considerable longevity. A dark wood interior is obscured by shingles and license plates from many businesses on Cape Cod. Newspapers hang from a line between pillars separating the bar and dining area. Red-and-black checkered tablecloths and checked napkins complete the scene. The menu features sandwiches, seafood and homemade desserts. Entrees are priced daily. A late night menu is available until midnight. Casual dress. **Bar:** Full bar. **Hours:** 11:30 am-10 pm; Sunday brunch. Closed: 12/25. **Address:** 38 Main St 02653 **Location:** Corner of SR 6A and Main St; center. **Parking:** on-site.

THE LOBSTER CLAW   *Menu on AAA.com*

Seafood
$8-$30

Phone: 508/255-1800   (33)

Hearty portions of fresh seafood, along with some burgers and sandwiches, are served in the casual family restaurant. The bustling atmosphere contributes to this place's popularity. Casual dress. **Bar:** Full bar. **Hours:** Open 5/1-11/15 & 4/1-4/30; 11:30 am-9 pm. **Address:** 42 Rt 6A 02653 **Location:** Jct SR 28. **Parking:** on-site.

LOBSTER POUND

Seafood
$8-$23

Phone: 508/240-1234   (39)

Appointed in nautical decor, the family restaurant offers options for dining inside or outside. This place is popular for lobsterbakes and clambakes that can be eaten here or taken out, in addition to fried and baked seafood dishes, such as fried clam platter, baked native scrod, fried seafood platter and baked seafood medley. Guests can pick their own market-priced lobster from the tank. Casual dress. **Bar:** Full bar. **Reservations:** accepted. **Hours:** Open 5/25-10/12; 11:30 am-10 pm. **Address:** 157 Cranberry Hwy (SR 6A) 02653 **Location:** Just w of center on SR 6A. **Parking:** on-site.

MAHONEY'S ATLANTIC BAR & GRILL

American
$16-$27

Phone: 508/255-5505   (35)

The fun and vibrant place features live music in its jazz bar on some nights. The comfortable, cozy dining room has a subtle sophistication. Popular appetizers include soft-shell crabs and drunken shellfish—a combination of cherrystone clams and mussels steamed in brown ale. American entrees range from filet mignon and rack of lamb to barbecue ribs, broiled scallops and grilled tuna. Diners top off the meal with. Casual dress. **Bar:** Full bar. **Reservations:** not accepted. **Hours:** 5 pm-9 pm, Fri & Sat-9:30 pm. Closed: 4/4, 11/25, 12/24, 12/25. **Address:** 28 Main St 02653 **Location:** Village center; 0.7 mi w of rotary; just n of jct SR 6A and Main St. **Parking:** on-site.

OLD JAILHOUSE TAVERN

American
$7-$26

Phone: 508/255-5245   (40)

Experience casual family dining in a contemporary atmosphere with Victorian accents at the Old Jailhouse Tavern. Daily saute specials, seafood primavera, prime rib, sandwiches, baked brie and lighter fare at the bar are served in a lively setting. Casual dress. **Bar:** Full bar. **Hours:** 11:30 am-11 pm, Sun from 11 am; seasonal hours vary. Closed: 11/25, 12/25. **Address:** 28 West Rd 02653 **Location:** US 6, exit 12, just e on SR 6A, then just n. **Parking:** on-site. CALL 🛗M

(See map and index starting on p. 458)

ORLEANS INN RESTAURANT   Phone: 508/255-2222   32

Seafood
$9-$20

From a great location on the water, diners can watch boats come and go as they unwind in the main dining room. The more casual pub has a beautiful mahogany back bar. The all-weather deck opens seasonally, including for lunch. The cuisine—which includes choices such as scallops with peaches, grilled duck breast and a vegetarian selection—goes beyond typical New England fare. Guests can order from a lighter menu of starters and sandwiches in the pub at dinner. Service is friendly. Casual dress. **Bar:** Full bar. **Reservations:** accepted. **Hours:** 11 am-9 pm; winter hours may vary. Closed: 12/25. **Address:** 21 Rt 6A 02653 **Location:** On SR 28 and 6A, exit rotary, just w; in Orleans Inn. **Parking:** on-site.

OSTERVILLE   (See map and index starting on p. 458)

———— **WHERE TO DINE** ————

WIMPY'S SEAFOOD CAFE   Phone: 508/428-6300   104

American
$9-$26

Beginning in 1938 as a hamburger stand with five seats, the popular restaurant has grown to include two dining rooms, a sunroom patio, a cozy tavern and a fish market. A large stone fireplace adds warmth to the dining room, while another accents the tavern. Heavy on fresh seafood, the menu offerings are wholesome, healthy American. Servers are friendly and efficient. A line of spices based on seaweed is available for purchase. Casual dress. **Bar:** Full bar. **Reservations:** suggested. **Hours:** Open 5/1-12/31 & 2/1-4/30; 11:30 am-9 pm, Fri & Sat-9:30 pm, Sun 11 am-9 pm; Sunday brunch; hours may vary off season. **Address:** 752 Main St 02655 **Location:** 2.1 mi s of SR 28 via S Country Rd; 6 mi e on SR 28 S from airport rotary in Hyannis. **Parking:** on-site.

PROVINCETOWN pop. 3,192   (See map and index starting on p. 458)

ANCHOR INN BEACH HOUSE   Phone: 508/487-0432   10

Hotel
$150-$400 5/1-1/2

Address: 175 Commercial St 02657 **Location:** 2 blks se of SR 6A, just sw of post office; center. Located on harbor. **Facility:** Designated smoking area. 23 one-bedroom standard units, some with whirlpools. 3 stories (no elevator), interior/exterior corridors. **Bath:** combo or shower only. **Parking:** on-site. **Terms:** open 5/1-1/2, office hours 8 am-8 pm, 2-5 night minimum stay - seasonal and/or weekends, age restrictions may apply, 21 day cancellation notice-fee imposed. **Amenities:** CD players, dual phone lines, voice mail, irons, hair dryers. **Guest Services:** wireless Internet.
⊠ / SOME UNITS ▯

BAYSHORE & CHANDLER   Phone: 508/487-9133   7

Condominium
$105-$325 All Year

Address: 493 Commercial St 02657 **Location:** Oceanfront. 0.8 mi e of Town Hall. **Facility:** Smoke free premises. 25 units. 2 one-bedroom standard units with kitchens. 19 one- and 4 two-bedroom suites with kitchens. 2-3 stories (no elevator), exterior corridors. **Bath:** combo or shower only. **Parking:** on-site. **Terms:** office hours 10 am-5 pm, 2 night minimum stay - seasonal and/or weekends, 30 day cancellation notice-fee imposed. **Amenities:** irons. *Some:* DVD players. **Leisure Activities:** limited beach access. **Guest Services:** wireless Internet. ⊠ ▯ ▭ / SOME UNITS FEE 🐾 🎿

(See map and index starting on p. 458)

CAPE COLONY INN   Phone: 508/487-1755  5

Motel
$119-$269 6/26-10/17
$89-$139 5/18-6/25

Address: 280 Bradford St 02657 **Location:** SR 6A, 1 mi e of Town Hall. **Facility:** Smoke free premises. 57 units. 49 one- and 8 two-bedroom standard units. 2 stories (no elevator), exterior corridors. *Bath:* combo or shower only. **Parking:** on-site. **Terms:** open 5/18-10/17, office hours 8 am-11 pm, 2-3 night minimum stay, 7 day cancellation notice-fee imposed. **Pool(s):** heated outdoor. **Leisure Activities:** grills, picnic tables, horseshoes, shuffleboard, volleyball. **Guest Services:** wireless Internet. **Free Special Amenities: continental breakfast and high-speed Internet.**

CHATEAU PROVINCETOWN   *Book great rates at AAA.com*   Phone: (508)487-1286 11

Motel
$99-$269 5/2-11/15

Address: 105 Bradford St Ext 02657 **Location:** SR 6A, 0.8 mi w of Town Hall. **Facility:** Designated smoking area. 54 one-bedroom standard units. 1-2 stories (no elevator), exterior corridors. **Parking:** on-site. **Terms:** open 5/2-11/15, office hours 7 am-11 pm, 2 night minimum stay - seasonal and/or weekends, 14 day cancellation notice-fee imposed. **Amenities:** voice mail, irons, hair dryers. *Some:* safes. **Pool(s):** heated outdoor. **Guest Services:** wireless Internet. *(See color ad below)*

FREE continental breakfast and high-speed Internet

▼ *See AAA listing above* ▼

Travel Basics: Keep a AAA Atlas in
every vehicle in the household.

(See map and index starting on p. 458)

CROWNE POINTE HISTORIC INN & SPA
Phone: 508/487-6767 **8**

Country Inn
$129-$499 5/1-10/15
$99-$399 10/16-4/30

Address: 82 Bradford St 02657 **Location:** On SR 6A, just w of Town Hall. **Facility:** The property's picturesque grounds, atop a bluff in the middle of Provincetown, include a landscaped garden courtyard. Smoke free premises. 40 units. 36 one-bedroom standard units, some with kitchens and/or whirlpools. 4 one-bedroom suites with kitchens and whirlpools. 2 stories (no elevator), interior/exterior corridors. *Bath:* combo or shower only. **Parking:** on-site. **Terms:** office hours 7 am-11 pm, age restrictions may apply, 21 day cancellation notice-fee imposed. **Amenities:** video library, DVD players, CD players, high-speed Internet, voice mail, safes, honor bars, irons, hair dryers. **Pool(s):** heated outdoor. **Leisure Activities:** sauna, whirlpools, steamroom, gardens, spa. **Guest Services:** valet laundry, wireless Internet. **Business Services:** PC. **Free Special Amenities:** full breakfast and high-speed Internet. ⬛ ⬛ ⬛ ⬛ ⬛ ⬛ ⬛ / SOME UNITS ⬛

THE MASTHEAD
Phone: (508)487-0523 **12**

Motel
$137-$517 All Year

Address: 31-41 Commercial St 02657 **Location:** 0.8 mi w of Town Hall. Located on ocean. **Facility:** Smoke free premises. 21 units. 14 one-bedroom standard units, some with efficiencies or kitchens. 2 one- and 3 two-bedroom suites with kitchens. 2 cottages. 1-2 stories (no elevator), exterior corridors. *Bath:* some shared or private, combo or shower only. **Parking:** on-site and street. **Terms:** office hours 8 am-8 pm, check-in 4 pm, 14 day cancellation notice-fee imposed. **Amenities:** safes, irons. *Some:* DVD players, hair dryers. **Leisure Activities:** beach access, fishing, charcoal grills, picnic area, beach towels, sun deck. **Guest Services:** wireless Internet. **Free Special Amenities:** local telephone calls and newspaper. ⬛ ⬛ ⬛ ⬛ ⬛

SURFSIDE HOTEL & SUITES
Book at AAA.com
Phone: (508)487-1726 **6**

Hotel
$139-$329 5/1-10/31
$139-$250 4/1-4/30

Address: 542-543 Commercial St 02657 **Location:** Oceanfront. 1 mi e of Town Hall. **Facility:** Smoke free premises. 88 units. 84 one-bedroom standard units. 3 one- and 1 two-bedroom suites, some with kitchens and/or whirlpools. 3-4 stories (no elevator), interior/exterior corridors. **Parking:** on-site. **Terms:** open 5/1-10/31 & 4/1-4/30, office hours 8 am-midnight, 28 day cancellation notice-fee imposed. **Amenities:** voice mail, irons, hair dryers. **Pool(s):** heated outdoor. **Leisure Activities:** beach access. **Guest Services:** wireless Internet. **Business Services:** PC. ASK ⬛ ⬛ ⬛ ⬛ ⬛ ⬛ ⬛ / SOME UNITS FEE ⬛

WHITE WIND INN
Phone: 508/487-1526 **9**

Bed & Breakfast
Rates not provided

Address: 174 Commercial St 02657 **Location:** Just w of Town Hall. **Facility:** Located in the busy tourist section, this mid-1800s New England-style mansion was once the home of a prosperous ship builder. Smoke free premises. 13 units. 12 one-bedroom standard units, some with whirlpools. 1 one-bedroom suite with whirlpool. 2 stories (no elevator), interior corridors. *Bath:* combo or shower only. **Parking:** on-site. **Terms:** office hours 9 am-8 pm. **Amenities:** video library, DVD players, CD players, voice mail, hair dryers. **Guest Services:** wireless Internet. ⬛ ⬛ ⬛ / SOME UNITS FEE ⬛ ⬛

─── *The following lodging was either not evaluated or did not* ───
meet AAA rating requirements but is listed for your information only.

HARBOR HILL AT PROVINCETOWN CONDOMINIUMS
Phone: 508/487-0541

[fyi]

Not evaluated. **Address:** 4 Harbor Hill Rd 02657 **Location:** SR 6A, 0.7 mi w of Town Hall. Facilities, services, and decor characterize a mid-scale property.

─── **WHERE TO DINE** ───

CIRO & SAL'S RESTAURANT
Phone: 508/487-6444 **8**

Italian
$15-$35

The funky Italian restaurant is in a residential neighborhood, with the entrance down the alley just off Commercial Street. Guests should duck their head as they make their way into the basement of a large home and navigate under low ceiling beams to their table. Table spacing is a bit tight, but the food is excellent. Casual dress. **Bar:** Full bar. **Reservations:** suggested. **Hours:** Open 5/1-12/31 & 2/1-4/30; 5:30 pm-10 pm. **Address:** 4 Kiley Ct 02657 **Location:** 1 mi e of Town Hall on Commercial St. **Parking:** on-site (fee).

(See map and index starting on p. 458)

DEVON'S   Phone: 508/487-4773   10

New American
$9-$30

This trendy restaurant features a covered patio with hanging lanterns or tables in a narrow, intimate dining room with exposed wood beams from the original fish market that once stood there. A good starter is the lobster cake, followed by mouthwatering roasted organic Niman Ranch pork tenderloin with rhubarb compote, grilled asparagus and stone-ground grits. Not to be missed is the pastry chef's signature creation: Callebaut chocolate truffle terrine with candied pecans and creme anglaise. Dressy casual. **Bar:** Full bar. **Reservations:** suggested. **Hours:** Open 5/1-10/31; 8 am-1 & 6-10 pm. Closed: major holidays, 12/24, 12/26; also Wed; Mon, Tues & Thurs 5/1-5/31 & 10/1-10/31. **Address:** 401 1/2 Commercial St 02657 **Location:** Between Washington Ave and Law St; center. **Parking:** street.

FANIZZI'S BY THE SEA   *Menu on AAA.com*   Phone: 508/487-1964   7

American
$6-$24

The pleasant setting along the bay offers views of the ocean and nautical activity. On the varied menu is traditional New England fare, from meatloaf to chicken dishes to fried, broiled or baked seafood. The staff is friendly, and this popular spot can be bustling. Casual dress. **Bar:** Full bar. **Reservations:** suggested. **Hours:** 11:30 am-10 pm; Sunday brunch 10 am-2 pm; hours vary off season. Closed: 11/25, 12/25. **Address:** 539 Commercial St 02657 **Location:** Just s of SR 6A. **Parking:** on-site and street.

FRONT STREET RESTAURANT   Phone: 508/487-9715   12

New Continental
$19-$32

The local institution features an eclectic yet well-rounded menu accented with Mediterranean and Italian flavors. Casual dress. **Bar:** Full bar. **Reservations:** required. **Hours:** Open 5/1-12/1; 5:30 pm-10:30 pm; hours vary in fall. Closed major holidays; also Tues; Mon 9/10-11/30. **Address:** 230 Commercial St 02657 **Location:** Just w of Town Hall. **Parking:** on-site (fee).

THE LOBSTER POT   Phone: 508/487-0842   11

Seafood
$6-$24

A full menu of pan roasted lobster, lobster rolls, steak and salads are served in a two-level dining room, with the top floor offering great views of Provincetown Harbor. Their homemade salad dressing is available for purchase. Casual dress. **Bar:** Full bar. **Hours:** Open 5/1-11/30 & 4/1-4/30; 11:30 am-10 pm. **Address:** 321 Commercial St 02657 **Location:** Center. **Parking:** no self-parking.

THE MEWS   Phone: 508/487-1500   9

Continental
$18-$34

A relaxed atmosphere and dining rooms overlooking the harbor and bay create a peaceful, pleasant setting. In the off-season, the coffeehouse offers Monday entertainment. Lighter American fare is served in the cafe. Casual dress. **Bar:** Full bar. **Reservations:** suggested. **Hours:** 6 pm-10 pm; Sunday brunch 11 am-2:30 pm 4/15-10/15. Closed: 12/25. **Address:** 429 Commercial St 02657 **Location:** 0.5 mi e of Town Hall. **Parking:** street.

SANDWICH pop. 3,058   (See map and index starting on p. 458)

COUNTRY ACRES MOTEL   Phone: 508/888-2878   106

Motel
$74-$129 5/1-10/31
$65-$75 11/1-4/30

Address: 187 Rt 6A 02563 **Location:** Jct SR 6A and Main St, just e. **Facility:** Smoke free premises. 18 units. 17 one-bedroom standard units. 1 cottage. 1 story, exterior corridors. *Bath:* shower only. **Parking:** on-site. **Terms:** office hours 7 am-10 pm, 2 night minimum stay - seasonal and/or weekends, 7 day cancellation notice. **Amenities:** voice mail, irons, hair dryers. **Pool(s):** outdoor. **Leisure Activities:** croquet, shuffleboard. **Guest Services:** wireless Internet. **Business Services:** PC. **Free Special Amenities:** continental breakfast and high-speed Internet.

(See map and index starting on p. 458)

THE DAN'L WEBSTER INN & SPA   *Book at AAA.com*   **Phone:** (508)888-3622   `104`

Country Inn
$179-$399 5/1-10/18
$159-$329 10/19-4/30

Address: 149 Main St 02563 **Location:** US 6, exit 2, 2 mi n; center. **Facility:** Part of a quaint historic village, the service-oriented, Colonial-style inn radiates a casual elegance. Smoke free premises. 48 units. 43 one-bedroom standard units, some with whirlpools. 5 one-bedroom suites, some with whirlpools. 2 stories (no elevator), interior/exterior corridors. *Bath:* combo or shower only. **Parking:** on-site. **Terms:** 2 night minimum stay - weekends, 4 day cancellation notice. **Amenities:** voice mail, irons, hair dryers. *Some:* DVD players. **Dining:** restaurant, see separate listing. **Pool(s):** heated outdoor. **Leisure Activities:** whirlpool, spa. **Guest Services:** wireless Internet. **Business Services:** meeting rooms, fax (fee). *(See color ad p 482)* ⓐⓢⓚ 🍴 🛏 🏊 👪 ✕ 💻 / SOME UNITS 🏢

THE EARL OF SANDWICH MOTEL   **Phone:** (508)888-1415   `107`

AAA SAVE

Motel
$75-$129 5/1-11/27
$65-$99 11/28-4/30

Address: 378 SR 6A 02537 **Location:** At MM 5.1. **Facility:** Smoke free premises. 24 one-bedroom standard units. 1 story, exterior corridors. **Parking:** on-site. **Terms:** office hours 8 am-10 pm, 7 day cancellation notice. **Amenities:** *Some:* irons, hair dryers. **Pool(s):** outdoor. **Leisure Activities:** firepit, playground. **Guest Services:** wireless Internet. *(See color ad below)* 🍴 🏊 ✕ 💻

FREE expanded continental breakfast and high-speed Internet

ISAIAH JONES HOMESTEAD   **Phone:** (508)888-9115   `105`

Bed & Breakfast
$190-$300 5/1-10/31
$165-$220 11/1-4/30

Address: 165 Main St 02563 **Location:** US 6, exit 2, 2 mi n; center. **Facility:** The 1849 Victorian inn is located in the historic village; a library is stocked with tourist information. A hot breakfast is served 8:30 to 10 am. Smoke free premises. 7 one-bedroom standard units, some with whirlpools. 2 stories (no elevator), interior corridors. *Bath:* combo or shower only. **Parking:** on-site. **Terms:** office hours 10 am-10 pm, 1-2 night minimum stay - seasonal and/or weekends, 14 day cancellation notice-fee imposed. **Amenities:** video library, DVD players, CD players, hair dryers. **Guest Services:** wireless Internet. **Business Services:** PC. ⓐⓢⓚ ✕ ☎

SANDY NECK MOTEL   **Phone:** 508/362-3992   `109`

Motel
$65-$129 5/1-10/31 &
4/15-4/30

Address: 669 Rt 6A 02537 **Location:** 5.3 mi e on SR 6A; at entrance road to Sandy Neck Beach. **Facility:** Designated smoking area. 12 units. 11 one-bedroom standard units. 1 one-bedroom suite with kitchen. 1 story, exterior corridors. *Bath:* combo or shower only. **Parking:** on-site. **Terms:** open 5/1-10/31 & 4/15-4/30, office hours 8 am-10 pm, 7 day cancellation notice-fee imposed. **Amenities:** irons. *Some:* hair dryers. **Guest Services:** wireless Internet.
ⓐⓢⓚ 🍴 ✕ 🏢 📺 💻

(See map and index starting on p. 458)

SHADY NOOK INN & MOTEL

Motel
Rates not provided

Phone: 508/888-0409   **103**

Address: 14 Old Kings Hwy (SR 6A) 02563 **Location:** On SR 6A, 1.5 mi w. **Facility:** Smoke free premises. 30 units. 29 one-bedroom standard units, some with kitchens. 1 two-bedroom suite with kitchen. 1 story, exterior corridors. *Bath:* combo or shower only. **Parking:** on-site. **Terms:** office hours 9 am-9 pm. **Amenities:** *Some:* irons, hair dryers. **Pool(s):** outdoor.

SPRING GARDEN INN

Motel
$79-$130 All Year

Phone: 508/888-0710   **108**

Address: 578 SR 6A 02537 **Location:** 4.5 mi e. **Facility:** Smoke free premises. 11 units. 9 one-bedroom standard units, some with kitchens. 2 one-bedroom suites, some with kitchens. 2 stories (no elevator), exterior corridors. *Bath:* combo or shower only. **Parking:** on-site. **Terms:** office hours 8 am-10 pm, 2 night minimum stay - seasonal and/or weekends, 7 day cancellation notice. **Amenities:** voice mail. *Some:* DVD players, irons, hair dryers. **Pool(s):** outdoor. **Guest Services:** wireless Internet.

—— WHERE TO DINE ——

A CAFE

American
$5-$12

Phone: 508/888-5220   **95**

With a six-seat counter in addition to a dozen or so tables, the small eatery serves breakfast and lunch. Whiteboard specials supplement the regular menu, on which house specialties include turkey pot pie, fish and chips and a Mexican-style burrito. Also listed are pizza, pasta, soups and a selection of sandwiches. Casual dress. **Bar:** Beer & wine. **Reservations:** not accepted. **Hours:** 6 am-2:30 pm. Closed: 11/25, 12/25. **Address:** 415 SR 6A 02537 **Location:** 3 mi e. **Parking:** on-site.

AMARI BAR & RISTORANTE

Italian
$11-$31

Phone: 508/375-0011   **97**

Guests who patronize the upscale bistro are treated to delicious contemporary Italian cooking and an atmosphere made cozy by a three-sided fireplace. The menu lists pizzas cooked in a wood-fired oven, grilled chops, six pasta dishes and a 14-ounce sirloin, as well as chicken, veal or shrimp made in scampi, piccata or Marsala style. Portions are generous. Desserts include chocolate thunder and homemade flan. The service pace, at times, is leisurely. Casual dress. **Bar:** Full bar. **Reservations:** suggested. **Hours:** 4:30 pm-9 pm. Closed: 11/25, 12/25. **Address:** 674 SR 6A 02537 **Location:** 5.3 mi e. **Parking:** on-site.

AQUA GRILLE

American
$9-$25

Phone: 508/888-8889   **90**

Sandwiched between the Coast Guard station and the Sandwich Marina, this bistro-style restaurant overlooks the northern end of the Cape Cod Canal. In addition to local seafood, a variety of salads, sandwiches, pastas and a couple of chicken and beef dishes are offered. The desserts are tempting. Portions are generous. A porch, on two sides of the restaurant, provides outdoor dining, weather permitting. Restaurant hours vary off-season. Casual dress. **Bar:** Full bar. **Reservations:** suggested. **Hours:** 11:30 am-3 & 4-9 pm, Sat & Sun noon-close; 4 pm-close 11/1-4/14. Closed: Mon-Wed 11/1-4/14. **Address:** 14 Gallo Rd 02563 **Location:** 1.5 mi n of SR 6A via Tupper and Town Neck rds; adjacent to Sandwich Marina. **Parking:** on-site.

THE BEE-HIVE TAVERN

American
$6-$22

Phone: 508/833-1184   **96**

In a quiet, rural setting is this casual Colonial tavern, which prepares fresh, homemade Cape Cod cuisine. Diners can choose from the menu or daily blackboard specials. Specialty desserts range from traditional New England treats to original selections such as the schnee ball—homemade ice cream rolled in toasted coconut and served on a bed of raspberry sauce. The decor is evocative of an 18th-century roadhouse. Casual dress. **Bar:** Full bar. **Hours:** 11:30 am-9 pm, Sun from 9 am. Closed: 12/25; also Super Bowl Sun. **Address:** 406 Rt 6A 02537 **Location:** 3 mi e. **Parking:** on-site.

BOBBY BYRNE'S RESTAURANT AND PUB

American
$7-$16

Phone: 508/888-6088

The popular establishment provides dependably good food—from light salads and soups to sandwiches and burgers. Plenty of parking and a nearby shopping center make this restaurant an easy stop for lunch or dinner. Casual dress. **Bar:** Full bar. **Reservations:** not accepted. **Hours:** 11 am-11 pm. Closed: 11/25, 12/25. **Address:** 65 Rt 6A 02563 **Location:** Just n of SR 6A, 0.9 mi w; in Stop & Shop Plaza. **Parking:** on-site.

THE BRITISH BEER COMPANY RESTAURANT & PUB

British
$6-$19

Phone: 508/833-9590   **91**

On a grassy knoll under shade trees, the pub is within walking distance to motels and a shopping center. Roughly 20 draft beers and more than 50 bottled brews come from around the world. A BSA motorcycle is displayed. Two of the four dining areas have a fireplace, and one is in a sun room extension. On the menu is a wide selection of hot and cold sandwiches, half-pound burgers and traditional British fare, such as fish and chips and shepherd's pie. Entertainers perform on Friday and Saturday. Casual dress. Entertainment. **Bar:** Full bar. **Reservations:** not accepted. **Hours:** 11:30 am-10 pm, Sun from noon. Closed: 4/4, 11/25, 12/25. **Address:** 46 Rt 6A 02563 **Location:** 1 mi w. **Parking:** on-site.

(See map and index starting on p. 458)

THE DAN'L WEBSTER INN

American
$7-$33

Phone: 508/888-3622   93

Guests can dine in the delightful, plant-filled, glass-paned conservatory or in one of the restaurant's other cozy dining rooms. The innovative chef's selections include local seafood and sinfully delicious desserts. The acclaimed wine list and gracious service make this restaurant one of the first choices for anyone visiting or living in the mid-Cape area. For a more casual dining experience, The Tavern fills the bill with a wide selection of traditional and lighter entrées. Casual dress. **Bar:** Full bar. **Reservations:** suggested. **Hours:** 8-11 am, 11:30-3 & 4:30-9 pm, Sun 8-11 am, 11:30-2:30 & 3:30-9:30 pm. Closed: 12/25. **Address:** 149 Main St 02563 **Location:** US 6, exit 2, 2 mi n; center; in The Dan'l Webster Inn & Spa. **Parking:** on-site.

MARSHLAND RESTAURANT

American
$5-$17

Phone: 508/888-9824   92

While the restaurant is known for hearty breakfast plates, satisfying lunches and dinners focused on comfort food, the adjacent bakery pleases patrons with its great muffins, in addition to cookies, cakes and pies. Representative of the eatery fare are eggs Benedict, omelets and Belgian waffles for breakfast; the Marshland Harvest salad with cranberries, apples and crumbled blue cheese for lunch; and dinners of meatloaf, roasted chicken and seafood ranging from baked seafood to stuffed scrod. Casual dress. **Bar:** Beer & wine. **Hours:** 6 am-8 pm, Fri & Sat-8:30 pm. **Address:** 109 SR 6A 02563 **Location:** 0.5 mi e of center. **Parking:** on-site.

SEAFOOD SAM'S

Seafood
$7-$18

Phone: 508/888-4629   89

Guests order at the counter and are given a faux lobster pager that goes off when it's time to pick up their food. Seating is available indoors or at picnic tables that face the water. Offerings include Atlantic haddock or salmon, whole belly clams, native oysters and lobster that is fried, broiled, steamed or baked. Children will be satisfied with choices ranging from popcorn shrimp to peanut butter and jelly sandwiches, not to mention the "Sam's lollipop" they'll get as thanks for stopping in. Casual dress. **Bar:** Full bar. **Reservations:** not accepted. **Hours:** 11 am-9 pm. Closed: 1/1, 11/25, 12/24. **Address:** 6 Coast Guard Rd 02563 **Location:** From SR 6A, just nw on Tupper Rd, 0.4 mi ne on Town Neck Rd, then just n. **Parking:** on-site. CALL &M

SOUTH DENNIS pop. 3,679   (See map and index starting on p. 454)

—— **WHERE TO DINE** ——

BANGKOK THAI CUISINE II

Thai
$7-$17

Phone: 508/394-7699   23

Near the end of a shopping area close to theaters and marked by a simple "Thai Food" sign over the door is a cozy, 40-seat restaurant with crisp, linen-draped tables covered with glass. A life-size statue of a Thai lady in the traditional welcoming pose greets guests. The forte is the vegetables, which are fresh, bright and crisp. On the menu are soups, noodle dishes and curries, which are served with chicken, beef, tofu or vegetables. Specialties include duck, salmon and seafood ginger. Casual dress. **Reservations:** no accepted. **Hours:** 11 am-10 pm, Sun 4 pm-9 pm. Closed: 11/25, 12/25. **Address:** 8 Enterprise Rd 02660 **Location:** US 6, exit 9, 0.3 mi s; south end of Patriot Square shopping area. **Parking:** on-site. CALL &M

SOUTH WELLFLEET   (See map and index starting on p. 458)

THE EVEN'TIDE MOTEL & COTTAGES

AAA SAVE

Motel
$75-$310 5/1-10/28

Phone: 508/349-3410   15

Address: 650 Rt 6 02663 **Location:** On US 6, 4.5 mi n of National Seashore Visitor's Center. **Facility:** Smoke free premises. 38 units. 22 one-bedroom standard units, some with efficiencies. 8 one-bedroom suites. 8 cottages. 1-2 stories (no elevator), exterior corridors. *Bath:* combo or shower only. **Parking:** on-site. **Terms:** open 5/1-10/28, office hours 8 am-10 pm, 2-4 night minimum stay seasonal and/or weekends, 14 day cancellation notice-fee imposed. **Amenities:** hair dryers. **Pool(s):** heated indoor. **Leisure Activities:** miniature golf, badminton, table tennis, barbecue picnic area, billiards, hiking trails, jogging, playground, exercise room, basketball, horseshoes, shuffleboard. **Guest Services:** wireless Internet. **Business Services:** meeting rooms, PC. **Free Special Amenities:** newspaper and high-speed Internet.

See map and index starting on p. 458)

WELLFLEET MOTEL AND LODGE

 Book great rates at AAA.com   **Phone:** (508)349-3535   **16**

(AAA) (SAVE)
▽▽ ▽▽
Motel
$75-$220 5/1-11/30 & 4/1-4/30

Address: 170 US 6 02663 **Location:** On US 6, 3.5 mi n of National Seashore Visitor's Center. **Facility:** Smoke free premises. 65 units. 57 one-bedroom standard units. 8 one-bedroom suites. 1-2 stories (no elevator), exterior corridors. **Parking:** on-site. **Terms:** open 5/1-11/30 & 4/1-4/30, office hours 8 am-10 pm, check-in 3:30 pm, 2-3 night minimum stay - seasonal, 14 day cancellation notice-fee imposed. **Amenities:** voice mail, hair dryers. **Pool(s):** heated outdoor, heated indoor. **Leisure Activities:** whirlpool. *Fee:* game room. **Guest Services:** wireless Internet. **Business Services:** meeting rooms, fax (fee). *(See color ad p 508)*

🍴 🍸 🏊 ✕ 🎦 📞 💻 / SOME UNITS FEE 📷

FREE high-speed Internet

―――― **WHERE TO DINE** ――――

CATCH OF THE DAY RESTAURANT & SEAFOOD MARKET

Phone: 508/349-9090   **21**

(AAA)
▽▽
Seafood
$9-$20

A combined fish market and full-service eatery, this cozy restaurant gives guests options for dining inside or outside. Local fresh seafood is the showcased item here. From 3 to 5 pm, buckets of steamers, mussels, littlenecks and chicken wings are half price. Delicious entrees include grilled fish, including salmon, swordfish, tuna and striped bass. Fried seafood platters and the fisherman's stew are also popular. Casual dress. **Bar:** Beer & wine. **Hours:** Open 5/1-11/1 & 4/1-4/30; 11:30 am-9 pm. **Address:** 975 Rt 6 02667 **Location:** 5.1 mi n of National Seashore Visitor's Center. **Parking:** on-site.

VAN RENSSELAER'S RESTAURANT & RAW BAR

Phone: 508/349-2127   **20**

(AAA)
▽▽ ▽▽
American
$14-$32

Zuppa di pesce—a melange of scallops, shrimp, chopped clams, sausage and mussels in garlic, tomato and white wine broth over linguine—is well worth trying, but also good are chicken, veal and prime rib selections, in addition to other fresh seafood dishes. Tempting desserts make it hard to say no. Screened-porch seating is offered when the weather warms. Early-bird specials are offered from 4:30 to 6 pm daily, and guests can get smaller portions from the bistro menu. Casual dress. **Bar:** Full bar. **Reservations:** accepted. **Hours:** Open 5/1-10/24 & 4/14-4/30; 4:30 pm-9 pm; also 8 am-noon 6/10-9/30; hours vary off season. **Address:** 1019 Rt 6 02663 **Location:** On US 6, 5.3 mi n of National Seashore Visitor's Center. **Parking:** on-site. CALL 🅿M

SOUTH YARMOUTH pop. 11,603   (See map and index starting on p. 454)

AMBASSADOR INN & SUITES

 Book great rates at AAA.com   **Phone:** (508)394-4000   **29**

(AAA) (SAVE)
▽▽ ▽▽
Hotel
$60-$190 All Year

Address: 1314 Main St 02664 **Location:** On SR 28, just w of Bass River Bridge. **Facility:** 89 units. 87 one- and 2 two-bedroom standard units. 2 stories (no elevator), interior corridors. **Parking:** on-site. **Amenities:** irons, hair dryers. **Pool(s):** outdoor, heated indoor. **Leisure Activities:** sauna, whirlpool. *Fee:* game room. **Guest Services:** wireless Internet. **Business Services:** meeting rooms, PC. **Free Special Amenities:** expanded continental breakfast and early check-in/late check-out.

🏊 ✕ 📞 💻 / SOME UNITS FEE 🐾 ✕ 📷

BLUE ROCK GOLF RESORT

Phone: 508/398-6962   **28**

(AAA) (SAVE)
▽▽ ▽▽
Motel
$95-$215 5/1-10/16 & 4/9-4/30

Address: 39 Todd Rd 02664 **Location:** SR 28, 1 mi ne via N Main St and High Bank Rd, then 0.5 mi nw on Country Club Dr, follow signs. **Facility:** Smoke free premises. 45 units. 44 one-bedroom standard units, some with whirlpools. 1 one-bedroom suite with kitchen. 2 stories (no elevator), exterior corridors. **Parking:** on-site. **Terms:** open 5/1-10/16 & 4/9-4/30, office hours 7 am-10 pm, 10 day cancellation notice-fee imposed. **Amenities:** voice mail, irons, hair dryers. *Some:* DVD players. **Pool(s):** heated outdoor. **Leisure Activities:** putting green, tennis court, basketball. *Fee:* golf-18 holes. **Guest Services:** wireless Internet. **Business Services:** meeting rooms, PC. **Free Special Amenities:** local telephone calls and high-speed Internet.

🍴 🍸 🏊 ✕ ✕ 📞 💻 / SOME UNITS FEE 🐾

BLUE WATER ON THE OCEAN

Phone: 508/398-2288   **33**

(AAA) (SAVE)
▽▽ ▽▽
Hotel
$90-$199 5/1-10/17 & 4/9-4/30

Address: 291 S Shore Dr 02664 **Location:** Oceanfront. 1 mi s off SR 28. **Facility:** Smoke free premises. 110 units. 95 one-bedroom standard units, some with efficiencies and/or whirlpools. 5 one- and 10 two-bedroom suites with kitchens. 1-3 stories (no elevator), interior/exterior corridors. *Bath:* combo or shower only. **Parking:** on-site. **Terms:** open 5/1-10/17 & 4/9-4/30, 30 day cancellation notice-fee imposed. **Amenities:** video library, voice mail, irons, hair dryers. *Some:* DVD players. **Dining:** 2 restaurants. **Pool(s):** heated outdoor, heated indoor. **Leisure Activities:** whirlpool, beach access, putting green. *Fee:* watersport equipment. **Guest Services:** coin laundry, wireless Internet. **Business Services:** meeting rooms, PC. **Free Special Amenities:** local telephone calls and high-speed Internet. 🍴 🍸 🏊 ✕ ✕ 📞 💻 / SOME UNITS FEE 🐾 📷

(See map and index starting on p. 454)

CLARION INN   Phone: 508/394-7600   **31**

Hotel
$79-$249 All Year

Address: 1199 Main St 02664 **Location:** On SR 28, 0.5 mi w of Bass River Bridge. **Facility:** Smoke free premises. 114 one-bedroom standard units. 2 stories (no elevator), interior corridors. *Bath:* combo or shower only. **Parking:** on-site. **Amenities:** video library (fee), DVD players, irons, hair dryers. **Pool(s):** heated outdoor, heated indoor. **Leisure Activities:** saunas, whirlpool, playground, exercise room. *Fee:* game room. **Guest Services:** valet and coin laundry, wireless Internet. **Business Services:** business center. *(See color ad below)*

CALL 🛏M 🛆 ⊠ ⊠ 🎥 🖥 🖵

FREE expanded continental breakfast and high-speed Internet

OCEAN MIST RESORT   Phone: 508/398-2633   **3**

Hotel
Rates not provided

Address: 97 S Shore Dr 02664 **Location:** Oceanfront. 1 mi s off SR 28. **Facility:** 63 one-bedroo standard units, some with efficiencies. 3 stories (no elevator), interior/exterior corridors. **Parking:** o site. **Terms:** open 5/1-11/11 & 4/7-4/30, office hours 7 am-11 pm. **Amenities:** hair dryer **Pool(s):** heated indoor. **Leisure Activities:** whirlpool, limited beach access.

🏌 🛆 🖥 / SOME UNITS ⊠ 🖵

▼ *See AAA listing above* ▼

(See map and index starting on p. 454)

ED JACKET BEACH

Phase: (508)398-6941

Hotel
$125-$430 5/1-10/24
$125-$295 4/3-4/30

Address: 1 S Shore Dr 02664 **Location:** Oceanfront. 2 mi s off SR 28. **Facility:** Smoke free premises. 164 units. 148 one-bedroom standard units, some with whirlpools. 2 two-bedroom suites. 14 cottages. 2 stories (no elevator), interior/exterior corridors. **Parking:** on-site. **Terms:** open 5/1-10/24 & 4/3-4/30, 10 day cancellation notice-fee imposed. **Amenities:** voice mail, irons, hair dryers. *Some:* DVD players. **Pool(s):** heated outdoor, heated indoor. **Leisure Activities:** whirlpool, limited beach access, rental boats, rental sailboats, boat dock, fishing, tennis court, recreation programs in summer, playground, limited exercise equipment, spa, basketball, shuffleboard, volleyball. *Fee:* parasailing, kayaks, personal watercraft. **Guest Services:** coin laundry, wireless Internet. **Business Services:** meeting rooms, PC. **Free Special Amenities: local telephone calls and high-speed Internet.**

IVIERA BEACH RESORT

Book great rates at AAA.com

Phone: (508)398-2273

Hotel
$135-$550 5/15-10/12

Address: 327 S Shore Dr 02664 **Location:** Oceanfront. 1 mi s off SR 28. **Facility:** Smoke free premises. 125 units. 123 one-bedroom standard units, some with efficiencies and/or whirlpools. 2 one-bedroom suites with kitchens. 2 stories (no elevator), interior/exterior corridors. **Parking:** on-site. **Terms:** open 5/15-10/12, 10 day cancellation notice-fee imposed. **Amenities:** video library, dual phone lines, voice mail, irons, hair dryers. *Some:* DVD players. **Pool(s):** heated outdoor, heated indoor. **Leisure Activities:** whirlpool, putting green, basketball. *Fee:* watersport equipment, watersport equipment. **Guest Services:** wireless Internet. **Business Services:** PC. **Free Special Amenities: local telephone calls and high-speed Internet.**

URFCOMBER ON THE OCEAN

Phone: 508/398-9228

Motel
Rates not provided

Address: 107 S Shore Dr 02664 **Location:** Oceanfront. 1 mi s off SR 28. Located on the ocean. **Facility:** Smoke free premises. 33 units. 30 one- and 2 two-bedroom standard units, some with efficiencies. 2 stories (no elevator), exterior corridors. *Bath:* combo or shower only. **Parking:** on-site. **Terms:** open 5/15-10/12, office hours 8:30 am-9 pm. **Amenities:** voice mail, hair dryers. *Some:* DVD players. **Pool(s):** heated outdoor. **Leisure Activities:** limited beach access, shuffleboard. **Guest Services:** wireless Internet.

------ **WHERE TO DINE** ------

RDEO

Phone: 508/760-1500

Mediterranean
$7-$23

Good thin-crust pizzas come with many varieties of toppings and in many specialties, including fire-roasted garlic and artichoke, four white cheese and shrimp. Also on the menu are pasta dishes, salads and Mediterranean favorites. Casual dress. **Bar:** Full bar. **Reservations:** not accepted. **Hours:** 11:30 am-11 pm. Closed: 11/25, 12/25. **Address:** 23V Whites Path 02664 **Location:** US 6, exit 8, just se; in Union Station Plaza. **Parking:** on-site.

HRISTOPHER'S RIBS AND SEAFOOD

Phone: 508/394-8006

Seafood
$9-$22

With its whimsical Caribbean theme and reasonable prices, the upbeat, sometimes noisy, restaurant is a hit with families. Guests who arrive early can wait for a table in one of several giant hand-shaped chairs. The menu centers on ribs and seafood. A favorite is the "round-up," a half-rack of ribs, half of a boiled lobster and fried clams. Casual dress. **Bar:** Full bar. **Reservations:** accepted. **Hours:** Open 5/1-10/31 & 4/1-4/30; 4 pm-11 pm. Closed: 4/4. **Address:** 769 Main St 02664 **Location:** On SR 28, 3.7 mi e of Hyannis. **Parking:** on-site.

ERARDI'S CAFE

Phone: 508/394-3111

Italian
$12-$22

Quite the find, the cafe is a must-stop for all who appreciate homemade Italian fare. Diners who listen closely may well hear other patrons raving about the chef/owner's wonderful piccata, parmigiana and ravioli dishes, in addition to splendid homemade desserts. Casual dress. **Bar:** Beer & wine. **Reservations:** accepted. **Hours:** 4 pm-9 pm; seasonal hours vary. Closed major holidays; also Mon. **Address:** 902 Main St 02664 **Location:** On SR 28, just w of SR 134. **Parking:** on-site.

EARTH 'N KETTLE RESTAURANT

Phone: 508/394-2252

American
$5-$15

Traditional Cape Cod cooking is served in an informal, family-friendly atmosphere. The diverse menu has the standards, from bacon, eggs and omelets for breakfast and sandwiches, chowders and salads for lunch to old favorites such as meatloaf and chicken pot pie for dinner. Fresh seafood is the forte. Finish the meal with one of the traditional New England desserts, such as Indian pudding or a distinctive treatment of strawberry shortcake. A few vegetarian selections are offered. Casual dress. **Bar:** Full bar. **Reservations:** not accepted. **Hours:** 7 am-9 pm; closing hour may vary. Closed: 12/25. **Address:** 1196 Main St 02664 **Location:** 0.8 mi w of Bass River Bridge. **Parking:** on-site. CALL [GM]

HE PANCAKE MAN

Phone: 508/398-9532

American
$6-$12

This simple, full-service family breakfast restaurant with a relaxed, friendly feel offers an array of unique pancake combinations, from sausage-wrapped apple cinnamon to peanut butter and chocolate chip. For a different twist, try breakfast nachos or corned-beef hash omelets. Casual dress. **Bar:** Beer & wine. **Reservations:** not accepted. **Hours:** Open 5/1-11/28 & 2/15-4/30; 7 am-2 pm. **Address:** 952 Rt 28 at Long Pond Dr 02664 **Location:** On SR 28. **Parking:** on-site.

CCADILLY DELI & CAFE

Phone: 508/394-9018

American
$5-$12

Red and white striped awnings mark the location of this casual cafe and deli. Bright cafe curtains and pictures of clowns highlight the interior. Sit at simple tables or at the lime green counter. Breakfasts, including omelets and lox from Nova Scotia, and lunches of soups, salads and specialty sandwiches are popular. Desserts and pastries are homemade. Service is folksy and friendly. Casual dress. **Bar:** Beer & wine. **Reservations:** not accepted. **Hours:** 6 am-2 pm. Closed: 12/25. **Address:** 1105 SR 28 02664 **Location:** Just e of Forest and US Post Office. **Parking:** on-site. CALL [GM]

(See map and index starting on p. 454)

RIVERWAY LOBSTER HOUSE   **Phone:** 508/398-2172

Seafood
$9-$25

This well-established restaurant has been serving the public since 1943, and its New England decor—including white linen, wood accents and seafaring artwork—has changed little over the years. The menu features items such as ocean-fresh lobster, filet mignon, pasta and prime rib. **Casual dress. Bar:** Full bar. **Reservations:** suggested. **Hours:** 4 pm-10 pm. Closed: 11/25, 12/25; also 2/14 & 12/31. **Address:** 133 Main St (SR 28) 02664 **Location:** Just w of Bass River Bridge. **Parking:** on-site.

THE SKIPPER RESTAURANT & CHOWDER HOUSE   **Phone:** 508/394-7406

Seafood
$7-$28

Within walking distance of many seaside lodging establishments and the beach, the restaurant amuses with the nautical puns identifying its widely varied breakfast, lunch and dinner menu items. Good choices include the cooked-to-order breakfasts, homemade soups and desserts and variations of standard fare. **Casual dress. Bar:** Full bar. **Hours:** Open 5/1-10/31 & 4/1-4/30; 11:30 am-10 pm, Fri & Sat-11 pm. **Address:** 152 Shore Dr 02664 **Location:** 1.5 mi s of SR 28; across from ocean. **Parking:** on-site.

SKIPPY'S PIER 1 RESTAURANT   **Phone:** 508/398-9556

American
$8-$27

Overlooking a small marina, the restaurant presents a menu of mostly seafood but also serves landlubber favorites of burgers, pasta and more. A children's menu makes this a nice spot for families. **Casual dress. Bar:** Full bar. **Hours:** Open 5/1-10/31 & 3/15-4/30; 11:30 am-11 pm; hours vary off season. **Address:** 1 Neptune Ln 02664 **Location:** On SR 28, 3.7 mi e of Hyannis. **Parking:** on-site.

TRURO   (See map and index starting on p. 458)

—— WHERE TO DINE ——

THE WHITMAN HOUSE RESTAURANT   **Phone:** 508/487-1740

American
$7-$26

Patrons discover charming fine dining amid traditional Early American decor. Fresh seafood and prime rib are featured stars. Family operated for more than 30 years, the restaurant boasts quality, well-prepared fare including Portuguese kale soup. Lunch is available in the Bass Tavern. **Casual dress. Bar:** Full bar. **Reservations:** suggested. **Hours:** Open 5/1-12/24 & 4/1-4/30; noon-3 & 5-9:30 pm; hours may vary off season. Closed: 12/24, 12/25. **Address:** 5 Great Hollow Rd 02666 **Location:** On US 6, 0.8 mi s of SR 6A/Shore Rd. **Parking:** on-site.

WELLFLEET   (See map and index starting on p. 458)

—— WHERE TO DINE ——

BEACHCOMBER   **Phone:** 508/349-6055

Seafood
$4-$20

Live entertainment is offered most evenings at this local institution. It's hard to beat this location for an on-the-beach spot. The fare is appropriately seafood—fried, baked, salads and even a separate raw bar—but fans of landlubber fare need not worry. This is a perfect spot to hang out at Cahoon Hollow Beach and wander up the dunes for a bite to eat, beverage or both. **Casual dress. Entertainment. Bar:** Full bar. **Reservations:** not accepted. **Hours:** Open 5/25-9/7; noon-8 pm. **Address:** 1120 Cahoon Hollow Rd 02667 **Location:** US 6 E, 2.5 mi ne via LeCount Hollow Rd and Ocean View Dr. **Parking:** on-site.

▼ See AAA listing p 505 ▼

(See map and index starting on p. 458)

MOBY DICK'S FAMILY RESTAURANT

Seafood

$6-$22

Phone: 508/349-9795   (15)

Enjoy very informal dining in the old Cape Cod tradition with paper plates and plastic utensils. Fresh cape lobster, clam bakes, steamers, mussels, sandwiches and burgers are served in a screened picnic area. Certain items can be fried or broiled. You are welcome to bring your own bottle. Casual dress. **Reservations:** not accepted. **Hours:** Open 5/5-10/12; 11:30 am-9 pm; to 10 pm 7/1-8/31. **Address:** 3225 US 6 02667 **Location:** On US 6; opposite Gull Pond Rd. **Parking:** on-site.

WINSLOW'S TAVERN   *Menu on AAA.com*

Mediterranean

$9-$27

Phone: 508/349-6450   (17)

Built in 1865 as a sea captain's house, this recently renovated establishment has several dining areas: a tavern-like setting upstairs, a well-appointed main dining room and a patio for al fresco meals. Dishes centered on local seafood include starters of bacon-wrapped scallops with mango chutney or savory curried mussels; a wide selection of daily specials; and entrees of roasted cod, organic salmon and grilled swordfish. Casual dress. Entertainment. **Bar:** Full bar. **Hours:** Open 5/15-10/15; noon-3 & 5:30-close. **Address:** 316 Main St 02667 **Location:** US 6, exit Wellfleet Center, just e to town center. **Parking:** on-site. **Historic**

WEST BARNSTABLE   (See map and index starting on p. 458)

BURSLEY MANOR

Bed & Breakfast

$195 5/1-10/31
$175 11/1-4/30

Phone: 508/362-7788   (99)

Address: 651 Main St 02668 **Location:** SR 6A, 0.7 mi w of SR 149. **Facility:** Dating to 1640, this B&B offers individually decorated rooms with a romantic glimpse into yesteryear. Smoke free premises. 5 one-bedroom standard units with whirlpools. 2 stories (no elevator), interior corridors. **Parking:** on-site. **Terms:** office hours 8:30 am-9 pm, 2 night minimum stay - seasonal and/or weekends, age restrictions may apply, 14 day cancellation notice-fee imposed. **Amenities:** video library, CD players, hair dryers. *Some:* DVD players. **Guest Services:** wireless Internet.

HONEYSUCKLE HILL BED & BREAKFAST

Historic Bed
& Breakfast

$167-$294 All Year

Phone: 508/362-8418   (98)

Address: 591 Old Kings Hwy 02668 **Location:** On SR 6A, 0.7 mi w of jct SR 149. **Facility:** Set amid lush grounds, the 1810 Queen Anne-style farmhouse features comfortable guest rooms with feather beds. Smoke free premises. 4 units. 3 one-bedroom standard units. 1 one-bedroom suite. 2 stories (no elevator), interior corridors. *Bath:* shower only. **Parking:** on-site. **Terms:** office hours 6 am-9 pm, 2 night minimum stay - weekends, 14 day cancellation notice-fee imposed. **Amenities:** hair dryers. *Some:* DVD players. **Guest Services:** wireless Internet.

THE MAPLE STREET INN

Bed & Breakfast

$135-$249 All Year

Phone: (508)362-2980   (100)

Address: 208 Maple St 02668 **Location:** 0.7 mi w of SR 149, then 0.5 mi s. **Facility:** Each room is decorated in eye-appealing colors and equipped with modern-day conveniences; breakfast is served daily 8-9 am. Smoke free premises. 3 units. 1 one-bedroom standard unit. 2 one-bedroom suites, some with whirlpools. 2 stories (no elevator), interior/exterior corridors. *Bath:* combo or shower only. **Parking:** on-site. **Terms:** office hours 9 am-9 pm, 2-3 night minimum stay - seasonal and/or weekends, age restrictions may apply, 10 day cancellation notice-fee imposed. **Amenities:** DVD players, CD players, hair dryers. **Guest Services:** wireless Internet. **Free Special Amenities: full breakfast and high-speed Internet.**

WEST DENNIS   pop. 2,570   (See map and index starting on p. 454)

INN AT SWAN RIVER   *Book at AAA.com*

Motel

$110-$259 5/1-9/3
$89-$119 9/4-4/30

Phone: (508)394-5415   (39)

Address: 829 Main St 02670 **Location:** On SR 28, just w of SR 134. **Facility:** Smoke free premises. 26 one-bedroom standard units, some with efficiencies. 2 stories (no elevator), exterior corridors. **Parking:** on-site. **Terms:** 2 night minimum stay, 14 day cancellation notice-fee imposed. **Amenities:** irons. **Pool(s):** heated outdoor. **Leisure Activities:** shuffleboard. **Guest Services:** wireless Internet.

─── WHERE TO DINE ───

KREAM' N KONE

Seafood

$5-$16

Phone: 508/394-0808   (46)

An area institution for more than 50 years, this place has enjoyed acclaim from locals and tourists who herald it for having the "best fried clams, onion rings and seafood," and its lobster rolls aren't too shabby either. Burgers and hot dogs appeal to those who seek an alternative to the main fare. Diners may sit inside or on the patio or order food for take-out. Although it's not beside the beach or ocean, this eatery takes on all challengers for top-notch, well-prepared seafood. Casual dress. **Hours:** Open 5/1-10/15 & 2/20-4/30; 11 am-9 pm. **Address:** 961 SR 28 02670 **Location:** At SR 134. **Parking:** on-site.

WEST FALMOUTH   pop. 1,867   (See map and index starting on p. 458)

CHAPOQUOIT INN BED & BREAKFAST

Historic Bed
& Breakfast

$225-$275 5/1-10/31
$150-$200 11/1-4/30

Phone: 508/540-7232   (122)

Address: 495 W Falmouth Hwy (Rt 28A) 02574 **Location:** SR 28, 0.5 mi w on Brick Kiln Rd, then just n. **Facility:** Two units in the outbuilding include a gas fireplace. A full-breakfast starts each day; complimentary in-room water and snacks is offered. Smoke free premises. 7 one-bedroom standard units. 2 stories (no elevator), interior corridors. *Bath:* combo or shower only. **Parking:** on-site. **Terms:** office hours 9 am-11 pm, 2-3 night minimum stay - weekends, age restrictions may apply, 14 day cancellation notice-fee imposed. **Amenities:** video library, hair dryers. **Leisure Activities:** bicycles. **Guest Services:** wireless Internet.

(See map and index starting on p. 458)

—— WHERE TO DINE ——

CHAPOQUOIT GRILL   Phone: 508/540-7794   (11:)

American
$10-$23

Offerings of eclectic New American cuisine with diverse international influences include brick-oven pizza cooked over a wood fire, steaks, chops and seafood cooked on the grill. Excellent, artistically presente desserts are made on the premises. Substantial waits, sometimes on the order of one to two hours, can b anticipated during prime dining hours in the summer season. Casual dress. **Bar:** Full bar. **Hours:** 5 pm-1 pm. Closed: 9/6, 11/25, 12/24, 12/25. **Address:** 410 W Falmouth Hwy 02574 **Location:** 0.3 mi w of SR 28 exit Brick Kiln Rd, just s. **Parking:** on-site. CALL

WEST YARMOUTH pop. 6,460   (See map and index starting on p. 454)

BAYSIDE RESORT HOTEL   *Book great rates at AAA.com*   Phone: (508)775-5669   **45**

Hotel
$80-$180 5/1-10/30
$70-$110 10/31-4/30

Address: 225 Main St (SR 28) 02673 **Location:** 1.8 mi e of jct SR 132. **Facility:** Smoke free premises. 128 one-bedroom standard units, some with whirlpools. 2 stories (no elevator), interior corridors. *Bath:* combo or shower only. **Parking:** on-site. **Terms:** 2 night minimum stay - seasonal and/or weekends, 3 day cancellation notice. **Amenities:** high-speed Internet, irons, hair dryers. **Pool(s):** outdoor, heated indoor. **Leisure Activities:** saunas, whirlpool, exercise room, volleyball. *Fee:* game room. **Guest Services:** wireless Internet. **Business Services:** meeting rooms, PC, fax (fee). *(See color ad p 483)*

FREE expanded continental breakfast and high-speed Internet

THE CAPE POINT HOTEL   Phone: (508)778-1500   **48**

Hotel
$60-$170 5/1-10/31
$60-$120 11/1-4/30

Address: 476 Main St 02673 **Location:** Just e of Higgins Crowell Rd on SR 28. **Facility:** Smoke free premises. 116 units. 110 one- and 4 two-bedroom standard units. 2 one-bedroom suites. 2 stories, interior corridors. **Parking:** on-site. **Terms:** 2-3 night minimum stay - seasonal and/or weekends, 3 day cancellation notice. **Amenities:** video library (fee), DVD players, safes, irons, hair dryers. **Pool(s):** heated outdoor, heated indoor. **Leisure Activities:** saunas, whirlpool, exercise room. *Fee:* game room. **Guest Services:** wireless Internet. **Business Services:** meeting rooms, PC. *(See color ad p 487)*

FREE early check-in/late check-out and high-speed Internet

THE COVE AT YARMOUTH   *Book great rates at AAA.com*   Phone: (508)771-3666   **4:**

Condominium
$200 5/1-9/4
$135 9/5-4/30

Address: 183 Main St (SR 28) 02673 **Location:** 1 mi e of jct SR 132. **Facility:** Select from tradition condo suites and townhouses; extensive recreational facilities offer plenty of activities for everyon Smoke free premises. 229 one-bedroom suites. 2 stories (no elevator), interior corridors. **Parking:** o site. **Terms:** check-in 4 pm, 10 day cancellation notice-fee imposed. **Amenities:** DVD players, C players, voice mail, irons, hair dryers. *Fee:* video library, high-speed Internet. **Pool(s):** outdoor, heate indoor. **Leisure Activities:** saunas, whirlpool, steamrooms, 5 tennis courts (3 indoor), racquetba courts, recreation programs, playground. *Fee:* game room. **Guest Services:** wireless Interne **Business Services:** PC.

GREEN HARBOR ON THE OCEAN   Phone: (508)771-1126   **5**

Condominium
$95-$800 5/17-9/5
$95-$375 9/6-10/11

Address: 182 Baxter Ave 02673 **Location:** 0.5 mi e of jct SR 132 on SR 28, 0.8 mi **Facility:** Situated on spacious, manicured grounds overlooking Nantucket Sound. Smoke fre premises. 53 units. 8 one-bedroom standard units with efficiencies. 12 one-, 24 two- and 9 thre bedroom suites with kitchens. 1-2 stories (no elevator), exterior corridors. *Bath:* combo or shower onl **Parking:** on-site. **Terms:** open 5/17-10/11, office hours 8:30 am-10 pm, 2 night minimum stay seasonal and/or weekends, 10 day cancellation notice-fee imposed. **Amenities:** DVD players, voic mail, irons, hair dryers. **Pool(s):** heated outdoor. **Leisure Activities:** limited beach access, boatin canoeing, boat dock, fishing, 2 moorings, miniature golf, recreation programs in summer, charco grills, bicycles, playground, basketball, shuffleboard. **Guest Services:** coin laundry, wireless Interne **Free Special Amenities:** local telephone calls and high-speed Internet.

See map and index starting on p. 454)

HAMPTON INN & SUITES CAPE COD

Phase: (508)862-9010   **42**

Hotel
$109-$289 All Year

Address: 99 Main St/Rt 28 02673 **Location:** On SR 28, 0.5 mi e of jct SR 132. **Facility:** Smoke free premises. 136 one-bedroom standard units. 3 stories, interior corridors. *Bath:* combo or shower only. **Parking:** on-site. **Terms:** 1-7 night minimum stay, cancellation fee imposed. **Amenities:** high-speed Internet, voice mail, irons, hair dryers. **Pool(s):** outdoor, heated indoor. **Leisure Activities:** exercise room. **Guest Services:** coin laundry, wireless Internet. **Business Services:** meeting rooms, business center.

AAA Benefit:
Members save up to
10% everyday!

INN AT LEWIS BAY

Phone: 508/771-3433   **51**

Bed & Breakfast
$128-$158 5/1-11/1
$108-$118 11/2-4/30

Address: 57 Maine Ave 02673 **Location:** Jct SR 28, 0.7 mi s on Berry Ave, just w on Broadway, then just n. **Facility:** Located within walking distance of the beach, this 1920s Dutch Colonial inn features individually decorated guest rooms. Smoke free premises. 6 one-bedroom standard units. 2 stories (no elevator), interior corridors. *Bath:* combo or shower only. **Parking:** on-site. **Terms:** office hours 9 am-9 pm, 2 night minimum stay - seasonal and/or weekends, age restrictions may apply, 14 day cancellation notice-fee imposed. **Amenities:** hair dryers. *Some:* irons. **Leisure Activities:** beach towels & chairs. **Guest Services:** wireless Internet.

THE MARINER MOTOR LODGE

Phone: 508/771-7887   **49**

Hotel
$40-$140 All Year

Address: 573 Main St 02673 **Location:** On SR 28, 2.8 mi e of jct SR 132. **Facility:** Smoke free premises. 100 one-bedroom standard units. 2 stories (no elevator), interior corridors. **Parking:** on-site. **Terms:** 2 night minimum stay - seasonal and/or weekends, 3 day cancellation notice-fee imposed. **Amenities:** safes, irons, hair dryers. **Pool(s):** heated outdoor, heated indoor. **Leisure Activities:** saunas, whirlpool, miniature golf, picnic area, playground. *Fee:* game room. **Guest Services:** wireless Internet. **Business Services:** meeting rooms. *(See color ad p 487)*

FREE early check-in/late check-out and high-speed Internet

TIDEWATER INN

Book great rates at AAA.com

Phone: (508)775-6322   **43**

Motel
$69-$159 5/1-8/31
$59-$129 9/1-4/30

Address: 135 Main St 02673 **Location:** On SR 28, 0.8 mi e of jct SR 132. **Facility:** Smoke free premises. 101 one-bedroom standard units, some with whirlpools. 2 stories (no elevator), interior/exterior corridors. **Parking:** on-site. **Terms:** office hours 7 am-9 pm, cancellation fee imposed. **Amenities:** irons, hair dryers. **Pool(s):** outdoor, heated indoor. **Leisure Activities:** whirlpool, barbecue grills & picnic areas, playground, horseshoes, volleyball. *Fee:* game room. **Guest Services:** wireless Internet. **Business Services:** PC. *(See color ad p 488)*

TOWN 'N COUNTRY MOTOR LODGE

Phone: 508/771-0212   **47**

Motel
$34-$178 5/1-10/18
$34-$79 4/10-4/30

Address: 452 Main St 02673 **Location:** On SR 28, 2.5 mi e of jct SR 132. **Facility:** 141 one-bedroom standard units. 2 stories (no elevator), exterior corridors. **Parking:** on-site. **Terms:** open 5/1-10/18 & 4/10-4/30, office hours 7 am-11 pm, 3 day cancellation notice-fee imposed. **Pool(s):** outdoor, heated outdoor, heated indoor. **Leisure Activities:** saunas, whirlpool, charcoal grills, picnic area, playground. *Fee:* game room. **Guest Services:** wireless Internet. *(See color ad p 487)*

FREE early check-in/late check-out and preferred room (subject to availability with advance reservations)

(See map and index starting on p. 454)

THE YARMOUTH RESORT   *Book at AAA.com*   Phone: 508/775-5155

Motel
Rates not provided

Address: 343 Main St 02673 **Location:** On SR 28, 2 mi e of jct SR 132. **Facility:** 95 units. 93 one bedroom standard units. 2 one-bedroom suites. 2 stories (no elevator), interior/exterior corridors. **Parking:** on-site. **Terms:** office hours 9 am-9 pm. **Amenities:** *Some:* irons, hair dryers. **Pool(s):** outdoor, heated indoor. **Leisure Activities:** saunas, whirlpool, exercise room. *Fee:* game room. **Guest Services:** coin laundry. **Business Services:** meeting rooms.

WHERE TO DINE

ANN & FRAN'S KITCHEN   Phone: 508/775-7771   51

American
$4-$9

The terrific breakfast spot serves memorable eggs Benedict and plenty more. Patrons should allow for a bit of wait at peak times, as there is a loyal local following. Casual dress. **Hours:** 7 am-2 pm; seasonal hours vary. Closed: 11/25, 12/25. **Address:** 471 Main St 02673 **Location:** On SR 28, 2.5 mi e of jct SR 132. **Parking:** on-site.

CAPTAIN PARKER'S PUB & RESTAURANT   *Menu on AAA.com*   Phone: 508/771-4266   53

Seafood
$5-$20

Captain Parker's is a locally popular, casual pub and eatery specializing in clam chowder, steaks, chops and seafood. There is also a daily vegetarian offering. The informal dining rooms are lined with cedar paneling and each has a wood stove. The larger of the rooms has a vaulted ceiling with skylights and overlooks a marsh. Of note is the large collection of shoulder patches, most of which are from police departments across the country. The same captain has been at the helm since 1981. Casual dress. **Bar:** Full bar. **Reservations:** not accepted. **Hours:** 11:30 am-10 pm; seasonal hours may vary. **Address:** 668 Main St 02673 **Location:** 3.3 mi e of Hyannis on SR 28. **Parking:** on-site.

KELTIC KITCHEN   Phone: 508/771-4835   54

American
$3-$10

Kissed by an Irish influence, the diner serves cooked-to-order eggs, freshly perked coffee and baked goods. The casual spot has a solid local following. Casual dress. **Reservations:** not accepted. **Hours:** 7 am-2 pm. Closed: 12/25. **Address:** 415 Main St 02673 **Location:** On SR 28, 2 mi e of jct SR 132. **Parking:** on-site.

LOBSTER BOAT   Phone: 508/775-0486   55

Seafood
$7-$29

Fresh, traditional New England seafood is fried, broiled or baked. Rustic appointments decorate the dining room. The waterside location offers outdoor seating, weather permitting. Casual dress. **Reservations:** not accepted. **Hours:** Open 5/1-10/31 & 4/15-4/30; 11:30 am-9:30 pm. Closed major holidays. **Address:** 681 Main St 02673 **Location:** On SR 28, 3.5 mi e of Hyannis. **Parking:** on-site.

MOLLY'S RESTAURANT & PUB   Phone: 508/778-1927   52

Irish
$9-$25

Bright awnings and leaded lights in heavy oak doors lead to a mahogany and brass pub with billiards and darts and a pleasant, almost frilly dining room with sheer cloths draped between pillars and walls decorated with dried vines and country art. Self-proclaimed "American cuisine with an Irish accent" includes dishes such as fish and chips, prime rib, pasta, sandwiches and shepherd's pie. Additionally, there are daily blackboard specials and live entertainment on weekends. Casual dress. **Bar:** Full bar. **Hours:** 11:30 am-close; from 7:30 am 6/1-8/31. Closed: 11/25, 12/25. **Address:** 585 Main St 02673 **Location:** On SR 28, 2 mi e of jct SR 132. **Parking:** on-site.

(See map and index starting on p. 454)

YARMOUTH HOUSE RESTAURANT

Phone: 508/771-5154 (49)

AAA

WWW WWW

American
$6-$27

The large restaurant has several rooms decorated in equestrian and garden themes and one with a water wheel and wishing pond. Among entrees are sauteed dishes and fresh lobster. The many dessert tray offerings shouldn't be passed up. Casual dress. **Bar:** Full bar. **Reservations:** suggested. **Hours:** 11:30 am-close. Closed: 1/1, 12/25. **Address:** 335 W Main St (Rt 28) 02673 **Location:** 2 mi e of Hyannis. **Parking:** on-site.

WOODS HOLE pop. 935 (See map and index starting on p. 458)

SANDS OF TIME MOTOR INN

Phone: 508/548-6300 (137)

AAA SAVE

WWW WWW

Motel
$95-$225 5/1-11/15 &
4/15-4/30

Address: 549 Woods Hole Rd 02543 **Location:** 0.3 mi n, 3.8 mi s of SR 28. Overlooking Vineyard Sound. **Facility:** Smoke free premises. 33 units. 32 one-bedroom standard units, some with kitchens. 1 one-bedroom suite with kitchen. 2-3 stories (no elevator), interior/exterior corridors. *Bath:* combo or shower only. **Parking:** on-site. **Terms:** open 5/1-11/15 & 4/15-4/30, 7 day cancellation notice-fee imposed. **Amenities:** dual phone lines, voice mail, irons, hair dryers. **Pool(s):** heated outdoor. **Guest Services:** wireless Internet. **Free Special Amenities:** newspaper and high-speed Internet.

SLEEPY HOLLOW MOTOR INN

Phone: 508/548-1986 (138)

AAA SAVE

WWW WWW

Motel
$90-$225 5/1-11/16

Address: 527 Woods Hole Rd 02543 **Location:** 0.3 mi n, 3.5 mi s of SR 28. **Facility:** Smoke free premises. 24 one-bedroom standard units. 1-2 stories, exterior corridors. *Bath:* combo or shower only. **Parking:** on-site. **Terms:** open 5/1-11/16, office hours 8 am-11 pm, 2-3 night minimum stay - seasonal and/or weekends, 7 day cancellation notice-fee imposed. **Pool(s):** outdoor. **Guest Services:** wireless Internet.

—— WHERE TO DINE ——

FISHMONGER'S CAFE

Phone: 508/540-5376 (133)

WWW WWW

Seafood
$7-$25

On the canal at the east end of the bridge in the center of Woods Hole, you will find this popular rustic eatery. Sit at wooden tables, some with a view of the water, or at the bar. Dinner is slightly more formal as paper napkins are replaced with cloth. This 3-meal "natural foods" restaurant features soups, salads, sandwiches and seafood along with daily blackboard specials. Service is informal. Casual dress. **Reservations:** not accepted. **Hours:** 7:30 am-10 pm; seasonal hours vary. Closed major holidays. **Address:** 56 Water St 02543 **Location:** Center. **Parking:** street.

PHUSION GRILLE

Phone: 508/457-3100 (132)

WWW WWW

International
$18-$28

In the center of Woods Hole at the drawbridge, the restaurant is a short walk from the ferry terminal. Lending to the casual atmosphere is a deck, some of which is covered, on the two waterfront sides of the building. On the menu are the likes of steak au poivre, ginger- and soy-marinated salmon, garlic-rubbed pork tenderloin, seafood and chicken dishes and a couple of pizzas. Among starter possibilities are Cajun fried calamari and chicken and Chinese sausage fried dumplings. Casual dress. **Bar:** Full bar. **Hours:** Open 5/1-10/15 & 4/15-4/30; 5 pm-10 pm, Sat also 8 am-2 pm, Sun also 8 am-3 pm; Saturday & Sunday brunch. Closed: Mon. **Address:** 71 Water St 02543 **Location:** Center; at drawbridge. **Parking:** street.

PIE IN THE SKY BAKERY & INTERNET CAFE

Phone: 508/540-5475 (134)

WWW

American
$5-$8

A short walk from the ferry terminal, the eatery sits on a compact lot and has a walk-up counter and simple seating inside and several tables in the garden streetside. Homemade soups and deli sandwiches precede baked-from-scratch pies, cakes, bread and pastries, which go great with the organic coffee. Casual dress. **Hours:** 5 am-9 pm; to 11 pm in summer. Closed: 12/25; also for dinner 11/26. **Address:** 10 Water St 02543 **Location:** Center. **Parking:** street.

YARMOUTH PORT pop. 5,395 (See maps and indexes starting on p. 454, 458)

INN AT CAPE COD

Phone: 508/375-0590 (86)

WWW WWW

Historic Bed
& Breakfast
$195-$345 All Year

Address: 4 Summer St 02675 **Location:** US 6, exit 7 (Willow St/Yarmouth Port), 1 mi n on Willow St, then 0.5 mi e. **Facility:** Massive ionic columns define the front porch of this Colonial-style mansion, which is on grounds shaded by mature trees of equally impressive stature. Smoke free premises. 9 units. 7 one-bedroom standard units. 2 one-bedroom suites. 3 stories (no elevator), interior corridors. *Bath:* combo or shower only. **Parking:** on-site. **Terms:** office hours 9 am-8 pm, 2-3 night minimum stay - seasonal and/or weekends, age restrictions may apply, 21 day cancellation notice-fee imposed. **Amenities:** hair dryers. *Some:* DVD players. **Guest Services:** wireless Internet.

ONE CENTRE STREET INN

Phone: 508/362-9951 (85)

WWW WWW

Historic Bed
& Breakfast
$145-$250 5/1-10/31
$125-$225 11/1-4/30

Address: One Center St 02675 **Location:** 1 mi e on SR 6A, just w of jct Union St. **Facility:** In a quaint seaside village, this restored 1824 Colonial inn once served as a parsonage for the First Congregational Church of Yarmouth Port. Smoke free premises. 5 units. 3 one-bedroom standard units. 2 one-bedroom suites. 3 stories (no elevator), interior corridors. *Bath:* combo or shower only. **Parking:** on-site. **Terms:** office hours 9 am-7 pm, 2 night minimum stay - seasonal and/or weekends, age restrictions may apply, 15 day cancellation notice-fee imposed. **Amenities:** video library, DVD players, CD players, irons, hair dryers. **Guest Services:** wireless Internet.

(See maps and indexes starting on p. 454, 458)

——— WHERE TO DINE ———

INAHO JAPANESE RESTAURANT   Phone: 508/362-5522   ⑧⓪

🔻🔻 🔻🔻   On historic route 6A, this popular Japanese restaurant in an unassuming, expanded cape is highly regarded
Japanese   locally for its sushi. Also offered are tempura and teriyaki dishes with fish, meat or vegetables. Casual dress.
$14-$27   **Bar:** Full bar. **Reservations:** accepted. **Hours:** 4:30 pm-9 pm; seasonal hours vary. Closed major holidays;
              also Sun. **Address:** 157 Main St 02675 **Location:** US 6, exit 7 (Willow St/Yarmouth Port), 2 mi n to SR 6A,
              then just e. **Parking:** street.

Heritage Museums and Gardens, Sandwich / © David Lyons / Alamy

This ends listings for Cape Cod.
The following page resumes the alphabetical listings of cities in Massachusetts.

CENTERVILLE—See Cape Cod p. 470.

CHARLEMONT

THE OXBOW RESORT MOTEL

Phone: 413/625-6011

Motel

$65-$89 5/1-10/23
$55-$79 10/24-4/30

Address: 1741 Mohawk Tr (SR 2) 01370 **Location:** On SR 2, 2.8 mi w of jct SR 112 S. **Facility:** Smoke free premises. 25 one-bedroom standard units. 1 story, exterior corridors. *Bath:* combo or shower only. **Parking:** on-site, winter plug-ins. **Terms:** office hours 8 am-8 pm, 2-3 night minimum stay - seasonal and/or weekends, 7 day cancellation notice. **Pool(s):** outdoor. **Leisure Activities:** 2 tennis courts, basketball. **Guest Services:** wireless Internet.

CHATHAM—See Cape Cod p. 470.

CHELMSFORD—See Boston p. 405.

CHELSEA—See Boston p. 406.

CHESTNUT HILL—See Boston p. 406.

CHICOPEE pop. 54,653

HAMPTON INN   *Book great rates at AAA.com*

Phone: (413)593-1500

Hotel

$99-$189 All Year

Address: 600 Memorial Dr 01020 **Location:** I-90, exit 5. **Facility:** 90 units. 88 one-bedroom standard units, some with whirlpools. 2 one-bedroom suites with whirlpools. 3 stories, interior corridors. *Bath:* combo or shower only. **Parking:** on-site. **Terms:** 1-7 night minimum stay, cancellation fee imposed. **Amenities:** high-speed Internet, dual phone lines, voice mail, irons, hair dryers. **Pool(s):** heated indoor. **Leisure Activities:** whirlpool, exercise room. **Guest Services:** valet and coin laundry, area transportation, wireless Internet. **Business Services:** meeting rooms, business center. CALL / SOME UNITS

AAA Benefit:
Members save up to
10% everyday!

QUALITY INN-CHICOPEE   *Book great rates at AAA.com*

Phone: (413)592-6171

Hotel

$72-$79 All Year

Address: 463 Memorial Dr 01020 **Location:** I-90, exit 5, just ne, use jug handle overpass to SR 33 N. **Facility:** 100 units. 99 one-bedroom standard units. 1 one-bedroom suite. 2 stories (no elevator), interior corridors. **Parking:** on-site. **Amenities:** voice mail, irons, hair dryers. **Pool(s):** outdoor. **Leisure Activities:** exercise room. **Guest Services:** valet and coin laundry, wireless Internet. **Free Special Amenities: continental breakfast and high-speed Internet.**
/ SOME UNITS FEE FEE FEE

COHASSET—See Boston p. 406.

CONCORD—See Boston p. 407.

COTUIT—See Cape Cod p. 474.

DANVERS—See Boston p. 407.

DARTMOUTH

------ **WHERE TO DINE** ------

NOT YOUR AVERAGE JOE'S

Phone: 508/992-5637

American
$7-$19

This eatery exemplifies the "in-trend" style of high-art contemporary design through vibrant color schemes, comfortable seating and smartly dressed staff. However, the high point is the food. The cooking team whips up gourmet comfort foods of homemade meatloaf with a flavorful twist, creative hand-made pizzas, sandwiches, salads and more. Casual dress. **Bar:** Full bar. **Reservations:** not accepted. **Hours:** 11 am-10 pm, Fri & Sat-11 pm, Sun noon-9 pm. Closed: 11/25, 12/25. **Address:** 61 State Rd 02747 **Location:** US 6, just w of SR 140. **Parking:** on-site.

DEDHAM—See Boston p. 409.

DEERFIELD —See also South Deerfield.

DEERFIELD INN

Phone: (413)774-5587

Historic
Country Inn
$155-$250 All Year

Address: 81 Old Main St 01342 **Location:** Center. **Facility:** The guest rooms at this handsome New England-style 1884 country inn offer period decor with modern conveniences. Smoke free premises. 24 units. 23 one-bedroom standard units. 1 one-bedroom suite. 2 stories, interior corridors. *Bath:* combo or shower only. **Parking:** on-site. **Terms:** office hours 8 am-9 pm, 2 night minimum stay - seasonal and/or weekends, 7 day cancellation notice-fee imposed. **Amenities:** video library, DVD players, CD players, voice mail, irons, hair dryers. **Dining:** Champney's Restaurant & Tavern, see separate listing. **Guest Services:** wireless Internet. **Business Services:** meeting rooms, PC.

—— WHERE TO DINE ——

CHAMPNEY'S RESTAURANT & TAVERN   Phone: 413/774-5587

Continental
$10-$25

In a traditional 1884 New England country inn, the charming dining room is filled with authentic antiques as well as reproductions. Dishes on the creative menu use fresh local ingredients. The preparation is excellent, and presentation is attractive. Dressy casual. **Bar:** Full bar. **Reservations:** suggested. **Hours:** 7:30 am-10, noon-2:30 & 6-9 pm. Closed: 12/23-12/27. **Address:** 81 Old Main St 01342 **Location:** Center; in Deerfield Inn. **Parking:** street.

DENNIS—See Cape Cod p. 474.

DENNIS PORT—See Cape Cod p. 474.

EAST FALMOUTH—See Cape Cod p. 476.

EASTHAM—See Cape Cod p. 476.

EAST HARWICH—See Cape Cod p. 477.

EAST LONGMEADOW

—— WHERE TO DINE ——

PANDA SOUTH   Phone: 413/525-1820

Chinese
$8-$19

In the small Heritage Village Shoppes strip mall, this restaurant prepares traditional fare: hot and sour soup, spicy Szechuan and Hunan dishes and an array of other familiar items. The traditional decor doesn't detract from the good cuisine. Casual dress. **Bar:** Full bar. **Hours:** 11:30 am-9:30 pm, Fri & Sat-10:30 pm, Sun noon-9:30 pm. Closed: 11/25. **Address:** 31 Harkness Ave 01028 **Location:** I-91, exit 2 northbound, 4 mi se on SR 83; in Heritage Village Shoppes. **Parking:** on-site.

EAST ORLEANS—See Cape Cod p. 478.

EAST WAREHAM   (See map and index starting on p. 458)

ATLANTIC MOTEL   *Book great rates at AAA.com*   Phone: (508)295-0210   [112]

AAA [SAVE]

Motel
$90-$200 5/1-10/23
$80-$150 10/24-4/30

Address: 7 Depot St 02538 **Location:** Between eastbound and westbound lanes of US 6/SR 28; jct SR 25, exit 1. **Facility:** 24 one-bedroom standard units. 2 stories (no elevator), exterior corridors. **Parking:** on-site. **Terms:** office hours 7:30 am-10 pm, 10 day cancellation notice-fee imposed. **Amenities:** hair dryers. *Some:* irons. **Pool(s):** outdoor. **Guest Services:** wireless Internet. Free **Special Amenities:** preferred room (subject to availability with advance reservations) and high-speed Internet.

—— WHERE TO DINE ——

CHARLIE'S PLACE A FAMILY RESTAURANT   Phone: 508/295-6656   [100]

American
$8-$17

This restaurant is perfect for families and casual dining. Traditional American fare of burgers, steak and pizza makes up the menu. Casual dress. **Bar:** Full bar. **Hours:** 11:30 am-9 pm. **Address:** 3073 Cranberry Hwy 02538 **Location:** On SR 28. **Parking:** on-site.

(See map and index starting on p. 458)

LINDSEY'S FAMILY RESTAURANT *Menu on AAA.com*   Phone: 508/759-5544   101

American
$6-$25

A favorite restaurant with locals since 1948, the old-fashioned, home-style cooking centers on fresh, local seafood and folksy, friendly service. Lindsey's comfortable dining rooms, varied menu and ample portions make families feel right at home. Casual dress. **Bar:** Full bar. **Reservations:** not accepted. **Hours:** 11:30 am-9 pm. Closed: 11/25, 12/25. **Address:** 3138 Cranberry Hwy 02532 **Location:** US 6 and SR 28; 2 mi nw of Bourne rotary. **Parking:** on-site. CALL

EDGARTOWN—See Martha's Vineyard p. 531.

ESSEX—See Boston p. 410.

FAIRHAVEN

HAMPTON INN   *Book great rates at AAA.com*   Phone: (508)990-8500

Hotel
$109-$169 All Year

Address: 1 Hampton Way 02719 **Location:** I-195, exit 18, 0.8 mi s on SR 240, just w on Bridge St, then s on Alden St. **Facility:** 107 units. 89 one-bedroom standard units. 18 one-bedroom suites, some with whirlpools. 3 stories, interior corridors. *Bath:* combo or shower only. **Parking:** on-site. **Terms:** 1-7 night minimum stay, cancellation fee imposed. **Amenities:** dual phone lines, voice mail, irons, hair dryers. **Pool(s):** outdoor. **Leisure Activities:** exercise room. **Guest Services:** valet laundry, wireless Internet. **Business Services:** meeting rooms, business center.

AAA Benefit:
Members save up to
10% everyday!

SEAPORT INN L.L.C   *Book great rates at AAA.com*   Phone: (508)997-1281

Hotel
$119-$159 5/1-11/1
$89-$119 11/2-4/30

Address: 110 Middle St 02719 **Location:** I-195, exit 15, 1 mi s, then just off US 6. **Facility:** 88 one-bedroom standard units. 2 stories (no elevator), interior corridors. **Parking:** on-site. **Amenities:** video games (fee), high-speed Internet, voice mail, irons, hair dryers. **Leisure Activities:** exercise room. *Fee:* game room. **Guest Services:** valet and coin laundry. **Business Services:** conference facilities, business center. **Free Special Amenities:** expanded continental breakfast and high-speed Internet.

—— WHERE TO DINE ——

HUTTLESTON HOUSE RESTAURANT   Phone: 508/999-1791

Continental
$7-$25

The menu lists an extensive selection of fresh local seafood, including lobster, as well as specialty lunch "burgers" and prime beef, veal, pasta and duck dishes. Portions are ample, quality good, service cheerful and atmosphere cozy and sophisticated with a touch of the frilly. Low ceilings, barn-board walls and exposed ceiling beams contribute to the rustic nature of the dining room. Glass and artificial flowers top the tables, which are draped with double linens. The owner-chef has operated the restaurant for more than 25 years. The staff decorates the restaurant extensively for the Christmas holiday. Service is upbeat and friendly. Casual dress. **Bar:** Full bar. **Reservations:** accepted. **Hours:** 11:30 am-9 pm, Fri & Sat-10 pm, Sun noon-9 pm. Closed: 1/1, 11/25, 12/25. **Address:** 111 Huttleston Ave (Rt 6) 02719 **Location:** SR 240, exit 18, 1 mi w. **Parking:** on-site.

MIKE'S RESTAURANT   Phone: 508/996-9810

American
$5-$40

Locals often gather for drinks and meals at the laid-back neighborhood restaurant, which has a somewhat dated look but serves good food at reasonable prices. The menu lists lobster, prime rib and plenty of burgers and sandwiches for those who prefer lighter fare. Pleasant servers treat even first-timers as though they are regulars. Casual dress. **Bar:** Full bar. **Reservations:** not accepted. **Hours:** 11:30 am-10 pm, Fri & Sat-11 pm, Sun noon-10 pm. Closed: 11/25, 12/25; also for dinner 12/24. **Address:** 390 Huttleston Ave 02719 **Location:** US 6, 1.8 mi e of jct SR 240. **Parking:** on-site.

THE PASTA HOUSE   Phone: 508/993-9913

Italian
$12-$26

Renovated in 2009, this local institution now thrives as an amazing contemporary space with a dual-sided stone fireplace, attractive light fixtures and modern tables and chairs. Something of a "place to be seen," it seems to be crowded with patrons enjoying cocktails at the bar or delicious Italian specialties or fire deck oven pizzas in the dining room. Guests line up for items such as butternut squash ravioli. Luscious creme brulee is topped with fresh cream, mint and strawberries. Dressy casual. **Bar:** Full bar. **Reservations:** accepted. **Hours:** 4 pm-9 pm, Thurs-Sat to 10 pm. Closed: 11/25, 12/24, 12/25. **Address:** 100 Alden Rd 02719 **Location:** I-195, exit 18, just sw via Bridge St. **Parking:** on-site. CALL

FALL RIVER pop. 91,938

COMFORT INN & SUITES   *Book at AAA.com*   Phone: (508)672-0011

Hotel
$80-$110 All Year

Address: 360 Airport Rd 02720 **Location:** SR 79 and 24, exit 8; at Fall River Airport. Located in an industrial park. **Facility:** Smoke free premises. 82 units. 80 one-bedroom standard units. 2 one-bedroom suites with whirlpools. 4 stories, interior corridors. **Parking:** on-site. **Terms:** cancellation fee imposed. **Amenities:** irons, hair dryers. **Pool(s):** heated indoor. **Leisure Activities:** whirlpool, exercise room. **Guest Services:** valet laundry, wireless Internet. **Business Services:** meeting rooms, business center.

—— WHERE TO DINE ——

LE PAGE'S SEAFOOD & GRILLE   Phone: 508/677-2180

Seafood
$6-$22

Humble beginnings of tasty fried New England seafood expanded to a full variety of baked and broiled fare, pasta, steak and some gourmet dishes at Le Page's, overlooking the scenic Watuppa Pond. Outdoor seating is available in season. Modest surroundings understate the quality of the food. Servers in polo shirts provide attentive, friendly service. Casual dress. **Bar:** Full bar. **Reservations:** accepted. **Hours:** 11:30 am-9 pm, Fri & Sat-10 pm. Closed: 4/4, 11/25, 12/25. **Address:** 439 Martine St (US 6) 02723 **Location:** I-195, exit 9, 0.8 mi w to US 6; at Fall River/Westport line. **Parking:** on-site.

T A RESTAURANT   Phone: 508/673-5890

Portuguese
$7-$16

Popular with locals, particularly the Portuguese community, the downtown restaurant prepares traditional Portuguese preparations of pork, beef and rabbit, as well as hearty sandwiches and some American standards. Guests can opt for the daily luncheon buffet, except on Sunday. Casual dress. **Bar:** Full bar. **Hours:** 11 am-10 pm, Sun noon-9 pm. Closed major holidays. **Address:** 408 S Main St 02721 **Location:** Corner of Morgan St; downtown. **Parking:** on-site.

FALMOUTH—See Cape Cod p. 478.

FISKDALE pop. 2,156

—— WHERE TO DINE ——

STURBRIDGE COFFEE HOUSE   Phone: 508/347-2288

Coffee/Tea
$1-$7

A favorite local haunt for coffee, the coffee house is in the Sturbridge tourist area. The espresso bar provides cappuccinos, cafe mochas and the like. Baked-in-house items include muffin tops, pastries, scones and croissants. The contemporary spot features nice art pieces on the walls, and musicians play some nights of the week. Casual dress. **Reservations:** not accepted. **Hours:** 5 am-4 pm, Fri-9 pm, Sat 6 am-9 pm, Sun 7 am-4 pm. **Address:** 479 Main St 01518 **Location:** I-84, exit 3B westbound, 1.8 mi w on US 20; exit 2 eastbound, 1.1 mi nw on SR 15, then 1.4 mi w on US 20. **Parking:** on-site.

FITCHBURG pop. 39,102

COURTYARD BY MARRIOTT FITCHBURG   *Book great rates at AAA.com*   Phone: (978)342-7100

Hotel
$122-$149 All Year

Address: 150 Royal Plaza Dr 01420 **Location:** SR 2, exit 28, just s on SR 31. **Facility:** Smoke free premises. 245 one-bedroom standard units. 6 stories, interior corridors. **Parking:** on-site. **Terms:** cancellation fee imposed. **Amenities:** high-speed Internet, voice mail, irons, hair dryers. **Pool(s):** heated indoor. **Leisure Activities:** whirlpool, exercise room. **Guest Services:** valet and coin laundry, wireless Internet. **Business Services:** conference facilities, business center. *(See color ad p 380)*

AAA Benefit:
Members save a minimum 5% off the best available rate.

 CALL ⚕M 🏊 ✕ 🐾 🍽 / SOME UNITS FEE 🐕

FREE expanded continental breakfast and high-speed Internet

FORT DEVENS

SPRINGHILL SUITES DEVENS COMMON CENTER   *Book great rates at AAA.com*   Phone: (978)772-3030

Hotel
$157-$191 All Year

Address: 27 Andrews Pkwy 01434 **Location:** SR 2, exit 37B, 1.9 mi ne on Jackson Rd. **Facility:** Smoke free premises. 121 units. 120 one-bedroom standard units. 1 one-bedroom suite with whirlpool. 3 stories, interior corridors. **Bath:** combo or shower only. **Parking:** on-site. **Terms:** cancellation fee imposed. **Amenities:** high-speed Internet, voice mail, irons, hair dryers. **Pool(s):** heated indoor. **Leisure Activities:** whirlpool, limited exercise equipment. **Guest Services:** valet and coin laundry, wireless Internet. **Business Services:** conference facilities, business center.

AAA Benefit:
Members save a minimum 5% off the best available rate.

🏨 CALL ⚕M 🏊 ✕ 🐾 📠 🖥 🖥

—— WHERE TO DINE ——

THE DEVENS GRILL   Phone: 978/862-0060

American
$8-$24

A comfortable place for lunch or dinner, the restaurant employs friendly servers in black T-shirts and khaki pants. Bar area TVs can be viewed from most tables in the dining room. Each table has a jar filled with fresh garden flowers. A meal might include a steaming bowl of spinach and artichoke dip, a buffalo chicken or grilled Reuben sandwich and hot apple crisp topped with vanilla ice cream. Popular dinner choices include a fried haddock dinner and meatloaf. Casual dress. **Bar:** Full bar. **Reservations:** not accepted. **Hours:** 11 am-10 pm, Sun 8 am-9 pm. Closed major holidays. **Address:** 4 Ryans Way 01434 **Location:** SR 2, exit 37B, 1.9 mi ne on Jackson Rd. **Parking:** on-site. CALL ⚕M

FOXBORO—See Boston p. 410.

FRAMINGHAM—See Boston p. 412.

FRANKLIN—See Boston p. 413.

GARDNER pop. 20,770

COLONIAL HOTEL *Book at AAA.com*

Hotel
$99-$139 All Year

Phone: (978)630-2500

Address: 625 Betty Spring Rd 01440 **Location:** SR 2, exit 24 eastbound; exit 24B, 0.9 mi n on SR 140, then 0.5 mi w. **Facility:** 112 units. 111 one-bedroom standard units, some with whirlpools. 1 one-bedroom suite with whirlpool. 2 stories, interior corridors. **Parking:** on-site. **Terms:** cancellation fee imposed. **Amenities:** voice mail, irons, hair dryers. **Pool(s):** heated indoor. **Leisure Activities:** whirlpool, exercise room. *Fee:* game room. **Guest Services:** valet and coin laundry, wireless Internet. **Business Services:** conference facilities, PC.

ASK ⓘ 🍸 🏊 ✕ 📹 📶 💻 / SOME UNITS FEE 🛏 ✕ FEE 📠

SUPER 8 *Book at AAA.com*

Motel
$79-$110 All Year

Phone: (978)630-2888

Address: 22 Pearson Blvd 01440 **Location:** SR 2, exit 23, just n. **Facility:** 47 one-bedroom standard units. 2 stories (no elevator), interior corridors. **Parking:** on-site. **Terms:** cancellation fee imposed. **Amenities:** hair dryers. **Guest Services:** wireless Internet.

ASK ⓘ⁺ 📹 📶 📠 💻 / SOME UNITS FEE 🛏 ✕

——— WHERE TO DINE ———

YEN YEN CHINESE RESTAURANT & COCKTAIL LOUNGE

Chinese
$6-$18

Phone: 978/630-1535

In a small shopping center, the restaurant sets up luncheon buffets daily, with the exception of major holidays. Choices span the breadth of Chinese cooking styles. Casual dress. **Bar:** Full bar. **Reservations:** accepted. **Hours:** 11:30 am-10 pm, Fri & Sat-11 pm, Sun noon-10 pm. Closed: 11/25. **Address:** 42 Pearson Blvd 01440 **Location:** SR 2, exit 23, just n. **Parking:** on-site.

GLOUCESTER—See Boston p. 414.

GREAT BARRINGTON pop. 2,459

COMFORT INN & SUITES *Book great rates at AAA.com*

ⒶⒶⒶ SAVE

Hotel
$120-$360 All Year

Phone: (413)644-3200

Address: 249 Stockbridge Rd, Rt 7 01230 **Location:** I-90, exit 2, SR 102 W to US 7, then 5.5 mi s. **Facility:** Smoke free premises. 93 units. 88 one-bedroom standard units, some with whirlpools. 5 one-bedroom suites. 3 stories, interior corridors. *Bath:* combo or shower only. **Parking:** on-site. **Terms:** 2 night minimum stay - seasonal and/or weekends, 3 day cancellation notice. **Amenities:** high-speed Internet, voice mail, irons, hair dryers. *Some:* DVD players (fee). **Pool(s):** heated indoor. **Leisure Activities:** whirlpool, playground, exercise room. *Fee:* game room. **Guest Services:** valet and coin laundry, wireless Internet. **Business Services:** meeting rooms, business center. *(See color ad p 520)*

ⓘ⁺ CALL 🅼 🏊 ✕ ✕ 📹 📶 📠 💻

FREE expanded continental breakfast and high-speed Internet

HOLIDAY INN EXPRESS HOTEL & SUITES *Book great rates at AAA.com*

ⒶⒶⒶ SAVE

Hotel
$149-$325 5/1-9/7
$139-$299 9/8-4/30

Phone: (413)528-1810

Address: 415 Stockbridge Rd 01230 **Location:** On US 7, 1 mi s of jct SR 183. **Facility:** Smoke free premises. 58 units. 55 one-bedroom standard units, some with whirlpools. 3 one-bedroom suites. 2 stories, interior corridors. *Bath:* combo or shower only. **Parking:** on-site. **Amenities:** high-speed Internet, dual phone lines, voice mail, irons, hair dryers. **Pool(s):** heated indoor. **Leisure Activities:** whirlpool, exercise room. **Guest Services:** valet laundry, wireless Internet. **Business Services:** meeting rooms, PC. **Free Special Amenities:** full breakfast and high-speed Internet.

CALL 🅼 🏊 ✕ 📹 📶 📠 💻

LANTERN HOUSE MOTEL

Phone: 413/528-2350

Motel
$55-$189 5/1-10/31
$55-$150 11/1-4/30

Address: 256 Stockbridge Rd 01230 **Location:** On US 7, 1.2 mi s of jct SR 183. **Facility:** Smoke free premises. 14 one-bedroom standard units, some with whirlpools. 1 story, exterior corridors. **Parking:** on-site. **Terms:** office hours 7 am-10 pm, 21 day cancellation notice-fee imposed. **Amenities:** voice mail. **Leisure Activities:** playground. **Guest Services:** wireless Internet. **Free Special Amenities:** high-speed Internet.

▼ See AAA listing p 519 ▼

MONUMENT MOUNTAIN MOTEL   *Book great rates at AAA.com*   Phone: (413)528-3272

Motel
$59-$199 All Year

Address: 247 Stockbridge Rd (Rt 7) 01230 **Location:** On US 7, 1.2 mi s of jct SR 183. **Facility:** Smoke free premises. 17 one-bedroom standard units. 1 story, exterior corridors. *Bath:* combo or shower only. **Parking:** on-site, winter plug-ins. **Terms:** office hours 7 am-10 pm, 2-3 night minimum stay - seasonal and/or weekends, 14 day cancellation notice-fee imposed. **Amenities:** voice mail, hair dryers. **Pool(s):** outdoor. **Leisure Activities:** playground, horseshoes. **Guest Services:** wireless Internet. **Free Special Amenities:** local telephone calls and high-speed Internet.

WINDFLOWER INN   Phone: (413)528-2720

Historic Bed
& Breakfast
$125-$250 All Year

Address: 684 S Egremont Rd 01230 **Location:** On SR 23, 3 mi w of jct US 7. **Facility:** Antiques and collectibles decorate the guest rooms and common areas of the 1800s Federal-style inn; located across from an 18-hole public golf course. Smoke free premises. 13 one-bedroom standard units. 2 stories (no elevator), interior corridors. *Bath:* combo or shower only. **Parking:** on-site. **Terms:** office hours 7:30 am-9 pm, 2-3 night minimum stay - seasonal and/or weekends, 21 day cancellation notice-fee imposed. **Pool(s):** outdoor. **Guest Services:** wireless Internet.

The following lodging was either not evaluated or did not meet AAA rating requirements but is listed for your information only.

STONEGATE MANSION   Phone: 413/528-9554

[fyi]

Not evaluated. **Address:** 111 West Ave 01230. Facilities, services, and decor characterize a mid-scale property.

WHERE TO DINE

AEGEAN BREEZE   Phone: 413/528-4001

Greek
$6-$35

Contemporary details punctuate the Mediterranean restaurant's warm decor. The menu lists both traditional and new interpretations of favorite Greek dishes. Hearty portions can be paired with wines from this celebrated mythic land. Outdoor seating is a seasonal option. Casual dress. **Bar:** Full bar. **Reservations:** suggested, weekends. **Hours:** 11 am-10 pm. **Address:** 327 Stockbridge Rd 01230 **Location:** On US 7, 1.3 mi s of jct SR 183. **Parking:** on-site.

BARRINGTON BREWERY & RESTAURANT   Phone: 413/528-8282

American
$8-$20

The restaurant's house-specialty microbrews match well with traditional pub fare, including burgers, fish and chips, pasta and pizza. The patio is open during nice weather. Casual dress. **Bar:** Beer & wine. **Reservations:** not accepted. **Hours:** 11:30 am-9:30 pm, Fri & Sat-10 pm, Sun-9 pm; to 10 pm 7/1-8/31. Closed: 4/4, 11/25, 12/25. **Address:** 420 Stockbridge Rd 01230 **Location:** On US 7, 1 mi s of jct SR 183. **Parking:** on-site.

BIZEN GOURMET JAPANESE RESTAURANT & SUSHI BAR   Phone: 413/528-4343

Japanese
$8-$21

In many rooms here, patrons can sit on the floor or at a low table that gives off the same impression. Authentic Kaiseki tea ceremonies and a long list of sake offerings enhance the authentic Japanese experience, as does the tatami room. Fresh sushi, sashimi and tempura preparations are at the heart of the menu. Dressy casual. **Bar:** Full bar. **Reservations:** accepted. **Hours:** noon-2:30 & 5-9:30 pm, Fri-10 pm, Sat & Sun noon-3 & 5-10 pm. Closed major holidays. **Address:** 17 Railroad St 01230 **Location:** Jct SR 23, 0.5 mi s on US 7, then just nw. **Parking:** street.

THE NEIGHBORHOOD DINER   Phone: 413/528-8226

American
$5-$15

The charming, typical village restaurant offers what folks love best about diners: good, simple food, all-day breakfast items and a warm, friendly staff that welcomes everyone. This place is popular with locals and visitors alike. Lines on summer weekends aren't unusual. Casual dress. **Hours:** 7 am-9 pm; hours vary in summer. Closed: 12/25. **Address:** 282 Main St 01230 **Location:** Center. **Parking:** street.

GREENFIELD pop. 13,716

THE BRANDT HOUSE B&B   Phone: 413/774-3329

Historic Bed
& Breakfast
$95-$295 5/1-10/31
$95-$245 11/1-4/30

Address: 29 Highland Ave 01301-3605 **Location:** I-91, exit 26, 1.8 mi e on SR 2A, then se via Crescent St. **Facility:** The wraparound porch accenting the Colonial Revival mansion or the Zen garden's pergola are both great spots for taking in the scenic mountain views. Smoke free premises. 9 one-bedroom standard units. 3 stories (no elevator), interior corridors. *Bath:* some shared or private. **Parking:** on-site. **Terms:** office hours 6:30 am-10 pm, 30 day cancellation notice-fee imposed. **Amenities:** hair dryers. **Guest Services:** wireless Internet. **Business Services:** PC.

DAYS INN   *Book at AAA.com*   Phone: (413)774-5578

Motel
$89-$180 5/1-10/31
$79-$109 11/1-4/30

Address: 21 Colrain Rd 01301 **Location:** I-91, exit 26, just n of SR 2 W. **Facility:** 59 one-bedroom standard units. 2 stories (no elevator), interior corridors. **Parking:** on-site. **Amenities:** high-speed Internet, irons, hair dryers. **Guest Services:** wireless Internet. **Business Services:** PC.

HAMPTON INN & SUITES   *Book great rates at AAA.com*

Phone: (413)773-0057

Hotel
$109-$219 All Year

Address: 184 Shelburne Rd 01301 **Location:** I-91, exit 26, just n of SR 2W. **Facility:** 68 one-bedroom standard units, some with whirlpools. 4 stories, interior corridors. *Bath:* combo or shower only. **Parking:** on-site. **Terms:** 1-7 night minimum stay, cancellation fee imposed. **Amenities:** video games (fee), high-speed Internet, dual phone lines, voice mail, irons, hair dryers. **Pool(s):** heated indoor. **Leisure Activities:** limited exercise equipment. **Guest Services:** valet and coin laundry, wireless Internet. **Business Services:** meeting rooms, business center.

CALL [icons] / SOME UNITS [icons]

AAA Benefit:
Members save up to 10% everyday!

------ **WHERE TO DINE** ------

CHINA GOURMET CHINESE & JAPANESE CUISINE

Phone: 413/774-2299

Asian
$6-$16

Right out of downtown, the popular restaurant prepares varied Chinese dishes and sushi bar items. The dining room picks up on the Orient and has wood separators and live plants. Casual dress. **Bar:** Full bar. **Reservations:** accepted. **Hours:** 11 am-10 pm, Fri & Sat-11 pm. Closed: 11/25. **Address:** 78 Mohawk Tr (SR 2A) 01301 **Location:** I-91, exit 26, just e. **Parking:** on-site.

HADLEY

COMFORT INN   *Book great rates at AAA.com*

Phone: (413)584-9816

Hotel
$81-$160 All Year

Address: 237 Russell St 01035 **Location:** I-91, exit 19 northbound; exit 20 southbound, 3 mi e on SR 9. **Facility:** 86 one-bedroom standard units. 1-3 stories (no elevator), interior corridors. *Bath:* combo or shower only. **Parking:** on-site. **Terms:** check-in 4 pm, cancellation fee imposed. **Amenities:** voice mail, irons, hair dryers. **Pool(s):** heated indoor. **Leisure Activities:** exercise room. **Guest Services:** coin laundry, wireless Internet. **Business Services:** meeting rooms, business center. **Free Special Amenities: expanded continental breakfast and high-speed Internet.**

[icons] / SOME UNITS FEE [icons]

COURTYARD HADLEY/AMHERST   *Book great rates at AAA.com*

Phone: (413)256-5454

Hotel
$129-$139 All Year

Address: 423 Russell St 01035 **Location:** I-91, exit 19 (northbound), 5 mi e on SR 9. **Facility:** Smoke free premises. 96 units. 92 one-bedroom standard units. 4 one-bedroom suites. 1-3 stories, interior corridors. *Bath:* combo or shower only. **Parking:** on-site. **Terms:** cancellation fee imposed. **Amenities:** high-speed Internet, voice mail, irons, hair dryers. *Some:* DVD players (fee). **Pool(s):** heated indoor. **Leisure Activities:** whirlpool, exercise room. **Guest Services:** valet and coin laundry, wireless Internet. **Business Services:** meeting rooms, business center.

[icons] CALL [icons] / SOME UNITS [icons]

AAA Benefit:
Members save a minimum 5% off the best available rate.

ECONO LODGE   *Book at AAA.com*

Phone: (413)582-7077

Hotel
$79-$179 All Year

Address: 329 Russell St 01035 **Location:** I-91, exit 19 northbound, 4 mi e on SR 9; exit 20 southbound, 2.5 mi s on SR 10/US 5 (King St), then 5.5 mi ne on SR 9 (Bridge St becoming Russell St after the bridge). Adjacent to Hampshire Mall. **Facility:** 63 one-bedroom standard units. 3 stories, interior corridors. *Bath:* combo or shower only. **Parking:** on-site. **Terms:** cancellation fee imposed. **Amenities:** high-speed Internet, voice mail, irons, hair dryers. **Pool(s):** heated indoor. **Guest Services:** coin laundry, wireless Internet. **Business Services:** PC, fax (fee).

[ASK] [icons] / SOME UNITS [icons] FEE [icons] FEE [icons]

HAMPTON INN   *Book great rates at AAA.com*

Phone: (413)586-4851

Hotel
$109-$189 All Year

Address: 24 Bay Rd 01035 **Location:** I-91, exit 19 northbound, 0.7 mi ne on SR 9, then just se; exit 20 southbound, 0.9 mi e on Damon Rd, 0.7 mi ne on SR 9, then just se. **Facility:** 73 one-bedroom standard units, some with whirlpools. 3 stories, interior corridors. *Bath:* combo or shower only. **Parking:** on-site. **Terms:** 1-7 night minimum stay, cancellation fee imposed. **Amenities:** high-speed Internet, dual phone lines, voice mail, irons, hair dryers. **Pool(s):** heated indoor. **Leisure Activities:** exercise room. **Guest Services:** valet and coin laundry, wireless Internet. **Business Services:** business center. **Free Special Amenities: full breakfast and high-speed Internet.**

CALL [icons] / SOME UNITS [icons]

AAA Benefit:
Members save up to 10% everyday!

HOLIDAY INN EXPRESS & SUITES   *Book at AAA.com*

Phone: (413)582-0002

Hotel
$89-$199 5/1-11/6
$89-$149 11/7-4/30

Address: 400 Russell St 01035 **Location:** I-91, exit 19 northbound, 4.3 mi e on SR 9; exit 24 southbound, 10 mi s on SR 116, then just w on SR 9. **Facility:** 100 units. 93 one-bedroom standard units. 7 one-bedroom suites, some with whirlpools. 3 stories, interior corridors. *Bath:* combo or shower only. **Parking:** on-site. **Amenities:** high-speed Internet, dual phone lines, voice mail, irons, hair dryers. *Some:* video games (fee). **Pool(s):** heated indoor. **Leisure Activities:** whirlpool, exercise room. **Guest Services:** coin laundry, wireless Internet. **Business Services:** meeting rooms, PC.

[ASK] CALL [icons] / SOME UNITS [icons]

HOWARD JOHNSON INN   *Book at AAA.com*

Hotel
$79-$209 All Year

Phone: (413)586-0114

Address: 401 Russell St 01035 **Location:** I-91, exit 19 northbound, 4.3 mi e on SR 9; exit 24 southbound, 10 mi s on SR 116, then just w on SR 9. **Facility:** 100 one-bedroom standard units, some with whirlpools. 2-5 stories, interior corridors. **Parking:** on-site. **Terms:** 2 night minimum stay - seasonal and/or weekends, cancellation fee imposed. **Amenities:** voice mail, irons, hair dryers. *Some:* video games (fee), high-speed Internet. **Pool(s):** outdoor. **Leisure Activities:** exercise room. **Guest Services:** valet and coin laundry, wireless Internet. **Business Services:** meeting rooms, business center. (ASK) CALL (&M) / SOME UNITS FEE

------ **WHERE TO DINE** ------

CARMELINAS RISTORANTE

Italian
$10-$29

Phone: 413/584-8000

Flavorful bruschetta and excellent zuppa di pesce-assorted seafood on angel-hair pasta-exhibit nice attention to plate arrangement, color and texture. Other equally distinctive dishes are served in an informal, pleasant atmosphere. Casual dress. **Bar:** Full bar. **Reservations:** suggested. **Hours:** 5 pm-10 pm. Closed major holidays; also Mon. **Address:** 96 Russell St 01035 **Location:** I-91, exit 19, 1.5 mi e on SR 9. **Parking:** on-site.

ESSELON CAFE

American
$8-$15

Phone: 413/585-1515

This popular cafe is known for its great brunches and fast counter-service lunches, which include freshly baked items, salads, soups, burgers and sandwiches. Varied seating options include cafe-style tables, long communal tables and a covered porch overlooking the nicely landscaped garden. A coffee theme, incorporating large coffee barrels and sacks, weaves through the nicely decorated restaurant. Casual dress. **Reservations:** not accepted. **Hours:** 7 am-9 pm, Sat from 8 am, Sun 8 am-5 pm, Mon 7 am-3 pm. Closed: 1/1; also 12/23-12/29. **Address:** 99 Russell St 01035 **Location:** I-91, exit 19, 1.3 mi ne on SR 9. **Parking:** on-site.

HANCOCK

THE COUNTRY INN AT JIMINY PEAK   *Book great rates at AAA.com*

Resort
Hotel
$129-$509 All Year

Phone: (413)738-5500

Address: 37 Corey Rd 01237 **Location:** US 7, 3 mi w on Brodie Mountain Rd. **Facility:** The inn occupies an 800-acre wooded site at the base of a ski resort; find condo-style rooms, many with decks and fireplaces, and a country store. Smoke free premises. 100 one-bedroom suites with efficiencies and kitchens. 3 stories, interior/exterior corridors. **Parking:** on-site. **Terms:** check-in 4 pm, 2-3 night minimum stay - seasonal and/or weekends, 14 day cancellation notice-fee imposed. **Amenities:** video library (fee), DVD players, voice mail, irons, hair dryers. **Pool(s):** heated outdoor. **Leisure Activities:** saunas, whirlpools, 3 tennis courts, mountain bike trails, hiking trails, playground, exercise room, sports court. *Fee:* miniature golf, downhill skiing, Alpine slide, bouncy-bounce, climbing wall, euro-bungee, scenic summit ride, giant swing, mountain coaster, bicycles, game room. **Guest Services:** coin laundry, wireless Internet. **Business Services:** meeting rooms. **Free Special Amenities:** local telephone calls.

------ *The following lodging was either not evaluated or did not* ------
meet AAA rating requirements but is listed for your information only.

WYNDHAM BENTLEY BROOK

(fyi)

Phone: 413/738-8600

Not evaluated. **Address:** 1 Corey Rd 01237. Facilities, services, and decor characterize a mid-scale property.

HANOVER

—— WHERE TO DINE ——

JOE'S AMERICAN BAR & GRILL
Phone: 781/878-1234

American
$9-$24

If it's Americana you want, you'll get all that and more at Joe's, where the bill of fare includes all-American favorites like hearty burgers, fresh-from-the-oven chicken pot pies, Maryland lump crab cakes, and Joe's classic meatloaf. Pizzas, pastas, steaks and salads round out the extensive menu, giving diners the freedom to choose from a vast selection of offerings. There's nothing more American than that, except, of course, for apple pie, so save some room. Casual dress. **Bar:** Full bar. **Reservations:** not accepted. **Hours:** 11:30 am-10:30 pm, Fri & Sat-11:30 pm, Sun 11 am-10:30 pm. Closed: 12/25. **Address:** 2087 Washington St 02339 **Location:** SR 3, exit 13, 0.5 mi n on SR 53. **Parking:** on-site. CALL 🅢🅜

PAPA RAZZI
Phone: 781/982-2800

Northern Italian
$10-$26

Italy has changed and so has authentic Italian food. It's lighter, fresher, more exciting Italian, and it's just what you'll find amid the elegant yet comfortable atmosphere that is Papa Razzi. If the steamy bowls of pasta don't tempt you, one of the aromatic pizzas or a warm panini sandwich definitely will. In addition there is a fine wine list, an array of salads, chicken, and fish options to choose from. Dressy casual. **Bar:** Full bar. **Reservations:** suggested. **Hours:** 11:30 am-10 pm, Fri & Sat-11 pm; Sunday brunch. Closed: 11/25, 12/25. **Address:** 2087 Washington St 02339 **Location:** SR 3, exit 13, 0.5 mi n on SR 53. **Parking:** on-site. CALL 🅢🅜

HARWICH PORT—See Cape Cod p. 480.

HAVERHILL—See Boston p. 416.

HINGHAM—See Boston p. 417.

HOLLAND pop. 1,444

THE INN AT RESTFUL PAWS
Phone: 413/245-7792

Bed & Breakfast
$174 All Year

Address: 70 Allen Hill Rd 01521 **Location:** SR 20, 2.1 mi s on E Brimfield Rd, 0.4 mi on Alexander Rd, then 0.7 mi n. Located in a quiet area. **Facility:** This is a one-of-a-kind, pet-oriented lodge where dogs and cats are happily welcomed; a unique feature here is the bone-shaped, "dogs only" pool area. Smoke free premises. 4 one-bedroom standard units. 1 story, interior corridors. **Parking:** on-site. **Terms:** age restrictions may apply, 14 day cancellation notice-fee imposed. **Amenities:** video library, hair dryers. *Some:* DVD players. **Leisure Activities:** hiking trails. **Guest Services:** TV in common area. ASK ✕ 🆆 ☎ 🖵 / SOME UNITS 🐾

HOLYOKE pop. 39,838

COUNTRY INN & SUITES BY CARLSON   *Book at AAA.com*
Phone: 413/533-2100

Hotel
Rates not provided

Address: 1 Country Club Rd 01040 **Location:** I-91, exit 18, 2.8 mi s. **Facility:** 62 units. 42 one-bedroom standard units, some with efficiencies. 20 one-bedroom suites. 6 stories, interior corridors. *Bath:* combo or shower only. **Parking:** on-site. **Amenities:** high-speed Internet, voice mail, irons, hair dryers. **Dining:** The Delaney House, see separate listing. **Pool(s):** heated indoor. **Leisure Activities:** whirlpool, exercise room. **Guest Services:** valet and coin laundry. **Business Services:** meeting rooms. 🍴 CALL 🅢🅜 🚐 📹 🍽 🖵 / SOME UNITS ✕ 🛗 📠

HOLIDAY INN SPRINGFIELD-HOLYOKE   *Book at AAA.com*
Phone: (413)534-3311

Hotel
$119-$179 All Year

Address: 245 Whiting Farms Rd 01040 **Location:** I-91, exit 15. **Facility:** 209 one-bedroom standard units. 4 stories, interior corridors. *Bath:* combo or shower only. **Parking:** on-site. **Amenities:** video games (fee), voice mail, irons, hair dryers. *Some:* safes. **Pool(s):** heated indoor. **Leisure Activities:** whirlpool, exercise room. **Fee:** game room. **Guest Services:** valet and coin laundry, area transportation, wireless Internet. **Business Services:** conference facilities, business center.
ASK 🍴 🍽 CALL 🅢🅜 🚐 ✕ 📹 🖵 / SOME UNITS ✕ 🛗 📠

HOMEWOOD SUITES BY HILTON HOLYOKE-SPRINGFIELD   *Book great rates at AAA.com*
Phone: (413)532-3100

Extended Stay
Hotel
$96-$169 All Year

Address: 375 Whitney Ave 01040 **Location:** I-91, exit 15, just w on Lower Westfield Rd, then 0.4 mi s. **Facility:** 114 units. 29 one-bedroom standard units with efficiencies. 81 one- and 4 two-bedroom suites with efficiencies. 5 stories, interior corridors. *Bath:* combo or shower only. **Parking:** on-site. **Terms:** 1-7 night minimum stay, cancellation fee imposed. **Amenities:** video games (fee), high-speed Internet, dual phone lines, voice mail, irons, hair dryers. *Some:* DVD players. **Pool(s):** heated indoor. **Leisure Activities:** whirlpool, exercise room, sports court. **Guest Services:** valet and coin laundry, area transportation, wireless Internet. **Business Services:** meeting rooms, business center.
CALL 🅢🅜 🚐 ✕ 📹 🛗 📠 🖵 / SOME UNITS FEE 🐾 ✕

—— WHERE TO DINE ——

THE DELANEY HOUSE *Menu on AAA.com*
Phone: 413/532-1800

American
$23-$45

Four distinctively decorated dining rooms enhanced by pleasant background music nestle in the refurbished 1880 manor. A carving station, omelet station, Belgian waffle station and Viennese table are offered at Sunday brunch. Dressy casual. **Bar:** Full bar. **Reservations:** suggested. **Hours:** 5 pm-9 pm, Sun 10 am-1:30 & 4-8 pm; Sunday brunch. Closed: 1/1, 12/24, 12/25. **Address:** 3 Country Club Rd 01040 **Location:** I-91, exit 18, 2.8 mi s; in Country Inn & Suites By Carlson. **Parking:** on-site.

HUDSON—See Boston p. 417.

HULL—See Boston p. 417.

HYANNIS—See Cape Cod p. 481.

IPSWICH—See Boston p. 418.

LANESBOROUGH pop. 2,990

THE WEATHERVANE MOTEL
Phone: (413)443-3230

Motel
$65-$110 5/1-10/31
$35-$65 11/1-4/30

Address: 475 S Main St 01237 **Location:** 1.3 mi s on US 7. **Facility:** 12 one-bedroom standard units, some with kitchens. 1 story, exterior corridors. **Bath:** combo or shower only. **Parking:** on-site. **Terms:** 15 day cancellation notice. **Amenities:** hair dryers. **Guest Services:** wireless Internet. **Free Special Amenities:** local telephone calls and early check-in/late check-out.

LAWRENCE—See Boston p. 418.

LEE pop. 2,021

AMERICAS BEST VALUE INN *Book great rates at AAA.com*
Phone: (413)243-0501

Motel
$59-$199 5/1-10/31
$49-$129 11/1-4/30

Address: 980 Pleasant St (SR 102) 01238 **Location:** I-90, exit 2, 1.8 mi w. **Facility:** 26 one-bedroom standard units, some with whirlpools. 2 stories (no elevator), exterior corridors. **Parking:** on-site. **Terms:** 2 night minimum stay - seasonal and/or weekends, 3 day cancellation notice. **Amenities:** hair dryers. *Some:* irons. **Guest Services:** wireless Internet. **Free Special Amenities:** continental breakfast and high-speed Internet.

APPLEGATE INN
Phone: (413)243-4451

Bed & Breakfast
$150-$385 All Year

Address: 279 W Park St 01238 **Location:** I-90, exit 2, 0.8 mi nw on US 20, then 0.5 mi w. **Facility:** This circa 1920 Georgian Colonial is reminiscent of "grandmother's house" with wonderful antiques, fine linens and comfortable surroundings. Smoke free premises. 11 units. 10 one-bedroom standard units, some with whirlpools. 1 two-bedroom suite with kitchen and whirlpool. 2 stories (no elevator), interior corridors. **Bath:** combo or shower only. **Parking:** on-site. **Terms:** office hours 8 am-9 pm, 2-3 night minimum stay - seasonal and/or weekends, cancellation fee imposed. **Amenities:** video library, CD players, voice mail, irons, hair dryers. *Some:* DVD players. **Pool(s):** heated outdoor. **Leisure Activities:** bicycles, volleyball. **Guest Services:** wireless Internet. **Business Services:** PC.

THE PILGRIM INN *Book at AAA.com*
Phone: (413)243-1328

Motel
$95-$225 5/1-10/31
$65-$125 11/1-4/30

Address: 165 Housatonic St (Rt 20) 01238 **Location:** I-90, exit 2, 0.3 mi w. **Facility:** 37 units. 36 one- and 1 two-bedroom standard units, some with whirlpools. 2 stories (no elevator), interior/exterior corridors. **Bath:** combo or shower only. **Terms:** 14 day cancellation notice-fee imposed. **Amenities:** irons, hair dryers. **Pool(s):** outdoor. **Guest Services:** coin laundry, wireless Internet.

RODEWAY INN *Book great rates at AAA.com*
Phone: 413/243-0813

Motel
Rates not provided

Address: 200 Laurel St 01238 **Location:** I-90, exit 2, 1.8 mi w on US 20. **Facility:** Smoke free premises. 23 one-bedroom standard units, some with efficiencies and/or whirlpools. 1 story, exterior corridors. **Bath:** combo or shower only. **Parking:** on-site. **Amenities:** irons, hair dryers. **Pool(s):** outdoor. **Guest Services:** wireless Internet. **Free Special Amenities:** continental breakfast and high-speed Internet.

SUNSET MOTEL
Phone: 413/243-0302

Motel
$90-$225 5/1-9/3
$60-$170 9/4-4/30

Address: 150 Housatonic St (Rt 20) 01238 **Location:** I-90, exit 2, 0.3 mi w. **Facility:** 27 one-bedroom standard units, some with whirlpools. 1 story, exterior corridors. **Parking:** on-site. **Terms:** 14 day cancellation notice-fee imposed. **Amenities:** hair dryers. *Some:* DVD players. **Pool(s):** outdoor. **Guest Services:** wireless Internet. **Free Special Amenities:** local telephone calls and high-speed Internet.

SUPER 8 *Book at AAA.com*

Motel
$65-$195 5/1-10/31
$55-$95 11/1-4/30

Phone: (413)243-0143

Address: 170 Housatonic St (Rt 20) 01238 **Location:** I-90, exit 2, 0.3 mi w. **Facility:** 49 one-bedroom standard units. 2 stories (no elevator), interior corridors. **Parking:** on-site. **Terms:** 3 day cancellation notice. **Amenities:** irons, hair dryers. **Guest Services:** wireless Internet.

(ASK) ☐ / SOME UNITS ⊠ ☐ 🖵

------ WHERE TO DINE ------

CHEZ NOUS

French
$12-$30

Phone: 413/243-6397

The delightful French bistro prepares a terrific sampling of homemade dishes and wonderful pastries. Casual dress. **Bar:** Full bar. **Reservations:** suggested, weekends. **Hours:** Open 5/1-2/28 & 4/1-4/30; 5 pm-9 pm; expanded hours 7/1-8/31. Closed major holidays; also 3/1-3/31 & Mon-Wed 1/1-2/28. **Address:** 150 Main St 01238 **Location:** On US 20 at Academy St; center. **Parking:** on-site.

CORK 'N HEARTH

American
$19-$26

Phone: 413/243-0535

Overlooking the serenity of Laurel Lake, the restaurant prepares fresh seafood, steak, veal, chicken and pork, as well as a nice selection of homemade desserts. Of note is an exceptional lemon-lime chicken with assorted vegetables and roasted potatoes. Casual dress. **Bar:** Full bar. **Reservations:** suggested. **Hours:** 5 pm-9 pm, Sun 4 pm-8 pm. Closed: 11/25, 12/24, 12/25; also Mon. **Address:** US 20 01238 **Location:** 1.3 mi s of jct US 7. **Parking:** on-site.

THE MORGAN HOUSE

American
$8-$27

Phone: 413/243-3661

This downtown restaurant serves homestyle New England fare: Caesar salad, roast beef, New England bouillabaisse, assorted seafood dishes and wonderful desserts. Traditional decor is displayed around a dining room marked by original-style wood floors and colorful area rugs. Casual dress. **Bar:** Full bar. **Reservations:** accepted. **Hours:** 11:30 am-8 pm, Fri & Sat-9 pm; seasonal hours may vary. Closed: 12/25; also Mon & Tues. **Address:** 33 Main St 01238 **Location:** I-90, exit 2, 0.5 mi n. **Parking:** on-site.

SULLIVAN STATION RESTAURANT

American
$8-$21

Phone: 413/243-2082

Nestled off the main street, the nifty little find was once a train depot and now offers locals and travelers New England-style fare. Lunch offerings include salads, baked Boston scrod and the signature station burger. Hearty dinner selections range from chicken parmigiana to baked stuffed sole. The decor is a reminder of a bygone era: walls of pictures map out the history of the station and the townspeople. A restored caboose for family dining and a screened deck recently were added. Casual dress. **Bar:** Full bar. **Reservations:** suggested. **Hours:** 11:30 am-4 & 4:30-close; seasonal hours may vary. Closed: 4/4, 11/25, 12/25; also Mon & Tues 11/1-5/1. **Address:** 109 Railroad St 01238 **Location:** I-90, exit 2, 1.5 mi w on US 20. **Parking:** on-site.

LEICESTER

------ WHERE TO DINE ------

THE CASTLE RESTAURANT

Continental
$7-$35

Phone: 508/892-9090

Guests can choose from two menus: one lighter, the other more classical. Typical tasty findings include crab cakes, tortellini and Chateaubriand. The castle-like atmosphere also incorporates terrace seating in summer. The extensive wine list is impressive. Dressy casual. **Bar:** Full bar. **Reservations:** suggested. **Hours:** 11:30 am-9:30 pm, Sun 2 pm-9 pm. Closed: 1/1, 11/25, 12/25; also Mon & Tues. **Address:** 1230 Main St 01524 **Location:** SR 9, 0.4 mi w of jct SR 56. **Parking:** on-site. CALL (&M)

LENOX pop. 1,667

BLANTYRE *Book great rates at AAA.com*

(AAA) (SAVE)

Boutique Country Inn
$600-$1850 All Year

Phone: (413)637-3556

Address: 16 Blantyre Rd 01240 **Location:** US 20, 1 mi s from jct SR 183. **Facility:** Luxurious rooms, a conservatory, croquet courts and a music room comprise this 1902 Tudor-style mansion, which replicates a grand Scottish manor. Smoke free premises. 23 units. 16 one-bedroom standard units. 5 one- and 2 two-bedroom suites, some with whirlpools. 2 stories (no elevator), interior corridors. **Bath:** combo or shower only. **Parking:** on-site. **Terms:** 2 night minimum stay - weekends, age restrictions may apply, 30 day cancellation notice-fee imposed. **Amenities:** video library, DVD players, CD players, voice mail, safes, irons, hair dryers. **Dining:** Blantyre Main Dining Room, see separate listing. **Pool(s):** heated outdoor. **Leisure Activities:** sauna, whirlpool, steamroom, 4 tennis courts, cross country skiing, ice skating, snow shoeing, croquet, hiking trails, exercise room, spa, shuffleboard. *Fee:* bicycles. **Guest Services:** area transportation-within 10 mi, wireless Internet. **Business Services:** meeting rooms, business center.

(🍴) (🏊) (⊠) (⊠) (🎦) (☐) / SOME UNITS FEE (🐕) (🖵) (🖵)

FREE full breakfast and high-speed Internet

BROOK FARM INN

Historic Bed
& Breakfast
$165-$425 5/1-9/1
$165-$400 9/2-4/30

Phone: 413/637-3013

Address: 15 Hawthorne St 01240 **Location:** From town hall, just s on Old Stockbridge Rd, just w. Located in a residential area. **Facility:** Built in 1850, rooms at the converted farmhouse feature antiques and reproductions. Some rooms are designed for guests with reduced mobility. Smoke free premises. 15 units. 14 one-bedroom standard units, some with whirlpools. 1 one-bedroom suite with whirlpool. 2-3 stories (no elevator), interior corridors. **Bath:** combo or shower only. **Parking:** on-site. **Terms:** office hours 8 am-7 pm, age restrictions may apply, 30 day cancellation notice-fee imposed. **Amenities:** video library, voice mail, hair dryers. *Some:* DVD players, CD players, irons. **Pool(s):** heated outdoor. **Guest Services:** wireless Internet.

CALL (&M) (🏊) (⊠) / SOME UNITS (W) (☐) (🖵)

HAMPTON INN & SUITES

Phone: (413)499-1111

Hotel
$119-$359 All Year

Address: 445 Pittsfield Rd 01240 **Location:** I-90, exit 2, 8.6 mi n on US 7/20. **Facility:** Smoke free premises. 79 one-bedroom standard units, some with whirlpools. 3 stories, interior corridors. *Bath:* combo or shower only. **Parking:** on-site. **Terms:** 1-7 night minimum stay, cancellation fee imposed. **Amenities:** high-speed Internet, voice mail, irons, hair dryers. **Pool(s):** heated indoor. **Leisure Activities:** exercise room. **Guest Services:** complimentary and valet laundry. **Business Services:** meeting rooms, business center. *(See color ad below)*

AAA Benefit:
Members save up to 10% everyday!

FREE expanded continental breakfast and high-speed Internet

▼ See AAA listing p 543 ▼

▼ See AAA listing above ▼

THE KEMBLE INN   *Book at AAA.com*   Phone: (413)637-4113

Bed & Breakfast
$225-$455 5/25-9/7
$115-$385 9/8-4/30

Address: 2 Kemble St 01240 **Location:** Jct SR 183 and 7A. **Facility:** Built as a private home, the 1881 Georgian-style mansion now functions as a bed and breakfast, with guest rooms named after well-known authors. Smoke free premises. 13 one-bedroom standard units, some with whirlpools. 3 stories (no elevator), interior corridors. *Bath:* combo or shower only. **Parking:** on-site. **Terms:** open 5/25-4/30, office hours 8:30 am-7 pm, 2-3 night minimum stay - seasonal and/or weekends, 15 day cancellation notice-fee imposed. **Guest Services:** wireless Internet. ASK ⊠ / SOME UNITS FEE 🛏

THE LENOX INN   *Book great rates at AAA.com*   Phone: (413)499-0324

AAA SAVE
▽▽▽
Motel
$75-$165 5/1-10/31
$55-$75 11/1-4/30

Address: 525 Pittsfield Rd 01240 **Location:** 4 mi n on US 7/20. **Facility:** 17 one-bedroom standard units. 1 story, exterior corridors. **Parking:** on-site. **Terms:** 2-3 night minimum stay - seasonal and/or weekends, 10 day cancellation notice-fee imposed. **Amenities:** hair dryers. **Pool(s):** outdoor. **Free Special Amenities: local telephone calls and high-speed Internet.**
🍴 🏊 🖥 / SOME UNITS ⊠

THE SUMMER WHITE HOUSE   Phone: 413/637-4489

▽▽▽
Historic Bed
& Breakfast
$160-$225 All Year

Address: 17 Main St 01240 **Location:** On SR 183; center. **Facility:** This 1885 Berkshire cottage is located in the historic district and one mile from Tanglewood; guest rooms feature a four-poster, canopy bed. Smoke free premises. 6 one-bedroom standard units. 3 stories (no elevator), interior corridors. *Bath:* combo or shower only. **Parking:** on-site. **Terms:** office hours 8:30 am-9 pm, 3 night minimum stay - seasonal and/or weekends, 14 day cancellation notice. **Amenities:** *Some:* DVD players. 🍴 ⊠ ☎

WHEATLEIGH   *Book at AAA.com*   Phone: (413)637-0610

▽▽▽ ▽▽▽
Historic Boutique
Country Inn
$715-$2100 All Year

Address: 11 Hawthorne Rd 01240 **Location:** 1.8 mi s on SR 183, then 1 mi e. **Facility:** During the Gilded Age, Wheatleigh was constructed in the style of an Italian palazzo. It is decorated with quiet elegance throughout. Smoke free premises. 19 units. 17 one-bedroom standard units. 2 one-bedroom suites. 2 stories (no elevator), interior corridors. *Bath:* combo or shower only. **Parking:** on-site and valet. **Terms:** check-in 4 pm, 2-3 night minimum stay - seasonal and/or weekends, age restrictions may apply, 28 day cancellation notice-fee imposed. **Amenities:** video library, DVD players, CD players, high-speed Internet, dual phone lines, safes, hair dryers. *Some:* irons. **Dining:** restaurant, see separate listing. **Pool(s):** heated outdoor. **Leisure Activities:** tennis court, bicycles, jogging, exercise room. *Fee:* massage. **Guest Services:** valet laundry, area transportation, wireless Internet. **Business Services:** meeting rooms, PC. 🍴 24 🏊 ⊠ ⊠ 🎥 / SOME UNITS 🖥 📺

——————— *The following lodging was either not evaluated or did not* ———————
meet AAA rating requirements but is listed for your information only.

CANYON RANCH IN THE BERKSHIRES   Phone: 413/637-4100

fyi

Not evaluated. **Address:** 165 Kemble St 01240. Facilities, services, and decor characterize an upscale property.

▼ See AAA listing p 544 ▼

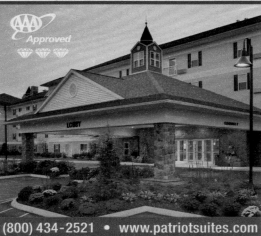

——— WHERE TO DINE ———

ARIZONA PIZZA CO.

Pizza
$6-$12

Phone: 413/442-9746

On a major byway, the fine eatery prepares more than just pizza, but the pizza alone is worth the trip. Casual dress. **Bar:** Full bar. **Reservations:** not accepted. **Hours:** 11 am-10 pm, Fri & Sat-11 pm. Closed: major holidays, 12/24. **Address:** 395 Pittsfield Rd 01240 **Location:** 3 mi n on US 7/20. **Parking:** on-site.

BISTRO ZINC

French
$8-$31

Phone: 413/637-8800

The trendy French bistro pairs its extensive wine selection with offerings of fine cuisine. Casual dress. **Bar:** Full bar. **Reservations:** accepted. **Hours:** 11:30 am-3 & 5:30-10 pm. Closed: 11/25, 12/25. **Address:** 56 Church St 01240 **Location:** Just n of SR 183. **Parking:** on-site.

BLANTYRE MAIN DINING ROOM

French
$50-$165

Phone: 413/637-3556

Patrons discover an exquisite, one-of-a-kind dining experience amid a breathtaking setting with incredible artwork, antiques and pastoral grounds. Guests are made to feel comfortable by first enjoying a glass of wine and classical music in the parlor or on the terrace, then are escorted into the spacious private dining room. After dinner, enjoy coffee and dessert in the parlor. Semi-formal attire. Entertainment. **Bar:** Full bar. **Reservations:** required. **Hours:** 12:30 pm-2 & 5:45-8:45 pm. Closed: Mon. **Address:** 16 Blantyre Rd 01240 **Location:** US 20, 1 mi s from jct SR 183; in Blantyre. **Parking:** on-site and valet.

CHURCH STREET CAFE

American
$11-$28

Phone: 413/637-2745

The tasteful bistro provides leisurely paced dining, with jazz music playing in the background. The eclectic, seasonally changing menu blends gourmet American, Southwestern and Asian flavors. The décor is simple yet elegant, with fresh flowers on every table and soft candlelight. Dressy casual. **Bar:** Full bar. **Reservations:** suggested. **Hours:** Open 5/1-11/1; 11:30 am-2 & 5:30-9 pm. Closed: Sun & Mon 5/1-6/1 & 9/1-11/1. **Address:** 65 Church St 01240 **Location:** Just n of SR 183. **Parking:** on-site.

GATEWAYS INN

American
$8-$30

Phone: 413/637-2532

This lovely Victorian inn offers a gracious atmosphere for enjoying an excellent selection of entrées featuring fresh seafood, prime beef, lamb and game. The décor is rich with antiques, reproductions and Oriental rugs. Casual dress. **Bar:** Full bar. **Reservations:** required. **Hours:** 5 pm-midnight; Sat & Sun also noon-2:30 pm 6/1-9/30. Closed: Mon off season. **Address:** 51 Walker St 01240 **Location:** On SR 183; center. **Parking:** on-site.

LUAU HALE

Asian
$4-$17

Phone: 413/443-4745

Just south of Pittsfield, this restaurant serves Chinese, Polynesian and Szechuan dishes, in addition to some American choices, amid rain forest decor. Everything here is fresh. Casual dress. **Bar:** Full bar. **Reservations:** accepted. **Hours:** 11:30 am-10 pm. Closed: 11/25. **Address:** 569 Pittsfield Rd 01240 **Location:** 2.9 mi n on US 7/20. **Parking:** on-site.

PANDA HOUSE

Chinese
$7-$25

Phone: 413/499-0660

Convenient to many hotels, the restaurant prepares slightly more complex interpretations of famous Chinese dishes, and beautiful, traditional presentations of carved animals and flowers decorate the service platters. Peking duck is a specialty. Casual dress. **Bar:** Full bar. **Reservations:** accepted. **Hours:** 11:30 am-10 pm, Fri & Sat-11 pm, Sun noon-10 pm. Closed: 11/25, 12/25. **Address:** 664 Pittsfield Rd 01240 **Location:** 3.6 mi n on US 7/20. **Parking:** on-site.

SLOANE'S TAVERN

American
$8-$25

Phone: 413/637-1364

The tavern is ensconced on the grounds of a popular 18-hole golf course and school, along with a full-service hotel and spa. The casual restaurant is a great place to relax after a day of golf. Outdoor seating is available. Casual dress. **Bar:** Full bar. **Reservations:** not accepted. **Hours:** 11:30 am-9 pm, Fri & Sat-10 pm. **Address:** 55 Lee Rd 01240 **Location:** I-90, exit 2, 3.5 mi n on US 7/20; in Cranwell Resort, Spa & Golf Club. **Parking:** on-site. CALL 🚬M

TRATTORIA "IL VESUVIO"

Italian
$17-$33

Phone: 413/637-4904

The attractive eatery serves traditional Italian dishes in a comfortable and friendly atmosphere. Casual dress. **Bar:** Full bar. **Reservations:** suggested, in summer. **Hours:** 5 pm-9 pm. Closed: 11/25, 12/25. **Address:** 242 Pittsfield Rd 01240 **Location:** 2.6 mi n on US 7/20. **Parking:** on-site.

WHEATLEIGH'S DINING ROOM

French
$125-$165

Phone: 413/637-0610

Originally designed by Frederick Law Olmsted, the grounds remain magnificent, especially their wonderful decorative facade. Built in 1893, the recently restored replica French chateau is breathtaking. Diners savor fabulous concoctions and confections prepared for their delight, such as Scottish salmon and black truffles wrapped in puff pasty with foie gras or possibly gateau of wild mushrooms and roasted winter vegetables with an intense vegetable reduction. Dressy casual. **Bar:** Full bar. **Reservations:** suggested. **Hours:** 6 pm-9 pm, Fri & Sat-9:30 pm, Sun 9:30 am-1 & 5-9 pm. **Address:** 11 Hawthorne Rd 01240 **Location:** 1.8 mi s on SR 183, then 1 mi e; in Wheatleigh. **Parking:** on-site and valet. **Historic**

WYNDHURST

Continental
$29-$39

Phone: 413/637-1364

In an historic Gilded Age mansion, the elegant dining room offers magnificent views of the Berkshire Mountains. Tables are dressed with linen and fresh flowers and appointed with upscale carved-wood chairs. The room features a fireplace and floral wallpaper above wood wainscoting. Seasonally changing menu selections may include refreshing gazpacho in the summer and goat cheese-filled ravioli with exotic mushrooms, cognac cream sauce, spinach and garlic. Dressy casual. **Bar:** Full bar. **Reservations:** suggested. **Hours:** 5 pm-9:30 pm. **Address:** 55 Lee Rd 01240 **Location:** I-90, exit 2, 3.5 mi n on US 7/20; in Cranwell Resort, Spa & Golf Club. **Parking:** on-site. CALL 🚬M

LEOMINSTER pop. 41,303

FOUR POINTS BY SHERATON LEOMINSTER   *Book great rates at AAA.com*   Phone: (978)534-9000

Hotel
$95-$185 All Year

Address: 99 Erdman Way 01453 **Location:** Jct SR 2 and 12. **Facility:** Smoke free premises. 187 one-bedroom standard units. 7 stories, interior corridors. *Bath:* combo or shower only. **Parking:** on-site. **Terms:** cancellation fee imposed. **Amenities:** video games (fee), dual phone lines, voice mail, irons, hair dryers. **Dining:** 2 restaurants. **Pool(s):** heated indoor. **Leisure Activities:** whirlpool, exercise room. **Guest Services:** valet laundry, wireless Internet. **Business Services:** conference facilities, business center.

FOUR POINTS
BY SHERATON

AAA Benefit:
Members get up to
15% off, plus
Starwood Preferred
Guest® bonuses.

SUPER 8   *Book great rates at AAA.com*   Phone: (978)537-2800

Motel
$69-$96 All Year

Address: 482 N Main St 01453 **Location:** SR 2, exit 31B, just n on SR 12. **Facility:** 101 one-bedroom standard units. 4 stories, interior corridors. **Parking:** on-site. **Terms:** cancellation fee imposed. **Amenities:** irons, hair dryers. **Guest Services:** coin laundry, wireless Internet. **Business Services:** PC. **Free Special Amenities: continental breakfast and high-speed Internet.**

—————— WHERE TO DINE ——————

WEATHERVANE SEAFOOD RESTAURANT   Phone: 978/345-2877

Seafood
$7-$24

The popular, family-oriented restaurant presents a large menu with lobster, fried clams and crisp Cape Cod apple-cranberry cobbler. Flavorful dishes are served in large portions. A fish market is on the premises. Casual dress. **Bar:** Full bar. **Reservations:** accepted. **Hours:** 11 am-9 pm. Closed: 11/25, 12/25. **Address:** 1290 Main St 01453 **Location:** SR 2, exit 32, 2 mi n on SR 13. **Parking:** on-site.

LEXINGTON—See Boston p. 418.

LOWELL—See Boston p. 420.

LUDLOW

COMFORT INN & SUITES   *Book great rates at AAA.com*   Phone: (413)589-9300

Hotel
$84-$145 All Year

Address: 321 Center St 01056 **Location:** I-90, exit 7, 0.4 mi s on SR 21. **Facility:** 71 units. 69 one-bedroom standard units, some with efficiencies. 2 one-bedroom suites, some with whirlpools. 3 stories, interior corridors. *Bath:* combo or shower only. **Parking:** on-site. **Terms:** cancellation fee imposed. **Amenities:** high-speed Internet, dual phone lines, voice mail, safes, irons, hair dryers. **Pool(s):** heated indoor. **Leisure Activities:** exercise room. **Guest Services:** valet and coin laundry, wireless Internet. **Business Services:** meeting rooms, PC. **Free Special Amenities: expanded continental breakfast and high-speed Internet.**

LYNN—See Boston p. 420.

MALDEN—See Boston p. 420.

MANSFIELD

HOLIDAY INN MANSFIELD   *Book at AAA.com*   Phone: (508)339-2200

Hotel
$99-$159 All Year

Address: 31 Hampshire St 02048 **Location:** I-95, exit 7A, 0.5 mi s on SR 140, then 1 mi w on Forbes Rd; I-495, exit 12, 2 mi n on SR 140, then w on Forbes Rd. Located in the I-95 Industrial Center. **Facility:** 202 one-bedroom standard units, some with whirlpools. 2-3 stories, interior corridors. *Bath:* combo or shower only. **Parking:** on-site. **Terms:** cancellation fee imposed. **Amenities:** video games (fee), dual phone lines, voice mail, irons, hair dryers. **Pool(s):** heated indoor. **Leisure Activities:** saunas, whirlpool. *Fee:* racquetball court. **Guest Services:** valet and coin laundry, wireless Internet. **Business Services:** conference facilities, business center.

—————— WHERE TO DINE ——————

PIKE'S PEAK MINING CO   Phone: 508/339-2200

Steak
$6-$20

Diners walk through a mining shaft into this Northwestern-themed restaurant complete with barn-board and stone walls filled with jars, shovels and mining pans. New England clam chowder is made fresh each day. The house specialty is steak served with sweet potato fries or another side. A decadent finish is the luscious chocolate torte. Casual dress. **Bar:** Full bar. **Reservations:** accepted. **Hours:** 11:30 am-10 pm. **Address:** 31 Hampshire St 02048 **Location:** I-95, exit 7A, 0.5 mi s on SR 140, then 1 mi w on Forbes Rd; I-495, exit 12, 2 mi n on SR 140, then w on Forbes Rd; adjacent to Holiday Inn. **Parking:** on-site.

MARBLEHEAD—See Boston p. 420.

MARLBOROUGH—See Boston p. 421.

Martha's Vineyard

Schedules for ferry service to Martha's Vineyard are available from your local AAA office, but are subject to change on short notice.

EDGARTOWN

ASHLEY INN

Historic Bed & Breakfast

$195-$345 5/1-12/15
$150-$250 4/1-4/30

Phone: 508/627-9655

Address: 129 Main St 02539 **Location:** 2 blks w; center. **Facility:** Distinguishing the 1800s sea captain's home are a Chinese Chippendale fence and a cloverleaf window; a gourmet breakfast is served 8:20 to 10 am. Smoke free premises. 10 one-bedroom standard units. 3 stories (no elevator), interior corridors. *Bath:* combo or shower only. **Parking:** on-site. **Terms:** open 5/1-12/15 & 4/1-4/30, office hours 8 am-9 pm, 3 night minimum stay - seasonal and/or weekends, age restrictions may apply, 14 day cancellation notice-fee imposed. **Amenities:** *Some:* irons, hair dryers. **Business Services:** PC.

ASK 📶 ✖

CLARION MARTHA'S VINEYARD   *Book great rates at AAA.com*

Hotel
$190-$400 5/1-9/11
$130-$300 9/12-4/30

Phone: (508)627-5161

Address: 227 Upper Main St 02539 **Location:** 0.8 mi nw; center. **Facility:** Smoke free premises. 34 one-bedroom standard units. 2 stories (no elevator), interior corridors. **Parking:** on-site. **Terms:** 3 night minimum stay - seasonal and/or weekends, cancellation fee imposed. **Amenities:** high-speed Internet, voice mail, safes (fee), irons, hair dryers. **Guest Services:** wireless Internet. **Business Services:** business center. *(See color ad below)* 🍴 🍸 ✖ 🖥 📞 🛏 📺

FREE continental breakfast and local telephone calls

Visit AAA.com for one-stop travel planning and reservations.

COLONIAL INN OF MARTHA'S VINEYARD

Book great rates at AAA.com

Phone: (508)627-4711

Historic
Country Inn
$95-$425 5/1-11/28 &
4/8-4/30

Address: 38 N Water St 02539 **Location:** Just n from Main St. **Facility:** Off the fourth floor of this inn, which has operated continuously since 1911, is a small covered deck that overlooks the harbor. Smoke free premises. 28 units. 26 one-bedroom standard units. 2 one-bedroom suites. 4 stories (no elevator); interior corridors. *Bath:* combo or shower only. **Parking:** no self-parking. **Terms:** open 5/1-11/28 & 4/8-4/30, office hours 8 am-8 pm, 2-3 night minimum stay - seasonal and/or weekends, 14 day cancellation notice-fee imposed. **Amenities:** voice mail, irons, hair dryers. *Some:* DVD players, CD players. **Leisure Activities:** exercise room. **Guest Services:** wireless Internet. **Business Services:** meeting rooms. *(See color ad below)*

FREE local telephone calls and high-speed Internet

THE HARBOR VIEW HOTEL

Book great rates at AAA.com

Phone: (508)627-7000

Historic
Hotel
$125-$2100 All Year

Address: 131 N Water St 02539 **Location:** 0.3 mi n; center. **Facility:** The hotel's brick-trimmed pool area is surrounded by a spacious lawn and flower gardens. The hotel is walking distance from numerous shops. Smoke free premises. 114 units. 94 one-bedroom standard units. 6 one-, 13 two- and 1 three-bedroom suites with efficiencies. 2-4 stories, interior/exterior corridors. *Bath:* combo or shower only. **Parking:** on-site and valet. **Terms:** check-in 4 pm, 2-3 night minimum stay - seasonal and/or weekends, 21 day cancellation notice-fee imposed. **Amenities:** CD players, voice mail, safes, irons, hair dryers. *Some:* DVD players. **Pool(s):** heated outdoor. **Leisure Activities:** *Fee:* boat dock. **Guest Services:** wireless Internet. **Business Services:** conference facilities.

KELLEY HOUSE

Book great rates at AAA.com

Phone: (508)627-7900

Hotel
$200-$335 5/14-10/11

Address: 23 Kelley St 02539 **Location:** At N Water St; center. **Facility:** Smoke free premises. 54 units. 43 one-bedroom standard units. 6 one-, 4 two- and 1 three-bedroom suites, some with kitchens. 2-3 stories (no elevator); interior/exterior corridors. **Parking:** on-site. **Terms:** open 5/14-10/11, check-in 4 pm, 2-3 night minimum stay - seasonal and/or weekends, 21 day cancellation notice-fee imposed. **Amenities:** CD players, voice mail, irons, hair dryers. **Pool(s):** outdoor. **Leisure Activities:** beach privileges. **Guest Services:** wireless Internet. **Business Services:** PC. **Free Special Amenities:** continental breakfast and high-speed Internet.

--- **WHERE TO DINE** ---

ATRIA

Phone: 508/627-5850

New American
$30-$48

Named for the brightest star in the Southern Triangle, the eatery is just a short walk from downtown. Subdued lighting, mellow surroundings and soft jazz combine to soothe the spirit. The New American menu changes daily based on fresh ingredients: seafood just off the boat, locally grown organic produce and aged meats. A five-course tasting menu also is offered. Service is casual yet correct. Valet parking is an option from Memorial Day to Labor Day. Dressy casual. Entertainment. **Bar:** Full bar. **Reservations:** suggested. **Hours:** Open 5/1-10/31; 5:30 pm-10 pm. Closed: Wed. **Address:** 137 Main St 02539 **Location:** 2 blks w. **Parking:** on-site. CALL

--- ▼ *See AAA listing above* ▼ ---

DAVID RYANS

American
$8-$26

Phone: 508/627-4100

Fresh seafood, clam chowder and innovative pasta dishes prevail in an informal, lively and decidedly hip atmosphere, made so by a cheery and contemporary decor. One distinctive choice is fried chevre atop greens. Service is prompt and professional. Casual dress. **Bar:** Full bar. **Reservations:** not accepted. **Hours:** 11:30 am-10 pm, Fri & Sat-11 pm. Closed major holidays. **Address:** 11 N Water St 02539 **Location:** Just n of Main St, just off harbor. **Parking:** street.

LATTANZI'S RESTAURANT, PIZZERIA AND CAFFE

Italian
$13-$48

Phone: 508/627-8854

At the Old Post Office Square, the restaurant features Italian dishes and pizza. The setting is cozy, and service is friendly and knowledgeable. Casual dress. **Bar:** Full bar. **Reservations:** suggested, weekends. **Hours:** 6 pm-10 pm. Closed: 12/25; also Sun & Mon 10/1-6/30. **Address:** Church St - Old Post Office Square 02539 **Location:** Just n; center. **Parking:** street.

MAIN STREET DINER

American
$7-$17

Phone: 508/627-9337

Near the center of town with entry through the movie theater hallway, the popular eatery has close quarters, so there may be a crowd and a wait. The diner serves "homemade comfort food" along the lines of meatloaf, real turkey and mashed potatoes, chicken pot pie and lots of burgers, sandwiches and breakfast plates. Casual dress. **Bar:** Beer & wine. **Hours:** 7 am-7 pm, Fri & Sat-8 pm, Sun-4 pm; to 9 pm in summer. Closed: 11/25, 12/25. **Address:** 65 Main St 02539 **Location:** Downtown. **Parking:** on-site.

THE SEAFOOD SHANTY

Seafood
$12-$35

CALL

Phone: 508/627-8622

The popular, informal, waterfront restaurant features a tiered dining room and an upstairs lounge with an outdoor deck. The 270-degree view includes the harbor and Chappaquiddick Island beyond. Seafood—fried, grilled or blackened—is the specialty, but patrons also find beef, chicken and vegetable risotto. Service is friendly. Casual dress. **Bar:** Full bar. **Reservations:** accepted. **Hours:** Open 5/15-10/15; 11 am-close; hours vary off season. **Address:** 31 Dock St 02539 **Location:** At base of Kelley St; center. **Parking:** street.

THE SQUARE RIGGER RESTAURANT

Seafood
$18-$42

Phone: 508/627-9968

Seafood lovers flock to the restaurant for its warm and cozy nautical ambience. The cooks can be watched as they grill seafood and prepare other entrees. In addition to lobster plates and fresh seafood, the menu lists pasta linguine, chicken and steak. Casual dress. **Bar:** Full bar. **Reservations:** suggested. **Hours:** 5 pm-10 pm; 5:30 pm-9 pm off season. Closed: 11/25, 12/24, 12/25; also Mon & Tues 2/1-5/17. **Address:** 225 State Rd 02539 **Location:** 1.3 mi w, on Upper Main St at Beach and Edgartown rds; at the Point of "The Triangle". **Parking:** on-site.

MENEMSHA

——— WHERE TO DINE ———

BEACH PLUM RESTAURANT

New American
$36-$45

Phone: 508/645-9454

Peaceful surroundings and excellent food characterize the restaurant. Breathtaking views of Menemsha Harbor are available from the window-filled dining room. Diners who desire wine must bring their own, as this is a dry village. Prix-fixe menus average $68 in season and $50 off-season. **Reservations:** accepted. **Hours:** Open 5/1-10/31; 8 am-10 & 5:30-8:30 pm; seasonal hours vary. **Address:** 50 Beach Plum Ln 02552 **Location:** Just nw of North Rd; center. **Parking:** on-site.

OAK BLUFFS

THE DOCKSIDE INN

Bed & Breakfast
$150-$450 5/1-10/11

Phone: (508)693-2966

Address: 9 Circuit Ave Ext 02557 **Location:** Center. Opposite ferry dock. **Facility:** This Victorian inn, which has some small rooms, features a welcoming front porch area with great views. Smoke free premises. 22 units. 17 one-bedroom standard units. 4 one- and 1 two-bedroom suites, some with efficiencies, kitchens and/or whirlpools. 3 stories (no elevator), exterior corridors. *Bath:* combo or shower only. **Parking:** on-site. **Terms:** open 5/1-10/11, office hours 8 am-8 pm, 2-3 night minimum stay - seasonal, 21 day cancellation notice. **Amenities:** video library, voice mail, hair dryers. *Some:* DVD players. **Leisure Activities:** hot tub, recreation room. **Guest Services:** wireless Internet. **Business Services:** PC. **Free Special Amenities: expanded continental breakfast and high-speed Internet.**

——— WHERE TO DINE ———

LINDA JEAN'S

American
$6-$22

Phone: 508/693-4093

Known as the best place for a hot breakfast in this tourist town, this place employs friendly servers and puts forth a large menu. Diners may need to wait on weekends for a table. At lunch, offerings include great-tasting sandwiches, burgers and seafood. The dining room has a fresh look, with contemporary earth tone paint colors and art mixed with country flair. Casual dress. **Reservations:** not accepted. **Hours:** 6 am-8 pm. Closed major holidays. **Address:** 25 Circuit Ave 02557 **Location:** Just sw of Lake Ave; center. **Parking:** street. CALL

SWEET LIFE CAFE

New American
$32-$44

Phone: 508/696-0200

The restaurant is on the upper end of popular Circuit Avenue, a nice street to stroll before or after dinner. The restored home has secluded patio seating and a cozy atmosphere inside with tasteful artwork, candlelight and enjoyable background music. French-inspired entrées are a showcase for the chef's creativity. Open and close dates vary from year to year. Casual dress. **Bar:** Beer & wine. **Reservations:** suggested. **Hours:** Open 5/10-10/15; 5:30 pm-9:30 pm; seasonal hours & days may vary. **Address:** 63 Circuit Ave 02557 **Location:** In Oaks Bluff. **Parking:** street.

─────── *The following restaurant has not been evaluated by AAA* ───────
but is listed for your information only.

MEDITERRANEAN RESTAURANT   Phone: 508/693-1617

(fyi) Not evaluated. The waterfront restaurant affords views of the bay, luxury private yachts and other marina activity, particularly from the screened porch. The menu features fabulous Mediterranean cuisine; the ingredients used are the freshest available and the seafood is memorable. **Address:** 15 Island Inn Rd 02557 **Location:** Just w of Beach Rd.

VINEYARD HAVEN pop. 2,048

1720 HOUSE   *Book at AAA.com*   Phone: 508/693-6407

Historic Bed
& Breakfast
Rates not provided

Address: 152 Main St 02568 **Location:** 0.5 mi n of town center and ferry dock. **Facility:** A 350-year-old copper beech tree shades the grounds of this historic B&B, where the congenial innkeeper is a wealth of local information. Smoke free premises. 6 one-bedroom standard units. 2 stories (no elevator), interior corridors. *Bath:* some shared or private, combo or shower only. **Parking:** on-site. **Terms:** office hours 7 am-10 pm. **Amenities:** *Some:* DVD players. **Leisure Activities:** bicycles.

THE CLARK HOUSE AT TWIN OAKS   Phone: 508/693-6550

Bed & Breakfast
Rates not provided

Address: 20 Edgartown Rd 02568 **Location:** 0.5 mi sw of ferry dock; on road to Edgartown. **Facility:** Smoke free premises. 5 one-bedroom standard units. 2 stories (no elevator), interior/exterior corridors. *Bath:* combo or shower only. **Parking:** on-site. **Terms:** office hours 7:30 am-10 pm. **Amenities:** irons, hair dryers. **Leisure Activities:** bicycles. **Guest Services:** wireless Internet.

CROCKER HOUSE INN   Phone: 508/693-1151

Bed & Breakfast
$265-$425 5/1-11/1
$185-$385 11/2-4/30

Address: 12 Crocker Ave 02568 **Location:** N of ferry dock via Main St. Located in a residential area. **Facility:** A wraparound porch with rocking chairs enhances the inn, which is in a residential setting not far from town. Smoke free premises. 8 one-bedroom standard units, some with whirlpools. 3 stories (no elevator), interior/exterior corridors. *Bath:* combo or shower only. **Parking:** on-site. **Terms:** office hours 8 am-10 pm, age restrictions may apply, 30 day cancellation notice-fee imposed. **Amenities:** DVD players, CD players, voice mail, honor bars, irons, hair dryers. **Guest Services:** valet laundry, wireless Internet. **Business Services:** PC.

THE DOCTOR'S HOUSE BED & BREAKFAST   Phone: 508/696-0859

Bed & Breakfast
$150-$340 All Year

Address: 60 Mt. Aldworth Rd 02568 **Location:** 0.4 mi sw to road to Edgartown, 1 blk e. Located in a quiet residential area. **Facility:** This stately home sits on two acres close to the village but offers a secluded feel; attention to detail is evident in the inn's warm, inviting decor. Smoke free premises. 7 one-bedroom standard units. 2 stories (no elevator), interior corridors. *Bath:* combo or shower only. **Parking:** on-site. **Terms:** office hours 10 am-10 pm, 2 night minimum stay - seasonal, 21 day cancellation notice-fee imposed. **Amenities:** video library, irons, hair dryers. *Some:* DVD players. **Leisure Activities:** bicycles, basketball. **Guest Services:** wireless Internet.

GREENWOOD HOUSE B & B   Phone: (508)693-6150

Bed & Breakfast
$179-$289 5/1-10/15
$119-$199 10/16-4/30

Address: 40 Greenwood Ave 02568 **Location:** 4 blks n of town center and ferry docks. Located in a residential area. **Facility:** Situated in a residential area, the large home features attractive gardens and is within walking distance of many shops and restaurants. Smoke free premises. 4 units. 2 one-bedroom standard units. 2 one-bedroom suites. 3 stories (no elevator), interior corridors. *Bath:* shower only. **Parking:** on-site. **Terms:** office hours 9 am-10 pm, 2 night minimum stay - seasonal and/or weekends, 21 day cancellation notice-fee imposed. **Amenities:** hair dryers. *Some:* DVD players. **Guest Services:** wireless Internet.

THE HANOVER HOUSE INN AT TWIN OAKS   Phone: 508/693-1066

(AAA) (SAVE)

Bed & Breakfast
$155-$315 5/1-10/31
$105-$180 11/1-4/30

Address: 28 Edgartown Rd 02568 **Location:** 0.5 mi sw of ferry dock; on road to Edgartown. **Facility:** A cozy country theme adorns the home; accommodations include a patio or deck that overlooks the picturesque garden. Smoke free premises. 15 units. 13 one-bedroom standard units. 2 one-bedroom suites with kitchens. 2 stories (no elevator), interior/exterior corridors. *Bath:* combo or shower only. **Parking:** on-site. **Terms:** office hours 7:30 am-11 pm, 2 night minimum stay - seasonal and/or weekends, 22 day cancellation notice-fee imposed. **Amenities:** video library, voice mail, irons, hair dryers. *Some:* DVD players. **Leisure Activities:** bicycles. *Fee:* beach chairs. **Guest Services:** wireless Internet.

MANSION HOUSE INN, HEALTH CLUB & SPA   *Book at AAA.com*   Phone: (508)693-2200

Hotel
$99-$509 All Year

Address: 9 Main St 02568 **Location:** W of ferry dock; corner of Beach Rd and Main St. **Facility:** Smoke free premises. 40 units. 36 one-bedroom standard units. 4 one-bedroom suites. 4 stories, interior corridors. *Bath:* combo or shower only. **Parking:** on-site. **Terms:** office hours 6 am-10 pm, 14 day cancellation notice-fee imposed. **Amenities:** dual phone lines, voice mail, irons, hair dryers. **Dining:** Zephrus Restaurant at Mansion House, see separate listing. **Pool(s):** heated indoor. **Leisure Activities:** sauna, whirlpool, steamroom, spa. **Guest Services:** wireless Internet. **Business Services:** meeting rooms, PC.

THORNCROFT INN   *Book great rates at AAA.com*   Phone: (508)693-3333

AAA SAVE

◆◆◆ ◆◆◆
Bed & Breakfast
$225-$550 All Year

Address: 460 Main St 02568 **Location:** 1 mi n of ferry dock. Located in a quiet area. **Facility:** In a tranquil setting on more than three acres, the inn offers fireplaces, antique furniture and rooms with a hot tub; a private cottage is available. Smoke free premises. 14 one-bedroom standard units, some with whirlpools. 2 stories (no elevator), interior/exterior corridors. *Bath:* combo or shower only. **Parking:** on-site. **Terms:** office hours 9 am-9 pm, 2 night minimum stay - seasonal and/or weekends, 30 day cancellation notice-fee imposed. **Amenities:** high-speed Internet, irons, hair dryers. *Some:* DVD players. **Guest Services:** wireless Internet. **Free Special Amenities:** full breakfast and high-speed Internet.   FEE 🛜 ☒ / SOME UNITS 🔲 🖥

—— WHERE TO DINE ——

BLACK DOG TAVERN   Phone: 508/693-9223

◆◆◆ ◆◆◆
American
$7-$33

One of the more popular and frequented dining spots on the island, the rustic, harborfront restaurant presents an eclectic, changing menu of fresh local seafood. Homemade bread and tempting pastries are among bakery treats. Casual dress. **Reservations:** not accepted. **Hours:** 7 am-11, noon-4 & 5-10 pm; seasonal days & hours may vary. Closed: 11/25, 12/25. **Address:** Beach St 02568 **Location:** On harbor, 1st wharf s of Steamship Authority Ferry Wharf. **Parking:** on-site. 🎵

LE GRENIER   Phone: 508/693-4906

◆◆◆
French
$24-$36

This bustling bistro offers candlelit dining where guests are welcome to bring their own alcoholic beverages; setups are available for a nominal charge. The chef is extremely cordial and is more likely than not to issue invitations to tour his kitchen. Overlooking the busy street, the second-floor restaurant with exposed wood ceilings is located in what they call the "space under the attic." Hundreds of wine corks top the numerous windows. Casual dress. **Reservations:** suggested. **Hours:** 5:30 pm-10 pm. **Address:** 96 Main St 02568 **Location:** Just n of ferry dock; center. **Parking:** street.

ZEPHRUS RESTAURANT AT MANSION HOUSE   *Menu on AAA.com*   Phone: 508/693-3416

AAA

◆◆◆
American
$6-$35

The dining experience here is terrific. Diners can watch the chef and staff prepare delectable selections of fresh fish, shellfish and meat from the open-concept kitchen. Creative dishes are prepared with a high level of skill. Outdoor cafe seating is available in season. Dressy casual. **Hours:** 11:30 am-9:30 pm; hours vary off season. Closed: 12/25. **Address:** 9 Main St 02568 **Location:** W of ferry dock; corner of Beach Rd and Main St; in Mansion House Inn, Health Club & Spa. **Parking:** street.

WEST TISBURY

—— *The following lodging was either not evaluated or did not* ——
meet AAA rating requirements but is listed for your information only.

LAMBERTS COVE INN & RESTAURANT   Phone: 508/693-2298

[fyi]
Hotel

Did not meet all AAA rating requirements for locking devices in some guest rooms at time of last evaluation on 05/23/2007. **Address:** 90 Manaquayak Rd 02568 **Location:** 3 mi se on Lambert Cove Rd, 0.5 mi e. Facilities, services, and decor characterize a mid-scale property.

The previous listings were for Martha's Vineyard.
This page resumes the alphabetical listings of cities in Massachusetts.

MASHPEE—See Cape Cod p. 491.

MEDFORD—See Boston p. 422.

MENEMSHA—See Martha's Vineyard p. 533.

METHUEN—See Boston p. 423.

MIDDLEBORO

FAIRFIELD INN PLYMOUTH/MIDDLEBORO   *Book great rates at AAA.com*   Phone: (508)946-4000

◆◆◆
Hotel
$89-$109 All Year

Address: 4 Chalet Rd 02346 **Location:** I-495, exit 6, 0.3 mi on US 44. **Facility:** Smoke free premises. 102 one-bedroom standard units. 4 stories, interior corridors. *Bath:* combo or shower only. **Parking:** on-site. **Terms:** cancellation fee imposed. **Amenities:** voice mail, irons, hair dryers. **Pool(s):** outdoor. **Leisure Activities:** exercise room. **Guest Services:** valet and coin laundry, wireless Internet. **Business Services:** business center. ☒ 📷 🖥 / SOME UNITS 🔲 🖥

AAA Benefit:
Members save a
minimum 5% off the
best available rate.

HOLIDAY INN EXPRESS HOTEL & SUITES — *Book at AAA.com*

Phone: (508)946-3398

Hotel
$109-$159 5/1-11/24
$89-$139 11/25-4/30

Address: 43 Harding St 02346 **Location:** I-495, exit 6, just w. **Facility:** 83 one-bedroom standard units, some with whirlpools. 4 stories, interior corridors. *Bath:* combo or shower only. **Parking:** on-site. **Amenities:** high-speed Internet, voice mail, irons, hair dryers. **Pool(s):** heated indoor. **Leisure Activities:** whirlpool, exercise room. **Guest Services:** valet and coin laundry, wireless Internet. **Business Services:** meeting rooms, business center.

—— WHERE TO DINE ——

FIRESIDE GRILLE & SPIRITS

Phone: 508/947-5333

American
$8-$23

Off the interstate, the family-owned-and-operated restaurant occupies a rural setting. Two stone fireplaces anchor the country decor in the lounge and one of the dining rooms. Brass rails, floral prints, ceiling fans and walls hung with memorabilia set the tone. Populating the menu is a range of New England favorites, including homemade turkey pot pie, baked stuffed chicken, fish and chips, London broil, steak tips, filet mignon, fried clams, baked scrod, lobster and pasta. Service is friendly. Casual dress. **Bar:** Full bar. **Reservations:** accepted. **Hours:** 11:30 am-10 pm, Sun 10 am-9 pm; Sunday brunch. Closed: 7/4, 12/25. **Address:** 30 Bedford St 02346 **Location:** I-495, exit 6, just e on US 44 to traffic circle, then just s on SR 18. **Parking:** on-site.

LORENZO'S ITALIAN RESTAURANT

Phone: 508/947-3000

Italian
$6-$19

Fresh-daily pasta and sauces, as well as fresh herbs, are central to the homemade Italian fare Lorenzo and family have been providing since 1950. The recipes are traditional and the service friendly. When the weather warms, the screened patio is opened. Guests can sit in one of the dining rooms or serve themselves from the walk-up window area. The menu includes pizza, sandwiches, veal, chicken, seafood and beef, plus some homemade desserts. Some items can be prepared to be lower in fat. Casual dress. **Bar:** Full bar. **Reservations:** accepted. **Hours:** 11 am-9 pm, Fri & Sat-10 pm. Closed: 11/25, 12/25. **Address:** 500 W Grove St 02346 **Location:** SR 28, 0.3 mi s of jct US 44 and SR 18. **Parking:** on-site.

CALL

MILFORD pop. 24,230

COMFORT INN — *Book great rates at AAA.com*

Phone: (508)634-2499

Hotel
$81-$91 All Year

Address: 3 Fortune Blvd 01757 **Location:** I-495, exit 20, 0.3 mi s on SR 85, then just e. **Facility:** 65 one-bedroom standard units. 2 stories, interior corridors. *Bath:* combo or shower only. **Parking:** on-site. **Amenities:** voice mail, irons, hair dryers. **Leisure Activities:** exercise room. **Guest Services:** valet and coin laundry, wireless Internet. **Business Services:** meeting rooms, PC. **Free Special Amenities:** continental breakfast and high-speed Internet.

COURTYARD BOSTON MILFORD — *Book great rates at AAA.com*

Phone: (508)634-9500

Hotel
$143-$175 All Year

Address: 10 Fortune Blvd 01757 **Location:** I-495, exit 20, 0.3 mi s on SR 85. **Facility:** Smoke free premises. 152 units. 140 one-bedroom standard units. 12 one-bedroom suites. 4 stories, interior corridors. *Bath:* combo or shower only. **Parking:** on-site. **Terms:** cancellation fee imposed. **Amenities:** high-speed Internet, voice mail, irons, hair dryers. **Pool(s):** heated indoor. **Leisure Activities:** whirlpool, exercise room. **Guest Services:** valet and coin laundry, area transportation. **Business Services:** meeting rooms, business center.

AAA Benefit:
Members save a minimum 5% off the best available rate.

DOUBLETREE HOTEL BOSTON/MILFORD — *Book great rates at AAA.com*

Phone: (508)478-7010

Hotel
$99-$189 All Year

Address: 11 Beaver St 01757 **Location:** I-495, exit 19, jct SR 109. **Facility:** Smoke free premises. 177 one-bedroom standard units. 5 stories, interior corridors. *Bath:* combo or shower only. **Parking:** on-site. **Terms:** 1-7 night minimum stay, cancellation fee imposed. **Amenities:** dual phone lines, voice mail, irons, hair dryers. *Some:* high-speed Internet. **Pool(s):** heated indoor. **Leisure Activities:** exercise room. **Guest Services:** valet laundry, wireless Internet. **Business Services:** conference facilities, business center.

DOUBLETREE
HOTELS·SUITES·RESORTS·CLUBS

AAA Benefit:
Members save 5% or more everyday!

FAIRFIELD INN & SUITES BOSTON MILFORD — *Book great rates at AAA.com*

Phone: (508)478-0900

Hotel
$135-$144 All Year

Address: 1 Fortune Blvd 01757 **Location:** I-495, exit 20, 0.3 mi s on SR 85, then just e. **Facility:** Smoke free premises. 72 one-bedroom standard units. 3 stories, interior corridors. *Bath:* combo or shower only. **Parking:** on-site. **Terms:** cancellation fee imposed. **Amenities:** high-speed Internet, voice mail, irons, hair dryers. *Some:* CD players. **Pool(s):** heated indoor. **Leisure Activities:** whirlpool, exercise room. **Guest Services:** valet and coin laundry, wireless Internet. **Business Services:** meeting rooms, PC, fax (fee). CALL

AAA Benefit:
Members save a minimum 5% off the best available rate.

HOLIDAY INN EXPRESS

Book great rates at AAA.com

Phone: (508)634-1054

Hotel
$79-$159 All Year

Address: 50 Fortune Blvd 01757 **Location:** I-495, exit 20, just sw on SR 85, then just se. **Facility:** 117 one-bedroom standard units. 4 stories, interior corridors. *Bath:* combo or shower only. **Parking:** on-site. **Amenities:** video games (fee), dual phone lines, voice mail, irons, hair dryers. **Pool(s):** heated indoor. **Leisure Activities:** whirlpool, exercise room. **Guest Services:** complimentary and valet laundry, wireless Internet. **Business Services:** meeting rooms, PC. **Free Special Amenities: full breakfast and high-speed Internet.**

LA QUINTA INN

Book at AAA.com

Phone: (508)478-8243

Hotel
$75-$139 All Year

Address: 24 Beaver St 01757 **Location:** I-495, exit 19, just w on SR 109. **Facility:** 89 units. 88 one-bedroom standard units. 1 one-bedroom suite with kitchen. 5 stories, interior corridors. *Bath:* combo or shower only. **Parking:** on-site. **Amenities:** high-speed Internet, dual phone lines, voice mail, irons, hair dryers. **Guest Services:** complimentary and valet laundry, wireless Internet. **Business Services:** meeting rooms, fax (fee).

—— WHERE TO DINE ——

MANGO THAI CUISINE

Phone: 508/482-9779

Thai
$6-$15

Less than a mile off the interstate in a shopping center storefront, the restaurant welcomes diners into a cheerful, bright dining room. Thai tapestries and art objects grace the walls. The menu lists the expected array: satay, Thai rolls, lemongrass shrimp and numerous seafood, beef, pork, chicken and noodle dishes. Also offered are 10 curries with assorted meats, dishes from Thailand's neighbors and a vegetarian menu. Service is efficient and upbeat. Casual dress. **Bar:** Full bar. **Reservations:** accepted. **Hours:** 11:30 am-3 & 4-10 pm, Fri & Sat-10:30 pm. **Address:** 9 Medway Rd 01757 **Location:** I-495, exit 19, 0.7 mi w; in Victory Plaza. **Parking:** on-site.

NANTUCKET ISLAND

THE CARRIAGE HOUSE

Phone: 508/228-0326

Historic Bed
& Breakfast
$120-$180 5/1-12/31
$90-$150 1/1-4/30

Address: 5 Ray's Ct 02554 **Location:** Just s of Main St via Fair St. Located in a quaint residential area. **Facility:** This B&B is located on a seashell lane shaded by trees; a wealth of information, the innkeeper is eager to assist with a day trip on Nantucket. Smoke free premises. 7 one-bedroom standard units. 2 stories (no elevator), interior corridors. *Bath:* shower only. **Parking:** street. **Terms:** office hours 9 am-11 pm, 30 day cancellation notice-fee imposed. **Amenities:** hair dryers. **Guest Services:** TV in common area.

NANTUCKET INN

Phone: (508)228-6900

Hotel
$140-$390 5/21-10/16

Address: One Millers Way 02554 **Location:** Opposite Nantucket Memorial Airport terminal. **Facility:** Smoke free premises. 100 one-bedroom standard units. 1-2 stories (no elevator), exterior corridors. **Parking:** on-site. **Terms:** open 5/21-10/16, check-in 4 pm, 7 day cancellation notice-fee imposed. **Amenities:** voice mail, safes, irons, hair dryers. *Some:* CD players. **Pool(s):** outdoor, heated indoor. **Leisure Activities:** whirlpools, 2 lighted tennis courts, exercise room. *Fee:* game room. **Guest Services:** coin laundry, area transportation, wireless Internet. **Business Services:** conference facilities, business center.

SEVEN SEA STREET INN

Book great rates at AAA.com

Phone: (508)228-3577

Bed & Breakfast
$99-$339 All Year

Address: 7 Sea St 02554 **Location:** Center. **Facility:** Furnished in the Early American-style and topped by a widow's walk, the inn offers modern comforts and conveniences. Smoke free premises. 15 units. 13 one-bedroom standard units. 2 one-bedroom suites, some with kitchens. 3 stories (no elevator), interior corridors. *Bath:* combo or shower only. **Parking:** on-site. **Terms:** office hours 7:30 am-9 pm, 2-3 night minimum stay - seasonal and/or weekends, 15 day cancellation notice-fee imposed. **Amenities:** video library, irons, hair dryers. *Some:* DVD players, voice mail. **Leisure Activities:** whirlpool. **Guest Services:** wireless Internet. **Business Services:** business center. **Free Special Amenities: expanded continental breakfast and high-speed Internet.**

SHERBURNE INN

Phone: 508/228-4425

Historic Bed
& Breakfast
$250-$375 5/1-10/19
$115-$250 10/20-4/30

Address: 10 Gay St 02554 **Location:** Just w of jct Broad and Center sts. **Facility:** Founded as the Atlantic Silk Company headquarters in 1835, the property was converted to a guest house in 1872. Smoke free premises. 8 one-bedroom standard units. 2 stories (no elevator), interior corridors. *Bath:* combo or shower only. **Parking:** street. **Terms:** office hours 8 am-9 pm, 2-3 night minimum stay - seasonal and/or weekends, 15 day cancellation notice-fee imposed. **Amenities:** video library, DVD players, hair dryers. **Leisure Activities:** beach chairs, towels, umbrellas. **Guest Services:** wireless Internet. **Business Services:** PC. **Free Special Amenities: continental breakfast and high-speed Internet.**

THE WAUWINET

Phone: 508/228-0145

Country Inn
Rates not provided

Address: 120 Wauwinet Rd 02554 **Location:** Oceanfront. From center of town, 4.5 mi ne on Polpis Rd, then 2.5 mi n. **Facility:** The Nantucket-style inn offers richly-appointed rooms and cottages, thoughtful service, impeccable ocean beaches and a great lawn overlooking the bay. Smoke free premises. 32 units. 30 one-bedroom standard units. 2 one-bedroom suites with whirlpools. 3 stories (no elevator), interior/exterior corridors. *Bath:* combo or shower only. **Parking:** on-site. **Terms:** open 5/4-10/26, check-in 4 pm, age restrictions may apply. **Amenities:** video library, DVD players, CD players, voice mail, safes, irons, hair dryers. **Dining:** Topper's, see separate listing. **Leisure Activities:** beach access, boating, sailboats, fishing, 2 tennis courts, recreation programs, bicycles, limited exercise equipment, spa. **Guest Services:** valet laundry, area transportation, wireless Internet. **Business Services:** business center.

WHITE ELEPHANT

Classic Historic
Hotel
$225-$900 5/1-11/1 &
11/25-12/6

Book at AAA.com

Phone: (508)228-2500

Address: 50 Easton St 02584 **Location:** Just n of ferry dock, between Willard St and Hulbert Ave. **Facility:** A 5-minute walk from downtown shops, the waterfront hotel features luxury accommodations and attentive service from the well-trained staff. Smoke free premises. 67 units. 38 one-bedroom standard units. 29 one-bedroom suites. 3 stories, interior/exterior corridors. *Bath:* combo or shower only. **Parking:** on-site. **Terms:** open 5/1-11/1 & 11/25-12/6, 3 night minimum stay - seasonal and/or weekends, 14 day cancellation notice-fee imposed. **Amenities:** voice mail, safes, irons, hair dryers. **Dining:** Brant Point Grill, see separate listing. **Leisure Activities:** spa. **Guest Services:** valet laundry, area transportation, wireless Internet. **Business Services:** meeting rooms, business center.

The following lodgings were either not evaluated or did not meet AAA rating requirements but are listed for your information only.

THE COTTAGES & LOFTS AT BOAT BASIN

[fyi]

Phone: 508/325-1499

Not evaluated. **Address:** 24 Old South Wharf 02554 **Location:** Oceanfront. Just n of town pier; center. Facilities, services, and decor characterize a mid-scale property.

JARED COFFIN HOUSE

[fyi]

Phone: 508/228-2400

Not evaluated. **Address:** 29 Broad St 02554 **Location:** Center. Facilities, services, and decor characterize a mid-scale property.

--- **WHERE TO DINE** ---

ARNO'S AT 41 MAIN ST

American
$12-$26

Phone: 508/228-7001

In the heart of the historic downtown district, the modern restaurant keeps its original exposed brick walls and hardwood flooring intact. The lively atmosphere makes this a fun stop for eclectic American cuisine, including traditional fish and chips, high-quality steaks, blueberry-glazed duckling and wild mushroom ravioli. Some rave that this place serves the best breakfast in town. Casual dress. **Bar:** Beer & wine. **Reservations:** accepted. **Hours:** Open 5/1-1/1; 8 am-9 pm; hours vary off season. Closed: 12/25. **Address:** 41 Main St 02554 **Location:** Between S Water and Union sts; center. **Parking:** street.

BOARDING HOUSE

New American
$28-$38

Phone: 508/228-9622

In the basement of an historic home, the award-winning restaurant sports low, honey-colored ceilings. The outdoor patio-the "to-be-seen" spot on the island-demands advance reservations. Although the menu changes seasonally, many guests enjoy house-made tagliatelle with butternut squash, sage and speck, or return for a staple chicken dish featuring Parmesan farro, lemon and arugula. Servers can help choose a wine from their list of organic, bio-dynamic and sustainable options. Casual dress. **Bar:** Full bar. **Reservations:** suggested. **Hours:** 5:30 pm-10 pm; Saturday & Sunday brunch 10 am-2 pm. Closed: 1/1, 12/25; also Sun 10/1-4/30 & Mon 9/1-6/30. **Address:** 12 Federal St 02554 **Location:** Corner of India St; center. **Parking:** street.

BRANT POINT GRILL

New England
$15-$45

Phone: 508/325-1320

An elegant dining experience awaits at this place, which affords views of the hotel's gardens and Nantucket harbor filled with boats and an active ferry dock. Diners might start with New England clam chowder topped with a fried clam, smoked bacon and chives, then indulge in a certified Angus flat-iron steak, Colorado lamb chops or skillet-roasted clambake with mussels, littlenecks, sweet corn, chorizo and Boston brown bread steamed in beer broth. The wait staff suggests suitable bottles. Dressy casual. **Bar:** Full bar. **Reservations:** suggested. **Hours:** Open 5/1-12/6 & 4/22-4/30; 8-11 am, 11:30-3 & 5:30-9 pm. Closed: 11/2-11/24. **Address:** 50 Easton St 02584 **Location:** Just n of ferry dock, between Willard St and Hulbert Ave; in White Elephant. **Parking:** street. CALL &M

THE BROTHERHOOD OF THIEVES

American
$7-$28

Phone: 508/228-2551

Evocative of an old 1840s whaling bar, the downstairs tavern/restaurant opens for lunch and features exposed brick walls, original wood flooring, low lighting and a cavernous dining area. Guests also may opt to sit on the patio. The menu consists mainly of great-tasting sandwiches, burgers and some Asia-inspired seafood. Casual dress. **Bar:** Full bar. **Reservations:** not accepted. **Hours:** 11:30 am-10 pm. Closed: 1/1, 11/25, 12/25. **Address:** 23 Broad St 02554 **Location:** Between Centre & N Water sts; downtown. **Parking:** street.

DEMARCO RESTAURANT

Italian
$20-$37

Phone: 508/228-1836

Cozy dining is what patrons expect in the restored 19th-century home. The menu of well-prepared Northern Italian entrees changes regularly to take advantage of Nantucket's fresh produce and seafood. Casual dress. **Bar:** Full bar. **Reservations:** suggested. **Hours:** Open 5/1-10/31; 6 pm-10 pm. **Address:** 9 India St 02554 **Location:** Center. **Parking:** street.

DUNE

New American
$11-$29

Phone: 508/228-5550

The two-story Federal-style home has been renovated into an elegant beach house restaurant with designer sea grass wallpaper, hardwood flooring and upscale original art. The menu changes often to incorporate seasonal local produce, fish and meats from regional farms. Menu offerings may include lamb chops with goat cheese polenta, organic chicken with truffled potatoes and hen of the woods mushrooms, or roasted beet salad with aged goat cheese, pistachios and 10-year-old balsamic vinegar. Dressy casual. **Bar:** Full bar. **Reservations:** suggested. **Hours:** noon-3 & 6-10 pm. Closed: 1/1, 11/25, 12/24, 12/25; also for lunch 10/1-5/30. **Address:** 20 Broad St 02554 **Location:** Between Federal & Central sts; downtown. **Parking:** street.

THE ROPEWALK
Phone: 508/228-8886

Seafood
$10-$18

In a great location at the end of a pier, this family-friendly spot offers panoramic views of Nantucket harbor. It features a large, nautically inspired dining room and patio seating. Fresh items from the seafood and raw bar are a must. Diners might start with Portuguese mussels steamed with linguica sausage, tomatoes, garlic, saffron and white wine, then enjoy bourbon-peach barbecue statler chicken breast or steamed Nantucket lobster. Casual, friendly service matches this place's theme. Casual dress. **Bar:** Full bar. **Reservations:** not accepted. **Hours:** Open 5/1-10/1; 11 am-3 & 5:30-10 pm. Closed major holidays. **Address:** 1 Straight Wharf 02554 **Location:** Just e of Main St. **Parking:** street.

SLIP 14
Phone: 508/228-2033

American
$9-$28

On a pier with some views of Nantucket Harbor, the small room has light-colored walls, contemporary art and an airy feel. Many guests enjoy unwinding on the good-size covered patio on the dock. Choices may include grilled chicken cobb salad; pan-roasted halibut with fennel, dried apricot and toasted pine nuts; and grilled New York strip steak with a potato pastry and creamed spinach. Casual dress. **Bar:** Full bar. **Reservations:** suggested. **Hours:** Open 5/15-9/24; 11 am-4 & 5-9 pm. Closed major holidays. **Address:** 14 Old S Wharf 02554 **Location:** Just s of ferry dock. **Parking:** street.

THE TAVERN RESTAURANT
Phone: 508/228-1266

American
$10-$30

On a wharf near the Hy-Line ferry terminal, this restaurant has a double deck that seems to be the spot for enjoying a wide variety of salads, grilled sandwiches and burgers while sipping a frozen cocktail. Casual dress. **Bar:** Full bar. **Reservations:** not accepted. **Hours:** Open 5/15-10/8; 11:30 am-9:30 pm. **Address:** 1 Straight Wharf 02554 **Location:** Just w of Hyline ferry dock. **Parking:** street.

TOPPER'S
Phone: 508/228-0145

Regional American
$25-$89

Inside the beachside Wauwinet Inn, this extraordinary gem pampers patrons with impeccable service as they feast on choices from a seasonally changing prix fixe menu. Selections may include fine caviars, lobster, rack of lamb or tender Kobe sirloin. Beautiful sculptures separate linen-draped tables in the elegant, upscale dining room, which features long, flowing window treatments and fresh floral arrangements. In season, a complimentary boat cruise travels from the town center to the restaurant. Dressy casual. **Bar:** Full bar. **Reservations:** suggested. **Hours:** Open 5/1-10/12; noon-3 & 6-9:30 pm. **Address:** 120 Wauwinet Rd 02554 **Location:** From center of town, 4.5 mi ne on Polpis Rd, then 2.5 mi n; in The Wauwinet. **Parking:** on-site.

The following restaurant has not been evaluated by AAA but is listed for your information only.

NANTUCKET PHARMACY
Phone: 508/228-0180

Not evaluated. One of two side-by-side pharmacies, this place boasts one of the last counter-service diners within a pharmacy. **Address:** 45 Main St 02554 **Location:** Center.

NATICK—See Boston p. 424.

NEEDHAM—See Boston p. 424.

NEW ASHFORD

——— WHERE TO DINE ———

MILL ON THE FLOSS
Phone: 413/458-9123

French
$27-$34

Patrons can enjoy the elegant simplicity of French country cuisine in the charm of an 18th-century farmhouse with an open kitchen and cozy fireplace. Menu items include flavorful and nicely presented sweetbreads and a delightfully satisfying apple crisp. Casual dress. **Bar:** Full bar. **Reservations:** suggested. **Hours:** 5 pm-9 pm; closing hours may vary. Closed: 11/25, 12/25; also Mon. **Address:** US 7 N 01237 **Location:** 4.1 mi s of jct SR 43. **Parking:** on-site.

NEW BEDFORD pop. 93,768

——— WHERE TO DINE ———

ANTONIO'S RESTAURANT & CAFE
Phone: 508/990-3636

Portuguese
$4-$15

Popular with locals, the reputable Portuguese restaurant is busy, particularly on weekends. Its energetic mood feels like a party looking to happen. Decor in the pleasant and bright main dining room only hints at the Portuguese culture. The menu lists a good variety of traditional dishes, most centered on fresh local seafood, along with some American standards. Portions are enormous. Credit cards are not accepted. Casual dress. **Bar:** Full bar. **Reservations:** not accepted. **Hours:** 11:30 am-9:30 pm, Fri & Sat-10 pm. Closed: 7/4, 11/25, 12/25. **Address:** 267 Coggeshall St 02746 **Location:** I-195, exit 16 eastbound via Washburn St; exit 17 westbound, 0.3 mi w; jct N Front St. **Parking:** on-site.

THE CANDLEWORKS
Phone: 508/997-1294

Italian
$8-$34

In the historic downtown district, the restaurant occupies the former 1810 Rodman Candleworks factory. The menu is primarily Italian, and servers don tuxedos. A pianist entertains nightly. Dressy casual. **Bar:** Full bar. **Reservations:** suggested. **Hours:** 11:30 am-3:30 & 5-9 pm, Thurs & Fri-10 pm, Sat 5 pm-10 pm, Sun 5 pm-9 pm. Closed major holidays. **Address:** 72 N Water St 02740 **Location:** I-195, exit 15, 1.2 mi s on SR 18. **Parking:** on-site.

DAVY'S LOCKER   Phone: 508/992-7359

Seafood
$8-$21

The restaurant tempts patrons with fresh local seafood, a nautical motif and quick, friendly service. Fish entrees are prepared grilled over an open flame, broiled, fried or Cajun, similar to how it's done at K-Paul's Kitchen of New Orleans. Also on the menu is a good selection of beef, ribs, chicken and pasta. The deck and some windows of the bar and dining room overlook the harbor and Butter Flats Lighthouse. This place is open one hour later in summer. Casual dress. **Bar:** Full bar. **Reservations:** accepted. **Hours:** 11:30 am-9 pm, Fri & Sat-10 pm. Closed: 12/25. **Address:** 1480 E Rodney French Blvd 02744 **Location:** I-195, exit 15, 2.7 mi s on SR 18, then 0.9 mi e, follow ferry signs. **Parking:** on-site.

FREESTONE'S CITY GRILL   Phone: 508/993-7477

American
$7-$22

In a restored 1877 bank building, the informally upscale dining room is surrounded in marble, brass and mahogany. The specialty is seafood, but sandwiches, meal-size salads and beef, chicken, ribs and vegetarian dishes also are offered. Some dishes have an Asian flavor. The location is near Whaling National Historic Park and associated attractions from the days of the whaling trade. Casual dress. **Bar:** Full bar. **Reservations:** not accepted. **Hours:** 11:30 am-10:30 pm, Sun noon-9 pm. Closed: 11/25, 12/25. **Address:** 41 William St 02740 **Location:** I-195, exit 15, 1.4 mi s on SR 18, w on Union to 2nd St, then just n; corner of William and 2nd sts; in downtown historic district. **Parking:** street.

NEWBURYPORT—See Boston p. 425.

NEW MARLBOROUGH

——— **WHERE TO DINE** ———

THE OLD INN ON THE GREEN   Phone: 413/229-7924

Regional American
$26-$65

Dining at the sophisticated establishment is like taking a step back in time. The dining room is set in a quiet old Berkshire village inside a restored 1760 country inn. Flickering candlelight, wood plank floors, crisp white linen tabletops and vines stretching across the ceiling make for a romantic atmosphere. The menu features superbly prepared and cleverly presented regional American cuisine with Italian and Mediterranean influences. Dressy casual. **Bar:** Full bar. **Reservations:** suggested. **Hours:** 5:30 pm-9:30 pm. Closed: Tues, also Mon 11/1-7/1. **Address:** 134 Hartsville New Marlborough Rd 01230 **Location:** US 7, 3.4 mi e on SR 23, then 5.7 mi se. **Parking:** on-site. **Historic**

NEWTON—See Boston p. 426.

NORTH ADAMS pop. 14,681

HOLIDAY INN BERKSHIRES   *Book at AAA.com*   Phone: (413)663-6500

Hotel
$100-$229 All Year

Address: 40 Main St 01247 **Location:** Jct SR 8; downtown. **Facility:** Smoke free premises. 89 one-bedroom standard units. 7 stories, interior corridors. *Bath:* combo or shower only. **Parking:** on-site. **Terms:** 3 day cancellation notice. **Amenities:** dual phone lines, voice mail, irons, hair dryers. *Some:* high-speed Internet. **Pool(s):** heated indoor. **Leisure Activities:** sauna, whirlpool. **Guest Services:** coin laundry, wireless Internet. **Business Services:** meeting rooms, business center.

ASK CALL &M 🏊 🛝 ✕ 🎥 📖 / SOME UNITS ♿

JAE'S INN   AAA SAVE   Phone: 413/664-0100

Motel
$135-$160 5/1-10/31
$95-$125 11/1-4/30

Address: 1111 S State St 01247 **Location:** 2 mi s on SR 8; center. **Facility:** Smoke free premises. 11 one-bedroom standard units with whirlpools. 3 stories (no elevator), interior corridors. **Parking:** on-site. **Terms:** office hours 8 am-midnight, 3 day cancellation notice. **Amenities:** DVD players, voice mail, irons, hair dryers. **Pool(s):** heated outdoor. **Leisure Activities:** sauna, tennis court, exercise room, spa, sports court. **Guest Services:** wireless Internet, beauty salon. **Business Services:** meeting rooms. **Free Special Amenities:** continental breakfast and high-speed Internet.

🍸 🏊 ✕ ✕ ♿ / SOME UNITS FEE 🐕

——— *The following lodging was either not evaluated or did not* ———
meet AAA rating requirements but is listed for your information only.

THE PORCHES INN   Phone: 413/664-0400

fyi

Not evaluated. **Address:** 231 River St 01247. Facilities, services, and decor characterize an upscale property.

——— **WHERE TO DINE** ———

THE FREIGHT YARD RESTAURANT & PUB   Phone: 413/663-6547

American
$7-$16

In a restored railroad station with historical museums, galleries and shops, the casual restaurant displays a pub-style decor. Traditional American fare includes burgers, deli sandwiches, beef, soup and salad. Casual dress. **Bar:** Full bar. **Reservations:** suggested. **Hours:** 11:30 am-11 pm. Closed: 12/25. **Address:** Heritage State Park, Bldg 4 01247 **Location:** SR 8, just s of Main St and SR 2, follow signs to Heritage State Park. **Parking:** on-site.

GRAMERCY BISTRO   *Menu on AAA.com*   Phone: 413/663-5300

American
$18-$26

The long, skinny dining room allows for intimate dining. Tasty dishes are presented attractively. Casual dress. **Bar:** Beer & wine. **Reservations:** suggested. **Hours:** 5 pm-9 pm, Fri & Sat-10 pm, Sun 10 am-1 & 5-9 pm. Closed major holidays; also Tues, 1/21 & 9/11. **Address:** 24 Marshall St 01247 **Location:** On SR 8; downtown. **Parking:** street.

NORTHAMPTON pop. 28,978

CLARION HOTEL & CONFERENCE CENTER   *Book at AAA.com*   Phone: (413)586-1211

Hotel
$99-$265 5/1-11/15
$79-$265 11/16-4/30

Address: One Atwood Dr 01060 **Location:** I-91, exit 18, just s on US 5. **Facility:** 122 one-bedroom standard units, some with whirlpools. 2 stories (no elevator), interior corridors. *Bath:* combo or shower only. **Parking:** on-site. **Amenities:** voice mail, safes (fee), irons, hair dryers. **Pool(s):** outdoor, heated indoor. **Leisure Activities:** 2 lighted tennis courts, horseshoes, volleyball. *Fee:* game room. **Guest Services:** valet laundry, wireless Internet. **Business Services:** conference facilities, business center.

HOTEL NORTHAMPTON   *Book at AAA.com*   Phone: (413)584-3100

Historic
Hotel
$175-$799 5/1-10/31
$155-$799 11/1-4/30

Address: 36 King St 01060 **Location:** Jct US 5 and SR 9; center. **Facility:** With a gas fireplace and piped-in jazz, this 1927 hotel has a nostalgic ambience; room are nicely appointed, and a summer patio overlooks downtown. 106 units. 100 one-bedroom standard units, some with whirlpools. 6 one-bedroom suites with whirlpools. 5 stories, interior/exterior corridors. *Bath:* combo or shower only. **Parking:** on-site. **Amenities:** voice mail, safes, irons, hair dryers. *Some: Fee:* DVD players, high-speed Internet. **Leisure Activities:** exercise room. **Guest Services:** valet laundry, wireless Internet. **Business Services:** conference facilities, business center.

QUALITY INN & SUITES   *Book at AAA.com*   Phone: (413)586-1500

Motel
$79-$289 All Year

Address: 117 Conz St 01060 **Location:** I-91, exit 18, just n on US 5. **Facility:** 88 units. 81 one-bedroom standard units, some with whirlpools. 7 one-bedroom suites with efficiencies. 2-3 stories (no elevator), interior/exterior corridors. **Parking:** on-site. **Amenities:** voice mail, irons, hair dryers. **Pool(s):** heated indoor. **Leisure Activities:** whirlpool, exercise room. **Guest Services:** valet and coin laundry, wireless Internet. **Business Services:** meeting rooms, PC.

—— WHERE TO DINE ——

GREEN STREET CAFE   Phone: 413/586-5650

American
$6-$25

The chef prepares creative fish, beef, chicken and pasta dishes in the setting of a quaint, restored, turn-of-the-20th-century rooming house. Casual dress. **Bar:** Beer & wine. **Reservations:** suggested. **Hours:** noon-10 pm, Sun 10 am-9 pm; Sunday brunch. Closed major holidays. **Address:** 64 Green St 01060 **Location:** Just n of SR 66 (West St); on Smith College campus. **Parking:** street.

PIZZERIA PARADISO   Phone: 413/586-1468

Pizza
$10-$18

The youthful and bustling downtown eatery serves contemporary pizza topped with fresh and unusual ingredients. Daily specials showcase fragrant creations on an Italian theme. Beverages include an attractive list of wines by the glass and a good beer selection. Casual dress. **Bar:** Full bar. **Reservations:** suggested. **Hours:** 5 pm-9:30 pm, Fri-10:30 pm, Sat 4:30 pm-10:30 pm, Sun 4:30 pm-9 pm. Closed: 11/25, 12/25. **Address:** 12 Crafts Ave 01060 **Location:** Just se of Main St; center. **Parking:** street.

SOO RA RESTAURANT   Phone: 413/387-6333

Asian
$7-$15

Specializing in Korean and Japanese cuisine, the extensive menu lines up fresh sushi and sashimi, as well as traditional dishes. Light wood tones and distinctive artwork accent the appealing dining room, which has a large sushi bar at its center. Casual dress. **Bar:** Full bar. **Reservations:** accepted. **Hours:** 11:30 am-3 & 5-10 pm, Sat 11:30 am-10 pm, Sun noon-9:30 pm, Mon & Tues 5 pm-10 pm. Closed: 7/4, 11/25, 12/25. **Address:** 1 Roundhouse Plaza 01060 **Location:** Corner of Crafts Ave; downtown. **Parking:** street.

UNION STATION   Phone: 413/586-5366

American
$15-$25

A fun stop for steak and seafood dishes, the beautifully restored train station has a large room with a fireplace that burns daily. Many homemade dressings line the salad bar. A convenient metered parking lot is beside the restaurant. Casual dress. **Bar:** Full bar. **Reservations:** not accepted. **Hours:** 4:30 pm-9 pm, Fri & Sat-10 pm, Sun 10 am-2 & 4:30-9 pm; Sunday brunch. Closed: 7/4, 12/25; also Mon. **Address:** 125A Pleasant St 01060 **Location:** I-91, exit 18, 0.8 mi n on US 5. **Parking:** on-site.

NORTH ANDOVER—See Boston p. 426.

NORTH ATTLEBORO   (See map and index starting on p. 606)

HOLIDAY INN EXPRESS-PROVIDENCE/NORTH ATTLEBORO   *Book at AAA.com*   Phone: (508)643-9900   🔟⑤

Hotel
$109-$129 5/1-11/15
$69-$89 11/16-4/30

Address: 707 S Washington St 02760 **Location:** I-295, exit 1B, 0.6 mi n on US 1. **Facility:** 65 one-bedroom standard units, some with whirlpools. 2 stories, interior corridors. *Bath:* combo or shower only. **Parking:** on-site. **Amenities:** high-speed Internet, dual phone lines, voice mail, irons, hair dryers. **Pool(s):** heated indoor. **Leisure Activities:** exercise room. **Guest Services:** valet and coin laundry, wireless Internet. **Business Services:** meeting rooms, business center.

NORTH CHELMSFORD—See Boston p. 427.

NORTH DARTMOUTH

COMFORT INN

Hotel
$119-$149 5/1-10/15
$89-$119 10/16-4/30

Book great rates at AAA.com   Phone: (508)996-0800

Address: 171 Faunce Corner Rd 02747 **Location:** I-195, exit 12A westbound; exit 12 eastbound, then s. **Facility:** 84 one-bedroom standard units. 2 stories (no elevator), interior corridors. **Parking:** on-site. **Amenities:** irons, hair dryers. **Pool(s):** outdoor. **Guest Services:** valet laundry, wireless Internet. **Business Services:** business center. **Free Special Amenities: high-speed Internet.**

RESIDENCE INN NEW BEDFORD DARTMOUTH   *Book great rates at AAA.com*   Phone: (508)984-5858

Extended Stay Hotel
$130-$190 All Year

Address: 181 Faunce Corner Rd 02747 **Location:** I-195, exit 12A westbound; exit 12 eastbound, just s. **Facility:** Smoke free premises. 96 units. 33 one-bedroom standard units with efficiencies, some with whirlpools. 47 one- and 16 two-bedroom suites, some with efficiencies or kitchens. 3 stories, interior corridors. *Bath:* combo or shower only. **Parking:** on-site. **Terms:** cancellation fee imposed. **Amenities:** dual phone lines, voice mail, irons, hair dryers. *Some:* high-speed Internet. **Pool(s):** heated indoor. **Leisure Activities:** whirlpool, exercise room, sports court. **Guest Services:** valet and coin laundry, wireless Internet. **Business Services:** meeting rooms, business center. **Free Special Amenities: full breakfast and high-speed Internet.**

AAA Benefit:

Members save a minimum 5% off the best available rate.

------ WHERE TO DINE ------

THAI TASTE   Phone: 508/997-2109

Thai
$7-$17

You will find all of the expected Thai offerings here from satay and Siam rolls to tom kar gai soup to an assortment of noodle dishes and curries. Chicken, beef, pork, and duck supplement the fresh vegetables and spices or there are several selections from the "Vegetarian Corner." Coconut and green tea flavored ice creams. The service is friendly. Popular with diners and take-out as well. Casual dress. **Bar:** Full bar. **Reservations:** not accepted. **Hours:** 11:30 am-9:30 pm, Fri & Sat-10:30 pm, Sun noon-9 pm. Closed major holidays. **Address:** 634 State Rd 02747 **Location:** Jct SR 177, 1.7 mi e on US 6. **Parking:** on-site.

NORTH FALMOUTH—See Cape Cod p. 492.

NORTH GRAFTON

------ WHERE TO DINE ------

THE OLD POST OFFICE PUB   Phone: 508/839-6106

American
$8-$22

This American pub serves daily specials and prime rib, a specialty of the house, in a decor featuring antiques and other memorabilia of the postal and travel businesses. The lounge boasts a sports theme. A Sunday buffet is available 8 am-12:30 pm. Casual dress. **Bar:** Full bar. **Hours:** 11:30 am-9 pm, Fri & Sat-10 pm, Sun 9 am-9 pm. Closed: 12/25. **Address:** 1 Ray St 01536 **Location:** I-90 (Massachusetts Tpke), exit 11, 2 mi n, then just e of SR 140. **Parking:** on-site.

NORTH TRURO—See Cape Cod p. 492.

NORTON

EXTENDED STAYAMERICA-FOXBORO-NORTON   *Book at AAA.com*   Phone: (508)285-7800

Extended Stay Hotel
$60-$85 All Year

Address: 280 S Washington St 02766 **Location:** I-495, exit 9, 0.3 mi se on Bay St, then 0.5 mi nw via Industrial Park Rd. **Facility:** 101 one-bedroom standard units with efficiencies. 3 stories, interior corridors. *Bath:* combo or shower only. **Parking:** on-site. **Terms:** office hours 7 am-11 pm, cancellation fee imposed. **Amenities:** voice mail, irons. *Some:* hair dryers. **Guest Services:** coin laundry, wireless Internet.

NORWELL

------ WHERE TO DINE ------

NOT YOUR AVERAGE JOE'S   Phone: 781/616-6160

American
$9-$18

This eatery exemplifies the "in-trend" style of high-art contemporary design through vibrant color schemes, comfortable seating and smartly dressed staff. However, the high point is the food. The cooking team whips up gourmet comfort foods of homemade meatloaf with a flavorful twist, creative hand-made pizzas, sandwiches, salads and more. Casual dress. **Reservations:** not accepted. **Hours:** 11:30 am-10 pm, Fri & Sat-11 pm, Sun noon-10 pm. Closed: 11/25, 12/25. **Address:** 111 Pond St 02061 **Location:** On SR 228; between SR 3 and 53. **Parking:** street.

STRAWBERRY FAIR RESTAURANT
Phone: 781/878-7878

American
$7-$18

Homespun New England cuisine and homemade dessert are served in a single-story farmhouse with rough-hewn beams and barnboard walls adorned with namesake memorabilia. This has been a family operation since 1975 and is both a great find and a good value. Casual dress. **Bar:** Full bar. **Hours:** 8 am-9 pm, Sun 8:30 am-2 pm, Mon 8 am-4 pm. Closed: 11/25, 12/25. **Address:** 14 Pond St 02061 **Location:** SR 228, just s of jct SR 53. **Parking:** on-site.

NORWOOD—See Boston p. 427.

OAK BLUFFS—See Martha's Vineyard p. 533.

ORANGE pop. 3,945

EXECUTIVE INN
Phone: (978)544-8864

(AAA) (SAVE)

Motel
$45-$80 All Year

Address: 110 Daniel Shays Hwy 01364 **Location:** US 202, exit 16, just n of jct SR 2. **Facility:** 28 one-bedroom standard units. 1 story, interior/exterior corridors. *Bath:* combo or shower only. **Parking:** on-site. **Terms:** 7 day cancellation notice-fee imposed. **Guest Services:** coin laundry, wireless Internet. **Free Special Amenities: continental breakfast and early check-in/late check-out.**

ORLEANS—See Cape Cod p. 493.

OSTERVILLE—See Cape Cod p. 498.

PEABODY—See Boston p. 428.

PITTSFIELD pop. 45,793

BERKSHIRE INN
Book at AAA.com
Phone: (413)443-3000

Motel
$89-$219 5/1-10/31
$69-$119 11/1-4/30

Address: 150 W Housatonic St 01201 **Location:** On US 20, 0.4 mi w of jct US 7. **Facility:** 32 one-bedroom standard units. 1 story, exterior corridors. *Bath:* combo or shower only. **Parking:** on-site. **Terms:** office hours 8 am-9 pm, 7 day cancellation notice-fee imposed. **Amenities:** *Some:* hair dryers. **Pool(s):** outdoor.

COMFORT INN
Book great rates at AAA.com
Phone: (413)443-4714

Hotel
$79-$309 5/1-10/15
$79-$259 10/16-4/30

Address: 1055 South St 01201 **Location:** On US 7 and 20, 3 mi s. **Facility:** Smoke free premises. 57 one-bedroom standard units. 3 stories, interior corridors. *Bath:* combo or shower only. **Parking:** on-site. **Terms:** 2 night minimum stay - seasonal and/or weekends, 3 day cancellation notice-fee imposed. **Amenities:** irons, hair dryers. **Pool(s):** outdoor. **Guest Services:** valet and coin laundry, wireless Internet. **Business Services:** PC. *(See color ad p 527)*

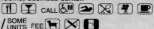

PATRIOT SUITES HOTEL   *Book great rates at AAA.com*   Phone: (413)997-3300

Hotel
$145-$295 All Year

Address: 8 Dan Fox Dr 01201 **Location:** I-90, exit 2, 9 mi nw on US 20, then just w. **Facility:** 146 one-bedroom suites. 5 stories, interior corridors. *Bath:* combo or shower only. **Parking:** on-site. **Terms:** check-in 4 pm, 3 day cancellation notice. **Amenities:** DVD players, voice mail, safes, irons, hair dryers. **Pool(s):** heated indoor. **Leisure Activities:** exercise room, pet path. *Fee:* game room. **Guest Services:** wireless Internet. **Business Services:** meeting rooms, business center. *(See color ad p 528)*

CALL ... / SOME UNITS FEE ...

FREE expanded continental breakfast and local telephone calls

RAMADA LIMITED INN & SUITES   *Book great rates at AAA.com*   Phone: (413)442-8714

Hotel
$79-$309 5/1-10/15
$79-$259 10/16-4/30

Address: 1350 W Housatonic St 01201 **Location:** US 20, 2.9 mi w of jct US 7. **Facility:** 59 units. 49 one-bedroom standard units. 10 two-bedroom suites. 3 stories, interior corridors. *Bath:* combo or shower only. **Parking:** on-site. **Terms:** 2 night minimum stay - seasonal and/or weekends, 3 day cancellation notice-fee imposed. **Amenities:** dual phone lines, voice mail, irons, hair dryers. *Some:* high-speed Internet. **Leisure Activities:** exercise room. **Guest Services:** valet and coin laundry, wireless Internet. **Business Services:** meeting rooms, PC. *(See color ad below)*

CALL ... / SOME UNITS ...

FREE continental breakfast and high-speed Internet

THE THADDEUS CLAPP HOUSE   Phone: 413/499-6840

Historic Bed
& Breakfast
$125-$295 5/1-10/31
$100-$195 11/1-4/30

Address: 74 Wendell Ave 01201 **Location:** Just e of US 7; between E Housatonic and East sts; downtown. **Facility:** Reminiscent of the Arts and Crafts movement, the inn's rooms feature luxurious bedding and fine amenities; numerous jogging trails are within a half mile. Smoke free premises. 8 units. 2 one-bedroom standard units. 6 one-bedroom suites, some with whirlpools. 3 stories (no elevator), interior corridors. **Parking:** on-site. **Terms:** office hours 8 am-8 pm, 2-3 night minimum stay - seasonal and/or weekends, age restrictions may apply, 30 day cancellation notice-fee imposed. **Amenities:** CD players, irons, hair dryers. *Some:* DVD players. **Guest Services:** wireless Internet. **Free Special Amenities:** full breakfast and high-speed Internet.

▼ *See AAA listing above* ▼

—— **WHERE TO DINE** ——

DAKOTA

American

$12-$29

Phone: 413/499-7900

The restaurant presents a warm, inviting atmosphere with a touch of Southwest feel and Aboriginal artifacts. The steak is served juicy, hot and sizzling, and the fish and seafood are ocean fresh. Casual dress. **Bar:** Full bar. **Reservations:** suggested. **Hours:** 4:30 pm-9 pm, Fri & Sat-10 pm. Closed: 11/25, 12/26. **Address:** 1035 South St 01201 **Location:** 3 mi s on US 7 and 20. **Parking:** on-site. CALL Ⓜ

THE LANTERN BAR & GRILL

American

$3-$17

Phone: 413/448-2717

A bright red neon sign marks this small restaurant in the center of town. Burgers and delicatessen sandwiches are specialties here. Casual dress. **Reservations:** not accepted. **Hours:** 8 am-11 pm. Closed major holidays; also Sun. **Address:** 455 North St 01201 **Location:** Jct North and Linden sts; center. **Parking:** street.

PATRICK'S PUB

American

$5-$16

Phone: 413/499-1994

A local favorite, the friendly neighborhood pub serves everything from burgers to chicken parmigiana to baked haddock. Casual dress. **Bar:** Full bar. **Hours:** 4:30 pm-11:30 pm, Fri & Sat 11:30 am-12:30 pm, Sun 11:30 am-11:30 pm. Closed major holidays. **Address:** 26 Bank Row St 01201 **Location:** Center; in Park Square. **Parking:** street.

PLYMOUTH pop. 7,658   (See map and index starting on p. 458)

BEST WESTERN COLD SPRING   *Book great rates at AAA.com*   **Phone:** (508)746-2222   **39**

Motel

$99-$199 5/1-11/28 & 3/11-4/30

Address: 188 Court St 02360 **Location:** Jct US 44, 0.5 mi n on SR 3A. **Facility:** Smoke free premises. 58 units. 53 one- and 2 two-bedroom standard units. 3 one-bedroom suites. 1-2 stories, exterior corridors. *Bath:* combo or shower only. **Parking:** on-site. **Terms:** open 5/1-11/28 & 3/11-4/30, office hours 7 am-10 pm, 2 night minimum stay - seasonal and/or weekends, 3 day cancellation notice. **Amenities:** voice mail, irons, hair dryers. *Some:* high-speed Internet. **Pool(s):** heated outdoor. **Guest Services:** coin laundry, wireless Internet. **Business Services:** meeting rooms, PC. **Free Special Amenities: local telephone calls and high-speed Internet.** FEE 🛒🍳 ✕ 🖥 📷 💻

AAA Benefit:
Members save up to 20%, plus 10% bonus points with rewards program.

BLUE SPRUCE MOTEL & TOWNHOUSES   *Book at AAA.com*   **Phone:** (508)224-3990   **46**

Motel

$89-$149 5/1-11/29
$79-$129 11/30-4/30

Address: 710 State Rd 02360 **Location:** 6.5 mi s on SR 3A. **Facility:** 28 units. 24 one-bedroom standard units. 4 one-bedroom suites with efficiencies. 1 story, exterior corridors. *Bath:* combo or shower only. **Parking:** on-site. **Terms:** office hours 8 am-9 pm, 3 day cancellation notice-fee imposed. **Amenities:** voice mail, hair dryers. **Pool(s):** outdoor. **Guest Services:** wireless Internet. 🛜➕ 🏊 🖥 / SOME UNITS ✕ 📷

· ٧ ⚘ **Three generations and they all have the same ears.** ⚘ ᷄·

There's so much in life worth celebrating. But often, our "day to day" has to come before those things that truly last. This is the year to gather with all the people who make you the happiest and celebrate at the place where dreams come true.

Enjoy EXCLUSIVE benefits when you book your *AAA Vacations®* *Disneyland®* Resort package at your local AAA Travel office, or online at **AAA.com**.

What will you celebrate?
Disneyland
RESORT

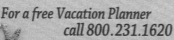

(See map and index starting on p. 458)

COMFORT INN   *Book great rates at AAA.com*   Phone: 508/746-2800 42

Hotel
Rates not provided

Address: 155 Samoset St 02360 **Location:** SR 3, exit 6, 0.3 mi w on US 44. **Facility:** 67 one-bedroom standard units. 3 stories, interior corridors. *Bath:* combo or shower only. **Parking:** on-site. **Amenities:** voice mail, irons, hair dryers. **Pool(s):** heated indoor. **Guest Services:** wireless Internet. **Business Services:** meeting rooms, PC. **Free Special Amenities: expanded continental breakfast and high-speed Internet.** 🍴 CALL 📶 🏊 📺 💻 / SOME UNITS ✕ 🗄 📷

HAMPTON INN & SUITES - PLYMOUTH KINGSTON   *Book great rates at AAA.com*   Phone: (508)747-5000 43

Hotel
$99-$159 All Year

Address: 10 Plaza Way 02360 **Location:** SR 3, exit 7. **Facility:** 122 one-bedroom standard units. 4 stories, interior corridors. *Bath:* some combo or shower only. **Parking:** on-site. **Terms:** 1-7 night minimum stay, cancellation fee imposed. **Amenities:** video games (fee), voice mail, irons, hair dryers. *Some:* high-speed Internet. **Pool(s):** heated indoor. **Leisure Activities:** whirlpool, exercise room. **Guest Services:** valet and coin laundry, area transportation, wireless Internet. **Business Services:** meeting rooms, business center. *(See color ad p 547)* 🍴 CALL 📶 🏊 📺 💻 / SOME UNITS ✕ 🗄 📷

Hampton Inn & Suites

AAA Benefit:
Members save up to
10% everyday!

HILTON GARDEN INN PLYMOUTH   *Book great rates at AAA.com*   Phone: (508)830-0200 45

Hotel
$99-$199 All Year

Address: 4 Home Depot Dr 02360 **Location:** SR 3, exit 5, just s. **Facility:** Smoke free premises. 130 one-bedroom standard units. 5 stories, interior corridors. *Bath:* combo or shower only. **Parking:** on-site. **Terms:** 1-7 night minimum stay, cancellation fee imposed. **Leisure Activities:** video games (fee), high-speed Internet, voice mail, irons, hair dryers. **Pool(s):** heated indoor. **Leisure Activities:** whirlpool, exercise room. **Guest Services:** valet and coin laundry, wireless Internet. **Business Services:** meeting rooms, business center. 🍴 CALL 📶 🏊 ✕ 📺 🗄 📷 💻

Hilton Garden Inn

AAA Benefit:
Members save 5% or
more everyday!

JOHN CARVER INN & SPA   *Book at AAA.com*   Phone: (508)746-7100 41

Hotel
$99-$329 All Year

Address: 25 Summer St 02360 **Location:** Center. **Facility:** Smoke free premises. 80 units. 74 one-bedroom standard units. 6 one-bedroom suites with whirlpools. 3 stories, interior corridors. *Bath:* combo or shower only. **Parking:** on-site. **Terms:** 2 night minimum stay - seasonal and/or weekends. **Amenities:** video games (fee), voice mail, irons, hair dryers. *Some:* DVD players, CD players. **Dining:** Hearth 'n Kettle Restaurant, see separate listing. **Pool(s):** heated indoor. **Leisure Activities:** sauna, whirlpool, waterslide, exercise room, spa. *Fee:* game room. **Guest Services:** wireless Internet. **Business Services:** conference facilities, business center. *(See color ad p 547)* ASK 🍴 CALL 📶 🏊 ✕ 📺 / SOME UNITS FEE 🗄

PILGRIM SANDS ON LONG BEACH   Phone: 508/747-0900 44

Motel
$84-$195 All Year

Address: 150 Warren Ave 02360 **Location:** On SR 3A. Located on Cape Cod Bay. **Facility:** Smoke free premises. 64 units. 62 one-bedroom standard units. 2 two-bedroom suites with kitchens. 2 stories (no elevator), interior/exterior corridors. **Parking:** on-site. **Terms:** 3 day cancellation notice-fee imposed. **Amenities:** voice mail, hair dryers. *Some:* irons. **Pool(s):** outdoor, heated indoor. **Leisure Activities:** whirlpool. **Guest Services:** wireless Internet. **Business Services:** PC, fax. *(See color ad p 547)* ASK 🍴 🏊 ✕ 📺 🗄 / SOME UNITS 🐾 📷

RADISSON HOTEL PLYMOUTH HARBOR   *Book great rates at AAA.com*   Phone: (508)747-4900 40

Hotel
$144-$414 5/1-10/18
$126-$364 10/19-4/30

Address: 180 Water St 02360 **Location:** Just e of SR 3A, follow signs; center. **Facility:** Smoke free premises. 175 units. 172 one-bedroom standard units, some with whirlpools. 3 one-bedroom suites with whirlpools. 4 stories, interior corridors. **Parking:** on-site. **Terms:** 2-3 night minimum stay - seasonal and/or weekends. **Amenities:** video games (fee), voice mail, irons, hair dryers. **Pool(s):** heated indoor. **Leisure Activities:** saunas, whirlpool, exercise room. **Guest Services:** valet and coin laundry, wireless Internet. **Business Services:** conference facilities, business center. *(See color ad p 547)* 🍴 🍸 CALL 📶 🏊 ✕ ✕ 📺 💻 / SOME UNITS 🗄 FEE 📷

———— **WHERE TO DINE** ————

EAST BAY GRILLE   Phone: 508/746-9751 44

Seafood
$9-$28

On the north end of the harbor near the charter and cruise boats, the dining room and lounge provide water views from most areas. Commemorative racing shell oars, open beam ceilings and generous use of fine wood combine with the location to further the yacht club feel. Casual dress. **Bar:** Full bar. **Reservations:** not accepted. **Hours:** 11 am-4 & 4:30-10 pm; Sunday brunch. Closed: 12/25. **Address:** 173 Water St 02360 **Location:** On Plymouth Harbor at Town Wharf. **Parking:** on-site. CALL 📶

(See map and index starting on p. 458)

HEARTH 'N KETTLE RESTAURANT   **Phone: 508/747-7405**

Regional American
$5-$15

Traditional Cape Cod cooking is served in an informal, family-friendly atmosphere. The diverse menu has the standards, from bacon, eggs and omelets for breakfast and sandwiches, chowders and salads for lunch to old favorites such as meatloaf and chicken pot pie for dinner. Fresh seafood is the forte. Finish the meal with one of the traditional New England desserts, such as Indian pudding or a distinctive treatment of strawberry shortcake. A few vegetarian selections are offered. Casual dress. **Bar:** Full bar. **Reservations:** accepted. **Hours:** 7 am-9 pm, Fri & Sat-10 pm. Closed: 12/25. **Address:** 25 Summer St 02360 **Location:** Center; in John Carver Inn. **Parking:** on-site. CALL ⑤M

ISAAC'S ON THE WATERFRONT   **Phone: 508/830-0001** ㊽

Seafood
$7-$23

It's worth the wait for a memorable dining experience in the upscale, contemporary dining room, which affords panoramic views of Plymouth Harbor from its second-floor vantage point. The food is tasty and varied, ranging from sandwiches and pasta to seafood, poultry and meat dishes, all of which are served with the signature hazelnut squash. Homemade desserts also merit consideration. Outdoor patio seating is available in season. Dressy casual. **Bar:** Full bar. **Reservations:** suggested. **Hours:** 11:30 am-10:30 pm, Sun from 11 am. Closed: 12/25. **Address:** 114 Water St 02360 **Location:** Opposite harbor. **Parking:** street. CALL ⑤M

LOBSTER HUT   **Phone: 508/746-2270** ㊺

Seafood
$7-$20

Overlooking a marina and harbor, the restaurant is a terrific spot for families seeking a quick bite of fried seafood. Outdoor seating is an option. Casual dress. **Bar:** Beer & wine. **Hours:** Open 5/1-12/31 & 2/15-4/30; 11 am-9 pm; to 8 pm in winter. **Address:** 25 Town Wharf 02360 **Location:** At Plymouth Harbor. **Parking:** on-site.

MAMMA MIA'S RESTAURANT ON THE
WATERFRONT   **Phone: 508/747-4670** ㊼

Italian
$5-$19

Offering a great view of the north end of the harbor, this eatery is a favorite haunt of locals and tourists. Regionally brewed beer, homemade pasta and subs are served at this popular, bustling restaurant, which focuses on authentic recipes for varied veal, chicken and seafood. Dishes are simply presented and served in ample portions; even the 13-inch small pizza seems large. The dining room surrounds a small bar, which is separated by a shoulder-high oak wall. Casual dress. **Bar:** Full bar. **Hours:** 11 am-10 pm. Closed: 4/4, 11/25, 12/25. **Address:** 122 Water St 02360 **Location:** Opposite harbor. **Parking:** street. CALL ⑤M

(See map and index starting on p. 458)

NINETY NINE RESTAURANT

American
$7-$18

Phone: 508/732-9932

This popular pub is committed to serving large portions of great food at reasonable prices. Guest favorites include hot wings, burgers, seafood, barbecue ribs and chicken. While reservations are not taken, call-ahead seating is offered. A children's menu is also available. Casual dress. **Bar:** Full bar. **Reservations:** not accepted. **Hours:** 11 am-10:30 pm, Fri & Sat-11 pm, Sun-10 pm. Closed: 11/25, 12/24, 12/25. **Address:** 21 Home Depot Dr 02360 **Location:** SR 3, exit 5, just s. **Parking:** on-site.

THE ROOBAR

American
$12-$30

Phone: 508/746-4300 [43]

Works by local artists, offset by white table linens covered with butcher paper, provide a whimsical touch to the décor. Creative American food, including clam chowder, lobster bisque, grilled salmon with citrus beurre blanc and polenta, pork tenderloin and seafood Provençal, is prepared in the open kitchen. The restaurant occupies an historic mill building with high ceilings and original brick work and beams. Casual dress. **Bar:** Full bar. **Reservations:** accepted. **Hours:** 5 pm-10 pm. Closed major holidays; also Mon. **Address:** 10 Cordage Pk, Suite 253 02360 **Location:** Off SR 3A. **Parking:** on-site.

SAM DIEGO'S MEXICAN COOKERY AND BAR

Mexican
$6-$20

Phone: 508/747-0048

The lively and colorful Mexican restaurant is inside a converted firehouse. Multilevel dining areas are accented by beautiful oak woodwork and a swirling central staircase. The menu lists traditional hot and spicy dishes, such as burritos, enchiladas and fajitas, along with burgers and sandwiches. Smoking is allowed only in the patio dining area. Casual dress. **Bar:** Full bar. **Reservations:** not accepted. **Hours:** 11:30 am-midnight. Closed: 12/24, 12/25. **Address:** 51 Main St 02360 **Location:** Center. **Parking:** street. CALL 🅶🅼

STONEFORGE PLYMOUTH

American
$7-$29

Phone: 508/747-7887 [50]

The dining room affords an expansive view of the Atlantic: breathtaking and lively depending on the tides. The menu focuses on fresh seafood and a few landlubber favorites, which are served by the pleasant staff. Casual dress. **Bar:** Full bar. **Reservations:** accepted. **Hours:** 11:30 am-9 pm, Sun from noon. Closed: 12/25. **Address:** 140 Warren Ave 02360 **Location:** 3 mi s; on SR 3A. **Parking:** on-site.

WATER STREET CAFE

American
$6-$9

Phone: 508/746-2050 [49]

A popular spot for both locals and tourists, the casual atmosphere makes the cafe a great stop for breakfast or lunch. Homemade desserts and a take-out menu are also available. Casual dress. **Reservations:** not accepted. **Hours:** 5:30 am-3 pm. Closed major holidays. **Address:** 25 Water St 02360 **Location:** At Union St. **Parking:** on-site.

WEATHERVANE SEAFOOD RESTAURANT

Seafood
$8-$25

Phone: 508/746-4195

The popular, family-oriented restaurant presents a large menu with lobster, fried clams and crisp Cape Cod apple-cranberry cobbler. Flavorful dishes are served in large portions. A fish market is on the premises. Casual dress. **Bar:** Full bar. **Reservations:** not accepted. **Hours:** 11 am-9 pm. Closed: 11/25, 12/25. **Address:** 6 Town Wharf 02360 **Location:** On the harbor. **Parking:** street. CALL 🅶🅼

WOOD'S SEAFOOD

Seafood
$5-$30

Phone: 508/746-0261 [46]

Open year round, the Plymouth Harbor seafood institution is a favorite of locals and tourists alike. Offerings include great fried seafood, in addition to terrific broiled off-the-boat fish. Guests order at the counter and wait for their number to be called. Casual dress. **Reservations:** not accepted. **Hours:** 11 am-7 pm, Fri & Sat-8 pm; to 9 pm in summer. Closed major holidays. **Address:** 15 Town Pier 02360 **Location:** At Plymouth Harbor. **Parking:** on-site.

PRINCETON

—— WHERE TO DINE ——

MOUNTAIN BARN

American
$6-$18

Phone: 978/464-2044

Dine in a remotely-located yet popular red barn eatery located in a scenic area with a simple, rustic interior of natural wood paneling and railings. A friendly staff serves steak, ribs, chicken, fish and pasta in good portions and at a good price. Casual dress. **Bar:** Full bar. **Hours:** 4:30 pm-10 pm, Sun noon-9 pm, Thurs 4:30 pm-9 pm. Closed: 12/25; also Mon-Wed. **Address:** 174 Worcester Rd 01541-0327 **Location:** 1.6 mi s on SR 31. **Parking:** on-site.

PROVINCETOWN—See Cape Cod p. 498.

QUINCY—See Boston p. 430.

RANDOLPH—See Boston p. 430.

RAYNHAM

COURTYARD BOSTON/RAYNHAM   *Book great rates at AAA.com*

Phone: (508)822-8383

Hotel
$116-$142 All Year

Address: 37 Paramount Dr 02767 **Location:** SR 24, exit 13A, 0.3 mi e on US 44. **Facility:** Smoke free premises. 120 units. 118 one-bedroom standard units, some with whirlpools. 2 one-bedroom suites. 3 stories, interior corridors. *Bath:* combo or shower only. **Parking:** on-site. **Terms:** cancellation fee imposed. **Amenities:** high-speed Internet, dual phone lines, voice mail, irons, hair dryers. **Pool(s):** heated indoor. **Leisure Activities:** whirlpool, exercise room. **Guest Services:** valet and coin laundry, wireless Internet. **Business Services:** meeting rooms, business center.

AAA Benefit:
Members save a minimum 5% off the best available rate.

HAMPTON INN RAYNHAM - TAUNTON   *Book great rates at AAA.com*

Phone: (508)822-6222

Hotel
$139-$199 All Year

Address: 600 New State Hwy 02767 **Location:** SR 24, exit 13A, just e on US 44. **Facility:** 87 units. 84 one-bedroom standard units. 3 one-bedroom suites. 4 stories, interior corridors. *Bath:* combo or shower only. **Parking:** on-site. **Terms:** 1-7 night minimum stay, cancellation fee imposed. **Amenities:** video games (fee), high-speed Internet, voice mail, irons, hair dryers. **Pool(s):** heated indoor. **Leisure Activities:** whirlpool, exercise room. **Guest Services:** valet and coin laundry, wireless Internet. **Business Services:** meeting rooms, business center.

AAA Benefit:
Members save up to 10% everyday!

QUALITY INN OF RAYNHAM-TAUNTON   *Book great rates at AAA.com*

Phone: (508)824-8647

Motel
$74-$115 5/1-10/31
$55-$89 11/1-4/30

Address: 164 New State Hwy 02767 **Location:** SR 24, exit 13B, 0.8 mi w on US 44. **Facility:** 68 one-bedroom standard units. 1-2 stories (no elevator), interior/exterior corridors. *Bath:* combo or shower only. **Parking:** on-site. **Amenities:** irons, hair dryers. **Pool(s):** outdoor. **Guest Services:** coin laundry, wireless Internet. **Business Services:** PC. **Free Special Amenities:** continental breakfast and high-speed Internet.

——— **WHERE TO DINE** ———

STONEFORGE TAVERN

Phone: 508/977-9845

American
$6-$24

This more casual side to the adjacent Publick House restaurant features plenty of televisions broadcasting the latest sporting events. Seafood preparations such as the award-winning clam chowder and clams casino are excellent choices. Typical pub food consists of sandwiches, burgers and salads. Casual dress. **Bar:** Full bar. **Reservations:** not accepted. **Hours:** 11:30 am-11 pm, Fri & Sat-1 am, Sun from noon. Closed: 12/25. **Address:** 90 Paramount Dr 02767 **Location:** SR 24, exit 13A, 0.4 mi e on US 44. **Parking:** on-site.

STONEFORGE TAVERN & PUBLICK HOUSE

Phone: 508/977-9845

American
$16-$29

A short distance off the highway in a building that looks like a turn-of-the-20th-century seaside cottage with an attached carriage house, the restaurant has two personalities: one upscale and a touch refined, the other rustic and less formal. Beef is certified Angus, and seafood is delivered daily. Homemade soups, salads and side dishes, tempting desserts and an extensive wine list complement the main course offerings. A massive bar covers most of one wall. Servers are friendly and efficient. Dressy casual. **Bar:** Full bar. **Reservations:** suggested. **Hours:** 5 pm-9:30 pm, Fri & Sat-10 pm. Closed: 12/25. **Address:** 90 Paramount Dr 02767 **Location:** SR 24, exit 13A, 0.4 mi e on US 44. **Parking:** on-site.

READING—See Boston p. 431.

REHOBOTH (See map and index starting on p. 606)

FIVE BRIDGE INN BED & BREAKFAST

Phone: 508/252-3190 **26**

Bed & Breakfast
$98-$145 All Year

Address: 154 Pine St 02769 **Location:** 1.6 mi n of US 44; 3.3 mi w of jct SR 118; US 44, n on Blanding, e on Broad, n on Salisbury, then w. Located in a quiet area. **Facility:** A Georgian Colonial house on some 80 acres in a forest preserve, the retreatlike B&B has a large family suite, a lap pool and a screened gazebo. Smoke free premises. 5 one-bedroom standard units, some with whirlpools. 3 stories (no elevator), interior corridors. *Bath:* some shared or private, combo or shower only. **Parking:** on-site. **Terms:** office hours 7 am-10 pm, 2 night minimum stay - seasonal and/or weekends, 3 day cancellation notice. **Amenities:** irons, hair dryers. **Pool(s):** outdoor. **Leisure Activities:** tennis court, playground, exercise room. *Fee:* yoga & pilates classes. **Guest Services:** wireless Internet.

REVERE—See Boston p. 431.

RICHMOND

THE INN AT RICHMOND

Phone: 413/698-2566

Historic Bed
& Breakfast

$160-$380 All Year

Address: 802 State Rd (SR 41) 01254 **Location:** 2.5 mi s of jct US 20. **Facility:** On 27 acres, this restored 18th-century farmhouse features gardens, a reflecting pool and some fireplace suites. Public areas have pine plank floors. Smoke free premises. 9 units. 3 one-bedroom standard units. 3 one-bedroom suites, some with whirlpools. 3 cottages. 2 stories (no elevator), interior/exterior corridors. **Bath:** combo or shower only. **Parking:** on-site. **Terms:** 2 night minimum stay - seasonal and/or weekends, 15 day cancellation notice-fee imposed. **Amenities:** video library, CD players, irons, hair dryers. **Some:** DVD players. **Leisure Activities:** cross country skiing, hiking trails. **Fee:** massage. **Guest Services:** wireless Internet. **Business Services:** meeting rooms.

(A$K) ⊠ ⊠ / SOME UNITS FEE 🐾 🖥 🖾 🖵

ROCKLAND

BEST WESTERN ROCKLAND   *Book great rates at AAA.com*

Phone: (781)871-5660

(AAA) (SAVE)

Hotel

$119-$169 5/1-10/31
$109-$149 11/1-4/30

Address: 909 Hingham St 02370 **Location:** SR 3, exit 14, 0.3 mi sw on SR 228. **Facility:** 76 one-bedroom standard units. 2 stories (no elevator), interior corridors. **Parking:** on-site. **Amenities:** video games (fee), voice mail, irons, hair dryers. **Leisure Activities:** exercise room. **Guest Services:** complimentary and valet laundry, wireless Internet. **Business Services:** meeting rooms, PC. **Free Special Amenities: expanded continental breakfast and high-speed Internet.**

🍴 🎥 🖵 / SOME UNITS FEE 🐾 ⊠ 🖥 🖾

AAA Benefit:
Members save up to
20%, plus 10%
bonus points with
rewards program.

COMFORT INN   *Book at AAA.com*

Phone: (781)982-1000

Hotel

$79-$249 All Year

Address: 850 Hingham St 02370 **Location:** SR 3, exit 14, 0.5 mi sw on SR 228. **Facility:** 101 units. 100 one-bedroom standard units, some with whirlpools. 1 one-bedroom suite with whirlpool. 3 stories, interior corridors. **Parking:** on-site. **Amenities:** voice mail, safes (fee), irons, hair dryers. **Leisure Activities:** limited exercise equipment. **Guest Services:** valet and coin laundry, wireless Internet. **Business Services:** meeting rooms, business center.

(A$K) 🍴 CALL 📞 🎥 🐾 🖵 / SOME UNITS ⊠ 🖥 🖾

HOLIDAY INN ROCKLAND-BOSTON SOUTH   *Book at AAA.com*

Phone: 781/871-0545

Hotel

Rates not provided

Address: 929 Hingham St 02370 **Location:** SR 3, exit 14, 0.3 mi sw on SR 228. **Facility:** Smoke free premises. 127 one-bedroom standard units, some with whirlpools. 5 stories, interior corridors. **Bath:** combo or shower only. **Parking:** on-site. **Amenities:** dual phone lines, voice mail, irons, hair dryers. **Some:** high-speed Internet. **Pool(s):** heated outdoor. **Leisure Activities:** exercise room. **Guest Services:** valet and coin laundry, wireless Internet. **Business Services:** meeting rooms, business center.

🍴 🍸 🏊 ⊠ 🎥 🖵 / SOME UNITS FEE 🖥 FEE 🖾

------ **WHERE TO DINE** ------

BELLA'S

Italian
$8-$33

Phone: 781/871-5789

The bustling dining room is partitioned with planters and partial walls. Good portions of varied fare, mostly Italian, are served at the popular eatery. Pasta choices include linguine, ziti, angel hair, bowtie and homemade ravioli, while other entree options might be veal, chicken or eggplant parmigiana, scaloppine or Marsala, pork tenderloin, swordfish or scrod. Pizza and carry-out service are not available on Saturday. Rustic wreaths, dried flower arrangements and posters grace the walls. Casual dress. **Bar:** Full bar. **Reservations:** suggested. **Hours:** 11:30 am-10 pm, Sat from 4 pm, Sun 4 pm-9 pm. Closed major holidays. **Address:** 933 Hingham St 02370 **Location:** SR 3, exit 14, 0.3 mi sw on SR 228. **Parking:** on-site.

CALL 👤M

ROCKPORT—See Boston p. 432.

ROWLEY—See Boston p. 435.

SALEM—See Boston p. 435.

SALISBURY—See Boston p. 437.

SANDWICH—See Cape Cod p. 501.

SAUGUS—See Boston p. 438.

SCITUATE pop. 5,069

------ **WHERE TO DINE** ------

THE MILL WHARF

New American
$7-$28

Phone: 781/545-3999

Roasted and fried items ranging from pizza to sandwiches to seafood are served in the lounge and dining room and on seasonal decks that overlook the picturesque harbor. A pub menu is offered at lunch and in the lounge, where smoking is permitted. Servers, casually uniformed in tan shorts or slacks and blue tennis shirts, provide down-home service. Casual dress. **Bar:** Full bar. **Reservations:** accepted. **Hours:** 11:30 am-10 pm; seasonal hours vary. Closed: 12/25. **Address:** 150 R Front St 02066 **Location:** On Scituate Harbor; behind Welch Company. **Parking:** on-site.

P J'S COUNTRY HOUSE RESTAURANT

American
$10-$28

Phone: 781/545-1340

Fairly close to the water, the restaurant allows patrons to breathe the ocean air. On the menu are traditional New England comfort foods, including seafood, steak and poultry. The decent selection is sure to please most folks. Casual dress. **Bar:** Full bar. **Hours:** 11:30 am-4 & 5-9:30 pm, Sun 12:30 pm-9 pm. Closed major holidays; also Mon. **Address:** 227 Chief Justice Cushing Hwy 02066 **Location:** Just se of SR 123. **Parking:** on-site.

SEEKONK (See map and index starting on p. 606)

BEST WESTERN PROVIDENCE-SEEKONK INN   *Book great rates at AAA.com*   **Phone:** (508)336-4927 **38**

Hotel
$100-$135 All Year

Address: 45 Mink St 02771 **Location:** I-195, exit 1, 0.6 mi e on SR 114A. **Facility:** Smoke free premises. 50 one-bedroom standard units. 3 stories, interior corridors. **Parking:** on-site. **Amenities:** high-speed Internet, voice mail, irons, hair dryers. **Pool(s):** heated indoor. **Leisure Activities:** whirlpool, exercise room. **Guest Services:** valet and coin laundry, wireless Internet. **Business Services:** meeting rooms, business center. **Free Special Amenities: expanded continental breakfast and high-speed Internet.** 🍴 CALL 👤M 🏊 ✕ 📹 🔌 🖥 🖥

AAA Benefit:
Members save up to 20%, plus 10% bonus points with rewards program.

COMFORT INN PROVIDENCE/SEEKONK   *Book great rates at AAA.com*   **Phone:** (508)336-7900 **37**

Hotel
$90-$130 All Year

Address: 341 Highland Ave 02771 **Location:** I-195, exit 1, just s; on SR 6. **Facility:** 90 one-bedroom standard units. 2 stories (no elevator), interior corridors. **Parking:** on-site. **Amenities:** voice mail, safes, irons, hair dryers. *Some:* high-speed Internet. **Pool(s):** outdoor. **Leisure Activities:** exercise room. **Guest Services:** valet and coin laundry, wireless Internet. **Business Services:** meeting rooms, business center. *(See color ad p 612)*
🍴 🏊 📹 🖥 / SOME UNITS ✕ 🔌 🖥

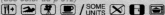

(See map and index starting on p. 606)

HAMPTON INN   *Book great rates at AAA.com*   Phone: (508)336-9000 36

Hotel
$84-$169 All Year

Address: 1030 Fall River Ave 02771 **Location:** I-195, exit 1, just s. **Facility:** 91 one-bedroom standard units. 3 stories, interior corridors. *Bath:* combo or shower only. **Parking:** on-site. **Terms:** 1-7 night minimum stay, cancellation fee imposed. **Amenities:** video games (fee), high-speed Internet, voice mail, irons, hair dryers. **Pool(s):** heated outdoor. **Leisure Activities:** exercise room. **Guest Services:** valet laundry, wireless Internet. **Business Services:** meeting rooms, business center.

AAA Benefit:
Members save up to
10% everyday!

HISTORIC JACOB HILL INN   Phone: 508/336-9165 32

Historic Bed
& Breakfast
$199-$459 All Year

Address: 120 Jacob St 02771 **Location:** Jct US 44 and SR 114A, 1.7 mi e on US 44, then 0.5 mi n. Located in a residential area. **Facility:** In a pastoral setting, the B&B features many romantic rooms with a whirlpool tub and gas fireplace; complimentary snacks are offered. Smoke free premises. 12 units. 10 one-bedroom standard units, some with whirlpools. 2 one-bedroom suites, some with whirlpools. 2-3 stories (no elevator), interior corridors. **Parking:** on-site. **Terms:** 2 night minimum stay, age restrictions may apply, 15 day cancellation notice-fee imposed. **Amenities:** video library, CD players, irons, hair dryers. *Some:* DVD players. **Pool(s):** outdoor. **Leisure Activities:** tennis court, billiards, table tennis, game room. **Guest Services:** wireless Internet. **Business Services:** meeting rooms. **Free Special Amenities: full breakfast and high-speed Internet.**

JOHNSON & WALES INN   *Book great rates at AAA.com*   Phone: (508)336-8700 33

Hotel
$109-$139 5/1-10/31
$99-$129 11/1-4/30

Address: 213 Taunton Ave 02771 **Location:** On US 44, 0.3 mi e of jct SR 114A. **Facility:** Smoke free premises. 86 units. 65 one-bedroom standard units, some with whirlpools. 21 one-bedroom suites with whirlpools. 3-4 stories, interior corridors. *Bath:* combo or shower only. **Parking:** on-site. **Amenities:** high-speed Internet, voice mail, irons, hair dryers. **Dining:** Audrey's Restaurant, see separate listing. **Leisure Activities:** exercise room. **Guest Services:** valet and coin laundry, wireless Internet. *Fee:* airport transportation-TF Greene Airport, area transportation-within 5 mi, Amtrak & bus stations. **Business Services:** conference facilities, business center. *(See color ad p 614)*

FREE continental breakfast and high-speed Internet

MOTEL 6 - 1289   *Book at AAA.com*   Phone: (508)336-7800 34

Motel
$55-$65 All Year

Address: 821 Fall River Ave 02771 **Location:** I-195, exit 1, just n on SR 114A. **Facility:** 85 one-bedroom standard units. 2 stories (no elevator), interior corridors. *Bath:* combo or shower only. **Parking:** on-site. **Guest Services:** coin laundry, wireless Internet.

RAMADA INN-PROVIDENCE   *Book at AAA.com*   Phone: (508)336-7300 35

Hotel
$89-$150 All Year

Address: 940 Fall River Ave 02771 **Location:** I-195, exit 1, just s. **Facility:** 128 units. 127 one-bedroom standard units. 1 one-bedroom suite. 2 stories (no elevator), interior corridors. **Parking:** on-site. **Amenities:** irons, hair dryers. **Dining:** Darling's Restaurant & Lounge, see separate listing. **Pool(s):** heated indoor. **Leisure Activities:** putting green, playground, shuffleboard. **Guest Services:** valet laundry, wireless Internet. **Business Services:** conference facilities, business center.

—— WHERE TO DINE ——

AUDREY'S RESTAURANT   Phone: 508/336-4636 70

American
$5-$30

This restaurant, which also serves as a training facility, offers an excellent, varied menu that changes with the seasons. Desserts are artistically presented. The rich, English-style dining room has mahogany, cherry and brass accents. There's one special table for two in the glass-walled wine room. Dressy casual. **Bar:** Full bar. **Reservations:** suggested. **Hours:** 6:30 am-10 pm, Sun 7:30 am-1 & 4-10 pm. Closed: 12/25. **Address:** 213 Taunton Ave 02771 **Location:** On US 44, 0.3 mi e of jct SR 114A; in Johnson & Wales Inn. **Parking:** on-site. *(See color ad p 614)*

CHARDONNAY'S   Phone: 508/336-0967 69

American
$9-$26

This casually elegant restaurant serves eclectic New American cuisine along with a carefully chosen wine list that includes 20 by-the-glass choices and many more by the bottle. Among the house favorites are Zippy Shrimp, marinated in Cajun-teriyaki sauce, grilled and served over sautéed Asian spinach; lobster ravioli with vodka-tomato-cream sauce; and chicken piccata, which is sautéed with lemon, butter and capers. Fresh sushi also is available. Dressy casual. **Bar:** Full bar. **Hours:** 4 pm-close, Sun from 2 pm; seasonal hours may vary. Closed: 11/25, 12/25. **Address:** 393 Taunton Ave (SR 44) 02771 **Location:** I-195, exit 4 eastbound, 2.7 mi e; exit 1 westbound, 1.5 mi nw on SR 114A, then 0.6 mi ne. **Parking:** on-site.

(See map and index starting on p. 606)

DARLING'S RESTAURANT & LOUNGE   *Menu on AAA.com*   Phone: 508/336-9222

American
$7-$18

Jimmy Carter put this restaurant, which has been operated by the same family since 1929, on the map when he ate here during his presidency. Diners appreciate its steak and seafood specialties, combination platters and homestyle fare along the lines of chicken pot pie and other New England-style favorites. Interesting desserts range from apple and prune pie to the ice cream puff drizzled with chocolate syrup. This place is part of a hotel. Service is folksy and efficient. Casual dress. **Bar:** Full bar. **Reservations:** suggested, weekends. **Hours:** 7 am-10 pm. Closed: 12/25. **Address:** 940 Fall River Ave 02771 **Location:** I-195, exit 1, just s; in Ramada Inn-Providence. **Parking:** on-site. CALL

NEWPORT CREAMERY   Phone: 508/336-4519

American
$6-$9

A New England tradition since the 1940s, the creamery is known for its "awful, awful" milk shakes and homemade ice cream. Families will be comfortable visiting for a good meal, friendly service and a delicious sundae for dessert. Casual dress. **Hours:** 7 am-10 pm, Fri & Sat-11 pm. Closed: 11/25, 12/25. **Address:** 701 Fall River Ave 02771 **Location:** I-95, exit 7 eastbound, 0.4 mi e on US 6, just ne on Warren Ave, then just se; exit 1 westbound, 0.4 mi nw on SR 114A. **Parking:** on-site. CALL

THE OLD GRIST MILL TAVERN   Phone: 508/336-8460   (71)

American
$7-$26

Prime rib and fresh local seafood reign supreme in the restored Colonial tavern's charming, rustic dining room, which is adjacent to a peaceful duck pond. Stuffed mushroom caps, crab cakes, shrimp cocktail, baked onion soup, white clam chowder and lobster are favorites. The restaurant can be busy on weekends. Filet mignon—which, like the prime rib, comes in three sizes—joins sirloin and lamb chops among meat offerings. Casual dress. **Bar:** Full bar. **Reservations:** suggested. **Hours:** 11:30 am-10 pm, Sun 10 am-9 pm. Closed: 11/25, 12/25. **Address:** 390 Fall River Ave 02771 **Location:** I-195, exit 1, 1.3 mi n on SR 114A. **Parking:** on-site.

TITO'S CANTINA   Phone: 508/336-2400   (73)

Mexican
$4-$15

Accenting the Mexican cantina theme are tile floors and colorfully painted murals of tropical birds and flora. Diners can sip a large margarita while contemplating such choices as freshly prepared enchiladas, burritos and quesadillas, including spinach and lobster varieties. Homemade salsa pairs with organic chips. Casual dress. **Bar:** Full bar. **Hours:** 11:30 am-10 pm. Closed: 4/4, 11/25, 12/25. **Address:** 1379 Fall River Ave (SR 6) 02771 **Location:** I-195, exit 1 eastbound, 0.9 mi se on SR 114A; exit 2 westbound, 0.5 mi sw on SR 136, then 3.2 mi ne on SR 6. **Parking:** on-site. CALL

VINNY T'S OF BOSTON   Phone: 508/336-8488

Italian
$11-$22

The Old World-themed family restaurant is decorated with elegant chandeliers, rich wood floors, Roman sculptures and an abundance of framed photos and artwork set in Italy. Meals, which are freshly prepared on site, might include chicken Marsala, lasagna and mussels fra diavolo. Casual dress. **Bar:** Full bar. **Reservations:** suggested. **Hours:** 11 am-10 pm, Sun from 11:30 am. Closed: 11/25, 12/25. **Address:** 353 Highland Ave (US 6) 02771 **Location:** I-195, exit 1, 0.4 mi s. **Parking:** on-site. CALL

SHARON—See Boston p. 439.

SHIRLEY—See Boston p. 439.

SHREWSBURY

DAYS INN WORCESTER/SHREWSBURY   *Book at AAA.com*   Phone: (508)842-8500

Hotel
$75-$80 All Year

Address: 889 Boston Tpke (SR 9) 01545 **Location:** I-495, exit 23B (SR 9 W), 6 mi; I-90, exit 11A (I-495 N), 1 mi to exit 23B (SR 9 W). **Facility:** 101 one-bedroom standard units. 2 stories (no elevator), interior corridors. *Bath:* combo or shower only. **Parking:** on-site. **Amenities:** voice mail, irons, hair dryers. *Fee:* safes. **Guest Services:** coin laundry, wireless Internet. **Business Services:** business center. ASK FEE

SOMERSET pop. 18,234

QUALITY INN-FALL RIVER/SOMERSET   *Book great rates at AAA.com*   Phone: (508)678-4545

Hotel
$80-$165 5/1-10/11
$75-$155 10/12-4/30

Address: 1878 Wilbur Ave 02725 **Location:** Jct SR 103 and I-195, exit 4 eastbound; exit 4A westbound. **Facility:** 104 units. 102 one-bedroom standard units, some with whirlpools. 2 one-bedroom suites with whirlpools. 2 stories (no elevator), interior corridors. **Parking:** on-site. **Terms:** cancellation fee imposed. **Amenities:** high-speed Internet, voice mail, irons, hair dryers. *Some:* DVD players (fee). **Pool(s):** heated indoor. **Leisure Activities:** fishing, soccer area, exercise room, basketball, volleyball. **Guest Services:** valet and coin laundry, wireless Internet. **Business Services:** meeting rooms, business center. **Free Special Amenities: full breakfast and high-speed Internet.**

 WHERE TO DINE

MA RAFFA'S   Phone: 508/324-0909

Italian
$4-$11

The simple and exceptionally clean Italian restaurant has a large menu and generous portions. Thin-crust pizza is a specialty. Chicken Messina sauteed with fresh spinach, broccoli, mushrooms, olives, red peppers, ziti and a touch of garlic is excellent. Casual dress. **Bar:** Full bar. **Hours:** 11 am-9 pm, Fri & Sat-10 pm. Closed major holidays. **Address:** 1142 County St 02726 **Location:** Jct US 6, 1.7 mi n on SR 138; center. **Parking:** on-site. CALL

SOMERVILLE—See Boston p. 439.

SOUTH ATTLEBORO (See map and index starting on p. 606)

—— WHERE TO DINE ——

HEARTH 'N KETTLE RESTAURANT Phone: 508/399-6677

American
$5-$15

Traditional Cape Cod cooking is served in an informal, family-friendly atmosphere. The diverse menu has the standards, from bacon, eggs and omelets for breakfast and sandwiches, chowders and salads for lunch to old favorites such as meatloaf and chicken pot pie for dinner. Fresh seafood is the forte. Finish the meal with one of the traditional New England desserts, such as Indian pudding or a distinctive treatment of strawberry shortcake. A few vegetarian selections are offered. Casual dress. **Bar:** Full bar. **Reservations:** accepted. **Hours:** 7 am-close. Closed: 12/25. **Address:** 250 Washington St 02703 **Location:** I-295, exit 1A, 1.8 mi s on US 1. **Parking:** on-site. CALL [M]

SHANGHAI GARDENS Phone: 508/761-9339 [53]

Chinese
$6-$16

This modern Chinese restaurant is easy to spot from the road with its dramatic Asia-inspired exterior, complete with a koi pond. Patrons can enjoy a mai tai while tasting traditional favorites such as General Tso's chicken, kung pao chicken or the pu pu platter. Meals are served either family style or as individual combination plates. Lunch specials are reasonable. Casual dress. **Bar:** Full bar. **Reservations:** not accepted. **Hours:** 11:30 am-1 am, Fri & Sat-2 am, Sun noon-1 am. Closed: 11/25. **Address:** 901 Washington St 02703 **Location:** I-95, exit 30 northbound, 0.6 mi ne on Fountain St, then 0.6 mi n on US 1; exit 1 southbound, just n on US 1. **Parking:** on-site. CALL [M]

SOUTHBOROUGH

RED ROOF INN # 7075 *Book great rates at AAA.com* Phone: (508)481-3904

Motel
$76-$100 5/1-10/31
$66-$100 11/1-4/30

Address: 367 Turnpike Rd 01772 **Location:** I-495, exit 23A, just e on SR 9. **Facility:** 108 one-bedroom standard units. 2 stories (no elevator), exterior corridors. *Bath:* combo or shower only. **Parking:** on-site. **Amenities:** video games (fee), voice mail. **Guest Services:** wireless Internet. **Free Special Amenities:** local telephone calls.

SOUTHBRIDGE pop. 12,878

SOUTHBRIDGE HOTEL & CONFERENCE CENTER *Book at AAA.com* Phone: (508)765-8000

Hotel
$105-$189 All Year

Address: 14 Mechanic St 01550 **Location:** Off SR 169, just n of rotary; downtown. **Facility:** 203 units. 199 one-bedroom standard units. 4 one-bedroom suites. 4 stories, interior corridors. *Bath:* combo or shower only. **Parking:** on-site. **Terms:** cancellation fee imposed. **Amenities:** high-speed Internet, dual phone lines, voice mail, irons, hair dryers. **Pool(s):** heated indoor. **Leisure Activities:** saunas, whirlpool, steamrooms, racquetball courts, exercise room, sports court. **Guest Services:** valet and coin laundry, wireless Internet. **Business Services:** conference facilities, business center.

(ASK) [Y] CALL [M]

SOUTH DEERFIELD pop. 1,868—See also Deerfield.

—— WHERE TO DINE ——

CHANDLER'S TAVERN RESTAURANT Phone: 413/665-1277

American
$9-$29

Part of the enormous Yankee Candle Company complex, the restaurant features a stylish, rustic dining room lit by more than 200 candles. Well-prepared New England cuisine is made with only the freshest of ingredients. Each dish is presented with a variety of brilliant colors. Casual dress. **Bar:** Full bar. **Reservations:** suggested, for dinner. **Hours:** 10:30 am-4 pm, Wed-Sun to 8 pm. Closed: 12/25. **Address:** Rt 5 & 10 01373 **Location:** I-91, exit 24, 0.6 mi n; behind Yankee Candle Company. **Parking:** on-site.

SOUTH DENNIS—See Cape Cod p. 504.

SOUTH EGREMONT

WEATHERVANE INN Phone: 413/528-9580

Historic Bed
& Breakfast
$135-$350 All Year

Address: 17 Main St 01258 **Location:** On SR 23, 3.4 mi w of jct US 7. **Facility:** Befitting the age of the building, some guest rooms in this 1785 converted farmhouse are on the small side. Smoke free premises. 10 units. 8 one-bedroom standard units. 2 one-bedroom suites. 2 stories (no elevator), interior corridors. *Bath:* combo or shower only. **Parking:** on-site. **Terms:** office hours 8 am-9 pm, 2-3 night minimum stay - seasonal and/or weekends, 15 day cancellation notice-fee imposed. **Amenities:** video library. **Pool(s):** outdoor. **Leisure Activities:** *Fee:* massage.

SOUTH WELLFLEET—See Cape Cod p. 504.

SOUTH YARMOUTH—See Cape Cod p. 505.

SPRINGFIELD pop. 152,082—See also West Springfield.

HILTON GARDEN INN *Book great rates at AAA.com*

Phone: (413)886-8000

Hotel
$99-$199 All Year

Address: 800 W Columbus Ave 01105 **Location:** I-91, exit 7 southbound, exit 4 northbound, follow signs to Basketball Hall of Fame. **Facility:** 143 units. 141 one-bedroom standard units. 2 one-bedroom suites with whirlpools. 6 stories, interior corridors. *Bath:* combo or shower only. **Parking:** on-site. **Terms:** 1-7 night minimum stay, cancellation fee imposed. **Amenities:** video games (fee), high-speed Internet, dual phone lines, voice mail, irons, hair dryers. **Pool(s):** heated indoor. **Leisure Activities:** whirlpool, exercise room. *Fee:* game room. **Guest Services:** valet and coin laundry, wireless Internet. **Business Services:** meeting rooms, business center.

Hilton Garden Inn

AAA Benefit:
Members save 5% or more everyday!

MARRIOTT SPRINGFIELD *Book great rates at AAA.com*

Phone: (413)781-7111

Hotel
$184-$194 All Year

Address: 2 Boland Way 01115 **Location:** I-91, exit 6 northbound; exit 7 southbound, just n; downtown. Located in a shopping mall. **Facility:** Smoke free premises. 265 units. 262 one-bedroom standard units. 3 one-bedroom suites. 16 stories, interior corridors. *Bath:* combo or shower only. **Parking:** on-site (fee). **Terms:** check-in 4 pm, cancellation fee imposed. **Amenities:** voice mail, irons, hair dryers. *Fee:* video games, high-speed Internet. **Dining:** 2 restaurants. **Pool(s):** heated indoor. **Leisure Activities:** whirlpool. **Guest Services:** valet and coin laundry, wireless Internet. **Business Services:** conference facilities, business center.

Marriott
HOTELS & RESORTS

AAA Benefit:
Members save a minimum 5% off the best available rate.

SHERATON SPRINGFIELD MONARCH PLACE *Book great rates at AAA.com*

Phone: (413)781-1010

Hotel
$99-$229 All Year

Address: 1 Monarch Pl 01144 **Location:** I-91, 6 northbound; exit 7 southbound, just n; downtown. **Facility:** Smoke free premises. 325 units. 313 one-bedroom standard units, some with whirlpools. 12 one-bedroom suites, some with efficiencies and/or whirlpools. 12 stories, interior corridors. **Parking:** on-site (fee) and valet. **Terms:** cancellation fee imposed. **Amenities:** video games (fee), voice mail, irons, hair dryers. *Some: Fee:* high-speed Internet. **Dining:** 2 restaurants. **Pool(s):** heated indoor. **Leisure Activities:** sauna, whirlpools, steamrooms, racquetball court. *Fee:* massage, game room. **Guest Services:** valet and coin laundry, wireless Internet. **Business Services:** conference facilities, business center. **Free Special Amenities: local telephone calls and newspaper.**

Sheraton
HOTELS & RESORTS

AAA Benefit:
Members get up to 15% off, plus Starwood Preferred Guest® bonuses.

——— **WHERE TO DINE** ———

PAZZO RISTORANTE

Phone: 413/737-5800

Italian
$7-$29

In a great location across from the Basketball Hall of Fame, this contemporary Italian trattoria is decorated with Tuscan-style chandeliers, tapestries and elegant framed mirrors on warm yellow walls. Brick-oven pizzas, a multitude of homemade pastas, and Italian favorites including chicken francese and spaghetti and meatballs are offered. A children's menu also is available. Dressy casual. **Bar:** Full bar. **Reservations:** suggested. **Hours:** 11 am-10 pm, Fri & Sat-11 pm, Sun 1 pm-8 pm. Closed: 1/1, 11/25, 12/25. **Address:** 1000 W Columbus Ave 01105 **Location:** I-91, exit 4 northbound; exit 7 southbound, follow signs to Basketball Hall of Fame. **Parking:** on-site.

STUDENT PRINCE & FORT RESTAURANT

Phone: 413/788-6682

German
$7-$28

The popular restaurant prepares fresh and flavorful German and American fare, such as schnitzel and sauerkraut. Contributing to the casual and comfortable atmosphere is a good collection of steins along the upper perimeter of the dining room. Casual dress. **Bar:** Full bar. **Reservations:** suggested. **Hours:** 11 am-10 pm, Sun noon-8 pm. Closed: 12/25. **Address:** 8 Fort St 01103 **Location:** Between Main St and Columbus Ave. **Parking:** street.

STOCKBRIDGE —See also West Stockbridge.

THE INN AT STOCKBRIDGE

Phone: (413)298-3337

Historic Bed
& Breakfast
$195-$375 5/1-10/31
$160-$280 11/1-4/30

Address: 30 East St, US 7 01262 **Location:** 1.7 mi n. **Facility:** Cottages at this 1906 Georgian-style inn are spacious and have fireplaces; visitors enjoy candlelight breakfasts and nightly wine and cheese. Smoke free premises. 15 one-bedroom standard units, some with whirlpools. 2 stories (no elevator), interior/exterior corridors. *Bath:* combo or shower only. **Parking:** on-site. **Terms:** office hours 9 am-9 pm, 2-3 night minimum stay - seasonal and/or weekends, 14 day cancellation notice-fee imposed. **Amenities:** video library, CD players, irons, hair dryers. *Some:* DVD players. **Pool(s):** heated outdoor. **Leisure Activities:** exercise room. *Fee:* massage. **Guest Services:** wireless Internet. **Business Services:** PC. **Free Special Amenities: full breakfast and room upgrade (subject to availability with advance reservations).**

—— WHERE TO DINE ——

THE RED LION INN   Phone: 413/298-5545

American
$9-$32

In the center of the lovely little village is a pleasant country inn where contemporary New England dishes are prepared with thoughtful creativity and flavor. Jackets are appreciated in the dining room, but tavern seating is more casual. Entertainment. **Bar:** Full bar. **Reservations:** suggested. **Hours:** 7 am-10:30, noon-4 & 5:30-9 pm, Fri & Sat-10 pm, Sun 7 am-10:30, noon-4 & 5-8:30 pm; hours may vary off season. **Address:** 30 Main St 01262 **Location:** Center. **Parking:** on-site.

STONEHAM—See Boston p. 440.

STOUGHTON—See Boston p. 440.

STURBRIDGE pop. 2,047

COMFORT INN & SUITES COLONIAL   *Book great rates at AAA.com*   Phone: (508)347-3306

Hotel
$109-$269 5/1-10/31
$89-$189 11/1-4/30

Address: 215 Charlton Rd 01566 **Location:** I-90 (Massachusetts Tpke), exit 9, 0.5 mi e; I-84, exit 3A. **Facility:** Smoke free premises. 77 units. 73 one-bedroom standard units. 4 one-bedroom suites, some with whirlpools. 1-3 stories, interior/exterior corridors. *Bath:* combo or shower only. **Parking:** on-site. **Amenities:** dual phone lines, voice mail, irons, hair dryers. *Some:* high-speed Internet. **Pool(s):** outdoor, heated indoor. **Leisure Activities:** whirlpool, exercise room. **Guest Services:** valet and coin laundry, wireless Internet. **Business Services:** meeting rooms, PC. *(See color ad below)*

FREE expanded continental breakfast and high-speed Internet

DAYS INN   *Book at AAA.com*   Phone: 508/347-3391

Motel
Rates not provided

Address: 66-68 Haynes St (SR 15) 01566 **Location:** I-84, exit 2, 0.5 mi n, follow signs to SR 131, on I-84 service road. **Facility:** 32 units. 30 one- and 2 two-bedroom standard units. 1-2 stories (no elevator), interior/exterior corridors. *Bath:* combo or shower only. **Parking:** on-site. **Amenities:** irons, hair dryers. **Pool(s):** outdoor. **Guest Services:** wireless Internet.

ECONO LODGE   *Book at AAA.com*   Phone: (508)347-2324

Motel
$65-$140 5/1-10/31
$50-$75 11/1-4/30

Address: 682 Main St 01518 **Location:** I-84, exit 3B, 2.6 mi w on US 20. **Facility:** 52 units. 51 one-bedroom standard units. 1 one-bedroom suite. 1-2 stories (no elevator), exterior corridors. **Parking:** on-site. **Terms:** cancellation fee imposed. **Amenities:** irons, hair dryers. **Pool(s):** outdoor. **Leisure Activities:** playground. **Guest Services:** coin laundry, wireless Internet.

▼ See AAA listing above ▼

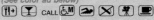

HAMPTON INN

Book great rates at AAA.com

Phone: 508/347-6466

AAA [SAVE]
▽▽▽▽
Hotel
Rates not provided

Address: 328 Main St 01566 **Location:** I-84, exit 3B, just w on US 20, then just s on SR 131. **Facility:** 84 one-bedroom standard units, some with whirlpools. 3 stories, interior corridors. *Bath:* combo or shower only. **Parking:** on-site. **Amenities:** high-speed Internet, dual phone lines, voice mail, irons, hair dryers. **Pool(s):** heated indoor. **Leisure Activities:** whirlpool, exercise room. **Guest Services:** valet and coin laundry, wireless Internet. **Business Services:** meeting rooms, PC. *(See color ad below)*

AAA Benefit: Members save up to 10% everyday!

PUBLICK HOUSE HISTORIC INN & COUNTRY LODGE   *Book at AAA.com*

Phone: (508)347-3313

▽▽ ▽▽
Hotel
$119-$299 5/1-10/31
$79-$179 11/1-4/30

Address: 295 Main St 01566 **Location:** I-90 (Massachusetts Tpke), exit 9; I-84, exit 3B, 0.5 mi s of jct US 20. Located on the Common. **Facility:** 103 units. 94 one-bedroom standard units. 8 one- and 1 two-bedroom suites. 2 stories (no elevator), interior/exterior corridors. *Bath:* combo or shower only. **Parking:** on-site. **Terms:** cancellation fee imposed. **Amenities:** irons. *Some:* hair dryers. **Dining:** restaurant, see separate listing. **Pool(s):** outdoor. **Leisure Activities:** playground. **Guest Services:** wireless Internet. **Business Services:** conference facilities.

QUALITY INN-STURBRIDGE   *Book at AAA.com*

Phone: 508/347-5141

▽▽ ▽▽
Hotel
Rates not provided

Address: 478 Main St 01566 **Location:** I-90, exit 9, 1.4 mi w on US 20; 1 mi w of jct US 20 and SR 131. **Facility:** 64 one-bedroom standard units, some with whirlpools. 3 stories, interior corridors. *Bath:* combo or shower only. **Parking:** on-site. **Amenities:** voice mail, irons, hair dryers. **Leisure Activities:** limited exercise equipment. **Guest Services:** coin laundry, wireless Internet. **Business Services:** meeting rooms, PC.

SCOTTISH INNS   *Book great rates at AAA.com*

Phone: (508)347-9514

AAA
▽▽▽
Motel
$59-$79 5/1-10/31
$50-$59 11/1-4/30

Address: 142 Main St 01566 **Location:** On SR 131, 1.5 mi s of jct US 20. **Facility:** 20 one-bedroom standard units. 1 story, exterior corridors. *Bath:* combo or shower only. **Parking:** on-site. **Terms:** cancellation fee imposed. **Amenities:** high-speed Internet. **Free Special Amenities:** continental breakfast and local telephone calls.

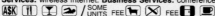
▼ See AAA listing above ▼

A friendly place. A great value.

Going to a new town? You will find a friend in Hampton. We value our strong partnership with AAA and are delighted to offer special rates* for AAA members.

we love having you here.®

Hampton Inn
328 Main St.
Sturbridge, MA 01566
508-347-6466 • www.hampton.com

AAA Approved
▽▽▽

The Hilton Family

*Subject to availability. Special rates for AAA members are not transferable. AAA card required at check-in.

©2009 Hilton Hotels Corporation

SUPER 8 *Book great rates at AAA.com*   Phone: (508)347-9000

 SAVE

Motel
$79-$169 5/1-10/23
$59-$89 10/24-4/30

Address: 358 Main St 01566 **Location:** I-90 (Massachusetts Tpke), exit 9; I-84, exit 3B on US 20. **Facility:** 56 one-bedroom standard units, some with whirlpools. 3 stories (no elevator), exterior corridors. **Parking:** on-site. **Terms:** cancellation fee imposed. **Amenities:** high-speed Internet, irons, hair dryers. **Pool(s):** outdoor. **Guest Services:** wireless Internet. **Business Services:** meeting rooms.

TRAVELODGE *Book great rates at AAA.com*   Phone: (508)347-1978

SAVE

Hotel
$80-$130 5/1-10/31
$60-$70 11/1-4/30

Address: 400 Haynes Rd (SR 15) 01566 **Location:** I-84, exit 1, 0.5 mi w. **Facility:** 78 one-bedroom standard units. 3 stories, interior corridors. *Bath:* combo or shower only. **Parking:** on-site. **Amenities:** irons, hair dryers. **Pool(s):** heated outdoor. **Leisure Activities:** exercise room. **Guest Services:** wireless Internet. **Business Services:** meeting rooms. **Free Special Amenities:** continental breakfast and high-speed Internet.

─── WHERE TO DINE ───

CEDAR STREET RESTAURANT   Phone: 508/347-5800

Continental
$21-$32

The leisurely paced experience is memorable. The menu centers on creative fare, including homemade desserts. Dressy casual. **Bar:** Full bar. **Reservations:** suggested. **Hours:** 5 pm-9:30 pm, Sat-10 pm; hours may vary off season. Closed: 9/6, 12/25. **Address:** 12 Cedar St 01566 **Location:** I-90, exit 9; I-84, exit 3B, 0.8 mi w on US 20, then just n. **Parking:** on-site.

EMPIRE VILLAGE

Chinese
$5-$14

Phone: 508/347-6588

On US 20, the restaurant prepares Chinese food with an American twist, many dishes of which line the daily lunch buffet. A large lounge with a large flat-screen TV is adjacent to the open dining room. Casual dress. **Bar:** Full bar. **Reservations:** accepted. **Hours:** 11 am-10 pm, Fri & Sat-11 pm. Closed: 11/25. **Address:** 446 Main St (US 20) 01566 **Location:** I-90 (Massachusetts Tpke), exit 9, 1 mi w on US 20; I-84, exit 3B. **Parking:** on-site.

OXHEAD TAVERN

American
$7-$25

Phone: 508/347-7393

"New England country casual" best describes the atmosphere in a dining room enhanced with local memorabilia. The staff is competent. Traditional comfort foods include fish and chips, chicken pot pie and other favorites. Casual dress. **Bar:** Full bar. **Hours:** 11 am-9 pm, Sun noon-9 pm. Closed: 12/25. **Address:** 366 Main St 01566 **Location:** I-90 (Massachusetts Tpke), exit 9, just w on US 20; I-84, exit 3B; in Sturbridge Host Hotel and Conference Center on Cedar Lake. **Parking:** on-site.

PICCADILLY PUB

American
$8-$15

Phone: 508/347-8189

Patrons at the informal, folksy restaurant range from families to neatly pressed professionals. Fish and chips, clam chowder in a bread bowl, burgers, sandwiches, and special dinners, such as Yankee pot roast and homemade meatloaf, are well-complemented by a selection of microbrews. Portions are ample, and the service is efficient. Casual dress. **Bar:** Full bar. **Reservations:** not accepted. **Hours:** 11 am-10 pm, Thurs-Sat to 11 pm, Sun noon-9 pm. Closed: 11/25, 12/25. **Address:** 362 Main St 01566 **Location:** I-90 (Massachusetts Tpke), exit 9, just w on US 20. **Parking:** on-site.

PUBLICK HOUSE HISTORIC INN

American
$8-$32

Phone: 508/347-3313

Diners can step back in time at the 1771 inn. The menu centers on innovative New England fare and old standbys such as New England clam chowder, baked onion soup with three cheeses, lobster pie and traditional turkey dinner. Dishes are supported by a notable American wine list. The bakery basket of breads and all desserts are made on the premises. Staff in period costume provide bright, cheery service in the inn, which was founded by Col. Ebenezer Crafats. Casual dress. **Bar:** Full bar. **Reservations:** suggested. **Hours:** 7:30 am-10 pm. **Address:** 277 Main St 01566 **Location:** I-90 (Massachusetts Tpke), exit 9; I-84, exit 3B, 0.5 mi s of jct US 20; in Publick House Historic Inn & Country Lodge. **Parking:** on-site. **Historic**

ROVEZZI'S RISTORANTE

Italian
$14-$24

Phone: 508/347-0100

The eatery features contemporary Italian cuisine. The upscale dining rooms have white tablecloths, candlelight and bold colors for a romantic atmosphere. Casual dress. **Bar:** Full bar. **Reservations:** suggested. **Hours:** 11:30 am-2 & 5-9 pm, Fri & Sat-10 pm, Sun 4 pm-8 pm. Closed: major holidays, 12/24; also Mon. **Address:** 2 School St 01566 **Location:** I-84, exit 3B, 2.5 mi w on US 20; at jct SR 148. **Parking:** on-site.

THAI PLACE RESTAURANT

Thai
$4-$14

Phone: 508/347-2999

The small, inviting restaurant prepares authentic Thai cuisine and continues the motif with Thai art. Locals love this place. Casual dress. **Reservations:** not accepted. **Hours:** 11:30 am-9 pm, Sat & Sun from noon. Closed: 11/25, 12/25. **Address:** 371 Main St 01566 **Location:** I-90 (Massachusetts Tpke), exit 9, 0.5 mi w on US 20. **Parking:** on-site.

SUDBURY—See Boston p. 440.

SWANSEA

HOLIDAY INN EXPRESS & SUITES   *Book great rates at AAA.com*

Hotel
$89-$129 All Year

Phone: (508)672-6857

Address: 1400 GAR Hwy 02777 **Location:** I-195, exit 3, 1 mi nw on US 6. **Facility:** 80 one-bedroom standard units. 3 stories, interior corridors. *Bath:* combo or shower only. **Parking:** on-site. **Amenities:** high-speed Internet, dual phone lines, voice mail, irons, hair dryers. **Pool(s):** heated indoor. **Leisure Activities:** whirlpool, exercise room. **Guest Services:** valet and coin laundry, wireless Internet. **Business Services:** meeting rooms, business center. **Free Special Amenities: expanded continental breakfast and high-speed Internet.**

-------- **WHERE TO DINE** --------

TICKLE'S TEA ROOM

American
$6-$12

Phone: 508/379-0717

Design elements of the small, country-style tea room include a fireplace mantel, French doors overlooking gardens, rustic hardwood floors and a corner hutch displaying china. Traditional homestyle country cuisine mixed with fresh seafood dishes is the main draw. The roasted turkey dinner, chicken pot pie and lobster roll are great selections. Casual dress. **Bar:** Beer & wine. **Hours:** 10:30 am-3 pm, Sun from 11 am. Closed major holidays. **Address:** 2219 GAR Hwy (US 6) 02777 **Location:** I-195, exit 2, just sw on SR 136, then just se. **Parking:** on-site.

VENUS DE MILO RESTAURANT

American
$6-$30

Phone: 508/678-3901

The lively restaurant has good food and a pleasant staff. Because this place offers primarily function space, gatherings are popular here. Casual dress. **Bar:** Full bar. **Reservations:** suggested. **Hours:** 11 am-2:30 & 4:30-8:30 pm, Fri-9:30 pm, Sat 5 pm-9:30 pm, Sun 11 am-8:30 pm. Closed: 12/25. **Address:** 75 GAR Hwy 02777 **Location:** I-195, exit 3, 1.8 mi e. **Parking:** on-site.

TAUNTON pop. 55,976

HOLIDAY INN TAUNTON/FOXBORO   *Book great rates at AAA.com*   Phone: (508)823-0430

Hotel
$109-$189 5/1-8/31
$109-$159 9/1-4/30

Address: 700 Myles Standish Blvd 02780 **Location:** I-495, exit 9, just sw. Located in Myles Standish Industrial Park. **Facility:** 155 units. 154 one-bedroom standard units. 1 one-bedroom suite. 7 stories, interior corridors. **Parking:** on-site. **Terms:** cancellation fee imposed. **Amenities:** video games (fee), dual phone lines, voice mail, irons, hair dryers. *Some:* high-speed Internet. **Pool(s):** heated indoor. **Leisure Activities:** saunas, whirlpool, steamrooms, racquetball court. **Guest Services:** valet and coin laundry, wireless Internet, tanning facilities. **Business Services:** meeting rooms, business center. **Free Special Amenities: local telephone calls and high-speed Internet.**

------ WHERE TO DINE ------

BENJAMIN'S RESTAURANT & FUNCTION FACILITY   Phone: 508/824-6313

American
$10-$30

A well-established, family dining tradition, the restaurant has a warm country decor with relaxed garden rooms and a library lounge with sweeping staircases. Diners are treated to ample portions of smoked Norwegian salmon, escargot Florentine, crab cake, homemade soup and chowder starters, not to mention entrees of chicken Marsala, scampi, duck a l'orange, veal piccata, grilled veal chop, steaks and prime rib. The homemade desserts are divine. The current owners acquired the property in 1966. Dressy casual. **Bar:** Full bar. **Reservations:** accepted. **Hours:** 11:30 am-9 pm, Fri-10 pm, Sat 4:30 pm-10 pm, Sun 10 am-9 pm; Sunday brunch. Closed: 12/24, 12/25. **Address:** 698 Bay St 02780 **Location:** I-495, exit 9, 2.8 mi se. **Parking:** on-site.

TEWKSBURY—See Boston p. 441.

TRURO—See Cape Cod p. 508.

TYNGSBORO—See Boston p. 441.

VINEYARD HAVEN—See Martha's Vineyard p. 534.

WAKEFIELD—See Boston p. 442.

WALTHAM—See Boston p. 442.

WATERTOWN—See Boston p. 445.

WEBSTER pop. 11,600

------ WHERE TO DINE ------

COLONIAL RESTAURANT   Phone: 508/943-4040

American
$6-$21

Pasta, beef and seafood dishes make up the restaurant's menu. Casual dress. **Bar:** Full bar. **Reservations:** suggested. **Hours:** 11:30 am-9 pm, Fri & Sat-10 pm, Sun-8:30 pm. Closed: 12/25. **Address:** 290 Thompson Rd 01570 **Location:** I-395, exit 1, 0.5 mi s. **Parking:** on-site.

THE LODGE   Phone: 508/949-0000

American
$6-$22

Simple-style dishes make up a menu of mostly comfort foods. Casual dress. **Bar:** Full bar. **Reservations:** accepted. **Hours:** 11:30 am-9:30 pm, Fri-10:30 pm, Sat-11 pm. Closed: 12/25; also Mon. **Address:** 148 Gore Rd 01570 **Location:** I-395, exit 2. **Parking:** on-site.

WELLESLEY—See Boston p. 445.

WELLFLEET—See Cape Cod p. 508.

WEST BARNSTABLE—See Cape Cod p. 509.

WESTBOROUGH pop. 3,983

COURTYARD BOSTON WESTBOROUGH   *Book great rates at AAA.com*   Phone: (508)836-4800

Hotel
$170-$208 All Year

Address: 3 Technology Dr 01581 **Location:** I-495, exit 23B, just w on SR 9, exit Computer and Research drs; 0.5 mi ne; within the Westborough Technology Park. **Facility:** Smoke free premises. 98 units. 95 one-bedroom standard units, some with whirlpools. 3 one-bedroom suites. 3 stories, interior corridors. *Bath:* combo or shower only. **Parking:** on-site. **Terms:** cancellation fee imposed. **Amenities:** voice mail, irons, hair dryers. **Pool(s):** heated indoor. **Leisure Activities:** whirlpool, exercise room. **Guest Services:** valet and coin laundry, wireless Internet. **Business Services:** meeting rooms, business center.

DOUBLETREE HOTEL BOSTON/WESTBOROUGH   *Book great rates at AAA.com*   Phone: (508)366-5511

Hotel
$99-$219 All Year

Address: 5400 Computer Dr 01581 **Location:** I-495, exit 23B, just w on SR 9, exit Computer and Research drs. **Facility:** 223 units. 222 one-bedroom standard units. 1 one-bedroom suite. 4 stories, interior corridors. *Bath:* combo or shower only. **Parking:** on-site. **Terms:** 1-7 night minimum stay, cancellation fee imposed. **Amenities:** high-speed Internet (fee), dual phone lines, voice mail, irons, hair dryers. **Pool(s):** heated indoor. **Leisure Activities:** whirlpool, exercise room. **Guest Services:** valet laundry, wireless Internet. **Business Services:** conference facilities, business center. *(See color ad below)*

AAA Benefit:

Members save 5% or more everyday!

EXTENDED STAY DELUXE-BOSTON-WESTBOROUGH   *Book at AAA.com*   Phone: (508)616-9213

Extended Stay Hotel
$70-$90 All Year

Address: 180 E Main St 01581 **Location:** I-495, exit 23B, 1.4 mi w, then just sw on SR 30. **Facility:** 86 units. 80 one-bedroom standard units with kitchens. 6 one-bedroom suites with kitchens. 3 stories, interior corridors. *Bath:* combo or shower only. **Parking:** on-site. **Terms:** office hours 7 am-11 pm, cancellation fee imposed. **Amenities:** DVD players, dual phone lines, voice mail, irons, hair dryers. **Leisure Activities:** exercise room. **Guest Services:** coin laundry, wireless Internet.

EXTENDED STAY DELUXE BOSTON-WESTBOROUGH-COMPUTER DR   *Book at AAA.com*   Phone: (508)366-6100

Extended Stay Hotel
$70-$90 All Year

Address: 1800 Computer Dr 01581 **Location:** I-495, exit 23B, just w; north side of SR 9. **Facility:** 112 one-bedroom standard units with efficiencies. 3 stories, interior corridors. *Bath:* combo or shower only. **Parking:** on-site. **Terms:** cancellation fee imposed. **Amenities:** DVD players, dual phone lines, voice mail, irons, hair dryers. **Pool(s):** heated outdoor. **Leisure Activities:** exercise room. **Guest Services:** coin laundry, wireless Internet.

RESIDENCE INN BY MARRIOTT BOSTON/WESTBOROUGH   *Book great rates at AAA.com*   Phone: (508)366-7700

Extended Stay Hotel
$152-$186 All Year

Address: 25 Connector Rd 01581 **Location:** I-495, exit 23B, just w on SR 9, exit Computer and Research drs, then 0.3 mi s. **Facility:** Smoke free premises. 109 units. 85 one- and 24 two-bedroom suites with efficiencies. 3 stories, interior/exterior corridors. *Bath:* combo or shower only. **Parking:** on-site. **Terms:** cancellation fee imposed. **Amenities:** high-speed Internet, dual phone lines, voice mail, irons, hair dryers. **Pool(s):** heated outdoor. **Leisure Activities:** exercise room, sports court. **Guest Services:** valet and coin laundry, wireless Internet. **Business Services:** meeting rooms, PC.

AAA Benefit:

Members save a minimum 5% off the best available rate.

▼ *See AAA listing above* ▼

WESTBOROUGH INN   *Book at AAA.com*   Phone: (508)836-1900

Bed & Breakfast
$114-$129 All Year

Address: 4 Boardman St 01581 **Location:** SR 9, 1.4 mi sw on SR 30, then just w on SR 135. Close to central square. **Facility:** Smoke free premises. 26 one-bedroom standard units. 3 stories (no elevator), interior corridors. *Bath:* combo or shower only. **Parking:** on-site. **Terms:** office hours 7 am-10 pm. **Amenities:** voice mail, irons, hair dryers. *Some:* DVD players. **Leisure Activities:** exercise room. **Guest Services:** valet and coin laundry, wireless Internet.

———— WHERE TO DINE ————

ARTURO'S RISTORANTE   Phone: 508/366-1881

Italian
$7-$30

In a strip shopping center just a quarter mile east of the town central square, the restaurant is marked by bright-yellow awnings. Dark woods, high ceilings and an open kitchen contribute to the casual feel. In addition to the expected Northern Italian dishes, guests can try grilled salmon, haddock roasted in a wood-fired oven and numerous salads and pizzas. Service is quick and friendly. Casual dress. **Bar:** Full bar. **Reservations:** suggested. **Hours:** 11:30 am-3 & 5-9 pm, Fri-10 pm, Sat 4:30 pm-10 pm. Closed: major holidays, 12/24; also Sun. **Address:** 54 E Main St 01581 **Location:** SR 9, 1.2 mi sw on SR 30. **Parking:** on-site.

THE CHATEAU ITALIAN FAMILY DINING   Phone: 508/366-5959

Italian
$8-$27

Since 1933, this family-owned local chain has been serving traditional Italian dishes, thin-crust pizzas, entree salads and calzones. The attractive dining room is accented with romantic chandeliers and walls covered with framed pictures from Italy circa 1930s. Toasted ravioli topped with delicious red meat sauce is a fitting lead-in to veal cutlet parmigiana and a topper of tiramisu. Casual dress. **Bar:** Full bar. **Reservations:** accepted. **Hours:** 11:30 am-10 pm, Fri-11 pm, Sat noon-11 pm, Sun noon-9 pm. Closed: 7/4, 11/25, 12/25. **Address:** 95 Turnpike Rd 01581 **Location:** I-495, exit 23B, 1.4 mi w. **Parking:** on-site.

HISA JAPANESE CUISINE & SUSHI BAR   Phone: 508/898-9262

Japanese
$8-$20

Just east of the central square at the end of a building with green awnings, the restaurant features tables surrounding a nine-seat circular bar in a room that might be called industrial minimalist. Guests might start with sashimi, ikura oroshi, salmon roe or gyoza before moving on to such chef specials as ginger chicken, orange shrimp or grilled salmon. Also available are tempura, sushi and sashimi dinners. Portions are generous. Casual dress. **Bar:** Beer & wine. **Hours:** 11:30 am-2:30 & 4:30-9 pm, Fri-10 pm, Sat 4:30 pm-10 pm, Sun 4:30 pm-9 pm. Closed major holidays. **Address:** 21 South St 01581 **Location:** Just e on SR 135; center. **Parking:** street. CALL 🅶M

PICCADILLY PUB   Phone: 508/366-9262

American
$8-$17

Patrons at the informal, folksy restaurant range from families to neatly pressed professionals. Fish and chips, clam chowder in a bread bowl, burgers, sandwiches, and special dinners, such as Yankee pot roast and homemade meatloaf, are well-complemented by a selection of microbrews. Portions are ample, and the service is efficient. Casual dress. **Bar:** Full bar. **Reservations:** not accepted. **Hours:** 11 am-10 pm, Thurs-Sat to 11 pm, Sun noon-9 pm. Closed: 11/25, 12/25. **Address:** 17 Connector Rd 01581 **Location:** I-495, exit 23B, just w; on south side of SR 9. **Parking:** on-site. CALL 🅶M

WEST BOYLSTON

CLASSIC SUITES & INNS   Phone: 508-835-4456

Hotel
$80-$90 5/1-10/1
$70-$80 10/2-4/30

Address: 181 W Boylston St 01583 **Location:** I-190, exit 4, 0.8 mi ne on SR 12. **Facility:** 48 one-bedroom standard units, some with efficiencies and/or whirlpools. 2 stories (no elevator), interior corridors. **Parking:** on-site. **Amenities:** voice mail, safes, hair dryers. *Some:* DVD players. **Guest Services:** coin laundry, wireless Internet. **Free Special Amenities: continental breakfast and newspaper.**

WEST BROOKFIELD pop. 1,610

———— WHERE TO DINE ————

SALEM CROSS INN   Phone: 508/867-8337

American
$7-$30

Dating back to 1705, this beautifully restored 600-acre country homestead affords pretty views of wooden fence-lined pastures. Inside, displays of exceptional Colonial American antique implements and furnishings line the walls of many rooms. One dining room is the original kitchen, with its large open-hearth fireplace. Meals of New England fare, served by the solid staff, often wrap up with one of the homemade desserts. Portions tend to be generous. Casual dress. **Bar:** Full bar. **Reservations:** suggested. **Hours:** 11:30 am-9 pm, Sat from 5 pm, Sun noon-8 pm; hours may vary in winter. Closed: 12/24, 12/25; also Mon. **Address:** 260 W Main St (SR 9) 01585 **Location:** 1.8 mi w. **Parking:** on-site. **Historic** CALL 🅶M

WEST DENNIS—See Cape Cod p. 509.

WEST FALMOUTH—See Cape Cod p. 509.

WESTFIELD pop. 40,072

ECONO LODGE & SUITES   *Book great rates at AAA.com*
Phone: (413)568-2821

(AAA) (SAVE)

Hotel
$69-$129 5/1-11/20
$64-$109 11/21-4/30

Address: 2 Southampton Rd 01085 **Location:** I-90, exit 3, at US 202 and SR 10. **Facility:** 57 one-bedroom standard units. 2 stories (no elevator), interior/exterior corridors. **Parking:** on-site. **Terms:** cancellation fee imposed. **Amenities:** voice mail, irons, hair dryers. **Pool(s):** outdoor. **Guest Services:** coin laundry, wireless Internet. **Business Services:** PC. **Free Special Amenities:** expanded continental breakfast.

ELM MOTEL   *Book great rates at AAA.com*
Phone: (413)562-9727

(AAA) (SAVE)

Motel
$60-$72 All Year

Address: 50 Russell Rd 01085 **Location:** I-90, exit 3, 1.2 mi s on US 202, 0.9 mi w on Franklin Rd. **Facility:** 17 one-bedroom standard units. Exterior corridors. **Parking:** on-site. **Guest Services:** wireless Internet. **Free Special Amenities:** local telephone calls and high-speed Internet.

HOLIDAY INN EXPRESS HOTEL & SUITES
WESTFIELD   *Book at AAA.com*
Phone: (413)564-6900

Hotel
$129-$199 5/1-10/31
$119-$179 11/1-4/30

Address: 39 Southampton Rd 01085 **Location:** I-90, exit 3. **Facility:** Smoke free premises. 86 units. 67 one-bedroom standard units. 19 one-bedroom suites. 3 stories, interior corridors. *Bath:* combo or shower only. **Parking:** on-site. **Amenities:** high-speed Internet, voice mail, irons, hair dryers. **Pool(s):** heated indoor. **Leisure Activities:** exercise room. **Guest Services:** valet and coin laundry, wireless Internet. **Business Services:** meeting rooms, business center.

WESTFORD—See Boston p. 445.

WESTMINSTER

WACHUSETT VILLAGE INN & CONFERENCE
CENTER   *Book great rates at AAA.com*
Phone: (978)874-2000

(AAA) (SAVE)

Hotel
$99-$169 All Year

Address: 9 Village Inn Rd 01473 **Location:** 0.7 mi w on Village Inn Rd; SR 2, exit 27 westbound, 0.3 mi e; exit 26 eastbound. **Facility:** 74 units. 58 one-bedroom standard units. 16 one-bedroom suites. 1-2 stories (no elevator), interior/exterior corridors. *Bath:* combo or shower only. **Parking:** on-site. **Terms:** cancellation fee imposed. **Amenities:** dual phone lines, voice mail, irons, hair dryers. **Dining:** 2 restaurants. **Pool(s):** outdoor. **Leisure Activities:** hiking trails, exercise room, volleyball. *Fee:* dog sledding, hayrides, massage. **Guest Services:** valet and coin laundry, wireless Internet. **Business Services:** meeting rooms, PC.

---- WHERE TO DINE ----

THE OLD MILL
Phone: 978/874-5941

(AAA)

American
$7-$23

Picturesque dining rooms make up the old mill, which overlooks a pond, falls and covered bridge. Specialties are corn fritter-pecan rolls and chicken vegetable pie. Appetizers, onion soup, sandwiches, shrimp linguine, prime rib and fish are served. Casual dress. **Bar:** Full bar. **Reservations:** suggested. **Hours:** 11:30 am-9 pm, Fri & Sat-9:45 pm, Sun 10 am-8 pm. Closed: 9/6, 12/25; also Mon. **Address:** 69 SR 2A E 01473 **Location:** SR 2, exit 25, 0.8 mi e. **Parking:** on-site.

WESTPORT

HAMPTON INN-FALL RIVER-WESTPORT   *Book great rates at AAA.com*
Phone: (508)675-8500

Hotel
$99-$169 All Year

Address: 53 Old Bedford Rd 02790 **Location:** I-195, exit 9 eastbound; exit 10 westbound, just s to US 6, then 1.3 mi w. **Facility:** 129 one-bedroom standard units. 4 stories, interior corridors. *Bath:* combo or shower only. **Parking:** on-site. **Terms:** 1-7 night minimum stay, cancellation fee imposed. **Amenities:** video games (fee), dual phone lines, voice mail, irons, hair dryers. **Pool(s):** heated indoor. **Leisure Activities:** whirlpool, lighted tennis court, exercise room, basketball. **Guest Services:** valet and coin laundry, wireless Internet. **Business Services:** meeting rooms, business center.

AAA Benefit:
Members save up to
10% everyday!

WESTPORT POINT

—— **WHERE TO DINE** ——

THE BACK EDDY Phone: 508/636-6500

Seafood
$19-$30

The bustling and surprisingly contemporary restaurant offers a refreshing change from the traditional preparations of fish and seafood offered by many regional eateries. Although the menu lists some simple and more traditional items, most choices appeal to a more creative palate. The raw bar satisfies fans of clams and oysters. Casual dress. **Bar:** Full bar. **Reservations:** not accepted. **Hours:** noon-10 pm, Mon & Tues from 5 pm; seasonal hours vary. Closed: 11/25, 12/25; also Mon & Tues 9/6-5/27. **Address:** 1 Bridge Rd 02790 **Location:** I-195, exit 10, 11.5 mi s, just w of SR 88, s of the drawbridge. **Parking:** on-site.

WEST SPRINGFIELD pop. 27,899—See also Springfield.

CANDLEWOOD SUITES *Book great rates at AAA.com* Phone: (413)739-1122

(AAA) (SAVE)
▼▼▼▼
Hotel
$108-$117 All Year

Address: 572 Riverdale St 01089 **Location:** I-91, exit 13B, 1.3 mi s. **Facility:** 71 units. 55 one-bedroom standard units with efficiencies. 16 one-bedroom suites with efficiencies. 5 stories, interior corridors. *Bath:* combo or shower only. **Parking:** on-site. **Terms:** cancellation fee imposed. **Amenities:** video library, DVD players, CD players, high-speed Internet, dual phone lines, voice mail, irons, hair dryers. **Pool(s):** heated indoor. **Leisure Activities:** whirlpool, grill, picnic area, exercise room. **Guest Services:** complimentary and valet laundry, wireless Internet. **Business Services:** PC. **Free Special Amenities: local telephone calls and high-speed Internet.**

CALL 🔤 🏊 ✕ 🎥 📶 📠 💻 / SOME UNITS FEE 🐕 ✕

CLARION HOTEL & CONFERENCE CENTER *Book great rates at AAA.com* Phone: (413)781-8750

(AAA) (SAVE)
▼▼▼ ▼
Hotel
$89-$299 5/1-10/31
$82-$299 11/1-4/30

Address: 1080 Riverdale St 01089 **Location:** I-91, exit 13B, just s. **Facility:** 260 one-bedroom standard units, some with whirlpools. 2-4 stories, interior corridors. *Bath:* combo or shower only. **Parking:** on-site. **Amenities:** video games (fee), voice mail, irons, hair dryers. **Pool(s):** heated indoor. **Leisure Activities:** saunas, whirlpool, exercise room. **Fee:** game room. **Guest Services:** valet and coin laundry, wireless Internet. **Business Services:** conference facilities, business center. **Free Special Amenities: full breakfast and high-speed Internet.**

🍽 🍸 🏊 ✕ 🎥 📶 💻 / SOME UNITS ✕ 📠

COMFORT INN & SUITES *Book great rates at AAA.com* Phone: (413)736-5000

(AAA) (SAVE)
▼▼ ▼
Hotel
$81-$108 All Year

Address: 106 Capital Dr 01089 **Location:** I-91, exit 13A, just n on US 5, then just e on Ashley Ave. **Facility:** 75 units. 53 one-bedroom standard units. 22 one-bedroom suites with kitchens, some with whirlpools. 2 stories (no elevator), interior corridors. *Bath:* combo or shower only. **Parking:** on-site. **Amenities:** voice mail, irons, hair dryers. **Pool(s):** heated indoor. **Leisure Activities:** sauna, whirlpool, exercise room. **Fee:** game room. **Guest Services:** valet and coin laundry, wireless Internet. **Free Special Amenities: continental breakfast and high-speed Internet.**

CALL 🔤 🏊 ✕ 🎥 📶 📠 💻 / SOME UNITS ✕

HAMPTON INN *Book great rates at AAA.com* Phone: (413)732-1300

▼▼▼▼
Hotel
$109-$179 All Year

Address: 1011 Riverdale St (US 5) 01089 **Location:** I-91, exit 13B, 0.3 mi s. Located in a commercial area. **Facility:** 125 one-bedroom standard units. 4 stories, interior corridors. *Bath:* combo or shower only. **Parking:** on-site. **Terms:** 1-7 night minimum stay. **Amenities:** high-speed Internet, voice mail, irons, hair dryers. **Pool(s):** outdoor. **Leisure Activities:** exercise room. **Guest Services:** valet and coin laundry, wireless Internet. **Business Services:** business center.

🍴 CALL 🔤 🏊 🎥 📶 📠 💻 / SOME UNITS 🐕 ✕

AAA Benefit:
Members save up to
10% everyday!

RESIDENCE INN WEST SPRINGFIELD *Book great rates at AAA.com* Phone: (413)732-9543

▼▼▼
Hotel
$150-$190 All Year

Address: 64 Border Way 01089 **Location:** I-91, exit 13A, on US 5. **Facility:** Smoke free premises. 88 units. 32 one-bedroom standard units with efficiencies. 41 one- and 15 two-bedroom suites, some with efficiencies or kitchens. 4 stories, interior corridors. *Bath:* combo or shower only. **Parking:** on-site. **Terms:** cancellation fee imposed. **Amenities:** voice mail, irons, hair dryers. **Pool(s):** heated indoor. **Leisure Activities:** whirlpool, exercise room, sports court. **Guest Services:** valet and coin laundry, wireless Internet. **Business Services:** meeting rooms, business center.

CALL 🔤 🏊 ✕ ✕ 🎥 📶 📠 💻 / SOME UNITS FEE 🐕

AAA Benefit:
Members save a
minimum 5% off the
best available rate.

—— **WHERE TO DINE** ——

CAL'S WOOD FIRED GRILL & BAR Phone: 413/827-9353

▼▼▼
American
$8-$23

Varied preparation styles are evident in fish and shellfish dishes made at the family-owned restaurant. Traditional favorites also are available for landlubbers. The casual atmosphere promotes relaxed dining, and the staff is friendly and helpful. Casual dress. **Bar:** Full bar. **Hours:** 11:30 am-10 pm, Sat from 3:30 pm, Sun noon-9 pm; Sunday brunch. Closed: 11/25. **Address:** 1068 Riverdale St 01089 **Location:** I-91, exit 13B, just s. **Parking:** on-site.

HOFBRAUHAUS RESTAURANT   *Menu on AAA.com*   Phone: 413/737-4905

German
$13-$44

Costumed servers go along with this restaurant's Bavarian décor, which includes antiques and a German stein collection. Pride of place on the menu goes to veal shank, Jaeger schnitzel and table-side-prepared Caesar salad and flambé. Lighter fare is available in the tavern. Casual dress. **Bar:** Full bar. **Reservations:** suggested. **Hours:** 11:30 am-2:30 & 4-9 pm, Fri & Sat 4 pm-10 pm. Closed: 12/25; also Mon. **Address:** 1105 Main St 01089 **Location:** Jct US 5 and SR 147, just w on SR 147, just nw. **Parking:** on-site.

MONTE CARLO   Phone: 413/734-6431

Italian
$7-$24

Since 1933, lovers of Italian food have converged at the family-owned-and-operated restaurant for nightly changing specials and an extensive selection of pasta, meat and seafood dishes, as well as desserts. Casual dress. **Bar:** Full bar. **Reservations:** accepted. **Hours:** 11:30 am-10 pm, Sat & Sun from 4 pm. Closed: 11/25, 12/25; also Mon. **Address:** 1020 Memorial Ave 01089 **Location:** I-91, exit 13B, 0.6 mi s on US 5, 2.3 mi sw on Elm and Union sts, then 0.7 mi w. **Parking:** on-site.

PICCADILLY PUB   Phone: 413/746-2444

American
$8-$15

Patrons at the informal, folksy restaurant range from families to neatly pressed professionals. Fish and chips, clam chowder in a bread bowl, burgers, sandwiches, and special dinners, such as Yankee pot roast and homemade meatloaf, are well-complemented by a selection of microbrews. Portions are ample, and the service is efficient. Casual dress. **Bar:** Full bar. **Reservations:** not accepted. **Hours:** 11 am-10 pm, Thurs-Sat to 11 pm, Sun noon-9 pm. Closed: 11/25, 12/25. **Address:** 1506 Riverdale St 01089 **Location:** I-91, exit 13A northbound, 0.9 mi n on US 5; exit 14 southbound, 1.1 mi s on US 5. **Parking:** on-site. CALL ⟨M⟩

WEST STOCKBRIDGE —See Stockbridge.

WEST TISBURY—See Martha's Vineyard p. 535.

WEST YARMOUTH—See Cape Cod p. 510.

WEYMOUTH—See Boston p. 446.

WILLIAMSTOWN pop. 4,754

THE 1896 HOUSE COUNTRY MOTELS   Phone: 413/458-1896

Motel
$62-$172 5/1-10/29
$62-$132 10/30-4/30

Address: 910 Cold Spring Rd (Rt 7) 01267 **Location:** 1.8 mi s on US 7 and SR 2. **Facility:** Smoke free premises. 30 units. 29 one-bedroom standard units, some with whirlpools. 1 one-bedroom suite with kitchen and whirlpool. 1-2 stories (no elevator), exterior corridors. *Bath:* combo or shower only. **Parking:** on-site. **Terms:** office hours 8 am-9:30 pm, 2 night minimum stay - seasonal and/or weekends, 7 day cancellation notice-fee imposed. **Amenities:** irons, hair dryers. **Pool(s):** heated outdoor. **Leisure Activities:** fishing. **Guest Services:** wireless Internet. **Business Services:** meeting rooms. ⟨≈⟩ ⟨✕⟩ ⟨▯⟩ / SOME UNITS FEE ⟨▮⟩ ⟨▦⟩

THE 1896 HOUSE LUXURY INN   Phone: 413/458-1896

Country Inn
$179-$289 5/1-10/29
$179-$269 10/30-4/30

Address: 910 Cold Spring Rd (Rt 7) 01267 **Location:** 1.8 mi s on US 7 and SR 2. **Facility:** Lavish rooms feature vaulted ceilings, king-size pillow-top beds, gas fireplaces and a two-person whirlpool tub. Smoke free premises. 6 one-bedroom standard units with whirlpools. 1 story, exterior corridors. **Parking:** on-site. **Terms:** office hours 8 am-9:30 pm, 2 night minimum stay - seasonal and/or weekends, 7 day cancellation notice-fee imposed. **Amenities:** DVD players, CD players, dual phone lines, irons, hair dryers. **Dining:** The '6 House Pub, see separate listing. **Pool(s):** heated outdoor. **Leisure Activities:** fishing, shuffleboard. *Fee:* massage. **Guest Services:** wireless Internet. **Business Services:** meeting rooms. **Free Special Amenities: full breakfast and high-speed Internet.**
⟨▯⟩ ⟨≈⟩ ⟨✕⟩ ⟨✕⟩ ⟨▮⟩ ⟨▯⟩ / SOME UNITS ⟨▦⟩

BERKSHIRE HILLS MOTEL   Phone: (413)458-3950

Motel
$69-$169 5/1-10/27
$59-$129 10/28-4/30

Address: 1146 Cold Spring Rd 01267 **Location:** 2.3 mi s on US 7 and SR 2. **Facility:** Smoke free premises. 21 one-bedroom standard units. 2 stories (no elevator), exterior corridors. *Bath:* combo or shower only. **Parking:** on-site. **Terms:** office hours 8 am-9:30 pm, 5 day cancellation notice. **Amenities:** *Some:* irons, hair dryers. **Pool(s):** heated outdoor. **Guest Services:** wireless Internet. ⟨ASK⟩ ⟨▯⟩ ⟨≈⟩ ⟨✕⟩

COZY CORNER MOTEL   Phone: 413/458-8006

Motel
$65-$135 5/1-10/31
$50-$95 11/1-4/30

Address: 284 Sand Springs Rd (US 7) 01267 **Location:** On US 7, 1.5 mi n of jct SR 2. **Facility:** Smoke free premises. 12 one-bedroom standard units. 2 stories (no elevator), exterior corridors. *Bath:* shower only. **Parking:** on-site. **Terms:** office hours 8 am-10 pm, 2 night minimum stay - seasonal and/or weekends, 10 day cancellation notice-fee imposed. **Amenities:** voice mail, hair dryers. **Guest Services:** wireless Internet. **Business Services:** meeting rooms.
⟨▯⟩ ⟨✕⟩ ⟨▣⟩ ⟨▮⟩ ⟨▦⟩ / SOME UNITS FEE ⟨▮⟩

MAPLE TERRACE MOTEL   Phone: 413/458-9677

Motel
$58-$158 All Year

Address: 555 Main St 01267 **Location:** On SR 2, 1 mi e of jct US 7. **Facility:** Smoke free premises. 17 units. 15 one-bedroom standard units. 2 one-bedroom suites with kitchens. 1-2 stories (no elevator), exterior corridors. *Bath:* combo or shower only. **Parking:** on-site. **Terms:** office hours 7:30 am-10 pm, 2 night minimum stay - seasonal and/or weekends, 10 day cancellation notice-fee imposed. **Amenities:** DVD players, hair dryers. **Pool(s):** heated outdoor. **Guest Services:** wireless Internet.
⟨≈⟩ ⟨✕⟩ ⟨▮⟩ / SOME UNITS FEE ⟨▮⟩ ⟨▦⟩

THE ORCHARDS HOTEL   *Book great rates at AAA.com*   Phone: (413)458-9611

Country Inn
$139-$379 5/1-10/30
$139-$229 10/31-4/30

Address: 222 Adams Rd 01267 **Location:** 1 mi e on SR 2. **Facility:** The Orchards, which has undergone a three-year renovation project, offers well-appointed rooms and a high standard of service. Smoke free premises. 49 units. 48 one-bedroom standard units, some with whirlpools. 1 one-bedroom suite with whirlpool. 3 stories, interior corridors. **Parking:** on-site. **Terms:** check-in 4 pm, 7 day cancellation notice-fee imposed. **Amenities:** CD players, voice mail, irons, hair dryers. *Some:* DVD players, safes. **Dining:** Gala Restaurant & Bar, see separate listing. **Pool(s):** outdoor. **Leisure Activities:** sauna, exercise room. *Fee:* massage. **Guest Services:** valet laundry, wireless Internet. **Business Services:** meeting rooms, business center. **Free Special Amenities:** room upgrade (subject to availability with advance reservations) and high-speed Internet.

THE VILLAGER MOTEL   *Book great rates at AAA.com*   Phone: (413)458-4046

Motel
$55-$159 All Year

Address: 953 Simonds Rd 01267 **Location:** On US 7, 1.7 mi n of jct SR 2. Located in a semi-rural area. **Facility:** 13 one-bedroom standard units. 1 story, exterior corridors. **Parking:** on-site. **Terms:** office hours 8 am-11 pm, 2-3 night minimum stay - seasonal, 14 day cancellation notice-fee imposed. **Free Special Amenities:** expanded continental breakfast and high-speed Internet.

THE WILLOWS MOTEL   *Book at AAA.com*   Phone: (413)458-5768

Motel
$79-$149 5/1-11/15
$59-$109 11/16-4/30

Address: 480 Main St 01267 **Location:** 0.8 mi e on SR 2. **Facility:** Smoke free premises. 17 units. 16 one-bedroom standard units. 1 cottage. 1-2 stories (no elevator), exterior corridors. *Bath:* combo or shower only. **Parking:** on-site. **Terms:** office hours 7:30 am-midnight, 2-3 night minimum stay - seasonal and/or weekends, 7 day cancellation notice-fee imposed. **Amenities:** hair dryers. *Some:* DVD players, irons. **Pool(s):** heated outdoor. **Guest Services:** wireless Internet.

—— WHERE TO DINE ——

THE '6 HOUSE PUB   Phone: 413/458-1896

American
$6-$12

In a renovated old barn, this charming restaurant features tasteful early Americana and country decor. Guests are encouraged to mix and match their choices of soup, salad, pasta, sandwiches and burgers. The bar is lively, and the desserts are divine. Casual dress. **Bar:** Full bar. **Reservations:** not accepted. **Hours:** 5 pm-9 pm; closing hours may vary. **Address:** 910 Cold Spring Rd (Rt 7) 01267 **Location:** 1.8 mi s on US 7 and SR 2; in The 1896 House Luxury Inn. **Parking:** on-site.

CHOPSTICKS   Phone: 413/458-5750

Asian
$6-$27

Japanese, Chinese and Korean cuisine share space on the lively restaurant's menu. An extensive list of rolls and sushi are offered alongside bento lunch boxes, Korean barbecue and spicy noodles, not to mention extravagant cocktail presentations and all the favorite Chinese dishes. Casual dress. **Bar:** Full bar. **Hours:** 10:30 am-10:30 pm, Fri & Sat-11 pm, Sun 11 am-10:30 pm. Closed major holidays. **Address:** 412 Main St 01267 **Location:** 1 mi e on SR 2. **Parking:** on-site.

COZY CORNER RESTAURANT   Phone: 413/458-3854

American
$5-$15

Featuring a casual family atmosphere, friendly service and reasonable prices, the popular eatery serves a nice selection of homemade items, burgers, deli sandwiches, pizza, soups and salads. A cup of chowder is a good lead-in to the cheeseburger plate. Casual dress. **Bar:** Full bar. **Reservations:** accepted, except Fri. **Hours:** 11 am-9 pm, Sun from noon; Fri & Sat-10 pm in summer. Closed major holidays. **Address:** 850 Simonds Rd 01267 **Location:** 1.5 mi n on US 7. **Parking:** on-site.

GALA RESTAURANT & BAR   Phone: 413/458-9611

Continental
$8-$30

New England influences flavor the Continental cuisine presented in this finely appointed English dining room, which overlooks a courtyard garden. Beautiful food designs and tasteful creations contribute to make this experience a memorable one. Terrace seating is offered, weather permitting. Dressy casual. **Bar:** Full bar. **Reservations:** suggested. **Hours:** 7-10:15 am, 11:30-2 & 5:30-10:15 pm, Sun 7 am-2 & 5:30-9 pm. Closed major holidays. **Address:** 222 Adams Rd 01267 **Location:** 1 mi e on SR 2; in The Orchards Hotel. **Parking:** on-site. CALL

HOBSON'S CHOICE   Phone: 413/458-9101

Steak
$8-$25

Guests can settle in for a casual dining experience, complete with a rustic country decor, in the historic home. Blackened steak and seafood have made the restaurant a popular stop on the dining circuit, as have the pasta and various vegetarian specialties of the house. Dressy casual. **Bar:** Full bar. **Reservations:** suggested. **Hours:** 5 pm-9:30 pm. Closed: 1/1, 11/25, 12/25; also Super Bowl Sun. **Address:** 159 Water St 01267 **Location:** SR 43, 0.3 mi s of jct SR 2. **Parking:** on-site.

THE MOONLIGHT DINER AND GRILLE   Phone: 413/458-3305

American
$5-$15

In addition to serving breakfast all day, the '50s-style diner offers lunch and dinner choices, including hamburgers, sandwiches and milk shakes. Casual dress. **Bar:** Beer & wine. **Reservations:** not accepted. **Hours:** 7 am-10 pm, Fri & Sat-11 pm. Closed major holidays. **Address:** 408 Main St 01267 **Location:** Jct US 7, 1 mi e on SR 2. **Parking:** on-site.

SPICE ROOT MODERN INDIAN CUISINE Phone: 413/458-5200

Indian
$10-$22

On the main shopping road in a college town, this restaurant offers a comfortable and contemporary atmosphere. Terra cotta-colored walls are accented with Indian artwork and tapestries. Tandoori specials include shrimp malai kebabs (marinated shrimp with saffron) and chicken tikka (marinated in ginger and garlic then grilled). Authentic breads include naan and parantha. Guests may order off the menu or enjoy the popular lunch buffet. Casual dress. **Bar:** Full bar. **Reservations:** accepted. **Hours:** 11:30 am-2:30 & 5-10 pm. Closed: 11/25; also Mon for lunch. **Address:** 23 Spring St 01267 **Location:** Jct US 7, 0.4 mi e on SR 2, then just s. **Parking:** street.

THAI GARDEN Phone: 413/458-0004

Thai
$7-$17

Decorated with many pieces of Thai artwork, the small restaurant whips up many rice, noodle and vegetable dishes. Casual dress. **Bar:** Beer & wine. **Reservations:** accepted. **Hours:** 11:30 am-3 & 5-10 pm, Fri & Sat-10:30 pm. Closed: 11/25, 12/25. **Address:** 27 Spring St 01267 **Location:** 0.3 mi e on SR 2, just s. **Parking:** street.

THE WATER STREET GRILL Phone: 413/458-2175

American
$6-$18

The restaurant's menu is filled with comfort foods such as The Cattle Car, an abundant roast beef, cheddar and mushroom sandwich. The beer batter combo platter of mushrooms, zucchini and onions is another delicious choice. Casual dress. **Bar:** Full bar. **Reservations:** suggested. **Hours:** 11:30 am-11 pm. Closed: 4/4, 11/25, 12/25. **Address:** 123 Water St 01267 **Location:** On SR 43, just s of jct SR 2. **Parking:** on-site.

WILLIAMS INN Phone: 413/458-9371

American
$8-$27

Breakfast, lunch and dinner are served daily. Yankee pot roast, Shaker chicken with apple rings, and lighter fare of soups, salads and sandwiches are just a brief sampling of the menu options. Dressy casual. **Bar:** Full bar. **Reservations:** suggested. **Hours:** 7 am-2 & 5:30-9 pm. **Address:** 1090 Main St 01267 **Location:** On The Green. **Parking:** on-site.

WILMINGTON—See Boston p. 446.

WINTHROP—See Boston p. 446.

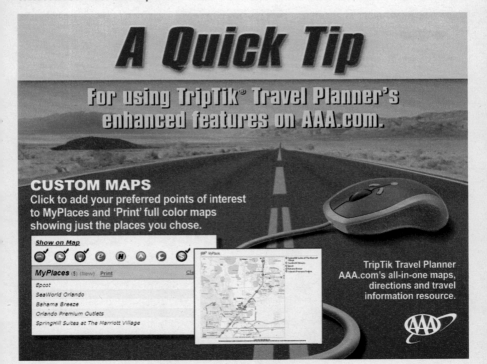
Create complete trip routings and custom place maps
with the TripTik® Travel Planner on AAA.com

WOBURN—See Boston p. 446.

WOODS HOLE—See Cape Cod p. 513.

WORCESTER pop. 172,648

BEECHWOOD HOTEL   *Book great rates at AAA.com*   Phone: (508)754-5789

Hotel
$159-$390 All Year

Address: 363 Plantation St 01605 **Location:** I-290, exit 22 westbound, 0.5 mi w on Lincoln St, then 1.5 mi s; exit 21 eastbound, 1.3 mi s. **Facility:** Smoke free premises. 73 units. 72 one-bedroom standard units. 1 one-bedroom suite. 2-5 stories, interior corridors. *Bath:* combo or shower only. **Parking:** on-site. **Terms:** cancellation fee imposed. **Amenities:** high-speed Internet, dual phone lines, voice mail, irons, hair dryers. **Dining:** Harlequin Restaurant, see separate listing. **Leisure Activities:** jogging, exercise room. *Fee:* golf privileges. **Guest Services:** valet laundry, area transportation-within 10 mi, wireless Internet. **Business Services:** meeting rooms, business center. *(See color ad below)*

FREE expanded continental breakfast and high-speed Internet

COURTYARD BY MARRIOTT WORCESTER   *Book great rates at AAA.com*   Phone: (508)363-0300

Hotel
$143-$175 All Year

Address: 72 Grove St 01605 **Location:** I-290, exit 18 westbound; exit 17 eastbound, just n of SR 9 via Salisbury St. **Facility:** Smoke free premises. 130 units. 126 one-bedroom standard units. 4 one-bedroom suites. 4 stories, interior corridors. *Bath:* combo or shower only. **Parking:** on-site. **Terms:** cancellation fee imposed. **Amenities:** high-speed Internet, dual phone lines, voice mail, irons, hair dryers. **Pool(s):** heated indoor. **Leisure Activities:** whirlpool, exercise room. **Guest Services:** valet and coin laundry, wireless Internet. **Business Services:** meeting rooms, business center.

AAA Benefit:
Members save a minimum 5% off the best available rate.

▼ *See AAA listing above* ▼

ALL THE COMFORTS OF HOME

Your home away from home, the Beechwood Hotel's old world charm and superior hospitality will help you rest easy. The Beechwood Hotel is the premier location in Central Mass.

 BEECHWOOD HOTEL
363 Plantation Street, Worcester MA
800.344.2589 | beechwoodhotel.com

CROWNE PLAZA HOTEL   *Book great rates at AAA.com*

(AAA) SAVE

Hotel
$119-$199 All Year

Phone: (508)791-1600

Address: 10 Lincoln Square 01608 **Location:** I-290, exit 17 eastbound; exit 18 westbound, 0.3 mi s. **Facility:** Smoke free premises. 243 units. 236 one-bedroom standard units. 7 one-bedroom suites. 9 stories, interior corridors. *Bath:* combo or shower only. **Parking:** on-site (fee) and valet. **Terms:** check-in 4 pm, cancellation fee imposed. **Amenities:** CD players, dual phone lines, voice mail, irons, hair dryers. **Pool(s):** heated indoor/outdoor. **Leisure Activities:** whirlpool, exercise room. **Guest Services:** valet and coin laundry, area transportation-within 10 mi, wireless Internet. **Business Services:** conference facilities, business center. **Free Special Amenities: newspaper and high-speed Internet.**

HAMPTON INN-WORCESTER   *Book great rates at AAA.com*

Hotel
$109-$149 All Year

Phone: (508)757-0400

Address: 110 Summer St 01608 **Location:** I-290, exit 16, just n. **Facility:** 97 one-bedroom standard units. 5 stories, interior corridors. *Bath:* combo or shower only. **Parking:** on-site. **Terms:** 1-7 night minimum stay, cancellation fee imposed. **Amenities:** video games (fee), dual phone lines, voice mail, irons, hair dryers. **Leisure Activities:** exercise room. **Guest Services:** valet laundry, wireless Internet. **Business Services:** meeting rooms, business center.

AAA Benefit:
Members save up to 10% everyday!

HILTON GARDEN INN WORCESTER   *Book great rates at AAA.com*

Hotel
$109-$239 All Year

Phone: (508)753-5700

Address: 35 Major Taylor Blvd 01608 **Location:** I-290, exit 16, just s. Located across from the DCU center. **Facility:** 199 units. 187 one-bedroom standard units. 12 one-bedroom suites. 8 stories, interior corridors. *Bath:* combo or shower only. **Parking:** on-site (fee) and valet. **Terms:** check-in 4 pm, 1-7 night minimum stay, cancellation fee imposed. **Amenities:** voice mail, irons, hair dryers. **Pool(s):** heated indoor. **Leisure Activities:** whirlpool, exercise room. **Guest Services:** valet and coin laundry, area transportation, wireless Internet. **Business Services:** meeting rooms, business center.

Hilton Garden Inn

AAA Benefit:
Members save 5% or more everyday!

RESIDENCE INN BY MARRIOTT WORCESTER   *Book great rates at AAA.com*

Extended Stay
Hotel
$164-$179 All Year

Phone: (508)753-6300

Address: 503 Plantation St 01605 **Location:** I-290, exit 21, 0.5 mi sw. **Facility:** Smoke free premises. 122 units. 56 one-bedroom standard units with kitchens. 54 one- and 12 two-bedroom suites with kitchens. 5 stories, interior corridors. *Bath:* combo or shower only. **Parking:** on-site. **Terms:** cancellation fee imposed. **Amenities:** high-speed Internet, dual phone lines, voice mail, irons, hair dryers. **Pool(s):** heated indoor. **Leisure Activities:** exercise room, billiards, sports court. **Guest Services:** valet and coin laundry, area transportation, wireless Internet. **Business Services:** meeting rooms, business center.

Residence Inn Marriott

AAA Benefit:
Members save a minimum 5% off the best available rate.

------ **WHERE TO DINE** ------

HARLEQUIN RESTAURANT

New American
$10-$32

Phone: 508/754-5789

A colorful carousel horse greets guests at the entrance to the restaurant, where tables are dressed with fine white linen, decorative napkin folds and candles. The strong menu lists starters such as butternut-squash soup with crabmeat and crème fraîche, and entrées along the lines of Atlantic farm-raised salmon steak over Mediterranean tomato couscous with caper pesto and tomato emulsion served on asparagus. Dressy casual. **Bar:** Full bar. **Reservations:** accepted. **Hours:** 6:30 am-2:30 & 5:30-10 pm, Sat from 7:30 am, Sun 7:30 am-2 & 5-9 pm; Sunday brunch. **Address:** 363 Plantation St 01605 **Location:** I-290, exit 22 westbound, 0.5 mi w on Lincoln St, then 1.5 mi s; exit 21 eastbound, 1.3 mi s; in Beechwood Hotel. **Parking:** on-site.

MAXWELL-SILVERMAN'S TOOLHOUSE

American
$7-$36

Phone: 508/755-1200

The restaurant occupies the space of the 1879 five-story building formerly occupied by the screw machine department of the Henry L. Hanson Company, a maker of taps and dies. The interior decor is highlighted by restored machinery, parts of a belt drive system and a 1905 Steward boiler set in one wall. Chicken, veal, beef and seafood follow a wide selection of starters and pasta dishes. Specialty breads, a raw bar and salads round out the menu. A sandwich and salad bar is available at lunch. Dressy casual. **Bar:** Full bar. **Reservations:** suggested. **Hours:** 11 am-10 pm, Fri & Sat-11 pm, Sun 10 am-2 & 4-10 pm; Sunday brunch. Closed: 5/31, 12/25. **Address:** 25 Union St 01608 **Location:** At Lincoln Square. **Parking:** on-site.

NANCY CHANG

Asian
$6-$15

Phone: 508/752-8899

Patrons will find a welcoming, casual and rustic atmosphere in which they can enjoy an extensive menu featuring a wide range of fresh and healthful Asian selections. Specialties include Thai, Malaysian and Polynesian dishes. Casual dress. **Bar:** Full bar. **Reservations:** accepted. **Hours:** 11:30 am-10 pm, Fri-11 pm, Sat noon-11 pm, Sun noon-10 pm. Closed: 11/25. **Address:** 372 Chandler St 01602 **Location:** Jct Park Ave/SR 9/12, 0.4 mi nw on SR 122. **Parking:** on-site.

O'CONNOR'S RESTAURANT & BAR

Menu on AAA.com

Phone: 508/853-0789

Irish
$8-$21

More than 5,000 pieces of Irish and pub memorabilia cover the walls of the popular dining spot. Traditional Irish dishes, in addition to American and European preparations, are served in ample portions. Casual dress. **Bar:** Full bar. **Hours:** 11:30 am-10 pm, Mon-9 pm. **Closed:** 7/4, 11/25, 12/25; also Sun. **Address:** 1160 W Boylston St 01606 **Location:** I-190, exit 4, just s on SR 12. **Parking:** on-site.

ONE ELEVEN CHOP HOUSE

Phone: 508/799-4111

Steak
$19-$40

Beef lovers relish the perfectly grilled steaks and chops that are house specialties here. The menu also lists a range of seafood entrees, including lobster and crab legs. Side dishes, such as broccoli with hollandaise sauce, are ample in size. The dining room, with its red leather chairs and view of the open kitchen, is upscale, but the noise level can be distracting. Dressy casual. **Bar:** Full bar. **Reservations:** suggested. **Hours:** 4 pm-10 pm, Fri & Sat-11 pm, Sun-9:30 pm. **Closed:** 7/4, 11/25, 12/24, 12/25; also Super Bowl Sun. **Address:** 111 Shrewsbury St 01604 **Location:** Jct Hill St. **Parking:** on-site. CALL &M

PICCADILLY PUB

Phone: 508/755-1808

American
$8-$15

Patrons at the informal, folksy restaurant range from families to neatly pressed professionals. Fish and chips, clam chowder in a bread bowl, burgers, sandwiches, and special dinners, such as Yankee pot roast and homemade meatloaf, are well-complemented by a selection of microbrews. Portions are ample, and the service is efficient. Casual dress. **Bar:** Full bar. **Reservations:** not accepted. **Hours:** 11 am-10 pm, Thurs-Sat to 11 pm, Sun noon-9 pm. **Closed:** 11/25, 12/25. **Address:** 480 Shrewsbury St 01604 **Location:** Jct US 20; in Piccadilly Plaza. **Parking:** on-site.

THE SOLE PROPRIETOR

Phone: 508/798-3474

Seafood
$7-$30

Representative of traditional New England fare, the menu includes a wide selection of fresh fish and shellfish in addition to several landlubber favorites. The excellent salmon entrée and fish chowder are served in generous portions. The newly renovated, nautical-themed dining room is attractive, with blue-and-white stained-glass chandeliers and a nautical theme. Friendly servers further enhance a pleasurable dining experience. Casual dress. **Bar:** Full bar. **Reservations:** accepted. **Hours:** 11:30 am-10 pm, Fri & Sat-11 pm, Sun 4 pm-9:30 pm; hours vary in summer. **Closed:** 11/25, 12/24, 12/25; also Super Bowl Sun. **Address:** 118 Highland St 01609 **Location:** I-290, exit 17, 0.7 mi w; downtown. **Parking:** on-site.

CALL &M

VIVA BENE ITALIAN RISTORANTE

Phone: 508/799-9999

Italian
$6-$25

Across from the DCU Center, the contemporary restaurant prepares a wide choice of Italian and some American cuisine. A broad wine and drink selection complements the food. The large bar is conducive to waiting or just hanging out. Casual dress. **Bar:** Full bar. **Reservations:** accepted. **Hours:** 10 am-9 pm, Fri 11 am-10 pm, Sat noon-10 pm, Sun 4 pm-8 pm, Mon 10 am-2 pm. **Closed:** 11/25, 12/25. **Address:** 144 Commercial St 01608 **Location:** Jct Commercial St and Worcester Center Blvd. **Parking:** on-site and street.

WRENTHAM—See Boston p. 449.

YARMOUTH PORT—See Cape Cod p. 513.

Rhode Island

Old Stone Mill, Newport
© Dean Fox / SuperStock

BARRINGTON pop. 16,819

—— WHERE TO DINE ——

CHIAZZA TRATTORIA & BAR   Phone: 401-247-0303

Italian
$7-$30

In a shopping plaza in historic downtown, the restaurant prepares excellent pasta, seafood, steak and pizza cooked in a wood-fired brick oven. Lending to the modern decor are marble-topped tables, mosaic-tiled columns and brightly colored accent walls. Dressy casual. **Bar:** Full bar. **Reservations:** suggested. **Hours:** 11:30 am-10 pm, Fri-11 pm, Sat noon-10 pm, Sun 4 pm-9 pm. Closed: 7/4, 11/25, 12/25. **Address:** 308 County Rd 02806 **Location:** I-195, exit 7 eastbound, 6 mi se on SR 114; exit 2 westbound, 3 mi s on SR 136, 0.5 mi sw on Market St, then 1.8 mi nw on SR 114. **Parking:** on-site.

NEWPORT CREAMERY   Phone: 401-245-2212

American
$6-$8

A New England tradition since the 1940s, the creamery is known for its "awful, awful" milk shakes and homemade ice cream. Families will be comfortable visiting for a good meal, friendly service and a delicious sundae for dessert. Casual dress. **Hours:** 7 am-9 pm, Fri & Sat-10 pm; hours vary off season. Closed: 11/25, 12/25. **Address:** 296 County Rd 02806 **Location:** I-195, exit 7 eastbound, 6 mi se on SR 114; exit 2 westbound, 3 mi s on SR 136, 0.5 mi sw on Market St, then 1.8 mi nw on SR 114. **Parking:** on-site.

CALL

TYLER POINT GRILLE   Phone: 401-247-0017

New Italian
$13-$26

The charming restaurant's location in the middle of a boat yard adds to its nautical appeal. The open-air kitchen turns out contemporary Italian and seafood dishes, including such seasonal entrees as capellini with lobster, pea pods and sun-dried tomatoes in lemon-butter sauce and double-cut pork chops with fresh sage and Madeira wine sauce. Young ones can order from the children's menu. Dressy casual. **Bar:** Full bar. **Reservations:** suggested. **Hours:** 4:30 pm-10 pm, Fri & Sat-11 pm, Sun-9:30 pm. Closed major holidays. **Address:** 32 Barton Ave 02806 **Location:** I-195, exit 7, 7.1 mi se on SR 114, then just s. **Parking:** on-site.

BLOCK ISLAND

—— *The following lodgings were either not evaluated or did not* —— *meet AAA rating requirements but are listed for your information only.*

THE 1661 INN   Phone: 401/466-2421

[fyi]   Not evaluated. **Address:** 1 Spring St 02807. Facilities, services, and decor characterize a mid-scale property.

THE ATLANTIC INN   Phone: 401/466-5883

[fyi]   Not evaluated. **Address:** High St 02807. Facilities, services, and decor characterize a mid-scale property.

THE BLUE DORY INN   Phone: 401/466-5891

[fyi]   Not evaluated. **Address:** Dodge St 02807. Facilities, services, and decor characterize a mid-scale property.

THE HOTEL MANISSES   Phone: 401/466-2421

[fyi]   Not evaluated. **Address:** 1 Spring St 02807. Facilities, services, and decor characterize a mid-scale property.

PAYNES HARBOR VIEW INN   Phone: 401/466-5758

[fyi]   Not evaluated. **Address:** 111 Beach Ave 02807. Facilities, services, and decor characterize an economy property.

SPRING HOUSE HOTEL   Phone: 401/466-5844

[fyi]   Not evaluated. **Address:** Spring St 02807. Facilities, services, and decor characterize a mid-scale property.

—— WHERE TO DINE ——

BALLARD'S   Phone: 401/466-2231

Seafood
$10-$27

This famous restaurant is known for their own gorgeous private sand beach and live entertainment every day in season as well as in the piano bar in the evenings. Guests can order one of the many frozen drinks right on the beach. The food is served on disposable plates but the quality is top notch especially the fresh seafood including lobster, clams, shrimp and scallops. Casual dress. **Bar:** Full bar. **Reservations:** not accepted. **Hours:** Open 5/13-10/1; 10 am-10 pm. Closed major holidays. **Address:** 42 Water St 02807 **Location:** Just e of ferry dock. **Parking:** on-site.

CHEESECAKE CASTLE & CAFE   Phone: 401/465-4740

Desserts
$6-$7

This full-service coffee bar is the place in town for a great cup of joe, latte or Italian soda. Classic New York-style cheesecakes are made from scratch and garnished with real whipped cream. Also tempting are distinctive frozen cheesecake pops and other desserts. Seating on the back patio overlooks Crescent Beach. The minimum credit card purchase is $15. Casual dress. **Reservations:** not accepted. **Hours:** 6:30 am-9 pm. **Address:** Dodge St 02807 **Location:** From ferry dock, just nw on Water St, then just w. **Parking:** street.

ELI'S RESTAURANT
Phone: 401/466-5230

New American
$19-$30

Diners in the mood for something other than clam cakes and chowder can come here for contemporary bistro fare made from fresh ingredients. A meal might start with arugula and warm goat cheese salad with dried cranberries, roasted red peppers and balsamic vinaigrette; progress to a pasta dish or Asian-inspired fried basmati rice with scallops and shrimp over sugar snap peas, carrots, celery and onions with sweet chili-peanut sauce; and end with a delicious homemade dessert. The wine list is vast. Casual dress. **Bar:** Full bar. **Reservations:** not accepted. **Hours:** Open 5/1-11/21 & 3/1-4/30; 5 pm-10 pm; hours vary off season. Closed major holidays; also Mon-Wed in fall & spring. **Address:** Chapel St 02807 **Location:** Between Water St and Weldons Way; center. **Parking:** street.

FINN'S SEAFOOD RESTAURANT
Phone: 401/466-2473

Seafood
$9-$29

You won't be disappointed in the portion sizes at Finn's, the lobster alone can weigh in at three pounds. While your meal is being prepared, sit back and relax in the informal dining room overlooking the harbor. Outdoor patio seating is also available in season. Casual dress. **Bar:** Full bar. **Reservations:** not accepted. **Hours:** Open 5/23-10/31; 11:30 am-9 pm, Fri & Sat-10 pm; hours may vary off season. **Address:** 212 Water St 02807 **Location:** At Old Harbor; opposite ferry docks. **Parking:** on-site.

MOHEGAN CAFE
Phone: 401/466-5911

Seafood
$8-$22

A seaside motif mixes with historical black-and-white pictures from around the island. Window seats provide a view of the water and Main Street. This place is known for its good seafood, especially calamari heralded by some as the best on the island. Fresh cod is used in the fish and chips, which features a light batter. There is also a long list of sandwiches available for lunch. The staff employs a casual yet friendly service style. Casual dress. **Bar:** Full bar. **Reservations:** not accepted. **Hours:** Open 5/1-10/25 & 3/17-4/30; 11:30 am-9 pm. Closed major holidays. **Address:** Water St 02807 **Location:** Between Chapel St and Fountain Square; center. **Parking:** street.

BRISTOL pop. 22,469   (See map and index starting on p. 588)

BRADFORD-DIMOND-NORRIS HOUSE BED & BREAKFAST
Phone: (401)253-6338   35

Historic Bed & Breakfast
$150-$250 All Year

Address: 474 Hope St 02809 **Location:** On SR 114; center. **Facility:** Four-poster or canopy beds are featured in tasteful rooms at this restored, Federal-style B&B with Victorian accents, antiques and reproductions. Smoke free premises. 4 units. 2 one- and 2 two-bedroom standard units. 2 stories (no elevator), interior corridors. *Bath:* shower only. **Parking:** on-site. **Terms:** 2 night minimum stay - weekends, age restrictions may apply, 3 day cancellation notice-fee imposed. **Amenities:** hair dryers. **Guest Services:** wireless Internet.

BRISTOL HARBOR INN   *Book at AAA.com*
Phone: (401)254-1444   36

Hotel
$135-$255 5/1-11/1
$95-$145 11/2-4/30

Address: 259 Thames St 02809 **Location:** Just w of SR 114; between State and Bradford sts; center. **Facility:** Smoke free premises. 40 units. 28 one-bedroom standard units. 12 one-bedroom suites. 3 stories, interior corridors. **Parking:** on-site. **Terms:** 2 night minimum stay - seasonal and/or weekends, 3 day cancellation notice. **Amenities:** high-speed Internet, voice mail, irons, hair dryers. **Dining:** DeWolf Tavern, see separate listing. **Leisure Activities:** spa. *Fee:* marina. **Guest Services:** valet laundry, wireless Internet. **Business Services:** meeting rooms, business center.

POINT PLEASANT INN & RESORT
Phone: (401)253-0627   38

Boutique Bed & Breakfast
$375-$675 5/1-10/31

Address: 333 Poppasquash Rd 02809 **Location:** 1.7 mi sw of SR 114. **Facility:** The all-inclusive, English-style manor offers a number of recreational activities and a spirits closet with serve-yourself alcohol and soft drinks. Smoke free premises. 5 units. 4 one-bedroom standard units. 1 one-bedroom suite. 3 stories, interior corridors. **Parking:** on-site. **Terms:** open 5/1-10/31, office hours 7 am-10 pm, 2-3 night minimum stay - seasonal and/or weekends, age restrictions may apply, 30 day cancellation notice-fee imposed. **Amenities:** video library, DVD players, CD players, safes, hair dryers. **Pool(s):** heated outdoor. **Leisure Activities:** sauna, whirlpool, boating, fishing, kayaks, golf privileges, tennis court, croquet, bocci, firepit, bicycles, exercise room, basketball, horseshoes, game room. *Fee:* massage. **Guest Services:** valet laundry, wireless Internet, personal trainer. **Business Services:** meeting rooms, administrative services, PC. **Free Special Amenities: full breakfast and high-speed Internet.**

ROCKWELL HOUSE INN
Phone: 401/253-0040   34

Historic Bed & Breakfast
$159-$379 5/1-10/31
$129-$259 11/1-4/30

Address: 610 Hope St 02809 **Location:** On SR 114; center. **Facility:** This restored 1809 B&B features several rooms with gas fireplaces as well as terry cloth robes and lighted make-up mirrors at a separate vanity area. Smoke free premises. 4 one-bedroom standard units. 2 stories (no elevator), interior corridors. *Bath:* combo or shower only. **Parking:** on-site. **Terms:** office hours 8 am-9 pm, 2-3 night minimum stay - seasonal and/or weekends, 21 day cancellation notice. **Amenities:** video library, safes, irons, hair dryers. **Guest Services:** TV in common area, wireless Internet.

WILLIAM'S GRANT INN
Phone: (401)253-4222   37

Historic Bed & Breakfast
$129-$199 5/1-10/31
$89-$179 11/1-4/30

Address: 154 High St 02809 **Location:** SR 114, just e on Constitution St, then just s. Located in a residential area. **Facility:** On a tree-lined street a few blocks from the waterfront, this 1808 Federal-style home has a back patio area, fish pond and hand-painted décor accents. Smoke free premises. 5 one-bedroom standard units, some with whirlpools. 2 stories (no elevator), interior corridors. *Bath:* combo or shower only. **Parking:** on-site. **Terms:** office hours 9 am-10 pm, 2 night minimum stay - seasonal and/or weekends, age restrictions may apply, 14 day cancellation notice-fee imposed. **Amenities:** video library, hair dryers. **Leisure Activities:** bicycles. *Fee:* massage. **Guest Services:** TV in common area, valet laundry, wireless Internet.

(See map and index starting on p. 588)

—— **WHERE TO DINE** ——

AIDAN'S

Irish
$7-$19

Phone: 401/254-1940   ㊷

Authentic Irish dishes include bangers and mash, shepherd's pie, corned beef and fish and chips. Casual dress. **Bar:** Full bar. **Reservations:** not accepted. **Hours:** 11:30 am-10 pm, Fri & Sat-11 pm. **Address:** 5 John St 02809 **Location:** Just w of SR 114; center. **Parking:** on-site.

BACKROAD GRILLE

American
$8-$20

Phone: 401/253-0553

The restaurant offers a wide range of food ranging from delicious barbecue ribs and pulled pork sandwiches to classic New England seafood dishes including baked scrod with butter, wine and cracker crumbs. The comfortable dining room is contemporary in style but lacks natural light since there are no windows. The casual, friendly wait staff provides attentive service. Casual dress. **Bar:** Full bar. **Reservations:** not accepted. **Hours:** 11 am-9 pm, Fri & Sat-10 pm, Sun 8 am-8:30 pm. Closed major holidays; also Mon. **Address:** 549 Metacom Ave 02809 **Location:** Jct SR 114, 3 mi n on SR 136. **Parking:** on-site. CALL ♿Ⓜ

BRISTOL HOUSE OF PIZZA

Pizza
$5-$12

Phone: 401/253-2550   ㊴

Near eclectic shops and historic homes, the centrally located restaurant is in the downtown shopping district. The main draw here is great-tasting pizza as well as Greek specialties, including gyros and other sandwiches. Casual dress. **Reservations:** not accepted. **Hours:** 11 am-9 pm, Sun from noon. Closed: 1/1, 11/25, 12/25. **Address:** 55 State St 02809 **Location:** Just sw of SR 114; downtown. **Parking:** street.

BRISTOL SUNSET CAFE

Breads/Pastries
$3-$8

Phone: 401/253-1910   ㊲

Guests can nibble on breakfast or a sandwich while overlooking the historic homes of downtown. Lines aren't a good reason to forgo a visit; waits are rarely long, and the reasonably priced food makes any wait worthwhile. Casual dress. **Hours:** 7 am-3 pm, Sun-2 pm. Closed major holidays; also Mon in winter. **Address:** 499 Hope St 02809 **Location:** On SR 114; between State and Bradford sts; downtown. **Parking:** street.

DEWOLF TAVERN

American
$15-$42

Phone: 401/254-2005   ㊳

At Thames Street Landing, the historic building has kept many integral architectural features, such as its stone facade and original hardwood floors, while adding contemporary decor and artwork. Fireplace and window seats afford great views of the waterfront. Entree choices might include grilled prime filet mignon, pan-fried pork cutlet with apples or seafood casserole with lobster-crab mashed potatoes, shrimp, lobster, mussels, sea scallops and fish. Dressy casual. **Bar:** Full bar. **Reservations:** accepted. **Hours:** 5 pm-10 pm, Sun-9 pm; hours vary off season. Closed: 1/1, 7/4, 12/25. **Address:** 259 Thames St 02809 **Location:** Just w of SR 114; center; in Bristol Harbor Inn. **Parking:** on-site.

JACKY'S GALAXIE & SUSHI BAR

Asian
$5-$25

Phone: 401/253-8818

The restaurant prides itself on serving "fine Asian cuisine," featuring an eclectic mix of dishes inspired by Chinese, Japanese and Southeast Asian flavors. Diners can choose from a great selection of fresh sushi and tempura. Each dish is individually cooked and prepared, enabling patrons to omit or add any ingredient or seasoning. Casual dress. **Bar:** Full bar. **Hours:** 11:30 am-10:30 pm, Fri & Sat-11 pm, Sun noon-10 pm. Closed: 11/25. **Address:** 383 Metacom Ave 02809 **Location:** I-195, exit 2, 3.4 mi s on SR 136. **Parking:** on-site. CALL ♿Ⓜ

LEO'S RISTORANTE

Italian
$5-$16

Phone: 401/253-9300   ㊸

On the city's tree-shaded main street, this restaurant occupies a historic brick building. Diners may relax and take in the beauty of the old Colonial homes around them while dining inside by a large window or outside on the sidewalk tables. Classic Italian favorites such as lasagna, veal and chicken with penne, along with great pizza and a long list of sandwiches, are available. Casual dress. **Bar:** Full bar. **Hours:** 11 am-9 pm, Fri & Sat-10 pm. Closed major holidays. **Address:** 365 Hope St 02809 **Location:** On SR 114, corner of Church St; center. **Parking:** street.

THE LOBSTER POT

Seafood
$10-$29

Phone: 401/253-9100   ㊺

Remarkable water views, along with delicious seafood and steak, make the restaurant a local favorite. Local artisans showcase their work on the walls. Diners may leave completely satisfied with a great meal and a new piece of artwork. Dressy casual. **Bar:** Full bar. **Reservations:** suggested. **Hours:** 11:30 am-9 pm, Fri & Sat-10 pm, Sun noon-9 pm. Closed major holidays; also Mon. **Address:** 119-121 Hope St 02809 **Location:** Jct SR 114 and High St; downtown. **Parking:** on-site. CALL ♿Ⓜ

PERSIMMON

New American
$20-$35

Phone: 401/254-7474   ㊵

The small, intimate bistro is a treasure among locals. Elegant tables, muted walls and original oil paintings set the mood. The menu may change daily based on the chef's selection of fresh ingredients. Dressy casual. **Bar:** Full bar. **Reservations:** suggested. **Hours:** 5 pm-9 pm, Fri & Sat-10 pm. Closed: 11/25, 12/25; also Mon & Sun 1/1-6/30. **Address:** 31 State St 02809 **Location:** Just e of SR 114; downtown. **Parking:** street.

QUITO'S
Seafood
$6-$20

Phone: 401/253-9042   ㊱

This little clam shack on the harbor front is the ideal place to stop before or after a ride on the East Bay bike path. It offers incredible views of Narragansett Bay and its many sailboats. The restaurant itself is a bit dated and basic looking, but the service is friendly and the local seafood is fresh. Favorites include the lobster roll, clam cakes, fried whole belly clams, littlenecks, chowder, fried calamari and fried shrimp. Casual dress. **Bar:** Full bar. **Reservations:** not accepted. **Hours:** 11:30 am-10 pm, Sun-9 pm. Closed: Mon & Tues in fall, winter & spring. **Address:** 411 Thames St 02809 **Location:** Between Bradford and Franklin sts; adjacent to Independence Park. **Parking:** on-site.

(See map and index starting on p. 588)

REDLEFSEN'S

Continental
$9-$27

Phone: 401/254-1188 ㉟

Themed after small-town European restaurants the owners frequented during their travels, the restaurant presents an eclectic menu of dishes inspired by Germany, France and Sweden. Dressy casual. **Bar:** Full bar. **Reservations:** suggested. **Hours:** 11:30 am-2:30 & 5-9 pm, Fri & Sat-10 pm, Sun noon-8 pm. Closed: 1/1. **Address:** 444 Thames St 02809 **Location:** Between Franklin and Bradford sts; downtown. **Parking:** street.

ROBERTO'S

Northern Italian
$14-$27

Phone: 401/254-9732 ㊹

A delightful surprise, the cozy eatery prepares creative Italian cuisine. The staff is knowledgeable about wines and dish preparations. Dressy casual. **Bar:** Full bar. **Reservations:** suggested. **Hours:** 5 pm-9 pm, Fri & Sat-9:30 pm. Closed major holidays. **Address:** 301 Hope St 02809 **Location:** On SR 114; between Constitution and Church sts; downtown. **Parking:** street.

S. S. DION RESTAURANT

Seafood
$15-$24

Phone: 401/253-2884 ㉞

Patrons enjoy picturesque views of Independence Park and Narragansett Bay, with its many sailboats, while dining on fresh selections of seafood. Dressy casual. **Bar:** Full bar. **Reservations:** suggested. **Hours:** 5 pm-9 pm. Closed: 11/25, 12/25; also Sun. **Address:** 520 Thames St 02809 **Location:** Jct SR 114, just s; between Oliver and Franklin sts. **Parking:** on-site.

THAMES WATERSIDE BAR & GRILL

American
$10-$25

Phone: 401/253-4523 ㊶

On a wharf overlooking beautiful Bristol harbor and its many sailboats and large private estates, the restaurant offers docking slips for guests who arrive via the water. The decor has an upscale pub feel. Rattan seating on the covered patio is casual yet sophisticated. Starters of New England clam chowder or Bristol-style steamed local littleneck clams with chorizo and kale are fitting lead-ins to outstanding marinated steak tips served with garlic mashed potatoes. Casual dress. **Bar:** Full bar. **Reservations:** not accepted. **Hours:** noon-8 pm, Fri & Sat-9 pm. Closed: 12/25. **Address:** 251 Thames St 02809 **Location:** Just w of SR 114, between State & Bradford sts; center. **Parking:** on-site. CALL 🖆Ⓜ

CHARLESTOWN

WILLOWS RESORT MOTEL

AAA SAVE
Motel
$99-$175 5/12-10/12

Phone: 401/364-7727

Address: 5310 Post Rd (US 1) 02813 **Location:** US 1, 8 mi n of jct SR 78 (Westerly Bypass). **Facility:** Smoke free premises. 50 units. 47 one-bedroom standard units, some with efficiencies. 3 cottages. 2 stories (no elevator), exterior corridors. *Bath:* combo or shower only. **Parking:** on-site. **Terms:** open 5/12-10/12, office hours 8 am-10 pm, 2 night minimum stay - weekends, 10 day cancellation notice-fee imposed. **Pool(s):** heated outdoor. **Leisure Activities:** rental boats, rental canoes, rental paddleboats, boat dock, fishing, chipping range, tennis court, horseshoes, shuffleboard, game room. *Fee:* kayaks. **Guest Services:** coin laundry, wireless Internet. **Free Special Amenities:** local telephone calls and high-speed Internet. 🍴 🏊 ✂ ✕ 🛢 / SOME UNITS 🖥

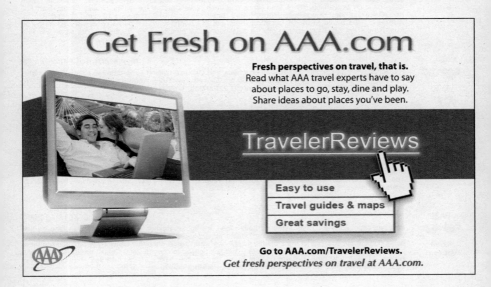

—— **WHERE TO DINE** ——

NORDIC LODGE RESTAURANT   Phone: 401/783-4515

Seafood
$80

The restaurant lays out a sprawling Viking smorgasbord with all-you-can-eat lobster, shrimp, beef and Italian entrees. The setting is rustic and jovial. Casual dress. **Bar:** Full bar. **Hours:** Open 5/1-12/12 & 4/28-4/30; 5 pm-8:30 pm, Sat from 4 pm, Sun 3 pm-6:30 pm. Closed: Mon-Thurs. **Address:** 178 E Pasquiset Tr 02813 **Location:** I-95, exit 3A, 1.8 mi e on SR 138, 5.4 mi s on SR 112, 1.2 mi n on SR 2, then 3 mi se, follow signs; US 1, exit Kenyon Ave, 4.8 mi n on SR 2, then 3 mi se, follow signs. **Parking:** on-site.

COVENTRY

FAIRFIELD INN & SUITES BY MARRIOTT
    COVENTRY   *Book great rates at AAA.com*   Phone: (401)821-3322

Hotel
$85-$103 All Year

Address: 4 Universal Blvd 02816 **Location:** I-95, exit 7, just ne; at center of New England Plaza. **Facility:** Smoke free premises. 91 one-bedroom standard units, some with whirlpools. 3 stories, interior corridors. *Bath:* combo or shower only. **Parking:** on-site. **Terms:** cancellation fee imposed. **Amenities:** video games (fee), high-speed Internet, dual phone lines, voice mail, safes, irons, hair dryers. **Pool(s):** heated indoor. **Leisure Activities:** whirlpool, exercise room. **Guest Services:** valet and coin laundry, wireless Internet. **Business Services:** meeting rooms, business center.

CALL

AAA Benefit:
Members save a minimum 5% off the best available rate.

HAMPTON INN COVENTRY   *Book great rates at AAA.com*   Phone: (401)823-4041

Hotel
$89-$119 All Year

Address: 850 Centre of New England Blvd 02816 **Location:** I-95, exit 7, just ne. **Facility:** 124 units. 120 one-bedroom standard units. 4 one-bedroom suites with whirlpools. 5 stories, interior corridors. *Bath:* combo or shower only. **Parking:** on-site. **Terms:** 1-7 night minimum stay, cancellation fee imposed. **Amenities:** high-speed Internet, dual phone lines, voice mail, irons, hair dryers. **Pool(s):** heated indoor. **Leisure Activities:** whirlpool, exercise room. **Guest Services:** valet and coin laundry, area transportation, wireless Internet. **Business Services:** meeting rooms, business center.

AAA Benefit:
Members save up to 10% everyday!

CRANSTON pop. 79,269   (See map and index starting on p. 606)

—— **WHERE TO DINE** ——

BASTA CAFE' & RESTAURANT   Phone: 401/461-0330   ⑨¹

Italian
$16-$28

On the casually elegant restaurant's menu are excellent homemade pasta dishes, as well as seafood and steak. Specific choices may include clams casino, tortellini in vodka-cream sauce and traditional Italian desserts such as tiramisu. White linen cloths and fresh flowers accent the tables. Dressy casual. **Bar:** Full bar. **Reservations:** suggested. **Hours:** 4:30 pm-8:30 pm, Fri-9 pm, Sat-10 pm. Closed: 12/25. **Address:** 2195 Broad St 02905 **Location:** I-95, exit 14A northbound, 0.6 mi ne on SR 37, 3.3 mi ne on Post Rd via exit 5B, then just nw; exit 18 southbound, 0.9 mi s on Eddy St, then 1.7 mi se on SR 117. **Parking:** on-site.

GALAXIE   Phone: 401/946-9464   ⑧⁹

Asian
$5-$15

Reasonably priced Cambodian, Thai, Vietnamese and Chinese cuisine lures patrons. Casual dress. **Bar:** Full bar. **Hours:** 11 am-10 pm, Fri & Sat-10:30 pm. Closed: 7/4, 11/25. **Address:** 957 Reservoir Ave 02910 **Location:** I-95, exit between 16 and 14B; on SR 2. **Parking:** on-site.

NICOLE'S TUSCANY GRILLE AND RESTAURANT   Phone: 401/944-2500   ⑧⁷

Northern Italian
$8-$29

Within a couple miles of the highway, the family-owned bistro provides a nice selection of specialty salads and desserts, which complement Northern Italian preparations of local veal, homemade pasta and chargrilled fish steaks and pork. Sauces are made fresh daily, and portions are generous. Alternatively, diners might try grilled pizza cooked in open-hearth, wood-fired ovens. Caesar salad is a signature item. Lunch hours vary on weekends. Dressy casual. **Bar:** Full bar. **Reservations:** suggested. **Hours:** 11:30 am-9:30 pm, Fri-10:30 pm, Sat 4:30 pm-10:30 pm, Sun 1 pm-8 pm. Closed: 11/25, 12/24, 12/25; also Mon & Tues. **Address:** 555 Atwood Ave 02920 **Location:** I-295, exit 4, 1.2 mi e on SR 114, then 0.6 mi s on SR 5. **Parking:** on-site. CALL

PAPA RAZZI   Phone: 401/942-2900

Italian
$8-$28

Italy has changed and so has authentic Italian food. It's lighter, fresher, more exciting Italian, and it's just what you'll find amid the elegant yet comfortable atmosphere that is Papa Razzi. If the steamy bowls of pasta don't tempt you, one of the aromatic pizzas or a warm panini sandwich definitely will. In addition there is a fine wine list, an array of salads, chicken, and fish options to choose from. Casual dress. **Bar:** Full bar. **Hours:** 11:30 am-10 pm, Fri & Sat-11 pm, Sun-9 pm. Closed: 11/25, 12/25. **Address:** 1 Paparazzi Way 02920 **Location:** S of SR 2; in Garden City Center. **Parking:** on-site. CALL

(See map and index starting on p. 606)

SPAIN RESTAURANT

Phone: 401/946-8686   (90)

Spanish
$12-$22

The main dining room is reminiscent of an outdoor Spanish-style courtyard with its stucco walls, arched entrances, ironwork gates and trim and two-story fountain wall. Attentive servers are professionally dressed in cummerbunds and bow ties. The menu consists mainly of seafood, chicken and steak. Great to try are any of the mariscadas: shellfish combinations consisting of lobster, clams, mussels, shrimp and scallops cooked in a choice of sauce. Dressy casual. **Bar:** Full bar. **Reservations:** not accepted. **Hours:** 4:30 pm-9:30 pm, Fri & Sat-10:30 pm, Sun 1 pm-9 pm. Closed: 7/4, 11/25, 12/24, 12/25; also Tues. **Address:** 1073 Reservoir Ave 02920 **Location:** I-295, exit 2 northbound, 3.7 mi n on SR 2; exit 3A southbound, 1.3 mi e on SR 37, then 1.8 mi n on SR 2. **Parking:** on-site and valet. CALL &M

TWIN OAKS

Phone: 401/781-9693   (88)

Italian
$5-$30

The Rhode Island institution is known for its tender steaks, fresh seafood and signature Italian dishes. The secret pasta sauces are so good that bottled versions are sold in local grocery stores. The casual atmosphere is family-friendly. Casual dress. **Bar:** Full bar. **Reservations:** not accepted. **Hours:** 11:30 am-11 pm, Fri & Sat-midnight, Sun from noon. Closed: 11/25, 12/25; also Mon. **Address:** 100 Sabra St 02910 **Location:** Jct SR 2, just sw on Frankfort St, ne on Niantic Ave, then just ne. **Parking:** on-site.

EAST GREENWICH   (See map and index starting on p. 606)

------ **WHERE TO DINE** ------

CHIANTI'S

Phone: 401/885-4999

Italian
$7-$23

Favorite Italian dishes include traditional lasagna, chicken Alfredo, shrimp fra diavolo (a spicy marinara sauce with hot pepper rings), cheese tortellini, gnocchi and pasta with sweet Italian sausage. Also on the menu are seafood, veal and beef options and children's choices of spaghetti and meatballs, grilled cheese and other classics. A large bar sits in the center of the dining room. Each table has a heated bowl of olive oil infused with fresh garlic and rosemary for great bread dipping. Casual dress. **Bar:** Full bar. **Reservations:** accepted. **Hours:** 11:30 am-9 pm, Fri-10 pm, Sat 4 pm-10 pm. Closed major holidays; also Mon. **Address:** 195 Old Forge Rd 02818 **Location:** From US 1, just se. **Parking:** on-site. CALL &M

THE GRILLE ON MAIN

Phone: 401/885-2200   (108)

American
$7-$22

Located on charming Main Street, this contemporary, hip restaurant is hard to miss with its brightly painted red walls and large colorful paintings. Two large glass doors are opened during warmer months so that diners may feel they are dining bistro style. Casual dress. **Bar:** Full bar. **Hours:** 11:30 am-10 pm, Wed & Thurs-11 pm, Fri & Sat-midnight. Closed: 7/4, 12/25. **Address:** 50 Main St 02812 **Location:** On US 1, between King and Division sts. **Parking:** on-site.

KON ASIAN BISTRO

Phone: 401/886-9200   (109)

Asian
$10-$30

A large Buddha statue in the center of the room seems to protect the tables that surround a pool of water. Multiple hanging lanterns made of orange silk fabric drape from the ceiling, and a water wall separates the hibachi area. It is always a spectacle watching the hibachi chefs show off their talents—from making a volcano with raw onion rings to flipping eggs in the air and spitting them perfectly to tossing pieces of broccoli into the mouths of any guest up for the challenge. Casual dress. **Bar:** Full bar. **Reservations:** suggested, for dinner. **Hours:** 11:30 am-10 pm, Fri & Sat-11 pm, Sun 12:30 pm-10 pm. Closed: 11/25, 12/25. **Address:** 553 Main St 02818 **Location:** Jct SR 401, just ne on US 1. **Parking:** street. CALL &M

MERITAGE

Phone: 401/884-1255

New American
$18-$26

This modern restaurant prepares eclectic New American cuisine, which pairs with selections from a carefully chosen wine list that includes 20 by-the-glass options. Chicken teriyaki skewers with Thai dipping sauce is a delicious way to keep occupied while waiting for lobster ravioli or another well-prepared dish. For dessert, it's hard to beat pizza Melba, a luscious fruit, cheese, cream and sauce delicacy. When making reservations, guests should ask about happy hour special in the lounge. Dressy casual. **Bar:** Full bar. **Reservations:** suggested. **Hours:** 4:30 pm-10 pm, Thurs-Sat to 11 pm. Closed: 11/25, 12/25. **Address:** 5454 Post Rd 02818 **Location:** Jct SR 401, 0.7 mi sw on US 1. **Parking:** on-site. CALL &M

POST OFFICE CAFE

Phone: 401/885-4444   (107)

Italian
$12-$24

Artistic, creative cuisine combines facets of classic Italian with the trendy. Interesting selections from the dessert tray are sure to tempt. Although the dining room retains the atmosphere of its former incarnation—that of a U.S. Post Office from 1934 to 1977—it is softened by heavy drapes on the 15-foot windows and white table linens. Valet parking is available Friday and Saturday. Casual dress. **Bar:** Full bar. **Reservations:** suggested. **Hours:** 4:30 pm-9:30 pm, Fri & Sat-10:30 pm, Sun 10 am-2 pm. Closed: 1/1, 11/25, 12/25; also Mon. **Address:** 11 Main St 02818 **Location:** On US 1 at Division St; center. **Parking:** on-site.

EAST PROVIDENCE pop. 48,688   (See map and index starting on p. 606)

EXTENDED STAYAMERICA PROVIDENCE-EAST
PROVIDENCE   *Book at AAA.com*

Phone: (401)272-1661   (41)

Extended Stay Hotel
$75-$149 All Year

Address: 1000 Warren Ave 02914 **Location:** I-195, exit 8 eastbound, just e; exit 6 westbound, 1.1 mi e via Warren Ave. **Facility:** 100 one-bedroom standard units with efficiencies. 4 stories, interior corridors. *Bath:* combo or shower only. **Parking:** on-site. **Terms:** office hours 7 am-11 pm, cancellation fee imposed. **Amenities:** voice mail, irons, hair dryers. **Guest Services:** coin laundry, wireless Internet. ASK CALL &M / SOME UNITS FEE

(See map and index starting on p. 606)

——— WHERE TO DINE ———

CATTAILS CITY GRILL
Phone: 401/434-2288   81

Mediterranean
$8-$24

This hip restaurant features excellent-quality dishes inspired by Italy, Portugal and Spain. Shrimp wrapped in prosciutto served with perfectly marinated tomatoes or chicken Marsala with wild mushrooms and homemade mashed potatoes are among great-tasting choices. The trendy bar area is a great place for an after-work cocktail. Dressy casual. **Bar:** Full bar. **Reservations:** not accepted. **Hours:** 4:30 pm-9:30 pm, Fri & Sat-10:30 pm, Sun 4 pm-9 pm. Closed major holidays. **Address:** 315 Waterman Ave 02914 **Location:** I-195, exit 4 eastbound, 0.7 mi e on US 44; exit 6 westbound, just n on Broadway, then just e. **Parking:** on-site. CALL (L)(M)

DAVENPORT'S RESTAURANT
Phone: 401/438-3381   80

American
$7-$15

The standout here is seafood chowder, which has won numerous local awards. Also on the menu are Italian dishes, burgers and chicken dinners, as well as children's favorites. Casual dress. **Bar:** Full bar. **Reservations:** accepted. **Hours:** 11 am-10 pm, Thurs-10:30 pm, Fri & Sat-11:30 pm. Closed: 11/25, 12/25. **Address:** 1925 Pawtucket Ave (SR 114) 02914 **Location:** Just n of jct US 44. **Parking:** on-site. CALL (L)(M)

GREGG'S RESTAURANT & PUB
Phone: 401/438-5700

American
$5-$15

It's well worth the short wait in line for Gregg's great daily specials, sandwiches, salads and various homemade pastries and wonderful desserts. Friendly, fast-paced service in the bustling, cheery dining room is attentive and fun. Casual dress. **Bar:** Full bar. **Reservations:** not accepted. **Hours:** 11:30 am-1 am; closing hours vary off season. Closed: 11/25, 12/25. **Address:** 1940 Pawtucket Ave 02914 **Location:** Jct Pawtucket Ave and US 44 (Taunton Ave). **Parking:** on-site.

HORTON'S SEAFOOD
Menu on AAA.com   **Phone:** 401/434-3116   82

Seafood
$7-$18

The restaurant is locally known for fresh seafood at economical prices. The decor is basic, but the service is friendly and the food good. Traditional New England favorites—such as lobster sandwiches, fried whole-belly clam plates and baked stuffed sole—are just some of the many fried and baked meals. Red, clear and white clam chowder are delicious. Casual dress. **Bar:** Beer & wine. **Hours:** 11 am-8 pm, Fri 10 am-9 pm. Closed: 1/1, 11/25, 12/25; also Sun-Tues. **Address:** 809 Broadway 02914 **Location:** I-195, exit 6 westbound, 0.3 mi n; exit 4 eastbound, just e on US 44, 0.3 mi se on Grosvenor Ave, then just n. **Parking:** street.

ICHIGO ICHIE HIBACHI & SUSHI BAR
Phone: 401/435-5511   84

Japanese
$9-$35

Guests enter this visually stunning dining area past an indoor waterfall and through etched-glass doors. Modern crystal chandeliers hang from the ceiling. Dining at the hibachi grill is sure to be a memorable experience, and chefs keep diners entertained as they prepare meals in front of them. It's not unusual for the chef to encourage a sake-drinking contest by use of squirt bottle. The fresh sushi bar tempts with choices such as the local Boston roll with shrimp, cucumber, lettuce and mayo. Casual dress. **Bar:** Full bar. **Reservations:** accepted. **Hours:** 11 am-2:30 & 4:30-9:30 pm, Fri-10:30 pm, Sat 1 pm-10:30 pm, Sun 1 pm-9:30 pm. Closed: 11/25, 12/25. **Address:** 5 Catamore Blvd 02914 **Location:** Jct SR 114A, 0.9 mi nw via US 6. **Parking:** on-site. CALL (L)(M)

MADEIRA RESTAURANT
Phone: 401/431-1322   83

Portuguese
$5-$27

The local favorite serves Portuguese cuisine in an upscale atmosphere. House specialties include Portuguese-style steak with fried egg and pork with littlenecks. Dressy casual. **Bar:** Full bar. **Reservations:** not accepted. **Hours:** 11:30 am-10 pm, Fri & Sat-11 pm, Sun noon-10 pm. Closed: 12/25. **Address:** 288 Warren Ave 02914 **Location:** I-195, exit 6, just w on Broadway, then just n. **Parking:** on-site.

RIVIERA II FAMILY RESTAURANT
Phone: 401/431-9231   79

Portuguese
$8-$17

The informal neighborhood family restaurant presents a menu of Portugal- and Spain-influenced dishes. Patio seating is available during warmer months. Casual dress. **Bar:** Full bar. **Reservations:** accepted. **Hours:** 11:30 am-10 pm, Fri & Sat-11 pm. Closed: 7/4, 12/24. **Address:** 580 N Broadway 02914 **Location:** I-195, exit 6 westbound, 0.7 mi n; exit 4 eastbound, just e on Taunton Ave, just se on Grosvenor Ave, then 0.5 mi n. **Parking:** on-site.

HARRISVILLE pop. 1,561

——— WHERE TO DINE ———

WRIGHT'S FARM RESTAURANT AND BANQUET FACILITY
Phone: 401/769-2856

American
$10-$19

Relaxed, all-you-can-eat, family-style chicken dinners are a tradition here. Casual dress. **Bar:** Full bar. **Hours:** 4 pm-9 pm, Sat noon-9:30 pm, Sun noon-8 pm. Closed: 12/25; also Mon-Wed. **Address:** 84 Inman Rd 02830 **Location:** Jct SR 7 and 102, 0.6 mi n on SR 102. **Parking:** on-site.

JAMESTOWN (See map and index starting on p. 588)

THE WYNDHAM BAY VOYAGE INN
Book at AAA.com   **Phone:** (401)423-2100   55

Hotel
$150-$300 5/1-10/1
$95-$275 10/2-4/30

Address: 150 Conanicus Ave 02835 **Location:** SR 138, exit Jamestown, 0.5 mi s; just w of bridge toll. **Facility:** Smoke free premises. 32 one-bedroom suites. 3 stories, interior corridors. **Parking:** on-site. **Terms:** check-in 4 pm, 2 night minimum stay - seasonal, 3 day cancellation notice-fee imposed. **Amenities:** CD players, voice mail, irons, hair dryers. **Dining:** Bay Voyage Restaurant, see separate listing. **Pool(s):** outdoor. **Leisure Activities:** sauna, exercise room. **Guest Services:** wireless Internet. **Business Services:** meeting rooms, PC (fee).

ECO (ASK) (🍴)(🍷)(🏊)(✕)(🎥)(🖥)(🖼)(💻)

(See map and index starting on p. 588)

———— *The following lodging was either not evaluated or did not* ————
meet AAA rating requirements but is listed for your information only.

WYNDHAM NEWPORT OVERLOOK   Phone: 401/423-1886

[fyi]   Not evaluated. **Address:** 150 Bayview Dr 02835. Facilities, services, and decor characterize a mid-scale property.

———— **WHERE TO DINE** ————

BAY VOYAGE RESTAURANT   Phone: 401/423-2100   66

New American
$13-$28

Guests are treated to amazing views from the wall of windows overlooking the Newport Bridge and Narragansett Bay. Well-known brunch and dinner items include lump crab cakes with sweet peppers and apple celery root remoulade or pan-seared duck with coconut rice, kimchee, honey, ginger and pineapple sauce. Rich flavor characterizes the dark chocolate Grand Marnier soufflé, which is served with white chocolate ganache, or banana strudel served with vanilla ice cream and caramel rum sauce. Dressy casual. **Bar:** Full bar. **Reservations:** accepted. **Hours:** 5 pm-9 pm, Sun also 10:30 am-1:30 pm. **Address:** 150 Conanicus Ave 02835 **Location:** SR 138, exit Jamestown, 0.5 mi s; just w of bridge toll; in The Wyndham Bay Voyage Inn. **Parking:** on-site. CALL [&M]

TRICIA'S TROPI-GRILLE   Phone: 401/423-1490   67

Caribbean
$10-$20

Key West's shabby chic tropical vibe comes to life in the decor, from the tiki bar to the pineapple-print chairs. An umbrella-topped frozen drink washes down the tiki pu pu platter with conch fritters, ponzu wings, coconut shrimp and mango-barbecue ribs. The friendly staff will gladly offer suggestions among entree choices such as the Cuban sandwich or Cudjoe Key crab cakes. A slice of Key lime pie rounds out the island experience. Casual dress. **Bar:** Full bar. **Reservations:** not accepted. **Hours:** 11:30 am-10 pm. Closed major holidays. **Address:** 14 Narragansett Ave 02835 **Location:** SR 138, exit Jamestown, 0.4 mi se on Shore Rd, 0.8 mi s on Conanicus Ave, then just w. **Parking:** street. CALL [&M]

LINCOLN   (See map and index starting on p. 606)

COURTYARD BY MARRIOTT
PROVIDENCE/LINCOLN   *Book great rates at AAA.com*   Phone: (401)333-3400   18

Hotel
$149-$169 All Year

Address: 636 George Washington Hwy 02865 **Location:** I-295, exit 9A (SR 146), just w on SR 116 S. **Facility:** Smoke free premises. 121 units. 119 one-bedroom standard units, some with whirlpools. 2 one-bedroom suites. 5 stories, interior corridors. *Bath:* combo or shower only. **Parking:** on-site. **Terms:** cancellation fee imposed. **Amenities:** high-speed Internet, dual phone lines, voice mail, irons, hair dryers. **Pool(s):** heated indoor. **Leisure Activities:** whirlpool, exercise room. **Guest Services:** valet and coin laundry, area transportation, wireless Internet. **Business Services:** meeting rooms, business center.

AAA Benefit:
Members save a minimum 5% off the best available rate.

———— **WHERE TO DINE** ————

FRED & STEVE'S STEAKHOUSE   Phone: 401/475-8400   57

Steak
$19-$40

Perfect for special occasions, this place offers great food and service that may be even greater. The attentive staff makes guests feel at home. Owners Fred Smerlas and Steve DeOssie, both retired NFL players, creatively mix football memorabilia into an upscale dining room. The $30 prix fixe menu—which includes an appetizer, entree, side, dessert and glass of house wine—is available most nights. Everyone raves about the tender prime rib with au jus, horseradish sauce and homemade creamed corn. Dressy casual. **Bar:** Full bar. **Reservations:** suggested. **Hours:** 5 pm-9 pm, Fri & Sat-11 pm, Sun 4 pm-8 pm. Closed: Mon & Tues. **Address:** 100 Twin River Rd 02865 **Location:** SR 146, exit Twin River Rd, 0.7 mi sw; in Twin River Casino. **Parking:** on-site and valet. CALL [&M]

THE LODGE PUB & EATERY   Phone: 401/725-8510   56

American
$6-$20

Diners enjoy friendly service at the rustic restaurant. Steak, pasta and fresh local seafood, such as baked stuffed fish or shrimp, are some examples of what the menu offers. Casual dress. **Bar:** Full bar. **Reservations:** not accepted. **Hours:** 11 am-11 pm, Thurs-Sat to 12:30 pm, Sun noon-10 pm. Closed: 7/4, 11/25, 12/25. **Address:** 40 Breakneck Hill Rd (SR 123) 02865 **Location:** SR 146, exit Breakneck Hill Rd, just ne. **Parking:** on-site.

MIDDLETOWN   (See map and index starting on p. 588)

THE CARRIAGE HOUSE INN, AN ASCEND
COLLECTION HOTEL   *Book great rates at AAA.com*   Phone: (401)841-0018   48

Hotel
$108-$258 5/1-10/31
$78-$128 11/1-4/30

Address: 93 Miantonomi Ave 02842 **Location:** Just e of jct SR 138 and 114. **Facility:** Smoke free premises. 23 one-bedroom standard units. 3 stories, interior corridors. *Bath:* combo or shower only. **Parking:** on-site. **Terms:** 2 night minimum stay - seasonal and/or weekends, 3 day cancellation notice. **Amenities:** voice mail, safes (fee), irons, hair dryers. *Some:* high-speed Internet. **Guest Services:** valet laundry, wireless Internet. **Business Services:** business center. **Free Special Amenities:** continental breakfast.

(See map and index starting on p. 588)

COMFORT INN NEWPORT
Book great rates at AAA.com

Phone: (401)619-2800 **51**

Hotel
$129-$329 5/1-10/31
$79-$149 11/1-4/30

Address: 28 Aquidneck Ave 02842 **Location:** Jct SR 214, just s on SR 138A; across from Easton Beach. **Facility:** Smoke free premises. 55 one-bedroom standard units. 3 stories, interior corridors. **Parking:** on-site. **Terms:** 2 night minimum stay - seasonal and/or weekends, 3 day cancellation notice. **Amenities:** voice mail, safes (fee), irons, hair dryers. *Some:* high-speed Internet. **Pool(s):** heated indoor. **Leisure Activities:** limited exercise equipment. **Guest Services:** valet laundry, wireless Internet. **Business Services:** meeting rooms. **Free Special Amenities: expanded continental breakfast.**

COURTYARD BY MARRIOTT-NEWPORT/MIDDLETOWN
Book great rates at AAA.com

Phone: (401)849-8000 **43**

Hotel
$119-$239 All Year

Address: 9 Commerce Dr 02842 **Location:** SR 114, 0.5 mi n of jct SR 138. Located in Newport Corporate Park. **Facility:** Smoke free premises. 148 units. 138 one-bedroom standard units. 10 one-bedroom suites. 2-3 stories, interior corridors. **Parking:** on-site. **Terms:** check-in 4 pm, cancellation fee imposed. **Amenities:** high-speed Internet, voice mail, irons, hair dryers. **Pool(s):** heated indoor/outdoor. **Leisure Activities:** whirlpool, exercise room. *Fee:* game room. **Guest Services:** valet and coin laundry, wireless Internet. **Business Services:** meeting rooms, business center. **Free Special Amenities: full breakfast and high-speed Internet.**

AAA Benefit:
Members save a minimum 5% off the best available rate.

ECONO LODGE
Book at AAA.com

Phone: (401)849-2718 **41**

Motel
$60-$210 5/1-10/31
$45-$80 11/1-4/30

Address: 1359 W Main Rd 02842 **Location:** On SR 114, just n of jct SR 214. **Facility:** 55 one-bedroom standard units. 2 stories (no elevator), interior corridors. **Parking:** on-site. **Terms:** 2 night minimum stay - seasonal and/or weekends, cancellation fee imposed. **Amenities:** irons, hair dryers. **Pool(s):** heated outdoor. **Guest Services:** wireless Internet.

HAMPTON INN & SUITES
Book great rates at AAA.com

Phone: (401)848-6555 **47**

Hotel
$99-$294 All Year

Address: 317 W Main Rd 02842 **Location:** On SR 114, 0.3 mi s of jct SR 138. **Facility:** 95 units. 91 one-bedroom standard units. 4 one-bedroom suites. 4 stories, interior corridors. *Bath:* combo or shower only. **Parking:** on-site. **Terms:** 1-7 night minimum stay, cancellation fee imposed. **Amenities:** video games (fee), high-speed Internet, voice mail, irons, hair dryers. *Some:* dual phone lines. **Pool(s):** heated indoor. **Leisure Activities:** whirlpool, exercise room. **Guest Services:** valet and coin laundry, wireless Internet. **Business Services:** meeting rooms, business center. *(See color ad p 596)*

AAA Benefit:
Members save up to 10% everyday!

See map and index starting on p. 588)

HOLIDAY INN EXPRESS MIDDLETOWN *Book great rates at AAA.com* **Phone:** (401)848-7128

(AAA) (SAVE)
▽▽▽
Hotel
$79-$289 5/1-10/31
$79-$209 11/1-4/30

Address: 855 W Main Rd 02842 **Location:** SR 114, 0.5 mi n of jct SR 138. **Facility:** Smoke free premises. 117 units. 111 one-bedroom standard units, some with efficiencies. 6 one-bedroom suites, some with efficiencies and/or whirlpools. 3 stories, interior corridors. *Bath:* combo or shower only. **Parking:** on-site. **Terms:** 3 day cancellation notice-fee imposed. **Amenities:** video library, DVD players, video games (fee), CD players, high-speed Internet, dual phone lines, voice mail, safes, irons, hair dryers. **Pool(s):** heated indoor. **Leisure Activities:** whirlpool, exercise room. **Guest Services:** valet and coin laundry, wireless Internet. **Business Services:** meeting rooms, business center. *(See color ad p 596)*

OWARD JOHNSON INN-NEWPORT *Book great rates at AAA.com* **Phone:** (401)849-2000 45

(AAA) (SAVE)
▽▽ ▽▽
Hotel
$79-$254 5/1-10/17
$49-$144 10/18-4/30

Address: 351 W Main Rd 02842 **Location:** On SR 114, 0.3 mi s of jct SR 138. **Facility:** 114 one-bedroom standard units. 2 stories (no elevator), interior corridors. *Bath:* combo or shower only. **Parking:** on-site. **Terms:** 2-3 night minimum stay - seasonal and/or weekends. **Amenities:** voice mail, safes (fee), irons, hair dryers. *Some:* DVD players (fee). **Pool(s):** heated indoor. **Leisure Activities:** sauna, whirlpool, exercise room. *Fee:* game room. **Guest Services:** valet and coin laundry, wireless Internet. **Business Services:** meeting rooms, business center. **Free Special Amenities:** newspaper and high-speed Internet. *(See color ad p 596)*

THE NEWPORT BEACH HOTEL & SUITES *Book great rates at AAA.com* **Phone:** (401)846-0310 52

(AAA) (SAVE)
▽▽▽
Hotel
$99-$599 5/1-9/30
$59-$259 10/1-4/30

Address: 30 Wave Ave 02842 **Location:** 1.5 mi ne on SR 138A. Located across from Easton Beach. **Facility:** Smoke free premises. 68 units. 28 one-bedroom standard units, some with whirlpools. 16 one- and 24 two-bedroom suites, some with kitchens and/or whirlpools. 4 stories, interior corridors. *Bath:* combo or shower only. **Parking:** on-site. **Terms:** 3 day cancellation notice-fee imposed. **Amenities:** video library, DVD players, CD players, voice mail, safes, irons, hair dryers. **Pool(s):** heated indoor. **Leisure Activities:** whirlpools, sun deck, firepit, exercise room, spa. *Fee:* beach cabanas. **Guest Services:** valet and coin laundry, wireless Internet. **Business Services:** meeting rooms, business center. *(See color ad p 599)*

UALITY INN & SUITES ATLANTIC BEACH HOTEL *Book at AAA.com* **Phone:** (401)847-5330 50

▽▽ ▽▽
Hotel
$99-$329 5/1-10/31
$69-$149 11/1-4/30

Address: 34 Wave Ave 02842 **Location:** 1.5 mi ne on SR 138A. Located across from Easton Beach. **Facility:** Smoke free premises. 43 one-bedroom standard units, some with whirlpools. 4 stories, interior corridors. **Parking:** on-site. **Terms:** 2 night minimum stay - seasonal and/or weekends, 3 day cancellation notice-fee imposed. **Amenities:** dual phone lines, voice mail, safes (fee), irons, hair dryers. **Leisure Activities:** exercise room, pool privileges. **Guest Services:** valet and coin laundry, wireless Internet. **Business Services:** meeting rooms, business center.

**ESIDENCE INN BY
MARRIOTT-NEWPORT/MIDDLETOWN** *Book great rates at AAA.com* **Phone:** (401)845-2005 46

(AAA) (SAVE)
▽▽▽
Extended Stay
Hotel
$139-$275 All Year

Address: 325 W Main Rd 02842 **Location:** On SR 114, 0.3 mi s of jct SR 138. **Facility:** Smoke free premises. 97 units. 52 one-bedroom standard units with kitchens. 33 one- and 12 two-bedroom suites, some with kitchens. 4 stories, interior corridors. **Parking:** on-site. **Terms:** check-in 4 pm, 3 day cancellation notice-fee imposed. **Amenities:** video games (fee), high-speed Internet, voice mail, irons, hair dryers. **Pool(s):** heated indoor. **Leisure Activities:** whirlpool, exercise room, sports court. **Guest Services:** valet and coin laundry, wireless Internet. **Business Services:** meeting rooms, business center. **Free Special Amenities:** newspaper and high-speed Internet. *(See color ad p 596)*

AAA Benefit:
Members save a minimum 5% off the best available rate.

HEA'S INN BY THE SEA *Book at AAA.com* **Phone:** (401)849-3548 49

▽▽ ▽▽
Bed & Breakfast
$139-$269 5/1-11/2
$79-$189 11/3-4/30

Address: 42 Aquidneck Ave (SR 138A) 02842 **Location:** 1.6 mi ne. **Facility:** Smoke free premises. 9 units. 7 one-bedroom standard units, some with whirlpools. 2 one-bedroom suites. 3 stories (no elevator), interior corridors. *Bath:* combo or shower only. **Parking:** on-site. **Terms:** office hours 7 am-9 pm, 2-3 night minimum stay - seasonal and/or weekends, 7 day cancellation notice-fee imposed. **Amenities:** hair dryers. *Some:* irons. **Guest Services:** wireless Internet.

(See map and index starting on p. 588)

TRAVELODGE *Book great rates at AAA.com* Phone: (401)849-4700    42

AAA SAVE

Motel
$60-$250 5/1-12/31
$50-$99 1/1-4/30

Address: 1185 W Main Rd 02842 **Location:** SR 114, 1.1 mi n of jct SR 138. **Facility:** 77 one-bedroom standard units. 2 stories (no elevator), interior/exterior corridors. **Parking:** on-site. **Terms:** office hours 7 am-11 pm, 2 night minimum stay - seasonal and/or weekends, cancellation fee imposed. **Amenities:** irons, hair dryers. **Pool(s):** heated outdoor. **Guest Services:** coin laundry, wireless Internet.

WHERE TO DINE

ANTHONY'S SEAFOOD GROUP Phone: 401/846-9620 59

Seafood
$5-$19

Guests order at the counter and wait for their number to be called. Terrific off-the-boat seafood is generally fried and tastes great. A lobster pound is on site. Casual dress. **Bar:** Beer & wine. **Reservations:** not accepted. **Hours:** 11 am-8 pm; hours vary off season. Closed major holidays. **Address:** 963 Aquidneck Ave 02842 **Location:** 0.7 mi s of SR 138. **Parking:** on-site.

ATIK GARDEN RESTAURANT Phone: 401/848-0663 58

Chinese
$7-$11

Guests can unwind in a pleasant family atmosphere to sample Szechuan, Hunan, Cantonese and other Asian dishes, including curries, satay entrees and a great, well-stocked buffet with more than 100 hot and fresh items. Casual dress. **Bar:** Full bar. **Reservations:** suggested. **Hours:** 11 am-3 & 4-10 pm, Sun 11:30 am-10 pm. **Address:** 11 E Main Rd (SR 138) 02842 **Location:** Jct SR 138 and 114. **Parking:** on-site.

BECKY'S REAL BBQ Phone: 401/841-9909 57

Barbecue
$4-$12

The small country-style restaurant is known for its fast service and hickory-smoked barbecue ribs, pulled pork, chicken and beef. Family-style platters also are available. Casual dress. **Hours:** 11 am-8 pm, Sun from noon. Closed major holidays. **Address:** 82 E Main Rd 02842 **Location:** On SR 138, just ne of jct SR 114. **Parking:** on-site.

BLUE PLATE DINER Phone: 401/848-9500 54

American
$5-$15

The retro-style 1950s diner is a standout with powder blue walls, white octagonal tile flooring and a jukebox. A creative spin on the 10 Commandments, written on the walls, amuses with clever rules such as "Thou shall not worship the Golden Arches." The on-site bar serves up milk shakes and martinis. Offerings range from all-day breakfast menu items to burgers, sandwiches, oversize salads and seafood dishes. Why not splurge on a banana split for dessert? Casual dress. **Bar:** Full bar. **Reservations:** not accepted. **Hours:** 6:30 am-10 pm, Fri & Sat-11 pm. Closed major holidays. **Address:** 665 W Main Rd 02842 **Location:** Jct SR 24, 6.1 mi s on SR 114. **Parking:** on-site. CALL

CODDINGTON BREWING CO Phone: 401/847-6690 56

American
$7-$23

A terrific selection of in-house brews and traditional beer is paired with tasty American fare, including burgers and barbecue. Casual dress. **Bar:** Full bar. **Reservations:** not accepted. **Hours:** 11 am-10 pm, Fri-Sun to 11 pm. Closed: 4/4, 11/25, 12/25. **Address:** 210 Coddington Hwy 02842 **Location:** Jct SR 138 and 114, just n, then just w. **Parking:** on-site. CALL

FLO'S CLAM SHACK Phone: 401/847-8141 61

Seafood
$7-$20

As the name implies, Flo's Clam Shack carries out a clam shack theme throughout with buoys, quirky signs and fishing nets adorning the walls and ceiling. A popular spot since 1936, it turns out tasty fried or steamed seafood, especially clam cakes, New England clam chowder and steamed crab legs. Casual dress. **Bar:** Full bar. **Reservations:** not accepted. **Hours:** 11 am-9 pm; hours vary off season. Closed major holidays; also Mon-Wed 9/7-5/25. **Address:** 4 Wave Ave 02842 **Location:** Jct SR 214, just w on SR 138A. **Parking:** on-site.

JOHNNY'S ATLANTIC BEACH CLUB Phone: 401/847-2750 63

American
$7-$25

The specialty is fresh local seafood, and the casual setting features numerous windows around the dining room that provide a lovely ocean view. The lunch menu is offered until 4 pm. Seasonally, the beachfront grill offers lighter fare. Casual dress. **Bar:** Full bar. **Reservations:** suggested. **Hours:** 11:30 am-10 pm, Sun from 10:30 am. Closed: 12/25. **Address:** 55 Purgatory Rd 02842 **Location:** SR 138A; at Easton Beach. **Parking:** on-site. CALL

SAIGON CAFE Phone: 401/848-2252 53

Vietnamese
$6-$25

Representative of traditional cuisine are noodle soup, sauteed lemongrass tofu and steamed vermicelli. Casual dress. **Bar:** Full bar. **Reservations:** accepted. **Hours:** 11 am-9 pm, Fri & Sat-10 pm. Closed major holidays; also Mon. **Address:** 823 W Main Rd 02842 **Location:** On SR 114, just n of SR 214. **Parking:** on-site.

(See map and index starting on p. 588)

SEA SHAI

Japanese
$5-$17

Phone: 401/849-5180

Meaning "quiet river," the restaurant provides serenity for sushi lovers or anyone looking for Japanese an Korean cuisine. Bento boxes are a great way to sample the menu; many include miso soup, salad wi homemade ginger dressing, rice, tempura and a choice of teriyaki-style meat, such as chicken or bee Casual dress. **Bar:** Full bar. **Reservations:** accepted. **Hours:** 11:30 am-2:30 & 5-10 pm, Sat & Sun from pm. Closed major holidays; also Mon. **Address:** 747 Aquidneck Ave (SR 138A) 02842 **Location:** Jct S 214, 0.3 mi ne on Green End Ave, just s. **Parking:** on-site.

SIAM SQUARE

Thai
$7-$17

Phone: 401/851-7988

In a strip mall, this restaurant offers fine Thai cuisine in an upscale environment. A meal might start wi steamed Thai dumplings stuffed with shrimp, chicken, bamboo shoots, water chestnuts and blac mushrooms and served with a signature soy sauce; move next to an entree of Bangkok beef stir-fried wi mushrooms, onions, scallions and sesame seed and served on a sizzling hot plate; and top off with th homemade honey fried banana. Casual dress. **Bar:** Full bar. **Reservations:** not accepted. **Hours:** 11:3 am-9 pm, Fri-10 pm, Sat noon-10 pm, Sun noon-9 pm. Closed: Mon. **Address:** 238 E Main Rd 0284 **Location:** Jct SR 138 and 214. **Parking:** on-site. CALL

See map and index starting on p. 588)

ICKET'S BAR & GRILL
Phone: 401/847-7678   (62)

WWW WWW
American
$7-$20

A sleek, upscale and modern design lends an air of distinction to this sports bar and restaurant, which has cappuccino-colored rustic wood tables, a long bar area, an elegant purple ceiling and carpet, cream leather-like wall coverings and an exposed stone accent wall. This place is as comfortable to the sports averse as it is to rabid fans. Crispy chicken wings come in a variety of sauces from barbecue to extra spicy. Casual dress. **Bar:** Full bar. **Reservations:** accepted. **Hours:** 11 am-10 pm. Closed major holidays. **Address:** 15 Aquidneck Ave 02842 **Location:** Jct SR 214, just s on SR 138A; across from Easton Beach. **Parking:** on-site. CALL (&M)

MISQUAMICUT

BREEZEWAY RESORT
Phone: 401/348-8953

AAA (SAVE)

WWW WWW
Vintage Motel
$127-$245 5/1-10/11

Address: 70 Winnapaug Rd 02891 **Location:** 0.3 mi s of SR 1A, 0.3 mi n of beach. **Facility:** Near Misquamicut Beach, the inn features a peaceful, parklike setting with fountains and flora; some rooms feature contemporary decor and furnishings. Smoke free premises. 55 units. 45 one-bedroom standard units, some with efficiencies and/or whirlpools. 5 one- and 4 two-bedroom suites, some with kitchens and/or whirlpools. 1 cottage. 1-2 stories (no elevator), exterior corridors. *Bath:* combo or shower only. **Parking:** on-site. **Terms:** open 5/1-10/11, office hours 7 am-11 pm, 2-3 night minimum stay - seasonal and/or weekends, 15 day cancellation notice-fee imposed. **Amenities:** voice mail, irons, hair dryers. **Pool(s):** heated outdoor. **Leisure Activities:** beach access, playground, shuffleboard. *Fee:* game room. **Guest Services:** coin laundry, wireless Internet. **Free Special Amenities: continental breakfast and local telephone calls.** / SOME UNITS

NARRAGANSETT

THE VILLAGE INN AT NARRAGANSETT PIER
RESORT & CONFERENCE CENTER   *Book great rates at AAA.com*   **Phone:** (401)783-6767

AAA (SAVE)

WWW WWW
Hotel
$90-$350 5/1-10/31
$69-$195 11/1-4/30

Address: 1 Beach St 02882 **Location:** On SR 1A; opposite town beach and post office. **Facility:** Smoke free premises. 62 one-bedroom standard units, some with whirlpools. 3 stories, interior corridors. *Bath:* combo or shower only. **Parking:** on-site. **Terms:** 2 night minimum stay - seasonal, 7 day cancellation notice-fee imposed. **Amenities:** CD players, voice mail, irons, hair dryers. **Dining:** entertainment. **Pool(s):** heated indoor. **Leisure Activities:** whirlpool, sun deck. **Guest Services:** wireless Internet. **Business Services:** meeting rooms, business center.

—— **WHERE TO DINE** ——

ASIL'S
Phone: 401/789-3743

WWWW
Continental
$18-$48

Close to the pier area, this intimate dining establishment resides in a cozy Victorian setting. Creative entrees emphasize French preparation, which are all well presented. Dressy casual. **Bar:** Full bar. **Reservations:** suggested. **Hours:** 5:30 pm-10 pm. Closed: 11/25, 12/25; also Mon & Tues 9/3-6/25. **Address:** 22 Kingstown Rd 02882 **Location:** Center; opposite shopping plaza. **Parking:** on-site.

COAST GUARD HOUSE
Phone: 401/789-0700

WWWW
American
$8-$29

The spectacular location, nearly in the ocean, can't be beat. On the menu are simple preparations of traditional New England comfort foods. Dressy casual. **Bar:** Full bar. **Reservations:** suggested. **Hours:** 11:30 am-3:30 & 5-10 pm, Fri & Sat-11 pm, Sun 10 am-2 & 4-10 pm; Sunday brunch; hours may vary off season. Closed: 12/25. **Address:** 40 Ocean Rd 02882 **Location:** On SR 1A, just s of Narragansett Pier. **Parking:** on-site.

CRAZY BURGER
Phone: 401/783-1810

WWW WW
American
$7-$18

The eclectic menu lists creative vegan dishes, in addition to pizza and burgers made with a Mexican flair. Casual dress. **Reservations:** not accepted. **Hours:** 8 am-9 pm, Fri & Sat-10 pm. Closed: 11/25, 12/25; also 12/31. **Address:** 144 Boon St 02882 **Location:** Just w of SR 1A; between Continental and Congdon sts. **Parking:** street.

GEORGES OF GALILEE
Phone: 401/783-2306

WWW
Seafood
$5-$23

The restaurant features fresh fish and great ocean views due to its location on the waterfront of Galilee. Patrons should call to inquire about live music dates. Casual dress. **Bar:** Full bar. **Hours:** 11:30 am-10 pm; hours & days vary off season. Closed: 11/25, 12/25. **Address:** 250 Sand Hill Cove Rd 02882 **Location:** At Port of Galilee. **Parking:** on-site.

SPAIN RESTAURANT
Phone: 401/783-9770

WWWW
Continental
$13-$22

Mediterranean-influenced European cuisine is served in an informally elegant setting reminiscent of a Spanish court. Mariscada Spain is a delicious seafood dish with spinach in a tomato-based sauce. A few tables are offered on the courtyard and second-floor deck. Dressy casual. **Bar:** Full bar. **Hours:** 4 pm-10 pm, Fri & Sat-11 pm, Sun 1 pm-9 pm; to 9 pm, Fri & Sat-10 pm, Sun 1 pm-9 pm in winter. Closed: 11/25, 12/24, 12/25; also Mon. **Address:** 1144 Ocean Rd 02882 **Location:** SR 108, exit Scarborough State Beach, 1.7 mi se. **Parking:** on-site. CALL (&M)

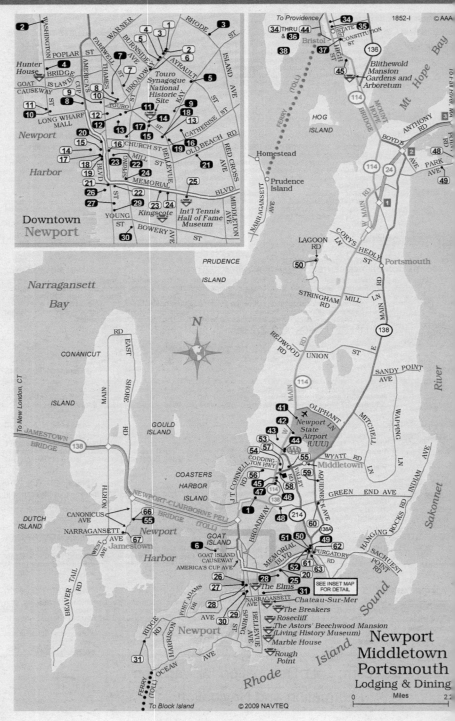

Downtown
Newport

Newport
Middletown
Portsmouth
Lodging & Dining

© 2009 NAVTEQ

Newport/Middletown/Portsmouth and Vicinity

This index helps you "spot" where approved lodgings and restaurants are located on the corresponding detailed maps. Lodging daily rate range is for comparison only and show the property's high season. Restaurant rate range is a combination of lunch and/or dinner. Turn to the listing page for more detailed rate information and consult display ads for special promotions.

NEWPORT

Map Page	OA	Lodgings	Diamond Rated	High Season	Page
1 / p. 588	AAA	Best Western Mainstay Inn - see color ad p 594	◈◈	$69-$230 SAVE	594
2 / p. 588	AAA	Stella Maris Inn	◈◈◈	$125-$225	600
3 / p. 588	AAA	Beech Tree Inn	◈◈	$139-$359 SAVE	593
4 / p. 588		Sarah Kendall House	◈◈◈	$100-$325	600
5 / p. 588		Hilltop Inn	◈◈◈	Rates not provided	595
6 / p. 588	AAA	Hyatt Regency Newport Hotel & Spa	◈◈◈	$109-$449 SAVE	597
7 / p. 588	AAA	Jail House Inn	◈◈◈	$99-$359 SAVE	597
8 / p. 588	AAA	Newport Marriott Hotel	◈◈◈	$249-$489 SAVE	599
9 / p. 588	AAA	La Farge Perry House	◈◈◈	$325-$525 SAVE	598
10 / p. 588		Wyndham Long Wharf Resort	◈◈◈	Rates not provided	600
11 / p. 588		The Clarkston	◈◈◈	Rates not provided	595
12 / p. 588		Cleveland House Inn	◈◈◈	Rates not provided	595
13 / p. 588		The Melville House	◈◈◈	Rates not provided	598
14 / p. 588	AAA	Abigail Stoneman Inn	◈◈◈◈	$250-$650 SAVE	593
15 / p. 588	AAA	Yankee Peddler Inn	◈◈	$79-$289 SAVE	600
16 / p. 588		Brinley Victorian Inn	◈◈	$109-$249	594
17 / p. 588		Pilgrim House Inn	◈◈	$125-$265	600
18 / p. 588	AAA	The Hotel Viking	◈◈◈	$99-$499 SAVE	595
19 / p. 588	AAA	Hydrangea House Inn	◈◈◈	$295-$495 SAVE	597
20 / p. 588	AAA	Newport Harbor Hotel & Marina - see color ad p 598	◈◈◈	$169-$469 SAVE	599
21 / p. 588		The Old Beach Inn	◈◈◈	$145-$375	599
22 / p. 588		Pelham Court Hotel	◈◈◈	$149-$449	599
23 / p. 588	AAA	Almondy Inn	◈◈◈	$200-$365 SAVE	593
24 / p. 588	AAA	The Burbank Rose	◈◈	$119-$240 SAVE	594
25 / p. 588		The Chanler at Cliff Walk	◈◈◈◈	$309-$1499	595
26 / p. 588	AAA	Harborside Inn	◈◈◈	$159-$459 SAVE	595
27 / p. 588		The Francis Malbone House Inn	◈◈◈	Rates not provided	595
28 / p. 588	AAA	Cliffside Inn	◈◈◈◈	$195-$675 SAVE	595
29 / p. 588		Admiral Fitzroy Inn	◈◈◈	$115-$355	593
30 / p. 588	AAA	Spring Street Inn	◈◈◈	$159-$299 SAVE	600
31 / p. 588	AAA	Ivy Lodge	◈◈◈	$159-$499 SAVE	597

Map Page	OA	Restaurants	Diamond Rated	Cuisine	Meal Range	Page
① / p. 588		Pop Kitchen & Cocktails	◆◆	New American	$7-$23	602
② / p. 588		Norey's	◆◆	American	$12-$28	602
③ / p. 588		Tucker's Bistro	◆◆◆	French	$21-$30	603
④ / p. 588		Salvation Cafe	◆◆	International	$10-$25	603
⑤ / p. 588	AAA	**Portabella**	◆	Italian	$4-$27	602
⑥ / p. 588		The Corner Cafe	◆◆	American	$3-$15	602
⑦ / p. 588		White Horse Tavern	◆◆◆	American	$14-$40	603
⑧ / p. 588	AAA	**Yesterday's Ale House**	◆◆	American	$7-$23	603
⑨ / p. 588		The Barking Crab	◆◆	Seafood	$12-$42	601
⑩ / p. 588		Jonathan's Ocean Coffee Roasters	◆	Coffee/Tea	$6-$9	602
⑪ / p. 588		Belle's	◆	American	$7-$9	601
⑫ / p. 588		Brick Alley Pub & Restaurant	◆◆	American	$8-$28	601
⑬ / p. 588		One Bellevue Restaurant	◆◆◆	American	$7-$32	602
⑭ / p. 588		Twenty-two Bowen's Wine Bar & Grille	◆◆◆	American	$10-$46	603
⑮ / p. 588	AAA	**The Wharf Pub & Restaurant**	◆◆	American	$7-$20	603
⑯ / p. 588		Rhode Island Quahog Company	◆◆	Seafood	$9-$25	602
⑰ / p. 588		The Mooring	◆◆◆	Regional American	$10-$35	602
⑱ / p. 588		The Black Pearl	◆◆	American	$8-$30	601
⑲ / p. 588		The Commodore's Room at the Black Pearl	◆◆◆	American	$20-$40	601
⑳ / p. 588	AAA	**Spiced Pear Restaurant**	◆◆◆◆	New Continental	$20-$65	603
㉑ / p. 588		Salas' Upstairs Dining Room & Salas' Down Under	◆◆	Italian	$4-$30	603
㉒ / p. 588		The Red Parrot	◆◆	American	$5-$29	602
㉓ / p. 588		Sardella's Italian Restaurant	◆◆	Italian	$9-$24	603
㉔ / p. 588		Puerini's	◆◆	Italian	$14-$22	602
㉕ / p. 588	AAA	**Canfield House**	◆◆◆	American	$18-$31	601
㉖ / p. 588		Bouchard Restaurant & Inn	◆◆◆	French	$20-$38	601
㉗ / p. 588		Scales & Shells	◆◆	Seafood	$19-$33	603
㉘ / p. 588		Cafe Zelda	◆◆◆	French	$8-$30	601
㉙ / p. 588		Ocean Breeze Cafe	◆◆	Breads/Pastries	$7-$10	602
㉚ / p. 588		Asterisk	◆◆◆	American	$20-$32	601
㉛ / p. 588		Castle Hill Inn & Resort Dining Room	◆◆◆	Regional American	$15-$110	601

BRISTOL

Map Page	OA	Lodgings	Diamond Rated	High Season	Page
㉞ / p. 588		Rockwell House Inn	◆◆◆	$159-$379	575
㉟ / p. 588		Bradford-Dimond-Norris House Bed & Breakfast	◆◆◆	$150-$250	575
㊱ / p. 588		Bristol Harbor Inn	◆◆◆	$135-$255	575

BRISTOL (cont'd)

Map Page	OA	Lodgings (cont'd)	Diamond Rated	High Season	Page
37 / p. 588		William's Grant Inn	◆◆◆	$129-$199	575
38 / p. 588	AAA	**Point Pleasant Inn & Resort**	◆◆◆◆	$375-$675 SAVE	575

Map Page	OA	Restaurants	Diamond Rated	Cuisine	Meal Range	Page
34 / p. 588		S. S. Dion Restaurant	◆◆	Seafood	$15-$24	577
35 / p. 588		Redlefsen's	◆◆◆	Continental	$9-$27	577
36 / p. 588		Quito's	◆◆	Seafood	$6-$20	576
37 / p. 588		Bristol Sunset Cafe	◆	Breads/Pastries	$3-$8	576
38 / p. 588		DeWolf Tavern	◆◆◆	American	$15-$42	576
39 / p. 588		Bristol House of Pizza	◆	Pizza	$5-$12	576
40 / p. 588		Persimmon	◆◆◆	New American	$20-$35	576
41 / p. 588		Thames Waterside Bar & Grill	◆◆	American	$10-$25	577
42 / p. 588		Aidan's	◆	Irish	$7-$19	576
43 / p. 588		Leo's Ristorante	◆◆	Italian	$5-$16	576
44 / p. 588		Roberto's	◆◆◆	Northern Italian	$14-$27	577
45 / p. 588		The Lobster Pot	◆◆◆	Seafood	$10-$29	576

MIDDLETOWN

Map Page	OA	Lodgings	Diamond Rated	High Season	Page
41 / p. 588		Econo Lodge	◆	$60-$210	582
42 / p. 588	AAA	**Travelodge**	◆◆	$60-$250 SAVE	585
43 / p. 588	AAA	**Courtyard by Marriott-Newport/Middletown**	◆◆◆	$119-$239 SAVE	582
44 / p. 588	AAA	**Holiday Inn Express Middletown** - see color ad p 596	◆◆◆	$79-$289 SAVE	583
45 / p. 588	AAA	**Howard Johnson Inn-Newport** - see color ad p 596	◆◆	$79-$254 SAVE	583
46 / p. 588	AAA	**Residence Inn by Marriott-Newport/Middletown** - see color ad p 596	◆◆◆	$139-$275 SAVE	583
47 / p. 588		Hampton Inn & Suites - see color ad p 596	◆◆◆	$99-$294	582
48 / p. 588	AAA	**The Carriage House Inn, an Ascend Collection hotel**	◆◆	$108-$258 SAVE	581
49 / p. 588		Rhea's Inn by the Sea	◆◆	$139-$269	583
50 / p. 588		Quality Inn & Suites Atlantic Beach Hotel	◆◆	$99-$329	583
51 / p. 588	AAA	**Comfort Inn Newport**	◆◆◆	$129-$329 SAVE	582
52 / p. 588	AAA	**The Newport Beach Hotel & Suites** - see color ad p 599	◆◆◆	$99-$599 SAVE	583

Map Page	OA	Restaurants	Diamond Rated	Cuisine	Meal Range	Page
53 / p. 588		Saigon Cafe	◆	Vietnamese	$6-$25	585
54 / p. 588		Blue Plate Diner	◆◆	American	$5-$15	585
55 / p. 588		Siam Square	◆◆	Thai	$7-$17	586
56 / p. 588		Coddington Brewing Co	◆◆	American	$7-$23	585
57 / p. 588		Becky's Real BBQ	◆	Barbecue	$4-$12	585

Map Page	OA	Restaurants (cont'd)	Diamond Rated	Cuisine	Meal Range	Page
58 / p. 588		Batik Garden Restaurant	◆◆	Chinese	$7-$11	585
59 / p. 588		Anthony's Seafood Group	◆	Seafood	$5-$19	585
60 / p. 588		Sea Shai	◆◆	Japanese	$5-$17	586
61 / p. 588		Flo's Clam Shack	◆	Seafood	$7-$20	585
62 / p. 588		Ticket's Bar & Grill	◆◆	American	$7-$20	587
63 / p. 588		Johnny's Atlantic Beach Club	◆◆◆	American	$7-$25	585

JAMESTOWN

Map Page	OA	Lodging	Diamond Rated	High Season	Page
55 / p. 588		The Wyndham Bay Voyage Inn	◆◆◆	$150-$300	580

Map Page	OA	Restaurants	Diamond Rated	Cuisine	Meal Range	Page
66 / p. 588		Bay Voyage Restaurant	◆◆◆	New American	$13-$28	581
67 / p. 588		Tricia's Tropi-Grille	◆◆	Caribbean	$10-$20	581

PORTSMOUTH

Map Page	OA	Restaurants	Diamond Rated	Cuisine	Meal Range	Page
48 / p. 588		15 Point Road Restaurant	◆◆	American	$15-$25	605
49 / p. 588		Graziano's 501 Cafe	◆◆	American	$7-$22	605
50 / p. 588		Melville Grille	◆◆	New England	$7-$23	605

NEWPORT pop. 26,475   (See map and index starting on p. 588)

ABIGAIL STONEMAN INN

AAA SAVE

▽▽▽ ▽▽▽

Historic Bed
& Breakfast

$250-$650 5/1-10/31
$195-$495 11/1-4/30

Phone: (401)847-1811   **14**

Address: 102 Touro St 02840 **Location:** At Mt. Vernon St. **Facility:** Built in 1866, this property offers many special, complimentary amenities: Guests receive a pillow menu, soap menu and an exotic water and tea menu. Smoke free premises. 5 units. 2 one-bedroom standard units with whirlpools. 2 one- and 1 two-bedroom suites with whirlpools, some with kitchens. 3 stories (no elevator), interior corridors. **Parking:** on-site. **Terms:** office hours 6:30 am-9 pm, age restrictions may apply, 15 day cancellation notice-fee imposed. **Amenities:** video library, CD players, voice mail, irons, hair dryers. *Some:* DVD players. **Leisure Activities:** *Fee:* massage. **Guest Services:** valet laundry, wireless Internet. **Free Special Amenities:** full breakfast and high-speed Internet.

✕ / SOME UNITS 🖥 📷 💻

ADMIRAL FITZROY INN

▽▽▽▽

Bed & Breakfast

$115-$355 5/1-9/14
$105-$355 9/15-4/30

Phone: (401)848-8000   **29**

Address: 398 Thames St 02840 **Location:** S of Memorial Blvd; between Brewer and Dennison sts; downtown. **Facility:** In the heart of the city, this comfortable inn is known for its rooftop deck with incredible views; rooms feature hand-painted walls. Smoke free premises. 18 units. 17 one-bedroom standard units, some with whirlpools. 1 one-bedroom suite. 3 stories, interior/exterior corridors. *Bath:* combo or shower only. **Parking:** on-site. **Terms:** 2 night minimum stay - weekends, 10 day cancellation notice-fee imposed. **Amenities:** voice mail, irons, hair dryers. **Guest Services:** wireless Internet. **Business Services:** meeting rooms, PC. 🍴► ✕ 🖥

ALMONDY INN

AAA SAVE

▽▽▽ ▽▽▽

Historic Bed
& Breakfast

$200-$365 5/1-10/28
$155-$270 10/29-4/30

Phone: (401)848-7202   **23**

Address: 25 Pelham St 02840 **Location:** Just n of Memorial Blvd (SR 138A) via Spring St, then just w. **Facility:** In the Historic Hill district and steps away from Brick Market, most rooms at this 1890s Victorian home have bay views, fireplaces and Jacuzzi tubs. Smoke free premises. 5 units. 3 one-bedroom standard units, some with whirlpools. 2 one-bedroom suites with whirlpools. 3 stories (no elevator), interior corridors. **Parking:** on-site. **Terms:** office hours 9 am-9 pm, 2 night minimum stay - weekends, 14 day cancellation notice-fee imposed. **Amenities:** video library, DVD players, CD players, voice mail, irons, hair dryers. **Guest Services:** valet laundry, wireless Internet. **Business Services:** meeting rooms, business center. **Free Special Amenities:** full breakfast and high-speed Internet. 🍴► ✕

BEECH TREE INN

AAA SAVE

▽▽▽ ▽▽

Bed & Breakfast

$139-$359 5/1-10/31
$99-$279 11/1-4/30

Book great rates at AAA.com   **Phone:** (401)847-9794   **3**

Address: 34 Rhode Island Ave 02840 **Location:** Just e of SR 114; 0.8 mi s of jct SR 138. Located in a residential area. **Facility:** Many of the third-floor rooms at the charming 1887 inn have decks overlooking the water; also find a garden, roof deck, games and a book collection. Smoke free premises. 8 units. 7 one-bedroom standard units, some with whirlpools. 1 one-bedroom suite with whirlpool. 3 stories (no elevator), interior corridors. *Bath:* combo or shower only. **Parking:** on-site. **Terms:** office hours 10 am-10 pm, 2-3 night minimum stay - seasonal and/or weekends, 14 day cancellation notice-fee imposed. **Amenities:** irons, hair dryers. **Leisure Activities:** *Fee:* massage. **Guest Services:** wireless Internet. **Free Special Amenities:** full breakfast and high-speed Internet. ✕ / SOME UNITS FEE 🛒 🖥

(See map and index starting on p. 588)

BEST WESTERN MAINSTAY INN

Book great rates at AAA.com

Phone: (401)849-9880   **1**

Hotel

$69-$230 5/1-10/31
$50-$109 11/1-4/30

AAA Benefit:
Members save up to 20%, plus 10% bonus points with rewards program.

Address: 151 Admiral Kalbfus Rd 02840 **Location:** SR 138; from Newport Bridge, 2nd exit. Opposite Jai Alai Fronton. **Facility:** 199 units. 198 one-bedroom standard units. 1 one-bedroom suite. 4 stories, interior corridors. *Bath:* combo or shower only. **Parking:** on-site. **Terms:** 2 night minimum stay - seasonal and/or weekends, 3 day cancellation notice-fee imposed. **Amenities:** voice mail, irons, hair dryers. **Pool(s):** outdoor. **Leisure Activities:** sun deck, exercise room. **Guest Services:** valet and coin laundry, wireless Internet. **Business Services:** meeting rooms, business center. *(See color ad below)*

FREE local telephone calls and high-speed Internet

BRINLEY VICTORIAN INN

Phone: 401/849-7645   **16**

Historic Bed & Breakfast

$109-$249 All Year

Address: 23 Brinley St 02840 **Location:** Just e of Bellevue Ave; between Kay and Catherine sts. Located in a residential area. **Facility:** Built between 1850 and 1870, the Victorian inn features a small library and antiques, soft linens, curtains and wallpapers reflecting period ambience. Smoke free premises. 16 one-bedroom standard units, some with whirlpools. 2 stories (no elevator), interior corridors. *Bath:* combo or shower only. **Parking:** on-site. **Terms:** office hours 9 am-9 pm, 2 night minimum stay - seasonal and/or weekends, age restrictions may apply, 14 day cancellation notice-fee imposed. **Amenities:** hair dryers. **Guest Services:** TV in common area, wireless Internet.

THE BURBANK ROSE

Phone: 401/849-9457   **24**

Historic Bed & Breakfast

$119-$240 5/1-11/1
$89-$180 11/2-4/30

Address: 111 Memorial Blvd W 02840 **Location:** Just e on SR 138A. **Facility:** With flower pots covering the front stoop, the 1850s-era inn is in a central location convenient to the pier, area restaurants and Brick Market. Smoke free premises. 5 units. 2 one-bedroom standard units. 3 one-bedroom suites with kitchens. 3 stories (no elevator), interior corridors. *Bath:* shower only. **Parking:** on-site. **Terms:** office hours 9 am-9 pm, 2 night minimum stay - seasonal and/or weekends, 7 day cancellation notice-fee imposed. **Amenities:** CD players, irons, hair dryers. **Guest Services:** wireless Internet. **Free Special Amenities:** expanded continental breakfast and high-speed Internet.

▼ *See AAA listing above* ▼

(See map and index starting on p. 588)

THE CHANLER AT CLIFF WALK   *Book at AAA.com*   Phone: (401)847-1300   25

Country Inn
$309-$1499 All Year

Address: 117 Memorial Blvd W 02840 **Location:** Oceanfront. On SR 138A, just e of Rhode Island Ave; at Cliff Walk entrance near Easton's Beach. **Facility:** An elegant brick and stucco mansion built in the 1870s, The Chanler commands a fine view of an ocean cove, and manicured gardens grace the grounds. Smoke free premises. 20 units. 11 one-bedroom standard units, some with whirlpools. 9 one-bedroom suites with whirlpools. 2-3 stories (no elevator), interior/exterior corridors. *Bath:* combo or shower only. **Parking:** on-site and valet. **Terms:** 2 night minimum stay - seasonal and/or weekends, 30 day cancellation notice-fee imposed. **Amenities:** video library, DVD players, CD players, dual phone lines, voice mail, safes, irons, hair dryers. **Dining:** Spiced Pear Restaurant, see separate listing. **Leisure Activities:** jogging. *Fee:* massage. **Guest Services:** valet laundry, area transportation, wireless Internet. **Business Services:** meeting rooms.

THE CLARKSTON   Phone: 401/848-5300   11

Historic Bed
& Breakfast
Rates not provided

Address: 28 Clarke St 02840 **Location:** Just e of Thames St via Touro St, follow right opposite Washington Square to narrow one-way Clarke St; downtown. **Facility:** Guest rooms at this 1705 Colonial inn feature antiques and optional feather beds; five units have a fireplace. Smoke free premises. 9 one-bedroom standard units, some with whirlpools. 3 stories (no elevator), interior corridors. *Bath:* combo or shower only. **Parking:** on-site. **Terms:** office hours 7 am-10 pm. **Amenities:** *Some:* hair dryers. **Guest Services:** wireless Internet.

CLEVELAND HOUSE INN   Phone: 401/848-5300   12

Historic Bed
& Breakfast
Rates not provided

Address: 27 Clarke St 02840 **Location:** Just e of Thames St via Touro St, follow right opposite Washington Square onto narrow one-way Clarke St; downtown. **Facility:** On a side street near Brick Market, this Victorian home has nicely decorated rooms with fine linens and canopy, sleigh or four-poster beds. Smoke free premises. 17 one-bedroom standard units, some with whirlpools. 3 stories (no elevator), interior corridors. *Bath:* combo or shower only. **Parking:** on-site. **Terms:** office hours 7 am-10 pm. **Amenities:** *Some:* hair dryers. **Guest Services:** wireless Internet.

CLIFFSIDE INN   Phone: (401)847-1811   28

[AAA] [SAVE]

Historic Bed
& Breakfast
$195-$675 5/1-10/31
$140-$425 11/1-4/30

Address: 2 Seaview Ave 02840 **Location:** Just s of Memorial Blvd via Cliff Ave. **Facility:** Built in 1876 by Maryland Governor Swann and later inhabited by artist Beatrice Turner, the inn is widely respected for its afternoon tea service. Smoke free premises. 16 units. 8 one-bedroom standard units, some with whirlpools. 8 one-bedroom suites with whirlpools. 1-3 stories (no elevator), interior/exterior corridors. *Bath:* combo or tub only. **Parking:** on-site. **Terms:** office hours 8 am-8 pm, 15 day cancellation notice-fee imposed. **Amenities:** video library, DVD players, CD players, voice mail, irons, hair dryers. **Guest Services:** wireless Internet. **Free Special Amenities: full breakfast and high-speed Internet.**

THE FRANCIS MALBONE HOUSE INN   Phone: 401/846-0392   27

Bed & Breakfast
Rates not provided

Address: 392 Thames St 02840 **Location:** Just s of Memorial Blvd; downtown. **Facility:** A 1760 Colonial-style mansion, the inn has antiques and reproductions, four guest parlors, a manicured courtyard, afternoon tea and homemade snacks. Smoke free premises. 20 one-bedroom standard units, some with whirlpools. 2-3 stories (no elevator), interior corridors. *Bath:* combo or shower only. **Parking:** on-site. **Terms:** office hours 7 am-11 pm, age restrictions may apply. **Amenities:** video library, DVD players, voice mail, irons, hair dryers. *Some:* CD players. **Guest Services:** valet laundry, wireless Internet. **Business Services:** meeting rooms.

HARBORSIDE INN   *Book great rates at AAA.com*   Phone: (401)846-6600   26

[AAA] [SAVE]

Bed & Breakfast
$159-$459 5/1-10/31
$99-$239 11/1-4/30

Address: Christie's Landing 02840 **Location:** Just w of Thames St; downtown. **Facility:** On the water near shops and restaurants, the inn has many rooms with harbor views; some suites have steep stairs that are somewhat difficult to climb. Smoke free premises. 15 units. 6 one- and 9 two-bedroom standard units. 3 stories (no elevator), interior corridors. **Parking:** on-site. **Terms:** 2-4 night minimum stay - seasonal and/or weekends, 7 day cancellation notice-fee imposed. **Amenities:** DVD players, irons, hair dryers. **Guest Services:** valet laundry, wireless Internet. **Free Special Amenities: expanded continental breakfast and high-speed Internet.**

HILLTOP INN   Phone: 401/846-0392   5

Bed & Breakfast
Rates not provided

Address: 2 Kay St 02840 **Location:** Corner of Touro St and Bellevue Ave. **Facility:** Blocks from the waterfront and wharves, the inn offers a mix of antiques and such modern appointments as marble showers, plasma TVs and CD players. Smoke free premises. 5 one-bedroom standard units with whirlpools. 2 stories (no elevator), interior corridors. **Parking:** on-site. **Terms:** office hours 7 am-10 pm, age restrictions may apply. **Amenities:** video library, DVD players, CD players, irons, hair dryers. **Leisure Activities:** exercise room. **Guest Services:** valet laundry, wireless Internet.

THE HOTEL VIKING   *Book great rates at AAA.com*   Phone: (401)847-3300   18

[AAA] [SAVE]

Historic
Hotel
$99-$499 All Year

Address: 1 Bellevue Ave 02840 **Location:** Corner of Kay and Church sts and Bellevue Ave. **Facility:** Flower pots decorate the gardens and windows of the hotel's elegant brick facade, and Georgian and Queen Anne furnishings create a graceful ambience. Smoke free premises. 209 units. 194 one-bedroom standard units. 13 one- and 2 two-bedroom suites. 4-5 stories, interior corridors. *Bath:* combo or shower only. **Parking:** on-site (fee) and valet. **Terms:** check-in 4 pm, 2 night minimum stay - seasonal and/or weekends, 7 day cancellation notice-fee imposed. **Amenities:** dual phone lines, voice mail, irons, hair dryers. *Fee:* high-speed Internet, safes. *Some:* CD players. **Dining:** One Bellevue Restaurant, see separate listing. **Pool(s):** heated indoor. **Leisure Activities:** whirlpool, exercise room, spa. *Fee:* bicycles. **Guest Services:** valet laundry, wireless Internet. **Business Services:** conference facilities, business center. **Free Special Amenities: newspaper and room upgrade (subject to availability with advance reservations).**

Plan. Map. Go.
TripTik® Travel Planner on AAA.com

(See map and index starting on p. 588)

HYATT REGENCY NEWPORT HOTEL & SPA

Book great rates at AAA.com

Phone: (401)851-1234 [6]

Resort Hotel
$109-$449 All Year

Address: 1 Goat Island 02840 **Location:** 0.8 mi w of America's Cup Ave, follow signs to Goat Island. **Facility:** Located on Goat Island, many rooms at the hotel offer views of the harbor, marina and downtown Newport. 257 units. 238 one-bedroom standard units, some with whirlpools. 19 one-bedroom suites, some with whirlpools. 2-9 stories, interior corridors. *Bath:* combo or shower only. **Parking:** on-site (fee) and valet. **Terms:** check-in 4 pm, 3 day cancellation notice-fee imposed. **Amenities:** voice mail, safes, irons, hair dryers. *Some:* DVD players (fee), CD players, dual phone lines. **Pool(s):** outdoor, heated indoor. **Leisure Activities:** bicycles, exercise room, spa. *Fee:* saunas. **Guest Services:** valet laundry, area transportation-downtown, wireless Internet. **Business Services:** conference facilities, business center. **Free Special Amenities: full breakfast.**

AAA Benefit:
Ask for the AAA rate and save 10%.

HYDRANGEA HOUSE INN

Phone: 401/846-4435 [19]

Historic Bed & Breakfast
$295-$495 All Year

Address: 16 Bellevue Ave 02840 **Location:** Corner of Kay and Church sts and Bellevue Ave. **Facility:** Elegantly renovated, the 1876 inn has such amenities as two-person hot tubs, heated towel racks, faux-painted wall treatments and luxurious fabrics. Smoke free premises. 10 one-bedroom standard units, some with whirlpools. 3 stories (no elevator), interior corridors. *Bath:* combo or shower only. **Parking:** on-site. **Terms:** office hours 9 am-9 pm, 3 night minimum stay - seasonal and/or weekends, 14 day cancellation notice-fee imposed. **Amenities:** CD players, high-speed Internet, irons, hair dryers. **Leisure Activities:** *Fee:* massage. **Guest Services:** wireless Internet. **Free Special Amenities: full breakfast and high-speed Internet.**

IVY LODGE

Phone: (401)849-6865 [31]

Historic Bed & Breakfast
$159-$499 5/1-10/31
$99-$429 11/1-4/30

Address: 12 Clay St 02840 **Location:** S on Bellevue Ave, e on Narragansett Ave, then n. **Facility:** An 1886 Victorian-style home in the mansion district of historic Newport, Ivy Lodge boasts antiques, richly detailed oak walls and a fireplace hearth. Smoke free premises. 8 one-bedroom standard units, some with whirlpools. 3 stories (no elevator), interior corridors. *Bath:* combo or shower only. **Parking:** on-site. **Terms:** office hours 8 am-9 pm, 2-3 night minimum stay - weekends, 14 day cancellation notice-fee imposed. **Amenities:** CD players, voice mail, irons, hair dryers. *Some:* DVD players. **Guest Services:** wireless Internet. **Free Special Amenities: full breakfast and high-speed Internet.**

JAIL HOUSE INN

Book great rates at AAA.com

Phone: (401)847-4638 [7]

Historic Bed & Breakfast
$99-$359 5/1-9/20
$79-$279 9/21-12/10

Address: 13 Marlborough St 02840 **Location:** 1.2 mi sw of SR 138 via Broadway. **Facility:** This historic city jail has been nicely converted into a B&B with a front porch overlooking the street; tea and cookies are served each afternoon. Smoke free premises. 23 units. 19 one-bedroom standard units. 4 two-bedroom suites. 3 stories (no elevator), interior corridors. **Parking:** on-site. **Terms:** open 5/1-12/10, office hours 7 am-11 pm, 2-4 night minimum stay - seasonal and/or weekends, 7 day cancellation notice-fee imposed. **Amenities:** irons, hair dryers. **Guest Services:** valet laundry, wireless Internet. **Free Special Amenities: expanded continental breakfast and high-speed Internet.**

(See map and index starting on p. 588)

LA FARGE PERRY HOUSE — *Book great rates at AAA.com* — Phone: (401)847-2223 — **9**

Historic Bed & Breakfast
$325-$525 5/1-10/15
$145-$395 10/16-4/30

Address: 24 Kay St 02840 **Location:** Corner of Kay and Bull sts. **Facility:** Wood floors, Oriental rugs and marble baths add elegance to this comfortable, historic home; afternoon refreshments and tasty macaroons are included. Smoke free premises. 5 units. 4 one- and 1 two-bedroom standard units. 3 stories (no elevator), interior corridors. *Bath:* combo or shower only. **Parking:** on-site. **Terms:** 2 night minimum stay - weekends, 7 day cancellation notice-fee imposed. **Amenities:** video library, DVD players, CD players, voice mail, irons, hair dryers. **Guest Services:** wireless Internet. **Free Special Amenities:** full breakfast and high-speed Internet. ⊠ 🎦 🖥 / SOME UNITS 🖥

THE MELVILLE HOUSE — Phone: 401/848-5300 — **13**

Historic Bed & Breakfast
Rates not provided

Address: 39 Clarke St 02840 **Location:** Just e of Thames St via Touro St, follow right opposite Washington Square onto narrow one-way Clarke St; downtown. Located in a quiet historic district. **Facility:** Antiques furnish many of the rooms at this comfortable B&B on a quiet street one and a half blocks from Brick Market Place and the harbor. Smoke free premises. 6 one-bedroom standard units. 2 stories (no elevator), interior corridors. *Bath:* shower only. **Parking:** on-site. **Terms:** office hours 7 am-10 pm, age restrictions may apply. **Amenities:** irons, hair dryers. **Guest Services:** wireless Internet. ⊠ 🎦 🆓

▼ See AAA listing p 599 ▼

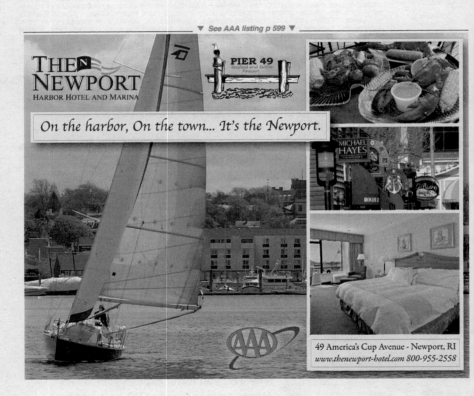

(See map and index starting on p. 588)

NEWPORT HARBOR HOTEL & MARINA *Book great rates at AAA.com* **Phone:** (401)847-9000 **20**

Hotel
$169-$469 5/1-10/31
$119-$229 11/1-4/30

Address: 49 America's Cup Ave 02840 **Location:** On Newport Harbor. **Facility:** Smoke free premises. 133 one-bedroom standard units. 4 stories, interior corridors. **Parking:** on-site (fee). **Terms:** check-in 4 pm, 2 night minimum stay - seasonal and/or weekends, 3 day cancellation notice-fee imposed. **Amenities:** video games (fee), high-speed Internet, voice mail, irons, hair dryers. **Pool(s):** heated indoor. **Leisure Activities:** saunas. *Fee:* marina. **Guest Services:** valet and coin laundry, wireless Internet. **Business Services:** meeting rooms, business center. *(See color ad p 598)*

 / SOME UNITS FEE

FREE newspaper and high-speed Internet

NEWPORT MARRIOTT HOTEL *Book great rates at AAA.com* **Phone:** (401)849-1000 **8**

Hotel
$249-$489 All Year

Address: 25 America's Cup Ave 02840 **Location:** Downtown; on the harbor. Adjacent to Newport Visitor Center. **Facility:** Smoke free premises. 317 units. 310 one-bedroom standard units, some with whirlpools. 7 one-bedroom suites, some with whirlpools. 7 stories, interior corridors. *Bath:* combo or shower only. **Parking:** on-site (fee) and valet. **Terms:** check-in 4 pm, cancellation fee imposed. **Amenities:** CD players, dual phone lines, voice mail, safes, irons, hair dryers. *Fee:* video games, high-speed Internet. **Pool(s):** heated indoor. **Leisure Activities:** sauna, whirlpool, racquetball courts. *Fee:* massage, game room. **Guest Services:** valet and coin laundry, wireless Internet. **Business Services:** conference facilities, business center. **Free Special Amenities:** newspaper.

Marriott
HOTELS & RESORTS

AAA Benefit:
Members save a minimum 5% off the best available rate.

THE OLD BEACH INN **Phone:** 401/849-3479 **21**

Historic Bed
& Breakfast
$145-$375 5/1-10/31
$95-$350 11/1-4/30

Address: 19 Old Beach Rd 02840 **Location:** Just e of Bellevue Ave. **Facility:** This 1879 Victorian home includes a manicured courtyard and is furnished with many period pieces; some rooms have fireplaces. Smoke free premises. 6 one-bedroom standard units. 3 stories (no elevator), interior/exterior corridors. *Bath:* combo or shower only. **Parking:** on-site. **Terms:** office hours 7:30 am-8 pm, 2 night minimum stay - weekends, age restrictions may apply, 15 day cancellation notice-fee imposed. **Amenities:** *Some:* irons, hair dryers. [ASK] / SOME UNITS

PELHAM COURT HOTEL **Phone:** 401/619-4950 **22**

Hotel
$149-$449 All Year

Address: 14 Pelham St 02840 **Location:** Just n of Memorial Blvd (SR 138A) via Spring St, then just w. **Facility:** Smoke free premises. 8 units. 1 one-bedroom standard unit with kitchen. 7 one-bedroom suites, some with kitchens. 2-3 stories (no elevator), interior corridors. *Bath:* combo or shower only. **Parking:** on-site. **Terms:** office hours 9 am-5 pm, 7 day cancellation notice-fee imposed. **Amenities:** DVD players, CD players, irons, hair dryers. **Guest Services:** coin laundry, wireless Internet.

▼ See AAA listing p 583 ▼

(See map and index starting on p. 588)

PILGRIM HOUSE INN

Phone: 401/846-0040 **17**

Historic Bed & Breakfast

$125-$265 5/1-11/2
$125-$160 11/3-4/30

Address: 123 Spring St 02840 **Location:** Just e of Thames St. **Facility:** Built circa 1809, this charming B&B offers views from a rooftop deck and some rooms that overlook a small garden and Newport Harbor. Smoke free premises. 11 one-bedroom standard units. 3 stories (no elevator), interior corridors. *Bath:* shower only. **Parking:** street. **Terms:** office hours 7 am-midnight, age restrictions may apply. **Amenities:** CD players, hair dryers. *Some:* DVD players. **Leisure Activities:** roof top deck. **Guest Services:** wireless Internet. [ASK] [X] [☎]

SARAH KENDALL HOUSE

Phone: 401/846-7976 **4**

Historic Bed & Breakfast

$100-$325 All Year

Address: 47 Washington St 02840 **Location:** Between Elm and Bridge sts; just n from Newport Harbor; just nw of Gateway Visitor's Center. Located in the historic district. **Facility:** This 1871 Victorian B&B offers many rooms with views of Newport Harbor and its sailboats, plus a 50-foot-tall Tower Sitting Room with dramatic views. Smoke free premises. 5 one-bedroom standard units. 3 stories (no elevator), interior corridors. *Bath:* combo or shower only. **Parking:** on-site. **Terms:** office hours 8 am-10 pm, 2 night minimum stay - weekends, 14 day cancellation notice-fee imposed. **Amenities:** CD players, irons, hair dryers. *Some:* DVD players. **Guest Services:** wireless Internet.

[ASK] [X] [🍴] [☎] [🖥]

SPRING STREET INN

Phone: (401)847-4767 **30**

[AAA] [SAVE]

Historic Bed & Breakfast

$159-$299 All Year

Address: 353 Spring St 02840 **Location:** Just e of Thames St; corner of Howard St. **Facility:** Antique prints adorn public areas in this 1858 Empire-style Victorian inn, with afternoon refreshments, welcome gifts and cozy, comfortable rooms. Smoke free premises. 7 units. 6 one-bedroom standard units. 1 one-bedroom suite with whirlpool. 3 stories (no elevator), interior corridors. *Bath:* combo or shower only. **Parking:** on-site. **Terms:** office hours 9 am-9 pm, 2 night minimum stay - weekends, 10 day cancellation notice-fee imposed. **Amenities:** high-speed Internet, hair dryers. **Guest Services:** wireless Internet. **Free Special Amenities: full breakfast and high-speed Internet.** [X] [☎]

STELLA MARIS INN

Phone: 401/849-2862 **2**

[AAA] [SAVE]

Historic Bed & Breakfast

$125-$225 5/1-10/31

Address: 91 Washington St 02840 **Location:** Jct Pine and Cherry sts; 1 blk from Newport Harbor, 0.3 mi nw of Gateway Visitor's Center. Located in a historic district. **Facility:** Tall ceilings and antique furnishings bring an elegant ambience to the red-stone, 1861 Victorian mansion; some rooms have ocean views and a fireplace. Smoke free premises. 9 one-bedroom standard units. 3 stories (no elevator), interior corridors. *Bath:* combo or shower only. **Parking:** on-site. **Terms:** open 5/1-10/31, office hours 8 am-10 pm, 2 night minimum stay - weekends, 6 day cancellation notice-fee imposed. **Amenities:** *Some:* irons, hair dryers. **Guest Services:** TV in common area, wireless Internet. **Free Special Amenities: expanded continental breakfast and high-speed Internet.**

[X] [K] [🐾] [☎]

WYNDHAM LONG WHARF RESORT   *Book at AAA.com*

Phone: 401/847-7800 **10**

Hotel

Rates not provided

Address: 5 Washington St 02840 **Location:** Just w of America's Cup Ave. Located behind transportation center. **Facility:** Smoke free premises. 101 units. 92 two- and 9 three-bedroom suites with kitchens and whirlpools. 4 stories, interior corridors. **Parking:** on-site. **Terms:** check-in 4 pm. **Amenities:** video library (fee), DVD players, voice mail, irons, hair dryers. **Pool(s):** outdoor, heated indoor/outdoor. **Leisure Activities:** whirlpools, exercise room. *Fee:* game room. **Guest Services:** complimentary laundry, wireless Internet. **Business Services:** meeting rooms.

[ECO] [📶] [🏊] [X] [X] [🍴] [🖥] [📷] [💻]

YANKEE PEDDLER INN   *Book great rates at AAA.com*

Phone: (401)846-1323 **15**

[AAA] [SAVE]

Historic Bed & Breakfast

$79-$289 5/1-11/9

Address: 113 Touro St 02840 **Location:** 1.2 mi sw of SR 138 via Broadway, just e. **Facility:** The 19th-century Greek Revival inn offers great views from a rooftop deck; rooms have period antique furniture, interesting fabrics and original art. Smoke free premises. 20 units. 17 one-bedroom standard units. 3 one-bedroom suites. 3 stories (no elevator), interior corridors. *Bath:* combo or shower only. **Parking:** on-site. **Terms:** open 5/1-11/9, office hours 7 am-11 pm, 2-4 night minimum stay - seasonal and/or weekends, 7 day cancellation notice-fee imposed. **Amenities:** *Some:* irons, hair dryers. **Leisure Activities:** sun deck. **Guest Services:** wireless Internet. **Free Special Amenities: expanded continental breakfast and high-speed Internet.** [📶] [X] [☎] / SOME UNITS [🖥]

The following lodgings were either not evaluated or did not meet AAA rating requirements but are listed for your information only.

CASTLE HILL INN & RESORT

Phone: 401/849-3800

[fyi]

Not evaluated. **Address:** 590 Ocean Dr 02840 **Location:** Oceanfront. Facilities, services, and decor characterize an upscale property.

NEWPORT ONSHORE

Phone: 401/849-1500

[fyi]

Not evaluated. **Address:** 405 Thames St 02840. Facilities, services, and decor characterize a mid-scale property. [ECO]

OCEANCLIFF HOTEL

Phone: 401/841-8868

[fyi]

Not evaluated. **Address:** 65 Ridge Rd 02840 **Location:** Oceanfront. Facilities, services, and decor characterize an upscale property.

WYNDHAM INN ON THE HARBOUR

Phone: 401/849-6789

[fyi]

Not evaluated. **Address:** 359 Thames St 02840. Facilities, services, and decor characterize an economy property. [ECO]

(See map and index starting on p. 588)

─── **WHERE TO DINE** ───

ASTERISK

Phone: 401/841-8833   30

American
$20-$32

The contemporary New York City-inspired restaurant displays an eclectic mix of furnishings and decor; many colorful paintings and distinctive lighting fixtures complete the look. Fresh ingredients factor into preparations of seafood, fish, chops and steaks. Complimentary on-site parking is limited. Dressy casual. **Bar:** Full bar. **Reservations:** suggested. **Hours:** 7 am-10 pm, Fri & Sat-11 pm; seasonal hours vary. **Address:** 599 Thames St 02840 **Location:** 0.5 mi s of Memorial Blvd; downtown. **Parking:** on-site.

THE BARKING CRAB

Phone: 401/846-2722   9

Seafood
$12-$42

Similar to the original restaurant in Boston, this place has patrons busily cracking crab legs with large river rocks. Other popular choices include fried Rhode Island calamari and steamer clam bake with red bliss potatoes, corn on the cob and coleslaw. On warm days most guests prefer to sit outside at a picnic table under the red-and-yellow-striped tent rather than in the nicely decorated dining room, which has a nautical feel. Service is casual but friendly and attentive. Casual dress. **Bar:** Full bar. **Reservations:** not accepted. **Hours:** 11:30 am-10 pm. Closed: 4/4, 11/25, 12/25. **Address:** 151 Swineburne Row 02840 **Location:** Jct SR 138A and Thames St; downtown. **Parking:** on-site (fee). CALL ⑤M

BELLE'S

Phone: 401/846-6000   11

American
$7-$9

Past the Newport Shipyard gates, this hidden jewel is a great place for a casual breakfast among the mega-yachts parked outside. Guests nibble on tasty omelets and sip on espresso or other specialty coffee as they check their e-mail at a computer kiosk. Casual dress. **Reservations:** not accepted. **Hours:** Open 12/1-3/1; 7 am-4 pm. Closed major holidays. **Address:** 1 Washington St 02840 **Location:** Between Marsh St & Long Wharf Mall Rd; within the Newport Shipyard; downtown. **Parking:** street.

THE BLACK PEARL

Phone: 401/846-5264   18

American
$8-$30

The more casual side to the adjacent Commodore's Room. This dining area and bar are reminiscent of the interior of a prized wooden sailboat with its high-gloss black walls adorned with old nautical maps, hardwood floors and views of the marina just outside. The fresh fish and seafood preparations are really the highlight here, though a large menu featuring sandwiches, burgers and salads will keep everyone happy. Casual dress. **Bar:** Full bar. **Reservations:** not accepted. **Hours:** Open 5/1-1/2 & 2/13-4/30; 11:30 am-11 pm; hours vary off season. Closed: 11/25, 12/24, 12/25. **Address:** Bannister's Wharf 02840 **Location:** Just w of America's Cup Ave. **Parking:** street.

BOUCHARD RESTAURANT & INN

Phone: 401/846-0123   26

French
$20-$38

French dishes are artistically presented at the upscale restaurant, which occupies an elegant 1785 Georgian-style house in the heart of the city. Dressy casual. **Bar:** Full bar. **Reservations:** suggested. **Hours:** 5:30 pm-9 pm. Closed: 11/25, 12/25; also Tues & 1/1-1/10. **Address:** 505 Thames St 02840 **Location:** Jct SR 138A, 0.5 mi s. **Parking:** street.

BRICK ALLEY PUB & RESTAURANT

Phone: 401/849-6334   12

American
$8-$28

After a busy day or evening of shopping, many scoot across the street to the bustling, casual eatery to peruse a menu of seafood, steak, nachos and varied appetizers. A salad buffet offers good variety, and Tex-Mex fare is featured on Tuesday. Dressy casual. **Bar:** Full bar. **Reservations:** accepted. **Hours:** 11:30 am-10 pm, Fri & Sat 11 am-10:30 pm, Sun 10:30 am-10 pm. Closed: 11/25, 12/25. **Address:** 140 Thames St 02840 **Location:** Opposite Brick Market Place. **Parking:** street.

CAFE ZELDA

Phone: 401/849-4002   28

French
$8-$30

Diners enter through a lively bar and then step into the intimate dining room. Creativity marks French-American dishes made from fresh regional ingredients. Casual dress. **Bar:** Full bar. **Reservations:** suggested. **Hours:** 3 pm-10 pm, Fri-10:30 pm, Sat 11 am-10:30 pm, Sun 11 am-10 pm. Closed: 11/25, 12/25. **Address:** 528 Thames St 02840 **Location:** S of Memorial Blvd; between Holland St and Dean Ave. **Parking:** on-site and street.

CANFIELD HOUSE

Phone: 401/847-0416   25

American
$18-$31

American cuisine is served in an 1860s building formerly owned by gambler Richard Canfield. Dressy casual. **Bar:** Full bar. **Reservations:** suggested. **Hours:** 5 pm-9 pm, Fri & Sat-10 pm. Closed: 12/25; also Mon. **Address:** 5 Memorial Blvd 02840 **Location:** Just e of Bellevue Ave; downtown. **Parking:** on-site. **Historic**

CASTLE HILL INN & RESORT DINING ROOM

Phone: 401/849-3800   31

Regional American
$15-$110

Overlooking Narragansett Bay is the 1874 summer home of Alexander Agassiz, the famous geologist. Here you'll enjoy modern New England cuisine from a seasonally changing menu that is driven by the availability of fresh ingredients. Dressy casual. **Bar:** Full bar. **Reservations:** suggested. **Hours:** 11:30 am-3 & 6-9 pm, Fri & Sat-10 pm; hours may vary off season. **Address:** 590 Ocean Ave 02840 **Location:** 4.5 mi se on Ocean Ave via Ocean Dr. **Parking:** on-site. **Historic**

THE COMMODORE'S ROOM AT THE BLACK PEARL

Phone: 401/846-5264   19

American
$20-$40

The more formal side of the adjacent Black Pearl, this place employs refined, attentive servers in professional attire. Accenting the New England ship atmosphere are dark-green walls, illustrations of late 19th-century sailing boats and white-linen-topped tables. The chef expertly prepares French-American cuisine centered on New England lobster tails, duck, veal and high-end steaks. Special occasions merit special meals, which is what diners can expect. Dressy casual. **Bar:** Full bar. **Reservations:** suggested. **Hours:** Open 5/1-1/2 & 2/13-4/30; 6 pm-10:30 pm. Closed: 11/25, 12/25. **Address:** Bannister's Wharf 02840 **Location:** Just w of America's Cup Ave. **Parking:** street.

(See map and index starting on p. 588)

THE CORNER CAFE
Phone: 401/846-0606 ⑥

American
$3-$15

This cafe boasts great curb appeal, with interesting signage and colorful banquette views from the window. Furthering the fun contemporary feel inside are tropical fans, sage walls, an exposed-brick accent wall and a central fireplace. An old stool counter area with a flat-panel TV viewable from all tables remains in service toward the back of the restaurant. Locals love this place for its delicious breakfast and brunch items. Casual dress. **Bar:** Full bar. **Reservations:** not accepted. **Hours:** 6:45 am-2:30 pm, Thurs-Sat also 5:30 pm-9:30 pm, Sun 6:45 am-2:45 pm. Closed: 12/25. **Address:** 110 Broadway 02840 **Location:** 1.1 mi sw of SR 138. **Parking:** street.

JONATHAN'S OCEAN COFFEE ROASTERS
Phone: 401/846-6060 ⑩

Coffee/Tea
$6-$9

Popular with locals and tourists for their morning cup of joe, the coffeehouse features homemade desserts and pastries. Lunch offerings include a number of soups and sandwiches, including ham, turkey and BLTs. The narrow dining area is accented with a black-and-white-tiled floor, yellow and red walls and colorful artwork that is also for sale. Casual dress. **Reservations:** not accepted. **Hours:** 6 am-5 pm. Closed: 12/25. **Address:** 22 Washington Square 02840 **Location:** Corner of Charles St, just e of Thames St; downtown. **Parking:** street.

THE MOORING
Phone: 401/846-2260 ⑰

Regional American
$10-$35

Contemporary New England cuisine and fine yachting memorabilia highlight the experience at the original New York Yacht Club station house. Seafood scampi, lobster, Key lime pie and bread pudding are specialties. A few steaks and chops also are featured. Patio seating overlooking the marina is available in season. Dressy casual. **Bar:** Full bar. **Reservations:** suggested. **Hours:** 11:30 am-10 pm, Fri & Sat-11 pm; hours vary off season. Closed: 12/25. **Address:** Sayer's Wharf 02840 **Location:** Downtown; on the waterfront. **Parking:** on-site (fee).

NOREY'S
Phone: 401/847-4971 ②

American
$12-$28

The fun, eclectic and trendy restaurant gives guests a choice of seating in a comfortable booths, at a wooden picnic table or at the counter. Freshly prepared meals offer a creative twist on grilled pizza, seafood and steak. Casual dress. **Bar:** Full bar. **Reservations:** accepted. **Hours:** 4:30 pm-11 pm. Closed: 11/25, 12/25. **Address:** 156 Broadway 02840 **Location:** Jct SR 138, 0.9 mi sw. **Parking:** street.

OCEAN BREEZE CAFE
Phone: 401/849-1750 ㉙

Breads/Pastries
$7-$10

The casual eatery prepares breakfast and lunch items using its homemade breads and pastries. Casual dress. **Reservations:** not accepted. **Hours:** 7 am-3 pm. Closed: 11/25, 12/25. **Address:** 580 Thames St 02840 **Location:** Corner of Thames St and Wellington Ave. **Parking:** on-site.

ONE BELLEVUE RESTAURANT
Phone: 401/848-4824 ⑬

American
$7-$32

The restaurant offers elegant dining and, weather permitting, al fresco dining as well. The chef prepares traditional New England fare such as clam chowder, steamed clams and lobster salad; however, more adventurous dishes include roasted duckling, soy and honey glazed salmon. The menu does change seasonally. Dressy casual. **Bar:** Full bar. **Reservations:** suggested. **Hours:** 7-11 am, 11:30-3 & 5:30-9 pm, Sat & Sun 7 am-noon, 12:30-3 & 5:30-10 pm. **Address:** One Bellevue Ave 02840 **Location:** Corner of Kay and Church sts and Bellevue Ave; in The Hotel Viking. **Parking:** valet.

POP KITCHEN & COCKTAILS
Phone: 401/846-8456 ①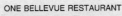

New American
$7-$23

The New York City-styled restaurant feels more like a lounge than a restaurant. In the dining room are boldly painted walls in hues of orange and red and rectangular nooks holding candles and pieces of art; comfortable sofas and banquettes sit near an inviting fireplace. Accentuating the homey feel is a doorbell that chimes when food is ready to be delivered. Menu options range from grilled pizza to high-quality steak to fresh seafood. Casual dress. **Bar:** Full bar. **Hours:** 5 pm-10 pm. Closed major holidays. **Address:** 162 Broadway 02840 **Location:** Jct SR 138, 0.9 mi sw. **Parking:** street.

PORTABELLA
Menu on AAA.com Phone: 401/847-8200 ⑤

Italian
$4-$27

The family-run Italian market and delicatessen serves delicious homemade soups, large salads and made-to-order sandwiches on a choice of freshly baked breads. Long glass counters are showcases for an array of prepared foods, such as lasagna, calzones and meatballs, which can be ordered at the counter then eaten in the dining room or taken home. Casual dress. **Reservations:** not accepted. **Hours:** 8:30 am-6 pm, Fri & Sat-10:30 pm. Closed: 1/1, 11/25, 12/25; also Sun in winter. **Address:** 136 Broadway 02840 **Location:** 1 mi sw of SR 138. **Parking:** on-site.

PUERINI'S
Phone: 401/847-5506 ㉔

Italian
$14-$22

This casual neighborhood restaurant and local favorite presents a menu of freshly made Northern and Southern Italian preparations of homemade pasta, veal, chicken, calamari and shrimp. The atmosphere is intimate and inviting. Casual dress. **Bar:** Beer & wine. **Reservations:** not accepted. **Hours:** 5 pm-10 pm. **Address:** 24 Memorial Blvd W 02840 **Location:** Just w of Bellevue Ave. **Parking:** street.

THE RED PARROT
Phone: 401/847-3800 ㉒

American
$5-$29

Built in 1898, the three-story building remains a downtown focal point due to its striking brick facade and colorful window flower boxes. Anyone dining here is bound to find something enjoyable on the expansive 22-page menu. Be sure to save room for one of the exotic desserts, which draw on Caribbean influences. Casual dress. **Bar:** Full bar. **Reservations:** not accepted. **Hours:** 11:30 am-10 pm, Fri & Sat-11 pm. Closed: 12/25. **Address:** 348 Thames St 02840 **Location:** Corner of Memorial Blvd; downtown. **Parking:** street.

RHODE ISLAND QUAHOG COMPANY
Phone: 401/848-2330 ⑯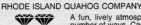

Seafood
$9-$25

A fun, lively atmosphere is nurtured at the popular restaurant. Seafood, the main draw, is prepared in a number of ways. Casual dress. **Bar:** Full bar. **Reservations:** suggested. **Hours:** Open 5/1-12/31 & 3/1-4/30; 11:30 am-10 pm, Fri & Sat-11 pm; hours may vary off season. Closed major holidays. **Address:** 250 Thames St 02840 **Location:** Between Mill and Pelham sts; downtown. **Parking:** street.

(See map and index starting on p. 588)

SALAS' UPSTAIRS DINING ROOM & SALAS' DOWN UNDER

Phone: 401/846-8772   ㉑

Italian
$4-$30

The bustling, casual, second-floor family restaurant offers an eclectic mix of Italian and Oriental dishes prepared in a refreshing way. Seafood and oriental spaghetti are favorites. The downtown eatery sports bay windows and seafaring artwork inside. Casual dress. **Bar:** Full bar. **Reservations:** accepted. **Hours:** 11 am-10 pm. **Closed:** 11/25, 12/24, 12/25. **Address:** 345 Thames St 02840 **Location:** Just off Memorial Blvd. **Parking:** street.

SALVATION CAFE

Phone: 401/847-2620   ④

International
$10-$25

The South Pacific meets 1960s retro at this local favorite. Eclectic decor fills every space of the distinctive restaurant. The inventive cuisine fuses Southeast Asian, Mediterranean, Indian and Mexican influences. The many rooms merit a quick tour. In warmer months, guests can enjoy a frozen drink at the tiki bar. Dressy casual. **Bar:** Full bar. **Hours:** 5 pm-11 pm; Sun-Thurs to 10 pm in winter. **Address:** 140 Broadway 02840 **Location:** 0.9 mi sw of SR 138. **Parking:** on-site.

SARDELLA'S ITALIAN RESTAURANT

Phone: 401/849-6312   ㉓

Italian
$9-$24

Italian dishes, complemented by a good list of reasonably priced wines, have been freshly prepared to order for 20 years. Many pasta dishes are available as half orders. The atmosphere is cozy and warm, particularly in winter when a fire is ablaze in the dining room fireplace. Dinner-for-two specials on Monday and Tuesday include a bottle of wine. During summer, validated parking is available in the shopping center parking lot to the rear of the restaurant. Dressy casual. **Bar:** Full bar. **Reservations:** suggested. **Hours:** 5 pm-10 pm, Fri & Sat-11 pm, Sun 4 pm-10 pm. **Closed:** 11/25. **Address:** 30 Memorial Blvd N 02840 **Location:** 0.3 mi e, just w of Bellevue Ave. **Parking:** on-site.

SCALES & SHELLS

Phone: 401/846-3474   ㉗

Seafood
$19-$33

The restaurant is known for its open kitchen concept. Guests can view fresh seafood as they walk by the wood-fire grill. Bright orange walls, dark hardwood flooring and a contemporary-style bar accent the casually elegant dining space. Casual dress. **Bar:** Full bar. **Reservations:** not accepted. **Hours:** Open 5/1-12/18 & 1/13-4/30; 5 pm-9 pm, Fri & Sat-10 pm; to 10 pm, Fri & Sat-11 pm, Sun 4 pm-10 pm in summer. **Closed:** 4/4; also Mon 1/1-5/1 & Super Bowl Sun. **Address:** 527 Thames St 02840 **Location:** Jct SR 138A and Memorial Blvd, 0.4 mi s. **Parking:** street.

SPICED PEAR RESTAURANT

Phone: 401/847-2244   ⑳

New Continental
$20-$65

Perched on a cliff, the restaurant affords breathtaking views of Newport Beach. Guests seeking an elegant dining experience might try the chef's tasting menu with a set wine pairing. Semi-formal attire. **Bar:** Full bar. **Reservations:** suggested. **Hours:** 7:30-10:30 am, 11:30-2:30 & 6-9 pm, Fri & Sat-9:30 pm. **Closed:** Mon & Tues in winter & spring. **Address:** 117 Memorial Blvd 02840 **Location:** On SR 138A, just e of Rhode Island Ave; at Cliff Walk entrance near Easton's Beach; in The Chanler at Cliff Walk. **Parking:** on-site and valet. CALL

TUCKER'S BISTRO

Phone: 401/846-3449   ③

French
$21-$30

The restaurant's slogan says it all: "Step through the door and you will be transported back to a 1930s Paris bistro". Dressy casual. **Bar:** Full bar. **Reservations:** accepted. **Hours:** 6 pm-10 pm, Fri & Sat-10:30 pm. **Closed:** 11/25, 12/25. **Address:** 150 Broadway 02840 **Location:** Jct SR 138, 1 mi sw. **Parking:** street.

TWENTY-TWO BOWEN'S WINE BAR & GRILLE

Phone: 401-841-8884   ⑭

American
$10-$46

Affording excellent views of the marina, the bustling two-level harborside setting is popular for its fresh seafood and hand-carved USDA Prime steaks. Popular choices include Duck Trap River smoked salmon, raw oysters, littlenecks, rib lamb chops and grilled swordfish. Upscale nautical appointments fill the dining room, which has dark wood ceiling beams, brick flooring, wainscoting and French doors that open onto the patio. Dressy casual. **Bar:** Full bar. **Reservations:** suggested, for dinner. **Hours:** 11:30 am-3:30 & 5-10 pm, Fri & Sat-11 pm; hours vary off season. **Closed:** 12/25. **Address:** 22 Bowen's Wharf 02840 **Location:** Just w of Thames St; between Market Square and Scotts Wharf; downtown. **Parking:** on-site (fee). CALL

THE WHARF PUB & RESTAURANT

Phone: 401/846-9233   ⑮

American
$7-$20

The atmosphere is laid-back and friendly at the brewpub, where patrons order from a menu of chowder, fresh raw bar items, deli sandwiches, burgers, fresh local fish and chips and fried clams. The dinner menu is presented after 5 pm. The outdoor deck affords a seating alternative. Casual dress. **Bar:** Beer & wine. **Reservations:** not accepted. **Hours:** 11:30 am-11 pm. **Closed:** 4/4, 11/25, 12/25. **Address:** 37 Bowens Wharf 02840 **Location:** Off America's Cup Ave. **Parking:** on-site (fee).

WHITE HORSE TAVERN

Phone: 401/849-3600   ⑦

American
$14-$40

A gracious, candlelit dining room with a formal setting in a historical residence awaits; you'll dine on a variety of fare including oysters and red snapper, and be catered to by a formally attired, skilled staff. Gentlemen are required to wear jackets. Semi-formal attire. **Bar:** Full bar. **Reservations:** suggested. **Hours:** 11:30 am-2:30 & 5:30-9 pm, Sun noon-3 & 5:30-9 pm; hours vary in winter. **Closed:** 12/25. **Address:** 26 Marlborough St 02840 **Location:** Corner of Marlborough and Farewell sts. **Parking:** on-site. **Historic**

YESTERDAY'S ALE HOUSE

Phone: 401/847-0116   ⑧

American
$7-$23

Part of two restaurants under one roof, Yesterday's is more casual, but the food remains memorable. Selections from the creative menu include delicious burgers, homemade soups and chowders, grilled steaks and herb-crusted lamp chops. Casual dress. **Bar:** Full bar. **Reservations:** accepted. **Hours:** 11:30 am-9 pm, Fri & Sat-10 pm. **Closed:** 11/25, 12/25. **Address:** 28 Washington Square 02840 **Location:** Just e of Thames St. **Parking:** street.

NORTH KINGSTOWN

HAMILTON VILLAGE INN

◈◈◈

Motel

$99-$139 5/1-10/31
$79-$109 11/1-4/30

Phone: 401/295-0700

Address: 642 Boston Neck Rd 02852 **Location:** SR 1A, 1.3 mi s of jct SR 102. **Facility:** 56 units. 52 one-bedroom standard units, some with efficiencies. 4 one-bedroom suites with kitchens. 2 stories (no elevator), exterior corridors. *Bath:* combo or shower only. **Parking:** on-site. **Terms:** office hours 8 am-10 pm, 2 night minimum stay - seasonal and/or weekends, 7 day cancellation notice-fee imposed. **Dining:** Sea View Station, see separate listing. **Guest Services:** coin laundry. **Business Services:** PC. ⊟ / SOME UNITS ⊟ ⊠ ⊟ ⊞ ⊟

———— WHERE TO DINE ————

THE CORNER TAVERN

◈◈

American

$5-$19

Phone: 401/294-9897

The cozy little restaurant offers traditional New England fare and friendly service. Prices are reasonable. Casual dress. **Bar:** Full bar. **Hours:** 11 am-8 pm, Fri & Sat-9 pm. Closed: 11/25, 12/25. **Address:** 20 S County Tr 02852 **Location:** On US 2 at SR 102. **Parking:** on-site.

GREGG'S RESTAURANT & PUB

◈◈◈

American

$7-$15

Phone: 401/294-5700

Popular with all age groups, the relaxed and cheery restaurant prepares a wide selection of sandwiches and full dinners. It's well worth a short wait in line for a seat, not only for the meal but also for a delicious homemade pastry. Casual dress. **Bar:** Full bar. **Reservations:** not accepted. **Hours:** 11:30 am-11 pm, Fri & Sat-midnight. Closed: 11/25, 12/25. **Address:** 4120 Quaker Ln (SR 2) 02852 **Location:** SR 4, exit 5A southbound, 2 mi s; exit 5B northbound, 0.5 mi ne. **Parking:** on-site.

SEA VIEW STATION

◈◈

American

$5-$12

Phone: 401/295-8666

The bright, airy restaurant presents a menu of preparations that appeal to all members of the family. Casual dress. **Bar:** Full bar. **Hours:** 7 am-2 pm, Fri & Sat 5 pm-8 pm. Closed: 11/25, 12/25. **Address:** 640 Boston Neck Rd 02852 **Location:** SR 1A, 1.3 mi s of jct SR 102; in Hamilton Village Inn. **Parking:** on-site.

CALL ♿Ⓜ

NORTH PROVIDENCE pop. 32,411   (See map and index starting on p. 606)

———— WHERE TO DINE ————

TWIN'S PIZZA

◈◈

Italian

$3-$17

Phone: 401/726-8978   (76)

The family-run restaurant prepares Italian favorites such as homemade lasagna, meatball sandwiches and pizza. The plain surroundings are comfortable. Guests should bring a stash of quarters to feed personal jukeboxes at almost every table. Casual dress. **Bar:** Full bar. **Hours:** 11 am-10 pm, Fri & Sat-11 pm, Sun 1 pm-9:30 pm, Tues 4 pm-10 pm. Closed major holidays; also Mon. **Address:** 1000 Mineral Spring Ave 02904 **Location:** SR 146, exit Mineral Spring Ave, just e. **Parking:** on-site.

NORTH SMITHFIELD

—— WHERE TO DINE ——

BEEF BARN INC

American
$2-$5

Phone: 401/762-9880

Since 1968, the restaurant has served sandwiches, homemade soup and pastries on paper plates. Casual dress. **Hours:** 11 am-10 pm, Sun from noon. Closed major holidays; also Mother's Day. **Address:** 1 Greenville Rd (Rt 104) 02896 **Location:** Jct SR 146A, 0.3 mi n of Park Square; SR 146, 0.8 mi ne. **Parking:** on-site.

PAWTUCKET pop. 72,958   (See map and index starting on p. 606)

COMFORT INN-PROVIDENCE/PAWTUCKET   *Book at AAA.com*   Phone: (401)723-6700   **29**

Hotel
$99-$175 All Year

Address: 2 George St 02860 **Location:** I-95, exit 27, just e, then just n. **Facility:** 138 units. 133 one-bedroom standard units. 5 one-bedroom suites. 5 stories, interior corridors. *Bath:* combo or shower only. **Parking:** on-site. **Amenities:** video games (fee), voice mail, irons, hair dryers. **Pool(s):** heated indoor. **Leisure Activities:** exercise room. **Guest Services:** coin laundry, wireless Internet. **Business Services:** meeting rooms, business center.

(ASK) [tableware] [drink] CALL [&M] [pool] [exercise] [video] / SOME UNITS [X] FEE [refrigerator] FEE [microwave]

—— WHERE TO DINE ——

MODERN DINER

American
$4-$7

Phone: 401/726-8390   **66**

The friendly neighborhood diner serves traditional comfort foods of burgers and more. Casual dress. **Bar:** Full bar. **Hours:** 6 am-2 pm, Sun from 7 am. Closed major holidays. **Address:** 364 East Ave 02860 **Location:** I-95, exit 27, just s on George St, then just se. **Parking:** on-site.

SPUMONI'S

Italian
$6-$16

Phone: 401/726-4449   **65**

Spumoni's is a lively, bright and colorful family restaurant that offers a wide selection of appetizers and seafood prepared with an Italian flair. Reasonably priced steaks, veal, chicken and seafood, as well as pasta by the pound, make this restaurant a popular and affordable place to take the entire family. Casual dress. **Bar:** Full bar. **Hours:** 11:30 am-10 pm, Fri & Sat-11 pm, Sun-9:30 pm. Closed: 11/25, 12/24, 12/25. **Address:** 1537 Newport Ave 02861 **Location:** I-95, exit 2A, just s. **Parking:** on-site.

PEACE DALE

—— WHERE TO DINE ——

PUMP HOUSE RESTAURANT

American
$10-$25

Phone: 401/789-4944

A comfortable, rustic ambience permeates the dining room in the beautifully restored stone water pumping site. The menu lists traditional American fare, with steak, fresh local seafood, chicken and duck as highlights. Smoking is permitted only in the lounge. Casual dress. **Bar:** Full bar. **Reservations:** not accepted. **Hours:** 4 pm-10 pm, Sun noon-9 pm. Closed: 12/25. **Address:** 1464 Kingstown Rd 02883 **Location:** 0.5 mi n on SR 108. **Parking:** on-site. **Historic**

PORTSMOUTH   (See map and index starting on p. 588)

—— WHERE TO DINE ——

15 POINT ROAD RESTAURANT

American
$15-$25

Phone: 401/683-3138   **48**

The Sakonnet River at Old Stone Bridge forms the backdrop for intimate, candlelight dining. On the menu are grilled meat, fresh local seafood and creative pasta entrees. Prix fixe meals are available off season. Casual dress. **Bar:** Full bar. **Hours:** 5 pm-9 pm, Fri & Sat-10 pm, Sun 4 pm-9 pm. Closed: 11/25, 12/24, 12/25; also Mon. **Address:** 15 Point Rd 02871 **Location:** SR 24, exit Island Park, 0.5 mi e on Boyd's Ln, then 1 mi n on Park Ave. **Parking:** on-site.

GRAZIANO'S 501 CAFE

American
$7-$22

Phone: 401/683-0750   **49**

The small local favorite serves an excellent breakfast that is available all day. Fresh seafood and American favorites such as burgers and chicken sandwiches are available for lunch and dinner on weekends. The restaurant sits on the banks of the Sakonnet River, but high windows in the dining room mean it's best to sit on the summer patio for the best views. Service is attentive and welcoming. The hospitable owner comes around to each table to make sure diners are content. Casual dress. **Bar:** Full bar. **Reservations:** accepted. **Hours:** 6 am-3:30 pm, Fri & Sat-10 pm, Sun-4 pm. Closed: 11/25, 12/25. **Address:** 501 Park Ave 02871 **Location:** SR 24, exit Island Park, 0.5 mi se on Boyd's Ln, then 0.5 mi ne. **Parking:** on-site.

MELVILLE GRILLE

New England
$7-$23

Phone: 401/683-4400   **50**

Overlooking Melville Marina and Narragansett Bay, the dining room and outdoor patio are appointed in nautical decor and feature a tin-roof ceiling and framed pictures of sailboats on the walls. Classic New England favorites include butter crumb-baked scrod and Portuguese fish chowder with cod, shrimp, scallops and chorizo in creamy broth. Ultra-thin-crust pizzas, burgers, pasta and sandwiches are also popular. Among choices on the kids menu are bowties and tomato sauce and macaroni and cheese. Casual dress. **Bar:** Full bar. **Reservations:** accepted. **Hours:** 11:30 am-8 pm; hours may vary off season. Closed: 11/25. **Address:** One Lagoon Rd 02871 **Location:** Jct SR 24, 1.7 mi s on SR 114, 1 mi w on Stringham Rd, then just n. **Parking:** on-site.

Read, Share, Ask, Plan. Join the travel
conversation at AAATravelViews.com

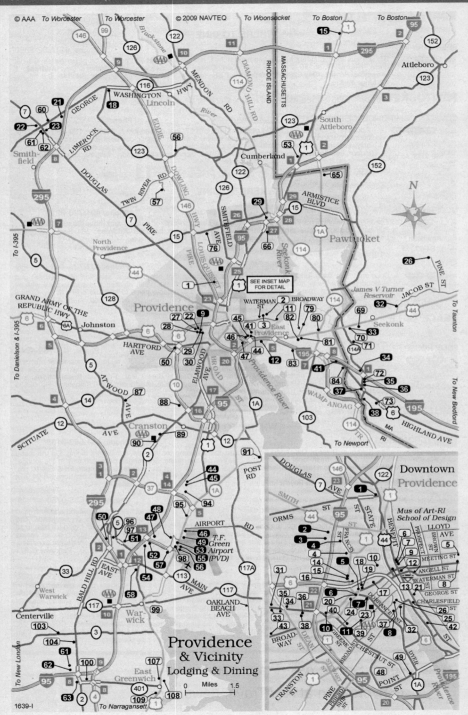

© AAA To Worcester   To Worcester   © 2009 NAVTEQ   To Woonsocket   To Boston   To Boston

Providence
& Vicinity
Lodging & Dining

0   Miles   1.5

Downtown
Providence

Mus of Art-RI
School of Design

SEE INSET MAP
FOR DETAIL

1639-I

✈ Airport Accommodations

Map Page	OA	THEODORE FRANCIS GREEN STATE	Diamond Rated	High Season	Page
49 / p. 606		Comfort Inn-Airport, 0.8 mi n of terminal	◆◆◆	$80-$149	625
55 / p. 606	AAA	**Hampton Inn & Suites Providence-Warwick Airport, just n of terminal**	◆◆◆	$89-$189 SAVE	626
54 / p. 606		Homestead Studio Suites-Providence/Airport/ Warwick, 2 mi w of terminal	◆◆	$75-$149	627
45 / p. 606		La Quinta Inn & Suites, 1.5 mi n of terminal	◆◆	$65-$159	627
53 / p. 606	AAA	**Radisson Hotel Providence Airport, 0.3 mi s of terminal**	◆◆◆	$109-$161 SAVE	628
47 / p. 606		Residence Inn Providence/Warwick, 1.5 mi w of terminal	◆◆◆	$159-$169	628
46 / p. 606	AAA	**Sheraton Providence Airport Hotel, 0.5 mi n of terminal**	◆◆◆	$79-$209 SAVE	628

Providence and Vicinity

This index helps you "spot" where approved lodgings and restaurants are located on the corresponding detailed maps. Lodging daily rate range is for comparison only and show the property's high season. Restaurant rate range is a combination of lunch and/or dinner. Turn to the listing page for more detailed rate information and consult display ads for special promotions.

PROVIDENCE

Map Page	OA	Lodgings	Diamond Rated	High Season	Page
1 / p. 606	AAA	**Marriott Providence Downtown**	◆◆◆	$251-$307 SAVE	615
2 / p. 606	AAA	**The Christopher Dodge House**	◆◆◆	$139-$179 SAVE	612
3 / p. 606	AAA	**The Mowry-Nicholson House**	◆◆◆	$139-$169 SAVE	616
4 / p. 606	AAA	**Renaissance Providence Hotel - see color ad p 616**	◆◆◆◆	$197-$241 SAVE	617
5 / p. 606		Courtyard by Marriott, Downtown Providence	◆◆◆	$158-$194	613
6 / p. 606	AAA	**The Westin Providence**	◆◆◆◆	$149-$419 SAVE	617
7 / p. 606		Providence Biltmore Hotel	◆◆◆	$119-$299	616
8 / p. 606		Hampton Inn & Suites Providence-Downtown	◆◆◆	$149-$229	613
9 / p. 606		Hotel Dolce Villa	◆◆◆	$129-$429	614
10 / p. 606		Hilton Providence	◆◆◆	$129-$289	614
11 / p. 606	AAA	**The Hotel Providence - see color ad p 615**	◆◆◆◆	$149-$399 SAVE	614
12 / p. 606	AAA	**Radisson Hotel Providence Harbor**	◆◆◆	$99-$169 SAVE	616

Map Page	OA	Restaurants	Diamond Rated	Cuisine	Meal Range	Page
1 / p. 606	AAA	**Pearl Restaurant & Lounge**	◆◆◆	New American	$10-$35	621
2 / p. 606		Twist on Angell	◆◆	New American	$13-$21	622
3 / p. 606		Red Stripe	◆◆◆	French	$8-$21	621
4 / p. 606		Temple Downtown	◆◆◆	New American	$10-$26	622
5 / p. 606		Andreas	◆◆	Greek	$7-$20	617
6 / p. 606		Cafe Noir	◆◆◆	French	$10-$22	618
7 / p. 606		Chinese Laundry	◆◆◆	Chinese	$17-$20	619
8 / p. 606		Cafe Paragon/Viva	◆◆	New American	$7-$20	618
9 / p. 606		Mills Tavern	◆◆◆	American	$18-$39	620
10 / p. 606		Cafe Nuovo	◆◆◆	Continental	$8-$39	618

Map Page	OA	Restaurants (cont'd)	Diamond Rated	Cuisine	Meal Range	Page
11 / p. 606		Waterman Grille	◆◆◆	New American	$18-$27	622
12 / p. 606		Cafe Choklad	◆	Breads/Pastries	$6-$8	618
13 / p. 606		New Rivers	◆◆	International	$16-$30	620
14 / p. 606		Napa Valley Grille	◆◆◆	American	$7-$28	620
15 / p. 606		The Cheesecake Factory	◆◆◆	American	$9-$30	619
16 / p. 606		Ruth's Chris Steak House	◆◆◆	Steak	$34-$45	622
17 / p. 606		Raphael Bar-Risto	◆◆◆	Italian	$14-$30	621
18 / p. 606		Citron Wine Bar & Bistro	◆◆◆	New American	$6-$25	619
19 / p. 606		Union Station Brewery	◆◆	Regional American	$7-$24	622
20 / p. 606		Agora	◆◆◆	American	$10-$38	617
21 / p. 606		Parkside Rotisserie & Bar	◆◆◆	American	$6-$30	621
22 / p. 606		Casertas Pizzeria	◆	Pizza	$2-$20	619
23 / p. 606		McCormick & Schmick's	◆◆◆	Seafood	$8-$30	620
24 / p. 606		The Capital Grille	◆◆◆	Steak	$9-$35	618
25 / p. 606		Pot Au Feu Restaurant & Bistro	◆◆◆	French	$6-$29	621
26 / p. 606		Hemenway's Seafood Grill & Oyster Bar	◆◆◆	Seafood	$7-$27	620
27 / p. 606		Don Jose Tequilas	◆◆	Mexican	$13-$22	619
28 / p. 606	AAA	**Providence Oyster Bar**	◆◆◆	Seafood	$10-$36	621
29 / p. 606		Providence Prime	◆◆◆	Steak	$29-$41	621
30 / p. 606		Walter's Ristorante d' Italia	◆◆◆	Regional Italian	$18-$25	622
31 / p. 606		Zooma Bar Ristorante	◆◆◆	Italian	$14-$29	623
32 / p. 606		Capriccio	◆◆◆	Continental	$12-$35	618
33 / p. 606		Siena	◆◆◆	Northern Italian	$12-$29	622
34 / p. 606		Cassarino's	◆◆	Italian	$8-$24	619
35 / p. 606		Blue Grotto Restaurant	◆◆◆	Italian	$8-$29	618
36 / p. 606		Joe Marzilli's Old Canteen	◆◆	Italian	$10-$28	620
37 / p. 606		10 Prime Steak & Sushi	◆◆◆	Steak	$6-$40	617
38 / p. 606		Camille's	◆◆◆	Italian	$7-$40	618
39 / p. 606		Aspire	◆◆◆	New American	$17-$59	617
40 / p. 606	AAA	**Gracie's**	◆◆◆	New American	$21-$38	619
41 / p. 606		Rue De L' Espoir	◆◆	New American	$10-$31	621
42 / p. 606		Bacaro Restaurant	◆◆◆	Italian	$19-$30	618
43 / p. 606		Nick's on Broadway	◆◆	New American	$9-$26	620
44 / p. 606		Blue Elephant	◆	Breakfast	$6-$15	618
45 / p. 606	AAA	**Taste of India**	◆◆	Indian	$7-$17	622
46 / p. 606		Fellini Cafe & Pizzeria	◆	Pizza	$4-$19	619

Map Page	OA	Restaurants (cont'd)	Diamond Rated	Cuisine	Meal Range	Page
47 / p. 606		Al Forno Restaurant	◆◆◆	Northern Italian	$25-$30	617
48 / p. 606	AAA	**CAV Restaurant**	◆◆◆	International	$10-$29	619
49 / p. 606		Olga's Cup and Saucer	◆	Breads/Pastries	$7-$10	620
50 / p. 606		Wes' Rib House	◆	Barbecue	$7-$17	622

NORTH ATTLEBORO, MA

Map Page	OA	Lodging	Diamond Rated	High Season	Page
15 / p. 606		Holiday Inn Express-Providence/North Attleboro	◆◆◆	$109-$129	541

LINCOLN

Map Page	OA	Lodging	Diamond Rated	High Season	Page
18 / p. 606		Courtyard by Marriott Providence/Lincoln	◆◆◆	$149-$169	581

Map Page	OA	Restaurants	Diamond Rated	Cuisine	Meal Range	Page
56 / p. 606		The Lodge Pub & Eatery	◆◆	American	$6-$20	581
57 / p. 606		Fred & Steve's Steakhouse	◆◆◆	Steak	$19-$40	581

SMITHFIELD

Map Page	OA	Lodgings	Diamond Rated	High Season	Page
21 / p. 606	AAA	**Quality Inn Smithfield**	◆◆	$120-$280 [SAVE]	623
22 / p. 606		Comfort Suites	◆◆◆	$99-$189	623
23 / p. 606	AAA	**Hampton Inn & Suites Smithfield**	◆◆◆	$119-$209 [SAVE]	623

Map Page	OA	Restaurants	Diamond Rated	Cuisine	Meal Range	Page
60 / p. 606		Cricket's of Smithfield	◆◆	Italian	$10-$20	623
61 / p. 606		D. Carlo Trattoria	◆◆◆	Italian	$8-$20	623
62 / p. 606		Faial Restaurant & Lounge	◆◆	Portuguese	$6-$25	623

REHOBOTH, MA

Map Page	OA	Lodging	Diamond Rated	High Season	Page
26 / p. 606		Five Bridge Inn Bed & Breakfast	◆◆◆	$98-$145	551

PAWTUCKET

Map Page	OA	Lodging	Diamond Rated	High Season	Page
29 / p. 606		Comfort Inn-Providence/Pawtucket	◆◆◆	$99-$175	605

Map Page	OA	Restaurants	Diamond Rated	Cuisine	Meal Range	Page
65 / p. 606		Spumoni's	◆◆	Italian	$6-$16	605
66 / p. 606		Modern Diner	◆	American	$4-$7	605

SEEKONK, MA

Map Page	OA	Lodgings	Diamond Rated	High Season	Page
32 / p. 606	AAA	**Historic Jacob Hill Inn**	◆◆◆◆	$199-$459 [SAVE]	554
33 / p. 606	AAA	**Johnson & Wales Inn -** see color ad p 614	◆◆◆	$109-$139 [SAVE]	554
34 / p. 606		Motel 6 - 1289	◆	$55-$65	554
35 / p. 606		Ramada Inn-Providence	◆◆	$89-$150	554
36 / p. 606		Hampton Inn	◆◆◆	$84-$169	554

SEEKONK, MA (cont'd)

Map Page	OA	Lodgings (cont'd)	Diamond Rated	High Season	Page
㊲ / p. 606	AAA	**Comfort Inn Providence/Seekonk** - see color ad p 612	◆◆◆	$90-$130 SAVE	553
㊳ / p. 606	AAA	**Best Western Providence-Seekonk Inn**	◆◆◆	$100-$135 SAVE	553

Map Page	OA	Restaurants	Diamond Rated	Cuisine	Meal Range	Page
(69) / p. 606		Chardonnay's	◆◆◆	American	$9-$26	554
(70) / p. 606		Audrey's Restaurant	◆◆◆	American	$5-$30	554
(71) / p. 606		The Old Grist Mill Tavern	◆◆	American	$7-$26	555
(72) / p. 606	AAA	**Darling's Restaurant & Lounge**	◆	American	$7-$18	555
(73) / p. 606	AAA	**Tito's Cantina**	◆◆	Mexican	$4-$15	555

EAST PROVIDENCE

Map Page	OA	Lodging	Diamond Rated	High Season	Page
㊶ / p. 606		Extended StayAmerica Providence-East Providence	◆◆	$75-$149	579

Map Page	OA	Restaurants	Diamond Rated	Cuisine	Meal Range	Page
(79) / p. 606		Riviera II Family Restaurant	◆◆	Portuguese	$8-$17	580
(80) / p. 606		Davenport's Restaurant	◆◆	American	$7-$15	580
(81) / p. 606		Cattails City Grill	◆◆◆	Mediterranean	$8-$24	580
(82) / p. 606	AAA	**Horton's Seafood**	◆	Seafood	$7-$18	580
(83) / p. 606		Madeira Restaurant	◆◆	Portuguese	$5-$27	580
(84) / p. 606		Ichigo Ichie Hibachi & Sushi Bar	◆◆◆	Japanese	$9-$35	580

WARWICK

Map Page	OA	Lodgings	Diamond Rated	High Season	Page
㊹ / p. 606		Courtyard by Marriott Providence-Warwick	◆◆◆	$125-$153	625
㊺ / p. 606		La Quinta Inn & Suites	◆◆	$65-$159	627
㊻ / p. 606	AAA	**Sheraton Providence Airport Hotel**	◆◆◆	$79-$209 SAVE	628
㊼ / p. 606		Residence Inn Providence/Warwick	◆◆◆	$159-$169	628
㊽ / p. 606		Hilton Garden Inn Providence Airport/Warwick	◆◆◆	$99-$219	626
㊾ / p. 606		Comfort Inn-Airport	◆◆◆	$80-$149	625
㊿ / p. 606		Extended StayAmerica Providence-Airport-Warwick	◆◆	$65-$149	626
(51) / p. 606	AAA	**NYLO Providence/Warwick** - see color ad p 615	◆◆◆	$89-$229 SAVE	627
(52) / p. 606		Homewood Suites by Hilton	◆◆◆	$85-$159	627
(53) / p. 606	AAA	**Radisson Hotel Providence Airport** - see color ad p 628	◆◆◆	$109-$161 SAVE	628
(54) / p. 606		Homestead Studio Suites-Providence/Airport/Warwick	◆◆	$75-$149	627
(55) / p. 606	AAA	**Hampton Inn & Suites Providence-Warwick Airport**	◆◆◆	$89-$189 SAVE	626

WARWICK (cont'd)

Map Page	OA	Lodgings (cont'd)	Diamond Rated	High Season	Page
56 / p. 606	AAA	**Best Western Airport Inn** - see color ad p 612	◆◆	$85-$125 SAVE	625
57 / p. 606		Holiday Inn Express Hotel & Suites	◆◆◆	$79-$129	627
58 / p. 606		Crowne Plaza Hotel at the Crossings	◆◆◆	$99-$149	626

Map Page	OA	Restaurants	Diamond Rated	Cuisine	Meal Range	Page
94 / p. 606		Shogun Steak & Seafood House	◆◆	Japanese	$12-$36	629
95 / p. 606		Thai Excursion	◆◆	Thai	$8-$16	629
96 / p. 606		Twist	◆◆◆	Italian	$7-$23	630
97 / p. 606		The Loft	◆◆◆	New American	$9-$22	629
98 / p. 606		Legal Sea Foods	◆◆◆	Seafood	$7-$24	629
99 / p. 606		Crow's Nest Restaurant	◆◆	Seafood	$6-$22	629
100 / p. 606	AAA	**Eleven Forty Nine**	◆◆◆	New American	$7-$36	629

WEST WARWICK

Map Page	OA	Lodgings	Diamond Rated	High Season	Page
61 / p. 606	AAA	**Comfort Suites Providence/West Warwick** - see color ad p 613	◆◆◆	$90-$145 SAVE	631
62 / p. 606		SpringHill Suites Providence West Warwick	◆◆◆	$98-$120	632
63 / p. 606		Extended StayAmerica Providence-Airport-West Warwick	◆◆	$69-$149	631

Map Page	OA	Restaurants	Diamond Rated	Cuisine	Meal Range	Page
103 / p. 606		Cowesett Inn	◆◆	American	$8-$22	632
104 / p. 606		Pinelli's Gourmet Deli/Cafe	◆	Deli	$4-$17	632

SOUTH ATTLEBORO, MA

Map Page	OA	Restaurant	Diamond Rated	Cuisine	Meal Range	Page
53 / p. 606		Shanghai Gardens	◆◆	Chinese	$6-$16	556

NORTH PROVIDENCE

Map Page	OA	Restaurant	Diamond Rated	Cuisine	Meal Range	Page
76 / p. 606		Twin's Pizza	◆	Italian	$3-$17	604

CRANSTON

Map Page	OA	Restaurants	Diamond Rated	Cuisine	Meal Range	Page
87 / p. 606		Nicole's Tuscany Grille and Restaurant	◆◆	Northern Italian	$8-$29	578
88 / p. 606		Twin Oaks	◆◆	Italian	$5-$30	579
89 / p. 606		Galaxie	◆◆	Asian	$5-$15	578
90 / p. 606		Spain Restaurant	◆◆◆	Spanish	$12-$22	579
91 / p. 606		Basta Cafe' & Restaurant	◆◆◆	Italian	$16-$28	578

EAST GREENWICH

Map Page	OA	Restaurants	Diamond Rated	Cuisine	Meal Range	Page
107 / p. 606		Post Office Cafe	◆◆◆	Italian	$12-$24	579
108 / p. 606		The Grille on Main	◆◆	American	$7-$22	579
109 / p. 606		Kon Asian Bistro	◆◆◆	Asian	$10-$30	579

PROVIDENCE pop. 173,618   (See map and index starting on p. 606)

THE CHRISTOPHER DODGE HOUSE   Phone: 401/351-6111   ❷

AAA SAVE

🔻🔻🔻🔻

Historic Bed
& Breakfast

$139-$179 5/1-10/31
$119-$149 11/1-4/30

Address: 11 W Park St 02908 **Location:** I-95, exit 22C to Kinsley Ave,
bear left Promenade St, then just w. **Facility:** The restored 1858 brick
Italianate home offers custom-made furnishings, upgraded amenities and
such preserved architectural features as tin ceilings. Smoke free
premises. 14 one-bedroom standard units, some with efficiencies. 4
stories (no elevator), interior corridors. *Bath:* combo or shower only.
Parking: on-site. **Terms:** office hours 9 am-9 pm, 7 day cancellation
notice-fee imposed. **Amenities:** voice mail, irons, hair dryers. **Guest
Services:** wireless Internet. **Business Services:** business center.

⊠ 📷 / SOME UNITS 🖥 📠 🖨

FREE full breakfast and high-speed Internet

▼ *See AAA listing p 625* ▼

▼ *See AAA listing p 553* ▼

(See map and index starting on p. 606)

COURTYARD BY MARRIOTT, DOWNTOWN PROVIDENCE   *Book great rates at AAA.com*   Phone: (401)272-1191   **5**

Hotel
$158-$194 All Year

Address: 32 Exchange Terrace Blvd 02903 **Location:** Downtown. **Facility:** Smoke free premises. 216 units. 210 one-bedroom standard units, some with whirlpools. 6 one-bedroom suites. 7 stories, interior corridors. *Bath:* combo or shower only. **Parking:** on-site (fee). **Terms:** cancellation fee imposed. **Amenities:** video games (fee), dual phone lines, voice mail, irons, hair dryers. *Some:* high-speed Internet. **Pool(s):** heated indoor. **Leisure Activities:** whirlpool, exercise room. **Guest Services:** valet and coin laundry, wireless Internet. **Business Services:** meeting rooms, business center.

AAA Benefit:
Members save a
minimum 5% off the
best available rate.

HAMPTON INN & SUITES PROVIDENCE-DOWNTOWN   *Book great rates at AAA.com*   Phone: (401)608-3500   **8**

Hotel
$149-$229 All Year

Address: 58 Weybosset St 02903 **Location:** Between Delta and Peck sts; downtown; across from The Arcade. **Facility:** 110 units. 107 one-bedroom standard units. 3 one-bedroom suites. 11 stories, interior corridors. *Bath:* combo or shower only. **Parking:** valet. **Terms:** check-in 4 pm, 1-7 night minimum stay, cancellation fee imposed. **Amenities:** video games, high-speed Internet, dual phone lines, voice mail, irons, hair dryers. **Leisure Activities:** exercise room. **Guest Services:** valet and coin laundry, area transportation, wireless Internet. **Business Services:** meeting rooms, business center.

AAA Benefit:
Members save up to
10% everyday!

▼ See AAA listing p 631 ▼

(See map and index starting on p. 606)

HILTON PROVIDENCE   *Book great rates at AAA.com*   Phone: (401)831-3900   **10**

Hotel
$129-$289 All Year

Address: 21 Atwells Ave 02903 **Location:** I-95, exit 21. Adjacent to civic center. **Facility:** 274 one-bedroom standard units. 14 stories, interior corridors. *Bath:* combo or shower only. **Parking:** valet. **Terms:** 1-7 night minimum stay, cancellation fee imposed. **Amenities:** video library, dual phone lines, voice mail, irons, hair dryers. **Pool(s):** heated indoor. **Leisure Activities:** exercise room. **Guest Services:** valet laundry, wireless Internet. **Business Services:** conference facilities, business center.

ECO ▯ ▯ ▯ ▯ ▯ / SOME UNITS FEE ▯ ▯ ▯

Hilton

AAA Benefit:
Members save 5% or
more everyday!

HOTEL DOLCE VILLA   Phone: 401/383-7031   **9**

Boutique
Hotel
$129-$429 5/1-10/31
$119-$399 11/1-4/30

Address: 63 De Pasquale Plaza 02903 **Location:** I-95, exit 21 (Broadway), just w on Atwells Ave, just n on Dean St, then just w on Spruce St. **Facility:** The ultra-modern, Mediterranean boutique hotel offers pure white-on-white decor throughout; guest room amenities include robes and slippers. Smoke free premises. 14 units. 9 one- and 5 two-bedroom suites with kitchens, some with whirlpools. 3 stories (no elevator), interior corridors. *Bath:* combo or shower only. **Parking:** valet. **Terms:** 7 day cancellation notice-fee imposed. **Amenities:** video library, DVD players, CD players, high-speed Internet, voice mail, safes, irons, hair dryers. **Guest Services:** valet laundry. ASK ▯ ▯ ▯ ▯ ▯ ▯

THE HOTEL PROVIDENCE   *Book great rates at AAA.com*   Phone: (401)861-8000   **11**

(AAA) SAVE

Boutique
Hotel
$149-$399 All Year

Address: 139 Mathewson St 02903 **Location:** I-95, exit 22A, 0.5 mi se on Memorial Blvd, then 0.3 mi sw; entrance on Mathewson St. **Facility:** This European-style boutique hotel features classically appointed rooms with comfortable duvet bedding and elegant marble flooring in the bathroom. Smoke free premises. 80 units. 61 one-bedroom standard units. 19 one-bedroom suites, some with whirlpools. 5-7 stories, interior corridors. *Bath:* combo or shower only. **Parking:** valet. **Terms:** check-in 4 pm, cancellation fee imposed. **Amenities:** high-speed Internet, dual phone lines, voice mail, safes, irons, hair dryers. **Dining:** Aspire, see separate listing. **Leisure Activities:** sun deck, exercise room. **Guest Services:** valet laundry, airport transportation (fee)-Theodore Francis Green State Airport, wireless Internet. **Business Services:** meeting rooms, business center. *(See color ad p 615)*

ECO FEE ▯ ▯ ▯ ▯ ▯ / SOME UNITS FEE ▯ FEE ▯ FEE ▯

FREE newspaper and high-speed Internet

▼ See AAA listing p 554 ▼

(See map and index starting on p. 606)

MARRIOTT PROVIDENCE DOWNTOWN *Book great rates at AAA.com* **Phone:** (401)272-2400 ❶

Hotel
$251-$307 All Year

Address: 1 Orms St 02904 **Location:** I-95, exit 23 to state offices. **Facility:** Smoke free premises. 351 units. 346 one-bedroom standard units. 5 one-bedroom suites. 5-6 stories, interior corridors. *Bath:* combo or shower only. **Parking:** on-site. **Terms:** cancellation fee imposed. **Amenities:** high-speed Internet (fee), dual phone lines, voice mail, irons, hair dryers. **Pool(s):** heated indoor/outdoor. **Leisure Activities:** whirlpool, fire pit, exercise room. **Guest Services:** valet laundry, airport transportation (fee)-Theodore Francis Green State Airport, area transportation-within 1 mi, wireless Internet. **Business Services:** conference facilities, business center. **Free Special Amenities: early check-in/late check-out and preferred room (subject to availability with advance reservations).**

ECO FEE 🚭 🍴 🍸 CALL 🅼 🛇 ✕ 🎥 📶 📷
📱 / SOME UNITS FEE 🐕

(See map and index starting on p. 606)

THE MOWRY-NICHOLSON HOUSE

Phone: 401/351-6111 **3**

AAA SAVE
▽▼▲▼▽
Historic Bed
& Breakfast
$139-$169 5/1-10/31
$119-$139 11/1-4/30

Address: 57 Brownell St 02908 **Location:** I-95, exit 22C to Kingsley Ave, left to Promenade St, just w to Holden, then just s. **Facility:** Built in 1865, this beautiful Victorian home features nicely decorated rooms and a large front porch with panoramic views of the historic district. Smoke free premises. 13 one-bedroom standard units, some with efficiencies. 3 stories (no elevator), interior corridors. *Bath:* combo or shower only. **Parking:** on-site. **Terms:** office hours 9 am-9 pm, 7 day cancellation notice. **Amenities:** voice mail, irons, hair dryers. **Guest Services:** wireless Internet. **Business Services:** business center. **Free Special Amenities: full breakfast and high-speed Internet.**

☒ 🎥 / SOME UNITS 🖥 📠 🖥

PROVIDENCE BILTMORE HOTEL   *Book at AAA.com*

Phone: (401)421-0700 **7**

▽▼▲▼▽
Historic
Hotel
$119-$299 All Year

Address: 11 Dorrance St 02903 **Location:** I-95, exit 22A; downtown. **Facility:** This 1922 downtown hotel is considered to be an architectural treasure; an Elizabeth Arden Red Door Spa and Starbucks are located on the premises. 292 units. 242 one-bedroom standard units, some with whirlpools. 50 one-bedroom suites, some with whirlpools. 17 stories, interior corridors. *Bath:* combo or shower only. **Parking:** valet. **Terms:** cancellation fee imposed. **Amenities:** dual phone lines, voice mail, irons, hair dryers. *Some:* DVD players, high-speed Internet. **Dining:** McCormick & Schmick's, see separate listing. **Leisure Activities:** exercise room, spa. **Guest Services:** valet laundry, wireless Internet. **Business Services:** conference facilities, business center.

ECO ASK 🍴 CALL 📶M 🎥 🖥 / SOME UNITS FEE 🐾 ☒ 🖥 📠

RADISSON HOTEL PROVIDENCE HARBOR   *Book great rates at AAA.com*

Phone: (401)272-5577 **12**

AAA SAVE
▽▼▲▼▽
Hotel
$99-$169 All Year

Address: 220 India St 02903 **Location:** I-195, exit 3 westbound, just s, follow signs; exit 2 eastbound. **Facility:** Smoke free premises. 136 one-bedroom standard units, some with whirlpools. 6 stories, interior corridors. *Bath:* combo or shower only. **Parking:** on-site. **Amenities:** video games (fee), dual phone lines, voice mail, irons, hair dryers. **Leisure Activities:** exercise room. **Guest Services:** valet laundry, area transportation (fee)-downtown, wireless Internet. **Business Services:** meeting rooms, business center. **Free Special Amenities: newspaper and high-speed Internet.**

ECO 🍴 🍸 CALL 📶M ☒ 🎥 🖥 / SOME UNITS 🖥 📠

▼ See AAA listing p 617 ▼

there's always something wonderfully new to be found!

Your senses will come alive as you discover this relaxing and inspiring destination. Experience provocative amenities and savvy service, that is distinctly Renaissance.

RENAISSANCE.
PROVIDENCE HOTEL
Inspiration Revealed

To begin your journey call 401.919.5000
or visit renaissanceprovidence.com

Renaissance Providence Hotel
5 Avenue of the Arts | Providence, RI

Marriott
REWARDS   Receive valuable Marriott Rewards®
            bonus points with every stay.

Get a Fresh Perspective on AAATravelViews.com

- Blogs from our experts on popular and unique destinations
- The latest in helpful travel advice and news
- Photos, videos, maps and special member offers
- Comments and Q&A with AAA experts

Share travel at
AAATravelViews.com

(See map and index starting on p. 606)

RENAISSANCE PROVIDENCE HOTEL

Book great rates at AAA.com

Phone: (401)919-5000   **4**

Hotel
$197-$241 All Year

Address: 5 Avenue of the Arts 02903 **Location:** US 1, just n on Francis St; opposite the State House. **Facility:** Located within the beautifully restored 1929 neoclassic Masonic Temple, this hotel features a modern yet lavish interior. Smoke free premises. 272 units. 265 one-bedroom standard units. 7 one-bedroom suites. 9 stories, interior corridors. *Bath:* combo or shower only. **Parking:** valet. **Terms:** cancellation fee imposed. **Amenities:** voice mail, safes, irons, hair dryers. *Fee:* video games, high-speed Internet. **Dining:** Temple Downtown, see separate listing. **Leisure Activities:** exercise room. **Guest Services:** valet laundry, wireless Internet. **Business Services:** conference facilities, business center. *(See color ad p 616)*

RENAISSANCE.
HOTELS & RESORTS

AAA Benefit:
Members save a minimum 5% off the best available rate.

THE WESTIN PROVIDENCE

Book great rates at AAA.com

Phone: (401)598-8000   **6**

Hotel
$149-$419 All Year

Address: One W Exchange St 02903 **Location:** I-95, exit 22A; downtown. Adjacent to the convention center. **Facility:** Guest rooms boast modern or neoclassic decor, and feature Westin signature heavenly beds and double shower heads. Providence Place Mall is attached. Smoke free premises. 564 units. 560 one-bedroom standard units. 4 one-bedroom suites, some with whirlpools. 25 stories, interior corridors. *Bath:* combo or shower only. **Parking:** on-site (fee) and valet. **Terms:** cancellation fee imposed. **Amenities:** dual phone lines, voice mail, safes, honor bars, irons, hair dryers. *Fee:* video games, high-speed Internet. *Some:* DVD players, CD players, fax. **Dining:** Agora, see separate listing. **Pool(s):** heated indoor. **Leisure Activities:** saunas, whirlpool, steamrooms, exercise room, spa. **Guest Services:** valet laundry, wireless Internet. **Business Services:** conference facilities, business center. **Free Special Amenities:** newspaper and early check-in/late check-out.

WESTIN
HOTELS & RESORTS

AAA Benefit:
Enjoy up to 15% off your next stay, plus Starwood Preferred Guest® bonuses.

WHERE TO DINE

---

10 PRIME STEAK & SUSHI

Phone: 401/453-2333   **37**

Steak
$6-$40

The eclectic decor incorporates contemporary art and velvet banquettes. The cuisine is a wonderful fusion of Asian fare and steak, hence the name. The wonderful bistro strikes a balance with creative cuisine and high art. Casual dress. **Bar:** Full bar. **Reservations:** suggested. **Hours:** 11:30 am-10 pm, Thurs & Fri-11 pm, Sat 4 pm-11 pm, Sun & Mon 4 pm-10 pm. Closed major holidays. **Address:** 55 Pine St 02903 **Location:** Between Orange and Peck sts. **Parking:** valet.

AGORA

Phone: 401/598-8011   **20**

American
$10-$38

Overlooking Providence Place Mall, the elegant restaurant presents a menu of creative American cuisine, emphasizing local seafood. Steaks are prepared over a natural wood grill or in skillets and come with a choice of sauces. Dressy casual. **Bar:** Full bar. **Reservations:** suggested. **Hours:** 6:30 am-2 pm. **Address:** One W Exchange St 02903 **Location:** I-95, exit 22A; downtown; in The Westin Providence. **Parking:** on-site (fee) and valet.

AL FORNO RESTAURANT

Phone: 401/273-9767   **47**

Northern Italian
$25-$30

Specialties of the house include grilled pizza, clams Al Forno, a selection of baked pasta and various Tuscany-style cuisine, emphasizing fresh, seasonal ingredients. Made-to-order dessert is evident in the tasty fruit tarts and fresh churned ice cream. Casual dress. **Bar:** Full bar. **Reservations:** not accepted. **Hours:** 5 pm-10 pm, Sat from 4 pm. Closed: 1/1, 12/24, 12/25; also Sun & Mon. **Address:** 577 S Main St 02903 **Location:** I-195, exit 2; downtown. **Parking:** on-site and valet.

ANDREAS

Phone: 401/331-7879   **5**

Greek
$7-$20

In the heart of the Brown University campus, the restaurant serves designer sandwiches, pasta and such popular Greek specialties as beef kebabs and souvlaki sandwiches. Grab one of the many window seats or outdoor bistro tables to people-watch and be part of the action. Casual dress. **Bar:** Full bar. **Reservations:** accepted. **Hours:** 11 am-midnight, Fri-1 am, Sat 9 am-1 am, Sun 9 am-midnight. **Address:** 268 Thayer St 02906 **Location:** Corner of Meeting St; downtown. **Parking:** street.

ASPIRE

Phone: 401/521-3333   **39**

New American
$17-$59

The varied menu ranges from make-your-own chopped salads and grilled halibut to braised short ribs and sushi. Contemporary decor and electronica music pumping through the restaurant make it a fun and lively place to be. The terrace befits an al fresco meal. Dressy casual. **Bar:** Full bar. **Reservations:** suggested. **Hours:** 5 pm-9 pm, Fri & Sat-10 pm. **Address:** 311 Westminster St 02903 **Location:** I-95, exit 22A, 0.5 mi se on Memorial Blvd, then 0.3 mi sw; entrance on Mathewson St; in The Hotel Providence. **Parking:** valet. *(See color ad p 615)*

(See map and index starting on p. 606)

BACARO RESTAURANT

Italian
$19-$30

Phone: 401/751-3700 ㊷

A team of chefs expertly prepares Italian favorites. Diners might start with the salumeria experience assortment served on a wood cutting board with honey-roasted nuts and assorted jams. When it comes time for the entree, it can be hard to choose among the signature crispy chicken covered in panko crumbs then lightly fried and served over buttered noodles; pasta fagioli; or the simple but superb pasta with European butter, cracked black pepper and pecorino Romano cheese. Dressy casual. **Bar:** Full bar. **Reservations:** suggested. **Hours:** 5 pm-10 pm. Closed major holidays; also Sun & Mon. **Address:** 262 S Water St 02903 **Location:** Just w of US 6; between Power and Williams sts. **Parking:** on-site.

BLUE ELEPHANT

Breakfast
$6-$15

Phone: 401/383-8149 ㊹

This artsy restaurant on the East Side is one of the best places for breakfast or brunch in the city. Inside a historic home, the two dining rooms are small in size and feel tight with a large number of tables sitting next to each other, but the atmosphere is fun with colorful comic book artwork on the laminated tables and jewelry hanging on the walls. Fresh ingredients go into the chef's broad menu. The children's menu features pancakes made into small shapes of stars, moons and the like. Casual dress. **Reservations:** not accepted. **Hours:** 7 am-3 & 5:30-9:30 pm, Sun-3 pm. Closed major holidays; also Mon-Wed. **Address:** 312 Wickenden St 02906 **Location:** I-195, exit 2 eastbound, 0.3 mi ne; exit 3 westbound, just s on Gano St, then 0.4 mi w. **Parking:** street.

BLUE GROTTO RESTAURANT

Italian
$8-$29

Phone: 401/272-9030 ㉟

In famous Federal Hill, the upscale restaurant prepares many appealing seafood and pasta dishes. Attentive servers are professionally dressed in tuxedos. Some dining rooms have chandeliers dangling from the ceiling and another offers a fireplace, while the rest have small windows decorated with white Christmas lights. Dressy casual. **Bar:** Full bar. **Reservations:** suggested. **Hours:** Open 5/1-7/31 & 9/1-4/30; 11:30 am-2:30 & 5-10 pm, Fri-10:30 pm, Sat 11:30 am-2:30 & 4:30-10:30 pm, Sun noon-9 pm. Closed major holidays. **Address:** 210 Atwells Ave 02903 **Location:** I-95, exit 21 northbound, just n on Service Rd No 8, then just w; exit southbound, just w. **Parking:** valet and street.

CAFE CHOKLAD

Breads/Pastries
$6-$8

Phone: 401/383-4764 ⑫

The colorful country cafe is near Rhode Island School of Design and the city's museum section. Homemade bakery items, specialty coffees and imported European chocolates are available throughout the day, while lunch items include a limited menu of sandwiches, soups and salads. Casual dress. **Hours:** 8 am-3 pm; Mon-Fri to 6 pm 6/1-10/11. Closed major holidays; also Sun. **Address:** 2 Thomas St 02903 **Location:** I-195, exit 2, 0.5 mi nw via S Main St. **Parking:** street.

CAFE NOIR

French
$10-$22

Phone: 401/272-2116 ⑥

Relatively inexpensive for the area, this brasserie keeps patrons coming back for its artisan cheese plate and specialties such as lamb shank with mushrooms bolognese over orecchiette pasta, fettuccine with crimini mushrooms and truffle essence and great steak frites. For dessert, it's hard to beat warm chocolate cake with peppermint ice cream. The restaurant is broken up into two rooms: one with a lively bar and the other with brick walls, needlepoint window treatments and hand-painted murals. Dressy casual. **Bar:** Full bar. **Reservations:** suggested. **Hours:** 5 pm-10 pm, Fri & Sat-11 pm. Closed: 1/1, 11/25, 12/25. **Address:** 125 N Main St 02903 **Location:** I-95, exit 22A, 0.7 mi e, just ne on Washington Pl, then just n. **Parking:** valet.

CAFE NUOVO

Continental
$8-$39

Phone: 401/421-2525 ⑩

The attractive and trendy eatery sits along the river on the first floor of Citizen's Plaza. The inventive menu shows an Asian influence, and desserts are works of art. Alfresco seating is an option when the weather is appropriate. Dressy casual. **Bar:** Full bar. **Reservations:** suggested. **Hours:** 11:30 am-3 & 5-10:30 pm, Sat 5 pm-11 pm. Closed major holidays; also Sun. **Address:** 1 Citizens Plaza 02903 **Location:** Between Exchange St and Park Row; on the river. **Parking:** on-site (fee) and valet. CALL ♿Ⓜ

CAFE PARAGON/VIVA

New American
$7-$20

Phone: 401/331-6200 ⑧

The eclectic restaurant offers seating in two very different rooms: the bright and colorful Paragon and the more dramatic Viva, which has dark-red walls and mosaic tiles. Both present the same menu, which boasts some delicious mixed-green salads, steaks and seafood. Viva also offers a sushi bar and has late-night dancing on weekends. Dressy casual. **Bar:** Full bar. **Reservations:** not accepted. **Hours:** 11 am-midnight, Sun from 10 am. **Address:** 234 Thayer St 02906 **Location:** Corner of Angell and Thayer sts; downtown. **Parking:** street.

CAMILLE'S

Italian
$7-$40

Phone: 401/751-4812 ㊳

One of the more upscale restaurants on Federal Hill, this place features trendy contemporary decor, including leopard-print carpeting, floral arrangements within a chainlike cage and a beautiful circular mosaic tile artwork. Representative of the creative and flavorful Italian food are antipasto with marinated vegetables and cured meats, homemade pasta and seafood dishes and high-quality steaks. Dressy casual. **Bar:** Full bar. **Reservations:** suggested. **Hours:** 11:30 am-3 & 5-10 pm, Fri-11 pm, Sat 5 pm-11 pm. Closed: Sun. **Address:** 71 Bradford St 02903 **Location:** Between Atwells Ave and Federal St; downtown. **Parking:** valet.

THE CAPITAL GRILLE

Steak
$9-$35

Phone: 401/521-5600 ㉔

Cherry wood and red leather assist in making this "clubby" dining room a beautiful spot to dine on excellent cuts of dry-aged beef. The staff is highly attentive and knowledgeable. Dressy casual. **Bar:** Full bar. **Reservations:** suggested. **Hours:** 11:30 am-3 & 5-10 pm, Fri-11 pm, Sat 5 pm-11 pm, Sun 4 pm-9 pm. Closed: 7/4, 11/25, 12/25; also Super Bowl Sun. **Address:** 1 Union Station 02903 **Location:** I-95, exit 22A, 0.7 mi e on Memorial Blvd, then just se; on lower level of former Union Train Station. **Parking:** on-site (fee).

CAPRICCIO

Continental
$12-$35

Phone: 401/421-1320 ㉜

Fare grounded in the traditional takes on a Northern Italian slant. Steak Diane and crepes flambé are skillfully prepped tableside in a quiet, romantic, almost formal setting. Pasta, seafood, steak, poultry and veal dominate. Dressy casual. **Bar:** Full bar. **Reservations:** suggested. **Hours:** 11:30 am-10:30 pm, Fri-11 pm, Sat 5 pm-11 pm, Sun 4 pm-9 pm. Closed major holidays. **Address:** 2 Pine St 02903 **Location:** I-195, exit 1; corner of Dyer and Pine sts; downtown. **Parking:** valet.

(See map and index starting on p. 606)

CASERTAS PIZZERIA

Phone: 401/621-3618 ㉒

Pizza
$2-$20

The busy Rhode Island institution has served outstanding pizza since 1946. Casual dress. **Bar:** Beer & wine. **Reservations:** not accepted. **Hours:** 9:30 am-10 pm, Fri & Sat-11:30 pm. Closed major holidays; also Mon. **Address:** 121 Spruce St 02903 **Location:** I-95, exit 21, just w on Atwells Ave, just n on Crout St, then just w. **Parking:** on-site.

CASSARINO'S

Phone: 401/751-3333 ㉞

Italian
$8-$24

This oldie but goodie on Federal Hill is hard to miss with its bright Broadway-like sign. This three-level restaurant offers good views of the city scene below, especially for those who request a table by a second-floor window. Those who play it safe will enjoy toasted ravioli, mozzarella sticks, chicken parmigiana or veal Marsala, while their adventurous counterparts can try a dish such as sea scallops topped with penne pasta and sun-dried tomatoes in pink vodka cream sauce. Dressy casual. **Bar:** Full bar. **Reservations:** accepted. **Hours:** 11:30 am-10 pm, Fri-11 pm, Sat noon-11 pm. Closed: Sun. **Address:** 177 Atwells Ave 02903 **Location:** I-95, exit 21, just w. **Parking:** valet and street. CALL [&M]

CAV RESTAURANT

Phone: 401/751-9164 ㊽

International
$10-$29

Located in an old historic industrial building, this restaurant fuses a creative menu with a unique atmosphere filled with antiques and artifacts from Africa and the Middle East. They also boast a 35-page menu of martinis and other international drinks. Dressy casual. **Bar:** Full bar. **Reservations:** suggested. **Hours:** 11:30 am-9:30 pm, Fri & Sat-11 pm, Sun 10:30 am-10 pm; Sunday brunch. Closed: 12/25. **Address:** 14 Imperial Pl 02903 **Location:** Between Elm and South sts; downtown; courtyard entrance faces parking lot. **Parking:** on-site.

THE CHEESECAKE FACTORY

Phone: 401/270-4010 ⑮

American
$9-$30

A display case of mouthwatering cheesecakes is the first thing visitors see as they walk through the door. The extensive menu incorporates many types of cuisine, including Asian, Italian, Greek and Spanish. Casual dress. **Bar:** Full bar. **Reservations:** not accepted. **Hours:** 11:30 am-11 pm, Fri & Sat-12:30 am, Sun 10 am-11 pm. Closed: 11/25, 12/25. **Address:** 94 Providence Pl 02903 **Location:** Downtown; in Providence Place Mall. **Parking:** on-site.

CHINESE LAUNDRY

Phone: 401/272-8676 ⑦

Chinese
$17-$20

This hip, contemporary spot has dark woodwork and pops of red color. The menu is limited mostly to sushi, noodle dishes and appetizers made from organic ingredients from local farms whenever possible. A flavorful meal might be built with the king crab tempura appetizer drizzled with honey and truffle aioli; a spicy entree of glass noodles with tenderloin, chilies, mint, scallions and red peppers; and a sweet finish of flourless chocolate cake with spiced pecans and five-spice anglaise. Dressy casual. **Bar:** Full bar. **Reservations:** suggested. **Hours:** 5 pm-10 pm, Fri & Sat-11 pm. Closed major holidays; also Sun & Mon. **Address:** 121 N Main St 02903 **Location:** I-95, exit 22A, 0.7 mi e, just ne on Washington St, then just n. **Parking:** street.

CITRON WINE BAR & BISTRO

Phone: 401/621-9463 ⑱

New American
$6-$25

Orange glass mosaic tiles make a bold statement on the bistro's exterior, while upgraded sconces lend to the trendy interior decor. Whenever possible, dishes combine organic locally grown produce and grains, as well as meats that are free of growth hormones and antibiotics. Free-range poultry fed a strict vegetarian diet is used exclusively. Travelers who don't want to leave their pups behind can browse the "dog menu" on the outdoor patio. Discounted parking is available with validation. Dressy casual. **Bar:** Full bar. **Reservations:** suggested. **Hours:** noon-2:30 & 4:30-10 pm, Fri-11 pm, Sat 4:30 pm-11 pm, Sun 4:30 pm-10 pm. Closed: 7/4, 11/25, 12/25; also Super Bowl Sun. **Address:** 5 Memorial Blvd 02903 **Location:** I-95, exit 22A, just e; entrance thru parking lot via Exchange St. **Parking:** on-site (fee). CALL [&M]

DON JOSE TEQUILAS

Phone: 401/454-8951 ㉗

Mexican
$13-$22

Outstanding food earns this place diners' votes as the city's best Mexican restaurant. A meal might comprise a sampler platter; fried or baked chimichanga burrito; and creamy flan. A romantic feel punctuates the dining room, especially at night with the pressed-tin lighting and unusual counter-lit bar top aglow. A hand-painted mural running across the restaurant serves as a piece of art, with large window-like mirrors breaking it up every few feet to make the dining room feel more spacious. Casual dress. **Bar:** Full bar. **Reservations:** accepted. **Hours:** 3 pm-10 pm, Thurs 11:30 am-11 pm, Fri & Sat 11:30 am-1 am, Sun 11 am-10 pm. Closed major holidays. **Address:** 351 Atwells Ave 02903 **Location:** I-95, exit 21 (Broadway), 0.5 mi w. **Parking:** street. CALL [&M]

FELLINI CAFE & PIZZERIA

Phone: 401/751-6737 ㊻

Pizza
$4-$19

Creative red and white pizzas, salads, soups and sandwiches are served at the local favorite. The late-night menu is popular with the young crowd who drop in after enjoying the nearby dance clubs. Casual dress. **Hours:** 11 am-midnight, Thurs-Sat to 2 am. Closed: 4/4, 11/25, 12/25. **Address:** 166 Wickenden St 02903 **Location:** I-195, exit 2 eastbound, just ne on Bridge St, then just e; exit westbound, just nw on S Main St, just sw on James St, just ne on Bridge St, then just e. **Parking:** street.

GRACIE'S   *Menu on AAA.com*

Phone: 401/272-7811 ㊵

New American
$21-$38

Located across the street from the popular Trinity Rep Play House, this elegant restaurant features sophisticated artwork, warm woodwork, a rich red and gold color scheme seen on the walls and drapes, and a "Star" theme which is subtly placed in different areas from the accent pillows to the wine glasses. The servers are very knowledgeable and sincere providing a comfortable dining experience. Dishes are creatively presented and taste as good as they look. Dressy casual. **Bar:** Full bar. **Reservations:** suggested. **Hours:** 5 pm-10 pm, Fri & Sat-11 pm, Sun 4 pm-9 pm. Closed: major holidays, 12/24; also Mon & Sun 7/15-8/31. **Address:** 194 Washington St 02903 **Location:** I-95, exit 21 (Broadway); between Empire and Aborn sts; downtown. **Parking:** valet.

(See map and index starting on p. 606)

GREGG'S RESTAURANT & PUB

American
$7-$15

Phone: 401/831-5700

It's well worth the short wait in line for Gregg's great daily specials, sandwiches, salad and well-known wide variety of homemade pastries and wonderful desserts. Friendly, fast-paced service in the bustling, cheery dining room is attentive and fun. Casual dress. **Bar:** Full bar. **Reservations:** not accepted. **Hours:** 11:30 am-midnight, Fri & Sat-1 am. Closed: 11/25, 12/25. **Address:** 1303 N Main St 02904 **Location:** I-95, exit 25, 0.8 mi ne. **Parking:** on-site. CALL ⬛M

HEMENWAY'S SEAFOOD GRILL & OYSTER BAR

Seafood
$7-$27

Phone: 401/351-8570   26

Adding to the upscale atmosphere are impressive mahogany and brass accents and serene views of the Providence River, city skyline and flower-filled park. A wide variety of fresh local seafood graces the menu, as do preparations of steak, chicken and pasta. Metered street parking is available, as is discounted parking at the garage next door with validation from the restaurant. Casual dress. **Bar:** Full bar. **Reservations:** suggested. **Hours:** 11:30 am-10 pm, Fri & Sat-11 pm, Sun noon-9 pm. Closed: 12/25. **Address:** 121 S Main St 02903 **Location:** On east side of the river at Crawford St bridge; at south end of Providence River Park; downtown; opposite Old Stone Bank. **Parking:** valet.

JOE MARZILLI'S OLD CANTEEN

Italian
$10-$28

Phone: 401/751-5544   36

The elegant and romantic restaurant offers a wide variety of traditional Italian favorites at a great value. Guests can ask for a table by one of the large windows for a view of historic Federal Hill. Dressy casual. **Bar:** Full bar. **Reservations:** suggested. **Hours:** 11:30 am-10 pm. Closed major holidays; also Tues & 7/1-7/14. **Address:** 120 Atwells Ave 02903 **Location:** I-95, exit 21, just w. **Parking:** valet.

JOE'S AMERICAN BAR & GRILL

American
$9-$24

Phone: 401/270-4737

If it's Americana you want, you'll get all that and more at Joe's, where the bill of fare includes all-American favorites like hearty burgers, fresh-from-the-oven chicken pot pies, Maryland lump crab cakes, and Joe's classic meatloaf. Pizzas, pastas, steaks and salads round out the extensive menu, giving diners the freedom to choose from a vast selection of offerings. There's nothing more American than that, except, of course, for apple pie, so save some room. Casual dress. **Bar:** Full bar. **Reservations:** accepted. **Hours:** 11 am-11 pm, Fri & Sat-midnight. Closed: 12/25. **Address:** 148 Providence Pl 02903 **Location:** Downtown; in Providence Place Mall. **Parking:** on-site.

MCCORMICK & SCHMICK'S

Seafood
$8-$30

Phone: 401/351-4500   23

This place is all about seafood, which is imported from all over the world. Among good choices are Washington state oysters, Maine clams, delicate Hawaiian escolar and tuna from Ecuador. The clublike decor is cozy, and expert staff provide able assistance. Casual dress. **Bar:** Full bar. **Reservations:** suggested. **Hours:** 6:30 am-11 pm. **Address:** 11 Dorrance St 02903 **Location:** I-95, exit 22A, downtown; in Providence Biltmore Hotel. **Parking:** valet. CALL ⬛M

MILLS TAVERN

American
$18-$39

Phone: 401/272-3331   9

Contemporary American cuisine, with an emphasis on wood-fire cooking, is the specialty at this spot. Among house favorites are rabbit ravioli and seared foie gras on a buttermilk biscuit. Dressy casual. **Bar:** Full bar. **Reservations:** suggested. **Hours:** 5 pm-10 pm, Fri & Sat-11 pm, Sun 4 pm-9 pm. Closed major holidays. **Address:** 101 N Main St 02903 **Location:** Between Meeting and Thomas sts; downtown. **Parking:** valet. CALL ⬛M

NAPA VALLEY GRILLE

American
$7-$28

Phone: 401/270-6272   14

Cutting-edge contemporary cuisine best describes the eatery's food. This place specializes in serving hard-to-find California wines. Casual dress. **Bar:** Full bar. **Reservations:** suggested. **Hours:** 11:30 am-10 pm, Fri & Sat-10:30 pm, Sun 11:30 am-9 pm. Closed: 12/25. **Address:** 111 Providence Pl 02903 **Location:** Downtown; in Providence Place Mall. **Parking:** on-site (fee).

NEW RIVERS

International
$16-$30

Phone: 401/751-0350   13

Portuguese, Thai, Caribbean and Tuscan cuisines grace a daily changing menu based on availability from local sources. Made-to-order desserts such as lemon tartlet are divine. Table spacing and acoustics make this an up-close and sometimes bustling eatery. Casual dress. **Bar:** Full bar. **Reservations:** suggested. **Hours:** 5:30 pm-10 pm. Closed major holidays; also Sun. **Address:** 7 Steeple St 02903 **Location:** Corner of N Main and Steeple sts, on eastbound one-way street, opposite end of Waterman St; I-195, exit 2, 0.7 mi n. **Parking:** on-site (fee).

NICK'S ON BROADWAY

New American
$9-$26

Phone: 401/421-0286   43

In the up-and-coming West Side district, this restaurant is slightly off the beaten path but well worth the trip. The trendy, new age diner catches eyes with its deep red laminate tabletops and tiled walls. Banquette table spacing is tight and so are areas near the counter that offer a good view of the chefs working in the open kitchen. Interesting takes on traditional diner fare include tofu scrambled eggs for breakfast and citrus-scented sea scallops with celery, vegetables and butter broth. Casual dress. **Bar:** Full bar. **Reservations:** accepted, for dinner. **Hours:** 7 am-3 & 5:30-10 pm, Sun 8 am-3 pm. Closed: major holidays, 12/24; also Mon & Tues. **Address:** 500 Broadway 02909 **Location:** I-95, exit 21(Broadway), just n via Service Rd, then 0.8 mi sw. **Parking:** street.

OLGA'S CUP AND SAUCER

Breads/Pastries
$7-$10

Phone: 401/831-6666   49

In the middle of the Jewelry district, the artsy coffee shop hums with the almost constant sound of the espresso machine as it turns out specialty coffees. Diners nosh on homemade bread, desserts, soup and salad, which they order at the counter. Guests bring a numbered art rock to their table, and a friendly, efficient staff member picks it up when the food is delivered. The outdoor gardens are a great respite from the city, but protesters at the nearby Planned Parenthood can be distracting. Casual dress. **Reservations:** not accepted. **Hours:** 7 am-4 pm, Sat & Sun 9 am-2 pm. Closed major holidays. **Address:** 103 Point St 02903 **Location:** Jct SR 1A, just sw; corner of Richmond St; downtown. **Parking:** street. CALL ⬛M

(See map and index starting on p. 606)

PARKSIDE ROTISSERIE & BAR

American
$6-$30

Phone: 401/331-0003   ㉑

Near Brown University and the Rhode Island School of Design, this Manhattan-style bistro seems to always be packed with creative minds from the campuses. The restaurant is owned by a talented chef who prepares favorites such as spicy crab cakes served with a roasted red pepper and lemon sauce. Also tempting are filet mignon with green peppercorn-cognac cream sauce or sirloin steak with chipotle pepper demi-glace. Professional servers gladly offer recommendations from the extensive wine list. Dressy casual. **Bar:** Full bar. **Reservations:** accepted. **Hours:** 11:30 am-10 pm, Fri-11 pm, Sat 5 pm-11 pm, Sun 4 pm-9 pm. Closed: 11/25, 12/25. **Address:** 76 S Main St 02903 **Location:** On US 44, between Hopkins and Planet sts; downtown. **Parking:** valet. CALL Ⓛ Ⓜ

PEARL RESTAURANT & LOUNGE   *Menu on AAA.com*

New American
$10-$35

Phone: 401/331-3000   ①

The dramatic atmosphere at this trendy spot is hard to compare to any other in the city. Distinctive cobalt blue and white lighting and high-tech appointments mixed with hand-blown glass sculptures and oversized black leather banquettes create the perfect backdrop for a Miami-like dining experience and after-dinner drinks. The menu is just as incredible, with exquisite steaks, chicken dishes and pasta preparations, in addition to a full sushi menu. Dressy casual. **Bar:** Full bar. **Reservations:** suggested, weekends. **Hours:** 5 pm-11 pm. Closed: Sun & Mon. **Address:** 393 Charles St 02904 **Location:** I-95, exit 24, just nw on Branch Ave, then just sw on Silver Spring St. **Parking:** valet.

POT AU FEU RESTAURANT & BISTRO

French
$6-$29

Phone: 401/273-8953   ㉕

The main dining salon is an elegant, uncluttered room with subdued lighting and soft music. The cuisine is typically French with rich creamy sauces and traditional dishes such as escargot and pates for starters and entrees of coquille St. Jacques and tournedos au Poivre among the many selections available. For those with a sweet tooth, the creme brulee is not only delicious but arrives at the table in a portion sufficient to satisfy at least three people. Dressy casual. **Bar:** Full bar. **Reservations:** suggested. **Hours:** 11:30 am-2 & 5-9 pm, Fri-10 pm, Sat 5 pm-10 pm. Closed: 11/25, 12/25; also Sun & 8/1-8/7. **Address:** 44 Custom House St 02903 **Location:** I-95, exit 22, 0.3 mi s on Dorrance St, then 3 blks e on Weybosset St; downtown. **Parking:** on-site.

PROVIDENCE OYSTER BAR

Seafood
$10-$36

Phone: 401/272-8866   ㉘

The contemporary bistro-like restaurant has dark hardwood flooring, a painted pressed-tin ceiling, large potted plants and unusual lighting fixtures. The raw bar features fresh selections from the East and West coasts, such as Nova Scotia and Oregon. Entree selections include grilled or lightly fried fish and seafood, along with some wonderful pasta dishes. Dressy casual. **Bar:** Full bar. **Reservations:** suggested. **Hours:** 5 pm-10 pm, Fri 11:30 am-4 & 5-11 pm, Sat noon-4 & 5-11 pm. Closed major holidays; also Sun. **Address:** 283 Atwells Ave 02903 **Location:** I-95, exit 21, 0.4 mi w. **Parking:** valet and street.

PROVIDENCE PRIME

Steak
$29-$41

Phone: 401/454-8881   ㉙

Warm red woods, stained glass and black-and-white industrial train photos accent the sophisticated setting, a long intimate room with an upscale bar that runs its length. Knowledgeable servers gladly go over the high-quality steak cuts lined up on a silver platter. Filets and bone-in rib selections are served a la carte, but additional sides are enough to fill two people. Diners might end the experience with campfire s'mores cooked over a table grill. Dressy casual. **Bar:** Full bar. **Reservations:** suggested. **Hours:** 5 pm-10 pm, Fri & Sat-11 pm. Closed major holidays; also Sun. **Address:** 279 Atwells Ave 02903 **Location:** I-95, exit 21, 0.3 mi w. **Parking:** valet and street.

RAPHAEL BAR-RISTO

Italian
$14-$30

Phone: 401/421-4646   ⑰

On the lower level of the original Union Station, the restaurant is a short walk from Waterplace Park. Decor is modern and minimalist, with natural woods, brushed aluminum and glass. Representative of progressive Italian cuisine are assorted pizzas and pasta dishes, as well as preparations of chicken, veal, tuna steak, roast pork, beef and salmon. From tiramisu to classic creme brulee, the desserts are uniformly tempting. Dressy casual. **Bar:** Full bar. **Reservations:** suggested. **Hours:** 5 pm-10 pm, Fri & Sat-11 pm. Closed: 11/25, 12/25. **Address:** 1 Union Station 02903 **Location:** I-95, exit 22A, on lower level of former Union Train Station. **Parking:** on-site (fee).

RED STRIPE

French
$8-$21

Phone: 401/437-6950   ③

In the Wayland Square area on the trendy East Side, this French bistro is hard to miss, especially with its oversize chrome fork hanging over the door. Although this is a popular restaurant for brunch, it also offers a delicious lunch and dinner menu. Among delicious "originals" are the grilled cheese created with prosciutto, poached pear and basil and served with oven-roasted tomato soup or hand-cut fries and aioli. Not to be missed are luscious desserts such as chocolate espresso cheesecake. Casual dress. **Bar:** Full bar. **Reservations:** accepted. **Hours:** 11:30 am-10 pm. Closed major holidays. **Address:** 465 Angell St 02906 **Location:** Between Wayland and Elmgrove aves; downtown. **Parking:** street. CALL Ⓛ Ⓜ

RI-RA IRISH PUB

Irish
$10-$21

Phone: 401/272-1953

The restaurant specializes in traditional Irish cuisine with a contemporary twist. Some examples include beef and Guinness pie and classic fish and chips. The noise level can be loud at times due to the pub's popularity and folk bands that regularly play. Casual dress. **Bar:** Full bar. **Reservations:** accepted. **Hours:** 11:30 am-10 pm. Closed: 12/25. **Address:** 52 Exchange Terr 02903 **Location:** I-95, exit 22A, 0.7 mi e on Memorial Blvd, then just se. **Parking:** on-site (fee).

RUE DE L' ESPOIR

New American
$10-$31

Phone: 401/751-8890   ㊶

This popular gourmet breakfast and weekend brunch spot serves New American cuisine prepared with a French twist. Favorites include crepes filled with blueberries and mascarpone, roasted line-caught salmon salad and the BLT with grilled yellow tomato, apple-wood-smoked bacon, baby arugula and homemade mozzarella on toasted multigrain bread with herb mayo. Warm wood paneling, contemporary framed art and green plants enhance the appeal of this friendly neighborhood restaurant. Casual dress. **Bar:** Full bar. **Reservations:** accepted. **Hours:** 7:30 am-11 & 11:30-9 pm, Fri-10:30 pm, Sat 8:30 am-2:30 & 5-10:30 pm, Sun 8:30 am-9 pm. Closed: 11/25, 12/25. **Address:** 99 Hope St 02906 **Location:** I-195, exit 3 eastbound, just s on Gano St, 0.3 mi w on Wickenden St, then just n; exit Gano St westbound, just n, 0.3 mi w on Wickenden St, then just n. **Parking:** on-site.

(See map and index starting on p. 606)

RUTH'S CHRIS STEAK HOUSE

Steak
$34-$45

Phone: 401/272-2337　16

The main fare is steak, which is prepared from several cuts of prime beef and cooked to perfection, but the menu also lists lamb, chicken and seafood dishes. Guests should come hungry because the side dishes, which are among the a la carte offerings, could make a meal in themselves. Dressy casual. **Bar:** Full bar. **Reservations:** suggested. **Hours:** 5 pm-10 pm, Fri & Sat-11 pm, Sun 5 pm-9 pm. Closed: 11/25, 12/25. **Address:** 10 Memorial Blvd 02903 **Location:** Corner of Memorial Square and Washington Blvd; downtown; in GTECH Center. **Parking:** valet. CALL &M

SIENA

Northern Italian
$12-$29

Phone: 401/521-3311　33

Serving "Tuscan soul food" on famous Federal Hill, this restaurant offers dishes such as a starter of baby blue mussels and littlenecks steeped in a flavorful broth and served over grilled Tuscan crostini, followed by an entree of pollo al diavolo, wood-grilled chicken breasts rubbed with crushed red pepper and herbs and oven-finished with olive oil, herbs and white wine. The must-have desserts are mini fried doughboys served with vanilla gelato and Nutella, chocolate and hazelnut spread. Dressy casual. **Bar:** Full bar. **Reservations:** suggested. **Hours:** 5 pm-10 pm, Sat 4:30 pm-11 pm, Sun 3 pm-10 pm. Closed major holidays. **Address:** 238 Atwells Ave 02903 **Location:** I-95, exit 21, just w. **Parking:** valet. CALL &M

TASTE OF INDIA　*Menu on AAA.com*

Indian
$7-$17

Phone: 401/421-4355　45

The family-owned-and-operated eatery builds its menu on tandoori specialties, delicious Indian breads and other delicacies. Casual dress. **Hours:** 11:30 am-2:30 & 5-10 pm, Sat noon-3 & 5-10 pm, Sun noon-3 & 5-9:30 pm. Closed: 11/25, 12/25. **Address:** 230 Wickenden St 02906 **Location:** I-195, exit 2, 0.3 mi e. **Parking:** street.

TEMPLE DOWNTOWN

New American
$10-$26

Phone: 401/919-5050　4

Inside the 1926 Masonic Temple, which remained unfinished between the Great Depression and now, the restaurant pays homage to the graffiti artists who frequented the magnificent structure while it was vacant with distinctive pieces of art. A meal here might start with a pretzel-crusted crab cake; move to an entree of excellent steak, such as the grilled filet served with crisp gnocchi with baby spinach and Gorgonzola cream; and end with the trip of mini cupcakes. Dressy casual. **Bar:** Full bar. **Reservations:** suggested. **Hours:** 6:30 am-10 pm, Fri & Sat-11 pm. **Address:** 106 Francis St 02903 **Location:** I-95, exit 22A (downtown); in Renaissance Providence Hotel. **Parking:** valet.

TWIST ON ANGELL

New American
$13-$21

Phone: 401/831-4500　2

On the East Side but off the beaten path in the basement level of a large apartment building, the modern restaurant is accented in a black, white and red color scheme. The extensive menu lists reasonably priced dishes ranging from gourmet pizzas, burgers and salads to traditional American favorites prepared with twists that draw in the flavors commonly found in Italian, Irish, Mexican and Pan-Asian food. Deep-fried ice cream is a perfect way to end a meal. Table service is casual but friendly. Casual dress. **Bar:** Full bar. **Reservations:** accepted. **Hours:** 4 pm-10 pm, Fri & Sat-11 pm. Closed: 1/1, 11/25, 12/25; also Mon. **Address:** 500 Angell St 02906 **Location:** From US 44, 1.1 mi e on Waterman Ave, just n via Wayland Ave; lower level of Wayland Square Complex. **Parking:** street.

UNION STATION BREWERY

Regional American
$7-$24

Phone: 401/274-2739　19

Regional and creative American cuisine, served in a casual, rustic atmosphere is what you'll discover at Union Station. Chicken pot pie, meatloaf, pasta and salad are just a few of the menu choices. A variety of microbrews complements your meal. Validated parking. Casual dress. **Bar:** Full bar. **Reservations:** suggested. **Hours:** 11:30 am-11 pm, Fri & Sat-12:30 am. Closed: 11/25, 12/25. **Address:** 36 Exchange Terrace 02903 **Location:** I-95, exit 22A, on lower level of former Union Train Station. **Parking:** on-site (fee).

WALTER'S RISTORANTE D' ITALIA

Regional Italian
$18-$25

Phone: 401/273-2652　30

Select from stylized Italian items—those prepared and served in clay pots—or cuisine of Italian-Jewish origin in an inviting decor. A seven-course tasting menu is available for the latter, $35. Outdoor dining is offered, weather permitting. Dressy casual. **Bar:** Full bar. **Reservations:** suggested. **Hours:** 4:30 pm-10 pm. Closed major holidays; also Sun & Mon. **Address:** 286 Atwells Ave 02903 **Location:** I-95, exit 21 southbound, 0.4 mi nw on Federal Hill; exit Broadway northbound; in DePasquale Plaza. **Parking:** valet and street.

WATERMAN GRILLE

New American
$18-$27

Phone: 401/521-9229　11

Located in the romantic setting of an old brick gatehouse overlooking the Seekonk River, this restaurant serves up casual, intimate ambience along with New England cuisine in New Orleans flair. The New Orleans barbecue shrimp and blackened yellowfin tuna are among the nods to the Jazz City. The Maine mussels risotto and daily fresh fish specials give the restaurant its taste of New England. Dressy casual. **Bar:** Full bar. **Reservations:** suggested. **Hours:** 5 pm-9 pm, Fri & Sat-10 pm, Sun 10 am-3 & 5-8 pm. Closed: 12/25. **Address:** 4 Richmond Square 02906 **Location:** I-195, exit 3, 1 mi ne via Gano and Pitman sts; on Seekonk River. **Parking:** on-site. CALL &M

WES' RIB HOUSE

Barbecue
$7-$17

Phone: 401/421-9090　50

Appointed in a Wild West theme, the casual, established eatery is known for its ribs, chicken and homemade cornbread. Casual dress. **Bar:** Full bar. **Reservations:** accepted. **Hours:** 11:30 am-2 am, Fri & Sat-4 am, Sun noon-2 am. Closed: 11/25, 12/25. **Address:** 38 Dike St 02909 **Location:** Just s of SR 6A. **Parking:** on-site.

(See map and index starting on p. 606)

ZOOMA BAR RISTORANTE

Italian
$14-$29

Phone: 401/383-2002 (31)

With its eggplant-colored exterior and beautiful overflowing flower boxes, this trattoria is hard to miss. The main dining room toward the back overlooks the wood oven, where delicious pizzas bake, while the front bar area features a flat-panel TV and views of bustling Federal Hill. Among good homemade pasta dishes is carmello di astice, featuring lobster and mascarpone cheese stuffed inside homemade ravioli and topped with a sauce of cherry tomatoes and dry vermouth. Dressy casual. **Bar:** Full bar. **Reservations:** suggested. **Hours:** 11:30 am-10 pm, Fri & Sat-11 pm. Closed: 1/1, 12/25. **Address:** 245 Atwells Ave 02903 **Location:** I-95, exit 21, 0.3 mi w. **Parking:** on-site.

SMITHFIELD (See map and index starting on p. 606)

COMFORT SUITES *Book at AAA.com*

Hotel
$99-$189 5/1-10/31
$89-$179 11/1-4/30

Phone: (401)231-6300 (22)

Address: 1010 Douglas Pike 02917 **Location:** I-295, exit 8B, 0.7 mi n on SR 7. **Facility:** Smoke free premises. 84 units. 81 one-bedroom standard units. 3 one-bedroom suites with kitchens. 3 stories, interior corridors. *Bath:* combo or shower only. **Parking:** on-site. **Amenities:** high-speed Internet, dual phone lines, voice mail, irons, hair dryers. **Leisure Activities:** exercise room. **Guest Services:** coin laundry, wireless Internet. **Business Services:** business center. (ASK) ⊠ 🎥 🛏 🖨 💻

HAMPTON INN & SUITES SMITHFIELD *Book great rates at AAA.com*

(AAA) (SAVE)

Hotel
$119-$209 All Year

Phone: (401)232-9200 (23)

Address: 965 Douglas Pike 02917 **Location:** I-295, exit 8B, 0.6 mi nw on SR 7. **Facility:** Smoke free premises. 101 one-bedroom standard units. 4 stories, interior corridors. *Bath:* combo or shower only. **Parking:** on-site. **Terms:** 1-7 night minimum stay, cancellation fee imposed. **Amenities:** video games (fee), high-speed Internet, voice mail, irons, hair dryers. **Pool(s):** heated indoor. **Leisure Activities:** exercise room. **Guest Services:** valet and coin laundry, wireless Internet. **Business Services:** meeting rooms, business center. **Free Special Amenities: full breakfast and high-speed Internet.** CALL 🛗M 🏊 ⊠ 🎥 🛏 🖨 💻

AAA Benefit:
Members save up to
10% everyday!

QUALITY INN SMITHFIELD *Book great rates at AAA.com*

(AAA) (SAVE)

Hotel
$120-$280 5/1-10/23
$100-$230 10/24-4/30

Phone: (401)232-2400 (21)

Address: 355 George Washington Hwy 02917 **Location:** I-295, exit 8B, 0.3 mi n on SR 7, then 0.6 mi e on SR 116. **Facility:** 111 one-bedroom standard units. 2 stories (no elevator), interior corridors. *Bath:* combo or shower only. **Parking:** on-site. **Terms:** 7 day cancellation notice-fee imposed. **Amenities:** safes (fee), irons, hair dryers. **Pool(s):** heated outdoor. **Leisure Activities:** whirlpool. **Guest Services:** valet and coin laundry, wireless Internet. **Business Services:** meeting rooms, business center. CALL 🛗M 🏊 🎥 🛏 💻 / SOME UNITS FEE 🛒 ⊠ 🖨

WHERE TO DINE

CRICKET'S OF SMITHFIELD

Italian
$10-$20

Phone: 401/232-0300 (60)

Convenient to the interstate, the charming, country-style restaurant offers simple, fresh seafood and Italian entrees. A good choice is the fresh and flavorful made-to-order Reuben sandwich. Dressy casual. **Bar:** Full bar. **Reservations:** suggested. **Hours:** 11:30 am-10 pm, Sun-9 pm; hours vary off season. Closed: 1/1, 12/25; also Mon. **Address:** 280 George Washington Hwy 02917 **Location:** I-295, exit 8B, 0.3 mi e of jct SR 7. **Parking:** on-site.

D. CARLO TRATTORIA

Italian
$8-$20

Phone: 401/349-4979 (61)

This trattoria brings the flavors of Tuscany and other Italian regional areas to town in a warm yet modern and stylish space. On the menu are many tasty dishes prepared from homemade pastas, seafood and chicken. Dressy casual. **Bar:** Full bar. **Hours:** 11:30 am-2:30 & 5-9:30 pm, Fri-10 pm, Sat 5 pm-10 pm. Closed: 11/25, 12/24, 12/25; also Sun. **Address:** 970 Douglass Pike 02917 **Location:** Jct SR 116, just se on SR 7. **Parking:** on-site. CALL 🛗M

FAIAL RESTAURANT & LOUNGE

Portuguese
$6-$25

Phone: 401/231-1100 (62)

Serving authentic Portuguese cuisine, the menu does feature a few American and fresh seafood dishes. A great starter is the littleneck clams steamed with Portuguese spices, chorizo and onions. Follow that with the grilled New York strip loin topped with a fried egg and served with seafood rice and Portuguese potatoes. For the grand finale, the Faial pudding is a mixture of chocolate pudding, mousse, whipped cream and a softened cookie. Casual dress. **Bar:** Full bar. **Reservations:** accepted. **Hours:** 11:30 am-9 pm. **Address:** 970 Douglas Pike 02917 **Location:** I-295, exit 8B, 0.7 mi nw on SR 7. **Parking:** on-site. CALL 🛗M

SOUTH KINGSTOWN

HAMPTON INN SOUTH KINGSTOWN/NEWPORT
AREA *Book great rates at AAA.com*

Phone: (401)788-3500

Hotel
$99-$159 All Year

Address: 20 Hotel Dr 02879 **Location:** Jct SR 138, 2 mi s on US 1; in South County Commons. **Facility:** 100 one-bedroom standard units. 4 stories, interior corridors. *Bath:* combo or shower only. **Parking:** on-site. **Terms:** 1-7 night minimum stay, cancellation fee imposed. **Amenities:** voice mail, irons, hair dryers. **Pool(s):** heated indoor. **Leisure Activities:** whirlpool, sun deck, exercise room. **Guest Services:** valet and coin laundry, wireless Internet. **Business Services:** meeting rooms, business center. **Free Special Amenities: expanded continental breakfast and high-speed Internet.**

AAA Benefit:
Members save up to
10% everyday!

HOLIDAY INN   *Book at AAA.com*

Phone: (401)789-1051

Hotel
$129-$269 5/15-4/30
$89-$139 5/1-5/14

Address: 3009 Tower Hill Rd 02874 **Location:** Just n of jct SR 138 W on US 1. **Facility:** 107 one-bedroom standard units. 4 stories, interior corridors. *Bath:* combo or shower only. **Parking:** on-site. **Terms:** cancellation fee imposed. **Amenities:** video games (fee), voice mail, irons, hair dryers. *Some:* high-speed Internet. **Pool(s):** outdoor. **Leisure Activities:** exercise room, volleyball. **Guest Services:** valet and coin laundry, wireless Internet. **Business Services:** meeting rooms, business center.

TIVERTON pop. 7,282

—— WHERE TO DINE ——

THE BOAT HOUSE

Phone: 401/624-6300

American
$12-$26

The bayfront location affords excellent water views from long paneled windows in its nautical dining room and from its seasonal cafe-style patio. Signature menu entrees include baked stuffed white shrimp with Jonah crab-sweet corn filling, warm spaghetti squash and wild arugula; grilled Scottish salmon with Israeli couscous, artichokes, spinach, roasted garlic, pepitas and grape compote; and roasted Murray's Statler chicken with fresh fettuccine, tomato, broccoli rabe and pine nut-cream. Dressy casual. **Bar:** Full bar. **Reservations:** suggested. **Hours:** 11:30 am-9 pm, Fri & Sat-10 pm, Sun 11 am-9 pm; hours vary off season. Closed: 12/25; also Mon. **Address:** 227 Schooner Dr 02878 **Location:** SR 24, exit 5, 0.4 mi n on SR 138, then just e; at The Villages of Mount Hope Bay. **Parking:** on-site.

WAKEFIELD

THE KINGS' ROSE INN

Phone: 401/783-5222

Historic Bed
& Breakfast
$110-$145 All Year

Address: 1747 Mooresfield Rd (SR 138) 02879 **Location:** I-95, exit 3A, 11 mi e on SR 138; 3.3 mi w of US 1. **Facility:** A 1930s colonial-style house with spacious lawns and English gardens, this inn is furnished with antiques and has one room with a working fireplace. Smoke free premises. 6 units. 5 one-bedroom standard units. 1 two-bedroom suite. 3 stories (no elevator), interior corridors. *Bath:* combo or shower only. **Parking:** on-site. **Terms:** office hours 7 am-10 pm. **Amenities:** irons, hair dryers. **Business Services:** meeting rooms.

WARREN

—— WHERE TO DINE ——

COUNTRY INN RESTAURANT

Phone: 401/245-8318

American
$5-$21

This restaurant is great for families due to the casual atmosphere and wide menu selection including sandwiches, fried and broiled seafood, steaks and chicken. Casual dress. **Bar:** Full bar. **Reservations:** not accepted. **Hours:** 11 am-9 pm, Fri & Sat-10 pm, Sun 11:30 am-9 pm. Closed: 12/25. **Address:** 382 Market St 02885 **Location:** I-195, exit 2, 2 mi s on SR 136. **Parking:** on-site.

CROSSROADS

Phone: 401/245-9305

American
$8-$18

The large restaurant is divided into several small rooms, each with its own individual feel. One is a bright sunroom filled with live plants; another is an early 1900s pub-like room with antique New York City pictures. Favorite American pasta and chicken dishes make up the large menu. Casual dress. **Bar:** Full bar. **Reservations:** not accepted. **Hours:** 11:30 am-11 pm. Closed major holidays; also Mon. **Address:** 133 Market St 02885 **Location:** Just e of SR 114. **Parking:** on-site.

JACK'S FAMILY RESTAURANT

Phone: 401/245-4052

Seafood
$6-$19

Since 1972, locals have returned to this hole in the wall for fresh seafood, Italian, Portuguese and American dishes. The food is cooked to order and the friendly, casual service makes guests feel right at home. Appetizers include fried calamari with hot peppers on the side. Guests rave about the "famous seafood special" consisting of spaghetti with chopped littlenecks, shrimp, langostinos, scallops and mushrooms in a choice of red or white sauce. Many dishes can be served in half portions. Casual dress. **Bar:** Full bar. **Reservations:** not accepted. **Hours:** 11 am-10 pm, Fri & Sat-11 pm, Sun noon-10 pm. Closed major holidays; also Tues. **Address:** 294 Child St 02885 **Location:** Jct SR 136, just w on SR 103. **Parking:** on-site.

LUKE'S INN

Phone: 401/247-0665

Chinese
$5-$17

The eatery is a local favorite for Chinese and Polynesian dishes at affordable prices. Teriyaki sticks, house chicken wings and General Tso's chicken are popular selections. Casual dress. **Bar:** Full bar. **Hours:** 11:30 am-10 pm, Fri & Sat-midnight. Closed: 11/25, 12/25. **Address:** 650 Metacom Ave (SR 136) 02885 **Location:** I-195, exit 2, 4.3 mi s. **Parking:** on-site.

STELLA BLUES

New England
$8-$20

Phone: 401/289-0349

In the historic waterfront district, the restaurant is nicely decorated with contemporary artwork. The enclosed sun porch offers views of the downtown area, while the seasonal patio has beautiful plants and foliage. Guests might start with a cup of Italian wedding soup, featuring chicken and meatballs, then enjoy Tuscan bruschetta with prosciutto or spinach and feta. New York sirloin alla Mama, a tasty choice, includes freshly chopped garlic and butter sauce. Casual dress. **Bar:** Full bar. **Reservations:** not accepted. **Hours:** 11:30 am-9:30 pm, Fri & Sat-10:30 pm, Sun noon-9 pm. Closed major holidays; also Mon. **Address:** 50 Miller St 02885 **Location:** Corner of Water St; downtown. **Parking:** street.

THE SUNNYSIDE DAYTIME DINING

American
$6-$10

Phone: 401/247-1200

If the food doesn't entice—which is highly unlikely given the tempting offering of classic dishes prepared with creative twists—the casual oceanside elegance and views will do the trick. The fantastic gourmet brunch menu lines up choices such as pumpkin and pecan pancakes with Vermont maple syrup or baked raisin French toast with grated apples and toasted almonds. Guests also can create their own grilled omelet. The chef's homemade jams are served with flavored bread at the start of the meal. Casual dress. **Bar:** Beer & wine. **Reservations:** not accepted. **Hours:** 7 am-2 pm. Closed major holidays; also Mon & Tues. **Address:** 267 Water St 02885 **Location:** Just w of SR 114; between Church and State sts; downtown. **Parking:** on-site.

TAV-VINOS

Seafood
$9-$16

Phone: 401/245-0231

Nestled along the bay, the nautically themed restaurant serves generous portions of fresh seafood and steaks. During warmer months, outdoor seating on a deck overlooking the water is available. Dressy casual. **Bar:** Full bar. **Reservations:** suggested. **Hours:** 8 am-2 pm, Sat & Sun from 7 am. Closed major holidays; also Mon & Tues. **Address:** 267 Water St 02885 **Location:** Just w of SR 114; between Church and State sts. **Parking:** on-site.

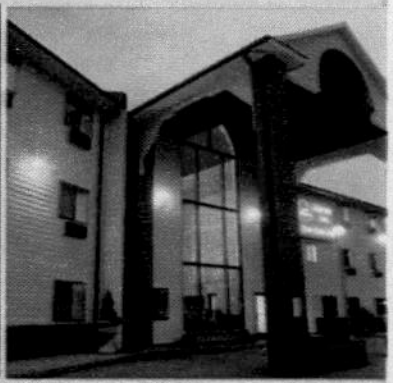

TUSCAN TAVERN

Northern Italian
$9-$26

Phone: 401/247-9200

Elegant yet relaxed decor, including rich wood paneling and colorful murals, accentuates the dining room. On the menu are tasty Italian favorites such as spicy penne arrabbiata, veal parmigiana and spaghetti pescatore: shrimp, clams and mussels in Mediterranean tomato herb sauce. Guests can view chefs preparing a wide variety of homemade pizzas and bruschettas in the wood-burning oven. Dressy casual. **Bar:** Full bar. **Reservations:** accepted. **Hours:** 4 pm-9:30 pm, Fri & Sat-10:30 pm, Sun 4 pm-9 pm. Closed: 7/4, 11/25, 12/25; also Mon. **Address:** 632 Metacom Ave 02885 **Location:** I-195, exit 2, 4.2 mi s on SR 136. **Parking:** on-site.

WARWICK pop. 85,808   (See map and index starting on p. 606)

(See map and index starting on p. 606)

CROWNE PLAZA HOTEL AT THE CROSSINGS   *Book at AAA.com*   **Phone:** (401)732-6000   58

▼▼▼
Hotel
$99-$149 All Year

Address: 801 Greenwich Ave 02886 **Location:** I-95, exit 12A southbound; exit 12 northbound, 0.3 mi se on SR 5. **Facility:** 266 one-bedroom standard units, some with whirlpools. 6 stories, interior corridors. **Parking:** on-site. **Amenities:** CD players, high-speed Internet, dual phone lines, voice mail, irons, hair dryers. **Pool(s):** heated indoor. **Leisure Activities:** sauna, whirlpool, exercise room. **Guest Services:** valet laundry, area transportation, wireless Internet. **Business Services:** conference facilities, business center.

EXTENDED STAYAMERICA
   PROVIDENCE-AIRPORT-WARWICK   *Book at AAA.com*   **Phone:** (401)732-2547   50

▼▼ ▼▼
Extended Stay
Hotel
$65-$149 All Year

Address: 245 W Natick Rd 02886 **Location:** I-295, exit 2 northbound, just sw; exit 3A southbound, 1.1 mi e on SR 37, 2 mi s on SR 2, then just sw. **Facility:** 104 one-bedroom standard units with efficiencies. 3 stories, interior corridors. *Bath:* combo or shower only. **Parking:** on-site. **Terms:** office hours 7 am-11 pm, cancellation fee imposed. **Amenities:** dual phone lines, voice mail, irons, hair dryers. **Guest Services:** coin laundry, wireless Internet.

HAMPTON INN & SUITES PROVIDENCE-WARWICK
   AIRPORT   *Book great rates at AAA.com*   **Phone:** (401)739-8888   55

(AAA) (SAVE)
▼▼▼
Hotel
$89-$189 All Year

Address: 2100 Post Rd 02886 **Location:** I-95, exit 13, e to US 1, then just n. **Facility:** 173 units. 126 one-bedroom standard units. 47 one-bedroom suites with efficiencies. 5 stories, interior corridors. *Bath:* combo or shower only. **Parking:** on-site. **Terms:** 1-7 night minimum stay, cancellation fee imposed. **Amenities:** video games (fee), voice mail, irons, hair dryers. *Some:* dual phone lines. **Pool(s):** heated indoor. **Leisure Activities:** whirlpool, exercise room. **Guest Services:** valet and coin laundry, airport transportation-Theodore Francis Green State Airport, area transportation-within 3 mi, wireless Internet. **Business Services:** meeting rooms, business center. **Free Special Amenities: expanded continental breakfast and high-speed Internet.**

AAA Benefit:
Members save up to
10% everyday!

HILTON GARDEN INN PROVIDENCE
   AIRPORT/WARWICK   *Book great rates at AAA.com*   **Phone:** (401)734-9600   48

▼▼▼
Hotel
$99-$219 All Year

Address: 1 Thurber St 02886 **Location:** I-95, exit 13, 0.4 mi on Airport Connector Rd, exit Jefferson Blvd, then 0.4 mi n. **Facility:** 160 one-bedroom standard units. 6 stories, interior corridors. *Bath:* combo or shower only. **Parking:** on-site. **Terms:** 1-7 night minimum stay, cancellation fee imposed. **Amenities:** video games (fee), high-speed Internet, dual phone lines, voice mail, irons, hair dryers. **Pool(s):** heated indoor. **Leisure Activities:** whirlpool, exercise room. **Guest Services:** valet and coin laundry, area transportation, wireless Internet. **Business Services:** meeting rooms, business center.

Hilton
Garden Inn
AAA Benefit:
Members save 5% or
more everyday!

(See map and index starting on p. 606)

HOLIDAY INN EXPRESS HOTEL & SUITES   *Book at AAA.com*   Phone: (401)736-5000   **57**

Hotel
$79-$129 All Year

Address: 901 Jefferson Blvd 02886 **Location:** I-95, exit 13, 0.4 mi on Airport Connector Rd, then exit Jefferson Blvd. **Facility:** 147 units. 116 one-bedroom standard units. 31 one-bedroom suites. 4 stories, interior corridors. *Bath:* combo or shower only. **Parking:** on-site. **Amenities:** video games (fee), dual phone lines, voice mail, irons, hair dryers. **Pool(s):** heated indoor. **Leisure Activities:** whirlpool, exercise room. **Guest Services:** valet laundry, area transportation, wireless Internet. **Business Services:** meeting rooms, business center.

[ASK] [✈] CALL [&M] [▨] [▣] / SOME UNITS FEE [🐕] [✕] [🛢] [▤]

HOMESTEAD STUDIO
SUITES-PROVIDENCE/AIRPORT/WARWICK   *Book at AAA.com*   Phone: (401)732-6667   **54**

Hotel
$75-$149 All Year

Address: 268 Metro Center Blvd 02886 **Location:** I-95, exit 12A, 0.4 mi e on SR 113, 0.4 mi n on SR 5, then 0.4 mi e. **Facility:** 94 units. 73 one-bedroom standard units with efficiencies. 21 one-bedroom suites with efficiencies. 3 stories, interior corridors. *Bath:* combo or shower only. **Parking:** on-site. **Terms:** cancellation fee imposed. **Amenities:** dual phone lines, voice mail, irons, hair dryers. **Leisure Activities:** whirlpool, exercise room, sports court. **Guest Services:** valet and coin laundry, area transportation, wireless Internet. **Business Services:** meeting rooms.

[ASK] [✈] CALL [&M] [✕] [🎦] [🛢] [▤] [▣] / SOME UNITS [🐕] [✕]

HOMEWOOD SUITES BY HILTON   *Book great rates at AAA.com*   Phone: (401)738-0008   **52**

Extended Stay
Hotel
$85-$159 All Year

Address: 33 International Way 02886 **Location:** I-95, exit 13, 0.4 mi n on Jefferson Blvd, 0.5 mi nw on Kilvert St, then 0.4 mi sw on Metro Center Blvd. **Facility:** 82 units. 39 one-bedroom standard units with efficiencies. 30 one- and 13 two-bedroom suites with efficiencies. 3 stories, interior corridors. *Bath:* combo or shower only. **Parking:** on-site. **Terms:** 1-7 night minimum stay, cancellation fee imposed. **Amenities:** dual phone lines, voice mail, irons, hair dryers. *Some:* DVD players, high-speed Internet. **Pool(s):** heated indoor. **Leisure Activities:** whirlpool, exercise room, sports court. **Guest Services:** valet and coin laundry, wireless Internet. **Business Services:** meeting rooms, business center.

CALL [&M] [▨] [✕] [🎦] [🛢] [▤] [▣] / SOME UNITS FEE [🐕] [✕]

AAA Benefit:
Members save 5% or
more everyday!

LA QUINTA INN & SUITES   *Book at AAA.com*   Phone: (401)941-6600   **45**

Hotel
$65-$159 All Year

Address: 36 Jefferson Blvd 02888 **Location:** I-95, exit 15, just se. **Facility:** 115 one-bedroom standard units. 5 stories, interior corridors. *Bath:* combo or shower only. **Parking:** on-site. **Amenities:** voice mail, irons, hair dryers. *Some:* high-speed Internet. **Pool(s):** outdoor. **Leisure Activities:** exercise room. **Guest Services:** valet and coin laundry, area transportation, wireless Internet. **Business Services:** business center.

[ASK] [✈] [🍴] [▨] [🎦] [▣] / SOME UNITS [🐕] [✕] [🛢] [▤]

NYLO PROVIDENCE/WARWICK   *Book great rates at AAA.com*   Phone: (401)734-4460   **51**

[ⒶⒶⒶ] [SAVE]

Boutique
Hotel
$89-$229 All Year

Address: 400 Knight St 02886 **Location:** Jct SR 5, just ne. Located across from Warwick Mall. **Facility:** This ultra-modern, boutique-style hotel is located in what looks to be an old, restored mill; though it is an entirely new building. Smoke free premises. 163 units. 159 one-bedroom standard units. 4 one-bedroom suites. 5 stories, interior corridors. *Bath:* shower only. **Parking:** on-site. **Terms:** cancellation fee imposed. **Amenities:** CD players, high-speed Internet, voice mail, safes, irons, hair dryers. **Dining:** The Loft, see separate listing. **Leisure Activities:** saunas, billiards, exercise room. **Guest Services:** airport transportation-Theodore Francis Green State Airport, wireless Internet. **Business Services:** meeting rooms, business center. *(See color ad p 615)*

[ECO] [✈] [🍴] [🍷] CALL [&M] [✕] [✕] [🎦] [▣]
/ SOME UNITS FEE [🐕] [🛢] [▤]

FREE local telephone calls and high-speed Internet

Now
That's
Refreshing
ⒶⒶⒶ ⒸⒶⒶ

Take the surprise out of
hotel and restaurant visits.
Let the simple, reliable
AAA/CAA Diamond Ratings
guide your decisions.

(See map and index starting on p. 606)

RADISSON HOTEL PROVIDENCE AIRPORT *Book great rates at AAA.com* Phone: (401)739-3000 **53**

Hotel
$109-$161 All Year

Address: 2081 Post Rd 02886 **Location:** I-95, exit 13, e to US 1, then just ne. **Facility:** Smoke free premises. 111 units. 72 one-bedroom standard units. 39 one-bedroom suites with whirlpools. 2 stories, interior corridors. *Bath:* combo or shower only. **Parking:** on-site. **Terms:** cancellation fee imposed. **Amenities:** high-speed Internet, dual phone lines, voice mail, irons, hair dryers. **Leisure Activities:** exercise room. **Guest Services:** valet laundry, airport transportation-Theodore Francis Green State Airport, wireless Internet. **Business Services:** conference facilities, business center. *(See color ad below)*

FREE newspaper and high-speed Internet

RESIDENCE INN PROVIDENCE/WARWICK *Book great rates at AAA.com* Phone: (401)737-7100 **47**

Extended Stay
Hotel
$159-$169 All Year

Address: 500 Kilvert St 02886 **Location:** I-95, exit 13 to Jefferson Blvd, 0.4 mi n, then 0.6 mi w. **Facility:** Smoke free premises. 96 one-bedroom standard units with kitchens. 2 stories (no elevator), exterior corridors. *Bath:* combo or shower only. **Terms:** cancellation fee imposed. **Amenities:** voice mail, irons, hair dryers. **Pool(s):** heated indoor. **Leisure Activities:** whirlpool, exercise room, sports court. **Guest Services:** valet and coin laundry, wireless Internet. **Business Services:** meeting rooms, business center.

AAA Benefit:
Members save a minimum 5% off the best available rate.

SHERATON PROVIDENCE AIRPORT HOTEL *Book great rates at AAA.com* Phone: (401)738-4000 **46**

Hotel
$79-$209 All Year

Address: 1850 Post Rd 02886 **Location:** I-95, exit 13, 0.6 mi n on US 1. **Facility:** Smoke free premises. 207 one-bedroom standard units. 5 stories, interior corridors. *Bath:* combo or shower only. **Parking:** on-site. **Amenities:** high-speed Internet (fee), dual phone lines, voice mail, irons, hair dryers. **Pool(s):** heated indoor. **Leisure Activities:** exercise room. **Guest Services:** valet laundry, airport transportation-Theodore Francis Green State Airport, wireless Internet. **Business Services:** meeting rooms, business center. **Free Special Amenities:** newspaper.

S Sheraton
HOTELS & RESORTS
AAA Benefit:
Members get up to 15% off, plus Starwood Preferred Guest® bonuses.

▼ See AAA listing above ▼

(See map and index starting on p. 606)

——— **WHERE TO DINE** ———

CHELO'S HOMETOWN BAR & GRILLE

American
$6-$25

Phone: 401/884-3000

The popular, lively restaurant is at an active marina. Diners often wait a bit during peak times to enjoy the homemade chowders, fresh seafood and a wide selection of landlubber dishes. The casual atmosphere appeals to families, large parties and just about anyone. Casual dress. **Bar:** Full bar. **Reservations:** not accepted. **Hours:** Open 5/1-10/12 & 4/15-4/30; 11:30 am-10:30 pm, Thurs-Sat to 11 pm. Closed major holidays. **Address:** 1 Masthead Dr 02886 **Location:** On US 1. **Parking:** on-site.

CROW'S NEST RESTAURANT
Seafood
$6-$22

Phone: 401/732-6575   99

Across from an active boat marina, the popular restaurant serves plentiful portions. Fresh seafood preparations are favorites. Casual dress. **Bar:** Full bar. **Reservations:** not accepted. **Hours:** Open 5/1-1/15 & 2/15-4/30; 11:30 am-10 pm, Fri & Sat-10:30 pm. Closed: 11/25, 12/24, 12/25. **Address:** 288 Arnold's Neck Dr 02886 **Location:** 0.5 mi s on US 1 from jct SR 117, then 0.5 mi e. **Parking:** on-site.

ELEVEN FORTY NINE
AAA
New American
$7-$36

Phone: 401/884-1149   100

Modern decor, great-tasting food and congenial service impress at the upscale restaurant, which features cloth-draped tables set with china and glass stemware. Striking architectural features, including stone-wall facades, slate flooring and dark wood moldings, elevate the space. The lunch menu offers salads, sandwiches and creative entrees, while top-quality steaks, seafood and brick oven pizzas delight for dinner. Live entertainment enhances the atmosphere Thursday through Saturday evenings. Dressy casual. **Bar:** Full bar. **Reservations:** suggested. **Hours:** 11:30 am-2:30 & 5-10 pm, Fri & Sat-11 pm, Sun 10 am-2 & 4-8 pm. Closed: 1/1, 11/25, 12/25. **Address:** 1149 Division St 02818 **Location:** On SR 401, just e of jct SR 2. **Parking:** on-site. CALL 🅛🅜

A Memorable Experience for Discriminating Diners

GREGG'S RESTAURANT & PUB
American
$5-$15

Phone: 401/467-5700

Gregg's popularity and its bustling, cheerful atmosphere can, at times, cause a wait in line during busy peak meal times. Daily specials, sandwiches, salad and a wide variety of homemade pastries and desserts are delivered by friendly and fast servers. Casual dress. **Bar:** Full bar. **Reservations:** not accepted. **Hours:** 11:30 am-midnight, Fri & Sat-1 am. Closed: 11/25, 12/25. **Address:** 1359 Post Rd (Rt 1) 02888 **Location:** Just n of jct SR 37. **Parking:** on-site.

LEGAL SEA FOODS

Seafood
$7-$24

Phone: 401/732-3663   98

Legal prides itself on a reputation for freshness and consistency. More than 40 varieties of seafood can be grilled, broiled, fried or prepared Cajun style. Try the clam chowder that has been served at every presidential inauguration since 1981. The nautically inspired dining room is upscale and attractive with its rich cherry wood paneling and intricately detailed model ships. Dressy casual. **Bar:** Full bar. **Reservations:** suggested, weekends. **Hours:** 11:30 am-10 pm, Fri-10:30 pm, Sat noon-10:30 pm, Sun noon-9 pm. Closed: 11/25, 12/25. **Address:** 2099 Post Rd 02886 **Location:** I-95, exit 13, on US 1. **Parking:** on-site.

THE LOFT
New American
$9-$22

Phone: 401/734-4460   97

Unique glass curio boxes filled with shells were handcrafted as tables, and blue and white director chairs and coral chandeliers provider further reminders of this place's Ocean State location. Chefs are accomplished in New England cooking such as the trio of Rhode Island sliders with a mini Angus beef burger, lobster salad and crab cake. Through the glass doors is a fabulous, 3,000-square-foot, resort-style patio deck that offers incredible views of the Pawtucket River. Casual dress. **Bar:** Full bar. **Reservations:** suggested. **Hours:** 6 am-11 & 11:30-10 pm, Fri-11 pm, Sat 6:30 am-11 pm, Sun 6:30 am-10 pm. **Address:** 400 Knight St 02886 **Location:** Jct SR 5, just ne; in NYLO Providence/Warwick. **Parking:** on-site. CALL 🅛🅜

SHOGUN STEAK & SEAFOOD HOUSE
Japanese
$12-$36

Phone: 401/270-3608   94

Diners looking for a show with dinner can take a seat at one of the many hibachi tables and let the chefs impress with their ability to flip anything into the air and have it land in the crease of their hat. Each dinner comes with traditional miso soup, a salad topped with homemade ginger dressing, white rice and grilled vegetables including zucchini, mushrooms, onions and bean sprouts. Then guests choose a protein from a long list of options that include filet mignon, swordfish or lobster. Casual dress. **Bar:** Full bar. **Reservations:** not accepted. **Hours:** 5 pm-10 pm, Fri & Sat-11 pm, Sun 4 pm-9 pm. Closed: 7/4, 11/25, 12/25. **Address:** 76 Jefferson Blvd 02888 **Location:** I-95, exit 15, 0.5 mi se. **Parking:** on-site. CALL 🅛🅜

THAI EXCURSION

Thai
$8-$16

Phone: 401/921-5582   95

Representative of nicely prepared authentic Thai cuisine are the shumai dumplings starter, which is steamed or pan fried with shrimp and vegetables and served with the house soy sauce, as well as entrees from the "curry corner" and create-your-own options with pad thai noodles, fried rice and unusual choices such as coconut and pineapple. The sticky rice dessert is a delicious end to the experience. The setting features colorful orchids painted on the walls and placed in vases on clothed tables. Casual dress. **Bar:** Full bar. **Reservations:** accepted. **Hours:** 11:30 am-10 pm, Sun from 5 pm. Closed major holidays. **Address:** 1565 Post Rd 02888 **Location:** 0.3 mi se on Airport Connector Rd, then 0.5 mi n on Jefferson Blvd. **Parking:** on-site.

(See map and index starting on p. 606)

TWIST

Italian
$7-$23

Phone: 401/734-4440   96

The dining room is accented with warm contemporary brown hues, laminate wood flooring and a twisted copper pipe made into an art piece that divides the space. High-quality dishes include a starter of Harpoon beer-steamed mussels with fennel, andouille sausage, tomato, thyme and leeks and homemade pasta specials such as ravioli stuffed with mushrooms, broccoli rabe and provolone cheese and served in saffron broth with sautéed spinach. Scrumptious desserts include the seasonal pumpkin cheesecake. Casual dress. **Bar:** Full bar. **Reservations:** accepted. **Hours:** 11:30 am-1 am. Closed: 11/25, 12/25. **Address:** 336 Bald Hill Rd 02886 **Location:** I-295, exit 2, 0.5 mi n. **Parking:** on-site. CALL ♿M

WESTERLY pop. 17,682

SHELTER HARBOR INN

Historic
Country Inn
$106-$258 5/1-9/6
$106-$198 9/7-4/30

Phone: 401/322-8883

Address: 10 Wagner Rd 02891 **Location:** 4 mi ne of jct SR 78 on US 1. **Facility:** This family-run country inn, a converted 1911 farmhouse with outbuildings, is near a historic state park. Smoke free premises. 24 one-bedroom standard units. 1-3 stories (no elevator), interior/exterior corridors. *Bath:* combo or shower only. **Parking:** on-site. **Terms:** office hours 7 am-10 pm, 2 night minimum stay - seasonal and/or weekends. **Amenities:** irons, hair dryers. **Dining:** restaurant, see separate listing. **Leisure Activities:** beach access, putting green, playground. **Guest Services:** wireless Internet. **Business Services:** meeting rooms, business center. 🍽 ✂

THE VILLA BED & BREAKFAST

Bed & Breakfast
$245-$320 5/1-9/30
$125-$245 10/1-4/30

Phone: 401/596-1054

Address: 190 Shore Rd 02891 **Location:** SR 1A, 2.5 mi e of US 1 via Airport and Winnapaug rds. Located in a quiet area. **Facility:** Minutes from Misquamicut Beach, this Mediterranean-style B&B makes for a perfect romantic hideaway with its lush flower gardens, porticos and verandas. Smoke free premises. 8 units. 7 one-bedroom standard units with whirlpools. 1 one-bedroom suite with whirlpool. 3 stories (no elevator), interior/exterior corridors. **Parking:** on-site. **Terms:** 2 night minimum stay - weekends, age restrictions may apply, 15 day cancellation notice-fee imposed. **Amenities:** video library, DVD players, CD players, voice mail, irons, hair dryers. **Pool(s):** heated outdoor. **Leisure Activities:** whirlpool, library. **Guest Services:** wireless Internet. **Business Services:** business center. **Free Special Amenities:** full breakfast and high-speed Internet. 🛏 ✂ 🐾 📶 🖥 💻

WINNAPAUG INN-MISQUAMICUT/WESTERLY   *Book great rates at AAA.com*   Phone: (401)348-8350

Hotel
$89-$199 5/1-9/6
$89-$169 9/7-4/30

Address: 169 Shore Rd 02891 **Location:** SR 1A, 2 mi e of US 1 via Airport and Winnapaug rds. **Facility:** Smoke free premises. 54 units. 49 one-bedroom standard units, some with whirlpools. 4 one-bedroom suites with whirlpools. 1 cottage. 4 stories, interior/exterior corridors. *Bath:* combo or shower only. **Parking:** on-site. **Terms:** office hours 8 am-9 pm, 2-3 night minimum stay - seasonal and/or weekends, 14 day cancellation notice-fee imposed. **Amenities:** voice mail, irons, hair dryers. **Dining:** Venice Restaurant & Lounge, see separate listing. **Pool(s):** heated outdoor. **Leisure Activities:** shuffleboard. **Guest Services:** wireless Internet. **Business Services:** meeting rooms. **Free Special Amenities:** continental breakfast and high-speed Internet.
🍽 🛏 ✂ 🐾 📶 / SOME UNITS 📺

———— WHERE TO DINE ————

PIZZA PLACE PIE & SUDS

Pizza
$7-$13

Phone: 401/348-1803

As the name entails, this is the place for a delicious pizza and cold beer from the incredibly large in-stock selection. Guests order at the counter and sit at tables dressed with vinyl green-and-white-checkered table covers. Soups, chili, pasta and a multitude of red and white pizzas are offered. Among gourmet toppings are Rhode Island favorite clams casino with red and yellow peppers, a hint of onion, garlic and fresh clams shucked on site with crispy bacon. Casual dress. **Bar:** Beer & wine. **Reservations:** not accepted. **Hours:** 11 am-9 pm; hours may vary in season. Closed major holidays. **Address:** 43 Broad St 02891 **Location:** On US 1; between High and Union sts; center; across from library. **Parking:** on-site (fee). CALL ♿M

SHELTER HARBOR INN

Regional New
England
$9-$29

Phone: 401/322-8883

Guests come here for gracious dining in a charming country inn dining room or in a quiet, comfortable candlelit garden setting. The service is cordial and attentive. The variety of homemade breads and pastries is pleasing. Dressy casual. **Bar:** Full bar. **Reservations:** suggested. **Hours:** 7:30 am-10 pm. **Address:** 10 Wagner Rd 02891 **Location:** 4 mi ne of jct SR 78 on US 1; in Shelter Harbor Inn. **Parking:** on-site.

VENICE RESTAURANT & LOUNGE

Italian
$9-$26

Phone: 401/348-0055

The restaurant nurtures an elegant yet informal atmosphere. The view from the dining room is pleasant; from the fourth floor lounge, it's spectacular. From there, on a clear day, Block Island and the tip of Long Island in New York are visible. Upscale Italian food leans heavily on seafood and light cream sauces. Portions are generally large. Staff members are friendly. Weekends are busy, in part due to the large ballroom and meeting facility. Casual dress. **Bar:** Full bar. **Reservations:** suggested, weekends. **Hours:** 4 pm-10 pm, Sat & Sun from noon. **Address:** 165 Shore Rd 02891 **Location:** SR 1A, 2 mi e of US 1 via Airport and Winnapaug rds; in Winnapaug Inn-Misquamicut/Westerly. **Parking:** on-site. CALL ♿M

WEST GREENWICH

BEST WESTERN WEST GREENWICH INN   *Book great rates at AAA.com*

Phone: (401)397-5494

AAA (SAVE)
WWW WWW
Hotel
$59-$139 All Year

Address: 99 Nooseneck Hill Rd 02817 **Location:** I-95, exit 6, 0.3 mi n on SR 3. Located in a quiet rural area. **Facility:** 56 one-bedroom standard units. 2 stories (no elevator), interior corridors. **Parking:** on-site. **Amenities:** voice mail, irons, hair dryers. **Pool(s):** heated indoor. **Leisure Activities:** whirlpool, picnic tables, limited exercise equipment. **Guest Services:** wireless Internet. **Business Services:** meeting rooms, business center. **Free Special Amenities:** expanded continental breakfast and high-speed Internet.

AAA Benefit:
Members save up to 20%, plus 10% bonus points with rewards program.

RESIDENCE INN BY MARRIOTT PROVIDENCE / COVENTRY   *Book great rates at AAA.com*

Phone: (401)828-1170

WWWW
Extended Stay Hotel
$117-$143 All Year

Address: 755 Center of New England Blvd 02817 **Location:** I-95, exit 7, just ne; center of New England Plaza. **Facility:** Smoke free premises. 100 units. 44 one-bedroom standard units, some with kitchens. 41 one- and 15 two-bedroom suites, some with kitchens. 4 stories, interior corridors. **Parking:** on-site. **Terms:** cancellation fee imposed. **Amenities:** voice mail, irons, hair dryers. **Pool(s):** heated indoor. **Leisure Activities:** whirlpool, exercise room, sports court. **Guest Services:** valet and coin laundry, wireless Internet. **Business Services:** meeting rooms, business center.

AAA Benefit:
Members save a minimum 5% off the best available rate.

SUPER 8   *Book at AAA.com*

Phone: (401)397-3381

WW WW
Motel
$59-$99 5/1-9/5
$49-$79 9/6-4/30

Address: 101 Nooseneck Hill Rd 02817 **Location:** I-95, exit 6, just n on SR 3 N. **Facility:** 47 one-bedroom standard units. 2 stories (no elevator), interior/exterior corridors. **Parking:** on-site. **Amenities:** voice mail, hair dryers. **Guest Services:** wireless Internet.

WEST WARWICK   pop. 29,581   (See map and index starting on p. 606)

COMFORT SUITES PROVIDENCE/WEST WARWICK   *Book great rates at AAA.com*

Phone: (401)826-1800   **61**

AAA (SAVE)
WWW
Hotel
$90-$145 All Year

Address: 10 Keyes Way 02893 **Location:** I-95, exit 8 southbound; exit 8B northbound, just n on Old Quaker Ln, 0.3 mi nw on J P Murphy Hwy, then just sw. **Facility:** Smoke free premises. 88 units. 86 one-bedroom standard units. 2 one-bedroom suites. 4 stories, interior corridors. *Bath:* combo or shower only. **Parking:** on-site. **Amenities:** high-speed Internet, dual phone lines, voice mail, irons, hair dryers. **Pool(s):** heated indoor. **Leisure Activities:** exercise room. **Guest Services:** valet and coin laundry, wireless Internet. **Business Services:** meeting rooms, business center. *(See color ad p 613)*

FREE continental breakfast and high-speed Internet

EXTENDED STAYAMERICA PROVIDENCE-AIRPORT-WEST WARWICK   *Book at AAA.com*

Phone: (401)885-3161   **63**

WW WW
Extended Stay Hotel
$69-$149 All Year

Address: 1235 Division Rd 02893 **Location:** I-95, exit 8A northbound, just s on SR 2, then just w; exit 8 southbound, just s on SR 2, then just w. **Facility:** 104 one-bedroom standard units with efficiencies. 3 stories, interior corridors. *Bath:* combo or shower only. **Parking:** on-site. **Terms:** office hours 7 am-11 pm, cancellation fee imposed. **Amenities:** dual phone lines, voice mail, irons, hair dryers. **Guest Services:** coin laundry, wireless Internet.

Travel Basics: Keep a AAA Atlas in every vehicle in the household.

(See map and index starting on p. 606)

SPRINGHILL SUITES PROVIDENCE WEST WARWICK *Book great rates at AAA.com*

Phone: (401)822-1244

Hotel
$98-$120 All Year

Address: 14 James P Murphy Industrial Hwy 02893 **Location:** I-95, exit 8 southbound, just nw; exit 8B northbound. **Facility:** Smoke free premises. 107 one-bedroom standard units. 4 stories, interior corridors. *Bath:* combo or shower only. **Parking:** on-site. **Terms:** cancellation fee imposed. **Amenities:** video games (fee), dual phone lines, voice mail, irons, hair dryers. **Pool(s):** heated indoor. **Leisure Activities:** whirlpool, exercise room. **Guest Services:** valet and coin laundry, area transportation, wireless Internet. **Business Services:** meeting rooms, business center.

AAA Benefit:
Members save a minimum 5% off the best available rate.

─────── **WHERE TO DINE** ───────

COWESETT INN

Phone: 401/828-4726   103

American
$8-$22

This casual restaurant serves traditional American and Italian food. All dishes are homemade, and the selections are both tasty and varied. Casual dress. **Bar:** Full bar. **Hours:** 11:30 am-11 pm, Thurs-Sat to midnight. Closed: 12/25. **Address:** 226 Cowesett Ave 02893 **Location:** I-95, exit 8 southbound, 1 mi n on SR 2 (Quaker Ln), then 0.5 mi w on SR 3. **Parking:** on-site.

PINELLI'S GOURMET DELI/CAFE

Phone: 401/821-8828   104

Deli
$4-$17

The delicatessen prepares fresh pasta salads, pastries and terrific made-to-order sandwiches. Casual dress. **Reservations:** suggested. **Hours:** 10 am-3 & 4:30-9 pm, Fri & Sat-10 pm. Closed major holidays; also Sun. **Address:** 701 Quaker Ln 02893 **Location:** On SR 2 (Quaker Ln), just s of SR 3; in Quaker Valley Mall. **Parking:** on-site.

WOONSOCKET pop. 43,224

HOLIDAY INN EXPRESS HOTEL & SUITES *Book great rates at AAA.com*

Phone: (401)769-5000

Hotel
$140-$160 All Year

Address: 194 Fortin Dr 02895 **Location:** I-295, exit 9 (SR 146/99/122), 3.5 mi n; on SR 122. **Facility:** 88 units. 80 one-bedroom standard units. 8 one-bedroom suites. 5 stories, interior corridors. *Bath:* combo or shower only. **Parking:** on-site. **Terms:** cancellation fee imposed. **Amenities:** video games (fee), dual phone lines, voice mail, irons, hair dryers. *Some:* high-speed Internet. **Pool(s):** heated indoor. **Leisure Activities:** exercise room. **Guest Services:** coin laundry, wireless Internet. **Business Services:** meeting rooms, business center. **Free Special Amenities: continental breakfast and high-speed Internet.**

WOONSOCKET MOTOR INN

Phone: (401)762-1224

Motel
$60-$78 All Year

Address: 333 Clinton St 02895 **Location:** SR 146, exit SR 146A northbound, 1.3 mi n on Park Ave, just w on Hamlet Ave, then just ne; exit Pound Hill Rd southbound, 1 mi ne, just se on SR 146A, 1.3 mi ne on S Main St, then just ne. **Facility:** 38 one-bedroom standard units. 2 stories (no elevator), interior corridors. **Parking:** on-site. **Guest Services:** wireless Internet. **Business Services:** meeting rooms, fax (fee). **Free Special Amenities: high-speed Internet.**

─────── **WHERE TO DINE** ───────

CHAN'S FINE ORIENTAL DINING

Phone: 401/765-1900

Chinese
$5-$14

Traditional cuisine—including Cantonese, Szechuan, Hunan, Mandarin and Shanghai dishes—has made Chan's a popular dining spot since 1905. Acclaimed jazz and blues entertainers perform on Friday and Saturday; guests should call for details. A luncheon buffet is set up on weekdays. Patrons within 2 miles can get delivery. Casual dress. **Bar:** Full bar. **Reservations:** suggested, weekends. **Hours:** 11:30 am-10 pm, Thurs & Sun-11 pm, Fri & Sat-12:30 am. Closed: 11/25. **Address:** 267 Main St 02895 **Location:** Jct Main and Railroad sts; 0.3 mi w of Monument Square; downtown; at Depot Square. **Parking:** on-site.

WYOMING

STAGECOACH HOUSE INN

Phone: (401)539-9600

Bed & Breakfast
$129-$199 5/1-1/1
$100-$199 1/2-4/30

Address: 1136 Main St (SR 138) 02898 **Location:** I-95, exit 3B northbound, 0.7 mi nw; exit southbound, 0.4 mi nw. **Facility:** The stagecoach inn has been transformed into a quaint B&B that offers nine guest rooms on the second floor and three rooms on the ground floor. Smoke free premises. 12 one-bedroom standard units, some with whirlpools. 3 stories, interior/exterior corridors. *Bath:* combo or shower only. **Parking:** on-site. **Terms:** office hours 8:30 am-9:30 pm, cancellation fee imposed. **Amenities:** hair dryers. *Some:* irons. **Guest Services:** wireless Internet. **Free Special Amenities: expanded continental breakfast and high-speed Internet.**

Travel Basics: Keep a AAA Atlas in every vehicle in the household.

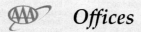

Offices

Cities with main offices are listed in **BOLD TYPE** and toll-free member service numbers in *ITALIC TYPE*.
All are closed Saturdays, Sundays and holidays unless otherwise indicated.
The addresses, phone numbers and hours for any AAA/CAA office are subject to change.
The type of service provided is designated below the name of the city where the office is located:

✦ Auto travel services, including books and maps, and on-demand TripTik ® routings.

● Auto travel services, including selected books and maps, and on-demand TripTik ® routings.

■ Books/maps only, no marked maps or on-demand TripTik ® routings.

▲ Travel Agency Services, cruise, tour, air, car and rail reservations; domestic and international hotel reservations; passport photo services; international and domestic travel guides and maps; travel money products; and International Driving Permits. In addition, assistance with travel related insurance products including trip cancellation, travel accident, lost luggage, trip delay and assistance products.

❂ Insurance services provided.

✖ Car Care Plus Facility provides car care services.

AAA NATIONAL OFFICE: 1000 AAA DRIVE, HEATHROW, FLORIDA 32746-5063, (407) 444-7000

CONNECTICUT

AVON—AAA ALLIED GROUP INC, 70 E MAIN ST, 06001. WEEKDAYS (M-F) 8:30-5:30, SAT 9:00-2:00. (860) 236-3261, *(800) 842-4320.* ✦ ▲ ❂

BRANFORD—AAA SOUTHERN NEW ENGLAND, 143 CEDAR ST, 06405. WEEKDAYS (M-F) 9:00-5:00, SAT 9:00-1:00. (203) 765-4222. ✦ ▲ ❂

CROMWELL—AAA ALLIED GROUP INC, 34 SHUNPIKE RD #20, 06416. WEEKDAYS (M-F) 8:30-5:30, SAT 9:00-2:00. (860) 236-3261, *(800) 842-4320.* ✦ ▲ ❂

DANBURY—AAA SOUTHERN NEW ENGLAND, 93 LAKE AVE, 06810. WEEKDAYS (M-F) 9:00-5:00, SAT 9:00-1:00. (203) 765-4222. ✦ ▲ ❂

ENFIELD—AAA ALLIED GROUP INC, 109 ELM ST, 06082. WEEKDAYS (M-F) 8:30-5:30, SAT 9:00-2:00. (860) 236-3261, *(800) 842-4320.* ✦ ▲ ❂

HAMDEN—AAA SOUTHERN NEW ENGLAND, 2276 WHITNEY AVE, 06518. WEEKDAYS (M-F) 9:00-5:00, SAT 9:00-1:00. (203) 765-4222. ✦ ▲ ❂

MANCHESTER—AAA ALLIED GROUP INC, 1153 TOLLAND TPK, 06042. WEEKDAYS (M-F) 8:30-5:30, SAT 9:00-2:00. (860) 236-3261, *(800) 842-4320.* ✦ ▲ ❂

MILFORD—AAA SOUTHERN NEW ENGLAND, 827 BRIDGEPORT AVENUE, 06460. WEEKDAYS (M-F) 9:00-5:00, SAT 9:00-1:00. (203) 765-4222. ✦ ▲ ❂

OLD SAYBROOK—AAA ALLIED GROUP INC, 210 MAIN ST, 06475. WEEKDAYS (M-F) 8:30-5:30, SAT 9:00-2:00. (860) 236-3261, *(800) 842-4320.* ✦ ▲ ❂

PLAINVILLE—AAA ALLIED GROUP INC, 17 FARMINGTON AVE, 06062. WEEKDAYS (M-F) 8:30-5:30, SAT 9:00-2:00. (860) 236-3261, *(800) 842-4320.* ✦ ▲ ❂

STAMFORD—AAA SOUTHERN NEW ENGLAND, 623 NEWFIELD AVE, 06905. WEEKDAYS (M-F) 9:00-5:00, SAT 9:00-1:00. (203) 765-4222. ✦ ▲ ❂

STRATFORD—AAA SOUTHERN NEW ENGLAND, 180 WATSON BLVD, 06615. WEEKDAYS (M-F) 8:30-5:30, SAT 8:30-12:00. (203) 765-4222. ✖

WATERBURY—AAA SOUTHERN NEW ENGLAND, 720 WOLCOTT ST, 06705. WEEKDAYS (M-F) 9:00-5:00, SAT 9:00-1:00. (203) 765-4222. ✦ ▲ ❂

WATERFORD—AAA ALLIED GROUP INC, 117 BOSTON POST RD, 06385. WEEKDAYS (M-F) 8:30-5:30, SAT 9:00-2:00. (860) 236-3261, *(800) 842-4320.* ✦ ▲ ❂

WEST HARTFORD—**AAA ALLIED GROUP INC**, 815 FARMINGTON AVE, 06119. WEEKDAYS (M-F) 8:30-5:30, SAT 9:00-2:00. (860) 236-3261. ✦ ▲ ❂

WESTPORT—AAA SOUTHERN NEW ENGLAND, 20 SAUGATUCK AVE, 06880. WEEKDAYS (M-F) 9:00-5:00, SAT 9:00-1:00. (203) 765-4222. ✦ ▲ ❂

MASSACHUSETTS

ACTON—AAA SOUTHERN NEW ENGLAND, 411 MASSACHUSETTS AVE, 01720. WEEKDAYS (M-F) 9:00-5:00, SAT 9:00-1:00. (978) 266-1000. ✦ ▲ ❂

AUBURN—AAA SOUTHERN NEW ENGLAND, 711 SOUTHBRIDGE ST, 01501. WEEKDAYS (M-F) 9:00-5:00, SAT 9:00-1:00. (508) 832-0200. ✦ ▲ ❂

BOSTON—AAA SOUTHERN NEW ENGLAND, 125 HIGH ST, 02110. WEEKDAYS (M-F) 9:00-5:00. (617) 443-9300. ✦ ▲ ❂

BURLINGTON—AAA SOUTHERN NEW ENGLAND, 34 CAMBRIDGE ST #140, 01803. WEEKDAYS (M-F) 9:00-5:00, SAT 9:00-1:00. (781) 272-3272. ✦ ▲ ❂

FAIRHAVEN—AAA SOUTHERN NEW ENGLAND, 32 FAIRHAVEN COMMONS, 02719. WEEKDAYS (M-F) 9:00-5:00, SAT 9:00-1:00. (508) 997-7811. ✦ ▲ ❂

FRAMINGHAM—AAA SOUTHERN NEW ENGLAND, 653 WORCESTER RD, 01701. WEEKDAYS (M-F) 9:00-5:00, SAT 9:00-1:00. (508) 875-2000. ✦ ▲ ❂

FRANKLIN—AAA SOUTHERN NEW ENGLAND, 260 FRANKLIN VILLAGE DR, 02038. WEEKDAYS (M-F) 9:00-5:00, SAT 9:00-01:00. (508) 528-9300. ✦ ▲ ❂

GREENFIELD—AAA PIONEER VALLEY, 91 MAIN ST, 01301. WEEKDAYS (M-F) 9:00-5:30. *(800) 622-9211.* ✦ ▲ ❂

HADLEY—AAA PIONEER VALLEY, 41 RUSSELL ST RT 9, 01035. WEEKDAYS (M-F) 9:00-5:30, THU 9:00-7:00. *(800) 622-9211.* ✦ ▲ ❂

HAVERHILL—AAA MERRIMACK VALLEY, 90 KENOZA AVE, 01830. WEEKDAYS (M-F) 9:00-5:30, SAT 9:00-1:00. (978) 373-3611. ✦ ▲ ❂

LAWRENCE—AAA MERRIMACK VALLEY, 155 PARKER ST, 01843. WEEKDAYS (M-F) 9:00-5:30, SAT 9:00-1:00. (978) 681-9200. ✦ ▲ ❂

LEOMINSTER—AAA SOUTHERN NEW ENGLAND, 20 COMMERCIAL RD STE #1, 01453. WEEKDAYS (M-F) 9:00-5:00, SAT 9:00-1:00. (978) 537-4000. ✦ ▲ ❂

LONGMEADOW—AAA PIONEER VALLEY, 8 BLISS RD, 01106. WEEKDAYS (M-F) 9:00-5:30. *(800) 622-9211.* ✦ ▲ ❂

LOWELL—AAA MERRIMACK VALLEY, 585 PAWTUCKET BLVD, 01854. WEEKDAYS (M-F) 9:00-5:30, SAT 9:00-1:00. (978) 937-3061. ✦ ▲ ❂

MARLBOROUGH—AAA SOUTHERN NEW ENGLAND, 197 BOSTON POST RD W, 01752. WEEKDAYS (M-F) 9:00-5:00, SAT 9:00-1:00. (508) 303-2400. ✦ ▲ ❂

NEWBURYPORT—AAA MERRIMACK VALLEY, 45 STOREY AVE RT 113, 01950. WEEKDAYS (M-F) 9:00-5:30, SAT 9:00-1:00. (978) 499-4222. ✦ ▲ ❂

NEWTON—AAA SOUTHERN NEW ENGLAND, 281 NEEDHAM ST, 02464. WEEKDAYS (M-F) 9:00-5:00, SAT 9:00-1:00. (617) 332-9900. ✦ ▲ ❂

NORTH ANDOVER—**AAA MERRIMACK VALLEY**, 49 ORCHARD HILL RD, 01845. WEEKDAYS (M-F) 9:00-5:30, SAT 9:00-1:00. (978) 946-0432. ✦ ▲ ❂

PITTSFIELD—AAA SOUTHERN NEW ENGLAND, 660 MERRILL RD, 01201. WEEKDAYS (M-F) 9:00-5:00, SAT 9:00-1:00. (413) 445-5635. ✦ ▲ ❂

PLYMOUTH—AAA SOUTHERN NEW ENGLAND, 29 HOME DEPOT DR, 02360. WEEKDAYS (M-F) 9:00-5:00, SAT 9:00-1:00. (508) 747-6100. ✦ ▲ ❂

QUINCY—AAA SOUTHERN NEW ENGLAND, 650 ADAMS ST UNIT C, 02169. WEEKDAYS (M-F) 9:00-5:00, SAT 9:00-1:00. (617) 472-4900. ✦ ▲ ❂

RAYNHAM—AAA SOUTHERN NEW ENGLAND, 350 NEW STATE HWY STE 3, 02767. WEEKDAYS (M-F) 9:00-5:00, SAT 9:00-1:00. (508) 823-6000. ✦ ▲ ❂

ROCKLAND—AAA SOUTHERN NEW ENGLAND, 900 HINGHAM ST, 02370. WEEKDAYS (M-F) 9:00-5:00, SAT 9:00-1:00. (781) 871-5880. ✛▲✿

SAUGUS—AAA SOUTHERN NEW ENGLAND, 214A BROADWAY RT 1, 01906. WEEKDAYS (M-F) 9:00-5:00, SAT 9:00-1:00. (781) 231-3000. ✛▲✿

SOMERSET—AAA SOUTHERN NEW ENGLAND, 869 GAR HWY, 02726. WEEKDAYS (M-F) 9:00-5:00, SAT 9:00-1:00. (508) 672-2600. ✛▲✿

SOUTH ATTLEBORO—AAA SOUTHERN NEW ENGLAND, 405 WASHINGTON ST, 02703. WEEKDAYS (M-F) 9:00-5:00, SAT 9:00-1:00. (508) 399-9000. ✛▲✿

SOUTH DENNIS—AAA SOUTHERN NEW ENGLAND, 500 RT 134, 02660. WEEKDAYS (M-F) 9:00-5:00, SAT 9:00-1:00. (508) 760-4778. ✛▲✿

SPRINGFIELD—AAA PIONEER VALLEY, 270 COOLEY ST-5 TOWN PLZ, 01128. WEEKDAYS (M-F) 9:00-5:30, THU 9:00-7:00, SAT 9:00-1:00 (INSURANCE OFFICE CLOSED ON SAT). *(800) 622-9211.* ✿

WALTHAM—AAA SOUTHERN NEW ENGLAND, 856 LEXINGTON ST, 02452. WEEKDAYS (M-F) 9:00-5:00, SAT 9:00-1:00. (781) 899-9000. ✛▲✿

WAREHAM—AAA SOUTHERN NEW ENGLAND, 2667-A CRANBERRY HWY, 02571. WEEKDAYS (M-F) 8:00-5:00. (508) 273-9940. ✿

WEBSTER—AAA SOUTHERN NEW ENGLAND, 400 S MAIN ST, 01570. WEEKDAYS (M-F) 9:00-5:00, SAT 9:00-1:00. (508) 943-0058. ✛▲✿

WEST PEABODY—AAA SOUTHERN NEW ENGLAND, 637 LOWELL ST STE A150, 01960. WEEKDAYS (M-F) 9:00-5:00, SAT 9:00-1:00. (978) 535-5300. ✛▲✿

WEST SPRINGFIELD—AAA PIONEER VALLEY, 150 CAPITAL DR, 01089. WEEKDAYS (M-F) 9:00-5:30, THU 9:00-7:00, SAT 9:00-1:00 (INSURANCE OFFICE CLOSED ON SAT). *(800) 622-9211.* ✛▲✿

WESTWOOD—AAA SOUTHERN NEW ENGLAND, 335 PROVIDENCE HWY, 02090. WEEKDAYS (M-F) 9:00-5:00, SAT 9:00-1:00. (781) 461-6800. ✛▲✿

WORCESTER—AAA SOUTHERN NEW ENGLAND, 25 MOUNTAIN ST E, 01606. WEEKDAYS (M-F) 9:00-5:00, SAT 9:00-1:00. (508) 853-7000. ✛▲✿

RHODE ISLAND

BARRINGTON—AAA SOUTHERN NEW ENGLAND, 180 COUNTY RD, 02806. WEEKDAYS (M-F) 9:00-5:00, SAT 9:00-1:00. (401) 245-1050. ✛▲✿

CRANSTON—AAA SOUTHERN NEW ENGLAND, 1035 RESERVOIR AVE, 02910. WEEKDAYS (M-F) 9:00-5:00, SAT 9:00-1:00. (401) 944-7300. ✛▲✿

CUMBERLAND—AAA SOUTHERN NEW ENGLAND, 2000 MENDON RD ST #3, 02864. WEEKDAYS (M-F) 9:00-5:00, SAT 9:00-1:00. (401) 333-9500. ✛▲✿

GREENVILLE—AAA SOUTHERN NEW ENGLAND, 445 PUTNAM PIKE, 02828. WEEKDAYS (M-F) 9:00-5:00, SAT 9:00-1:00. (401) 232-5100. ✛▲✿

MIDDLETOWN—AAA SOUTHERN NEW ENGLAND, 49 E MAIN RD, 02842. WEEKDAYS (M-F) 9:00-5:00, SAT 9:00-1:00. (401) 841-5000. ✛▲✿

NARRAGANSETT—AAA SOUTHERN NEW ENGLAND, 14 WOODRUFF AVE STE 15, 02882. WEEKDAYS (M-F) 9:00-5:00, SAT 9:00-1:00. (401) 789-3000. ✛▲✿

PROVIDENCE—AAA SOUTHERN NEW ENGLAND, 55 DORRANCE ST, 02903. WEEKDAYS (M-F) 9:00-5:00. (401) 272-7100. ✛▲✿

PROVIDENCE—AAA SOUTHERN NEW ENGLAND, 110 ROYAL LITTLE DR, 02904. WEEKDAYS (M-F) 9:00-5:00, SAT 9:00-1:00. (401) 868-2010. ✛▲✿

WARWICK—AAA SOUTHERN NEW ENGLAND, 501 CENTERVILLE RD, 02886. WEEKDAYS (M-F) 9:00-5:00, SAT 9:00-1:00. (401) 732-5000. ✛▲✿

Metric Equivalents Chart

TEMPERATURE

To convert Fahrenheit to Celsius, subtract 32 from the Fahrenheit temperature, multiply by 5 and divide by 9. To convert Celsius to Fahrenheit, multiply by 9, divide by 5 and add 32.

ACRES

1 acre = 0.4 hectare (ha)   1 hectare = 2.47 acres

MILES AND KILOMETERS

Note: A kilometer is approximately 5/8 or 0.6 of a mile. To convert kilometers to miles multiply by 0.6.

Miles/Kilometers		Kilometers/Miles	
15	24.1	30	18.6
20	32.2	35	21.7
25	40.2	40	24.8
30	48.3	45	27.9
35	56.3	50	31.0
40	64.4	55	34.1
45	72.4	60	37.2
50	80.5	65	40.3
55	88.5	70	43.4
60	96.6	75	46.6
65	104.6	80	49.7
70	112.7	85	52.8
75	120.7	90	55.9
80	128.7	95	59.0
85	136.8	100	62.1
90	144.8	105	65.2
95	152.9	110	68.3
100	160.9	115	71.4

Celsius ° / Fahrenheit °

Celsius		Fahrenheit
100	BOILING	212
37		100
35		95
32		90
29		85
27		80
24		75
21		70
18		65
16		60
13		55
10		50
7		45
4		40
2		35
0	FREEZING	32
-4		25
-7		20
-9		15
-12		10
-15		5
-18		0
-21		-5
-24		-10
-27		-15

LINEAR MEASURE

Customary	Metric
1 inch = 2.54 centimeters	1 centimeter = 0.4 inches
1 foot = 30 centimeters	1 meter = 3.3 feet
1 yard = 0.91 meters	1 meter = 1.09 yards
1 mile = 1.6 kilometers	1 kilometer = .62 miles

LIQUID MEASURE

Customary	Metric
1 fluid ounce = 30 milliliters	1 milliliter = .03 fluid ounces
1 cup = .24 liters	1 liter = 2.1 pints
1 pint = .47 liters	1 liter = 1.06 quarts
1 quart = .95 liters	1 liter = .26 gallons
1 gallon = 3.8 liters	

WEIGHT

If You Know:	Multiply By:	To Find:
Ounces	28	Grams
Pounds	0.45	Kilograms
Grams	0.035	Ounces
Kilograms	2.2	Pounds

PRESSURE

Air pressure in automobile tires is expressed in kilopascals. Multiply pound-force per square inch (psi) by 6.89 to find kilopascals (kPa).

24 psi = 165 kPa   28 psi = 193 kPa
26 psi = 179 kPa   30 psi = 207 kPa

GALLONS AND LITERS

Gallons/Liters				Liters/Gallons			
5	19.0	12	45.6	10	2.6	40	10.4
6	22.8	14	53.2	15	3.9	50	13.0
7	26.6	16	60.8	20	5.2	60	15.6
8	30.4	18	68.4	25	6.5	70	18.2
9	34.2	20	76.0	30	7.8	80	20.8
10	38.0	25	95.0	35	9.1	90	23.4

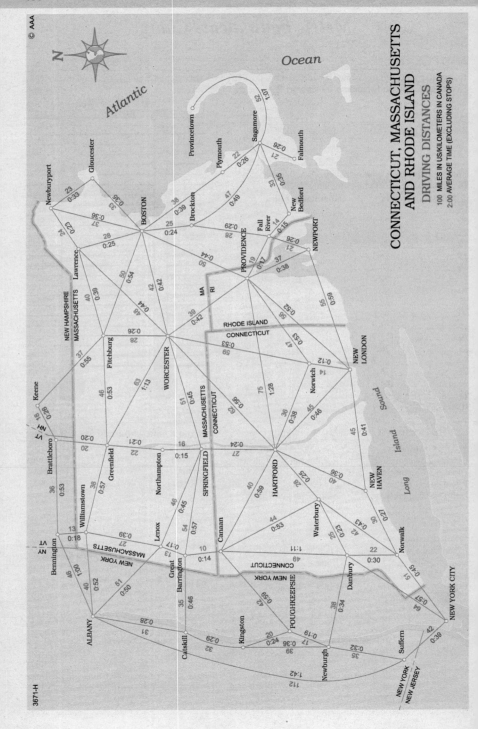

CONNECTICUT, MASSACHUSETTS
AND RHODE ISLAND
DRIVING DISTANCES
100 MILES IN US/KILOMETERS IN CANADA
2:00 AVERAGE TIME (EXCLUDING STOPS)

© AAA

3671-H

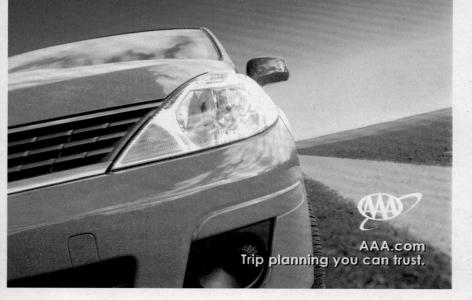

Points of Interest Index

Index Legend

⚘ GEM: Points of Interest Offering a *Great Experience for Members*®

EXHIBITS & COLLECTIONS-INDIAN

EXHIBITS & COLLECTIONS-MUSIC

SAVE *Attraction Admission Discount Index*

Bed & Breakfast Lodgings Index

Some bed and breakfasts listed below might have historical significance.
Those properties are also referenced in the Historical index.

Country Inns Index

Some of the following country inns can also be considered as bed-and-breakfast operations.

Historical Lodgings & Restaurants Index

Some of the following historical lodgings can also be considered as bed-and-breakfast operations.

Resorts Index

Many establishments are located in resort areas; however, the following
places have extensive on-premises recreational facilities:

Comprehensive City Index

Here is an alphabetical list of all cities appearing in this TourBook® guide. Cities are presented by state/province. Page numbers under the POI column indicate where points of interest text begins. Page numbers under the L&R column indicate where lodging and restaurant listings begin.

Comprehensive City Index (cont'd)

Comprehensive City Index (cont'd)

Theme park fun: SMART.

Theme park discounts: INGENIOUS.

Get more vacation for your dollar with valuable AAA member savings on attractions and entertainment. Look for colorful SAVE symbols in the printed TourBook guides and on AAA.com for locations that offer member discounts.

Savings at home and at play!
Visit AAA.com/discounts and
discover a new way to save.